MILLER'S

ANTIQUES

PRICE GUIDE 2007

MILLER'S ANTIQUES PRICE GUIDE 2007

Created and designed by
Miller's Publications
The Cellars, High Street
Tenterden, Kent, TN30 6BN
Tel: +44 (0) 1580 766411
Fax: +44 (0) 1580 766100

First published in Great Britain in 2006
by Miller's, a division of Mitchell Beazley,
imprints of Octopus Publishing Group Ltd,
2–4 Heron Quays, London E14 4JP
Miller's is a registered trademark of
Octopus Publishing Group Ltd

ISBN-13: 978-1-84533-250-1

ISBN-10: 1-84533-250-4

A CIP catalogue record for this book is available from the British Library

Set in Frutiger

Colour origination by Apex Press Ltd, Whitstable, Kent
Additional colour origination by Ian Williamson, Pevensey Scanning
Printed and bound: Rotolito Lombarda, Italy

Consultant Editor: Jonty Hearnden

General Editor: Elizabeth Norfolk
Managing Editor: Valerie Lewis
Production Co-ordinator: Philip Hannath
Editorial Co-ordinator: Deborah Wanstall
Editorial Assistants: Melissa Hall, Joanna Hill
Production Assistants: Charlotte Smith, Mel Smith, Ethne Tragett
Advertising Executives: Emma Gillingham, Michael Webb, Carol Woodcock
Advertising Co-ordinator & Administrator: Melinda Williams
Designer: Nick Harris
Advertisement Designer: Kari Moody
Indexer: Hilary Bird
Production: Jane Rogers
Jacket Design: Tim Foster
Additional Photographers: Elizabeth Field, Emma Gillingham,
Paul Harding, Jerermy Martin, Dennis O'Reilly, Robin Saker

Front cover illustrations:
A Whitefriars Banjo glass vase, c1968. Sotheby's Picture Library
An Art Deco bronze figure of a dancer, by J.Lormier, c1930. Sotheby's Picture Library
A maiolica dish, Italian, Montelupo, 17thC, 11¾in (30cm) diam. **£1,450–1,750** SWO

Back cover illustrations:
A Staffordshire model of a leopard, c1815, 8in (20.5cm) wide. **£3,150–3,500** HOW
A Minton cabinet cup and stand, c1830. **£1,450–1,650** JOR
A George IV mahogany breakfast library bookcase, c1825. Sotheby's Picture Library
A large and rare cast medal Golden Arrow Record Car, English, 1930s. Sotheby's Picture Library

Photographs of Jonty Hearnden by Adrian Pope

Half title illustration:
A Dutch Delft plate, c1740, 9in (23cm) diam. **£170–190** PeN

Contents illustration:
A Whitefriars Ears glass vase, by Geoffrey Baxter, No. 9416, c1969, 9in (23cm) high. **£165–185** HUN

MILLER'S

ANTIQUES PRICE GUIDE 2007

ELIZABETH NORFOLK *GENERAL EDITOR*

JONTY HEARNDEN
CONSULTANT EDITOR

2007
VOLUME XXVIII

HOW TO USE

To find a particular item, consult the contents list on page 7 to determine it can be found under the main heading – for example, Decorative Arts. You will find that larger sections have been sub-divided into more focused collecting areas. If you are looking for a particular factory, designer or craftsman, consult the index which starts on page 756.

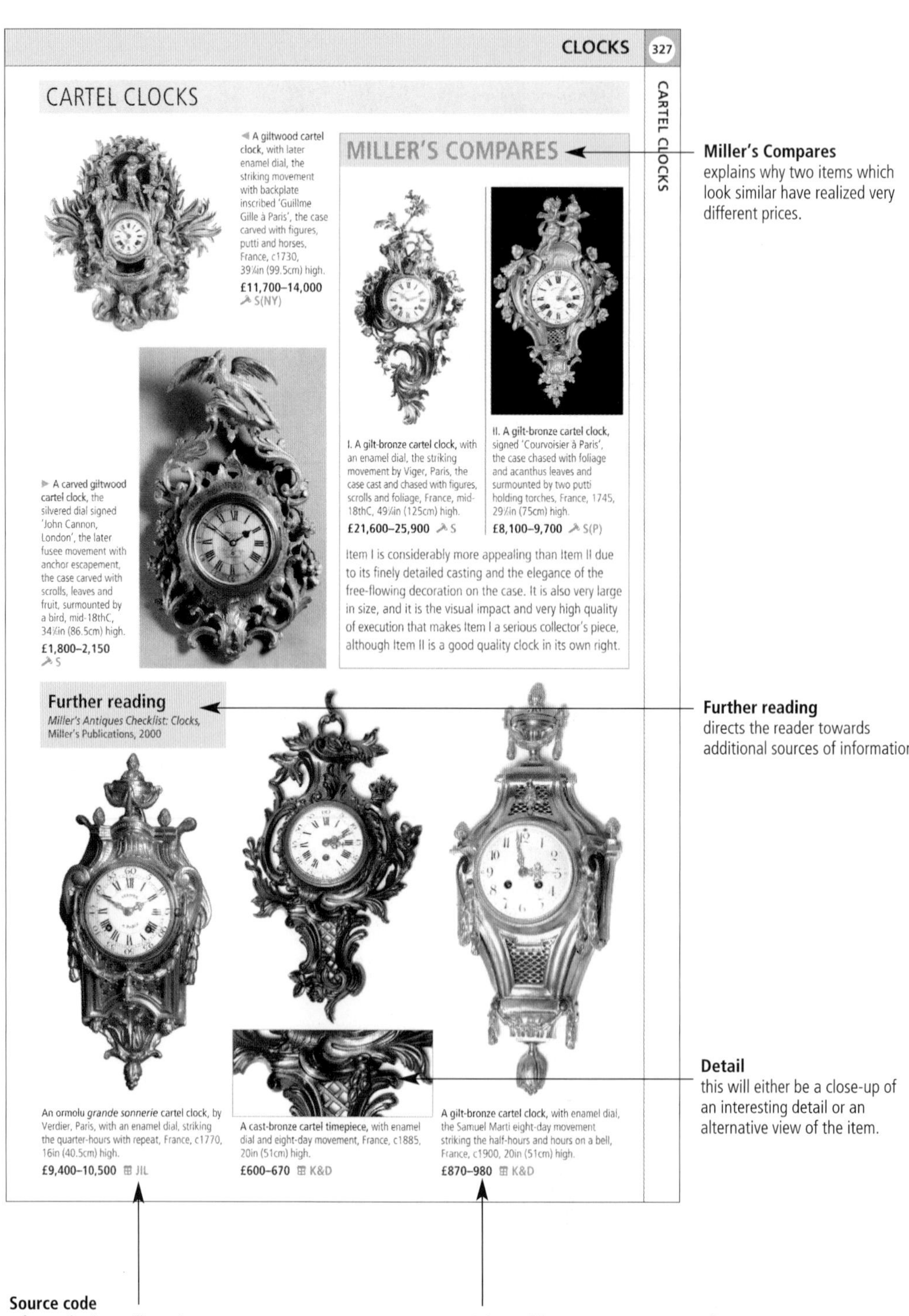

CLOCKS 327

CARTEL CLOCKS

CARTEL CLOCKS

◄ A giltwood cartel clock, with later enamel dial, the striking movement with backplate inscribed 'Guillme Gille à Paris', the case carved with figures, putti and horses, France, c1730, 39¼in (99.5cm) high.
£11,700–14,000 S(NY)

► A carved giltwood cartel clock, the silvered dial signed 'John Cannon, London', the later fusee movement with anchor escapement, the case carved with scrolls, leaves and fruit, surmounted by a bird, mid-18thC, 34¼in (86.5cm) high.
£1,800–2,150 S

MILLER'S COMPARES

I. A gilt-bronze cartel clock, with an enamel dial, the striking movement by Viger, Paris, the case cast and chased with figures, scrolls and foliage, France, mid-18thC, 49¼in (125cm) high.
£21,600–25,900 S

II. A gilt-bronze cartel clock, signed 'Courvoisier à Paris', the case chased with foliage and acanthus leaves and surmounted by two putti holding torches, France, 1745, 29½in (75cm) high.
£8,100–9,700 S(P)

Item I is considerably more appealing than Item II due to its finely detailed casting and the elegance of the free-flowing decoration on the case. It is also very large in size, and it is the visual impact and very high quality of execution that makes Item I a serious collector's piece, although Item II is a good quality clock in its own right.

Further reading
Miller's Antiques Checklist: Clocks, Miller's Publications, 2000

An ormolu *grande sonnerie* cartel clock, by Verdier, Paris, with an enamel dial, striking the quarter-hours with repeat, France, c1770, 16in (40.5cm) high.
£9,400–10,500 JIL

A cast-bronze cartel timepiece, with enamel dial and eight-day movement, France, c1885, 20in (51cm) high.
£600–670 K&D

A gilt-bronze cartel clock, with enamel dial, the Samuel Marti eight-day movement striking the half-hours and hours on a bell, France, c1900, 20in (51cm) high.
£870–980 K&D

Miller's Compares
explains why two items which look similar have realized very different prices.

Further reading
directs the reader towards additional sources of information.

Detail
this will either be a close-up of an interesting detail or an alternative view of the item.

Source code
refers to the Key to Illustrations on page 746 that lists the details of where the item was photographed. The icon indicates the item was sold at auction. The icon indicates the item originated from a dealer.

Price guide
this is based on actual prices realized. Remember that Miller's is a price guide not a price list and prices are affected by many variables such as location, condition, desirability and so on. Don't forget that if you are selling it is quite likely you will be offered less than the price range. Price ranges for items sold at auction tend to include the buyer's premium and VAT if applicable.

190 POTTERY

AMERICAN REDWARE

AMERICAN REDWARE

Experts details shows the authenticator's photograph and a brief biography.

George Allen

George is a partner at Raccoon Creek Antiques, Oley, PA. They specialize in American Folk Art, specifically ceramics.

George has a Teaching Degree; he majored in Ceramics, and became a potter working in stoneware, redware and porcelain.

REDWARE IS A LOW-FIRED CLAY. It was used by potters from the late 17th century throughout the American northeast and south and into

tool to incise a design when the clay scratching off coloured slip layers, kr colouring the wares with a brushed using a quilled slip cup – a moulded quills – to apply lines of coloured sli

With the advancement of technolo popularity of earthenware items, it c distinguish the old from the new. Th experience is to look, touch and feel pieces develop a patina and surface hard to copy. When buying, it is advi dealer or collector who already has a of the subject.

Folk Art pottery continues to rise in set records in the antiques market –

DOLLS 629

A Jumeau bisque-headed doll, with fixed eyes, original wig, France, late 19thC, 20in (51cm) high.
£990–1,100 BaN

Bébés
Bébés are dolls that are idealized version of a young girl, with chubby limbs and a rounded stomach. They are probably the most popular of all dolls – early examples, which usually had closed mouths and fixed wrists, can command extremely high prices if in exceptional condition. The French company Jumeau produced the first *bébé* in 1855 but the golden age of French production was from c1860 to the 1890s. After 1899 the quality declined due to the proliferance of less expensive examples from Germany, leading to the formation of the S. F. B. J. (Société Française de Bébés et Jouets).

Information box covers relevant collecting information such as factories, makers, care and restoration, fakes and alterations.

A Jumeau *bébé* doll, minor damage, France, early 20thC, 24in (61cm) high.
£750–900 JAA

KÄMMER & REINHARDT / SIMON & HALBIG

Feature Box shows two or more similar items by the same maker, together with information about the maker's product and history.

As well as producing entire dolls, Simon & Halbig (c1869–c1930) was one of the most prolific manufacturers of bisque and china shoulder heads, which they supplied to other manufacturers such as Kämmer & Reinhardt, Schmidt & Dressel, Jumeau and Roullet & Descamps. These dolls will usually bear the marks of both companies and also a mould number, which can be important as it will identify rare or desirable series.

A Kämmer & Reinhardt doll, with a Simon & Halbig bisque head, with weighted glass eyes, mohair wig, Germany, c1910, 23in (58.5cm) high.
£630–700 DOAN

A Kämmer & Reinhardt bisque-headed soldier doll, with intaglio eyes, Germany, c1910, 11in (28cm) high.
£1,050–1,200 DOAN

A Kämmer & Reinhardt bisque-headed walking doll, with weighted eyes, mohair wig, composition body, with head turning/walking mechanism, Germany, early 20thC, 21in (53.5cm) high.
£520–580 BaN

A Kestner bisque child doll, with weighted glass eyes, possibly human hair wig, repaired, incised mark and stamp, Germany, c1914, 27in (69cm) high.
£280–330 Bert

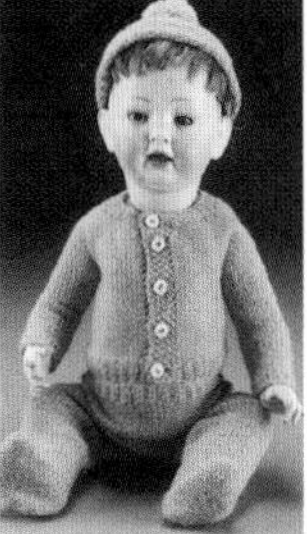

A Kestner character baby doll, mould No. 150, with weighted eyes, minor wear, Germany, early 20thC, 17in (43cm) high.
£200–240 JAA

A Kley & Hahn Walküre bisque doll, with weighted eyes, Germany, early 20thC, 28in (71cm) high.
£220–260 JAA

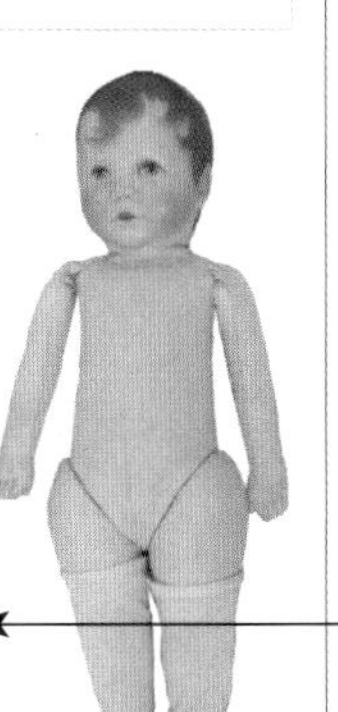

▶ A Käthe Kruse doll, the sewn-on muslin head with painted hair and features, the cloth body with wide, disc-jointed hips, signed, Germany, 1910–29, 14in (35.5cm) high.
£1,650–1,950 G(L)

Caption provides a brief description of the item including the maker's name, medium, size, year it was made and in some cases condition.

Dates	British Monarch	British Period	French Period	German Period	U.S. Period	Style	Woods
1558–1603	Elizabeth I	Elizabethan	Renaissance			Gothic	Oak Period (to c1670)
1603–1625	James I	Jacobean		Renaissance			
1625–1649	Charles I	Carolean	Louis XIII (1610–1643)		Early Colonial	Baroque (c1620–1700)	
1649–1660	Common-wealth	Cromwellian	Louis XIV (1643–1715)	Renaissance/ Baroque (c1650–1700)			
1660–1685	Charles II	Restoration					Walnut period (c1670–1735)
1685–1689	James II	Restoration			William & Mary		
1689–1694	William & Mary	William & Mary			Dutch Colonial	Rococo (c1695–1760)	
1694–1702	William III	William III		Baroque (c1700–1730)	Queen Anne		
1702–1714	Anne	Queen Anne					
1714–1727	George I	Early Georgian	Régence (1715–1723)	Rococo (c1730–1760)	Chippendale (from 1750)		Early mahogany period (c1735–1770)
1727–1760	George II	Early Georgian	Louis XV (1723–1774)	Neo–classicism (c1760–1800)	Early Federal (1790–1810)	Neo–classical (c1755–1805)	
1760–1811	George III	Late Georgian	Louis XVI (1774–1793) Directoire (1793–1799) Empire (1799–1815)	Empire (c1800–1815)	American Directoire (1798–1804) American Empire (1804–1815)	Empire (c1799–1815)	Late mahogany period (c1770–1810)
1812–1820	George III	Regency	Restauration Charles X (1815–1830)	Biedermeier (c1815–1848)	Late Federal (1810–1830)	Regency (c1812–1830)	
1820–1830	George IV	Regency					
1830–1837	William IV	William IV	Louis Philippe (1830–1848)	Revivale (c1830–1880)		Eclectic (c1830–1880)	
1837–1901	Victoria	Victorian	2nd Empire Napoleon III (1848–1870) 3rd Republic (1871–1940)	Jugendstil (c1880–1920)	Victorian	Arts & Crafts (c1880–1900)	
1901–1910	Edward VII	Edwardian			Art Nouveau (c1900–1920)	Art Nouveau (c1900–1920)	

contents

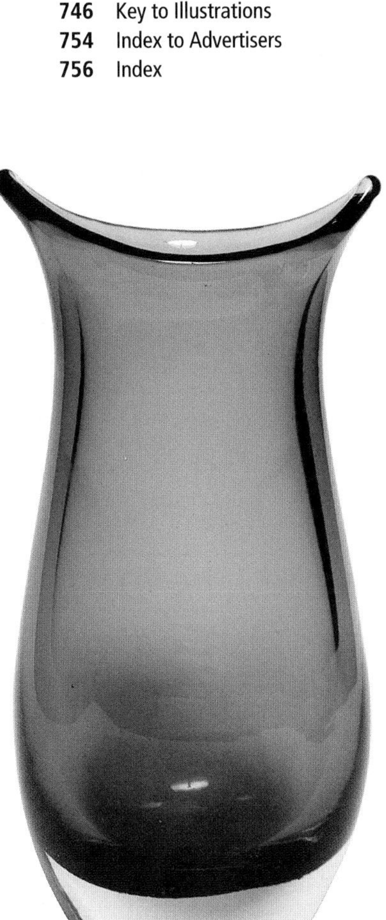

MEET THE EXPERTS

The publishers would like to acknowledge the great assistance given by our consultants. We would also like to extend our thanks to all auction houses and their press offices, as well as dealers and collectors, who have assisted us in the production of this book.

FURNITURE: **Leslie Gillham,** who has more than 35 years' experience in the world of auctioneering, is consultant to Gorringes in Tunbridge Wells, Kent and senior auctioneer at their Bexhill-on-Sea, East Sussex, auction rooms. Gorringes have four salerooms in southeast England, holding over 70 scheduled auction sales per year of Antiques, Fine Art and Collectables, together with occasional specialist and house sales.

Leslie Gillham, Gorringes, The Pantiles, Tunbridge Wells, Kent TN2 5TD

POTTERY: **John Howard** has been a dealer of English pottery for 30 years. His specializations are creamware, lustreware and animal figure groups manufactured in the British Isles in the 18th and 19th centuries. He has a showroom in Woodstock, near Oxford, and is a member of the British Antique Dealers' Association and the Cotswolds Art and Antique Dealers' Association. John also exhibits at major antiques fairs in the UK and USA, such as Olympia in London and the New York Ceramics Fair. He is Chairman of the Ceramics Vetting Committee at Olympia Fine Art and Antiques Fairs and is a member of the vetting team at many UK and USA antiques fairs.

John Howard, 6 Market Place, Woodstock, Oxon OX20 1TE

PORCELAIN: **John Axford** worked for Phillips Auctioneers in London before joining Woolley and Wallis, Salisbury, in 1993 to become head of the Ceramics, Glass and Oriental departments. He writes and lectures on ceramics and Oriental art and has been a member of the BBC's *Antiques Roadshow* team since 2000. In 2005 John discovered the first Limehouse figure and discovered and identified The Alexander Vase.

John Axford, Woolley & Wallis, 50–51 Castle Street, Salisbury, Wilts SP1 3SU

GLASS: **Jeanette Hayhurst** was European fine art photographer for Sotheby's and a collector of 18th-century drinking glasses. Together with her husband Malcolm they established their business in 1980 when their collecting habit got out of control and opened their present shop in 1986, specializing in most aspects and periods of British and European antique glass together with post-war design. Jeanette has lectured extensively on the identification of glass, appeared on television and radio, written and edited articles and books and was Special Consultant for *Miller's Glass of the '20s and '30s*. She has also curated several innovative exhibitions.

Jeanette Hayhurst, 32a Kensington Church Street, London W8 4HA

OAK & COUNTRY FURNITURE: **Robert Young** trained at Sotheby's and started his antiques business 1976. He specializes in Oak and Country furniture and is committee Chairman for Fine Art and Antiques Fairs at Olympia, London. He is on the vetting committee at Grosvenor House Antiques Fair, Chelsea Antiques Fairs, Birmingham NEC Antiques for Everyone and San Francisco Fall Antiques Show. Robert has also written many articles on country and folk subjects and is the author of *Folk Art* published by Mitchell Beazley.

Robert Young, 68 Battersea Bridge Road, London SW11 3AG

AMERICAN CERAMICS: **George R. Allen** is co-partner wth Gordon L. Wyckoff of Raccoon Creek Antiques, LLC, Oley, PA. They have been in business for 20 years and focus on American Folk Art with a specialized interest in Ceramics. George is also a potter working in stoneware, redware and porcelain, and lectures at colleges and civic organizations. He has also appeared on national television.

George Allen, Raccoon Creek Antiques, 208 Spangsville Road, Oley, PA 19547

CHINESE CERAMICS AND ASIAN WORKS OF ART: **Peter Wain** is a leading specialist in Chinese and Japanese ceramics and works of art. He lived in Hong Kong for several years and is a frequent visitor to China. He has written numerous books, catalogues and articles, has broadcast on radio and television and given many lectures in the UK, USA and Australia. Peter has been the Chairman of the Oriental Vetting Committees for many of the top international antiques fairs. He has recently curated an exhibition on Chinese Art of the Chairman Mao era for the Royal Museum of Scotland, Edinburgh.

Peter Wain, Anglesey

SILVER & SILVER PLATE: **Daniel Bexfield** has been dealing and specializing in antique silver for 25 years, and is based in Burlington Arcade, Mayfair, London, where he carries an extensive range of fine quality silver from the 18th century to the 1940s. He regularly contributes to television and radio programmes and a variety of publications, including *Miller's Silver & Plate Buyer's Guide*, and is editor of *The Finial*, a magazine solely related to silver spoons. He is also a supporter of The Silver Society, The Society of Caddy Spoon Collectors, The Writing Equipment Society, LAPADA, CINOA and is a council member of BADA.

Daniel Bexfield, 26 Burlington Arcade, London W1V 9AD

ADDITIONAL AMERICAN SILVER INFORMATION: **Mike Weller**

Argentum, The Leopard's Head, 472 Jackson Street, San Francisco, CA 94111

CLOCKS: **Robert Wren** started his own business specializing in clocks in 1983. In the mid-1990s he joined the workshops of Derek Roberts Antiques, Tonbridge, and is now the marketing manager, responsible for exhibitions, catalogues and assisting with running the business. Since 1997 he has been a consultant to Christie's South Kensington clocks department helping with the production of condition reports. Between 1998 and 2003 Robert assisted with the cataloguing and conservation of pre-balance spring watches in the collection at the British Museum. Robert is also the assistant tutor on the Antique Clocks Conservation and Restoration programme at West Dean College, Chichester, a Liveryman of the Worshipful Company of Clockmakers and a Member of the British Horological Institute.

Robert Wren, Derek Roberts Antiques,
25 Shipbourne Road, Tonbridge,
Kent TN10 3DN

AMERICAN CLOCKS: **Robert Schmitt** is a graduate of UCLA School of Management. He started collecting clocks in 1969, and 11 years later he took over a retail shop in Big Bear, California, and began holding semi annual clock auctions. In late 1983 he established a base in Nottingham, England, from which he sent thousands of clocks to the US. In November of 1985 he moved to New England, re-establishing his consignment clock auctions, which continue to this day. He is also active with the National Association of Watch & Clock Collectors, based in Columbia, PA.

Robert Schmitt, P O Box 162,
Windham, NH 03087

BAROMETERS: **Derek & Tina Rayment**

Orchard House, Barton Road, Nr Farndon,
Cheshire, SY14 7HT

DECORATIVE ARTS: **Keith Baker** is an independent consultant, valuer and art dealer, concentrating on all aspects of late 19th- and 20th-century Decorative Arts. He headed the Art Nouveau and Decorative Arts Department at Bonhams, London for 23 years and, with his wife Fiona, has co-authored *Twentieth Century Furniture*, published in 2001 by Carlton Books.

Keith Baker, keithbaker@yahoo.co.uk

TWENTIETH-CENTURY DESIGN: **Lisanne Dickson** is head of 1950s Modern Design for Treadway/Toomey Auctions, a Chicago-based auction house established in 1987 which holds four 20th-Century Design sales per year. In her seven years with the firm she has personally catalogued more than 6000 examples of furniture, pottery, glass, sculpture, lighting, jewellery and textiles dating from 1930 to 1980.

Lisanne Dickson, Treadway/Toomey
Auctions, 2029 Madison Road,
Cincinnati, Ohio 45208

TEXTILES: **Patricia T. Herr** is a researcher, author, lecturer, and dealer in the field of American historic textiles. She has curated exhibits sponsored by the Philadelphia Museum of Art, Winterthur Museum, Heritage Center Museum of Lancaster County, and Landis Valley Museum. Dr. Herr is author of several books on Lancaster County quilts, Amish decorative arts, and Moravian schoolgirl needlework. She has also written articles on textiles for *Early American Life*, *The Quilt Digest*, *The Magazine Antiques*, and other symposium and museum publications. Dr Herr received her Doctor of Veterinary Medicine from Cornell University and has been a practising companion animal veterinarian for over 40 years.

Patricia Herr, Lancaster, PA

BOOKS & BOOK ILLUSTRATIONS: **Dr Philip W. Errington** is Deputy Director of Printed Books and Manuscripts at Sotheby's, London. His specialized areas are Children's Books, Illustrated Books and Drawings and English Literature. He has published widely on the author John Masefield: his edition of Masefield's *Sea-Fever: Selected Poems*, was published in 2005 by Carcanet and his major bibliography of the author was published in 2004 by The British Library and nominated for the 14th ILAB bibliography prize. In 2000 he was appointed a visiting research fellow within the University of london and in 2004 was made an honorary research fellow of the Department of English Language and Literature, University College of London.

Dr Philip Errington, Sotheby's,
34–35 New Bond Street, London W1A 2AA

DOLLS: **Florence Theriault** is a magna cum laude researcher and member of the prestigious Phi Beta Kappa society. She has been researching, cataloguing and appraising dolls for 30 years and, with her husband George, founded Theriault's the Dollmasters, an auction house specializing in antique dolls. For over 35 years Theriault's has produced a monthly catalogue of antique dolls. Florence is a well-known lecturer and seminar leader in the study of dolls and is the author of a number of doll books, including *The Beautiful Jumeau*, *The Way They Wore* and *In Character, the Portrayal of Mood in Antique Dolls*.

Florence Theriault, Theriault's,
PO Box 151, Annapolis, MD 21404

SCIENTIFIC INSTRUMENTS: **Bill Higgins** has been a specialist dealer in Antique Scientific and Medical instruments for many years and has supplied collectors, dealers and museums as well as individual buyers on a worldwide basis. He has acted as an independent consultant and is on the vetting committee for 'Antiques for Everyone' fairs at Birmingham NEC. Bill has been interviewed for a number of national and international publications and television programmes including the *Telegraph*, and an hour-long programme for Russian television.

Bill Higgins, Fossack & Furkle,
PO Box 733 Abington, Cambridge CB1 6BF

INTRODUCTION

BEING INVOLVED in the antiques world, whether you're a novice or an old hand, is a truly exciting adventure. The thrill of finding that unique item, that perfect object for your collection or to enhance your home, cannot be bettered. No matter how long you have been visiting antiques shops, salerooms, car boot sales or trawling through the internet, there is always more to learn and always the chance of acquiring that amazing bargain.

Knowledge is indeed vital when it comes to buying antiques. Dealers' showrooms, antiques fairs and auction rooms are great places in which to delve. Never be afraid to ask for advice, for many dealers are more than happy to share their knowledge with the general public. Ask first, but always feel free to pick up, turn over and look inside the object, as many questions will be answered by this process.

Antiques fairs give you the chance to view the widest possible variety of items under one roof, with time to choose and compare, while dealers' own shops and galleries will afford you the opportunity to ask questions before making the crucial decision to purchase. Many dealers are experts in their particular fields and the selection of items they offer for sale will be based on their taste and the knowledge they have acquired over the years.

Auction sales always offer the hope and excitement of finding a true bargain. Try to visit a sale before auction day, as this will allow you to view properly and, even more importantly, ask the auctioneer for any further information you may require. Be aware that some items entered for sale may need restoration to a greater or lesser degree, which can add to your overall outlay. Remember, too, that all auctions carry a surcharge, known as the buyer's premium; in some cases this can be as much as 20 per cent of the hammer price, so take this into account when deciding what you are able to pay.

Here's where *Miller's Antiques Price Guide* can help you. Every item shown has either recently been sold at auction or is on offer in a dealer's showroom, thus providing an accurate reflection of what is actually happening in the marketplace today. Remember that antiques are unique items and values are affected by both supply and demand; as tastes change, prices rise and fall. You will find your Miller's Guide an indispensable tool that will keep you up to date with these variations, it will whet your appetite, teach you and guide you as you find your way through what is an incredibly varied and vibrant market – and your journey will be made much easier.The advice given here is by some of the best and most knowledgeable people in the trade today.

It is, of course, important to keep an eye on the fluctuating state of the antiques market, as what was fashionable yesterday may not be so desirable today. For example, the dramatic growth in the Chinese economy has encouraged new buyers into the field of Chinese ceramics and other works of art, as a result of which the international market has recently seen hugely inflated prices paid for items of high quality and good provenance. According to Peter Wain in his introduction to this section of the (see p233), international attention has in particular been focused on good-quality Imperial works, culminating in a world record fee for a single piece of Chinese porcelain at Christie's, London, where a Yuan Dynasty vase was sold for £14 million. Three days later, probably riding on the crest of the wave, another Yuan vase reached £3 million at Woolley & Wallis, Salisbury – a record price for a provincial auction house (see p252).

A double gourd vase, Yuan Dynasty, c1350, 18¾in (47.5cm) high.
£3,000,000–3,600,000 WW

Other Chinese works of art with good provenance have benefited from this new frenzy, reaching 'never before seen' levels on the international markets. Chinese jade cloisonné and enamel ware have reached record prices, while a large 300-year-old lacquered gilt-bronze figure representing the Buddha Amitabha recently sold at Sotheby's for £200,000. Although some Asian furniture is now struggling to sell in auction rooms as interior decorators move away from a style once regarded as high fashion, New York recently witnessed the sale of a pair of Wanli Imperial lacquer cabinets for over £500,000. The steadying of the Japanese economy has also seen buyers returning to the market, where there is increased interest in fine quality Japanese arms and armour in particular.

The new wealth in Russia has rekindled interest in Russian works of art across the board. Highlights of the year include the sale at Sotheby's of a pair of

St Petersburg vases from the stupendous Royal House of Hanover collection (see p224). Not to be outdone, on Valentine's Day 2006, Sworders of Stanstead Mountfitchet sold a small silver-gilt and cloisonné box by Fabergé for £50,000 (see p510). The grandfather of

A Fabergé silver-gilt and cloisonné enamel box, by Fedor Ruckert, the hinged cover decorated with 'A Knight at the Crossroads', after Viktor Vasnetsov, Fabergé and Imperial Warrant marks, London import marks, Russia, Moscow 1908–17,
£50,000–60,000 SWO

the vendor's husband, who had lived and worked in St Petersburg up to the time of the Russian revolution, had actually met Carl Fabergé in person.

It is interesting to note that, although there was plenty of Russian interest in the box, it ultimately went to a UK buyer, demonstrating that there is still a very strong market for Fabergé in this country. A further Fabergé item – a pill box – was sold in March 2006 by Moore, Allen & Innocent of Cirencester for the princely sum of £75,000.

The value of exports from the UK to the US remains mixed. Some dealers have experienced increases in sales while others have seen the market decline. A recent survey of some of the UK's top dealers suggests that their main sales have been through their shops and galleries, with only a small percentage of sales taking place on the internet. In many other areas of the market, however, quite the reverse has occurred, with eBay and the internet attracting huge new swathes of both buyers and sellers.

A recent furniture price index suggests that prices have fallen overall for the fourth year running, although as indicated by Leslie Gillham in his introduction (see p12), there have been unusual twists and turns in this particular field. The main casualty has been Victorian and Edwardian furniture, which has become as affordable as it has ever been in real terms. Clearly there has never been a better time to pick up a bargain in this area than right now.

Following the example of major auction houses that have been influenced by new buying trends in the field of decorative arts, provincial rooms have started in earnest to change tack and are holding back items for specialist sales. Lalique glass maintains its appeal in the international market, while Art Deco bronze and ivory figures continue to be popular, along with French Art Deco furniture. Arts and Crafts designs remain winners among British and American buyers. Hot areas for collectors of UK ceramics include signed Royal Worcester pieces, for which Australian and Canadian buyers are paying high prices. A further development in the ceramics market is the increase in price of early 18th-century pieces from British factories.

Twentieth-Century Design remains a strong growth area. Interior designers can often be seen outbidding dealers, as their now discerning clients are swayed by emotion rather than price when it comes to a purchase.

One of the best things about the antiques market is that it can be indulged in by almost anyone – for there can be just as much satisfaction in finding that delightful object that costs no more than a few pounds as there is in spending thousands on a superb piece of furniture and, the more knowledge you acquire, the more chance you have of unearthing something really special. I have found one of the greatest thrills of being in the antiques business is the joy of sharing knowledge, and this is what I love above anything else when presenting antiques on television. There is always more to learn, always something unexpected to discover – and it's always fun! I hope you will find it as enjoyable as I do.

Jonty Hearnden

A Chamberlain's Worcester dinner service, the Duke of Cumberland Service, comprising 189 pieces, decorated in the Imari style, 1802–06.
£376,000–451,000 S(Han)

Jonty Hearnden

FURNITURE

Leslie Gillham

Leslie is senior auctioneer at Gorringes auction house, Bexhill-on-Sea, East Sussex and consultant to Gorringes, Tunbridge Wells, Kent.

He has over 35 years experience in the world of auctioneering.

IT WOULD BE FOOLISH TO SUGGEST that the furniture market is any less of an enigma than it was a year ago. There is still strong demand for the very best pieces while the less distinguished 18th- and 19th-century stalwarts are not doing so well. Yet underlying this is an extraordinary turbulence in the auction rooms that can toss prices about on what often seems to be a week-by-week basis.

At the upper end of the scale, although not quite rivalling the spectacular £1,800,000 obtained by Christie's for an early 18th-century Florentine *pietra dura* table top on what was almost certainly a base by George Bullock, the Lincolnshire auctioneers Golding Young have had their own recent success. Called to a terraced house in Stamford, they found themselves confronted by a fine mahogany breakfront side cabinet with glorious gilt-metal mounts. An added bonus was an invoice dating from when the vendor's parents had purchased the piece from local dealers in 1942 for the sum of 25 guineas (£785 at today's values.) Unable to make up their minds whether the cabinet should be attributed to Thomas Hope or George Smith, the auctioneers left the matter open and let prospective purchasers decide. This decision certainly resulted in no dampening of enthusiasm for the item since on the day, after spirited bidding and despite serious interest from the US, a London dealer eventually secured the heirloom for a somewhat unexpected £155,250.

It is true that results are unlikely to grab the headlines in quite the same way at the other end of the market but this does not mean that what is happening there is any less important for buyer and seller alike. Watchful buyers can currently do extremely well – if you see a piece that you like and the price seems right then buy it. Stories are now legion of pieces being offered with estimates of, say, £800–1,200 and failing to sell. When re-offered in the next sale at a reduced estimate of £400–600 the same item then soars to £1,200, bid up by the same people who ignored it last time.

Such happenings are not as absurd as they may sound. When the market is difficult and unpredictable, dealers are reluctant to hold too much stock so they will only buy when they know they can sell a piece quickly. Whether you buy at auction, retail or both you should keep a weather eye open for real bargains at the moment – they are out there, but probably not for long.

Leslie Gillham

BEDS & CRADLES

A mahogany four-poster bed, with leaf-carved and painted decoration, America, New Hampshire, c1805, 51in (129.5cm) wide.
£3,500–4,200 SK(B)

A mahogany and ebony-inlaid swinging cradle, with turned pillars and hooped canopy, c1810, 44in (112cm) wide.
£2,150–2,400 YOX

An early Victorian mahogany and cane cradle, with canopy, on a ring-turned stand with outswept end supports, 50¾in (129cm) high.
£490–580 DN

◀ **A tiger maple bed,** with turned side posts and scalloped head and footboard, side rails missing, America, c1820, 52in (132cm) wide.

£175–210 JAA

A Victorian carved mahogany bed, 60in (152.5cm) wide.

£175–210 G(B)

A Victorian French-style brass and iron bed, with brass finials and pine base, with receipt headed 'W. Newton & Co, 165 Westgate Road', 56in (142cm) wide.

£530–630 PFK

Newton & Co are recorded as retailers of bicycles and furniture in Newcastle from 1860 to 1899.

A Renaissance revival walnut and burr-walnut highback bed, the headboard and footboard with framed and raised burr panels and shell and foliate crest, the posts with carved finials, the rails with carved returns, America, 1850–75, 68in (172.5cm) wide.

£1,400–1,650 NOA

A mahogany four-poster bed, with turned and tapered posts, panelled headboard and veneered canopy, the posts on brass ball feet, America, 1875–1900, 87in (221cm) wide.

£3,050–3,650 NOA

A rococo revival rosewood bed, the triple-panel headboard with a foliate-carved crest supported by tapering posts, the footboard with turned finials, America, 1850–75, 63½in (161.5cm) wide.

£1,000–1,200 NOA

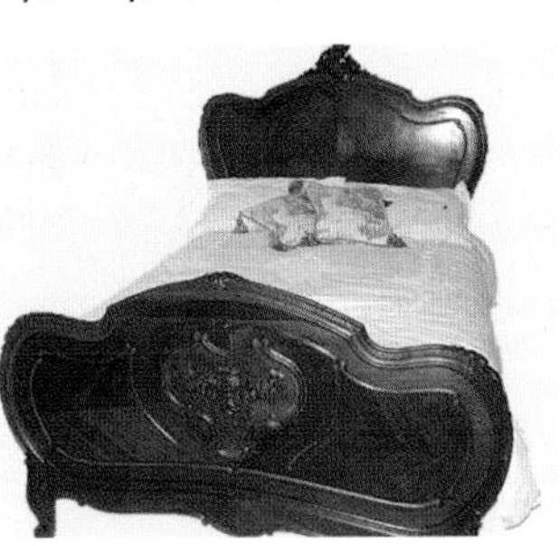

A Louis XV-style walnut bed, with quarter-veneered panels and carved detail to the footboard, France, c1900, 52in (132cm) wide.

£1,050–1,200 SWA

A Henri II-style walnut bed, with quarter-veneered panels and brass details, France, c1910, 60in (152.5cm) wide.

£1,350–1,500 SWA

A brass bed, with bowed top rail and foot rail, early 20thC, 54in (137cm) wide.

£340–400 PFK

◀ **A mahogany, amboyna and satinwood-banded bed,** the head and footboards with moulded crests above a panelled frieze with a central garrya gilt-metal mount, flanked by scrolled brackets, France, early 20thC, 61½in (156cm) wide.

£330–390 DN

BENCHES

A mahogany bench, on turned legs, c1820, 46in (117cm) wide.
£2,850–3,200 GEO

► **A William IV mahogany hall bench,** the shaped back with a central cartouche, above a solid seat flanked by turned arms, on baluster front legs, 52in (132cm) wide.
£1,350–1,600 MEA

A carved walnut hall bench, Italy, c1880, 41in (104cm) wide.
£1,350–1,500 BURA

BONHEURS DU JOUR

◄ **A *vernis Martin* bonheur du jour,** 19thC, 60in (152.5cm) high.
£2,450–2,750 SPUR

In the early 18th century, Guillaume Martin and his brothers obtained a patent for vernis Martin, *a French imitation of Oriental lacquer finishes and decoration applied to furniture. The term denotes pictorial lacquer applied in numerous successive coats to pieces of furniture, the panels being hand-painted and decorated with 18th-century romantic or courting scenes. Vernis Martin-style pieces were reproduced throughout the 19th and early 20th centuries by some of the most notable French and Continental cabinet-makers such as Linke and Sormani.*

An inlaid mahogany bonheur du jour, with a fitted upper section and fold-out writing surface, c1880, 33in (84cm) wide.
£1,450–1,650 TRED

A satinwood bonheur du jour, by Edwards & Roberts, decorated with tortoiseshell inlay, with a fitted writing slide, c1880, 44½in (113cm) wide.
£27,000–30,000 GEO

This piece is made of the more desirable satinwood and is by one of the most prestigious 19th-century cabinet makers.

► **A rosewood bonheur du jour,** with boxwood inlay and floral motifs, c1880, 40in (101.5cm) high.
£1,150–1,300 HEM

A Louis XVI-style mahogany bonheur du jour, with brass line inlay, a leather top and a fitted writing drawer, France, c1880, 32in (81.5cm) wide.
£1,750–1,950 CSM

BOOKCASES

A mahogany bookcase, the upper section with two glazed doors, the base with two panelled doors, c1810, 57in (145cm) wide.

£2,200–2,450 PICA

GLAZING BARS

The upper sections of early 18th-century bookcases were glazed with simple rectangular panes framed by solid glazing bars. After c1750, they were usually replaced by astragals (a semi-circular moulding), which, being lighter, could be arranged in more elaborate patterns. A more attractive design will generally add value. Small panes continued to be popular long after it was possible to manufacture large sheets of glass.
In early bookcases, individual panes of glass are set into the glazing bar framework whereas later 19th-century examples tend to consist of a single piece of glass onto which the bars have been applied.

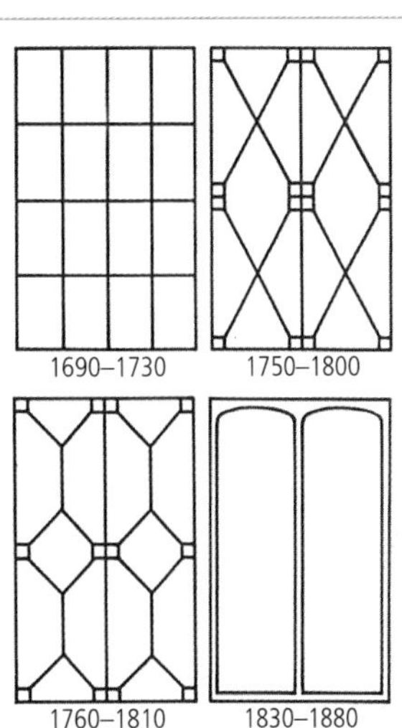

A library breakfront bookcase, c1840, 108in (274.5cm) wide.

£5,600–6,700 S(O)

► A Victorian mahogany bookcase, with two glazed doors enclosing adjustable shelving, the base with two cushion drawers above two panelled doors flanked by pilasters, 56¼in (143cm) wide.

£1,400–1,650 AH

A walnut bookcase, the upper section with two glazed doors, the base with two drawers and two panelled doors, c1890, 47in (119.5cm) wide.

£710–790 MTay

It was not until the reign of Charles II that the bookcase began to feature as a piece of domestic furniture. Until then, books had been regarded as items of great luxury and the ownership of any more than a handful of volumes had been confined largely to the church or colleges. Despite competition from modern information technology, books remain an essential component of most homes and the bookcase has therefore retained its popularity while so many other pieces of furniture seem to be no longer required in the 21st-century setting. Despite this there are still bargains to be had, particularly if you are prepared to accommodate late 19th-century Georgian-style offerings rather than original 18th-century pieces. When buying traditional tall two-section bookcases, always make sure that both the glazed upper part and the cupboard base began life together rather than being a later 'marriage'.

An Edwardian mahogany bookcase, the two astragal-glazed doors enclosing adjustable shelves, over two panelled cupboard doors, on bracket feet, 48in (122cm) wide.

£1,350–1,600 SWO

A mahogany bookcase, the three glazed doors enclosing two shelves, flanked by carved pilasters, America, c1910, 58in (147.5cm) wide.

£600–720 JAA

BUREAU BOOKCASES

A George III mahogany bureau bookcase, the boxwood and harewood patera-inlaid frieze over two astragal-glazed doors enclosing shelves, above a fall-front enclosing a fitted interior, over four long graduated cockbeaded drawers, on shaped bracket feet, damaged, top associated, 44in (112cm) wide.

£590–700 Hal

A mahogany cylinder bureau bookcase, with two glazed doors above a fall-front and two panelled doors, c1840, 42in (106.5cm) wide.

£3,200–3,600 TRED

A rococo revival rosewood cylinder bureau bookcase, the two glazed doors enclosing a maple-veneered interior, the cylinder opening with a mechanical action extending the writing surface as the top is raised, the base with a frieze drawer over two recessed cupboard doors, America, 1850–75, 49in (124.5cm) wide.

£2,250–2,700 JDJ

LOW BOOKCASES

A carved rosewood low bookcase, with adjustable shelves, c1830, 51in (129.5cm) wide.

£3,550–4,000 MALT

A Victorian crossbanded figured walnut breakfront bookcase, the three glazed doors enclosing two shelves, 66in (167.5cm) wide.

£3,650–4,350 G(L)

A Victorian walnut bookcase, the two glazed doors enclosing adjustable shelves, 48¼in (122.5cm) wide.

£320–380 WW

A late Victorian mahogany low bookcase, the two astragal-glazed doors with inlaid stringing, on splayed feet, 34in (86.5cm) wide.

£240–280 WW

A late Victorian mahogany breakfront low bookcase, the ribbed frieze and inlaid paterae above three astragal-glazed doors enclosing adjustable shelves, the central section with later glass shelves, 59¼in (150.5cm) wide.

£1,350–1,600 WW

OPEN BOOKCASES

An early Victorian rosewood breakfront open bookcase, with adjustable shelves flanked by panelled doors, 81½in (207cm) wide.

£3,500–4,200 CHTR

A Victorian walnut open bookcase, the carved gallery above a quarter-veneered ebony-strung and walnut-crossbanded top, over a frieze drawer and two adjustable shelves, on bun feet, 29in (73.5cm) wide.

£1,400–1,650 CAG

A walnut open bookcase, with gilt-bronze mounts, c1870, 29in (73.5cm) wide.

£3,700–4,400 S(O)

A pair of Regency-style satinwood open bookcases, with brass lion-paw feet, c1890, 23in (58.5cm) wide.

£4,400–4,900 NoC

A pair of Edwardian open bookcases, with a fretwork frieze above three shelves over two panelled doors, on bracket feet, 41¾in (106cm) wide.

£940–1,100 JAd

REVOLVING BOOKCASES

A walnut two-tier revolving bookcase, with a table top, c1870, 35in (89cm) high.

£1,350–1,500 GEO

A walnut revolving bookcase, possibly Gillows, the top inlaid with ebony, sycamore and fruitwood, above a carved frieze drawer, early 20thC, 25½in (65cm) wide.

£1,400–1,650 DN

An Edwardian satinwood revolving bookcase, the upper section decorated with crossbanding and stringing, on a stand with an undertier, 18in (45.5cm) wide.

£640–760 AG

SECRETAIRE BOOKCASES

A George III mahogany secretaire bookcase, with two carved astragal-glazed doors enclosing adjustable shelves, the base with a secretaire and fitted interior above two panelled doors enclosing a shelf, with boxwood stringing, 41in (104cm) wide.

£6,300–7,500 CAG

A George III mahogany secretaire bookcase, the swan-neck cornice with an urn stand, over two astragal-glazed doors enclosing three adjustable shelves, the base with a fitted secretaire drawer, above two doors, on outswept bracket feet, 47¾in (121.5cm) wide.

£6,100–7,300 BAM(M)

A George III mahogany and harewood secretaire bookcase, with two astragal-glazed doors enclosing adjustable shelves, the inlaid fall-front enclosing a fitted interior, above three long graduated drawers, detachable cornice later, handles and feet replaced, 44¾in (113.5cm) wide.

£1,750–2,100 WW

A Regency mahogany secretaire bookcase, with two astragal-glazed doors, over a secretaire drawer and two doors, on paw feet, 48¾in (124cm) wide.

£2,800–3,350 SWO

A mahogany secretaire bookcase, with two glazed doors over a fall-front with a fitted interior, over two doors, America, New York State, c1820, 45in (114.5cm) wide.

£2,900–3,450 JAA

A mahogany secretaire bookcase, with two astragal-glazed doors enclosing three adjustable shelves, above a fitted secretaire drawer and two panelled doors enclosing three sliding trays, c1830, 48½in (123cm) wide.

£2,250–2,700 Hal

A William IV mahogany secretaire bookcase, with two glazed doors flanked by rope-twist columns, above a secretaire drawer and two panelled doors, 48in (122cm) wide.

£1,650–1,950 DN(HAM)

A mahogany secretaire bookcase, c1880, 49in (124.5cm) wide.

£1,650–1,850 TRED

A Victorian mahogany secretaire bookcase, with two glazed doors flanked by columns, the base with a cushion drawer, fitted secretaire drawer and two graduated drawers, 51½in (131cm) wide.

£1,250–1,500 SWO

BUREAUX

◄ **A Queen Anne figured walnut and featherbanded bureau,** the fall-front enclosing a fitted interior and well, over two short and two long drawers, on bracket feet, 36¼in (92cm) high.

£1,350–1,600 SWO

A walnut bureau, with a fitted interior, on bun feet, 18thC, 35in (89cm) wide.

£6,100–6,800 AGI

A walnut and jacaranda-veneered bureau, with gilt-brass mounts, the fall-front enclosing a fitted interior, above three drawers, Sweden, Stockholm, c1750, 17in (43cm) wide.

£4,250–5,100 BUK

A Chippendale-style figured maple bureau, the fall-front over four graduated drawers, America, Massachusetts, c1780, 36in (91.5cm) wide.

£3,250–3,900 S(NY)

Ex-Estate of Laurance S. Rockefeller. Laurance S. Rockefeller, the grandson of the oil magnate John D. Rockefeller, was a pioneering venture capitalist, a dedicated conservationist and a visionary philanthropist. The sale of property from his estate included objects from his Fifth Avenue apartment, his Rockefeller Center office and his residences in Pocantico Hills, New York, Vermont and Wyoming, realizing a total of approximately £4,348,000.

A Chippendale-style cherrywood bureau, the fall-front enclosing a fitted interior, above four graduated cockbeaded drawers, America, late 18thC, 39in (99cm) wide.

£2,550–3,000 SK(B)

A Louis XV-style kingwood ***bureau de dame*****,** with chased gilt-bronze mounts and floral marquetry, on cabriole legs, France, 19thC, 29¼in (74.5cm) wide.

£1,050–1,250 LAY

A mahogany cylinder bureau, with a fitted interior, c1860, 48in (122cm) wide.

£900–1,000 HEM

One of the most dramatic falls from grace in this age of minimalism is the poor old bureau. A few years ago, it seemed that almost any half-decent George III example would command in excess of £1,000 at auction, whereas now it is not unusual to find them languishing in country sale catalogues at half that amount. Of course, while the received wisdom is that they are no longer popular because you cannot put a computer on a bureau, it is hard to believe that their day is really over, not least of all because they are such a boon to the sloppy manager of household correspondence and bills – all you need do is force the flap shut and lock it to complete six month's filing in one easy action, transforming your home from squalid pit to designer heaven in the process. For the lover of good Georgian furniture the bureau has to be a real bargain at the moment.

A rosewood bureau, with ivory inlay, the cylinder enclosing a fitted interior and pull-out writing surface, above a drawer, with trade plate 'H. Mawer and Stephenson, Fulham Road, South Kensington', late 19thC, 31in (78.5cm) wide.

£1,000–1,200 E

CABINETS

A walnut serpentine cabinet, with ormolu mounts, crossbanded, with floral marquetry, lattice- and strapwork-inlaid decoration, France, 19thC, 40½in (103cm) wide.

£2,100–2,500 CHTR

A walnut and ebonized cabinet, the two doors with applied ebonized panels, the base with two drawers, on toupie feet, Portugal, mid-19thC, 50in (127cm) wide.

£2,150–2,550 NOA

An inlaid mahogany cabinet, by Maple & Co, with flame mahogany panels, c1910, 82in (208.5cm) high.

£3,800–4,250 GEO

BEDSIDE CABINETS

A mahogany tray-top bedside cabinet, c1780, 21in (53.5cm) wide.

£1,300–1,450 PWA

A mahogany-veneered bedside cabinet, with a *faux* marble top and brass fittings, altered, Sweden, c1800, 18½in 47cm) wide.

£1,750–2,100 BUK(F)

A mahogany tray-top bedside cabinet, c1810, 19in (48.5cm) wide.

£1,350–1,500 MALT

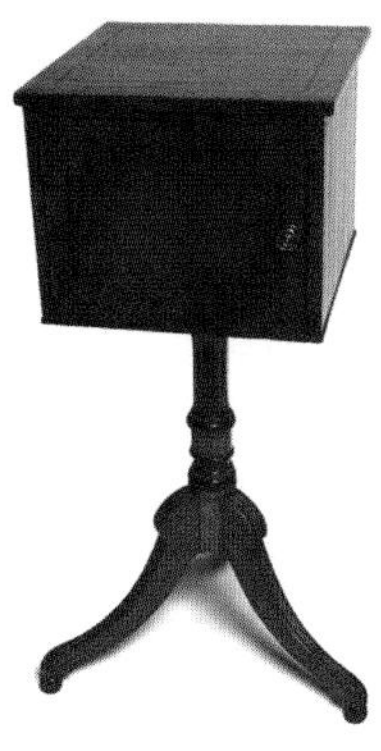

A mahogany bedside cabinet, with ebony inlay, on a pedestal and tripod base, Scotland, c1815, 12in (30.5cm) wide.

£1,050–1,200 CSM

A Victorian pollarded oak bedside cabinet, 31in (78.5cm) wide.

£310–350 MCB

A pair of mahogany fluted clyindrical bedside cabinets, 1850–1900, 30in (76cm) high.

£1,400–1,600 ⊞ GEO

A pair of mahogany bedside cabinets, each with a marble top, c1880, 16in (40.5cm) wide.

£610–680 ⊞ OCA

A satinwood and crossbanded bedside cabinet, late 19thC, 33in (84cm) high.

£340–380 ⊞ BURA

A pair of walnut bedside cabinets, each with a marble top above a drawer, over a cupboard, France, c1890, 20½in (52cm) high.

£810–900 ⊞ PSA

A pair of Henri II-style walnut bedside cabinets, each with a marble top and brass fittings, France, c1900, 16½in (42cm) wide.

£810–900 ⊞ SWA

An Edwardian mahogany bedside cabinet, by Gill & Reigate, London, 17in (43cm) wide.

£175–195 ⊞ PWA

An Edwardian mahogany bedside cabinet, with neo-classical marquetry and a satinwood-crossbanded border, 20in (51cm) wide.

£90–105 ⚒ GTH

A flame mahogany bedside cabinet, with a panelled door, c1910, 17in (43cm) wide.

£300–330 ⊞ HEM

BUREAU CABINETS

A George I walnut and burr-walnut bureau cabinet, with crossbanding and feather banding, the two bevelled mirror doors enclosing shelves, above candle slides, the fall-front enclosing a fitted interior with a secret compartment, brass fittings replaced, 40½in (103cm) wide.

£5,400–6,500 WW

A George I walnut bureau cabinet, the two bevelled mirror doors enclosing adjustable shelves, mirrors replaced, restored, 43¼in (110cm) wide.

£3,350–4,000 S(O)

A walnut-veneered bureau cabinet, the upper section with two mirror doors, above two candle slides, brass mounts replaced, restored, Sweden, Stockholm, c1775, 40½in (103cm) wide.

£13,700–16,400 BUK

◄ **A George III mahogany bureau cabinet,** the two panelled doors enclosing a fitted interior, above two candle slides, the fall-front enclosing a fitted interior, above four long graduated drawers, on bracket feet, 39in (99cm) wide.

£3,750–4,500 AG

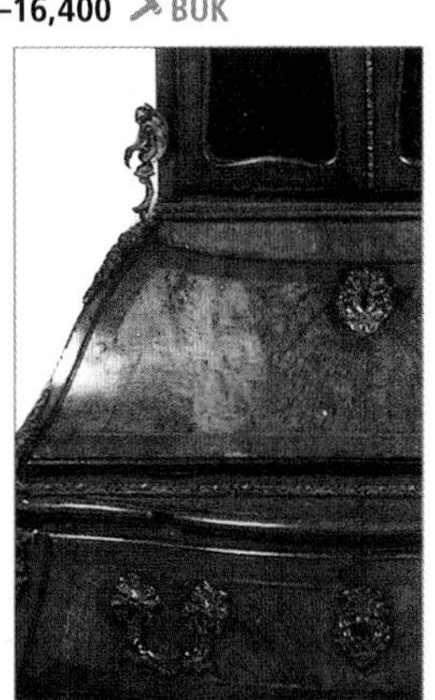

A walnut bureau cabinet, with ormolu mounts, Italy, 18thC and later, 40in (101.5cm) wide.

£4,700–5,600 HYD

CABINETS-ON-CHESTS

A walnut cabinet-on-chest, with a cushion frieze drawer above two doors enclosing a fitted interior, the base with four drawers, c1710, 40¼in (102cm) wide.

£4,200–5,000 S(O)

A mahogany collector's cabinet-on-chest, with later gallery, c1790, 20in (51cm) wide.

£14,400–16,000 HA

A rosewood and marquetry cabinet-on-chest, the two doors enclosing shelves and drawers, over a bowfronted chest of four long graduated drawers, some inlay later, damaged, Holland, c1800, 44in (112cm) wide.

£3,650–4,350 Hal

CORNER CABINETS

A walnut corner cabinet, the glazed door enclosing three shelves, the base with a panelled door enclosing a shelf, America, 18thC, 44½in (113cm) wide.

£1,850–2,200 JDJ

A Sheraton-style mahogany hanging corner cabinet, with boxwood inlay, Scotland, c1810, 30in (76cm) wide.

£630–700 CSM

A mahogany bowfronted hanging corner cabinet, with brass mounts, the two panelled doors enclosing two shelves, c1820, 23¼in (59cm) wide.

£1,450–1,650 JC

◄ **A Louis XV-style kingwood corner cabinet,** in the manner of François Linke, with ormolu mounts, with a glazed door above a drawer and two cupboard doors, 19thC, 31in (78.5cm) wide.

£8,200–9,800 G(L)

The Parisian cabinet-maker François Linke, who worked between 1882 and 1935, was one of the major producers of luxury furniture in the Belle Epoque style. At the International Exhibition of 1900 in Paris, he exhibited a lavish display of furniture in the Louis XV style with overtones of Art Nouveau, using the finest mounts applied to simple carcasses quarter-veneered in kingwood or tulipwood.

From the meticulous records he kept, one can see the enormous number of hours he put into each piece of furniture.

A mahogany corner cabinet, with ormolu mounts, the marble top above a drawer, over two doors, France, early 19thC, 33in (84cm) wide.

£1,500–1,800 NOA

A lacquered hanging corner cabinet, the two bowfronted doors decorated with flowers, birds and Oriental figures, Holland, 19thC, 24in (61cm) wide.

£490–580 HYD

A Victorian mahogany corner cabinet, with two glazed doors and two foliate-moulded doors, 40in (101.5cm) wide.

£420–500 PF

An Edwardian mahogany standing corner cabinet, with stringing and crossbanded inlay, the astragal-glazed door above a panelled door inlaid with a marquetry roundel, on bracket feet, 28in (71cm) wide.

£590–700 AH

An Edwardian inlaid mahogany corner cabinet, the astragal-glazed door above a cupboard door, 27½in (70cm) wide.

£290–340 AMB

DISPLAY CABINETS

A Biedermeier cherry-veneered display cabinet, Germany, c1830, 52½in (133.5cm) wide.

£1,850–2,200 DORO

A bone-inlaid and part-ebonized vitrine, the frieze inlaid with plaques of putti, the stiles carved with beasts, the case inlaid with scrolling foliage, with two glazed doors, Italy, 19thC, 44in (112cm) wide.

£760–910 SK

A kingwood display cabinet, with ormolu mounts, the marble top above two glazed doors, on splayed feet, France, 1850, 40in (101.5cm) wide.

£2,150–2,550 NOA

A mahogany and ebony-veneered display cabinet, with brass mounts and a mirror back, Russia, 1880–90, 33½in (85cm) wide.

£2,350–2,800 BUK(F)

An Empire-style mahogany vitrine, with gilt-bronze mounts, France, c1890, 39½in (100.5cm) wide.

£3,000–3,600 S(O)

An Edwardian mahogany and parquetry-inlaid display cabinet, the central astragal-glazed door enclosing glass shelves, the base with an inlaid door, 54in (137cm) wide.

£1,300–1,550 WW

An Edwardian mahogany bowfronted display cabinet, with boxwood inlay, the leaded light door above an undertier, 22in (56cm) wide.

£900–1,000 SWA

A Sheraton-style mahogany corner display cabinet, the glazed door enclosing glass shelves, c1910, 73in (185.5cm) high.

£2,600–2,900 YOX

A mahogany display cabinet, early 20thC, 58in (147.5cm) high.

£610–680 MTay

HANGING CABINETS

A mahogany and marquetry hanging cabinet, the astragal-glazed door enclosing a mirror back, Holland, c1800, 35in (89cm) wide.

£640–760 SWO

An Edwardian satinwood hanging cabinet, the two astragal-glazed doors enclosing two shelves, 28¾in (73cm) wide.

£800–960 WW

A rosewood and satinwood hanging cabinet, c1915, 18in (45.5cm)wide.

£270–300 OCA

MUSIC CABINETS

A George III mahogany two-tier music cabinet, the interior with two adjustable shelves, 25in (63.5cm) wide.

£1,950–2,350 CAG

A Victorian rosewood music cabinet, with a mirror above a glazed door enclosing shelves, 21½in (54.5cm) wide.

£110–130 G(B)

A Victorian inlaid rosewood music cabinet, with a part-glazed door, c1890, 53in (134.5cm) high.

£1,150–1,300 WAA

An ebonized music cabinet, the upper section with a pierced brass gallery above a glazed door enclosing shelves, the lower section with a cupboard door, c1900, 52in (132cm) high.

£300–340 MCB

An Edwardian mahogany music cabinet, the tambour front enclosing 88 pianola music rolls, 54in (137cm) high.

£140–165 GTH

An Edwardian rosewood music cabinet, with inlaid decoration, the pierced three-quarter gallery above a mirror, the glazed drop cupboard door above a pull-out cupboard, 18¼in (46.5cm) wide.

£470–560 SWO

The Shipping Company

- Worldwide Air & Sea Freight
- UK & European Transport
- Full & Part Container Shipments
- Specialist Packing for Export & Hand Carriage
- Casemaking & Storage

Nobody does it better

Bourton Industrial Park, Bourton-on-the-Water
Cheltenham, Gloucestershire GL54 2HQ
Tel: +44 (0)1451 822451 Fax: +44 (0)1451 810985
www.theshippingcompanyltd.com

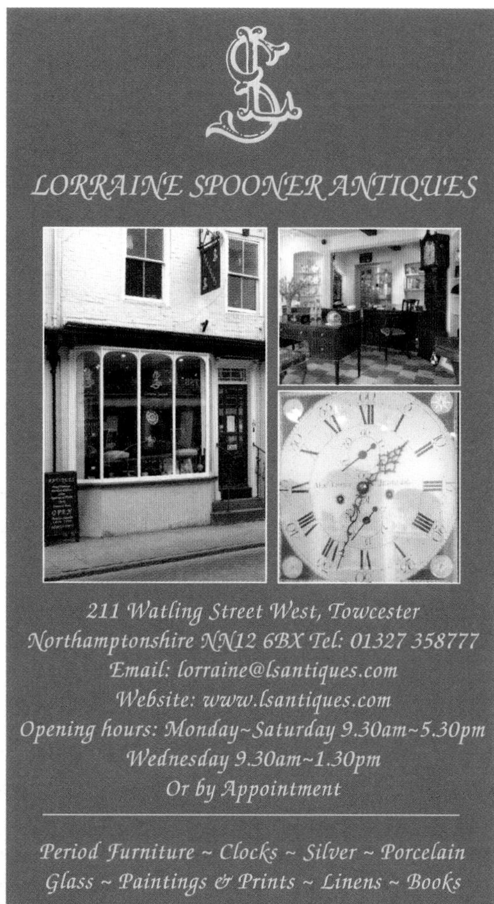

LORRAINE SPOONER ANTIQUES
211 Watling Street West, Towcester
Northamptonshire NN12 6BX Tel: 01327 358777
Email: lorraine@lsantiques.com
Website: www.lsantiques.com
Opening hours: Monday~Saturday 9.30am~5.30pm
Wednesday 9.30am~1.30pm
Or by Appointment
Period Furniture ~ Clocks ~ Silver ~ Porcelain
Glass ~ Paintings & Prints ~ Linens ~ Books

Pugh's Antiques

Pugh's Farm, Monkton
Nr. Honiton, Devon EX14 9QH
3 miles north of Honiton on A30
Tel: 01404 42860 Fax: 01404 47792
Email: sales@pughsantiques.com
Internet: www.pughsantiques.com

There are six barns of furniture (6,000 sq. feet) Edwardian to Victorian. Furniture imported fortnightly from France = Louis XV - country - French - armoires - dressers, etc. Speciality antique beds

OPEN MONDAY-SATURDAY

RELOCATING TO:
Portley House, Old Ludlow Road
Leominster H36 0AA
Tel: 01568 616646

PIER CABINETS

A pair of brass-inlaid and ebonized pier cabinets, with ormolu mounts, the marble tops above panelled doors depicting mythological scenes, France, mid-19thC, 29in (73.5cm) high.

£2,900–3,450 G(L)

A walnut and marquetry pier cabinet, with ormolu mounts, c1870, 40in (101.5cm) high.

£1,950–2,200 NoC

A pair of walnut pier cabinets, with ormolu mounts, c1880, 43in (109cm) high.

£1,600–1,800 MCB

SECRETAIRE CABINETS

A walnut secretaire cabinet, the fall-front enclosing a fitted interior, on later bracket feet, losses and later veneer, c1700, 37¼in (94.5cm) wide.

£1,800–2,150 DN(BR)

A George III mahogany and marquetry-inlaid secretaire cabinet, the fall-front enclosing a fitted interior, above two panelled doors enclosing three fitted trays, later inlay to doors, 46½in (118cm) wide.

£1,350–1,600 DN(BR)

Suffering from the same problem as the bureau, the secretaire cabinet is just not easily compatible with the computer, but what a waste it would be if this piece of furniture ended up in the doldrums with its cousin. Good walnut examples from the first half of the 18th century can be wonderful practical pieces of furniture offering a substantial writing surface and a lot of drawer space. When the flap is closed you have the benefit of good colour, banding and inlaid work and, when it is lowered, an intricate interior of drawers, cupboards and secret compartments is revealed. Once again, like the bureau, it is hard to believe that they will remain unfashionable for long.

A kingwood, tulipwood and marquetry secretaire cabinet, the marble top above a fall-front and two drawers, on inlaid and tapered legs, France, late 18thC, 31in (78.5cm) wide.

£2,000–2,400 NOA

A brass-mounted mahogany secretaire cabinet, the marble top above a door enclosing a fitted interior, above two doors enclosing a document box, France, 19thC, 29in (73.5cm) wide.

£1,500–1,800 NOA

A mahogany and marquetry secretaire cabinet, Holland, c1840, 39in (99cm) wide.

£3,050–3,400 MTay

SIDE CABINETS

A painted wood side cabinet, decorated with motifs in the manner of Jean Berain, after the Antique, Italy, early 18thC, 39¾in (101cm) wide.

£9,000–10,800 S

Jean Berain worked as French court designer from 1674 and was one of the originators of the Louis XIV style. His published symmetrical designs influenced ornamentation on contemporary furniture, carpets and silverware.

A mahogany side cabinet, with two drawers above two panelled doors, c1790, 45in (114.5cm) wide.

£1,100–1,300 S(O)

A mahogany breakfront side cabinet, with nine drawers, c1800, 65in (165cm) wide.

£9,000–10,800 S

A mahogany and marquetry side cabinet, the frieze drawer above two tambour shutters, Holland, late 18thC, 29in (73.5cm) wide.

£610–730 GTH

Side cabinets first appeared in the 18th century and usually consisted simply of shelves and drawers, with few decorative features. Later, the lower part was often enclosed by cupboard doors, and by the late 18th century good-quality examples featured silk-lined doors that were often protected by a brass grille. The golden age of the side cabinet was the 19th century, when increased prosperity led to a need for furniture for both storage and display. Of particular influence was the French chiffonier – a small shallow cabinet with an open shelf or shelves above, and sometimes a drawer, and the Italian credenza – a long low cabinet with shelves at either end.

A Regency mahogany chiffonier, with two drawers above two cupboard doors flanked by spiral-reeded pilasters, with ebony stringing, on ring-turned feet, 36in (91.5cm) wide.

£3,100–3,450 LGr

◄ **An early Victorian mahogany chiffonier,** 43in (109cm) wide.

£810–900 OCA

► **A rococo revival rosewood side cabinet,** attributed to John Henry Belter, the marble top above four glazed doors enclosing adjustable shelves, with carved decoration, America, New York, mid-19thC, 66¼in (168.5cm) wide.

£3,300–3,950 GTH

A Victorian walnut side cabinet, with gilt-metal mounts, the central mirrored door flanked by two glazed doors, 80in (203cm) wide.

£1,650–1,950 HYD

A Victorian walnut side cabinet, the central inlaid door flanked by two glazed doors enclosing shelves, 59¼in (150.5cm) wide.

£1,800–2,150 TRM(D)

A Victorian walnut and crossband side cabinet, with gilt-metal mounts, the central mirrored door flanked by two glazed doors, 72in (183cm) wide.

£2,350–2,800 AH

A Victorian ebonized side cabinet, with brass and tortoiseshell boulle decoration and gilt-metal mounts, c1870, 83in (211cm) wide.

£2,150–2,550 S(O)

A Victorian walnut side cabinet, the three open shelves with pierced galleries, above three glazed doors enclosing a shelf, 49in (124.5cm) wide.

£520–620 WW

A mid-Victorian burr-walnut side cabinet, the mirrored recess above a panelled door, decorated with satinwood stringing, Sèvres plaques and ormolu mounts, 23¾in (60.5cm) wide.

£680–810 SPF

A late Victorian mahogany side cabinet, the central cupboard flanked by mirrored panels and galleried shelves, above two doors carved with vases of flowers, 34½in (87.5cm) wide.

£260–310 FHF

◄ **A Louis XVI-style mahogany side cabinet,** the marble top above four drawers and panelled doors, late 19thC, 69¾in (177cm) wide.

£1,150–1,350 NOA

CABINETS-ON-STANDS

A japanned cabinet-on-stand, the two doors decorated with chinoiserie figures and enclosing an arrangement of drawers, the later silvered wood stand carved with putti and seraphims, decoration restored, Low Countries, 17thC, 43in (109cm) wide.

£10,800–12,900 S

A rosewood cabinet-on-stand, the hinged cover above two panelled doors enclosing 12 drawers and three secret drawers, decorated with ivory and tortoiseshell veneers carved with foliage, on a later ebonized stand, south Europe, probably Portugal, 17thC, 22in (56cm) wide.

£23,500–28,200 E

◀ **An ivory-inlaid, tortoiseshell and marquetry cabinet-on-stand,** with 12 drawers and two cupboard doors opening to reveal nine drawers, decorated with birds and stylized flowers, on a later ebonized stand with a frieze drawer panelled to simulate three drawers, on spiral-turned legs with bun feet, restored, Spain, 1650–1700, 43¾in (111cm) wide.

£9,000–10,800 S

▶ **A William and Mary laburnum oyster-veneered and marquetry cabinet-on-stand,** with satinwood crossbanding, the two doors with inlaid satinwood panels enclosing a cupboard and an arrangement of 12 drawers, the stand with two frieze drawers, altered and restored, 40¼in (102cm) wide.

£3,200–3,800 RTo

TABLE CABINETS

A mahogany table cabinet, with brass handles, c1800, 19in (48.5cm) wide.

£4,300–4,800 SPUR

A Victorian mahogany collector's table cabinet, with a central glazed door flanked by two glazed doors enclosing 26 drawers, 32¼in (82cm) wide.

£490–590 SWO

A Victorian mother-of-pearl and papier-mâché table cabinet, the hinged cover with a painted and inlaid castle scene, enclosing a fitted interior, above two doors enclosing two long and four short drawers, 8¼in (21cm) high.

£470–560 MA&I

CANTERBURIES

A mahogany canterbury, c1800, 20in (51cm) wide.
£2,450–2,750 GEO

A Regency mahogany canterbury, with a drawer, 18in (45.5cm) wide.
£1,750–2,100 JNic

A Regency mahogany canterbury, with a drawer, 20in (51cm) wide.
£1,750–1,950 WAA

A mahogany canterbury, with a drawer, c1825, 35¾in (91cm) wide.
£3,000–3,600 S(O)

A simulated rosewood canterbury, with a drawer, c1845, 23in (58cm) wide.
£540–640 Hal

A rococo revival simulated rosewood canterbury, with a serpentine drawer, stencilled label 'Mitchell and Rammelsburg Furniture Co, Cininnati, Oî,' America, 1850–75, 27½in (70cm) wide.
£510–610 NOA

◀ A Victorian walnut canterbury, with a drawer, 20½in (52cm) wide.
£580–650 PSA

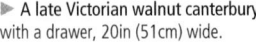

▶ A late Victorian walnut canterbury, with a drawer, 20in (51cm) wide.
£830–930 PFS

A walnut whatnot canterbury, c1860, 25in (63.5cm) wide.
£1,550–1,750 TRED

LOCATE THE SOURCE
The source of each illustration in Miller's can be found by checking the code letters below each caption with the Key to Illustrations, pages 746–753.

OPEN ARMCHAIRS

A carved walnut open armchair, late 17thC.
£2,050–2,300 APO

A George II walnut open armchair, the back carved with shells and leaves above shepherd's crook arms and an embroidered seat, on claw-and-ball feet, possibly Ireland.
£2,350–2,800 NSF

A George III mahogany open armchair, c1775.
£1,350–1,500 GGD

A pair of rococo painted wood armchairs, restored, Swedish, 1750–1800.
£3,300–3,950 BUK

A beech open armchair, with silk upholstery, c1780.
£1,050–1,200 ChS

◀ **A mahogany open armchair,** on sabre legs, Scotland, c1810.
£760–850 CSM

▶ **A pair of mahogany and parcel-gilt open armchairs,** upholstered in 'Portrait Gallery' fabric designed by Gianni Versace, Italy, c1810.
£13,000–15,600 S(NY)

Ex-Gianni Versace collection.

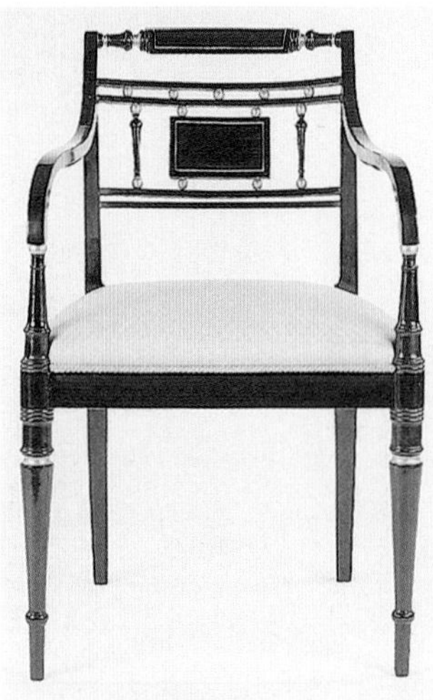

An ebonized and gilt open armchair, c1820.
£1,050–1,200 ChS

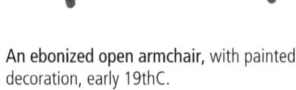

An ebonized open armchair, with painted decoration, early 19thC.
£230–270 PICA

A pair of mahogany library open armchairs, c1825.
£6,700–7,500 SPUR

A cherrywood open armchair, France, c1830.
£540–600 PFS

A carved mahogany *fauteuil*, France, c1850.
£350–390 MCB

A pair of Louis XV-style carved giltwood open armchairs, on cabriole legs with scroll feet, mid-19thC.
£1,200–1,400 G(L)

A pair of carved walnut open armchairs, with tapestry upholstery, France, 19thC.
£2,250–2,500 CGA

A Victorian walnut open armchair, with leaf-carved knees and cabriole legs.
£470–560 HYD

A rococo revival laminated rosewood open armchair, attributed to J. & J. W. Meeks, New York, America, 1850–75.

£1,900–2,250 NOA

A mahogany library open armchair, with leather upholstery, c1860.

£810–900 OCA

A Victorian carved walnut open armchair, reupholstered.

£1,300–1,450 LGr

A brass-inlaid rosewood open armchair, c1880.

£1,250–1,400 GGD

A carved mahogany open armchair, with matching footstool, c1890.

£260–290 HEM

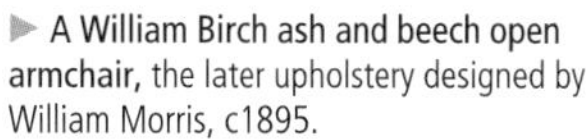

► **A William Birch ash and beech open armchair,** the later upholstery designed by William Morris, c1895.

£1,450–1,650 JuA

For more Arts & Crafts furniture, please see the Decorative Arts section on pages 367–440.

A Sheraton revival inlaid mahogany armchair, c1900.

£540–600 GEO

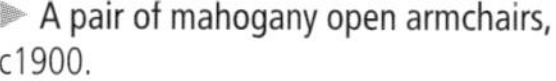

► **A pair of mahogany open armchairs,** c1900.

£450–500 SWA

A pair of mahogany and gilt open armchairs, Sweden, c1920.

£1,050–1,200 PI

UPHOLSTERED ARMCHAIRS

A pair of rococo-style carved and stained beechwood **armchairs,** with arched serpentine rails, on carved cabriole legs with cloven-hoof feet, Italy, early 18thC.

£1,900–2,250 NOA

Further reading

Miller's Buying Affordable Antiques Price Guide 2006, Miller's Publications, 2006

A Chippendale-style mahogany armchair, upholstery stripped, America, probably New York, 18thC.

£5,600–6,700 JDJ

Dealers are always keen to acquire pieces that can be restored to their own standards.

A mahogany armchair, America, late 18thC and later.

£280–330 NOA

A carved mahogany armchair, c1820.

£1,400–1,650 PBA

A mahogany armchair, c1835.

£2,150–2,550 S(O)

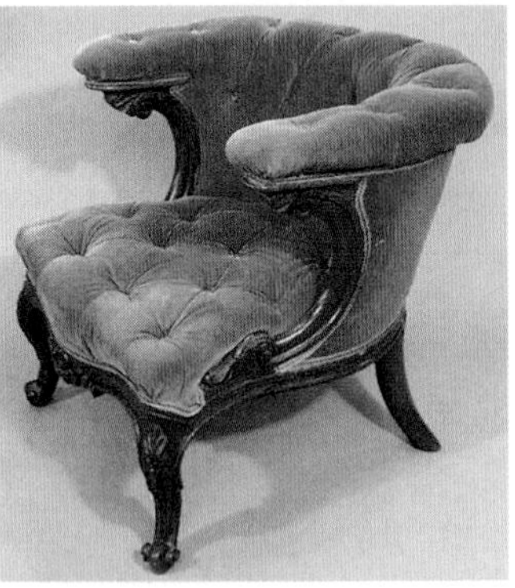

An early Victorian carved rosewood tub armchair, on scrolled legs.

£230–270 WilP

▶ **A pair of Victorian mahogany spoon-back armchairs,** with buttoned leather upholstery.

£1,300–1,550 BeFA

A mahogany wing armchair, by Howard & Sons, c1900.

£1,450–1,650 AGI

The fact that this chair is by Howard & Sons would enhance its value. Howard & Sons were throne makers and manufacturers of high-quality, deep-seated armchairs. The casters are usually stamped.

An Edwardian mahogany armchair, on sabre legs.

£240–280 SWO

▶ **A Knoll Associates Womb 70 chair and Ottoman 74,** designed by Eero Saarinen, with tubular steel frames, reupholstered, America, 1945–48.

£650–780 JDJ

For more 20thC furniture, please see the Twentieth-Century Design section on pages 441–470.

BERGERES

A painted beechwood bergère, on leaf-carved tapered legs, late 18thC.
£560–670 DN(HAM)

A mahogany bergère, on turned and reeded front legs, c1825.
£2,550–2,850 JC

A Regency-style mahogany and cane bergère, c1900.
£1,050–1,250 MTay

CHILDREN'S CHAIRS

A Louis XV-style child's beechwood chair, on cabriole legs, 19thC.
£125–150 SK

A child's mahogany bergère, c1870.
£630–700 GEO

A child's ebonized chair, with a rush seat, c1880.
£175–195 PENH

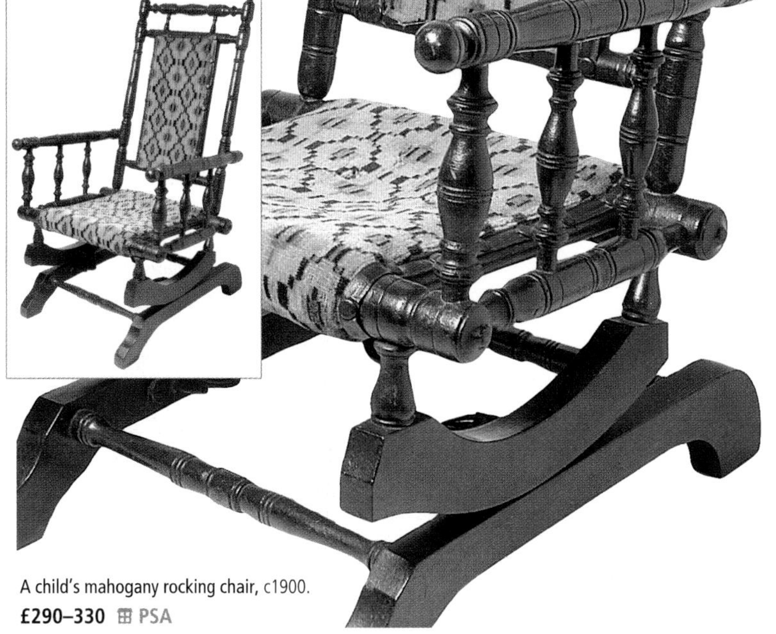

A child's mahogany rocking chair, c1900.
£290–330 PSA

A child's bentwood correction chair, c1910.
£240–270 PICA

CORNER CHAIRS

A mahogany corner chair, Ireland, c1740.

£1,150–1,350 HOK

A George III carved mahogany corner chair, with a cabriole front leg.

£2,150–2,550 S(O)

A pair of George III mahogany corner chairs, with cabriole front legs and turned rear legs.

£2,900–3,450 MAL(O)

An Edwardian mahogany corner chair, with inlaid decoration.

£420–490 PFS

DESK CHAIRS

A mahogany desk chair, with a leather back, on turned and fluted legs, c1870.

£430–480 TRED

An Edwardian inlaid mahogany revolving desk chair.

£300–360 SWO

An oak desk chair, with a swivel and tilt mechanism, c1920.

£490–550 QA

DINING CHAIRS

A set of six George II mahogany dining chairs, with pierced splats and stuff-over seats, on cabriole legs with pad feet.

£6,600–7,900 SWO

A set of four mahogany dining chairs, with pierced splats and reupholstered drop-in seats, c1760.

£2,450–2,750 LGr

A set of ten dining chairs, including two carvers, carvers restored, America, 1790–1800.

£10,200–12,200 SK(B)

◀ **A set of six mahogany dining chairs,** on square tapered legs, c1810.

£590–700 M

A set of eight Regency rosewood dining chairs, with brass inlay and caned seats, with cushions, on sabre legs.

£3,500–4,200 G(L)

◀ **A set of eight Regency mahogany dining chairs,** including two carvers, with ebony-strung decoration and tapestry upholstery, on sabre legs.

£2,900–3,450 Oli

STYLES OF LEGS

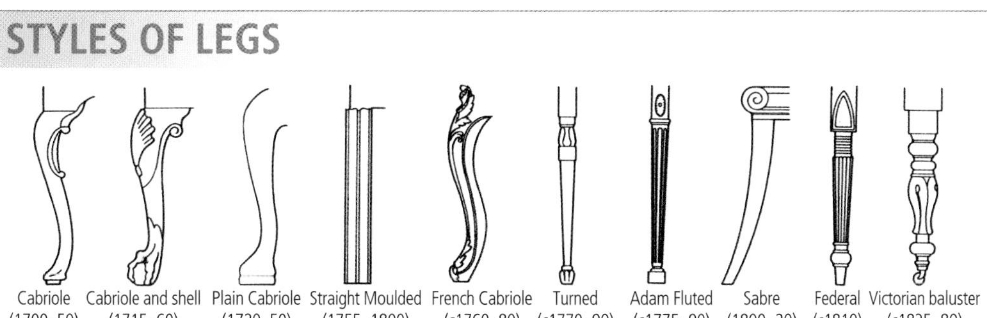

A set of 12 Regency rosewood dining chairs, with brass inlay, on sabre front legs.

£8,500–9,500 GEO

A set of six George IV mahogany dining chairs, with tapestry upholstered drop-in seats, on sabre front legs.

£1,650–1,950 CAG

A set of ten mahogany dining chairs, with leather seats, on turned and reeded front legs, c1825.

£9,900–11,000 NoC

A set of six mahogany dining chairs, on turned front legs, c1830.

£1,800–2,000 NAW

◄ **A set of six mahogany dining chairs,** with drop-in seats, on square tapered legs, 19thC.

£350–420 CGC

A set of six Victorian mahogany dining chairs, with upholstered backs and seats, on turned front legs.

£230–270 CHTR

A set of six Chippendale-style mahogany chairs, on cabriole legs with claw-and-ball feet, c1860.

£5,400–6,000 MALT

A set of six mahogany bar-back dining chairs, c1870.

£1,550–1,750 PFS

► **A set of eight Chippendale-style mahogany dining chairs,** on cabriole legs with claw-and-ball feet, late 19thC.

£5,400–6,000 ChS

A set of 12 Victorian oak dining chairs, with leather upholstery.

£2,850–3,200 HiA

A set of 12 dining chairs will include two carvers, which were placed at each end of a long table. Intended for the heads of the household or more important guests, they were larger and more imposing than the examples without arms.

► **A set of eight Victorian balloon-back mahogany dining chairs,** with leather upholstery, one chair with impressed maker's mark 'T. Wright', on turned and fluted legs.

£2,050–2,450 LAY

A set of four walnut dining chairs, on cabriole legs, c1880.

£1,250–1,400 MALT

A set of eight mahogany dining chairs, with pierced splats and stuff-over seats, c1885.

£1,250–1,500 PF

A set of eight Chippendale-style dining chairs, including two carvers, with pierced splats and drop-in seats, late 19thC.

£1,450–1,700 DN(HAM)

The rise of the kitchen as the main dining area for a large proportion of households has been reflected in a reduction in demand for more formal dining room furniture. True, there is still a call for larger sets of chairs and the longer extending tables, but this leaves some real bargains to be had among the more modest offerings. There is certainly a tendency to reject sets of chairs that are less than robust, so delicate Victorian walnut balloon-back examples on slender cabriole legs are currently very reasonable. They usually come in sets of six, which makes them a double bargain since many buyers only start to become interested when there are no fewer than eight. Sets of four chairs of almost any description (other than the most academic pieces) remain cheap, which leaves an opening for the non-purist to build up a 'matched' or 'harlequin' set of similar but not actually identical examples.

A set of six Hepplewhite-style mahogany dining chairs, with shield backs and stuff-over seats, the legs with carved capitals, late 19thC.

£590–700 ROS

A set of eight Chippendale-style ladder-back dining chairs, including two carvers, c1920.

£4,400–4,900 PWA

HALL CHAIRS

A George II oak hall chair.
£350–390 NoC

A pair of Regency mahogany hall chairs, on turned front legs.
£900–1,000 GGD

A mahogany hall chair, with a fluted back, on sabre legs, c1830.
£400–450 MALT

Hall chairs were introduced into Britain in the late 17th century, possibly influenced by similar chairs known as *sgabelli* that were to be found in the great Italian palaces during the 16th century. They were placed in the entrance halls of large houses and, since they were not intended for comfort but rather for use by tradesmen and messengers who would be wearing outdoor clothing that was likely to be damp and grubby, they were not upholstered and generally lacked arms. The backs often bore the painted coat-of-arms of the owner and sometimes were carved with motifs to emphasize his social status.

◄ **A pair of William IV mahogany hall chairs,** with acanthus-scrolled carving and turned front legs.
£440–520 ROS

A pair of Victorian oak hall chairs, with pierced arched backs and shaped seats, on turned front legs.
£230–270 SWO

A pair of carved mahogany hall chairs, on barley-twist legs, 19thC.
£1,400–1,600 GEO

A carved walnut hall chair, on turned front legs, dated 1892.
£180–200 HEM

A pair of fruitwood hall chairs, the backs painted with an armorial crest, c1900.
£760–850 PICA

NURSING CHAIRS

A Victorian mahogany nursing chair, by Ross & Co, Dublin, Ireland.

£640–760 SWO

► A Victorian walnut nursing chair, with embroidered upholstery, on ring-turned front legs, mid-19thC.

£210–250 Hal

A walnut nursing chair, on cabriole legs, c1860.

£360–400 SWA

A carved walnut nursing chair, on carved cabriole legs, c1870.

£530–590 PFS

A Victorian oak nursing chair, on turned legs.

£450–500 SWA

SIDE CHAIRS

A carved walnut side chair, on cabriole legs, France, c1720.

£2,850–3,200 AUB

A walnut side chair, on cabriole legs, early 18thC.

£880–980 AGI

► A Queen Anne walnut side chair, on cabriole front legs with pad feet, slight damage, America, Boston, 1740–60.

£3,500–4,200 SK(B)

Queen Anne

American furniture termed, for example, 'Queen Anne' does not necessarily date from the actual period of Queen Anne. This is because the latest fashions took about 20 years to cross the Atlantic from Britain to America, but the style is nevertheless of that period.

A set of six rococo-style painted wood side chairs, with gilt decoration, Sweden, 1750–1800.
£4,700–5,600 BUK

◀ A rococo-style carved fruitwood side chair, on carved cabriole legs, Portugal, mid-18thC.
£630–750 SK

A set of four rococo painted side chairs, Italy, Venice, mid-18thC.
£3,550–4,250 S(NY)

A pair of walnut and cane side chairs, 19thC.
£790–880 AGI

A pair of mahogany side chairs, with brass mounts, Russia, c1820.
£2,250–2,650 S(NY)

A pair of walnut and marquetry side chairs, Holland, c1830.
£1,100–1,250 GEO

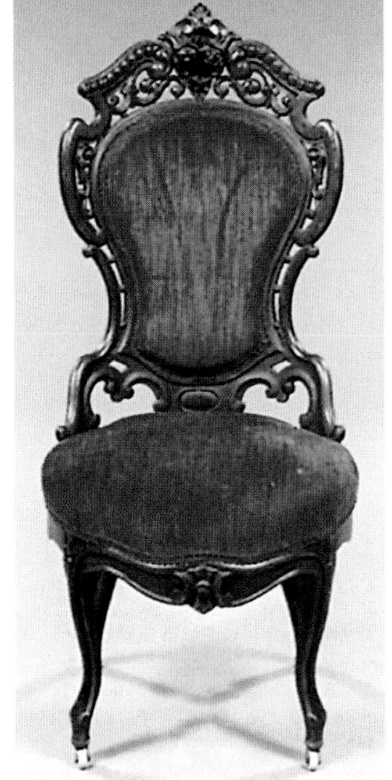

◀ A laminated rosewood side chair, attributed to J. & J. W. Meeks, with floral-carved and pierced crest, America, New York, mid-19thC.
£200–240 NOA

J. & J. W. Meeks of New York (1797–1868) produced fine furniture in the rococo style during the 1850s and early 1860s.

A pair of Napoleon III giltwood side chairs, with lyre-shaped splats, France.
£720–800 ChS

A pair of Louis XIV-style side chairs, with original paint, on reeded legs, c1900.
£380–430 PWA

CHESTS & COFFERS

A walnut coffer-on-stand, with a drawer, France, c1680, 27in (68.5cm) high.

£13,500–15,000 HWK

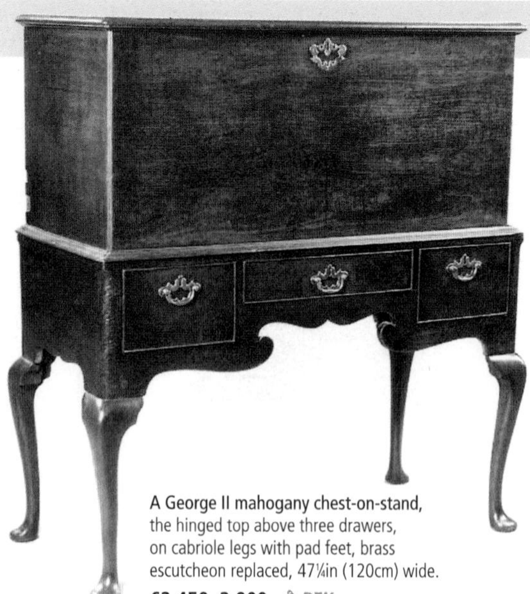

A George II mahogany chest-on-stand, the hinged top above three drawers, on cabriole legs with pad feet, brass escutcheon replaced, 47¼in (120cm) wide.

£2,450–2,900 PFK

A lacquered blanket box, decorated with chinoiserie scenes, with a drawer and carrying handles, c1750, 41¼in (105cm) wide.

£2,000–2,400 BAM(M)

A George III mahogany mule chest, the hinged top above five dummy drawers and four drawers, 70in (178cm) wide.

£1,250–1,500 PBA

A camphorwood chest, with brass stringing, 19thC, 43in (109cm) wide.

£750–900 DN

CHESTS-ON-CHESTS

A mahogany chest-on-chest, the upper section with two short and three long drawers, the base with three long graduated drawers, c1800, 42in (106.5cm) wide.

£1,250–1,400 NORTH

MILLER'S COMPARES

I. A mahogany chest-on-chest, with brass-inlaid decoration, the upper section with three short and three long drawers, the base with four long graduated drawers, Channel Islands, c1820, 36in (91.5cm) wide.

£3,200–3,600 TRED

II. A mahogany chest-on-chest, the upper section with two short and three long graduated drawers, the base with three long graduated drawers, Channel Islands, c1830, 42in (106.5cm) wide.

£1,750–1,950 TRED

Item I is in excellent condition, its quality emphasized by the attractive brass inlay in the cornice. It also retains its original handles. Item II is a lesser piece – it is plainer in design and lacks the canted corners to the upper case and decoratively shaped apron of Item I. Moreover, as often occurred with Channel Islands furniture produced for a lower budget market, the sides of Item II are constructed of grain-painted pine rather than veneered mahogany.

LOCATE THE SOURCE

The source of each illustration in Miller's can be found by checking the code letters below each caption with the Key to Illustrations, pages 746–753.

CHESTS OF DRAWERS & COMMODES

An early Georgian crossbanded and strung walnut batchelor's chest, the fold-over top above four long graduated drawers, the top drawer with pen and ink presentation inscription, 36in (91.5cm) wide.

£26,000–31,000 L&E

Catalogued as 19th century in the George I style, this chest of drawers was initially given a low estimate as it was thought to have had later alterations to an early 18th-century carcass. However, it created a lot of interest and the final selling price indicated that it was thought to be a genuine 18th-century piece.

A Louis XV walnut commode, with three drawers and a shaped apron, on splayed feet, remounted, France, mid-18thC, 48in (122cm) wide.

£4,200–5,000 S(NY)

A rococo painted commode, with three drawers, on cabriole legs, redecorated, Sicily, mid-18thC, 46in (117cm) wide.

£5,200–6,200 S(NY)

A George III mahogany and line-inlaid bowfronted chest of drawers, with three frieze drawers above two short and three long graduated drawers, with bone escutcheons, 43in (109cm) wide.

£560–670 ROS

A walnut chest of drawers, the moulded cornice above an arrangement of five short drawers over four long graduated drawers, 1750–75, America, 41in (104cm) wide.

£1,750–2,100 NOA

An inlaid mahogany serpentine chest of drawers, the four long graduated drawers decorated with stringing, top restored, slight damage, America, Massachusetts, c1780, 36in (91.5cm) wide.

£15,300–18,300 SK(B)

The price of this chest reflects the fact that it is a fine quality piece that has retained its original brasswork. It is also quite rare in that it was made in America – much 18th-century furniture was made in England.

A George III mahogany serpentine chest of drawers, with four long graduated drawers, slight damage, 46½in (118cm) wide.

£1,650–1,950 MCA

A fruitwood commode, the crossbanded quarter-veneered top inlaid with foliate roundels, Malta, c1780, 38½in (98cm) wide.

£3,750–4,500 BAM(M)

A jacaranda, rosewood, amaranth and birch chest of drawers, with a limestone top, Sweden, c1780, 44in (112cm) wide.

£6,800–8,150 BUK

A mahogany bowfronted chest of drawers, with four graduated drawers, America, c1790, 42in (106.5cm) wide.

£2,600–3,100 S(NY)

Ex-Estate of Laurance S. Rockefeller.

An inlaid maple chest of drawers, with four graduated drawers, America, New York, c1800, 39in (99cm) wide.

£4,600–5,500 S(NY)

Ex-Estate of Laurance S. Rockefeller.

A Regency mahogany and boxwood-strung bowfronted chest of drawers, with two short drawers and three long drawers, 43in (109cm) wide.

£810–900 MCB

A cherrywood chest of drawers, inlaid with mahogany veneer, the four long graduated drawers flanked by ring-turned reeded posts, America, probably Massachusetts, 1815–20, 45in (114.5cm) wide.

£1,450–1,700 SK(B)

DECORATION TECHNIQUES

Decoration on furniture became more sophisticated from the 16th century and the best pieces are a testament of the master craftsman's art. Shown below are some commonly found decorative techniques:

Oyster veneering
So-called because the grain resembles an oyster shell, this type of veneering was executed by slicing the veneer transversely across the end grain of smaller branches. The most frequently used woods were walnut, kingwood, laburnum and olivewood.

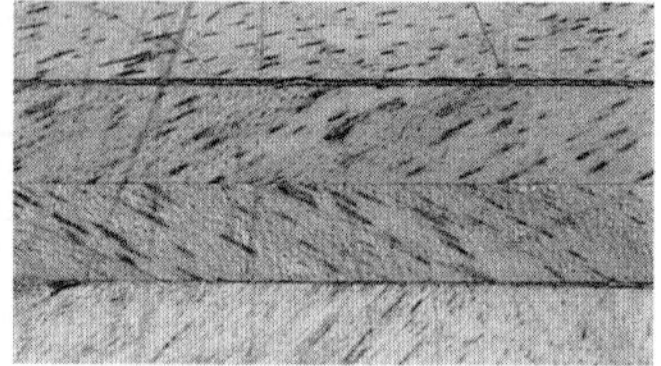

Herringbone veneering
A refinement of the technique of crossbanding, herringbone veneering is characterized by the use of two strips of opposing straight-grained veneer cut on a diagonal and laid side by side. The strips are usually cut from the same piece of timber, and present a mirror image.

Crossbanding and stringing
The technique of framing edges on both solid and veneered furniture. Matching timber was initially used; later, contrasting and more exotic banding veneers were employed, often laid with the grain at right angles to the principal veneer or timber, a technique known as crossbanding. In stringing and chequerbanding, the banding is framed with metal or wooden 'strings' or thin strips.

Marquetry
This is veneer composed of numerous woods, often further enriched by the use of staining, colouring and engraving, applied to a plain surface to create a pictorial mosaic.

Inlay
While marquetry is always applied as a veneer, inlay is formed from materials cut into solid ground wood. Inlays were originally of bone or ivory. Later, hardstones (*pietre dure*), fruitwoods, exotic timbers, pewter and brass were used.

Parquetry
This employs geometric designs, as opposed to the figurative or foliate motifs of marquetry. The most popular form of parquetry are the cube, lozenge, trellis and dot trellis.

A Biedermeier ebony-inlaid maple chest of drawers, with three long graduated drawers, c1820, 32in (81.5cm) wide.

£700–840 SK

A mahogany chest of drawers, with one overhanging drawer above three long drawers flanked by turned columns, America, c1820, 46in (117cm) wide.

£280–330 JAA

A cherrywood chest of drawers, with two short and three long drawers, America, probably Kentucky, 1820, 41½in (105.5cm) wide.

£2,850–3,400 SK(B)

A walnut commode, the marble top above a frieze drawer and three long drawers, with a concealed apron drawer, on block feet, France, early 19thC, 50¼in (127.5cm) wide.

£1,400–1,650 NOA

A walnut commode, the banded and quarter-veneered top above two frieze drawers and two long drawers, Italy, early 19thC, 45in (114.5cm) wide.

£1,050–1,250 NOA

◀ **A karelian birch veneer commode,** with four drawers, Russia, 1820s–30s, 35½in (90cm) wide.

£2,150–2,550 BUK(F)

An early Victorian mahogany bowfronted chest of drawers, with two short and three long drawers, 46in (117cm) wide.

£710–790 WiB

A Sheraton-style mahogany bowfronted chest of drawers, the top with two recessed drawers, above four long drawers flanked by turned columns, America, early 19thC, 39½in (100.5cm) wide.

£1,000–1,200 NOA

A mahogany and line-inlaid bowfronted chest of drawers, c1830, 52in (132cm) wide.

£1,650–1,850 MTay

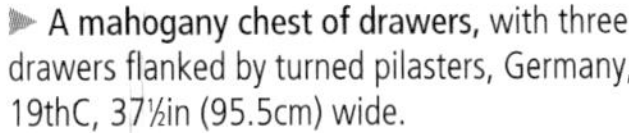

▶ **A mahogany chest of drawers,** with three drawers flanked by turned pilasters, Germany, 19thC, 37½in (95.5cm) wide.

£470–560 DN

A mahogany dressing chest, with carved side posts, on claw feet, America, c1840, 45in (114.5cm) wide.

£280–330 JAA

A rosewood chest of drawers, by Gillows of Lancaster, with two short drawers and three long graduated drawers, signed and dated 1859, 36in (91.5cm) wide.

£5,800–6,500 AGI

It is unusual for a Gillows piece to be dated.

A satin birch chest of drawers, by Heal & Sons, with two short drawers and four long graduated drawers, c1870, 45in (114.5cm) wide.

£850–950 TRED

A Victorian figured mahogany-veneered chest of drawers, with boxwood stringing, the cross-banded top above two short and three long drawers, with pine sides, 38¼in (97cm) wide.

£210–250 DD

A fiddle-back veneered mahogany chest of drawers, by Heal & Sons, with two short drawers above three long graduated drawers, c1880, 42in (106.5cm) wide.

£1,200–1,350 SAT

A Renaissance revival rosewood dressing chest, the foliate-carved mirror supports each with two candle stands and a small drawer, the base with a marble top and three graduated drawers lined with bird's-eye maple, America, New York, 1875–1900, 49in (124.5cm) wide.

£2,000–2,400 NOA

A Louis XVI-style commode, the banded top above three panelled drawers, on toupie feet, France, late 19thC, 41½in (105.5cm) wide.

£600–720 NOA

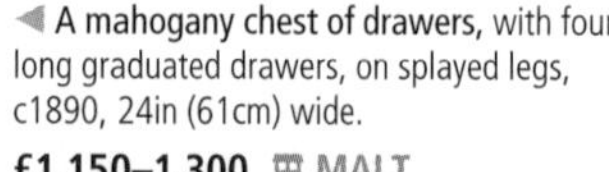

◀ **A mahogany chest of drawers,** with four long graduated drawers, on splayed legs, c1890, 24in (61cm) wide.

£1,150–1,300 MALT

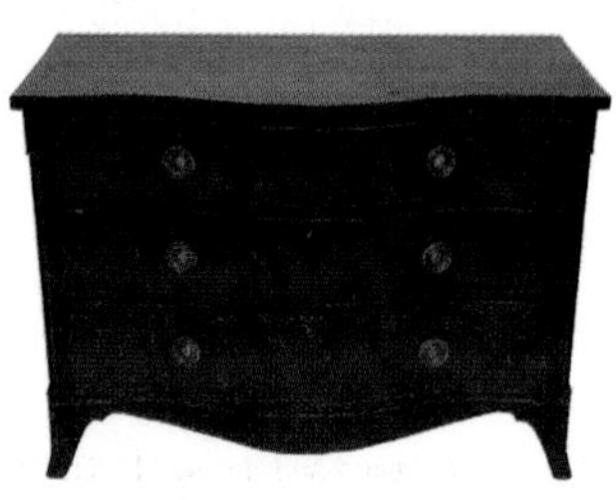

A mahogany serpentine chest of drawers, with two short and two long drawers, on splayed legs, c1890, 42in (106.5cm) wide.

£2,350–2,650 MCB

A walnut and marquetry commode, with a marble top and ormolu mounts, France, c1900, 52in (132cm) wide.

£3,050–3,400 BURA

A mahogany chest of drawers, with two short drawers and two long drawers, c1915, 36in (91.5cm) wide.

£360–400 OCA

MILITARY CHESTS

A teak and brass-bound military chest, the upper section with two short drawers, the base with three long drawers, early 19thC, 36¾in (93.5cm) wide.
£1,700–2,000 DN(BR)

A mahogany and brass-bound military secretaire chest, the fall-front enclosing a fitted interior, c1820, 39½in (100.5cm) wide.
£4,500–5,000 WALP

A mahogany campaign chest, with two short and three long drawers, with brass corner mounts, 19thC, 35½in (90cm) wide.
£560–670 GTH

A mahogany military chest, the upper section with two short drawers, the base with three long drawers, mid-19thC, 39½in (100.5cm) wide.
£820–980 ROS

► A teak and brass-bound chest, c1860, 42in (106.5cm) wide, on original packing case.
£2,150–2,400 WALP

SECRETAIRE CHESTS

An inlaid mahogany secretaire chest, the upper section with two doors enclosing a fitted interior, above a fold-over writing surface over four long graduated drawers, on splayed feet, slight damage, America, c1800, 40¾in (103.5cm) wide.
£1,150–1,350 JDJ

A mahogany secretaire chest, the crossbanded ebony- and boxwood-strung top above a fall-front enclosing a fitted interior, over three drawers, on splayed feet, early 19thC, 39¾in (101cm) wide.
£540–640 DMC

A walnut and kingwood secretaire chest, the marble top above a fall-front over three short drawers, France, late 19thC, 25in (63.5cm) wide.
£1,000–1,200 G(L)

CHESTS-ON-STANDS

A featherbanded and crossbanded walnut chest-on-stand, the upper section with three short and three long drawers, the later base with a drawer and turned supports, damaged, early 18thC, 41¾in (106cm) wide.

£4,450–5,300 MA&I

A George II walnut chest-on-stand, the later top above two short and three long drawers, the base with three drawers, handles later, stand later, 41½in (105.5cm) wide.

£1,050–1,250 WW

An inlaid and figured walnut chest-on-stand, with two short and three long graduated drawers, the base with three drawers, on cabriole legs, America, Boston, c1735, 39in (99cm) wide.

£6,600–7,900 S(NY)

Ex-Estate of Laurance S. Rockefeller.

◄ **A George III mahogany chest-on-stand,** the later top above four long graduated drawers, on cabriole legs, stand later, 39in (99cm) wide.

£350–420 WW

► **A painted wood chest-on-stand,** the moulded top above four long drawers flanked by quarter pilasters, on cabriole legs, Continental, 19thC, 49in (124.5cm) wide.

£175–210 WW

WELLINGTON CHESTS

A Victorian mahogany Wellington chest, with a fitted secretaire drawer above five drawers and a dummy drawer, 54½in (138.5cm) high.

£1,650–1,950 E

◄ **A Victorian walnut and burr-walnut Wellington chest,** the secretaire drawer with a fitted fruitwood interior, above five drawers, 51in (129.5cm) high.

£1,750–2,100 DN

► **A mahogany Wellington chest,** with seven drawers, c1870, 48in (122cm) high.

£2,000–2,250 TRED

► **A Victorian mahogany Wellington chest,** with seven drawers, 49in (124.5cm) high.

£2,000–2,250 MCB

The Wellington chest usually contains 6–12 drawers and is tall and narrow. Sometimes it is fitted with a secretaire drawer with a dummy front that makes it appear to be two drawers rather than one. Dating from the early part of the 19th century, these chests were designed to contain collectors' items or personal papers. The name probably dates from the time they were first produced, although there is no evidence to suggest that they were directly associated with the Iron Duke. It is more likely that they were named in accordance with the common practice of furniture makers after 1815 to label items 'Waterloo' or 'Wellington' in an attempt to cash in on the great victory. Whatever the origins of the name, the Wellington chest remains popular today.

CLOTHES & LINEN PRESSES

A mahogany clothes press, the two panelled doors enclosing hanging space, the base with two long graduated drawers, damaged, c1775, 52in (132cm) wide.

£1,100–1,300 Hal

A George III mahogany linen press, the two panelled doors enclosing slides, the base with two short and three long graduated drawers, on bracket feet, 50in (127cm) wide.

£1,000–1,200 GTH

A George III mahogany linen press, the two brass-trimmed doors with applied panelling enclosing slides, the base with two short and three long drawers, 57in (145cm) wide.

£940–1,100 AH

A burr-ash linen press, Scandinavia, c1800, 55in (139.5cm) wide.

£1,800–2,000 BURA

A late Georgian mahogany linen press, the two panelled doors with crossbanding and boxwood stringing, enclosing sliding shelves, the base with two short and two long drawers, 49in (124.5cm) wide.

£1,050–1,250 AG

A late Georgian mahogany linen press, on splayed feet, 81in (205.5cm) wide.

£2,600–2,900 PFS

A Regency mahogany linen press, with two panelled doors above two short and two long drawers, c1820, 50in (127cm) wide.

£3,250–3,650 OCA

A mahogany linen press, with two panelled doors flanked by turned pilasters, above two short and two long drawers, on turned feet, c1830, 48in (122cm) wide.

£1,700–1,900 HEM

A mahogany linen press, with two panelled doors above two short and two long drawers, on turned feet, c1880, 47in (119.5cm) wide.

£720–800 NORTH

DAVENPORTS

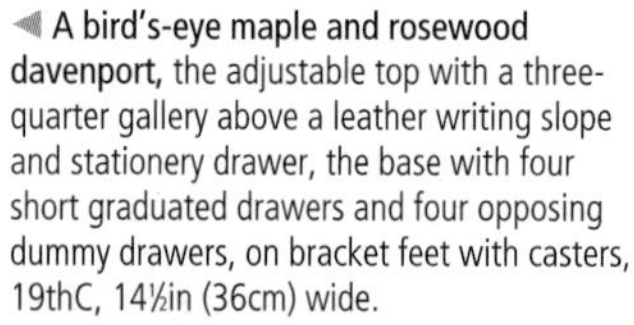

◄ **A bird's-eye maple and rosewood davenport,** the adjustable top with a three-quarter gallery above a leather writing slope and stationery drawer, the base with four short graduated drawers and four opposing dummy drawers, on bracket feet with casters, 19thC, 14½in (36cm) wide.

£2,250–2,700 CGC

► **An oak davenport,** on barley-twist legs, 19thC, 25in (63.5cm) wide.

£720–800 OCA

A rosewood davenport, with fretwork sides, stamped 'Stratham, Dublin', Ireland, c1850, 22in (56cm) wide.

£2,350–2,650 NoC

A walnut davenport, c1860, 22in (56cm) wide.

£670–750 NORTH

The first recorded example of this type of small writing cabinet is thought to be an entry made in the 1790s in the records of Gillows of Lancaster. It states simply 'Captain Davenport, a desk' and indeed this would be a useful piece of furniture on board a ship, although for most of the 19th century the davenport was generally used by women. Early examples are narrow and compact but from the 1830s they are broader and more ornate in design.

Most davenports have four drawers in the base section, with simulated drawer fronts on the opposite side. Just above the drawers there may be pull-out slides to hold papers or finished letters. The base is often fitted with casters for ease of movement. The top section typically comprises a desk with sloping lid inset with a leather writing surface. In the earliest examples the top section slides forward to accommodate the writer's legs, but later the desk section was more often fixed in the writing position. As the Victorian period progressed various design variations occurred, the most popular being the slope in the form of a piano lid, and the 'harlequin' top, by which a superstructure could be raised and lowered by pulling a button on one of the drawers in the compartment below the reading slope.

A Victorian inlaid walnut davenport, with a maple-lined fitted interior and rear stationery compartment, above four drawers opposing four dummy drawers, 21¼in (54cm) wide.

£420–500 WilP

A Victorian burr-walnut piano-top harlequin davenport, fitted with pigeonholes and drawers over a hinged top enclosing a pull-out leather writing surface, on leaf-capped scroll supports, 37½in (95.5cm) high.

£1,000–1,200 JAd

A Victorian rosewood piano-top harlequin davenport, with satinwood-veneered drawers and pigeon-holes and a pull-out writing compartment, the base with four drawers and four opposing dummy drawers, on leaf-carved scrolled front supports, 22½in (57cm) wide.

£1,900–2,250 WW

DESKS

A George III mahogany kneehole desk, 31¼in (79.5cm) wide.
£1,000–1,200 DN

A George III mahogany and rosewood crossbanded partners' desk, with a parquetry-inlaid top, c1790, 46¼in (143cm) wide.
£2,400–2,850 S(O)

◀ **A Regency mahogany kneehole desk,** on bracket feet, 42in (106.5cm) wide.
£760–850 MCB

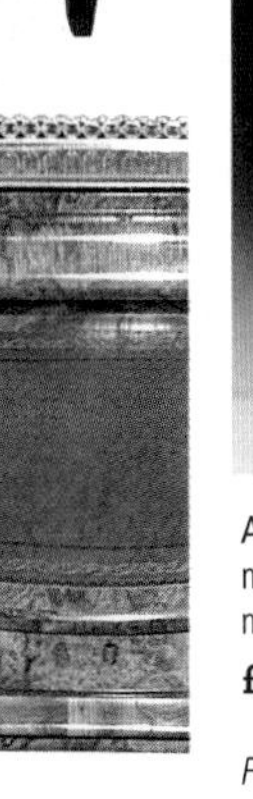

A burr-walnut desk, the carved supports united by a turned stretcher, c1850, 42in (106.5cm) wide.
£3,300–3,700 CGA

A satinwood lady's writing desk, in the manner of Holland & Sons, with gilt-bronze mounts, c1870, 42¼in (107.5cm) wide.
£3,600–4,300 S(O)

Founded c1803 as Taprell, Stephen & Holland, the firm of Holland & Sons became one of London's most distinguished cabinet-makers in Victorian times. Employing some of the leading designers of the day, they carried out many commissions for the Royal family and the government.

A rococo revival rosewood desk, possibly by J. & J. W. Meeks, New York, the upper section with three shelves with mirrored backs, the base with a hinged writing slope enclosing a fitted interior, the pierced scrolled ends flanking bookshelves, America, c1875, 33in (84cm) wide.
£760–910 NOA

A Victorian light oak writing desk, the upper section with six drawers and a hinged compartment, above three frieze drawers and a kneehole flanked by six small drawers, 59in (150cm) wide.
£3,050–3,400 MCB

A rosewood partners' desk, with a leather-inset top above carved columns and 18 drawers, France, c1880, 70in (178cm) wide.
£7,200–8,000 BURA

▶ **A Sheraton-style mahogany lady's desk,** c1880, 38in (96.5cm) high.
£1,200–1,350 GEO

A Renaissance-revival walnut, fruitwood and parcel-ebonized combination desk and chair, by Joseph Moore, the galleried top above a leather writing surface, the base with two moulded burr-walnut-veneer panelled doors enclosing a fitted interior, the hinged side enclosing a further fitted interior with a pull-out writing surface, America, Indiana, c1882, 58¾in (149cm) wide.

£45,000–54,000 S(NY)

Crafted upon the conception and designs of William Wooton's 'Extra Grade' desk patented in 1874, this monumental cabinet desk, patented in 1882, is a symbol of the prosperity of the period.

◀ **A rosewood lady's writing desk,** by James Shoolbred & Co, inlaid with foliate designs and stringing, the arched mirrored back with two pairs of short drawers above an inset leather writing surface, over two pairs of short drawers flanking a centre drawer, on cabriole legs, c1890, 45in (114.5cm) wide.

£1,450–1,700 PF

James Shoolbred & Co, established c1870, became one of the first great department stores in London, situated on Tottenham Court Road. The firm was renowned for the quality of its wares and was awarded a Royal warrant in the mid-1880s.

A Sheraton-style painted satinwood Carlton House desk, with rosewood crossbanding, late 19thC, 45¼in (115cm) wide.

£6,000–7,200 S(O)

A late Victorian walnut pedestal desk, the top with a leather cloth writing surface, above three short frieze drawers, each pedestal with pull-out hinged units enclosing stationery drawers and file partitions, 60in (152.5cm) wide.

£1,900–2,250 AG

▶ **A mahogany lady's writing desk,** with marquetry inlay and a leather top, c1890, 47in (119.5cm) wide.

£8,350–9,300 YOX

A satinwood-veneered, double-sided kneehole writing desk, by Edwards & Roberts, with brass string inlay and beading and brass drop handles, the frieze drawer stamped 'Edwards & Roberts', c1900, 60¼in (153cm) wide.

£1,200–1,400 HOLL

The firm of Edwards & Roberts was among the foremost English cabinet-makers of the second half of the 19th century, founded in 1845 and trading as 'Edwards & Roberts, 21 Wardour Street, Antique and Modern Cabinet Makers and Importers of Ancient Furniture'.

A walnut writing desk, France, c1900, 44in (112cm) wide.

£1,000–1,150 TRED

DUMB WAITERS

A Victorian mahogany metamorphic dumb waiter, with three tiers, damaged, 48in (122cm) wide.

£880–1,050 DN(BR)

◄ A mahogany dumb waiter, with two tiers, Ireland, c1800, 42in (106.5cm) high.

£2,100–2,350 GEO

A Victorian mahogany metamorphic dumb waiter, with a carved scroll back and three tiers, 54in (137cm) wide.

£640–760 SWO

JARDINIERES

A satinwood-veneered jardinière, with lacquered inserts and original brass liner, Holland, c1830, 11in (28cm) wide.

£560–630 CSM

A walnut jardinière, with ormolu gallery and mounts, on a carved oak column, c1860, 36in (91.5cm) diam.

£5,400–6,000 NoC

A Victorian carved mahogany jardinière, the *bombé* container with a metal liner, 37in (94cm) wide.

£430–510 PBA

A satinwood and polychrome-decorated jardinière, slight damage, late 19thC, 15in (38cm) square.

£195–230 WW

An Edwardian mahogany jardinière, inlaid with marquetry swags, with an undertier, 18in (45.5cm) wide.

£290–340 GTH

An Edwardian inlaid satinwood jardinière, with painted decoration and metal liner, 37¾in (96cm) high.

£940–1,100 SWO

LOWBOYS

A walnut and featherbanded lowboy, with a quarter-veneered top above three drawers, on leaf-carved cabriole legs, c1720, 28¼in (72cm) high.

£7,900–8,800 ⊞ RGa

► **A walnut lowboy,** with three drawers, on plain turned legs with pad feet, c1740, 30in (76cm) wide.

£1,500–1,700 ⊞ CSM

A Queen Anne walnut-veneered lowboy, with three drawers, on cabriole legs with pad feet, America, Massachusetts, 1730–50, 33½in (85cm) wide.

£3,000–3,600 SK(B)

A George III mahogany lowboy, the moulded edge above two short drawers and one long drawer, 31in (78.5cm) wide.

£630–750 CAG

A mahogany bowfronted lowboy, the cockbeaded frieze drawer above two short drawers and an arched kneehole, 19thC, 36in (91.5cm) wide.

£330–390 PF

MINIATURE FURNITURE

◄ **A baroque burr-walnut miniature bureau bookcase,** the upper section with two glazed cupboard doors enclosing a fitted interior, the lower section with a fall-front over three drawers, Italy, Venice, 18thC, 10in (25.5cm) wide.

£2,600–3,100 S(NY)

► **A crossbanded walnut miniature *bombé* commode,** the three drawers with brass rococo escutcheons, Germany, late 18thC, 14½in (36cm) wide.

£1,400–1,650 S(O)

A mahogany miniature chest of drawers, with four drawers, on ogee bracket feet, c1760, 8in (20.5cm) wide.

£2,000–2,250 ⊞ TIM

A mahogany miniature bowfronted chest, with two short and three long graduated cockbeaded drawers, 19thC, 12in (30.5cm) wide.

£350–420 BAM(M)

A pine miniature chest of drawers, with grained decoration, c1860, 16in (40.5cm) high.

£430–480 SAT

A mahogany miniature chest of drawers, the top with a burrwood edge, c1870, 11in (28cm) wide.

£360–400 GSA

A kingwood miniature commode, with a marble top, France, c1880, 13in (33cm) wide.

£2,200–2,450 TIM

A mahogany-veneered miniature settee, the rolled crest rail over an upholstered back, seat and side panels, with scrolling arms and moulded curved legs, pencil inscription on base 'July 1839', America, c1839, 17¾in (45cm) wide.

£570–680 SK(B)

A mahogany miniature set of hanging graduated shelves, c1840, 12in (30.5cm) wide.

£210–240 MB

Most pieces of miniature furniture were made as travelling salesmen's samples. They were used to show prospective customers the workshop's current stock and were made in the same way, in the same materials and in the exact proportions of their full-sized counterparts. Some examples were made by apprentices as a way of testing their ability and workmanship without wasting large amounts of valuable materials. Occasionally pieces would be produced as individual commissions for display or storage.

A mahogany miniature tilt-top breakfast table, c1850, 12in (30.5cm) diam.

£400–450 MB

An early Victorian maple miniature linen press, the two arched panelled doors enclosing four slides and four drawers, 21¼in (54cm) high.

£420–500 CGC

CHEVAL MIRRORS

◄ A George III mahogany cheval **mirror,** with a satinwood, purple heart and kingwood-banded frame, 70¼in (178.5cm) high.

£1,200–1,400 WW

A mahogany cheval mirror, with gilt Corinthian capitals and two ormolu two-light sconces in the form of winged caryatids, France, 1800–25, 77½in (197cm) high.

£2,300–2,750 NOA

◄ **A Sheraton revival satinwood cheval mirror,** with chequer line inlay and roundels, 19thC, 69½in (176.5cm) high.

£2,800–3,350 GTH

A mahogany cheval mirror, c1880, 49in (124.5cm) high.

£700–780 NoC

TOILET MIRRORS

A walnut and featherbanded toilet mirror, with a parcel-gilt slip, on bracket feet, c1750, 18½in (47cm) wide.

£1,250–1,500 DN

Further reading

Miller's Antiques Checklist: Furniture, Miller's Publications, 1994

MILLER'S COMPARES

I. A satinwood and mahogany-inlaid gentleman's toilet mirror, with a serpentine front, 1780–1810, 17in (43cm) wide.

£2,250–2,500 GGD

II. A mahogany and boxwood-inlaid toilet mirror, with a serpentine front, 1790–1820, 18in (45.5cm) wide.

£1,500–1,700 GGD

Item I is made of satinwood, a scarce and desirable timber from the West Indies that is as sought after today as it was in the 18th century. Consequently pieces made in this wood are far less common than pieces made of mahogany, such as Item II, and will invariably command a premium.

A mahogany toilet mirror, c1780, 25½in (65cm) high.

£360–400 PSA

A George III mahogany toilet mirror, with brass finials and mounts, 15¾in (40cm) wide.

£140–165 PFK

A mahogany toilet mirror, with line inlay, 19thC, 21in (53.5cm) high.

£175–195 DEB

A rosewood toilet mirror, with bone banding, handles and feet, c1820, 21in (53.5cm) wide.

£530–590 TRED

► A mahogany and marquetry toilet mirror, Holland, c1820, 26in (66cm) high.

£810–900 GEO

A mahogany toilet mirror, c1835, 24in (61cm) wide.

£340–380 SPUR

A mahogany toilet mirror, with a convex drawer, c1850, 27in (68.5cm) high.

£240–270 HEM

A mahogany toilet mirror, with barley-twist supports, c1880, 27in (68.5cm) wide.

£340–380 NoC

WALL MIRRORS

A baroque part-ebonized walnut mirror, with gilt-metal mounts, Franco-Flemish, late 17thC, 26in (66cm) wide.

£2,900–3,450 S(NY)

A giltwood mirror, surmounted by a carved shell, the corners with acanthus leaf-carved C-scrolls, France, c1740, 37¼in (94.5cm) wide.

£7,800–9,300 S(NY)

A rococo giltwood mirror, north Italy, mid-18thC, 64½in (164cm) wide.

£6,500–7,800 S(NY)

A carved giltwood wall mirror, Italy, 18thC, 57in (145cm) high.

£12,500–14,000 AUB

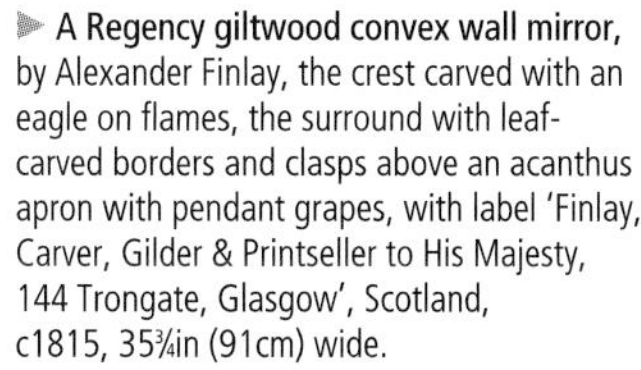

A Regency giltwood convex wall mirror, by Alexander Finlay, the crest carved with an eagle on flames, the surround with leaf-carved borders and clasps above an acanthus apron with pendant grapes, with label 'Finlay, Carver, Gilder & Printseller to His Majesty, 144 Trongate, Glasgow', Scotland, c1815, 35¾in (91cm) wide.

£9,600–11,500 S

Alexander Finlay first appears as a carver and gilder in the 1803 Glasgow directory at 144 Trongate. He is recorded at this address until 1820 when he appears as Alexander 'Findlay' at 622 Argyle Street, the western extension of Trongate. In 1824 he added to his business by taking on a picture gallery in South Maxwell Street, before disappearing from the directories in 1826, either as the consequence of death or the financial crisis of that year.

A pair of giltwood and gesso wall mirrors, each with moulded cornices with floral devices above spiral bands and tablets, with a grapevine and rope-twist border, the plate flanked by spiral-twist columns, slight damage, America, Massachusetts, 1815–20, 25in (63.5cm) wide.

£3,800–4,550 SK(B)

A giltwood and gesso wall mirror, with a *verre eglomisé* panel depicting a woman and her son, slight damage, America, Massachusetts, 1815–20, 21¾in (55.5cm) wide.

£440–520 SK(B)

A mahogany, ebonized fruitwood and gilt-plaster wall mirror, north Europe, c1825, 32½in (82.5cm) wide.

£540–640 NOA

A carved mahogany wall mirror, c1835, 15in (38cm) wide.

£580–650 JC

A pair of Chippendale-style giltwood mirrors, 19thC, 21in (53.55cm) high.

£720–800 Lfo

A mahogany and giltwood wall mirror, with retailer's label 'Bought of J. F. Calvin, 21 Van Houton Street, Patterson, NJ', America, c1850, 21¾in (55.5cm) wide.

£600–720 NOA

A pair of carved giltwood wall mirrors, with mirrored borders, some with blue tinted glass, Italy, 19thC, 27½in (70cm) wide.

£4,950–5,900 DN

A Renaissance revival wood and copper wall mirror, with embossed and openwork copper fittings of foliage, satyr heads and fruit garlands, Continental, 19thC, 35½in (90cm) wide.

£1,100–1,300 BERN

A giltwood wall mirror, in the manner of A. M. E. Fournier, 19thC, 43¼in (110cm) wide.

£760–910 ROS

A. M. G. Fournier was a Parisian cabinet maker. In 1867 he exhibited at the Exposition Universelle *in Paris.*

A neo-classical giltwood wall mirror, with a Wedgwood plaque of a dancing Muse and applied foliate decoration, late 19thC, 28½in (72.5cm) wide.

£1,250–1,500 SK

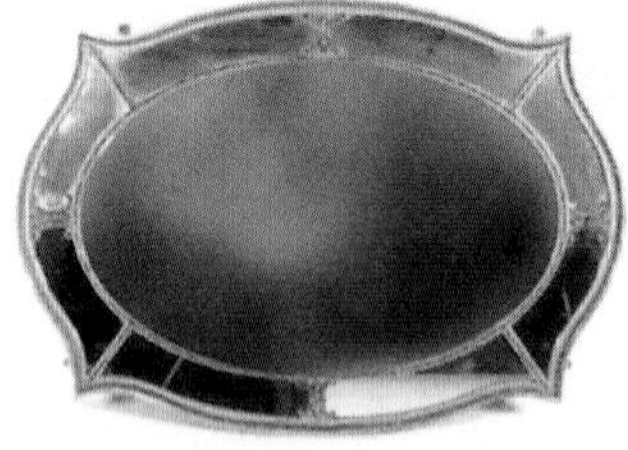

A Victorian George III-style gilt wall mirror, the bevelled plate within a mirrored border spaced by acanthus leaves and mouldings, 44in (112cm) wide.

£640–760 Hal

The appeal of wall mirrors seems to continue undimmed. With much of the furniture market being led by interior decorators, mirrors can always seem to find a place, even in a shockingly modern interior. Damaged frames, including major loss of gesso, will greatly devalue the piece, so pay particular attention to condition. Regency mirrors are always popular, especially the three-panelled overmantel variety, and so too are good quality convex mirrors, which were designed to permit the butler to have a full view of the diners around a table so that he could judge when courses should be served and glasses recharged. Mirrors with their original glass plates are desirable but many have been replaced or resilvered.

◀ **A kingwood wall mirror,** with ormolu mounts, c1920, 27in (68.5cm) wide.

£400–450 OCA

OTTOMANS

A upholstered rosewood ottoman, with a hinged lid, c1835, 18½in (47cm) high.

£850–950 RGa

A mahogany ottoman, with an upholstered seat, c1840, 23in (58.5cm) wide.

£360–400 DOA

A Victorian rosewood ottoman, with upholstered hinged lid and sides, the corners with spiral-turned pillars, 25½in (65cm) wide.

£370–440 DN

PEDESTALS

A pair of rococo painted and parcel-gilt pedestals, refreshed, south German, mid-18thC, 35½in (90cm) high.

£5,800–6,900 S(NY)

A pair of *faux* marble, parcel-gilt and composition pedestals, slight damage, Italy, early 19thC, 44in (112cm) high.

£6,000–7,200 S

A Louis XV-style ormolu-mounted pedestal, attributed to François Linke, with a marble top and parquetry sides, 19thC, 43in (109cm) high.

£3,750–4,500 G(L)

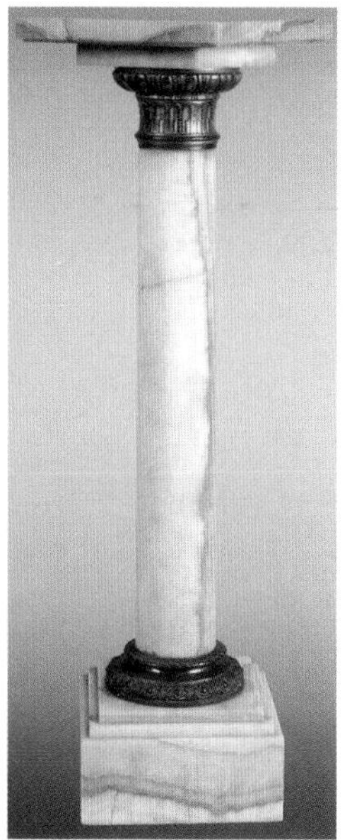

A Victorian marble pedestal, with a revolving top, the column with a brass capital, 42in (106.5cm) high.

£520–620 Mit

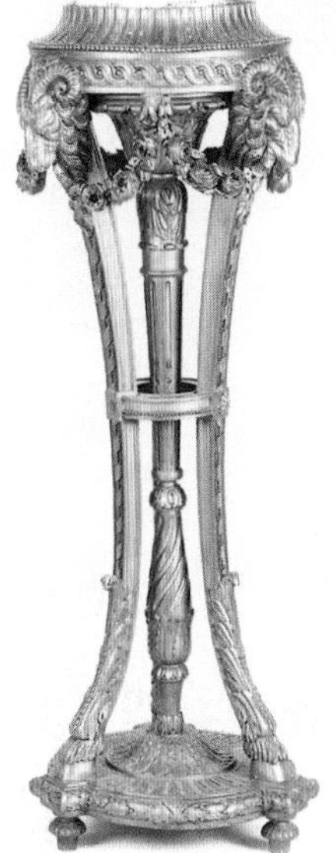

A Louis XVI-style giltwood pedestal, carved with rams' heads and rose garlands, late 19thC, 48in (122cm) high.

£1,000–1,200 BERN

An Empire-style amboyna and rosewood pedestal, with a marble top and gilt-metal mounts, France, c1890, 44in (112cm) high.

£1,400–1,650 S(O)

A pair of marble pedestals, with gilt-bronze mounts, France, c1900, 43¼in (110cm) high.

£3,700–4,400 S(O)

SCREENS

A leather four-fold screen, painted with panels of Watteauesque figures and animals on a gilt ground, the reverse ebonized and with painted borders, 19thC, panels 21in (53.5cm) wide.

£3,900–4,650 DN

An ash three-fold screen, each panel with a pierced crest and painted with a Continental riverscape, signed and dated 'Ct. S. Spink, Aug 1883', the reverse applied with Victorian scraps within a giltwood moulding, late 19thC, each panel 25½in (65cm) wide.

£880–1,050 DN

A three-fold screen, the arched panels with chinoiserie decoration, mid-20thC, each panel 20in (51cm) wide.

£270–300 SWA

FIRE SCREENS

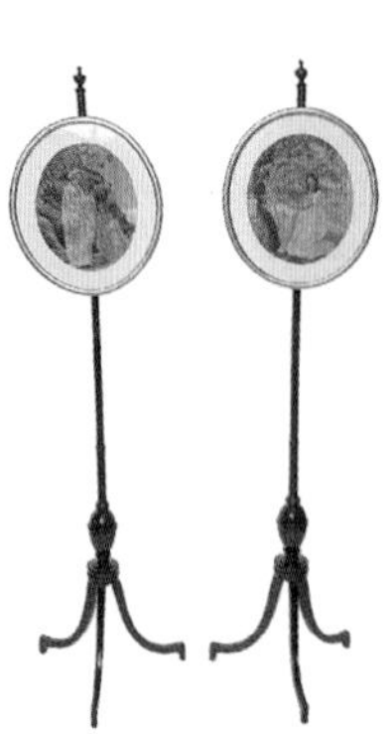

A pair of mahogany pole screens, each panel with silkwork in a gilt frame, 1810–20, 60in (152.5cm) high.

£900–1,000 YOX

Pole screens protected the face from the heat of the fire.

A mahogany pole screen, the panel with fretwork decoration, c1835, 56in (142cm) high.

£290–330 NoC

A rosewood fire screen, the panel embroidered with Sir Walter Raleigh laying down his cloak for Queen Elizabeth I, in a barley-twist frame, c1840, 27in (68.5cm) wide.

£370–440 Hal

A carved rosewood fire screen, with a needlework panel, Scotland, c1845, 56in (142cm) high.

£700–780 CSM

A carved walnut fire screen, with a glazed needlework panel, c1860, 32in (81.5cm) wide.

£580–650 MCB

A carved mahogany fire screen, with a glazed fabric panel, c1870, 27in (68.5cm) wide.

£420–480 TRED

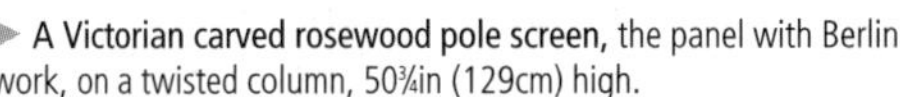

► **A Victorian carved rosewood pole screen,** the panel with Berlin work, on a twisted column, 50¾in (129cm) high.

£220–260 DN(HAM)

A Victorian carved rosewood fire screen, with a needlework panel, 36in (91.5cm) wide.

£440–520 AH

SETTEES & SOFAS

A George I walnut settee, on cabriole front legs with pad feet, 55¼in (140.5cm) high.
£13,000–15,600 SWO

A rococo giltwood canapé, on cabriole legs, Italy, Venice, mid-18thC, 77in (195.5cm) wide.
£5,200–6,200 S(NY)

A mahogany-veneered sofa, on ogee bracket feet, reupholstered, America, 1825–50, 80½in (203cm) wide.
£1,900–2,250 NOA

An Empire-style mahogany sofa, with gilt-bronze mounts, France, c1825, 70in (178cm) wide.
£1,400–1,650 S(O)

A mahogany sofa, on bracket feet, reupholstered, America, 1825–50, 79in (200.5cm) wide.
£630–750 NOA

A karelian birch settee, Russia, 1825–50, 77in (195.5cm) wide.
£4,200–5,000 S(NY)

◀ **A Biedermeier satin-birch and inlaid sofa,** by Johan Uddbye, with four cushions, Sweden, c1825, 99¾in (253.5cm) wide.
£1,550–1,850 S(O)

Johan Uddbye was born and brought up in Denmark and served his apprenticeship as a cabinet-maker in Copenhagen. He emigrated to Sweden in 1814, working first in the Swedish naval town of Karlshamn and afterwards moving to Stockholm where he was recognized as a master cabinet-maker in 1816. He died in 1847. The inlay on the back of this sofa is one of a number of inlays that he always used on his furniture.

A rosewood settee, with button-back upholstery, on cabriole legs, c1850, 73in (185.5cm) wide.

£1,550–1,750 SWA

A rococo-revival laminated rosewood sofa, with pierced carved panels of leaves, grapes and vines, on carved cabriole legs, reupholstered, America, mid-19thC, 69in (175.5cm) wide.

£2,300–2,750 NOA

A mid-Victorian walnut salon settee, with two button-upholstered backs and padded arms, on cabriole legs, 45in (114.5cm) wide.

£700–840 SWO

A Victorian carved walnut settee, with button-back upholstery, on turned legs, 71in (180.5cm) wide.

£350–420 WW

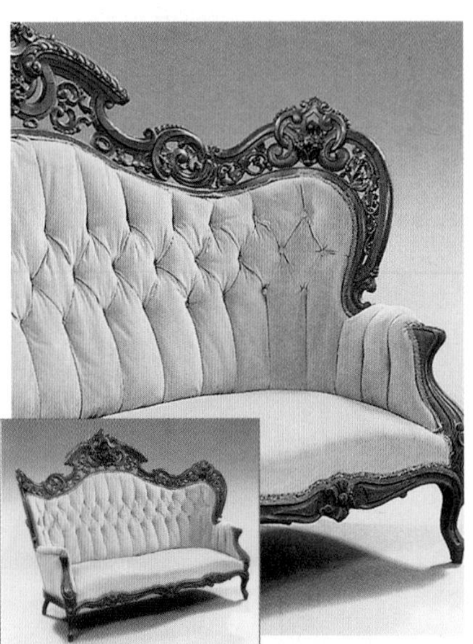

A pair of Victorian French-style gilded and carved sofas, with bolster cushions, on scroll legs, 76in (193cm) wide.

£2,350–2,800 NSF

◄ **A rococo revival laminated rosewood sofa,** attributed to J. & J. W. Meeks, New York, the foliate and scroll-carved back with a crest, with a serpentine seat rail and cabriole front legs, America, 1850–75, 77in (195.5cm) wide.

£5,700–6,800 NOA

A leather Chesterfield sofa, c1880, 70in (178cm) wide.

£1,700–1,900 PFS

A painted and carved wood sofa, on cabriole legs with scroll feet, reupholstered, c1880, 75in (190.5cm) wide.

£1,250–1,500 Hal

A Louis XVI-style settee, France, c1880, 80in (203cm) wide.
£3,150–3,500 HA

An Edwardian Chippendale-style mahogany settee, on square legs with pierced corner brackets, 86½in (219.5cm) wide.
£1,000–1,200 DMC

A carved mahogany settee, 1920s, 76½in (194.5cm) wide.
£800–960 SWO

SHELVES

A set of Victorian mahogany hanging shelves, with pierced ends, 42¼in (107.5cm) wide.
£230–270 WW

A pair of mahogany bowfronted hanging corner shelves, with mirrored backs, c1890, 38in (96.5cm) high.
£330–370 SPUR

A set of Victorian rosewood hanging shelves, with spiral-turned supports, 21in (53.5cm) wide.
£370–440 DN

SIDEBOARDS

A George III inlaid mahogany bowfronted sideboard, the frieze drawer above a concealed drawer, with a cupboard and a cellaret, on tapered legs with spade feet, 72in (183cm) wide.
£3,000–3,600 MEA

A Georgian mahogany sideboard, with two short and two deep drawers, on turned legs, 91in (231cm) wide.
£2,600–2,900 OCA

A mahogany bowfronted sideboard, with tulipwood banding and inlaid paterae, on tapered legs with spade feet, c1790, 35in (89cm) high.

£7,300–8,300 ⊞ RGa

A mahogany and mahogany-veneered sideboard, with two long drawers over two recessed hinged doors and four short drawers, on tapered legs, restored, slight damage, America, probably Massachusetts, c1800, 69½in (176.5cm) wide.

£5,100–6,100 SK(B)

A mahogany sideboard, with ebony line inlay, on tapered legs with spade feet, c1810, 54in (137cm) wide.

£2,700–3,000 ⊞ CGA

A Regency mahogany pedestal breakfront sideboard, with lion mask handles, on turned legs, 78in (198cm) wide.

£1,200–1,400 PBA

Alterations

Pedestal sideboards and serving tables have often been altered in width and depth to make them more commercial. When purchasing a sideboard check that the proportions are correct, drawers or veneers have not been replaced, the back has not been altered or the legs moved, and the legs should always be constructed of one piece. Cuts are often hidden behind decorative moulding or crossbanding below the upper section, but alterations can often be detected by differences in the colour of the timber or the timber itself.

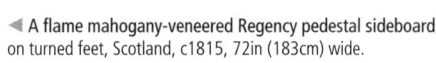

◄ **A flame mahogany-veneered Regency pedestal sideboard,** on turned feet, Scotland, c1815, 72in (183cm) wide.

£760–850 ⊞ CSM

A Regency mahogany sideboard, with a cellaret to one side, on turned legs, 55in (139.5cm) wide.

£4,500–5,000 ⊞ YOX

◄ **A late Georgian boxwood-strung mahogany bowfronted sideboard,** the back with a brass rail, with two central drawers and two cupboards, on tapered legs with spade feet, 72in (183cm) wide.

£1,000–1,200 AG

A mahogany sideboard, with two deep drawers, on turned legs, Scotland, c1820, 74in (188cm) wide.

£3,900–4,400 ⊞ Fai

A mahogany pedestal sideboard, with carved decoration, c1820, 73in (185.5 cm) wide.

£2,000–2,250 ⊞ OCA

A mahogany sideboard, the parquetry top above three mahogany-lined drawers, over six drawers and two panelled doors enclosing a shelf, on bun feet, c1830, 55½in (141cm) wide.

£3,450–3,850 ⊞ JC

A William IV mahogany sideboard, with carved decoration of fruiting vines, 78in (198cm) wide.

£3,350–3,750 ⊞ PWA

A mahogany pedestal sideboard, on carved feet, c1835, 68in (172.5cm) wide.

£1,750–1,950 ⊞ BURA

A mahogany sideboard, with four doors, on bun feet, c1850, 74in (188cm) wide.

£1,800–2,000 ⊞ Fai

A Victorian mahogany inverted breakfront sideboard, the back carved with acanthus leaves, above three frieze drawers and three cupboard doors, on bun feet, 54¼in (138cm) wide.

£490–580 RTo

An Edwardian crossbanded mahogany bowfronted sideboard, with a frieze drawer over tambour doors flanked by cupboards, on tapered legs with spade feet, with an undertier, 55¼in (140.5cm) wide.

£430–510 CGC

FOLIO STANDS

A Regency mahogany adjustable folio stand, with brass terminals and casters, 30¾in (78cm) wide.
£1,500–1,800 DN

◄ **A William IV rosewood folio stand,** with gadrooned toupie feet, 26½in (67.5cm) wide.
£3,000–3,600 G(B)

▲ **A walnut and brass folio stand,** with a carved pedestal, c1860, 47in (119.5cm) high.
£3,200–3,600 GEO

MUSIC STANDS

A Regency rosewood adjustable duet music stand, with two brass sconces, on a fluted and carved column, 48in (122cm) high.
£3,300–3,950 G(L)

A mahogany music stand, with a brass extender, on a barley-twist column, mid-19thC, 46in (117cm) high.
£230–260 NAW

A Victorian walnut music stand, with two turned brass sconces and an adjustable turned brass stem within a baluster-turned column, 57in (145cm) high unextended.
£690–820 WW

A carved and turned walnut music stand, c1880, 59in (150cm) high.
£610–680 PFS

READING STANDS

A **mahogany reading stand,** c1800, 38in (96.5cm) high.
£530–590 NAW

◄ **A mahogany reading stand,** with two candle stands, on an adjustable column with three reeded downswept legs and brass casters, c1800, 32in (81.5cm) high.
£5,200–5,800 RGa

A Regency mahogany reading stand, 18¼in (46.5cm) wide.
£540–640 DN(HAM)

► **A Regency mahogany reading stand,** with a brass sconce, on later legs, 29¾in (75.5cm) high.
£200–240 WW

◄ **A Victorian walnut and cast-iron adjustable reading stand,** patented as John Carter's Patent Literary Machine, with animal paw feet and enamel maker's label, top 14in (35.5cm) diam.
£350–420 HYD

URN STANDS

◄ **An inlaid and figured maple and mahogany urn stand,** with a single drawer, on square tapered legs, America, c1800, 20in (51cm) wide.
£1,700–2,000 S(NY)

Ex-Estate of Laurance S. Rockefeller.

► **A cherrywood urn stand,** with a single drawer, on square tapered legs, America, New England, c1800, 17in (43cm) wide.
£920–1,100 S(NY)

Ex-Estate of Laurance S. Rockefeller.

A late George III yew-wood urn stand, the top above a slide, the legs with pierced brackets and two mahogany X-stretchers, 11¼in (28.5cm) wide.
£420–500 WW

A George III mahogany urn stand, the pierced gallery above a slide, the legs with pierced lattice brackets, damaged, replacements, 12in (30.5cm) wide.
£560–670 WW

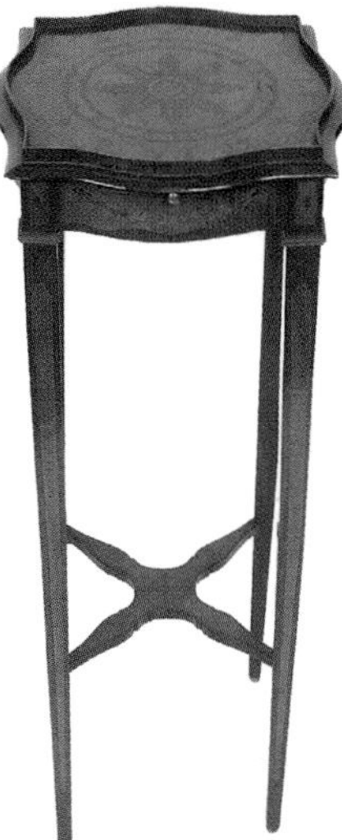

◄ **A Sheraton-style satinwood and marquetry urn stand,** c1880, 31in (78.5cm) high.
£1,550–1,750 GEO

MISCELLANEOUS STANDS

A cherrywood candle stand, with a vase- and ring-turned support, slight damage, America, New England, early 19thC, 28½in (72.5cm) high.

£400–480 SK(B)

A mahogany shaving stand, with two lidded compartments, the turned column on three leaf-carved scroll legs, c1860, 61½in (156cm) high.

£470–560 N

A carved walnut stand, with a figural column, Italy, 19thC, 31in (78.5cm) high.

£490–550 AMG

A Victorian mahogany jardinière stand, with a bead-work top on a spiral-carved column, 30in (76cm) high.

£580–650 GEO

A mahogany jardinière stand, with gilt-metal mounts, the marble top with a pierced gallery over a carved frieze, the supports united by a platform and splayed legs, late 19thC, 32¾in (83cm) high.

£220–260 JAd

A pair of mahogany offertory stands, each with a brass bowl and turned column, c1880, 34¼in (87cm) high.

£2,250–2,500 GEO

A mahogany cake stand, c1900, 33in (84cm) high.

£175–195 QA

An Edwardian inlaid mahogany plant stand, 37in (94cm) high.

£160–180 NAW

STEPS

A set of Regency mahogany bed steps, with a cupboard and bidet compartment, c1830, 32in (81.5cm) high.

£1,250–1,400 GSA

A mahogany step commode, c1860, 28in (71cm) high.

£1,800–2,000 MALT

A set of Victorian mahogany metamorphic library steps, with leather insets, folding to a scroll-arm elbow chair with a cane seat.

£1,650–1,950 MAL(O)

STOOLS

A pair of carved beechwood stools, with serpentine tops, the pierced rails carved with shell and foliate motifs, on carved cabriole legs with scrolled toes, France, c1720, 20½in (52cm) wide.

£9,100–10,900 S(NY)

A pair of giltwood 'rope twist' stools, after A. M. E. Fournier, with buttoned seats, France, c1860, 23½in (59.5cm) diam.

£7,800–9,300 S(NY)

A giltwood stool, with an X-frame, 19thC, 17in (43cm) wide.

£340–380 NoC

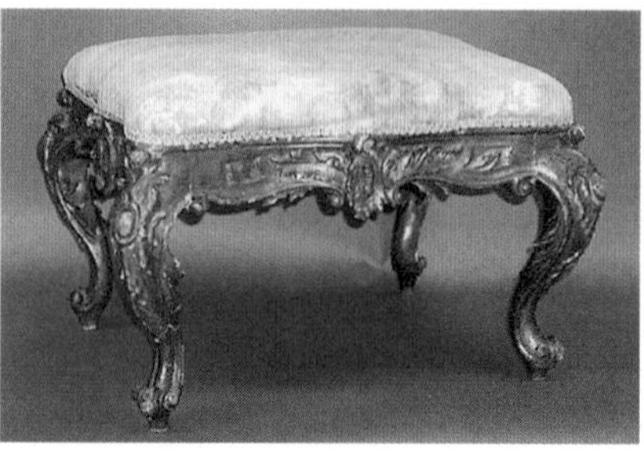

A carved giltwood and gesso stool, with a foliate-carved frieze, the acanthus-carved and moulded cabriole legs on scroll feet, 19thC, 24in (61cm) wide.

£300–360 MA&I

A needlework stool, with a pleated silk base, on bun feet, c1870, 15in (38cm) wide.

£125–140 PICA

A Victorian leather and mahogany gout stool, 14in (35.5cm) high.

£145–160 MCB

A Victorian rosewood dressing stool, with a woolwork top, on carved and faceted legs, 41in (104cm) wide.

£910–1,050 Mit

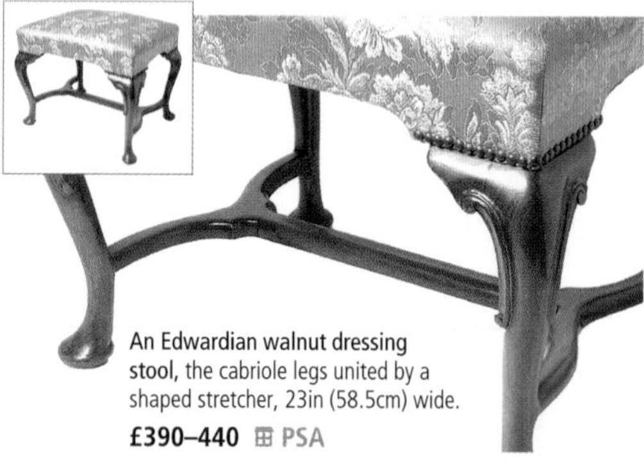

An Edwardian walnut dressing stool, the cabriole legs united by a shaped stretcher, 23in (58.5cm) wide.

£390–440 PSA

MUSIC STOOLS

A Regency rosewood adjustable piano stool, with reeded legs.

£530–630 SWO

An ebonized harpist's stool, c1830, 24in (61cm) high.

£360–400 RBM

A lacquer and gilt piano stool, with chinoiserie decoration and a hinged top, c1880, 21in (53.5cm) wide.

£130–145 PEC

BEDROOM SUITES

A rococo revival carved rosewood bedroom suite, attributed to Mitchell and Rammelsberg Furniture Co, Ohio, comprising a bed, wardrobe, dressing table and wash stand, America, Ohio, 1850–75, bed 69in (175.5cm) wide.

£12,700–15,200 NOA

A rococo revival *faux* rosewood bedroom suite, attributed to Mitchell & Rammelsberg Furniture Co, comprising a bed, dressing chest with a tilting mirror and marble top and a washstand with a marble top and three drawers, America, Ohio, c1875, bed 95in (241.5cm) high.

£1,750–2,100 NOA

An Edwardian mahogany bedroom suite, comprising a wardrobe, dressing table and bedside cabinet, on cabriole legs.

£940–1,100 TRM(D)

A japanned bedroom suite, with polychrome and gilt chinoiserie decoration, comprising a wardrobe, chest of drawers, dressing table with a mirror, bedside cabinet, bedroom chair, easel mirror and two single headboards, early 20thC.

£820–980 DN(BR)

A burr-walnut crossbanded bedroom suite, comprising a chest, tallboy, dressing table, two bedside chests and a single bed, 1920s.

£640–760 G(B)

SALON SUITES

A mahogany salon suite, comprising a canapé and two bergères, on later feet, France, c1810, canapé 72in (183cm) wide

£5,800–6,900 S(NY)

A rococo revival laminated rosewood salon suite, attributed to J. & J. W. Meeks, New York, comprising a button-backed settee, two armchairs and two side chairs, with pierced foliate and scroll carving, each piece reupholstered, America, 1850–75, settee 64½in (164cm) wide.

£22,300–26,700 NOA

An Edwardian inlaid rosewood salon suite, comprising a sofa and two open armchairs.

£660–790 TRM(D)

A walnut bergère salon suite, comprising a sofa and two chairs with loose cushions, on cabriole feet, c1920, sofa 54in (137cm) wide.

£400–450 MCB

BREAKFAST TABLES

A rosewood breakfast table, on a carved support, c1835, 43¾in (111cm) diam.

£1,550–1,800 S(O)

A mahogany tilt-top breakfast table, on a carved column and platform base with paw feet, c1850, 44in (112cm) wide.

£610–680 MTay

A Victorian walnut breakfast table, the burr-figured top above a leaf-carved column, on leaf-carved scrolled legs, 52¾in (134) wide.

£390–460 DN(BR)

CARD TABLES

A mahogany card and tea table, with a fold-over triple top, on cabriole legs with pad feet, c1740, 32in (81.5cm) wide.

£5,200–5,800 CGA

A George III mahogany card table, the baize-lined top above a frieze drawer, on square moulded legs with carved leaf brackets, refreshed, 26in (66cm) wide.

£1,400–1,650 CAG

A Chippendale-style carved mahogany card table, with a serpentine top, the frieze carved with a shell, on moulded and chamfered tapered legs, America, Massachusetts, 1760–80, 34½in (87.5cm) wide.

£3,800–4,500 SK(B)

A mahogany card table, with inlaid decoration, on tapered legs with spade feet, Scotland, c1800, 36in (91.5cm) wide.

£670–750 CSM

A mahogany card table, the fold-over top above inlaid panels, on turned and reeded legs with tapered feet, America, Boston, c1810, 36in (91.5cm) wide.

£2,100–2,500 JAA

A William IV rosewood card table, the fold-over top on a reeded column and carved lion-paw feet, 36in (91.5cm) wide.

£1,200–1,400 PWA

A Victorian walnut card table, the quarter-veneered baize-lined fold-over top above carved supports joined by a central urn, on carved scrolled legs, 42¼in (107.5cm) extended.

£1,100–1,300 GIL

A Victorian walnut card table, with line-inlaid decoration, with a fold-over and swivel top, on turned tapered legs, 35½in (90cm) wide.

£1,700–2,000 E

A rosewood and marquetry-inlaid envelope card table, on square tapered legs, c1880, 21in (53.5cm) wide.

£1,600–1,800 BURA

CENTRE TABLES

◄ **A baroque rosewood and mahogany centre table,** with gilt-lacquer mounts, on turned legs with turned stretchers, Portugal, mid-18thC, 53½in (148.5cm) wide.

£8,400–10,000 S(NY)

A mahogany centre table, with a revolving top, on a tapered triform base with lion-paw feet, c1825, 42in (106.5cm) diam.

£550–660 JBe

A rococo revival walnut centre table, with a marble top, the carved legs joining a central platform with a carving in the form of a squirrel, America, Ohio, Cincinnati, 1850–75, 41in (104cm) wide.

£1,050–1,250 NOA

A Victorian goncalo alves centre table, attributed to Gillows, the tilt-top with a moulded edge and crossbanded frieze, on a column with three downswept scroll feet, 52in (132cm) diam.

£2,700–3,200 Mit

A rococo revival laminated rosewood centre table, attributed to J. and J. W. Meeks, New York, the marble top over a pierced and carved frieze, on pierced and carved cabriole legs, the pierced stretcher with a basket of fruit, America, 1850–75, 45in (114.5cm) wide.

£18,500–22,200 NOA

Furniture attributable to a prestigious American furniture company such as Meeks will usually command a premium in the home market.

A Victorian burr-walnut centre table, with boxwood and ebony line inlay and amboyna and kingwood crossbanding, the tilt-top inlaid with eight Tunbridge ware panels, on a carved base with four downswept scroll feet, 53in (134.5cm) diam.

£3,100–3,450 LGr

A mahogany centre table, with a granite top and ormolu mounts, c1900, 28in (71cm) diam.

£1,000–1,150 ALCH

CONSOLE & PIER TABLES

A rococo giltwood pier table, the top veneered with marble, Italy, Venice, mid-18thC, 55in (139.5cm) wide.

£5,800–6,900 S(NY)

A painted wood console table, with a marble top, on scroll supports, France, late 18thC, 44in (112cm) wide.

£11,700–13,000 AUB

◄ **A giltwood console table,** with a *faux* marble top and carved decoration of leaves and flowers, Sweden, Stockholm, mid-18thC, 26¾in (68cm) wide.

£2,500–3,000 BUK

A carved wood bowfronted console table, the marble top above a guilloche frieze with floral swags, on leaf-carved turned legs united by a stretcher with an urn, with later paint, Italy, 19thC, 37in (94cm) wide.

£2,500–3,000 WW

A giltwood console table, the marble top over a carved frieze and carved scroll supports, mid-19thC, 21in (53.5cm) wide.

£540–640 G(L)

Made from the 18th century onwards, console tables have no back legs to support them and were permanently fixed to a wall in an entrance hall or salon, while pier tables were designed to stand in the wall space between two windows and have a back support. They were both often made in pairs. Console tables are frequently found in giltwood with marble tops – look out for original marble and attractive carving. Pier tables are usually constructed in expensive woods such as rosewood, mahogany and giltwood, and Regency versions often have mirrors below to reflect light. Desirable features are original mirror glass, a semi-circular or serpentine shape and original gilding.

◄ **A giltwood pier table,** with a marble top, on carved legs united by a stretcher with an urn, c1850, 47in (119.5cm) wide.

£11,200–12,500 PWA

This table is a highly desirable piece as it is constructed of giltwood and marble and has ornate carved decoration.

A pair of Empire-style mahogany pier tables, the tops inset with *verde antico* marble, on gilt-metal mounted column supports with undertiers, on bun feet, mid-19thC, 36½in (92.5cm) wide.

£1,000–1,200 NOA

► **A rococo revival laminated rosewood pier table,** with a scroll and foliate-carved frieze, on shell and floral-carved cabriole legs with shelves, with label for 'T. Brooks Cabinet and Upholstery Warehouse, Brooklyn', America, 1850–75, 59in (150cm) wide.

£4,600–5,500 NOA

A George III-style satinwood pier table, the top with segmented veneers and portrait medallions within kingwood banding and stringing, with parcel-gilt decoration, c1900, 55½in (141cm) wide.

£5,400–6,400 S

DINING TABLES

A mahogany dining table, with brass mounts, on tapered legs, with two later leaves, France, c1780, 29½in (75cm) wide.

£6,500–7,900 S(NY)

A George III mahogany dining table, the frieze with line-inlaid decoration, with central drop-leaf section, on tapered legs, 72in (183cm) extended.

£2,200–2,600 HOLL

A late George III mahogany dining table, Thomas Butler's patent, with one extra leaf, brass patent label, on turned and reeded tapered legs, 84in (213.5cm) extended.

£7,700–9,200 CAG

Thomas Butler of 13/14 Catherine Street, Strand, London, is recorded as working between 1787 and 1814. He specialized in patented bedsteads, dining tables and chair beds, which often bore a brass patent label as with this piece. His handbills advertise 'Bed Furniture and Mattresses calculated for the East and West Indies. Ship cabbins furnished. Articles particularly adapted for Travelling and Exportation.'

◀ **A George III mahogany dining table,** with two extra leaves, on three turned tapered pillars with down-swept legs, 142in (360.5cm) extended.

£14,000–16,800 HYD

▶ **A late George III mahogany dining table,** in two sections, on tapered square legs, 47¼in (120cm) diam.

£370–440 AMB

A mahogany drop-leaf dining table, the flame mahogany ends inset with acanthus-carved panels, on rope-twist legs, America, New York, c1800, 82in (208.5cm) extended.

£1,250–1,500 JAA

A Regency mahogany dining table, with drop-leaf ends, a concertina base and four extra leaves, on turned tapered legs, 135in (343cm) extended.

£4,700–5,600 SWO

▶ **A George IV mahogany drop-leaf dining table,** in the manner of Gillows, with two extra leaves, 191in (486cm) extended.

£6,000–7,200 S

Gillows was founded in Lancaster in 1695 by Robert Gillows, a joiner. A branch was opened in what is now Oxford Street in London in 1761. By the 19th century, the company was one of the foremost cabinet-makers in the country.

A George IV mahogany dining table, the drop-leaf centre section with a frieze drawer, on four turned columns with splay feet, together with a pair of 'D'-shaped ends on turned tapered legs, 76in (193cm) extended.

£1,900–2,250 AG

An early Victorian mahogany dining table, with a plain frieze, on turned tapered legs, with three extra leaves and a leaf cabinet, 122½in (311cm) extended.

£3,650–4,300 GIL

A Victorian mahogany dining table, on cabriole legs with armorial and leaf-scroll carving, 65½in (166.5cm) wide.

£810–970 JAd

A Victorian mahogany dining table, with an extra leaf, on baluster-turned tapered legs, 84¼in (224cm) extended.

£1,200–1,400 CHTR

A mahogany dining table, with four extra leaves, on gadrooned baluster legs, 19thC, 146in (371cm) extended, together with a contemporary mahogany leaf cabinet.

£7,600–9,100 CGC

A mahogany dining table, with an extra leaf, 19thC and later, on turned and reeded legs, 93in (236cm) wide.

£3,000–3,600 HYD

A mahogany dining table, with two extra leaves, on turned and reeded legs, c1870, 72in (183cm) extended.

£3,850–4,600 PFS

A mahogany dining table, with one extra leaf, on cabriole legs with claw-and-ball feet, c1920, 53in (134.5cm) wide.

£420–480 MTay

DISPLAY TABLES

A kingwood *bijouterie* **table,** with ormolu mounts, on cabriole legs, France, 19thC, 36¾in (93.5cm) wide.

£1,750–2,100 WilP

A Louis XVI-style gilt-brass vitrine/display table, the superstructure with two glazed cupboard doors enclosing a mirrored and shelved interior, the lower section with a glazed hinged top, on fluted tapered legs, c1870, 33½in (85cm) wide.

£540–640 NOA

A Louis XV-style kingwood and marquetry ***bijouterie*** **table,** on cabriole legs, c1900, 17in (43cm) wide.

£2,200–2,450 MTay

◄ **A Louis XVI-style mahogany display table,** with ormolu mounts, on fluted tapered legs, c1900, 31¾in (80.5cm) wide.

£1,900–2,250 NOA

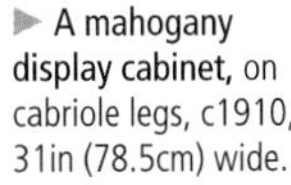

► **A mahogany display cabinet,** on cabriole legs, c1910, 31in (78.5cm) wide.

£360–400 MCB

DRESSING TABLES

A George III mahogany dressing table, the hinged top enclosing a recess, above a dummy drawer, a drawer and a cupboard, on tapered legs with spade feet, 15¾in (40cm) wide.

£330–390 DN

A figured walnut dressing table, the mirror flanked by candle shelves, above a marble top and six drawers, America, 1850–75, 48½in (123cm) wide.

£310–370 NOA

A mahogany dressing table, with a cheval mirror, the pedestals each with a drawer and cupboard, c1905, 48in (122cm) wide.

£630–700 HEM

DROP-LEAF TABLES

A mahogany drop-leaf table, Sweden, c1800, 58¾in (149cm) wide.

£2,000–2,400 BUK

◄ A mahogany **drop-leaf table,** the tapered legs inlaid with bellflowers, America, 1800–25, 48in (122cm) wide.

£700–840 NOA

◄ **A mahogany drop-leaf table,** on turned tapered legs with pad feet, c1820, 51in (129.5cm) wide.

£510–580 BURA

► **A mahogany and marquetry drop-leaf table,** with a drawer, on cabriole legs with pad feet, Holland, c1830, 54in (137cm) wide.

£1,800–2,000 NoC

DRUM TABLES

A mahogany drum table, with four drawers and four dummy drawers, leather top replaced, c1800, 36¼in (92cm) diam.

£7,200–8,600 S

A George III mahogany drum table, the leather-inset top above four drawers, 42in (106.5cm) diam.

£2,900–3,450 MA&I

A George IV rosewood drum table, with satinwood beading, the revolving leather-inset top above four drawers and four dummy drawers, 47in (119.5cm) diam.

£2,700–3,200 WW

A mahogany drum table, the revolving top above drawers and a cupboard, on brass lion-paw feet, c1830, 50in (127cm) diam.

£5,200–5,800 PWA

An inlaid mahogany drum table, with three drawers and three dummy drawers, 1880–1900, 18in (45.5cm) diam.

£880–980 DEB

GAMES TABLES

A rococo games table, the top with a later gilt-tooled leather inset, Italy, mid-18thC, 30in (76cm) wide.

£2,900–3,450 S(NY)

A games table, the sycamore top with penwork sides and inlaid with a boxwood and ebony chessboard, on an ebonized column and base, c1820, 21in (53.5cm) wide.

£1,000–1,150 CSM

A walnut games/work table, the fold-over top with burr veneers and inlaid for chess and backgammon, above a frieze drawer and sliding workbox, on turned supports and stretchers and leaf-carved outscrolled legs, mid-19thC, 21in (53.5cm) wide.

£840–1,000 N

An early Victorian rosewood games table, the fold-over top inlaid with a chessboard, enclosing a leather-lined surface, on turned tapered legs, slight damage, 33in (84cm) wide.

£860–1,000 MCA

◀ **A walnut games table,** the tilt-top inlaid with a chessboard and marquetry, on a carved tripod base, c1860, 24in (61cm) diam.

£1,350–1,500 PSA

In the 18th century numerous tables were produced specifically for playing cards or games such as backgammon, chess and tric trac (a form of backgammon). Tops were often reversible with a games board on one side and a plain surface on the other. By c1810, games tables were often incorporated with work tables. As the century progressed, designs became increasingly ingenious, with tops that opened, revolved around 90 degrees revealing boards for different games, with perhaps a fitted drawer below and a bag underneath for holding needlework accessories.

LIBRARY TABLES

A Regency rosewood library table, with three drawers, on carved and turned supports united by a carved and turned stretcher, the legs with paw feet, stamped 'Gillingtons 4965', Ireland.

£1,650–1,950 AMB

The brothers George and Samuel Gillington are recorded at several addresses in Dublin and in various partnerships from 1815 to 1838.

A George IV mahogany library table, on reeded legs, 60in (152.5cm) wide.

£2,850–3,200 OCA

A rosewood library table, with two frieze drawers, mid-19thC, 52in (132cm) wide.

£1,700–2,000 Bea

▶ **A walnut and carved oak library table,** the quarter-veneered and crossbanded top above four drawers and four dummy drawers, carved with scrolling foliage, the supports carved in the form of lions, 19thC, 60¾in (154.5cm) wide.

£1,750–2,100 DN

NESTS OF TABLES

A Regency nest of four quarter-veneered satinwood and burr-walnut tables, on turned legs with downswept feet, largest 19½in (49.5cm) wide.

£2,700–3,200 SWO

A Victorian nest of three walnut tables, on bobbin-turned legs with scroll-carved feet, 20in (51cm) wide.

£790–880 PSA

A nest of four crossbanded mahogany tables, on turned legs with downswept feet, c1890, 19in (48.5cm) wide.

£2,150–2,400 MALT

OCCASIONAL TABLES

A carved walnut occasional table, on foliate-carved feet, Continental, 19thC, 35½in (90cm) wide.

£1,200–1,400 SK

◄ **A Regency rosewood and ebonized tilt-top occasional table,** with parcel-gilt decoration, 16in (40.5cm) wide.

£3,850–4,300 HA

A mahogany occasional table, the later top with a leather inset on a tapered column and leaf-carved bun feet, France, 19thC, 22in (56cm) diam.

£300–360 DN

A carved mahogany occasional table, with specimen marble top, c1830, 25in (63.5cm) wide.

£1,950–2,200 NoC

A rosewood occasional/writing table, on a carved column, c1840, 22in (56cm) wide.

£2,050–2,300 MALT

A mahogany occasional table, c1870, 19in (48.5cm) diam.

£510–580 TRED

A walnut and parquetry occasional table, c1890, 22in (56cm) diam.

£250–280 ⊞ MCB

A marble and *pietra dura* occasional table, the top inset with a butterfly, late 19thC, 18½in (47cm) diam.

£2,000–2,400 ⚒ S(O)

An inlaid walnut occasional table, on tapered legs, c1900, 20in (51cm) wide.

£300–340 ⊞ QA

PEMBROKE TABLES

A George III satinwood Pembroke table, the quarter-veneered top with inlaid decoration above a frieze drawer, on square tapered legs, 24in (61cm) high.

£1,700–2,000 ⚒ SWO

An inlaid mahogany Pembroke table, on square tapered legs, altered, America, New England, c1790, 18¾in (47.5cm) wide.

£820–980 ⚒ S(NY)

Ex-Estate of Laurance S. Rockefeller.

A plum pudding mahogany and kingwood-crossbanded Pembroke table, with line-inlaid decoration and a drawer, on square tapered legs, c1790, 37½in (95.5cm) wide.

£2,150–2,400 ⊞ YOX

'Plum pudding' is a type of figuring in some veneers, characterized by dark spots in the wood. This indicates a piece of quality, as does the kingwood used in the crossbanding.

A late Georgian mahogany Pembroke table, with ebony and boxwood stringing, a drawer and a dummy drawer to each end, on turned tapered legs, 29¼in (74.5cm) open.

£350–420 ⚒ PFK

A rosewood Pembroke table, with satinwood crossbanding, c1810, 39in (99cm) wide.

£1,750–1,950 ⊞ WAA

An inlaid mahogany Pembroke table, with a drawer, on square tapered legs, 19thC, 35½in (90cm) wide.

£470–560 ⚒ TRM(E)

Insurance values

Always insure your valuable antiques for the cost of replacing them with similar items, regardless of the original price paid. Both dealers and auctioneers can provide a valuation service for a fee.

SERVING TABLES

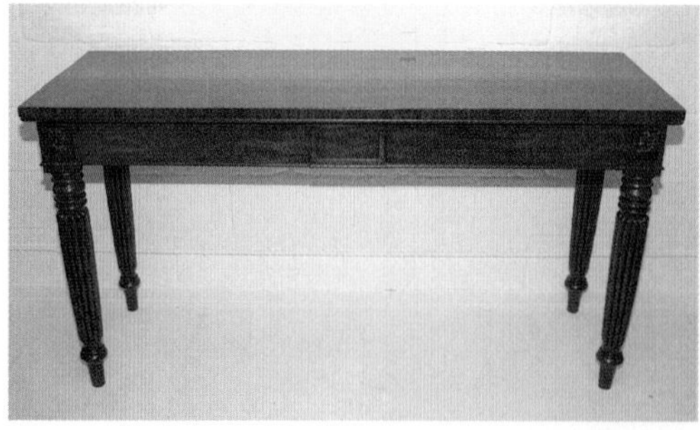

A **mahogany serving table,** with two drawers, on reeded legs, c1825, 72in (183cm) wide.

£4,300–4,800 BURA

A **George IV mahogany serving table,** the frieze with two concealed drawers, on carved scrolled supports, 77in (195.5cm) wide.

£2,350–2,800 TRM(C)

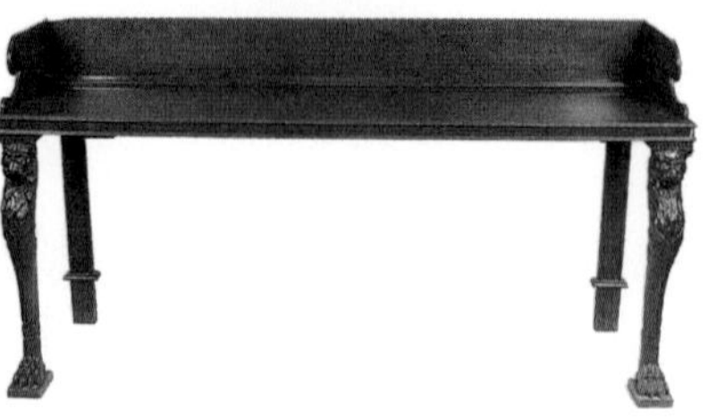

► A **William IV mahogany serving table,** the legs carved with lion masks, 48in (122cm) wide.

£4,900–5,800 JAd

SIDE TABLES

A **walnut single drop-leaf gateleg side table,** on spindle- and cup-turned legs, late 17thC, 28¼in (72cm) wide.

£940–1,100 PFK

A **Louis XV fruitwood-inlaid walnut side table,** with a frieze drawer, on cabriole legs with hoof feet, France, 32½in (82.5cm) wide.

£1,450–1,700 SK

A **George II mahogany side table,** the marble top above a carved frieze, on carved cabriole legs with hairy paw feet, Ireland, 48in (122cm) wide.

£37,500–45,000 DN

A wonderful example of Irish interpretation of the rococo style, this table with its beautiful carving and marble top was the focus of eight telephone bidders, although it eventually sold to a dealer in the room.

► A **George III cherrywood bowfronted side table,** with three drawers, on square tapered legs, 36in (91.5cm) wide.

£620–700 PSA

A **rosewood side table,** with a drawer, on turned legs and stretchers, c1810, 30in (76cm) high.

£1,650–1,850 GEO

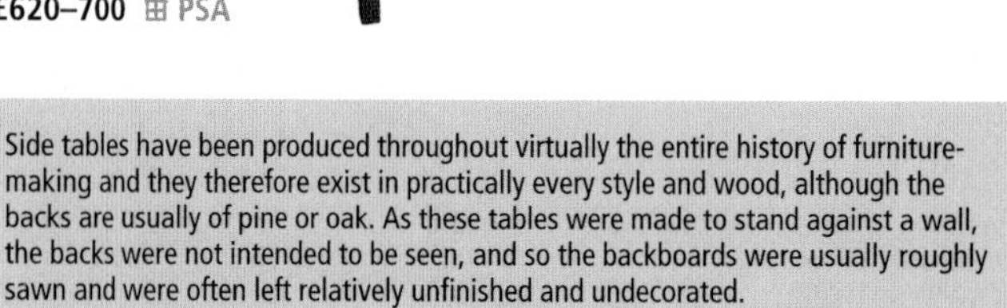

Side tables have been produced throughout virtually the entire history of furniture-making and they therefore exist in practically every style and wood, although the backs are usually of pine or oak. As these tables were made to stand against a wall, the backs were not intended to be seen, and so the backboards were usually roughly sawn and were often left relatively unfinished and undecorated.

A burr-elm side table, mahogany lined, with two drawers, on turned legs, c1830, 42in (106.5cm) wide.

£2,500–2,800 AGI

A walnut side table, by Heal & Sons, with a drawer, on turned legs, c1860, 36in (91.5cm) wide.

£620–700 BURA

▶ **A Victorian mahogany side table,** with two drawers, on reeded legs, 48in (122cm) wide.

£540–610 MCB

A maple side table, with two drawers, on ring-turned tapered legs, America, 19in (48.5cm) wide.

£920–1,100 S(NY)

Ex-Estate of Laurance S. Rockefeller.

▶ **A mahogany side table,** with a drawer, on turned columns and bow supports united by a turned stretcher, stamped 'Wilkinson, London', c1870, 24in (61cm) wide.

£850–950 TRED

The firm of Wilkinson was founded c1790 by William and Thomas Wilkinson. By 1808 William had established his own business in London, and by 1825 his two sons had joined the company. They built up a flourishing trade, winning commissions from distinguished clients such as the Goldsmiths company. Wilkinson produced furniture in the Egyptian, rococo and Grecian styles among others.

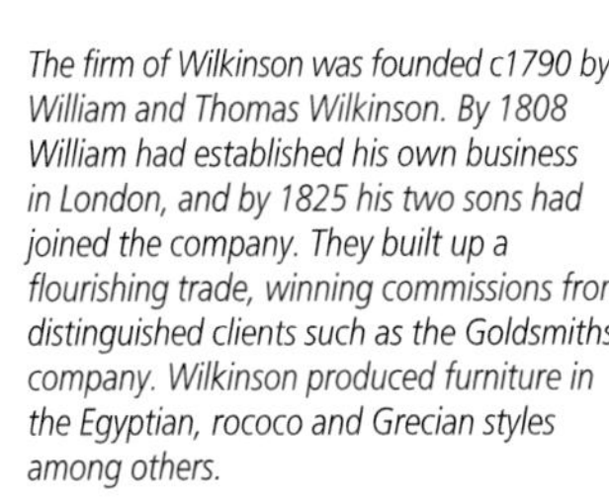

A walnut, kingwood and rosewood fold-over side table, with marquetry decoration and gilt-bronze mounts, on cabriole legs, c1890, 36in (91.5cm) wide.

£8,800–9,800 PWA

A mahogany side table, with a tambour shutter top and serpentine front, on tapered legs, c1900, 41in (104cm) wide.

£720–800 HEM

A pair of Sheraton revival walnut, satinwood and giltwood demi-lune side tables, with inlaid geometric decoration, on tapered legs, early 20thC, 38in (96.5cm) wide.

£5,900–7,000 G(L)

SOFA TABLES

A mahogany sofa table, the top with boxwood stringing and rosewood crossbanding, with a frieze drawer, on a turned column with reeded sabre legs, c1790, 28¾in (73cm) wide.

£850–950 RGa

A late George III mahogany and satinwood-inlaid sofa table, with drop flaps and two drawers, on downswept supports, damaged, 38¼in (97cm) wide.

£1,350–1,600 SWO

A Regency mahogany and satinwood-crossbanded sofa table, with drop flaps and two drawers, the supports with geometric inlay and scroll feet, possibly Channel Islands, 42in (106.5cm) wide.

£3,500–4,200 G(L)

A Regency mahogany sofa table, with brass line inlay, a drop flap and two frieze drawers, the supports with acanthus leaf-capped scroll toes, 58¼in (148cm) wide.

£3,000–3,600 CHTR

A calamander sofa table, with two drawers, on supports with splayed feet, c1810, 27in (68.5cm) high.

£20,700–23,000 RGa

Calamander is a particularly attractive and desirable timber.

◄ **A Regency brass-inlaid rosewood sofa table,** with a frieze drawer, on a lotus-carved stem with a gilt-brass collar and splayed feet, slight damage, 59in (150cm) wide,

£2,350–2,800 Bea

A Regency mahogany and ebonized sofa table, the top with an ebonized band, with later applied gilt-brass decoration, with two frieze drawers, the legs with brass paw sabots, damaged, 36½in (92.5cm) wide.

£1,150–1,350 WW

A mahogany sofa table, with drop-leaf ends, c1920, 36in (91.5cm) wide.

£610–680 MTay

SUTHERLAND TABLES

A Victorian burr-walnut Sutherland table, with a shaped top, on turned end supports, 36in (91.5cm) wide.

£640–760 HYD

A burr-walnut Sutherland table, with a shaped top, on turned end supports c1870, 36in (91.5cm) wide.

£780–880 TRED

An Edwardian mahogany Sutherland table, 33in (84cm) wide.

£310–350 PFS

TEA TABLES

A mahogany tea table, the fold-over top enclosing a well, c1730, 31¼in (79.5cm) wide.

£7,800–9,400 S

A mahogany serpentine tea table, on cabriole legs with claw-and-ball feet, 18thC, 32in (81.5cm) wide.

£1,400–1,650 G(L)

A mahogany tea table, with satinwood crossbanding, on square tapered legs, c1790, 36¼in (92cm) wide.

£2,150–2,550 S(O)

A Regency mahogany tea table, the swivel top above a breakfront frieze, on a ring-turned column, 35½in (90cm) wide.

£610–730 FHF

A mahogany tea table, the fold-over top enclosing a recess, on turned tapered legs with pad feet, late 18thC, 23¾in (60.5cm) high.

£1,000–1,200 SWO

A mahogany tea table, with a fold-over top, on turned legs, c1830, 36in (91.5cm) wide.

£1,150–1,300 OCA

◄ **A rococo revival rosewood tea table,** the fold-over top with a burr-veneered mahogany moulded edge, on a fluted column, c1850, 36in (91.5cm) wide.

£1,950–2,200 LGr

► **A rosewood tea table,** with a fold-over top and cabriole legs, c1900, 38in (96.5cm) wide.

£1,750–1,950 PWA

TRIPOD TABLES

◀ **A mahogany tilt-top tripod table,** on a baluster column and cabriole legs, 18thC, 28in (71cm) diam.

£450–500 WWH

▶ **A rosewood and gilt tripod table,** c1800, 29in (73.5cm) high.

£1,950–2,200 HA

A figured mahogany tilt-top tripod table, on a baluster ring-turned column, c1825, 18in (45.5cm) diam.

£830–930 JC

A pair of Victorian oak tripod tables, with marble tops, on turned columns, 15½in (39.5cm) diam.

£1,650–1,950 S(O)

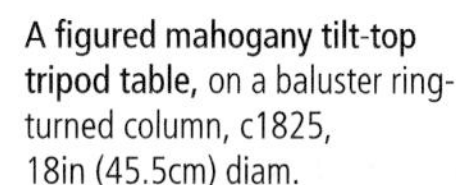

◀ **A mahogany tripod table,** with carved decoration, c1915, 29in (73.5cm) high.

£620–700 PFS

TWO-TIER TABLES

A Victorian satinwood two-tier table, with crossbanding and stringing, the removable tray top with brass handles, 34¾in (88.5cm) wide.

£520–620 AH

A mahogany two-tier table, with a brass gallery, France, c1880, 29in (73.5cm) high.

£800–890 GEO

An inlaid mahogany two-tier table, c1890, 25in (63.5cm) wide.

£1,150–1,300 MALT

◀ **A Louis XV-style kingwood and gilt-bronze two-tier table,** by P. Sormani, the upper tier with a removable glazed tray, stamped mark, France, late 19thC, 39½in (100.5cm) wide.

£9,600–11,500 S(O)

Paul Sormani traded from rue Charlot, Paris. The company produced high quality furniture predominantly in the Louis XV and Louis XVI styles.

▶ **A satinwood-veneered two-tier table,** with ormolu mounts, c1900, 23in (58.5cm) high.

£990–1,100 CSM

WORK TABLES

A mahogany work table, on lyre end supports, Holland, c1820, 21in (53.5cm) wide.

£890–1,000 ⊞ CSM

A figured mahogany work table, with brass inlay, with two drawers above a sliding pouch, 19thC, 20in (51cm) wide.

£1,100–1,300 ⚒ NSF

A tiger maple and bird's-eye maple work table, with two drawers, slight damage, America, 1825–35, 21in (53.5cm) wide.

£1,750–2,100 ⚒ SK(B)

A Sheraton-style rosewood-veneered work table, with two frieze drawers above a deep drawer, on turned legs, America, 1825–50, 21½in (54.5cm) wide.

£500–600 ⚒ NOA

A mahogany work table, inlaid with specimen woods, c1850, 21½in (54.5cm) wide.

£1,550–1,750 ⊞ GEO

A Napoleon III crossbanded fruitwood work table, with a frieze drawer, on columnar supports, France, 1848–70, 27½in (70cm) wide.

£400–480 ⚒ SK

► **A mahogany work table,** the hinged top enclosing a fitted interior, c1860, 22in (60cm) wide.

£1,150–1,300 ⊞ HEM

A Victorian walnut work table, the hinged top with a tooled-leather inset and marquetry decoration, enclosing a fitted interior, 18in (45.5cm) diam.

£680–810 ⚒ Mit

A Victorian pâpier-mâché work table, with painted and mother-of-pearl decoration, the hinged top enclosing a fitted interior, on a turned tripod base, 18½in (47cm) wide.

£210–250 ⚒ WilP

► **A satinwood and painted work table,** the hinged top with a tulipwood-crossbanded border, enclosing a lined interior, above a silk bag, late 19thC, 17½in (44cm) wide.

£940–1,100 ⚒ DN

WRITING TABLES

A Louis XVI walnut and mahogany *bureau plat*, with ormolu mounts, the sides with gilt-tooled leather-inset writing slides, on reeded legs, adapted, France, 56in (142cm) wide.

£3,900–4,650 S(NY)

▶ **A kingwood and rosewood writing table,** with a hinged quarter-veneered top over a leather-inset writing slide, a drawer to one side, on cabriole legs with ormolu sabots, Italy, Genoa, mid-18thC, 18¼in (46.5cm) wide.

£8,400–10,000 S(NY)

The design of this table with its quarter-veneered top is typical of the work of Genoese cabinet-makers imitating the French taste of the 1750s.

A tulipwood, kingwood, amaranth and parquetry *bureau plat*, with three drawers and three dummy drawers, with later mounts, stamped 'P. Roussel', France, c1780, 51in (129.5cm) wide.

£22,800–27,300 S

Pierre Roussel was received master in 1745 at the age of 22 and established his business in Paris. He was an extremely successful cabinet-maker and was regarded among his peers as the finest in the city. He enjoyed great success in his trade guild and was elected to various high offices. He enjoyed an illustrious client list which included the Prince de Condé, providing furniture for the Palais-Bourbon and the Château de Chantilly.

A neo-classical mahogany *bureau plat,* with brass mounts, the leather-inset top above three drawers, on square tapered legs, with two paper labels, one inscribed in Russian 'St Petersburg, English Avenue 28', Russia, St Petersburg, c1800, 58¼in (148cm) wide.

£10,400–12,400 S(NY)

▶ **A Victorian rosewood writing table,** with a leather-inset top, 45in (114cm) wide.

£500–560 MCB

MISCELLANEOUS TABLES

A late Victorian Eclipse patent walnut-veneered drinks table/humidor, with a rise-and-fall compartment fitted with two cut-glass decanters and eight tumblers, above a revolving shelf, 24in (61cm) closed.

£1,150–1,300 Mit

An Edwardian George II-style mahogany supper table, the top with nine dishes, 32in (81.5cm) diam.

£680–810 AMB

A painted wood corner table, with a drawer, c1920, 33in (84cm) wide.

£500–560 ALCH

TEAPOYS

A mahogany teapoy, c1810, 30in (76cm) high.
£2,350–2,650 GEO

A William IV rosewood teapoy, with a fitted interior, 18in (45.5cm) wide.
£470–560 GTH

A Victorian rosewood teapoy, with a fitted interior, 17in (43cm) wide.
£540–640 SWO

TORCHERES

A George III mahogany torchère, on a baluster-turned column and tripod base, 18½in (47cm) wide.
£760–910 DN

A pair of Regency painted and parcel-gilt torchères, on reeded legs, with gilt-metal paw feet, tops replaced, 38¾in (98.5cm) high.
£4,100–4,900 WW

A carved walnut torchère, restored, c1850, 48in (122cm) high.
£720–860 S(O)

A mahogany torchère, late 19thC, 43in (109cm) high.
£350–390 PFS

TRAYS

A pâpier-maché tray, by Jennens & Bettridge, London, c1860, 31in (78.5cm) wide.
£720–800 NoC

A Victorian mahogany butler's tray, 29½in (75cm) wide.
£370–440 JAd

An Edwardian satinwood tray, on a later mahogany stand, 28in (71cm) wide.
£600–670 PWA

WARDROBES

An early Victorian inverted breakfront wardrobe, the central panelled doors enclosing slides, above three drawers, flanked by two further panelled doors enclosing hanging space, 103¼in (262.5cm) wide.

£700–840 WW

An early Victorian figured mahogany inverted breakfront wardrobe, the central panelled doors over five drawers, flanked by two further panelled doors, 80¾in (205cm) wide.

£1,250–1,500 DD

A walnut wardrobe, the moulded cornice over two panelled doors, on ogee bracket feet, America, probably Louisiana, mid-19thC, 66in (167.5cm) wide.

£1,650–1,950 NOA

A walnut and marquetry-inlaid wardrobe, with a single drawer above a pair of panelled doors, on tapered feet, Holland, mid-19thC, 63in (160cm) high.

£2,000–2,300 GEO

A bird's-eye maple wardrobe, with a mirrored door, America, probably Philadelphia, 1850–75, 59in (150cm) wide.

£1,250–1,500 NOA

A burr-walnut wardrobe, the central mirrored door flanked by two panelled doors, c1860, 71in (180.5cm) wide.

£1,900–2,150 BURA

A Victorian walnut wardrobe, the central section with five graduated drawers, flanked by mirrored cupboard doors enclosing hanging space, 98in (249cm) wide.

£1,100–1,300 AH

A Victorian breakfront wardrobe, the mirrored door enclosing five drawers, flanked by panelled doors, 86½in (220cm) wide.

£1,200–1,400 SWO

A Victorian mahogany wardrobe, the two panelled doors over a base drawer, 72¾in (185cm) high.

£370–440 SWO

A mahogany wardrobe, the two doors enclosing three drawers and hanging space, c1880, 47in (119.5cm) wide.

£1,150–1,300 OCA

A carved cherrywood wardrobe, America, late 19thC, 51in (129.5cm) wide.

£270–320 JAA

An Edwardian mahogany wardrobe, with two parquetry panelled doors and one mirrored door, enclosing drawers, trays and hanging space, 75in (190.5cm) wide.

£1,350–1,500 SWA

An inlaid mahogany wardrobe, by Wylie & Lochhead, the two doors above two drawers, Scotland, Glasgow, c1910, 50in (127cm) wide.

£1,250–1,400 HEM

A mahogany wardrobe, with ormolu mounts and quarter-veneer and marquetry panels to the three doors and three drawers, c1910, 69½in (176.5cm) wide.

£1,800–2,000 SWA

WASHSTANDS

A George III mahogany corner washstand, 43in (109cm) high.

£760–850 PENH

A George III mahogany washstand, with a shaped frieze, 13in (33cm) square.

£280–330 WW

A Georgian mahogany washstand, 28in (71cm) high.

£270–300 Fai

MILLER'S COMPARES

I. **A George III mahogany washstand,** with original retractable mirror, 36in (91.5cm) high.
£990–1,100 PENH

II. **A George III mahogany washstand,** 33in (84cm) high.
£540–600 PENH

When considering these two washstands, it is immediately apparent that Item I has a more imposing appearance than Item II. Both the colour and the grain of the timber in Item I are superior and it is larger in size than Item II. The front of Item I is particularly attractive in design, with its two dummy drawers over a pair of cupboard doors and a real drawer beneath. Item I also has better quality moulded edges and moulding around the doors. The recessed mirror of Item I is a very desirable feature and the interior has been finished to a higher standard overall.

A George III yew-wood washstand, the dummy drawer above a door with a drawer below, legs reduced, 18in (45.5cm) wide.
£280–330 GTH

A Sheraton-style mahogany and boxwood-inlaid corner washstand, Scotland, c1805, 26in (66cm) wide.
£270–300 CSM

A Regency mahogany washstand, the scalloped splash-back and apron above a shelf with a drawer, on ring-turned supports and legs 23½in (59.5cm) wide.
£600–670 PSA

A mahogany washstand, in the form of an architectural column, the hinged lid enclosing a fitted interior, the fluted column with a cupboard door, 19thC, 33in (84cm) high.
£3,200–3,800 HOLL

A tiger maple washstand, the scrolled splash-back over a single drawer, slight damage, some repair, America, 1830s, 31in (78.5cm) wide.
£3,150–3,750 SK(B)

A mahogany corner washstand, c1860, 39in (99cm) high.
£210–240 NORTH

A mahogany washstand, with painted and mother-of-pearl decoration, the splash-back with a shelf above a marble insert, the base with a marble top above a drawer and two cupboards, c1900, 49in (124.5cm) wide.
£260–310 TRM(C)

A Victorian walnut washstand, the top with a marble insert, on three reeded column legs and bun feet, 31in (78.5cm) high.
£400–450 MCB

WHATNOTS

A carved rosewood four-tier whatnot, c1835, 50in (127cm) high.

£1,200–1,350 GSA

MILLER'S COMPARES

I. A mahogany four-tier whatnot, with a drawer to the base, c1790, 54in (137cm) high.

£2,000–2,250 GEO

II. A mahogany three-tier whatnot, with a drawer to the base, c1800, 45in (114.5cm) high.

£1,050–1,200 GEO

Item I is of more elegant proportions than Item II, and three of the four tiers have a gallery whereas Item II only has a gallery around the highest tier. The turned finials on Item I are another attractive feature. A further very important factor determining value is that the surfaces of the upper two tiers of Item II have been replaced, whereas Item I is in original condition.

WINDOW SEATS

A neo-classical painted and parcel-gilt window seat, Italy, late 18thC, 92in (233.5cm) long.

£6,200–7,400 S(NY)

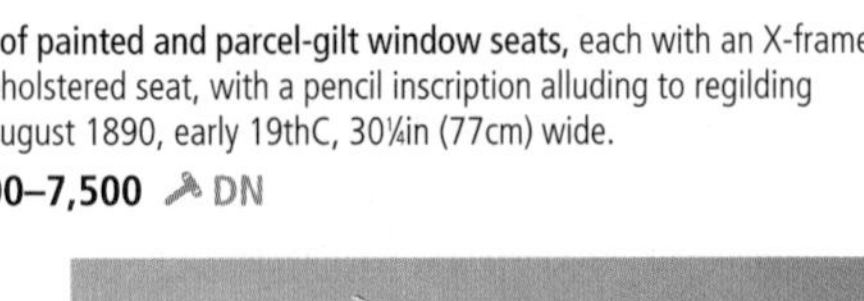

A pair of painted and parcel-gilt window seats, each with an X-frame and upholstered seat, with a pencil inscription alluding to regilding 17th August 1890, early 19thC, 30¼in (77cm) wide.

£6,300–7,500 DN

A mahogany window seat, with turned legs, c1880, 45in (114.5cm) wide.

£370–420 MCB

A pair of gilt-willow window seats, with upholstered seats, America, c1900, 20in (51cm) wide.

£510–610 NOA

A walnut window seat, with a button-backed top rail over acanthus and stop-fluted splats, the supports united by plain and cartouche-moulded stretchers, c1905, 84½in (215cm) wide.

£1,100–1,300 ROS

WINE COOLERS & CELLARETS

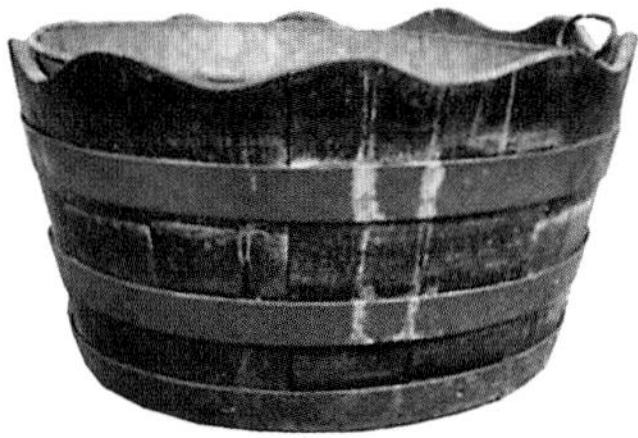

A George III coopered oak wine cooler, with brass binding and a tin liner, 20½in (52cm) wide.

£190–220 SWO

◀ **A George III inlaid mahogany cellaret,** with chequer and feather stringing, inlaid with husk swags, with a side drawer, 15in (38cm) high.

£940–1,100 SWO

A mahogany cellaret, with ebony stringing, c1800, 22in (56cm) wide.

£1,000–1,150 GSA

A Regency mahogany cellaret, with a moulded top, the swivel-front enclosing a baize-lined three-bottle carrier, 24in (61cm) wide.

£1,300–1,550 TEN

A Regency pollarded oak wine cooler, with brass lion-head handles, 19in (48.5cm) wide.

£1,350–1,500 NoC

A mahogany cellaret, with satinwood stringing, the top with a marquetry-inlaid medallion enclosing a six-section interior, early 19thC, 24in (61cm) wide.

£590–700 MA&I

A figured mahogany wine cooler, enclosing a lead-lined interior, with a panelled front, the corners with carved and shaped corbels, on lion-paw feet, c1825, 28½in (72.5cm) wide.

£3,350–3,750 JC

A William IV carved oak and pollarded oak wine cooler, c1825, 37½in (95.5cm) wide.

£2,400–2,850 S(O)

◀ **A mahogany wine cooler,** with a lead liner, on turned feet with inset brass casters, c1830, 27in (68.5cm) wide.

£1,750–1,950 YOX

GOTHIC REVIVAL

THE WORD GOTHIC WAS FIRST USED in the 17th century to distinguish medieval from classical architecture and was generally used in a disparaging sense, linking the style to a period regarded as dark and barbaric. Fortunately, despite this prejudice , the founding of the Society of Antiquaries in London in 1707 promoted interest in Gothic art and design and an appreciation of the many Gothic ruins around the country that were being dismantled for their raw materials and ornament.

By the middle of the 18th century, the revival of taste for medieval architecture had begun in earnest. When, between 1747 and 1753, Horace Walpole (1717–97) turned his Twickenham home, Strawberry Hill, into a compact Gothic villa, both the house and its contents did much to increase the popularity of the style. His whimsical approach however did not sit well with the great exponents of Gothic revival – Sir George Gilbert Scott (1811–78) and A. W. N. Pugin (1812–52 – see p104) regarded such early efforts as far too flippant and lacking in accuracy to deserve the epithet 'Gothic revival'.

There is now a mass of furniture varying hugely in both quality of design and manufacture that lays claim to the term. From the great confections of Pugin and John Gregory Crace (1809–89) to the humble 'Eastlake' and 'Wycombe' woodseat parlour chairs there seems to be something for everybody.

A good example of the former was offered recently in London by Sotheby's. It was a carved oak reading stand with a tracery superstructure over three hinged sloping flaps, supported on a tripod base, which came from Sutton Place, the home of J. Paul Getty until his death in 1976. It also had an additional piece of invaluable provenance – a hand-written label that stated: 'This piece of carved oak furniture from the exhibition in Hyde Park 1851 was given to Jemima Wyburd by her affectionate father Edward Corbould at Christmas 1900'. Corbould (1815–1905), whose daughter, Jemima, was married to the artist Francis Wyburd (1829–1909), was a prominent watercolour painter who would certainly have attended the Great Exhibition. Consequently, although the auctioneers were unable to identify the maker of the piece, this scrap of paper and the obvious quality of the item itself resulted in it shaking off the £7,000–10,000 estimate and eventually selling for a hammer price of £18,000.

Leslie Gillham

◄ **A Victorian Gothic revival oak hall bench,** the pierced rail over a hinged seat, with a shaped and pierced apron, 60¾in (154.5cm) wide.

£800–960 SWO

► **A Gothic revival mahogany and mahogany-veneered bookcase,** with glazed tracery-barred and panelled doors, repolished, America, New York, c1830, 51½in (131cm) wide.

£8,500–9,500 JBT

► **A Gothic revival oak bookcase,** in the manner of Cottingham, the crenellated cornice above a foliate-carved cavetto, the glazed upper doors with ogee arches and quatrefoil mullioned bars, flanked by pinnacle buttresses, the base doors with blind ogee arches, with carved animal heads, with initials 'H.L.', dated 1847, 40in (101.5cm) wide.

£20,700–23,000 AV

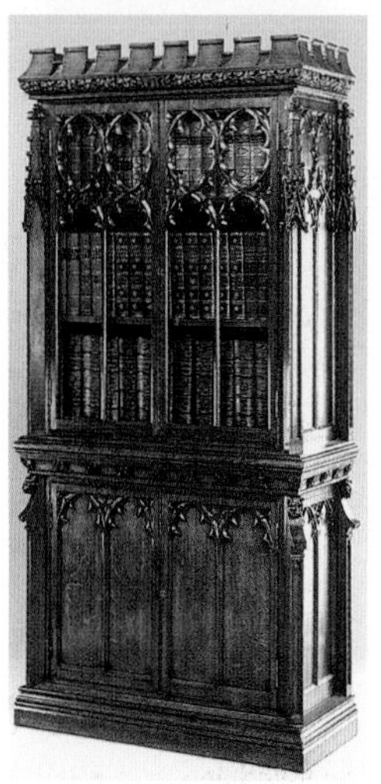

A Gothic revival carved oak buffet, the two doors carved with 'Romayne' heads, the base with three carved panels at the rear, with earlier elements, France, 19thC, 41¼in (104.5cm) wide.

£1,200–1,400 S(O)

A Gothic revival mahogany bow-fronted hanging corner cupboard, the fretwork cornice with obelisks, above a panelled door, 1805–20, 29in (73.5cm) wide.

£10,800–12,000 AV

A **Gothic revival rosewood side cabinet,** with carved linenfold panels, the two doors enclosing two drawers and a shelf, c1870, 41¾in (106cm) wide.
£3,450–4,100 S(O)

A **Victorian Gothic revival oak miniature corner cabinet,** with a carved and pierced door and carved initials 'CG', 13½in (34.5cm) wide.
£350–420 PFK

► A **pair of Gothic revival oak hall chairs,** c1850.
£580–650 NoC

A **pair of Gothic revival mahogany and mahogany-veneered chairs,** attributed to A. Roux, repairs to legs, America, New York, mid-19thC.
£990–1,100 JBT

These chairs were used by President Lincoln in the White House when he signed the Emancipation Proclamation

A **Gothic revival walnut side chair,** the pierced back with a central spire, with a tapestry seat, on turned legs, America, 1850–75.
£230–270 NOA

A **Gothic revival oak throne chair,** with button back upholstery, c1870.
£2,700–3,000 GEO

A **Gothic revival oak hall chair,** designed by Charles Bevan, manufactured by Marsh, Jones & Cribs, Leeds, with turned front and splayed back legs, c1870.
£900–1,000 PVD

For clocks in the Gothic revival style please see the Clocks section on pages 311–355.

A **Gothic revival oak hall chair,** with a pierced back, c1870.
£145–165 HEM

A **pair of Gothic revival mahogany hall chairs,** with solid seats and turned front legs, c1875.
£140–165 PF

◄ A **set of four Gothic revival carved oak hall chairs,** c1875.
£5,400–6,000 PVD

A set of six Gothic revival pitch pine dining chairs, including two carvers, c1880.

£3,500–4,000 TDG

A pair of Gothic revival mahogany armchairs, the arms carved with rams'-head terminals, c1880.

£1,850–2,100 RML

A Victorian Gothic revival carved mahogany writing desk, 30in (76cm) wide.

£3,800–4,550 S(O)

◄ A set of Gothic revival pine fretwork folding shelves, c1840, 22in (56cm) wide.

£440–490 PICA

► A set of Gothic revival wall shelves, with pierced back and sides, late 19thC, 20½in (52cm) wide.

£330–390 DN

A Gothic revival walnut sideboard, by the Robert Mitchell Furniture Company, with tile mounts, the upper section with a shelf, the base with six drawers and two cupboards, with stencilled maker's label, America, St Louis, c1875, 56in (142cm) wide.

£2,150–2,550 NOA

The firm of Robert Mitchell and Frederick Rammelsberg was established in 1847 in Cincinnati, Ohio. In 1855 they opened a factory in St Louis which was managed by Robert's brother, William. In 1846, William sold half of his interests in the St Louis company to Robert, making them equal partners. After the Civil War, Robert Mitchell travelled to New Orleans from Cincinnati and founded the firm of Mitchell, Craig and Company.

A Gothic Revival oak table, with a frieze drawer, the legs supported by carved figures of monks, France, c1870, 24¾in (63cm) wide.

£5,200–6,200 S(P)

◄ A Gothic revival figured rosewood wardrobe, the mirrored door enclosing a figured maple interior with maple shelves, mirror replaced, America, New York, c1840, 42in (106.5cm) wide.

£8,500–9,500 JBT

A. W. N. Pugin

Augustus Welby Northmore Pugin (1812–52) was the leading force behind the 19th-century Gothic revival in England, drawing his inspiration from the 15th century in particular. He based his designs on Gothic forms and, through his pursuit of archeological accuracy, the Gothic style became a vehicle of reform which would be echoed in the later Arts & Crafts movement. Pugin produced mainly robust utilitarian highly ornamented furniture, usually in oak. He insisted on following medieval styles and methods, so that all minor details and joints were hand made. When he decorated the interior of the newly rebuilt Houses of Parliament in London in the 1840s, he started a trend that led to Gothic being adopted as the national style.

◄ An early Victorian Gothic revival oak wardrobe, by Gillows, the design attributed to A. W. N. Pugin, the three six-panel linenfold doors enclosing slides, drawers and hanging space, stamped and initialled, 84¼in (214cm) wide.

£9,400–11,200 CGC

A sketch for a wardrobe of this pattern, designed by A. W. N. Pugin, features in the 1852 Estimate Sketch Book of Gillows of Lancaster and London.

OAK & COUNTRY FURNITURE

EARLY OAK AND COUNTRY FURNITURE was invariably made for 'minimalist' interiors and is therefore naturally compatible with today's sparse designs. This furniture was made for the purposes of function and practicality and was made to last. Over the course of time it would develop a rich patina, an intriguing surface texture, scars and bruises, showing evidence of its age and use and ultimately a unique character. These qualities are what the market cherishes. At a time when more traditional 'formal' antique furniture has been struggling to maintain popular support, early oak and country pieces have been flourishing and prime examples have achieved some remarkable prices.

Fall-front bureaux are still rather unfashionable, and case furniture, which by necessity needs to be situated against a wall, must have qualities of particular merit to attract strong demand. Even the classic dressers have not been achieving the extraordinary prices of a few years ago unless they are the very best examples. Fine quality, early carved and decorated furniture, however, is enjoying a renaissance. Particularly rare pieces with expressive, figurative or eccentric regional motifs dating from the 17th century or earlier, are commanding a huge premium.

Genuine paint-decorated and Folk Art furniture from the 18th and early 19th century continues to attract serious interest as well as charming primitive pieces such as dug out chairs and coffers, Windsor chairs, tavern and cricket tables and pieces bearing original carved or painted initials, names and dates. A growing interest in our vernacular heritage and folk art traditions has led to increased awareness in regional and local provenance. Pieces carrying a genuine and substantiated provenance are now also at a premium.

Robert Young

Robert trained at Sotheby's and started his antiques business in 1976. He is committee Chairman for Fine Art and Antiques Fairs at Olympia and a member of the vetting committee.

He has written many articles on country and folk subjects and is the author of Folk Art *published by Mitchell Beazley.*

Well-figured and unusual timbers, particularly yew, mulberry, fruitwoods and almost all specimen burr woods command a premium, as does original hardware and lack of visible interference. Pieces with later secondary carving, evidence of alterations, clumsy proportions and lack of genuine surface and patination still meet with little demand.

Free standing, 'sculptural' furniture, with an interesting graphic line and appealing silhouette, unusual charm and character are the examples to look out for but increasingly are hard to find. Subject to the natural market forces of supply and demand the best pieces are currently enjoying a high profile, although the sums involved are still relatively small and I suspect that prices will continue to rise. **Robert Young**

BOXES

◀ **A Charles I carved oak desk box,** the hinged top inlaid with banding and enclosing a fitted interior, the front with flowerhead carving and inlaid with guilloche, 25¼in (64cm) wide.

£2,400–2,850 S

◀ **An oak Bible box,** the hinged top above an iron lock and clasp, 17thC, 20½in (52cm) wide.

£500–600 GTH

◀ **An oak Bible box,** with carved decoration, 17thC, 28in (71cm) wide.

£270–300 CGA

An oak candle box, with a sliding front, c1780, 15in (38cm) high.

£210–240 WAA

BUFFETS

A cherrywood buffet, with brass fittings, France, 18thC, 49in (124.5cm) wide.
£1,500–1,700 ⊞ PENH

A chestnut buffet, France, c1800, 52in (132cm) wide.
£1,400–1,550 ⊞ GD

An ash buffet, with carved decoration, France, c1830, 52in (132cm) wide.
£1,350–1,500 ⊞ Lfo

BUREAUX

A George III oak kneehole bureau, with a fitted interior above seven drawers and a central cupboard, 38in (96.5cm) wide.
£1,350–1,600 MAL(O)

An oak bureau, the fall-front enclosing a fitted interior, above three drawers, c1790, 36in (91.5cm) wide.
£2,200–2,450 ⊞ RED

A George III oak bureau, the fall-front enclosing a fitted interior, above two drawers and two cupboard doors, 35¾in (91cm) wide.
£410–490 PFK

BUREAU BOOKCASES & CABINETS

An oak and crossbanded bureau cabinet, with ebony and boxwood stringing, the upper section with two doors enclosing a fitted interior, the fall-front enclosing a fitted interior, inlaid with initials and date 1747, on later ogee bracket feet, 48½in (123cm) wide.
£8,400–10,000 S

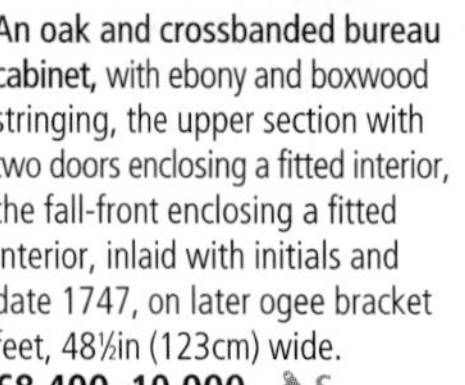

▶ **An elm and pine bureau cabinet,** the upper section with two cupboard doors, the base with a fall-front above five drawers, 18thC, 32½in (82.5cm) wide.
£4,900–5,500 ⊞ RED

An oak bureau cabinet, the upper section with two cupboard doors, the base with a fall-front above four drawers, 18thC, 41¾in (106cm) wide.
£2,350–2,800 RTo

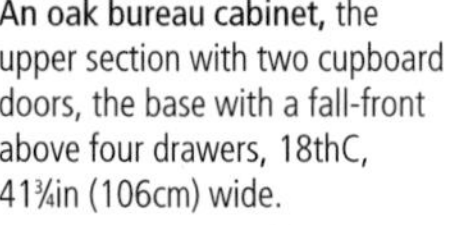

▶ **An oak and mahogany-crossbanded bureau bookcase,** the upper section with two astragal-glazed doors enclosing shelves, the base with a fall-front enclosing a fitted interior, over five drawers, losses, c1800, 41in (104cm) wide.
£1,500–1,800 Hal

◀ **An oak and mahogany-crossbanded bureau cabinet,** the upper section with two panelled doors enclosing adjustable shelves, the base with a fall-front enclosing a fitted interior, over two frieze drawers and two panelled doors, 19thC, 41in (104cm) wide.
£960–1,150 DA

CHAIRS

An oak wainscot chair, the panelled and carved back above turned supports, 17thC.

£2,800–3,350 CGC

A pair of oak hall chairs, both with a barley-twist stretcher, c1660.

£2,250–2,500 SPUR

A pair of carved oak side chairs, 1680–90.

£4,500–5,000 KEY

A pair of oak side chairs, c1680.

£610–680 NAW

A maple and ash armchair, with a rush seat and turned stretchers, height reduced, America, probably Massachusetts, 1690s.

£2,000–2,400 SK(B)

A William and Mary beech armchair, with a caned back, restored, late 17thC.

£1,400–1,650 S(O)

► **A painted side chair,** the cresting rail carved with feather plumes and scrolls, the back with block, vase and ring-turned stiles, on block, vase and ring-turned legs, America, Massachusetts, 1710–25.

£3,200–3,850 SK

◄ **An oak armchair,** initialled 'WRH' and dated '1712', North Yorkshire.

£4,400–4,900 KEY

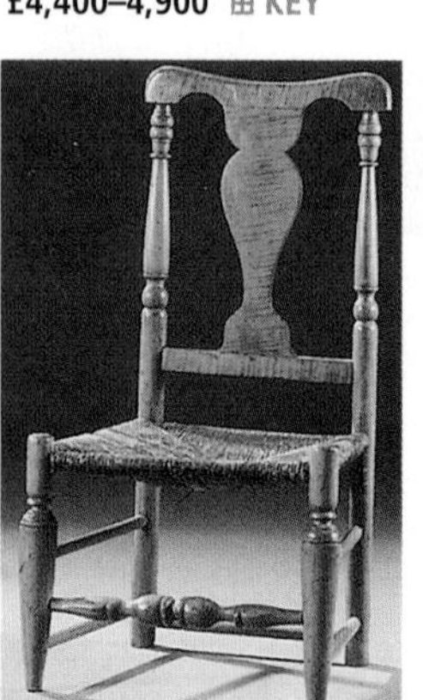

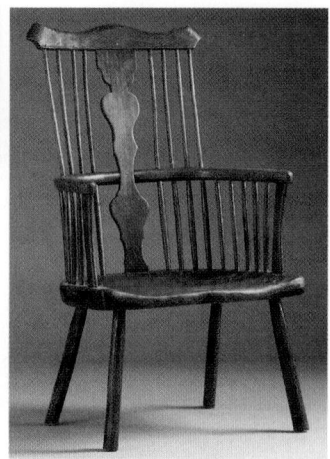

An elm and ash Windsor chair, probably Thames Valley, c1750.

£2,500–2,800 RYA

◄ **A Queen Anne tiger maple chair,** with a rush seat, on turned legs, America, probably Hudson Valley, c1740.

£150–180 JAA

A Queen Anne carved, joined and painted chair, with a rush seat, on Spanish feet, America, New England, c1765.

£4,900–5,400 ⊞ GIAM

A set of four elm country chairs, c1780.

£800–900 ⊞ PSA

An elm and ash ladder-back Windsor armchair, late 18thC.

£400–480 SWO

A pair of Hepplewhite-style elm chairs, 1790–1800.

£300–340 ⊞ ALCH

A pair of oak side chairs, Wales, 18thC.

£380–430 ⊞ WWH

An ash and fruitwood primitive back stool, c1800.

£1,900–2,200 ⊞ RYA

An ash and oak primitive chair, Isle of Man, c1800.

£2,450–2,750 ⊞ MMA

An oak and other woods bow-back Windsor side chair, America, probably Philadelphia, c1800.

£175–210 JAA

A Hepplewhite-style elm country chair, with a needlework seat, 19thC.

£165–185 ⊞ SPUR

A set of eight painted wood chairs, with rush seats, the ring-turned legs with bun feet, slight damage, majority of rush seats replaced, America, New England, 1815–30.

£1,150–1,350 SK(B)

► **A fruitwood and elm Windsor chair,** the back with turned spindles, c1820.

£880–980 HWK

A fruitwood and elm elbow chair, the back with reeded rails, on tapered legs, early 19thC.

£440–520 DN

A fruitwood elbow chair, c1830.

£200–230 BURA

A yew-wood Windsor chair, with a crinoline stretcher, c1840.

£850–950 MIN

A set of eight ash and elm spindle-back chairs, with turned legs, Lancashire, c1840.

£3,600–4,000 ChS

An ash rocking chair, with a rush seat, c1840.

£310–350 GD

An elm armchair, mid-19thC.

£250–280 WV

A set of six yew-wood Windsor **armchairs,** with elm seats, c1850.

£6,400–7,200 ⊞ PeN

This set of chairs is particularly desirable because of the unusual design, the timber and the colour.

An oak **armchair,** with pierced splat and sides and a leather seat, c1870.

£1,350–1,500 ⊞ NoC

A set of seven Carolean-style oak **dining chairs,** including two carvers, moulded and carved with masks and trailing flowers, with padded backs and stuff-over seats, on barley-twist supports, c1880.

£590–700 PF

CHILDREN'S CHAIRS

A child's carved ash **high chair,** c1615.

£12,100–13,500 ⊞ KEY

▶ A child's ash and elm **chair,** c1800.

£240–270 ⊞ NoC

A child's elm **Windsor chair,** 19thC.

£340–380 ⊞ SPUR

A child's ash and elm **Windsor high chair,** c1850.

£990–1,100 ⊞ CGA

A child's beech **chair,** the seat with a hole and a removable cover, c1880.

£340–380 ⊞ SAT

A child's fruitwood **chair,** with a rush seat, France, c1900.

£80–90 ⊞ MLL

CHESTS & COFFERS

An oak chest, the front inlaid with arabesque motifs and figural panels, the interior with an inlaid beech till, with two later drawers, bracket feet later, Anglo-German, 1600–25, 60¼in (153cm) wide.

£5,800–6,900 S

The origin of the design of this piece owes much to craftsmen who emigrated to England from France, Holland and Cologne in Germany in the late 16th and 17th centuries. Chests such as these are also known as 'Nonsuch chests' as they depict elements of the famous Nonsuch Palace built by Henry VIII, which was subsequently lost to fire.

A carved oak chest, with three panels, c1620, 50in (127cm) wide.

£3,250–3,900 S(NY)

An oak coffer, with bog oak and holly inlay, c1670, 48in (122cm) wide.

£850–950 REF

A panelled oak coffer, the front with carved decoration, West Country, c1680, 43in (109cm) wide.

£1,350–1,500 KEY

An oak coffer, the front with carved decoration, late 17thC, 45½in (115.5cm) wide.

£470–560 GTH

An oak coffer, the panelled top above a lunette-carved frieze, late 17thC, 39in (99cm) wide.

£1,250–1,400 DEB

A walnut chest, inlaid with bone and mother-of-pearl, the front with three carved panels, Anglo-Dutch, c1680, 67in (170cm) wide.

£4,550–5,400 S(O)

An oak coffer, the panelled front with carved decoration, Dorset, c1700, 38in (96.5cm) wide.

£350–400 CSM

An oak coffer, with plank top and sides, c1700, 48¾in (124cm) wide.
£1,300–1,550 BAM(M)

An oak coffer, the panelled top above a carved front, initialled 'W.C.' and dated '1729', some restoration, early 18thC, 41¾in (106cm) wide.
£350–420 Bea

Items in the Oak & Country Furniture section have been arranged in date order within each subsection.

An oak coffer, with a panelled top and front, 18thC, 43in (109cm) wide.
£580–650 HEM

▶ An oak mule chest, the panelled front with three drawers, on shaped bracket feet, c1780, 61in (155cm) wide.
£1,200–1,350 BURA

An oak coffer, dated 1720, 55in (139.5cm) wide.
£490–550 NoC

An oak chest, the panelled top above a carved frieze and two panels, on stile supports, damaged, early 18thC, 51½in (131cm) wide.
£290–340 Hal

◀ An oak coffer, with a panelled top and sides, on stile supports, early 18thC, 34in (86.5cm) wide.
£1,200–1,400 G(L)

An oak mule chest, the hinged top enclosing a candle box, above a panelled front with two drawers, 18thC, 44½in (113cm) wide.
£500–600 SWO

An oak coffer, with a panelled front, 1790–1800, 46in (117cm) wide.
£1,100–1,250 WWH

A burr-elm coffer, with a two-plank top, France, c1800, 56in (142cm) wide.
£810–900 ALCH

◄ A tiger-maple sugar box, with a drawer, slight damage, America, southern states, 1820–30, 42¾in (108.5cm) wide.
£4,150–4,900 SK(B)

An oak and metal-bound chest, with brass studs, Continental, c1900, 39in (99cm) wide.
£330–370 PEC

◄ A beech chest, Romania, c1850, 38in (96.5cm) wide.
£290–330 ERA

CHESTS-ON-CHESTS

A George III oak chest-on-chest, the top with two short and two long drawers, the base section with three long drawers, on shaped bracket feet, 44in (112cm) wide.
£570–680 HYD

A George III oak chest-on-chest, the top with three short drawers and three long drawers and fluted angles, the base with a slide over three long drawers, on bracket feet, 43½in (110.5cm) wide.
£840–1,000 AH

An oak chest-on-chest, the top with three short and three long drawers, the base with three long drawers, damaged, late 18thC, on bracket feet, 38in (96.5cm) wide.
£1,900–2,250 Hal

CHESTS OF DRAWERS

A Charles II oak and fruitwood chest of drawers, with four drawers and panelled sides, on later bracket feet, 37in (94cm) wide.

£520–620 HYD

An oak chest of drawers, with four panelled drawers, on bracket feet, the handles later, 17thC, 37in (94cm) high.

£880–1,050 SWO

An oak and yew-wood chest of drawers, with ebonized yew-wood mouldings, on bun feet, c1680, 40in (101.5cm) wide.

£1,750–1,950 PICA

MILLER'S COMPARES

I. **A William and Mary pearwood and snakewood chest of drawers,** with two graduated drawers above a further two drawers, 38½in (98cm) wide.

£5,900–7,000 HYD

II. **A Charles II oak chest of drawers,** with three short and three long drawers and panelled sides, on later feet, 39in (99cm) wide.

£640–760 HYD

Snakewood originates from the West Indies and is used in small quantities on the highest quality 17th-century furniture. The use of this rare timber and the combination of the originality, surface and colour of Item I ensured that it attracted a great deal of interest at auction. The cushion-moulded second drawer is another desirable feature as is the bold waist moulding. The fact that the chest is in two parts gives the side panels a more interesting appearance than the plainer sides of Item II. The bun feet, which are correct for the period, are also more pleasing than the later bracket feet on Item II. Moreover, the small vertical panels on each side of the drawers on Item I are more attractive than the simple 'D' moulding on Item II. In addition, Item I has an elegant moulded top and stepped base moulding.

An oak chest of drawers, c1690, 44in (112cm) wide.

£1,100–1,250 NoC

A Georgian crossbanded oak chest of drawers, with five drawers, 43¾in (111cm) wide.

£330–390 WilP

◄ **A crossbanded oak chest of drawers,** with two short and two long drawers, c1740, 33in (84cm) wide.

£2,000–2,250 WWH

► **An oak chest of drawers,** with four graduated drawers, early 18thC, 33in (84cm) wide.

£2,700–3,000 RED

A George II oak chest of drawers, with two short and three long graduated drawers, on bracket feet, 27in (68.5cm) wide.

£370–440 HYD

A burr-yew-wood chest of drawers, with later brass handles, c1740, 37in (94cm) wide.

£4,900–5,500 RYA

An oak bachelor's chest of drawers, the folding top with inlaid starburst decoration, above one long drawer over two short and two long drawers, on bracket feet, c1760, 32in (81.5cm) wide.

£3,700–4,200 NoC

It is most unusual to find bachelor's chests of this type in oak.

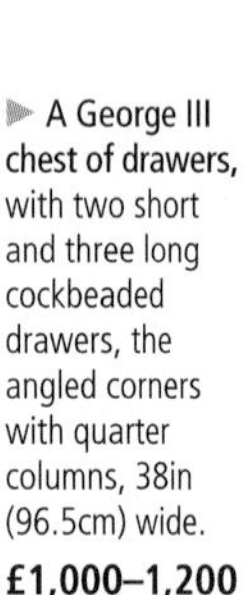

► **A George III chest of drawers,** with two short and three long cockbeaded drawers, the angled corners with quarter columns, 38in (96.5cm) wide.

£1,000–1,200 AH

A cherrywood chest of drawers, with four long drawers, c1790, 41½in (105.5cm) wide.

£800–960 Hal

Fruitwood furniture generally achieves higher prices than oak pieces.

An oak chest of drawers, with two short and three long graduated drawers, on bracket feet, with later handles, early 19thC, 36½in (92.5cm) wide.

£230–270 WW

► **An oak chest of drawers,** Denmark, c1820, 35in (89cm) wide.

£1,450–1,650 BURA

A cherrywood chest of drawers, with an overhanging top drawer on turned supports, with later pulls, America, c1830, 41in (104cm) wide.

£175–210 JAA

Traditionally, early chests of drawers are considered more desirable when under 36in (91.5cm) wide. An overhanging top with a moulded edge is a sign of quality, as is a good 'D' or double 'D' moulding between the drawers. Examples with attractive or exotic timber facings such as fruitwood, snakewood, olivewood, figured or burr-walnut are all cherished and add value.

Original feet, usually straight through stiles or turned bun feet, are now rare and add value. Examples with bracket feet are either very late or the feet will most likely be replacements. Examples prior to 1680 should have side-hung drawers with a broad groove cut into the outside edge of the thick drawer linings to house the internally fitted runners.

CHESTS-ON-STANDS

An oak chest-on-stand, the plank top above two short and three long drawers, the base with three short drawers, on eight legs, stand and handles later, later, 17thC, 40½in (103cm) wide.

£560–670 Hal

An oak chest-on-stand, with two short and three long drawers, the base with a panelled frieze drawer, 17thC, 48in (122cm) wide.

£1,200–1,400 ROS

An oak chest-on-stand, with two short and three long drawers, the base with three short drawers, on cabriole legs, stand possibly later, early 18thC, 41¾in (106cm) wide.

£640–760 DN

► **An oak chest-on-stand,** with two panelled drawers, 18thC, 26½in (67.5cm) wide.

£340–400 ROS

◄ **A George II oak chest-on-stand,** with two short and three long drawers, the base with three drawers and a shaped apron, 41in (104cm) wide.

£2,350–2,800 HYD

CLOTHES & LINEN PRESSES

An oak linen press, the arched panelled doors above six graduated drawers, Wales, 18thC, 50in (127cm) wide.

£2,250–2,500 WWH

An oak and mahogany-crossbanded linen press, with two panelled doors enclosing two shelves, the lower section with six drawers, repaired, probably Wales, 1750–1800, 50in (127cm) wide.

£840–1,000 Hal

An oak clothes press, with two panelled doors above three drawers, on claw-and-ball feet, Holland, c1820, 63in (160cm) wide.

£4,050–4,500 GD

CUPBOARDS

A carved oak mural cupboard, the two foliate-carved panelled doors enclosing a divided interior with shelves, 1625–50, 40¼in (102cm) wide.

£8,400–10,000

This piece was originally built into an architectural recess.

An oak wall cupboard, with two panelled doors, North Country, c1680, 26in (66cm) wide.

£1,500–1,700 PeN

A William and Mary oak press cupboard, the later moulded cornice above a carved frieze dated 1689, above panelled doors carved with Westmorland scrolls, over a shelf and panelled cupboard doors, 97in (246.5cm) wide.

£1,200–1,400 Mit

Westmorland style

In the 17th and early 18th centuries, the isolated rural areas of Westmorland and the Lake District were populated mainly by yeomen farmers, and a particular style of vernacular architecture and carved decoration developed. The carving on pieces from this region have a strong Celtic influence, typically with stylized lace strapwork motifs, often incorporating details of animal or human form, stylized ferns and bold serpent mofits, as well as dates and often initials. It is an area that is associated with built-in furniture from this period and, as a result, furniture historians have been able to examine fitted spice cupboards, housekeepers' and court cupboards, bread oven doors and decorated architectural elements *in situ* in order to establish a knowledge of this regional style.

A William III Westmorland-style oak press cupboard, the later moulded cornice above a carved frieze inscribed 'IGT 1695', over two carved panelled doors, the base with two doors above a further door, 50in (127cm) wide.

£2,600–3,100 PFK

An oak cupboard, 1720–30, 51½in (131cm) wide.

£4,650–5,200 RED

▶ **An oak corner cupboard,** in two parts, c1740, 76in (193cm) high.

£8,000–8,800 HWK

The unusual narrowness of this cupboard is a desirable feature.

A cherrywood wall cupboard, with two star-inlaid panelled doors, c1740, 36in (91.5cm) high.

£2,250–2,500 PEN

An oak cupboard, the moulded cornice above two panelled doors and two drawers, on ogee bracket feet, mid-18thC, 56in (142cm) wide.

£730–870 DN

An oak cupboard, the carved frieze over four fielded carved panelled doors and two drawers, carved decoration later, mid-18thC, 54in (137cm) wide.

£2,300–2,600 PSA

An elm hanging corner cupboard, the moulded cornice above an inlaid door, 18thC, 27¼in (69cm) high.

£960–1,150 SWO

An oak cupboard, with two doors over a drawer, 18thC, 20in (51cm) wide.

£580–650 CGA

An oak wall cupboard, 18thC, 19in (48.5cm) high.

£410–460 PSA

An oak wall cupboard, with a scroll pediment, 18thC, 28in (71cm) wide.

£850–950 WWH

◀ **An oak hanging corner cupboard,** the dentil cornice above a panelled door enclosing three shelves, Wales, Carmarthenshire, c1770, 38in (96.5cm) wide.

£630–750 PF

The fluted detail to the sides of this cupboard is a desirable feature.

Further reading

John Bly's Antiques Masterclass, Miller's Publications, 2005

▶ **An oak armoire,** the panelled cornice with carved masks over two panelled doors, above a panelled and lion-mask base, Continental, 18thC, 69¼in (176cm) high.

£820–980 SWO

A George III housekeeper's oak cupboard, the upper section with two doors, the base with four drawers, 57in (145cm) wide.

£4,000–4,500 NoC

A George III figured oak hanging corner cupboard, the two panelled doors enclosing shelves, 39in (99cm) wide.

£1,650–1,950 HYD

The attractive figuring to the timber and the two doors are desirable features on this cupboard.

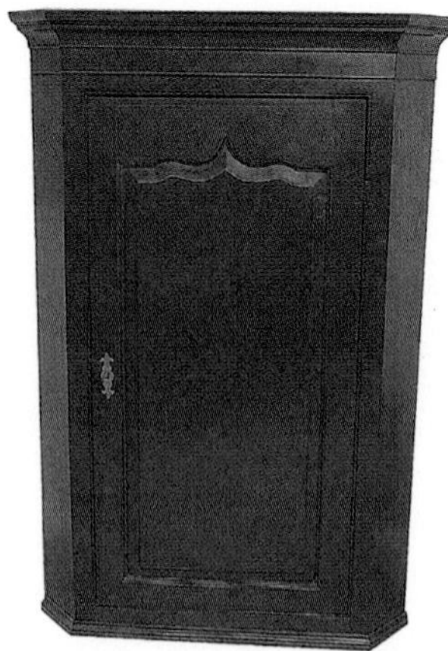

An oak and mahogany-banded corner cupboard, c1780, 43in (109cm) high.

£1,350–1,550 HWK

Corner cupboards

Both wall-hanging and floor-standing corner cupboards are more desirable with two opening doors rather than single doors. Exposed original 'H' or butterfly hinges, which appear on earlier examples up to c1750, are good features to find. In 18th-century examples, doors with multi-fielded (two or more) panels are also a sign of quality. It is wise to view carved decoration to fielded panels with suspicion as this is invariably a Victorian 'improvement' in the 'Jacobean style'. A curved or 'barrel' back within a corner cupboard is another sign of quality and floor-standing examples with barrel backs and internal 'architectural' details that can be left open to display glass and ceramics are the most sought after.

An oak bowfronted corner cupboard, decorated with crossbanding, with a dentil cornice, c1780, 47in (119.5cm) high.

£540–600 MCB

A burr-elm hanging corner cupboard, c1790, 39in (99cm) wide.

£3,350–3,750 HWK

◄ **A corner cupboard,** grained to imitate tiger maple, the top section with a smoke-painted glazed door enclosing shelves, the lower section with a panelled door, America, possibly Pennsylvania or Ohio, early 19thC, 47in (119.5cm) wide.

£6,300–7,500 SK

A cherrywood corner cupboard, with two glazed doors over two cupboard doors, America, c1820, 51in (129.5cm) wide.

£510–610 JAA

A burr-ash armoire, the two doors enclosing a fitted interior, France, 19thC, 82in (208.5cm) high.

£1,650–1,850 WWH

A carved oak cabinet, with two glazed doors, France, c1880, 48in (122cm) wide.

£2,000–2,250 ARCA

DRESSERS

An oak dresser, the base with three drawers above three cupboard doors, North Wales, 1730–40, 61¾in (157cm) wide.

£12,100–13,500 RED

Cupboard, or enclosed base dressers are considered more desirable when they feature three frieze drawers above the wing cupboards and, better still, a column of drawers or blind drawer fronts between these cupboards. Spice drawers or cupboards fitted into the base of a rack add interest and merit and are usually associated with the better quality examples. Racks with original backboards also carry a premium.

With open base or pot board dressers it is desirable to find shaped and open fret-cut decoration to the apron beneath the drawers. It is wise to view with suspicion open or serving dressers with only two frieze drawers because, although some were made, they are often three drawer pieces that have been reduced. Check that both ends of the serving surface are identical and that there is no evidence of having been cut and reduced.

An oak dresser, the cavetto cornice above a pierced apron and three shelves flanked by inset panelled cupboard doors, over three short cockbeaded drawers, above a pierced apron, West Midlands, c1780, 79½in (202cm) wide.

£5,300–6,300 Hal

The wide fitted cupboards within the rack and the shaped frieze to the cornice and apron are typical features of furniture from the West Midlands/Shropshire area.

An oak dresser, the coved cornice and shaped apron above two shelves, the base with two drawers above two panelled doors, 18thC, 53in (134.5cm) wide.

£4,350–5,200 NSF

An oak dresser, the base with eight drawers, with an associated rack and later brass handles, on cabriole front legs, possibly Cheshire/ Derbyshire, c1750, 96in (244cm) wide.

£3,500–4,200 Hal

The features associated with dressers from Cheshire and Derbyshire are the double row of drawers instead of cupboards, short cabriole legs and a proportionally high rack.

A George III oak dresser, the rack with three shelves, the base with three drawers above three fielded panelled doors,on bracket feet, restored, 61in (155cm) wide.

£2,800–3,350 MAL(O)

An oak dresser, with five spice drawers, North Wales, 18thC, 65in (165cm) wide.

£10,600–11,800 WWH

These slightly canopied racks with 'belly' sides and high, shaped shoes (the part of the rack where it meets the base), are typical of North Wales dressers of the mid-18th century, as are the shaped, overlaid plank panels to the doors. Spice drawers are a desirable feature.

An oak and mahogany-crossbanded dresser, the canopied rack with a later cornice and backing boards, above five cockbeaded drawers and two panelled doors, later handles, slight damage, northwest England, c1780, 72½in (184cm) wide.

£4,000–4,800 Hal

A George III inlaid oak and mahogany-crossbanded dresser, the shaped apron over two shelves and two cupboards, the base with eight drawers over a shaped apron, on cabriole legs, 98in (248cm) wide.

£4,450–5,300 SWO

The bank of double drawers to the base and the short cabriole legs indicate that this dresser may originate from Cheshire.

A George III Cumberland dresser, with three shelves above three frieze drawers, over three drawers flanked by two panelled doors, 60in (152.5cm) wide.

£2,700–3,200 Mit

Note the excellent wide boards to the back of the rack.

A George III oak dresser, with four shelves over three short drawers, above a pot board, 68in (172.5cm) wide.

£940–1,100 HYD

An oak and mahogany-crossbanded dresser, with brass handles and escutcheons and moulded fruitwood front legs, late 18thC, 68¼in (173.5cm) wide.

£2,250–2,700 DD

An oak dresser, the top with pierced frieze and sides and three shelves, the base with five drawers above three panelled doors, late 18thC, 94in (239cm) wide.

£11,300–13,500 DN

This is a very rare form of dresser with alternating wide and narrow drawers. It has a wonderful colour, original handles, good waist moulding and a very attractive rack. It appears to be lacking feet, although it may have small 'straight through' stile feet beneath the plinth.

An oak and pine dresser, the top section with three shelves above four drawers, the base with three drawers, late 18thC, 65¾in (167cm) wide.

£1,050–1,250 DN

An oak dresser, with three shelves above three drawers and a shaped fret, on turned supports and feet united by a pot board, c1800, 60¾in (154.5cm) wide.

£1,750–2,100 DN

▶ **An oak dresser,** with three long and three short drawers above a pot board, South Wales, c1810, 64in (162.5cm) wide.

£4,050–4,500 GD

◀ **An oak and pine dresser,** the upper section with three shelves and iron hooks, the base with three frieze drawers above a pot board, early 19thC, 55½in (141cm) wide.

£1,700–2,000 Bea

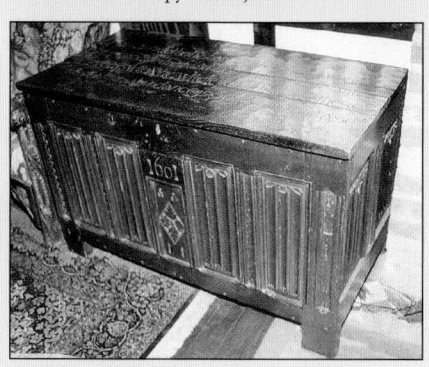

A late Georgian oak dresser, with three cockbeaded and mahogany-crossbanded drawers and two doors, on bracket feet, the associated contemporary rack with three shelves, 73¼in (186cm) wide.

£1,300–1,550 PFK

A fruitwood dresser, with two shelves over three frieze drawers, above three drawers flanked by two panelled doors, c1820, 63in (160cm) wide.

£2,950–3,300 NoC

An oak dresser, with three shelves above three drawers and a dog kennel recess flanked by two cupboards, early 19thC, 61½in (156cm) wide.

£2,200–2,600 JAd

An oak dresser, with two shelves above two drawers over turned supports and a pot board, with later brass plate handles and feet, rack associated, 19thC, 75in (190.5cm) wide.

£1,050–1,250 WW

An oak dresser, with three shelves over three drawers, above a pot board, Wales, Carmarthenshire, 19thC, 62in (157.5cm) wide.

£2,000–2,400 PF

A honey oak dresser, the upper section with two glazed cupboards and three shelves, the base with three frieze drawers above a dog kennel recess and two cupboards, Wales, Carmarthenshire, c1875, 60in (152.5cm) wide.

£940–1,100 PF

An oak crossbanded dresser, the upper section with three shelves and two cupboards, the base with three drawers and a pot board, c1860, 75in (190.5cm) wide.

£2,700–3,000 Fai

A Louis XV-style fruitwood dresser, with floral- and ribbon-carved decoration, the upper section with three shelves, the base with two drawers over two panelled cupboard doors, France, c1875, 51in (129.5cm) wide.

£2,500–3,000 NOA

LOW DRESSERS

An oak low dresser, with three panelled drawers, on turned baluster legs, some drawer linings replaced, c1690, 76in (193cm) wide.

£1,750–2,100 PF

An oak low dresser, with three frieze drawers, on square chamfered supports, the brass handles and escutcheons later, early 18thC, 71¾in (182.5cm) wide.

£2,000–2,400 WilP

MILLER'S COMPARES

I. A George II oak low dresser, with three drawers over two panelled cupboard doors, 60in (152.5cm) wide.

£3,400–4,050 HYD

II. A George II oak low dresser, with three drawers over two panelled cupboard doors, 62in (157.5cm) wide.

£1,500–1,800 HYD

Item I is slightly earlier in date than Item II, and is more 'honest' and attractive-looking, with twin panelled doors and twin panels between them. Item I has good, straight-through stile feet, compared to the awkward-looking bracket feet of Item II. The block-moulded drawers of Item I are pleasing to the eye, whereas on Item II the drawer moulding is laid over the escutcheons, which indicates a later alteration. Item II also has internal brass butt hinges, which are not correct for the period.

An oak low dresser, with seven drawers and a cupboard, c1740, 81½in (207cm) wide.

£8,100–9,000 RED

An oak low dresser, with three drawers over three cupboard doors, c1750, 71in (180.5cm) wide.

£9,000–10,000 CGA

An oak low dresser, with three drawers, on pad feet, 18thC, 85in (216cm) wide.

£1,650–1,950 HOLL

An oak low dresser, with three drawers over two panelled cupboard doors, 18thC, 63in (160cm) wide.

£5,600–6,700 JNic

► **A George III oak low dresser,** with three drawers, on turned front legs, 66in (167.5cm) wide.

£2,800–3,350 HYD

LOWBOYS

An ash lowboy, with a drawer, on cabriole legs, 18thC, 31in (78.5cm) wide.
£1,050–1,200 ⊞ CGA

A George II oak lowboy, with one long and three short drawers, on cabriole legs, 32in (81.5cm) wide.
£2,900–3,450 HYD

◄ A George II burr-oak lowboy, with three drawers above a shaped apron, on cabriole legs, 36in (91.5cm) wide.
£2,350–2,800 HYD

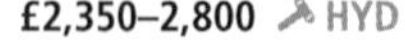

Well-defined and shaped aprons are a sign of quality and desirability. Carved details to the knees of cabriole legs and elegant shaped pad feet are also value points, as are shapely legs and slightly eccentric forms. Check for originality of the 'ears' at the top of cabriole legs as these are often replaced. The tops of earlier examples tend to have a more generous overhang and a well moulded edge is a desirable feature. Original brass fittings, locks and excellent colour and patination add to value.
The classic Queen Anne configuration of a shallow central drawer flanked by two deeper, often square, drawers is the most popular design. Early examples have overlapping moulded drawer fronts rather than cockbeaded edges.

An oak lowboy, with three cockbeaded drawers over a shaped apron, on cabriole legs, c1770, 32in (81.5cm) wide.
£3,000–3,600 BAM(M)

A George III oak lowboy, with three drawers, on chamfered legs, 32in (81.5cm) wide.
£820–980 Mit

An oak lowboy, with three drawers, on tapered legs, c1790, 32in (81.5cm) wide.
£1,300–1,450 ⊞ AGI

A George III oak lowboy, with three drawers above a shaped apron, on cabriole legs, 29¼in (74.5cm) wide.
£540–640 WilP

A Georgian oak lowboy, with three drawers above a shaped apron, 30in (76cm) wide.
£560–670 WilP

An oak lowboy, with one long and two short drawers, on turned fruitwood legs, Wales, c1860, 36in (91.5cm) wide.
£350–390 ⊞ PEC

RACKS & SHELVES

A set of carved and painted shelves, the pierced foliate and floral-carved cresting centred with a putto, flanked by eagle heads above three shelves, decoration refreshed, possibly Dutch, 1675–1700, 41in (104cm) wide.

£3,000–3,600 S

An oak plate rack, 18thC, 54in (137cm) wide.

£520–620 DD

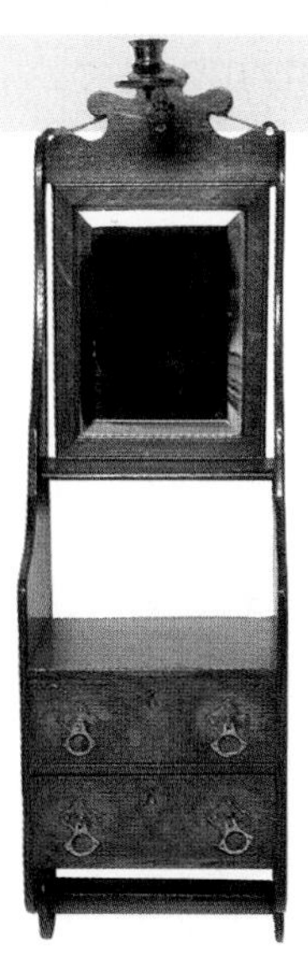

► **An oak shelf,** with a brass candle sconce over a mirror, a shelf and two drawers, 19thC, 33in (84cm) high.

£175–195 SPUR

SETTLES

An oak settle, with a niche-carved top rail above a panelled back, the front with a guilloche-carved frieze above three panels, box seat later, late 17thC, 57½in (146cm) wide.

£540–640 PFK

An oak settle, with a panelled back over a plank seat, c1720, 56in (142cm) wide.

£590–700 Hal

An oak settle, with a panelled back, c1760, 74in (188cm) wide.

£360–400 PWS

An oak settle, the back with five fielded panels over a slatted seat, on cabriole legs, on pad feet, c1780, 72in (183cm) wide.

£700–840 Hal

A painted wood settee, the crest rail above three splats, over a plank seat with a rolled front rail, inscribed 'BH. Hombroek' to base, slight damage, America, Pennsylvania, 1830–40, 77½in (197cm) wide.

£1,850–2,200 SK(B)

◄ **An oak settle,** with carved decoration, c1880, 52in (132cm) wide.

£1,050–1,200 BURA

► **An oak settle,** with carved decoration, c1900, 44in (112cm) wide.

£310–350 NORTH

STOOLS

An Elizabethan oak boarded stool, the moulded apron with a pierced arch, on shaped feet, 20in (51cm) wide.

£8,400–10,000 S

Stools such as this are seldom seen.

A joined oak stool, with carved decoration, 1660–80, 18in (45.5cm) wide.

£2,700–3,000 KEY

A joined oak stool, on turned legs, 17thC, 18in (45.5cm) wide.

£1,350–1,500 CGA

An oak stool, with tapestry upholstery, c1690, 20in (51cm) wide.

£3,800–4,250 HWK

A joined oak stool, with carved decoration, on turned legs, one stretcher replaced, late 17thC, 17¼in (44cm) wide.

£610–730 SWO

A joined oak stool, with a carved frieze and turned legs, c1700, 20in (51cm) high.

£470–560 G(L)

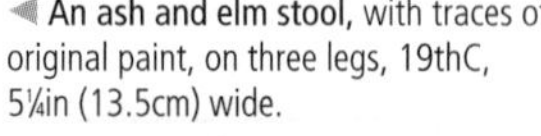

◄ **An ash and elm stool,** with traces of original paint, on three legs, 19thC, 5¼in (13.5cm) wide.

£120–140 AH

A wooden stool, with a burr-elm seat and ash legs, c1820, 12in (30.5cm) diam.

£270–300 PeN

A James I-style joined oak stool, c1880, 16in (40.5cm) wide.

£630–700 PeN

◄ **An elm, oak and beech adjustable stool,** c1900, 21in (53.5cm) high.

£700–780 HWK

TABLES

An elm gateleg table, with an end drawer, on barley-twist and block supports, 17thC, 38½in (98cm) wide.

£6,100–7,300 ROS

An oak refectory table, with a moulded and carved frieze rail, on turned legs with moulded and carved stretchers, c1670 and later, 103in (261.5cm) long.

£3,750–4,500 HYD

An oak side table, with a drawer, on turned legs, 17thC, 34in (86.5cm) wide.

£1,500–1,700 WWH

An oak gateleg table, with an end drawer, c1670, 50½in (128.5cm) diam.

£900–1,000 PSA

An oak side table, with a plank top above turned legs, c1670, 29½in (75cm) wide.

£940–1,100 HYD

An oak side table, with a drawer, c1670, 36in (91.5cm) wide.

£3,300–3,700 PeN

A cherrywood double gateleg table, with turned spindles, France, c1710, 45in (114.5cm) diam.

£8,100–9,000 AUB

An oak side table, with a drawer, on turned legs and stretcher, c1720, 30in (76cm) wide.

£400–450 CSM

◄ **An oak side table,** with two drawers, Wales, early 18thC, 25in (63.5cm) wide.

£830–930 NoC

► **An oak two-tier cricket table,** West Country, c1740, 25in (63.5cm) diam.

£2,500–2,800 RYA

◀ **A carved cherrywood tripod table,** on a turned column, America, Connecticut, c1765, 27in (68.5cm) high.

£4,900–5,400 ⊞ GIAM

An **oak cricket table,** 18thC, 26in (66cm) diam.

£850–950 ⊞ CGA

Tripod tables

Small single pedestal occasional tables are frequently found as marriages where the top and the pedestal base are from different periods. It is imperative to inspect the underside of the top for signs of assocation. Where there is a tilt top or a birdcage action, check that the bearers are fitted with original screws. Check for shadow marks of previous fittings, that there is a 'footprint' of the original block on the underside of the top and that the positioning of any catches has not been changed. Single plank tops are generally more sought after than multi-boards. Burr or specimen figured timbers are also a sign of quality but, above all, pieces that are original from top to bottom carry the highest premium. Married items have much lower value.

An oak table, the scrolled top over a shelf with pierced sides, above a drawer, on cabriole legs, Continental, 18thC, 14½in (37cm) wide.

£230–270 ⚒ SWO

An oak gateleg table, with an end drawer, on vase-turned legs, restored, 18thC, 73¼in (186cm) diam.

£3,500–4,200 ⚒ Bea

An oak farmhouse table, France, 18thC, 78in (198cm) long.

£1,050–1,200 ⊞ CGA

An oak and elm side table, with two drawers, c1780, 30in (76cm) wide.

£450–500 ⊞ CGA

An oak wine table, c1780, 20in (51cm) diam.

£1,050–1,200 ⊞ PeN

A George III oak tilt-top tripod table, 34in (86.5cm) diam.

£700–780 ⊞ TRED

◀ **An elm cricket table,** c1800, 36in (91.5cm) diam.

£1,600–1,800 ⊞ AGI

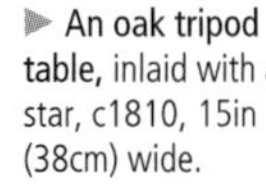

▶ **An oak tripod table,** inlaid with a star, c1810, 15in (38cm) wide.

£400–450 ⊞ CSM

An oak side table, with two drawers, Wales, early 18thC, 25in (63.5cm) wide.

£830–930 NoC

An oak and applewood farmhouse table, Wales, c1820, 65in (165cm) long.

£610–680 GD

An ash dairy table, c1820, 20in (51cm) diam.

£880–980 PeN

A Shaker painted cherrywood and pine table, on block-turned tapered legs, America, New England, early 19thC, 48¾in (124cm) wide.

£4,150–4,950 SK

A burr-elm cricket table, on associated ring-turned legs, early 19thC, 25½in (65cm) diam.

£1,300–1,550 AH

A walnut work table, with a drawer, on turned legs, America, c1830, 30in (76cm) wide.

£60–65 JAA

A cherrywood farmhouse table, France, 1800–50, 79½in (202cm) long.

£1,700–2,000 DN(BR)

◄ **A walnut table,** with a drawer, on splayed legs, restored, America, probably Pennsylvania, early 19thC, 20in (51cm) wide.

£5,700–6,800 SK(B)

► **A walnut side table,** with a drawer, France, c1830, 36in (91.5cm) wide.

£490–550 GD

A beechwood farmhouse table, c1840, 85in (216cm) long.
£1,750–1,950 PENH

An oak farmhouse table, France, c1840, 75in (190.5cm) long.
£3,000–3,400 RED

An elm tripod table, on a baluster-turned column, 19thC, 18in (45.5cm) diam.
£330–390 DN

► **A Victorian 17th century-style refectory table,** the plank top above a carved lunette frieze, on turned legs, 83½in (212cm) long.
£590–700 SWO

An oak and mahogany-crossbanded side table, with two drawers, c1870, 32in (81.5cm) wide.
£580–650 PICA

An oak wind-out dining table, with two leaves, on barley-twist legs, c1880, 93in (236cm) long.
£2,250–2,500 BURA

A carved oak side table, with two foliate-moulded frieze drawers, on baluster-turned legs, c1890, 42in (106.5cm) wide.
£240–280 PF

An ash and elm farmhouse table, France, late 19thC, 78¾in (200cm) long.
£1,150–1,350 NOA

◄ **An oak side table,** with a drawer, Continental, c1890, 28in (71cm) wide.
£250–280 PICA

A beechwood table, with splayed legs, France, c1890, 22in (56cm) square.
£145–165 PEC

PINE FURNITURE

BEDS & CRADLES

A pine rocking cradle, with original paint, c1840, 37in (94cm) long.
£80–90 ⊞ SPUR

A pitch pine *faux* bamboo bed, France, c1870, 51in (129.5cm) wide.
£1,350–1,500 ⊞ BURA

A pine sleigh bed, Continental, c1880, 47in (119.5cm) wide.
£220–250 ⊞ B2W

A pine rocking cradle, Hungary, c1890, 30in (76cm) long.
£85–95 ⊞ PEC

BENCHES

A pine bench, 19thC, 72in (183cm) long.
£1,050–1,200 ⊞ AQ

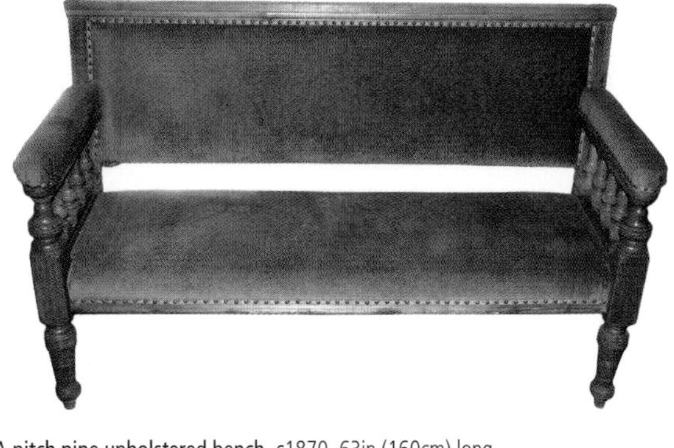

A pitch pine upholstered bench, c1870, 63in (160cm) long.
£330–370 ⊞ HAV

▶ **A pine bench,** with painted trestle legs, late 19thC, 62in (157.5cm) long.
£105–120 ⊞ WV

BOOKCASES

► A painted pine bookcase, c1890, 46in (117cm) wide.

£490–550 ARCA

◄ **A pine bookcase,** the upper section with glass doors and adjustable shelves, the base with two cupboard doors, Ireland, 1855–65, 91in (231cm) high.

£1,100–1,250 CLAR

A Regency-style stained pine breakfront open library bookcase, with adjustable shelves, the stiles carved with reeding and lions' masks, on paw feet, c1900, 58in (147.5cm) wide.

£2,050–2,450 SK

BOXES

A carved and painted pine candle box, America, Maine, c1840, 11½in (29cm) wide.

£16,300–19,500 GIAM

Attractive examples of American folk art such as this are very popular in the United States.

A pine box, with a domed top, Continental, c1860, 21in (53.5cm) wide.

£50–60 HRQ

A pine blanket box, c1890, 30in (76cm) wide.

£310–350 MIN

► **A painted pine linen box,** decorated with swags, Continental, c1890, 23in (58.5cm) wide.

£195–220 ALCH

CHAIRS

A pine chair, France, Savoie, 19thC.
£145–165 MLL

A pair of pine chairs, with original paint, Sweden, c1850.
£280–320 ALCH

A Black Forest carved pine and beech hall seat, Germany, c1860.
£4,950–5,900 G(B)

CHESTS & COFFERS

A carved pine coffer, with a side door enclosing three carved drawers, restored, losses, possibly Spanish Colonial, 17thC, 22in (56cm) wide.
£830–990 JAA

A carved and painted pine board chest, with crease-moulding to the front and sides, till missing, America, 1675–1725, 49in (124.5cm) wide.
£12,100–14,500 SK(B)

This is a very early piece and therefore highly desirable.

◄ **A George II pine mule chest,** the panelled front above a drawer, with later tortoiseshell effect paint finish, 42in (106.5cm) wide.
£230–270 HYD

► **A pine coffer,** France, 18thC, 33in (84cm) wide.
£320–360 TOP

A pine chest, with a domed top and wrought-iron mounts, c1840, 37½in (95.5cm) wide.
£95–110 JAA

A painted pine marriage chest, the front with two painted panels, central Europe, dated 1776, 40in (101.5cm) wide.

£3,350–3,750 RYA

A pine panelled blanket chest, with an inverted bowfront, Ireland, c1800, 56in (142cm) wide.

£600–670 CLAR

◄ **A painted pine chest,** on block feet, early 19thC, Canada, Quebec, 36in (91.5cm) wide.

£240–280 WAD

◄ **A pine dowry chest,** with painted decoration, the hinged lid enclosing a well and a till, above two short drawers, slight damage, America, Pennsylvania, early 19thC, 44in (112cm) wide.

£5,100–6,100 SK(B)

A pine dowry chest, with painted Pennsylvania-style decoration, the hinged lid enclosing a fitted compartment with a lid, decoration possibly not original, slight damage, America, early 19thC, 46in (117cm) wide.

£650–780 JDJ

► **A pine chest,** with painted decoration, the hinged top enclosing a well, over a drawer, slight damage, America, possibly Rhode Island, early 19thC, 33¼in (84.5cm) wide.

£18,500–22,200 SK(B)

A pine blanket chest, the hinged lid enclosing a fitted interior, above a drawer, Continental, c1870, 43in (109cm) wide.

£370–420 MIN

A painted pine mule chest, the drawer with recessed brass handles, c1890, 45in (114.5cm) wide.

£220–250 NWE

CHESTS OF DRAWERS

A pine chest of drawers, with a hinged top over two dummy drawers and two further drawers, brass mounts later, America, New England, 1700–50, 39½in (100.5cm) wide.
£950–1,100 SK(B)

A pine dowry chest, with three drawers, Ireland, 19thC, 54in (137cm) high.
£600–670 CLAR

A pine wedding chest, with carved and painted decoration and four drawers, Denmark, north-west Jutland, dated 1817, 49in (124.5cm) wide.
£7,600–8,500 RYA

An early Victorian pine chest of drawers, with five drawers, 40in (101.5cm) wide.
£540–600 TPC

A Victorian painted pine chest of drawers, decorated with gilt swags, with four drawers, 36¼in (92cm) wide.
£1,000–1,200 WW

A Queen Anne-style pine chest of drawers, with applied decoration and three drawers, on cabriole legs, 19thC, 25½in (65cm) wide.
£75–90 JAA

◀ **A painted pine chest of drawers,** with three drawers, Continental, c1880, 42in (106.5cm) wide.
£290–330 AIN

A pine chest of drawers, with original paint, the four drawers with brass handles, c1890, 36in (91.5cm) wide.
£180–200 NWE

◀ **A pine chest of drawers,** with four drawers, on turned feet, late 19thC, 42in (106.5cm) wide.
£155–185 JAA

CUPBOARDS

A painted pine hanging cupboard, the door enclosing two shelves, America, New England, 18thC, 10in (25.5cm) wide.

£5,400–6,400 SK(B)

This piece is desirable because of its early date and the fact that it retains the original paint.

◄ **A pine marriage cupboard,** with original painted decoration, inscribed 'A.S.S.', central Europe, dated '1773', 39½in (100.5cm) wide.

£3,400–3,800 RYA

It is unusual to find a marriage cupboard of such small proportions and with such an engaging primitive landscape panel, possibly inspired by decoration found on delftware ceramics of the same period.

A pine cupboard, with two pairs of doors, Sweden, 18thC, 46in (117cm) wide.

£3,500–3,900 AQ

A Georgian pine corner cupboard, the upper section with a glazed door enclosing shelves, the base with two panelled doors, 58in (147.5cm) wide.

£2,200–2,500 PENH

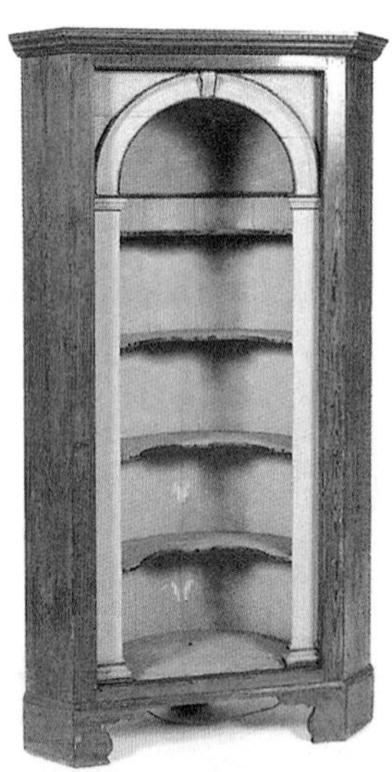

A pine corner cupboard, with four shaped shelves, early 19thC, 40in (101.5cm) wide.

£500–600 GTH

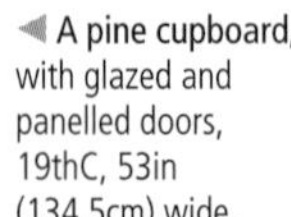

◄ **A pine cupboard,** with glazed and panelled doors, 19thC, 53in (134.5cm) wide.

£140–165 JAA

► **A pine cupboard,** with a scalloped gallery above two doors enclosing three shelves, 19thC, 42in (106.5cm) wide.

£200–240 JAA

An early Victorian pine corner cupboard, the astragal-glazed upper section enclosing shelves, above two panelled cupboard doors, 87in (221cm) high.

£1,250–1,400 ⊞ TPC

A Victorian pine cupboard, with two panelled doors over two drawers and two further cupboard doors, 47in (119.5cm) wide.

£640–760 G(L)

A pine cupboard, with four panelled doors enclosing shelves, Ireland, Galway, 1860s, 81in (205.5cm) high.

£720–810 ⊞ CLAR

A pine cupboard, with a curved top and four panelled doors, c1870, 95in (241.5cm) high.

£850–950 ⊞ MIN

A pine corner cupboard, the upper section with a glazed door over a drawer and a panelled door, Ireland, County Antrim, c1870, 80in (203cm) high.

£1,300–1,450 ⊞ HeR

A pine linen press, with two doors enclosing shelves, over two short and two long drawers, c1880, 51in (129.5cm) wide.

£990–1,100 ⊞ PWS

DESKS

A pine desk, with five drawers, on turned legs, Continental, c1870, 49in (124.5cm) wide.

£620–700 ⊞ HRQ

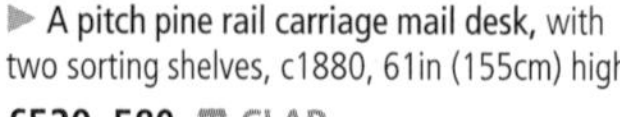

▶ **A pitch pine rail carriage mail desk,** with two sorting shelves, c1880, 61in (155cm) high.

£520–580 ⊞ CLAR

A pine school desk, with a lift-up top, c1890, 26in (66cm) wide.

£165–185 ⊞ AIN

DRESSERS

A pine dresser, with open shelves above three drawers, on cabriole legs, 18thC, 63in (160cm) wide.

£4,500–5,000 ⊞ CGA

A pine dresser, with open shelves above two drawers and two cupboard doors, 19thC, 80in (203cm) high.

£570–640 ⊞ HON

A pine dresser, with original paint, Ireland, c1820, 61in (155cm) wide.

£990–1,100 ⊞ CLAR

A painted pine dresser, with three drawers and two doors, Wales, c1870, 51in (129.5cm) wide.

£1,750–1,950 ⊞ ARCA

A pine dresser, the upper section with two doors, the base with three drawers and three doors, c1880, 60in (152.5cm) wide.

£900–1,000 ⊞ NORTH

◀ **A pine dresser,** the upper section with four glazed doors and four drawers, the base with a slide above two drawers and two doors, eastern Europe, c1900, 80in (203cm) high.

£600–680 ⊞ MIN

A pine dresser, with eight doors, Continental, c1900, 83½in (212cm) wide.

£2,250–2,500 ⊞ B2W

LOW DRESSERS & SIDE CABINETS

A pine dresser base, painted to simulate oak, the moulded top above three short drawers, on baluster profile front legs, drawer handles later, formerly with a plate rack, Ireland, 1720–40, 74in (188cm) wide.
£6,900–8,300 DN(BR)

A pine low dresser, with original paint and a scrubbed top over three drawers, c1750, 86½in (219.5cm) wide.
£6,700–7,500 & RYA

This rare early dresser has the seemingly unique feature of an unusually narrow frieze drawer at each end. It is assumed that this piece was a special commission.

A pine dresser base, with five drawers and two doors, c1750, 66in (167.5cm) wide.
£1,400–1,600 MIN

A pine dresser base, with seven drawers and one door, on turned feet, c1780, 66in (167.5cm) wide.
£740–830 HRQ

A pine side cabinet, the top with four drawers, over three graduated drawers and one door, on bun feet, 1850–1900, 48in (122cm) wide.
£540–600 WV

A pine side cabinet, with a single drawer over two doors, Ireland, 1860–80, 65in (165cm) high.
£400–440 CLAR

A pine side cabinet, the ends each with a drawer and a cupboard, Norway, 19thC, 34in 86.5cm) wide.
£110–130 JAA

▶ **A pine dresser base,** with two drawers over two doors, France, c1870, 51in (129.5cm) wide.
£240–270 AIN

A pine low dresser, the superstructure with four drawers, over three drawers and two doors, c1890, 54in (137cm) wide.
£540–600 TPAS

RACKS & SHELVES

► **A pine rack,** with notches for roasting spits, c1800, 48in (122cm) wide.
£160–180 CLAR

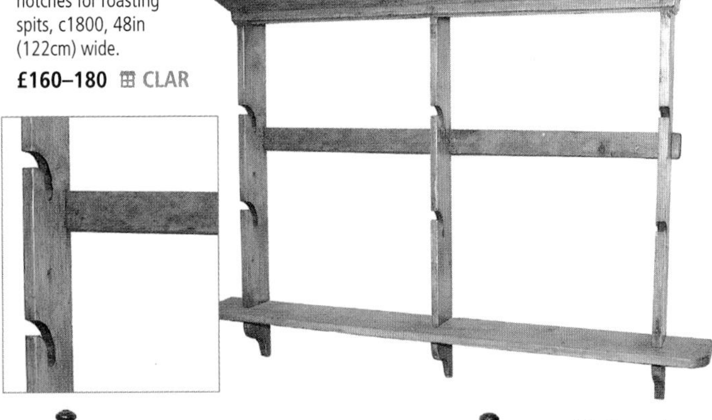

A **pine wall shelf,** painted to simulate oak, 19thC, 31¾in (80.5cm) wide.
£150–180 DN

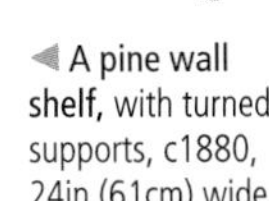

◄ **A pine wall shelf,** with turned supports, c1880, 24in (61cm) wide.
£125–140
PEC

► **A pine wall shelf,** Ireland, c1900, 45in (114.5cm) wide.
£90–100
CLAR

SETTLES

► **A pine settle,** early 18thC, 71in (180.5cm) wide.
£760–850
AIN

A Georgian stained pine farmhouse settle, with a curved back, 63½in (161.5cm) wide.
£470–560 DD

◄ **A pine settle,** with a box seat, c1875, 38in (96.5cm) wide.
£680–810 PF

► **A pine and elm settle,** with a curved back, solid seat and three drawers, 19thC, 77¼in (196cm) wide.
£410–490
DN

A **pine settle bed**, Ireland, County Clare, 1845–65, 74in (188cm) wide.
£450–500 ⊞ CLAR

A **painted pine settle bed**, Ireland, c1850, 71in (180.5cm) wide.
£450–500 ⊞ CLAR

A **pine settle bed**, Ireland, 1850–1880, 74in (188cm) wide.
£520–580 ⊞ CLAR

A **pine settle**, with a lift-up seat, Continental, c1930, 41in (104cm) wide.
£290–330 ⊞ HRQ

STOOLS

A **painted pine footstool**, the top covered with 18thC crewelwork, slight damage, early 19thC, 14in (35.5cm) wide.
£1,700–2,000 JDJ

▶ A **joined pine stool**, c1870, 22in (56cm) wide.
£310–350 ⊞ PeN

A **pine stool**, with original paint, c1890, 13in (33cm) wide.
£20–25 ⊞ AIN

A **pine stool**, with carved decoration, Ireland, c1900, 12in (30.5cm) high.
£70–80 ⊞ CLAR

TABLES

A pine stand, the chamfered support on a cross base, America, New England, late 18thC, 29¾in (75.5cm) high.

£480–570 SK(B)

A Regency pine *faux* bamboo side table, with original paint, 35¼in (89.5cm) wide.

£1,050–1,200 AQ

A pine farmhouse table, c1850, 39in (99cm) diam.

£120–135 PWS

A pine side table, with two drawers and turned legs, Ireland, c1865, 42in (106.5cm) wide.

£240–270 CLAR

▶ **A pine cricket table,** c1870, 25in (63.5cm) diam.

£470–530 PICA

A pine trestle table, on an X-frame, Continental, c1880, 82in (208.5cm) wide.

£670–750 MIN

A pine drop-leaf table, with a drawer, on turned legs, c1880, 43in (109cm) wide.

£270–300 HAV

A pine *faux* bamboo side table, with a drawer, France, c1890, 32in (81.5cm) wide.

£300–340 PICA

WARDROBES

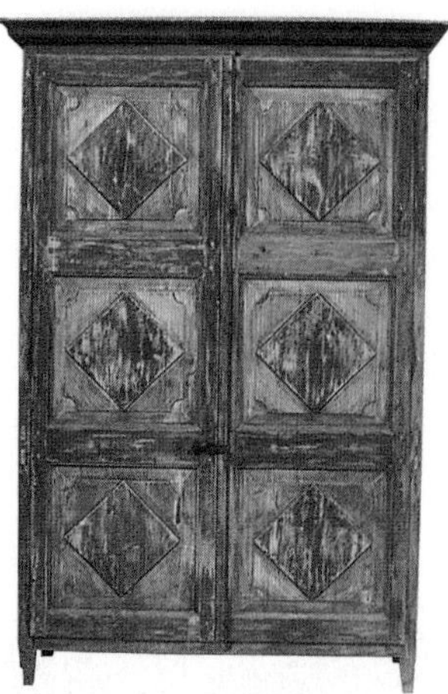

A painted pine armoire, with two panelled doors, France, late 18thC, 99¼in (252cm) high.

£590–700 DN(BR)

A pine wardrobe, with two doors, 19thC, 72in (183cm) high.

£340–380 HON

A pine wardrobe, with two doors flanked by fluted pilasters, Continental, mid-19thC, 76in (193cm) high.

£610–680 WV

A pine wardrobe, the mirrored door above a single drawer, on bun feet, mid-19thC, 77in (195.6cm) high.

£400–450 WV

A pine wardrobe, the two arch-panelled doors over a single drawer, on bun feet, mid-19thC, 72in (183cm) high.

£530–600 WV

A pine door, with a panelled door above a single drawer, eastern Europe, c1860, 42in (106.5cm) high.

£530–600 HRQ

A pine wardrobe, the upper section with a panelled door, the base with a drawer, Ireland, County Limerick, c1880, 80in (203cm) high.

£460–510 CLAR

A pine wardrobe, with three doors above three drawers, Continental, c1890, 61in (155cm) wide.

£490–550 AIN

A pine wardrobe, with two doors, Holland, c1900, 45in (114.5cm) wide.

£470–530 B2W

WASHSTANDS

A pine washstand, Ireland, County Mayo, 19thC, 1865–75, 36in (91.5cm) high.

£160–180 CLAR

A pine washstand, with two drawers and a central dummy drawer, on turned legs, mid-19thC, 34in (86.5cm) wide.

£190–220 WV

► **A pine washstand,** with drawers, c1890, 42in (106.5cm) wide.

£230–270 TPAS

A pine washstand, with original paint and *faux* bamboo legs, c1880, 34in (86.5cm) wide.

£240–280 MIN

A pine washstand, with original paint and two drawers, c1880, 41in (104cm) wide.

£600–680 PICA

◄ **A child's painted pine washstand,** c1880, 18in (45.5cm) wide.

£360–400 MALT

A pine washstand, the tiled back above a marble top, over a drawer, c1890, 36in (91.5cm) wide.

£310–350 HAV

A pine washstand, with a drawer, c1900, 27in (68.5cm) wide.

£270–300 HRQ

BAMBOO & WICKER FURNITURE

A Victorian bamboo table, the top with an oil painting, 25in (63.5cm) diam.

£270–300 NoC

◄ **A Victorian bamboo side cabinet,** the lacquer top above a glazed door, 23¼in (59cm) wide.

£260–310 WilP

A bamboo folding dumb waiter, with a rattan tray and an undertier, c1870, 23in (58.5cm) wide.

£310–350 BURA

A bamboo and lacquered occasional table, with a frieze drawer and two extending shelves, the lower shelf with a hinged compartment, c1900, 25in (63.5cm) wide.

£600–720 NOA

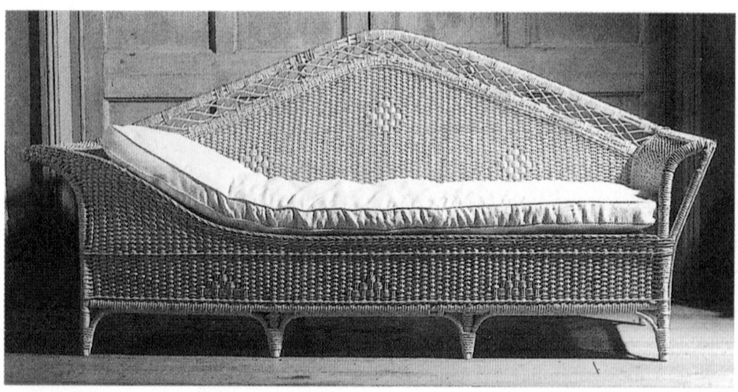

A suite of wicker furniture, comprising a pair of armchairs, a pair of smaller armchairs, a chaise longue and a table, late 19thc.

£12,000–14,400 S(O)

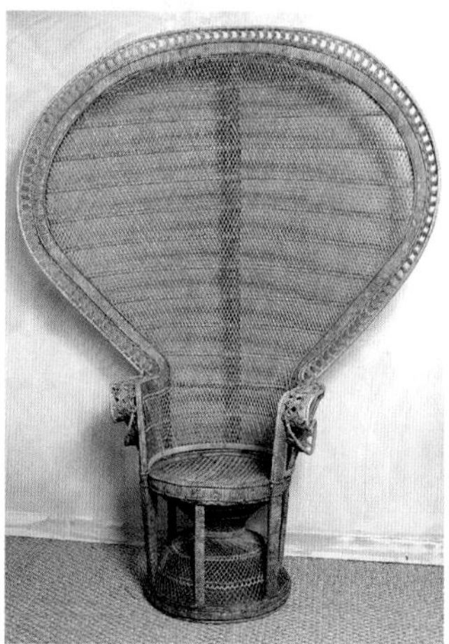

A wicker 'peacock' chair, 1920s–30s.

£250–290 AQ

A wicker rocking chair, with a caned seat, early 20thC.

£45–50 JAA

► **A Lloyd Loom armchair,** with oak supports, dated 1931.

£140–165 AMB

KITCHENWARE

A copper mixing bowl, c1870, 11in (28cm) diam.
£135–150 GSA

A pine churn, with cover and plunger, 1865–80, 35in (89cm) high.
£370–340 CLAR

A lignum vitae coffee mill, in the form of a barrel, with a brass handle, late 18thC, 8¾in (22cm) high.
£370–440 DN

A copper colander, with an iron handle and three ball feet, c1770, 21in (53.5cm) long.
£450–500 PeN

An oak cutlery box, Wales, c1780, 13in (33cm) wide.
£450–500 SEA

◄ A Grimwades ceramic jar, inscribed 'Sago', c1910, 9in (23cm) high.
£135–150 SMI

A wrought-iron lark spit, 18thC, 25in (63.5cm) high.
£340–390 KEY

► An iron and brass ladle, c1790, 21in (53.5cm) long.
£330–380 SEA

A counter display brass milk churn, c1860, 22in (56cm) high.

£1,800–2,000 SMI

A ceramic milk pail, with a brass cover, c1880, 16in (40.5cm) high.

£1,800–2,000 SMI

◀ A Wedgwood pearlware jelly mould, painted with flowers, slight damage, impressed mark, early 19thC, 9in (23cm) long.

£1,550–1,850 WW

A sycamore cheese mould, 18thC, 16½in (42cm) diam.

£580–650 AQ

A Staffordshire pottery mould, in the form of a recumbent ram, early 19thC, 10¾in (27.5cm) wide.

£150–180 ROS

A carved wood double-sided gingerbread mould, Holland, c1870, 19in (48.5cm) high.

£195–220 PeN

A Grimwades ceramic Quick-Cooker, c1910, 5in (12.5cm) high.

£135–150 SMI

POTTERY

A LARGE GULF BETWEEN 'the best and the rest' still remains in the market for antique pottery. The top end of the market is still very strong and shows no signs of weakening and, in fact, will almost certainly gather strength. Rarity, condition and demand from collectors and interior designers are all factors influencing prices. The main demand is still from the British home market and the USA. Early English pottery from the 18th century and very rare examples from the 19th century are the most popular areas, as well as exceptional quality art pottery from the early 20th century.

John Howard

John deals in English pottery, specializing in creamware, lustreware and animal figure groups.

He is Chairman of the Ceramics Vetting Committee at Olympia and is a member of the vetting teams at many UK and USA antiques fairs.

The middle and lower sections of the pottery market are less popular and common examples of middle and late 19th-century Staffordshire figures in particular have seen a significant reduction in values. This is particularly relevant to the items produced after c1870, such as general decorative figures and untitled examples. Many American and British collectors have upgraded and refined their collections, disposing of lesser quality items and pieces that were over-restored. The collector of the 21st century is more discriminating and the criteria for purchase are quality, condition and rarity, unlike in the past when many collections were formed mainly by volume. Values at the low end of the market have seen a major shift downwards; prices are now at a level where it is unlikely that there will be any further downward trend in this area in the forseeable future.

World events, a strong sterling rate against the US dollar and changes in home decorating fashions are major influences in the world of ceramics. The increased use of the internet has also influenced trading patterns and all these various features have contributed to the continuing polarity of the market.

There is no doubt that the best examples of good quality pottery will rise in value, fuelled by demand from wealthy connoisseur collectors and the growing influence of interior designers who are looking for a ceramic item that 'makes a statement' to enhance a room setting and show a sophistication of taste.

Bargains can still be found at the lower end of the market and some areas in the pottery field are still under-valued such as blue and white English delftware. However, the trend appears to be established and prices for the best pieces will no doubt continue to strengthen.

John Howard

ANIMALS

A Staffordshire salt-glazed stoneware teapot, in the form of a camel, slight damage, c1750, 7in (18cm) high.

£3,600–4,300 S(O)

▶ **A Staffordshire pearlware model of a squirrel,** c1790, 7in (18cm) high.

£2,700–3,000 HOW

A Nottingham stoneware mustard pot and cover, in the form of a bear, with a loop handle, repaired, c1800, 3½in (9cm) high.

£2,600–3,100 LFA

A Staffordshire pipe, in the form of a serpent, decorated in Pratt-coloured glazes, c1800, 9in (23cm) long.

£300–360 LAY

Prattware

Prattware is a lightweight pottery made from c1775 in Staffordshire, Yorkshire, the northeast of England and in Scotland. It is characterized by the use of high temperature underglaze colours, typically yellow-ochre, a sludgey green, cobalt blue, manganese and brown. Named after a family of Staffordshire potters that later became prolific producers of colour-printed pots for cosmetics and ointments, the wares mostly date from the late 18th and early 19th centuries and include figures, jugs, tea canisters, plates and bowls.

A Prattware pearlware model of a cockerel, c1820, 8¼in (21cm) high.

£1,250–1,400 HIS

Staffordshire dogs

The main criterion for buying Staffordshire dogs is the appeal factor – if the dogs have good looking faces you are buying something which will bring enjoyment every time you look at them. Earlier examples often have separately moulded legs, are crisply modelled and well painted with extra attention to details such as whiskers and noses. Dogs seated on bases or with children often command higher prices as they have extra appeal.

A pair of treacle-glazed models of hounds, c1840, 12in (30.5cm) wide.

£1,550–1,750 HUN

A pearlware model of a cat, c1840, 11in (28cm) wide.

£2,700–3,000 HOW

A Staffordshire porcellaneous inkwell, in the form of a nest and eggs with a bird being attacked by a snake, 1830–50, 3¼in (8.5cm) high.

£260–310 DN

A Staffordshire model of a monkey holding a trumpet, possibly part of a monkey band, c1845, 4in (10cm) high.

£950–1,050 RGa

A Staffordshire spill vase, with a cow, c1850, 4in (10cm) high.

£290–330 SER

A pair of Staffordshire models of whippets, c1850, 3¾in (9.5cm) high.

£730–820 RGa

A Staffordshire model of a Royal child on a St Bernard, c1860, 9in (23cm) high.

£690–770 HOW

A Victorian Staffordshire model of a greyhound, with a hare lying on a naturalistic base, 10¾in (27.5cm) wide.

£1,000–1,200 PFK

Origins of majolica

Majolica is a heavily-potted moulded earthenware covered in rich lustrous polychromatic glazes. It was first produced in the late 1840s in England, although the inspiration for it came from Italian Renaissance pottery, the 16th-century wares of the Frenchman Bernard Palissy and the pottery of the 18th-century Staffordshire makers Thomas Whieldon and Ralph Wood. Majolica was also made in the US, France and Germany.

► **A Minton majolica jug,** in the form of a cat, with a paw resting on a mouse, the tail forming the handle, impressed mark, No. 1924, registration mark, decorator's mark '34', c1875, 9¾in (25cm) high.

£3,500–4,200 TEN

A Staffordshire model of a camel, with a water bottle at its feet, c1875, 7in (18cm) high.

£900–1,000 HOW

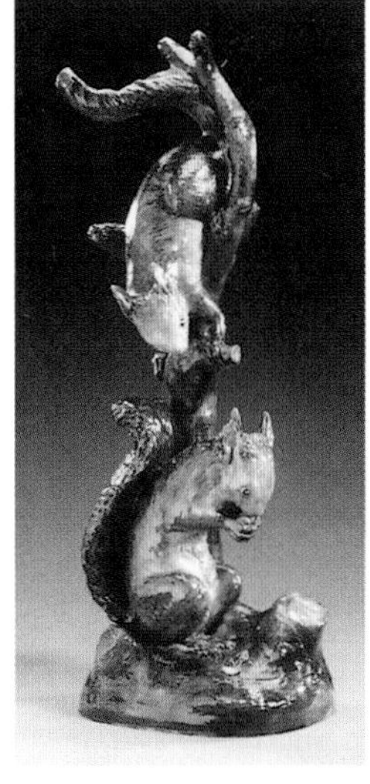

A Copeland majolica group of two squirrels on a branch, modelled by Louis Auguste Malempré, impressed marks, restored, c1878, 22½in (57cm) high.

£1,650–1,950 S(O)

A Palissy ware model of a snake, Portugal, c1880, 3in (7.5cm) wide.

£360–400 BGe

A Delphin Massier majolica jardinière, in the form of a caparisonned elephant, decorated with enamels, damaged, repaired, incised mark, France, late 19thC, 35½in (90cm) wide.

£3,900–4,650 DN

The Massier family, Clément, Delphin and Jérôme, produced ceramics at their factory in Golfe-Juan, France, during the 19th and early 20th centuries.

◄ **A Wemyss model of a pig,** impressed mark, Scotland, c1890, 6½in (16.5cm) wide.

£620–690 Fai

A Staffordshire egg crock, in the form of a hen on a nest, c1890, 8in (20.5cm) wide.

£200–230 CHAC

For more 20thC pottery, please see the Twentieth-Century Design section on pages 441–470.

◄ **A Pablo Picasso earthenware vase,** in the form of an owl, entitled 'Chouette', hand-painted and part-glazed, No. eight of edition of 350, stamped 'Edition Picasso, Madoura Plein Feu', inscribed and numbered, designed in 1969, France, 11¾in (30cm) high.

£3,900–4,650 S(O)

This vase was made to Picasso's original design in the workshop of Suzanne and George Ramié in Madoura, near Vallauris in the south of France.

BOUGH POTS

A pair of Staffordshire pearlware demi-lune bough pots, painted with panels of leaves and fruiting vine, slight damage, c1800, 4¾in (12cm) wide.

£940–1,100 DN

A Staffordshire garniture of three pearlware demi-lune bough pots and covers, each lustre-painted with landscape views above a band of foliate scrollwork, the pierced covers lustre-painted with flowers, c1820, largest 7½in (19cm) wide.

£2,150–2,550 S(O)

A Staffordshire demi-lune bough pot, by Bott & Co, printed with country house vignettes between moulded and enamelled arches, damaged and repaired, impressed mark, c1810, 9½in (24cm) wide.

£230–270 DN

BOWLS

◀ **An English delft punchbowl,** the interior inscribed 'Success to the British Arms', the exterior decorated with florets and trellis, c1750, 10¾in (27.5cm) diam.

£1,300–1,550 TEN

A Mason's Ironstone punchbowl, decorated with Japan pattern, 1820–25, 13in (33cm) diam.

£1,250–1,400 WAn

A footed bowl, transfer-printed with Canadian views of 'Outlet of Lake Memphremagog', the interior with a view of Chaudière Bridge, gilded, impressed and printed marks, Canada, c1850, 6in (15cm) high.

£180–210 WAD

A Sunderland lustre bowl, c1860, 6in (15cm) diam.

£105–120 GSA

A Wemyss bowl, painted with daffodils, Scotland, c1890, 6½in (16.5cm) diam.

£370–420 SDD

A Booth's Sèvres-style earthenware bowl, printed and painted with floral sprays and sprigs alternating with panels of exotic birds within foliate panels, c1900, 11½in (29cm) diam.

£340–400 WAD

BUILDINGS

A Brameld model of a castle keep, inscribed 'Connisburgh Castle', c1820, 9¾in (25cm) high.

£790–940 DA

A Staffordshire model of a cottage, dated 1846, 7in (18cm) high.

£270–300 TYE

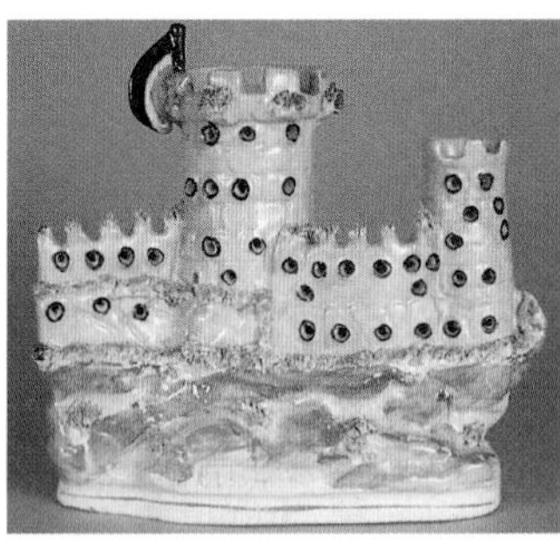

A Staffordshire model of Malakoff, c1854, 8¾in (22cm) high.

£490–550 RGa

Malakoff was a Russian fort near Sebastopol in the Crimea, the capture of which in 1854 marked the end of the Crimean war.

BUSTS

A Staffordshire pearlware bust of Matthew Prior, possibly by Neale & Co, c1790, 9in (23cm) high.

£1,700–1,900 RdV

Matthew Prior, 1664–1721, was an English diplomat and poet.

A Wedgwood black basalt bust of William Shakespeare, on a socle base, 19thC, 12in (30.5cm) high.

£720–800 LGr

Insurance values

Always insure your valuable antiques for the cost of replacing them with similar items, regardless of the original price paid. Both dealers and auctioneers can provide a valuation service for a fee.

◄ **A Wedgwood black basalt bust of Mercury, on a socle base,** impressed date code for 1873, 18in (45.5cm) high.

£2,000–2,250 LGr

This bust was originally modelled by John Flaxman in 1782.

A salt-glazed stoneware pin-tidy, in the form of a double-sided bust of a lady, on a pedestal base, c1850, 4in (10cm) high.

£370–440 G(L)

► **A bust of George Washington,** on a socle base, late 19thC, 8½in (21.5cm) high.

£150–180 BWL

COW CREAMERS

A Yorkshire cow creamer, with milkmaid, c1800, 6in (15cm) high.
£790–880 RdV

A Staffordshire pearlware cow creamer, with milkmaid, c1820, 5½in (14cm) high.
£1,250–1,400 HIS

A Staffordshire pearlware cow creamer, with milkmaid, c1820, 5½in (14cm) high.
£540–600 HIS

A Swansea Pottery lustre cow creamer, restored, early 19thC, 5½in (14cm) high.
£210–250 G(L)

A pair of Staffordshire cow creamers, with milkmaids, c1855, 7in (18cm) high.
£740–830 HOW

DISHES

A maiolica dessert dish, the panelled border with a shaped edge decorated with foliage, the centre decorated with a putto, the reverse moulded with scallop shells, on a spreading foot, drilled later, Italy, 17thC, 10¾in (27.5cm) diam.
£630–750 NSal

Maiolica

Maiolica is tin-glazed earthenware produced in Italy from the 15th to the 18th century. Pieces were typically decorated in bold, high-fired colours and often depicted biblical, mythological or historical themes (*istoriato* wares). Maiolica should not be confused with majolica, a heavily-potted moulded ware first produced in the mid-19th century in England.

A Magdeburg faïence reticulated dish, painted with floral sprays within a trellis border with flowerhead bosses, repaired, script mark 'M', Germany, c1760, 10in (25.5cm) diam.
£105–125 DN

A Staffordshire pearlware toy dish, moulded with a lobster, c1800, 4¾in (12cm) wide.
£360–400 HIS

▶ A pair of Mason's Ironstone dessert dishes, decorated with Bamboo pattern, 1820–30, 9in (23cm) wide.
£660–740 WAn

A George Jones majolica strawberry dish, c1860, 15in (38cm) wide.
£4,400–4,900 BRT

A pair of Minton majolica oyster dishes, each with a central well surrounded by nine oyster wells with shell divisions, one with slight damage, impressed factory marks, c1867, 9¾in (25cm) diam.
£610–730 RTo

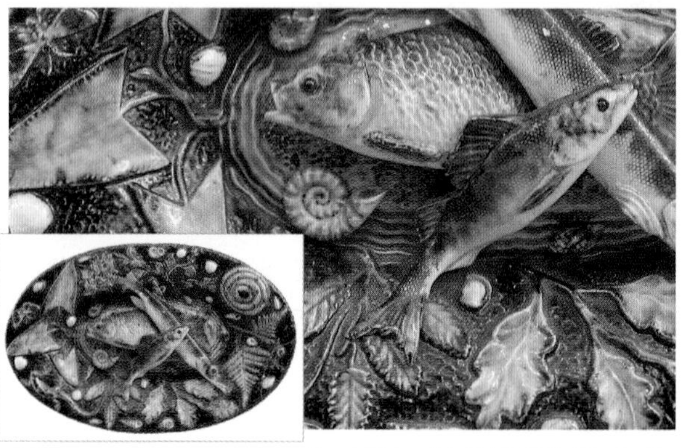

A Palissy-style dish, moulded with shells and fish in relief, 19thC, 12½in (32cm) wide.
£610–730 DA

A Palissy-style dish, moulded with fish, France, c1860, 15in (38cm) wide.
£1,800–2,000 BRT

A Quimper dish, France, c1860, 15in (38cm) wide.
£250–280 SAAC

◄ **A Wedgwood majolica oyster dish,** c1870, 9in (23cm) diam.
£180–200 GSA

► **A Thomas Forester majolica nut dish,** in the form of a bird on a begonia leaf, c1880, 15in (38cm) wide.
£200–230 CHAC

A Luneville asparagus cradle and dish, France, c1880, 14in (35.5cm) wide.
£420–470 MLL

A J. Fischer serving dish, painted with gypsies on a horse-drawn cart within a gilt and foliate border, impressed and printed marks, Hungary, Budapest, early 20thC, 22½in (57cm) wide.
£230–270 RTo

A Wemyss saucer, painted with dog roses, Scotland, c1920, 5in (12.5cm) diam.
£195–220 Fai

COVERED DISHES

◀ **A George Jones majolica cheese dish,** c1860, 12in (30.5cm) diam.
£4,400–4,900 ⊞ BRT

A Minton majolica game pie dish, the cover moulded as dead game on a bed of leaves with a twig handle, the body moulded with basket weave, oak leaves and acorns, impressed marks, c1864, 12½in (32cm) wide.
£870–1,000 RTo

A majolica pâté dish and cover, possibly by George Jones, modelled as a miniature game pie dish, 19thC, 5in (12.5cm) wide.
£530–630 PBA

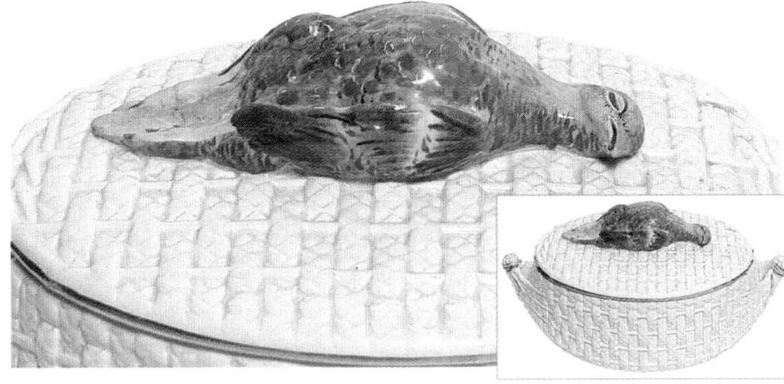

A George Jones game pie dish, c1900, 14in (35.5cm) wide.
£175–195 ⊞ BGe

FIGURES

A Staffordshire salt-glazed stoneware arbour group, in the form of a seated couple in contemporary costume, arbour missing, c1760, 4in (10cm) wide.
£1,900–2,250 S(O)

▶ **A Ralph Wood pearlware figure of a woman holding a tambourine,** c1790, 11½in (29cm) high.
£1,100–1,250 ⊞ AUC

A Wedgwood black basalt group of Bacchus and a faun, impressed mark, late 18thC, 17½in (44.5cm) high.
£2,650–3,150 NSF

Fauns were the friends and worshippers of Bacchus, the Roman god of wine.

A Staffordshire pearlware group of musicians with a flock of sheep, c1810, 9in (23cm) high.
£1,250–1,400 RdV

Pearlware

Pearlware was developed c1779 by Josiah Wedgwood as an improvement on his creamware, being whiter and therefore more porcelain-like in appearance. Pearlware is a misleading term as it implies iridescence – in fact the addition of cobalt oxide to the glaze imparts a bluish-white cast which can be seen most clearly where the glaze 'pools' (ie gathers more thickly), for example around the footrim. Pieces were often decorated with underglaze blue chinoiserie or floral subjects.

► A Yorkshire pottery group of a milkmaid with a ram and lambs, c1810, 6in (15cm) wide.
£1,450–1,650 HOW

A Staffordshire pearlware figure of Juno and the Peacock, early 19thC, 6in (15cm) high.
£160–180 IW

The story of Juno and the Peacock is one of Aesop's Fables. The peacock complained to Juno of his unattractive song, to which she replied that the lot of each bird was assigned by the Fates – to the peacock, beauty; to the nightingale, song; to the eagle, strength; to the raven, favourable omens and to the crow, unfavourable omens.

A Staffordshire pearlware figure of Wellington on a horse, c1820, 10in (25.5cm) high.
£2,850–3,200 HOW

A Dixon & Co lustre figure of Flora holding a cornucopia, entitled 'Summer', c1820, 9in (23cm) high.
£790–880 RdV

A pair of Staffordshire figures of actors, c1830, 5¼in (13.5cm) high.
£270–300 SER

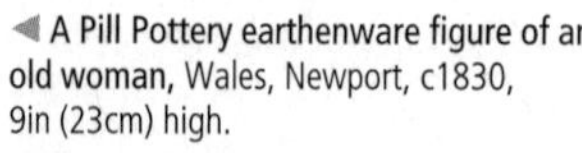

◄ A Pill Pottery earthenware figure of an old woman, Wales, Newport, c1830, 9in (23cm) high.
£450–500 IW

Figures and animals of this type were often attributed to a non-existent pottery at Pill near Bristol, or to north Devon. Evidence now confirms their place of manufacture to be the Pill Pottery at Newport, Gwent and dating to the first half of the 19th century.

► A pair of Staffordshire porcellaneous figures of Milton and Shakespeare, 1835–40, 12in (30.5cm) high.
£520–620 PBA

A Staffordshire pen holder, in the form of a sleeping man leaning on a barrel, c1840, 3½in (9cm) high.

£200–230 ⊞ SER

A pair of Staffordshire figures of Queen Victoria with a baby and Prince Albert, c1850, 6½in (16.5cm) high.

£230–260 ⊞ PICA

A pair of Staffordshire figures of children, decorated with copper lustre detail, c1850, 7in (18cm) high.

£220–250 ⊞ SER

Collecting themes

Many figures produced by the Staffordshire potters in the 19th century were made as a comment on the news of the day and commemorated celebrities of the day and special events such as murders, Royal christenings, weddings and military operations. Items of decorative value were also very popular and large numbers of dogs and other animals were manufactured for the burgeoning British and American middle classes that resulted from the expansion of the Empire and the industrial revolution. This vast output has resulted in specialist collecting areas: Admiral Lord Nelson, John Wesley, Queen Victoria, lions, dogs and Welsh costume figures are all particularly strong at the moment.

◄ **A faïence figure of an angel playing a viola,** Continental, c1850, 15in (38cm) high.

£320–380 ⚒ BWL

A Victorian Staffordshire figure of Benjamin Franklin holding his hat and a speech, the base inscribed 'Franklin', 14in (35.5cm) high.

£440–520 ⚒ PFK

A pair of Staffordshire figures of children sleeping with their dogs, c1855, 6in (15cm) wide.

£900–1,000 ⊞ HOW

◄ **A Staffordshire figure of Red Riding Hood,** c1860, 14½in (37cm) high.

£210–250 ⚒ LAY

A Staffordshire group of a dancing couple, c1860, 9in (23cm) high.

£180–200 IW

▶ **A Victorian Staffordshire group of the Siamese twins Chang and Eng Bunker,** standing beneath a bower, another figure beside them, 9½in (24cm) high.

£130–155 PFK

The Siamese twins, born in 1811, were shown as a curiosity at Barnum's Circus and appeared at Sadler's Wells in 1831. Their names translate as 'left' and 'right'. They married English sisters and settled as farmers in North Carolina, USA. Chang, a heavy drinker, fathered ten children and Eng nine, spending three nights in one twin's house and the next three in the other's, a mile and a half away.

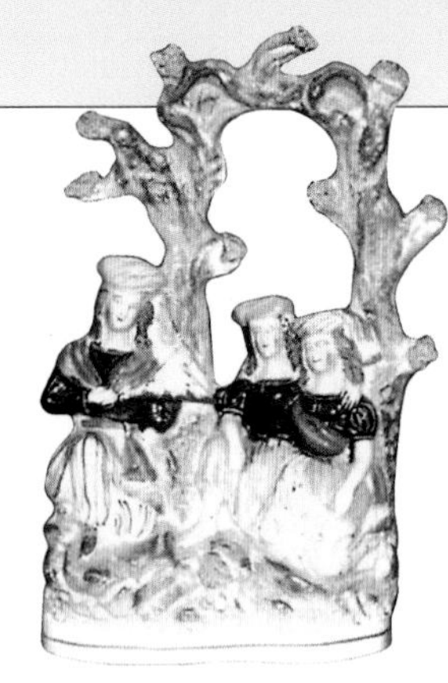

Reproduction Staffordshire figures

Reproduction of Staffordshire figures has been commonplace since the 1960s. In the last 15 years a large percentage of reproduction figures on the market has emanated from China, where figures have been produced on behalf of British wholesalers. Some of the examples can deceive the unwary. Below are some of the points to look out for:

- Staffordshire pottery has a standard palette of colours so developing a familiarity with this range will help distinguish fakes from the real thing.
- Many of the reproductions are of a crude and often dirty and distressed looking porcelain. Originals would have been made with a clay earthenware body, which is generally much lighter in weight.
- All-over crazing to the glaze indicates an attempt to fake the age of a piece. There is in fact very little crazing on original figures.
- Reproductions are sometimes made by taking moulds from original pieces. The result is that the copied items are approximately ten per cent smaller, due to shrinkage in the firing process.
- Most original 19th-century figures were made by pressing two moulded pieces together; this can be confirmed by the presence of a seam down the side of the item. Later versions made in the 20th century are slip-cast in one piece and there will be no seam.
- Bright metallic coloured gilding is usually indicative of items made in the 20th century.

◀ **A Victorian Staffordshire figure of the Reverend Christmas Evans,** the title inscribed to the base, 13¼in (33.5cm) high.

£470–560 PFK

Reverend Christmas Evans was a well-known Baptist who ministered in Wales in the late 18th and the early 19th centuries.

▶ **A Minton majolica sweetmeat basket,** in the form of cherubs holding a pail, slight damage, impressed mark and date cypher for 1866, 11½in (29cm) wide.

£250–300 WW

A Staffordshire box, in the form of a figure believed to be Jenny Lind holding a King Charles spaniel, late 19thC, 9in (23cm) high.

£210–250 DA

A majolica figure of a boy with a basket, late 19thC, 7½in (19cm) high.

£70–80 Hal

A pair of Staffordshire portrait figures of Moody and Sankey, named to bases, late 19thC, 17½in (44.5cm) high.

£260–310 PF

Dwight Moody and Ira Sankey were American evangelists.

FLATWARE

A Bristol delft charger, decorated with tulips within a stylized band, repaired, c1720, 13¾in (35cm) diam.

£2,000–2,400 Bea

A London delft plate, decorated with initials and date to the centre, dated 1721, 8¾in (22cm) diam.

£1,050–1,200 HIS

Restoration

Most items of British pottery were made for ordinary working folk for domestic use or decoration in the home and were not generally intended to be displayed in glass cases.

Naturally, pieces that are 100 to 200 years old will often have suffered some damage and as a result many items found on the market will have been restored. Of course it is always good to find perfect examples but allowances have to be made and restoration is inevitable with many examples of antique pottery. Professional restoration is acceptable if the item is rare and not over restored. It is less acceptable if a common item is poorly or over restored. Professional restoration is often invisible and it is always wise to confirm the extent of restoration when buying – reputable dealers will specify this on their price labels.

A Castelli maiolica plate, painted with a scene of Cupid overcoming Pan in a wooded landscape, within a border of putti and flowers, Italy, 18thC, 7½in (19cm) diam, in a fitted tooled-leather case inscribed in gilt 'Guido Reni Pinxit'.

£3,600–4,300 S(O)

A Hispano-Moresque charger, decorated with a stylized foliate ground enclosing a central raised boss, slight damage, Spain, 18thC, 15½in (39.5cm) diam.

£760–910 DN

A Dutch Delft plate, c1740, 9in (23cm) diam.

£170–190 PeN

Delftware

Delft is tin-glazed earthenware made in Holland since the 16th century and England from the 17th century and was named after the Dutch town where so much of it was produced. Decoration is blue or polychrome. In order to distinguish between the two types of delftware, it has become customary to use 'Delft' for Dutch wares and 'delft' or 'delftware' for English wares.

An English delft plate, c1760, 8in (20.5cm) diam.

£450–500 HOW

A De Porceleyne Klaeuw charger, painted with Peacock pattern, Holland c1760.

£165–195 DN

A Liverpool delft plate, painted in the Oriental manner with a river scene and a dwelling, 18thC, 8¾in (22cm) diam.

£110–130 DA

An English delft charger, c1780, 14in (35.5cm) diam.

£290–330 PeN

A pearlware plate, decorated with the American seal, repaired, c1800, 6in (15cm) diam.

£850–950 KUR

This plate was made in England for the American market.

A plate, decorated with the American eagle, repaired, 1800–20, 7¼in (18.5cm) diam.

£790–880 KUR

This plate was made in England for the American market.

A Davenport pearlware plate, with transfer-printed and enamel decoration, c1815, 9¾in (25cm) diam.

£80–90 HIS

A pair of pearlware dishes, decorated with flowers, c1820, 12in (30.5cm) wide.

£1,350–1,500 HOW

A Mason's Ironstone plate, decorated with Waterlily pattern, 1820–25, 9in (23cm) wide.

£135–155 WAn

A Jackson plate, transfer-printed with a view of Hartford, Connecticut, c1835, 9in (23cm) diam.

£95–105 KUR

This plate was made in England for the American market.

◄ **A Joseph Heath & Co plate,** transfer-printed with the residence of the late Richard Jordan, New Jersey, c1835, 9in (23cm) diam.

£160–180 KUR

This plate was made in England for the American market.

A Wemyss Gordon plate, painted with dog roses, Scotland, c1890, 8in (20.5cm) diam.

£620–690 Fai

◄ **A Spode plate,** with an impressed blue mark, c1840, 10in (25.5cm) diam.

£50–55 GSA

A Newcombe College pottery charger, incised by Charlotte Payne with clusters of fruit and foliage, slight damage, marked, America, New Orleans, 1904, 9½in (24cm) diam.

£2,550–3,050 DRO(C)

For more Arts & Crafts ceramics, please see the Decorative Arts section on pages 367–440.

JARS

◄ **An English delft syrup jar,** with flared spout, the strapwork label inscribed 'S:Spin:Cerv', within a cherub, shell, mask and scrolled surround, restored, 1720–30, 7½in (19cm) high.

£1,450–1,650 G&G

A pair of English delft drug jars, each with a blank cartouche above a pestle and mortar and leaves, surmounted with entwined serpents, c1770, 5in (12.5cm) high.

£300–360 DN

An iron-glazed jar, early 19thC, 10in (25.5cm) high.

£105–120 IW

A maiolica *albarello*, decorated with two portrait roundels, inscribed 'Isisdiga', Italy, 19thC, 8¼in (21cm) high.

£120–140 DMC

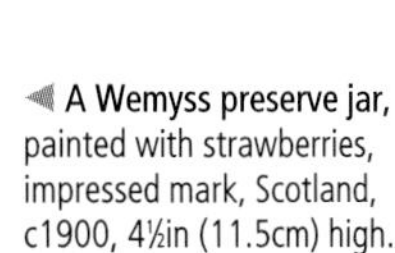

◄ **A Wemyss preserve jar,** painted with strawberries, impressed mark, Scotland, c1900, 4½in (11.5cm) high.

£270–300 RdeR

JARDINIERES

A glazed jardinière, probably Minton, each side moulded in high relief with turtles or swimming fish within ogee panels, with bamboo-moulded corners, on compressed bun feet, 19thC, 18in (45.5cm) high.

£470–560 Hal

A Minton jardinière, decorated with wicker and ribbon pattern, impressed mark, numbered '2721 14', registered July 1890, 12¼in (31cm) high.

£230–270 DD

A Minton majolica jardinière, modelled as a nautilus shell, c1880, 15in (38cm) high.

£400–450 HUM

JUGS & EWERS

A glazed jug, the neck applied with lion-mask medallions, the handle with overlapping scale detail, with roulette bandings enclosing named saints: S. Philippus, S. Thomas, S. Johannes and S. Salvator, slight damage, Germany, 17thC, 8in (20.5cm) high.

£350–420 TEN

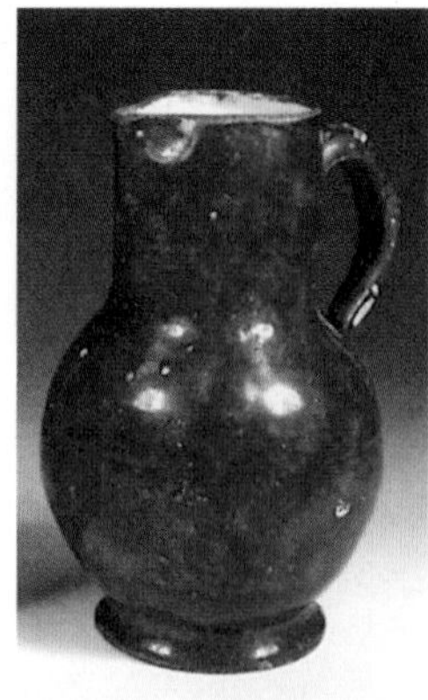

A *bleu de Nevers*-style **tin-glazed jug,** with white interior, France, mid-18thC, 9¼in (23.5cm) high.

£330–390 CGC

A pottery jug, printed and enamelled with 'The Archeress', c1805, 5in (12.5cm) high.

£220–250 IW

A pearlware commemorative jug, inscribed 'Admiral Nelson and Captain Berry', decorated in Pratt colours, slight damage, early 19thC, 6in (15cm) high.

£140–165 GTH

A Bacchus jug, c1820, 7in (18cm) high.

£720–800 HOW

A Staffordshire copper lustre marriage jug, inscribed 'Thomas & Nancy Hallworth', dated 1820, 7in (18cm) high.

£490–550 RdV

A silver resist lustre jug, c1820, 6in (15cm) high.

£400–450 HOW

The decorative technique of silver resist is normally found on pearlwares, particularly jugs and mugs, c1800–20. To achieve the effect, a design is painted onto the object in wax, then the silver lustre is applied to the surface. When the wax is burned off in the kiln, the painted design appears on a silver lustre ground. Examples in good condition today are scarce, as the silver resist is very prone to rubbing through use.

A jug, depicting a lion and lioness, c1820, 6in (15cm) high.

£490–550 HOW

A silver resist lustre pearlware jug, c1820, 5½in (14cm) high.

£90–100 OD

◀ **A jug,** commemorating the visit of the French soldier and statesman General Lafayette to the United States in 1824, c1825, 7in (18cm) high.

£820–920 KUR

In 1777, Lafayette assembled a band of men to sail to America and fight in the Revolution against the British, resulting in several victories. Two years later, he persuaded the French government to send aid to the Americans, thereby becoming a hero in their eyes. He returned to Paris after the British surrendered at Yorktown.

A Staffordshire pearlware jug, bat printed in puce with a pastoral country house scene, on a silver lustre ground, early 19thC, 6in (15cm) high.

£175–210 Bea

Bat printing is a type of transfer printing used to produce fine detail on ceramics by English factories in the early 19th century. The design was conveyed from an engraved copper plate to a glazed surface by means of slabs of glue or gelatin (bats). Tiny dots of oil were transferred to the porcelain and a fine coloured powder was then dusted on to the surface of the glaze. This powder stuck to the oil, rendering the design onto the article.

A Sunderland lustre jug, printed with a depiction of the 'Sailor's Farewell' and a verse, c1830, 7in (18cm) high.

£720–800 HOW

An American Manufacturing Pottery Company earthenware pitcher, commemorating the Landing of Lafayette at Castle Garden, New York City, August 16, 1824, America, 1825–30, 9in (23cm) high.

£5,700–6,800 SK

Lustrewares

Lustre is a type of decoration formed when metallic oxides are applied to pottery after an original firing, then reheated at a lower temperature to produce a metallic-type glaze. First used in the Middle East around the 7th century AD, these glazes were made popular again in England at the beginning of the 19th century. The main centres of production in England were Staffordshire, northeast England, Yorkshire and South Wales.

A Sunderland lustre jug, printed and painted with Masonic devices and a verse, 19thC, 9in (23cm) high.

£380–450 PF

A Sunderland lustre jug, printed and enamelled with a depiction of the 'Sailor's Farewell' and a verse, early 19thC, 5½in (14cm) high.

£210–250 G(L)

A Sunderland lustre jug, by the Garrison Pottery, printed with a compass, c1835, 7in (18cm) high.

£250–280 CHAC

▶ **Four conjoined pottery jugs,** painted with petal and leaf decoration, one jug with an incised floral spray, with an applied handle, impressed 'Orson C. Warner', slight damage, America, 19thC, 9in (23cm) wide.

£1,200–1,400 SK

A jug, commemorating the birth of Sarah Ann Law, Scotland, dated 1842, 8in (20.5cm) high.

£175–195 ⊞ CHAC

A Rockingham jug, relief-decorated with game, the handle modelled as a dog, c1850, 9in (23cm) high.

£160–180 ⊞ IW

A pair of Staffordshire copper lustre jugs, decorated with embossed figures, c1850, 7in (18cm) high.

£100–110 ⊞ ACAC

A Victorian ewer, with applied lion's mask, acanthus-moulded lip and scroll handle with a rosette decoration, pattern No. 244, 11¼in (28.5cm) high.

£140–165 PFK

◄ **A Palissy-style jug,** by Caldao, Portugal, c1860, 15in (38cm) high.

£990–1,100 ⊞ BRT

A jug, printed with cycling scenes, c1870, 6in (15cm) high.

£145–165 ⊞ CHAC

A ewer and basin, by John Marshall & Co, Bo'ness Pottery, transfer-printed with 13 vignettes of Canadian sports, impressed and printed marks, Scotland, c1880, jug 12½in (32cm) high.

£2,400–2,850 WAD

An Aller Vale pottery jug, incised with a four-line verse above a frieze of flowerheads, incised No. 906, late 19thC, 7in (18cm) high.

£165–195 PFK

The Aller Vale Pottery at Kingskerswell in Devon was owned by John Phillips. Wares were made from local clay and decorated with slips and glazes made at the pottery.

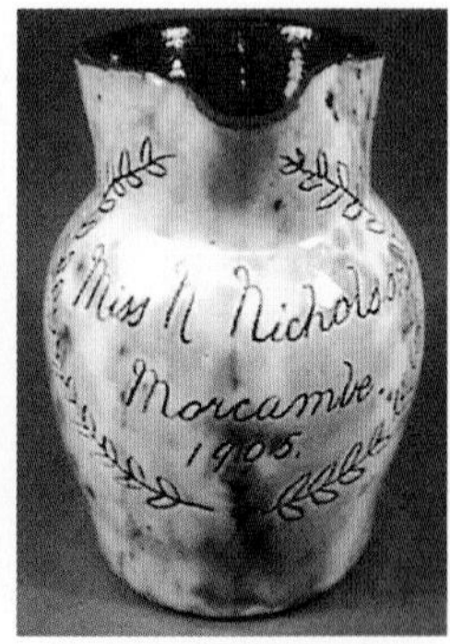

An Edwardian Wetheriggs Pottery jug, incised 'Miss N. Nicholson/ Morcambe 1905', within a foliate wreath, 4in (10cm) high.

£200–240 PFK

The Wetheriggs Pottery in Cumbria was founded by John Schofield and Margaret Thorburn. It is still in production and is the only steam-powered pottery in the UK.

MUGS & TANKARDS

A Vauxhall stoneware tankard, applied with a portrait of Queen Anne flanked by two soldiers and trees, above a stag hunt, inscribed 'John Sabine', dated 1723, 7½in (19cm) high.

£1,900–2,250 S(O)

An English delft mug, with strap handle and flange base, damaged, c1750, 5in (13cm) high.

£1,650–1,950 S(O)

A documentary scratch blue salt-glazed stoneware porter mug, inscribed 'H.S. & M', on a spreading ribbed foot, dated 1763, 4¾in (12cm) high.

£880–1,050 TEN

The decoration on this mug is scratched into the wet clay and then coloured blue.

Stonewares

Stonewares are ceramic wares fired at a high temperature (1200–1400°C), so that the body becomes vitrified and impervious to liquids. The earliest stonewares were made in China in the 7th century AD and did not appear in Europe until the 15th century, initially in northern Germany. Wares can be grey, red, brown, black or white and are often decorated with a salt glaze with a characteristic 'orange peel' surface.

◀ **A Jackfield pottery tankard,** c1770, 4½in (11.5cm) high.

£220–250 IW

A Mortlake-style salt-glazed stoneware tankard, sprigged with smokers and drinkers, a hunting scene and trees, the strap handle with a leaf terminal, the silver cover with shell thumbpiece and maker's mark GR, London 1821, 8¼in (21cm) high.

£230–270 DN(BR)

◀ **A silver resist lustre mug,** c1820, 4in (10cm) diam.

£450–500 HOW

A child's pearlware pottery mug, inscribed 'A Present from My Uncle', c1830, 3in (7.5cm) diam.

£175–195 RdV

A pottery mug, transfer-printed with the Oddfellows' arms, c1840, 4¾in (12cm) high.

£180–200 IW

◀ **A child's pottery mug,** with transfer-printed decoration, c1840, 2¾in (7cm) diam.

£135–150 HUM

A Sunderland lustre pottery mug, c1845, 4in (10cm) high.
£240–270 GSA

A pottery spongeware tankard, c1860, 6in (15cm) high.
£270–300 HUM

A Wemyss 'Earlshall' pottery mug, painted with rooks perching in trees with rabbits below, slight damage, impressed mark, Scotland, c1900, 6in (15cm) high.
£3,200–3,800 DN

The catalogue for specialist dealer Rogers de Rin's exhibition of Wemyss ware at Sotheby's in 1976 states 'Mr R. W. Mackenzie, the eccentric owner of Earlshall, created designs to be painted by Wemyss decorators. These products were sold at fairs held at the great house near Leuchars (Fife). Rooks in trees, rabbits, peacocks and topiary were subjects taken from familiar scenes in the grounds...'

Frog mugs

Frog mugs were drinking mugs with a small model of a frog on the inside, usually near the base. They were made at Leeds, Sunderland, Nottingham and other northern English potteries.

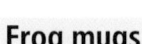

◄ A Halifax frog mug, c1900, 4in (10cm) high.
£195–220 IW

PLAQUES

A maiolica votive plaque, depicting Christ crucified, flanked by the Virgin and Child and the Angel Gabriel, inscribed 'VF/GR', probably southern Italy, 1600–50, 10 x 8½in (25.5 x 21.5cm).
£1,000–1,200 S(O)

A pair of Castelli maiolica plaques, from the workshops of the Grue family, depicting the Crucifixion and Deposition of Christ, damaged, Italy, 1750–1800, 12½in (32cm) wide.
£4,550–5,400 S(NY)

A Sunderland lustre pottery wall plaque, depicting the Reverend John Wesley, c1820, 7in (18cm) wide.
£220–250 GSA

A Minton plaque, painted by R. Coleman with the head and shoulders of a young Renaissance lady, impressed marks, date code for 1875, 19¾in (50cm) diam.
£2,350–2,800 CGC

A Della Robbia plaque, by Hannah Jones, c1900, 18in (45.5cm) diam.
£1,250–1,400 BKJL

A painted plaque, depicting a street scene with a town hall, signed, Holland, c1900, 22½ x 17in (57 x 43cm), in an ebonized and painted carved wood frame.
£820–980 TEN

POTS

An English delft drug or ointment pot, possibly Lambeth, painted with horizontal bands, repaired, 17th or early-18thC, 4¾in (12cm) high.

£340–400 WW

A Lambeth delft ointment pot, inscribed 'Valle 21 Hay Market', 18thC, 1½in (4cm) high.

£1,100–1,300 CAu

Valle was a well-known London retailer or 'oil man'.

A slipware honey pot, decorated with cream slip numerals, handle missing, slight damage, early 18thC, 5¼in (13.5cm) high.

£1,800–2,150 S(O)

A Sunderland lustre pot and cover, c1840, 6in (15cm) diam.

£530–590 GSA

A Wemyss pomade pot, painted by Karel Nekola with roses, Scotland, c1900, 4in (10cm) diam.

£450–500 RdeR

POT LIDS

'Bear in Ravine', Ball No. 14, restored, c1845, 2½in (6.5cm) diam.

£1,650–1,850 SAS

◀ **'Pheasant Shooting',** Ball No. 261, with mottled border and flange, c1855, 5in (12.5cm) diam.

£190–220 SAS

'The Fish Barrow', decorated with Pratt colours, c1870, 5in (12.5cm) diam.

£190–220 DHA

◀ **'Genuine Beef Marrow Pomatum',** slight damage, America, Philadelphia, late 19thC, 3in (7.5cm) diam.

£190–220 BBR

Pot lid numbers

The numbers in the captions refer to the system used by A. Ball in his reference work *The Price Guide to Pot Lids,* Antique Collectors Club, 1980.

◀ **'Maidens Decorating a Bust of Homer'**, Ball No. 380A, c1880, 3in (7.5cm) diam.

£3,500–4,200 SAS

▶ **A Prattware ceramic pot lid,** depicting a begging dog and a young boy, c1880, 3in (7.5cm) diam.

£130–145 DHA

'Aromatic Quinine Tooth Powder', depicting the Assembly Rooms, Malvern, 1890–1900, 3½in (9cm) diam.

£1,650–1,950 BBR

▶ **'The Administration Building, World's Fair, Chicago 1893',** Ball No. 146, 4in (10cm) diam.

£400–480 SAS

SERVICES

A Hicks, Meigh & Johnson stone china part dinner service, comprising 61 pieces, printed and enamelled with peony and blossoming branches within a cell diaper border with floral vignettes, the gadrooned rim overlaid in gold, faults, printed Royal Arms factory mark, painted pattern No. 58, slight damage, 1822–35.

£760–910 RTo

A Mason's Ironstone part dessert service, comprising 25 pieces, printed and painted in the *famille verte* palette with a Chinese garden scene with exotic birds, two plates damaged, printed crown and ribbon marks, c1840.

£1,950–2,300 Bea

Insurance values

Always insure your valuable antiques for the cost of replacing them with similar items, regardless of the original price paid. Both dealers and auctioneers can provide a valuation service for a fee.

▶ **A Samuel Alcock part dessert service,** comprising 27 pieces, painted and gilded with floral specimens interspersed with scrolling foliage, slight damage, painted mark 3/2042, c1855.

£940–1,100 Hal

An Ashworth Bros Ironstone China part dinner service, comprising 48 pieces, each with a gilt flowerhead centre within a painted and gilded rim, printed factory marks, 1862–90.

£350–420 RTo

A Luneville majolica asparagus set, comprising 17 pieces, France, c1880, plates 9in (23cm) diam.

£1,450–1,600 MLL

TEA & COFFEE POTS

A Staffordshire salt-glazed heart-shaped teapot, c1750, 4¾in (12cm) wide.

£1,350–1,500 HIS

A Staffordshire lead-glazed redware teapot and cover, with white slip decoration, slight damage, mid-18thC.

£590–700 DN

A glazed redware coffee pot, with engine-turned decoration, c1770, 10in (25.5cm) high.

£310–350 IW

A stoneware coffee pot, attributed to Brampton, the cover with relief-moulded flowers, the body modelled in relief with a pheasant in a cornfield, the reverse with a hare in a landscape, beneath a floral frieze, spout repaired, c1790, 7½in (19cm) high.

£90–105 PFK

A teapot and cover, with a bird's-head spout and C-scroll handle, slight damage, knop missing, painted mark, Italy, 18thC, 4½in (11.5cm) high.

£90–105 DMC

► **A pearlware teapot,** c1810, 7in (18cm) high.

£220–250 OD

A salt-glazed coffee pot, c1820, 11in (28cm) high.

£160–180 IW

A Thomas Till & Son majolica teapot, 1850–60, 6in (15cm) high.
£130–145 CHAC

A majolica teapot, with moulded sweetcorn decoration, c1860, 9in (23cm) high.
£105–120 ACAC

A Minton majolica teapot and cover, in the form of a flat iron, the sides moulded with a frieze of mice, the cover with a knop in the form of a mouse holding a carrot, the cable handle surmounted by a cat, handle repaired, impressed model No. 622, moulded lozenge and impressed marks, c1875, 8in (20.5cm) high.
£27,000–32,000 N

This is a very rare item and the whimsical nature of the decoration ensured a high price.

◀ **A Joseph Holdcroft majolica teapot and cover,** in the form of a Chinese boy on a coconut, cover damaged, c1875, 5¼in (13.5cm) high.
£300–360 SWO

Majolica manufacturers

The word majolica is derived from mailoica, the term for tin-glazed earthenwares produced in Italy during the Renaissance. Majolica was introduced into England in 1847 by Joseph Arnoux, the art director for Minton. The pieces he produced were a huge commercial success and other manufacturers soon began producing their own wares, such as George Jones, Wedgwood and Joseph Holdcroft.

A pottery teapot, relief-decorated with flowers, inscribed 'Chesterfield July 1896', 8in (20.5cm) high.
£230–260 GSA

A Wileman & Co *intarsio* teapot, in the form of S. J. P. Kruger, c1910, 5in (12.5cm) high.
£580–650 GaL

S. J. P. Kruger was a South African soldier and statesman, and President of Transvaal 1883–99. His opposition to Cecil Rhodes and his denial of civil rights to the Uitlanders led to the Boer War 1899–1902.

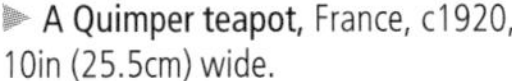

▶ **A Quimper teapot,** France, c1920, 10in (25.5cm) wide.
£180–200 MLL

TILES

A London delft tile, painted in manganese with a rural scene, 1725–60, 5in (12.5cm) square.

£85–95 ⊞ SAAC

A Dutch Delft tile, depicting a warrior on horseback, 18thC, 6in (15cm) square.

£85–95 ⊞ SAAC

A Dutch Delft polychrome tile, depicting a musketeer, c1750, 5in (12.5cm) square.

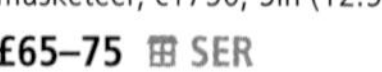

£65–75 ⊞ SER

A Dutch Delft tile, depicting a seated man, 18thC, 6in (15cm) square.

£95–110 ⊞ SAAC

A set of 13 Dutch Delft tiles, with hand-painted decoration, c1870, 5¼in (13.5cm) square.

£230–260 ⊞ DHA

A Minton majolica tile, depicting a bird on a fruiting branch, c1880, 8in (20.5cm) square.

£90–100 ⊞ CHAC

◄ **A Minton tile,** painted with two gentlemen fencing, the reverse with artist's painted monogram 'SK' and No. 253, impressed marks, c1880, 15¾in (40cm) wide.

£190–220 CGC

Sets/pairs

Unless otherwise stated, any description which refers to 'a set' or 'a pair' includes a guide price for the entire set or the pair, even though the illustration may show only a single item.

A set of nine Wedgwood tiles, transfer-printed with months of the year, depicting figures involved in country pursuits and seasonal activities, some damaged, June, August and October missing, moulded marks to reverse, stamped 'Old English', late 19thC, 6in (15cm) square.

£370–440 PFK

A Rozenburg tile plaque, comprising six tiles, hand-painted with a shepherd and sheep in a rural landscape, after Anton Mauve, Holland, c1900, each tile 6in (15cm) square.

£350–420 SK

TOBY & CHARACTER JUGS

A pearlware Martha Gunn Toby jug, her hat decorated with Prince of Wales feathers, c1790, 11in (28cm) high.

£2,600–3,000 JBL

A pearlware warty-faced Toby jug, holding a jug of ale, c1800, 9½in (24cm) high.

£400–480 TEN

A black-faced Toby jug, 1810–20, 10in (25.5cm) high.

£1,050–1,200 JBL

A Hearty Goodfellow Toby jug, c1820, 11½in (29cm) high.

£600–680 DHA

► **A pearlware pottery Toby jug,** with cover, northeast England, c1830, 8in (20.5cm) high.

£530–590 RdV

A faïence character jug, in the form of the head and shoulders of a naval officer wearing uniform, the handle modelled as rope, maker's cypher 'A.G.', France, 19thC, 8in (20.5cm) high.

£190–220 PFK

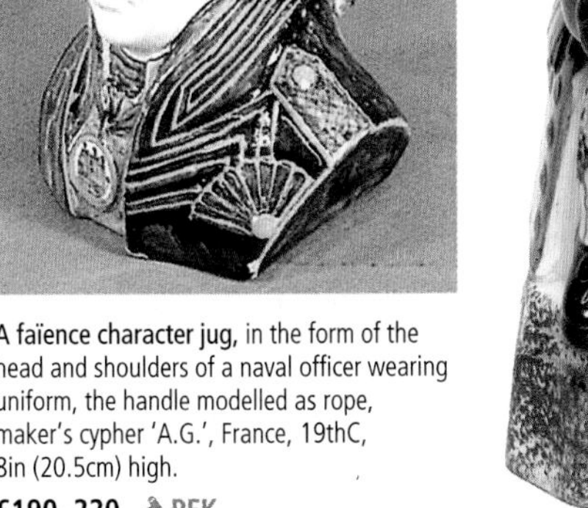

A Yorkshire Toby jug, 1830–40, 10in (25.5cm) high.

£350–390 DHA

Faïence

Faïence is the French term for tin-glazed earthenware. It was introduced into France by itinerant Italian potters at the beginning of the 16th century. Early wares resembled maiolica made in the Italian town of Faenza, hence the name.

► **A Staffordshire character jug,** 'The Landlord', c1880, 9¼in (23.5cm) high.

£95–110 SWO

A pair of Staffordshire Punch and Judy character jugs, slight damage, registration marks, c1900, 9½in (24cm) high.

£175–210 SWO

VASES

A pair of faïence vases, each with mask handles, Continental, 18thC, 8¼in (21cm) high.

£1,750–2,100 CGC

A Wedgwood jasper ware spill vase, decorated with a coat-of-arms and a bust of Josiah Wedgwood, impressed mark, 1730–95, 2¼in (5.5cm) high.

£50–60 BWL

A Dutch Delft vase, painted with birds among flowers, foliage and rockwork, c1750, 9in (23cm) high.

£230–270 WW

A black basalt neo-classical vase, probably Wedgwood, moulded with a band of laurel above swags of fabric suspended from six rings, slight damage, late 18thC, 14½in (37cm) high.

£1,050–1,250 S(O)

A pair of Mason's Ironstone covered vases, 1815–20, 26in (66cm) high.

£5,700–6,400 WAn

A pair of Sewell & Donkin pearlware quintals, with lustre decoration, slight damage, impressed marks, 1828–52, 8½in (21.5cm) high.

£1,400–1,650 WW

A quintal is a flower holder with five sockets rising from a square base, in the shape of a fan. They were listed as flower horns by Leeds, and by the Staffordshire potters as flower tubes.

A Mason's Ironstone vase, decorated with Pagoda pattern, seal mark to base, c1835, 5in (12.5cm) high.

£500–550 RdV

Ironstone

'Ironstone' or 'Ironstone China' is a trade name for a hard, durable earthenware patented by Charles Mason in 1813. It was claimed to contain slag of iron but it was subsequently proved to consist of earthenware strengthened by the addition of silica, probably in the form of calcined flint, which allowed the body to be fired at a higher temperature. Competitors were not fooled for long and soon many manufacturers were producing Ironstone, including Davenport, Spode, Ridgway and the Ashworth brothers. Early examples are highly sought after by collectors and can be very expensive.

◄ **A Palissy-style vase,** the handles surmounted by frogs, Portugal, c1860, 10in (25.5cm) high.

£990–1,100 BRT

A pair of Wedgwood jasper ware pedestal urns and covers, each decorated with figural medallions, with gilt-brass mounts and classical face mask handles, date code for 1871, 11in (28cm) high.

£1,450–1,700 MA&I

An E. B. Fishley vase, decorated with classical figures, north Devon, c1878, 18in (45.5cm) high.

£1,600–1,800 BKJL

Edwin Beer Fishley took over the running of his grandfather's pottery in Fremington, north Devon, in 1860. It was he who inspired the renowned studio potter, Michael Cardew, to take up the craft.

A two-handled vase, the handles in the form of entwined snakes with grotesque mask finials, Continental, late 19thC, 17¾in (45cm) high.

£120–140 ROS

A Wemyss Grosvenor vase, painted with tulips, Scotland, c1890, 5½in (14cm) high.

£430–480 SDD

A pair of Dutch Delft covered vases, painted with panels of Oriental birds and plants, the covers with lion and ball knops, pseudo PAK monogram mark, 253/4in (65.5cm) high.

£3,900–4,650 S(NY)

A Quimper vase, France, c1920, 9in (23cm) high.

£250–280 MLL

MISCELLANEOUS

A pair of faïence drug bottles, painted in Faenza-style with scrolling foliage, repaired, Mexico, 17thC, 9in (23cm) high.

£960–1,150 S(O)

A pair of Wemyss Kantor candlesticks, decorated with cherries, impressed mark, Scotland, c1900, 10in (25.5cm) high.

£580–650 RUSK

A pair of centrepieces, each ribbed bowl interior decorated with a pastoral scene, the exteriors decorated with flowers and insects, the foot in the form of three dolphins, slight damage, France, probably Moustiers, 19thC, 9½in (24cm) high.

£510–610 BERN

A pearlware cradle, decorated in Pratt colours, c1800, 13in (33cm) long.

£1,950–2,200 HOW

An English delft flower brick, painted with a river scene, 18thC, 6in (15cm) wide.

£820–980 HYD

A Mason's Ironstone footbath, with two leaf-moulded scroll handles, painted in Imari-style with a tobacco leaf design, the interior decorated with a band of flowers and leaves, repaired, c1815, 19¼in (49cm) wide.

£3,900–4,650 LFA

A Minton majolica Renaissance garden seat, damaged, date mark for 1862, 18in (45.5cm) high.

£230–270 LAY

A Wedgwood majolica Argenta ware Corinthian pedestal, decorated in relief with neo-classical portrait pendants suspended from ribbons, above a fruiting grapevine garland terminating with leopard masks with trophy drops below, damaged and restored, impressed mark, c1878, 33½in (85cm) high.

£760–910 SK

A Wedgwood jasper cameo ware scent bottle, each side with a portrait bust within a floral swag surround, with a yellow-metal screw top, c1800, 2½in (6.5cm) high.

£590–700 Hal

A Spode supper set, comprising a covered dish, four segmental plates and the original mahogany tray, painted in the Imari palette, slight damage and restoration, c1810, 22½in (57cm) wide.

£760–910 SWO

A faïence wine cistern, painted in the Transitional style with Oriental figures in landscapes within floral borders, with two lion's-head masks with ring handles, on bun feet, repaired, France, possibly Nevers, possibly late 17thC, 21¾in (55.5cm) wide.

£1,100–1,300 DN

An English delft tea canister, Bristol or London, painted with flower- and diaper-patterned panels, the cover inscribed 'A P 1753' above a band of scrolls, damage and restoration, incised mark 'BP E Q 1753', dated 1753, 4½in (11.5cm) high.

£10,800–12,900 S(O)

This piece realized a high price because of the initials and date on the cover, which are seldom seen.

CREAMWARE

CREAMWARE, with its refined cream-coloured body and transparent lead glaze, virtually replaced delftware and became the ceramic of choice for the middle and upper classes in the late 18th and early 19th centuries. Its fineness and lightness made it an ideal form for expressing in ceramic the neo-classical art influences and the new genteel style that was a result of the fashion for the Grand Tour and typified in the designs of Robert Adam and George Hepplewhite.

Thomas Whieldon is regarded as one of the great English potters and his influence on his contemporaries such as Wedgwood, Greatbatch and Spode was very strong. Examples of his creamware are known from c1750 – it was often decorated with mottled coloured glazes sometimes referred to as 'tortoiseshell'. Enamel decoration was introduced in the 1760s and colourful floral chinoiserie pictures were hand-decorated onto pots. One of the most famous enamellers was David Rhodes who was originally commissioned by Josiah Wedgwood.

Several factories produced creamware including Wedgwood, the Leeds Pottery, Warburtons of Cobridge, Cockpit Hill Derby and others in Staffordshire, Yorkshire and South Wales, the first two of these being the largest producers. Josiah Wedgwood was commissioned to produce a set of creamware tableware for Queen Charlotte; it was so popular that more requests were received from the Royal household giving Wedgwood the opportunity to name his creamware Queen's ware. The stunning impact of Wedgwood's glaze on a creamy white body without any decoration was such that numerous factories copied his lead. The Leeds Pottery with its bold shapes and famous reticulated work was so successful and prolific in their output that creamware is often called Leeds ware to this day.

All forms of tableware were produced, both plain and coloured, and designs often replicated silver items. Delicate strapwork handles with floral motifs, rams' heads, acanthus leaves, trellis work, sphinxes and Greek classical symbols were incorporated in the designs.

The impact of the introduction of creamware in the 18th century cannot be understated and there is no doubt that it is the direct ancestor of the domestic tableware we use today. The market for it is very strong, fuelled today by a demand from collectors and interior designers, especially in the United States. When buying, it is wise to acquire fine clean pieces from the 18th century. Creamware is often collected by shape or factory although a varied collection or assemblage looks stunning and makes an unsurpassable statement of taste and appreciation of design in ceramics.

John Howard

A creamware basket, with a pierced border and entwined rope-twist handles terminating in moulded leaves and flowers, the centre printed with a vignette of fishermen by a river, on a pedestal foot, 18thC, 10½in (26.5cm) wide.

£175–210 HYD

A creamware basket, cover and stand, the knop in the form of a cherub, c1780, 11in (28cm) wide.

£1,350–1,500 HOW

► **A creamware bowl and cover,** probably Staffordshire, enamelled with sprays of flowers, the entwined handles with foliate terminals, slight damage, c1780, 6¼in (16cm) wide.

£230–270 DN

A Leeds creamware coffee pot, decorated with a chintz pattern, impressed triangle mark, c1775, 9in (23cm) high.

£590–700 ROS

A pair of creamware candlesticks, 1893–1906, 12in (30.5cm) high.

£110–125 ⊞ CHAC

A creamware dish, with pierced decoration, c1785, 13in (33cm) wide.

£810–900 ⊞ HOW

A creamware dish, with pierced decoration, c1780, 8¾in (22cm) diam.

£125–140 ⊞ HIS

A Leeds creamware ewer and basin, c1780, 10in (25.5cm) high.

£1,700–1,900 ⊞ HOW

A Wedgwood creamware egg cup and cover, c1790, 4¾in (12cm) high.

£540–600 ⊞ HIS

A Wedgwood creamware footbath and jug, with banded decoration, slight damage, early 19thC, footbath 18½in (47cm) wide.

£260–310 ⚒ DN(BR)

What is creamware?

Creamware is a mixture of very fine clay and flint, glazed with a smooth lead cream-tinted composition. It was invented by Josiah Wedgwood c1760. Objects produced often replicate silver shapes, with intricate and finely textured moulding and attention to detail.

A pair of creamware goblets, possibly Swansea, with painted decoration, c1820, 4in (10cm) high.

£310–350 ⊞ ReN

A creamware jug, in the style of William Greatbatch, moulded and glazed with berries and leaves, above moulded basketwork, c1770, 4½in (11.5cm) high.

£330–390 ⚒ WW

A creamware jug, attributed to Neale & Co, transfer-printed with symbols of Peace and Plenty, c1790, 8½in (21.5cm) high.

£580–650 ⊞ OCH

A Yorkshire creamware puzzle jug, c1790, 9½in (24cm) high.

£630–700 ⊞ HIS

A creamware jug, decorated with a panel depicting George Washington, surrounded by a banner inscribed with the names of the American states, c1800, 8in (20.5cm) high.

£810–900 ⊞ KUR

This jug was made in England for the American market.

A creamware jug, decorated with copper lustre, depicting two ships and entitled 'The *Wasp & Reindeer*', 1815–20, 7in (18cm) high.

£1,250–1,400 ⊞ KUR

This jug was made in England for the American market.

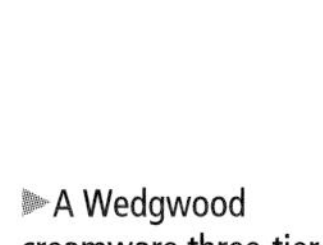

◀ **A creamware mould,** impressed with a cherub, c1800, 8in (20.5cm) wide.

£400–450 ⊞ HOW

A creamware ladle, the bowl in the form of a shell, slight damage, Staffordshire or south Yorkshire, c1780, 11½in (29cm) long.

£370–440 ⚒ DN

▶ **A Wedgwood creamware three-tier mould,** impressed mark, c1795, 8in (20.5cm) wide.

£570–680 ⚒ GTH

A creamware plate, with a pierced border, Wales, c1765, 9in (23cm) diam.

£200–230 ⊞ HOW

A creamware plate, decorated with a peafowl, France, c1810, 9½in (24cm) diam.

£135–150 ⊞ HIS

A creamware plate, decorated with an underglaze transfer-print of a rural scene, c1780, 9½in (24cm) diam.

£135–150 ⊞ HIS

A Hartley Green & Co **creamware plate,** commemorating the coronation of George IV, dated July 19 1821, 9in (23cm) diam.

£990–1,100 RdV

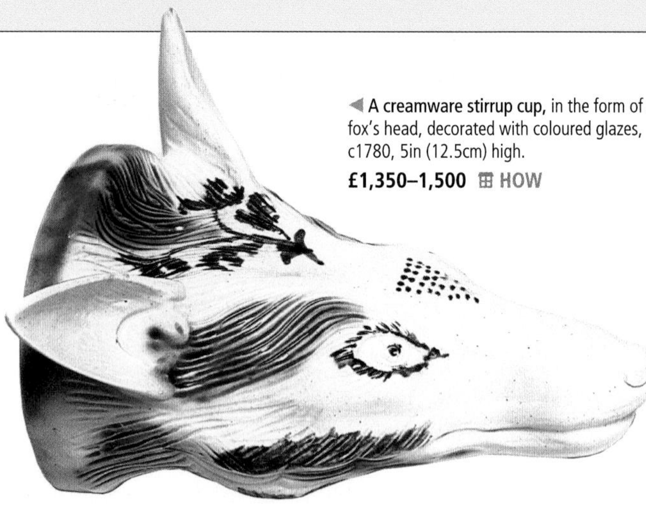

◀ **A creamware stirrup cup,** in the form of a fox's head, decorated with coloured glazes, c1780, 5in (12.5cm) high.

£1,350–1,500 HOW

◀ **A creamware tea canister and cover,** transfer-printed in the manner of Hancock with lovers taking tea, the reverse with a shepherd and his flock, c1780, 5½in (14cm) high.

£150–180 HYD

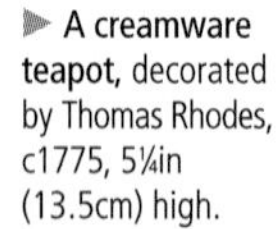

▶ **A creamware teapot,** decorated by Thomas Rhodes, c1775, 5¼in (13.5cm) high.

£1,350–1,500 HIS

A creamware teapot and cover, painted with fruit and flower sprays, c1800, 5½in (14cm) high.

£140–165 RTo

A creamware tureen and ladle, in the form of a melon, with pierced and moulded decoration, c1780, 9in (23cm) wide.

£1,700–1,900 HOW

◀ **A Petrus Regout & Co creamware tureen,** Continental, 1836–70, 6in (15cm) wide.

£45–50 CHAC

▶ **A creamware wine cistern and cover,** possibly Joseph Hannong, painted with an armorial above figures watching the departure of the ship *Le Neptune*, the shoulders and cover with applied fish, blue mark 'JH/39', France, late 18thC, 17in (43cm) high.

£840–1000 CGC

BLUE & WHITE TRANSFER-PRINTED WARE

A pair of Spode baskets, transfer-printed with Willow pattern, c1810, 8in (20.5cm) wide.
£510–570 GSA

A dairy bowl, transfer-printed with lovers in a rustic scene, c1820, 15in (38cm) diam.
£3,150–3,500 GN

A Wedgwood Ferrara bowl, with transfer-printed decoration, c1895, 9in (23cm) diam.
£75–85 GSA

A Minton cake or cheese stand, transfer-printed with a rural scene of travellers passing a thatched gatehouse within a floral border, from the Monk's Rock series, 1820–25, 10¾in (27.5cm) diam.
£260–310 DN

A Spode egg cup, transfer-printed with Tower pattern, c1820, 2in (5cm) diam.
£155–175 GN

A pair of Mason's Ironstone dishes, decorated with Blue Pheasants pattern, 1815–25, 21in (53.5cm)wide.
£1,150–1,300 WAn

English-made pottery for the American market

The Staffordshire potters of the late 18th and early 19th centuries were skilled entrepreneurs always looking for new markets to develop. Naturally many Staffordshire potters such as Adams, Woods, Rogers, Podmore Walker and Clews gave attention to the developing market in the United States. These factories forged a strong export business with the US. In 1837 James Clews even went to America and joined the Indiana Pottery Co as one of its three principals. Much of the ware destined for the United States was specially produced for the American market. Associations with individual retailers was established and such wares often bear the name of the US importer such as R. Ludlow, Charleston, SC.

American views such as the Boston State House were produced, as well as commemoratives of the defeat of the British in the War of Independence and aspects of interest relating to Washington and Lafayette. The Staffordshire potters also catered for the taste of the American public by developing a deep cobalt blue decoration for much of their export ware. Later in the 19th century this dark blue process was developed with great commercial success with the introduction of flow blue wares where the dark cobalt bled into the glaze giving a unique and appealing blurred effect.

A Staffordshire dish, transfer-printed with the 'Landing of Lafayette', c1825, 16in (40.5cm) wide.
£1,400–1,550 KUR

This dish was made in England for the American market. Please see page 167 for information on Lafayette.

A dish, decorated with an underglaze transfer-printed pattern, early 19thC, 15in (38cm) wide.
£210–240 IW

A Jones & Son dish, transfer-printed with the 'Death of Lord Nelson' within a border of flowers, patriotic symbols and accoutrements, from the British History series, slight damage, printed marks, 1826–28, 14½in (37cm) wide.
£2,250–2,700 DN

A John William Ridgway meat dish, transfer-printed with Japan Flowers pattern, c1830, 11in (28cm) wide.

£130–145 GSA

A Pountney & Goldney meat dish, transfer-printed with a view of 'Bristol Hot Wells' within a floral border, from the Bristol Views series, printed title and impressed maker's name, c1835, 18¼in (46.5cm) wide.

£1,050–1,250 DN

A Maddock Ironstone meat dish with a gravy well, transfer-printed with figures in a garden with a pagoda, impressed marks, c1855, 20in (51cm) wide.

£195–220 IW

John Maddock of Burslem produced wares from 1842 to 1855.

A J. & R. Riley drainer, transfer-printed with the arms of the Coventry Drapers, c1828, 14½in (37cm) wide.

£990–1,100 GN

A Spode electioneering jug, transfer-printed with Italian pattern and an overglaze wreath with the inscription 'Lord Anson for Ever, Huzza, 1826', 9¾in (25cm) high.

£2,350–2,800 G(L)

◀ **An Enoch Wood & Sons jug,** transfer-printed with 'Lafayette at Franklin's Tomb', slight damage, c1835, 5in (12.5cm) high.

£450–510 KUR

This jug was made in England for the American market.

A Victorian jug, transfer-printed with Persian pattern, mark to base, 10½in (26.5cm) high.

£370–440 PFK

A Staffordshire loving cup, transfer-printed with a Paisley pattern and a verse, the interior with two lizards, c1845, 5½in (14cm) high.

£110–130 DA

A lustre mug, with transfer-printed decoration, c1820, 3½in (9cm) high.

£500–600 HOW

A Staffordshire pearlware commemorative mug, transfer-printed with a portrait of Admiral Lord Nelson and inscription, slight damage, c1806, 5¼in (13.5cm) high.

£150–180 DN

A mug, transfer-printed with Grazing Rabbits pattern, early 19thC, 3¼in (8.5cm) diam.

£190–220 PFK

A Staffordshire meat dish and six plates, by John Rogers & Son, Longport, the meat dish transfer-printed with a scene of the defeat of the frigate *Chesapeak* by the frigate HMS *Shannon* within a border of marine life and shells, the plates transfer-printed with a scene of a ship within borders of marine life and shells, 1814–36, meat dish 21½in (53.5cm) wide.

£2,000–2,400 JDJ

A soup plate, transfer-printed with Beemaster pattern within a border of flowers and animals, 1820–30, 9½in (24cm) diam.

£150–180 DN

A J. & R. Clews soup plate, transfer-printed with a border ribbon naming the States of the USA, c1825, 7in (18cm) diam.

£240–270 KUR

This bowl was made in England for the American market.

A Staffordshire plate, by Thomas Mayer, Stoke, transfer-printed with the Arms of New York within a floral and foliate border, marked, c1825, 10in (25.5cm) diam.

£570–680 SK

This plate was made in England for the American market.

◀ **An Enoch Wood plate,** transfer-printed with a view of the City of Albany, State of New York, c1825, 9in (23cm) diam.

£380–430 KUR

This plate was made in England for the American market.

A Staffordshire plate, transfer-printed with a winter view of Pittsfield, Massachusetts, c1835, 9½in (24cm) diam.

£280–320 KUR

This plate was made in England for the American market.

An Enoch Wood plate, transfer-printed with 'Commodore MacDonnough's Victory', c1835, 9in (23cm) diam.

£240–270 KUR

This plate was made in England for the American market. Commodore Thomas MacDonnough defeated a British Naval squadron on Lake Champlain in Vermont in 1814. The British had been intending to invade from Canada and attack New York.

An Enoch Wood plate, transfer-printed with the Baltimore & Ohio Railroad, c1835, 7in (18cm) diam.

£580–650 KUR

This plate was made in England for the American market.

A Wedgwood plate, transfer-printed with Boston Library, USA, c1900, 9in (23cm) diam.

£50–60 GSA

This sauce boat was made in England for the American market.

An Enoch Wood & Sons sauce boat, transfer-printed with an American ship off the British coast, c1825, 7in (18cm) wide.

£680–760 KUR

This sauce boat was made in England for the American market.

An Enoch Wood vegetable tureen, with transfer-printed decoration, from the Grapevine Border series, c1820, 11in (28cm) wide.

£570–640 GN

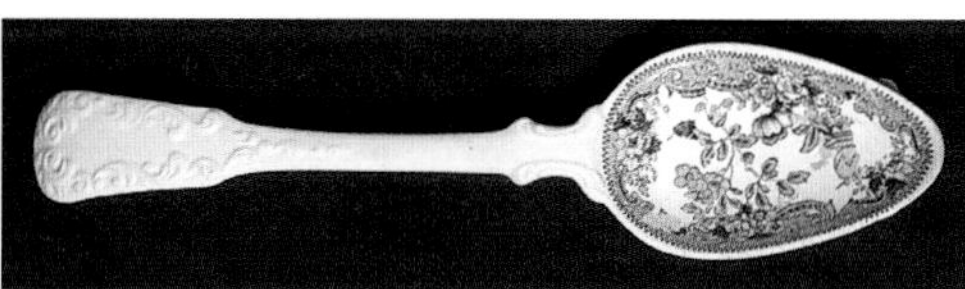

A serving spoon, attributed to William Smith, the bowl transfer-printed with Basket of Flowers pattern, c1830, 8in (20.5cm) long.

£250–280 GN

A smoker's set, attributed to Minton, comprising a candlestick, ashtray, tobacco jar, snuff box, snuffer and weight, transfer-printed with Dresden Opaque pattern, c1825, 14in (35.5cm) high, assembled.

£1,350–1,500 GN

A Herculaneum Pottery pearl-glazed supper set, comprising a covered bowl containing a pierced stand with six egg cups and a salt cellar, together with four covered dishes, transfer-printed with classical figures, one cover missing, impressed No. 37, c1815.

£1,250–1,500 Bea

If this supper set were complete it could sell for £2,000.

A Minton vase, transfer-printed with a scene of Ripon cathedral, from the English Scenery series, c1825, 5½in (14cm) high.

£360–400 GN

◄ **A Ralph Stevenson soup tureen and cover,** transfer-printed with Holliwell Cottage pattern, the cover with a flower knop, the body with two leaf-moulded handles, slight damage, early 19thC, 15¾in (40cm) wide.

£300–360 RTo

AMERICAN REDWARE

George Allen

George is a partner at Raccoon Creek Antiques, Oley, PA. They specialize in American Folk Art, specifically ceramics.

George has a Teaching Degree; he majored in Ceramics, and became a potter working in stoneware, redware and porcelain.

REDWARE IS A LOW-FIRED CLAY. It was used by potters from the late 17th century throughout the American northeast and south and into the mid-west to make utilitarian objects such as bricks, roof tiles, crocks, jugs, bowls, plates and pitchers.

Redware items can vary in appearance depending upon the glazing and firing. In many cases, redware is used without a glaze so when it is fired it appears red or orange in colour and rough to the touch. If glazed, it appears smooth and has a gloss or sheen to the surface. Household wares are usually glazed on the interior with a lead glaze that appears clear and shiny, to prevent absorption of liquids; the exterior may also be glazed, and is sometimes decorated. It is important to note that potters decorated pieces for several reasons, such as to attract a buyer, to impress an owner, to distinguish a special example or just to demonstrate their talent. Decoration was carried out in various ways, such as scratching the surface with a tool to incise a design when the clay was wet, scratching off coloured slip layers, known as sgraffito, colouring the wares with a brushed or dipped glaze or using a quilled slip cup – a moulded cup applied with quills – to apply lines of coloured slip design.

With the advancement of technology and the popularity of earthenware items, it can be difficult to distinguish the old from the new. The best way to gain experience is to look, touch and feel objects – older pieces develop a patina and surface quality that is hard to copy. When buying, it is advisable to consult a dealer or collector who already has a good knowledge of the subject.

Folk Art pottery continues to rise in popularity and set records in the antiques market – for instance a Pennsylvania bicolour redware food mould in the form of a fish recently sold for £1,000. The private collector who purchased this was able to distinguish it from other food moulds because of the rarity of form and unusual glaze combination. Another example of the popularity of Folk Art pieces was a rare charger decorated with a charming depiction of a bird which recently sold for £6,800. Prices like these will have an effect on the prices achieved by other special pieces such as a covered sugar bowl distinguished by an unusual design and strong graphics that recently commanded a market price of £1,900 – double what it was just five years ago.

George Allen

◀ **A redware jar,** the glaze with spotted decoration, slight damage, America, Connecticut, 19thC, 13¼in (33.5cm) high.
£280–330 JDJ

▶ **A redware jar and cover,** crackle-glazed and mottled, the jar with incised line decoration, slight damage, America, 19thC, 8in (20.5cm) high.
£280–330 JDJ

A redware jug, with sponged decoration, America, Delaware Valley, 1840–60, 7in (18cm) high.
£720–800 RCA

A redware jug, attributed to Norcross Pottery, America, Maine, 19thC, 6¾in (17cm) high.
£620–740 JDJ

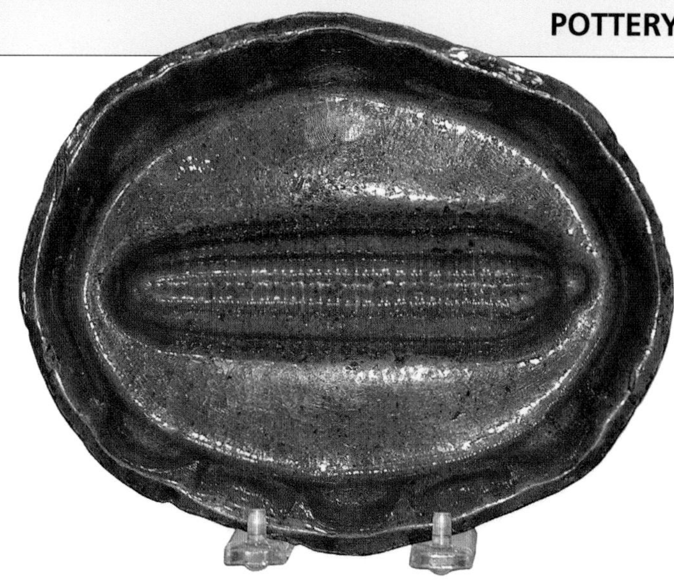

A redware corn pudding mould, impressed with a corn cob, America, c1860, 7in (18cm) wide.
£210–240 RCA

Three redware tart plates, with slip decoration, America, south-east Pennsylvania, c1850, 3½in (9cm) diam.
£3,350–3,700 RCA

A redware plate, with two-colour slip-trail decoration, America, Berks County, Pennsylvania, c1850, 5in (12.5cm) diam.
£1,250–1,400 RCA

Auction or dealer?

All the pictures in our price guides originate from auction houses and dealers. When buying at auction, prices can be lower than those of a dealer, but a buyer's premium and VAT will be added to the hammer price. Equally, when selling at auction, commission, tax and photography charges must be taken into account. Dealers will often restore pieces before putting them back on the market. Both dealers and auctioneers can provide professional advice, so it is worth researching both sources before buying or selling your antiques.

◀ **A redware plate,** attributed to the Smith Pottery, Norwalk, Connecticut, decorated with a slip-trail inscription 'Norwalk feb'y the 13 1854', slight damage, America, c1854, 12¼in (31cm) diam.
£10,800–12,900 SK(B)

A redware pie plate, the lead glaze with slip-trail decoration, America, New Jersey, c1860, 10in (25.5cm) diam.
£1,000–1,150 RCA

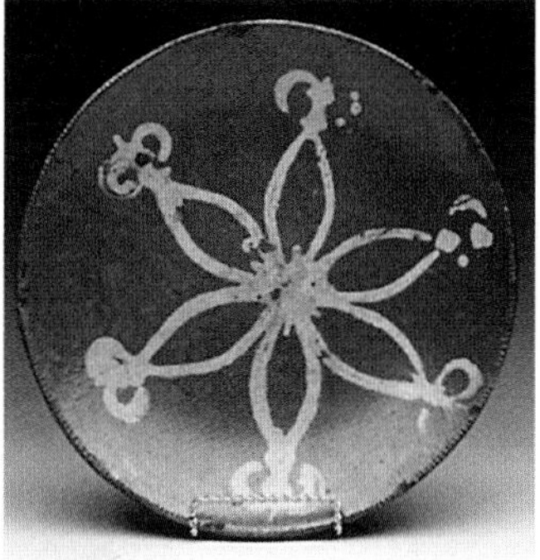

A redware plate, with a crimped edge and slip-trail decoration, damaged, America, 19thC, 11in (28cm) diam.
£370–440 JDJ

A redware stewing pot and cover, attributed to Norcross Pottery, slight damage, America, Maine, 19thC, 7½in (19cm) high.
£1,250–1,500 JDJ

AMERICAN STONEWARE

THERE IS AN INCREASING interest in American stoneware and more people are developing an appreciation for its historical value. Since the 18th century, clay found in northern New Jersey and shipped throughout the eastern states has been used to make utilitarian objects and for the storage of preserved foods, as well as items such as jugs, crocks, cake and butter pots that were intended for daily use.

The majority of stoneware items were salt-glazed during firing – a method used traditionally in Germany. This process sealed the pots with a clear, often textured, surface. Sometimes a milky-white Bristol glaze was used as an alternative to salt glazing. Various techniques were used for decorating, such as scratching or incising the surface with a design, brushing or quilling on oxide, or stencilling designs or names with colours. Prospective purchasers should beware of reproductions, which can be quite convincing since methods and techniques have not changed much over the years, although old pieces do develop their own patina and character.

The stoneware market in America continues to rise with unique pieces leading the pack and it appears that there will be little slow down. Auction prices in New York City and those in rural America continue to rise with the recent addition of bi-annual auctions devoted solely to redware and stoneware. Collectors love those special pieces and two purchased within the year by our client are now housed in The Doherty Collection. The first is a salt-glazed stoneware inkwell with a moulded figural frog, accented with cobalt, which came from The Anna Pottery and sold at auction for £3,500. The second is a rare and early New Jersey water cooler with profuse cobalt accented incised decoration, which recently sold at a major New York auction house for a hammer price of £35,000. It is unique and special pieces such as these that break the records and help set the market for stoneware in America. These prices also bring to the public's awareness the importance of these items as historic art objects, and cause otherwise unknown or unrecognized examples to surface. Prices are definitely rising as the number of collectors increase.

George Allen

► **A figural salt-glazed stoneware cooler,** with cobalt and manganese decoration, inscribed 'Betsy Baker is my name, Taunton, Mass. 1834', America, 1834, 15in (38cm) high.

£65,000–73,000 RCA

This figure, which is missing its head, was originally found in a house in Massachusetts. Its importance in the history of American stoneware is so great that her missing head, which could have been stoneware or even carved wood, does not matter. Figural examples of stoneware such as this are very rare and cross over into the category of Folk Art sculpture. Items of this size and importance are significant in the understanding of early American potters and their wares.

A Williams stoneware churn, with hand-painted decoration and stencilled with 'R. T. Williams New Geneva, PA' and a bird, America, Pennsylvania, 19thC, 15in (38cm) high.

£470–560 JAA

A stoneware churn, probably by Martin Wright, with floral decoration and applied handles, impressed 'Cedar Falls Iowa 3', America, 19thC, 14in (35.5cm) high.

£2,700–3,200 JAA

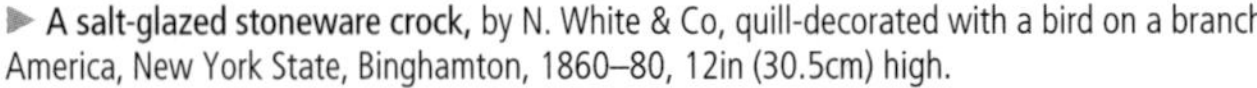

► **A salt-glazed stoneware crock,** by N. White & Co, quill-decorated with a bird on a branch, America, New York State, Binghamton, 1860–80, 12in (30.5cm) high.

£900–1,000 RCA

The thin lines were executed using a quill and the thicker lines painted with a brush.

A stoneware crock, decorated with a dog carrying a basket, America, c1880, 11½in (29cm) high.

£8,800–9,800 RCA

An advertising butter crock, by Fulper Bros, America, New Jersey, 1880–1900, 4in (10cm) diam.

£1,150–1,300 RCA

Further reading

Miller's Treasure or Not? How to Compare & Value American Art Pottery, Miller's Publications, 2001

A stoneware crock, by Fulper Bros, decorated with a running man in a hat, America, New Jersey, 1880–95, 8½in (21.5cm) high.

£11,700–13,000 RCA

◄ **A salt-glazed stoneware inkwell,** possibly by Henry Remmey, New York or Crolius Pottery, New York, the top with a central hole and three dipping holes decorated and incised with cobalt bell flowers, the side with incised and glazed inscriptions 'P.B. 1797', 'N.Y.' and 'R', America, c1797, 3½in (9cm) diam.

£12,700–15,200 SK(B)

The decoration on this inkwell resembles the incised and cobalt-filled decoration found on pottery made by two early New York potteries near the end of the 18th century: the Remmey family of potters, and the Crolius Pottery, both located close to each other on Potter's Hill, Manhattan Island. The rounded leaf tips on this inkwell are similar in decoration to that of stoneware items decorated by Henry Remmey, one of two grandsons of the original pottery owner John Remmey, working at the time this inkwell was made.

A stoneware jar, the cobalt-glazed band decorated with incised fish and berries, America, northern New Jersey, 1820–30, 6in (15cm) high.

£1,800–2,050 RCA

The incised decoration on this jar has been executed using an implement called a coggle wheel.

A stoneware jar, depicting a lady holding a money bag, America, 1860–80, 10in (25.5cm) high.

£20,500–22,800 RCA

Four conjoined stoneware jugs, by Absalom Stedman and Frederick Seymour, highlighted with cobalt blue decoration, with a reeded strap handle, slight damage, each jug impressed 'Stedman & Seymour' and 'New Haven', America, Connecticut, c1825, 9in (23cm) wide.

£5,400–6,400 SK(B)

A stoneware jug, stamped 'Beck Pottery Parish, Iowa' and '3', America, 19thC, 15in (38cm) high.

£95–110 JAA

A stoneware jug, with cobalt underglaze decoration, America, Baltimore, c1870, 10in (25.5cm) high.

£1,800–2,050 RCA

◄ **A stoneware presentation jug,** inscribed 'John Spuck, August 8th, 1874' to the front, handle and base, the base marked 'PHILA', America, c1874, 10in (25.5cm) high.

£13,600–15,200 RCA

This rare jug has the classic decoration of brushed tulips and sprigs generally associated with Richard Clinton Remmey, who was working in Philadelphia at this time.

A stoneware beer mug, inscribed 'Harry', America, New Jersey, c1880, 5in (12.5cm) high.

£360–400 RCA

PORCELAIN

John Axford

John worked for Phillips Auctioneers in London before joining Woolley and Wallis, Salisbury, in 1993 to become head of the Ceramics, Glass and Oriental departments.

He writes and lectures on ceramics and Oriental art, and has been a member of the BBC's Antiques Roadshow *team since 2000.*

WHILE THE LAST YEAR has proved difficult for many parts of the antiques trade, there are areas that seem immune to the vicissitudes of fashion. To some extent, porcelain falls into this category as was demonstrated by Bonhams' second sale of 18th-century coloured Worcester from the Zorensky collection, and we are looking forward to the third sale. This sale kicked off the year for porcelain enthusiasts as it proved a near sell-out. This great American collection was well known to dealers and collectors from the Antique Collectors' Club landmark reference work *Worcester Porcelain, The Zorensky Collection* by Simon Spero and John Sandon, published in 1996. Not only has First Period Worcester made the headlines, but Royal Worcester, particularly signed pieces, have been making record prices and is a field particularly popular with a number of Australian enthusiasts. This trend was demonstrated at a small saleroom in West Yorkshire where £27,000 was bid by an Australian collector for a pair of oval plaques dated 1921 and painted with highland cattle scenes by Harry Davis.

In May, a small damaged blue and white porcelain model of a seated Chinaman made headlines in the British tabloids. It was sent for auction in a box of junk and turned out to be the only Limehouse porcelain figure known to exist. Dating to circa 1747, it was identified as the Old Viceroy of Canton from a 17th-century Dutch print and sold to a Canadian collector for £22,000.

The new wealth in Russia has resulted in huge interest in Russian works of art across the board. This accounts for the top price achieved by the pair of St Petersburg vases, illustrated on page 224, that originated from the magnificent collections of the Royal House of Hanover and sold at Sotheby's in October 2005.

However, over the last 12 months both the American and German markets have been slower than usual, although there have been some notable exceptions. The market does feel polarized and the following pages illustrate this well. As we have seen, some huge prices are being paid in certain sectors, such as Russian and Welsh porcelains, as well as for Lowestoft, Chelsea and Worcester and for other good pieces offered with an important provenance. Collecting is not only for the super-rich. The good news now is that many pieces of porcelain are cheaper than ever before, so if you find pieces you like, now might be a good time to buy. **John Axford**

ANIMALS

A Belleek Sea Horse and Shell vase, restored, Ireland, Second Period, 1891–1926, 5in (12.5cm) wide.

£165–185 ⊞ BtoB

A Bow model of a parrot, 18thC, 6in (15cm) high.

£1,900–2,250 HYD

A Chelsea model of a tawny owl, 1748–50, 7¾in (19.5cm) high.

£22,500–27,000 WW

Only a small number of Chelsea models of owls are known, all of which are white glazed.

A pair of Meissen models of jays, by J. J. Kändler, decoration possibly later, restored, Germany, 1740–45, 15½in (39.5cm) high.

£28,800–34,500 S(NY)

Ex-Laurance Rockefeller collection. Laurance Rockefeller's collection of 18th-century Meissen birds was assembled over at least 30 years and is one of the finest of such collections to appear at auction. Jays, and also roller canaries, were first modelled by Kändler for the Japanese palace in 1735.

A Meissen model of a sheep, by J. J. Kändler and P. Reinicke, restored, Germany, c1750, 7in (18cm) long.

£780–930 S(O)

► **A Meissen Monkey Band figure,** Germany, c1860, 5in (12.5cm) high.

£1,100–1,250 MAA

The Monkey Band (Affenkapelle) *is a series of figures produced by Meissen in the middle of the 18th century. Believed to be a parody of the Dresden Court Orchestra, the set was modelled by Johann Kändler and Peter Reinicke after engravings by the French artists Jean-Antoine Watteau and Christopher Huet. The whole set may have consisted of 25 pieces and many were copied by the Chelsea, Derby and Samson factories. This piece is a 19th-century issue of an 18th-century design.*

A Meissen model of a magpie, beak damaged, Germany, late 19thC, 14in (35.5cm) high.

£450–500 HUM

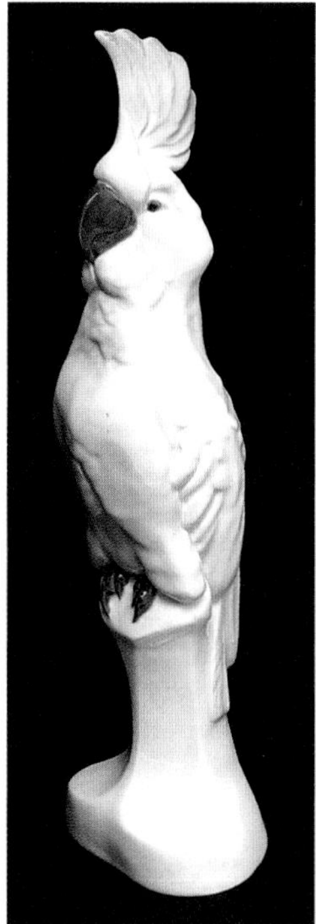

A Meissen model of a cockatoo, by Paul Walther, marked, Germany, c1925, 12¼in (31cm) high.

£1,800–2,000 DAV

◄ **A Meissen-style model of a pug,** Germany, late 19thC, 4¾in (12cm) wide.

£200–240 DN

► **A Rockingham model of a hare,** model No. 106, ears missing, impressed marks, c1830, 2½in (6.5cm) wide.

£610–730 DN

Rockingham is the most sought after of all English factories that produced porcelain animals in the 19th century.

► **A Royal Dux model of an elephant,** Bohemia, c1890, 15in (38cm) long.

£450–500 GSA

A Samson tureen, in the form of two lovebirds, pseudo Chelsea mark, France, 19thC, 14½in (37cm) wide.

£280–330 Mit

BASKETS

◄ A Belleek Twig basket, Ireland, First Period, 1863–90, 9in (23cm) wide.
£940–1,050 DeA

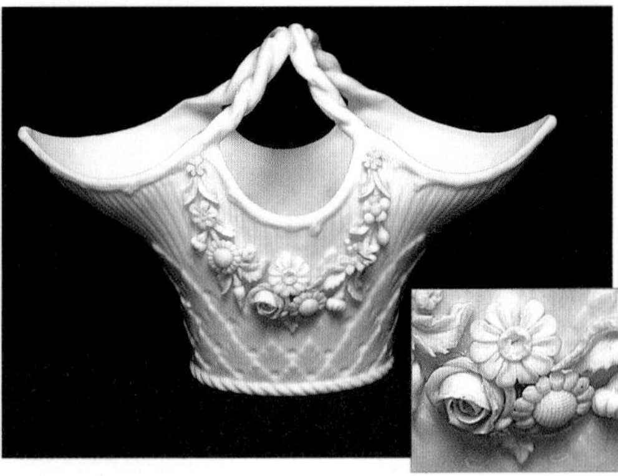

A Belleek Erne basket, Ireland, Second Period, 1891–1926, 9in (23cm) wide.
£760–850 BtoB

◄ **A pair of Worcester baskets, covers and stands,** with applied leaf and flower sprays, heightened in gilt, c1775, 10½in (26.5cm) wide.
£840–1,000 Mit

These baskets would be more valuable decorated in polychrome or blue and white.

A Chamberlain's Worcester basket, encrusted with shells, repaired, script mark, early 19thC, 4in (10cm) wide.
£220–260 DN

A Worcester basket, probably Grainger, Lee & Co, painted with a view of Worcester within a gilt border, c1830, 4in (10cm) wide.
£150–180 DN

A Worcester basket, decorated with a crest, slight wear to gilding, early 19thC, 11½in (28.5cm) diam.
£1,250–1,500 WAD

BOWLS

A Berlin bowl, from the Grand Duke Paul service, printed with the arms of the Russian Empire and of Holstein-Gottorp, marked, Germany, c1778, 9½in (24cm) diam.
£8,400–10,100 S(NY)

◄ **A Sèvres bowl,** painted with flowers, slight damage, date mark for 1773, France, 9¾in (25cm) wide.
£195–230 WW

► **A Worcester slop bowl,** printed and painted with Oriental figures, water buffalo and rockwork, 1760–70, 4in (10cm) diam.
£300–360 HYD

COVERED BOWLS & DISHES

A Chantilly bowl and cover, decorated with a bouquet of flowers, the cover with applied lemon knop and leaves, slight damage, France, c1750, 5in (12.5cm) high.

£1,550–1,850 S(O)

A Dresden bowl and stand, decorated in the workshops of Helena Wolfshon with courting couples and flowers, marked, Germany, 19thC, 7in (18cm) high.

£520–620 Mit

A Lowestoft Worcester-style butter dish, cover and stand, printed with a version of Fence pattern, slight damage, marked, c1780.

£1,450–1,700 DN

A Swansea sugar bowl, cover and stand, decorated with Kingfisher pattern, Wales, 1815–17, 6in (15cm) high.

£1,200–1,450 BWL

◄ **A Worcester sugar bowl and cover,** decorated with Jabberwocky pattern, the cover with a flower finial, painted mark, 1755–75, 4¾in (12cm) high.

£280–330 DN(HAM)

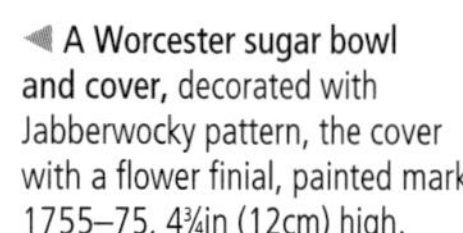

The Jabberwocky pattern is a brightly enamelled design derived from Japanese Kakiemon porcelain and used on fluted Worcester tea wares and plates of c1770. The design features a winged dragon, flowers and foliage all within turquoise borders. The name Jabberwocky from Lewis Carroll's famous poem was attached to this pattern by 20th-century dealers and collectors.

BOXES

A Meissen ormolu-mounted box, Germany, c1770, 4in (10cm) wide.

£2,550–2,850 MAA

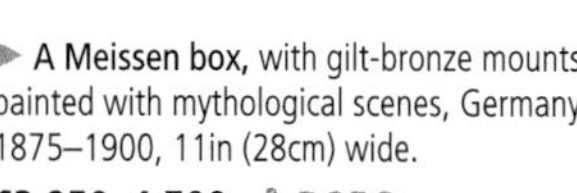

► **A Meissen box,** with gilt-bronze mounts, painted with mythological scenes, Germany, 1875–1900, 11in (28cm) wide.

£3,950–4,700 DORO

A box, painted with classical scenes, the interior of the cover with a portrait of Elizabeth I of Russia, Russia, probably St Petersburg, late 18thC, 3¼in (8.5cm) diam.

£8,100–9,700 DORO

BUSTS

► **A Sèvres biscuit porcelain bust of a young woman,** by Agathon Leonard, impressed marks, signed, France, dated 1903, 18½in (47cm) high.

£800–960 WAD

◄ **A pipe tamper,** Lowestoft or Liverpool, in the form of a bust of a man, damaged and repaired, inscribed 'C. W. S***, 1763', 2¾in (7cm) high.

£5,200–6,200 WW

A mould for a pipe tamper with a female bust was found during excavations on the Lowestoft factory site, but no models of this form are recorded. The calligraphy of the date '1763', bears close similarities to a Lowestoft teabowl dated 1763. Early dated ceramics such as this are rare.

A bust of Lord Byron, on a gilt and titled plinth, mid-19thC, 6in (15cm) high.

£140–165 DN

To find out more about Parian busts see our special feature on pages 229–231.

CANDLESTICKS & CHAMBERSTICKS

A pair of Berlin candlesticks, slight damage, marked, Germany, 1764–65, 7½in (19cm) high.

£960–1,150 S(O)

A pair of Berlin candlesticks, decorated with courting couples, flowers and insects, marked, Germany, late 19thC, 8in (20.5cm) high.

£210–250 Mit

A Nantgarw chamberstick, the handle in the form of a dolphin, painted with roses and moulded with acanthus leaves, slight damage, Wales, c1820, 2¾in (7cm) wide.

£2,600–3,100 S(O)

A pair of Worcester chambersticks, painted with floral sprays, with gilt decoration, one nozzle restored, c1770, 5½in (14cm) diam.

£2,000–2,400 S(O)

A chamberstick, painted with a bullfinch and fruit, c1820, 5¼in (13.5cm) wide.

£350–420 WW

CENTREPIECES

◀ **A pair of Coalport comports,** each painted by Frederick H. Chivers with fruit, printed, painted and impressed marks, signed, date code for 1920, 9½in (24cm) diam.

£400–480 WAD

A Dresden centrepiece, Germany, late 19thC, 18in (45.5cm) high.

£400–450 MRA

A Meissen centrepiece, by J. Eberlein, Germany, c1740, 14in (35.5cm) high.

£3,400–3,800 YA

A Minton centrepiece, modelled with two cherubs and two lovebirds, c1873, 11in (28cm) wide.

£580–650 JAK

A Nantgarw tazza, probably London decorated, painted with flowers and decorated with beading, Wales, c1820, 4¼in (11cm) wide.

£5,200–6,200 S(O)

A Sitzendorf centrepiece, Germany, early 20thC, 12¼in (31cm) high.

£120–140 DD

CUPS

A Belleek Celtic cup and saucer, Ireland, Second Period, 1891–1926.

£220–250 BtoB

▶ **A Berlin chocolate cup, cover and *trembleuse* saucer,** painted with hunting scenes, applied with two handles, damage to saucer, marked, Germany, late 19thC.

£120–140 DN(BR)

▶ **A Bristol cup and saucer,** painted with floral swags, with gilt rim, restored, marked, c1775.

£150–180 ROS

A Chelsea cup and *trembleuse* saucer, decorated in relief with prunus sprigs, marked, 1749–52.

£1,300–1,550 G(L)

A Coalport miniature cup and saucer, with 'jewelled' decoration, c1900, 1½in (4cm) high.

£500–560 Scot

A set of six Cozzi cups and saucers, with gilt decoration, three saucers restored, marked, Italy, c1770.

£800–960 DN

A Derby cup and saucer, the saucer decorated with a country scene in the manner of Zachariah Borman, pattern No. 119, marked, c1790.

£590–700 N

A Derby chocolate cup, painted with a peacock, a peahen and two birds, with entwined handle, painted marks, c1790.

£1,500–1,800 S(O)

Porcelain

Porcelain is a term used to cover a wide range of white high-fired ceramics. It is hard, translucent (unless thickly potted), it rings when struck and is vitreous. The Chinese first developed porcelain over a thousand years ago using a recipe of china clay (kaolin) and china stone (petuntse). There are many types of porcelain including soft paste, bone china, phosphatic and phelspatic. The term porcelain is said to derive from *porcella,* a Portuguese term for the cowrie shell, probably because the shell surface is similar to porcelain.

An Isleworth coffee cup, printed with Rose pattern, c1775.

£1,100–1,300 N

An Isleworth teabowl and saucer, painted with a version of Cannonball pattern, c1775.

£940–1,100 N

A Liverpool coffee cup, painted with figures on an island, slight damage, c1760.

£100–120 WW

A Liverpool teabowl and saucer, painted with flower sprays, c1770.

£270–320 N

◄ **A Longton Hall teabowl,** painted with flowers by the Trembly Rose painter, c1758.

£240–280 PBA

The Trembly Rose painter was the name given to a decorator at the Longton Hall Porcelain factory in Staffordshire, (1750–60). Like many porcelain modellers and painters in the 18th century, he remains anonymous and is identified by his use of thin cotton-like stems and crinkled petals after which he is named.

A Meissen teabowl, decorated with Lotus pattern, crossed swords mark, Germany, c1750, 1½in (4cm) high.

£350–420 GTH

A Meissen two-handled cup and saucer, decorated with harbour scenes and landscapes, Germany, 18thC.

£1,050–1,250 MAL(O)

A Meissen chocolate cup and cover, decorated with figures in gilt reserves, with moulded handles and applied flowers, crossed swords mark, Germany, c1740.

£1,000–1,200 PBA

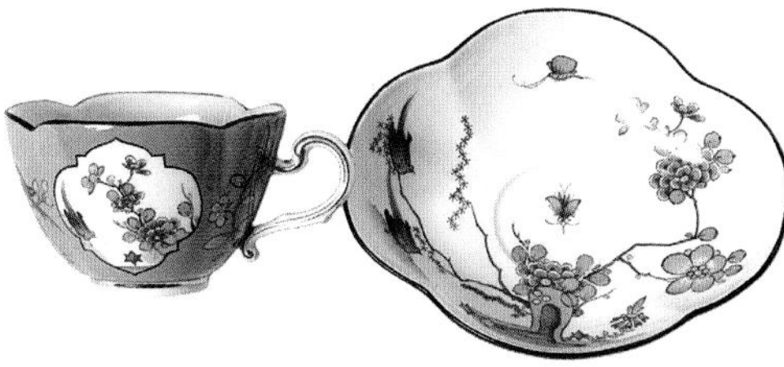

A Meissen cup and saucer, decorated in the Kakiemon style, Germany, c1870.

£400–450 MAA

A Nantgarw miniature cup and saucer, painted with roses within gilt borders, Wales, c1820, saucer 4¼in (11cm) diam.

£3,350–4,000 S(O)

◄ **A Sèvres two-handled cup and saucer,** decorated by Fumez with military trophies and agricultural implements within gilt borders, one handle restored, painted marks 'RF', 'FX' and 'IN', France, c1795.

£490–580 Hal

► **A Sèvres cup,** painted with a portrait of Jeanne d'Albret within a gilt reserve, printed marks, France, date code for 1846.

£680–810 N

Jeanne d'Albret was Queen of Navarre from 1555 to 1572.

A Sèvres coffee can and saucer, decorated with a portrait of Marie Antoinette, France, c1860.

£1,450–1,650 MAA

A set of four Spode New Shape cups and saucers, printed with pattern No. 1185, c1810.

£140–165 DN

A Copeland Spode trio, with painted and gilt decoration, made for Harrods, London, c1910.

£175–195 HEM

A Swansea coffee can and saucer, printed and enamelled with Parakeets in a Tree patttern, Wales, c1820.

£270–320 Bea

A Vienna cup and saucer, painted with leaves and laurel sprays, Austria, date code for 1807.

£1,000–1,200 DORO

A Vauxhall coffee can, painted with a garden scene, damaged and repaired, c1762.

£300–360 N

A Worcester *famille-verte* teabowl and saucer, painted with panels of plants, slight damage, c1753.

£1,900–2,250 S(O)

A Worcester coffee can, painted with an island, incised 'X', c1754.

£1,450–1,700 N

A Worcester cup and saucer, painted with flowers, fruit and insects, within gilt borders, c1770.

£300–360 BWL

A Worcester two-handled cup and saucer, painted with vignettes of exotic birds and insects, restored, square mark, c1770.

£165–195 DN(HAM)

A Worcester two-handled cup, cover and saucer, c1770, 4¼in (11cm) high.

£820–980 MAL(O)

A Worcester chocolate cup, cover and saucer, decorated with a version of Hop Trellis pattern, with a flower knop, slight damage, c1772, 5in (12.5cm) high.

£910–1,050 LFA

A Worcester tea cup and saucer, painted with a flower spray, crescent marks, c1772.

£420–500 N

► **A Worcester teabowl and saucer,** painted with narcissi and other flowers, crescent mark, 1775–80.

£2,800–3,350 LFA

◄ **A Worcester coffee cup and saucer,** painted by H. Stinton, c1914.

£650–730 Scot

DESSERT & DINNER SERVICES

A Coalport part dessert service, comprising 29 pieces, decorated with Japan pattern, one cover missing, early 19thC.

£1,450–1,700 Oli

A Coalport dessert service, comprising 22 pieces, decorated in the Imari style, slight damage, 19thC.

£750–900 JH

◄ **A Davenport service,** comprising 33 pieces, decorated in gilt with floral sprays, painted '276', slight damage, printed marks, c1830.

£1,700–2,000 WAD

A Victorian Davenport tea and coffee service, comprising 39 pieces, decorated with Japan pattern, slight damage, impressed and printed marks.

£370–440 CDC

A Derby part dessert service, comprising 12 pieces, with gilt decoration, one handle repaired, painted marks, c1815.

£590–700 Bea

A Royal Crown Derby dessert service, comprising 15 pieces, with gilt decoration, printed and impressed marks, date code for 1896.

£490–580 Mit

► **A Meissen part dinner service,** comprising 70 pieces, damaged, crossed swords mark, Germany, 1780–85.

£11,700–14,000 S(NY)

A Meissen part dinner service, comprising 91 pieces, painted with flowers and insects, damaged, crossed swords mark, Germany, late 19thC.

£1,950–2,300 S(NY)

A Spode part dessert service, comprising 13 pieces, painted with flowers within a gilt foliate border, slight damage, c1828.

£1,100–1,300 S(NY)

Ex-Gianni Versace collection.

A Chamberlain's Worcester dinner service, the Duke of Cumberland Service, comprising 189 pieces, decorated in the Imari style, 1802–06.

£376,000–451,000 S(Han)

Ex-Royal House of Hanover Sale.
This dinner service was commissioned from the Chamberlain's Worcester factory in 1802 by Prince Ernest August, the Duke of Cumberland, who was the brother of George IV and became King of Hanover in 1837. It was sold in a ten-day dispersal of property of the Royal House of Hanover from their castle, Schloss Marienburg, in Lower Saxony. Great Britain was ruled from 1714 to 1837 by the Hanoverian kings, George I, II, III, IV and William IV and property that had belonged to them was included in the sale. The pieces on sale had been stored unseen at the castle for generations after the family had lost various castles, including Cumberland and Blankenburg, due to wars and social upheavals in the late 19th and 20th centuries.

◄ **A dessert service,** comprising 11 pieces, decorated with pastoral scenes, 19thC.

£360–430 MAL(O)

DISHES

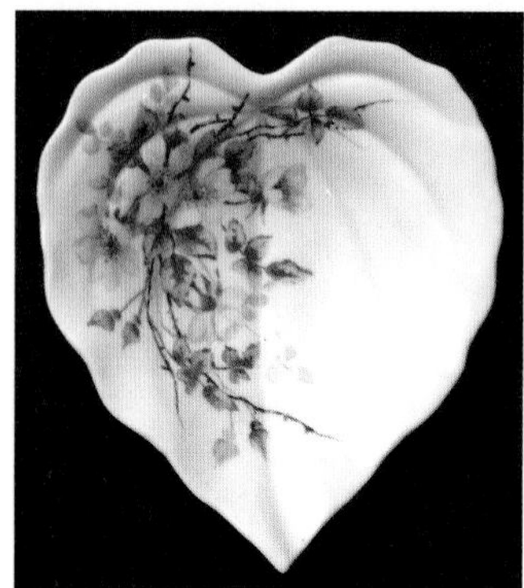

A Belleek Erne dish, with floral decoration, Ireland, Second Period, 1891–1926, 7in (18cm) wide.

£145–165 BtoB

A Bow dish, after a Japanese original, decorated in the Kakiemon stylye, slight damage, c1755, 8½in (21.5cm) diam.

£1,400–1,650 S(O)

A Caughley dish, decorated with underglaze blue and gilt with looped bands, impressed Salopian mark, c1790, 2½in (6.5cm) diam.

£960–1,150 LFA

◀ A Chelsea dish, with moulded grape and vine leaf decoration, red anchor mark, 1755–60, 9½in (24cm) wide.

£700–840 BWL

A Derby dish, painted with flower sprays, slight damage, 1755–60, 9½in (24cm) wide.

£290–340 WW

◀ A Royal Crown Derby butter dish, c1880, 8in (20.5cm) wide.

£270–300 Fai

A pair of Royal Crown Derby dishes, by A. Gregory, with anthemion handles and gadrooned rims, the centres painted with flowers, signed, date code for 1906, 10¾in (27.5cm) wide.

£1,500–1,800 ROS

A Meissen cheese dish, the bowl with a pierced interior and three scroll handles and three feet, on a plate painted with flowers and insects, slight damage, impressed '21', crossed swords mark, Germany, 1740–45, 8in (20.5cm) diam.

£3,800–4,550 S

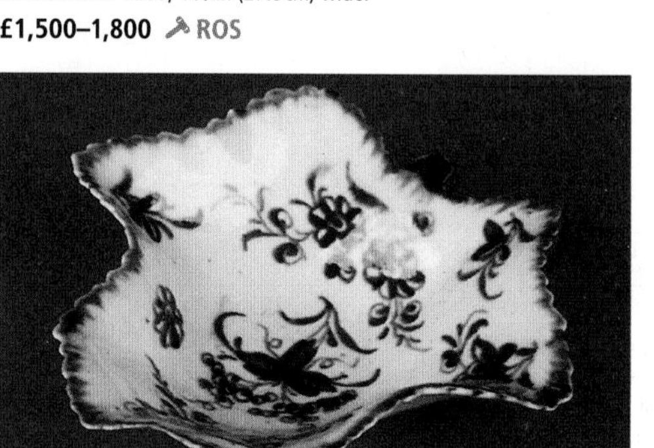

◀ A Worcester pickle dish, decorated with floral sprays, crescent mark, 1751–74, 3½in (9cm) wide.

£150–180 HYD

▶ A Worcester dish, enamelled with flowers and an insect, c1760, 7in (18cm) wide.

£760–910 TEN

FIGURES

◀ **A Belleek figure of Erin Awakening from her Slumbers,** Ireland, First Period, 1863–90, 17½in (44.5cm) high.

£3,600–4,300 JAd

This iconic piece of pure Victorian romanticism was designed by William Boyden Kirk (1824–1900). The figure of Erin is shown standing on the flagstone ford of the River Erne's falls at Belleek removing a drape over an urn with the name 'Belleek Pottery' written on it. This commemorates Ireland's embryonic entry into the world of industry. Further symbols of Ireland include shamrocks laced through her hair, the Celtic cross and the Irish harp embossed with Celtic designs.

To find out more about Parian figures and models please see our special feature on pages 229–231.

A Berlin figural group of Bacchus and Ariadne, with two leopards, restored, underglaze sceptre mark, Germany, late 19thC, 9¾in (25cm) high.

£130–155 ROS

An Ernst Bohne figural candelabra, with a figure of a young woman, German, c1890, 16in (40.5cm) high.

£310–350 MRA

▶ **A Derby figure of an Italian farmer holding a cockerel,** slight damage, patch marks, c1760, 8¾in (22cm) high.

£590–700 Bea

A pair of Derby figures of musicians, each seated on a flowering stump, the man playing bagpipes with a dog by his side, the woman playing a lute with a lamb by her side, late 18thC, 7¾in (19.5cm) high.

£470–560 ROS

A pair of Derby Samson & Hancock figures, entitled 'Laughing and Crying Philosophers', crown, crossed baton and dot marks, c1915, 5in (12.5cm) high.

£260–310 N

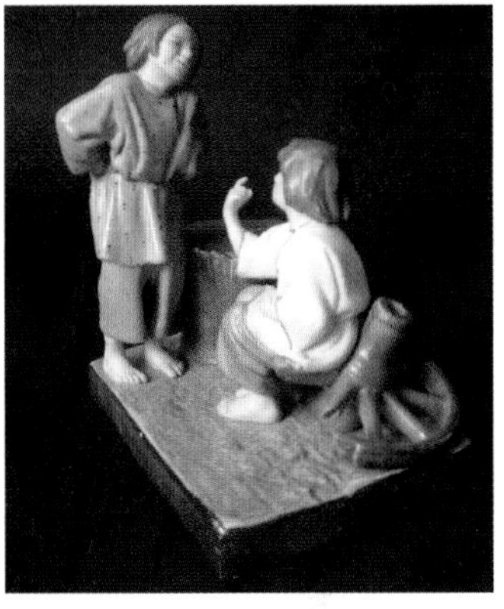

A Gardner figural group of two boys, one seated on a broken cart wheel, the other leaning against a tree stump, repaired, Russia, late 19thC, 5¾in (14.5cm) high.

£350–420 ROS

A Dresden figural group, Germany, late 19thC, 8in (20.5cm) high.

£175–195 MRA

A Höchst figure of a beggar, possibly by J. C. L. von Lücke, restored, marked, Germany, c1760, 10¼in (26cm) high.

£1,400–1,650 S(O)

A Limbach figural group of a beggar-woman and child, damaged, losses, Germany, c1775, 6in (15cm) high.

£1,050–1,250 S(O)

A Ludwigsburg figure of an old lady, with a cat on her shoulder, damaged, marked, Germany, 18thC, 6in (15cm) high.

£230–270 DMC

A Ludwigsburg figure of Plenty, holding a cornucopia and a bowl, marked, restored, Germany, late 18thC, 11in (28cm) high.

£230–270 ROS

A Meissen figural group of a lady and two children, from the Cries of London series, Germany, c1750, 6in (15cm) high.

£2,900–3,250 RGa

A Meissen figure of a boy in Turkish costume, from the Nationalities series, Germany, c1755, 5in (12.5cm) high.

£2,400–2,700 YA

A Meissen figure of a musician, Germany, c1760, 7in (18cm) high.

£2,550–2,850 MAA

A Meissen figure of Peace, modelled as Minerva seated on two cannons beneath an obelisk inscribed 'Pax', crossed swords, asterisk and two dashes marks, inscribed mark '1660', Germany, late 18thC, 6½in (16.5cm) high.

£560–670 ROS

A Meissen figure of a gardener, Germany, c1870, 5in (12.5cm) high.

£760–850 MAA

A pair of Meissen figures of children, slight damage, crossed swords mark, inscribed '1' and incised 'F31', Germany, c1870, 6¼in (16cm) high.

£1,050–1,250 SWO

A Meissen Pagoda figure of a Chinese woman, Germany, c1890, 6in (15cm) high.

£3,800–4,550 ⊞ ALEX

'Pagoda' figures are seated models of Chinese, often with nodding heads.

► **A Niderviller figure of a water seller,** carrying a cistern on his back, impressed 'NB' and 'NI', slight damage, France, 1765–70, 7¾in (19.5cm) high.

£1,200–1,400 S(O)

A pair of Nymphenburg Commedia dell'Arte figures, entitled 'Captain Spavento' and 'Leda', minor restoration, Germany, c1900, larger 7½in (19cm) high.

£1,750–2,100 DORO

A pair of Royal Dux figures of a young lady and man carrying baskets, model Nos. 1830 and 1831, Bohemia, early 20thC, larger 16¼in (41.5cm) high.

£390–460 MA&I

► **A Sitzendorf figural group of a couple with sheep,** Germany, c1890, 6in (15cm) high.

£240–270 ⊞ MRA

► **A Volkstedt figure of a cherub on a chariot,** Germany, c1880, 4in (10cm) wide.

£120–135 ⊞ OAK

A pair of Royal Worcester Mansion House figures of dwarfs, after Derby, one repaired, printed and impressed marks and date code for 1883, larger 7in (18cm) high.

£280–330 SWO

A pair of Royal Worcester Kate Greenaway-style figural salts, modelled as a boy and a girl with a wicker basket, impressed and printed factory marks, c1886, 9½in (24cm) high.

£1,000–1,200 RTo

A Royal Worcester figure of the Bather Surprised, modelled by James Hadley, No. 486, printed marks, c1924, 15½in (39.5cm) high.

£1,000–1,200 TEN

FLATWARE

◀ **A Berlin plate,** with an underglaze blue sceptre mark and painter's iron-red mark and impressed marks, Germany, 1817–22, 9¾in (25cm) diam.

£2,800–3,350 S(Han)

Ex-Royal House of Hanover sale. This plate is painted with a scene of Frederick the Great and the Duke of York on manoeuvres near Potsdam.

A Caughley dish, printed with a garden scene within a Fitzhugh-style border, blue 'S' mark, c1780, 14¼in (36cm) wide.

£800–960 Hal

A pair of Coalport cabinet plates, painted with landscape panels entitled 'Windermere' and 'Arran Isle', within a tooled gilt surround and gadrooned rim, printed and painted marks, late 19thC, 9in (23cm) diam.

£470–560 RTo

A Derby plate, painted with a bouquet of flowers, pattern No. 151, marked, c1800, 9½in (24cm) diam.

£200–240 WW

A Derby meat dish, decorated with Japan Pattern, crossed batons and 'D' mark, early 19thC, 25½in (65cm) wide.

£410–490 CDC

A Crown Derby porcelain plate, date code for 1888, 9in (23cm) diam.

£125–140 Fai

A Royal Crown Derby plate, c1890, 9in (23cm) diam.

£220–250 CHO

A Derby plate, painted by Cuthbert Gresley, c1911, 9in (23cm) diam.

£900–1,000 Scot

A Frankenthal plate, painted and relief-moulded with flowers within a gilt border, painted blue mark, Germany, 18thC, 9½in (24cm) diam.

£220–260 G(L)

◀ **An Imperial Porcelain Manufactory plate,** decorated with flowers and gilt, Russia, St Petersburg, 1825–55, 9in (23cm) diam.

£670–800 BUK(F)

An Imperial Porcelain Manufactory dish, decorated with flowers, repaired, Russia, St Petersburg, 1825–55, 14¼in (36cm) diam.

£470–560 BUK(F)

An Isleworth saucer, printed with a house, trees and rockwork, c1775, 4¼in (11cm) diam.

£1,550–1,850 N

A Meissen stand, painted with drapery and a bird within a border with landscapes, slight damage, crossed swords mark, Germany, c1725, 8¾in (22cm) diam.

£7,600–9,100 S(NY)

A Minton plate, hand-painted by Antoine Boullemier, c1886, 9½in (24cm) diam.

£1,650–1,850 MAA

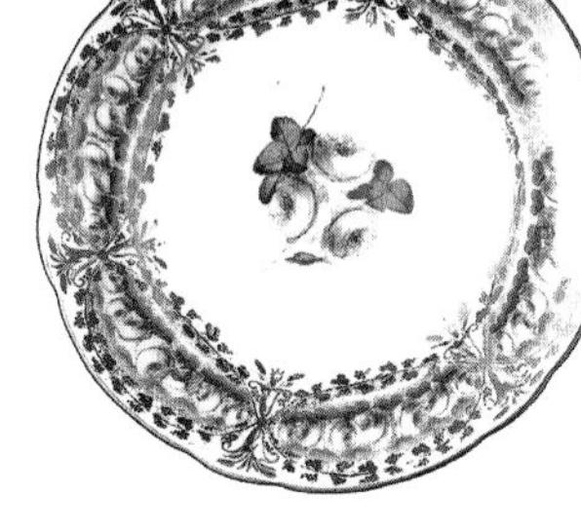

A Nantgarw plate, London-decorated with Three Roses pattern, Wales, 1813–22, 9½in (24cm) diam.

£1,450–1,600 DMa

A Nantgarw plate, attributed to Moses Webster, with floral decoration, Wales, c1819, 8½in (21.5cm) diam.

£2,150–2,400 DAP

A Nantgarw plate, decorated with cornflowers, impressed mark, Wales, c1822, 9½in (24cm) diam.

£1,150–1,300 DAP

A Meissen plate, the decoration after Raphael's 'Sistine Madonna', Germany, c1880, 5in (12.5cm) square.

£760–850 MAA

A Minton plate, hand-painted by Henry Mitchell, c1883, 10in (25.5cm) diam.

£1,100–1,250 MAA

◄ **A set of 19 Rockingham dessert plates,** c1830, 9¼in (23.5cm) diam.

£73,500–88,200 S(Han)

Ex-Royal House of Hanover sale. This set was commissioned by Frederica, Duchess of Cumberland, for her house at Kew.

Two Royal Copenhagen plates, one painted with a squirrel, the other a bear, marked, Denmark, 19thC, 10¼in (26cm) diam.

£1,000–1,200 S(NY)

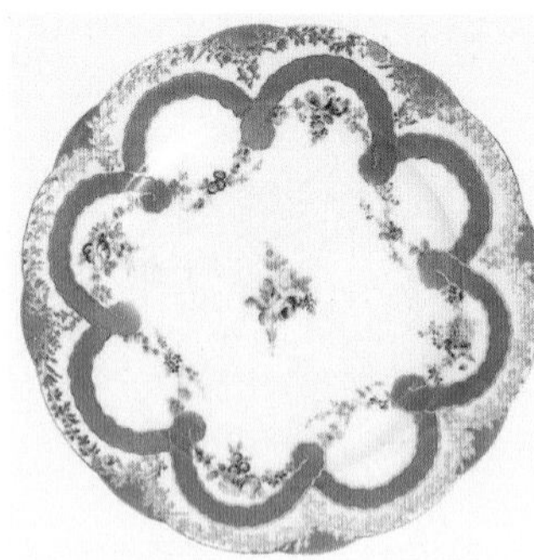

A Sèvres plate, painted with flowers and a gilt border, restored, painter's mark, France, 1756–57, 9¾in (25cm) diam.

£4,850–5,800 S(NY)

A Sèvres plate, painted with a view of Château de Saint Cloud, painter's mark 'LM', incised mark, France, 1823, 9¼in (23.5cm) diam.

£1,750–2,100 S(NY)

◄ **A Sèvres-style platter,** hand-painted with the *Bataille de Ravenne* within a gilt border with portraits, France, c1860, 13in (33cm) wide.

£2,250–2,500 MAA

A Swansea plate, painted by David Evans, with a bouquet of flowers, stencilled mark, c1815, 8in (20.5cm) diam.

£1,300–1,550 PBA

A Vienna Du Paquier plate, painted and gilded with birds, flowers and insects, slight restoration, Austria, c1725, 8½in (21.5cm) diam.

£4,800–5,700 S

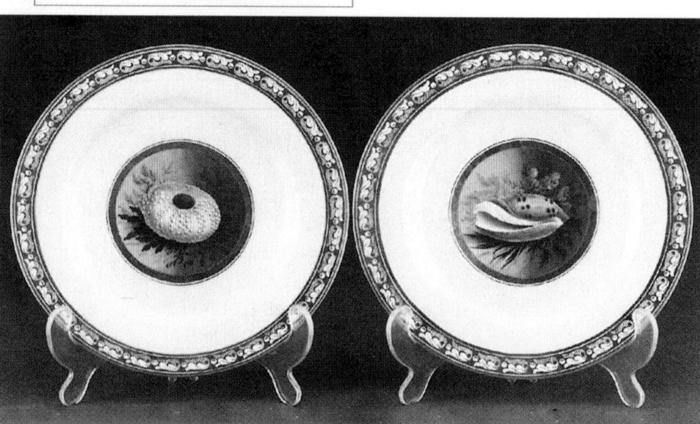

A pair of Worcester Flight, Barr & Barr plates, impressed marks, 1813–19, 8in (20.5cm) diam.

£2,750–3,300 WAD

◄ **A set of five plates,** decorated with floral sprays and gilt borders, c1840, 9in (23cm) diam.

£175–210 ROS

► **A cabinet plate,** by J. Bond, signed, 1911, 8½in (21.5cm) diam.

£100–115 HEM

JARDINIERES & CACHEPOTS

A pair of Coalport cachepots and stands, painted with flowers, c1800, 6¼in (16cm) high.

£2,000–2,400 Bea

Yellow is the most desirable ground colour.

A Derby jardinière, on a base, c1810, 6½in (16.5cm) high.

£760–850 JAK

A George Jones *pâte-sur-pâte* jardinière, by Frederick Schenk, c1890, 5in (12.5cm) high.

£1,400–1,600 WAC

Frederick Schenk was the chief pâte-sur-pâte *designer and sculptor working for the George Jones factory in Staffordshire in the mid-19th century, signing his pieces 'Schenk Sc'. He also worked freelance for companies including Wedgwood and Brown-Westhead & Moore. His designs depicting Cupid, nymphs and cherubs, that were so popular in Victorian England, are competent, but not of the same quality as those of Marc Louis Solon.*

A pair of Paris porcelain cachepots, decorated with palmettes, swans in lozenges and stylized foliage, with lion's-head handles, France, 1805–10, 7¾in (19.5cm) high.

£3,050–3,650 S(P)

A pair of Sèvres jardinières, with gilt decoration, stands and liners missing, repaired, France, dated 1847, 8in (20.5cm) high.

£10,400–12,400 S(NY)

A Vienna jardinière, signed 'Tataun', Austria, Vienna, c1880, 18in (45.5cm) wide.

£2,700–3,000 MAA

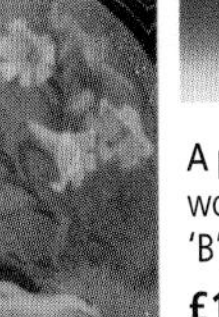

A pair of Barr Worcester jardinières, possibly decorated in the workshop of Thomas Baxter, depicting shells within gilt frames, incised 'B', c1805, 6¼in (16cm) high.

£12,000–14,400 RTo

A Royal Worcester two-handled jardinière, painted with flowers, shape No. 1523, printed marks, date code for 1894, 10¼in (26cm) wide.

£500–600 BAM(M)

◄ **A Royal Worcester jardinière,** by F. Roberts, painted with orchids and leaves, pattern No. 1976, damaged and restored, signed, marked, date code for 1899, 15in (38cm) wide.

£5,200–6,200 GIL

This jardinière was given a low estimate because the footrim has been broken and repaired. However, the piece attracted much interest due to the quality of the decoration and its large size. In perfect condition it could well have sold for twice the amount.

JUGS & EWERS

A Belleek jug, Ireland, First Period, 1863–90, 6½in (16.5cm) high.

£320–360 ⊞ DeA

A Coalport ewer, decorated with a bird, c1900, 9in (23cm) high.

£530–600 ⊞ CHO

A Royal Crown Derby ewer, painted with a botanical study, signed 'Leroy', marked, date code for 1891, 8in (20.5cm) high.

£530–630 ⚒ ROS

◀ **A Liverpool ewer,** decorated in relief with shells and dolphins, painted with birds, insects and flowers, c1775, 3¾in (9.5cm) high.

£210–250 ⚒ Hal

◀ **A Nantgarw cream jug,** painted by Thomas Pardoe, Wales, c1820, 6in (15cm) wide.

£5,400–6,400 ⚒ S(O)

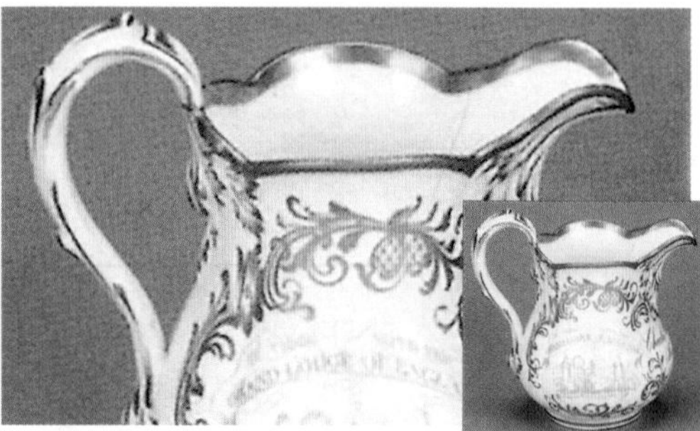

◀ **A Staffordshire bone china jug,** printed with Masonic panels, with inscription and motto, mid-19thC, 8¾in (22cm) high.

£230–270 ⚒ DN

Bone china

Bone china is a type of porcelain developed by Josiah Spode II c1794. The recipe uses up to 40 per cent bone ash, giving a clean, bright white body, which is stable in the kiln. While China, Japan and continental Europe produced hard-paste porcelain, by the 19th century most English factories were producing bone china, a material almost exclusively British.

A pair of Royal Worcester Tusk jugs, c1903, 7in (18cm) high.

£490–550 ⊞ HKW

A Royal Worcester blush ivory jug, painted with flower sprays, model No. 1507, date code for 1908, 8¾in (22cm) high.

£230–270 ⚒ PFK

LOVING CUPS & TYGS

A Royal Worcester blush ivory miniature tyg, No. 15, printed mark, date code for 1904, 1½in (3cm) high.
£80–95 PFK

A Royal Worcester blush ivory loving cup, painted with floral sprays, printed mark, date code for 1906, 6in (15cm) high.
£260–310 PFK

A Royal Worcester loving cup, painted by Raymond Rushton with a church and riverside, with gilt decoration, slight damage, date code for 1912, 6in (15cm) high.
£120–140 LAY

MUGS & TANKARDS

A Derby mug, painted with a vignette of exotic birds, handle restored, c1760, 6in (15cm) high.
£350–420 DN

A Derby mug, decorated in the manner of Edward Withers with floral decoration, c1780, 3¾in (9.5cm) high.
£400–480 Bea

A Gaudy Welsh mug, decorated with Sunflower pattern, c1850, 3¼in (8.5cm) high.
£130–145 DHA

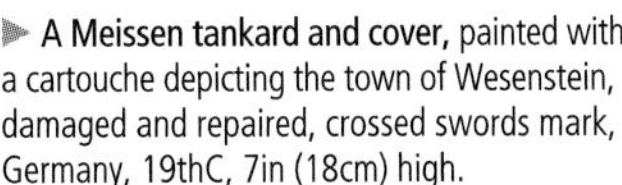

► **A Meissen tankard and cover,** painted with a cartouche depicting the town of Wesenstein, damaged and repaired, crossed swords mark, Germany, 19thC, 7in (18cm) high.
£540–640 WAD

A Plymouth mug, enamelled with a pair of exotic birds and insects, painted mark, 1768–70, 3¾in (9.5cm) high.
£3,300–3,950 Bea

A Vienna tankard, painted with a cartouche depicting Alpine dancers, Austria, c1880, 9in (23cm) high.
£1,350–1,550 MAA

◄ **A child's mug,** decorated in gilt with vines, inscribed 'Samuel', early 19thC, 3in (7.5cm) diam.
£155–175 HUM

PLAQUES

◄ **A Berlin plaque,** depicting an allegorical scene after Titian, signed 'W. Städtler', impressed mark, late 19thC, Germany, 10½ x 12½in (26.5 x 32cm).

£2,350–2,800 DORO

Wenzel Städtler, painter at the Springer & Co factory, Elbogen, was awarded the silver order of merit in 1896.

A Berlin plaque, entitled 'Lute Player after Kaulbach', impressed KPM mark, Germany, late 19thC, 8¼ x 4¼in (21 x 11cm).

£750–900 DD

A pair of Davenport plaques, enamelled with topographical scenes by Richard Ablott, one depicting The Valois and Montigny, the other a view of Lake Thun, framed and inscribed, one signed, c1875, 5¼in (13.5cm) wide.

£400–480 Bea

A Limoges *pâte-sur-pâte* plaque, entitled 'Night', France, early 20thC, 8in (20.5cm) square.

£200–230 SER

A pair of Sèvres-style plaques, one painted with a portrait of the Princesse de Condé, the other a portrait of the Comtesse du Maine, framed, France, late 19thC, 9¾in (25cm) high.

£680–810 WAD

A Volkstedt bisque plaque, entitled 'The Storm', Germany, 1890–1900, 13in (33cm) high.

£400–450 OAK

A plaque, painted with a portrait of a gentleman, 19thC, 6 x 4¾in (15 x 12cm), framed.

£310–370 WAD

A plaque, painted with a cherub after Raphael, Germany, late 19thC, 7½in (19cm) high.

£490–580 DN(HAM)

A plaque, depicting Cleopatra holding an asp, 19thC, 5 x 4¼in (12.5 x 11cm), in a giltwood frame.

£350–420 G(B)

POTPOURRI VASES

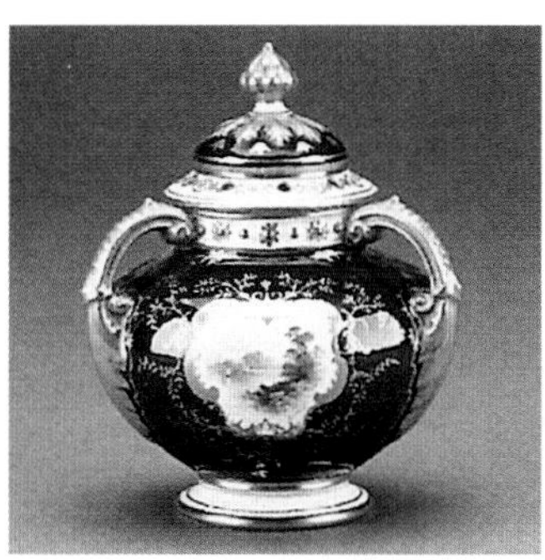

◄ **A Coalport potpourri vase and cover,** painted by E. O. Ball, with a view of Loch Earn, signed, printed marks, early 20thC, 5½in (14cm) high.

£510–610 WAD

Condition

The condition is absolutely vital when assessing the value of an antique. Damaged pieces on the whole appreciate much less than perfect examples. However, a rare desirable piece may command a high price even when damaged.

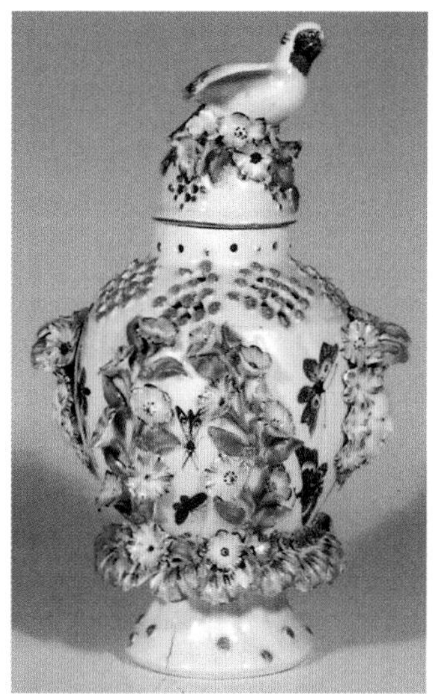

A Derby potpourri vase and cover, painted in 'Moth Painter' style with insects and applied with flowers and leaves, with a bird knop and female mask handles, some restoration, c1760, 11½in (29cm) high.

£1,050–1,250 LFA

A Spode potpourri vase and cover, painted with chinoiserie decoration of figures, birds and flowers, No. 4014, painted mark, early 19thC, 12½in (32cm) high.

£760–910 DN(HAM)

◄ **A Royal Worcester bone china potpourri jar and cover,** painted with daffodils, printed factory marks, c1909, 4¼in (11cm) high.

£330–390 RTo

SAUCE BOATS

A Lowestoft sauce boat, moulded and painted with a fisherman in a river landscape, painter's mark, c1760, 6in (15cm) wide.

£200–240 PBA

A Lowestoft Worcester-style sauce boat, printed and moulded with flowers and C-scrolls, c1780, 6¼in (16cm) wide.

£410–490 DN

A Worcester sauce boat, moulded and decorated with Little Fisherman pattern, c1765, 5½in (14cm) wide.

£210–250 HYD

A Worcester sauce boat, painted with flowers, crescent mark, 1770–80, 5½in (14cm) wide.

£150–180 WW

TEA & COFFEE POTS

A Belleek Tridacna teapot and cover, Ireland, Second Period, 1891–26, 7in (18cm) high.

£380–430 EAn

A teapot, cover and stand, probably Caughley or Worcester, painted with floral sprays, swags and pendants, crescent marks, c1780, 6in (15cm) high.

£320–380 PFK

A Derby coffee pot and cover, decorated in gilt with acanthus leaves, with a bud finial, restored, c1800, 8¾in (22cm) high.

£270–320 BAM(M)

A teapot and cover, possibly Liverpool, painted with sprays of flowers, c1770, 5½in (14cm) high.

£700–840 HYD

A Ludwigsburg teapot and cover, painted with sprays of *deutsche Blumen*, marked, slight damage, Germany, c1770.

£410–490 DN

A New Hall teapot, cover and stand, pattern No. N173, c1800, 6in (15cm) high.

£165–195 DD

A Nymphenburg teapot and cover, painted with *deutshce Blumen*, with an animal head spout, slight damage, Germany, 18thC, 7¼in (18.5cm) wide.

£170–200 WW

A Paris coffee pot and stand, decorated with flowers and garlands, with gilt-metal mounts, marked, France, 1800–10, coffee pot 8¼in (21cm) high.

£1,450–1,700 S(P)

A Sèvres teapot and cover, the cover with a chrysanthemum knop, later-decorated with exotic birds, France, date letter for 1760, 4¾in (12cm) high.

£700–840 Hal

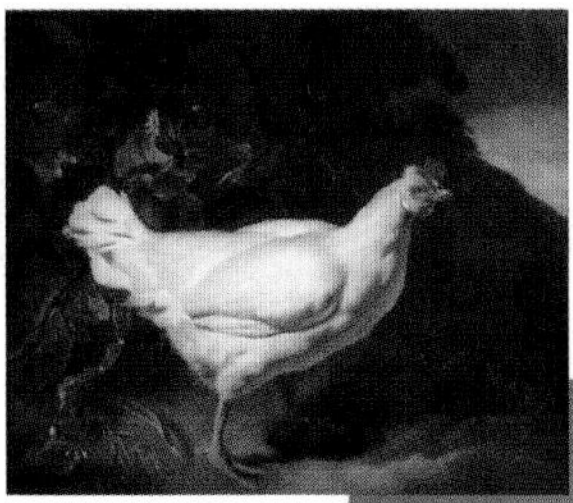

◀ **A Regency Spode teapot, cover and stand,** decorated with foliage, slight damage, 8in (20.5cm) diam.

£190–220 NSal

A Worcester teapot, decorated with Rock Warbler pattern, the cover with a flower knop, 1754–60, 4in (10cm) high.

£590–700 HYD

◀ **A Worcester teapot,** decorated with Putai and other Chinese figures, cover missing, 1755–60, 8in (20.5cm) wide.

£330–390 WW

A Worcester teapot and cover, painted with Prunus Root pattern, artist's mark, c1756, 7in (18cm) wide.

£1,350–1,600 N

A Worcester coffee pot and cover, decorated with Mansfield pattern, cover possibly associated, crescent mark, 1757–80, 7in (18cm) high.

£260–310 HYD

▶ **A teapot and cover,** probably Mansfield-decorated, each side painted with a country house and gardens within a gilt frame, the cover painted with a crest, c1800, 6¾in (17cm) high.

£1,650–1,950 S(O)

TEA & COFFEE SERVICES

A London-shape tea service, possibly Coalport, comprising 21 pieces, decorated with an Imari pattern, early 19thC.

£140–165 GTH

A Victorian Gaudy Welsh tea service, comprising 45 pieces, decorated with Tulip pattern, damaged.

£400–480 PF

A Meissen part tea service, comprising nine pieces, Germany, 19thC.
£2,700–3,000 YA

A tea service, possibly New Hall, comprising 19 pieces, decorated in the Mandarin pattern, early 19thC.
£420–500 G(L)

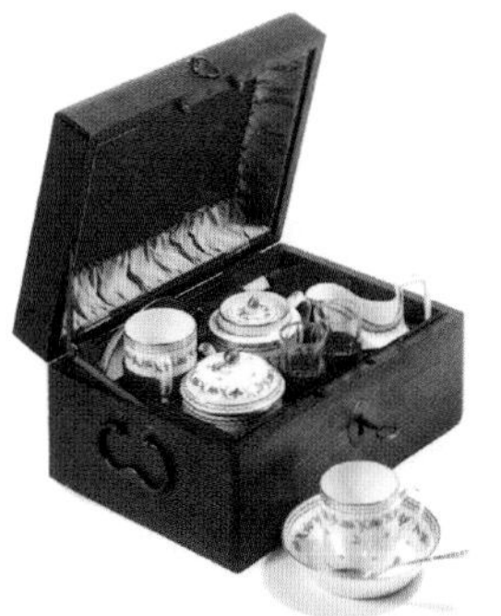

◀ A Paris travelling service, comprising 14 pieces, painted with bands of flowerheads, sugar bowl repaired, one spoon and one liqueur glass replaced, marked 'V. M. & C.', France, c1790.
£2,250–2,700 S(NY)

▶ A Paris tête-à-tête, comprising eight pieces, decorated with panels of figures, France, 19thC.
£1,500–1,800 E

A Sèvres part tea service, comprising 11 pieces, decorated with floral bouquets within gilt borders, damaged, painted and incised marks, France, c1764, teapot 5in (12.5cm) high.
£1,900–2,250 S(O)

A Spode part tea service, comprising 17 pieces, painted with peonies and phoenixes within gilt borders, c1810.
£230–270 ROS

A Vienna tête-à-tête, comprising eight pieces, decorated with gilt vine leaves, restored, Austria, date code for 1820.
£1,950–2,300 DORO

▶ A Worcester part tea service, comprising 33 pieces, painted with floral borders and sprigs, c1800.
£500–600 DN(HAM)

▶ A Chamberlain's Worcester tea service, comprising 28 pieces, decorated with Kylin pattern, painter's mark, 19thC.
£2,000–2,400 NSF

TRAYS

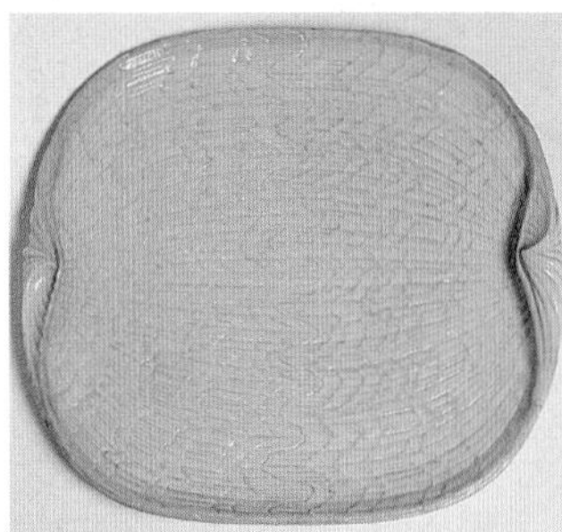

A Belleek Tridacna tray, Ireland, Second Period, 1891–26, 15in (38cm) high.

£490–550 EAn

A Meissen tray, painted and encrusted with a spray of flowers, slight damage, crossed swords mark, Germany, late 19thC, 17¼in (44cm) high.

£1,050–1,250 RTo

A Vienna tray, decorated with dancing couples and musicians at an encampment, after a Dutch painting, slight damage, restored, shield mark, Austria, c1760, 12in (30.5cm) wide.

£430–510 DORO

TUREENS

A Bow tureen and cover, painted with trees, rockwork and foliage, the cover with a lion knop, damaged, repaired, c1750, 12½in (32cm) wide.

£1,450–1,700 N

A Chamberlain's Worcester tureen and cover, decorated with botanical studies and gilt borders, the cover with a pineapple knop, c1830, 10¼in (26cm) diam.

£230–270 ROS

A pair of Chamberlain's Worcester sauce tureens, each surmounted and supported by gilt dolphins, covers restored, early 19thC, 9in (23cm) high.

£640–760 ROS

VASES

A Belleek Hippiritus vase, Ireland, First Period, 1863–90, 7in (18cm) high.

£490–550 BtoB

Further reading

Miller's Collecting Porcelain,
Miller's Publications, 2003

A Belleek Tulip vase, Ireland, First Period, 1863–90, 12½in (32cm) high.

£630–750 JAd

A pair of Bow vases, painted and encrusted with flowers and cherub masks, c1762, 9½in (24cm) high.

£1,450–1,650 RGa

◀ **A Coalport vase,** painted with a view of Buckingham Palace with Marble Arch, c1835, 9in (23cm) high.

£1,050–1,200 ⊞ JOR

Marble Arch was built in 1821 as the main entrance to Buckingham Palace. It was moved to its present location as an entrance to Hyde Park when Queen Victoria and Prince Albert extended the Palace in 1851.

A pair of Derby soft-paste porcelain vases and covers, possibly painted by William Pegg or Joseph Bancroft with flowers within gilt reserves, painted mark, 1800–25, 8in (20.5cm) high.

£820–980 HOLL

◀ **A Derby vase,** c1892, 6in (15cm) high.

£340–380 ⊞ CHO

A Royal Crown Derby vase and cover, painted by Charles Harris with flowers and leaves, knop repaired, signed, printed marks, date code for 1900, 9¾in (25cm) high.

£1,700–2,000 LFA

▶ **A Royal Crown Derby vase and cover,** painted with panels of flowers within gilt borders with 'jewelling', signed 'Leroy', date code for 1905, 6¼in (16cm) high.

£1,900–2,250 ROS

A Royal Crown Derby vase and cover, painted by Charles Harris with exotic birds within gilt borders, signed, date code for 1911, 9½in (24cm) high.

£1,300–1,550 ROS

A Royal Crown Derby vase, painted by Cuthbert Gresley with a view of Lake Menteith, Scotland, signed, c1920, 6½in (16.5cm) high.

£2,000–2,200 ⊞ JUP

A Dresden vase and cover, Germany, c1890, 16in (40.5cm) high.

£420–470 ⊞ MRA

A Fürstenberg vase and cover, hand-painted with flowers, the cover with a rose knop, slight damage, Germany, c1775, 14½in (37cm) high.

£960–1,150 S(O)

A pair of Imperial Porcelain Factory vases, depicting paintings after Rubens and Gerrit von Honthurst, Russia, St Petersburg, dated 1842 and 1849, 8in (20.5cm) high.

£1,144,000–1,372,000 S(Han)

Ex-Royal House of Hanover Sale. These vases commanded the highest price at the sale of works of art from the Royal House of Hanover.

A pair of vases, possibly Mason's, decorated in gilt with figures, c1820, 6¼in (16cm) high.

£1,100–1,300 WW

A Meissen campana vase, Germany, c1890, 5½in (14cm) high.

£380–430 MAA

A Minton double gourd vase, decorated with sparrows and bands of peaches, printed mark, late 19thC, 26¾in (68cm) high.

£1,200–1,400 TEN

A Minton *pâte-sur-pâte* vase, by Alboin Birks, c1900, 12in (30.5cm) high.

£2,800–3,200 Scot

A Nantgarw spill vase, London-decorated with panels of flowers, slight damage, Wales, c1820, 4½in (11.5cm) high.

£2,150–2,500 S(O)

A pair of Paris vases and stands, decorated with gilt scrolls, fountains and caduceus devices, one damaged and repaired, France, c1800, 9¾in (25cm) high.

£3,900–4,650 S(NY)

A pair of Paris vases, each painted with a tavern scene and baskets of flowers, slight damage, France, c1830, 11¾in (30cm) high.

£960–1,150 S(O)

◄ **A pair of Louis XVI-style Samson celadon vases,** with ormolu mounts, covers missing, France, 19thC, 13¼in (33.5cm) high.

£6,200–7,400 S(NY)

The French ceramics firm of Samson was established in 1845 by Edmé Samson at 7 rue Vendôme in Paris. The firm's initial purpose was to reproduce ceramics from museums and private collections and the factory claimed that all such reproductions would be distinctly marked to avoid confusion with the originals. In 1864, the factory was moved to Montreuil by Samson's son Emile. The range of wares included copies of 18th-century porcelain from such factories as Sèvres, Chelsea, Meissen and Derby, and Chinese-export wares. All items were reproduced in a glossy, hard-paste porcelain, which helps distinguish the copies from any originals in soft-paste or Chinese porcelain. The colours used were often innacurate and, in many cases, were incorrect in scale and heavily decorated and gilded. Although the company disclaimed any intention to deceive, many of its products have been passed off as originals, since the overglaze factory mark can be removed and substituted with false marks. The Samson factory continued to produce ceramics until 1969.

A near pair of Popov vases, decorated with horsemen and peasants within gilt borders, marked, Russia, c1850, 8¼in (21cm) high.

£880–1,050 ROS

A pair of Sèvres *pâte-sur-pâte* vases, France, 19thC, 9in (23cm) high.

£10,800–12,900 DuM

A Sèvres-style vase and cover, with gilt decoration and ormolu mounts, damaged, marked, France, mid-19thC, 16¼in (41.5cm) high.

£350–420 RTo

A pair of Sèvres-style vases and covers, France, c1870, 14in (35.5cm) high.

£2,250–2,500 MAA

A pair of Sèvres-style vases and covers, painted with panels of cherubs within gilt and 'jewelled' borders, slight restoration, painted marks, France, late 19thC, 19in (48.5cm) high.

£2,750–3,300 WAD

A pair of Sèvres-style vases, painted with bands of flowers above panels of figures within gilt borders, with gilt-metal mounts, Continental, 19thC, 18in (45.5cm) high.

£1,700–2,000 GIL

A Spode vase, with gilt decoration of Oriental foliage, pattern No. 967, early 19thC, 8½in (21.5cm) high.

£270–320 NSal

A Worcester vase, painted with flowers and insects, damaged, c1755, 4¾in (12cm) high.

£290–340 WW

A Swansea vase, painted with a band of garden flowers, with bee handles, restored and repaired, impressed mark, Wales, 1815–20, 6¾in (17cm) high.

£2,000–2,400 S(O)

A Swansea vase and cover, applied with floral garlands, the cover with a bud finial, damaged and repaired, Wales, 1815–20, 6in (15cm) high.

£1,050–1,250 S(O)

► **A pair of Worcester Barr, Flight & Barr vases,** painted with views of Middleham Castle, Yorkshire and Powis Castle, Powys, within gilt borders, with drop-ring handles, impressed mark, 1804–13, 4in (10cm) high.

£2,000–2,400 HYD

A pair of Royal Worcester vases, painted with roses, with gilt decoration, printed marks, date code for 1899, 9in (23cm) high.

£480–570 WAD

◄ **A Royal Worcester vase,** printed and painted with thistles and foliage within gilt borders and bands, model No. 1839, printed marks, date code for 1897, 10½in (26.5cm) high.

£390–460 BAM(M)

A pair of Royal Worcester vases, c1901, 13in (33cm) high.

£2,700–3,000 HKW

A Hadley's Worcester vase, painted by A. Shuck, signed, 1902–05, 9in (23cm) high.

£1,350–1,550 Scot

It is unusual for an artist to sign a Hadley's piece.

A pair of Royal Worcester vases, painted by Harry Davis, decorated with figures and animals in landscapes, shape No. 2331, covers missing, signed, c1909, 11½in (29cm) high.

£6,300–7,600 WW

A vase, painted with flowers and gilt anthemia, slight damage, c1820, 4¼in (11cm) high.

£120–145 WW

A pair of vases, decorated with stylized bands, France, early 19thC, 8¾in (22cm) high.

£340–400 WW

A pair of vases, painted with panels of landscapes within gilt borders, mid-19thC, 11in (28cm) high.

£920–1,100 WAD

A vase, painted with love birds and grapes, France, 1850–1900, 20in (51cm) high.

£250–300 WW

Sets/pairs

Unless otherwise stated, any description which refers to 'a set' or 'a pair' includes a guide price for the entire set or the pair, even though the illustration may show only a single item.

◄ **A pair of Chinese export-style armorial vases and covers,** decorated with flowers and faun masks, France, late 19thC, 12in (30.5cm) high.

£400–480 Mit

MISCELLANEOUS

A Meissen beaker, decorated with flowers, Germany, c1750, 3in (7.5cm) high.
£670–750 YA

A Royal Worcester biscuit barrel and cover, painted with floral sprays, shape No. 1412, impressed and painted marks, date code for 1892, 7in (18cm) high.
£280–330 PFK

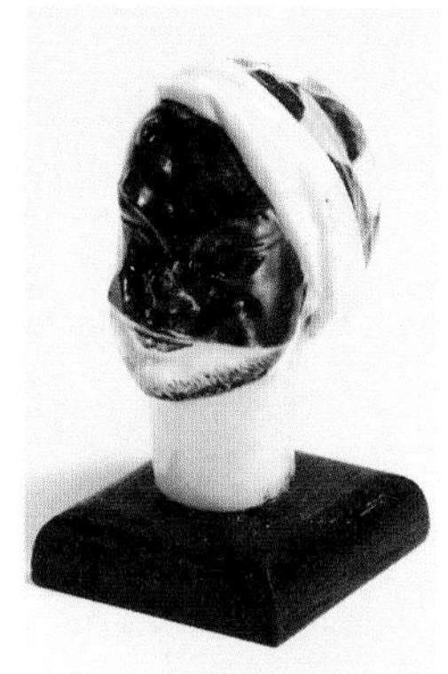

A cane handle, probably Doccia, in the form of a young man's head, slight damage, Italy, 1770–85, 2¾in (7cm) high.
£1,950–2,300 S(NY)

A Sèvres mantel clock, with gilt-bronze mounts, decorated with allegorical figures representing Geography and Reading, on a marble base, damage and losses, early 19thC, 19½in (49.5cm) high.
£2,250–2,700 S(P)

An egg, probably St Petersburg, painted with a portrait of the Madonna and Child, Russia, 19thC, 3½in (9cm) high.
£2,950–3,500 BUK

A Nantgarw egg cup, painted with a band of roses, Wales, c1820, 2in (5cm) high.
£1,900–2,250 S(O)

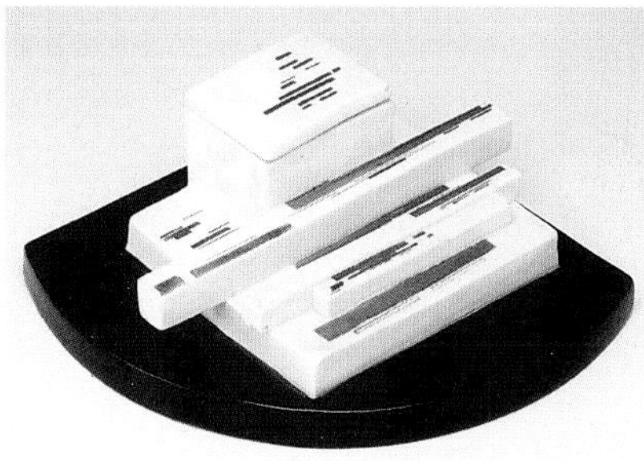

An inkstand, by Nikolai M. Suetin, painted with Suprematism pattern, impressed mark, Russia, 1920s, 7in (18cm) wide.
£8,700–10,400 BUK(F)

Nikolai M. Suetin is considered to be one of the leading Suprematism artists.

◀ **A Nantgarw inkwell,** painted with flowers, with gilt decoration, slight damage, Wales, c1820, 2¼in (5.5cm) high.
£2,000–2,400 S(O)

To find out more about 20thC Porcelain, please see the Decorative Arts section on pages 367–440 and the Twentieth-Century Design section on pages 441–470.

▶ **A Belleek honey pot and stand,** Ireland, Third Period, 1926–46, 6½in (16.5cm) high.
£620–700 SCH

A Meissen toilet mirror, surmounted by cherubs, restored, marked, Germany, mid-19thC, 9¾in (25cm) high.
£510–610 DORO

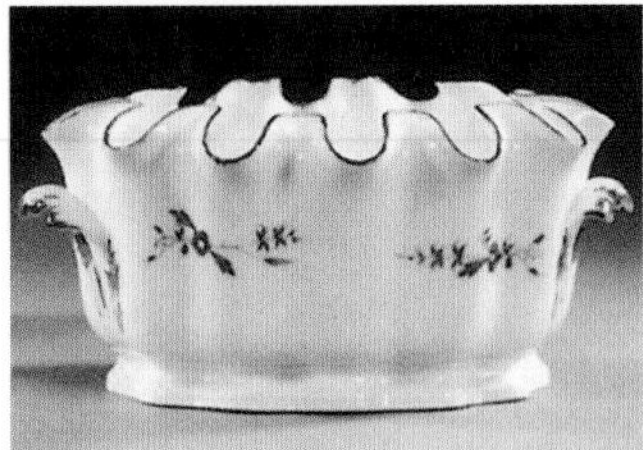

A pair of Caughley monteiths, painted with floral sprigs, with acanthus-leaf handles, slight damage and repair, impressed 'H', marked, 1775–90, 11¾in (30cm) wide.

£2,600–3,100 S(O)

A monteith is a wine glass cooler. It is normally found in silver or glass and takes the form of a bowl with a notched rim in which the stems of glasses can be held allowing the bowls to dip into the cooling water within. The name reputedly comes from a Scotsman who wore a cloak with a scalloped edge.

A Copenhagen pastille burner and cover, moulded with masks, supported on three dolphin feet, slight damage, Denmark, 1775–80, 5½in (14cm) high.

£960–1,150 S(O)

A Royal Crown Derby pot and cover, painted by John Porter Wale with a thatched cottage and landscape, signed, printed mark, date code for 1919, 3¼in (8.5cm) high.

£390–460 BAM(M)

A pair of Meissen salt and pepper shakers, Germany, c1770, 7in (18cm) high.

£2,000–2,300 YA

A Rockingham scent bottle, encrusted with flowers, marked, c1835, 4in (10cm) high.

£810–900 TYE

A Worcester rice spoon, painted with Maltese Cross pattern, with flower terminal, c1768, 5½in (14cm) long.

£680–810 N

A Baddeley Littler tea canister, painted with *famille rose* flowers and leaves, c1780, 5in (12.5cm) high.

£940–1,100 LFA

A pair of Meissen-style wall brackets, painted with flowers and figures, on Chinese-style dog of *Fo* supports, with wooden covers, Germany, 19thC, 13in (33cm) high.

£630–750 Mit

A Swansea miniature watering can, painted by William Pollard with scattered flowers, repaired, Wales, 1817–20, 3½in (9cm) high.

£1,300–1,550 S(O)

► **A pair of Worcester Flight, Barr & Barr wine coolers,** painted with panels of flowers and gilt borders, impressed marks, c1815, 8½in (21.5cm) wide.

£4,250–5,100 WW

PARIAN FIGURES & MODELS

PARIAN IS A QUINTESSENTIAL Victorian porcelain, developed to imitate the classical marble statues of antiquity, but its origins date back to the 18th-century biscuit porcelains of Sèvres and Derby. These were not ideal as they were absorbent when left unglazed, and so tended to stain and become dirty. As the biscuit body was difficult to work, we see only small figures and models produced.

In the second quarter of the 19th century, production at the Derby factory began to decline and Minton replaced them as the largest manufacturer of figures. The race was now on for an improved material, and so Parian appeared c1845. By the early 1850s both Minton and Copeland & Garrett were claiming to have invented Parian, which initially was marketed under a number of different names. Minton used the term Parian, derived from the marble mined in Roman times in the Greek island of Paros, whereas at Copeland & Garrett it was known as Statuary Porcelain, and at Wedgwood, Carrara Ware. Parian came to be used for all manner of sculptural ceramics with a vast array of busts and statues copied from contemporary marble and bronze models, works from the Renaissance, Gothic period and the 18th century, as well as from antique works that had arrived as Grand Tour souvenirs. Benjamin Cheverton's reducing machine, a type of three-dimensional pantograph, patented in 1844, was vital to this success, by enabling the reproduction of original works to be made comparatively quickly. The Great Exhibition of 1851 first brought Parian to public attention, but it also featured heavily at later exhibitions in Paris and Vienna.

Another important part of the Parian story is the association with the Art Union of London. This was the largest and most influential of the many Art Unions, the first of which were founded in the 1830s as a form of an 'improving' lottery but instead of winning cash, the prizes were contemporary works of art by British artists and designers, with tickets generally costing one guinea. From their first appearance, Parian statuettes were popular prizes. Public competitions were held for new sculptures, which would then be duplicated on a small scale in Parian. Some of the most popular Parian models were Art Union prizes, such as Narcissus by John Gibson, Psyche by Theed and Sabrina by Calder Marshall. Many were scantily-veiled maidens or sentimental subjects – so popular in Victoria's reign.

Today, as the following pages show, a wide array of models, often of excellent quality, can be bought fairly cheaply, and for the enthusiast, the excellent monograph *The Parian Phenomenon* edited by Paul Atterbury is an absolute must. **John Axford**

◄ **A Parian model of a dog,** c1860, 8in (20.5cm) high.
£390–440 ⊞ GAN

A Copeland Parian bust of Ophelia, c1850, 12¼in (31cm) high.
£200–230 ⊞ SER

A Copeland Parian bust of Alexandra, Princess of Denmark, inscribed 'Art Union of Crystal Palace', slight damage, dated 1863, 12¼in (31cm) high.
£200–240 DN

A Copeland Parian bust of William Shakespeare, by Rafael Monti, inscribed 'Art Union of Crystal Palace', dated 1864, 14in (35.5cm) high.
£450–500 ⊞ LGr

◄ **A Worcester Parian bust of Professor Wilson,** c1855, 11½in (29cm) high.
£320–360 ⊞ DHA

Professor John Wilson was an author, professor and moral philosopher at Edinburgh University who contributed to Blackwood's Magazine.

A Parian bust of Richard Cobden, by E. W. Wyon, impressed title and date, 1865, 16½in (42cm) high.

£270–320 SK

◄ A Parian bust of the Duke of Wellington, c1860, 9in (23cm) high.

£340–380 GAN

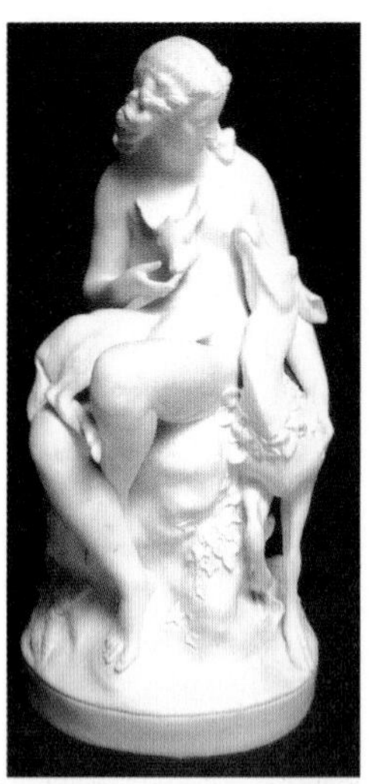

► A Parian figure of a wood nymph, by Birch, c1860, 20in (51cm) high.

£2,350–2,650 GAN

A Copeland Parian figural group of Uncle Toby and the Widow Wadman, dated 1873, 8½in (21.5cm) high.

£430–480 DHA

Uncle Toby and the Widow Wadman are characters in Laurence Sterne's Tristram Shandy.

A Copeland Parian figure of Beatrice, by Edgar Papworth, impressed marks, dated 1860, 22¼in (56.6cm) high.

£370–440 GTH

A Copeland Parian figure, by Edgar Papworth, entitled 'Fairy Cap', c1860, 14in (35.5cm) high.

£2,350–2,650 GAN

This figure is also known as 'Psyche Disguised'.

Parian is an unglazed or bisque porcelain developed in the 1840s by both Minton and Copeland & Garrett, and later produced by many English and American factories. It is named after the marble that was mined on the Greek island of Paros, and was used extensively in the manufacture of busts and figures. The principal makers were Copeland, Minton and Wedgwood.

► A Copeland Parian figure of Egeria, c1865, 28in (71cm) high.

£1,400–1,600 JAK

Egeria is a female adviser. She is supposed to have advised Numa Pompilius, the legendary second king of Rome, who is said to have lived at the turn of the 7th century BC.

A Copeland Parian figure of Master Tom, by J. Durham, inscribed 'Master Tom Vide Water Babies', impressed marks, dated 1872, 21in (53.5cm) high.

£530–630 TEN

A Copeland Parian figure of Robinette, 19thC, 14¼in (36cm) high.

£175–210 ROS

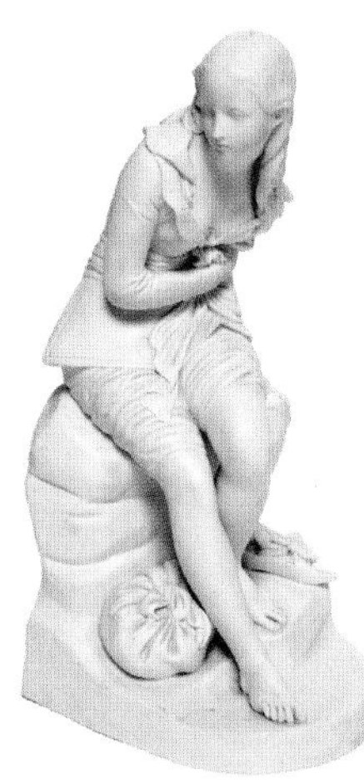

A Minton Parian figure of **Dorothea,** by John Bell, signed, c1847, 14in (35.5cm) high.

£690–780 GSA

A Minton Parian figure of **Temperance,** after Filippo Della Valle, slight damage, impressed marks, date code for 1861, 21in (53.5cm) high.

£590–700 DN

A Robinson & Leadbeater Parian figure of a young woman, c1880, 15in (38cm) high.

£450–500 MRA

A pair of Robinson & Leadbeater Parian figures of women, c1880, 13in (33cm) high.

£540–600 MRA

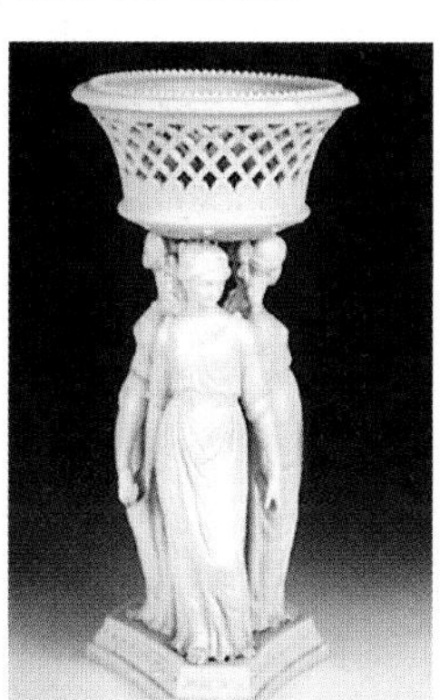

◄ A Copeland Parian figural **group,** in the form of the Three Graces supporting a basket, mid-19thC, 21in (53.5cm) high.

£590–700 CGC

A Parian figural group of **Ino and Bacchus,** c1860, 21in (53.5cm) high.

£2,700–3,000 GAN

Bacchus, the Roman god of wine and son of Jupiter was nursed through childhood by Ino.

A Parian figural group of the **Three Graces,** c1860, 14in (35.5cm) high.

£700–780 GAN

A Parian figural **group,** by John Rogers, entitled 'Wounded to the Rear, One More Shot', impressed mark, America, New York, c1864, 20in (51cm) high.

£2,350–2,800 NAAW

A Parian **figure,** after the Spinario, early 20thC, 8¾in (22cm) high.

£110–125 SER

This is a copy of an antique statue known as Spinario the Thornpuller, which portrays a young boy drawing a thorn from his foot.

A Parian figure of **Lord Roberts,** c1900, 13½in (34.5cm) high.

£150–175 SER

Lord Roberts of Kandahar commanded the British forces in Afghanistan (1881–82) and was Commander-in-Chief in India (1885–93) and in the Boer War (1899–1902). He was also Commander-in-Chief of the British Army (1901–04).

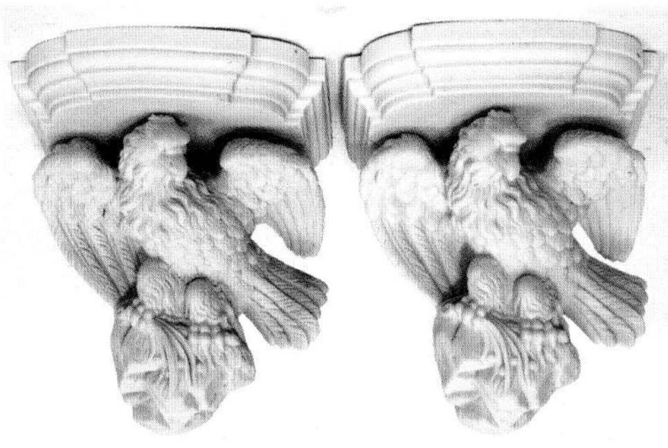

◄ A pair of Victorian Parian **wall brackets,** in the form of eagles, 7¼in (18.5cm) high.

£330–390 AH

A SELECTION OF CHINESE DYNASTIES & MARKS

EARLY DYNASTIES

Neolithic	10th – early 1st millennium BC
Shang Dynasty	16th century–c1050 BC
Zhou Dynasty	c1050–221 BC
Warring States	480–221 BC
Qin Dynasty	221–206 BC
Han Dynasty	206 BC – AD 220
Six Dynasties	AD 222–589
Wei Dynasty	AD 386–557
Sui Dynasty	AD 581–618
Tang Dynasty	AD 618–907
Five Dynasties	AD 907–960
Liao Dynasty	AD 907–1125
Song Dynasty	AD 960–1279
Northern Song	AD 960–1127
Southern Song	AD 1127–1279
Xixia Dynasty	AD 1038–1227
Jin Dynasty	AD 1115–1234
Yuan Dynasty	AD 1279–1368

MING DYNASTY MARKS

洪武年製
Hongwu
1368–1398

永樂年製
Yongle
1403–1424

大明宣德年製
Xuande
1426–1435

大明成化年製
Chenghua
1465–1487

大明弘治年製
Hongzhi
1488–1505

大明正德年製
Zhengde
1506–1521

大明嘉靖年製
Jiajing
1522–1566

大明隆慶年製
Longqing
1567–1572

大明萬曆年製
Wanli
1573–1619

大明天啟年製
Tianqi
1621–1627

崇禎年製
Chongzhen
1628–1644

QING DYNASTY MARKS

大清順治年製
Shunzhi
1644–1661

大清康熙年製
Kangxi
1662–1722

大清雍正年製
Yongzheng
1723–1735

大清乾隆年製
Qianlong
1736–1795

嘉慶年製
Jiaqing
1796–1820

大清道光年製
Daoguang
1821–1850

大清咸豐年製
Xianfeng
1851–1861

大清同治年製
Tongzhi
1862–1874

大清光緒年製
Guangxu
1875–1908

大清宣統年製
Xuantong
1909–1911

洪憲年製
Hongxian
1916

CHINESE CERAMICS

THE PHENOMENAL RISE IN THE VALUE of Chinese-taste ceramics continues, fuelled largely by its popularity in mainland China. However, the market is truly international and even the most remote provincial auction room can now expect a visit from mainland Chinese dealers. The recent world record of £14,000,000 for a single piece of Chinese porcelain, a Yuan Dynasty *guan* sold in London, shows that a well-researched item of exceptional quality and provenance will reach its full potential in the current market place. This piece heads a long list of Chinese porcelain items that have realized over £500,000 recently. The rapid rise in the market for fine Chinese ceramics has attracted private and corporate investors from both the East and West but deciding exactly which pieces are worthy of investment is not easy. Good quality Chinese-taste Imperial works will continue to command the field, particularly if they are well provenanced. Most of us, however, have to content ourselves with 'middle ground' collecting. Fortunately, the output of Chinese non-Imperial but high quality porcelain has been huge over the past four centuries and the discerning collector can still find good quality pieces at modest prices.

Chinese porcelain collecting has also been influenced by the current trends of Chinese dealers, many of whom have only recently come into the market place and their limited knowledge promotes copycat buying. In 2004 it was items of Transitional period blue and white that were sought after and in 2005 monochrome wares were fashionable.

Peter Wain

Peter is a leading specialist in Chinese and Japanese ceramics and works of art. He has also been the Chairman of the Oriental Vetting Committees for many of the top international antiques fairs.

He has written numerous books on this subject and given many lectures in the UK, USA and Australia.

One area as yet ignored by the Chinese is that of fine export porcelain, which is still led by the Western market. Exceptional, rare and well-provenanced export pieces are showing an increase in value as interior decorators from both the East and the West continue to use them. What is not Chinese taste at the moment may well become so in the future.

Oriental tomb ceramics struggle to find buyers unless they have good provenance, style and condition. This faltering market relies upon European and American collectors, as many Asian buyers believe tomb artefacts to be unlucky. For the same reason, demand has also been patchy for middle quality Song ceramics.

Mainland Chinese dealers are now sourcing objects via auctioneers' websites and are prepared to travel the world in search of fine pieces; the increase in values is set to continue.

Peter Wain

ANIMALS

An ash-glazed proto-porcelain jar, in the form of an owl, Zhou Dynasty, Warring States period, 480–221 BC, 17¼in (44cm) high.

£11,700–14,000 S(NY)

A pottery model of an ox, Han Dynasty, 206 BC– AD 220, 9in (23cm) long.

£720–800 GLD

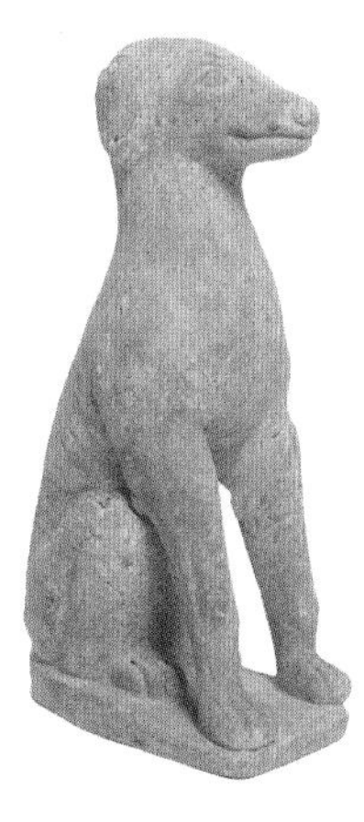

A pair of pottery models of dogs, Han Dynasty, 206 BC–AD 220, 7in (18cm) high.

£450–500 GLD

A pottery model of a pig, Han Dynasty, 206 BC–AD 220, 18in (45.5cm) wide.

£1,250–1,400 BOW

A pottery model of a seated lion dog, probably Six Dynasties, AD 222–589, 8in (20.5cm) high.

£230–270 WW

A pottery model of a horse, Tang Dynasty, AD 618–907, 12in (30.5cm) high.

£1,050–1,200 BOW

A pottery model of a horse and rider, Tang Dynasty, AD 618–907, 14in (35.5cm) high.

£1,850–2,100 A&C

A pair of pottery models of wolves, one tail repaired, Han Dynasty, 206 BC – AD 220, 11in (28cm) high.

£540–600 GLD

A pottery model of a war horse, Western Jin Dynasty, AD 265–317, 13¾in (35cm) high.

£820–980 DN(BR)

► A pottery figure of an earth spirit, Tang Dynasty, AD 618–907, 15in (20.5cm) high

£2,700–3,000 SOO

Earth spirit figures were left in tombs to ward off evil spirits so that the soul of the dead could ascend into Heaven without obstruction.

A pottery model of a Bactrian camel, Oxford T/L tested, Tang Dynasty, AD 618–907, 19½in (49.5cm) high.

£3,600–4,300 S

T/L Test

Oxford T/L test refers to a test certificate awarded by Oxford Authentication Ltd to those genuine pieces of ceramics that have passed their thermoluminescence test which is accurate to plus or minus 200 years.

A pottery model of a horse, made in two pieces, Western Han Dynasty, 40–71 BC, 19in (48.5cm) high.

£3,400–3,800 SOO

A pottery model of a horse and rider, Tang Dynasty, AD 618–907, 16in (40.5cm) high.

£1,600–1,800 BOW

A **pottery wine jug and cover,** in the form of a dog, with *sancai* glaze, slight damage, Kangxi period, 1662–1722, 4¼in (11cm) high.

£330–390 CDC

◀ **A pair of Meissen-style porcelain models of pug dogs,** slight damage, Qianlong period, 1736–95, 10¾in (27.5cm) high.

£14,100–16,900 BUK

A **porcelain model of a cat,** Kangxi period, 1662–1722, 6¼in (16cm) wide.

£1,750–2,100 BUK

This would be filled with oil and a wick floated in it. When lit, the porcelain would glow and the eyes would shine brightly, which was believed to scare away rats.

A **pair of *famille rose* models of cows,** slight damage, Qianlong period, 1736–95, 8¼in (21cm) wide.

£14,800–17,700 BUK

◀ **A terracotta model of a lion dog,** 19thC, 8in (20.5cm) long.

£130–155 GTH

A **biscuit-glazed model of a lion and two birds,** 19thC, 8½in (21.5cm) high.

£1,950–2,300 S(NY)

◀ **A *blanc-de-Chine* model of a European riding a horse,** restored, c1690, 3½in (9cm) high.

£540–640 WW

A **pair of Chinese export porcelain elephant tureens and covers,** each knop in the form of a recumbent hound, with later ormolu mounts, c1770, 6¼in (16cm) high.

£31,000–37,000 S(NY)

In the late 18th century it was quite common for people in the West to order tureens from China in the form of animals and birds. Some shapes were more popular than others. The shapes that were less popular then, such as these elephants, are today quite rare.

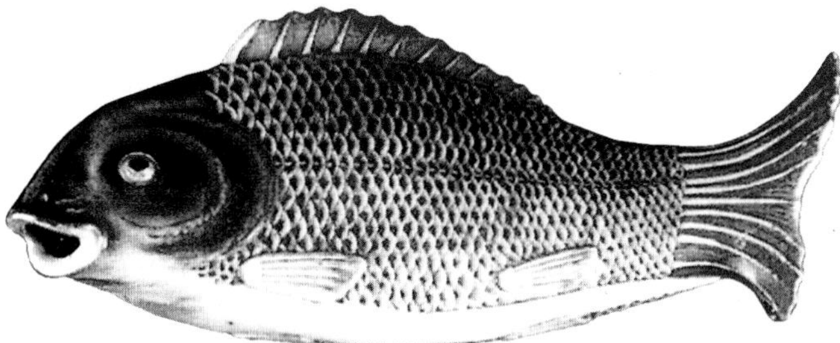

A **porcelain tureen and cover,** in the form of a carp, inscribed 'Dan ran ju shi zhi', slight damage, 19thC, 17in (43cm) long.

£1,500–1,800 WW

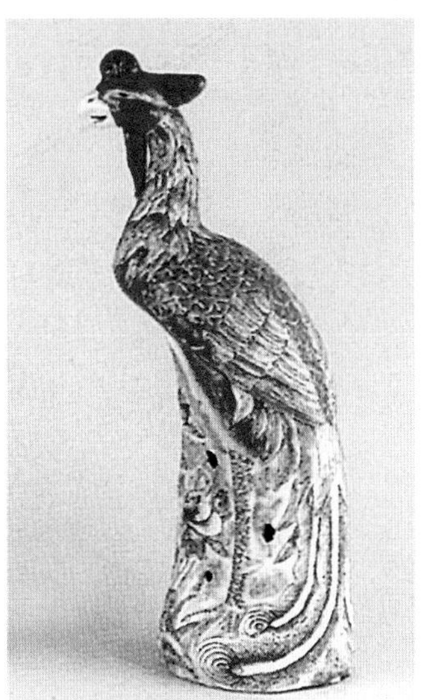

A **pair of *famille rose* porcelain models of phoenix,** 19th/20thC, 14¼in (36cm) high.

£370–440 DN(BR)

BOWLS

A marbled bowl, decorated to imitate wood, with an everted mouth, on a ring foot, Tang Dynasty, AD 618–907, 4in (10cm) diam.

£2,600–3,100 S(NY)

A kiln waster of a celadon bowl, Song Dynasty, AD 960–1279, 8in (20.5cm) wide.

£540–600 GLD

► **A Henan pottery bowl,** decorated with metallic glazes, Northern Song Dynasty, AD 960–1127, 7in (18cm) diam.

£2,600–3,100 S(NY)

Henan is the province in central China where this distinctive type of stoneware was produced.

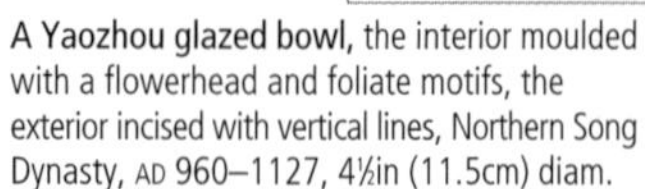

A Yaozhou glazed bowl, the interior moulded with a flowerhead and foliate motifs, the exterior incised with vertical lines, Northern Song Dynasty, AD 960–1127, 4½in (11.5cm) diam.

£7,800–9,300 S(NY)

Yaozhou is typically Northern Song green ware. The decoration was mainly moulded and incised before the pieces were completely dry. The pieces were then bisque fired before they were glazed, the process producing different shades of thick green glaze. Yaozhou wares are still made today in the mountainous area of Chenlu, one of the sites of the old Yaozhou kilns.

A Qingbai bowl, the interior carved with figures of boys, Southern Song Dynasty, 1127–1279, 7¾in (19.5cm) diam.

£2,600–3,100 S(NY)

Qingbai, also [illegible] is a type of porc[illegible] [illegible]ce, firs[illegible] during [illegible]

◄ **A Zhejiang Longquan bowl,** Southern Song Dynasty, 1127–1279, 7in (18cm) diam.

£540–600 BOW

Longquan wares usually have a pale grey body covered by a thick, opaque, bluish-green glaze that is slightly bubbly. Typical examples are bowls, vases, archaic forms and items for the scholar's desk.

► **A Cizhou teabowl,** the interior decorated with a leaf, Southern Song Dynasty, 1127–1279, 4in (10cm) diam.

£5,200–6,200 S(NY)

Cizhou wares came from many different kilns in northern China, although Cixian (Cizhou) itself was the most important site. They are characterized by bold shapes and decoration on a slip-covered body.

A Henan stoneware bowl, Yuan Dynasty, 1280–1368, 7in (18cm) diam.

£720–800 BOW

► **A Longquan celadon bulb bowl,** the sides incised with a lattice design, on three tapered feet, Ming Dynasty, 14th–15thC, 11½in (29cm) diam.

£300–360 NSal

A bowl, painted with two dragons among clouds chasing a flaming pearl, the interior with a further flaming pearl, 17thC, 9½in (24cm) diam.

£2,000–2,400 S

A bowl, the interior decorated with a dragon medallion, Kangxi period, 1662–1722, 4½in (11.5cm) diam.

£1,800–2,100 S

Wares for the female court

The decoration of Qing Imperial domestic wares for use by the Empress and concubines was stipulated under Palace regulations. In general, the higher the ranks, the greater the use of yellow and dragons. Yellow was reserved for the Empress while a third-rank concubine would have yellow with a green dragon and a seventh-rank concubine would have general polychrome decoration. The lowest ranking concubine was not allowed the use of any vessel with yellow or dragons on.

A bowl, decorated with The Three Friends of Winter, pine, prunus and bamboo, marked, Ming Dynasty, Chongzhen mark period, 1628–44, 2¾in (7cm) diam.

£2,000–2,400 WW

A footed bowl, incised with four medallions separated by *ruyi* clouds, marked, Kangxi period, 1662–1722, 4¾in (12cm) diam.

£1,600–1,900 S(NY)

A bowl, decorated with a scholar painting a scroll, marked 'Yu tang jia qi' (Beautiful vessel for the Jade Hall'), 17thC, 5¼in (13.5cm) diam.

£1,200–1,400 WW

A pair of porcelain *famille rose* bowls, decorated in the European style, Qianlong period, 1736–95, 10in (25.5cm) diam.

£4,000–4,800 BUK

A Chinese export *famille rose* bowl, decorated with figures and chicken-skin borders, damaged, Qianlong period, 1736–95, 16in (40.5cm) diam.

£470–560 Hal

Chicken skin is an American term for the use of a thick, opaque white glaze used for the background of ceramic items.

► **A Batavian-style bowl,** from the Nanking cargo, decorated with landscapes, c1750, 6in (15cm) diam.

£310–350 RBA

A soup bowl, from the Nanking cargo, painted with Willow and Terrace pattern, Qing Dynasty, c1750, 9in (23cm) diam.

£360–400 RBA

The Dutch East India Company's ship Geldermalsen *sank near Java in 1751. Included in its cargo was a particular type of Chinese blue and white porcelain known as Nanking, hence the name. Although there was little in the cargo to excite the purist collector of Asian ceramics, the story of the salvage attracted intense public interest, which was reflected in the prices achieved when the pieces were sold at auction in 1986. Items from this cargo still command a premium over comparable pieces of Chinese export porcelain.*

A glazed bowl, late 18thC, 4in (10cm) wide.

£530–630 WW

The shoe shape of an ingot is a traditional Chinese symbol of wealth.

A porcelain bowl, decorated with family groups, with a gilt border, late 18thC, 6¾in (17cm) diam.

£130–155 NSal

Colour codes

Qing Imperial vessels for ritual (altar) and official ceremonies were normally monochrome in colour. Specific colours were for use in the main temples – red for the Temple of the Sun, yellow for the Temple of the Earth, white for the Temple of the Moon and blue for the Temple of Heaven.

◀ **A bowl,** decorated with a garden scene, c1800, 10in (25.5cm) square.

£610–730 DN(BR)

A bowl and stand, from the *Diana* cargo, decorated with Chess Players pattern, 1817, stand 6¼in (16cm) diam.

£310–350 RBA

The Diana *sank off the coast of Malacca in 1817 and the cargo was recovered in 1985.*

A porcelain bowl, painted with a deer beneath a peach tree, with a bird and bats, six-character Daoguang mark, Daoguang period, 1821–1850, 7in (18cm) diam.

£900–1,050 WAD

▶ **A Canton porcelain punchbowl,** 19thC, 14¼in (36cm) diam.

£700–840 MAL(O)

A Chinese export punchbowl, decorated with figures, birds and flowers, mid-19thC, 13½in (34.5cm) diam.

£780–930 JDJ

A bowl, decorated with a *café-au-lait* glaze, marked, Guangxu period, 1875–1908, 6in (15cm) diam.

£700–840 WW

A bowl, decorated with bats, swastikas and *zhou*, marked, Guangxu period, 1875–1908, 7in (18cm) diam.

£1,750–2,100 DN

COVERED BOWLS

A porcelain Red Cliff bowl and cover, late Ming Dynasty, 1600–50, 6in (15cm) diam.

£1,000–1,200 BUK

This piece bears a narrative decoration illustrating the prose poem 'Red Cliff' by Su Shi, also known as Su Dong Po, in which the poet and his friends are setting off on a journey accompanied by the moon and their shadows. Chinese poems and paintings are closely related.

A bowl and cover, decorated with chrysanthemum sprays, slight damage, marked, Guangxu period, 1875–1908, 10¾in (27.5cm) diam.

£1,100–1,300 DN

A porcelain *famille rose* sugar bowl, cover and stand, decorated in the European style, cracks, restored, Qianlong period, 1736–95, 8¾in (22cm) wide.

£5,000–6,000 BUK

BOXES

A box and cover, moulded with a flowerhead formed by a five-petal floret set within two eight-petal blossoms, with *sancai* glaze, Tang Dynasty, 618–907, 4in (10cm) diam.

£4,500–5,400 S(NY)

Small sancai*-glazed covered boxes with impressed designs were most likely modelled after metal prototypes, particularly those with floret medallion motifs.* Sancai *literally translates as 'three colour' and refers to the splashed colours of green and brown that turn yellow when lightly applied over a white slip. This haphazard application of colour is often referred to as 'egg and spinach'.*

A porcelain box and cover, Ming Dynasty, Wanli period, 1573–1619, 11in (28cm) diam.

£2,700–3,200 DN

A sweetmeat box and cover, painted with flowers, the interior with seven segments, marked, Qianlong period, 1736–95, 6in (15cm) diam.

£2,000–2,400 WW

A box and cover, from the *Tek Sing* cargo, decorated with a peony and scrolling foliage, 1822, 3in (7.5cm) diam.

£760–850 RBA

The Tek Sing *sank in the Gaspar Straits in the Pacific Ocean in1822.*

A Canton *famille rose* box and cover, decorated with figures and flowers, 19thC, 7½in (19cm) wide.

£175–210 WW

BRUSHPOTS

A brushpot, in the form of bamboo, Kangxi period, 1662–1722, 4¾in (12cm) high.

£2,400–2,850 S

MILLER'S COMPARES

I. **A brushpot,** painted with a riverscape, hair crack, Kangxi period, 1662–1722, 7in (18cm) wide.

£1,900–2,250 WW

II. **A brushpot,** painted with a riverscape, slight damage, six-character Kangxi mark, 19thC, 7in (18cm) diam.

£350–420 WW

Item I is a Kangxi period piece with particularly good painting. Item II is a later copy and moreover the painting is not as strong and flowing as that in Item I.

◄ **A brushpot,** painted with two panels depicting a butterfly and a bird among chrysanthemums, Kangxi period, 1662–1722, 7in (18cm) high.

£7,800–9,300 S

Buying and selling

All the pictures in our price guides originate from auction houses and dealers. When buying at auction, prices can be lower than those of a dealer, but a buyer's premium and VAT will be added to the hammer price. Equally, when selling at auction, commission, tax and photography charges must be taken into account. Dealers will often restore pieces before putting them back on the market. Both dealers and auctioneers can provide professional advice, so it is worth researching both sources before buying or selling your antiques.

CENSERS

A Jun censer, applied with two masks and ring handles, on three feet, feet restored, Song Dynasty, AD 960–1280, 3½in (9cm) diam.

£4,300–4,800 G&G

The glazing process on Jun wares was so complicated that each piece fired differently and no one knew how it would look until it came out of the kiln. For each successful piece hundreds were rejected and perhaps only one in five was a masterpiece. Such pieces will sell for well in excess of £50,000.

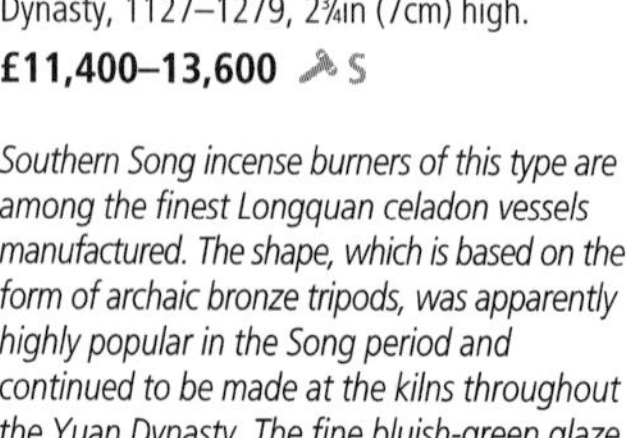

A Lonquan celadon censer, Southern Song Dynasty, 1127–1279, 2¾in (7cm) high.

£11,400–13,600 S

Southern Song incense burners of this type are among the finest Longquan celadon vessels manufactured. The shape, which is based on the form of archaic bronze tripods, was apparently highly popular in the Song period and continued to be made at the kilns throughout the Yuan Dynasty. The fine bluish-green glaze colour and the harmonious proportions of the censer were, however, achieved only in the Southern Song period and declined thereafter.

A censer, painted with a garden scene, on three animal-head feet, Ming Dynasty, Wanli period, 1573–1619, 9¾in (25cm) diam.

£2,900–3,450 S(NY)

► **A Guan-style censer,** with a pierced wood cover and stand, 18thC, 3¼in (8.5cm) high.

£1,050–1,250 S

Qing potters tried to recreate the glazes applied to the archaistic pieces of the Song period; these included the thick, crackled glazes used on guan wares. The Qing copies are generally smoother and shinier than the originals.

CUPS

A lobed cup, Tang Dynasty, AD 618–907, 3¾in (9.5cm) high.
£3,900–4,600 S(NY)

A Ding Yao cup, with a dragon handle, Song Dynasty, AD 960–1279, 3¼in (8.5cm) diam.
£630–700 BOW

Ding wares have a creamy white glaze and originate from Hebei province in northern China. Manufactured from the 10th to the 13th century, this was one of the first true porcelains to be made.

A Jun cup and stand, Jin Dynasty, 1115–1234, 3¾in (9.5cm) diam.
£5,200–6,200 S(NY)

A Qingbai stem cup, Southern Song Dynasty, 1127–1279, 4¾in (12cm) high.
£2,750–3,300 S(NY)

Qingbai is a white ware produced by potters in the Jingdezhen area throughout the Song Dynasty. Qingbai stem cups of this form are extremely unusual.

A Longquan celadon teabowl, Southern Song Dynasty, 1127–1279, 4in (10cm) diam.
£1,950–2,300 S(NY)

A *blanc-de-Chine* cup, London-decorated with flowers, slight damage, c1710, 2½in (6.5cm) high.
£175–210 WW

A teabowl and saucer, decorated with cranes, on a wooden display stand, slight damage, early 18thC.
£120–140 WW

A teabowl and saucer, from the Nanking cargo, decorated with a pagoda, c1750, bowl 3in (7.5cm) diam.
£310–350 RBA

A pair of *famille rose* wine cups, painted with flowers, marked, Xianfeng period, 1851–61, 2¾in (7cm) high.
£3,800–4,550 S

A pair of *famille rose* wine cups, painted with a fishing scene, inscribed with a poem and two seals, marked, Tongzhi period, 1862–74, 2in (5cm) high.
£2,100–2,500 S

DISHES

A pair of Henan dishes, with persimmon glaze, Song Dynasty, AD 960–1279, larger 4¼in (11cm) diam.

£18,200–21,800 S(NY)

It is rare to find a pair of plain-rim persimmon-glazed dishes as they are more commonly found with lobed rims.

A Canton warming dish, early 19thC, 9½in (24cm) diam.

£160–180 DHA

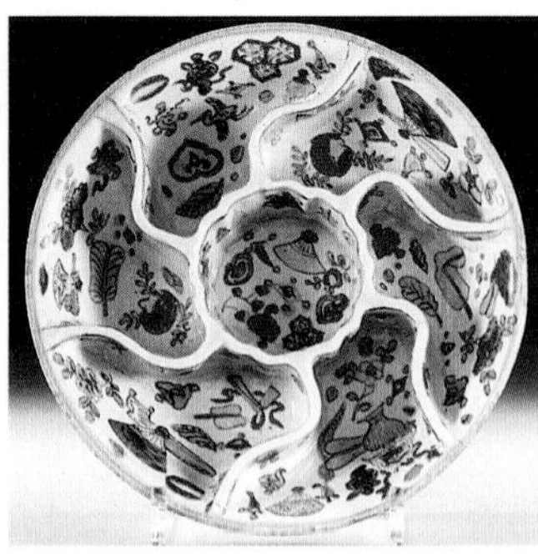

A *wucai* segmented sweetmeat dish, decorated with precious objects, marked, Ming Dynasty, Wanli period, 1573–1619, 8¾in (22cm) diam.

£5,400–6,400 S

A Chinese export dish, painted with butterflies and flower sprays, slight damage, Ming Dynasty, Tianqi period, 1621–27, 6½in (16.5cm) wide.

£590–700 WW

This dish, made for the Japanese market, is to Japanese taste of shape and decoration and would have been used in tea ceremonies. Japanese tea ceremony wares were a major export during the Tianqi period.

◄ **A *famille rose* warming dish and cover,** decorated with figures and a coat-of-arms, Daoguang period, 1821–50, 9¾in (25cm) diam.

£280–330 BERN

EWERS & JUGS

A *sancai*-glazed pottery ewer, the body moulded on both sides with a dragon among foliage, Liao Dynasty, AD 907–1125, 7in (18cm) high.

£9,600–11,500 S

Liao pottery ewers of this shape are rare.

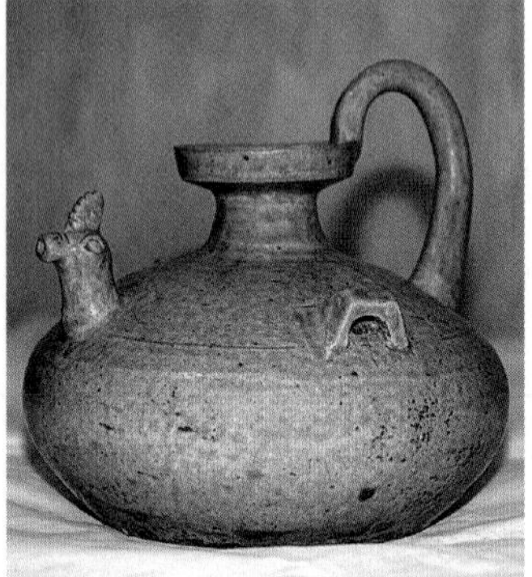

A pottery wine pourer, the spout in the form of a chicken's head, Jin Dynasty, 1115–1234, 5½in (14cm) high.

£3,250–3,650 A&C

A Yingqing ewer, Southern Song Dynasty, 1127–1279, 7in (18cm) high.

£1,050–1,200 BOW

A Chinese Imari ewer and basin, in the form of a shell, c1730, ewer 12¼in (31cm) high.

£13,200–15,800 S

► **A Chinese export porcelain covered cider jug,** decorated with two American eagles with stars, cannons and symbols of armed might beneath a band of flowers and fruit, gilt initials 'HC' under spout, with a strap handle, 1800–25, 11in (28cm) high.

£71,000–85,000 NAAW

Chinese export cider jugs, with original covers, are quite rare. Porcelain decorated with such a fine example of the American eagle is even rarer. This exceptional jug, dating from the early 19th century, is a superb example of export porcelain for the American market.

FIGURES

A pottery figure of a soldier, Han Dynasty, 206 BC – AD 220, 18½in (47cm) high.

£2,400–2,700 A&C

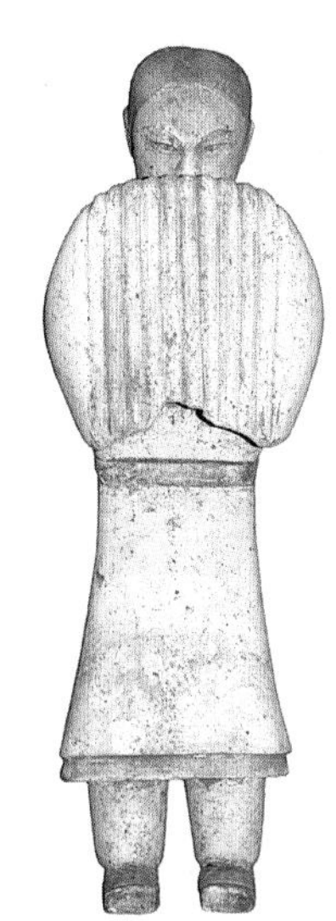

A pottery figure of a man, Han Dynasty, 206 BC – AD 220, 21in (54cm) high.

£720–820 A&C

A pottery figure of a kneeling maiden, decorated with earth pigments, Oxford T/L tested, slight damage and restoration, Han Dynasty, 206 BC – AD 220, 13in (33cm) high, on a wooden stand.

£2,700–3,200 WW

A cream-glazed figure of a man, Sui Dynasty, AD 581–618, 12in (30.5cm) high.

£2,700–3,000 GLD

A pottery figure of a lady, coated with slip and detailed with paint, Tang Dynasty, AD 618–907, 14in (35.5cm) high.

£1,350–1,500 SOO

A pottery figure of an attendant, with painted decoration, Tang Dynasty, AD 618–907, 9½in (24cm) high.

£175–210 DN(BR)

A Qingbai figure of a Daoist deity, in a pierced grotto, the entrance flanked by a bird and a candlestick, Song Dynasty, AD 960–1279, 5½in (14cm) high.

£6,000–7,200 S

Beginning with the Song Dynasty, devotional shrines and figures became a very popular product in the Jingdezhen kilns; however, it is rare to find a Qingbai shrine of this unusual design.

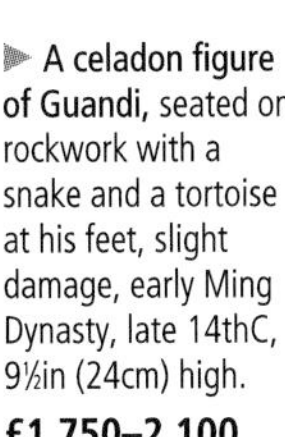

▶ **A celadon figure of Guandi,** seated on rockwork with a snake and a tortoise at his feet, slight damage, early Ming Dynasty, late 14thC, 9½in (24cm) high.

£1,750–2,100 WW

Guandi (Guan Yu) was a great general in the 2nd century AD, who later became worshipped as Guandi, the Chinese God of War.

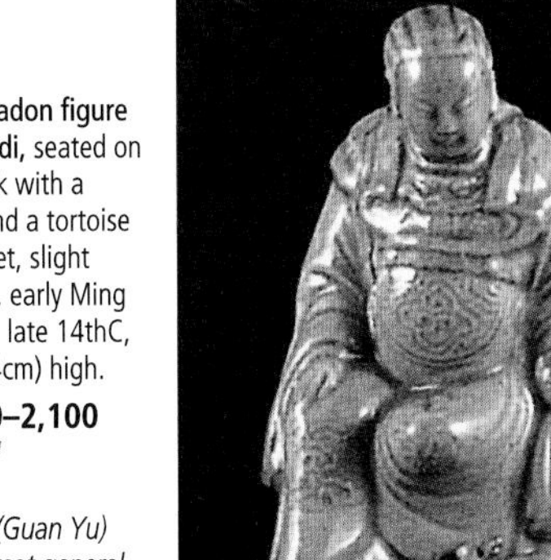

◀ **A terracotta figure,** Ming Dynasty, 8in (20.5cm) high.

£160–180 BOW

A terracotta figure, Ming Dynasty, 7½in (19cm) high.

£160–180 BOW

A *famille verte* biscuit figural group of He He Erxien, restored, Kangxi period, 1662–1722, 5½in (14cm) high.

£1,150–1,300 G&G

The He He Erxien are the twin genii of mirth and harmony, and patron deities of merchants, potters and lime burners.

A *blanc-de-Chine* figure of Buddha, Kangxi period, 1662–1722, 7in (18cm) high.

£2,900–3,450 WW

Blanc-de-Chine *is a white, or near-white, porcelain with a thick, rich glaze. It was made in the Dehua area of China from the late Ming Dynasty, particularly in the manufacture of figures for export during the 17th and 18th centuries.*

A Dehua figure of Guanyin, marked, Qianlong period, 1736–95, 20in (51cm) high.

£11,000–13,200 S(NY)

Dehua Guanyin figures wearing such elaborately carved crowns are rare. This piece, with its naturalistic and detailed sculpting of the Goddess of Mercy is especially fine.

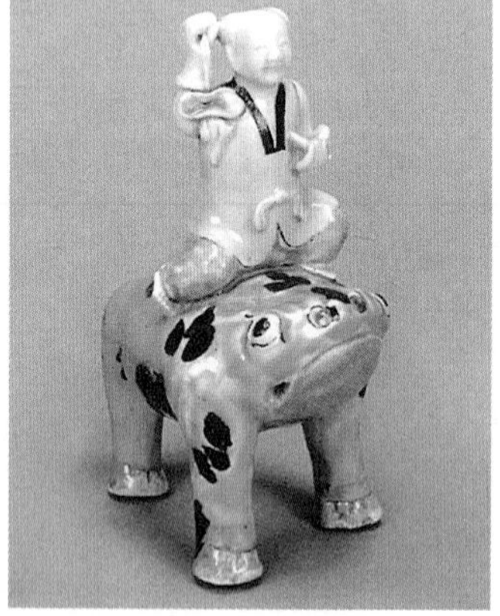

A *famille rose* figure of Liu Hai seated on a toad, Qianlong period, 1736–95, 6¼in (16cm) high.

£330–390 DN

Lui Hai was the God of Wealth and Successful Undertakings and, according to legend, was a government minister in the 10th century. It was claimed that he had a three-legged toad, a symbol of making money, on which he could ride anywhere.

A figure of a seated Buddha, holding a sack at his side, with enamelled decoration, Qianlong period, 1736–95, 5¾in (14.5cm) high.

£7,200–8,600 S

In Chinese Buddhism the figure of Budai is also known as the Loving or Friendly One. Budai was a wandering monk from the 9th century who, upon his death, revealed himself as the Bodhisattva Maitreya in disguise. He is believed to be the incarnation of the Future Buddha. His pleasing human features combined with the population's wish for hope and salvation make him one of the most popular Buddhist deities. During the 16th century Budai was canonized as the 16th and last Chinese bodhisattva. Budai is also associated with children as he often carries a sack filled with presents and is frequently depicted with children. He is worshipped as a god of good luck and prosperity and is also called the Laughing Buddha. Budai's good nature is a symbol of philosophical contentment and figures of Budai are always placed in the most prominent hall of the Buddhist temples.

A porcelain *famille rose* figural censer, one hand missing, Qing Dynasty, 18thC, 10in (25.5cm) high.

£1,000–1,200 BUK

A porcelain group of a happy couple, from the *Diana* cargo, partially glazed, Jiaqing period, 1817, 2½in (6.5cm) high.

£95–110 RBA

◀ A figure of a seated boy, from the *Tek Sing* cargo, with a glazed stomach, Daoquang period, 1822, 3in (7.5cm) high.

£1,350–1,500 RBA

FLATWARE

A **Longquan celadon charger,** with carved decoration, Ming Dynasty, 16½in (42cm) diam.

£2,100–2,500 S(NY)

A **charger,** painted with floral decoration, Ming Dynasty, 14in (35.5cm) diam.

£1,600–1,800 RGa

A ***Ko-Sometsuke* dish,** the centre decorated with a branch of peaches enclosed by a brown rim, Ming Dynasty, Tianqi period, 1621–27, 8in (20.5cm) diam.

£1,000–1,200 DN

Ko-Sometsuke is a Japanese term for old blue and white decoration. These pieces were made for the Japanese market for use in the tea ceremony.

A **moulded dish,** the centre painted with a cockerel and hen among lotus and bamboo, *fuku* mark, Ming Dynasty, Tianqi period, 1621–27, 6½in (16.5cm) diam.

£1,750–2,100 WW

A **porcelain saucer dish,** decorated with dragons on an enamel ground, six character mark, Kangxi period, 1662–1722, 8¾in (22cm) diam.

£3,650–4,350 DN

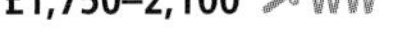

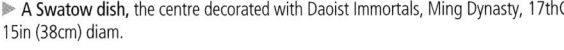

▶ A **Swatow dish,** the centre decorated with Daoist Immortals, Ming Dynasty, 17thC, 15in (38cm) diam.

£4,550–5,450 S(NY)

Swatow dishes with this type of design are quite rare. The scene illustrated on this dish is of Zhong Lijian, the head of the Eight Immortals. He is depicted as a fat man with a magic fan that revives people who have died.

◀ A ***famille verte* dish,** the centre painted with blue flowers, slight damage, Kangxi period, 1662–1722, 13¾in (35cm) diam.

£1,400–1,600 G&G

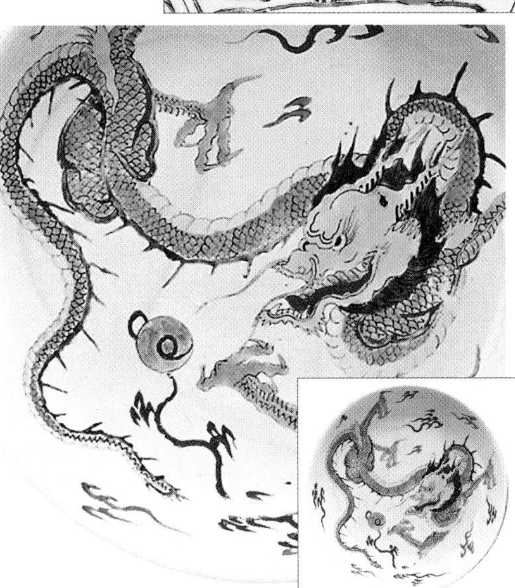

A ***famille verte* charger,** painted with a dragon chasing a flaming pearl, on a channelled foot, Kangxi period, 1662–1722, 13½in (34.5cm) diam.

£2,900–3,450 S(NY)

▶ A ***famille verte* charger,** painted with figures and panels of mythical beasts, slight damage, fungus mark, Kangxi period, 1662–1722, 14¾in (37.5cm) diam.

£2,600–3,100 WW

A *famille verte* **dish,** with a pie-crust rim, decorated with a lady and attendant boy, within a floral border with cartouches containing butterflies, Kangxi period, 1662–1722, 13¾in (35cm) diam.

£990–1,100 G&G

A *famille verte* **dish,** with a moulded rim, decorated with two figures in a garden, slight damage, Kangxi period, 1662–1722, 9½in (24cm) diam.

£530–630 DN

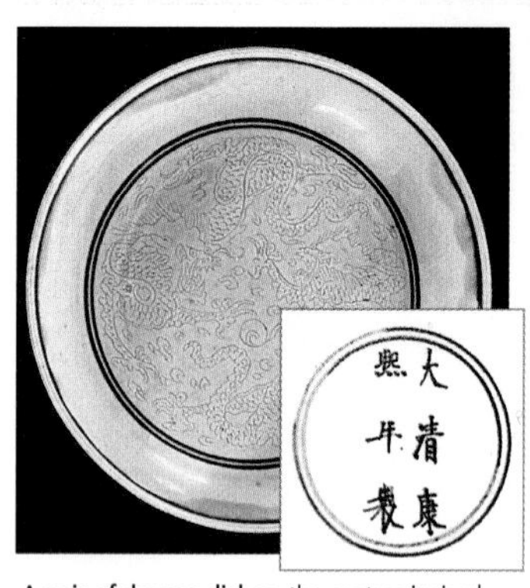

A pair of dragon dishes, the centres incised with two dragons in pursuit of a flaming pearl, the exterior with four sprays of grapevines, marked, Kangxi period, 1662–1722, 5¼in (13.5cm) diam.

£4,800–5,700 S

These dishes are Imperial pieces and consequently are sought after.

A charger, decorated with birds, insects and flowers, Kangxi period, 1662–1722, 14½in (37cm) diam.

£470–560 JNic

A saucer dish, decorated with scholars examining a scroll, slight damage, Kangxi period, 1662–1722, 6½in (16.5cm) diam.

£400–450 G&G

A ruby-backed ***famille rose*** **dish,** painted with a seated maiden and three children playing with rabbits, within a scale and trellis border, slight damage, repaired, Yongzheng period, 1723–35, 8in (20.5cm) diam.

£175–210 RTo

◄ **An armorial plate,** decorated with a coat-of-arms, Qing Dynasty, Yongzheng period, c1724, 8¾in (22cm) diam.

£820–980 WW

► **A pair of Chinese export porcelain** ***famille rose*** **tureen stands,** each painted with two birds, a tree and a peony in a fenced garden, Qianlong period, 1736–95, 9¾in (25cm) wide.

£730–870 RTo

A Chinese export meat dish, decorated with a river landscape within a Fitzhugh-type border, Qianlong period, 1736–95, 19¼in (49cm) wide.

£530–630 DN

The Fitzhugh pattern is characterized by a border of four split pomegranates and butterflies and was made for the American market, being named after the person first who ordered it.

A Chinese export charger, the body decorated with an island landscape within a floral and cell diaper border, Qianlong period, 1736–95, 18in (45.5cm) diam.

£400–480 Hal

A plate, from the Nanking cargo, painted with a peony and flowering pomegranate, Qianlong period, c1750, 9in (23cm) diam.

£340–380 RBA

A pair of Chinese export soup dishes, c1800, 8¾in (22cm) diam.

£270–300 WALP

A *famille rose* porcelain dish, the centre painted with flowers within a fruit, flower and insect border, damaged, Qianlong period, 1736–95, 16½in (42cm) diam.

£120–140 DN(BR)

A Nanking charger, Qianlong period, c1770, 15in (38cm) diam.

£290–330 PeN

A dish, from the *Tek Sing* cargo, decorated with chrysanthemums issuing from rockwork, inscribed with a poem, 1822, 6in (15cm) diam.

£115–130 RBA

A set of four *famille rose* plates, each enamelled with a central spray of flowers within a gilt chain border, Qianlong period, 1736–95, 9¾in (25cm) diam.

£210–250 HYD

A Nanking porcelain plate, Qianlong period, c1790, 17in (43cm) wide.

£340–380 GSA

Chinese porcelain was made in Jingdezhen and then shipped to Nanking for loading onto the tea clippers, for sale in Europe. As the wares were exported from Nanking they became known by the generic term 'Nanking' which referred to this standard underglaze blue type of decoration. The 'Nanking cargo' was so named because the porcelain on board the Dutch East India Company's ship Geldermalsen *was of this type. See page 237 for further information on the Nanking cargo.*

A set of five Canton *famille rose* graduated meat plates, decorated with figures within borders of flowers, foliage, fruit and insects, Qing Dynasty, early 19thC, largest 16¾in (42.5cm) wide.

£4,450–5,300 WW

A pair of saucer dishes, decorated with panels of flower sprigs on a sgraffito ground, one with slight damage, marked, Guangxu period, 1875–1908, 7¾in (19.5cm) diam.

£410–490 WW

GARDEN SEATS

A *famille rose* **garden seat,** the top pierced with a cash medallion, painted in enamels with stylized chrysanthemums among *lingzhi* scrolls with a key-fret border, the sides decorated with precious objects, Qianlong period, c1750, 8¾in (22cm) high.

£6,000–7,200 S

A pair of garden seats, decorated with pierced cash symbols and scrolling lotus, one with slight damage, Qing Dynasty, 18thC, 18½in (47cm) high.

£3,300–3,900 WW

A pair of Canton garden seats, decorated with figural courtyard scenes flanked by pierced medallions, Qing Dynasty, 19thC, 18in (45.5cm) high.

£760–910 SK

JARS

◀ **A Yue funerary jar,** the cover in the form of a pavilion, above a roof with four turrets and a flock of birds, over an architectural tier with two gateways guarded by crouching bears, flanked by haloed figures of Buddha, the body applied with moulded riders and *faux* mask-and-ring handles, Western Jin Dynasty, 3rdC AD, 16in (40.5cm) high.

£13,000–15,600 S(NY)

The Yue district is in northern Zhejiang Province in eastern China.

▶ **A Qingbai jar,** Southern Song Dynasty, 1127–1279, 4in (10cm) high.

£11,700–14,000 S(NY)

This exquisite form appears to be very rare.

◀ **A Ding jar and cover,** the body incised with two lotus heads and foliage, Northern Song Dynasty, AD 960–1127, 4¾in (12cm) high.

£12,300–14,700 S(NY)

A stoneware amphora, with a partial cream glaze, Tang Dynasty, AD 618–906, 18in (45.5cm) high.

£1,500–1,700 SOO

Longquan celadons

The Longquan kilns were the most prolific of the Song Dynasty, established after 1127 when the capital was established at Hangzhou. Over 50 kilns have been located. The output of these kilns was enormous – not only to supply the home market but also large quantities were exported to Japan and throughout southeast Asia. The body of the wares is stoneware and the glaze is an opaque celadon green with great depth and can be crackled or smooth. The ware is reduction fired at a temperature of 1200 degrees centigrade, which brings out the colour from a small quantity of iron oxide. The kilns continued production throughout the Yuan Dynasty and into the Ming Dynasty.

A Longquan celadon jar, carved with vertical ribs, the interior base plate moulded with a three-leaf medallion, with a wooden cover, Yuan/Ming Dynasty, 14thC, 12¾in (32.5cm) diam.

£7,100–8,500 S(NY)

A Fahua jar, decorated with the legend of the Eight Daoist Immortals' visit to Shoulao, between a *ruyi* lappet band enclosing the Eight Precious Things and a lotus-lappet band, with a wooden cover and stand, Ming Dynasty, Hongzhi/Zhengde period, 1488–1521, 16in (40.5cm) high.

£18,000–21,600 S

Shoulao is the Star God of Longevity. The three star gods (Health, Wealth and Longevity) are the three most senior gods.

A porcelain jar, slight damage, Ming Dynasty, Wanli period, 1573–1619, 9¾in (25cm) high.

£3,550–4,250 BUK

A jar, painted with lotus blooms on scrolling leaf stems, Ming Dynasty, Wanli period, 1573–1619, 13¼in (33.5cm) high.

£3,600–4,300 S

A jar, painted with lotus flowers, foliage and *chilong* within leaf-shaped bands, Transitional period, c1650, 8½in (21.5cm) high.

£2,850–3,400 S

A porcelain jar and cover, slight damage, Kangxi period, c1670, 18in (45.5cm) high.

£3,150–3,500 GLD

◀ **A jar and cover,** with floral decoration and emblems, the foot with upright lappets, 17thC, 31½in (80cm) high.

£11,000–13,200 S(NY)

This jar achieved a high price because of its large size, very attractive decoration with even colour, it is in excellent condition and has retained its original cover.

▶ **A jar,** painted with a continuous rocky landscape and figures in a lakeside scene, Kangxi period, 1662–1722, 8½in (21.5cm) high.

£1,900–2,250 S

JARDINIERES

A *famille rose* **jardinière,** the panelled sides painted with birds and insects among tree peonies and blossoms, on a pierced base, damaged, Qing Dynasty, Qianlong period, 1736–95, 15in (38cm) diam.

£1,650–1,950 N

A porcelain jardinière, decorated with reserves of birds and peonies, Qing Dynasty, late 18thC, 21¼in (54cm) diam.

£1,750–2,100 S(P)

A Chinese export *famille rose* **jardinière,** painted with vases of flowers, baskets of fruit, censers and precious objects, with a metal liner, drilled for drainage, 19thC, 9½in (24cm) high.

£1,450–1,700 S(NY)

TEAPOTS & WINE POTS

A teapot and cover, painted with vases and flowers, restored, gold wax seal for Duveen, Liverpool, Kangxi period, 1662–1722, 6½in (16.5cm) high.

£1,400–1,650 WW

A Yixing teapot and cover, decorated with robin's-egg glaze, the cover with a lotus-bud knop, indistinct seal mark, Qing Dynasty, 18thC, 5½in (14cm) high.

£1,400–1,650 S

The Yixing area is particularly famous for purple clay teapots and scholars' tableware. The high kaolin content of the clay used allowed pieces to be fired to a high temperature to give a strong, stone-like quality.

A *famille rose* wine pot and cover, the body decorated with lotus flowers and Buddhist knots, the neck with a band of cloud scrolls, the base with a band of stiff leaves, restored, gilt mark, Qianlong period, 1736–95, 5¾in (14.5cm) high.

£36,000–43,000 DN

This is an Imperial wine pot, made for the use of the Emperor, and therefore rare.

A teapot and cover, from the Nanking cargo, decorated in the Imari palette with flowers, some wear, Qianlong period, c1750, 4½in (11.5cm) high.

£450–500 RBA

A Chinese export teapot and cover, decorated with a version of the Valentine pattern depicting two love birds and a quiver of arrows, slight damage, Qianlong period, 1736–95, 8in (20.5cm) wide.

£270–320 Hal

A Canton *famille rose* teapot and cover, decorated with panels of figures, birds and insects, 19thC, 5½in (14cm) high.

£120–140 WW

TUREENS

A pair of Chinese export porcelain *famille rose* tureens, covers and stands, the covers with knops in the form of a rose, damaged and restored, Qianlong period, 1736–95, 10¾in (27.5cm) wide.

£6,200–7,400 BUK

A tureen, cover and stand, with lotus-pod handles and painted with scenes of figures among garden pavilions, the cover with a pomegranate knop, Qianlong period, 1736–95, stand 15in (38cm) wide.

£1,400–1,650 S

A porcelain tureen, cover and stand, painted with flowers and gilt bands, Qing Dynasty, late 18thC, 11in (28cm) diam.

£280–330 AH

► **A Canton *famille rose* tureen and cover,** decorated with figures within borders of flowers, leaves, insects and fruit, knop regilded, Qing Dynasty, early 19thC, 13¾in (35cm) wide.

£2,350–2,800 WW

A Canton *famille rose* tureen and cover, the exterior and interior decorated with figures within borders of flowers, fruit, foliage and insects, Qing Dynasty, early 19thC, 13in (33cm) wide.

£1,050–1,250 WW

VASES

A double gourd vase, Tang Dynasty, AD 618–907, 10in (25.5cm) high.

£4,550–5,400 S(NY)

It is unusual to find gourd-shaped bottles covered in such a vibrant green glaze.

A Cizhou-style vase, with sgraffito decoration of peonies, T/L tested, Jin Dynasty, 1115–1234, 11½in (29cm) high.

£8,400–10,000 S(NY)

MILLER'S COMPARES

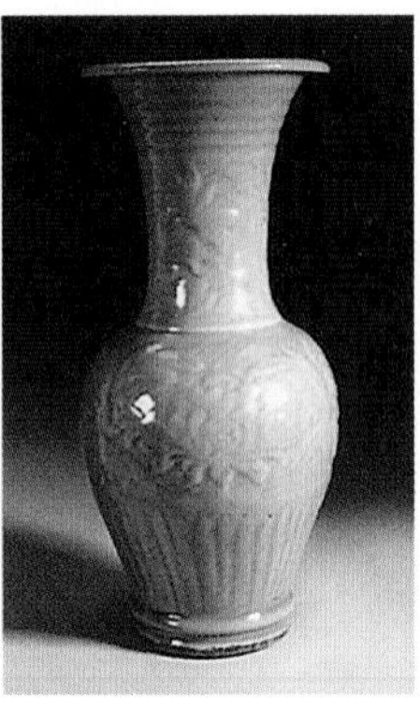

I. A celadon *yenyen* vase, moulded with lotus blooms, impressed flower mark, Ming Dynasty, 16thC, 19¼in (49cm) high.

£9,600–11,500 S

II. A celadon *yenyen* vase, incised with two medallions enclosing lotus blooms, Ming Dynasty, Wanli period, c1600, 18¾in (47.5cm) high.

£1,900–2,250 S

Item I is slightly larger and is better potted than Item II, which shows slight irregularities of shape. The decoration on Item I is much finer and encompasses the whole vase whereas Item II bears a medallion on each side on a diaper ground. Item I also has a very even glaze which is stylistic of earlier manufacture.

◄ **A vase,** painted with panels of stylized deer, slight damage, Ming Dynasty, 17thC, 3¼in (8.5cm) high.

£350–420 WW

► **A silver-mounted vase and cover,** decorated with a dragon, a fence and bamboo, Transitional period, c1650, 11in (28cm) high.

£1,400–1,650 JNic

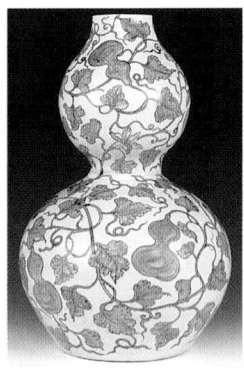

A double gourd vase, Yuan Dynasty, c1350, 18¾in (47.5cm) high.

£3,000,000–3,600,000 WW

Ex-Alexander Collection. William Cleverley Alexander was one of the most noted connoisseurs of his day, an accomplished draughtsman and a member of the Burlington Fine Arts Club. He was renowned for his taste in Western paintings and Asian works of art. His collection was started in 1867 and included items from the Tang, Song, Ming and Qing Dynasties. This piece was purchased in 1900 which was a very early time for a piece of Yuan blue and white to have reached England and an adventurous choice for a collector at the time. Yuan blue and white had not then been identified and the vase would probably have puzzled the authorities of the day. The beauty, rarity, condition and provenance of this vase all contributed to a price considerably higher than the estimate set by the auctioneers. Good Yuan Dynasty porcelain rarely comes on the open market, but by chance, just three days earlier, another exceptional Yuan jar was sold at Christie's in London for £14,000,000. This probably contributed to this vase achieving a record price for a provincial auction house.

Further reading

Miller's Chinese & Japanese Antiques Buyers Guide, **Miller's Publications, 2004**

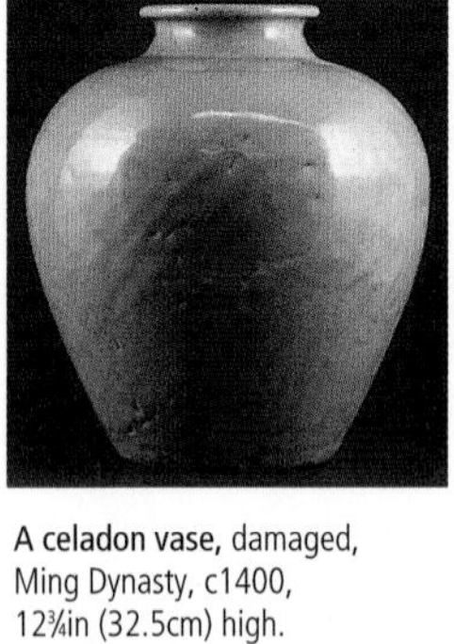

A celadon vase, damaged, Ming Dynasty, c1400, 12¾in (32.5cm) high.

£330–390 WW

A pair of *meiping* vases, one depicting dragons, the other with phoenix, Ming Dynasty, Wanli period, 1573–1619, 12½in (32cm) high.

£3,550–4,250 S(NY)

A *rouleau* vase, decorated with fish, Kangxi period, 1662–1722, 10¼in (26cm) high.

£4,250–5,100 WW

A *rouleau* vase, decorated with The Three Friends of Winter in a garden, Kangxi period, 1662–1722, 17¼in (44cm) high.
£4,800–5,700 S

The Three Friends of Winter are pine, prunus and bamboo. The prunus (wild plum) is the first to flower, often as early as January.

A pair of soft-paste beaker vases, incised with peonies, impressed mark, Kangxi period, 1662–1722, 16¼in (41.5cm) high.
£4,850–5,800 S(NY)

A pair of vases, painted with maidens in palace gardens, adapted for electricity, one damaged and repaired, Kangxi period, 1662–1722, 12in (30.5cm) high.
£3,300–3,950 L

A porcelain baluster vase, painted with lotus blossoms, damaged, Kangxi period, 1662–1722, 15½in (39.5cm) high.
£470–560 G(L)

► **A porcelain vase,** from the Vung Tau cargo, decorated with donkeys, figures and a rocky cove, Kangxi period, c1690, 5in (12.5cm) high.
£450–500 RBA

The Vung Tau cargo was salvaged from a Chinese junk that foundered off the coast of Vietnam, south of Vung Tao c1696.

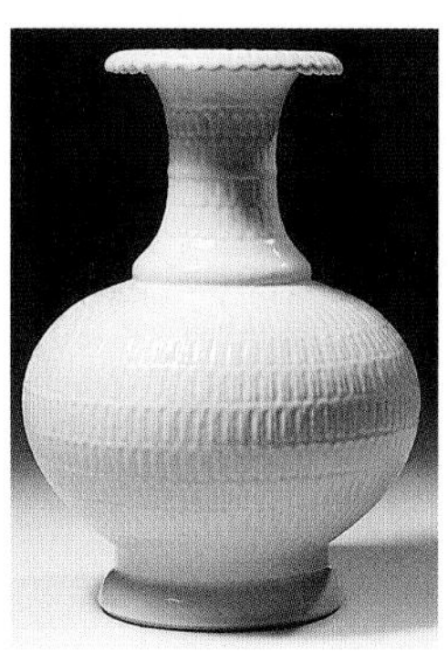
A bottle vase, with incised decoration, Qing Dynasty, 18thC, 12½in (32cm) high.
£5,200–6,200 S(NY)

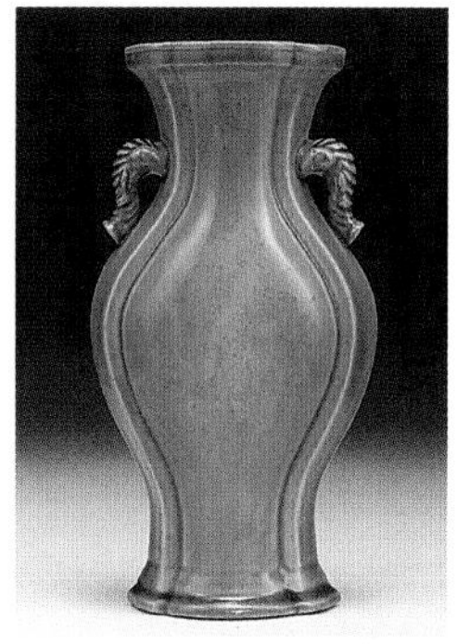
A *hu* vase, with two handles in the form of stylized elephant heads, 18thC, 9¾in (25cm) high.
£2,250–2,700 S(NY)

◄ **A pair of Canton porcelain baluster vases,** decorated with figural panels, Qing Dynasty, 18thC, 11in (28cm) high.
£870–1,050 MA&I

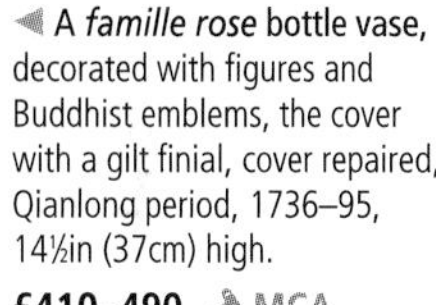
◄ **A *famille rose* bottle vase,** decorated with figures and Buddhist emblems, the cover with a gilt finial, cover repaired, Qianlong period, 1736–95, 14½in (37cm) high.
£410–490 MCA

A garniture of five *famille rose* baluster vases, decorated with panels of figures, on a chicken skin ground, one damaged, one repaired, Qianlong period, 1736–95, 9¾in (25cm) high.
£2,700–3,200 DN

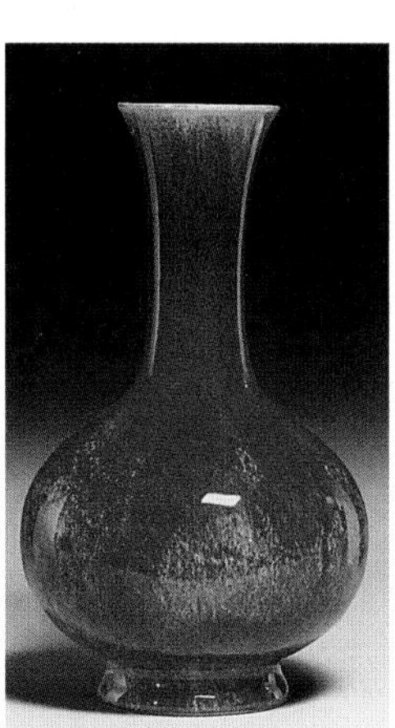
► **A flambé bottle vase,** seal mark, Qianlong period, 1736–95, 10½in (26.5cm) high.
£5,200–6,200 S(NY)

It is extremely rare to find a flambé glazed vase of this form with the mark and of the period of Qianlong. This vase is particularly striking with its vivid contrasting glaze colours.

A *famille rose* baluster vase, decorated with a figure on horseback and a lady in a carriage, Qianlong period, 1736–95, 14½in (37cm) high.
£1,500–1,800 DN

A Chinese export vase, decorated with peonies, Qianlong period, 1736–95, 7in (18cm) high.
£370–440 HYD

A pair of vases, with lotus decoration, mounted as lamps, Qing Dynasty, 18th–19thC, 21in (53.5cm) high.
£6,500–7,800 S(NY)

► **A Ming-style vase,** painted with lotus flowerheads on a foliate vine, 18th–19thC, 19¼in (49cm) high.
£4,850–5,800 S(NY)

A pair of porcelain bottle vases, decorated with stylized *mon* within panelled borders, Guangxu mark, 1875–1908, 15½in (39.5cm) high.
£5,200–6,200 DN(BR)

► **A pair of Canton vases,** enamelled with insects, flowers and leaves, with gilt handles and pierced covers, one vase restored, Qing Dynasty, 19thC, 8½in (21.5cm) high.
£1,000–1,200 G(L)

A Canton vase, painted with figures, the two handles in the form of mythological beasts, Qing Dynasty, 19thC, 25in (63.5cm) high.
£730–870 CGC

A baluster vase, decorated with scribes and prophets in a garden, marked, Qing Dynasty, 19thC, 14in (35.5cm) high.
£940–1,100 Hal

A *famille rose yenyen* vase, painted with floral sprigs beneath a basket weave lattice, potter's mark, 19thC, 17¾in (45cm) high.
£1,100–1,300 S(NY)

A Canton vase and cover, the finial in the form of a seated figure with a barrel seat and a wine pot, with two handles in the form of seated figures on lotus plinths, Qing Dynasty, 1850–1900, 22in (56cm) high.
£3,500–4,200 DN

A pair of Canton porcelain *famille rose* vases, decorated with panels of flowers, precious objects and butterflies, each applied with four gilt lion-mask handles, Qing Dynasty, mid-19thC, 18in (45.5cm) high.
£960–1,150 RTo

◄ **A pottery vase,** decorated with panels of figures and birds, pseudo Chenghua mark, Qing Dynasty, c1900, 23½in (59.5cm) high.
£530–630 Hal

► **A celadon baluster vase,** incised with a dragon, drilled for conversion to a lamp, on a carved hardwood stand, Qing Dynasty, c1900, 17½in (44.5cm) high.
£120–140 PFK

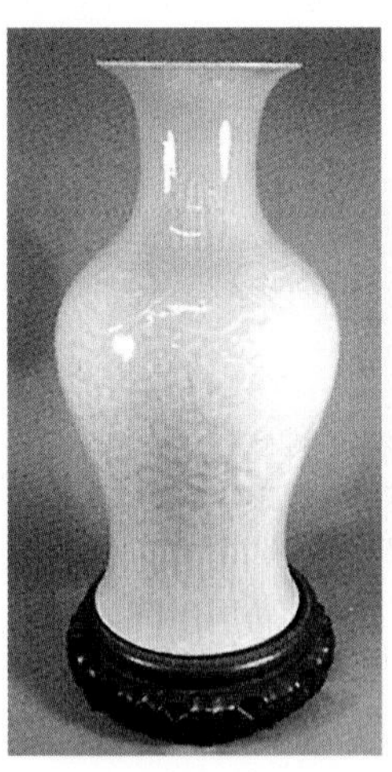

MISCELLANEOUS

A Chinese export porcelain *famille rose* basket, painted with lotus and peonies, slight damage, Qianlong period, c1750, 15in (38cm) wide.

£3,450–4,100 S(NY)

Ex-Estate of Laurance S. Rockefeller. For information on this collection please see page 20.

A Chinese export miniature chamber pot, from the Nanking cargo, decorated with branches of peonies and stylized foliage, Qianlong period, c1750, 6½in (16.5cm) wide.

£350–420 HYD

A gilt-metal-mounted porcelain cistern, decorated with birds and flowers, damaged, early 17thC, 14½in (37cm) high.

£1,750–2,100 G(L)

A food pot, painted with furniture and utensils, with two bronze handles, cover missing, Kangxi period, 1662–1722, 8½in (21.5cm) high.

£820–980 BWL

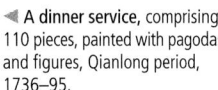

A dinner service, comprising 110 pieces, painted with pagodas and figures, Qianlong period, 1736–95.

£9,000–10,800 S

A porcelain *famille rose* plaque, painted with two ladies in a garden, Qing Dynasty, 19thC, in a gilt frame, 9¼ x 14½in (23.5 x 37cm).

£260–310 AH

A set of pottery miniature furniture, comprising two chairs and a table, Ming Dynasty, table 8in (20.5cm) wide.

£810–900 BOW

A pair of Canton porcelain *famille rose* tazze, one with slight damage, engraved marks, Qing Dynasty, c1870, 7in (18cm) wide.

£165–195 SWO

A Chinese export tray, decorated with herons in a garden, Qianlong period, 1736–95, 13¾in (35cm) wide.

£1,000–1,200 BUK

An artist's porcelain paintbrush wall pocket, decorated in enamels with figures on a veranda, Qing Dynasty, 18thC, 4½in (11.5cm) high.

£470–560 MAL(O)

A pair of Chinese export Meissen-style porcelain wine coolers, with painted and gilt floral decoration, damaged, restored, Qianlong period, c1780, 8¼in (21cm) high.

£1,900–2,250 S(NY)

Ex-Estate of Laurance S. Rockefeller.

JAPANESE CERAMICS

ANIMALS

A pair of Hirado models of tigers, 19thC, 6in (15cm) long.

£1,250–1,400 GLD

A porcelain *netsuke*, in the form of a monkey, 19thC, 1¼in (3cm) high.

£430–480 BOW

A Hirado porcelain model of a seated monkey, with incised detail, impressed seal mark, Meiji period, 1868–1911, 5½in (14cm) high.

£960–1,150 RTo

BOWLS

An Arita bowl, c1700, 11in (28cm) diam.

£430–480 K&M

A stoneware bowl, painted with a stylized prunus tree, damaged and repaired, 18thC, 8¼in (21cm) diam.

£140–165 WW

A porcelain bowl, decorated with a *shishi* and a tree, 19thC, 15¾in (40cm) diam.

£175–210 DMC

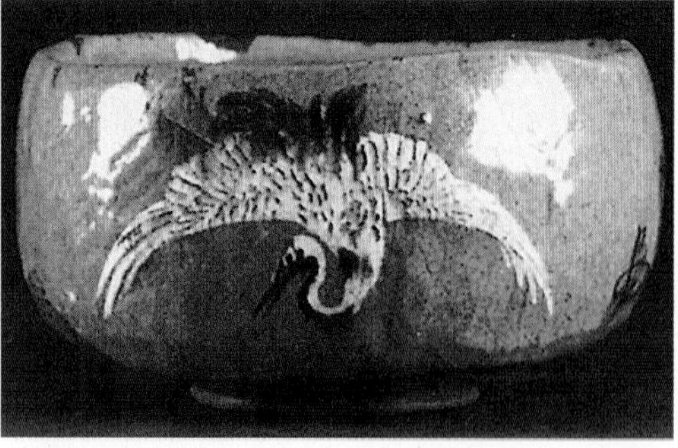

A pottery bowl, decorated with a crane and two *minogame*, repaired, 19thC, 5½in (14cm) diam.

£190–220 WW

A Satsuma bowl, by Yabu Meizan, decorated with flowers, the interior decorated with butterflies, signature seal, Meiji period, 1868–1911, 4¾in (12cm) diam.

£3,650–4,350 HYD

Yabu Meizan (1853–1934) was a famous Kyoto porcelain painter who specialized in the Satsuma brocade style.

Japanese chronology chart

Jomon (Neolithic) period	c10,000–100 BC
Yayoi period	c200 BC–AD 200
Tumulus (Kofun) period	200–552
Asuka period	552–710
Nara period	710–794
Heian period	794–1185
Kamakura period	1185–1333
Muromachi (Ashikaga) period	1333–1568
Momoyama period	1568–1600
Edo (Tokugawa) period	1600–1868
Genroku period	*1688–1703*
Meiji period	1868–1911
Taisho period	1912–1926
Showa period	1926–1989

FLATWARE

A pair of Arita Kakiemon-style porcelain plates, painted with a pair of long-tailed birds, the rim with birds and flowering branches, one with slight damage, c1700, 8¼in (21cm) diam.

£1,350–1,600 RTo

A set of four Imari dishes, decorated with gourds, flowers, cranes and trees, one restored, 19thC, 11¾in (30cm) diam.

£260–310 WW

An Imari charger, decorated with two *bijin* in a garden and panels of phoenix, 19thC, 16in (40.5cm) diam.

£350–420 Hal

A Satsuma bowl, decorated with figures, Meiji period, 1868–1911, 6¼in (16cm) diam.

£300–360 WW

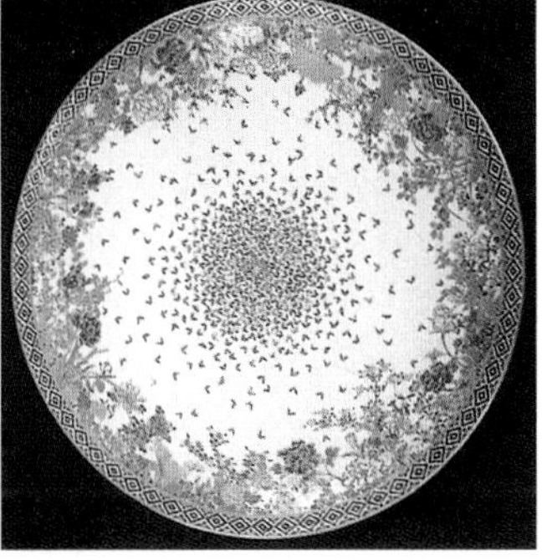

A Satsuma plate, by Yabu Meizan, decorated with butterflies and flowers, signature seal, Meiji period, 1868–1911, 8½in (21.5cm) diam.

£3,000–3,600 HYD

A pair of Imari chargers, decorated with panels of flowers and landscapes, 19thC, 17¾in (45cm) diam.

£470–560 L&E

◄ **An Imari dish,** c1890, 22in (56cm) diam.

£450–500 GSA

► **An Imari charger,** painted with a jardinière, flowers and birds, Meiji period, 1868–1911, 24in (61cm) diam.

£820–980 BAM(M)

KOROS

A Satsuma *koro* and cover, decorated with ladies and children looking at an aquarium, the reverse with a lakeside scene, slight damage, Meiji period, 1868–1911, 5½in (14cm) high.

£470–560 WW

A Satsuma *koro* and cover, with serpent handles, painted with figures in a garden, on a hardwood stand, Meiji period, 1868–1911, 9in (23cm) high.

£470–560 G(L)

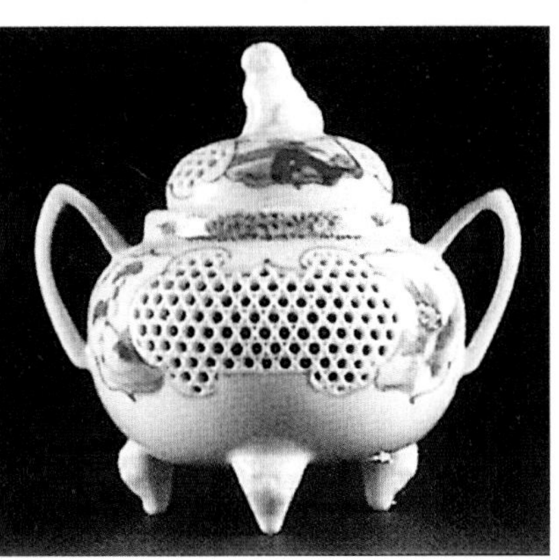

A Hirado *koro* and cover, with pierced decoration and painted with landscapes, c1900, 5in (12.5cm) high.

£140–165 WW

VASES

An Arita vase, decorated with a tiger and a dragon, with a replacement Delft cover, c1700, 20¾in (52.5cm) high.

£4,550–5,400 S

An Arita vase and cover, painted with exotic birds in gardens, c1700, 18¾in (47.5cm) high.

£1,400–1,650 CGC

An Imari inverted baluster vase, 19thC, 17¾in (45cm) high.

£175–210 AMB

A Satsuma pottery vase and cover, painted with birds and flowers, moulded with ribbon-tied *faux* drapes, on a hardwood stand, signed, 19thC, 12¾in (32.5cm) high.

£400–480 AH

A Satsuma vase, painted with cockerels, hens and chicks, impressed marks for Kinkozan, Meiji period, 1868–1911, 14¼in (36cm) high.

£3,750–4,500 WW

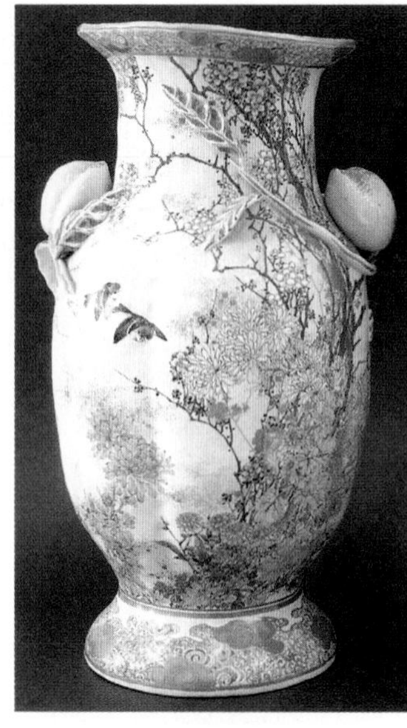

► **A pair of Satsuma vases,** painted with birds and flowers, each with two peach handles, impressed marks, Meiji period, 1868–1911, 13½in (34.5cm) high.

£230–270 G(L)

An Imari vase and cover, decorated with figures in a pavilion, pseudo seal mark, late Meiji period, c1900, 37¾in (96cm) high.

£4,250–5,100 TEN

A Satsuma vase, decorated with a Samurai warrior, signed, c1890, 13in (33cm) high.

£740–830 GSA

A pair of vases, decorated with panels of geisha, children and Samurai warriors, signed, late 19thC, 15in (38cm) high.

£1,000–1,200 HAD

An Arita porcelain vase, decorated with birds and peonies, c1900, 30¾in (78cm) high.

£500–600 Bea

A pair of Kaburagi Kutani vases, painted with figures, maker's mark, c1900, 10¼in (26cm) high.

£210–250 WAD

Kaburagi is a workshop in Kutani.

A pair of vases, with banded decoration, c1900, 12¼in (31cm) high.

£330–390 DN

A pair of Satsuma vases, decorated with panels of figures before Mount Fuji within gilt borders, signed, early 20thC, 8in (20.5cm) high.

£165–195 Hal

A pair of Fukagawa vases, painted with phoenix, early 20thC, 10¼in (26cm) high.

£100–120 WAD

A pair of porcelain vases, decorated with birds, flowers and prunus trees, 14¾in (37.5cm) high.

£430–510 WAD

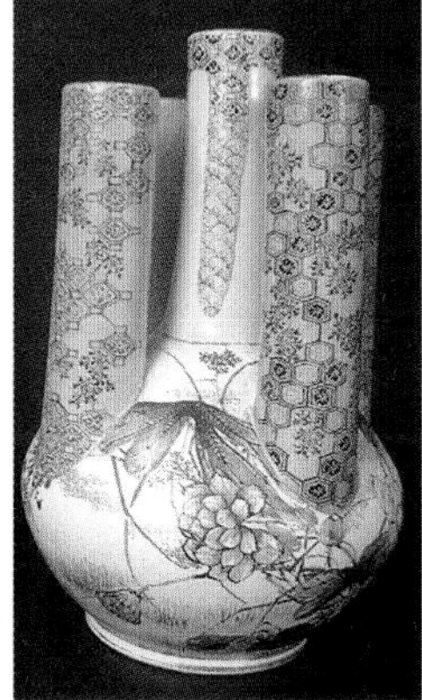

A pair of Satsuma crocus vases, each with five necks, decorated with lotus flowers and seed heads, signed, early 20thC, 8in (20.5cm) high.

£175–210 ROS

A pair of Kutani porcelain double gourd vases, decorated in underglaze blue, the panels enamelled with flowers, seal mark, early 20thC, 9¾in (25cm) high.

£1,450–1,700 S(NY)

A near pair of bottle vases, painted with sparrows and flowers, early 20thC, larger 10¼in (26cm) high.

£370–440 ROS

MISCELLANEOUS

A pair of Kutani beakers, each decorated with cranes and a fisherman, impressed mark, c1915, 4in (10cm) high.

£95–110 BAC

A Hirado porcelain figure of a man, holding a bowl, c1900, 5½in (14cm) high.

£230–270 DN

An Arita tankard, painted with figures and birds, damaged, with later metal cover, late 17thC, 7¾in (19.5cm) high.

£410–490 RTo

GLASS

Jeanette Hayhurst

Jeanette deals in British and European antique glass, and has a shop in Kensington Church Street, London.

She has lectured extensively on the identification of glass, appeared on television and radio and written numerous articles and books. She has also curated several exhibitions.

THE STATE OF THE MARKET report for this year is difficult to evaluate by comparing auction prices, as there have been so few auctions of glass due to the high minimum lot values and the high charges of the seller's and buyer's commission.

Christie's of South Kensington sale on 2 July, the day of the London bombings, could have been a disaster, but it was not so. It included a set of four small Beilby enamelled Masonic tumblers which were bought from a boot sale for a few pounds and achieved £22,200. There was a dark green shallow cut dish, the earliest I had ever seen, catalogued as early 19th century and priced at £100–200; it made over £5,000.

Continental glass especially finely engraved Silesian examples from the mid-18th century have been incredibly under-valued, thanks to the prices achieved at sale of the Royal House of Hanover conducted by Sotheby's, we hope to see a re-emergence of interest in this group. Most dealers in the 18th-century drinking glasses are suffering, there are plenty of avid collectors, but too many people chasing too little stock and when we replace stock we often pay as much as we charged for the last example. A few years ago we could sell a grape and vine leaf enamelled Beilby for £2,000. Providing it is in perfect condition, it will now be worth around £3,000, this proportion of increase applies to any good glass.

The enthusiasm for all glass collecting in America is still highly buoyant. A group of UK glass collectors visited a number of very busy fairs and conventions on a recent trip. At the uranium glass collectors convention, everyone was checking that everything fluoresced green with little ultraviolet lamps and when the selling took place it was like the opening of Harrod's sale. There is an increased use of internet selling, but please be very careful when buying from the auctions. There are many secure and safe sites, as the dealers abide by their local Trading Standards. Online auctions are 'buyer beware', all categories suffer misdescription and often reproduction 18th-century glasses are listed as genuine. The expression 'perfect' is subjective, glass needs to be handled.

My advice has always been to only buy what you like at a price that you can afford by remember the pleasure of the purchase always outweighs the pain of the price.

Jeanette Hayhurst

ALE, SPIRIT & WINE GLASSES

◀ **A Saxon filigree goblet,** decorated with an enamelled armorial, Germany, Dresden, dated 1620, 4¾in (12cm) high.
£6,900–8,200 S(Han)

Ex-Royal House of Hanover sale. For information about this sale, please see p205.

▶ **A Venetian wine glass,** with *latticinio* decoration, Italy, c1700, 3¼in (8.5cm) high.
£450–500 BrW

A goblet, the thistle bowl on a moulded pedestal stem with diamond studs to the shoulders, the enclosed tear above a folded conical foot, c1715, 7in (18cm) high.
£1,300–1,550 S(O)

A Bohemian goblet and cover, the funnel bowl with engraved decoration, on an inverted baluster stem enclosing ruby spiral threads on a conical foot, the associated cover with a faceted spear finial enclosing ruby thread spirals, slight damage to finial, c1720, 11½in (29cm) high.

£960–1,150 S(O)

A wine flute or ale glass, the bell bowl on an annular knop over an inverted baluster and ball and flattened ball knops, on a folded conical foot, 1725, 8¼in (21cm) high.

£2,250–2,700 S(O)

A goblet, the thistle bowl engraved with a house, hound and stag, and an inscription, above an inverted faceted baluster stem, on a folded conical foot, Germany or Bohemia, 1725–50, 8¼in (21cm) high.

£280–330 DN

A gin glass, the bell bowl on a flattened shoulder knop and inverted baluster stem with a base knop, on a conical foot, c1740, 4in (10cm) high.

£210–240 FD

◀ **A light baluster goblet,** the engraved bowl on a baluster stem, Holland, c1740, 8in (20.5cm) high.

£1,900–2,150 BrW

▶ **A goblet,** the bucket bowl on an air-twist stem and a conical foot, c1750, 7in (17.5cm) high.

£530–630 DN

A Bohemian goblet, the bowl engraved with *Laub- und Bandelwerk* and a dancing cupid in a cartouche, on a knop with red air-twist and aventurine inclusions, the base cut with olives, flutes and *Bandelwerk*, chips ground out, 1750–1800, 6¼in (16cm) high.

£350–420 DORO

A Lauenstein goblet and cover, engraved with the arms of King George II of Great Britain and N. Ireland, Germany, c1750, 13in (33cm) high.

£2,850–3,400 S(Han)

Ex-Royal House of Hanover sale.

◀ **A wine glass,** the funnel bowl engraved with the crowned arms of the Republic of the Seven United Provinces, inscribed 'Concordia Res Parvae Crescunt', the reverse with a monogram 'VOC' within martial trophies, above a cushion knop and an inverted baluster stem with air beads on a conical foot, slight restoration, Netherlands, c1750, 7½in (19cm) high.

£1,050–1,250 S(O)

'VOC' denotes the Verenigde Oostindische Compagnie, or the Dutch East India Company, which was granted a monopoly on trade in the East Indies in 1602 by representatives of the Dutch republic. The company was also supposed to fight enemies of the republic and prevent other European nations from participating in trade in the East Indies.

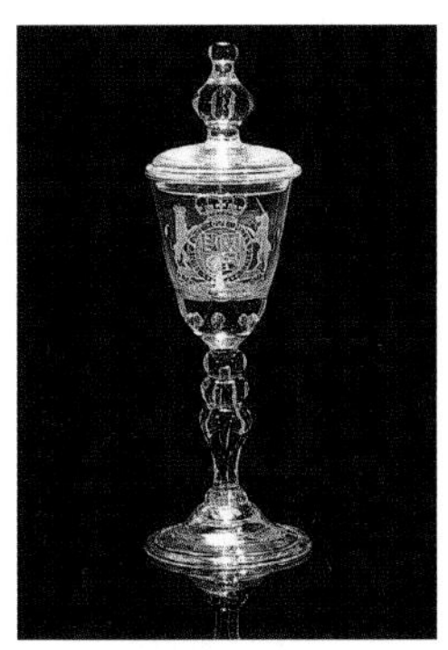

A Lauenstein goblet and cover, engraved with the arms of King George III of Great Britain and N. Ireland, Germany, c1760, 12½in (31.5cm) high.

£1,800–2,150 S(Han)

Ex-Royal House of Hanover sale.

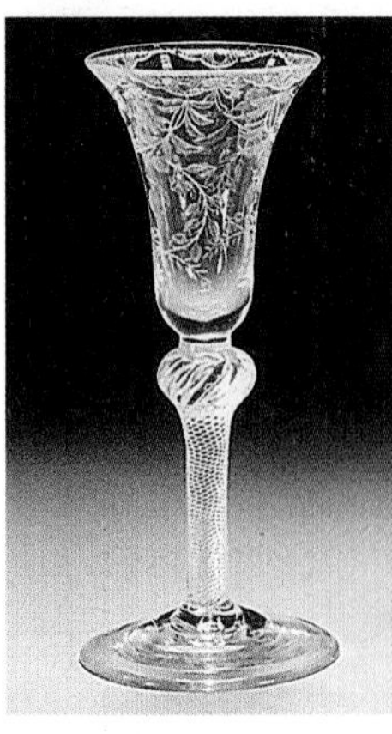

A cider glass, the bell bowl engraved and polished with a drapery border hung with tassels above scrolling foliate fruit branches, each with an apple, on a shoulder-knopped multi-spiral air-twist stem and conical foot, slight damage, c1760, 6¾in (17cm) high.

£1,550–1,850 S(O)

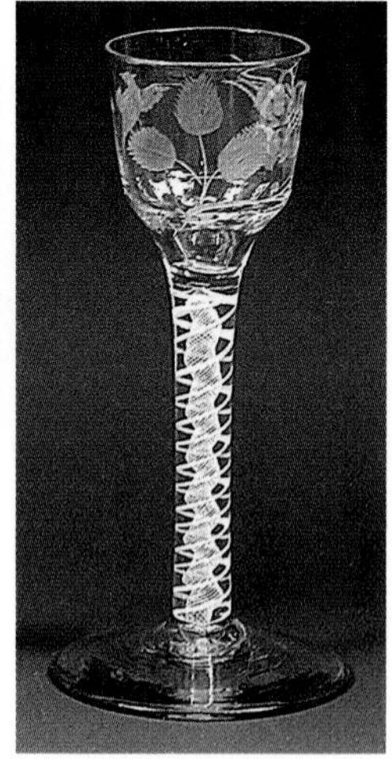

A wine glass, the ogee bowl engraved with flowers and a bird, on a double-series air-twist stem with a gauze inclusion, on a conical foot, c1760, 6in (15cm) high.

£280–330 SWO

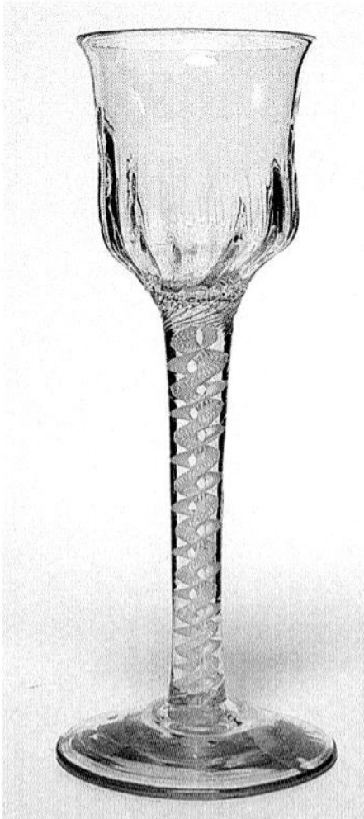

A wine glass, the ogee bowl with fluted ribbing, on a double-series opaque-twist stem, foot rim polished, c1760, 6in (15cm) high.

£400–450 BrW

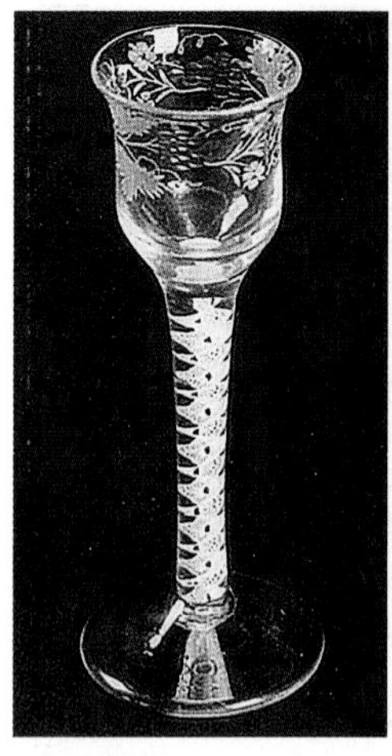

A wine glass, the ogee bowl with an everted rim, engraved and polished with a foliate band, on a double-series opaque-twist stem with a conical foot, c1760, 6in (15cm) high.

£410–490 DN

A light baluster trick wine glass, the flared bowl engraved with a band of flowerheads, eight of which are pierced, above two floral sprigs, on a knopped stem and a conical foot, Holland, c1760, 7½in (19cm) high.

£1,200–1,400 S(O)

It is the holes in the flowers that makes this a trick wine glass.

A wine glass, the bell bowl on a solid base with bead inclusions, on a triple-knopped double-series stem and conical foot, c1765, 7in (18cm) high.

£590–700 DN

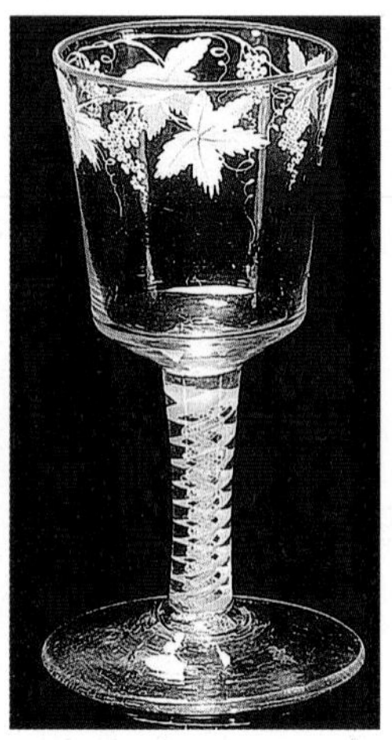

A Beilby goblet, the bucket bowl painted in enamel with a band of vine leaves and grapes, the rim with traces of gilding, on a double-series opaque-twist stem and conical foot, slight damage, c1765, 7¼in (18.5cm) high.

£7,800–9,300 S

A wine glass, the bell bowl on a three-colour-twist stem and conical foot, c1765, 6¼in (16cm) high.

£4,200–5,000 S(O)

A firing glass, the ogee bowl on a stem inset with a cobalt blue cord within an opaque spiral thread, on a terraced conical foot, c1765, 4¼in (11cm) high.

£2,150–2,550 S(O)

A wine glass, with a plain stem and folded foot, c1770, 3½in (9cm) high.

£75–85 BrW

A wine glass, the pan-topped bowl engraved with a band of fruiting vine, on an opaque-twist stem and a conical foot, c1770, 6in (15cm) high.

£700–840 DN

A wine glass, the petal-cut conical bowl on a double-series opaque-twist stem, c1770, 6in (15cm) high.

£240–280 PBA

◄ **A wine glass,** the gilt-decorated ogee bowl with a diamond band suspending lappets, on a double-series opaque-twist stem and a conical foot, c1770, 6in (15cm) high.

£1,000–1,200 DN

A set of four Kungsholm Glassworks glasses, engraved with turtle doves, hearts and inscriptions, slight damage, Sweden, 18thC, 5½in (14cm) high.

£970–1,150 BUK

A two-piece wine glass, the faceted ogee bowl with a gilt rim on a faceted stem and scalloped foot, slight damage, 18thC, 7in (18cm) high.

£165–195 BWL

A glass rummer, gilded by William Absolon, inscribed 'From rocks and sands and dangers free may God protect the ship and we', c1800, 5¼in (13.5cm) high.

£1,350–1,550 BrW

Coloured wine glasses

Prices for simple, green, late 18th-century and early 19th-century wine glasses have changed little over the last five years. This is due partly to a fall in their popularity in America and also to the fact that there has been a downturn in the popularity of coloured glass, as it is not easy to see the colour or the quality of the wine. Now is the time to start a collection of these delightful decorative glasses, with all types of bowls, stems and colours, as they can be bought for as little as £20–50. They can look wonderful on shelves with light behind them or placed before a frosted bathroom window. Blue and amethyst glasses are considerably more expensive – they are comparatively rare because they were not popular at the time of production. Blue decanters and finger bowls were produced in great numbers as they were made to be set on the table with blue and white dinner services.

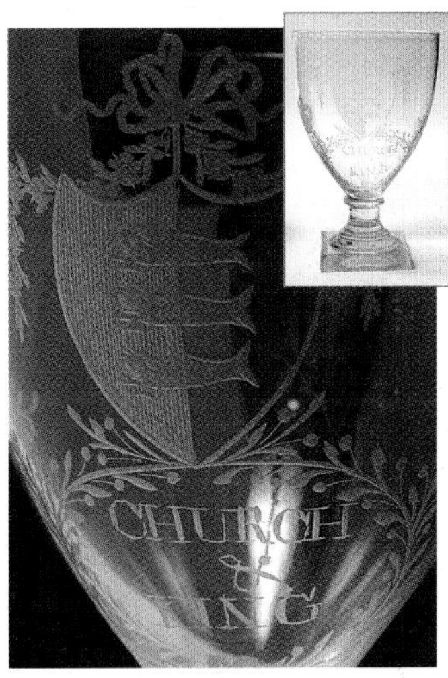

A rummer, engraved by William Absolon with the arms of Great Yarmouth and inscribed 'Church and King', c1800, 6¼in (16cm) high.

£1,750–1,950 BrW

Items in the Glass section have been arranged in date order within each sub-section.

A rummer, engraved with a ship sailing under Sunderland Bridge, inscribed 'Sunderland Bridge over the Wear', the back with initials 'JSW' under a basket of flowers, between hops and barley, c1800, 6½in (16.5cm) high.

£300–360 SWO

A wine glass, with a tulip bowl, c1840, 5in (12.5cm) high.

£50–55 PeN

A Bohemian glass Kiddush cup, the bowl inscribed with gilt Hebrew letters and etched in German, on a solid stem with an air bubble and splayed foot, 19thC, 5½in (14cm) high.

£110–130 WAD

Kiddush is a special Jewish blessing said before a meal on sabbaths and festivals, usually including the blessing for wine and bread.

A rummer, with double bowls, 1840–60, 5¾in (14.5cm) high.

£70–80 CHar

A wine glass, with an optic-moulded bowl and bladed knops, c1845, 4¼in (11cm) high.

£40–45 ⊞ Getc

A goblet, with an engraved bowl on an inverted baluster stem, c1850, 8in (20.5cm) high.

£140–160 ⊞ PeN

A Bohemian goblet, with gilded cut leaf-and-ball decoration, with applied green glass beads, two beads missing, 1850–1900, 6in (15cm) high.

£240–280 DORO

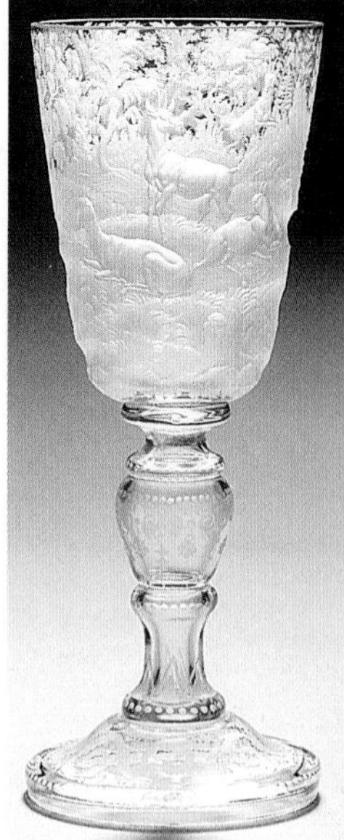

A Bohemian goblet, the bowl with intaglio-engraved ibex in a woodland scene, on a hollow multi-knopped stem and conical foot engraved with leaf scroll and other formal banding, c1850, 11¼in (28.5cm) high.

£1,400–1,650 S(O)

A pair of marriage rummers, the bowls engraved with roses and initials, on facet-cut stems, c1860, 6in (15cm) high.

£105–120 ⊞ FD

◄ **A mould-blown rummer,** with a coiled stem, 1860–80, 4¾in (12cm) high.

£25–30 ⊞ Getc

A Bohemian overlaid and cut-glass goblet, with engraved panels depicting castles, 19thC, 8in (20.5cm) high.

£220–260 WilP

A Moser Glassworks Bohemian römer, with enamel and gilt decoration, c1890, 12in (30.5cm) high.

£2,250–2,500 ⊞ BHA

A pressed-glass goblet, the three panels embossed with a cat, a rabbit and a horse, America, Iowa City, late 19thC, 6½in (16.5cm) high.

£530–630 JAA

A Bohemian goblet, the octagonal bucket bowl engraved with deer in a forest landscape, on a knopped stem and octagonal foot, late 19thC, 12in (30.5cm) high.

£470–560 DN

◄ **A set of three wine glasses,** from Edward VII's Royal Drinking Suite, the funnel bowls with gilded rims and lozenge-cut bases, enamelled 'E VII' enclosing a crown, on hexagonal tapered stems and circular feet, one repaired, c1905, 6¼in (16cm) high.

£140–165 TEN

BEAKERS & TUMBLERS

A Calcedonio *trembleuse* beaker and stand, the marbled opalescent glass with aventurine inclusions, Italy, Venice, c1725, 3½in (9cm) high.
£2,250–2,700 S(O)

It is rare for both the beaker and its original stand to have survived. Calcedonio is marbled glass imitating chalcedony or agate.

A blown tumbler, engraved with rose sprays, c1760, 3½in (9cm) high.
£180–200 Getc

A beaker, engraved with flowers and the initial 'V', France, c1810, 4in (10cm) high.
£200–230 BrW

A pair of whisky tumblers, cut with panels, rays and round printies, c1815, 4in (10cm) high.
£80–90 FD

► **A beaker,** possibly by Anton Kothgasser, enamelled with a spray of orange blossom, fruit and flowers, inscribed 'Mein Liebstes' within stained and gilt borders, the cogwheel base cut with palisade flutes edged in gilding, rim possibly regilt, Austria, Vienna, 1820–25, 4¼in (11.5cm) high.

£1,200–1,450 S(O)

A set of six Bohemian glass beakers, probably by Josef Richter, decorated with lake scenes, the reverse with sprays of forget-me-nots, Kreibitz, 1825–30, 4¼in (11cm) high.
£470–560 DORO

A commemorative tumbler, inscribed 'JEF' within a thistle and a rose, the reverse engraved with a house and a bridge in a river landscape, c1830, 5in (12.5cm) high.
£200–240 DN

◄ **A Bohemian glass beaker,** with pink staining and cobalt blue and white enamel overlay, c1840, 4¾in (12cm) high.
£400–480 DORO

A Bohemian glass beaker, decorated and gilt with flowers, leaves and *rocaille*, slight damage, c1840, 4¾in (12cm) high.
£360–430 DORO

A tumbler, the slice-cut sides decorated with four engraved Masonic symbols, the base containing three dice, late 19thC, 4½in (11.5cm) high.
£150–180 PF

LOCATE THE SOURCE

The source of each illustration in Miller's can be found by checking the code letters below each caption with the Key to Illustrations, pages 746–753.

◄ **A Bohemian glass tumbler,** cut with a coat-of-arms and a knight on horseback, late 19thC, 5in (12.5cm) high.
£400–480 DORO

BOTTLES

A sealed onion wine bottle, with an applied string rim, the body moulded with a baron's coronet above a fox, c1700, 5in (12.5cm) high.

£3,500–4,200 BBR

This is an important, well-documented and classic early English onion wine bottle. Pieces such as this rarely come onto the market.

► **An onion wine bottle,** with a 'kick-in' base, slight damage, early 18thC, 6½in (16.5cm) high.

£210–250 DN(HAM)

A wine bottle, with an applied seal inscribed 'B. Greive', dated 1727, 6½in (16.5cm) high.

£3,300–3,950 LFA

► **A sealed bottle,** with a string neck and seal inscribed 'Loop 1777', deep relief under base, late 18thC, 9in (23cm) high.

£730–870 PBA

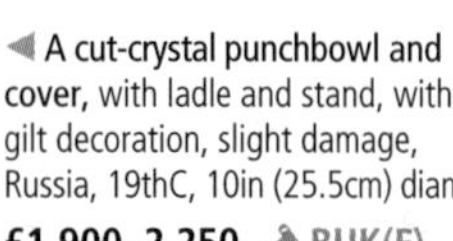

► **A sealed wine bottle,** the neck with a flared lip, the body with eight applied rigaree and the seal inscribed 'DN 1826', traces of white enamel near the pontilled base, Scotland, early 19thC, 12¾in (32.5cm) high.

£1,750–2,100 BBR

Rigaree is applied decoration of a crimped or pinched glass ribbon.

BOWLS

A cut-glass finger bowl, with neo-classical decoration, possibly Irish, 1790–1800, 3½in (9cm) high.

£135–150 Getc

A sugar bowl, on a fold-over pedestal foot, probably Bristol, early 19thC, 5in (12.5cm) high.

£80–95 NSal

A cut-glass pedestal bowl, the upper section with a gadrooned turnover rim, the lower section with frosted decoration and an armorial, on a gadrooned knop stem and petal-cut foot, slight damage, c1850, 14¼in (36cm) diam.

£370–440 DN

◄ **A cut-crystal punchbowl and cover,** with ladle and stand, with gilt decoration, slight damage, Russia, 19thC, 10in (25.5cm) diam.

£1,900–2,250 BUK(F)

► **A cut-glass footed punchbowl,** with intaglio cutting, in the Alhambra pattern, America, 1900–25, 13½in (34.5cm) high.

£1,400–1,650 NOA

BOXES

An ormolu-mounted opaline casket, the hinged cover and body with bevelled edges, the body on four acanthus and hoof feet, France, 1815–25, 3¾in (9.5cm) wide.

£1,550–1,850 S(O)

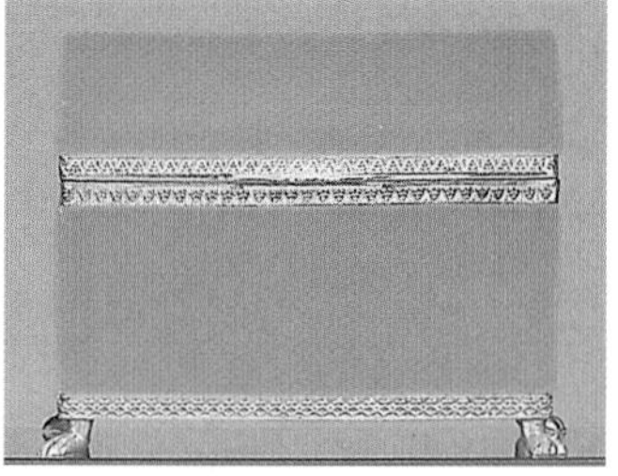

A Bohemian glass chrysoprase sugar box, with gilt mounts, c1860, 5½in (14cm) wide.

£360–430 DORO

Chrysoprase is an opaque green glass, first made by Baccarat in 1843.

A glass trinket box, with gilt-metal mounts, the sides enamelled with flower swags, 19thC, 5¼in (13.5cm) wide.

£270–320 DN

A pair of ruby glass caskets, with gilt-metal mounts, late 19thC, 4¼in (11cm) high.

£590–700 DN(HAM)

A cut-glass casket, decorated with hobnails and stars, with gilt-metal masks, Continental, 19thC, 5½in (14cm) wide.

£350–420 GIL

A glass box, with enamel decoration and ormolu mounts, c1880, 4in (10cm) wide.

£530–600 BHA

CANDLESTICKS & CANDELABRA

A shield-cut faceted candlestick, with a swollen knop, on a domed foot, c1770, 9½in (24cm) high.

£1,100–1,250 BrW

◄ **A pair of candlesticks,** decorated in gilt with birds and musical instruments, probably in the atelier of James Giles, with ormolu mounts, 1775–80, 12¼in (31cm) high.

£11,500–13,800 WW

A pair of cut-glass candelabra, with silver-plated mounts, late 19thC, 15¾in (40cm) high.

£1,600–1,900 S(NY)

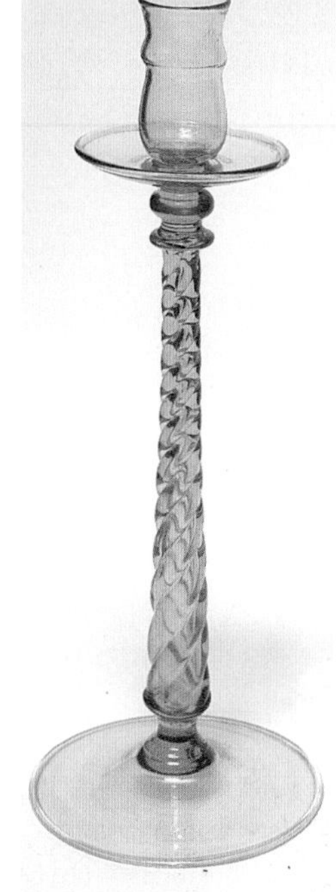

► **A pair of Venetian glass candlesticks,** Italy, late 19thC, 13in (33cm) high.

£320–370 BHA

◄ **A pair of vaseline glass candlesticks,** c1880, 5in (12.5cm) wide.

£220–250 JG

CENTREPIECES

A tazza, on a Silesian stem and folded foot, late 18thC, 8½in (21.5cm) diam.

£150–180 CGC

A Bohemian glass centrepiece, with overlay decorated with sprays of flowers and gilt, slight damage, c1840, 6½in (16.5cm) high.

£280–330 DORO

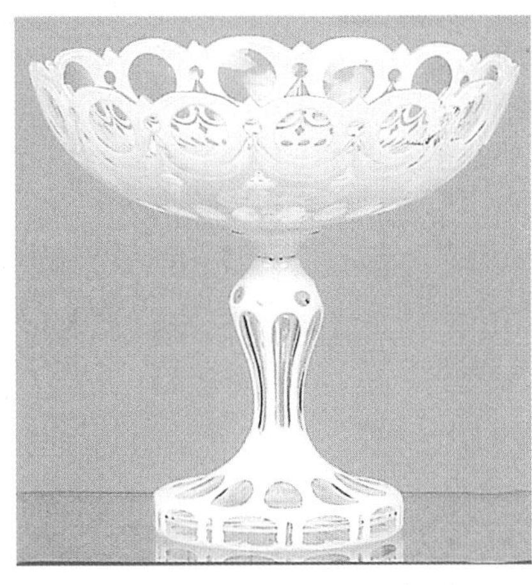

A Bohemian glass centrepiece, with enamel overlay, 1850–1900, 9in (23cm) high.

£280–330 DORO

A Bohemian glass centrepiece, with gilt decoration, slight damage, c1850, 7in (18cm) high.

£310–370 DORO

A Victorian epergne, the vases with undulating rims, 21¾in (55.5cm) high.

£400–480 G(L)

Buying epergnes

Epergnes were originally designed as centrepieces to hold desserts and fruit, but by the Victorian period they had become table centrepieces for flowers, comprising a number of vases, called trumpets. These were usually made in sections and can be taken apart – the central trumpet unscrews and then the other vases can be lifted out. This made it easier to clean but often resulted in pieces being lost. When buying an epergne it is wise to dismantle it, both to check the quality and that it is complete, as damage will seriously affect the value. If made of coloured glass, check that the colour is uniform – later additions will be a different shade.

▶ **A Victorian opaline epergne,** with four vases and a hanging basket, 22½in (57cm) high.

£240–280 PF

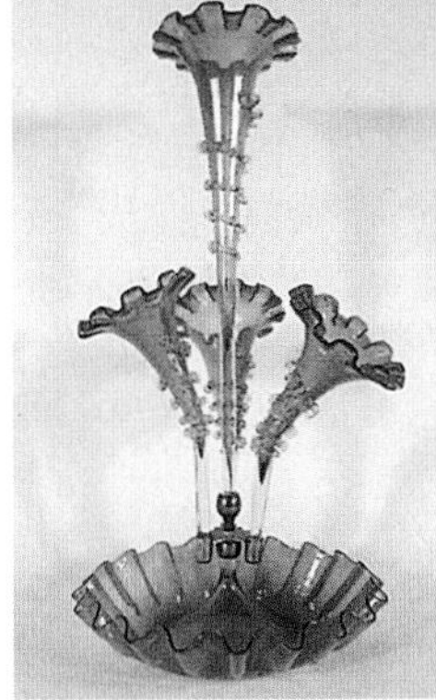

◀ **A cranberry glass epergne,** with trailed decoration, late 19thC, 18¼in (46.5cm) high.

£210–250 Hal

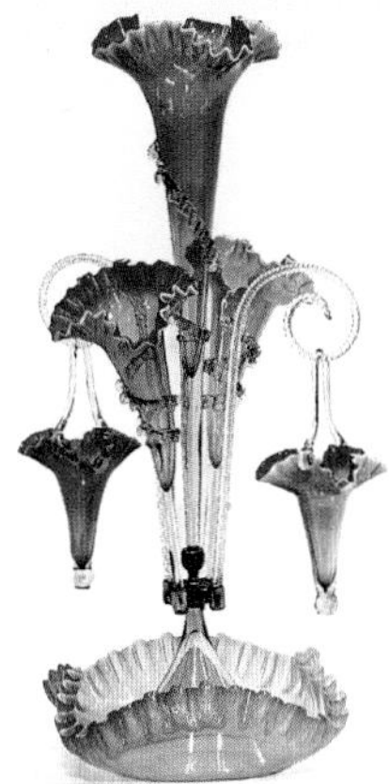

A Victorian epergne, with three vases and two hanging baskets, 9in (23cm) high.

£560–670 AH

▶ **A Venetian glass comport,** possibly by Salviati, in the form of a swan, with gold inclusions, c1880, 5½in (14cm) long.

£105–120 FD

A Stourbridge vaseline glass epergne, late 19thC, 18½in (47cm) high.

£400–480 DN

DECANTERS

A set of three George III glass decanters, by Isaac Jacobs, signed in gilt 'Holland', 'Brandy' and 'Rum', within gilt simulated labels, 9½in (24cm) high.

£760–910 G(L)

A decanter, engraved with flowers, late 18thC, 11in (28cm) high.

£180–210 FD

A set of three decanters, cut with diamonds and flutes, c1790, 7½in (19cm) high.

£220–250 Getc

A decanter, with a mushroom stopper, c1800, 10in (28cm) high.

£180–210 FD

A decanter, with a bevelled lozenge stopper, c1810, 11in (28cm) high.

£170–190 FD

A bell decanter, 1845–60, 12½in (32cm) high.

£65–75 Getc

A pair of Bohemian cased glass decanters, c1860, 16in (40.5cm) high.

£360–400 JG

Collecting decanters

Jeanette Hayhurst, specialist glass dealer, thinks that antique decanters are extremely good value when compared to their modern counterparts, with late 18th- or early 19th-century examples costing between £150 and £200. Only buy decanters that are clean and dry – it is likely that damp examples will have a whitish cloudy interior once they have dried, and usually this can only be removed by a professional cleaner. There are numerous old wives' tales about cleaning; some methods may work on one example but not on the next, so if clouding offends your eye then avoid buying such pieces, even if they are cheap. Stoppers should be appropriate for the decanter as it is almost impossible to find a replacement since there are more decanters than stoppers. If you do find a stopper in the right shape and colour it will probably not fit. Remember to make sure your decanter is dry before replacing the stopper to avoid future cloudiness.

A pair of Bohemian opaque glass decanters, with tulip stoppers, decorated with floral panels and gilt flowers, one damaged, late 19thC, 9½in (24cm) high.

£370–440 SWO

A Stevens & Williams decanter, attributed to John Orchard, engraved with leaves and flowerheads, with a spire stopper, c1885, 12½in (32cm) high.

£1,400–1,650 S(O)

JARS

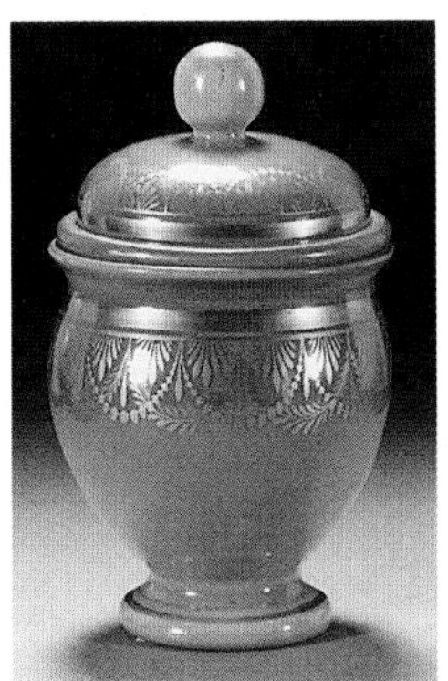

An opaline sugar jar and cover, decorated with gilt palmettes and foliate swags, on an everted foot, France, c1820, 5¾in (14.5cm) high.

£1,200–1,400 S(O)

A cranberry glass ginger jar, c1880, 8in (20.5cm) high.

£115–130 JG

A Bohemian glass jar, engraved with a hunting scene, the base engraved with leaf sprays, late 19thC, 12in (30.5cm) high.

£320–380 MCA

A Moser Glassworks jar and cover, with enamel decoration and prunts, engraved mark, Austria, 1880–90, 13in (33cm) high.

£160–180 FD

JUGS & EWERS

An opaque glass jug, enamelled with flowers, slight damage, c1770, 3½in (9cm) high.

£350–420 DN

A water jug, c1830, 7in (18cm) high.

£310–350 BrW

A ewer, with diamond-cut bands, on a lemon-squeezer foot, c1800, 10in (25.5cm) high.

£140–165 MEA

A George III beer jug, engraved with hops and barley, inscribed 'Coventry Atkins', 9in (23cm) high.

£330–390 CGC

A pair of claret ewers, cut with Greek-key decoration and cartouches, 19thC, 10¾in (27.5cm) high.

£700–840 Bea

A Bohemian glass ewer and pedestal, applied with a plaque depicting women, the pedestal decorated with flowers, damaged, mid-19thC, 30in (76cm) high.

£1,700–2,000 Bea

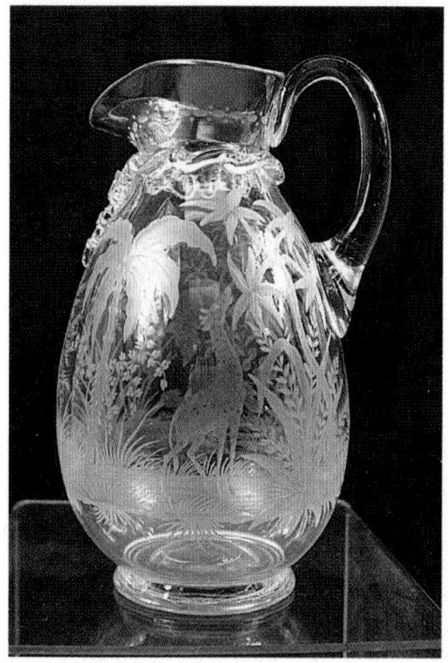

A jug, engraved with a giraffe, bird and spider in a web, the neck applied with a trail in the form of a tied ribbon, c1880, 8½in (21.5cm) high.

£500–600 SWO

◀ **A pair of cut-glass claret jugs,** with silver-gilt mounts, Russia, Moscow 1883, 14in (35.5cm) high, with a fitted display case.

£9,100–10,900 S(NY)

▶ **A Lobmeyr Islamic-style ewer,** by F. Schmoranz and M. Knab, from the Alhambra series, painted with birds and stylized flowers, painted monogram, Austria, Vienna, c1888, 9¼in (23.5cm) high.

£1,800–2,150 S(O)

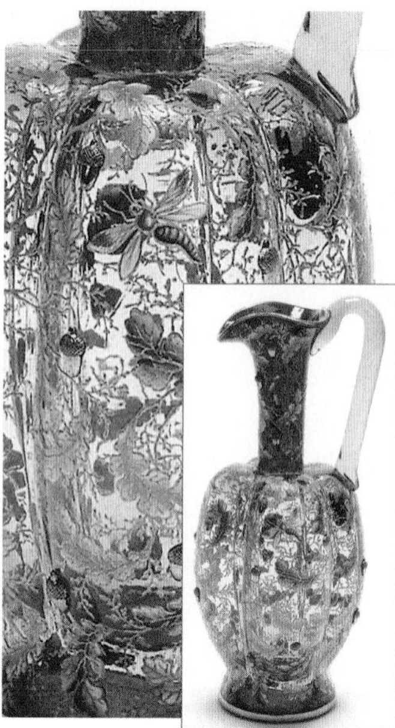

A Moser Glassworks jug, enamelled with oak leaves and insects, applied with acorns, c1885, 12½in (32cm) high.

£1,600–1,900 DN

LUSTRES

A pair of cut-glass and gilt-brass candelabra lustres, damage and losses, 19thC, 14¼in (36cm) high.

£1,600–1,900 WW

A pair of Victorian lustres, with blue overlay, 10in (25.5cm) high.

£400–480 G(L)

A pair of lustres, painted with floral swags, 19thC, 11in (28cm) high.

£590–700 WW

A pair of Bohemian glass lustres, overlaid in opaque white and cut with stylized leaves, late 19thC, 10in (25.5cm) high.

£910–1,100 WAD

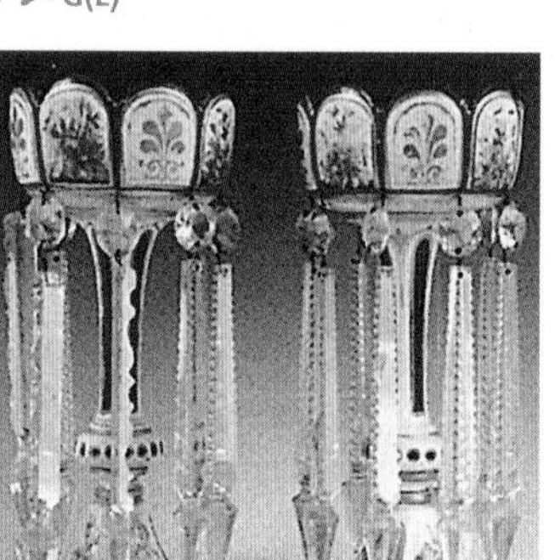

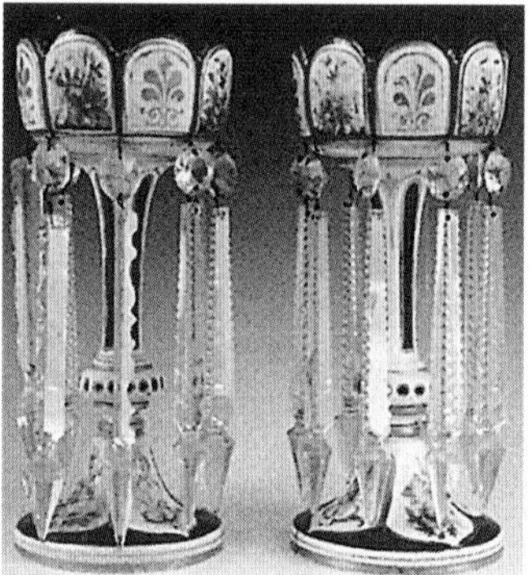

A pair of Bohemian cranberry glass lustres, painted with flowers and gilt scrolls, damaged, late 19thC, 11in (28cm) high.

£440–520 RTo

A pair of Bohemian glass lustres, painted with portraits of children and flowers, late 19thC, 12½in (32cm) high.

£1,300–1,550 SWO

PAPERWEIGHTS

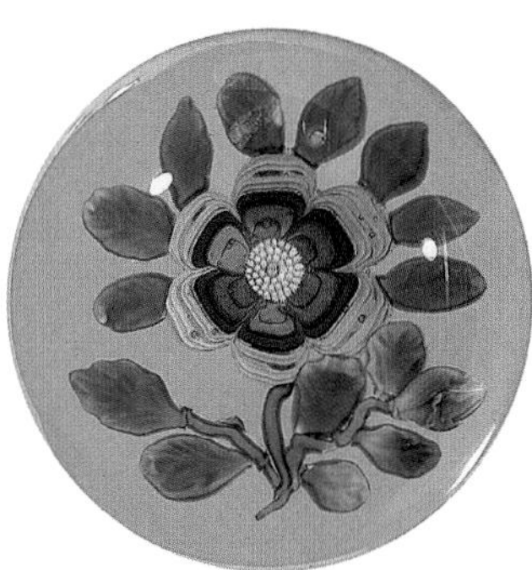

A Baccarat paperweight, with a primrose, France, c1850, 3in (7.5cm) diam.
£2,400–2,700 ⊞ DLP

A Baccarat paperweight, France, c1850, 2¾in (7cm) diam.
£4,850–5,400 ⊞ DLP

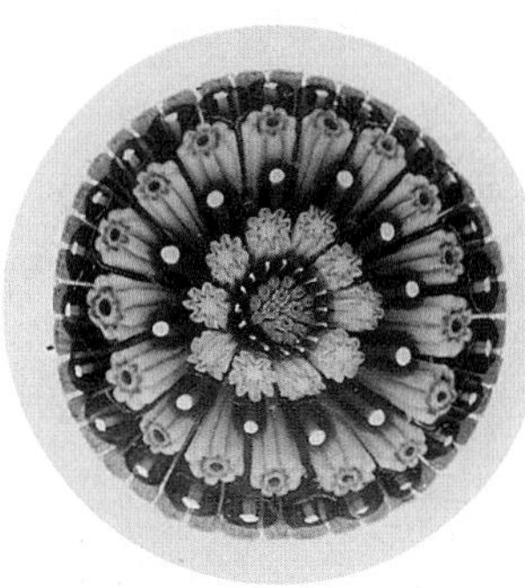

A Bacchus & Co concentric millefiori paperweight, 1850–1900, 4in (10cm) diam.
£2,250–2,700 ⚒ S(O)

A Clichy paperweight, with a violet, France, 1845–60, 3in (7.5cm) diam.
£4,950–5,500 ⊞ SWB

A Clichy paperweight, with a camellia, France, c1850, 3in (7.5cm) diam.
£3,400–3,800 ⊞ DLP

A Clichy concentric millefiori paperweight, the canes on an 'upset muslin' ground, France, c1850, 2½in (6.5cm) diam.
£540–640 ⊞ DLP

A New England Glass Co paperweight, with nosegay leaves, America, Massachusetts, c1850, 3in (7.5cm) diam.
£1,350–1,500 ⊞ SWB

The nosegay leaves in this paperweight were made by a maker who had moved from the St Louis factory in France to the New England Glass Co, which operated in Cambridge, Massachusetts from 1818 to 1888. .

A New England Glass Co scrambled paperweight, with silhouette canes of an eagle and three rabbits, America, c1850, 3in (7.5cm) diam.
£490–550 ⊞ SWB

A New England Glass Co millefiori paperweight, with a *latticinio* ground, America, c1850, 2¾in (7cm) diam.
£850–950 ⊞ SWB

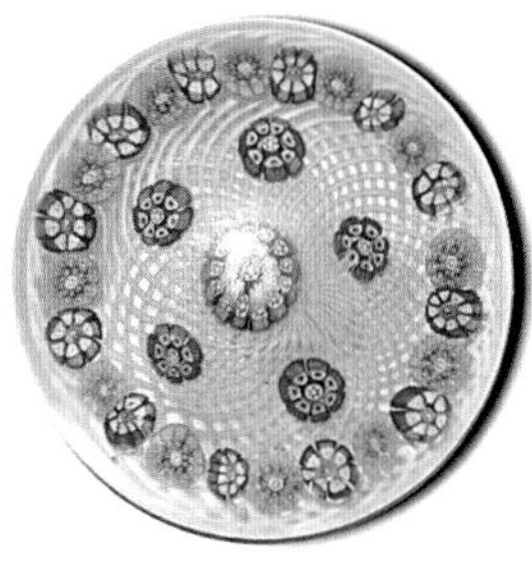

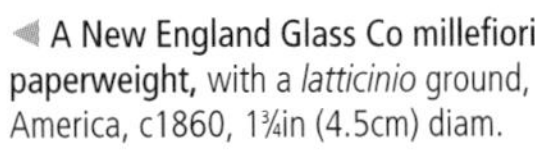

◄ **A New England Glass Co millefiori paperweight,** with a *latticinio* ground, America, c1860, 1¾in (4.5cm) diam.
£400–450 ⊞ SWB

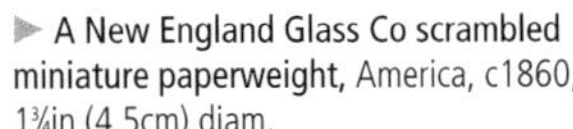

► **A New England Glass Co scrambled miniature paperweight,** America, c1860, 1¾in (4.5cm) diam.
£280–320 ⊞ SWB

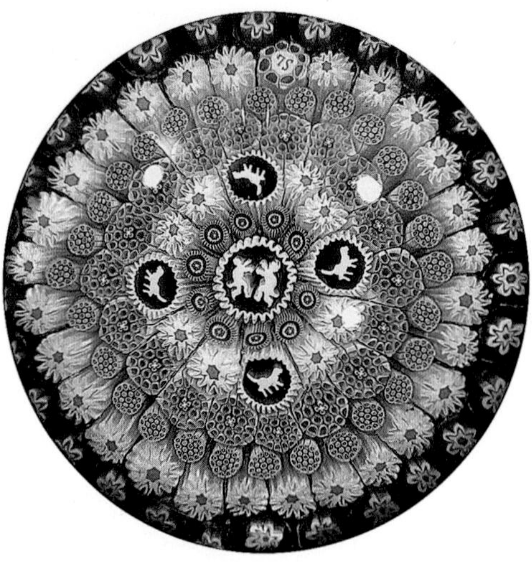

A St Louis close concentric paperweight, with silhouettes, France, c1850, 3in (7.5cm) diam.

£2,900–3,250 DLP

A St Louis bouquet paperweight, France, c1850, 2¾in (7cm) diam.

£1,450–1,650 DLP

A St Louis crown paperweight, France, 1845–60, 2¾in (7cm) diam.

£3,150–3,500 SWB

A St Louis crown paperweight, France, 1845–60, 2½in (6.5cm) diam.

£2,100–2,350 SWB

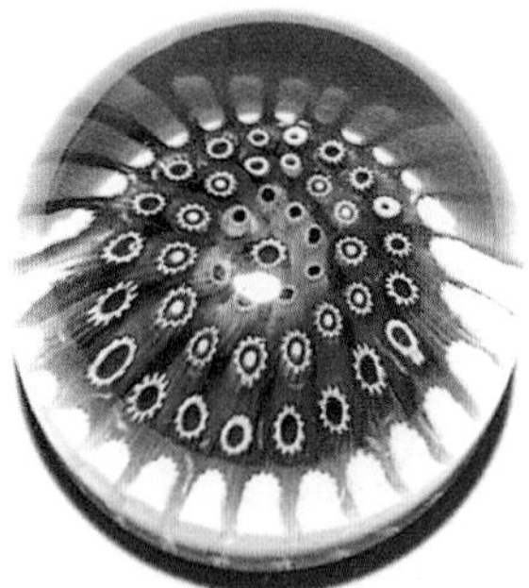

A concentric millefiori paperweight, possibly by John Walsh Walsh, late 19thC, 3½in (9cm) diam.

£130–155 DN

PICTURES

A picture, reverse-painted with a boy holding flowers, 18thC, 17 x 11¼in (43 x 28.5cm).

£1,700–2,000 DN

An optical box, comprising three glass panes depicting boats, in a wooden frame, damaged, Holland, late 18thC, 12¼ x 15½in (31 x 39.5cm).

£940–1,100 BERN

This optical box consists of three panes of glass which, when placed one behind the other, creates a 3D effect.

A picture, reverse-painted with a family, inscribed 'Saturday Night or the Reward of Industry', c1805, in an ebonized frame, 10 x 14in (25.5 x 35.5cm).

£2,900–3,450 AH

▶ **A mezzotint applied to glass,** entitled 'Sheep Shearing', 19thC, 10¼ x 14¼in (26 x 36cm), in a frame.

£390–460 WW

In the late 18th century the look of reverse glass painting was so popular in England that mezzotints and prints were applied to glass, with famous people and sporting scenes among the subjects depicted. Many of these were exported to America.

SCENT BOTTLES

A Pellatt & Green scent bottle and stopper, with a sulphide inclusion, the bust possibly depicting Princess Caroline of Brunswick, slight damage, impressed marks, c1820, 4¼in (11cm) high.

£700–840 DN

A Bohemian glass scent bottle, etched with baskets of flowers, with presentation inscription, 1830s, 4in (10cm) high.

£175–210 CAu

▶ A turquoise glass scent bottle, with gilt decoration, slight damage, probably Russia, 19thC, 4in (10cm) wide.

£550–660 BUK(F)

A wrythen-ribbed amethyst glass scent bottle, France, 19thC, 3in (7.5cm) long.

£85–95 BHA

A Thomas Webb & Sons scent bottle, in the form of a swan's head, the silver-gilt mount engraved with a crown by Sampson Mordan & Co, c1884, 8¾in (22cm) long, in original case.

£10,600–12,700 HYD

This was a world record price for such a scent bottle. It is said to have been a wedding gift given by Prince Henry of Battenberg to his valet.

▶ A gilt-metal-mounted scent bottle box, the hinged cover opening to reveal four scent bottles with covers depicting Parisian monuments, France, late 19thC, 7¾in (19.5cm) high.

£1,250–1,500 WAD

SETS & SERVICES

A Boston & Sandwich Glass Co Champagne service, comprising five pieces, engraved 'WW', America, Massachusetts, 1850–75, jug 10in (28cm) high.

£220–260 NOA

A Lobmeyr drinking set, with cypher for Marie Queen of Hanover, Austria, c1870, jug (30.5cm) high.

£13,000–15,600 S(Han)

Ex-Royal House of Hanover sale.

◀ A table service, comprising 24 pieces, the bowls gilt with swags and applied 'ruby' beads, with star-cut feet, America, c1900.

£4,200–5,000 S

▶ A cut-glass table service, comprising 77 pieces, with faceted shoulder knops and star-cut feet, including 17 matched Champagne glasses, America, c1900.

£2,000–2,400 S

A Daum spirit decanter, with five matching glasses, with enamel decoration, France, Nancy, 1890s, 8in (20.5cm) high.

£540–600 MiW

SWEETMEAT & JELLY GLASSES

A sweetmeat glass, with a spiral-faceted bowl, slight damage, 18thC, 5¼in (13.5cm) high.

£120–140 WW

A panel-moulded jelly glass, with a handle and a panel-moulded domed foot, c1750, 4¼in (11cm) high.

£210–240 JHa

Jelly glasses

According to glass expert Jeanette Hayhurst, jelly glasses are both underrated and underpriced. Many of them can be used for desserts, ice cream dishes and drinking vessels, and can be picked up for as little as £30. The rare examples can be bought to supplement the bowl types in a collection of 18th-century drinking glasses. Hexagonal bowl wine glasses with opaque-twist stems command over £1,500, whereas a jelly glass with the same bowl shape will cost £100. A pan-top or domed foot increases the value of a wine glass dramatically, but these features are sometimes incorporated in the same jelly glass. Jelly glasses only become relatively expensive when they have one or two handles, but they must be undamaged. Check for small cracks at the top or bottom of the handles – they can be difficult to detect but devalue the item substantially.

◄ **A jelly glass,** the pan-topped bowl on a domed foot, mid-18thC, 4in (10cm) high.

£330–390 DN

► **A hexagonal jelly glass,** on a domed foot, mid-18thC, 3½in (9cm) high.

£105–120 JHa

A sweetmeat glass, the flared bowl on a double-series opaque-twist stem and a moulded foot, c1760, 3in (7.5cm) high.

£320–360 FD

TANKARDS

◄ **A tankard,** with the cypher of GB, NI and E of L King George II, c1750, Germany, possibly Laurenstein or Brunswickm 6¼in (16cm) high.

£2,100–2,500 S(Han)

Ex-Royal House of Hanover sale. A similar tankard without the royal provenance would be worth approximately half this amount.

A tankard, engraved with roses and initials, 'DMcH', c1850, 4in (10cm) high.

£75–85 FD

A Bohemian cut-glass tankard, with pewter mounts, c1880, 6in (10cm) high.

£400–450 BHA

VASES & URNS

A near pair of cut-glass urns, with ormolu mounts, 19thC, larger 14½in (37cm) high.

£4,200–5,000 S(NY)

◄ **A pair of Bohemian glass vases,** overlaid in white, with gilt and enamel decoration, one reduced in height, 19thC, larger 16¼in (41.5cm) high.

£530–630 Hal

► **A Bohemian glass vase,** overlaid in white over green, cut with stylized leaves and with outline gilding, 19thC, 15¼in (38.5cm) high.

£330–390 AMB

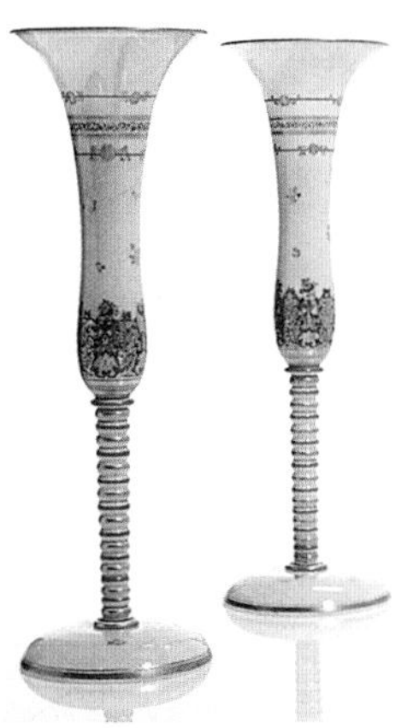

◀ **A pair of opaline vases,** enamelled with flowers, converted to lamps, France, mid-19thC, 23¼in (59cm) high.

£2,450–2,900 S(NY)

A garniture, each decorated with a parrot and flowers, Continental, c1870, largest 19in (48.5cm) high.

£290–340 ROS

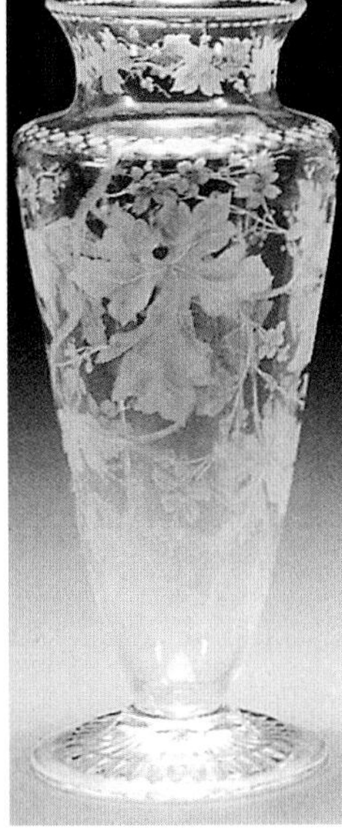

A Stourbridge vase, by George Woodall, engraved with a fruiting vine and flowers, signed, c1890, 14in (35.5cm) high.

£1,800–2,150 S(O)

The renowned cameo glass artist, George Woodall (1850–1925), is believed to have given vases of this type as presents to friends and relatives in the Stourbridge area where he worked for Thomas Webb & Sons.

A Bohemian glass vase, decorated in gilt with a flowering vine, France, 1880–1920, 19½in (49.5cm) high.

£1,300–1,550 S(NY)

A Bohemian glass vase, decorated with fruit, flowers, stylized foliage and gilt scrolls, slight damage, late 19thC, 36½in (92.5cm) high.

£5,100–6,100 WAD

This vase is very large and was made in three parts, so it can be taken apart. There is an enthusiastic market for imposing pieces such as this and it sold for many times in excess of its estimate.

◀ **A cut-glass vase,** America, c1900, 16in (40.5cm) high.

£230–270 JAA

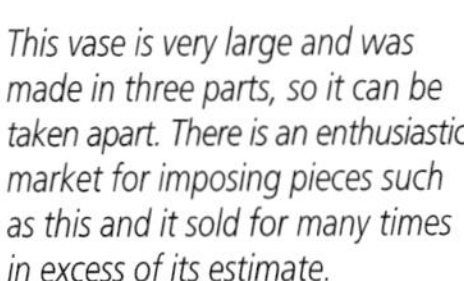

◀ **A pair of Imperial Glassworks vases and pedestals,** engraved with leaf swags, ribbons and wreaths, engraved marks, Russia, dated 1914, 8½in (21.5cm) high.

£3,600–4,300 S

◀ **A cut-glass vase,** America, early 20thC, 12in (30.5cm) high.

£60–70 JAA

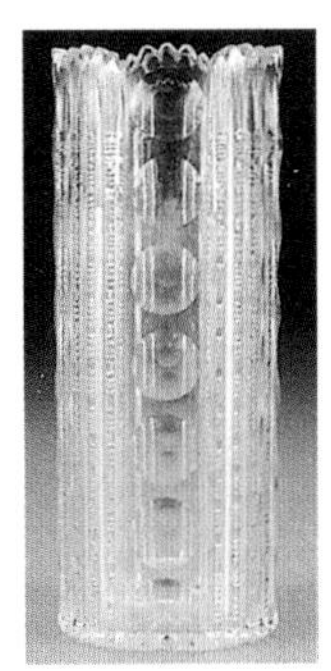

▶ **A cut-glass vase,** early 20thC, 10in (25.5cm) high.

£60–70 JAA

MISCELLANEOUS

A pair of Sunderland glass inkwells, c1870, 4in (10cm) high.

£330–380 GSA

An Iowa City Glass Co bread plate, decorated with a stork and deer, c1880, America, 11½in (29cm) wide.

£60–70 JAA

A *milchglas* teabowl and saucer, Germany, 18thC, saucer 4¼in (11cm) diam.

£280–320 G&G

SILVER

Daniel Bexfield

Daniel has been dealing and specializing in antique silver for 25 years. His shop is in the Burlington Arcade, in Mayfair, London.

He regularly contributes to television and radio programmes on silver and is editor of The Finial, *a magazine solely related to silver spoons.*

FOR THE MAJORITY of dealers and auctioneers times have been much leaner than we would have wished in the last few years. We have seen quite a drop in the price of showy pieces such as tea and coffee sets, epergnes and mass-produced silver made in the early 20th century, that in the past were quite easy to sell.

However, a new type of collector is entering the market: young single professionals who have purchased their own home and are conscious that to enhance their environment they would like to own a few individual pieces of quality that cannot be found in a regular high street outlet. It could be a beautiful Art Deco teapot for their herbal tea in the morning, a George II silver salt cellar to hold crushed peppercorns to embellish a dining table or a Chinese Export silver table snuff box to sit next to a glass vase by a modern designer. I would not refer to this type of customer as a collector, as I suspect their idea of a collector is one whose house is crammed to the brim with a hotch-potch of curios. Rather, they consider themselves to be discerning buyers appreciating works of art of all types and periods.

Antique silver cutlery is another area that is gaining strength and for as long as I can remember it has been very reasonably priced in comparison to new sets. You could own a 12-place setting of Georgian sterling silver cutlery in Old English pattern made by Richard Crossley, circa 1790, or a set by the prolific Victorian silversmith George Adams, for under £100 per piece. What a joy it is to sup your soup with a spoon made over 200 years ago while wondering who else may have used it in days gone by and knowing that if it is looked after well it could continue to be used by future generations!

The market for unusual or small pieces of very high quality silver continues to increase in price. Nutmeg graters are a good example, as they seem to go from strength to strength. Recently there has been a number of sales devoted to these items alone and a rare strawberry shaped grater sold for over £7,000. Only a few years ago it could have been bought for around £2,000 and that would have been thought of as expensive.

Clearly, quality and rare items continue to sell well, allowing for a reasonably optimistic outlook for the future. It is mediocre items that are still proving difficult to sell, however low the price.

Daniel Bexfield

ANIMALS

◄ **A silver pepper pot,** in the form of a duck, importer's mark of Joseph Morpurgo, London 1892, 3½in (9cm) high, 3oz.

£1,100–1,300 HYD

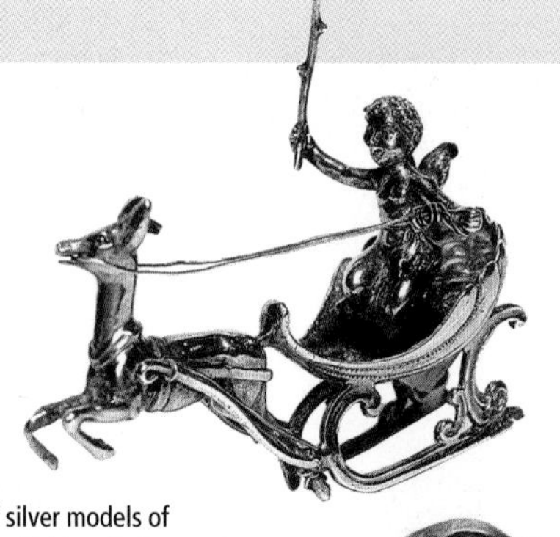

► **A silver model of a reindeer and sleigh,** by Berthold Müller, Holland, 1901, 2½in (6.5cm) long.

£260–290 BLm

◄ **A pair of silver models of pheasants,** with hinged wings and removable heads, Germany, early 20thC, 22½in (57cm) wide, 52oz.

£2,750–3,300 S(NY)

► **A set of four silver place card holders,** modelled as chicks, 1922, 1in (2.5cm) high.

£200–230 Fai

BASKETS

A silver basket, by Edward Aldridge, with a foliate scroll border, the body decorated with spiralling ears of corn with an engraved armorial to the centre, London 1768, 15in (38cm) wide, 33oz.

£1,550–1,850 S(O)

A silver sugar basket, by William Plummer, with a reeded border, London 1784, 5½in (14cm) wide, 6oz.

£230–270 N

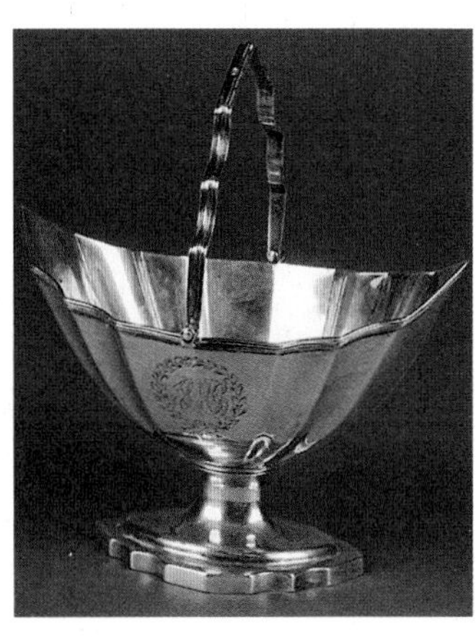

A silver sugar basket, with a reeded border, monogrammed, date letter rubbed, c1790, 6¼in (16cm) wide, 6oz.

£230–270 HYD

A silver cake basket, with pierced foliate decoration, the centre with a crest, Sheffield 1845, 14in (35.5cm) wide.

£820–980 BWL

A silver sweetmeat basket, possibly by G. Moltmann, America, c1850, 4½in (11.5cm) wide.

£950–1,100 DuM

A silver cake basket, with a reeded border, the body with an applied monogrammed shield, assay master Viktor Sawinkow 1866, mark of Alexander Nikolajewitsch Skolow, Russia, 19thC, 13in (33cm) wide.

£370–440 DN

► **A silver sugar basket,** the beaded rim and pierced body decorated with swags, the handle with bellflower decoration, Sheffield 1872, 5in (12.5cm) wide.

£190–220 Mit

A silver fruit basket, with pierced decoration, Birmingham 1902, 11in (28cm) diam.

£260–290 SPE

A silver fruit basket, by William Comyns, the beaded rim with pierced ribbon lug handles, the body pierced with trellis decoration, on bracket feet, London 1905, 11¾in (30cm) wide.

£460–550 AH

A silver basket, by Mappin & Webb, with pierced, repoussé and engraved decoration, Sheffield 1910, 16in (40.5cm) wide, 34½oz.

£680–810 WAD

BEAKERS

A pair of silver-gilt and enamel beakers, by Matthaus Baur II, decorated with scenes of children playing in landscape settings, on screw-on bases, Germany, Augsburg, 1710–12, 2½in (6.5cm) high.

£3,900–4,650 S(NY)

A silver and parcel-gilt beaker, engraved with a monogram within scrolls, with a parcel-gilt interior, Germany, Wolfenbüttel, c1735, 4¾in (12cm) high.

£1,900–2,250 TRM(E)

A silver beaker, with engraved decoration, Russia, c1800, 3in (7.5cm) high.

£1,100–1,250 SHa

BOWLS

A silver bowl, with a moulded leaf-and-dart border, the body with a crest, the two handles mounted with acanthus and fruiting oak, maker's mark JNS, France, Paris, 1798–1809, 14½in (37cm) wide, 55½oz.

£800–960 WAD

A silver bowl, by Henry Farnham, America, Boston, 1800–10, 7in (18cm) diam.

£1,700–2,000 ARG

A silver bowl, by Shiebler, with hammered decoration, America, New York, c1890, 7½in (19cm) diam.

£1,450–1,650 ARG

A silver punchbowl, by James Dixon & Son, Sheffield 1898, 10in (25.5cm) diam.

£990–1,100 ANC

A silver punchbowl, by Walker & Hall, Sheffield 1902, 12in (30.5cm) diam, 38oz.

£2,100–2,350 BEX

Repoussé silver from Baltimore

Around 1825, silversmiths in Baltimore developed a distinctive style. Surfaces were densely covered with floral and architectural patterns in high relief embossing and chasing, called repoussé in America. The chief proponent of the style was Samuel Kirk, followed later in the 19th century by A. E. Warner and others, and by competitors in Philadelphia. The style was and is still widely popular in the southern states. Makers used a standard mark of 11 or 10:15 fine (out of a 12 ounce pound). From 1814 to about 1830, Baltimore had its own assay office and date stamps using a complicated Dominical year mark. Kirk-Steiff Company continues to make repoussé silver today.

A silver footed bowl, by S. Kirk & Son, with repoussé decoration of flowers and leaves, America, Baltimore, Maryland, 1925–32, 10in (25.5cm) diam, 32½oz.

£700–840 WAD

COVERED BOWLS

A silver footed sugar bowl and cover, by William Tuite, the cover with a Watteauesque figural finial, the body decorated with embossed trailing roses within spiral flutes, London 1765, 8in (20.5cm) high, 21oz.

£840–1,000 DN

◀ **A silver sugar urn,** by Linderhill & Vernon, America, New York, 1785–87, 9½in (24cm) high.

£1,850–2,100 ARG

A silver bowl and cover, by E. Hugo, France, c1880, 9in (23cm) wide, 23oz.

£630–700 BEX

BOXES

A silver-gilt box, by Nicolaus Ostertag, decorated in baroque style, marked, Germany, Augsburg, 1716–19, 3¾in (9.5cm) wide, 5oz.

£1,750–2,100 DORO

A silver toothpick box, by John Piercy, with bright-cut decoration, Birmingham 1812, 3¼in (8.5cm) long.

£300–360 Hal

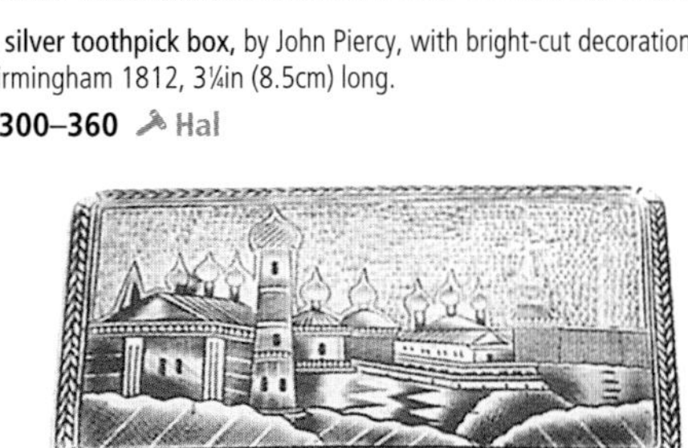

▶ **A silver and niello tinder box,** decorated with buildings within a chevron border, the reverse with a classical scene, maker's marks, Russian, Moscow 1834, 2½in (6.5cm) wide.

£370–440 DN

A silver sugar box, by Anders Lundqvist, Sweden, Stockholm 1838, 6¼in (16cm) wide.

£840–1,000 BUK(F)

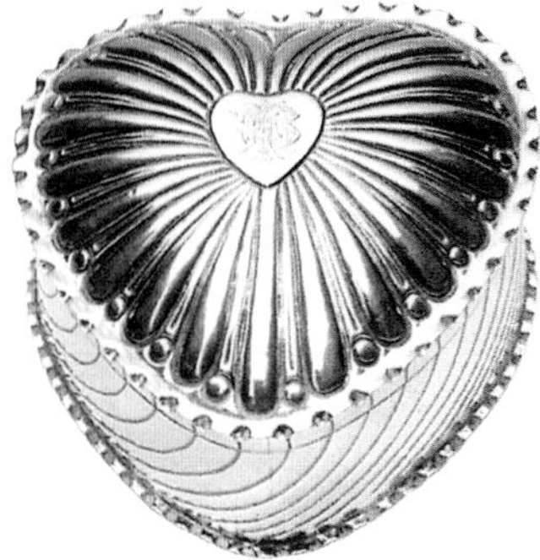

A silver trinket box, in the form of a heart, with fluted decoration, Birmingham 1870, 5in (12.5cm) wide.

£280–330 MAL(O)

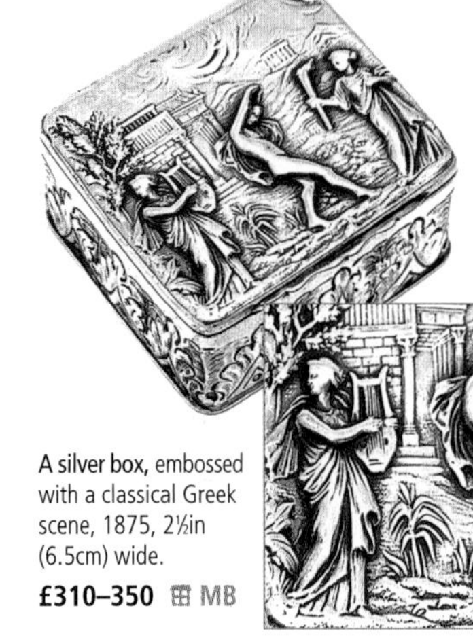

A silver box, embossed with a classical Greek scene, 1875, 2½in (6.5cm) wide.

£310–350 MB

A silver box, with embossed decoration, Birmingham 1886, 5in (12.5cm) wide.

£540–600 ⊞ ANC

A silver casket, decorated with glass cabochons and applied with figures of saints and embossed figural panels on a pierced ground, with a hinged cover, import marks for London 1902, importer's mark Aelly Miller, Continental, 5in (12.5cm) wide.

£760–910 ⚒ HYD

A silver table casket, the hinged cover with a monogrammed tablet flanked at each corner by a dolphin, the body embossed with thistles, the front with a scene of a Scottish lodge bordered by rococo reserves, on lion supports, Scotland, Glasgow 1903, 9¾in (25cm) wide, 50oz.

£2,900–3,450 ⚒ HOLL

CADDY SPOONS

A silver caddy spoon, London 1786, 2in (5cm) long.

£115–130 ⊞ SAT

A silver caddy spoon, by Joseph Taylor, in the form of a hand, Birmingham 1808, 2¼in (5.5cm) long.

£1,000–1,150 ⊞ BEX

A silver caddy spoon, by David Reid, Newcastle, 1856, 3¼in (8.5cm) long.

£570–640 ⊞ BEX

CANDLESTICKS & CHAMBERSTICKS

A pair of silver candlesticks, with filigree decoration, late 17thC, 5¾in (14.5cm) high.

£2,250–2,700 ⚒ S(NY)

A silver chamberstick, by John Cafe, the sconce with moulded borders, the handle with engraved decoration and arms in a rococo cartouche, London 1744, 8½in (21.5cm) long, 7½oz.

£1,450–1,700 ⚒ S(NY)

▶ **A silver chamberstick,** by John Crouch I and Thomas Hannam, with reeded borders and an extinguisher, London 1790, 4in (10cm) diam, 9.5oz.

£700–840 ⚒ DN

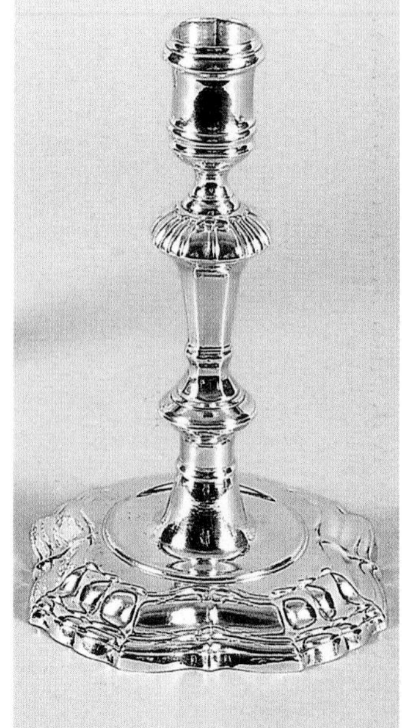

A pair of George III cast silver candlesticks, Ireland, 6¾in (17cm) high, 22oz.

£2,350–2,800 ⚒ JAd

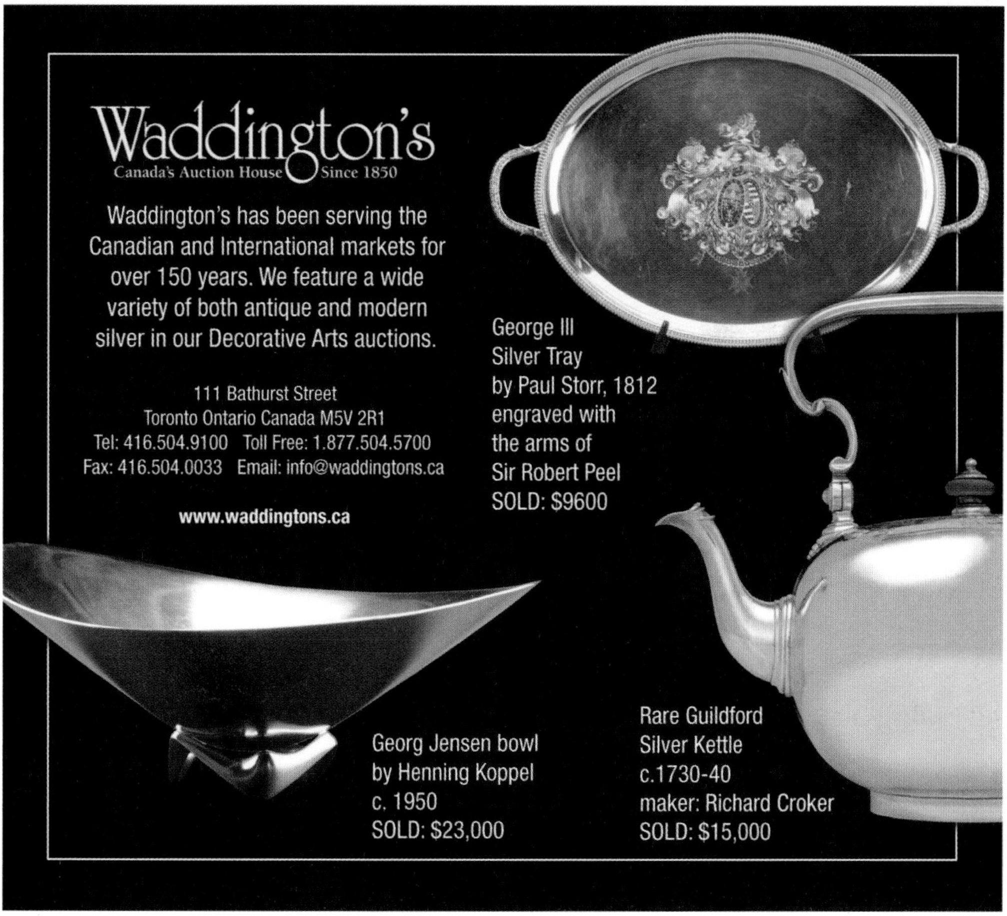

A silver 13-light candelabrum centrepiece, by Robert Garrard II, the base applied with St George and the Dragon, with the arms of Ernst August, King of Hanover, Duke of Cumberland and Brunswick-Luneberg, London 1843, 45¼in (115cm) high.

£376,000–451,000 S(Han)

Ex-Property of the Royal House of Hanover sale. For information about this sales please see p205.

A silver menorah, with embossed and engraved decoration, marked, mid-19thC, 30in (76cm) high.

£1,250–1,500 BERN

A pair of silver candlesticks, London 1896, 3½in (9cm) high.

£280–320 PSA

A pair of silver candlesticks, each column in the form of a lyre, Chester 1898, 8in (20.5cm) high.

£340–400 AMB

A pair of silver candlesticks, by T. Bradbury, decorated with embossed drapery festoons and beaded borders, loaded, London 1898, 7in (18cm) high.

£340–400 WW

A pair of silver Adam-style candlesticks, decorated with rams' head masks and ribbons, Birmingham 1902, 12in (30.5cm) high.

£940–1,100 BWL

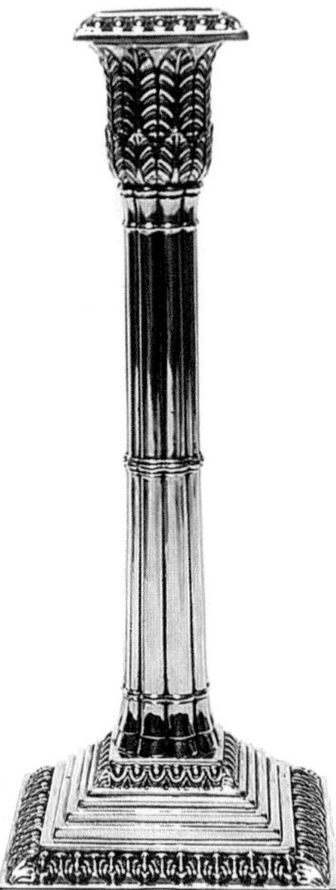

A pair of silver candlesticks, by James Deakin & Sons, with bamboo-style decoration, Sheffield 1908, 9in (23cm) high.

£790–880 ANC

A set of four silver candlesticks, by S. Kirk & Son, with repoussé decoration of flowers and leaves, America, Maryland, Baltimore, 1925–32, 9½in (24cm) high.

£1,200–1,450 WAD

For more Arts & Crafts silver, please see the Decorative Arts section on pages 367–440.

◀ **A silver chamberstick,** by Silvester Lenny-Smith, with hand-hammered decoration, Sheffield 1930, 6in (15cm) diam.

£720–800 DAD

Silvester Lenny-Smith first registered his mark in December 1930.

CARD CASES

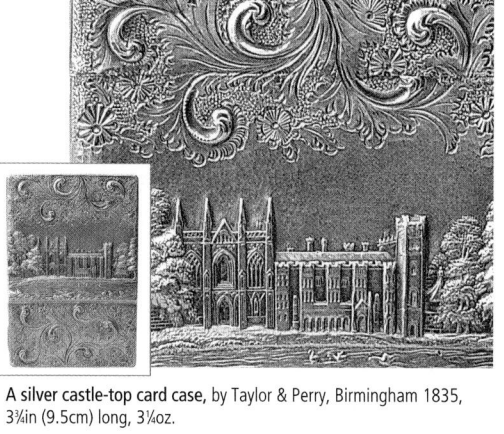

A silver card case, by Taylor & Perry, with embossed decoration, inscribed 'Cecilia', Birmingham 1829, 3½in (9cm) long.

£175–210 DN

A silver castle-top card case, by Taylor & Perry, Birmingham 1835, 3¾in (9.5cm) long, 3¼oz.

£1,300–1,450 BEX

A silver castle-top card case, by Nathaniel Mills, embossed with a castle gatehouse, Birmingham 1843, 4in (10cm) high.

£3,750–4,500 DN

◄ **A silver castle-top card case,** by Nathaniel Mills, decorated with a view of the Bevis Marks Synagogue within foliate scrolls, the reverse with scrolls and a cartouche, London 1845, 4in (10cm) high.

£9,400–11,200 DN

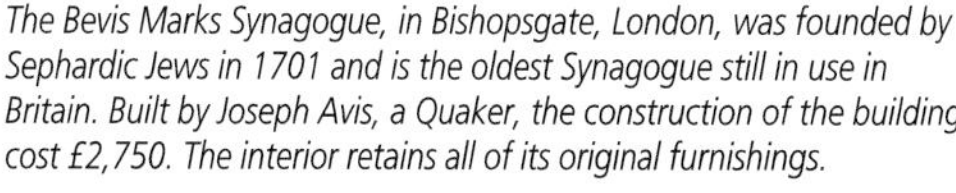

The Bevis Marks Synagogue, in Bishopsgate, London, was founded by Sephardic Jews in 1701 and is the oldest Synagogue still in use in Britain. Built by Joseph Avis, a Quaker, the construction of the building cost £2,750. The interior retains all of its original furnishings.

A silver card case, by Nathaniel Mills, chased with an image of Cupid and Venus, London 1846, 4in (10cm) high.

£270–320 PBA

LOCATE THE SOURCE

The source of each illustration in Miller's can be found by checking the code letters below each caption with the Key to Illustrations, pages 746–753.

◄ **A silver card case,** by Frederick Marson, engraved with flowers and leaf scrolls, slight damage, Birmingham 1857, 4in (10cm) high.

£150–175 DN

◄ **A silver card case,** by Walker & Hall, Sheffield 1905, 3¼in (8.5cm) high, 1½oz.

£360–400 BEX

CASTERS

A silver pepper caster, by Charles Adam, with an S-scroll handle, the cover pierced with foliage within a band of rosettes, the base engraved 'S' over 'DH', London 1708, 3¼in (8.5cm) high, 2½oz.

£2,100–2,500 S(NY)

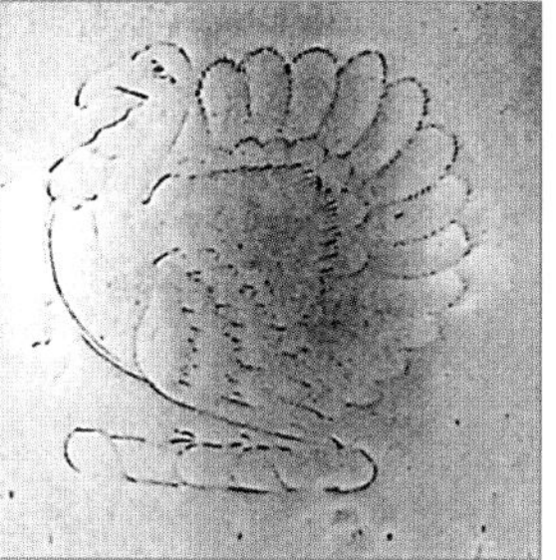

◄ **A silver caster,** by Simon Pantin I, the body engraved with a turkey crest, London 1710, 9in (23cm) high, 14oz.

£1,100–1,300 DN

A set of three silver casters, by Charles Adam, each engraved with a swan crest, London 1713, 6in (15cm) high, 18oz.

£2,750–3,300 S(NY)

Casters are popular items – they look good on the table as well as being useful; sets of three are quite rare.

CENTREPIECES

A Biedermeier silver centrepiece, by Josef Wastel, with pierced sides, Austria, Vienna 1824, 4¾in (12cm) high, 7¼oz.

£590–700 DORO

A pair of silver sweetmeat comports, with pierced and scrolling leaf decoration and bird-mask scroll handles, London 1908, 6¼in (16cm) wide.

£300–360 AH

◀ **A silver tazza,** the bowl with rope-work handles and a pierced rope-work border enclosing a gilded bowl, on four rope-mounted feet, Germany, Berlin, 19thC, 11in (28cm) high, 36oz.

£330–390 HYD

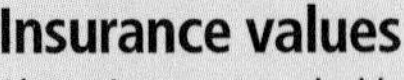

Insurance values

Always insure your valuable antiques for the cost of replacing them with similar items, regardless of the original price paid. Both dealers and auctioneers can provide a valuation service for a fee.

▶ **A silver epergne,** the central vase flanked by three smaller vases, maker's mark CC, Chester 1908, 12¼in (31cm) high.

£175–210 AG

A silver-gilt epergne, by Frederick Elkington, with a frosted glass bowl, the support modelled as a twisted vine on a rockwork base, London 1879, 10in (25.5cm) high.

£560–670 AH

CIGARETTE CASES

A Victorian silver cigarette case, with enamel decoration of a dog, hallmark incomplete, 2¼in (5.5cm) wide.

£330–390 FHF

A silver cigarette case and photograph frame, by William & George Neale, London 1900, 3¼in (8.5cm) wide.

£410–470 BEX

A silver cigarette case, with enamel decoration, Austria, c1900, 4½in (11.5cm) wide, 6¾oz.

£2,000–2,250 BEX

COFFEE & TEAPOTS

A silver teapot, by Samuel Willmott, the cover with a baluster finial, the interior pierced with foliate motifs at the spout, the base with engraved initials and date, Exeter 1730, 8¾in (22cm) wide, 13oz.

£2,250–2,700 S(NY)

Samuel Willmott (d1761) was apprenticed in London and afterwards lived in Plymouth, although his wares were marked in Exeter. Timothy Kent notes that he did not sell to the public but rather supplied the retail trade in Plymouth. This teapot would probably have realized a higher price if it had been sold in the UK.

A silver teapot, by Pierre Brun, embossed and chased with birds and fruit, the bird's-head spout cast and chased in the French manner, with an ivory handle, initialled 'RJW', Malta, 1775–97, 6in (15cm) high, 22½oz.

£5,400–6,400 S(O)

Pierre Brun, who intitially became a silversmith in St-Girons, near Toulouse, France, around 1745, is thought to have been influenced to go to Malta by Jean Lacère, to whom he had been apprenticed and who was connected to a number of Knights of St John. This maker's mark is found on a number of important pieces of Maltese silver in the French style.

A silver teapot, by Hester Bateman, with bright-cut borders, two foliate-mounted cartouches engraved with a crest and a monogram with beaded borders, with a scroll handle, London 1782, 5½in (14cm) high, 12oz.

£1,500–1,800 HYD

A silver teapot and stand, by Henry Chawner, with bright-cut swags, engraved with a shield and initials, London 1789, teapot 6in (15cm) high, 18oz.

£680–800 Mit

A silver teapot, by William Forbes, with engraved decoration and a wooden handle, America, New York, c1800, 7½in (19cm) high.

£1,750–1,950 ARG

A silver teapot, by William Hunterhand, decorated with a crest, the cover with a melon finial, on shell leaf-capped feet, c1849, 7in (18cm) high, 25½oz.

£230–270 SWO

American silver styles

American silversmiths, whatever their country of origin, mostly followed English provincial styles although, in New York, Dutch forms were popular during the 17th and 18th centuries. As the country became more sophisticated toward the end of the 18th century, current London styles were copied, particularly Adam-style designs with the Roman urn forms thought to be suitable for the new American Republic. The war of 1812 caused a break in this tradition and a new reliance on French design in the Empire taste followed. From the 1830s silver design followed a series of revivals including rococo, Renaissance and Gothic. In the 1870s these revival styles gave way to the Aesthetic style based on the newly popular Japanese wares that were first widely seen at the Philadelphia Centennial Celebration in 1876.

◀ **A silver teapot,** by Henry Salisbury, chased and embossed with leaves and flowers and scroll cartouches, the cover with a bud finial, America, New York, mid-19thC, 9in (23cm) high, 33oz.

£230–270 DN

A silver coffee pot, by Robert Hennell, engraved with scrolling acanthus leaves, London 1855, 10in (25.5cm) high, 28¼oz.

£340–400 WAD

A silver teapot, by Charles Boyton, with a moulded girdle and flower finial, monogrammed, London 1862, 6in (15cm) high, 28oz.

£200–240 SWO

An embossed silver coffee pot and milk jug, each with an applied shield engraved with a monogram, the cover with a chased leaf and flower finial, on four scroll feet, assay master Viktor Sawinkow 1866, mark of Alexander Nikolajewitsch Skolow, stamped '84', Russia, 19thC, coffee pot 8in (20.5cm) high, 47¼oz.

£400–480 DN

A silver coffee pot, by George Fox, with moulded borders and engraved with a crest and armorial, with a fruitwood handle, London 1879, 10in (25.5cm) high, 29oz.

£470–560 DN

The arms are of Thomas DeGrey, LLD, 6th Baron Walsingham, High Steward of Cambridge University.

► **A silver coffee pot,** by Marshall & Sons, engraved with foliate scrolls and cartouches, Scotland, Edinburgh 1892, 10½in (26.5cm) high.

£350–420 DN

A rococo-style silver coffee pot, by Charles Stuart Harris, with repoussé decoration and a crest, the cover with a fruit finial, London 1903, 11in (28cm) high, 28oz.

£480–210 WW

Charles Stuart Harris was a fine silversmith who copied many 18th-century designs. His pieces are normally made from thick gauge silver and are of good quality.

COFFEE & TEA SERVICES

◄ **A silver four-piece tea service,** by John Emes, engraved with Greek key borders and oak leaves, marked, London 1804, teapot 11¼in (28.5cm) wide, total weight 42oz.

£1,200–1,400 S(NY)

A silver three-piece tea service, by Andrew Fogelberg, with bright-cut key banding and floral-engraved reserves above key cartouches, on ball feet, London 1806.

£3,000–3,600 JAd

◄ **A silver four-piece coffee and tea service,** by William Elliott, with leaf-capped scroll handles, London 1825, total weight 80oz.

£1,000–1,200 WW

A silver three-piece tea service, probably by William Hewitt, with repoussé flowers and foliage surrounding a vacant cartouche, the teapot with a rose finial, London 1825, total weight 43oz.

£470–560 M

A silver five-piece coffee and tea service, by Grosjean & Woodward for Tiffany and Co, with repoussé and engraved decoration, crested and initialled, America, New York c1855, coffee pot 11in (28cm) high, total weight 119½oz.

£3,400–4,050 WAD

A silver four-piece coffee and tea service, by Elkington, Mason & Co, with engraved decoration and pierced galleries, Birmingham 1854, coffee pot 11½in (29cm) high.

£1,950–2,300 S(NY)

A silver four-piece coffee service, by W. S., with engraved decoration and inscription, coffee pot London 1858–59, with a matched teapot by Edward and John Barnard, London 1858, total weight 73¾oz.

£700–840 Bea

A silver six-piece coffee and tea service, by Gorham Manufacturing Co, the bodies engraved to one side with entwined initials below Oriental-style drapery panels of foliage and lotus blossom, the covers with bud finials, America, Providence, 1872, coffee pot 11¾in (30cm) high.

£1,400–1,650 S(O)

A silver eight-piece coffee and tea service, by Howard & Co, with shell and foliate rims, the bodies chased with flowers and foliage, on paw feet, America, New York, c1900, coffee pot 9¼in (23.5cm) high.

£2,600–3,100 S(O)

A silver five-piece coffee and tea service, by Gorham Manufacturing Co, with repoussé and engraved decoration, the rims and handles moulded with foliate scrollwork, initialled and inscribed, America, Providence, c1902, coffee pot 10in (25.5cm) high, total weight 88oz.

£1,450–1,700 WAD

The American tea and coffee service

A large tea and coffee service with tray was the ultimate American silver status symbol. Whether in sterling or silver plate, no middle-class family could be without one.

American sets produced after c1860 contain a coffee pot, one or two teapots (for black and green tea), a covered sugar bowl, a creamer and a waste or slop bowl. Often there was a kettle-on-stand and a sterling or plate tea tray ensuite. The major manufacturers could supply sets in any taste, from strictly traditional to avant-garde pieces that were already stocked in their vast factories and Tiffany & Co and Gorham Manufacturing Co could supply custom sets for presentation. Small three-piece black coffee sets became popular c1880.

Prices for complete sets can range from £400 for an attractive 19th-century plated set to £272,000 for a great custom-made set by Tiffany & Co in the Japanese taste.

A silver six-piece coffee and tea service, by Henry Birks & Sons, engraved with scrolling foliage, with ebonized wood scroll handles and finials, initialled, Canada, Montreal, 1929, coffee pot 8½in (21.5cm) high, total weight 111oz.

£1,450–1,700 WAD

CONDIMENT POTS

A silver trencher salt, by John Cory, with rope-work borders and engraved stylized decoration, London 1704, 2in (5cm) high, 1oz.

£500–600 HYD

A pair of silver salts, London 1809, 3in (7.5cm) diam.

£430–480 BHA

Trencher salt cellars

Trencher salt cellars have no feet and can be rectangular, circular or octagonal. They were first made in the last quarter of the 16th century. Prior to this date salts were mainly for ceremonial dinners and would be much larger and more elaborate. They would be placed next to distinguished guests or the host to show their importance, and certainly they would not be moved down the table. The term trencher – the wooden board that the lower orders would use as a plate – indicates the class difference between the 'low' salts and the tall imposing salts.

A silver mustard pot, by Diederick L. Bennewitz, with a hinged cover, the body with pierced decoration, with blue glass liner, Holland, Amsterdam 1801, 4½in (11.5cm) wide, 3¾oz.

£360–430 WW

A silver mustard pot, by Benoni Stephens, embossed with tulips, London 1835, 3½in (9cm) high, 5oz.

£300–360 DN

◄ **A silver mustard pot and spoon,** marked K, Austria, Linz, 1822, 2¾in (7cm) high, 2¼oz.

£1,150–1,350 DORO

CRUETS

A silver cruet, possibly by Robert Hennell, the stand with pierced and bright-cut decoration, with eight bottles, three later stoppers, one stopper missing, damage to handle, London 1783, 10in (25.5cm) high.

£260–310 Hal

► **A silver cruet,** by William Bateman, the reeded wirework frame on bun feet, with four later bottles, London 1815, 6¼in (16cm) high, 7½oz.

£230–270 SWO

◄ **A silver cruet,** with six silver-mounted and cut-glass bottles, maker's mark rubbed, stand London 1794, 7in (18cm) wide.

£350–420 DN

A set of four silver salts, by Martin, Hall & Co, relief-decorated with ribbon-tied floral swags, London and Sheffield, 1876–79, each 2½in (6.5cm) diam, with a set of salt spoons, in a fitted velvet-lined leather case.

£175–210 DD

CUPS & GOBLETS

A silver chinoiserie tea bowl, flat-chased with exotic birds, maker's mark D, London 1685, 3in (7.5cm) diam, 2oz.

£4,200–5,000 S(NY)

A silver two-handled cup and cover, with engraved cypher, maker's mark D, London 1691, 8in (20.5cm) high, 25oz.

£2,750–3,300 S(NY)

A William III silver tot cup, the base engraved 'AP' over '1699', maker's mark TS, c1699, 2in (5cm) diam.

£580–690 S(NY)

Silver markings in the United States

There is no American equivalent to the English hall-marking laws, with the small exception of Baltimore silver from about 1815 to 1835. Only the common law of fraud and some 20th-century consumer protection laws govern silver standards. Prior to the Revolution, American silversmiths used the sterling standard. Later, the 900/1000 of the Spanish colonial silver coinage was the legal standard in most US cities. This is often called coin-silver although the silverware was not necessarily made from coins directly. Most early American silver is struck only with the maker's name and initials, sometimes within the maker's working life. In 1868 Gorham Manufacturing Co adopted the sterling standard which quickly became the standard throughout the country. Marking for silver-plated wares was not regulated by law.

► **A silver two-handled cup,** by Joseph Johns, chased in relief with windmills, wheat sheaves, farm tools and flowers, Ireland, Limerick, 1730–75, 5in (12.5cm) high, 11oz.

£4,100–4,900 MEA

A silver tumbler cup, by John Swift, engraved with coat-of-arms and inscription, marked, London 1753, 2¾in (7cm) high, 6oz.

£6,200–7,400 S(NY)

◄ **A silver two-handled cup,** by Langlands & Robertson, with a reeded band, Newcastle 1783, 5½in (14cm) high, 11oz.

£440–520 DD

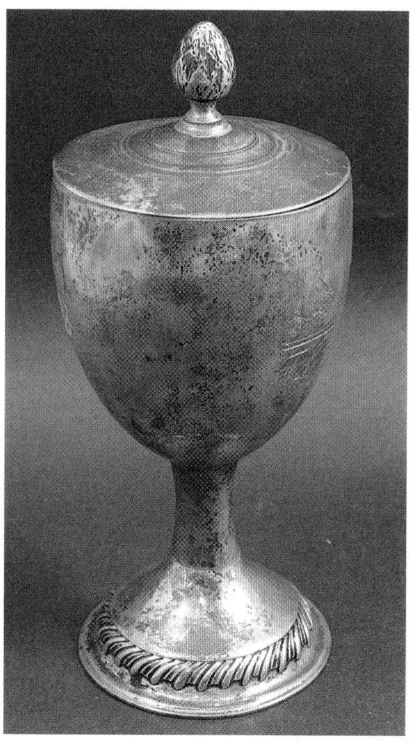

A George III silver goblet, by John Lloyd, with an engraved armorial, Irish, Dublin, together with an associated cover by Benjamin Godfrey, London 1732, 6¼in (16cm) high, 11oz.

£520–620 G(L)

A George III silver cup, later engraved with flowers and C-scrolls on a diaper ground, marker's mark WT, Ireland, Dublin, 5¼in (13.5cm) high.

£410–490 DN(BR)

A silver cup, by Chauldron's & Rasch, America, Philadelphia, c1812, 2¾in (7cm) diam.

£680–760 ARG

A silver goblet, by John Walton, Newcastle 1820, 7in (18cm) high.

£580–650 ANC

Goblets are often wrongly referred to as chalices, even though visually there is not much difference between them. A chalice would be used as a eucharist cup, whereas a goblet would be for the pleasure of drinking wine.

A pair of sterling silver goblets, by Grosjean & Woodward for Tiffany & Co, decorated in relief with flowers and leaves, marked, America, c1853, 6½in (16.5cm) high.

£2,500–3,000 JDJ

▶ **A silver goblet,** by Robert Hendery, with repoussé and engraved decoration of flowers and leaves and a cartouche with inscription, Canada, Quebec, c1860, 6in (15cm) high, 4½oz.

£1,700–2,000 WAD

A set of six silver-gilt and niello water goblets, each engraved with a city gate and a view of St Sophia, Constantinople, stamped '84', Russia, late 19thC, 5in (12.5cm) high.

£10,400–12,450 S(NY)

◀ **A silver and copper cup,** monogrammed, America, c1900, 9¼in (23.5cm) high.

£240–280 SWO

Further reading

Miller's Collecting Silver: The Facts at Your Fingertips, Miller's Publications, 1999

◀ **A silver two-handled trophy cup,** possibly by Whiting Manufacturing Co, with presentation inscription, on a wooden plinth, maker's mark W and a griffin, America, c1900, 11¾in (30cm) high, 74oz.

£1,000–1,200 WW

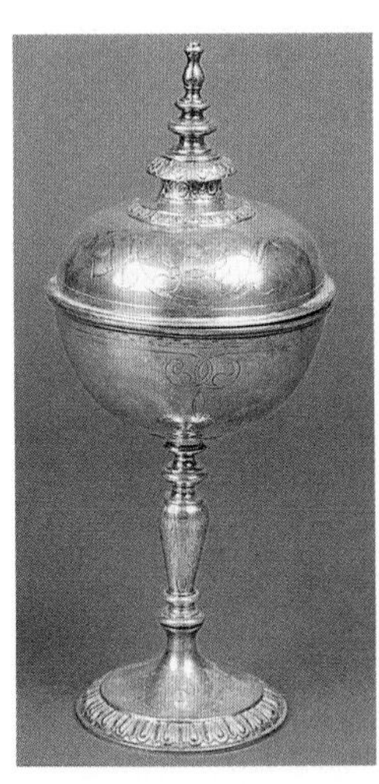

▶ **An Elizabethan-style silver cup and cover,** by D. & J. Welby, with engraved decoration, London 1909, 12½in (32cm) high, 26oz.

£350–420 HYD

CUTLERY

A silver seal top spoon, engraved 'MG', marked 'R' and 'B' within a shield, 17thC, 6in (15cm) long.

£2,050–2,450 TEN

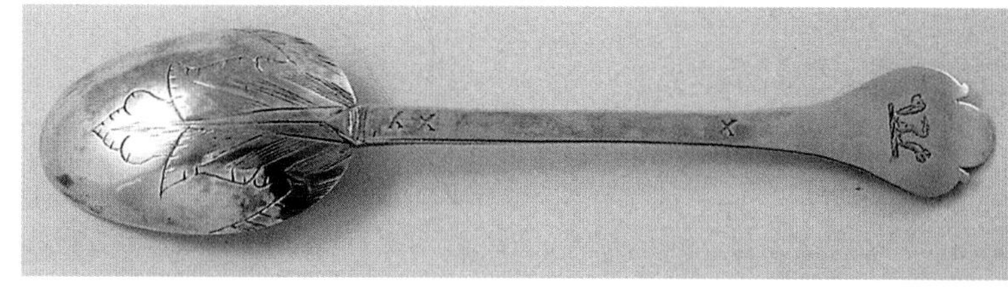

A silver trefid spoon, engraved with a tulip, crested, X marks, probably Exeter 1680–85, 8in (20.5cm) long, 1oz.

£570–680 WW

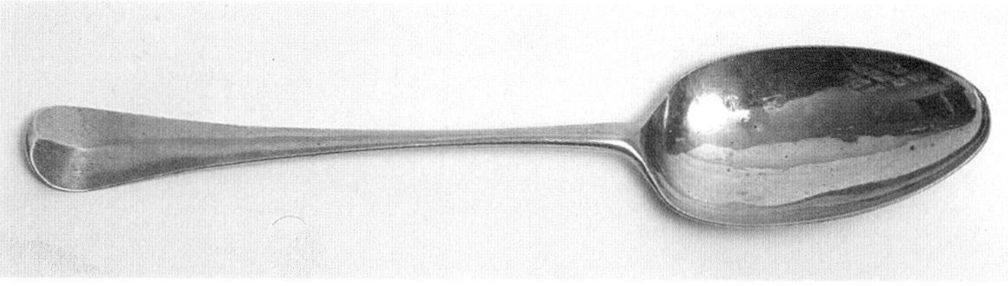

A silver spoon, by John Kentember, 1759, 8in (20.5cm) long.

£70–80 CoHA

A silver spoon, by Langlands & Robertson, Newcastle, c1780, 9in (23cm) long.

£65–75 GGD

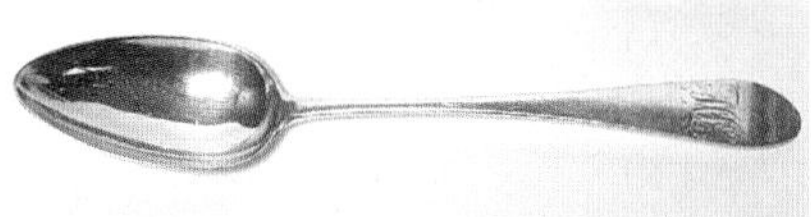

A pair of silver spoons, by Carden Terry and Jane Williams, Ireland, Cork, c1810, 9in (23cm) long.

£250–280 GRe

Silver from Cork in Ireland is very desirable.

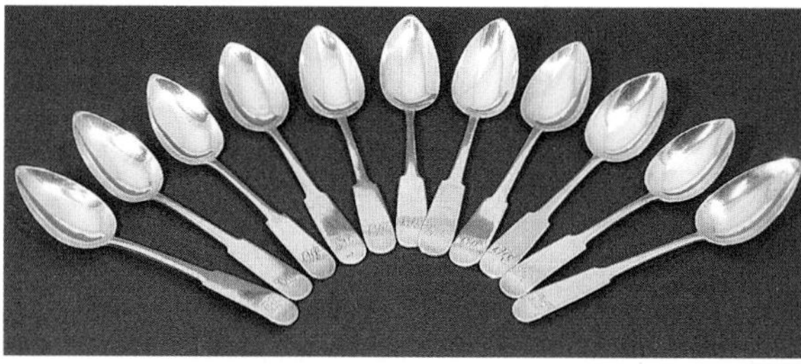

A set of 11 silver Fiddle pattern teaspoons, by Robert Keay, Scotland, Perth, early 19thC, 5in (12.5cm) long, 4½oz.

£220–260 G(L)

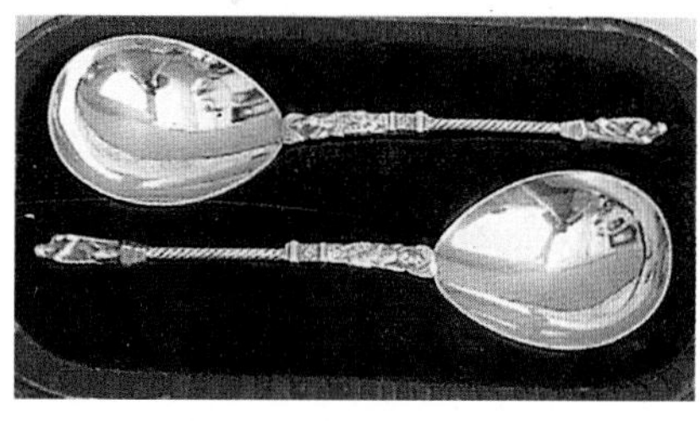

A pair of silver apostle spoons, by Edward Hutton, with twist handles and gilded bowls, London 1885, 7in (18cm) long, 4oz, in a case.

£120–140 PF

A silver dessert service, comprising 36 pieces, with ivory handles, Chester 1920, in mahogany case, 12 x 10in (30.5 x 25.5cm).

£175–195 SAT

When looking at ivory-handled cutlery, check for cracks in the ivory, as this lowers the price considerably.

APOSTLE SPOONS

Apostle spoons first appeared in the mid-15th century. They are so-called because the finials are cast in the form of the 12 apostles, each one identifiable by the emblem they are holding. Sets that comprise 13 pieces include the figure of Christ, but are very rare. Individual spoons were often given as a christening present, particularly if the child was named after one of the apostles. Very few full sets survive; they should all be made by the same maker in the same year.

left to right, top to bottom:
St Matthias, St James the Greater, St Jude, St Matthew, St Andrew, St Simon, St Thomas, St John, St Peter, St James the Less, St Philip and St Bartholomew.

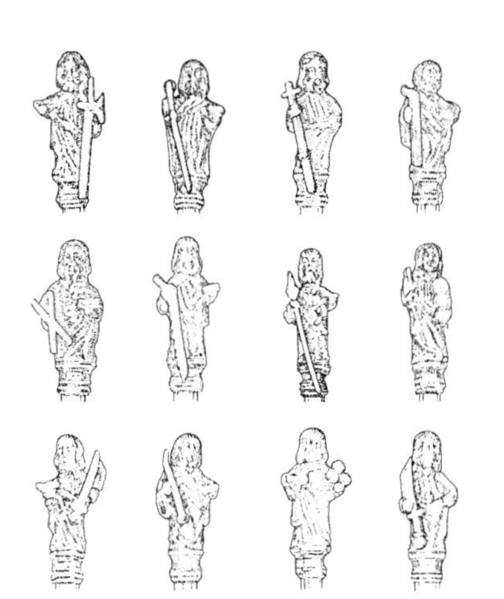

DISHES

► **A silver dish,** by William Williamson, Ireland, Dublin 1733, 6½in (16.5cm) wide.

£1,750–2,100 MEA

◄ **A silver-gilt two-handled dish,** with a central panel depicting a fruit picker, maker's mark HB and Augsburg mark, Germany, 17thC, 6in (15cm) wide, 3¾oz.

£700–840 Bea

◄ **A silver dish,** with chased and tooled rococo decoration, Assay Master's mark for José Antonio Lince Gonzalez, Mexico City, c1780, 16¾in (42.5cm) diam, 32oz.

£2,600–3,100 S(NY)

► **A silver olive dish,** by Gorham Manufacturing Co, America, Providence, c1885, 6in (15cm) wide.

£1,100–1,250 ARG

The Gorham Manufacturing Co

Jabez Gorham began making coin-silver spoons in the 1830s, but soon became interested in the technology of large scale silver production. By the 1860s Gorham was one of the largest manufacturers of silverware in the US, with many flatware patterns and full-scale production of hollow ware. European artists and designers were hired to ensure that the wares were stylish and contemporary. Gorham supplemented their mass-produced wares with smaller ranges of art silver such as the *martelé* line in the Art Nouveau taste. The Gorham trademark of a lion, an anchor and the letter G resembles British hallmarks. They used the coin silver standard of 900/1000 fine until 1863, after which they used the sterling standard of 925/1000. Gorham produced some of the finest silver made in America from 1860 to 1890.

A pair of silver strawberry dishes, retailed by The Goldsmiths & Silversmiths Co, stamped with game birds and hunting dogs, Ireland, Dublin 1908, 8¾in (22cm) diam, 23oz.

£820–980 N

COVERED DISHES

A silver and cut-glass butter dish, with engraved decoration, Sheffield 1850, 6in (15cm) wide.

£620–690 ANC

A silver butter dish and cover, by Kidney, Cann & Johnson, America, New York, 1863, 8½in (21.5cm) wide.

£1,300–1,450 ARG

A silver breakfast pan, the interior with three divisions, maker's mark 'TB', London 1903, 14in (35.5cm) diam, 58½oz.

£470–560 Hal

A pair of silver entrée dishes, by Turner Bradbury, London 1904, 11in (28cm) wide, 102oz.

£1,300–1,550 DN

◄ **A silver dish and cover,** chased with roses, marked 'S. Kirk & Sons', America, Baltimore, early 20thC, 13½in (34cm) wide, 50oz.

£870–1,050 DORO

DISH RINGS

A silver dish ring, by Benjamin Godfrey, marked, London 1740, 7¾in (19.5cm) diam, 12oz.
£4,200–5,000 S(NY)

A silver dish ring, by William Homer, with four cartouches depicting figures and animals, engraved with an hourglass crest, Ireland, Dublin 1771, 7¾in (19.5cm) diam, 11½oz.
£5,500–6,600 S(NY)

Fake hallmarks

The dish ring or cross was simply for keeping hot plates off the table. Some crosses will also have a burner in the centre to maintain the heat. The dish ring originates from Ireland in the 18th century and has commonly, but incorrectly, been described as a 'potato' ring. In the 19th century it became more fashionable to have blue glass liners made for rings to convert them into a more useful and decorative bowl. Around 1900, the fashion for these decorative 'bowls' increased and many good examples were made in the 18th-century style. However, this later led to a type of forgery wherein the hallmarks were cut out of the 19th-century examples and replaced with 18th-century Irish hallmarks taken from existing damaged pieces of silver, thus increasing the value considerably. This is probably one of the more common forms of faking but can be detected by close examination of the hallmarks and looking for the solder seam around the marks.

◀ A silver dish ring, decorated with chinoiserie motifs and scrollwork, with a glass liner, Ireland, Dublin 1892, 7½in (19cm) diam, 15½oz.
£1,050–1,250 JAd

▶ A silver dish ring, by Edmond Johnson, engraved with scroll and shell cartouches and birds and flowers among scrolling foliage, Ireland, Dublin 1914, 7in (18cm) diam, 8oz.
£910–1,100 WAD

FRAMES

A silver photograph frame, Birmingham 1892, 3in (7.5cm) high.
£135–150 SAT

A silver photograph frame, by H. Matthews, Birmingham 1900, 3½in (9cm) wide.
£360–410 RICC

A silver photograph frame, London 1903, 10in (25.5cm) wide.
£600–680 ANC

◀ A silver photograph frame, with pierced decoration, Birmingham 1903, 14½ x 9½in (37 x 24cm).
£330–390 SWO

▶ A silver photograph frame, with ribbon and reed pattern, Chester 1907, 7in (18cm) high.
£400–450 LUH

INKWELLS & STANDS

A silver and glass travelling inkwell, by George Reid, London 1839, 1¾in (4.5cm) square.

£270–300 LUH

A silver inkwell, in the form of a well with a bucket and a water barrel, slight damage, stamped 'E750', possibly Continental, 19thC, 5in (12.5cm) high, 8oz.

£140–165 Hal

A silver and hobnail cut-glass inkwell, by H. Matthews, Birmingham 1900, 4in (10cm) diam.

£350–390 ANC

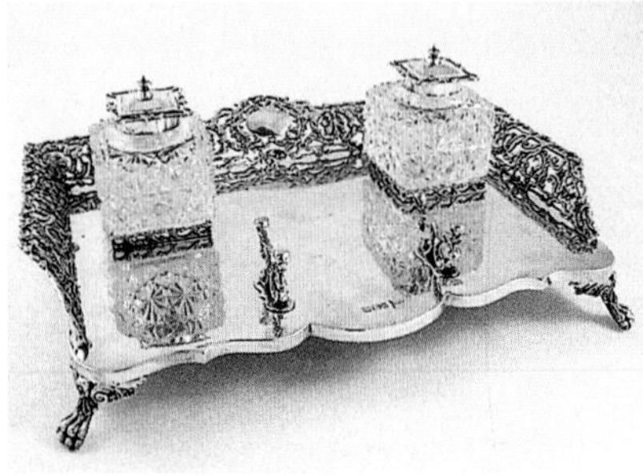

A silver inkstand, by Walker & Hall, with two cut-glass ink bottles with hinged covers, Sheffield 1900, 13¼in (33.5cm) wide, 41oz.

£960–1,150 WW

► **A silver inkstand,** by William Hutton & Sons, London 1900, 15in (38cm) wide.

£2,000–2,250 YOX

◄ **A silver inkwell,** by Simpson Benzie, in the form of a capstan, the hinged cover enamelled with an ensign, with a gilt interior, London 1914, 3¼in (8.5m) high, 4½oz.

£530–630 SWO

Simpson Benzie was listed as a jeweller at 61 High Street, Cowes, Isle of Wight.

JUGS & EWERS

A silver wine/hot water ewer, with acanthus-leaf decoration, London 1774, 12¼in (31cm) high, 26oz.

£700–840 MA&I

A sterling silver water jug, by Anthony Rasch, with engraved decoration, America, Philadelphia, early 19thC, 13¼in (33.5cm) high, 37oz.

£5,100–6,100 SK(B)

◄ **A silver cream jug,** by Thomas Wheather, Newcastle 1839, 5in (12.5cm) high.

£260–300 ANC

Water and whisky

Some silver forms are unique to America or have particular uses there. Large pitchers, elsewhere known as jugs, were used for iced water or lemonade, unlike the French ewer which really descends from pieces used to wash the hands over the basin. Many Americans converted their old beer tankards into jugs in response to the early 19th-century temperance movement. The jug by the German Anthony Rasch shown here was made in Philadelphia to the very latest French taste around 1815.

A silver-mounted glass claret jug, repoussé-decorated with flowers, by W. & G. Sissons, Sheffield 1864, 10in (25.5cm) high.

£1,400–1,650 PF

A silver wine ewer, by Messrs Barnard, London 1868, 12in (30.5cm) high.

£3,450–3,850 BEX

A silver wine jug, by Robert Hendery, engraved with the regimental badge of the Royal Canadian Rifles and a presentation inscription, the cover surmounted with a beaver finial, Canada, Quebec, c1868, 12in (30.5cm) high, 28oz.

£2,250–2,700 WAD

A silver-mounted claret jug, by W. & G. Sissons, Sheffield 1873–74, 11in (28cm) high.

£2,450–2,750 NS

A silver and parcel-gilt ewer, by Elkington & Co, chased and engraved with berries, fuchsias and foliage, with presentation inscription, Birmingham 1877, 14¼in (36cm) high.

£960–1,150 SWO

A pair of silver-gilt and crystal wine jugs, by Lars Larson & Co, slight damage, Sweden, Gothenburg 1885, 15in (38cm) high.

£5,400–6,400 BUK(F)

MIRRORS

A silver mirror, maker's mark CIB, Austria, Vienna, 17(?)9, 15½in (39.5cm) high.

£1,850–2,200 DORO

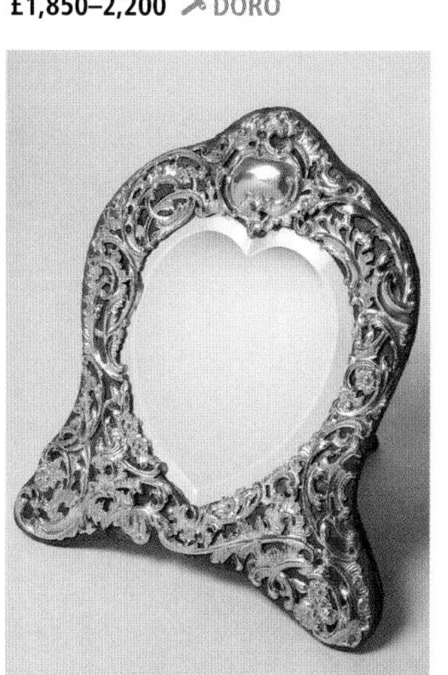

A silver mirror, London 1903, 12½in (32cm) high.

£350–390 PSA

A silver-mounted easel-back mirror, by Judah Rosenthal and Samuel Jacob, embossed with griffins, masks, scrolls and a cartouche, London 1884, 14in (36cm) high.

£360–430 DN

► **A silver mirror,** by William Comyns, pierced and embossed with figures, fairies, fauns, birds and Cupid, surmounted with a cartouche, London 1889, 27in (68.5cm) high.

£260–310 S(NY)

Prices

The price ranges quoted in this book reflect the average price a purchaser might expect to pay for a similar item. The price will vary according to the condition, rarity, size, popularity, provenance, colour and restoration of the item, and this must be taken into account when assessing values. Don't forget that if you are selling it is quite likely that you will be offered less than the price range.

◄ **A silver mirror,** by H. Matthews, pierced and embossed with scrolls and flowers, surmounted with a cartouche, Birmingham 1904, 20½ x 13¾in (52 x 35cm).

£280–330 DN

MINIATURE FURNITURE

A silver miniature cradle, Holland, 1890, 3in (7.5cm) wide.
£620–700 BLm

A silver miniature table, by Berthold Müller, Holland, London import marks for 1897, 2½in (6.5cm) wide.
£135–150 SAT

A set of silver miniature furniture, comprising table, chair and settee, each decorated with putti playing instruments, Birmingham 1901, table 2in (5cm) wide.
£270–300 CoHa

MUGS & TANKARDS

A silver tankard, by David Scheibner, chased with flowers, with a gilt interior, marked, Austria, Salzburg, c1670, 5½in (14cm) high, 9½oz.
£5,500–6,600 DORO

A silver mug, probably by Richard Syng, with part-fluted decoration and central cartouche, London 1704, 4in (10cm) high, 6oz.
£750–900 HYD

A silver tankard, by Jacob Hurd, engraved 'Samuel Whitney', 'Castine' and '1793', the base inscribed with Whitney family owners in the 18th and 19th centuries, slight damage, America, Boston 1728, 4¾in (12cm) high, 10oz.
£10,800–12,900 SK(B)

A silver mug, by Humphrey Payne, London 1739, 4in (10cm) high.
£1,450–1,650 BEX

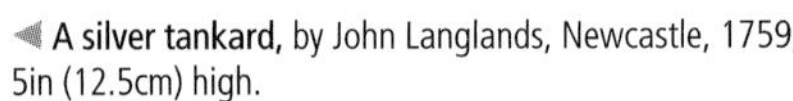

◄ **A silver tankard,** by John Langlands, Newcastle, 1759, 5in (12.5cm) high.
£850–950 ANC

A silver tankard, by Godbehere & Wigan, with a pierced thumbpiece, initialled 'G. & H. I.', London 1793, 8¾in (22cm) high, 23oz.
£1,100–1,300 TRM(E)

◄ **A silver christening mug,** with a gilt interior, London 1840, 4in (10cm) high.
£195–220 SPE

A silver christening mug, by Edward & John Barnard, with foliate-engraved cartouches, London 1857, 4in (10cm) high.
£120–140 MAL(O)

Christening mugs

As most christening mugs were given as presents, many were engraved with inscriptions and initials which may have been removed later, thereby reducing the value. By running your thumb and finger around the mug, it is easy to determine a change in thickness to the silver to discover if anything has been altered.

A silver mug, by Robert Harper, embossed with flowers and a scroll cartouche engraved with a crest and ribbon motto 'Res Non Verba', London 1873, 5¼in (13.5cm) high, 7½oz.
£240–280 DN

NAPKIN RINGS

◀ **A set of six silver napkin rings,** by James Dixon & Sons, with engine-turned decoration and applied numbers, Sheffield 1873, in a lined box, 10in (25.5cm) wide.

£230–270 HOLL

A set of six silver napkin rings, Birmingham 1907, 2in (5cm) diam, in a fitted case.

£470–530 ANC

◀ **A set of silver napkin rings,** engraved 'B', four London 1927, two Glasgow 1907, 6oz, in a leather case.

£240–280 Hal

▶ **A set of six silver napkin rings, each with a cartouche engraved with a number,** Sheffield 1936, 2in (5cm) diam, in a fitted case.

£630–700 BHA

NUTMEG GRATERS

A silver nutmeg grater, probably by Thomas Kedder, scratch-engraved with a tulip and border, with original grater, marked, London 1695–1700, 2½in (6.5cm) long, ½oz.

£1,950–2,350 WW

A silver nutmeg grater, by John Albright, London, c1700, 1½in (4cm) wide.

£2,000–2,400 S(O)

A silver nutmeg grater, by Michael Sculer Jr, Ireland, Kinsale, c1750, 1¾in (4.5cm) wide.

£3,600–4,000 WELD

Pieces from Kinsale are very rare.

PAPER KNIVES

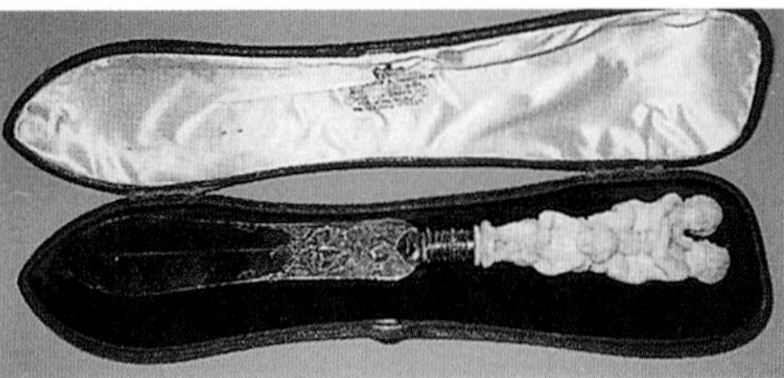

◀ **A silver-gilt paper knife,** with chased decoration and carved ivory handle in the form of cherubs, London 1858, 9in (23cm) long, in a fitted case.

£610–730 SPF

A silver paper knife, by R. D. & S, with a horn handle, Scotland, Glasgow 1872, 9in (23cm) long.

£390–440 BEX

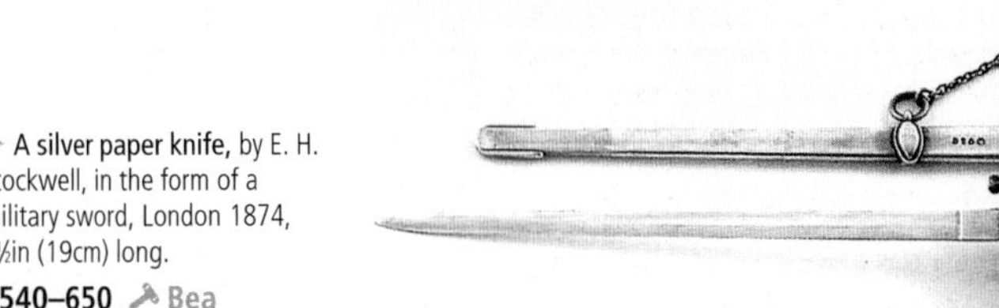

▶ **A silver paper knife,** by E. H. Stockwell, in the form of a military sword, London 1874, 7½in (19cm) long.

£540–650 Bea

PLATES & DISHES

A silver dinner plate, by N. O., Denmark, Copenhagen 1799, 26in (66cm) diam, 14¾oz.

£2,100–2,350 BEX

◀ **A set of ten silver dinner plates,** by William Bateman II for Rundell, Bridge & Co, the rim engraved with a cypher for Queen Adelaide, the centre engraved with later Greek Royal coat-of-arms, marked, London 1837, 10½in (26.5cm) diam, 232oz.

£7,800–9,350 S(NY)

These plates belong to a large service by William Bateman that was originally intended for William IV and Queen Adelaide. However, by the time these plates were delivered, William IV had died.

A pair of silver plates, each engraved with an armorial within a scrolled cartouche, London 1907, 9¾in (25cm) diam, 32oz.

£270–320 ROS

RATTLES

◀ **A baby's silver rattle,** by Hilliard & Thomason, decorated with three cherubs holding bells, with a whistle and a coral teether, Birmingham 1852, 4¾in (12cm) high.

£1,200–1,400 HYD

Rattles

Baby rattles are very popular as presents and highly collectable. However, they often have their bells missing, due to the nature of their use, and therefore it is common to find replacement bells. This does make a significant difference to their value, so check the bells for differing styles and colours. Coral was often used for the teether as it was thought to have soothing properties for the gums and, again, can often be broken or missing.

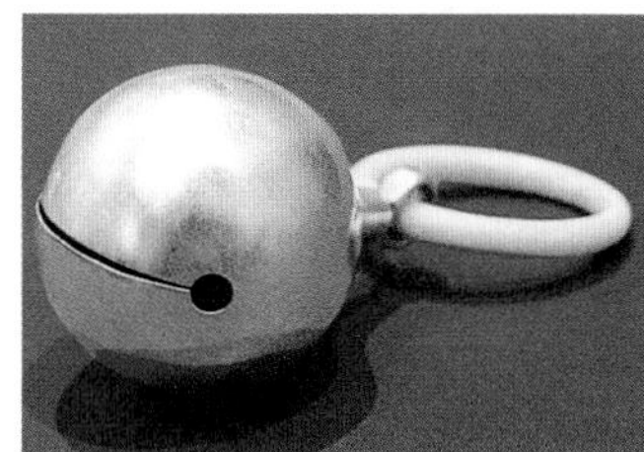

A baby's silver rattle, by G. S. Twist, in the form of a bell, with an ivory handle, Birmingham 1913, 4in (10cm) long.

£310–350 BEX

▶ **A baby's silver rattle,** by Crisford & Norris, in the form of a bear, with a bone handle and teether, slight damage, Birmingham 1922, 5¼in (13.5cm) long.

£390–440 BEX

SALVERS & TRAYS

◀ **A silver salver,** by Joseph Walker, with a moulded rim and capstan foot, engraved with a coat-of-arms, Ireland, Dublin 1696–8, 4½in (11.5cm) diam, 3½oz.

£2,100–2,500 S(NY)

▶ **A silver salver,** by Myer Myers, applied with shells, on cabriole legs, America, New York, mid-18thC, 8¼in (21cm) wide, 11¼oz.

£54,000–64,000 SK

Born in 1723 in New York City, Myer Myers was the most prolific silversmith in New York during the last half of the 18th century. After completing a seven-year apprenticeship with a master silversmith, he registered as a Goldsmith in 1746, making him the first native Jew within the British Empire to establish himself as a working silversmith since the incorporation of the Worshipful Company of Goldsmiths in 1327. Through a beneficial business partnership and marriage to the daughter of a wealthy merchant, Myers' business thrived. The clientele for his rococo-style objects included New York's wealthy elite. Myers' business suffered interruption in the summer of 1776, when the American Revolution came to New York. Myers and his family moved to Norwalk, Connecticut, thinking that the enemy would never come to such a small, insignificant place. Unfortunately, they were mistaken, and in 1779 British troops burned down the village, leaving Myers homeless and without his tools. Finally settling in Stratford, Connecticut, Myers started working again as a silversmith, adopting the neo-classical aesthetic of the New Republic. His business was not nearly as successful after the war, but his peers still held him in high regard, making him chairman of the newly formed Gold and Silver Smith's Society in 1785. He remained active in the Jewish community and died in 1795, at the age of 72. His works are now found in major museum collections in the US.

A silver tray, with a pierced border, on four ball feet, Portugal, Oporto, 1843–53, 26¾in (68cm) wide.

£1,700–2,000 WAD

A silver tray, by Frederick Elkington, engraved with stylized flowers and a coat-of-arms, Birmingham 1871, 28½in (72.5cm) wide, 130oz.

£2,250–2,700 HYD

A silver dressing table tray, by Elkington & Co, embossed and chased with swallows and a floral border, Birmingham 1900, 10¾in (27.5cm) wide.

£240–280 BWL

SAUCE BOATS

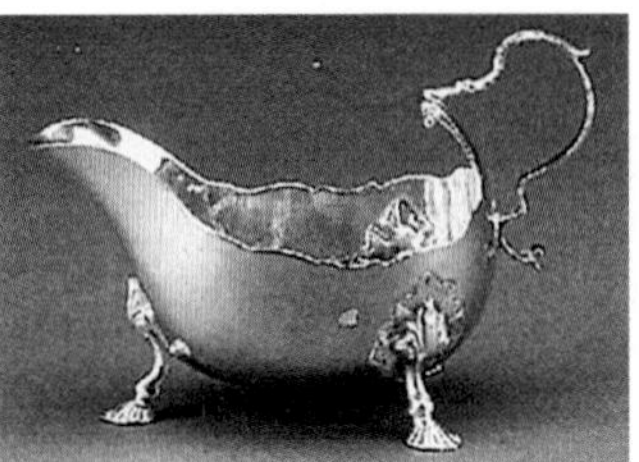

A silver sauce boat, with a leaf-capped scroll handle and shell feet, crested, maker's mark 'HW', Ireland, Dublin, c1770, 6in (15cm) wide.

£480–570 WAD

A silver sauce boat, by Fletcher & Gardiner, America, Philadelphia, c1820, 7in (18cm) long.

£590–660 ARG

A silver sauce boat, by Roberts & Belk, Sheffield 1899, 5in (12.5cm) high.

£340–380 ANC

SCENT BOTTLES

◀ **A parcel-gilt scent bottle,** the base engraved with initials 'WR' and a winged putto mask, with an ivory-mounted finial and screw cap, c1690, 3½in (9cm) high, 2½oz.

£690–820 WW

This scent bottle was sold with a piece of card, inscribed 'Curious ancient silver scent bottle and seal stamp, formerly belonging to King William III (Prince of Orange) many years in the museum of the late Dr Mcleish of Maryfield.'

A silver scent bottle, by Sampson Mordan & Co, with enamel floral decoration and a screw cap, London 1888, 2¾in (7cm) high, in a fitted leather case.

£640–760 RTo

Items in the silver section have been arranged in date order within each sub-section.

A silver scent bottle, by Sampson Mordan & Co, decorated with scrolls and birds, 1889, 3½in (9cm) high.

£600–680 BHA

A silver scent bottle, with foliate decoration and an inscription, and a hinged cover, maker's mark GW, Chester 1896, 3½in (9cm) high, in original fitted box.

£280–330 Bea

A silver-mounted cut-glass scent bottle, Birmingham 1906, 5in (12.5cm) high.

£270–300 ANC

A silver-mounted cut-glass scent bottle, by Mappin & Webb, Sheffield 1920, 6in (15cm) high.

£270–300 SAT

SERVING IMPLEMENTS

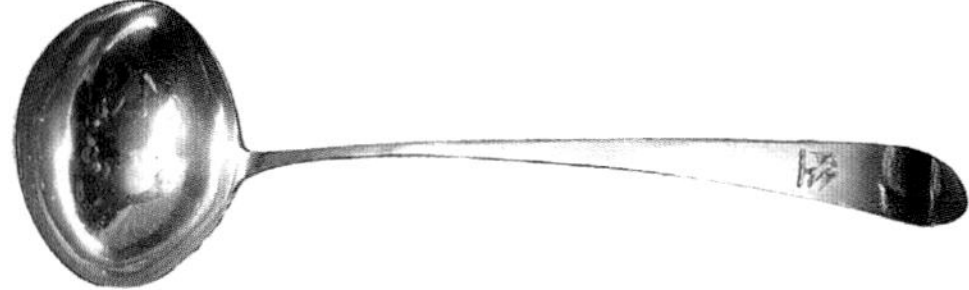

A silver ladle, by John Nicholson, Irish, Cork, c1775, 14in (35.5cm) long.
£1,950–2,200 WELD

If this ladle had been made in London it would be worth about £400. Cork silver is very hard to find, hence its value.

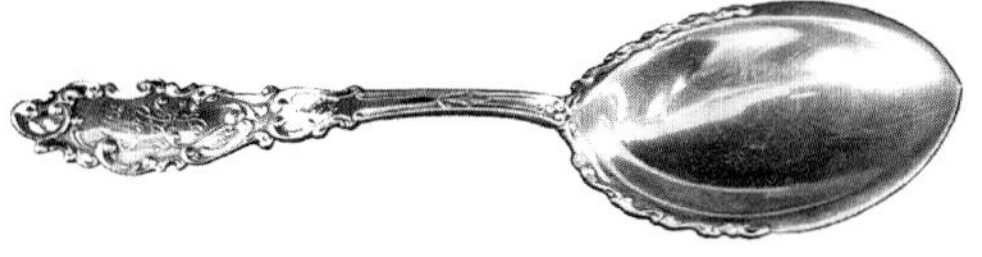

A silver-gilt and enamel serving spoon, by Gorham Manufacturing Co, America, Providence, 1880, 8¼in (21cm) long.
£250–280 ALT

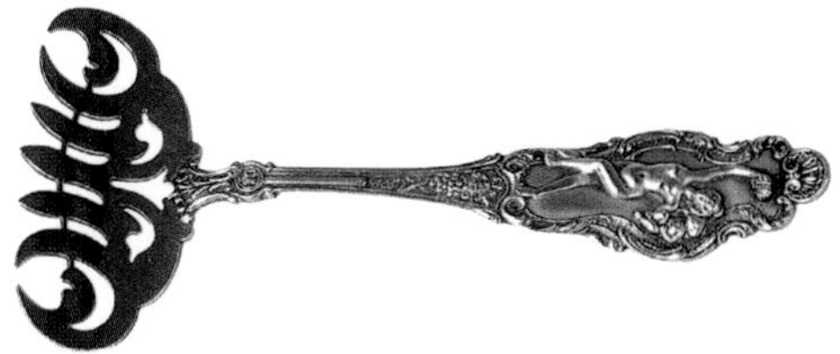

A silver basting spoon, by Stephen Adam, London 1784, 12in (30.5cm) long.
£220–250 GRe

American fancy goods

In the 1860s a vast flood of silver came out of the Comstock lode in Virginia City, Nevada. American manufacturers sensed the pent-up desire for fancy goods which arose after the Civil War and produced hundreds of proprietary flatware patterns and an infinite variety of fancy serving pieces. Terrapin forks, oyster ladles, fried-chicken tongs, sardine forks, mango forks and other exotic pieces competed for the attention of the public. Quality of design and workmanship are superb and such pieces are collected as art objects as much as for practical purposes. For a few decades American silver flatware was among the best in the world! Expect to pay from £80 for small fancy items up to £3,000 for important serving pieces.

◄ **A silver sardine fork,** by Watson Newell Co, decorated with Phoebe pattern, America, c1895, 4¾in (12cm) long.
£310–350 ARG

SNUFF BOXES

A Georgian silver snuff box, with reeded decoration, 2½in (6.5cm) wide.
£160–180 SAT

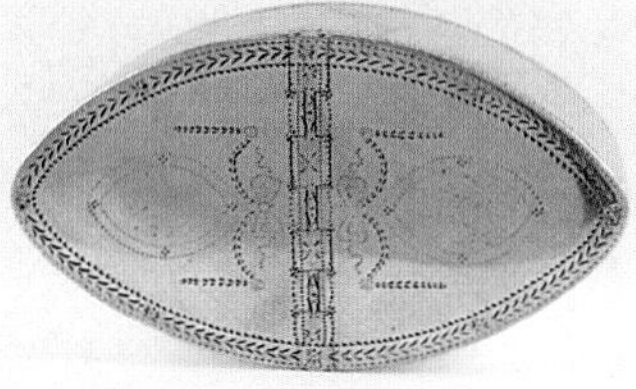

A silver double navette-shaped snuff box, with bright-cut decoration, the two covers with a single hinge enclosing gilt interiors, maker's mark 'IW', Scotland, Edinburgh, 1790–95, 4½in (11.5cm) wide, 6oz.
£1,550–1,850 WW

A silver-mounted shell snuff box, by Thomas Watson, Newcastle, c1793, 3in (7.5cm) wide.
£880–980 ANC

Further reading

Miller's Antiques Checklist: Silver and Plate, Miller's Publications, 1997

► **A silver snuff box,** c1860, Continental, 3in (7.5cm) wide.
£110–125 MB

A silver snuff box, with niello banding and engraved scrolling foliage, the hinged cover with a gold thumbpiece enclosing a gilt interior, Russia, Moscow 1849, 3½in (9cm) wide, 3½oz.
£470–560 NSal

◄ **A silver snuff box,** the cover inset with a mother-of-pearl panel and inscribed on both sides with details of 'The Great Eastern Steam Ship', Chester 1898, 7½in (19cm) wide.
£220–260 DD

STRAINERS

◄ **A silver punch strainer,** by John Albright, the bowl pierced with flowerheads, with openwork handles, London 1718, 7in (18cm) wide, 2oz.

£840–1,000 S(NY)

A silver tea strainer, by V. M. S, with an ivory handle, Austria, c1900, 6¾in (17cm) long, 3oz.

£200–230 BEX

◄ **A silver strainer,** engraved with crests and initials, maker's mark 'AB', 18thC, 6½in (16.5cm) wide, 3¼oz.

£2,350–2,800 BWL

TABLE BELLS

A silver table bell, possibly by Charles Frederick Kandler, later engraved to one side with a crest, maker's mark indistinct, London 1761, 5in (12.5cm) high, 7¼oz.

£3,250–3,900 S(NY)

A silver table bell, master's mark 'PM' for Paul Mayerhofer, Austria, Vienna 1806, 4in (10cm) high, 4½oz.

£470–560 DORO

A silver reception bell, with pierced scroll decoration, Sheffield 1875, 3in (7.5cm) high.

£340–400 MAL(O)

TEA CADDIES

A silver tea caddy, by William Plummer, with beaded borders and bright-cut ribbon-tied floral swags, vases and a cartouche with an armorial, the cover with an ivory finial, London 1783, 5¼in (13.5cm) diam, 12½oz.

£1,250–1,500 DN

A silver tea caddy, by William Robertson, with a hinged lid and engraved decoration with a vacant cartouche, Edinburgh 1792, 5in (12.5cm) wide.

£1,400–1,650 WilP

A silver tea caddy, embossed with a stag and boar hunting scene, Continental, import marks for London 1908, 5in (12.5cm) high, 7¼oz.

£125–150 WW

TUREENS

A silver soup tureen, by Alexander Johnson, engraved to one side of the cover and body with later arms and a shield in a rococo cartouche, London 1755, 15½in (39.5cm) wide, 87½oz.

£4,850–5,800 S(NY)

A silver soup tureen, by William Kerr Reid, London 1828, 17in (43cm) wide.

£14,100–15,700 ARG

◄ **A pair of silver soup tureens,** by John Robins, bodies later embossed with pineapples, flowers, C-scrolls and a cartouche with an armorial, the covers with cornucopia finials, London 1804, 16½in (42cm) wide, 150oz.

£5,200–6,200 DN

URNS

A silver tea urn, by Charles Kandler, London 1785, 21¼in (54cm) high, 87¼oz.

£1,200–1,400 S(O)

A silver urn, by Elkington & Co, London 1872, 8¼in (21cm) high.

£130–155 WilP

A pair of silver urns, by S. Blanckensee, the covers with vase finials, the pierced bowls with ram's-head mask ring handles, import marks for Chester 1905, 9in (23cm) high, 40¼oz.

£1,000–1,200 DN

VESTA CASES

A silver, gold and niello vesta and tobacco case, by A. Dubois, slight damage, France, c1870, 3¾in (9.5cm) diam.

£1,550–1,750 BEX

◄ **A silver vesta case,** the front with an enamelled vignette depicting a huntsman jumping a gate, marked SML, Birmingham 1901, 2in (5cm) high.

£370–440 SWO

Vestas

These pocket-sized cases for carrying matches took their name from Vesta, the Roman goddess of the hearth and home. A match was known as a 'vesta' up until the 20th century when 'match' became the favoured term. It was essential to carry the vestas in a case as they were highly flammable and needed to be kept dry. The inside of the case would often be gilded to protect the silver from the sulphur head of the match, which would otherwise tarnish the silver. Vesta cases were in general use between the 1860s and 1940s. They were carried predominantly by men in a waistcoat pocket on a 'double Albert' chain, which held a pocket watch on one side and a vesta case on the other. The invention of the pocket petrol lighter led to a decline in the need for the vesta case

A silver vesta case, with bright-cut decoration, Birmingham 1903, 2in (5cm) high.

£120–135 ANC

VINAIGRETTES

A silver vinaigrette, by Ledsam, Vale & Wheeler, engraved with flowers and leaves, the pierced grille embossed with leaves and beads, Birmingham 1827, 1in (2.5cm) wide.

£175–210 DN

A silver-gilt vinaigrette, by Ledsam, Vale & Wheeler, with engine-turned decoration, the grille pierced and engraved with a flower and foliate scrolls, Birmingham 1828, 1½in (4cm) wide.

£190–220 DN

A William IV silver vinaigrette, by Thomas Shaw, 1in (2.5cm) wide.

£350–390 BEX

Vinaigrettes

A vinaigrette is a small box with a hinged lid that opens to reveal a pierced grille which is also hinged. Underneath the grille would be a small sponge soaked in an oily, sweet-smelling substance. Vinaigrettes were used both by men and women and generally carried while travelling to produce a pleasant aroma, as streets and travelling companions could smell! All the interior surfaces would be gilded to protect the silver from staining.

A silver vinaigrette, by Nathaniel Mills, the cover engraved with a coastal scene, with a scroll border, Birmingham 1846, 3¼in (8.5cm) wide.

£330–390 G(L)

A silver vinaigrette, in the form of an egg, the hinged cover with a ring terminal, the body engraved with a crowned initial, the interior with a pierced grille, maker's mark obscured, London 1880, 1½in (4cm) high.

£260–310 HYD

WINE COOLERS

A silver-gilt wine cooler, the rim pierced with vine leaves and grapes, the body with an engraved monogram and presentation inscription, master's mark BB, Russia, Moscow 1851, 9in (23cm) high.

£3,550–4,250 DORO

A pair of silver wine coolers, by Brahmfeld & Gutruf, engraved with arms and a monogram within applied wreaths, screw-on bases and flower and twig handles, Germany, Hamburg, c1855, 10¼in (26cm) high, 114½oz.

£3,900–4,650 S(NY)

Items in the Silver section have been arranged in date order.

A silver wine cooler/soda syphon holder, Sheffield 1920, 7in (18cm) high.

£1,000–1,150 BHA

MISCELLANEOUS

A silver and parcel-gilt Bezoar stone holder, overlaid with scrolls, birds and deer, catch damaged, 17thC, 2¼in (5.5cm) diam, 2oz.

£2,800–3,350 Hal

A Bezoar stone is a hard mass found in the stomach or intestines of some animals, especially ruminants. Highly prized for their medicinal powers, these stones were believed to renew the owner's strength and health, and therefore they were usually kept in containers of great intrinsic value and fine craftsmanship.

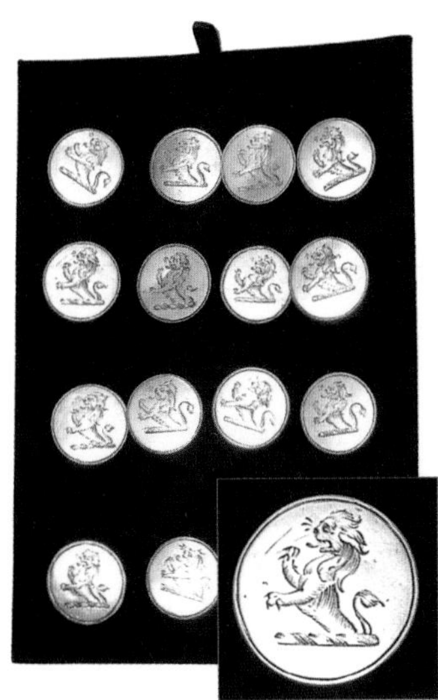

A set of 16 silver buttons, Ireland, c1765.

£3,900–4,400 WELD

A silver cream pail, by Benjamin West, the body with a crowned initial and a twisted bail handle, London 1739, 3¾in (9.5cm) high, 2oz.

£1,600–1,900 S(NY)

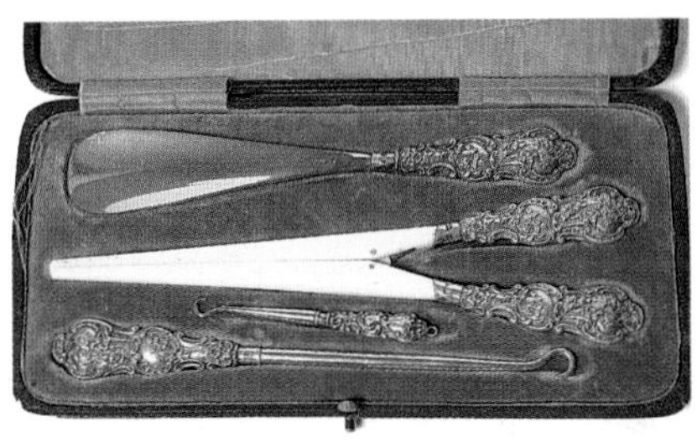

A silver dressing set, by Lister & Son, comprising a shoe horn, ivory and silver glove stretchers, boot hook, and glove hook, Birmingham 1899, with case 9in (23cm) wide.

£220–250 SAT

A silver-mounted rock crystal jar and cover, by C. T. & G. Fox, on a facetted stem, London 1889, 10in (25.5cm) high.

£400–480 G(L)

A silver tea kettle and stand, by Barnard & Sons, the cover with a three-flower finial, the body with embossed foliate swags and an engraved armorial and inscription, London 1837, 18½in (47cm) high, 94oz.

£2,150–2,550 S(O)

A silver spoon tray, by David Willaume II, with a fluted and scalloped rim, the centre engraved with a crest, London 1732, 6¾in (17cm) wide, 4¾oz.

£2,250–2,700 S(NY)

▶ **A Gerald Benney silver vase,** with a flared rim, the body with bark-effect decoration, London 1974, 10¼in (26cm) high, 18oz.

£1,050–1,250 Mit

This vase was purchased by the vendors directly from Gerald Benney on 15 April 1975. The vase comes with an original receipt, compliment slip and Benney's 1975 hardback catalogue in which the vase is photographed on page 23, plate number 51.

For more 20thC silver, please see the Twentieth-Century Design section on pages 441–470.

A silver wax jack, by John Hampston and John Prince, the handle and base with reeded borders, York 1796, 4½in (11.5cm) high, 6½oz.

£3,250–3,900 S(NY)

SILVER PLATE

A silver-plated and oak biscuit barrel, with a ceramic liner, c1880, 9in (23cm) high.

£360–400 WALP

A silver-plated cake stand, by Elkington & Co, decorated with panels from Greek mythology with applied cornucopiae between gadroon borders, 1865, 25¼in (64cm) diam.

£1,200–1,400 S(O)

A pair of silver-plated five-branch candelabra, by the Hartford Sterling Co, each with a nozzle in the form of a thistle, the central nozzle with a detachable flame finial, America, Philadelphia, c1925, 24in (61cm) high.

£410–490 NOA

A Sheffield plate centrepiece, by Matthew Boulton & Co, with five cut-glass bowls, 1784, 13in (33cm) high.

£5,200–5,800 BHA

A silver-plated centrepiece, decorated with swags, with a cut-glass bowl, c1900, 16in (40.5cm) wide.

£380–430 WAC

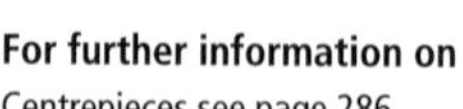

For further information on
Centrepieces see page 286

A silver-plated salver, by Pairpoint, with a gadrooned rim, on four scroll feet with engraved decoration, crested, America, New Bedford, late 19thC, 15½in (39.5cm) diam.

£80–95 WAD

A Victorian silver-plated and oak tray, 24½in (62cm) wide.

£165–185 PSA

A Victorian silver-plated urn, with two leaf-capped scrolling handles, 15in (38cm) high.

£190–220 PF

A pair of silver-plated vases, by Elkington & Co, c1860, 9in (23cm) high.

£800–890 ANC

◀ **A pair of Sheffield plate wine coolers,** by Matthew Boulton & Co, 1784, 9in (23cm) high.

£5,300–5,900 BHA

Matthew Boulton is an important maker. The fact that these wine coolers are a pair has added to their value, but had they been made of silver they would be worth at least four times this amount. For further information on Boulton please see p311.

WINE ANTIQUES

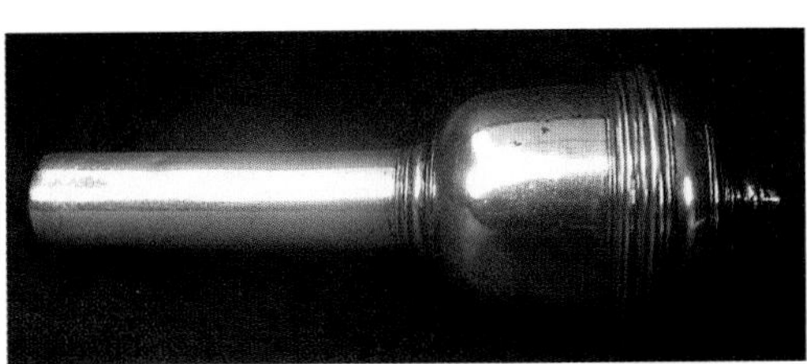

A silver corkscrew and nutmeg grater, with an acorn finial, 18thC, 7¾in (19.5cm) long.

£2,100–2,500 ROS

◀ **A pair of cast silver bottle stoppers,** by John S. Hunt, each in the form of a putto on a mound of vines, London 1848, 4¼in (11cm) high.

£1,050–1,250 WW

A Thomason-type corkscrew, with a bone handle and brush, applied with a gilt Royal coat-of-arms, c1810, 6in (15cm) long.

£160–180 CS

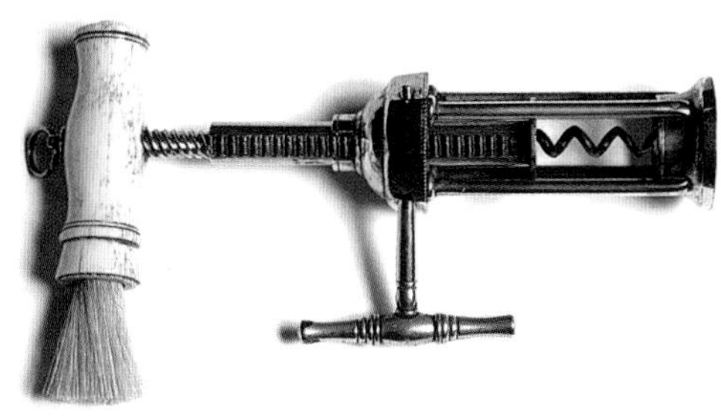

A steel King's Screw corkscrew, with a bone handle, c1820, 8in (20.5cm) long.

£370–420 CS

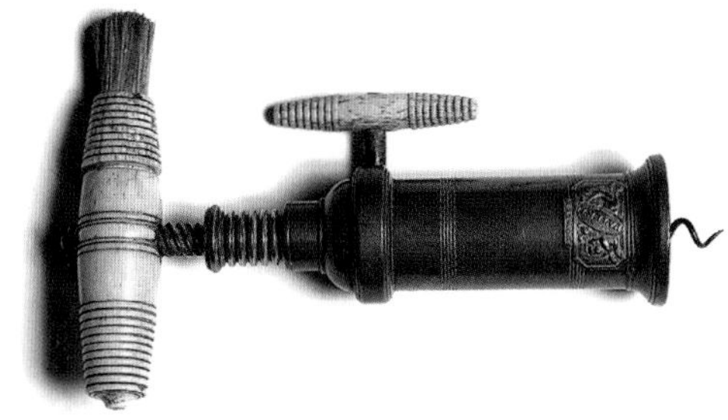

A Dowler gilt-bronze King's Screw corkscrew, c1820, 7in (18cm) long.

£400–450 CS

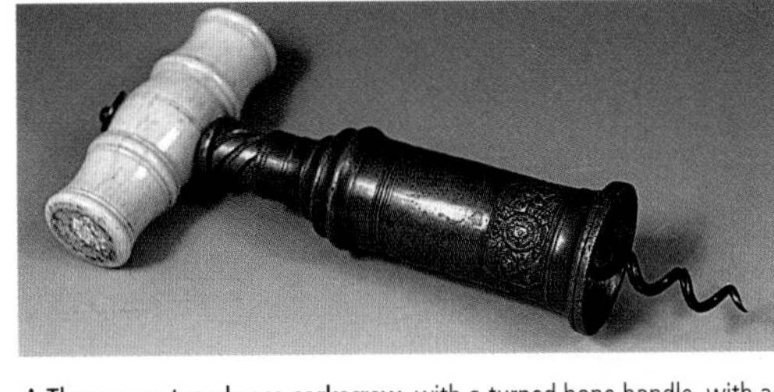

A Thomason-type brass corkscrew, with a turned bone handle, with a Royal coat-of-arms and motto 'Ne Plus Ultra', slight damage, 19thC, 6in (15cm) long.

£150–180 SWO

A silver pocket corkscrew, the handle and sheath with embossed decoration, Holland, c1850, 3in (7.5cm) long.

£400–450 CS

A Victorian brass corkscrew, embossed with fruiting vines, with a turned ivory handle, brush missing, 7½in (19cm) long.

£800–960 ROS

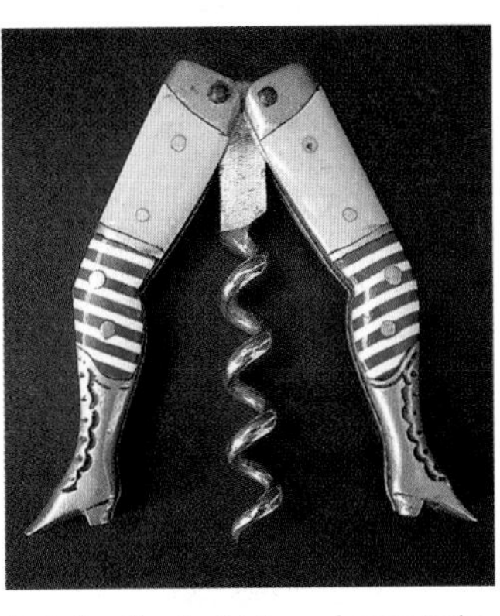

A steel and ivorine folding corkscrew, in the form of a pair of legs, France, early 20thC, 2½in (6.5cm) long.

£260–310 ROS

A late Victorian decanter box, adapted from a coco-de-mer, the hinged cover enclosing a cut-glass decanter and stopper, with a silver plaque inscribed 'Colombo to Paris 1898', one decanter missing, 13in (33cm) high, with a label for Thornhill & Co, London.

£520–620 MCA

A silver decanter stand, by Reily & Storer, engraved with a crest, with three cut-glass decanters, London 1837, 9½in (24cm) high, 15oz.

£280–330 HYD

A silver-plated decanter stand, with pierced decoration and three cut-glass decanters, late 19thC, 16in (40.5cm) high.

£340–400 Mit

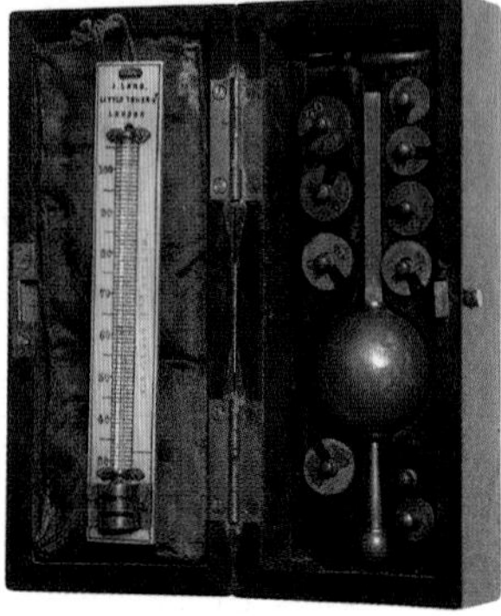

A Sikes hydrometer, by J. Long, in a burr-walnut box, c1900, 5in (12.5cm) wide.

£65–75 CS

A Sikes hydrometer was used to test the alcohol content in spirits.

A coromandel and satinwood tantalus, with cut-glass decanters and glasses, the base with a cigar drawer, c1850, 14in (35.5cm) wide.

£1,750–1,950 YOX

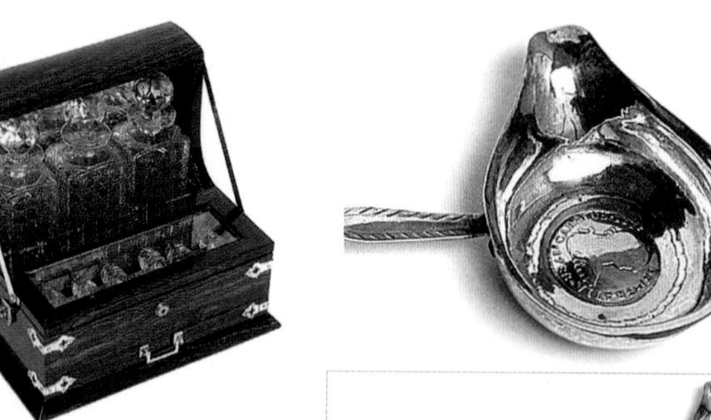

A silver toddy ladle, with a whalebone handle, c1788, 14½in (37cm) long.

£310–350 JAS

◀ **A silver wine funnel,** c1800, 7in (18cm) long.

£530–590 ANC

▶ **An English delft label,** inscribed 'Claret', 18thC, 5½in (14cm) wide.

£590–700 HYD

A set of eight silver wine labels, by Digby Scott & Benjamin Smith, decorated with putti, grapes and satyr masks, London 1806, 5oz.

£1,700–2,000 WW

A silver wine taster, maker's mark V. R., France, Dijon,-c1790, 3in (7.5cm) diam, 2¼oz.

£1,100–1,250 BEX

CLOCKS

BRITISH BRACKET, MANTEL & TABLE CLOCKS

An ebony table clock, by Samuel Aldworth, London, the dial with calendar and mock pendulum apertures and strike/silent lever, the signed fusee movement with verge escapement, striking the quarter-hours on five bells with eight hammers, the domed case with cast brass insets to the front and sides, restored, c1700, 14½in (37cm) high.

£9,600–11,500 S

Samuel Aldworth was born c1659 at Childrey in Buckinghamshire. He was apprenticed to John Knibb at Oxford between 1673 and 1680 and continued to work with him until 1689, at which time he set up on his own. He moved to London in 1697 and was admitted to the Clockmakers' Company as a Free Brother in December of that year. In 1703 he married Elizabeth Knibb. By 1720 he had returned to Childrey.

An ebony-veneered bracket clock, by Robert Williamson, London, the brass dial with a silvered chapter ring, strike/silent lever and calendar aperture, the twin fusee eight-day movement with restored verge escapement and pull quarter repeat on three bells with hour strike on a further bell, the case with a foliate pierced cherub and scroll-decorated repoussé basket and later pineapple finials, slight damage, c1700, 14½in (37cm) high.

£7,600–9,100 DN(HAM)

Robert Williamson is recorded in G. H. Baillie's Watchmakers & Clockmakers of the World *as working near the Royal Exchange, London, between 1666 and 1714.*

An ebonized bracket timepiece, by Jasper Taylor, Gray's Inn, London, the five-pillar movement with verge escapement, a mock bob pendulum and pull-wind quarter repeat striking on two bells, in an inverted bell-top case, c1705, 14½in (37cm) high.

£12,500–14,000 ALS

LOCATE THE SOURCE

The source of each illustration in Miller's can be found by checking the code letters below each caption with the Key to Illustrations, pages 746–753.

An ebonized bracket clock, by James Douglass, Chertsey, with strike/ silent dial in the arch, in a bell-top case, c1755, 19in (48.5cm) high.

£8,500–9,500 JeF

◄ **An ormolu musical table clock,** by Thomas Wright and Matthew Boulton, with enamel dial, the triple-train six-pillar fusee movement with verge escapement, the bell striking and chiming the quarter-hours on six bells and playing one of four tunes on the hour, the cylinder pinned for chimes and music driving 16 hammers playing on eight bells, the case surmounted by an ormolu urn above a blue john socle, with ewer finials above rams' mask corners and laurel garlands, with a pierced and engraved door, on a tortoiseshell-veneered wood base, socle damaged, c1772, 19in (48.5cm) high.

£411,000–493,000 S

Thomas Wright, watchmaker to the King, was Free of the Clockmakers' Company from 1770 and is recorded as working at 6 The Poultry, London, although a surviving watch paper gives his address as No. 13 The Poultry. He died in 1792 during a visit to Birmingham, probably while visiting Matthew Boulton.

Matthew Boulton, the greatest English metalworker of the 18th century, was born in 1728. His father was in business in Birmingham, making buttons, buckles and toys. At the age of 14 Matthew left school to begin working with his father and by 1750 had gone into partnership with him. In 1759 Matthew's father died and, in 1762, he was approached by John Fothergill with proposals for a partnership which lasted for 20 years. It was not an easy relationship, but Fothergill brought mercantile experience and useful overseas contracts to the business.

This clock is a combination of a type made for King George III in 1771 and a complicated 'Geographical' clock made in 1772. It was discovered in an attic where it had lain for over 100 years. Its popularity was greatly enhanced by the Boulton attribution.

An ebonized and brass-mounted musical bracket clock, by Green & Bentley, the brass dial and silvered chapter ring with strike/silent and tune selection dials and a silvered dial for forte and piano, the eight-day triple-train fusee movement with eight knopped pillars, the verge escapement playing one of four tunes with 12 hammers and 11 bells with two tones, the bell-top case with brass caryatids, c1775, 23in (58.5cm) high.

£17,800–19,800 DRA

A mahogany table clock, by Charles Howse, London, the dial with rococo spandrels, mock pendulum and calendar apertures, the arch with strike/silent dial, twin-train fusee striking movement and verge escapement, the bell-top case with cone finials, c1775, 18¾in (47.5cm) high.

£5,400–6,500 S

Charles Howse was Free of the Clockmakers' Company from 1761 and served as Master from October 1787. He worked at 5 Great Tower Street, London and it is thought that he died in 1804.

A mahogany bracket clock, by John Taylor, London, the dial with centre sweep calendar, the triple fusee, eight bell, hour-striking, quarter-chiming and repeating movement with verge escapement, in a bell-top case with brass finials, c1780, 24½in (62cm) high.

£20,700–23,000 ALS

A mahogany musical bracket clock, by Eardley Norton, London, the dial with date aperture and subsidiary dials for tune selection and strike/silent, the triple fusee movement with verge escapement playing four tunes on eight bells with 15 hammers, with music pull repeat and hour pull repeat, c1785, 28½in (72.5cm) high.

£27,900–31,000 ALS

Eardley Norton was undoubtedly one of the most talented clockmakers of the second half of the 18th century. The finest clock he made was the astronomical clock for George III for which he was paid £1,042. It is still in the Royal collection in Buckingham Palace.

A brass-mounted mahogany bracket clock, by William Chapman, London, the brass and enamel dial with foliate scroll and engraved gilt-brass spandrels, the arch with subsidiary strike/silent and regulation dials, the twin fusee five-pillar rack and bell-striking eight-day movement with rise and fall regulation, in a bell-top case on a brass-bound base, c1790, 19¼in (49cm) high.

£8,800–10,500 DN(HAM)

William Chapman is recorded in G. H. Baillie's Watchmakers & Clockmakers of the World *as working from 1756 to 1794.*

A brass-bound mahogany table clock, by Wightwick & Moss, London, the dial with rococo spandrels, the arch with subsidiary regulation and strike/silent dials, the twin-train trip repeating fusee movement striking on a bell, the half-deadbeat escapement with rise and fall regulation and lenticular bob to the pendulum, the case with a triple brass-bound pad top and scale side frets, c1790, 16in (40.5cm) high.

£9,000–10,800 S

A George III mahogany bracket clock, by George Ellecote, London, the silvered dial with engraved decoration and strike/silent dial above, eight-day twin fusee repeating movement, 21in (53.5cm) high.

£3,300–3,950 HYD

A George III mahogany musical bracket clock, by John Thwaites, London, the brass dial with silvered chapter ring and two subsidiary dials to the arch, the eight-day verge movement striking on a bell, the musical mechanism playing on eight bells, the case mounted with ormolu caryatid terminal figures and torch finials, the sides with ormolu frets, 24½in (62cm) high.

£6,800–8,100 G(L)

A gilt-brass mantel clock, by Henry Favre, London, the enamel dial with gold hands, the five pillar twin-train fusee and chain bell-striking movement with maintaining power and duplex escapement, the pull-wind alarm driving two hammers striking on a bell, the front door with a jasper ware roundel portrait of a young girl, the sides inset with scale frets, c1800, 7¼in (18.5cm) high.

£9,300–11,100 S

Henry Favre was Watchmaker to the Prince Regent, the Duke of York and the Duke of Cumberland and he worked at 27 Pall Mall, London between 1800 and 1824.

A Georgian bracket clock, by S. & C. Joyce, London, with convex dial and cast-brass bezel, the pad-top case with scale sides and brass fretting to the front, early 19thC, 13in (33cm) high.

£3,900–4,350 K&D

A mahogany table/bracket clock, by Joseph Payne, London, the dial with strike/silent facility, the eight-day movement with anchor escapement, striking and repeating the hours on a bell, the case with a broken arch top with a brass bordered pad and scale frets to the front and sides, c1810, 15in (38cm) high.

£7,200–8,000 PAO

An ebony-veneered, ebonized and brass-inlaid bracket clock, by Josiah Bartholomew, London, the enamel dial with fast/slow dial, the five-pillar twin fusee repeat striking movement with pendulum, with spirit level, on brass ball feet, c1815, 24in (61cm) high.

£9,400–10,500 ALS

An ebonized and brass-inlaid bracket clock, by John Osbertus Hamley, London, the painted dial with strike/silent mechanism, the twin-train movement with anchor escapement, the broken-arch case inset to the sides with scale frets and with stringing and decorative motifs to the front, with associated ebonized wall bracket, c1810, 17¼in (44cm) high.

£1,800–2,150 S

An ebonized pearwood bracket clock, by Webster, London, with strike/silent dial, the movement with anchor escapement and pendulum, c1810, 16½in (42cm) high.

£6,100–6,800 RGa

A mahogany ebony line-inlaid bracket clock, by Barraud, the eight-day movement with anchor escapement and striking on a bell, with brass mounts, early 19thC, 19¾in (50cm) high.

£1,750–2,100 MCA

Paul Philip Barraud and his sons Frederick Joseph and John were eminent clockmakers in London in the early 19th century.

A carved mahogany mantel clock, by James McCabe, London, with eight-day repeating and striking mechanism, c1810, 15in (38cm) high.

£7,200–8,000 SOS

James McCabe was born into a watch and clockmaking family in Belfast. He came to London in the 1770s, settling at Royal Exchange in 1804. He gained his Freedom of the Clockmakers' Company in 1786 and became a Warden in 1811, the year he died. James McCabe was succeeded by his son, also James, and it is he who must be regarded as one of the most successful English clock and watchmakers of the 19th century, producing many fine examples.

A rosewood and brass-inlaid bracket clock, the painted dial signed 'Mackie, London', the eight-day twin-train fusee movement striking on a bell with trip repeat, the case with a brass finial, c1810, 21in (53.5cm) high.

£4,300–4,800 YOX

A gilt-metal mantel timepiece, by Thomas Moss, with eight-day fusee movement, the marble base with a gilded floral swag, c1820, 7¼in (18.5cm) high.

£4,700–5,300 DRA

Thomas Moss was a well known clockmaker who was recorded as working in Ludgate Street, London between 1786 and 1827.

An ebonized and brass-inlaid bracket clock, by George Priest, with a porcelain dial, the twin-train movement with twin-gut fusees striking the quarter-hours on two bells, with anchor escapement pendulum and bob, c1820, 14¼in (36cm) high.

£13,500–15,000 ⊞ DRA

George Priest was noted as working in Norwich between 1796 and 1854.

A mahogany and satinwood-inlaid bracket clock, by John Farmer, London, the twin-train fusee movement with anchor escapement and trip repeat, c1825, 9½in (24cm) high.

£6,300–7,000 ⊞ GBD

A George IV mahogany and brass-inlaid clock, by Noakes, Burwash, the eight-day fusee striking movement probably by Thwaites & Reed, the case with a gilt-bronze pineapple finial and ebony inlay, 19½in (49.5cm) high.

£1,500–1,800 ⚒ G(B)

A Regency rosewood and brass-inlaid bracket clock, by William Braund, Dartford, the silvered dial signed, the double fusee movement striking the hours, with repeat and adjustable pendulum, c1825, 15in (38cm) high.

£8,000–8,900 ⊞ AV

An ebonized bracket clock, by Henry Wyatt, London, the silvered dial with engraved decoration, with an eight-day twin-train striking movement, c1830, 15in (38cm) high.

£6,100–6,800 ⊞ JeF

An ebony and ormolu clock, by Barraud & Lunds, London, the gilt dial with foliate-engraved surround, five-pillar fusee movement with anchor escapement and striking on a gong, the case with foliate mounts and trellis frets, c1850, 15½in (39.5cm) high.

£2,400–2,800 ⚒ S

A pollarded oak library timepiece, signed 'Dent, London', the case with bronze mounts, c1850, 9½in (24cm) high.

£4,700–5,300 ⊞ JeF

A mahogany, ebonized and brass-inlaid bracket clock, by Joseph Barling, Maidstone, the twin fusee movement striking the hours on a bell, 1850–75, 17in (43cm) high.

£2,650–2,950 ⊞ K&D

Joseph Barling is recorded as working in Maidstone, Kent, between 1847 and 1874.

A rosewood mantel clock, by Aldred & Son, Yarmouth, engraved brass dial, the eight-day double fusee movement with anchor escapement and striking on a bell, c1870, 9in (23cm) high.

£10,100–11,300 ⊞ PAO

The Clock-Work-Shop
Winchester

6A Parchment St., Winchester SO23 8AT
Tel: 01962 842331 Open 9.00–5.00 Mon–Sat
or Mobile 07885 954302 anytime
Website: www.clock-work-shop.co.uk

8 Day mahogany longcase clock by William Hall of Nottingham

- We offer for sale a wide range of lovingly restored quality antique clocks to suit most budgets.
- Full repair/restoration service.
- Delivery and set-up (or shipping) can be arranged.
- Good prices paid for quality/interesting clocks.

All work carries a 3 year written guarantee

WOODWARD ANTIQUE CLOCKS
CHELTENHAM

Specialists in the sale of:

- ★ Longcase Clocks
- ★ Decorative French mantel clocks
- ★ Wall clocks
- ★ Bracket clocks
- ★ Carriage clocks

21 Suffolk Parade, Cheltenham, Glos
Telephone: 01242 245667
www.woodwardclocks.com
Email: woodwardclocks@onetel.com

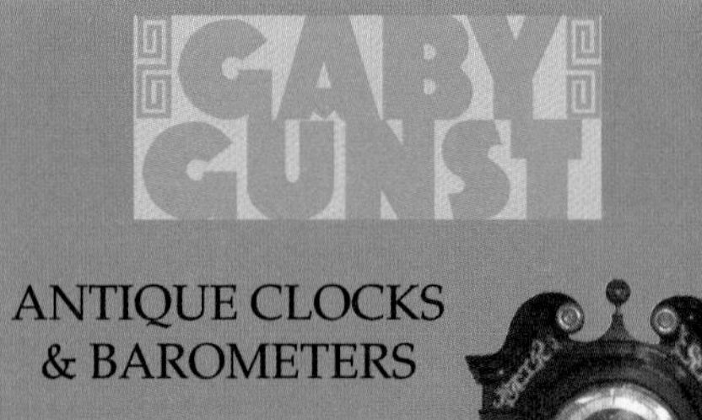

ANTIQUE CLOCKS
& BAROMETERS

140 High Street
Tenterden
Kent
TN30 6HT

Tel: 01580 765818

Email:
gabysclocks@tenterden
140.wanadoo.co.uk

3 showrooms of antique, Longcase, Grandmother, Skeleton, Bracket & Wall clocks all restored in our own workshop

Trading for 30 years

Mahogany longcase by Helm. Ormskirk, with sweep date hand, c1761, 85in high.

www.gabysclocks.co.uk

The Clock Clinic Ltd.
Antique Clocks

WILLIAM WALL, RICHMOND.
An 18th century bracket clock by this local maker, who also worked in Putney in 1791. Movement with original verge escapement and engraved backplate, with hour strike on a bell.

We undertake repairs and restorations
Valuations for Insurance

Tel: 020 8788 1407 Fax: 020 8780 2838
Website: www.clockclinic.co.uk
Email: clockclinic@btconnect.com

Open Tues–Fri 9am–6pm Sat 9am–1pm
Closed Mondays

85 Lower Richmond Road, Putney
London SW15 1EU

A mahogany mantel clock, the silvered dial with engine-turned decoration, 19thC, 9½in (24cm) high.

£530–630 BWL

An ebonized and gilt-metal table clock, the brass dial with subsidiary chime/ silent and Westminster/ chime, the triple fusee movement with anchor escapement chiming the quarter-hours on eight bells via eight hammers and striking on a gong, c1875, 48½in (123cm) high, with a pedestal.

£3,900–4,650 TEN

Bells and gongs

Victorian and Edwardian bracket and table clocks are starting to be appreciated by collectors. Once considered to be too large, their generous size no longer seems to be a problem. The cases are often in mahogany or ebonized, in the style of an earlier period and decorated with good quality gilt mounts. Sometimes they come with matching wall brackets. The beautifully engineered substantial triple-train chain fusee movements chime the quarters on a row of bells or gongs, or occasionally both. These clocks with all their Victorian excesses have started to increase in price at auction and now is a good time to find the best quality examples before the prices really start to rise. Examples with bells tend to fetch more money than gongs, but when originally made examples with gongs were at a premium.

A mahogany bracket clock, the silvered dial signed 'Dent, London', the eight-day movement striking the quarter-hours and the hours, c1890, 19in (48.5cm) high.

£3,100–3,500 SOS

A walnut bracket clock, the silvered dial with three subsidiary dials for chime/silent, slow/fast and Westminster/Cambridge/ Whittington chimes, the triple fusee movement chiming on four gongs and eight bells and striking on a gong, slight damage, the case with bracket feet, c1890, 23¾in (60.5cm) high.

£2,000–2,400 CGC

A mahogany table clock, the silvered dial signed 'Clerke, 1 Royal Exchange, London, 5102', with subsidiary chime/silent and chime selection dial, the triple-chain movement with anchor escapement, chiming and striking on nine gongs, the case inlaid with ivory and boxwood, c1900, 16in (40.5cm) high.

£1,400–1,650 S

A figured walnut and brass bracket clock, the eight-day twin-train movement chiming and striking on gongs, c1900, 14½in (37cm) high.

£1,150–1,350 N

A silver mantel timepiece, by William Comyns, London 1902, 5¾in (14.5cm) high.

£2,200–2,450 BEX

An Edwardian oak table clock, the brass dial with silvered chapter ring and three subsidiary dials for chime/silent, slow/fast and Westminster chimes/chime on eight bells, the eight-day triple-train movement striking on a gong and striking the quarter-hours on four gongs or eight bells, slight damage, 17in (43cm) high.

£1,000–1,200 DN

CONTINENTAL BRACKET, MANTEL & TABLE CLOCKS

◀ A gilt-brass *turmchenuhr*, the silvered chapter ring above a subsidiary dial for the quarter hours, the posted iron twin-train fusee and gut movement with verge escapement, south Germany, early 17thC, 11¾in (30cm) high.

£9,000–10,800 S

▶ **A tortoiseshell and gilt-bronze clock,** signed 'J. Le Doux à Paris', with embossed brass dial and twin-train striking movement, minor losses, France, 1643–1715, 20¾in (53cm) high.

£1,850–2,200 S(P)

Items in the Clock section have been arranged in date order.

▶ **A boulle *religieuse*,** by Pierre du Chesne, Paris, the gilt dial above a gilt-brass plaque, the plated movement with five baluster pillars and verge escapement with silk suspension striking the hours and half-hours, the case with pewter, brass and tortoiseshell decoration, signed, France, c1680, 22¼in (56.5cm) high.

£3,000–3,600 S

Pierre du Chesne was received as Master in the Guild of Faubourg Saint Germain in March 1675 and the city of Paris in June of the same year. A religieuse is a type of French clock made in the Dutch style, that copied the architectural decoration of the day. It is uncertain when they first acquired this name, but they were popular during the period of Louis XIV and Louis XV and the early examples were fairly plain with ebonized cases and gilt mounts. Later they became more flamboyant, often with boulle marquetry and tortoiseshell or lacquer casework, and with lavish gilt mounts.

A tortoiseshell and gilt-brass bracket clock, signed 'Chastelain à Paris', with embossed brass dial and striking movement, with gilt-brass mounts, France, 1715–23, 49¼in (125cm) high.

£3,100–3,700 S(P)

◀ **An ebonized fruitwood table clock,** by C. Engeringh, Dordrecht, the brass dial with mock pendulum and date apertures, with strike/silent dial, the eight-day twin-train movement with verge escapement striking on a bell, Holland, c1780, 18in (45.5cm) high.

£4,000–4,800 CAG

A stained horn bracket clock, by Balthazar Lieutaud, the ormolu dial with enamel reserves, with a striking movement, restored, signed, France, c1750, 41in (104cm) high.

£5,200–6,200 S(NY)

Balthazar Lieutaud's stamp is found on a number of wooden clock cases, particularly regulators, usually of high quality and often in collaboration with the leading bronziers of the day. He also produced a number of cartel clocks.

A Louis XVI-style Neuchâtel bracket clock, with gilt mounts and enamel dial, striking the quarter-hours on two bells, with repeat, signed and dated, Switzerland, 1777, 39in (99cm) high.

£7,000–7,800 JIL

▶ **A bronze and marble mantel clock,** by V. la Croix, Paris, with enamel dial and eight-day movement, France, c1795, 20in (51cm) high.

£10,800–12,000 JIL

A shagreen and ormolu-mounted bracket clock, the painted dial inscribed 'Nils Berg, Stockholm', with eight-day repeating movement, verge escapement and silk suspension striking on a bell, Sweden, c1800, 23¾in (60.5cm) high, with bracket.

£1,750–2,100 RTo

A bronze and ormolu clock, by Rieusse, with a twin-train striking movement, France, 1799–1815, 19in (48.5cm) high.

£700–840 JNic

An Empire-style porphyry and gilt-bronze mantel clock, by Jonas Cederlund, Stockholm, surmounted with a female bust, damaged and repaired, signed, Sweden, 1800–25, 15¾in (40cm) high.

£4,050–4,850 BUK

An ormolu and marble mantel clock, with enamel dial, the striking movement signed 'G. I. Champion à Paris', movement and case possibly associated, damaged, signed, France, c1800, 18½in (32.5cm) high.

£4,200–5,000 S(NY)

A bronze and ormolu mantel clock, the enamel dial signed 'Piolaine à Paris', with silk suspension movement striking on a bell, the case surmounted with a figure of Diana the Huntress, dial damaged, France, c1805, 19in (48.5cm) high.

£1,400–1,650 S

An ormolu and marble mantel clock, the enamel dial inscribed 'Le Nepreu à Paris', with striking movement, the case surmounted with doves and figures, France, c1810, 19in (48.5cm) high.

£9,100–10,900 S(NY)

An ormolu and marble mantel clock, the twin-train movement striking on a bell, France, c1810, 17in (43cm) high.

£8,500–9,500 JIL

An ormolu mantel clock, after Boizot, surmounted with figures depicting Father Time and Cupid, losses, on later feet, France, c1810, 21¾in (55.5cm) wide.

£7,100–8,500 S(NY)

This model is attributed to the sculptor Simon-Louis Boizot who succeeded Falconet as Directeur de la Sculpture at the Sèvres factory and worked with the bronzier Pierre-Philipe Thomire.

A gilt-bronze mantel clock, the enamel dial signed 'Farault à Paris', the eight-day movement with silk suspension and striking the half-hours and hours on a bell, the case surmounted by a figure with a lyre, France, 1815–30, 18in (45.5cm) high.

£1,300–1,450 K&D

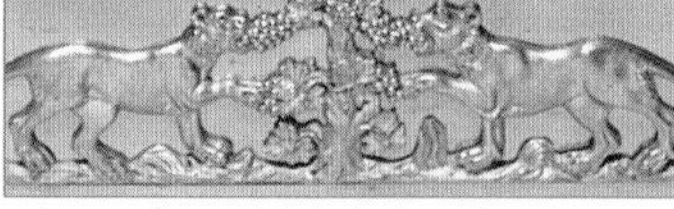

An ormolu mantel clock, the twin-train movement striking on a bell, France, c1818, 13in (33cm) high.

£3,750–4,200 JIL

A bronze and ormolu lyre clock, with enamel dial, the eight-day movement with platform escapement, France, c1820, 11in (28cm) high.

£830–930 K&D

An ormolu mantel clock, by Paul de Pons, Paris, No. 3173, the eight-day twin-train movement with silk suspension striking on a bell, the case surmounted with figures, slight damage, France, early 19thC, 18in (45.5cm) high.

£700–840 CAG

A simulated tortoiseshell, ivory and marble table clock, inscribed 'Redarde à Toulouse, No. 6590', France, c1825, 12¼in (31cm) high.

£7,100–8,500 S(NY)

Redarde was recorded working in rue de la Pomme, Toulouse, 1807–40.

A marble and gilt-bronze mantel clock, with enamel dial, striking movement and sunburst pendulum, signed 'Blanc Fils, Palais Royale', the case surmounted with an eagle and cherubs, France, early 19thC, 23in (58.5cm) high.

£2,000–2,400 MAL(O)

An ormolu mantel clock, the twin-train striking movement stamped '580', France, c1830, 28in (71cm) high.

£2,900–3,450 S(NY)

A rosewood and marquetry mantel clock, by Raingo Frères, Paris, the eight-day silk-suspended movement striking on a bell, France, c1835, 9in (23cm) high.

£1,700–1,900 JIL

An ormolu and green-patinated mantel clock, with silvered dial, the twin-train movement with silk-suspension, the case surmounted with a lady and a dog, France, 19thC, 15¼in (38.5cm) high.

£350–420 DMC

An ormolu and porcelain mantel clock, with twin-train striking movement, painted with landscapes, France, 19thC, 19in (48.5cm) high.

£2,250–2,700 G(L)

An ormolu mantel clock, with enamel dial, the eight-day Japy Frères-type movement with outside countwheel striking on a bell, the case with lion-mask handles, France, 19thC, 18in (45.5cm) high.

£590–700 HYD

A gilt-bronze mantel clock, with enamel dial and striking movement, the case with a figure of Cupid, France, 19thC, 14½in (37cm) high.

£860–1,000 WAD

An ormolu mantel clock, with enamel dial, the Japy Frères-type movement with outside countwheel striking on a bell, the case with leaf scrolls and swags and surmounted with an urn, France, 19thC, 16in (40.5cm) high.

£440–520 HYD

A gilt-bronze mantel clock, the twin-train movement striking on a bell, impressed 'R. & C. Paris & London', with a figure of a boy and a horse, France, 19thC, 15in (38cm) high.

£300–360 DN(BR)

Richard et Cie was founded in Paris in 1848 and opened a branch in London in 1857. By 1867, they were known as Richard & Co and traded until recently from 24 Cannon Street, London.

A rosewood clock, by Delhaye, Boulogne, with silvered dial, the movement with silk suspension and striking on a bell, slight damage, France, c1840, 10in (25.5cm) high.

£250–300 ROSc

A Black Forest carved oak mantel clock, the twin-train movement striking on a gong, the case decorated with game and a shotgun, Germany, 19thC, 23¾in (60.5cm) high.

£590–700 SWO

A brass mantel clock, the movement with silk suspension and striking on a gong, the case decorated with porcelain flowers, damaged, France, c1840, 19in (48.5cm) high.

£250–300 ROSc

A bronze and marble mantel clock, by Jean Jacques Pradier, with twin-train striking movement, the case surmounted with a figure of Sappho, signed and dated, France, 1848, 28¼in (72cm) high.

£3,200–3,800 S(P)

A rosewood portico mantel clock, the silvered dial signed 'Durant à Paris', with eight-day movement striking the half-hours and hours on a bell, the case with marquetry inlay, France, c1850, 20in (51cm) high.

£670–750 K&D

A gilt-bronze and boulle table clock, the Japy Frères movement striking on a bell, the Brocot escapement with sun mask pendulum, the case decorated with classical figures, France, c1850, 31¾in (80.5cm) high.

£2,150–2,550 S

An ormolu mantel clock, signed 'Sherer à Paris', the movement striking on a bell, the case inset with Sèvres-style porcelain panels, France, c1870, 15in (38cm) high.

£2,850–3,200 TUR

A Black Forest mantel cuckoo clock, the fusee and twin-train movement spring driven with twin bellows, the case carved with a hunter and a dog on a rocky base, stamped 'G.H.S.', Germany, 19thC, 23in (58.5cm) high.

£880–1,050 BWL

An ormolu mantel clock, the Japy Frères-type movement with mercury pendulum and Brocot escapement striking on a bell, the case surmounted with a classical urn, France, 1850–1900, 18½in (47cm) high.

£630–750 HYD

A Louis XV-style boulle mantel clock, the eight-day twin-barrel movement striking on a bell, with brass and ormolu mounts, France, c1870, 16in (40.5cm) high.

£3,600–4,000 JIL

A Louis XVI-style ormolu mantel clock, the movement by Martin & Co, No. 419, striking on a bell, the case decorated with Sèvres-style panels depicting figures and flowers, France, c1870, 15in (38cm) high, with glass dome.

£800–960 Hal

A burr-yew and ebonized mantel clock, by Victor-Athanase Pierret, the eight-day timepiece movement with pendulum, signed, France, c1875, 6½in (16.5cm) high.

£430–490 K&D

A boulle mantel clock, the eight-day movement striking the half-hours and hours on a bell, the case with gilt-bronze mounts and surmounted with a bird, c1875, 18in (45.5cm) high.

£1,800–2,000 K&D

A boulle mantel clock, with an enamel dial, the Japy Frères movement striking on a bell, France, c1880, 14½in (37cm) high.

£2,400–2,700 TUR

A gilt-bronze mantel clock, with enamel dial, the Samuel Marti movement with Brocot escapement and striking on a bell, France, c1880, 26¾in (68cm) high.

£2,150–2,550 S

An ormolu four-pillar mantel clock, with eight-day movement, on a mahogany base, France, c1880, with glass dome, 13in (33cm) high.

£1,800–2,000 SOS

A porcelain and ormolu timepiece, surmounted on a model of an elephant, flowers missing, France, c1880, 9in (23cm) high.

£820–980 SWO

A gilt-metal and enamel mantel clock, with twin-train striking movement, on a giltwood stand, c1880, 13¾in (35cm) high.

£1,050–1,250 S

A gilt-metal and marble mantel clock, the eight-day movement striking on a bell, France, c1880, 17in (43cm) high.

£1,600–1,800 YOX

An ebonized bracket clock, by Winterhalder & Hofmeier, with silvered dial and twin fusee ting tang movement, Germany, c1880, 12½in (32cm) high.

£1,300–1,450 FOF

Winterhalder & Hofmeier are arguably the most famous of the German 19th-century clockmakers. The firm was started by Anton Winterhalder in Schwarzenbach, Germany in 1810, taking Anton Hofmeier into partnership in 1850. The business ceased in 1910 on the death of Winterhalder's last son, Linus. They produced large numbers of high quality pieces for export to Britain, such as the example shown above.

A Black Forest table cuckoo clock, the twin fusee movement with countwheel striking on a gong, Germany, c1880, 14½in (37cm) high.

£440–520 TEN

A boulle and gilt-bronze mantel clock, the enamel dial signed 'K. Overstrijd, La Haye', the eight-day Japy Frères movement striking the half-hours and hours on a bell, France, Paris, c1890, 12in (30.5cm) high.

£870–980 K&D

A bronze, marble and gilt-metal clock, decorated with cherubs and floral swags, the eight-day movement striking the half hour and hours on a bell, inscribed 'Le Triomphe de l'Amour', France, c1890, 16in (40.5cm) high.

£860–970 K&D

A malachite-veneered mantel clock, by Paul Buhre, losses, Russia, St Petersburg, late 19thC, 12¾in (32.5cm) high.

£6,300–7,500 BUK(F)

A gilt-bronze and marble mantel clock, with twin-train striking movement, the case surmounted with a group of Bacchantes after Clodion, top and base possibly associated, France, late 19thC, 31½in (80cm) high.

£9,600–11,500 S

A Louis XVI-style gilt-bronze and porcelain mantel clock, the enamel dial decorated with floral garlands, the movement by Vincenti with platform lever escapement and striking on a bell, France, c1895, 17¼in (44cm) high.

£2,400–2,800 S

A gilt-metal mantel clock, dial inscribed 'Maple & Co', the eight-day twin-train movement striking on a bell, the case with *champlevé* enamel floral decoration, France, late 19thC, 11½in (29cm) high.

£880–1,050 PFK

A gilt-bronze and porcelain mantel clock, with twin-train striking movement, losses, France, late 19thC, 16½in (42cm) high.

£450–500 DORO

Further reading

Miller's Clocks & Barometers Buyer's Guide, Miller's Publications, 1997

A burr-walnut and gilt-metal bracket clock, with silvered chapter ring and subsidiary slow/fast dial, the eight-day movement stamped 'Lenzkirch', Germany, late 19thC, 15½in (39.5cm) high.

£910–1,050 SWO

Lenzkirch clocks are usually of very high quality. The Lenzkirch factory was founded by Eduard Hauser in 1849 and merged with Junghans in 1927.

A gilt-brass and *champlevé* enamel four-glass mantel clock, the porcelain dial with a paste-set bezel, the twin-train movement striking on a coiled gong, the pendulum set with a portrait, signed 'Medaille d'Argent', slight damage, France, c1900, 11½in (29cm) high.

£1,000–1,200 ROSc

A brass, onyx and *champlevé* enamel four-glass mantel clock, by Richard & Co, No. 14325, the eight-day twin-train movement striking on a gong, with a mercury pendulum, France, c1900, 11in (28cm) high.

£700–840 CAG

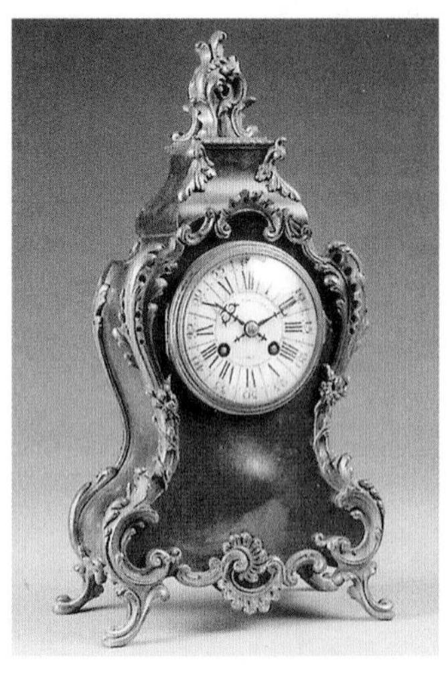

A tortoiseshell and ormolu mantel clock, the enamel dial inscribed 'Manoah Rhodes & Sons, Paris', the eight-day movement striking on a gong, France, c1900, 16¼in (41.5cm) high.

£610–730 N

A gilt-bronze four-glass mantel clock, the Samuel Marti eight-day movement striking the half-hours and hours on a bell, France, Paris, c1900, 13in (33in) high.

£1,100–1,250 K&D

▶ **A pewter mantel clock,** with an enamel dial, decorated with a snake and a frog, possibly Germany or Holland, c1900, 8in (20.5cm) high.

£1,350–1,500 PVD

For more Art Nouveau clocks, please see the Decorative Arts section on pages 367–440.

CARRIAGE CLOCKS

An ormolu *grande sonnerie* and alarm **travelling clock,** by Philipp Happacher, Vienna, with a silvered dial, the four-train movement with duplex and balance escapement striking the quarter-hours on a bell and the hours on a gong, Austria, c1820, 5in (12.5cm) high.

£3,000–3,600 S

A carriage clock, with porcelain dial, striking and repeating with alarm, the case with porcelain panels, case regilt, France, c1830, 7in (18cm) high.

£7,100–8,000 JeF

A brass carriage clock, the enamelled dial with subsidiary alarm dial, the repeating movement with alarm, France, 19thC, 6in (15cm) high.

£1,350–1,600 GIL

◀ **An ormolu and bronze carriage clock,** the enamel dial signed 'E. J. Dent, London', the eight-day twin fusee movement striking the half-hours and hours on a gong, c1850, 8½in (21.5cm) high.

£21,400–23,800 DRA

Edward John Dent was born in 1790 and was apprenticed to his grandfather. By 1814 he was becoming well known and was employed between 1815 and 1829 by a number of well established firms including Vulliamy, Barraud and McCabe. He went into partnership with John Roger Arnold in 1830 but by 1840 was in business himself. He died in 1853 and the business continued to prosper well into the 20th century. The quality of his carriage clocks is exceptional.

A brass carriage clock, with porcelain dial, the twin-train striking movement with Garnier escapement, France, 1835–40, 5in (12.5cm) high.

£3,200–3,800 ROSc

A brass carriage clock, the porcelain dial and movement signed 'Bolviller à Paris', the case cast with figures depicting the four seasons, the handle in the form of two mermaids, regilt, slight damage, France, c1875, 8¼in (21cm) high.

£1,250–1,500 ROSc

MILLER'S COMPARES

◀ **I. A gilt-brass carriage clock,** by Drocourt, with striking and repeating movement, France, c1880, 7in (18cm) high.

£3,050–3,400 BELL

▶ **II. A gilt-brass miniature carriage timepiece,** by Drocourt, with ivorine dial, France, c1880, 4in (10cm) high.

£1,600–1,800 BELL

The major difference between these two clocks is the size. Item I is a standard or 'full size' carriage clock at approximately 7in (18cm) high and the 'miniature' carriage clock is only about 4in (10cm) high. Normally the miniature would have a higher value but Item II is a simple timepiece with an engine-turned mask, simple handle and naïve shallow engraving. Item I, on the other hand, strikes the hour which can be repeated at will by depressing the button on top of the case and it also has the advantage of an alarm. The profusely engraved case, dial mask and shaped handle is far superior, having more depth with finer crisp detail, thereby increasing the value.

A brass carriage clock, the porcelain dial and panels depicting courting couples, the striking movement with repeat and alarm, France, c1880, 8in (20.5cm) high.

£2,500–2,800 ⊞ ROH

A brass carriage clock, by Margaine, with porcelain dial, five minute repeat and alarm, in a gorge case, slight damage, France, c1890, 7¼in (18.5cm) high.

£3,500–4,200 ⚒ ROSc

An embossed silver travelling timepiece, with enamel dial and French movement, maker's mark 'JB', London 1892, 3in (7.5cm) high.

£440–520 ⚒ AG

◀ **A mahogany and brass carriage clock,** by Barraud & Lunds, with silvered dial, the triple-train fusee movement striking the quarter-hours and hours on three gongs, with lever platform escapement, c1893, 8in (20.5cm) high, with original leather case and key.

£27,900–31,000 ⊞ DRA

The firm of Barraud & Lunds came into existence in 1870 following on from the firm of Barraud & Sons, which was formed in 1814 by the three sons of Paul Philip Barraud, himself a clockmaker. John Richard Lund joined the firm in 1838 and the firm became known as Barraud & Lunds. The company ceased trading in 1929.

▶ **A brass carriage clock,** the enamel dial with floral decoration, the eight-day movement striking the half-hours and hours on a gong, with lever platform escapement, France, c1900, 5in (12.5cm) high.

£640–720 ⊞ K&D

A brass carriage clock, by Couaillet, the dial within an engine-turned mask, the eight-day movement striking and repeating on a gong, in an *anglaise riche* case, France, c1900, 7in (18cm) high.

£1,250–1,400 ⊞ CPC

A gilt-brass carriage clock, with enamel dial, with alarm, striking the half-hours and hours on a gong, France, c1900, 5in (12.5cm) high, with leather carrying case.

£1,250–1,500 ⚒ WAD

A brass carriage clock, the enamel dial with a pierced and scrolled mask, the movement striking and repeating on a gong, France, early 20thC, 5¼in (13.5cm) high.

£330–390 ⚒ FHF

CARTEL CLOCKS

◄ **A giltwood cartel clock,** with later enamel dial, the striking movement with backplate inscribed 'Guillme Gille à Paris', the case carved with figures, putti and horses, France, c1730, 39¼in (99.5cm) high.

£11,700–14,000 S(NY)

Ornamentation

Cartel clocks originated in France during the 18th century and their appeal lies in the design and ornamentation of the case. The early examples are rococo in style but during the neo-classical period of Louis XVI they became more balanced in shape and decorated with bows, ribbons, etc. English cartel clocks are often asymmetrical and in the rococo, or occasionally Chinese, style. French cartel clocks are always in ormolu cases whereas English examples have gilded wooden cases with silvered dials and fusee movements.

A carved giltwood cartel clock, the silvered dial signed 'John Cannon, London', the later fusee movement with anchor escapement, the case carved with scrolls, leaves and fruit, surmounted by a bird, mid-18thC, 34¾in (86.5cm) high.

£1,800–2,150 S

MILLER'S COMPARES

I. A gilt-bronze cartel clock, with an enamel dial, the striking movement by Viger, Paris, the case cast and chased with figures, scrolls and foliage, France, mid-18thC, 49¼in (125cm) high.

£21,600–25,900 S

II. A gilt-bronze cartel clock, signed 'Courvoisier à Paris', the case chased with foliage and acanthus leaves and surmounted by two putti holding torches, France, 1745, 29½in (75cm) high.

£8,100–9,700 S(P)

Item I is considerably more appealing than Item II due to its finely detailed casting and the elegance of the free-flowing decoration on the case. It is also very large in size, and it is the visual impact and very high quality of execution that makes Item I a serious collector's piece, although Item II is a good quality clock in its own right.

An ormolu *grande sonnerie* cartel clock, by Verdier, Paris, with an enamel dial, striking the quarter-hours with repeat, France, c1770, 16in (40.5cm) high.

£9,400–10,500 JIL

A cast-bronze cartel timepiece, with enamel dial and eight-day movement, France, c1885, 20in (51cm) high.

£600–670 K&D

A gilt-bronze cartel clock, with enamel dial, the Samuel Marti eight-day movement striking the half-hours and hours on a bell, France, c1900, 20in (51cm) high.

£870–980 K&D

GARNITURES

An alabaster and ormolu garniture, the clock with gilt engine-turned dial, with twin-train striking movement, France, mid-19thC, clock 19in (48.5cm) high.

£4,650–5,200 D&D

A Louis XVI-style gilt-bronze garniture, the clock with twin-train striking movement, the candelabra converted for electricity, France, 1850–1900, clock 25¼in (64cm) high.

£8,100–9,700 BERN

A gilt-brass and porcelain garniture, the clock with twin-train striking movement signed 'Duplan et Garres, Paris', hand-painted with flowers and birds, restored, France, c1890, clock 14½in (37cm) high.

£950–1,100 ROSc

A gilt-bronze garniture, the clock with a painted porcelain dial and twin-train striking movement, inset with porcelain plaques and surmounted with fruit and flowers, France, c1900, clock 19¼in (49cm) high.

£1,600–1,900 WAD

LANTERN CLOCKS

A brass lantern clock, the dial with later pewter chapter ring and signed 'Andrew Prime, Londini fecit', the twin-train posted movement with early anchor escapement, alarm disc missing, c1665, 15¾in (40cm) high.

£2,250–2,700 S

Andrew Prime was the brother-in-law of Ahasuerus Fromanteel and through this connection used the same good quality frames as the Fromanteels. See p329 for more information about this family.

A brass lantern clock, the dial engraved with birds and flowers inscribed 'Cutbush, Maidstone', the later anchor escapement striking on a bell, late 17thC, 14¼in (36cm) high, on a later carved and pierced oak bracket.

£3,450–4,100 WW

There were at least 12 clock-makers from the Cutbush family in Maidstone, Kent, during a period of 150 years.

Is it original?

Traditionally lantern clocks could be bought fairly cheaply due to the fact that they are only 30-hour duration and had often suffered various alterations, losses and poor restoration. Today's collectors, however, have far more knowledge of the subject and can spot a fairly original example and are therefore prepared to pay a premium. This is why you occasionally see unknown makers achieving higher values than some of the better known makers. Two-handed lantern clocks are often later reproductions or the cases are original with a later movement and hands. A later clock with two hands should have a minute track with five divisions and a period clock will have a track and four divisions that show the quarters on a single-handed clock.

A brass mantel clock, the eight-day twin fusee movement striking the hours, c1900, on a mahogany plinth, 18¼in (46.5cm) high.

£760–910 PFK

LONGCASE CLOCKS

A walnut and marquetry longcase clock, by James Whiteman, London, the matted dial with date aperture and turned and punched decoration with cherub spandrels, the eight-day movement with turned pillars countwheel-striking the hours on a bell, the rising hood with barley-twist pillars, the case sides with boxwood-strung panels, c1680, 78in (198cm) high.

£27,000–30,500 DRA

James Whiteman was apprenticed in 1663 and was a member of the Clockmakers' Company between 1670 and 1684, a relatively short period of time.

An oak longcase clock, by Fromanteel, Amsterdam, the dial with a calendar aperture and seconds dial, the month-going movement with five ring-turned, knopped and latched pillars, five wheel trains and an outside countwheel, the formerly rising hood with spiral columns, the case with a carved lenticle, maintaining power missing, some carving probably later, Holland, c1695, 65in (165cm) high.

£12,600–15,100 S

The Fromanteel family was one of the most prominent in the field of horology during the 17th century. Although of Dutch stock Ahasuerus Fromanteel, the first clockmaker in the family, was born at Norwich in 1607 and apprenticed to a clockmaker. In 1631 he moved to London and was admitted to the Blacksmiths' Company, becoming known as a maker of great (i.e. large) clocks. In 1632, only a year after its foundation, he joined the Clockmakers' Company as a Free Brother. Fromanteel died in 1693 having established a dynasty of clockmakers working in both London and Amsterdam. It is likely that all the Fromanteels worked for the family firm and this is why many of the clocks made were signed just 'Fromanteel'.

An ebonized pine longcase clock, by James Brown, the brass dial with cherub and crown spandrels, silvered chapter ring and a single hand, 30-hour movement, the hood with gilded capitals, the trunk door with a lenticle, 1715–20, 88in (223.5cm) high.

£3,150–3,500 SOS

An oak longcase clock, by Joseph Butterworth, the brass dial with silvered chapter ring and apertures for date and lunar scale with penny moon, the 30-hour, four-pillar movement with anchor escapement and outside countwheel striking on a bell, the case door inlaid with a marquetry star, c1730, 82in (208.5cm) high.

£2,800–3,350 TEN

Joseph Butterworth of Cawthorne, Barnsley, was probably the son of John Butterworth who was also a clockmaker. Joseph is thought to have succeeded his father around 1720. Only half a dozen longcase clocks are known by Joseph, mostly 30-hour and eight-day examples. His dials display very fine engraving and unusual dial layouts.

The prices realized at auction may reflect the fact that the clocks have sometimes undergone alterations to their movements, or are in unrestored condition.

◄ **A walnut and crossbanded longcase clock,** the brass dial with strike/silent, seconds dial and date aperture, the four-pillar, eight-day movement striking on a bell, the case with pine sides, strike/silent damaged, 18thC, 84in (213.5cm) high.

£1,750–2,100 CGC

◄ **A chinoiserie lacquer longcase clock,** by Peter Dennis, London, the brass dial with silvered chapter ring and gilt-brass spandrels, date dial to the arch, the eight-day, five-pillar movement striking on a bell, the caddy-top hood with three brass finials and brass-capped pillars, c1725, 105in (266.5cm) high.

£11,500–12,800 PAO

A walnut-veneered and herringbone-inlaid longcase clock, by George Smith, Marshfield, Gloucestershire, the brass dial with seconds dial and date aperture, eight-day movement striking the hours, the trunk door with a bulls-eye lenticle with a brass bezel, 18thC, 84in (213.5cm) high.

£4,250–5,100 NSF

A mahogany longcase clock, by William Tomlinson, London, the brass dial with a silvered chapter ring, subsidiary seconds dial and date aperture, the twin-train movement with anchor escapement striking on a bell, the hood with brass-capped turned three-quarter columns, 18thC, 79½in (202cm) high.

£2,100–2,500 Bea

William Tomlinson was made Free of the Clockmakers' Company in 1699 and Master 1733–41.

A gilt japanned longcase clock, by James Scholefield, London, the dial with strike/silent, seconds dial and calendar aperture, eight-day movement striking the hours, with brass cased weights, c1750, 96in (244cm) high.

£15,100–16,800 AV

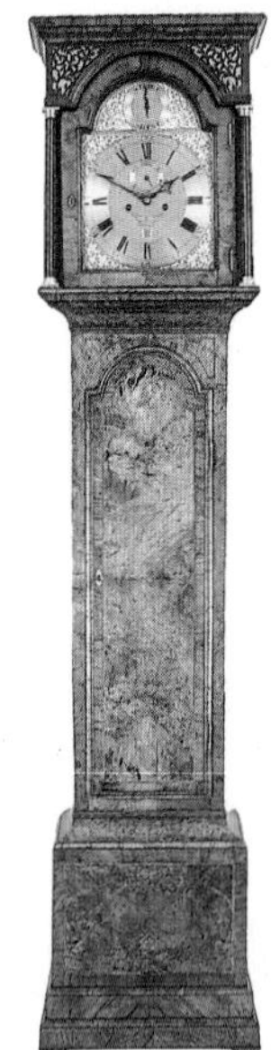

A walnut longcase clock, by Jasper Taylor, London, the brass dial with silvered chapter ring, seconds dial, date aperture and strike/silent to the arch, the eight-day five-pillar movement striking on a bell, the hood with brass-capped pillars, c1755, 89in (226cm) high.

£15,200–16,900 PAO

A Georgian oak longcase clock, by Webb, Thaxted, the dial decorated with a ship and lighthouse with subsidiary seconds and date ring, the eight-day twin-train movement striking on a bell, the hood with three finials, 80½in (204.5cm) high.

£1,500–1,800 DMC

A George II walnut longcase clock, by John Dixon, the brass dial with silvered chapter ring, subsidiary seconds, date aperture and silvered moonphase, the eight-day twin-train movement with anchor escapement and rack strike on a bell, the hood painted with a scrolling foliate frieze on an ebonized ground, with three ball finials, damage to case plinth, ball finials later, 96¾in (246cm) high.

£7,300–8,800 DN

See Britten's Old Clocks and Watches *where there is a John Dixon listed in the Clockmakers' Company 1748–56.*

A painted pine longcase clock, of sarcophagus shape, with twin-train striking movement, Sweden, 18thC, 87in (221cm) high.

£6,300–7,000 AUB

A japanned and gilt-decorated longcase clock, by William Harris, London, the brass dial with silvered chapter ring, subsidiary seconds dial, date aperture and ringed winding holes, the eight-day twin-train movement striking on a bell, c1760, 86in (218.5cm) high.

£3,000–3,600 CAG

This clock is possibly by William (Aaron), son of William Harris, apprenticed in 1735 and working in London 1743–73.

THE LARGEST GRANDFATHER CLOCK SHOP IN THE UK

ANTIQUE CLOCKS

Rare 8-day oval dial moonphase clock by Banister of Lichfield, 1783-95, in a fine mahogany and satinwood case

We have a high quality stock of 150 fine authentic longcases with automata, moonphase, chiming, musical, brass dial, painted dial 8-day clocks both by London and provincial makers. In addition we have music boxes, stick and banjo barometers, wall, bracket and carriage clocks.

Restoration by experienced craftsmen in our own workshops

Free delivery and setting up throughout the UK

OPEN ALL DAY MONDAY TO SATURDAY OR BY APPOINTMENT

CREDIT CARDS ACCEPTED

WORLDWIDE SHIPPING

A fine 8-day arched brass dial high water at Bristol moonphase clock by John Plumley of Bristol, 1746-71, in an exceptional flame mahogany case

Styles of Stow

The Little House, Sheep Street
Stow-on-the-Wold, Gloucestershire GL54 1JS
Telephone/Fax: 01451 830455
Website: www.stylesofstow.co.uk
Email: info@stylesofstow.co.uk

WRITTEN GUARANTEE AND INSURANCE VALUATION PROVIDED WITH EVERY PURCHASE

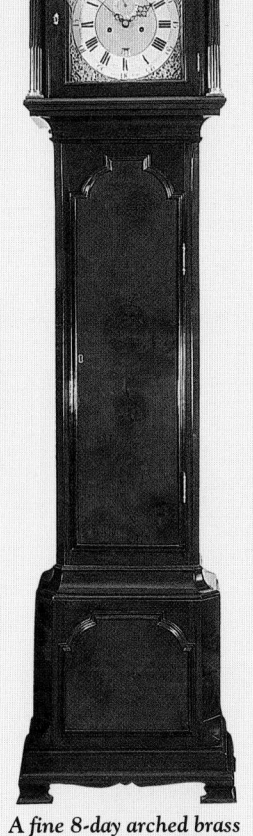

A walnut-veneered longcase clock, by Thomas Cox, Cromhall, the brass dial with silvered chapter ring and single hand, four-seasons spandrels, the date aperture with floral engraving, the 30-hour movement striking on a bell, c1770, 77in (195.5cm) high.

£1,800–2,000 ⊞ K&D

Thomas Cox of Cromhall is recorded in G. Dowler's Gloucestershire Clockmakers and Watchmakers *as working before 1784. The quality of his workmanship is noted in the book.*

An oak longcase clock, by J. Dyhous, the brass dial with a single hand, 30-hour movement, c1770, 77in (195.5cm) high.

£2,700–3,000 ⊞ SOS

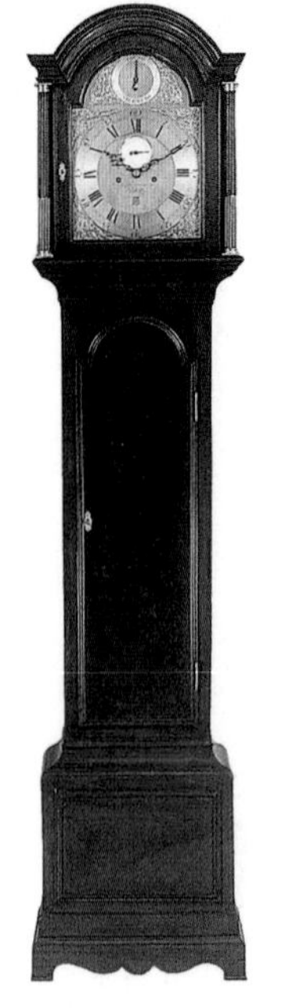

A mahogany longcase clock, by Thomas Lozano, London, the brass dial with silvered chapter ring, sunken seconds, date ring and strike/silent, the eight-day five-pillar movement striking on a bell, c1770, 90in (228.5cm) high.

£10,700–11,900 ⊞ PAO

The words 'Strike' and 'Silent' in the dial arch are inscribed in Spanish.

An oak longcase clock, by Thomas Blatchly, Bradford-on-Avon, the silvered-brass dial with moonphase and 'High Water at Bristol Key', with engraved four-seasons spandrels, eight-day striking movement, the hood with swan-neck pediment, c1770, 92in (233.5cm) high.

£7,900–8,800 ⊞ ALS

An oak longcase clock, by John Safley, Edinburgh, the brass dial with rococo spandrels, silvered chapter ring, sunken seconds dial and date aperture, with eight-day striking movement, Scotland, c1770, 87in (221cm) high.

£6,700–7,500 ⊞ JeF

A mahogany longcase clock, by Conyers Dunlop, London, the silvered-brass dial with strike/silent and date aperture, the eight-day five-pillar movement striking on a bell, c1775, 94in (239cm) high.

£13,000–14,500 ⊞ DRA

Conyers Dunlop was apprenticed in 1725 and was a member of the Clockmakers' Company from 1733 to his death in 1779 becoming Master in 1758. He is recorded as working at Spring Gardens, Charing Cross and was a noted maker of fine quality longcase and bracket clocks. He was a reasonably prolific maker and had a number of apprentices bound to him throughout his working life.

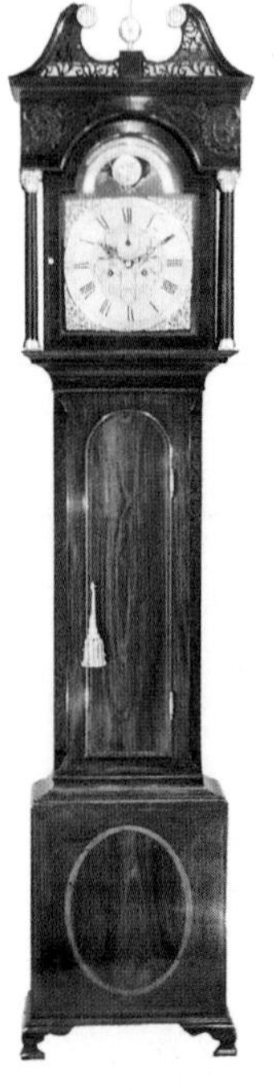

A Chippendale-style mahogany longcase clock, by William Tickle, Newcastle, the brass dial with moonphase, 'High Water at Home Port' and tidal indicators for homeward bound/outward bound ports with eight-day striking movement, c1780, 97in (246.5cm) high.

£12,100–13,500 ⊞ ALS

A mahogany longcase clock, by William Carter, Kingston, the silvered dial with moonphase, strike/silent and pendulum adjustment, with a silvered plaque painted with Chronos and engraved 'Sic Transit Gloria Mundi', the eight-day bell-striking movement with repeat lever, the swan-neck hood with ball finials, the case with reeded brass-inlaid columns and gilded Corinthian capitals, c1790, 96in (244cm) high.

£20,500–22,800 ⊞ DRA

The general style of this clock would suggest a Cheshire or North countlry maker and there is a Kingston in Staffordshire. However, the quality of the casework and the movement could point to a London maker. It is possible that although the case shows typical North Country style, this was a special commission from a clockmaker in Kingston-upon-Thames, close to London.

A mahogany longcase clock, by D. Michael & Sons, Swansea, the painted dial with moonphase and 'High Water at Swansea', with eight-day striking movement, the hood with swan-neck pediment, Wales, c1790, 92in (233.5cm) high.

£8,500–9,500 ALS

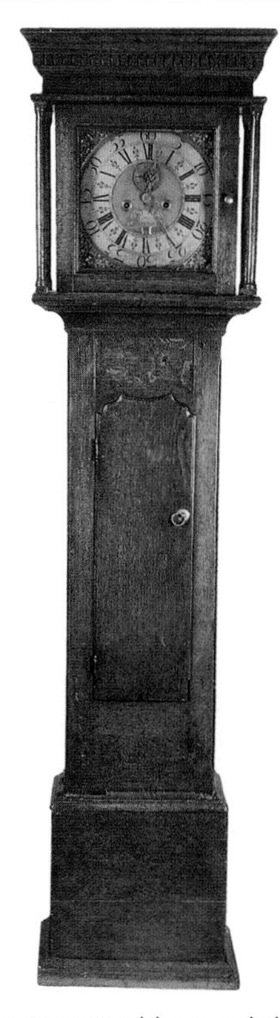

A George III oak longcase clock, by Barwise, Cockermouth, the brass dial with cherub and foliate spandrels and subsidiary seconds dial, with eight-day striking movement, 80in (203cm) high.

£1,250–1,500 Mit

A George III mahogany longcase clock, by Bromley, Horsham, the silvered dial engraved with bellflower festoons, with strike/silent, subsidiary seconds and date dials, the eight-day movement striking on a bell, the hood with brass finials, damage, 80¾in (205cm) high.

£2,000–2,400 RTo

A George III mahogany longcase clock, by Decka & Marsh, London, with silvered dial and eight-day striking movement, the case with gilt-brass mounts, 94in (239cm) high.

£3,000–3,600 WAD

A George III mahogany longcase clock, by O'Reilly, Dublin, with brass dial, the eight-day movement striking on a bell, the hood with swan-neck pediment and carved lion-mask frieze, Ireland, 92½in (235cm) high.

£4,000–4,800 JAd

A George III oak and mahogany-crossbanded longcase clock, by Thomas Holmes, Cheadle, with engraved brass dial and 30-hour movement, 76in (193cm) high.

£460–550 MAL(O)

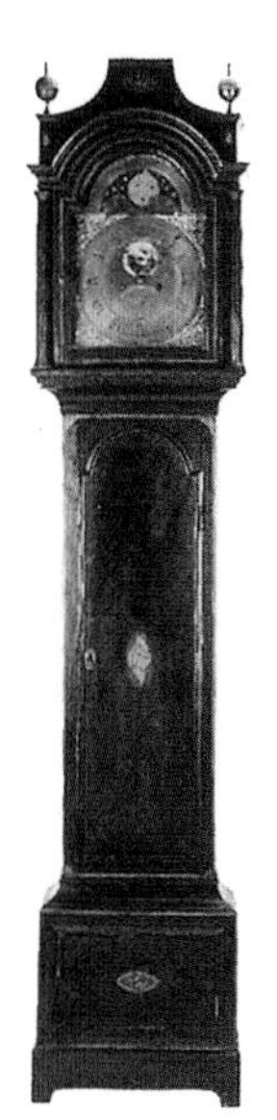

A George III mahogany longcase clock, by Robert Downse, London, the brass dial with moonphase, the eight-day movement striking on a bell, 91in (231cm) high.

£3,900–4,650 WAD

A George III oak longcase clock, by Adam Pringle, Edinburgh, with silvered and engraved dial, eight-day striking movement, the hood with swan-neck pediment and boxwood frets, Scotland, 87in (221cm) high.

£1,300–1,550 PBA

◀ **A George III mahogany and rosewood-crossbanded longcase clock,** by Andrew Rich, Bridgwater, with painted dial, Adam and Eve automaton movement and date aperture, eight-day striking movement, the case with carved shell and fan decoration, 93in (236cm) high.

£2,050–2,450 MAL(O)

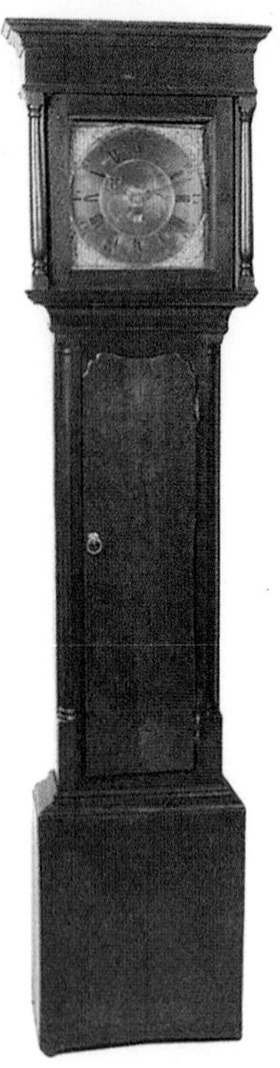

A George III oak longcase clock, by Simpson, Wigton, the brass dial with date aperture flanked by pierced cast spandrels, the 30-hour movement striking on a bell, 82in (208.5cm) high.

£820–980 HYD

A George III mahogany longcase clock, the painted dial with subsidiary seconds dial, the eight-day movement striking on a bell, the swan-neck pediment with ball and eagle brass finials above Corinthian capital reeded pilasters, movement later, 95in (241.5cm) high.

£2,500–3,000 WW

A mahogany longcase clock, by Edward Bird, Bristol, with silvered dial, eight-day movement rack-striking on a bell, late 18thC, 92in (233.5cm) high.

£7,600–8,500 JIL

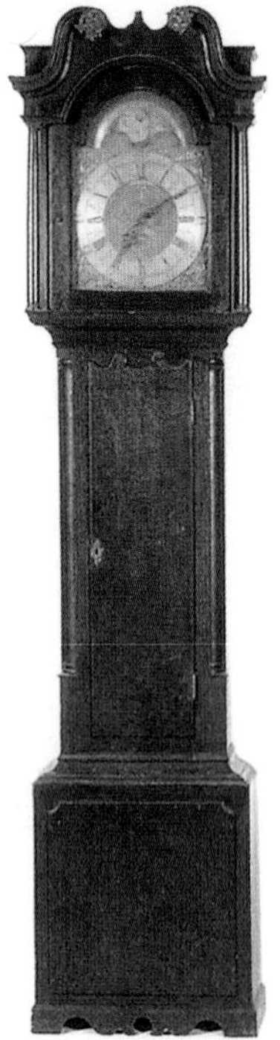

An oak longcase clock, by Thomas Lister, Halifax, the bird and foliate-engraved dial with silvered chapter ring, moonphase and date aperture, with 30-hour movement, late 18thC, 86½in (219.5cm) high.

£1,550–1,850 DMC

◀ **An oak longcase clock,** by John Harvey, Weymouth, with painted dial and eight-day striking movement, late 18thC, 76½in (194.5cm) high.

£4,250–4,750 ALS

A mahogany and boxwood-inlaid longcase clock, by B. Taylor, Birmingham, the foliate-engraved brass dial with later chapter ring, subsidiary seconds dial and cherub mask spandrels, the eight-day movement striking on a bell with a musical movement striking on eight graduated bells, late 18thC, 91in (231cm) high.

£1,900–2,250 Hal

A painted longcase clock, with brass dial and eight day rack and snail striking movement, restored, Denmark, c1791, 82in (208.5cm) high.

£1,250–1,500 ROSc

◀ **A mahogany longcase clock,** by William Avenell, Portsmouth, the engraved and silvered dial with moonphase and centre sweep date, with five-pillar eight-day movement, c1795, 88½in (225cm) high.

£8,800–9,800 ALS

An oak longcase clock, by Jackson of Boston, the dial depicting Nelson's victory on the Nile, August 1798, the arch with a portrait of Nelson, late 18thC, 85in (216cm) high.

£5,800–6,500 ⊞ SPUR

A mahogany and marquetry-inlaid longcase clock, by Alexander Kirkwood, Paisley, the decorated dial with gilt fan spandrels, seconds and date indicators, the eight-day movement striking on a bell, the hood with swan-neck pediment and glass apertures to the sides, Scotland, c1800, 90in (228.5cm) high.

£2,700–3,000 ⊞ K&D

Alexander Kirkwood of Paisley is recorded in Donald Whyte's book Clockmakers and Watchmakers of Scotland *as working 1788–1820.*

An oak longcase clock, the dial painted with a view of Loch Awe, with eight-day striking movement, Scotland, c1800, 80in (203cm) high.

£1,500–1,700 ⊞ CSM

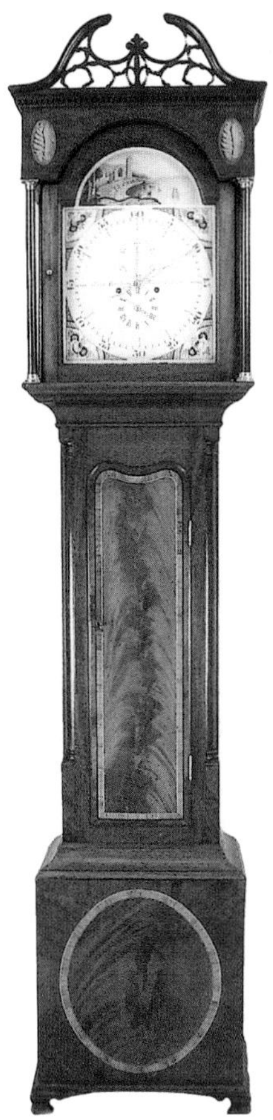

A mahogany and crossbanded longcase clock, by John Weston, the regulator-type painted dial painted with roses and flowers, the arch with a coastal scene, the eight-day movement with anchor escapement striking on a bell, the hood with a fretted frieze and shell inlay, c1800, 93in (236cm) high.

£6,100–6,800 ⊞ PAO

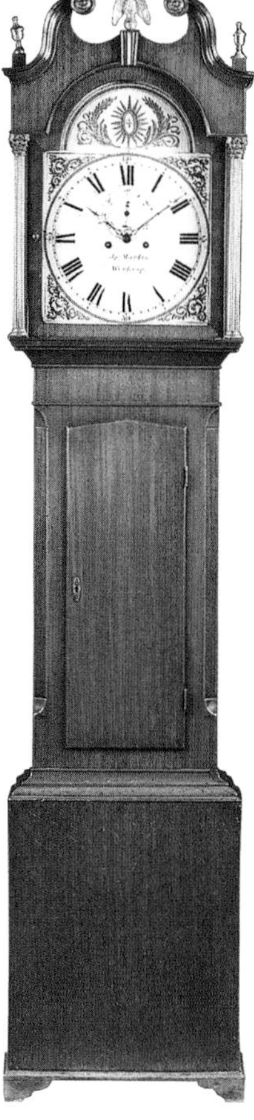

A mahogany longcase clock, by John Martin, Worksop, the painted dial with foliate spandrels and seconds dial, the arch decorated with a starburst, with eight-day striking movement, the hood with brass terminals and finials, c1805, 89¾in (228cm) high.

£960–1,150 S

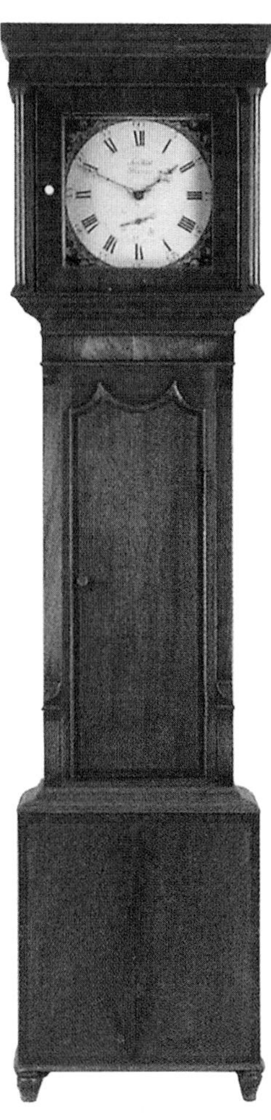

An oak and mahogany longcase clock, by Jos. Hall, Alston, the dial with painted spandrels and subsidiary date dial, with 30-hour striking movement, early 19thC, 83¾in (212.5cm) high.

£610–730 PFK

A figured mahogany longcase clock, by Richard Honeybone, Fairford, the painted dial with moonphase, with eight-day striking movement, c1810, 91½in (232.5cm) high.

£7,600–8,500 ⊞ ALS

An oak longcase clock, by Hancock & Son, Yeovil, with painted dial and eight-day striking movement, early 19thC, 76¼in (193.5cm) high.

£4,050–4,500 ⊞ ALS

Further reading

Miller's Antiques Checklist: Clocks,
Miller's Publications, 2000

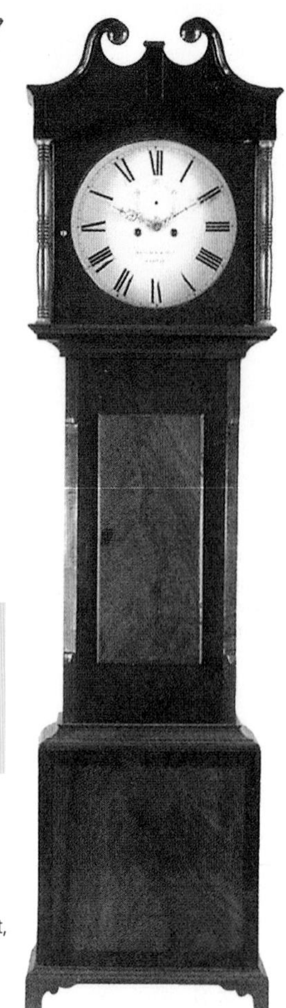

▶ **A mahogany longcase clock,** by Hancock & Son, Yeovil, the painted dial with seconds dial, with eight-day striking movement, seconds hand missing, early 19thC, 86in (218.5cm) high.

£1,100–1,200 PFK

An oak and mahogany longcase clock, the painted dial with subsidiary seconds and date dials, with eight-day striking movement, early 19thC, 96in (244cm) high.

£540–640 DD

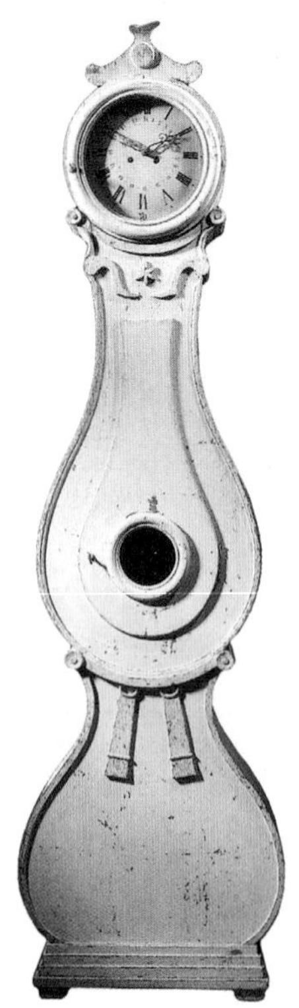

A painted longcase clock, the painted dial with a date hand, with eight-day striking movement, the case with a teardrop door with lenticle, Sweden, early 19thC, 84¼in (214cm) high.

£2,400–2,850 S

A mahogany longcase clock, by Thomas Dixon, Haddington, the dial, corners and arch painted with floral decoration, the eight-day movement striking on a bell, Scotland, c1820, 87in (221cm) high.

£4,400–4,900 ⊞ JIL

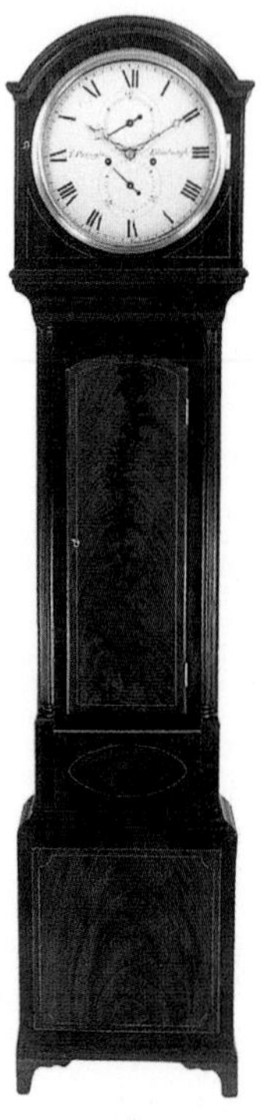

A mahogany and boxwood-strung longcase clock, by T. Pringle, Edinburgh, the dial with seconds and date dials, the eight-day movement striking on a bell, Scotland, c1820, 79in (200.5cm) high.

£7,200–8,000 ⊞ PAO

A mahogany longcase clock, by Withers, Bristol, the painted dial with subsidiary dial and date aperture, the arch and corners painted with a cottage scene, the eight-day movement rack striking on a bell, c1820, 87in (221cm) high.

£4,050–4,500 ⊞ JIL

A mahogany and ebony-inlaid longcase clock, by Sheppard & Potter, Wotton, the painted dial with the four seasons painted to the corners, the eight-day movement striking on a bell, the hood with brass finials, c1820, 82in (208.5cm) high.

£4,500–5,000 ⊞ K&D

William Potter and Thomas Sheppard of Wotton-under-Edge worked in the late 18th and early 19th centuries. They are recorded in G. Dowler's book Gloucestershire Clockmakers and Watchmakers.

An oak longcase clock, by W. Smith, Crowland, the dial with a painted hot-air balloon to the arch, with eight-day striking movement, finials missing, 1825–35, 81in (205.5cm) high.

£3,300–3,700 ⊞ SOS

A flame mahogany longcase clock, by James Duncan, London, the dial with seconds and date dials, the eight-day movement striking on a bell, the hood with cresting and three brass finials, c1830, 86in (218.5cm) high.

£8,300–9,300 ⊞ PAO

A flame mahogany longcase clock, by Ferris, Cirencester, the painted dial with moonphase, with eight-day striking movement, finials missing, c1830, 86in (218.5cm) high.

£8,900–9,900 ⊞ SOS

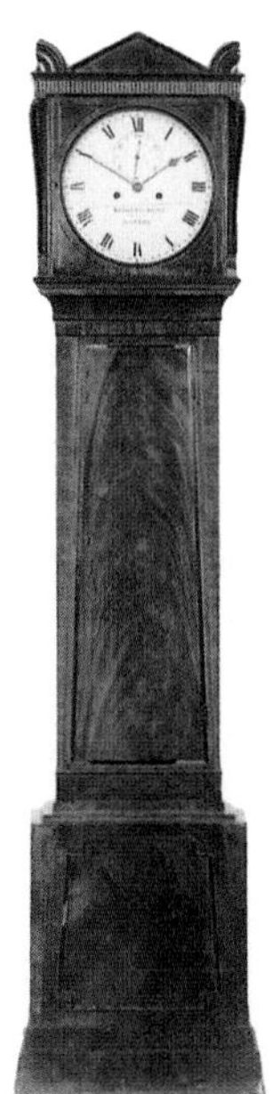

▶ **A William IV mahogany and crossbanded longcase clock,** by Arnold & Dent, London, the dial with subsidiary seconds and strike/silent above the XII, the twin-train movement with deadbeat escapement striking on a bell, the hood with arched pediment and moulded ear finials, 77¼in (196cm) high.

£11,000–13,200 Bea

Arnold & Dent was probably the most famous partnership of the 19th century, bringing together the eminent and well-established firm of Arnold, which had been run for several years by John Roger Arnold, the son of John Arnold of chronometer fame, and Edward John Dent, who had already established a fine reputation and was to become arguably the most famous English maker of the 19th century. This partnership lasted for ten years and ended in 1840.

◀ **A William IV mahogany drumhead longcase clock,** by J. Hamilton, Hamilton, with painted dial, the eight-day movement striking on a bell, Scotland, 85in (216cm) high.

£2,450–2,900 PBA

London clocks prices

Good quality eight-day striking mahogany longcase clocks by London makers have always been in demand and their prices have progressively risen over the years. Recently, however, they have been slower to sell, with the result that these longcase clocks, with their flame-veneered and canted corner cases and brass or silvered break-arch dials can now be bought a little more reasonably.

◀ **A mahogany longcase clock,** by William Barr, Hamilton, the gilded dial with subsidiary date and seconds dial and twin-train striking movement, the hood with a swan-neck pediment, Scotland, 19thC, 92in (233.5cm) high.

£1,550–1,850 DMC

▶ **A carved oak longcase clock,** by James Leigh, the matted dial with subsidiary seconds dial and gilt mask and scroll spandrels, the triple-train eight-day movement chiming on eight bells, with stepped top hood, the trunk door carved with a mask above a vase, the base carved with foliate scrolls, 19thC, 90¼in (229cm) high.

£1,650–1,950 RTo

A mahogany and satinwood-strung longcase clock, by D. Lloyd Price, Beaufort, the painted arched dial with subsidiary seconds dial and date aperture, with eight-day striking movement, Wales, 19thC, 88in (223.5cm) high.

£1,050–1,250 BWL

A mahogany and inlaid longcase clock, the dial with painted landscape vignettes, with eight-day striking movement, finials missing, 19thC, 84in (213.5cm) high.

£760–910 FHF

A mahogany and ebony-inlaid longcase clock, the dial with painted arch and spandrels, subsidiary seconds and date dials, with eight-day striking movement, finial missing, 19thC, 87½in (222.5cm) high.

£900–1,050 SWO

A mahogany longcase clock, by Donegan, Dublin, the painted dial with subsidiary seconds dial, the twin-train movement striking on a gong, the panel door with a silvered barometer and alcohol thermometer, Ireland, 19thC, 78¼in (199cm) high.

£2,600–3,100 Bea

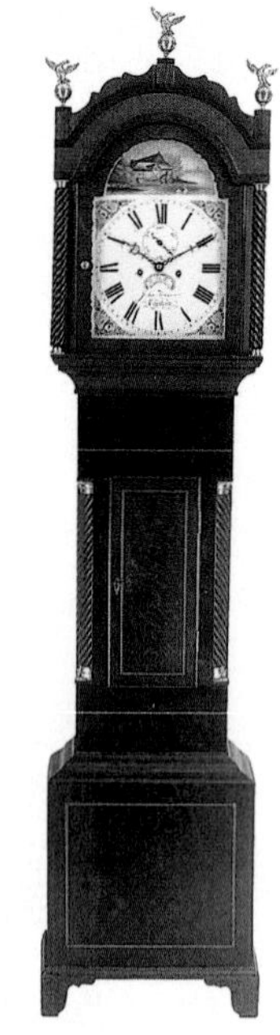

An ebony-inlaid mahogany longcase clock, by John Trevor, Topsham, the dial painted with a mill and country scene, the corners painted with flowers and foliage, with subsidiary seconds dial and date aperture, the eight-day movement striking on a bell, the hood with three brass eagle finials, c1840, 86in (218.5cm) high.

£5,300–5,900 PAO

◀ **An early Victorian mahogany longcase clock,** the dial painted with birds and foliage, with subsidiary seconds dial and date aperture, with eight-day striking movement, finial missing, 89in (226cm) high.

£820–980 ROS

Prices

The price ranges quoted in this book reflect the average price a purchaser might expect to pay for a similar item. The price will vary according to the condition, rarity, size, popularity, provenance, colour and restoration of the item, and this must be taken into account when assessing values. Don't forget that if you are selling it is quite likely that you will be offered less than the price range.

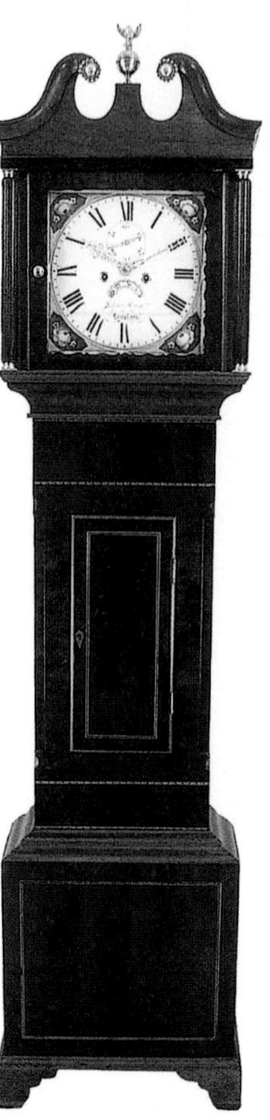

▶ **A mahogany and boxwood and ebony-inlaid longcase clock,** by John Morse, Lyneham, with subsidiary seconds and date dials, the eight-day movement striking the hours on a bell, the hood with brass paterae and brass eagle finial, c1845, 81in (205.5cm) high.

£4,700–5,200 PAO

A mahogany longcase clock, by Ballard, Cranbrook, the painted dial with subsidiary seconds and date dials and moonphase to the arch, the eight-day twin-train movement striking on a bell, damaged, c1850, 81in (205.5cm) high.

£3,000–3,600 CAG

Joseph Finney, Liverpool. An impressive mahogany longcase clock, with moonphase by this eminent maker. Circa 1770.

Ahasuerus Fromanteel II. A fine ebony-veneered and silver-mounted striking spring clock, with pull quarter repeat and alarm. Circa 1690.

John Johnson, London. An impressive and beautifully patinated mahogany bell top bracket clock, with original verge escapement and quarter chiming on eight bells. Circa 1780.

Books written by Derek Roberts:
British Longcase Clocks, Precision Pendulum Clocks – Volumes I, II & III, Carriage & Other Travelling Clocks, British Skeleton Clocks, Continental & American Skeleton Clocks and Mystery, Novelty & Fantasy Clocks.

A mahogany drumhead longcase clock, by D. Kiddie, Glasgow, the dial with subsidiary seconds and date dials, the four-pillar movement striking on a bell, Scotland, c1850, 82in (208.5cm) high.

£800–960 DN(HAM)

A metal-mounted tortoiseshell boulle longcase clock, the cast dial with enamel cartouche chapters, the twin-weighted movement with pinwheel escapement striking on a top-mounted bell, France, c1870, 91in (231cm) high.

£3,500–4,200 TEN

A late Victorian mahogany and satinwood-banded longcase clock, by Camerer Kuss & Co, London, the brass dial with silvered chapter ring, seconds and strike/silent dials with gilded mask spandrels, the triple-train movement with deadbeat escapement chiming and striking on five tubular chimes, with pull repeat, 84¾in (215.5cm) high.

£3,200–3,800 CGC

A bronze-mounted and ebonized oak longcase clock, by Lorenz Furtwangler & Sons, movement signed 'LFS', gong and some mouldings missing, damaged, Germany, c1890, 90in (228.5cm) high.

£1,900–2,250 ROSc

A flame mahogany longcase clock, by Maple & Co, London, the painted convex dial with strike/silent, the eight-day movement striking the half-hours and hours on a gong, the case with brass reeded pillars and fretwork, c1895, 83in (211cm) high.

£10,500–11,700 SOS

A mahogany and marquetry-inlaid longcase clock, the brass and silvered break-arch dial with strike/silent and chime/silent dials, the three-train Junghans movement chiming on five tubular gongs, Germany, 93in (236cm) high.

£2,100–2,500 DMC

An Edwardian mahogany and inlaid longcase clock, the dial with moonphase, with triple-train striking and chiming movement, retailed by the Association of Diamond Merchants, Jewellers and Silversmiths, 6 Grand Hotel Buildings, London, 104in (264cm) high.

£1,050–1,250 CAG

An Edwardian mahogany and crossbanded longcase clock, with chased brass dial and eight-day quarter-chiming German movement, with a brass-mounted pediment and glazed door, 78½in (199.5cm) high.

£1,200–1,400 AH

NOVELTY CLOCKS

An ormolu portico clock, with annular dial and silk suspension striking on a bell, France, c1790, 14in (35.5cm) high.

£4,750–5,700 ROSc

A brass night clock, with pierced chapter ring, spring-driven movement and crown wheel and verge escapement, cast with ormolu scrolls, France, c1800, 12¼in (31cm) high.

£840–1,000 DMC

A nightlight would sit behind the dial of this clock and illuminate the numerals on the rotating chapter ring.

A picture timepiece, by Thomas Brown, Birmingham, the clock driven by a fusee and chain movement, with verge escapement and ivory pullwind wheel, the movement connected to the windmill and causing the sails to revolve, early 19thC, in a giltwood frame, 14¼ x 19¼in (36 x 49cm).

£1,800–2,150 S

A picture clock, the eight-day movement by Samuel Marti with Brocot escapement, striking on a gong, with a further key-wound four-tune musical movement, France, mid-19thC, in a regilded wood and gesso frame with rococo decoration, 36½ x 44in (92.5 x 112cm).

£8,600–10,300 S

A ceramic clock, in the form of a painter's palette, with eight-day twin-train striking movement, France, 19thC, 9½in (24cm) high.

£165–195 WilP

Auction or dealer?

All the pictures in our price guides originate from auction houses and dealers. When buying at auction, prices can be lower than those of a dealer, but a buyer's premium and VAT will be added to the hammer price. Equally, when selling at auction, commission, tax and photography charges must be taken into account. Dealers will often restore pieces before putting them back on the market. Both dealers and auctioneers can provide professional advice, so it is worth researching both sources before buying or selling your antiques.

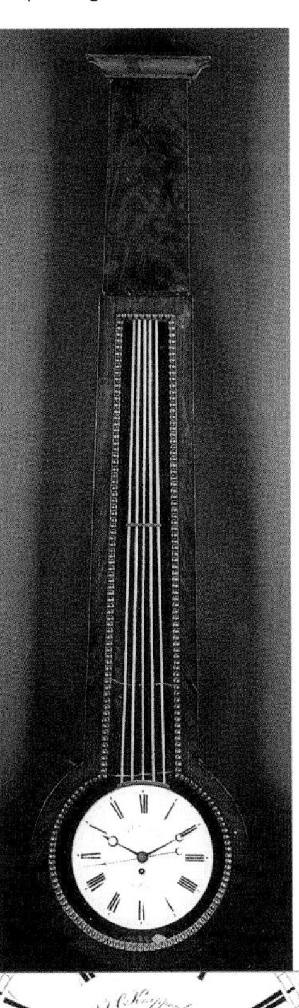

A mahogany window display clock, by A. J. C. Knippenberg, Leiden, the oscillating movement with dead-beat escapement, the gridiron-style pendulum hung from a knife-edge suspension, Holland, c1840, 53¼in (135.5cm) high.

£6,400–7,600 S(Am)

A terrestrial globe timepiece, with eight-day spring-driven movement, painted annual calendar, on a marble base, slight damage, France, c1870, 21in (53.5cm) high.

£5,700–6,800 ROSc

This timepiece has a unique movement with two levers for disengaging the Delamarche globe from the movement for demonstration purposes.

A gilt mystery clock, by Guilmet, the twin-train movement with countwheel and striking on a bell, the pendulum with a glass bob, the marble case with gilded mounts surmounted by a figure of a girl and a cherub, France, c1875, 22½in (57cm) high.

£7,600–8,500 DRA

A brass and copper timepiece, in the form of a boiler, with aneroid barometer dial and thermometer, the single barrel movement with platform cylinder escapement, France, c1880, 13in (33cm) high.

£1,050–1,250 TEN

A gilt, silvered and patinated bronze automaton clock, attributed to Guilmet, in the form of a ship's stern, the Samuel Marti movement striking on a gong, on a marble plinth and ebonized base, with glass dome, dome cracked, France, c1880, 11¾in (30cm) high.

£6,200–7,400 S

A bronze pendulum clock, with silvered dial and eight-day striking movement, surmounted by a figure of a woman holding an hourglass, signed 'Laurent, scpt', France, c1885, 37in (94cm) high.

£6,700–8,000 ROSc

A patinated spelter mystery timepiece, with eight-day movement, surmounted by a figure of Autumn Breeze, slight damage, figure signed 'Moreau', France, c1890, 29in (73.5cm) high.

£1,900–2,250 ROSc

A clock and barometer, in the form of a windmill, France, c1890, 19in (48.5cm) high.

£2,450–2,900 ROSc

A gilt-metal and marble mystery clock, the eight-day movement striking on a bell, the case surmounted by a figure of a Grecian maiden, the pendulum suspended from her arm, late 19thC, 25¼in (64cm) high.

£2,800–3,350 N

A cast-brass mantel clock, in the form of a bell, with French twin-train striking movementa, in a leaf- and scroll-moulded case inscribed with bands of Latin verse, late 19thC, 13in (33cm) high.

£410–490 Hal

◄ **A gilt-bronze and cut-glass urn clock,** the movement with club-tooth lever escapement, striking on a bell and driving two horizontal chapter rings, on a gilt socle supported by winged putti, on a marble plinth, France, c1900, 18in (45.5cm) high.

£6,000–7,200 S

A brass and papier-mâché 'Empiré' clock, in the form of a globe, damaged, France, early 20thC, 11½in (29cm) high.

£1,100–1,300 CAG

SKELETON CLOCKS

THIS LAST YEAR has been exceptional for skeleton clocks with some quite magnificent examples coming onto the market, including grand triple-train quarter-striking English skeleton clocks and even a rare world time example. The highlight of the year must surely be the complicated Belgian quarter-striking automaton skeleton clock with remontoire and calendar, dating from c1775, and sold by a Christie's London in 2005 for a six-figure sum.

The beautiful skeleton clocks made by James Condliff of Liverpool have continued to rise in value which is hardly surprising as they are exceptionally elegant with attractively designed frames and narrow silvered chapter rings. Although twin-train striking skeleton clocks are aesthetically more pleasing, triple-train quarter-striking clocks are commercially more valuable. However, this does not apply if the twin-train clock is of the balance wheel variety, for which large premiums are paid.

An impressive collection of skeleton clocks can be built for a reasonable amount, but it takes knowledge and a good eye to find the interesting and unusual pieces by individual makers. Occasionally a maker would design a skeleton clock as an example to display an innovative invention which could then be shown at one of the fashionable Great Exhibitions of the day. Such skeleton clocks are obviously very rare but research through the Patent Offices records can often help pinpoint the date of manufacture and increase its commercial value.

Robert Wren

Robert started his own business specializing in clocks in 1983. In the mid-1990s he joined the workshops of Derek Roberts Antiques, Tonbridge and is now the marketing manager.

He is a Liveryman of the Worshipful Company of Clockmakers and a Member of the British Horological Institute.

The simple timepiece skeleton clock with passing strike was made in large numbers and does not appeal to collectors, which make these a more reasonable prospect for someone who only wants one or two clocks in their home. But be warned, it should have a well fitting and undamaged glass dome, as these can be difficult and expensive to replace.

The 5th Lord Harris, who had an impressive collection of fine clocks, was known to say that he 'just liked to see the wheels go round'. This is just one of the many pleasures you can expect when you own a skeleton clock.

Robert Wren

A brass skeleton timepiece, the chain fusee movement with anchor escapement, on a rosewood base, with a glass dome, damaged, 19thC, 12¾in (32.5cm) high.
£560–670 Bea

◀ **A brass skeleton clock,** by G. Blakeborough, Ripon, with twin fusee striking movement, the wheels with six crossings, with a glass dome, 19thC, 11¾in (30cm) high.
£1,450–1,700 LAY

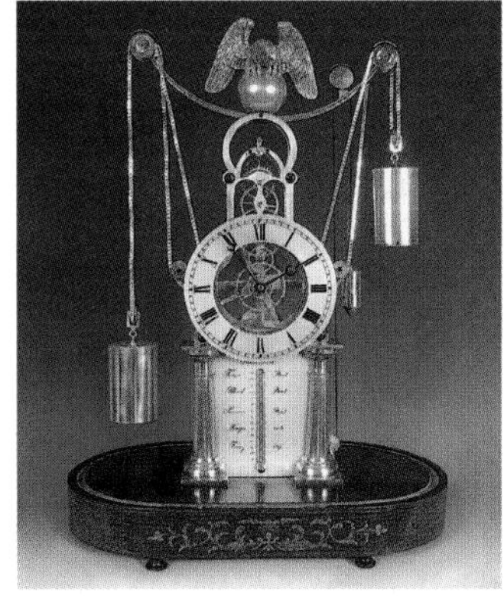

A brass skeleton clock, the silvered chapter ring with thermometer beneath, Huygen's principle weight-driven movement, the case surmounted by an eagle and a ball, France, c1845, 26in (66cm) high.
£6,300–7,000 DRA

◀ **A brass skeleton clock,** by Thomas Cox Savory, London, the eight-day twin fusee movement with anchor escapement and striking the hours on a bell, on a rosewood base, with a glass dome, c1840, 16½in (42cm) high.
£4,750–5,300 PAO

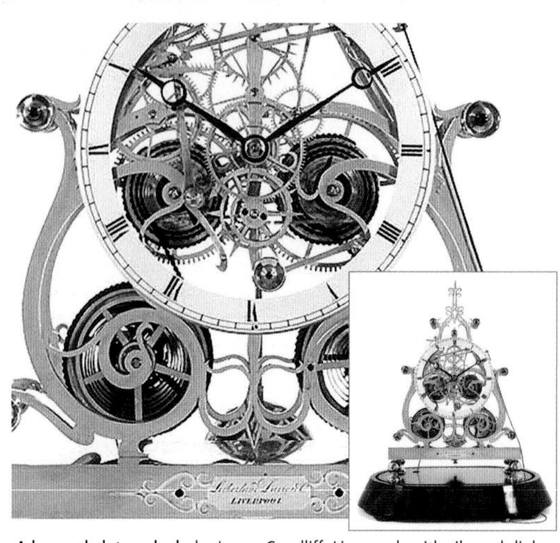

A brass skeleton clock, by James Condliff, Liverpool, with silvered dial, the twin-train movement striking the hours on a gong, with a pendulum, on a rosewood base, with a glass dome, c1850, 19in (48.5cm) high.

£26,000–29,000 DRA

A brass skeleton clock, by Evans of Handsworth, in the form of the Scott Memorial, on a marble base, c1850, 21in (53.5cm) high.

£5,600–6,300 DRA

John Houghton established his business, the Soho Clock Factory, in Soho Street, Handsworth, Birmingham, in 1805. Trade flourished and in due course his son-in-law, William Frederick Evans, joined him. Houghton retired in 1843 leaving Evans to run the business and died some 20 years later.

A brass skeleton clock, with silvered chapter ring, the fusee movement striking on a bell, with a glass dome, c1850, 20in (51cm) high.

£1,600–1,800 YOX

A brass skeleton timepiece, with silvered chapter ring, the fusee movement with anchor escapement and passing strike on a bell, on an ebonized plinth, with a glass dome, mid-19thC, 16½in (42cm) high.

£1,100–1,300 S(Am)

A skeleton timepiece, the silk thread suspension with later pendulum, later rosewood-veneered base and later glass dome, France, c1851, 8¾in (22cm) high.

£620–740 ROSc

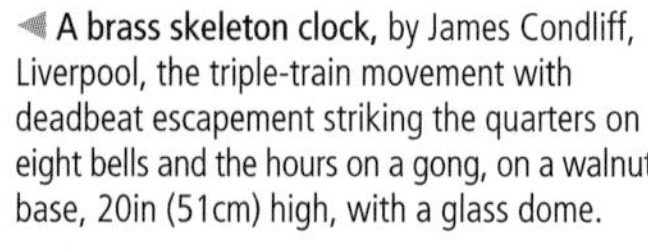

A brass skeleton clock, by James Condliff, Liverpool, the triple-train movement with deadbeat escapement striking the quarters on eight bells and the hours on a gong, on a walnut base, 20in (51cm) high, with a glass dome.

£37,800–42,000 DRA

James Condliff set up at 32 Gerrard Street, Liverpool in 1816, at which time the city was a thriving and important port. His manufacturing business produced many types of clocks but is best known for superb and distinctive skeleton clocks and for a few fine-quality regulators. From 1818 he occupied premises in Circus Street and from 1823 he moved to 5 Fraser Street where he continued for many years. He was joined by two other family members, Joseph and John, who were involved with the business from the mid-1820s. Finally, in the third quarter of the century the fourth Condliff, Thomas, appears in the business. The firm continued into the 1940s and the stock was then sold off by auction. James Condliff was highly talented and had a great technical ability which he combined with an artistic flair enabling him to produce high-quality clocks of exceptional beauty that are much sought-after today.

For further information on Clocks see pages 412–440

A brass skeleton timepiece, with silvered dial, the fusee movement with anchor escapement, on an ebonized plinth, with presentation inscription, with a glass dome, c1860, 8¼in (21cm) wide.

£880–1,050 TEN

SMITHS OF CLERKENWELL

Smiths of Clerkenwell were one of the most important makers of skeleton clocks of which many different designs and types were produced. Although Smiths produced large quantities of skeleton clocks, quarter-striking examples are less common, perhaps because of the massive difference in price shown in their catalogue. An hour strike skeleton clock could be purchased for £3 5s (about £205 at today's values), but there was a startling price rise to £20 (£1,263 today) for quarter-striking clocks.

A brass skeleton clock, by Smith & Sons, Clerkenwell, the movement striking the quarter-hours and hours on eight bells, with a glass dome, c1865, 25in (63.5cm) high, .

£19,800–22,000 DRA

A brass skeleton clock, possibly by Smith & Sons, Clerkenwell, with subsidiary dials for Canton, Madras, Port Natal, Paris, Dublin, New York, Edinburgh, St Petersburg, Sydney, Calcutta and Sebastopol, chiming the quarter-hours on a nest of bells, c1865, 24in (61cm) high.

£35,000–39,000 DRA

This is a difficult clock to date accurately. World time zones did not come into general usage until the early part of the 1880s, at which stage Greenwich was accepted worldwide as longitude zero. Prior to the advent of time zones the difference between areas of the globe were exact and based on the minute difference between solar time from one area to the next. Most world time clocks were manufactured after the change to time zones but it would appear that this was made earlier than that as there is little point in having the dial for Edinburgh which would have the same time as Greenwich after the advent of the time zone.

A brass skeleton timepiece, with silvered chapter ring, the fusee movement with anchor escapement and striking on a bell, on an ebonized plinth, with a glass dome, c1870, 10¼in (26cm) wide.

£880–1,050 TEN

A Victorian brass skeleton timepiece, with silvered chapter ring, the single chain fusee movement with anchor escapement, on a marble plinth, with a glass dome, dome damaged, 12¼in (31cm) high.

£560–670 Bea

A Victorian brass skeleton clock, with silvered chapter ring and single fusee movement, with later dome and base, 17¾in (45cm) high.

£500–600 CHTR

A brass skeleton timepiece, the eight-day fusee movement with anchor escapement, on a mahogany base, with a glass dome, dome cracked, c1880, 9¼in (23.5cm) high.

£520–620 ROS

A skeleton clock, by Smith & Sons, Clerkenwell, with silvered chapter ring, the triple-train fusee movement striking the quarter-hours on eight bells and the hours on a gong, on a later marble stand, late 19thC, 24¼in (61.5cm) high.

£28,000–33,000 GH

A skeleton clock, the chain fusee movement striking the hours on a bell, on a later wooden base, with a glass dome, c1900, 13in (33cm) high.

£380–450 ROSc

WALL CLOCKS

A japanned tavern wall clock, by John Johnson, Walton-on-Thames, the weight-driven timepiece movement with five-wheel train and anchor escapement, the case decorated with gilt trelliswork, with later base and trunk door, c1770, 58in (148cm) high.

£3,350–4,000 S

A George III mahogany wall clock, by H. Banister, Lichfield, the painted dial with subsidiary seconds dial and twin-train striking movement, the case with boxwood stringing and cockbeading, 59in (150cm) high.

£800–960 Mit

An Empire-style carved giltwood wall clock, by Israel Dahlström, slight damage, Sweden, Stockholm, 29½in (75cm) high.

£1,300–1,550 BUK

Israel Dahlström was working in Stockholm 1729–1829.

A mahogany wall clock, with painted enamel dial, the eight-day movement with anchor escapement, c1810, 49in (124.5cm) high.

£940–1,100 M

An ebonized drop dial wall clock, signed 'Desbois, Grays Inn Passage', with fusee movement, early 19thC, 23in (58.5cm) high.

£820–980 MAL(O)

A carved giltwood wall clock, by Paul Simeth, Vienna, in the form of an eagle carrying draped cloth, with later French painted dial and eight-day movement striking on a bell, Austria, c1820, 50in (127cm) high.

£1,400–1,650 S

A William IV mahogany drop dial wall clock, inscribed 'Drinkwater, Stockport', with single fusee movement, the case carved with leaves and foliate corbels, 30in (76cm) high.

£640–760 CDC

A carved giltwood wall clock, with enamel dial and twin-train striking movement, France, 19thC, 21 x 14in (53.5 x 35.5cm).

£740–880 WAD

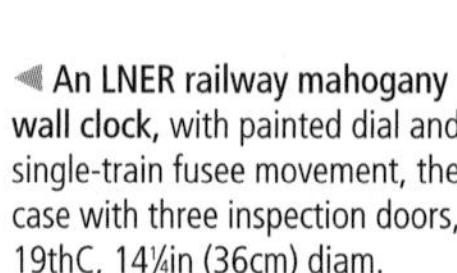

◀ **An LNER railway mahogany wall clock,** with painted dial and single-train fusee movement, the case with three inspection doors, 19thC, 14¼in (36cm) diam.

£1,250–1,500 DMC

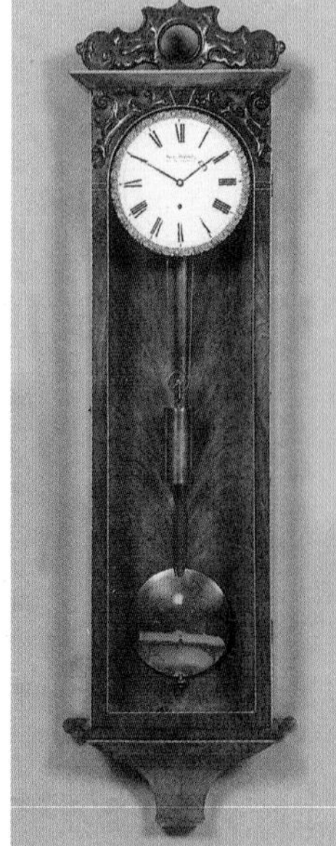

▶ **A walnut wall clock,** signed 'Ignaz Watchitz in WR Neustadt', the weight-driven month-going movement with deadbeat escapement and triangular plates, maintaining power, the case with a glazed door and satinwood inlay, Austria, c1840, 42½in (108cm) high.

£2,800–3,350 TEN

A figured mahogany drop-dial wall clock, by J. Hill, Bakewell, wih fusee movement, c1840, 25½in (65cm) high.

£470–560 DD

A rosewood drop-dial wall timepiece, with a single fusee movement, the case inlaid with mother-of-pearl, c1850, 20in (51cm) high.

£410–490 Hal

An oak wall timepiece, the enamel dial signed 'Arnsby, Northampton', with spring-driven key-wound movement, c1850, 13in (33cm) diam.

£190–220 Hal

A mahogany wall timepiece, by John Clappison, Hull, the fusee movement with anchor escapement, c1855, 11¾in (30cm) high.

£1,200–1,400 S

John Clappison is recorded working in Hull between 1851 and 1858.

A pressed-brass wall clock, by Antoine Ferrier, Luc-en-Dois, with enamel dial and twin weight-driven striking movement, the case with embossed decoration, France, 19thC, 18in (45.5cm) high.

£350–420 Hal

An American-style inlaid walnut wall clock, by Richard Iveson, Kirkby Stephen, with eight-day key-wound movement, the case with a glass panel and leaf-carved decoration, 19thC, 32¼in (82cm) high.

£700–840 PFK

Richard Iveson is recorded as working in Main Street, Kirkby Stephen, Cumbria from 1829.

A walnut wall year clock, by Anton Vogel, the six-wheel movement with grid pendulum, with later weights, Austria, Vienna, c1875, 32¾in (82cm) high.

£20,000–24,000 ROSc

A Black Forest carved wood cuckoo clock, with a 30-hour movement, damaged, Germany, c1875, 19in (48.5cm) high.

£230–270 ROSc

A Black Forest carved walnut wall clock, by Philip Haas, with eight-day movement and mock gridiron pendulum, Germany, c1890, 25in (63.5cm) high.

£570–680 ROSc

A gilt wall timepiece, with an eight-day movement, the patinated case with floral decoration, France, c1895, 7in (18cm) high.

£530–590 K&D

A gilt wall clock, with enamel dial, the eight-day movement striking the half-hours and hours on a bell, with swag and leaf decoration, France, c1900, 19in (48.5cm) high.

£730–820 K&D

A walnut wall clock, by Junghans, the dial decorated with a butterfly, the eight-day movement striking the half-hours and hours on a bell, with gilt pendulum, Germany, c1905, 42in (106.5cm) high.

£650–780 ROSc

AMERICAN CLOCKS

BEGINNER LEVEL ANTIQUE CLOCKS are among the most modestly priced antiques sold at auction in America today. As with other collectables, clocks made prior to the Industrial Revolution continue to be beyond the pocket of many buyers. However, after the assembly line arrived in the Connecticut River Valley, American clocks became the most affordable timekeepers available and helped to spell an end to English dominance in this field. These clocks were produced in tremendous quantities and exported around the world

Travellers continue to find old American clocks in India, Japan, England and other parts of the world. This voluminous production has left a legacy of many inexpensive clocks for the American collector. For instance, in a New Hampshire auction in October 2005, of the 570 lots sold, 114 clocks had a hammer price of £55 or less, 306 had a hammer price of under £270, and an additional 85 clocks had a hammer price lower than £540. No other field offers so much value for such a modest investment.

The Americans also brought practicality to their designs – the fragile marble and slate clocks produced in France were easily damaged, so the Americans produced similar cases in cast iron, painted to resemble marble; later, to reduce the weight, they used rubber that was treated to harden it.

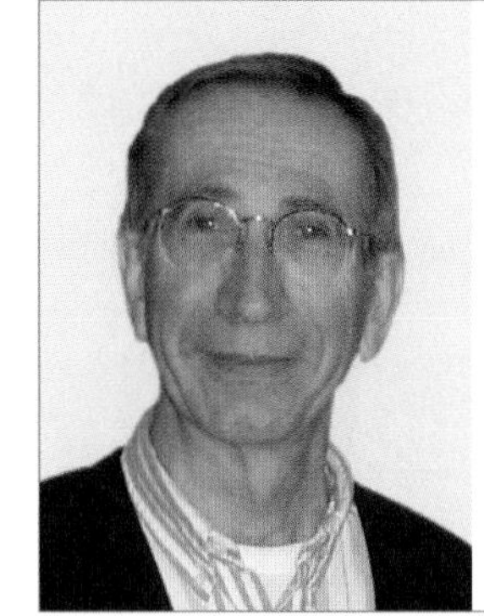

Robert Schmitt

Robert is a clock specialist and holds regular auctions from his base in New England, America.

He is active with the National Association of Watch & Clock Collectors, based in Columbia, PA.

Seth Thomas went a step further and produced clock cases in wood with a thin celluloid veneer that simulated marble or rosewood. American inventors such as B. B. Lewis made a calendar for clocks that was cheap and easy to produce and that corrected for short months and even for leap years, while D. J. Gale perfected a calendar that showed not only the day and date, but also the phases of the moon and a dial showing the lengthening days of summer and the shortening days of fall. The French and English had offered such options before, but with designs that were costly to produce. There is much interest in American clocks at auctions and markets, and that first purchase will result in a lifetime of enjoyment.

Robert Schmitt

A carved cherrywood tallcase clock, by William Crawford, Oakham, the floral-engraved dial with calendar aperture, the weight-driven movement with drop-strike mechanism, the hood with swan-neck cresting and pinwheel terminals with a brass finial, slight damage, Massachusetts, late 18thC, 83in (211cm) high.

£16,600–19,900 SK

A mahogany inlaid and string-inlaid tallcase clock, by Isaac Brokaw, Bridgetown, the engraved brass and silvered dial with moonphase, chapter ring, calendar aperture and gilt-metal spandrels, with eight-day weight-driven striking movement, the hood with swan-neck cresting, carved rosette terminals and three brass finials, New Jersey, late 18thC, 98in (249cm) high.

£5,400–6,400 SK(B)

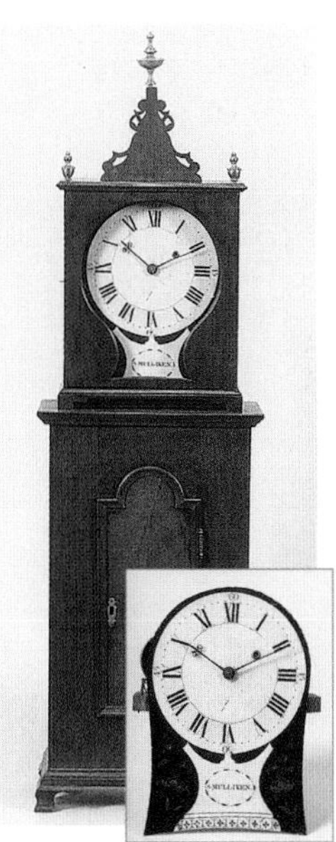

A mahogany shelf timepiece, by Samuel Mulliken, Salem or Lynn, the painted iron dial decorated with flowers, the weight-driven movement with drop-strike mechanism, the upper section with pierced shaped cresting with three brass urn finials, slight damage, Massachusetts, c1800, 40in (101.5cm) high.

£17,200–20,600 SK

A mahogany tallcase clock, by Martin Cheney, Windsor, with painted dial and seconds hand, with eight-day movement, the hood with three brass finials, damaged, Vermont, c1808, 86in (218.5cm) high.

£5,100–6,100 ROSc

An inlaid mahogany tallcase clock, the gilt and polychrome dial with seconds hand and calendar aperture, with brass eight-day weight-driven movement, New Jersey, c1810, 95in (241.5cm) high.

£8,300–9,900 SK

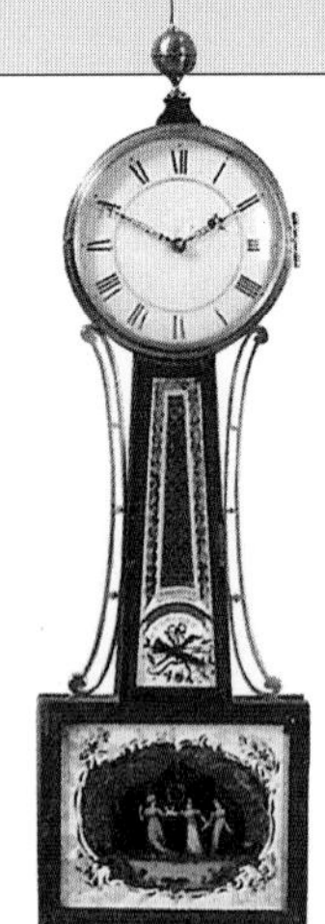

A mahogany inlaid banjo timepiece, by Lemuel Curtis, Concord, with painted iron dial and eight-day weight-driven movement, the crossbanded case with a brass bezel and pierced side arms, the lower tablet decorated with three women playing hide-and-seek, slight damage and restoration, Massachusetts, c1810, 34¼in (87cm) high.

£2,550–3,050 SK

A cherrywood tallcase clock, by Riley Whiting, Winchester, with painted and gilt wooden dial and 30-hour weight-driven movement, the hood with pierced fretwork and three brass urn finials, the case painted with simulated ebonized stringing, spreadwing eagle and an American flag, slight damage, Connecticut, c1820, 92¾in (235.5cm) high.

£2,350–2,800 SK(B)

A mahogany and mahogany-veneered pillar and scroll mantel clock, by Norris North, Torrington, with gilt and floral-painted dial, Torrington-type wooden 30-hour weight-driven striking movement, the door with *églomisé verre* panel depicting a sea battle, Connecticut, c1820, 29¾in (75.5cm) high.

£2,700–3,200 SK

A mahogany and mahogany-veneered pillar and scroll mantel clock, by Wadsworth & Turners, Litchfield, with gilt dial and a 30-hour striking weight-driven movement, the case with *églomisé verre* tablet depicting a house and landscape, Connecticut, c1825, 31in (78.5cm) high.

£1,050–1,250 SK

A mahogany and mahogany-veneered pillar and scroll mantel clock, by Eli & Samuel Terry, Plymouth, with gilt dial and 30-hour striking weight-driven movement, the case with *églomisé verre* tablet depicting a village, Connecticut, c1825, 31in (78.5cm) high.

£700–840 SK

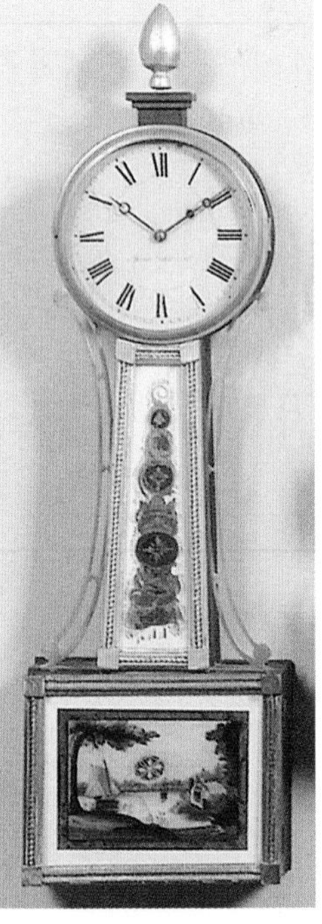

A mahogany and gilt gesso banjo timepiece, the painted metal dial inscribed 'Aaron Willard', with brass eight-day movement, the case with pierced brass sides, probably Massachusetts, early 19thC, 31½in (80cm) high.

£600–720 SK(B)

A painted pine tallcase clock, by Silas Hoadley, Plymouth, with seconds and calendar dials and 30-hour wooden weight-driven movement, the case with painted decoration, slight damage, Connecticut, c1825, 90in (228.5cm) high.

£6,300–7,500 SK

► **A mahogany pillar and scroll mantel clock,** by Eli & Samuel Terry, Plymouth, with 30-hour wooden weight-driven movement, the case with a glazed tablet depicting two urns, Connecticut, c1825, 31½in (80cm) high.

£3,800–4,500 SK(B)

► **A mahogany pillar and scroll mantel clock,** by Silas Hoadley, with a 30-hour wooden striking movement, c1825, 31½in (80cm) high.

£460–550 ROSc

A mahogany-veneered shelf clock, by Silas Hoadley, with inscription 'Time is Money' and 30-hour wooden striking movement, slight damage and losses, c1830, 35½in (90cm) high.

£360–430 ROSc

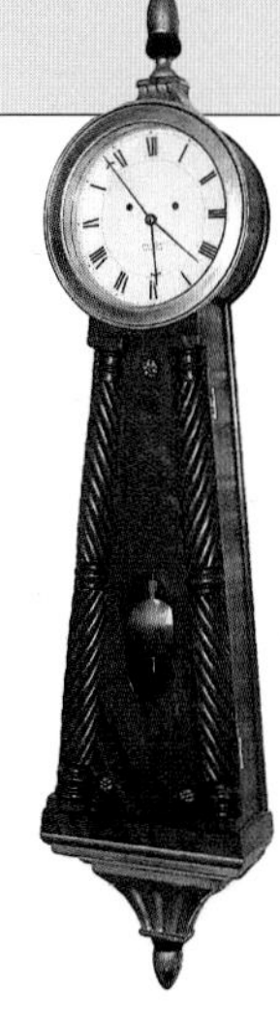

A mahogany and gilt wall clock, attributed to Joseph Dyar, Middlebury, with brass eight-day alarm movement, wooden spacer later, Vermont, c1832, 52in (132cm) high.

£2,350–2,800 ROSc

Clocks with truncated or tapered cases such as this are unique to the northern Vermont-Montreal area.

A carved wood clock, by Upson, Merrimans & Co, Bristol, with 30-hour wooden movement, the case top carved with a basket of fruit, damaged, Connecticut, c1832, 30in (76cm) high.

£320–380 ROSc

A gilt gesso banjo timepiece, by Samuel Abott, Montpelier, with eight-day weight-driven movement, signed, Vermont, c1835, 40in (101.5cm) high.

£3,300–3,950 ROSc

A mahogany-veneered mantel clock, by Hills, Goodrich & Co, Plainville, with 30-hour striking movement, the case with painted glass panels, Connecticut, c1842, 28in (71cm) high.

£220–260 ROSc

A mahogany wagon-spring shelf clock, by Birge & Fuller, Bristol, with painted zinc dial and eight-day lever-sprung movement, the case decorated with panels depicting a bee and beehive, inscribed 'By Industry We Thrive', Connecticut, c1845, 25½in (65cm) high.

£4,450–5,300 SK(B)

A wagon-spring is a large flat leaf spring used to power the movement.

An iron clock, by J. C. Brown, Forestville, with eight-day striking movement, the case inlaid with mother-of-pearl and a stencil of J. C. Brown, Connecticut, c1845, 18½in (47cm) high.

£380–450 ROSc

◀ **A rosewood shelf clock,** by Silas Burnham Terry, Terry's Ville, with engraved paper dial and brass 30-hour weight-driven striking movement, the case with a tablet depicting Hancock House, Boston, slight damage, Connecticut, 1845–50, 22¼in (56.5cm) high.

£700–840 SK

Silas Burnham Terry, a son of Eli Terry, made significant contributions to American clockmaking and the development of the American coiled clock spring.

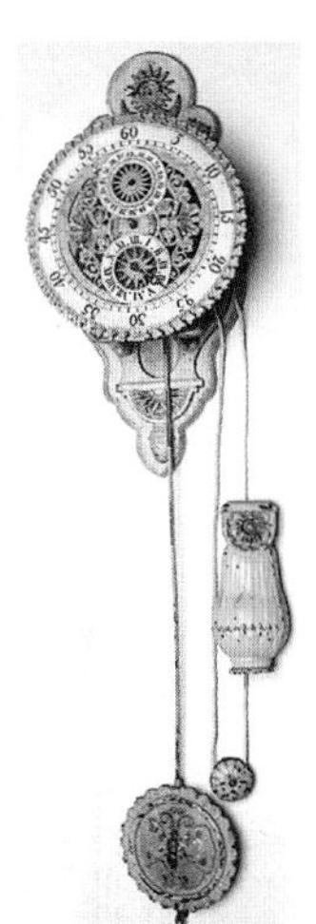

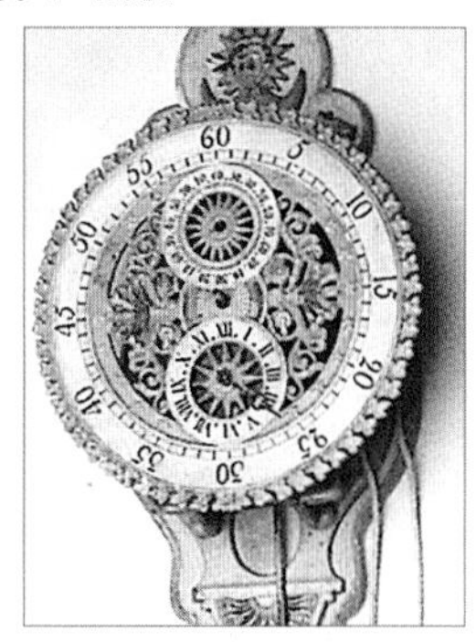

◀ **A painted cast-iron clock,** designed by Benjamin Franklin, with steel movement and cast-iron pendulum, repainted, 19thC, 22in (56cm) high.

£750–900 JDJ

A mahogany-veneered steeple clock, by Chauncey Jerome, New Haven, with an eight-day striking movement, damaged, repainted, Connecticut, c1855, 20in (51cm) high.

£110–130 ROSc

A rosewood cottage clock, by Seth Thomas, Thomaston, with 30-hour movement and alarm, Connecticut, c1868, 9in (23cm) high.

£150–180 ROSc

A rosewood-veneered cottage clock, by Terry Clock Co, Waterbury, with a 30-hour striking movement, slight damage, signed, Connecticut, c1870, 10¼in (26cm) high.

£650–780 ROSc

A plaster timepiece, by Seth Thomas, with double spring lever timepiece movement, moulded with plaster and horse hair, slight damage, c1870, 31in (78.5cm) wide.

£170–200 ROSc

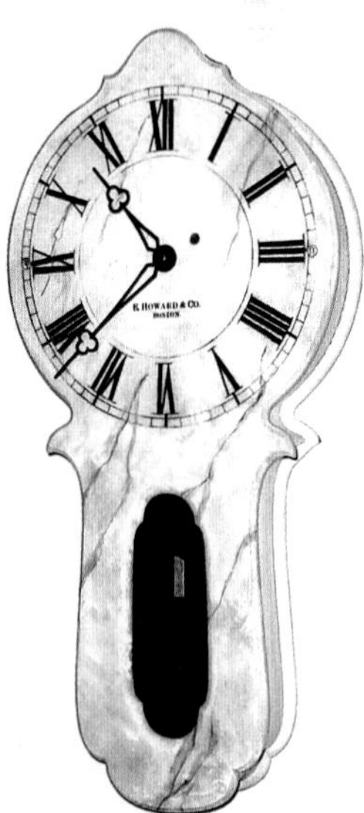

► **A marble dial clock,** by E. Howard & Co, Boston, with eight-day weight-driven movement, later tablet, Massachusetts, c1874, 29in (73.5cm) high.

£1,500–1,800 ROSc

A gilt-brass mantel clock, by Ansonia Clock Co, with enamel dial, the striking movement with visible escapement and double mercury pendulum, the case with glazed sides, New York, 1875–1900, 18in (45.5cm) high.

£890–1,050 NOA

A rosewood-veneered 'Oriental' shelf clock, by E. Ingraham & Co, with eight-day movement, slight damage, signed, c1880, 18¼in (46.5cm) high.

£840–1,000 ROSc

A mahogany wall clock, by Arizona Clock Co, New York, with a painted dial and eight-day striking movement, late 19thC, 32¼in (82cm) high.

£140–165 PFK

► **A walnut timepiece,** by Seth Thomas, with eight-day weight-driven movement and painted decoration, dial and pendulum repainted in places, c1895, 43½in (110.5cm) high.

£2,350–2,800 ROSc

A walnut steeple clock, by Seth Thomas, the eight-day key-wound movement striking on a bell, the glass door painted with a panel depicting children ice skating, Connecticut, late 19thC, 21in (53.5cm) high.

£130–155 PFK

A 'Rip Van Winkle' mantel clock, by Boston Clock Co, with porcelain dial, the eight-day tandem wind movement striking on a gong, c1895, 14½in (37cm) high.

£190–220 ROSc

A mahogany shelf clock, by Waterbury Clock Co, with brass striking movement and visible escapement, Connecticut, c1898, 12in (30cm) high.

£110–130 JAA

An oak school-house regulator, by Seth Thomas, c1900, 36in (91.5cm) high.

£370–440 JAA

A mahogany clock, by New Haven Clock Co, with painted metal dial, eight-day movement and a pendulum, c1900, 12in (30.5cm) diam.

£150–180 ROSc

A brass four-glass clock, by Ansonia Clock Co, the signed eight-day movement with rack striking on a gong, c1914, 11¾in (30cm) high.

£400–480 ROSc

A mahogany timepiece, by Seth Thomas, with painted dial and 30-day movement, slight damage, c1920, 21½in (54.5cm) diam.

£1,250–1,500 ROSc

CANADIAN CLOCKS

A mahogany bracket clock, by Joseph Petit Claire, Montreal, the silvered dial with subsidiary calendar ring, the eight-day striking movement with engraved backplate and trip repeat, c1800, 14½in (37cm) high.

£7,800–9,300 WAD

Joseph Petit Claire was known to be working in the lower town of Quebec City from at least 1790. In 1797, he moved to Montreal and announced his arrival in the Montreal Gazette. *He died in 1809.*

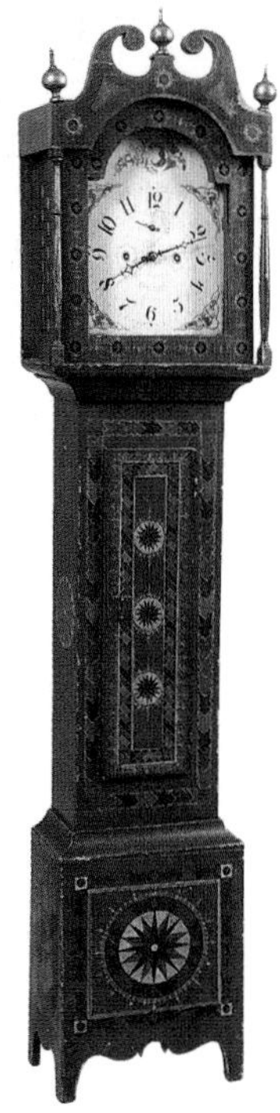

◄ **A painted wood tallcase clock,** by J. & H. Twiss, with wooden weight-driven striking movement, slight damage, dial signed, Montreal, early 19thC, 82in (208.5cm) high.

£4,150–4,900 SK

The Twiss family of clockmakers were natives of Meriden in Connecticut where they learned their trade. They established a clock factory in Montreal but it is believed they imported movements from Silas Hoadley in Connecticut.

A rosewood and gilt-gesso mantel clock, with painted zinc dial, tablets depicting the Merchant's Exchange, Philadelphia and an American eagle, slight damage, Toronto, c1860, 32½in (81.5cm) high.

£320–380 SK

BRITISH REGULATORS

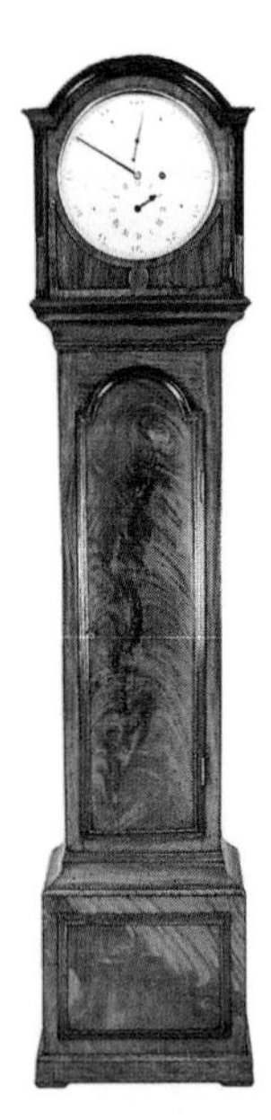

A mahogany longcase regulator, by Benjamin Knight, with silvered dial, the four-pillar eight-day movement with Harrison maintaining power and deadbeat escapement, the wooden pendulum with a brass bob, c1790, 76in (193cm) high.

£14,400–16,000 ⊞ PAO

A figured mahogany longcase regulator, by Thomas Ham, London, with silvered brass dial, eight-day six-pillar movement, high-count wheel train with six crossings, deadbeat escapement and Harrison's maintaining power, the wooden rod pendulum with a brass bob, c1820, 78in (198cm) high.

£14,800–16,500 ⊞ ALS

Further reading

Miller's Antiques Checklist: Clocks, Miller's Publications, 2000

A mahogany longcase regulator, by Richard D. Pugh, Liverpool, with silvered dial, the eight-day six-pillar movement with deadbeat escapement and woodem pendulum rod, c1850, 79in (200.5cm) high.

£7,800–8,800 ⊞ K&D

Richard D. Pugh is recorded as working in Liverpool between 1848 and 1851.

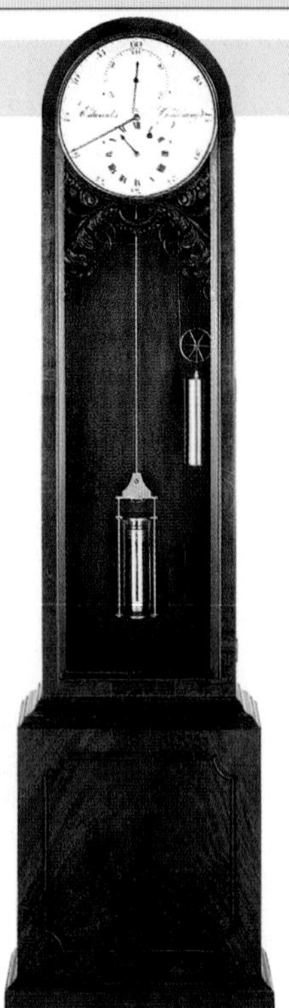

A mahogany longcase regulator, by James Edwards, with silvered dial, the movement with wheelwork and six crossings, c1860, 75¼in (191cm) high.

£12,600–14,000 ⊞ TUR

CONTINENTAL REGULATORS

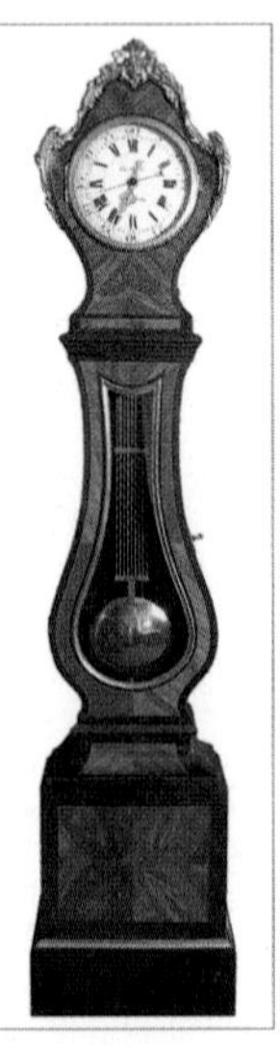

◀ **A kingwood, boxwood and mahogany longcase regulator,** by Platier, enamel dial signed 'Platier à Paris', the month-going movement with four pillars and four-wheel train and five crossings, with pinwheel escapement and gridiron pendulum, the case stamped by the *ebeniste* Jerôme Adrien Jollain, France, c1770, 81in (205.5cm) high.

£22,500–25,000 ⊞ JIL

Jerôme Adrien Jollain was from a family of clockmakers and he specialized in making fine cases using exotic wood and gilt-bronze mounts. He was received master on 1st August 1763 and died in 1788.

A fire-gilded bronze table regulator, by Ferdinand Berthoud, with enamel dial and month-going movement, France, c1775, 16in (40.5cm) high.

£19,800–22,000 ⊞ JIL

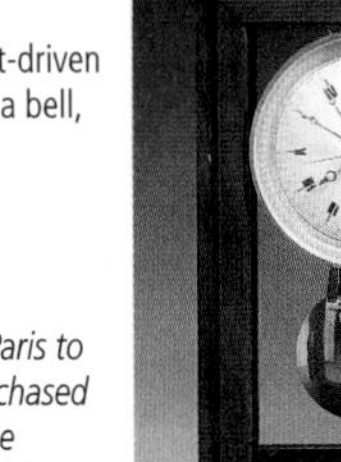

▶ **A mahogany table regulator,** the enamel dial signed 'Lépine hr de l'Impératrice', the 30-day weight-driven movement with Harrison's maintaining power and Graham-type deadbeat escapement and striking on a bell, with outside countwheel and gridiron pendulum, gilt-brass presentation plaque, France, c1809, 24¼in (61.5cm) high.

£57,000–68,000 ⚒ S

Pierre-Claude Raguet, known as Lépine, was the son of a cloth merchant at Dôle. In 1753 he came to Paris to work for the firm of Lépine. He married the daughter of Jean-Antoine Lépine, in 1782 and in 1783 purchased a one-third share of his father-in-law's business. He worked closely with Jean-Antoine and took over the business in June 1784 under the name Lépine à Paris, Horloger du Roi. By 1810, the year of his death, his clients included Napoleon, the Empress Joséphine, Jérôme, King of Westphalia, Charles IV, King of Spain and the Ambassadors for Russia and Austria. Soon after his death the firm was sold but continued to trade under the name of Lépine until the early 20th century.

THE CLOCK SHOP

· WEYBRIDGE ·

A comprehensive range of antique clocks and barometers from all periods bought, sold and restored.

64 CHURCH STREET, WEYBRIDGE
SURREY KT13 8DL
TEL: 01932 840407/855503
www.theclockshopweybridge.co.uk

10.00am–6.00pm Mon–Sat. Closed Wednesday

5 minutes from exit 11 on M25

The Old Clock Shop

63 HIGH STREET
WEST MALLING
KENT
Tel: 01732 843246

A Tavern Act of Parliament clock, weight-driven A-framed movement, inside counter balance, original lacquer case, signed by the maker Hancock, Bath. Circa 1785.

Visit our five showrooms and see a fine selection of modestly priced clocks and barometers

Restoration service provided

Open 9am–5pm Mon–Sat

Proprietor: Ms S. L. LUCK
Website: www.theoldclockshop.co.uk

The Clock House

Antiquarian Horology

75 Pound Street, Carshalton, Surrey SM5 3PG

SPECIALISTS IN LONGCASE CLOCK RESTORATION

◆

DIALS RESTORED

◆

CASE RESTORATION UNDERTAKEN

◆

CASES BOUGHT, ANY CONDITION

◆

PART CLOCKS AND MOVEMENTS CONSIDERED

CLOCKS SOLD FULLY RESTORED

◆

CLOCKS SOLD NEEDING RESTORATION

◆

RESTORATION MATERIALS STOCKED (Bushes, Gut, Pendulums, Suspension, Springs, etc.

◆

TRADE AND ENTHUSIASTS WELCOME

OPENING HOURS: TUESDAY to FRIDAY 9.30am–4.30pm, SATURDAY 9.00am–6.00pm, or at other times by appointment

TELEPHONE: MARK COCKLIN
+44 (0)20 8773 4844 • Mobile 07850 363 317
Email: markcocklin@theclockhouse.co.uk
Website: www.theclockhouse.co.uk

The only name you need to know
The world's largest dedicated antique watch website

WWW.ANTIQUE-WATCH.COM

Over 22,000 pages of

ANTIQUE AND PRECISION POCKET WATCHES IN FULL COLOUR SHOWING MOVEMENTS, CASES, ETC

WWW.ANTIQUE-WATCH.COM

All major credit cards accepted

PIECES OF TIME
1–7 DAVIES MEWS
LONDON W1K 5AB
Phone: +44 (0)20 7629 2422 Fax: +44 (0)20 7409 1625
email: info@antique-watch.com

Snail mail catalogue available
£10 for first catalogue
Subscription for 3 catalogues £20 or $50

See our affiliate website
www.cufflinksworld.com

Member of BADA

WATCHES

POCKET WATCHES

A brass pair-cased pocket watch, by Nathaniel Barrow, London, with two silvered regulation dials and a fusee verge movement, in a pierced case, the dial with later engine-turned decoration, damaged, c1690.

£2,050–2,450 DN

◀ **A 22ct gold consular cased verge pocket watch,** by Daniel Quare, London, with full-plate fire-gilt movement, the case back engraved with the date '1700' and a Bishop's mitre, case and dial replaced, hallmarked London 1774, 2in (5cm) diam.

£4,150–4,650 FOF

Daniel Quare was born in Somerset c1647 and came to London, where he worked at St Martin Le Grand and became Brother in the Clockmakers' Company in 1671. Besides being a very fine craftsman, he had an inventive mind and by 1676 had devised a motion that enabled the hour and minute hands to be set together. He became assistant to the Clockmakers' Company in 1700; a Warden from 1705 and its Master in 1708. He died in 1724 when the business was continued by Stephen Horseman whom he had taken into partnership c1705. Quare made the movement of this watch, but it was later re-cased and re-dialed to keep up with current fashion, as was common practice at the time.

A gold and diamond verge pocket watch, by Graham, London, with enamel dial, fusee and chain movement, the case with gold filigree decoration and gold inner sleeve, the back set with diamonds, c1720, 1¼in (3cm) diam.

£3,000–3,600 S

A gold and ruby cylinder watch, by Eardley Norton, London, with engine-turned dial, fire-gilt fusee and chain movement, c1775, 1¾ (4.5cm) diam.

£1,300–1,450 PT

A repoussé silver pair-cased verge watch, by W. Wood, the champlevé dial chased with satyr mask and a seated nude figure, with fusee movement, the outer case decorated with Adam and Eve in the Garden of Eden within a border of scrollwork, foliage and flower heads, signed, London 1787, 2in (5cm) diam.

£680–810 GTH

A silver-plated and tortoiseshell triple-cased verge watch, by George Charles, London, for the Turkish market, the enamel dial signed 'Eardley Norton, London', the silver inner and middle case with maker's mark 'WB', London 1794.

£800–960 AG

◀ **A leather and horn chatelaine watch,** by Charles Oudin, Paris, the dial with applied porcelain tablets, the cylinder escapement signed and marked 'Gold Medal Palais Royale', France, 1807–25, 1¾in (4.5cm) diam.

£540–600 FOF

Charles Oudin worked in Paris from 1807 to 1825. He was a highly respected maker of fine watches and a former student of Breguet.

A gold pair-cased pocket watch, by Vauchez, Paris, with an enamel dial, the case engraved and set with brilliant stones in silver ribbons enclosing a portrait of a young woman wearing a feathered tricorn hat, France, 18thC.

£1,400–1,650 PF

A gold and enamel digital cylinder pocket watch, by Ls Duchene et Fils, the signed engine-turned silver dial with an aperture at the top showing the hours on an enamel dial, the minutes showing through an aperture at the bottom, Switzerland, c1830, 2in (5cm) diam.

£2,700–3,000 PT

An early Victorian 18ct gold open-faced pocket watch, the case with milled and engine-turned floral decoration.

£300–360 DD

An 18ct gold keywind pocket watch, by Bonnardel, Nimes, with porcelain dial and engraved backplate, France, c1850.

£480–570 WAD

A pair of silver pocket watches, each with an enamel dial painted with Chinese characters to the centre, lever movement and key wind, c1850, each 1½in (4cm) diam, in original tooled leather presentation box.

£900–1,050 LJ

This pocket watch was made for the Chinese market.

◀ **A silver hunter pocket watch,** by the Elgin National Watch Co, Illinois, the enamel dial with subsidiary seconds, with keyless going barrel movement and club foot lever escapement, engraving worn, America, c1890, 2¼in (5.5cm) diam.

£540–600 PT

An enamel and diamond pendant watch, by A. Chopard, with a gold-plated dial, the guilloche enamel case with a floral reserve centred with a diamond and rose-cut diamond bail, Switzerland, early 20thC, 1in (2.5cm) diam.

£600–720 SK

An 18ct gold open-faced pocket watch, by Waltham Watch Co, with a subsidiary seconds dial, the Dennison case hallmarked Birmingham 1918, America, early 20thC, 2in (5cm) diam.

£300–360 FHF

A 9ct gold Traveller hunter pocket watch, by Waltham Watch Co, the enamel dial with subsidiary seconds, the keyless movement with going barrel and club foot lever escapement, the case hallmarked 'Birmingham 1919', maker's mark 'ALD', America, 2in (5cm) diam.

£670–750 PT

A gold pocket watch, by Breguet, the silver engine-turned dial with subsidiary seconds, with keyless lever movement, the back enamelled with the Egyptian Royal coat-of-arms, France, c1925, 2in (5cm) diam.

£3,500–4,200 TEN

The vendor purchased this watch in 1954 from Sotheby's 'The Palace Collections of Egypt' sale.

A 9ct gold Traveller hunter pocket watch, by Waltham Watch Co, the dial with subsidiary seconds, with keyless lever movement, the four-piece hinged case with a snap-on bezel and hallmarked Chester 1927, America, together with a 9ct rose gold curb albert chain and an 1895 sovereign.

£300–360 DN

A Rolex 14ct gold pocket watch, with '¼ Century Club' letters replacing the numerals on the dial, c1944, with a 10ct yellow and white gold watch chain.

£510–610 WAD

WRISTWATCHES

An 18ct gold half-hunter wristwatch, with a gilt-brass lever movement, signed 'J. W. Benson, 62 and 64 Ludgate Hill, London, Best London Make, by Warrant to H.M. the late Queen Victoria', London 1906, 1¼in (3cm) diam.

£1,150–1,300 FOF

A Harwood Watch Co silver automatic wristwatch, Switzerland, 1929.

£690–770 TEM

An International Watch Co 18ct gold wristwatch, with gold hands and sweep second, case, dial and 17-jewel movement signed, Switzerland, c1952.

£430–510 WAD

An International Watch Co 18ct white gold and diamond wristwatch, with silvered dial, 15-jewel enamel-wind movement, the gold and palladium case set with round and baguette-cut diamonds to the bezel with further diamonds to the lugs, Switzerland, c1960.

£600–720 LJ

A Jaeger LeCoultre 18ct gold Memovox alarm wristwatch, the gold dial with central alarm disc, gold hands and sweep second, case, dial and movement signed, Switzerland, 1950s.

£630–750 WAD

A Jaeger LeCoultre wristwatch, the black dial with subsidiary seconds dial, Switzerland, c1940.

£1,000–1,150 TEM

A Jaeger LeCoultre 14ct gold Mystery wristwatch, the textured dial with white gold markers and diamond numerals, the case and strap set with 42 single-cut diamonds, case, dial and movement signed, Switzerland, 1950s.

£310–370 WAD

A Longines 9ct gold wristwatch, the dial with subsidiary seconds dial, Switzerland, c1930.

£720–800 TEM

A Movado 18ct gold wristwatch, with time/date dial, moonphase dial and day and month apertures, Switzerland, c1940.

£3,150–3,500 TEM

An Omega 18ct gold Seamaster Autodate wristwatch, the enamel dial with a date aperture, the case with an inscription to the reverse, the 14ct gold mesh band with engraved initials, Switzerland, c1960.

£850–1,000 LJ

◀ A Patek Philippe 18ct pink **gold wristwatch,** the brushed silvered dial with subsidiary seconds dial, nickel lever movement, case, dial and movement signed, Switzerland, c1940, 1¼in (3cm) diam.

£3,350–4,000 S

▶ A Rolex Precision steel **wristwatch,** Switzerland, c1940.

£1,750–1,950 TEM

A Pierce 18ct gold chronograph **wristwatch,** with two subsidiary dials, Switzerland, 1940.

£810–900 TEM

A Rolex Precision 9ct gold **wristwatch,** Switzerland, 1950.

£1,000–1,150 TEM

A Rolex 18ct gold Cellini wristwatch, with 19-jewel movement, 18ct gold mesh strap, case, dial and movement signed, Switzerland, c1969.

£540–640 WAD

A Vacheron & Constantin 18ct gold **wristwatch,** with 20-jewel movement, 18ct gold mesh strap, Switzerland, c1975.

£390–460 WAD

A Waltham metal military wristwatch, the dial with luminous numerals and hands, 16-jewel movement, America, c1942.

£90–105 DN

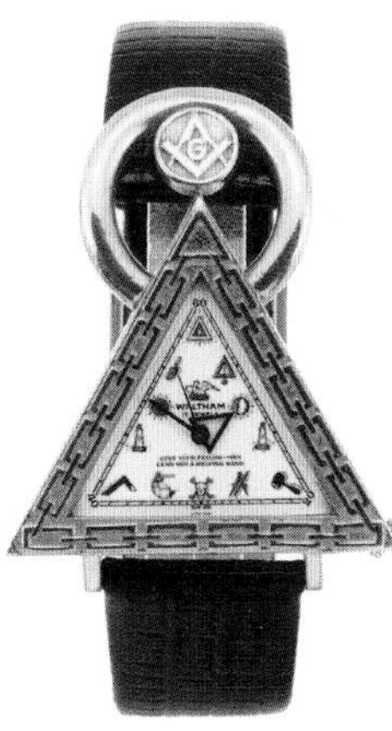

A Waltham gold-plated **Masonic wristwatch,** the dial inscribed 'Love your fellow-man lend him a helping hand' with Masonic symbol numerals, the case set with a loop and Masonic decoration, dial and movement signed, America, c1950, 1¾in (4.5cm) long.

£1,800–2,150 S

A Raymond Yard aquamarine **and diamond wristwatch,** with 17-jewel Swiss Movado movement and later 14ct white gold bracelet, America, c1940.

£1,550–1,850 SK

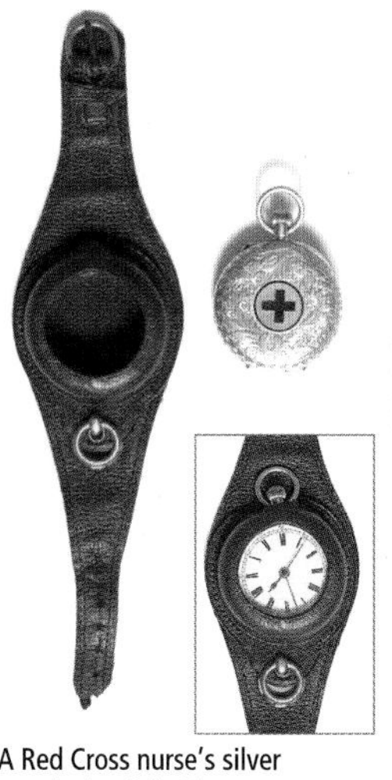

A Red Cross nurse's silver **watch,** the dial with sweep seconds, with fire-gilt 10-jewel keyless cylinder movement, the case with enamelled Red Cross logo to the reverse, patent leather wristlet strap with quick-release front, London 1914, 1½in (4cm) diam.

£290–330 FOF

An 18ct gold and rose diamond **wristwatch,** with silvered part engine-turned dial, 17-jewel movement, the two-piece case with single line bezel and leaf-engraved sides, case with import marks for London 1919, on a later gold-plated bracelet, Switzerland, c1930.

£120–140 DN

BAROMETERS

STICK BAROMETERS

A walnut stick barometer, by Ogden, Darlington, with two engraved brass registers and vernier, with a concealed tube above a turned cistern cover, 18thC, 37in (94cm) high.

£3,650–4,350 CGC

◀ **A George III mahogany stick barometer,** by Peter Clare, Manchester, with double enamel dial, the top with a reeded urn finial above a Greek key moulded cornice, the half-round and fluted reeded column on a moulded plinth, 44in (112cm) high.

£3,800–4,550 MEA

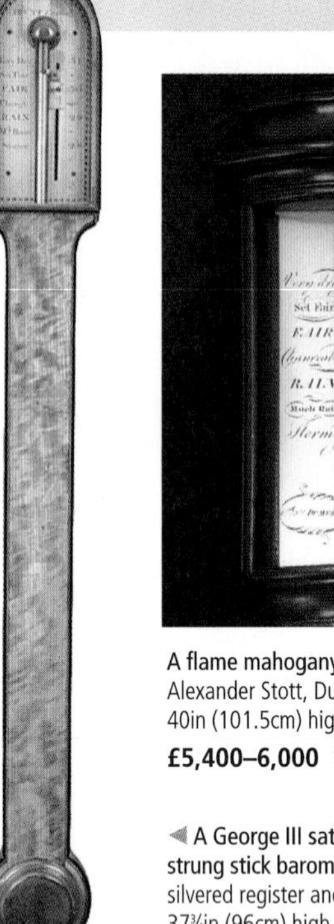

A flame mahogany stick barometer, by Alexander Stott, Dumfries, Scotland, c1790, 40in (101.5cm) high.

£5,400–6,000 AW

◀ **A George III satinwood and mahogany-strung stick barometer,** by Blunt, London, with silvered register and engraved banding, 37¾in (96cm) high.

£2,100–2,500 SWO

Market information

- Antique barometers have for the most part maintained their value over the recent year which, once again, has been difficult for the general antiques market.
- There are more wheel barometers in existence than stick barometers, and their prices have increased greatly. Stick barometers, after many years of gaining value, appear to have reached a price plateau.
- There has been more interest in unusual and decorative instruments, and barometers at the very highest price range have continued to be very sought after.

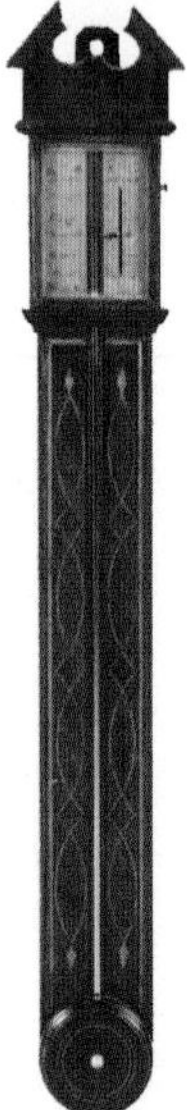

An inlaid walnut and boxwood-strung stick barometer, by Porthouse, Penrith, with printed paper dial and adjustable indicator, the trunk with an exposed tube, the cistern with an ivory stud, late 18thC, 40in (101.5cm) high.

£4,250–5,100 PFK

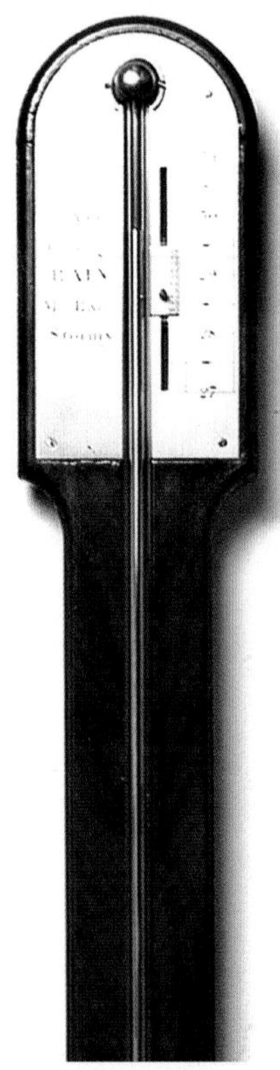

A mahogany stick barometer, by Cary, London, c1800, 36in (91.5cm) high.

£4,500–5,000 RAY

A mahogany stick barometer, by Anthony Tarony, London, signed 'A. Trony Fecit', the case with inlaid chequer stringing, c1800, 39in (99cm) high.

£2,950–3,300 AW

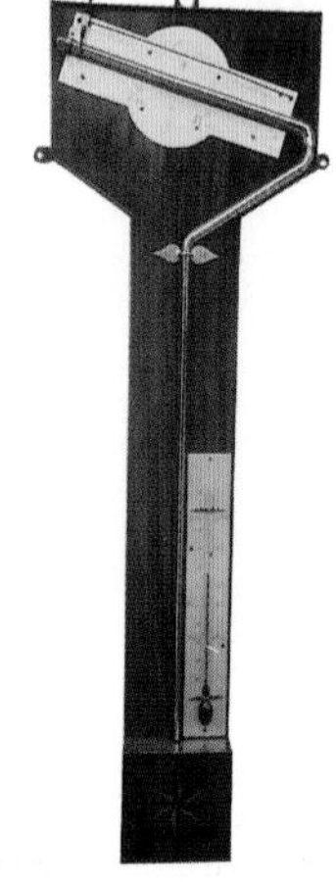

A mahogany double angle barometer, by William Robb, Montrose, with silvered engraved scales, Scotland, c1800, 36in (91.5cm) high.

£8,500–9,500 RAY

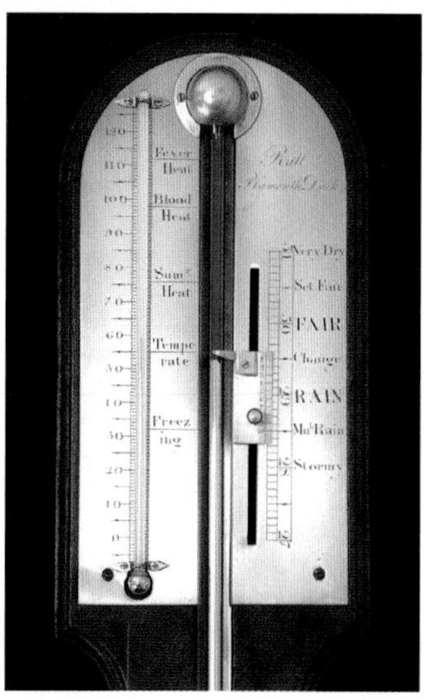

A mahogany stick barometer, by Richard Rutt, Plymouth Dock, c1810, 38in (96.5cm) high.

£3,400–3,800 AW

A mahogany angle barometer, signed 'Knie, Edinburgh', with silvered and engraved scales, Scotland, c1820, 36in (91.5cm) high.

£11,200–12,500 RAY

These are also known as signpost barometers.

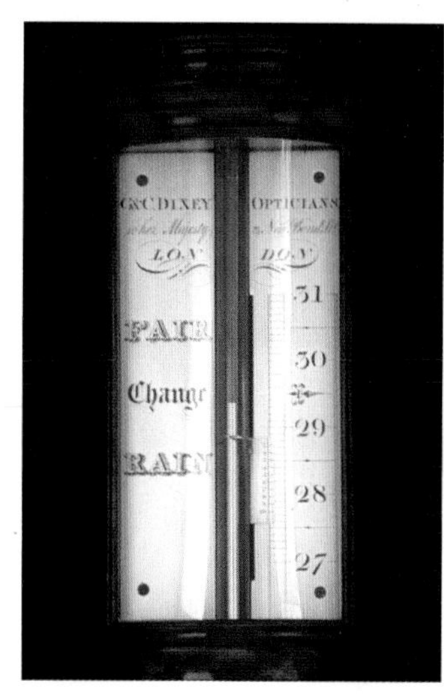

A figured rosewood stick barometer, by George & Charles Dixey, London, c1830, 39in (99cm) high.

£6,300–7,000 AW

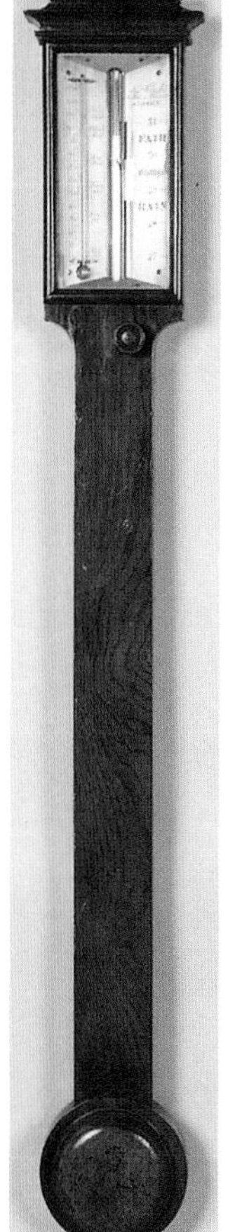

A rosewood stick barometer, by Thomas Clark, Walton-on-Thames, with faceted silver dial, vernier scale and thermometer, the case with a turned tortoiseshell adjuster, 19thC, 38¼in (97cm) high.

£1,750–2,100 WW

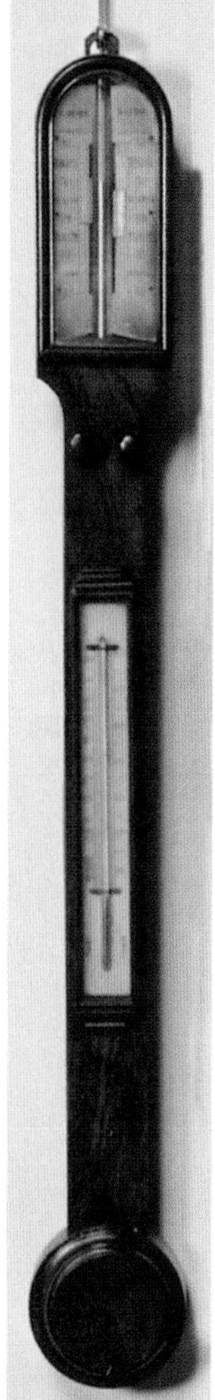

A walnut stick barometer, by J. Scott Walker, with mercury thermometer and ivory scale, 19thC, 36in (91.5cm) high.

£480–570 AG

A rosewood stick barometer, by Lewis Casartelli, Manchester, with a thermometer, c1850, 39in (99cm) high.

£3,400–3,800 AW

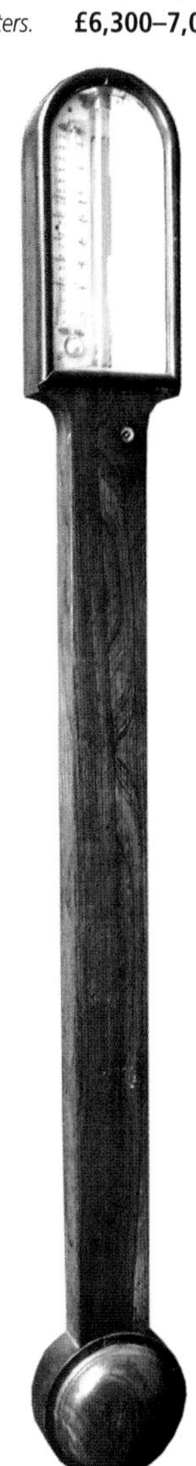

A rosewood stick barometer, by J. Tewson, Stamford, with a thermometer, the bone dial with vernier scale, c1850, 37in (94cm) high.

£730–870 ROS

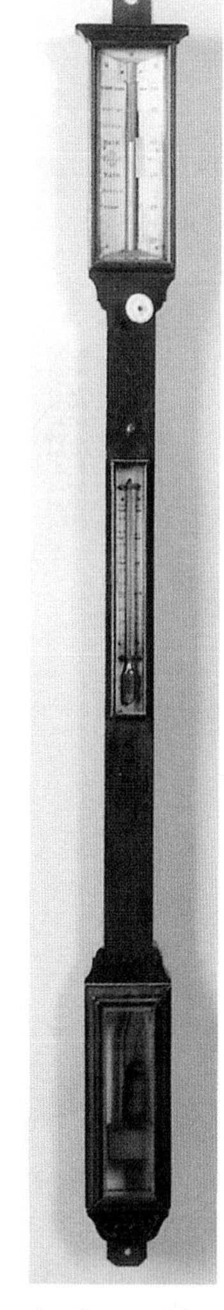

A mahogany stick barometer, by Eggert & Son, New York, with thermometer, America, late 19thC, 39in (99cm) high.

£1,750–2,100 SK

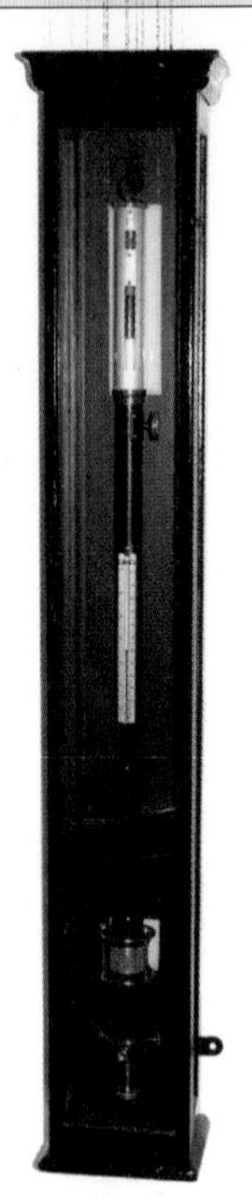

A painted Fortin stick barometer, by Bailey, Birmingham, restored, c1860, 50in (127cm) high.

£2,900–3,250 RTW

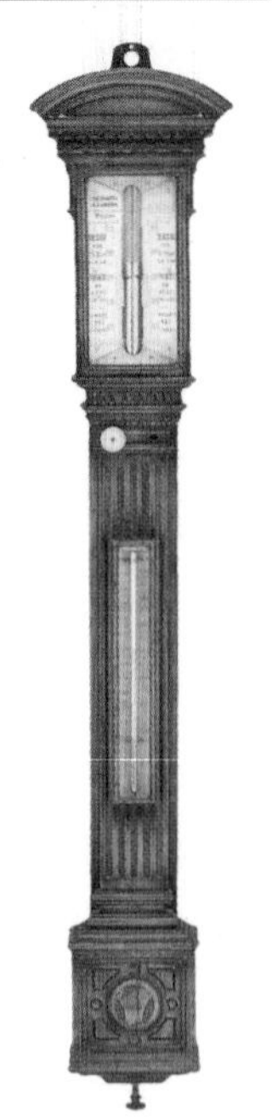

A carved oak stick barometer, by Negretti & Zambra, with thermometer, ivory plates and twin vernier, signed, c1870, 40½in (103cm) high.

£940–1,100 TEN

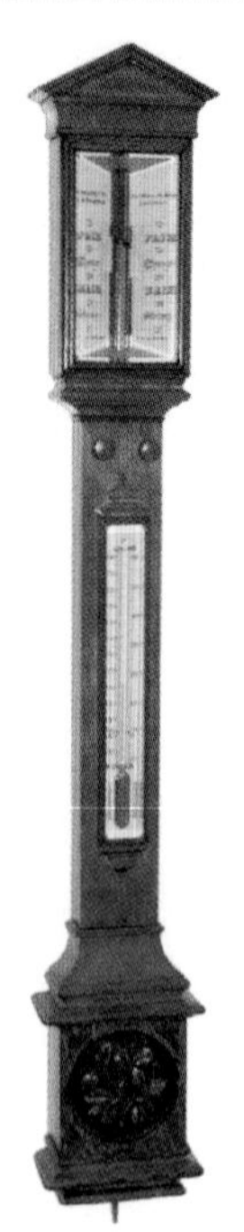

A carved oak stick barometer, by Negretti & Zambra, London, with two verniers, restored, c1880, 44in (112cm) high.

£2,700–3,000 RTW

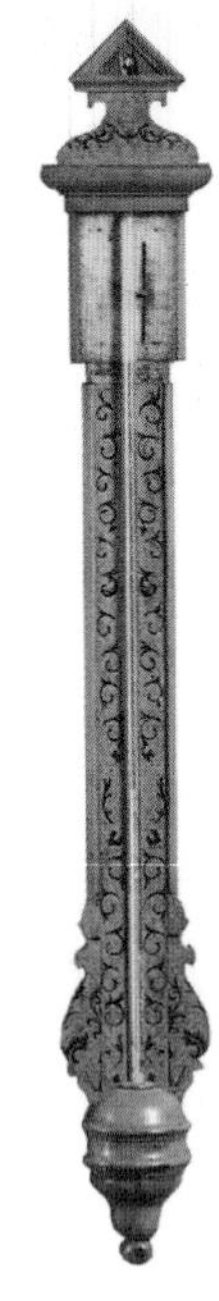

An 18th century-style marquetry stick barometer, the exposed tube with silvered plates, the case with oak mouldings, late 19thC, 43in (109cm) high.

£2,250–2,700 S

ADMIRAL FITZROY BAROMETERS

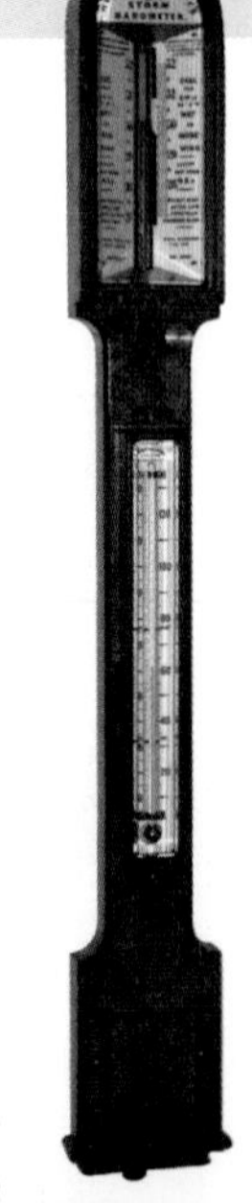

◄ **An oak Admiral Fitzroy storm barometer,** by Negretti & Zambra, with large bore mercury tube, c1880, 41in (104cm) high.

£2,700–3,000 RTW

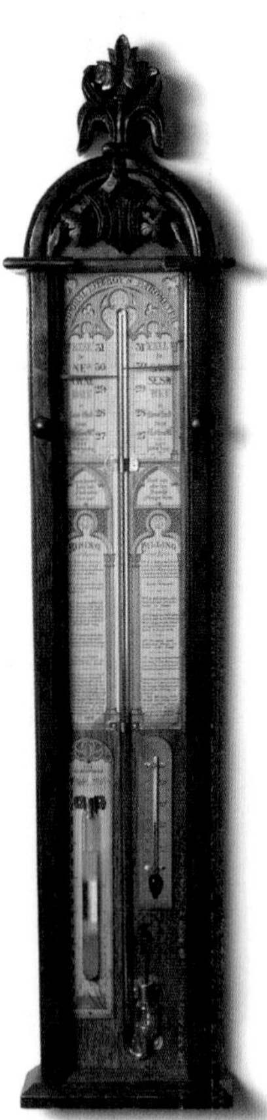

A carved oak Admiral Fitzroy barometer, c1860, 46in (117cm) high.

£1,200–1,350 TRI

A Victorian carved oak Admiral Fitzroy barometer, with paper dial and brass hands above a thermometer and hygrometer, 47in (119.5cm) high.

£760–910 GIL

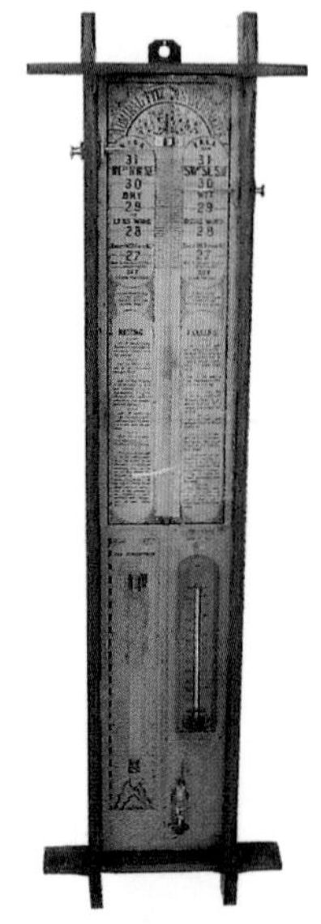

An oak Admiral Fitzroy barometer, with original charts, thermometer and storm bottle, c1880, 37in (94cm) high.

£670–750 RAY

Admiral Fitzroy joins the shipping forecast

The public interest in Admiral Fitzroy and the Darwin Expedition on the *Beagle* continues to maintain the popularity of Fitzroy barometers. There is now a designated shipping zone named after Fitzroy, situated west of the Bay of Biscay.

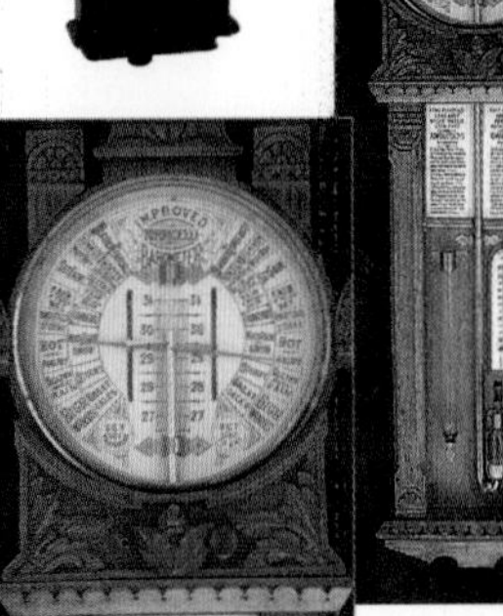

A carved oak Admiral Fitzroy Improved Torricelli barometer, by Joseph Davis, London, c1890, 42in (106.5cm) high.

£1,950–2,200 AW

WHEEL BAROMETERS

A George III mahogany and satinwood-crossbanded wheel barometer, by W. Squirrell, Bildeston, with silvered dial, 41½in (105.5cm) high.

£560–670 LAY

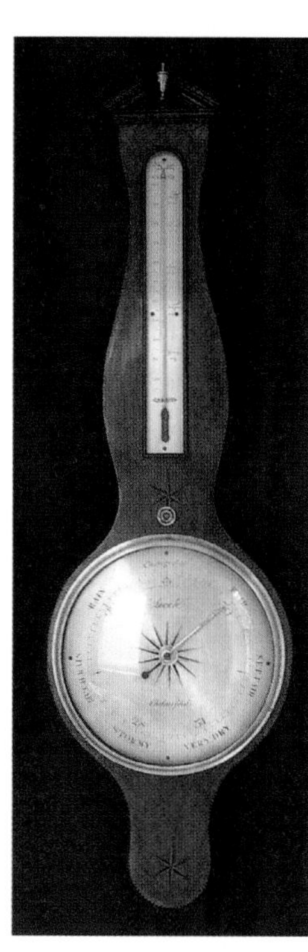

An inlaid satinwood wheel barometer, by James Leech, Chelmsford, c1800, 38in (96.5cm) high.

£3,200–3,600 AW

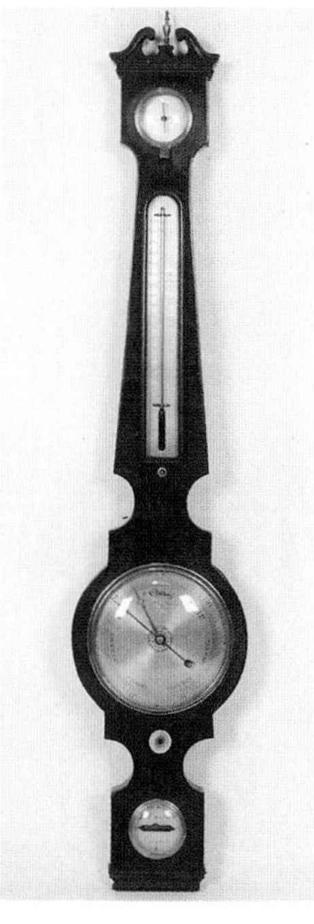

A Regency mahogany wheel barometer, by J. Ciceri & Co, London, with silvered dial, dry/damp gauge and level, the swan-neck pediment with a brass finial, 38in (96.5cm) high.

£730–870 HYD

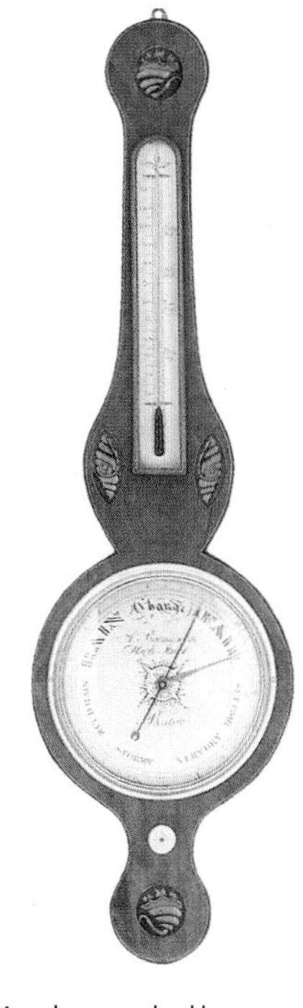

A mahogany wheel barometer, by A. Barnascone, Boston, with silvered dial, the arched pediment with shell inlay and strung borders, c1820, 35¾in (91cm) high.

£940–1,100 TEN

A satinwood wheel barometer, by Lione & Somalvico, London, c1820, 37in (94cm) high.

£2,250–2,500 RAY

A Sheraton-style mahogany wheel barometer, by Giovanni Stopani, London, with silvered-brass dial, the case with boxwood and ebony stringing and inlaid with a marquetry conch shell and flowerhead motif, c1820, 37in (94cm) high.

£1,050–1,200 AW

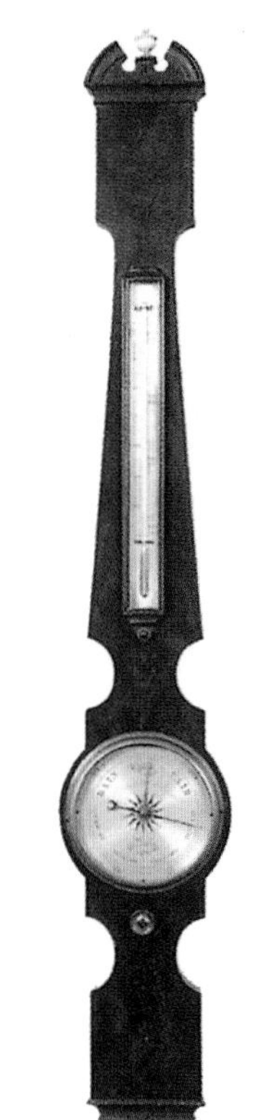

A mahogany wheel thermometer, by Dring & Fage, with 5in (12.5cm) silvered dial and brass adjuster, early 19thC, 38½in (98cm) high.

£1,800–2,150 WW

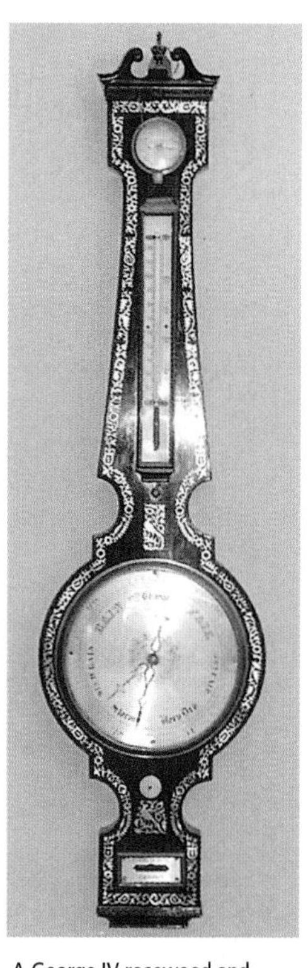

A George IV rosewood and mother-of-pearl inlaid wheel barometer, by G. Brachter, London, the silvered dial above a hygrometer and a later thermometer, 38½in (98cm) high.

£500–600 DN(HAM)

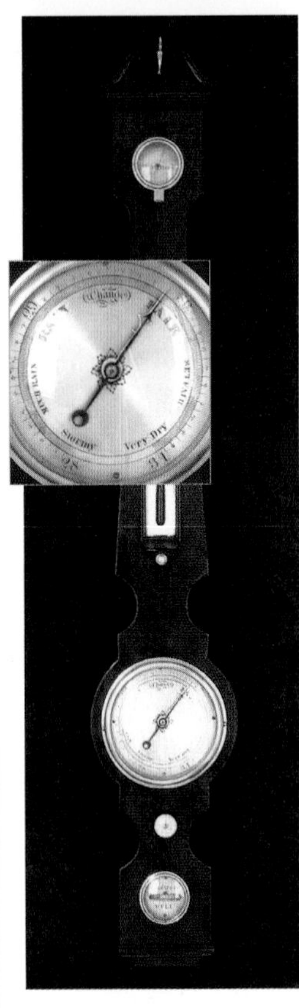

A flame mahogany wheel barometer, by Augustus Maspoli, Hull, c1830, dial 6in (15cm) diam.

£3,200–3,600 ⊞ AW

A mahogany and ebony-strung wheel barometer, by Atwood, Lewes, with engraved silvered-brass dial, hygrometer and level, c1835, dial 10in (25.5cm) diam.

£1,350–1,550 ⊞ PAO

A mahogany wheel barometer, by J. Mangacavalli, London, with silvered brass dial, thermometer scale and hygrometer, level and mirror, the top with a brass finial, c1835, dial 8in (20.5cm) diam.

£1,000–1,150 ⊞ PAO

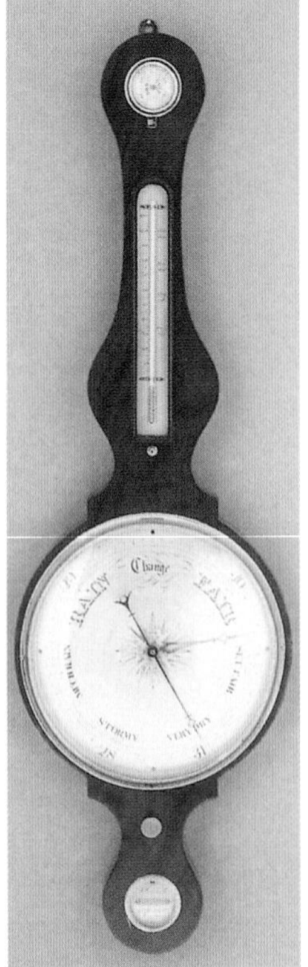

A mahogany wheel barometer, by Ronchetti, Manchester, with a silvered dial, hygrometer, thermometer and spirit level, c1835, 43¾in (111cm) high.

£1,300–1,550 TEN

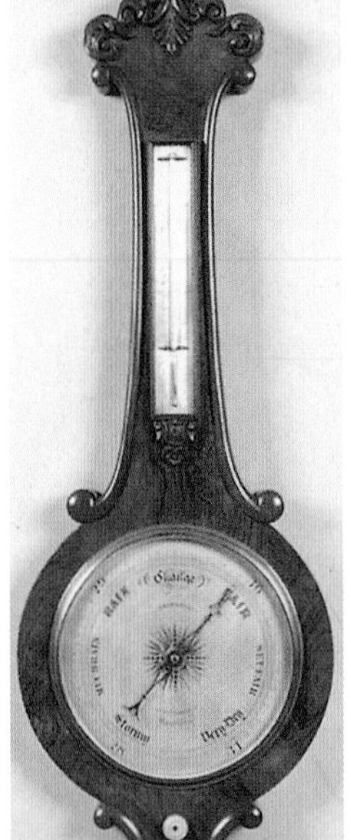

An early Victorian walnut wheel barometer, the dial inscribed 'Underhill, Manchester', the veneered case with applied carved foliage, 43in (109cm) high.

£460–550 WW

A carved softwood wheel barometer, inscribed 'Somalvico's, London', the dial flanked by winged mermaids, the case carved and pierced with leafy scrolls and masks, c1850, 50in (127cm) high.

£820–980 BAM

The prices realized at auction may reflect the fact that some barometers have undergone alterations, or are in unrestored condition.

A Victorian carved lacquered soft wood commemorative wheel barometer, with silvered register, the case carved with arms and motifs to commemorate the Duke of Wellington, repaired, 55in (139.5cm) high.

£1,200–1,400 Hal

A mahogany barometer, by Negretti & Zambra, with silvered dial, c1870, 37in (94cm) high.

£850–950 ⊞ FOF

The partnership between Henry Negretti and Joseph Zambra was formed in 1850. They were quickly established as a leading manufacturer of meteorological instruments and were awarded a medal at the 1851 Great Exhibition. As well as domestic pieces, the firm offered a comprehensive range of barometric instruments.

CONTINENTAL BAROMETERS

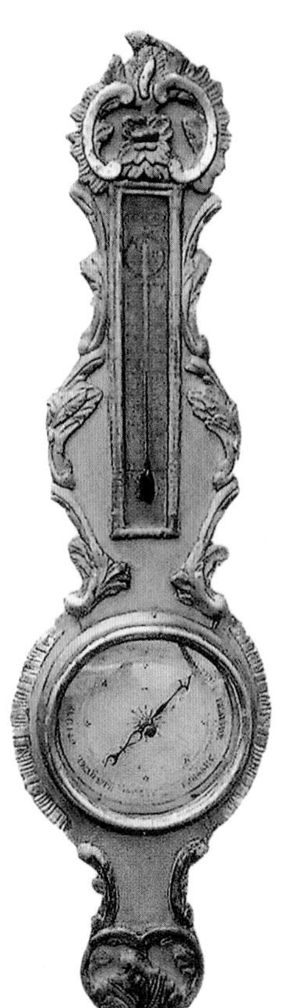

◄ **A giltwood barometer,** the hand-painted dial signed 'Par del Vecchio', France, c1760, 38in (96.5cm) high.

£4,950–5,500 RAY

A giltwood barometer, France, c1785, 39in (99cm) high.

£4,000–4,500 RAY

A giltwood barometer, the dial signed 'Repairer par Dijon', France, c1785, 35in (89cm) high.

£4,200–4,700 RAY

LOCATE THE SOURCE

The source of each illustration in Miller's can be found by checking the code letters below each caption with the Key to Illustrations, pages 746–753.

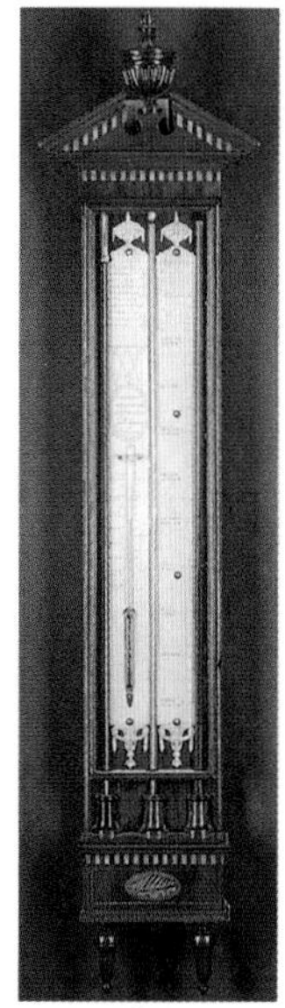

A mahogany barometer, signed 'Geb.s Lurasco Amsterdam', the broken pediment surmounted by a carved urn, with shell inlay, Holland, c1800, 50¾in (129cm) high.

£3,050–3,650 S(Am)

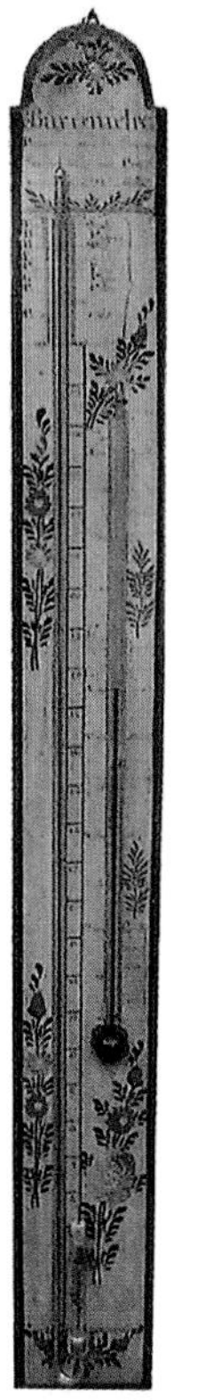

A painted stick barometer, signed 'Orlandy', France, c1810, 37in (94cm) high.

£1,800–2,000 RAY

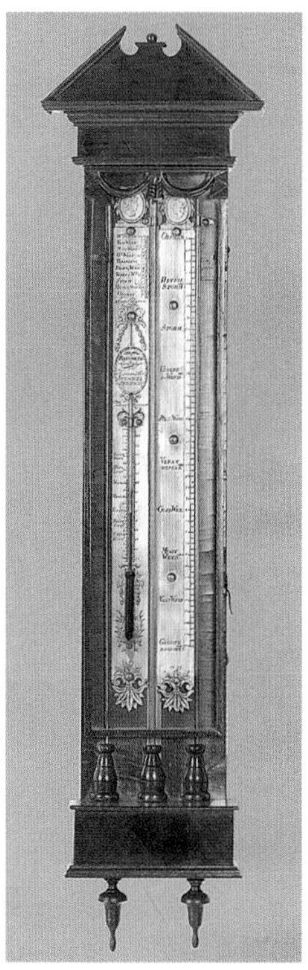

A mahogany-veneered and pewter barometer, signed 'Contraleur' and 'Thermometer J=Franzy Zericke', Holland, c1820, 47¼in (120cm) high.

£3,500–4,200 BERN

A giltwood barometer, the dial signed 'Quiltapace', France, early 19thC, 37in (94cm) high.

£4,500–5,000 RAY

► **A fruitwood folding barometer,** signed 'Baltazar, Paris', France, early 19thC, 39in (99cm) long.

£1,350–1,500 RAY

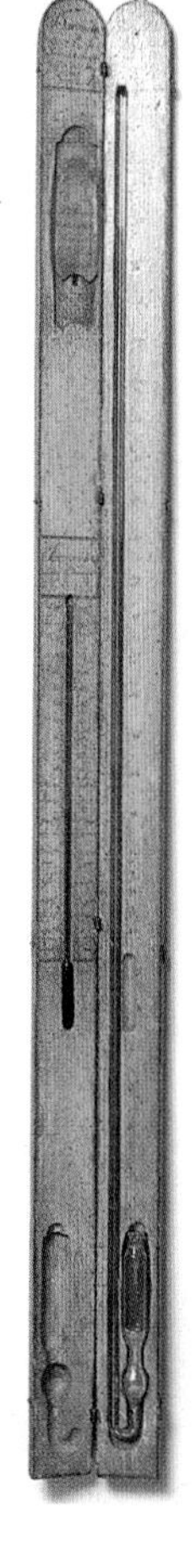

ANEROID BAROMETERS

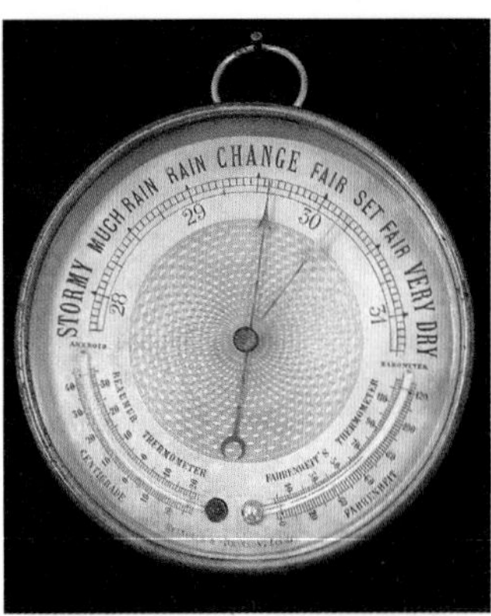

An engine-turned brass aneroid barometer/ thermometer, c1870, 6¾in (17cm) diam.

£540–600 AW

An ebonized aneroid barometer, by Stokes & Watson, Manchester, c1880, 10in (25.5cm) high.

£1,050–1,200 RTW

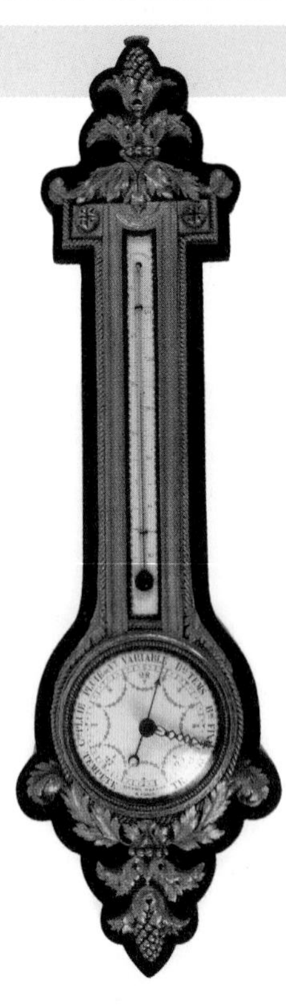

A mahogany barometer, by Henry Dasson, with enamel gauge and dial, ormolu mounts, signed and dated, France, dated 1887, 17½in (44.5cm) high.

£1,900–2,250 G(L)

A pocket aneroid barometer/ altimeter, with compass and thermometer, signed 'Dollond', c1900, 2¼in (5.5cm) diam, in original case.

£580–650 RAY

A mahogany aneroid barometer, with carved decoration, early 20thC, 13¼in (34cm) diam.

£200–230 ET

Not much room?

Pocket aneroid barometers and small travelling barometers continue to be popular as they are inexpensive to buy and a collection can be stored in a relatively small space.

BAROGRAPHS

◄ **A mahogany barograph,** by Negretti & Zambra, with aneroid barometer, eight-day fusee-pendulum clock, barograph and thermometer, dated 1874, 26in (66cm) wide.

£3,600–4,000 FOF

A Victorian oak barograph, by Short & Mason, 15in (38cm) wide.

£470–560 SWO

◄ **A late Victorian mahogany barograph,** by Chadburns, Liverpool, with chart drawer, the case with bevelled glass and boxwood stringing, 16in (40.5cm) wide.

£1,800–2,000 RTW

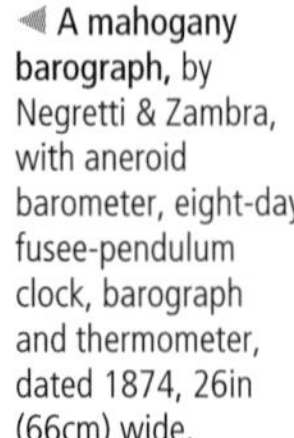

◄ **An oak barograph,** possibly by Short & Mason, the glass bottle with cut-glass stopper, with thermometer and chart drawer, c1890, 14½in (37cm) wide, with a box of charts.

£1,450–1,650 ALS

DECORATIVE ARTS

THE MAJOR AUCTION HOUSES have held specialist Decorative Arts sales for a long period of time but in recent years some of the provincial rooms have realized the financial advantage to be gained from diverting from their traditional fare. The result has been interesting and often important pieces are increasingly appearing away from the main centres, confirming that the provinces can be a good alternative for both seller and buyer. Pieces with international appeal such as Lalique glass and good Art Deco bronze and ivory figures have continued to perform well during the past year. The stunning and possibly unique Lalique 'Grenouilles et Nénuphars' vase, moulded with waterlily pads and applied with green glass frogs, realized over £160,000 at Christie's, New York. By contrast, the more common yet constantly popular 'Ceylan' vase moulded with budgerigars sells in excess of £2,000 whenever and wherever it appears.

Size and artist influence the Figures market. The works of Chiparus and Preiss are the most highly sought after although a lesser known artist's work sells well if the piece has a high degree of style and quality. Recently the figure 'Ankara Dancer' by Claire Colinet realized £70,000 at Sotheby's London and a Preiss 'Flame Leaper' reached £42,000 at Christie's, South Kensington.

High-quality French Art Deco furniture continues to sparkle in the salerooms. The work of French masters such as Ruhlmann, Jean Michel Frank, Pierre Chareau, Jean Prouvé and the superb metalworker and designer Edgar Brandt is always hotly contested.

Arts and Crafts have faithful British and American devotees, with US collectors buying British works but the trade does not generally seem to be reciprocal. The metal wares of John Pearson, Newlyn and Keswick continue to sell but seemingly slightly less fervently than in recent years. Good furniture by the likes of Gimson, the Barnsleys, Gordon Russell and Voysey are sufficiently rare that high prices are almost guaranteed when pieces become available.

The British fervently collect the studio ceramics of their own country. Doulton, Pilkington's Lancastrian, William de Morgan and Charles Vyse figures continue to be popular and also excite strong American interest. Moorcroft, which also has a very strong Australian following, continues to be buoyant and the rarer patterns by Clarice Cliff still, after all these years, cause a stir among would-be owners in the salerooms. French studio ceramics are widely admired outside France and particularly in the US as their influence inspired a whole raft of American potters. **Keith Baker**

Keith Baker

Keith Baker is an independent consultant, valuer and art dealer, concentrating on all aspects of late 19th- and 20th-century Decorative Arts.

He headed the Art Nouveau and Decorative Arts Department at Bonhams, London for 23 years and, with his wife Fiona, has co-authored Twentieth Century Furniture, *published in 2001 by Carlton Books.*

AESTHETIC MOVEMENT CERAMICS

◀ **A bottle and cover,** by John Bennett, painted with chrysanthemums, restored, chip, signed, America, dated 1888, 13½in (34.5cm) high.
£2,850–3,400 DRO(C)

▶ **A jar and cover,** by John Bennett, painted with roses, the cover interior painted with brown-eyed susans on a gilt ground, signed, America, dated 1881, 15½in (39.5cm) high.
£35,000–42,000 DRO(C)

This bottle and cover is exceptional in size, concept, condition, provenance and rarity. John Bennett worked out of a small studio in New York City for a short period of time. This is the best piece of his work to appear on the market in over a decade.

Items in the Decorative Arts section have been arranged alphabetically in factory order, with non-specific pieces appearing at the end of each sub-section.

THEODORE DECK

Théodore Deck (1823–91) was born in Guebwiller, France and began his working life as a maker of ceramic stoves. By 1856, he had set up Atelier Deck with his brother and nephew to produce art pottery. Deck was fascinated by the colours and designs of Islamic ceramics, both copying them and also creating his own variations. He even created his own deep turquoise glaze, called *bleu de Deck*, in 1861. Later in his career, he became fascinated with Asian ceramics and experimented with celadon and flambé glazes and the asymmetrical designs of Japanese wares. In 1887 he was made art director of the Sèvres factory, the first ceramist to be offered this post.

A stoneware charger, by Théodore Deck, with Iznik decoration, impressed marks, France, c1870, 19¾in (50cm) diam.
£1,600–1,900 G(B)

A pair of pottery vases, by Théodore Deck, decorated with birds, insects and flowers, with dragon-head handles, impressed mark, 19thC, 10¾in (27.5cm) high.
£980–1,150 Oli

A Faience Manufacturing Co pottery vase, decorated in enamels with prunus branches, America, New York, late 19thC, 16½in (42cm) high.
£510–610 SK

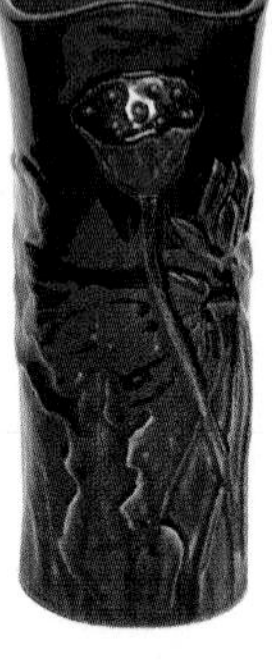

A Linthorpe vase, designed by Christopher Dresser, moulded with a lotus pod and leaves, c1882, 11in (28cm) high.
£880–980 HUN

A Minton flask, c1876, 9in (23cm) high.
£760–850 HUN

A Minton & Hollins tile, in the manner of Christopher Dresser, c1880, 8in (20.5cm) square.
£55–65 BKJL

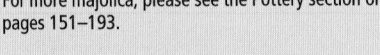

► **A majolica teapot and cover,** possibly Minton, attributed to Christopher Dresser, printed with Japanese fans and figures, impressed and painted marks, c1885, 5¼in (13.5cm) high.
£260–310 SWO

For more majolica, please see the Pottery section on pages 151–193.

A Wedgwood Marsden ware vase, with a pewter rim, 1883–88, 6in (15cm) high.
£230–260 WAC

A pair of Wedgwood earthenware garden seats, by Thomas Allen, transfer-printed with muses, slight damage and restoration, c1880, 17½in (44.5cm) high.
£1,200–1,400 SK

A Wedgwood wash set, by Thomas Allen, comprising four pieces, transfer-printed with flowers and figures, slight damage, c1885, jug 10½in (26.5cm) high.
£510–610 SK

► **A Royal Worcester flask,** decorated in relief with a butterfly, a frog and lily sprays, on a printed ground of Japanese-style *mons*, with gilt highlights, printed marks, date code for 1884, 11¾in (30cm) high.
£500–600 BAM(M)

◄ **A Royal Worcester flask,** decorated with floral sprigs and butterflies, with gilt highlights, c1884, 15in (38cm) high.
£500–600 G(L)

AESTHETIC MOVEMENT CLOCKS

A Japanese-style gilt and painted porcelain carriage clock, signed 'Gustave Sandoz Hger de la Marine, 147–148 Palais Royal, Paris', the repeating movement with a ratchet-tooth lever escapement striking on a gong, France, c1890, 6¾in (17cm) high.

£5,000–6,000 S

A late Victorian mantel clock, inscribed 'Payne & Co, London', with brass dial, eight-day movement with anchor escapement and striking on a gong, the case decorated with painted panels flanked by turned pilasters, 18½in (47cm) high.

£730–870 AG

A gilt-bronze carriage clock, with repeat chime, the case decorated with Japanesque-style lacquered glass panels, France, early 20thC, 7in (18cm) high.

£760–910 HOLL

AESTHETIC MOVEMENT FURNITURE

An ebonized carved-wood bookcase, with open shelves, the right pilaster carved with an owl, America, c1875, 33in (84cm) wide.

£120–140 SK

An ebonized wood side cabinet, the upper section with a pierced cupboard door, the base with glazed panels and a door, c1880, 32¼in (82cm) wide.

£3,600–4,300 S(O)

An ebonized amboyna cabinet, with painted panels, c1880, 75in (190.5cm) high.

£7,200–8,000 PVD

A late Victorian walnut and marquetry-inlaid bedside cabinet, the panelled door enclosing a shelf, ivorine labels for James Phillips & Sons, Bristol, 16½in (42cm) wide.

£500–600 WW

◀ **A James Peddle oak armchair,** designed by E. W. Godwin, with a leather seat, 1881.

£3,150–3,500 PVD

▶ **An ebonized chest of drawers,** with a marble top above seven drawers, c1880, 57in (145cm) high.

£4,500–5,000 PVD

An ebonized easel, with carved foliate panels, America, c1875, 76in (193cm) high.

£630–750 SK

A walnut dinner gong, with turned supports and carved cross sections, c1870, 23in (58.5cm) wide.

£170–190 HEM

A Japanesque ebonized settee, attributed to E. W. Godwin, c1880, 38in (96.5cm) wide.

£5,400–6,000 PVD

A late Victorian walnut, ebonized and parcel-gilt settee, in the manner of James Lamb, Manchester, with button-upholstered back and scroll arms, the turned supports with carved floral panels, 84in (213.5cm) wide.

£1,650–1,950 WW

A Liberty walnut settee, c1890, 42in (106.5cm) wide.

£1,800–2,000 PVD

A walnut sideboard, the extending top above a carved frieze and panelled doors, with brass mounts, America, probably Cincinnati, 1875–1900, 58in (147.5cm) wide.

£600–720 NOA

The over-expressed carving on the door panels together with the carved columns and mouldings suggest a strong link to the Cincinnati Art-Carved Furniture movement associated with Henry Fry and Benn Pitman.

A Moorish-style walnut and ebonized stool, possibly by Liberty & Co, with a leather seat above a carved frieze and panels, late 19thC, 15¾in (40cm) wide.

£540–640 DN

An ash bedroom suite, by Gillows of Lancaster, comprising a triple wardrobe, mirrored dressing table, toilet table and two bedside cabinets with marble tops, each with an ebonized surround enclosing a mahogany panel, c1880.

£2,350–2,800 PFK

◄ **An ebonized drop-leaf occasional table,** the shelf with a spindle gallery, 1875–1900, 24in (61cm) wide.

£120–140 NOA

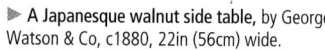

► **A Japanesque walnut side table,** by George Watson & Co, c1880, 22in (56cm) wide.

£2,700–3,000 PVD

A Japanesque ebonized centre table, c1880, 32in (81.5cm) wide.

£2,700–3,000 PVD

An ebonized writing table, designed by Bruce Talbot for Gillows of Lancaster, c1880, 48in (122cm) wide.

£7,600–8,500 PVD

A mahogany occasional table, c1890, 24in (61cm) wide.

£310–350 MTay

AESTHETIC MOVEMENT METALWARE

A silver-plated and glass claret jug, by Hukin & Heath, c1890, 8¾in (22cm) high.

£230–270 AG

A brass and copper kettle, attributed to Christopher Dresser, liner to cover possibly missing, c1876, 9in (23cm) high.

£4,500–5,000 StB

A silver posy holder, in the form of bamboo, maker's mark EF/HT, London 1888, 4in (10cm) high.

£210–250 DD

► **A silver tea service,** by Edward Brown, London, comprising three pieces, engraved with chinoiserie figures in a landscape, together with sugar tongs and two teaspoons, London 1875, with original case.

£1,050–1,250 BWL

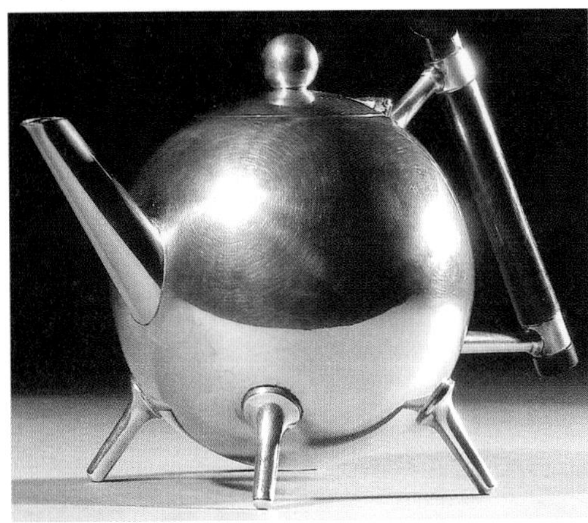

A silver teapot, by Christopher Dresser for James Dixon & Sons, with an ebonized handle, presentation inscription, stamped mark, Sheffield 1882, 5½in (14cm) high, 14oz.

£14,500–17,400 N

► **A silver tea service,** comprising three pieces, each chased with cranes and chinoiserie foliage, Sheffield 1888, teapot 9¼in (23.5cm) high, with a matching coffee pot, London 1892.

£440–520 AH

ARTS & CRAFTS CERAMICS

An Aller Vale pottery vase, designed by Blanche Vulliamy, c1900, 6in (15cm) high.

£270–300 BKJL

◄ **A pottery vase,** attributed to Ault, c1890, 9in (23cm) high.

£75–85 HUN

An Avon Faience Co hanging basket, by Rudolph Lorber, signed, America, dated 1900, 6½in (16.5cm) high.

£95–110 CINN

A Marblehead Pottery vase, by Arthur Baggs, marked, America, dated 1904, 4¾in (12cm) high.

£320–380 CINN

The Marblehead Pottery was set up in 1904 in Marblehead, Massachusetts, under the direction of Arthur Baggs as a therapeutic activity for the patients of Dr Herbert Hall's sanatorium. In 1908, the Pottery was separated from the sanatorium and established as a fully commercial outfit, with the profits benefiting the hospital. Baggs bought out the company in 1912 and it remained a small concern, as Baggs devoted more and more of his time to teaching. It finally closed in 1936. Marblehead produced five main lines of wares: hand-thrown vases in smooth, speckled monochrome glazes; similar ware that was incised or painted with designs in the Arts & Crafts and Art Deco styles; tin-glazed dishes; incised or matt-painted tiles and moulded commercial tiles.

Brannam ware

Charles Brannam established his pottery in Barnstaple, north Devon, in 1879. The pottery is often referred to as Barum ware after the Roman name for Barnstaple. Much of it is sgraffito-decorated, meaning that coloured slips were laid over the red clay and carved through by the artist. Popular Brannam subjects include fish and birds, often by key designers such as James Dewdney, Frederick Braddon and William Baron.

A Baron pottery jug, designed by Blanche Vulliamy, c1890, 6in (15cm) high.

£135–150 BKJL

A Brannam Pottery jug, sgraffito-decorated with panels of songbirds and stylized foliage, incised marks, monogrammed for James Dewdney, dated 1882, 6in (15cm) high.

£420–500 Bea

A Brannam Pottery vase, sgraffito-decorated with a dragon and fruit, incised signature and marks, dated 1889, 16¼in (41.5cm) high.

£175–210 MCA

A Castle Hedington pottery jug, by Edward Bingham, damaged, dated 1889, 12in (30.5cm) high.

£125–140 WAC

◀ **A Chelsea Keramik Art Works ewer,** marked, America, 1872–80, 11½in (29cm) high.

£190–220 CINN

The Chelsea Keramik Art Works was set up in 1872 by the Robertson family, who were already established as potters in Chelsea, Massachusetts. By 1875, they were creating copies of Greek urns and bronzes and in 1876 they developed a white clay body that allowed the full richness of clear tinted glazes. These transparent finishes were produced in light and spinach greens, soft and dark browns and light and deep blues. In 1889 the company ran out of money and had to close. It resurfaced two years later, backed by a consortium of wealthy collectors, as Chelsea Pottery US.

An Alexander Lauder earthenware vase, decorated with stylized leaves, 1891, 16in (40.5cm) high.

£420–470 MMc

▶ **A William de Morgan Persian-style pottery vase and cover,** by Joe Juster, c1888, 12in (30.5cm) high.

£9,900–11,000 POW

Joe Juster and the Passenger brothers were among the finest painters working in de Morgan's studio.

William de Morgan

William Frend de Morgan (1839–1917) was the most significant potter to be connected with the English Arts & Crafts Movement. He worked with many different artists throughout his life and many of his designs were executed by others. He is best known for his decorative tiles, but also created numerous chargers, plates, dishes and vases, hand-painted with all-over decoration.

An Elton Ware pottery jug, slip-decorated with flowers and leaves, c1910, 5in (12.5cm) high.

£105–120 HUN

Sir Edmond Elton set up a workshop and kiln on his estate at Clevedon, Somerset in 1881 with the help of an under gardener, George F. Masters, who later became his chief assistant. Elton was entirely self-taught and was more interested in creating new and challenging forms than in repeating designs he was sure of, therefore the quality of his output fluctuated.

A Farnham Pottery earthenware candlestick, c1900, 13in (33cm) high.

£90–100 IW

The Farnham Pottery was established in 1873 by Absalom Harris at Wrecclesham, near Farnham in Surrey. The wares were sold locally and also at Liberty's and Heal's in the late 19th and early 20th centuries.

A Fulper Pottery Vaz-bowl, marked, with label for Pan Pacific International Exposition, America, c1915, 6½in (16.5cm) diam.

£470–560 CINN

The Fulper Pottery evolved from a pottery originally set up in 1815 in Flemington, New Jersey. Around 1900, William Hill Fulper II began experimenting with coloured glazes and in 1909 introduced the Vasekraft line. Made of stoneware clay and fired at high temperatures, it was inspired by Oriental, Greek and Germanic forms, and was covered in spectacular flambé, mirrored, matt or crystalline glazes. Pieces were usually marked with a vertical, rectangular ink stamp.

An earthenware plate, painted by Jessie Marion King, Scotland, 1920s, 6½in (16.5cm) diam.

£590–660 SDD

Jessie Marion King, a prominent member of the Glasgow School, began her professional career primarily as a book illustrator and designer. She was, however, multi-talented and also produced some of the most exciting jewellery in the Cymric range for Liberty & Co, as well as designing ceramics, wallpapers, fabrics, murals and costume. She was married to the Glasgow School painter and furniture designer E. A. Taylor.

A Linthorpe plate, designed by Christopher Dresser, c1880, 16in (40.5cm) diam.

£880–980 HUN

The Linthorpe pottery was set up in 1879 in Middlesbrough, northern England, by Christopher Dresser, as artistic creator, and a local landowner and artist, Henry Tooth, as manager. Wares are marked with the pottery name, sometimes shown over an impressed outline of a squat vase. An incised facsimile of Dresser's signature appears on some pieces alongside Tooth's monogram.

Maw & Co lustre pottery vase, with foliate decoration, marked 'Floreat Salopia', c1890, 11½in (29cm) high.

£610–730 BWL

A Newcomb College vase, by Parkenson, decorated by Roberta Kennon, incised with a cotton flower bud, signed, America, c1904, 12in (30.5cm) high.

£24,400–27,200 CaF

American art pottery is very sought after in the home market.

A Newcomb College jug and cover, by Joseph Meyer, decorated by Henrietta Bailey, finial restored, signed, marked, America, dated 1908, 5in (12.5cm) high.

£1,050–1,250 CINN

A Newcomb College vase, decorated by Marie Ross with yellow poppies and leaves, slight damage, America, c1904, 7¾in (19.5cm) high.

£4,750–5,700 DRO(C)

Newcomb College

The pottery at Newcomb College, New Orleans, has produced some of the rarest and most valuable American art pottery. Operated mainly by women, the distinctive hand-thrown wares were hand-decorated with incised patterns of local flora and fauna highlighted in polychrome slip. Early pieces have a high glaze, while post-1910 wares usually have a semi-matt finish. Larger items are the most collectable along with pieces featuring landscape decoration or pieces decorated by the better artists such as Mary Sheerer, or the founder, Joseph Meyer.

A Newcomb College vase, decorated by Henrietta Bailey, slight damage, signed, marked, America, dated 1912, 9¼in (23.5cm) high.

£1,300–1,550 CINN

A Pilkington's Lancastrian jar and cover, by Gordon M. Forsyth, silver-lustre-painted with a band of deer and trees, slight damage, impressed mark, painted signature, date mark for 1911, 9½in (24cm) high.

£1,100–1,300 Bea

Items in the Decorative Arts section have been arranged in factory order.

Pilkington's Lancastrian

The Pilkington pottery, near Manchester, was founded in 1892, mainly for the production of tiles. The production of art pottery began in 1897 when William Burton joined the company from Wedgwood. The company is best known for its lustre-decorated wares, and won acclaim at the Paris exhibition in 1900. It employed a number of talented artist decorators including Gordon Forsyth, William Salter Mycock, Richard Joyce and Gladys Rodgers. The wares were known as Pilkington's Lancastrian, taking the 'Royal' title from 1913.

A Rookwood jug, by William McDonald, decorated with spiders and grasses with a Limoges glaze, marked, America, 1882, dated 4½in (11.5cm) high.

£410–490 TREA

A Rookwood Scenic Vellum plaque, painted by E. T. Hurley, depicting sheep grazing under apple trees, flame mark, America, dated 1914, 9 x 12¼in (23 x 31cm), with original frame.

£14,400–17,200 DRO(C)

This plaque is desirable because of its large size and unusual subject matter. Rookwood plaques usually feature misty scenes with tall trees and waterscapes. The rich colours and original Arts & Crafts frame contributed to the substantial price realised.

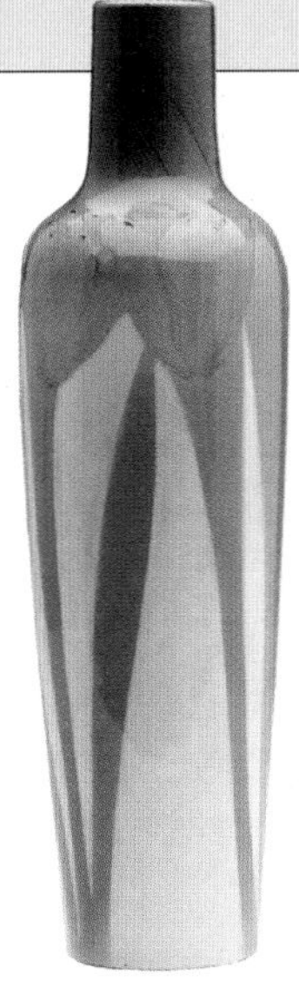

A Rookwood vase, possibly by Sara Sax, carved and slip-painted with tulips and celadon leaves, signed, marked, labelled, America, c1900, 13¼in (33.5cm) high.

£7,600–9,100 DRO(C)

◄ **A Rookwood vase,** with Native American-style decoration, marked, America, dated 1912, 3¼in (8.5cm) high.

£200–240 CINN

Rookwood Pottery

The Rookwood Pottery was established by Maria Longworth Nichols in 1880. It was situated in Cincinnati in the Ohio valley and was able to take advantage of the rich clay deposits and easy access to major water routes.

The factory employed many artists and expert technicians and imposed very high production standards. Wares were hand-painted with designs such as indigenous flora and fauna, landscapes, Native Americans and Oriental flowers on a naturalistic underglaze slip. 'Standard' glaze wares, featuring brown, yellow and ochre slips on dark grounds and covered with a clear, glossy glaze, were produced from 1883. 'Vellum' wares, produced from 1904, were typically decorated with stylized flora or forest landscapes and covered in a matt glaze.

A Rookwood vase, by Kataro Shirayamadani, depicting a nymph riding a fish, marked, artist's cypher, America, dated 1891, 14½in (37cm) high.

£3,200–3,800 CINN

Kataro Shirayamadani was a very important artist at Rookwood.

A Rookwood vase, by William Hentschel, incised with stylized flowers, America, dated 1913, 8¼in (21cm) high.

£1,850–2,200 TREA

A Rookwood Scenic Vellum vase, by Ed Diers, painted with trees, marked, America, dated 1914, 11in (28cm) high.

£2,700–3,200 DRO(C)

A Rookwood wall pocket, with leaf and bud decoration, America, dated 1920, 6in (15cm) high.

£200–240 TREA

Note that the style of this piece is rather angular and is showing the influence of the Art Deco style that was becoming increasing popular at the time.

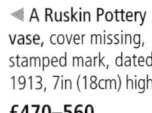

◄ **A Ruskin Pottery vase,** cover missing, stamped mark, dated 1913, 7in (18cm) high.

£470–560 DRO(C)

Ruskin Pottery

William Howson Taylor, an English art potter, set up his art pottery in West Smethwick, Birmingham, and began commercial production in 1901 under the trade name of Ruskin Pottery in honour of the artist John Ruskin. For an initial three-year period Taylor produced a lot of experimental pieces, and it was not until 1909 that he traded as Ruskin. His range of wares includes his soufflé pieces in a mottled, monochrome glaze, and lustre-decorated wares (both in earthenware), as well as an eggshell-thin bone china in crystalline glaze and his keenly sought-after high-fired stonewares.

◄ **A Saturday Evening Girls ceramic tea service,** comprising teapot, cream jug, sugar pot and teapot tile, slight damage, America, dated 1910, teapot 4¾in (12cm) high.

£1,050–1,250 CINN

Edith Guerrier and Edith Brown set up the Saturday Evening Girls Club in 1899 at the North Branch of Boston Library under the patronage of the philanthropist Mrs James Storrow, to teach arts and crafts to mainly Italian and Jewish immigrant girls. A kiln was acquired in 1906 and a pottery opened in 1907 for the production of domestic wares. The girls were paid for decorating the pottery and taught every aspect of the craft from design to chemistry, and for further edification they were read to while they worked. Mrs Storrow continued to fund the pottery until it closed in 1942.

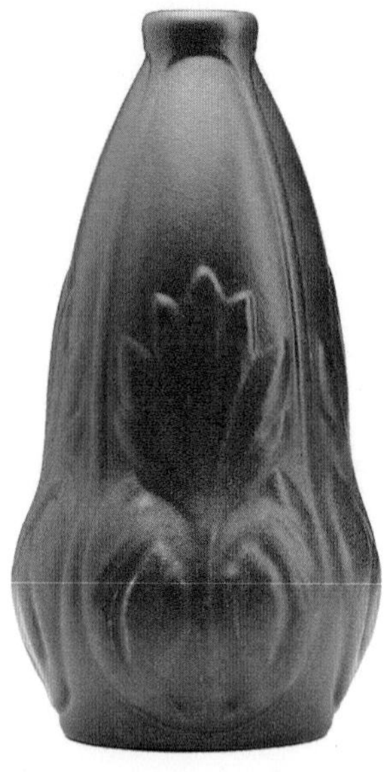

A Van Briggle Pottery vase, embossed with flowers and leaves, marked 'AA' for Anne and Artus, America, dated 1903, 10in (25.5cm) high.

£2,050–2,450 DRO(C)

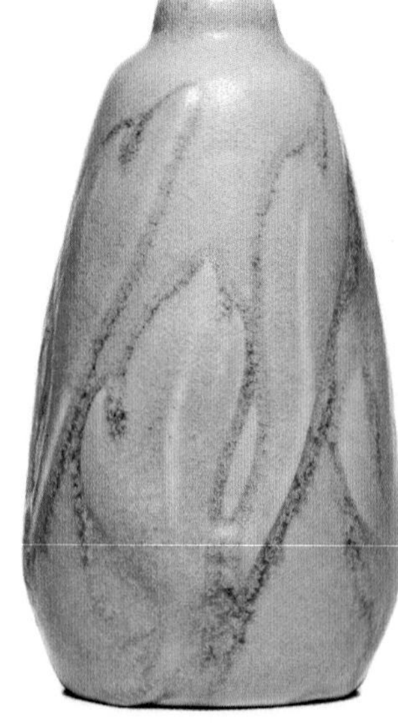

A Van Briggle Pottery vase, with raised design under a matt glaze, incised marks, America, dated 1903, 6in (15cm) high.

£1,450–1,700 TREA

A Van Briggle Pottery two-handled vase, damaged, incised marks, America, dated 1905, 6¼in (16cm) high.

£380–450 TREA

Van Briggle Pottery

The Van Briggle Pottery was opened in 1900 in Colorado Springs by Artus and Anne Van Briggle. Artus previously worked as a decorator at Rookwood Pottery. They won medals in the 1903 Paris Salon and the 1904 Louisiana Purchase Exposition. Wares were embossed with patterns reflecting the Colorado flora and fauna, or moulded with hand-detailing, bringing together elements of Art Nouveau and Native American designs. Natural colours and textures were employed to augment these organic designs. Artus died of tuberculosis in 1904 at the age of 35, but Anne continued to create fine pieces until 1912, when other potters took up the work.

A Van Briggle Pottery vase, embossed with trefoils, marked 'AA', America, dated 1906, 7in (18cm) high.

£1,500–1,800 DRO(C)

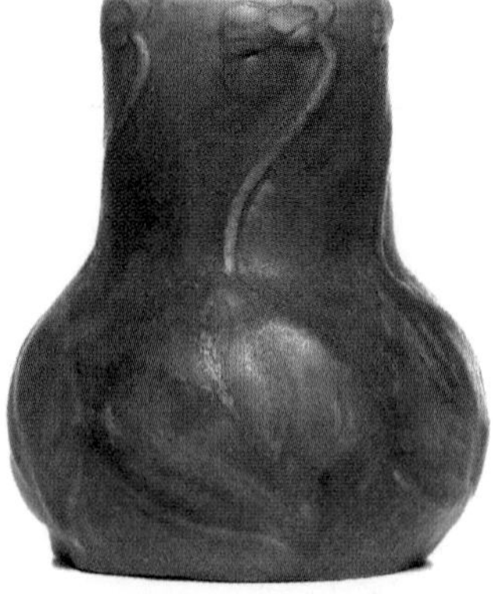

A Van Briggle Pottery vase, decorated with stylized flowers, incised marks, America, 1907–12, 3½in (9cm) high.

£350–420 TREA

A jug, by Elizabeth Mary Watt, decorated with a bird, Scotland, Glasgow, 1920s, 6in (15cm) high.

£310–350 SDD

◄ **A White Pines Pottery glazed earthenware Eucalyptus vase,** by Jane Byrd McCall Whitehead and Ralph Radcliffe-Whitehead, with printed label, America, 1914–26, 7¾in (19.5cm) high.

£650–780 S(NY)

Jane and Ralph Radcliffe-Whitehead established a pottery at White Pines, their home at the Byrdcliffe Arts and Crafts Colony in New York. At first Jane made pots at the Frederick Hurten Rhead studio, which was located close to the Whiteheads' California home. Her pots were shipped east to White Pines for Ralph to glaze. Most White Pines pottery was slip cast and the shapes were derived from photographs of ancient Oriental ceramics. Rare examples bear Jane's decorations, which were most often painted or applied with eucalyptus leaves inspired by Rhead's work. Ralph's glazes rival the best work of the Revere and Hampshire potteries, which he particularly admired. White Pines pottery is marked with either a paper label showing a stylized pine tree or an incised or painted wing and arrow cypher.

A Weller Pottery Lonhuda ewer, by Ed Abel, marked, America, c1895, 8¾in (22cm) high.

£440–520 CINN

The Weller Pottery was opened in Ohio in 1872 by Samuel A. Weller to produce utilitarian pots, and only in 1893 did he begin to produce art ware. Inspired by Lonhuda ware at the Chicago World's Fair, he persuaded its creator, William Long, to join the company and was soon producing Lonhuda himself. Jacques Sicard developed decoration in coloured lustres called 'sicardo', and by 1915 Weller Pottery was at the peak of its production. It operated until 1945, but its heyday was long since over.

ARTS & CRAFTS AND ART NOUVEAU CLOCKS

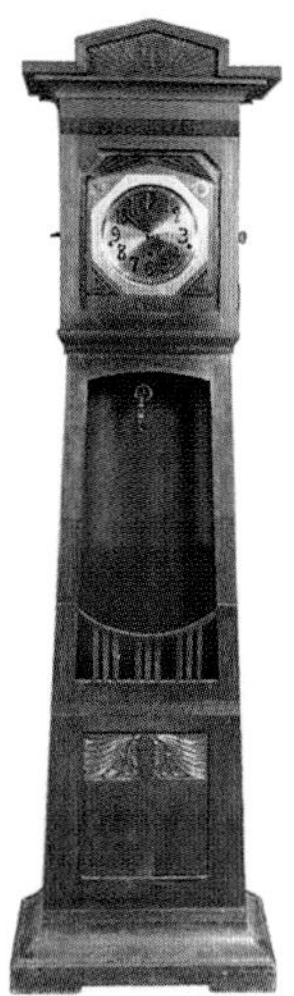

An oak longcase clock, the brass dial with chime/silent and chime selection dials, the triple-train movement with deadbeat escapement chiming on eight bells or four gongs, striking on a fifth, the case with an open gallery, the hood and base carved with stylized acanthus, c1900, 93in (236cm) high.

£800–960 TMA

An oak longcase clock, by H. Berthoud, Berne, with weight-driven movement, Switzerland, c1900, 85in (216cm) high.

£1,600–1,800 HEM

A silver and enamel desk timepiece, by J. G., on a wooden base, Birmingham 1905, 7in (18cm) high.

£1,600–1,800 TA2

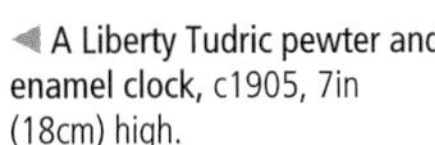

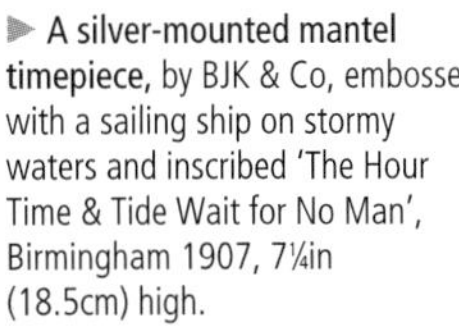

◀ **A Liberty Tudric pewter and enamel clock,** c1905, 7in (18cm) high.

£450–540 AAT

▶ **A silver-mounted mantel timepiece,** by BJK & Co, embossed with a sailing ship on stormy waters and inscribed 'The Hour Time & Tide Wait for No Man', Birmingham 1907, 7¼in (18.5cm) high.

£150–180 DN(HAM)

ARTS & CRAFTS FURNITURE

A Liberty-style oak bench, with pierced back and plank seat, the arms with spherical rests, late 19thC, 50in (127cm) wide.

£520–620 DN

A Roycrofters oak Ali Baba bench, with plank seat, marked, incised 'R 046', America, New York, c1905, 19½in (49.5cm) wide.

£7,800–9,300 S(NY)

The American craft community known as the Roycrofters (1895–1938) was founded by Elbert Hubbard to produce metalwork, textiles and furniture.

An oak bench, with pegged seat and shaped ends, c1900, 36½in (92.5cm) wide.

£410–490 PFK

An oak bureau bookcase, the back with two shelves, above a fall-front with anodized copper strap hinges, over an adjustable shelf, the sides with copper studs, c1900, 27½in (70cm) wide.

£210–250 DMC

An oak bookcase, with pierced top and slatted back, c1890, 21in (53.5cm) wide.

£150–170 OCA

An oak three-tier book stand, with pierced sides and back rails, decorated with copper panels, c1900, 15½in (39.5cm) wide.

£230–270 DMC

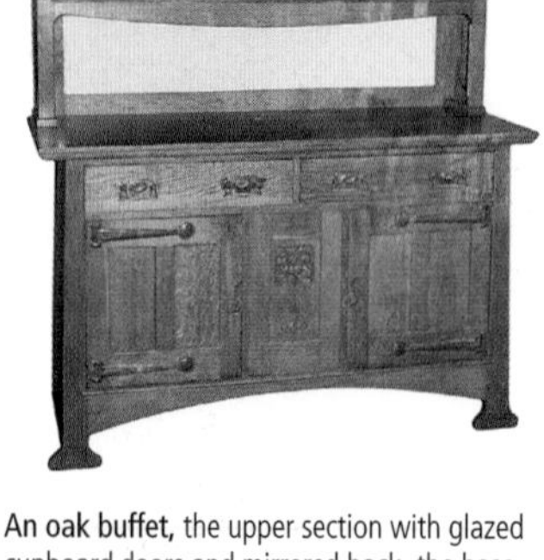

An oak buffet, the upper section with glazed cupboard doors and mirrored back, the base with two frieze drawers above two cupboards, 1880–1920, 60in (152.5cm) wide.

£2,000–2,250 STRA

A stained oak buffet, by Gustav Stickley, the two short drawers over one long drawer, with chamfered sides and pyramid-shape pulls, labelled, America, c1902, 59in (150cm) wide.

£32,000–38,000 DRO(C)

This server is early in date, in exceptional original condition and new to the market. The rarity and desirability of the form resulted in a high selling price.

An oak bureau, with a mirrored back above a fall-front, with a shipping tag for 'Northwestern Cabinet Co, Burlington, IA', America, c1910, 26in (66cm) wide.

£175–210 JAA

A Liberty oak coal cabinet, with a pierced back and wrought-iron hinges, c1905, 35in (89cm) high.

£900–1,000 TDG

An inlaid mahogany display cabinet, inlaid with trees and leaves, the glazed door enclosing three shelves, on claw-and-ball feet, c1890, 30¾in (78cm) wide.

£940–1,100 PFK

A walnut and marquetry cabinet, Denmark, c1900, 47in (119.5cm) wide.

£1,850–2,100 BURA

◄ **A mahogany display cabinet,** by Shapland & Petter, Barnstaple, the central glazed door with upper pierced foliate silvered-metal backing, above a frieze drawer, flanked by cupboard doors inlaid with mother-of-pearl, holly and chequer stringing, flowerheads and butterflies, c1900, 53½in (136cm) wide.

£4,800–5,700 S

Shapland & Petter was established in Barnstaple, Devon in 1864. The firm was a major manufacturer of furniture in the Arts & Crafts and Art Nouveau styles, supplying retailers such as Liberty and Waring & Gillow. The workers were highly skilled, serving seven-year apprenticeships and attending classes at the Barnstaple School of Art. The company's archives are deposited at the Museum of Barnstaple and North Devon.

► **An oak armchair,** by J. S. Henry, designed by G. M. Ellwood, 1895.

£2,700–3,000 PVD

A Liberty oak table cabinet, stamped to the reverse, c1900, 17½in (44.5cm) high.

£480–540 TDG

An oak wall cabinet, with leaded glass doors, 1880–1920, 22in (56cm) high.

£480–540 STRA

An oak armchair, with pierced back and solid seat, c1900.

£105–125 JAA

◄ **An armchair,** by Gustav Stickley, with a drop-in seat, with label, leather replaced, some refinishing, America, c1902.

£600–720 DRO(C)

Gustav Stickley

Gustav Stickley started a furniture business in1884 in New York with his two younger brothers. They made furniture with an Arts & Crafts feel, using mainly American white oak, stained either rich or light brown, or grey, using a fuming process developed at the factory. Traditional construction methods were used, as well as hand-made hardware, often with a hammered surface. The upholstery is mainly leather and typically brown, red or green.

◄ **A set of four dining chairs,** by William Birch, High Wycombe, with arched panelled backs and drop-in rush seats, c1905.

£165–195 Hal

An oak armchair, with a high bobbin back and turned supports, c1910.

£580–650 NAW

An oak high-back chair, by Frank Lloyd Wright, with leather upholstery, America, c1907.

£12,300–14,700 S(NY)

Recent information has revealed that the form and construction of this chair is nearly identical to the model designed by Wright for Browne's Bookstore in Chicago in 1907. Although the bookstore soon became established as a literary salon for Chicago's cultured readers, it struggled with profitability and was closed in 1912, being demolished shortly thereafter.

An oak high-back chair, designed by George Grant Elmslie for Jean B. Hassewer Co, with leather upholstery, America, Chicago, 1910–12.

£21,100–25,300 S(NY)

This chair was previously in use in the dining room of the Harold C. Bradley House, Madison, Wisconsin, designed by Louis Sullivan.

A chest of drawers, by Charles Rohlfs, with six graduated drawers, impressed signature and '07', America, 1907, 33½in (85cm) wide.

£7,000–8,400 DRO(C)

Charles Rohlfs was one of the American Arts & Crafts movement's most talented designers. He opened his first commercial workshop in Buffalo in 1898, and two years later a local department store held an exhibition of his work. He exhibited in Turin in 1902, and was made an honorary member of the Royal Society of Arts in London after having supplied a set of chairs to Buckingham Palace.

A Byrdcliffe Arts & Crafts Colony cherrywood chiffonier, the carved polychrome panels designed by Zulma Steele, with bronze handles, branded 'Byrdcliffe 1904', marked, America, 38½in (98cm) wide.

£98,000–118,000 S(NY)

Furniture bearing the Byrdcliffe Arts & Crafts Colony lily cypher was made from 1903 when the colony opened until the beginning of 1905. No credible theory about why production stopped has yet been put forth although some believe colony founder Ralph Whitehead might simply have lost interest. While some of the craft shops at Byrdcliffe were teaching facilities, the woodshop was run as a commercial venture. The small size of the shop and the short period of production limited the number of completed pieces. Today, fewer than one hundred pieces exist and most of those remained at Whitehead's home, White Pines, until 1984 when they were removed for exhibition. This chiffonier is among the very few pieces that did not descend to the Whitehead heirs. Zulma Steel's style as exemplified by the carved chestnut panel on this cabinet is now the most recognized and sought after of Byrdcliffe production.

An oak hall stand and seat, with a mirror and an umbrella stand, 1920s, 75in (190.5cm) high.

£195–220 MCB

A mahogany hall stand, with a dinner gong and striker, c1890, 53in (134.5cm) high.

£610–680 BURA

▶ **An oak breakfront overmantel,** inset with three prints and a mirror, the pediment with a plate groove, c1890, 58¼in (148cm) wide.

£175–210 PFK

An oak settle, by George Walton, with a solid seat, Scotland, c1900, 50in (127cm) wide.

£1,050–1,200 JSG

George Walton studied architecture and design at evening classes at the Glasgow School of Art. He started his own interior design firm, George Walton & Co, Ecclesiastical & House Decorators, in 1888. Among his commissions were chairs in ebonized wood for the photographic firm Kodak, and he began work for Liberty & Co in 1897.

An oak sideboard, by Harris Lebus, with copper mounts and Ruskin pottery plaques, 1880–1920, 49in (124.5cm) wide.

£2,350–2,650 STRA

The firm of Harris Lebus was founded in Tottenham, London in 1900 and many of its first products are in the Arts & Crafts style.

An oak sideboard, with a mirrored back, the centre cupboard with a turquoise leaf motif above two short drawers and two foliate-carved doors, c1910, 54in (137cm) wide.

£470–560 Hal

◄ **A Byrdcliffe Arts & Crafts Colony cherrywood Thistle stool,** the carved panels designed by Zulma Steele, America, c1904, 21in (53.5cm) wide.

£8,400–10,100 S(NY)

An oak stick stand, by Wylie & Lochhead, with copper strapwork and drip tray, Scotland, c1905, 29in (73.5cm) high.

£510–570 TDG

A Liberty walnut occasional table, the plank supports pierced with heart motifs, c1900, 36in (91.5cm) wide.

£1,350–1,500 PVD

Liberty & Co

Arthur Lasenby Liberty established Liberty & Co in Regent Street, London in 1875, selling Oriental goods such as Indian silks, Arabian furniture and Chinese porcelain. The craze for art furniture of the Aesthetic Movement led him to open a design studio in 1883, directed by Leonard F. Wyburd, and their own cabinet-making workshops four years later. The store stocked furniture from outside designers including Baillie Scott, Voysey and George Walton, as well as producing their own pieces that were influenced by these designers.

► **A Cotswold School walnut and chequer-inlaid wardrobe,** by Sidney Barnsley, the two cupboard doors enclosing an inlaid interior with sliding shelves and two drawers with compartments, the base with an apron drawer, early 20thC, 50in (127cm) wide.

£21,600–25,900 S

This wardrobe was designed by Sidney Barnsley for his friend, the architect Robert Weir Schultz. It forms part of a collection of furniture he designed for his house in Hartley Wintney, Hampshire. Schultz's various architectural projects were often occasion for collaboration with Barnsley as well as Ernest Gimson.

◄ **A tea table,** by Gustav Stickley, the top inset with twelve Grueby pottery tiles, restored, America, c1902, 26in (66cm) wide.

£17,600–21,000 DRO(C)

ARTS & CRAFTS GLASS

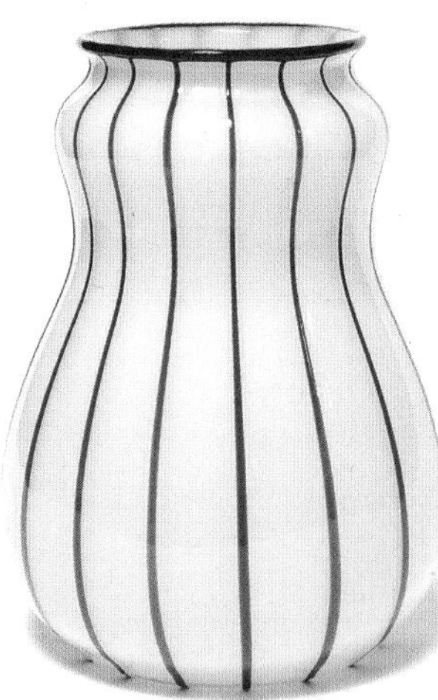

A Loetz glass vase, by Michael Powolny, c1914, 8in (20.5cm) high.
£810–900 MiW

Michael Powolny designs are among the most collectable of Loetz production, reproduced and imitated by Czechoslovakian firms and designers.

A pair of leaded glass panels, by George Walton, c1898, 13in (33cm) wide.
£2,700–3,000 JSG

These panels are from Miss Cranston's Tearooms in Glasgow, for which the interior was designed by Walton and Charles Rennie Mackintosh.

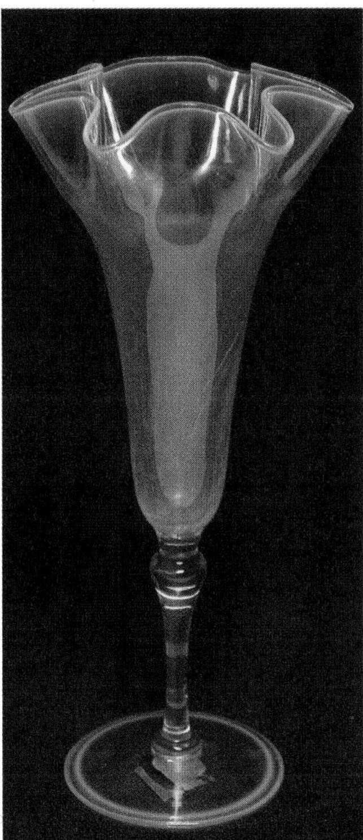

A Whitefriars uranium glass goblet, designed by Harry Powell, c1885, 8in (20.5cm) high.
£270–300 HUN

A Whitefriars glass vase, designed by Harry Powell, c1880, 9in (23cm) high.
£2,200–2,450 HUN

Harry Powell

Harry Powell, (1835–1922), protégé of William Morris and colleague of W. A. S. Benson, designed some of the most sinuous glass of the Arts & Crafts period. Typical of great 19th-century entrepreneurs, he combined running the Whitefriars glassworks with an interest in chemistry, continually developing new colours and techniques. He was also much loved by his workforce. He won posthumously a Gold Medal for modern design at the 1925 Paris Art Deco Exhibition for a glass table service designed in 1895.

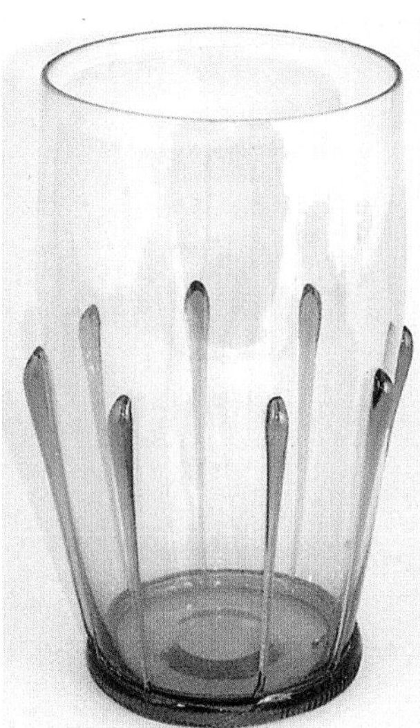

A Whitefriars glass Hugo van der Goes teardrop vase, designed by Harry Powell, pattern No. 1099, c1901, 9in (23cm) high.
£730–870 DN(HAM)

The design of this vase is based on a vase depicted in the Portinari Altarpiece *painted c1475 by Hug van der Goes. The altarpiece is now in the Uffizi Gallery in Florence.*

▶ **A set of six glasses,** designed by Otto Prutscher for the Wiener Werkstätte, probably made by Bakalowits, with amber glass decoration, Austria, c1910, 8¼in (21cm) high.
£8,000–9,600 G(L)

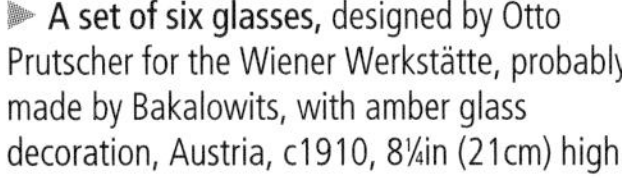

Although very Secessionist in style, the design of these glasses anticipates Art Deco.

ARTS & CRAFTS JEWELLERY

A Guild of Handicraft citrine and garnet **brooch,** c1900, 2in (5cm) long, with original box.

£1,400–1,650 S(O)

The jewellery market

Arts and Crafts jewellery continues to have a strong fan base. Pieces by lesser known makers are both popular and wearable and also very affordable. There is still a strong market for jewellery by high flyers such as Sibyl Dunlop, Dorrie Nossiter, the Gaskins, Guild of Handicraft, Archibald Knox for Liberty and H. G. Murphy.

A silver and enamel brooch, by Charles Horner, Chester 1910, 1in (2.5cm) diam.

£160–180 ANO

◄ **A white metal and amber pendant brooch,** the reverse stamped '826' and engraved 'EA 1915', probably Denmark.

£400–480 DN

◄ **A Liberty silver buckle,** with hammered decoration and enamel roundel, Birmingham 1910, 1¾in (4.5cm) square.

£190–220 DN(HAM)

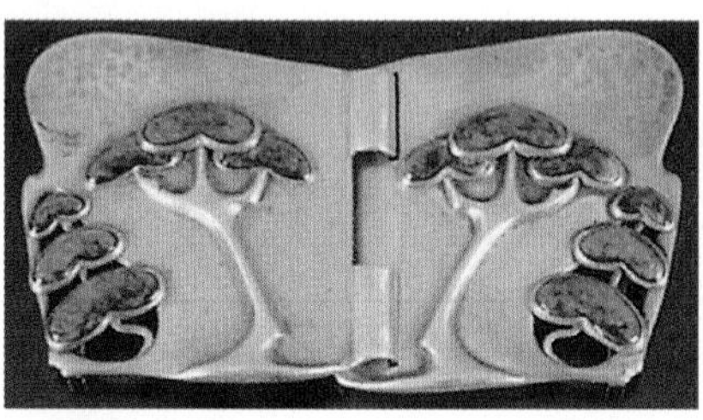

A Liberty & Co silver and enamel buckle, applied with stylized tree motifs inlaid with enamel panels, Birmingham 1908, 3½in (9cm) wide.

£440–520 DN

► **A pair of silver and enamel hat pins,** by Murrle, Bennett & Co, each with a cruciform motif, marked 'MB&Co', Birmingham 1908.

£260–310 DN

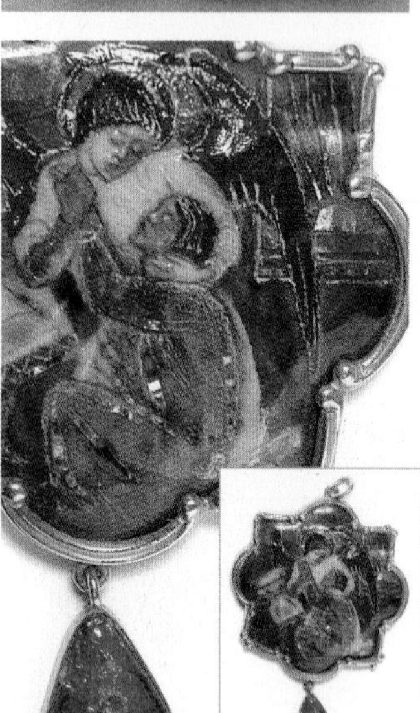

A gold and enamel pendant, by Phoebe Anna Traquair, entitled 'The Finished Task', signed and dated 1906 to the reverse, Scotland, 1½in (4cm) diam.

£4,500–5,000 JSG

Phoebe Anna Traquair (1852–1936) was one of the leading lights of the Arts & Crafts movement in Edinburgh. She was a woman of many talents, skilled in painting, manuscript illumination, enamelling and embroidery.

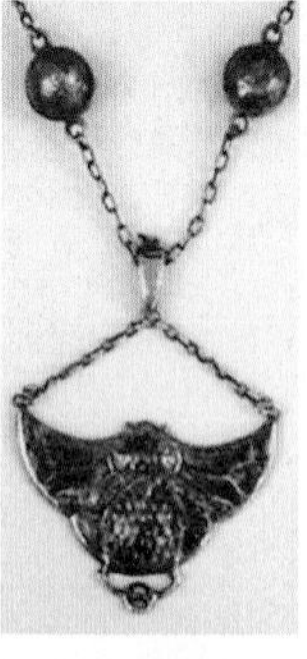

A silver and enamel pendant necklace, by Charles Horner, the pendant in the form of a winged insect, the chain with three pairs of enamelled divisions, Chester 1909.

£440–520 RTo

A silver pendant necklace, set with moonstones and pearl clusters within foliate wirework, the bifurcated beaded suspension loop with one gold bead, c1910, 3in (7.5cm) high, with original case.

£2,700–3,000 DAD

A sterling silver and labradorite pendant, by Robert R. Jarvie, stamped mark, America, 1910–16, 1½in (4cm) high.

£3,900–4,650 S(NY)

Robert Ridelle Jarvie and his wife Lillian opened the Jarvie shop in Chicago in 1904. They sold hand-made copper and brass pieces. It was not until 1905 that he began to work in silver and gold, producing holloware and trophies. His jewellery is extremely rare.

ARTS & CRAFTS LIGHTING

A wrought-iron hall lantern, c1880, 22in (56cm) high.
£400–450 ⊞ EAL

A Japanese-style plated-brass oil lamp, by Hukin & Heath, c1885, 14in (35.5cm) high.
£360–400 ⊞ HUN

A brass and copper oil lamp, by W. A. S. Benson, c1890, 28in (71cm) high.
£1,800–2,000 ⊞ PVD

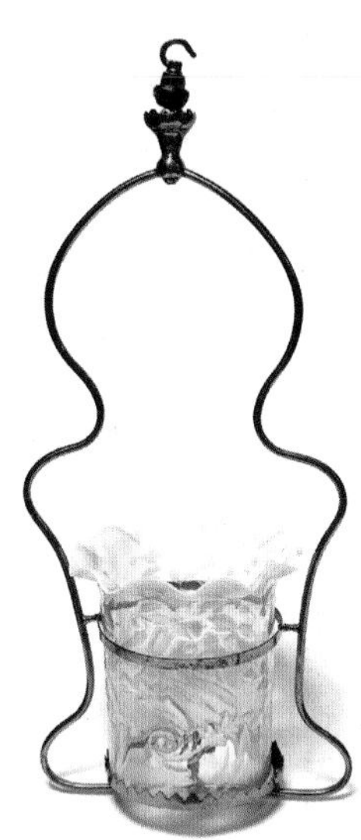

A brass lantern, with a vaseline glass shade, converted for electricity, c1890, 28in (71cm) high.
£850–950 ⊞ MiW

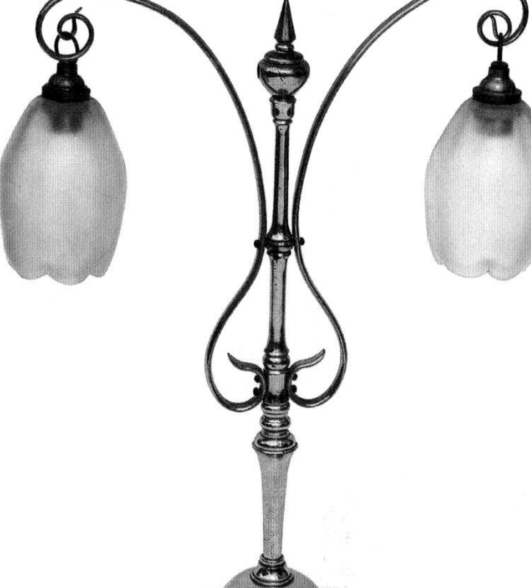

A brass and copper table lamp, by W. A. S. Benson, the two branches with original glass shades by James Powell & Sons, c1890, 18in (45.5cm) high.
£3,600–4,000 ⊞ PVD

◀ **A brass ceiling light,** with vaseline glass shades by James Powell & Sons, c1895, 13in (33cm) high.
£1,600–1,800 ⊞ MiW

▶ **A brass ceiling light,** with vaseline glass shades, c1895, 21in (53.5cm) high.
£1,600–1,800 ⊞ MiW

A copper and brass table lamp, by W. A. S. Benson, c1900, 24in (61cm) high.
£2,100–2,300 ⊞ HUN

A copper table lamp, by W. A. S. Benson, c1900, 20in (51cm) high.
£450–500 ⊞ TA2

An oxidized-copper five-branch ceiling light, c1900, 25in (63.5cm) diam.
£720–800 EAL

WILLIAM ARTHUR SMITH BENSON

W. A. S. Benson is recognized today as being perhaps the most important English designer and architect who produced commercial metalware and lighting. Benson helped to establish the Art Workers' Guild in 1883 and the Arts & Crafts Exhibition Society in 1888. Production at his Hammersmith workshop commenced in 1880 with emphasis on copper and brass, although silver wares were also produced. The workshop closed in 1920.

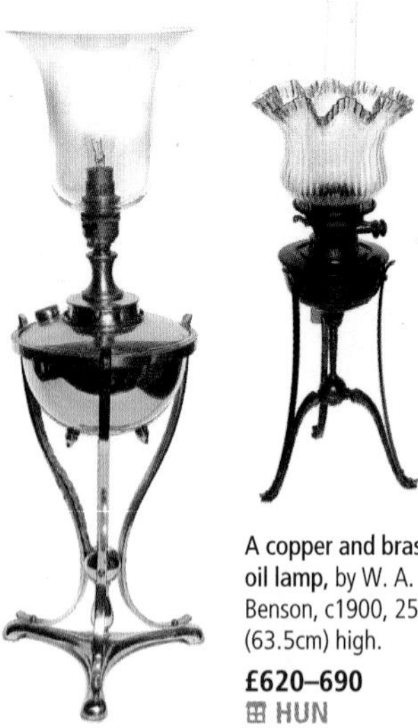

► **A copper and brass oil lamp,** by W. A. S. Benson, converted for electricity, c1900, 21in (53.5cm) high.
£720–800 HUN

A copper and brass oil lamp, by W. A. S. Benson, c1900, 25in (63.5cm) high.
£620–690 HUN

◄ **A brass and copper wall light,** set with Ruskin Pottery roundels, with a vaseline glass shade, c1900, 16in (40.5cm) high.
£1,800–2,000 PVD

A copper and brass three-branch ceiling light, with original holophane shades, c1904, 16in (40.5cm) diam.
£880–980 CHA

A patinated metal and leaded glass lantern, America, c1910, 31¼in (79.5cm) high.
£5,200–6,200 S(NY)

A copper and brass four-branch ceiling light, by W. A. S. Benson, the glass shade decorated with opalescent swirls, early 20thC, 13in (33cm) high.
£1,400–1,650 S(O)

A brass lamp, set with ruby glass roundels, c1910, 20in (51cm) high.
£270–300 WAC

► **A copper and mica ceiling light,** attributed to Dick van Erp, America, 1920s, 9in (23cm) high.
£1,600–1,900 DRO(C)

This piece has been passed down through the family of the original owner, who was given it by a relative who worked in the van Erp studio.

A Roycrofters copper and leaded glass table lamp, engraved with a presentation inscription, stamped mark, America, c1917, 20¼in (51.5cm) high.
£19,500–23,400 S(NY)

For more information on the Roycrofters see p377.

ARTS & CRAFTS METALWARE

A silver bowl, with three pierced handles, London 1903, 5½in (14cm) diam.

£670–750 SHa

◄ **A silver beaker,** embossed with stylized shells and applied with garnet cabochons, Russia, Moscow, 1908–17, 3¼in (8.5cm) high.

£350–420 BUK(F)

A copper and pewter bowl, by Hugh Wallis, monogrammed, c1905, 10in (25.5cm) diam.

£260–290 TDG

The coppersmith Hugh Wallis worked in Altringham, Cheshire, having studied at the Herkomer Art School in Bushey, Hertfordshire. He frequently exhibited at the Royal Academy.

A pair of copper and silver candlesticks, by A. E. Jones, c1900, 8in (20.5cm) high.

£580–650 WAC

A pair of wrought-iron candlesticks, by Coberg, Germany, c1905, 9in (23cm) high.

£175–195 TDG

A pair of silver candlesticks, by Wakely & Wheeler, London, 1908, 5in (12.5cm) high.

£610–680 ANC

A copper and brass casket, the cover with enamel decoration, 1880–1920, 5in (12.5cm) wide.

£490–550 STRA

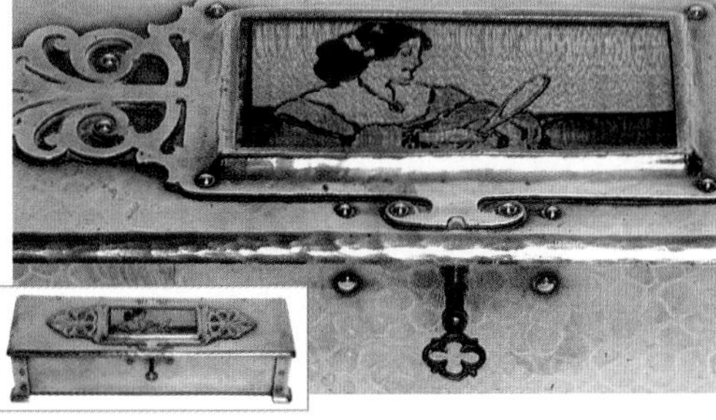

A copper casket, the cover with a painted wooden panel depicting a woman with a hand mirror, c1900, 12in (30.5cm) wide.

£350–390 RUSK

► **A Keswick School of Industrial Arts copper casket,** designed by Herbert Maryon, made by Thomas Spark and enamelled by Herbert Maryon and Thomas Clarke, the front and sides with fielded panels, signed 'John Peel' and 'T. Clarke', c1900, 14½in (37cm) wide.

£3,200–3,800 PFK

This casket was described in Vol. XX of Studio *magazine in 1900.*

A silver-plated copper casket, the cover set with a cloisonné enamel panel, Germany, Pforzheim, c1900, 5in (12.5cm) wide.

£1,100–1,250 ANO

A copper casket, with silver mounts and an enamel roundel depicting a landscape to the cover, 1900–10, 9in (23cm) wide.

£4,500–5,000 TA2

A silver cup, by Jess Barkentin, designed by William Burges, the bowl with a frieze of Lombardic script 'To H. Curzon Esq. in recognition of his services to the Arts Club 1878', above a calyx of feathers, the foot decorated with *champlevé* enamel motifs, the bowl interior set with an enamel boss with a character figure and the monogram 'HC', London 1877, 4½in (11.5cm) diam, 9oz.

£23,000–27,600 WW

Burges designed a group of these cups to be given to friends and associates in the Arts community. Each had an indication in the centre and around the rim as to who the recipient would be. A similar example but with a turned maplewood bowl and cover was made for Burges himself and is now in the British Museum. Pieces by Burges are always highly sought after and command high prices, but the selling figure of £23,000 seems quite moderate when compared to the price of a rare piece by a designer such as Christopher Dresser.

A silver, enamel and leather desk portfolio, by Khlebnikov, the applied silver plaque cast and chased with three warriors against an enamelled background painted with a monastery on an island, on four bun supports, silk interior, Russia, Moscow, c1910, 19¼in (49cm) high.

£11,700–14,000 S(NY)

A copper dish, the corners set with ceramic plaques, c1890, 13½in (34.5cm) wide.

£720–800 TDG

Prices

The price ranges quoted in this book reflect the average price a purchaser might expect to pay for a similar item. The price will vary according to the condition, rarity, size, popularity, provenance, colour and restoration of the item, and this must be taken into account when assessing values. Don't forget that if you are selling it is quite possible that you will be offered less than the price range.

A Guild of Handicraft silver covered dish and spoon, designed by C. R. Ashbee, the cover set with enamel, the knop set with a blister pearl, the dish with loop handles, London 1903, 9¾in (25cm) wide.

£21,000–25,200 SWO

This extremely attractive piece had been in the vendor's family since its purchase in 1904 and being fresh to the market was of particular interest to collectors.

The Guild of Handicraft was a school and cooperative workshop founded by Charles Robert Ashbee in 1888 in London. Ashbee's aim was to improve the quality of English applied arts and also, true to his socialist principles, to improve the quality of the common man through artistic endeavour. Their repertoire included furniture, silver, jewellery, enamel work, books and bindings, and in 1897 pieces were made to the designs of M. H. Baillie Scott for the Grand Duke of Hesse at Darmstadt, Germany. The Guild exhibited in Munich in 1898 and at the eighth Secession exhibition in Vienna in 1900, but closed in 1907, due to economic pressure caused by serious competition from other firms including Liberty & Co.

A silver bonbon dish, set with an enamelled plaque depicting a pre-Raphaelite maiden, Birmingham 1906, 7in (18cm) diam.

£900–1,000 PVD

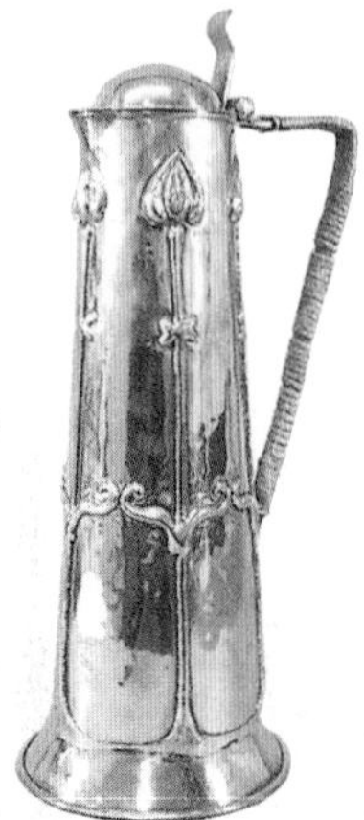

◄ **A Keswick School of Industrial Arts copper hot water jug,** by Thomas Spark, designed by Harold Stabler, the body decorated with stylized flowers, stem and leaf designs, the handle wound with string, c1899, 14in (35.5cm) high.

£1,200–1,400 PFK

This, and other similar designs, were exhibited at the Home Arts & Industries Exhibition of 1899.

A copper and brass kettle and stand, by W. A. S. Benson, c1900, 11in (28cm) high.

£300–350 HUN

A copper log box and cover, by John Pearson, the cover embossed with leaves and buds, the body embossed with birds on branches, signed and dated 1905 to base, 17in (43cm) high.

£540–640 DN

A hammered silver mustard pot and salt cellar, by A. E. Jones, Birmingham 1906, with a spoon, Birmingham 1921, pot 3in (7.5cm) high.

£450–500 DAD

A silver napkin ring, by Omar Ramsden and Alwyn Carr, the centre embossed with a band of Tudor roses, London 1913, 2¼in (5.5cm) high, 1oz.

£300–360 HYD

A pair of silver-gilt serving spoons, by Sibray, Hall & Co, London 1888, 8in (20.5cm) long.

£180–200 HEM

A Liberty Cymric silver Edward VII coronation spoon, designed by Archibald Knox, Birmingham 1902, 6½in (16.5cm) long.

£850–950 ANO

Further reading

Miller's Silver & Plate Buyer's Guide, Miller's Publications, 2002

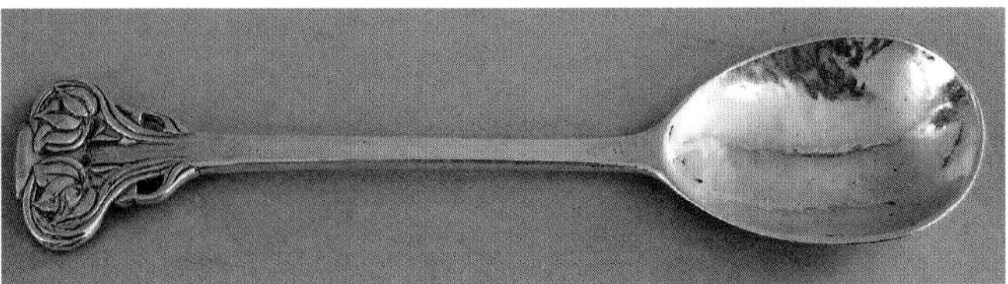

A silver preserve spoon, by Omar Ramsden, with a hammered bowl, London 1920, 6in (15cm) long.

£400–480 DA

► **A silver tea glass holder,** by Omar Ramsden, cast and chased with roses and briars, London 1926, 5in (12.5cm) high.

£1,350–1,550 DAD

◄ **A silver teapot,** by C. R. Ashbee, the cover with a hardstone cabochon finial, the spot-hammered body with a wicker-bound scroll handle, on a foot with a punched bead border, London 1899, 6in (15cm) high.

£9,400–11,200 HYD

This rare teapot of 1899 was made three years after Ashbee registered his mark on 29 January 1896. Stylistically, this early teapot shows all the major design elements that came to typify Ashbee's work in later years. The elongated wirework handle, subtle planishing, cabochon set finial and sparingly applied decoration are all key elements of his designs. Hollow ware from this period is uncommon, not only due to the cost of hand manufacture, but also due to the limited commercial success at this stage.

A pewter and copper tea service, comprising four pieces, Continental, early 1900s, tray 22in (56cm) wide.

£360–400 ⊞ STRA

A copper tray, in the manner of John Pearson, stamped with the motto 'Thy Yesterday is Thy Past, Thy Today is Thy Future, Tomorrow is a Secret', c1900, 16in (40.5cm) wide.

£270–300 ⊞ TOP

A silver and bronze vase, by Fine Art Metal Studios, marked, America, Chicago, c1900, 10in (25.5cm) high.

£860–1,000 ⚒ NOA

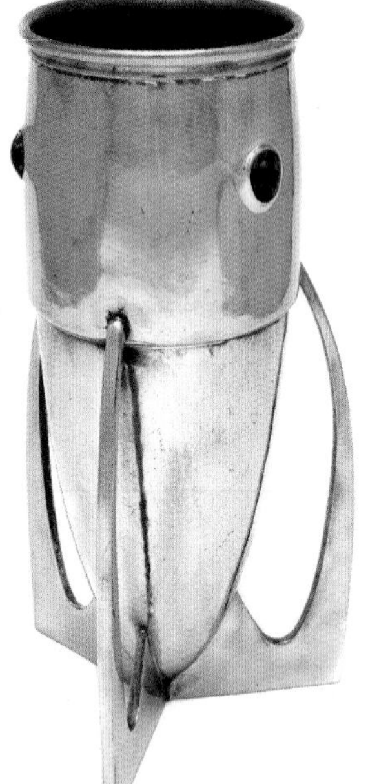

A Liberty pewter vase, designed by Archibald Knox, c1905, 11½in (29cm) high.

£1,550–1,750 ⊞ SHa

A School of Koloman Moser silver and glass bud vase, set with enamelled cabochon, c1905, 13in (33cm) high.

£360–400 ⊞ JSG

A Liberty & Co silver vesta case, by Archibald Knox, applied with an enamel Celtic knot, London 1904, 2in (5cm) high.

£480–570 ⚒ DN

ARTS & CRAFTS RUGS & TEXTILES

◄ **A Donegal rug,** with stylized flowers and palmettes, Ireland, c1900, 108¼ x 72¾in (275 x 185cm).

£3,500–4,200 ⚒ SWO

In the 1890s Alexander Morton began a carpet weaving business in Donegal, an area of Ireland that was depressed through lack of employment. They commissioned several well-known artists of the time, including Charles Voysey, to provide designs for hand-made carpets. The carpets were frequently found with large stylized leaves and flowers. It appears that these designs were also commissioned from weavers in Turkey, which seems to rather defeat the object of Morton's original scheme. Liberty & Co was one of their main customers.

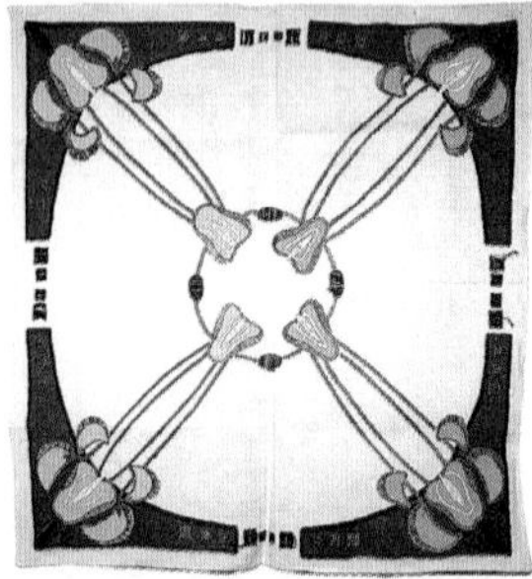

A Glasgow School of Art embroidered panel, by Ann Macbeth, c1900, 32in (81.5cm) square.

£400–450 ⊞ JSG

► **A batik on silk nursery panel,** by Jessie M. King, c1925, framed, 33in (84cm) wide.

£2,250–2,500 ⊞ JSG

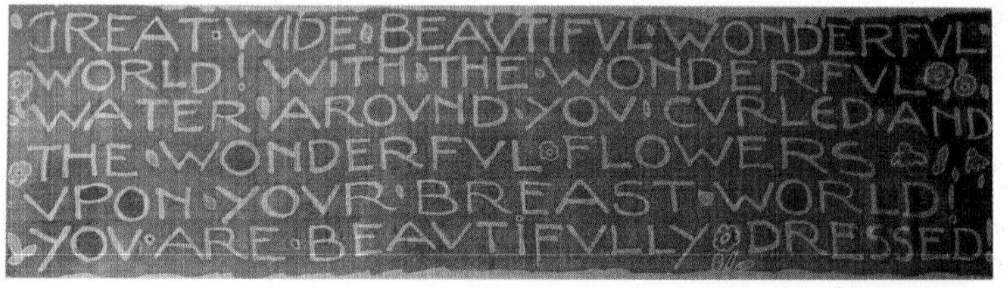

DOULTON

A Royal Doulton Kingsware model of a **tavern barrel,** with silver spigot and wooden stand, 1911–12, 7in (18cm) high.

£500–570 ⊞ BGe

A Royal Doulton **stoneware bowl,** with a silver rim inscribed 'Jean', Birmingham 1921, 5in (12.5cm) wide.

£75–85 ⊞ HTE

A Doulton Lambeth **sugar bowl,** with a silver cover and handle, c1879, 3in (7.5cm) high.

£200–230 ⊞ Scot

A Royal Doulton **bowl,** decorated with Arcady pattern, c1930, 10in (25.5cm) diam.

£135–150 ⊞ HUM

► A Doulton Lambeth **stoneware ewer,** by Frank Butler, lip restored, c1900, 12in (30.5cm) high.

£300–360 ⚒ ROS

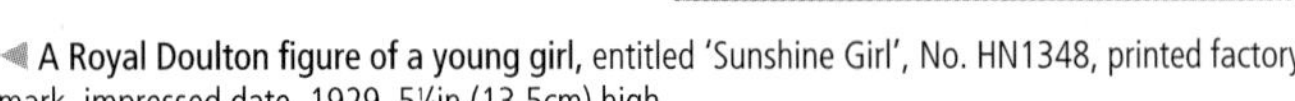

◄ A Royal Doulton **figure of a young girl,** entitled 'Sunshine Girl', No. HN1348, printed factory mark, impressed date, 1929, 5¼in (13.5cm) high.

£2,400–2,850 ⚒ S(O)

The HN numbers on Royal Doulton figures refer to Harry Nixon, the first manager of the factory's figure painting department.

A Royal Doulton **figure of a woman,** entitled 'Teresa', No. HN1682, slight damage, printed marks, 1935–49, 5¾in (14.5cm) high.

£350–420 ⚒ SWO

A Doulton Lambeth ***pâte-sur-pâte*** **tobacco jar and cover,** probably painted by Florence Barlow with a band of geese, 1880s, 5¼in (13.5cm) high.

£470–560 ⚒ G(L)

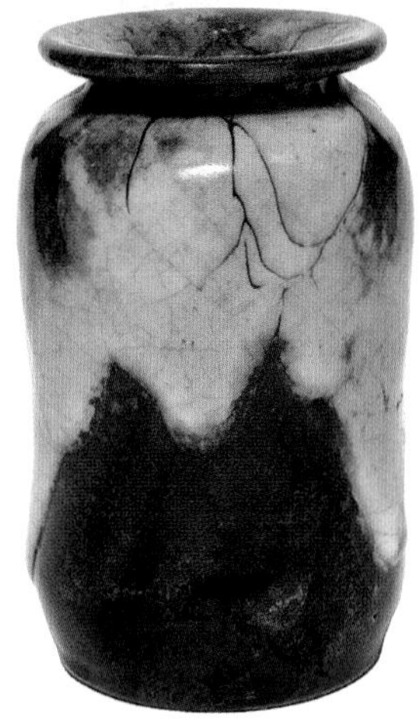

A Royal Doulton **Chang ware jar,** by Harry Nixon, 1920–25, 7in (18cm) high.

£1,850–2,100 ⊞ BWDA

A Doulton Lambeth stoneware **jardinière and stand,** decorated with flowers and foliage, c1900, 50in (127cm) high.

£640–760 E

A Royal Doulton jardinière and stand, by Eliza Simmance, c1902, 40in (101.5cm) high.

£4,100–4,600 POW

A Doulton jug, decorated with scenes from the Eglington Tournament, c1890, 6½in (16.5cm) high.

£260–290 DHA

During the 19th century, there was a resurgence of interest in the medieval period, due in some part to the popularity of the novels of Walter Scott. The high point of this fervour was the staging of the Eglington Tournament in Ayrshire in 1839 by the Earl of Eglington. This was an extravaganza of feasting, jousting and archery in rather belated honour of Queen Victoria's coronation in 1837, the celebrations for which the Earl felt should have been more redolent of the Age of Chivalry.

A Royal Doulton stoneware soap dish, surmounted by a bird, c1925, 5in (12.5cm) high.

£360–400 StB

A pair of Doulton stoneware vases, decorated by Hannah Barlow, Florence Barlow and Emily Stormer with a band of cattle, birds and flowers, repaired, impressed and incised marks, c1880, 12½in (32cm) high.

£2,000–2,400 Bea

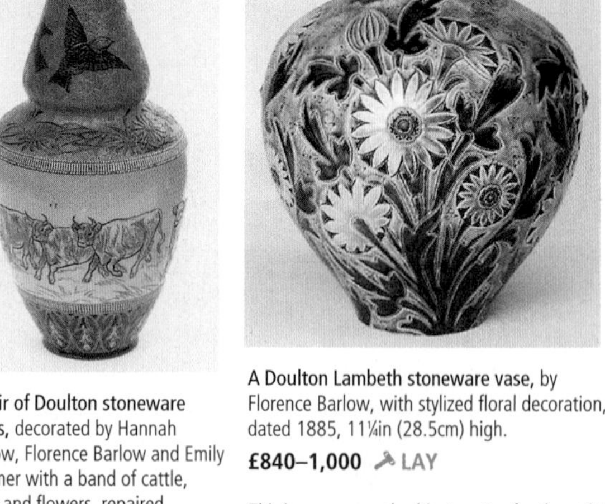

A Doulton Lambeth stoneware vase, by Florence Barlow, with stylized floral decoration, dated 1885, 11¼in (28.5cm) high.

£840–1,000 LAY

This is very unusual subject matter for the artist Florence Barlow. She was usually known for her pâte-sur-pâte birds and this vase is an example of her innovative and versatile style.

A pair of Doulton Lambeth stoneware vases, by Emily Stormer, decorated with leaves, incised monogram, dated 1886, 10½in (26.5cm) high.

£500–600 LT

▶ **A pair of Royal Doulton Lambeth vases,** by Eliza Simmance, c1905, 9½in (24cm) high.

£840–940 WAC

Although these vases do not fully illustrate what a fine artist Eliza Simmance was, especially in the Art Nouveau mode, this price reflects how highly desirable her work is among collectors.

A pair of Royal Doulton stoneware baluster vases, tube-lined with sunflowers, early 20thC, 14in (35.5cm) high.

£190–220 WilP

MARTIN BROTHERS

A Martin Brothers 'New Year' stoneware jar and cover, in the form of a grotesque bird, slight damage, incised marks, dated 1 January 1885, 11¼in (28.5cm) high.

£22,500–27,000 CAG

This piece is entitled 'New Year' due to its production on New Year's Day in 1885.

A Martin Brothers tyg, with incised decoration, marked, dated 1886, 7in (18cm) high.

£850–950 RUSK

A Martin Brothers stoneware vase, decorated with mythical beasts and scrolling foliage, dated 1892, 9in (23cm) high.

£3,550–3,950 BWDA

A Martin Brothers stoneware jar, entitled 'Toby', on an ebonized plinth, incised mark, dated 1894, 11½in (29cm) high.

£21,000–25,200 G(L)

Toby featured in Punch and Judy shows as Mr Punch's dog.

A Martin Brothers stoneware vase, painted and incised with stylized flowers, incised marks, dated 1890, 7¾in (19.5cm) high.

£1,450–1,700 DN

A Martin Brothers stoneware vase, incised and painted with grotesque fish and other sea creatures, dated 1903, 9in (23cm) high.

£4,300–4,800 BWDA

A Martin Brothers stoneware spoon warmer, in the form of a grotesque creature, incised mark, dated 1882, 6in (15cm) high.

£7,750–9,300 G(L)

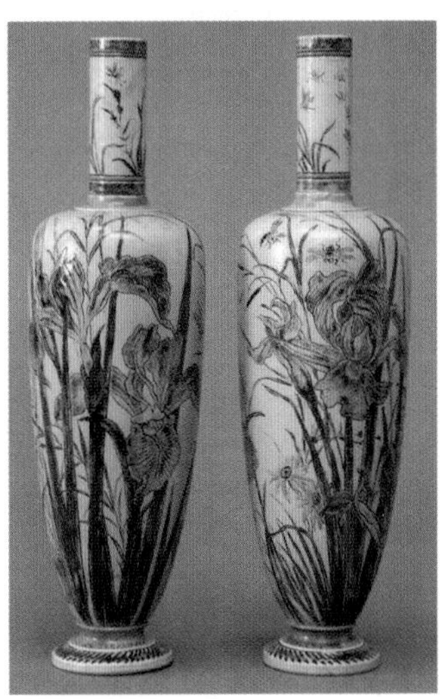

A pair of Martin Brothers salt-glazed stoneware vases, incised with irises, dragonflies and other flowers, damaged, incised marks, dated 1890, 13½in (34.5cm) high.

£1,200–1,400 CAG

A Martin Brothers stoneware vase, incised and moulded with jellyfish, damaged and repaired, incised mark, dated 1903, 10¼in (26cm) high.

£800–960 CAG

MOORCROFT

A Moorcroft Macintyre Florian ware bowl, designed by William Moorcroft, decorated with Honesty pattern, c1903, 3½in (9cm) high.

£990–1,100 ⊞ GOv

A Moorcroft Macintyre salad bowl, designed by William Moorcroft, decorated with Green and Gold Florian pattern, with a silver-plated rim, c1910, 10½in (26.5cm) wide, together with a pair of matching salad servers.

£560–670 AH

A Moorcroft bowl, designed by William Moorcroft, decorated with Hazeldene pattern, c1930, 4in (10cm) diam.

£800–900 ⊞ WAC

A Moorcroft Flamminian ware vase, designed by William Moorcroft for Liberty, impressed with stylized floral roundels, incised signature, printed mark, 1906–13, 12½in (32cm) high.

£600–720 Hal

For further information on vases see pages 222-226

A Moorcroft vase, designed by William Moorcroft, decorated with Pomegranate pattern, impressed Cobridge factory mark, painted signature, 1913–16, 5½in (14cm) high.

£270–320 CINN

A Moorcroft Macintyre vase, designed by William Moorcroft, decorated in gold with Eighteenth Century pattern, c1907, 9¼in (23.5cm) high.

£330–390 HAD

A Moorcroft vase, designed by William Moorcroft, tube-lined and decorated with Poppy pattern, painted signature, impressed marks, c1920, 7in (18cm) high.

£640–760 N

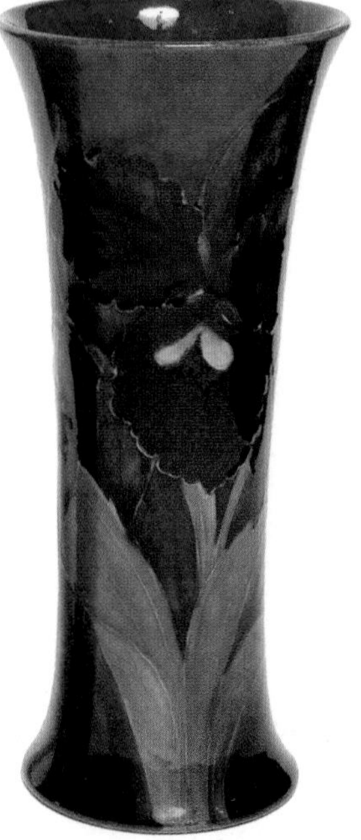

A pair of Moorcroft vases, designed by William Moorcroft, decorated with Orchid pattern, c1919, 10½in (26.5cm) high.

£4,500–5,000 ⊞ GaL

A Moorcroft vase, designed by William Moorcroft, decorated with leaves and fruit under a flambé glaze, signed 'Potter to HM The Queen', c1928, 10½in (26.5cm) high.

£440–520 SWO

ART NOUVEAU CERAMICS

◀ **A salt-glazed bowl,** by Jean Carriès, France, c1900, 6in (15cm) diam.

£360–400 ⊞ TA2

▶ **A Foley *intarsio* charger,** designed by Frederick Rhead, decorated with figures and flowers, c1898, 14½in (37cm) diam.

£1,400–1,650 ⚒ DD

◀ **A Foley *intarsio* bowl,** designed by Frederick Rhead, decorated with a scene from *Hamlet,* views of Glamis Castle and a seated clown, the exterior decorated with stylized foliage, with a silver-plated rim, printed marks, c1910, 11½in (29cm) diam.

£350–420 ⚒ N

Foley became the trade name for Wileman & Co, which was then known as Shelley from 1925. The name derived from their premises, 'The Foley' at Longton, Staffordshire. Their Art Nouveau wares included a range of earthenware, designed by Frederick Rhead, using a dramatic form of underglaze decoration known as intarsio.

A Foley *intarsio* jug and bowl, probably by Frederick Rhead, the jug decorated with geese and the bowl decorated with bands of flowers, slight damage, printed marks, c1910, jug 6½in (16.5cm) high.

£470–560 ⚒ DN

◀ **A Foley *intarsio* Temple jar and cover,** designed by Frederick Rhead, decorated with rabbits and flowers, c1910, 16in (40.5cm) high.

£1,600–1,800 ⊞ GaL

A pair of Thomas Forester & Sons vases, decorated with Mucha-style maidens, c1910, 16in (40.5cm) high.

£720–800 ⊞ HEW

A Roger Guerin vase, moulded with monkeys, with a waxy glaze, incised mark, Belgium, early 20thC, 11in (28cm) high.

£760–910 ⚒ CINN

A Langley ware jardinière, incised with poppies, c1900, 9in (23cm) high.

£220–250 ⊞ StB

▶ **A Minton Secessionist vase,** by Leon Solon and John Wadsworth, c1904, 5in (12.5cm) high.

£130–145 ⊞ WAC

A Morris ware vase, by George Cartlidge, decorated with flowers and berries, c1920, 10in (25.5cm) high.

£1,950–2,200 GaL

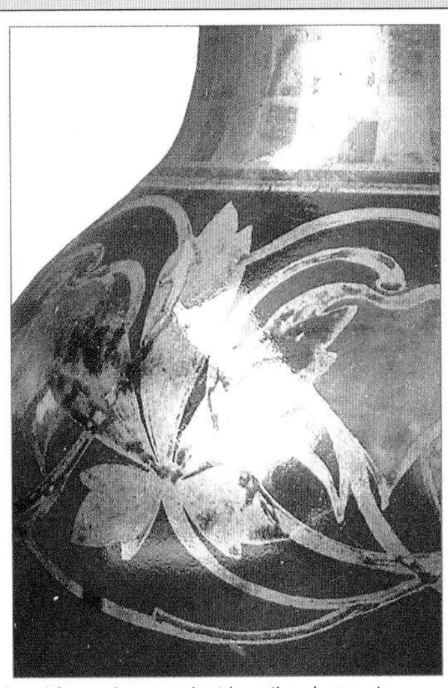

A Pilkington's Royal Lancastrian vase, of shouldered form, decorated with a silver lustre vine, early 20thC, 8¾in (22cm) high.

£700–840 ROS

A pair of Reissner, Stellmacher & Kessel Amphora vases, each moulded with branches and a pheasant, impressed and painted marks, Austria, c1900, 16½in (42cm) high.

£1,950–2,300 WAD

Reissner, Stellmacher & Kessel

The Austrian firm Reissner, Stellmacher & Kessel (established 1892) produced Art Nouveau sculpture from their factory in Turn-Teplitz. Most sought after is their mass-produced earthenware Amphora range of wares which are typically exotic in form with moulded organic decoration of berries, leaves and stems upon thick on-glaze enamels.

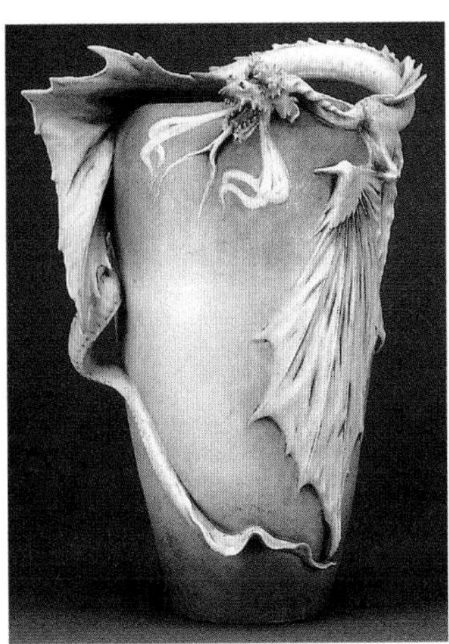

► **A Reissner, Stellmacher & Kessel Amphora vase,** modelled with a winged dragon, with gilt highlights, impressed and painted marks, Austria, c1900, 17in (43cm) high.

£8,900–10,600 WAD

A Reissner, Stellmacher & Kessel Amphora vase, decorated with flowers, chestnuts and 'jewels', slight damage, impressed marks, Austria, c1900, 10in (25.5cm) high.

£1,500–1,800 WAD

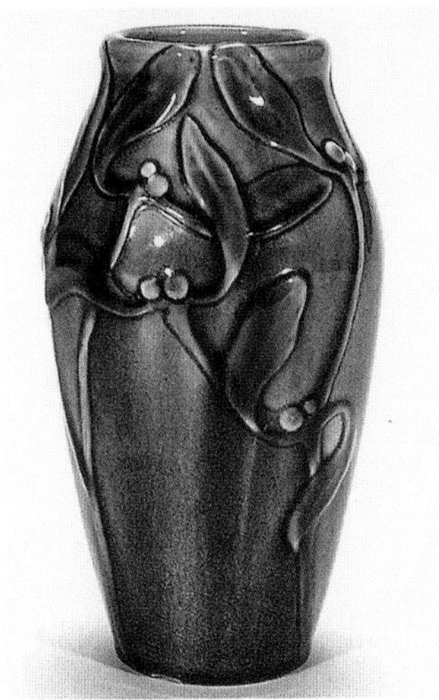

A Rookwood Iris Glaze vase, attributed to Matt Daly, slight damage, marked, America, 1901, 8in (20.5cm) high.

£1,550–1,850 CINN

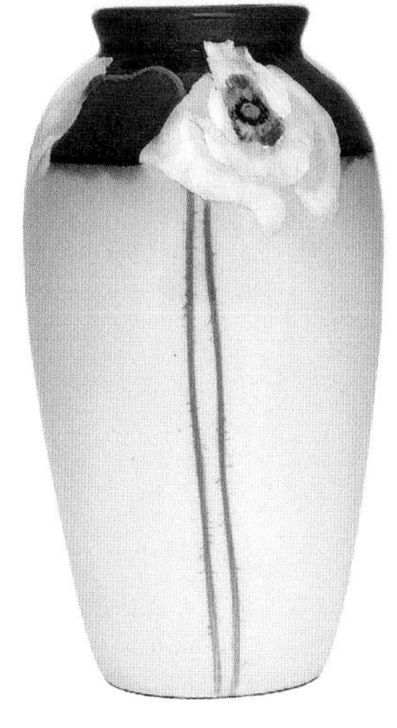

A Rookwood Iris Glaze vase, by Irene Bishop, decorated with poppies, America, 1908, 7in (18cm) high.

£1,700–2,000 TREA

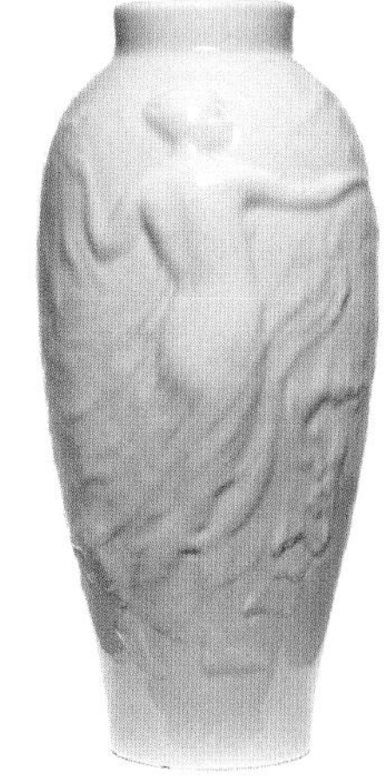

A Rookwood vase, by Harriet Wilcox, moulded with female figures, America, 1918, 17½in (44.5cm) high.

£2,700–3,200 TREA

A Rozenburg vase, by J. W. van Rossum, decorated with salamanders, Holland, c1892, 11in (28cm) high.

£1,600–1,800 JuA

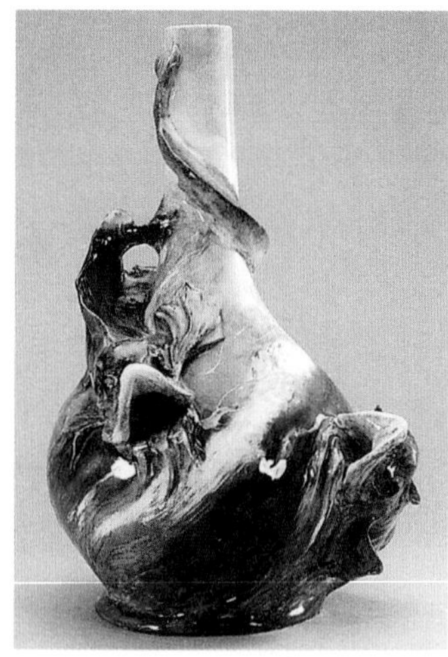

A Rörstrand vase, by Alf Wallander, slight damage, repaired, signed, Sweden, c1895, 18in (45.5cm) high.

£3,900–4,650 BUK

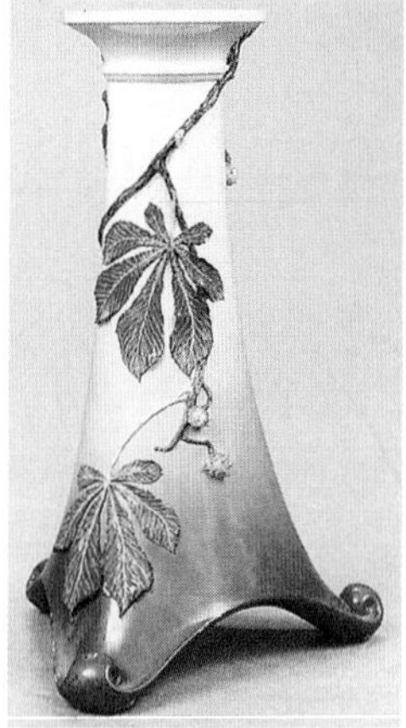

A Rörstrand vase, by Alf Wallander, decorated with horse chestnut branches, slight damage, signed and dated, Sweden, 1897, 43¼in (110cm) high.

£1,950–2,300 BUK

A Sitzendorf porcelain figural centrepiece, in the form of mermaids emerging from waves, Germany, 1900–10, 10in (25.5cm) wide.

£330–380 OAK

► **An Ernst Wahliss vase,** decorated with a maiden and flowers, Austria, c1900, 7in (28cm) high.

£440–500 ANO

An Ernst Wahliss vase, painted with flowers on a gilded ground, printed and incised marks, Austria, c1900, 12½in (32cm) high.

£1,000–1,200 WAD

An Intarsio pottery jug, possibly by Frederick Rhead, c1900, 6in (15cm) high.

£270–300 TA2

A Zuid Holland Etruscan-shape vase, initialled 'B', c1899, 9½in (24cm) high.

£370–420 JuA

Many Zuid Holland designs were based on Javanese batiks.

A Zuid Holland lamp base, c1899, 20¼in (51.5cm) high.

£460–520 JuA

ART NOUVEAU FIGURES & BUSTS

◄ **A bronze figure,** by Maurice Bouval, entitled 'Le Secret', France, c1900, 13in (33cm) high.

£3,150–3,500 MiW

A Daum *pâte-de-verre* figure of a woman, France, Nancy, c1910, 5in (12.5cm) high.

£1,800–2,000 MiW

A marble and patinated bronze bust of a woman, by Frederic, on a stone socle, inscribed, probably Austria or Germany, c1910, 11½in (29cm) high.

£1,400–1,650 DORO

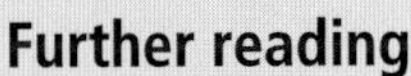

Further reading

Miller's Ceramic Figures Buyers Guide, Miller's Publications, 2006

► **A patinated and gilded-bronze figure of a woman with a mirror,** by Paul Philippe, with carved-ivory head and arms, on an onyx socle, France, Paris, c1900, 17¼in (44cm) high.

£5,900–7,000 DORO

A pair of Goldscheider terracotta wall plaques, in the form of women with flowers in their hair, impressed marks, signed 'Cherc', Austria, Vienna, c1900, 14¼in (36cm) high.

£1,600–1,900 S(O)

A Zsolnay lustre glazed figural vase, impressed and implied marks, Hungary, early 20thC, 9½in (24cm) high.

£2,750–3,300 S(O)

Established at Pêcs, Hungary, in 1862, Zsolnay became a leading producer of Art Nouveau ceramics in eastern Europe. After the appointment of Vinsce Wartha in 1893 as artistic director, the factory began to make wares of organic form with iridescent glazes in the style of Clément Massier.

A patinated bronze bust of a girl, by Piquemal, with a carved ivory face, on a stone socle, probably France, c1900, 10¾in (27.5cm) high.

£940–1,100 DORO

A bronze figure of a woman holding a fan, c1900, 9in (23cm) high.

£720–800 MiW

A bronze figural paperweight, entitled 'Judith', c1905, 6½in (16.5cm) high.

£300–340 TDG

ART NOUVEAU FURNITURE

An smoker's oak cabinet, with brass and enamel decoration, c1900, 17in (43cm) high.
£360–400 TA2

An inlaid mahogany chair, by Wylie & Lochhead, with later upholstery, Scotland, 1880–1920.
£860–970 STRA

A J. & J. Kohn stained bentwood and brass armchair, designed by Gustav Siegel, Austria, Vienna, c1900.
£1,950–2,300 S(NY)

This chair design won first prize at the Paris Exhibition of 1900.

A Thonet chair, by Otto Wagner, 1904–06.
£1,450–1,700 S(Am)

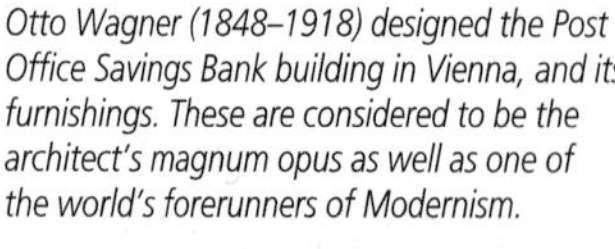

Otto Wagner (1848–1918) designed the Post Office Savings Bank building in Vienna, and its furnishings. These are considered to be the architect's magnum opus as well as one of the world's forerunners of Modernism.

A beechwood and marquetry-inlaid writing desk, by Emile Gallé, incised signature, France, Nancy, c1900, 28in (71cm) wide.
£2,600–3,100 S(O)

Gallé Furniture

Emile Gallé is probably best known for his wonderful Art Nouveau glass. His first venture into furniture production was in the mid-1880s with the earliest designs based on 18th-century models from the reign of Louis XV. The mouldings and supports of these pieces were often of organic forms with naturalistic outlines sometimes carved with florets or perhaps a snail. The flat surfaces were inlaid with landscapes and plant-forms which had interesting figuring or were stained the required colour. Some bore inscriptions, perhaps from works by the poet Baudelaire, and some were given titles appropriate to the decoration.

A J. & J. Kohn ebonized-beech and brass desk, by Josef Hoffmann, Austria, Vienna, c1901, 38½in (98cm) wide.
£24,400–29,200 S(NY)

This is a very stylish piece of furniture and has a very geometric appearance, far removed from typical French or Belgian 'Art Nouveau' pieces of the same date. This piece anticipates the geometry of what would become to be recognized as Art Deco.

An oak desk and chair, in the style of Louis Majorelle, probably Nancy School, France, c1905, 51in (129.5cm) wide.
£4,000–4,500 TDG

For further information on
Furniture see pages 12–104

◀ **An inlaid mahogany fire surround,** 1880–1920, 72in (183cm) high.
£2,300–2,600 STRA

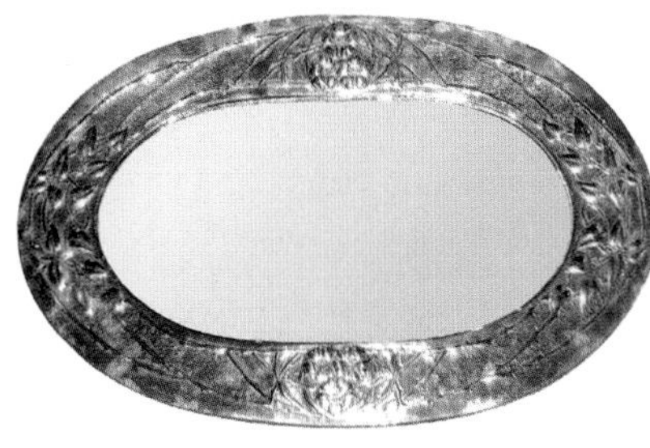

A brass mirror, 1880–1920, 32½in (83cm) wide.
£580–650 STRA

A mahogany and pewter mirror, France, c1900, 33in (84cm) wide.
£190–220 TOP

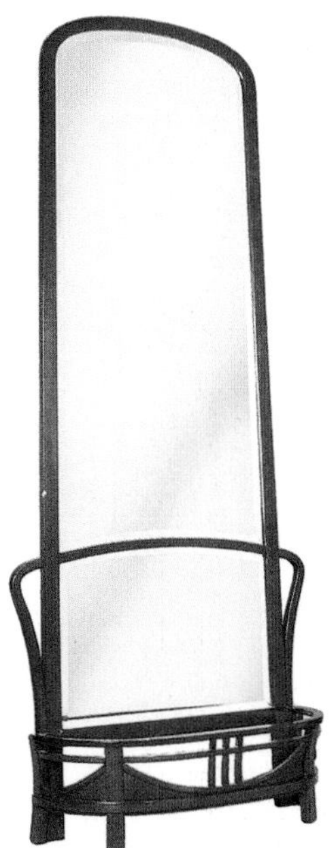

A mahogany salon suite, comprising sofa and six side chairs, early 20thC, sofa (120cm) wide.
£470–560 DN

◄ **A Thonet beechwood jardinière and mirror,** some losses, restored, Austria, Vienna, early 20thC, 98½in (250cm) high.
£1,150–1,350 DORO

A carved mahogany settee, by Henry van de Velde, with velvet upholstery, artist's cypher, Belgium, 1902, 63in (160cm) wide.
£65,000–78,000 S(NY)

This settee was part of an interior commissioned by Julius Stern, the banker and collector, for his Berlin residence. The project was ambitious and the interiors were published several times in trend-setting journals of the day. These designs were the most important and the largest commission that van de Velde received in Germany.

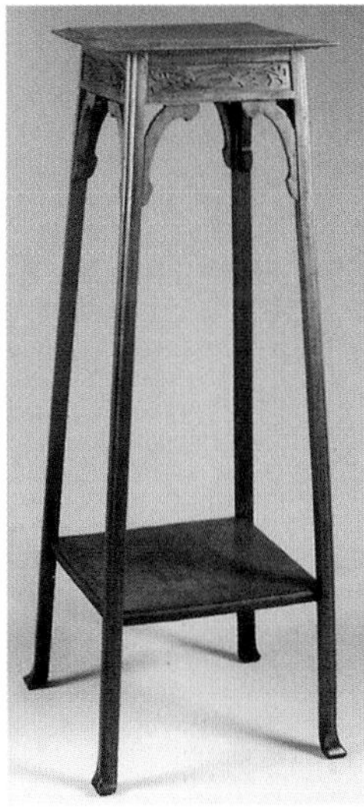

A mahogany plant stand, with brass decoration, slight damage, early 20thC, 44in (112cm) high.
£310–370 JDJ

A beechwood and marquetry-inlaid tilt-top table, by Emile Gallé, inlaid with foliage and butterflies, signed, France, Nancy, c1900, 29½in (75cm) wide.
£1,200–1,400 S(O)

A mahogany two-tier occasional table, by Louis Majorelle, inlaid with flowers and foliage, the supports with gilt sabots, signed, France, c1900, 29½in (75cm) wide.
£6,200–7,400 S

A Thonet ebonized-beechwood table, by Marcel Kammerer, with brass mounts, Austria, Vienna, c1904, 30½in (77.5cm) high.
£3,900–4,650 S(NY)

A mahogany whatnot, with ormolu mounts, France, c1900, 45in (114.5cm) high.
£1,350–1,500 PVD

ART NOUVEAU GLASS

A Daum miniature beaker, acid-etched with mistletoe, with gilded detailing, France, Nancy, c1900, 2in (5cm) high.

£360–400 MiW

A Daum glass cabinet bowl, parcel-gilt and enamelled with tulips, signed, France, Nancy, c1875, 4¼in (11cm) diam.

£1,000–1,200 NOA

◄ **A Daum glass bowl,** enamelled with violets, France, Nancy, c1900, 5in (12.5cm) diam.

£1,950–2,200 MiW

Pieces decorated with violets have been consistently popular with collectors and the price would indicate that this is still the case.

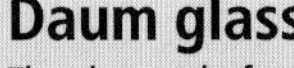

Daum glass

The glassworks factory of the brothers Auguste and Antonin Daum was located in Nancy, Lorraine, the same place as their contemporary Emile Gallé. Like Gallé, they produced multicoloured ornamental vessels and lamps. They created cameo pieces which often included multi-layered 'skins' of coloured glass that were acid-etched with floral or landscape scenes in relief. Sometimes added subtlety could be achieved by skilful cutting with a wheel. Pieces inspired by the four seasons were enamelled in naturalistic colours that reflected the particular time of year. The brothers collaborated with Alméric Walter to produce *pâte de verre* pieces embellished with creatures such as snails, fish and lizards and Louis Majorelle who produced gilt-bronze or wrought-iron mounts for stunning Art Nouveau lamps and armatures. During the Art Deco period, Daum produced single coloured heavy glass vessels acid-etched with geometric designs and in more recent times they created extraordinary pieces based on the designs of Salvador Dali, Philippe Starck and André Dubreuil.

A set of six Daum drinking glasses, designed by Edmond Lachenal, enamelled with sprigs of mistletoe, France, Nancy, c1895, 6in (15cm) high.

£1,250–1,400 MiW

Taught by Théodore Deck, Edmond Lachenal (1855–1930) became one of the great names of Art Nouveau design, mostly associated with ceramics and glass.

A Daum glass vase, acid-etched with foliage and applied with a poppy, France, Nancy, c1900, 9in (23cm) high.

£3,600–4,000 MiW

◄ **A Daum cameo glass vase,** overlaid with ruby glass acid-etched with lilies and foliage, France, Nancy, 1900–05, 13in (33cm) high.

£3,150–3,500 MiW

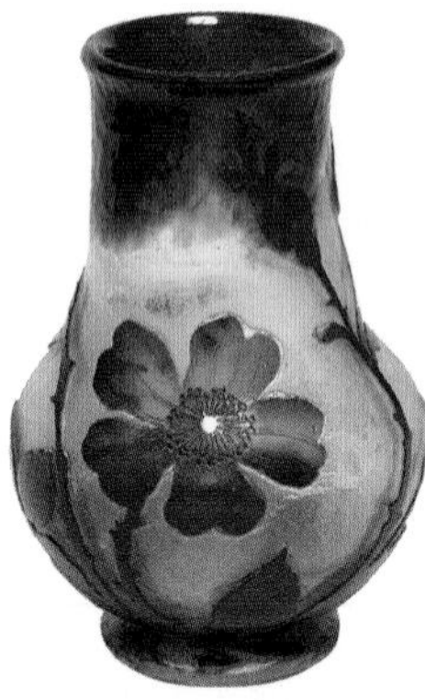

◄ **A Daum cameo glass vase,** decorated with flowers on a *martelé* ground, France, Nancy, c1900, 7in (18cm) high.

£3,600–4,000 MiW

The surface of the neck of this vase was carved with a wheel to give a 'hammered' appearance.

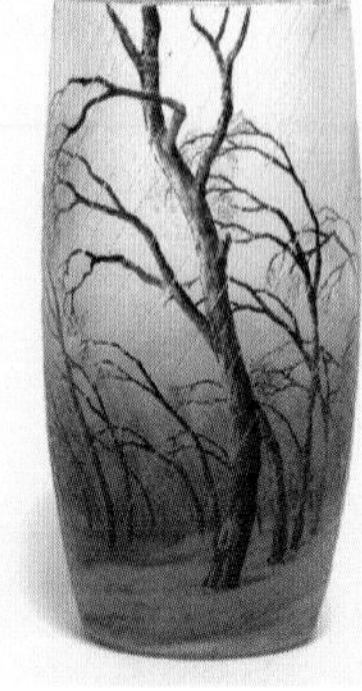

A Daum Seasons enamelled vase, entitled 'Rain', France, Nancy, c1900, 5in (12.5cm) high.

£5,400–6,000 MiW

This is from a series of Daum vases relating to the four seasons and has been acid-etched to give a relief image heightened with coloured enamels.

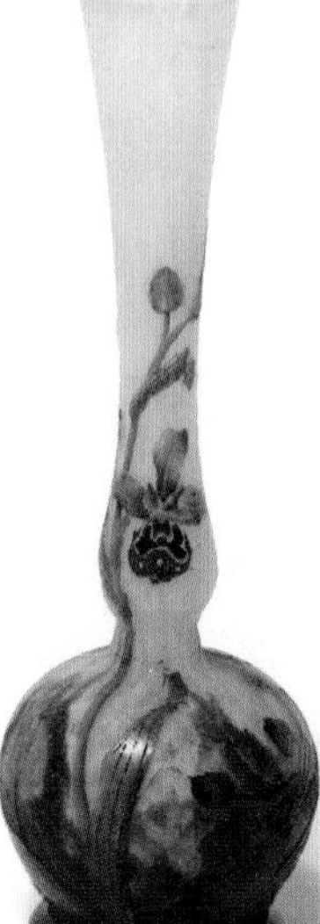

◄ **A Daum glass vase,** acid-etched and enamelled with an orchid, signed, France, Nancy, c1906, 6in (15cm) high.

£3,600–4,000 MI

A Daum opalescent glass vase, the *martelé* ground decorated with lilies, marked, France, Nancy, early 20thC, 8in (20.5cm) high.
£2,700–3,200 S(O)

A Daum cameo glass ***vide poche***, overlaid and acid-etched with bats, France, Nancy, c1900, 6in (15cm) wide.
£2,700–3,000 MiW

This might have been placed in a hallway to receive visiting cards left by guests.

A Durand iridescent glass vase, America, early 20thC, 8¼in (21cm) high.
£380–450 DuM

Victor Durand produced art glass at the Vineland Glass Manufacturing Co, New Jersey from 1897 until his death in 1931. Typical examples are vases of neo-classical form in gold or blue iridescence. He employed Quezal artists, and many of his products resemble Quezal pieces.

◄ **A Wilhelm Habel's Elizabethhütte Glassworks opalescent glass bowl,** with coloured glass stringing, on a gilded metal mount, Bohemia, c1885, 10in (25.5cm) high.
£510–570 BHA

The Pallme glassworks was first established in Steinschonau, Austria, in 1786 by Ignaz Pallme-König. In 1889 it merged with Wilhelm Habel's Elizabethhütte Glassworks near Teplitz and became Pallme-König & Habel. During the Art Nouveau period, this glass company produced high quality iridescent glass. In examples such as this piece, hot glass trails were wound around the body forming a network, and the piece was then blown into a mould.

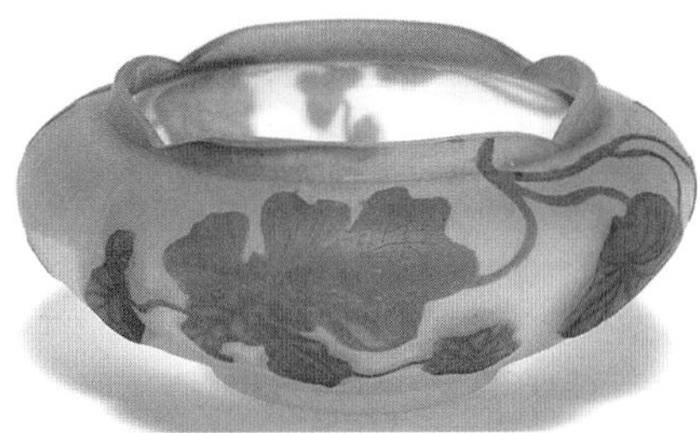

◄ **An Emile Gallé cameo glass bowl,** acid-etched with nasturtiums, France, Nancy, 1904–06, 8in (20.5cm) diam.
£1,400–1,600 MiW

► **An Emile Gallé silver-mounted *vase parlant*,** the body etched and enamelled with blossom, signed, France, Nancy, c1897, 4in (10cm) high.
£7,500–8,400 MI

Some Gallé vases bear an engraved verse, generally by a luminary of French literature such as Mallarmé or Baudelaire, and these are known as vases parlants.

A pair of Emile Gallé cameo glass bud vases, etched with cyclamen, signed, France, Nancy, c1900, 12¼in (31cm) high.
£2,600–3,100 S(NY)

Emile Gallé

Emile Gallé (1846–1904) studied botany at Weimar and trained as a glassmaker in Meissenthal, Germany and then at his father's glass and faïence factory in Saint-Clément, France. He quickly established himself not only as an outstanding designer, but also as a highly accomplished glass technician. His development of cameo glass in the 1880s – a technique first perfected by the Romans – was perhaps his most important contribution to the world of art glass. To create this effect, two or more layers of coloured glass are fused together and a design engraved or acid-etched with a wheel through to the layer below.

An Emile Gallé cameo glass footed vase, decorated with anemones, France, Nancy, c1900, 8in (20.5cm) high.
£2,700–3,000 MiW

An Emile Gallé silver-mounted cameo glass vase, decorated with a fruiting vine, the mounts cast with flowers and ivy leaves, signed, France, Nancy, c1900, 2¾in (7cm) high.
£960–1,150 S(O)

► **An Emile Gallé cameo glass vase,** decorated with flowers and leaves, France, Nancy, c1900, 6in (15cm) high.
£1,250–1,400 MiW

An Emile Gallé cameo glass vase, decorated with pine cones, France, Nancy, c1900, 12in (30.5cm) high.

£1,950–2,200 MiW

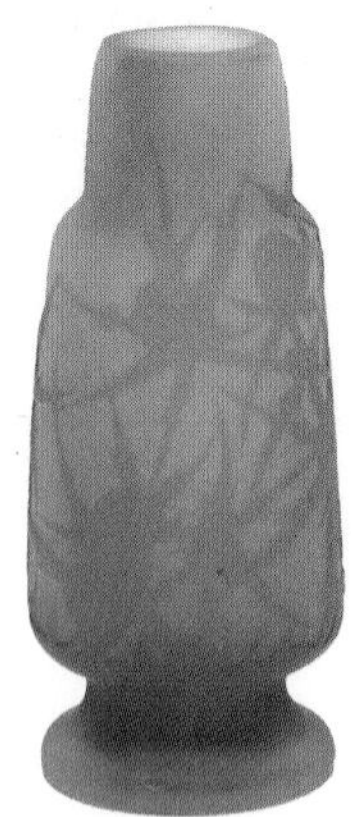

An Emile Gallé cameo glass vase, France, Nancy, c1900, 4in (10cm) high.

£540–600 MiW

An iridescent glass vase, probably by Harrach, decorated in gilt with flowering foliage, gilt-painted numerals, Bohemia, early 20thC, 10in (25.5cm) high.

£540–640 WAD

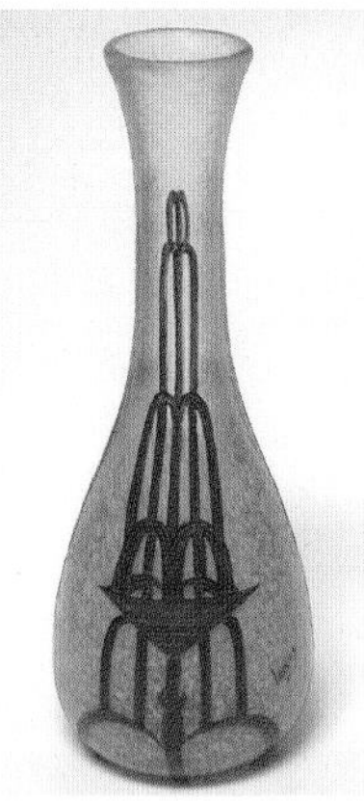

A Legras & Cie frosted glass jug, with acid-etched decoration, France, 1900–14, 15in (38cm) high.

£620–690 CHAC

◄ **A Loetz iridescent glass bowl,** Austria, c1900, 10in (25.5cm) diam.

£630–700 MiW

► **A Loetz iridescent glass and pewter bowl,** Austria, c1920, 8in (20.5cm) diam.

£670–750 BHA

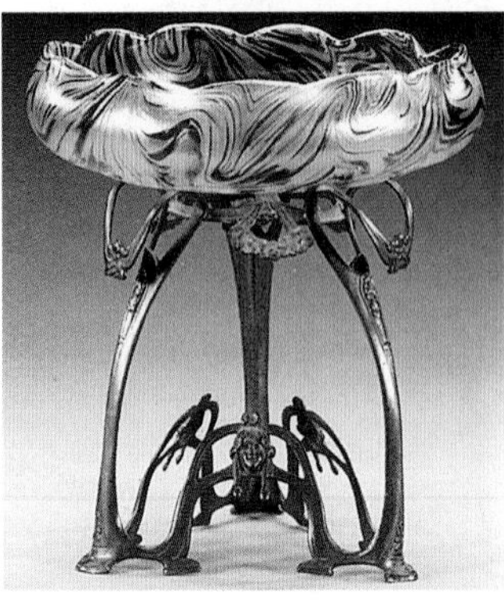

A Loetz iridescent glass bowl, with waved rim, on a patinated brass stand cast with floral designs and three maidens' heads, Austria, c1900, 10¼in (26cm) diam.

£2,150–2,550 S(O)

A Loetz iridescent glass vase, Austria, c1900, 7in (18cm) high.

£340–380 RUSK

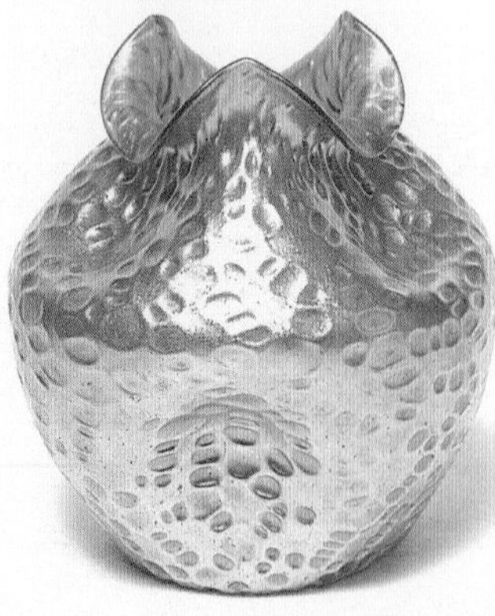

A Loetz iridescent glass vase, with a trefoil neck, Austria, c1900, 7in (18cm) high.

£670–750 MiW

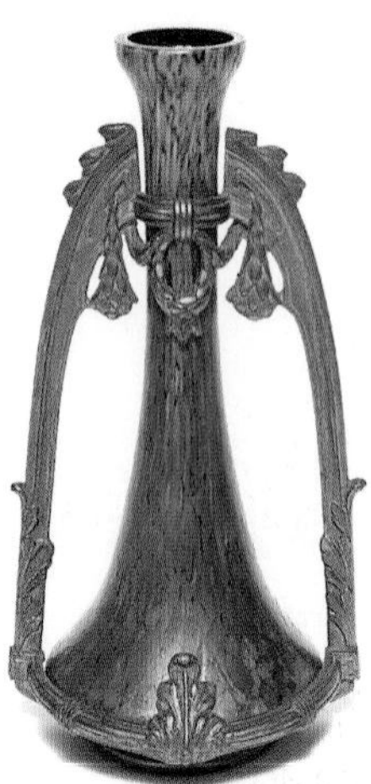

◄ **A Loetz glass vase,** held in a bronze mount, Austria, c1900, 9in (23cm) high.

£670–750 TA2

Further reading

Miller's Glass Buyers Guide, Miller's Publications, 2001

► **A Moser glass vase,** Bohemia, c1900, 10in (25.5cm) high.

£400–450 MiW

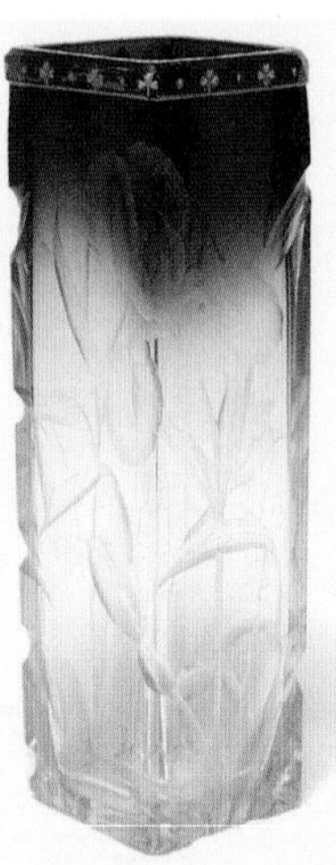

A Muller Frères cameo glass vase, acid-etched with a Geisha in a Japanesque scene, France, c1910, 11¾in (30cm) high.

£900–1,050 DuM

A Muller Frères cameo glass vase, internally decorated and overlaid with flowers, signed, France, c1915, 7in (18cm) high.

£950–1,100 JAA

A Pallme-König iridescent glass bowl, with banded decoration, Bohemia, c1905, 7in (18cm) diam.

£310–350 BHA

A Quezal Jack-in-the-Pulpit glass vase, decorated with pulled feather design, America, 1900–25, 15½in (39.5cm) high.

£5,900–7,000 JDJ

A Reijmyre Glassworks glass vase, by Axel Enoch Boman, etched with a woodland scene and birds in flight, signed, Denmark, 1917, 7½in (19cm) high.

£340–400 BUK

A Schneider cameo glass vase, etched with foxgloves, marked 'Le Verre Français', France, c1920, 9in (23cm) high.

£1,350–1,500 SAT

Charles Schneider founded the Verrerie Schneider in Epinay-sur-Seine near Paris in 1913. Many wares are signed 'Le Verre Français' or 'Charder', which is a combination of Charles and Schneider.

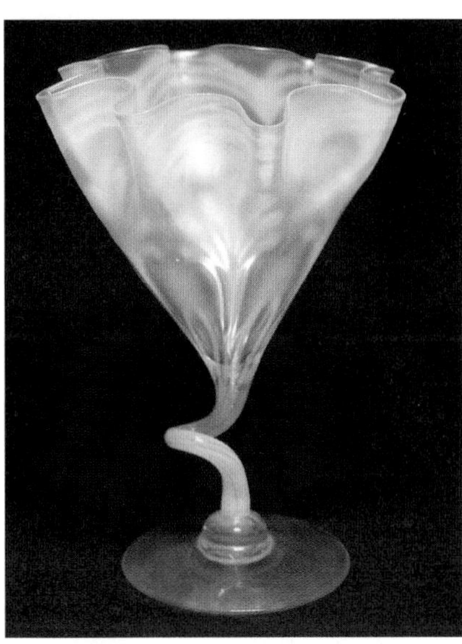

A John Walsh Walsh vaseline glass vase, on a spiralling stem, c1900, 7½in (18.5cm) high.

£670–750 MiW

LOCATE THE SOURCE

The source of each illustration in Miller's can be found by checking the code letters below each caption with the Key to Illustrations, pages 746–753.

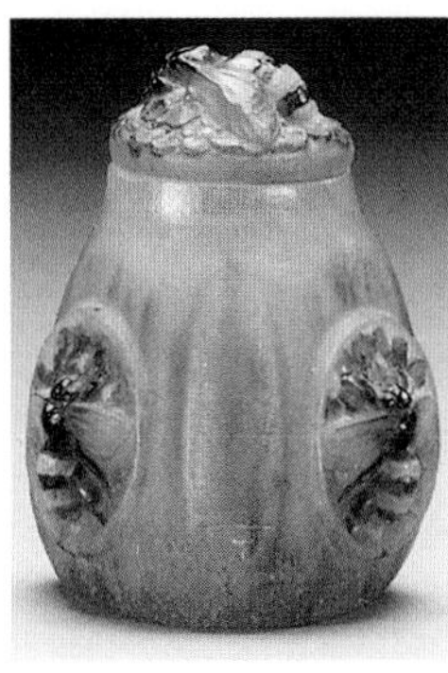

An Alméric Walter *pâte de verre* box and cover, designed by Henri Bergé, moulded with bees and flowers, moulded marks, France, Nancy, 1910–20, 4in (10cm) high.

£3,350–4,000 S(O)

A glass jug, with enamelled decoration, Bohemia, c1900, 12in (30.5cm) high.

£200–230 CHAC

A pair of silver-mounted iridescent glass vases, with applied foliate decoration, c1907, 6in (15cm) high.

£400–450 BHA

► **A pair of clear-cased tinted glass vases,** each mounted on an ebonized wood base, slight damage, c1900, 49¾in (126.5cm) high.

£1,300–1,550 S(NY)

ART NOUVEAU JEWELLERY

A gold, sapphire, diamond and pearl brooch, the sapphire surmounted by two cupids, each holding a diamond, probably Austro-Hungarian, 19thC, 1½in (4cm) diam, with a Wartzski box.

£7,000–8,400 CGC

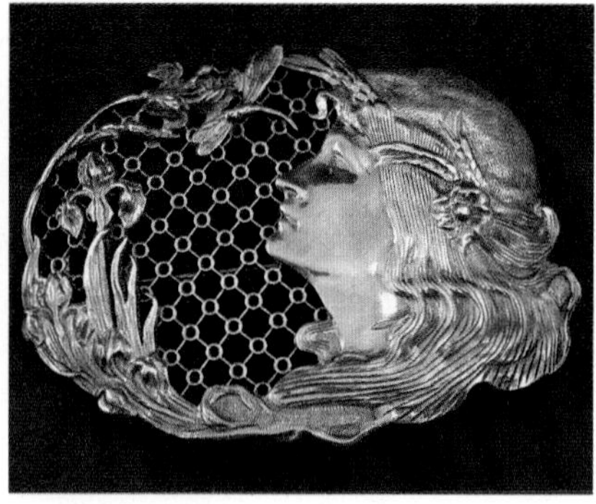

A silver brooch, by Arthur James Smith, in the form of a maiden's profile and a dragonfly on a lattice ground, marked, Birmingham 1900, 3¼in (8.5cm) wide.

£350–420 G(L)

A silver-gilt and *plique-à-jour* enamel brooch, attributed to Otto Prutscher, probably made by Heinrich Levanger, Pforzheim, in the form of a winged scarab, Germany, 1900–05, 1½in (4cm) wide.

£760–850 ANO

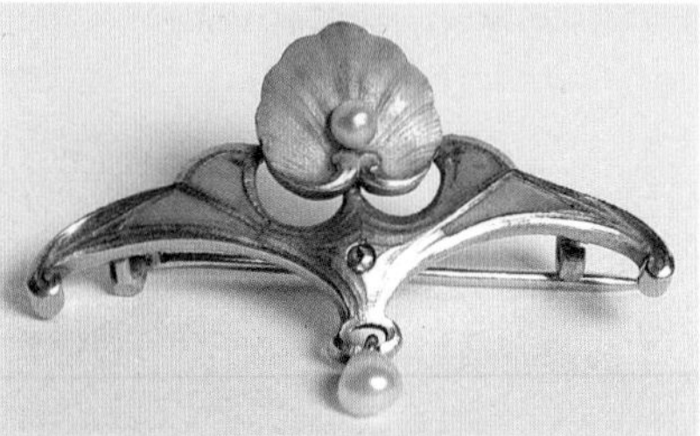

A 14ct gold and *plique-à-jour* enamel brooch, set with pearls and with a pearl drop, America, c1900, 1½in (4cm) wide.

£610–680 WIM

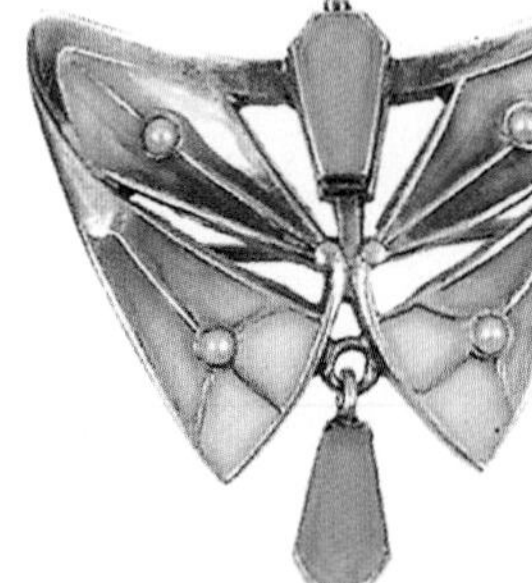

A *plique-à-jour* enamel and chrysoprase brooch, in the form of a stylized butterfly, the enamelled wings decorated with imitation pearl collets, slight damage, stamped '900', German, c1905.

£420–500 DN

A metal buckle, in the form of a beetle resting on leaves flanked by buds, c1900, 4in (10cm) wide.

£95–105 TDG

◄ **A silver and enamel buckle,** by Andrew Barrett & Sons, 1901, 3¾in (9.5cm) wide.

£100–120 SWO

A carved horn pendant, by Madame Bonté, carved with exotic leaves and berries, with a pendant glass bead, the double-strand cord set with glass beads, signed, France, Paris, c1920.

£730–870 DN(HAM)

Madame Bonté was a prominent Parisian jeweller and created jewels in the Art Nouveau tradition from unorthodox materials such as horn. She teamed up with the designer Georges Pierre to produce insect and foliate pendants and their collaboration lasted from about 1900 until 1936.

A set of six silver buttons, by W. J. F., each cast with the face of a maiden, Birmingham 1902, each 1in (2.5cm) diam.

£200–230 TDG

A gold pendant, with mother-of-pearl plaques and a pearl drop, signed 'H. M.' Birmingham 1905, 1½in (4cm) long.

£270–310 VDA

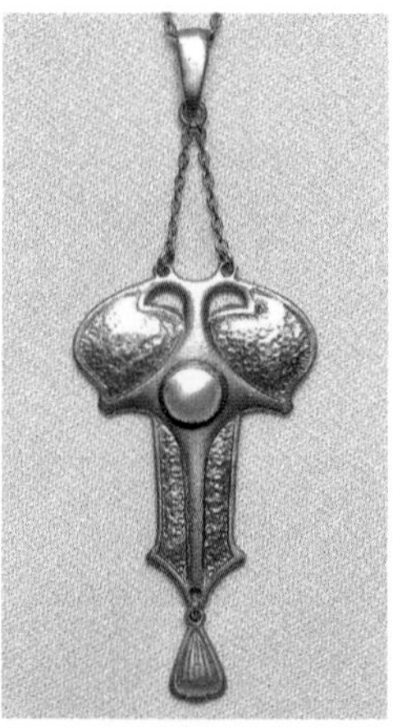

A silver, mother-of-pearl and enamel pendant, by Charles Horner, Chester 1908, 2in (5cm) long.

£290–320 ANO

Currently the fashion is for large, ostentatious jewellery, so this is a good time to buy beautiful, delicate pieces such as this.

ART NOUVEAU LIGHTING

A pair of patinated bronze and brass wall lights, by Friedrich Adler, each with three sconces before a mirror plate, Germany, c1900, 10¾in (27.5cm) wide.

£3,800–4,550 S

A bronze and slag glass lamp, probably by Bradley & Hubbard, America, early 20thC, 19in (48.5cm) high.

£220–260 JAA

A leaded glass lamp, attributed to the Chicago Mosaic Lamp Co, the shade with floral and leaf decoration, the base modelled in the form of a tree trunk, with label, America, c1925, 28in (71cm) high.

£2,300–2,750 NOA

A silvered-bronze table lamp, by Maurice Dufrène, the pierced foliate shade above a tapering stem, signed, France, early 20thC, 12½in (32cm) high.

£1,800–2,150 S(O)

A metal overlay lamp, by Handel, the shade decorated with trees, the base with a band of stylized flowers and leaves, signed, America, early 20thC, 25½in (65cm) high.

£9,600–11,500 JDJ

A silver-plated figural lamp, by J. P. Kayser & Söhne, Germany, c1900, 19in (48.5cm) high.

£1,800–2,000 TA2

A Pairpoint Puffy table lamp, the shade decorated with flowers and leaves, the base in the form of a tree trunk, America, 1900–25, 22½in (57cm) high.

£5,900–7,000 JDJ

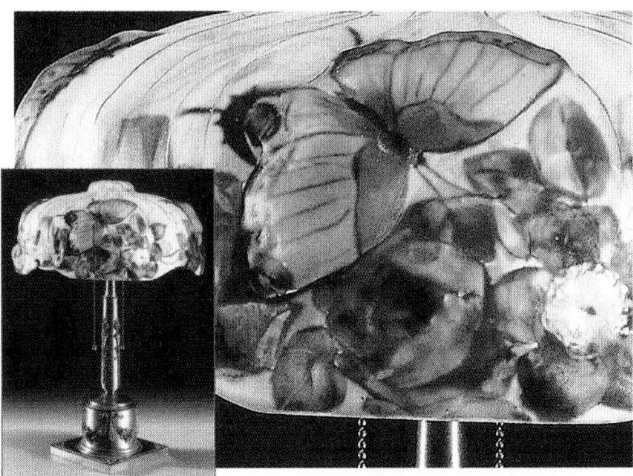

A Pairpoint Puffy table lamp, the shade decorated with sprays of roses, dogwood flowers and butterflies, shade and base signed, America, c1910, 21in (53.5cm) high.

£5,400–6,400 JAA

The Pairpoint Corporation

In the early 20th century, the Pairpoint Corporation of New Bedford, Massachusetts made a range of innovative, reverse-painted and moulded table and boudoir lamps called Puffy lamps, with uneven glass shades. Bases vary; some simulate bronze, some are designed to resemble tree trunks, or are ribbed, and others are made from gilt-metal.

► **A Reissner, Stellmacher & Kessel Esmarelda lamp,** in the form of the bust of a young woman, restored, Bohemia, c1900, 24in (61cm) high.

£2,550–3,050 WAD

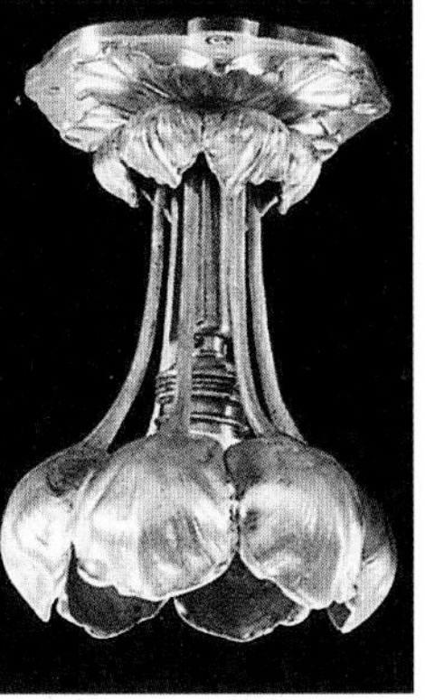

A pair of gilt-bronze ceiling lights, in the form of flowerheads, early 20thC, 8in (20.5cm) high.

£1,400–1,650 S(O)

A Classique glass table lamp, the shade reverse-painted with a scene of the setting sun, c1915, 23in (58.5cm) high.

£800–960 JAA

TIFFANY

A Tiffany & Co **silver bowl,** the rim cast in high relief with clover and leaves, America, c1895, 8in (20.5cm) diam.

£850–950 SHa

◀ **A Tiffany Studios Favrile glass and bronze Grapevine double photograph frame,** marked, with monogram 'W', America, c1910, 9½ x 15½in (24 x 39.5cm).

£3,900–4,650 S(NY)

A Tiffany Studios Favrile glass, silver and brass photograph frame, by Leslie Nash, inscribed mark, America, 1911, 9¼ x 7in (23.5 x 18cm).

£6,500–7,800 S(NY)

This is apparently a unique design by Leslie Nash.

A Tiffany Studios gilt and glass table lamp, shade stamped, impressed mark, slight damage, America, early 20thC, 25in (63.5cm) high.

£10,200–12,200 SK

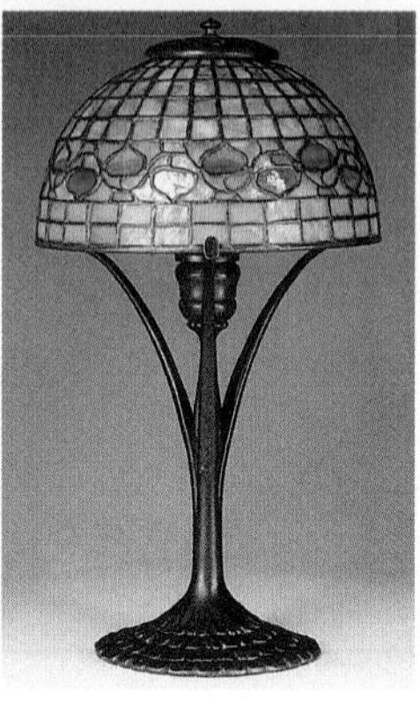

A Tiffany Studios Acorn lamp, slight damage, rewired, signed, America, early 20thC, 17in (43cm) high.

£5,300–6,300 JDJ

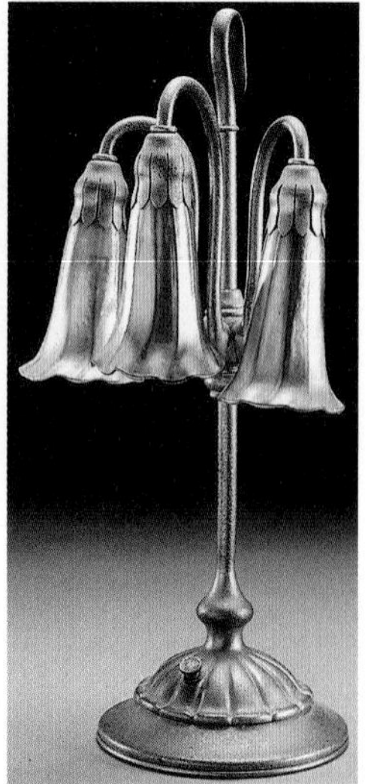

A Tiffany Studios Favrile gilt-bronze and glass Lily table lamp, each shade inscribed 'LCT Favrile', signed, America, c1910, 16½in (42cm) high.

£4,450–5,300 JAA

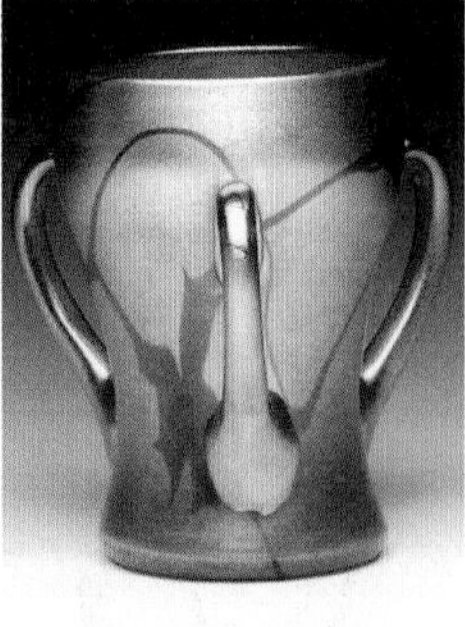

A Tiffany Studios Favrile glass loving cup, the iridescent glaze decorated with leaves and vines, applied with three handles, slight damage, signed, America, early 20thC, 5in (12.5cm) high.

£430–510 JDJ

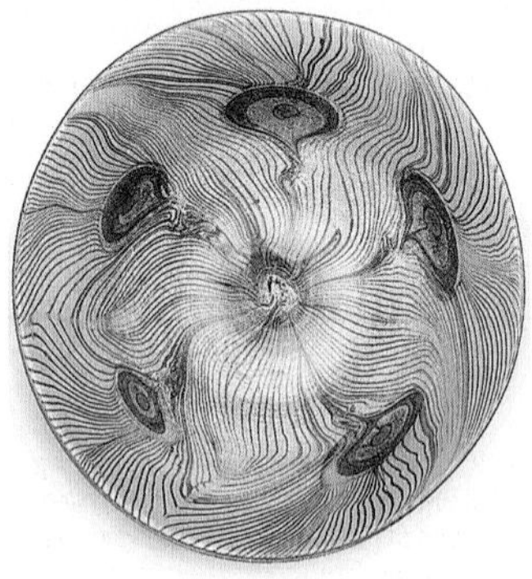

A Tiffany Studios Favrile glass Peacock plate, engraved 'L.C.T. K2409', America, c1896, 6¼in (16cm) diam.

£5,500–6,600 S(NY)

A set of 12 Tiffany & Co Century dinner plates and ten side plates, designed by Arthur L. Barney, with stepped applied blocks linked by incised lines, each monogrammed 'LSR' and marked and numbered to the reverse, America, c1940, dinner plate 9in (23cm) wide.

£13,000–15,600 S(NY)

Ex-Estate of Laurance S. Rockefeller.
For information about this sale please see p20.

◀ **A Tiffany & Co sterling silver and metal Japanese-style teapot,** America, 1877–78, 7½in (19cm) wide.

£2,700–3,000 ARG

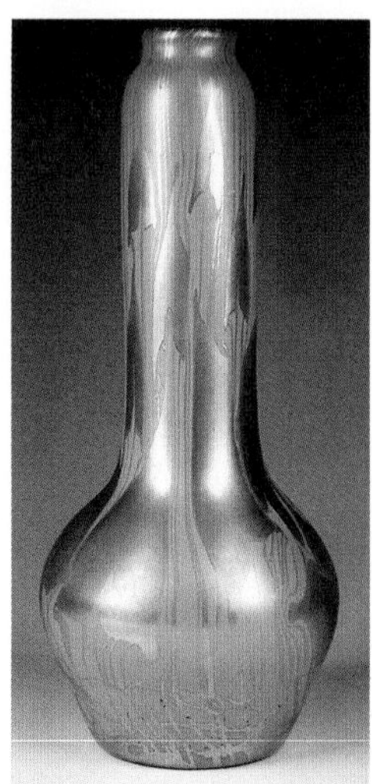

▶ **A Tiffany Studios Favrile glass vase,** the iridescent surface decorated with a pulled heart and vine design, slight damage, signed, American, early 20thC, 21in (53.5cm) high.

£9,350–11,200 JDJ

ART NOUVEAU METALWARE

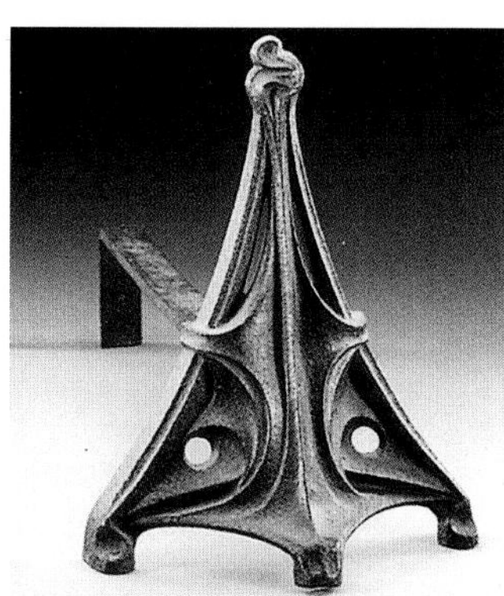

A pair of wrought-iron andirons, by Hector Guimard, with stylized foliate facings, stamped marks, France, c1900, 10½in (26.5cm) high.

£3,000–3,600 S(O)

Guimard is well known for his bronze entrances to the Paris Metro.

A pewter, silver-plated and glass biscuit barrel, Germany, 1900–10, 4½in (11.5cm) diam.

£400–450 TA2

A Kayserzinn pewter liquor bottle, by Hugo Leven, Germany, c1900, 9in (23cm) high.

£250–280 NAW

A silver two-handled bowl, by E. Connell, possibly designed by Kate Harris, the bowl with hammered decoration and an inscription, the scroll handles inset with harebells, with a glass liner, London 1903, 10in (25.5cm) wide, 9oz.

£1,750–2,100 HYD

A WMF silver-plated jewellery box, cast with scrolling tendrils and maidens' faces, Germany, c1900, 6in (15cm) wide.

£540–600 PVD

A Liberty Tudric pewter biscuit box, designed by Archibald Knox, impressed mark, c1902, 5in (12.5cm) high.

£630–700 RUSK

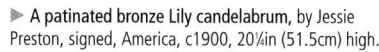

A patinated bronze Lily candelabrum, by Jessie Preston, signed, America, c1900, 20¼in (51.5cm) high.

£21,100–25,300 S(NY)

Jessie Preston was a well-known metalsmith and artist working in Chicago. She studied at the Art Institute of Chicago, where she exhibited her work between 1902 and 1911, and operated a studio in Chicago's Fine Arts Building from 1900 to 1918. Her repertoire is comparatively limited, and surviving examples of her metalwork are exceedingly rare. Although best known for her unique candlestick designs, Preston's elaborate floriform candelabra represent her most accomplished masterworks in the medium. Their sinuous, graceful lines clearly display her strong connection to the Art Nouveau style. This candelabrum represents the only known example executed by Preston in this impressive large size, although three smaller-scale examples of the design are currently known.

A silver dish, relief-decorated with poppies, with pierced sides, on three feet, marked, Austria, Vienna, c1900, 14in (35.5cm) wide.

£510–610 DORO

LOCATE THE SOURCE

The source of each illustration in Miller's can be found by checking the code letters below each caption with the Key to Illustrations, pages 746–753.

A La Société des Artistes Français gilt-bronze dish, by Albert Marionnet, France, c1905, 5in (12.5cm) diam.

£200–230 CHAC

A WMF pewter dish, with a figural handle, c1905, 12½in (32cm) wide.
£610–680 ⊞ SHa

WMF

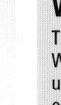

The German company Württembergische Metallwarenfabrik, usually known as WMF, was established in 1880 and was one of the most successful producers of commercial Art Nouveau wares in Continental pewter, an electroplated metal alloy similar to Britannia metal. They specialized in decorative pieces that were typically embellished with trailing foliage and sinuous women with tumbling locks and diaphanous garments.

A silver dish, by William Hutton & Sons, set with opals, London 1902, 4in (10cm) diam.
£850–950 ⊞ ANO

An embossed silver and enamel photograph frame, by William Hutton, with an easel back, Birmingham 1904, 8in (20.5cm) high.
£880–1,050 DN(HAM)

An embossed silver photograph frame, by William Comyns, decorated with clover, London 1908, 22 x 18in (56 x 45.5cm).
£450–500 ⊞ RICC

An Orivit gilded pewter-mounted jar, the glass acid-etched and decorated with enamels, Germany, c1905, 7in (18cm) high.
£290–330 ⊞ CHAC

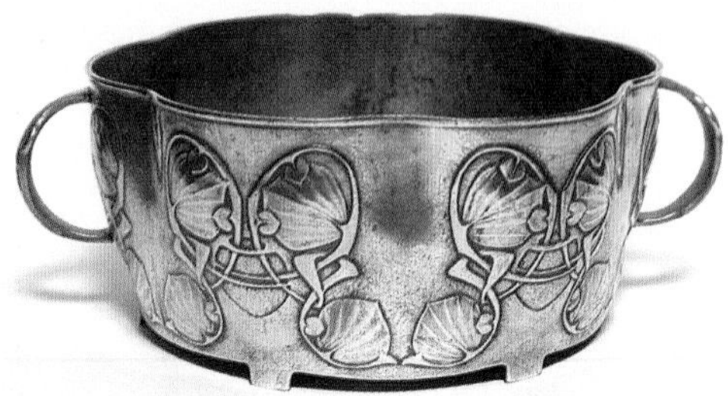

A Liberty Tudric pewter jardinière, designed by Archibald Knox, decorated with stylized foliage, impressed mark, c1904, 9in (23cm) diam.
£1,350–1,500 ⊞ RUSK

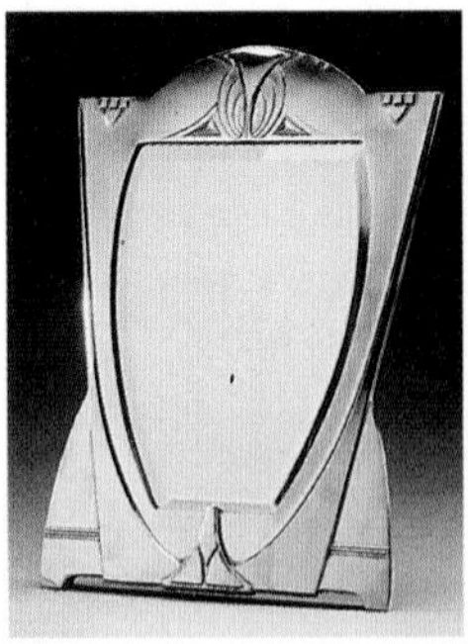

◄ **A WMF silvered-pewter Secessionist-style easel mirror,** with a bevelled plate, stamped mark, Germany, early 20thC, 15½in (39.5cm) high.
£1,200–1,400 S(O)

A silver-plated claret jug, by William Hutton & Sons, 1900–10, 11in (28cm) high.
£1,600–1,800 ⊞ TA2

A WMF copper jug, with brass finial and handle, Germany, c1900, 12in (30.5cm) high.
£145–165 ⊞ CHAC

► **A WMF silver-plated wall plaque,** Germany, c1905, 12in (30.5cm) diam.
£400–450 ⊞ NAW

A WMF copper and brass punchbowl and cover, Germany, c1900, 13in (33cm) high.
£310–350 ⊞ TA2

A silver coffee service, comprising six cup-holders with Royal Doulton flambé liners, six matching silver plates and spoons, one liner missing, another damaged, retailer's mark for James Ramsay, Dundee, Sheffield 1907, cups 2½in (6.5cm) high, in a fitted case.

£230–270 Hal

A WMF silvered-pewter tea and coffee service, comprising five pieces, decorated with ivy leaves and stylized foliate scrolls, stamped marks, Germany, early 20thC, tray 25¼in (64cm) wide.

£2,150–2,550 S(O)

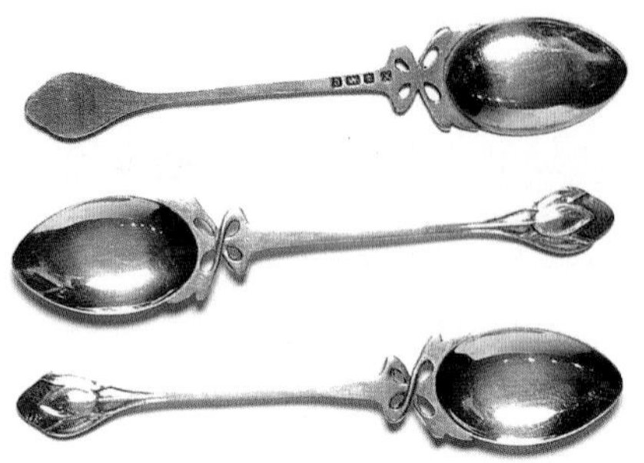

A set of six Liberty silver spoons, with pierced decoration, Birmingham 1902, 4½in (11.5cm) long.

£630–700 WAC

A silver Magnolia Blossom tea and coffee service, by Georg Jensen, comprising three pieces, with ivory handles, designed 1905, Denmark, Copenhagen, 1933–34, coffee pot 8in (20.5cm) high.

£3,900–4,650 BUK

An Orivit pewter and mahogany tray, Germany, c1900, 17in (43cm) wide.

£210–240 WAC

Orivit was founded in Cologne in 1894 by Wilhelm Schmitz. It was taken over by WMF in 1905.

For more silver antiques
see our Silver section on pages 278–307

A silver-mounted glass vase, by Bolin, Russia, Moscow, c1900, 6¼in (15.5cm) high.

£14,100–16,900 BUK(F)

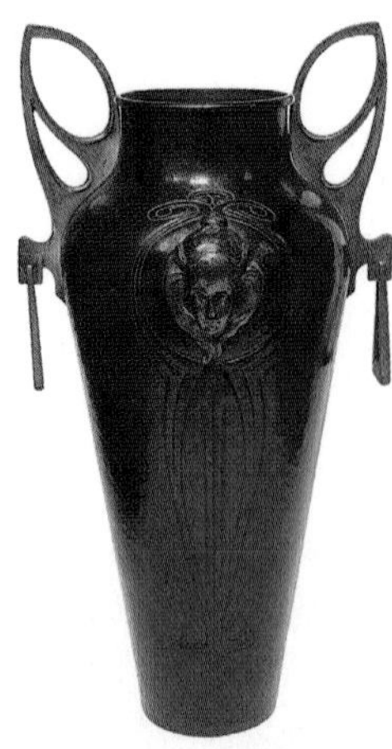

A WMF copper and bronze vase, by Albert Mayer, signed, Germany, c1900, 24in (61cm) high.

£1,400–1,600 TA2

A WMF pewter *vide poche*, Germany, c1906, 10in (25.5cm) wide.

£900–1,000 NAW

A WMF copper and brass wine cooler, Germany, c1900, 8in (20.5cm) high.

£145–165 CHAC

A WMF pewter wine cooler, cast with a mermaid, with associated glass liner, stamped marks, Germany, early 20thC, 12½in (32cm) high.

£2,150–2,550 S(O)

ART DECO CERAMICS

◄ **A Boch Frères earthenware vase,** designed by Charles Catteau, enamelled with a deer on a crackled ground, Belgium, c1925, 8¾in (22cm) high.

£330–390 G(L)

The Belgian ceramics firm Boch Frères (established 1841), was a branch of the German company Villeroy & Boch.

► **A Burleigh Ware jug,** by Harold Bennett, with tube-lined waterlily decoration, painted and printed marks to base, signed, 1930s, 9in (23cm) high.

£165–195 DN

A Burleigh Ware jug, the front decorated with guardsmen, the reverse with a sentry box, 1930s, 8in (20.5cm) high.

£1,950–2,200 GaL

CHARLOTTE RHEAD

Charlotte Rhead was employed by several Staffordshire pottery factories before joining her father Frederick Rhead at Wood & Sons of Burslem, producers of Bursley Ware, in 1912. In 1926 she moved to Burgess & Leigh who produced Burleigh Ware and by 1937 had moved again to A. G. Richardson, makers of Crown Ducal pottery. Finally, in 1941 she worked once more for Wood's, at H. J. Wood in Burslem.

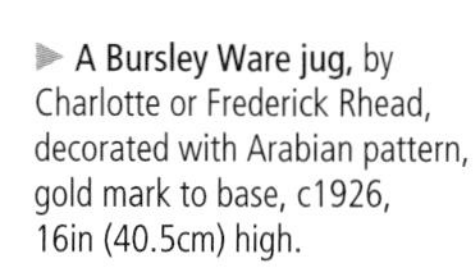

► **A Bursley Ware jug,** by Charlotte or Frederick Rhead, decorated with Arabian pattern, gold mark to base, c1926, 16in (40.5cm) high.

£370–440 LT

A Bursley Ware jug, by Charlotte Rhead, with tube-lined decoration, signed, c1930, 9¾in (24.5cm) high.

£140–165 AMB

A Carlton Ware Orchard lustre vase, 1920s, 11in (28cm) high.

£360–400 BEV

A Carter, Stabler & Adams jug, designed by Truda Carter, shape No. 897, probably painted by Mary Brown, impressed mark, 1926–34, 9¾in (25cm) high.

£390–460 DN(HAM)

Carter & Co was founded in Poole, Dorset in 1873, adopting the combined names of its partners, Carter, Stabler & Adams, upon its expansion in 1921. It was not until 1963 that the trade name of Poole Pottery was adopted.

A Carter, Stabler & Adams vase, designed by Truda Carter, decorated in EP pattern of stylized foliage by Mary Brown, impressed mark and shape no. 911, artist's monogram, 1921–34, 8¼in (21cm) high.

£590–700 Hal

A Susie Cooper jug, hand-painted with a geometric design, early 1930s, 8in (20.5cm) high.

£990–1,100 GaL

A Susie Cooper teapot, hand-painted with a geometric design, c1930, 5in (12.5cm) high.

£580–650 BEV

► **A Fieldings Crown Devon vase,** decorated with Spider's Web pattern, 1930s, 10in (25.5cm) high.

£450–500 EAn

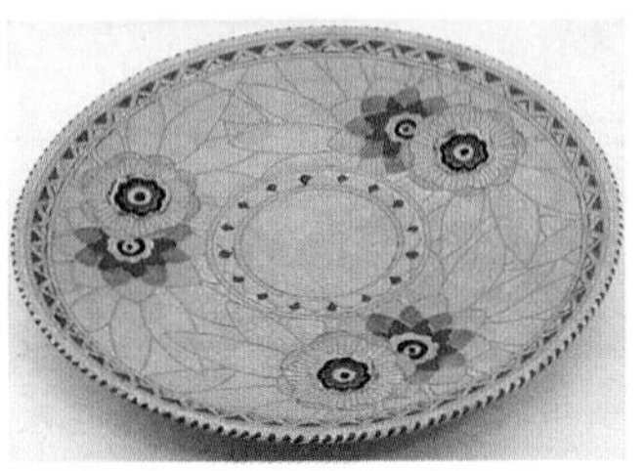

A Crown Ducal earthenware charger, by Charlotte Rhead, decorated with Rhodian pattern, c1933, 17½in (44.5cm) diam.

£220–260 L&E

A Crown Ducal vase, possibly by Charlotte Rhead, decorated with Persian Rose pattern, c1930, 8in (20.5cm) high.

£85–95 GSA

A Richard Ginori lamp base, probably designed by Gio Ponti, decorated with pipes, scissors, spectacles and keys on a chequered ground, printed mark 'S. Cristoforo', Italy, 1923–30, 11in (28cm) high.

£3,000–3,600 S

A Goldscheider wall mask, Austria, early 1930s, 11in (28cm) high.

£1,400–1,600 GaL

◄ **A Theodore Haviland & Co tea service,** designed by Edouard Marcel Sandoz, comprising four pieces, France, Limoges, c1930, teapot 8in (20.5cm) high.

£410–490 AAT

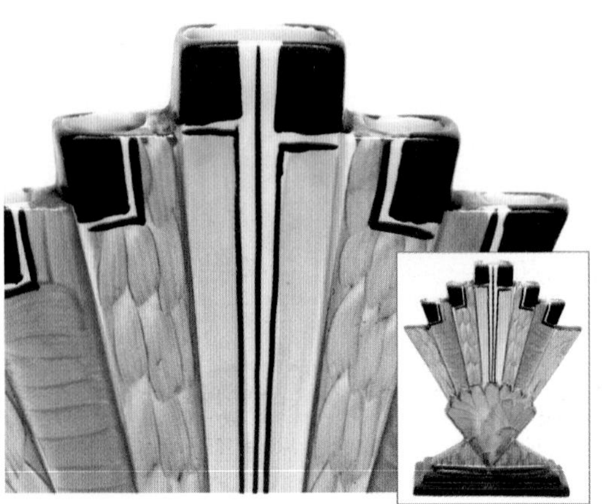

◄ **A Myott fan vase,** 1930s, 10in (25.5cm) high.

£490–550 GaL

► **A Newcomb College vase,** by Jonathan Hunt, decorated by Anna Frances Simpson, impressed mark, date code and artist's monogram, America, date code for 1929, 3¼in (8.5cm) high.

£1,700–2,000 CINN

A Newcomb College cabinet vase, carved by Sadie Irvine with Spanish moss and oak trees, America, 1931, 2¼in (5.5cm) high.

£1,250–1,500 DRO(C)

American Art pottery

Although American Art pottery doesn't have universal appeal it enjoys very strong interest in the home market. The most prestigious and prolific manufacturer was the Rookwood factory and there is an extraordinary variety of high-quality pieces available to the collector.

◄ **A Pilkington's Royal Lancastrian jar,** designed by William Salter Mycock, c1925, 7in (18cm) high.

£360–400 HUN

A Rookwood vase, decorated by Sara Sax, decorated with forsythia blossoms under French Red glaze, marked, artist's monogram, America, 1922, 9½in (24cm) high.

£11,400–13,600 CINN

A Rookwood vase, decorated by Kataro Shirayamadani with lobsters under a Black Opal glaze, shape No. 670 C, signed and marked, America, 1925, 9¾in (25cm) high.

£10,300–12,300 CINN

Works by this Japanese artist are very desirable, hence the high price of any piece of Rookwood decorated by him.

A Rookwood vase, decorated with an embossed design, impressed marks, America, dated 1925, 9½in (24cm) high.

£200–240 JAA

A Rookwood vase, by William Hentschel, decorated with a nude, antelopes and geese, hole drilled in base, marked, America, c1929, 13½in (34.5cm) high.

£3,000–3,600 DRO(C)

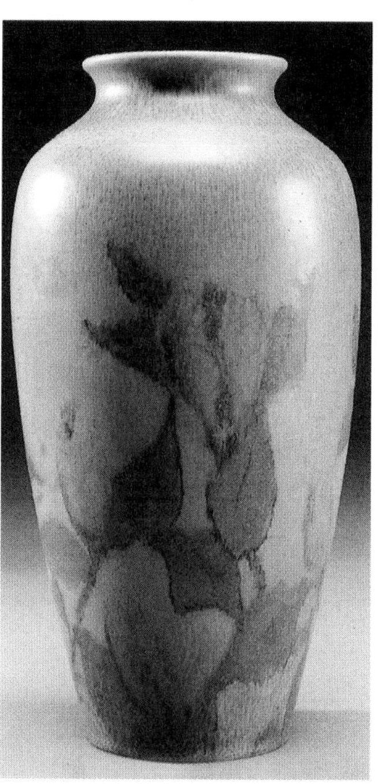

A Rookwood pottery vase, decorated by Jens Jensen with stylized flowers and leafy stems and a matt glaze, stamped mark, initialled, America, c1929, 13in (33cm) high.

£890–1,050 JAA

A Rookwood vase, painted by Lorinda Epply with four panels decorated with stylized floral designs, America, 1930, 12in (30.5cm) high.

£2,050–2,450 TREA

A Rookwood vase, moulded with floral decoration, with a matt glaze, marked, America, dated 1931, 4¼in (11cm) high.

£175–210 CINN

► **A Rookwood vase,** painted by Jens Jensen with hibiscus blooms and leaves, marked, America, dated 1931, 12½in (32cm) high.

£2,700–3,200 DRO(C)

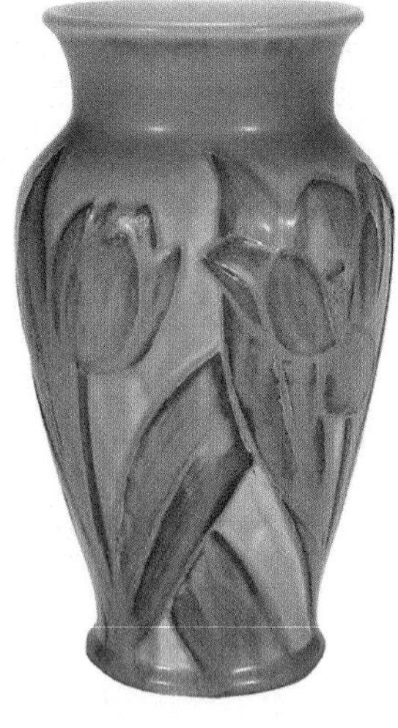

A Rookwood vase, decorated by Kataro Shirayamadani, carved and painted with tulips, incised marks, America, 1933, 7½in (19cm) high.

£2,000–2,400 CINN

A Victor Schreckengost earthenware Jazz bowl, by Cowan Pottery, impressed mark, America, c1931, 17in (43cm) diam.

£104,000–124,000 S(NY)

This fine example of Viktor Schreckengost's famous Jazz bowl from Cowan's second production series displays an elegantly fired rim and intensely saturated aqua blue glaze. This is one of three rare Jazz bowls offered at auction by Sotheby's since December 2003.

A Shelley part tea service, comprising 14 pieces, printed with stylized scrolling foliage and hand-painted with berries, pattern No. 11575, printed marks, 1925–40.

£260–310 PF

Style is very important with Shelley wares, as can be seen with this 14-piece tea service. This design is based on shapes often found in silver pieces and is not as popular as other Shelley tea or coffee services of a more quintessentially Art Deco style.

A Wedgwood black basalt vase, by Keith Murray, the upper body decorated with horizontal lines, signed, impressed marks, 1930s, 8in (20.5cm) high.

£1,100–1,300 FLDA

◄ **A Wedgwood lustre bowl,** decorated with Hummingbird pattern, 1914–30, 19in (48.5cm) diam.

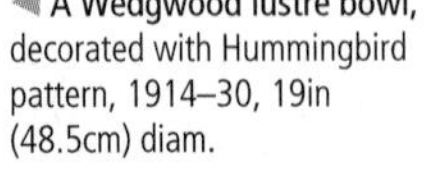

£810–900 Scot

► **A Weller LaSa vase,** with an iridescent glaze and decorated with mountains and trees, America, c1925, 8½in (21.5cm) high.

£260–310 JDJ

It was typical for art pottery and art glass companies to make up names for their wares. LaSa ware was designed by Weller's art director John Lessell and his assistant Art Wagner. It is possible that the name was made up of L for Lessell, a for Art and Sa, the initials of Samuel A. Weller's forenames. Another line produced by Weller was Louwelsa, Lou from the first three letters of his daughter's name, wel from Weller and sa from Weller's initials.

CLARICE CLIFF

A Clarice Cliff Conical bowl, decorated with Applique Orange Lucerne pattern, printed mark, 1930–31, 6in (15cm) diam.

£1,000–1,200 WW

A Clarice Cliff Fantasque bowl, decorated with Autumn pattern, 1930–34, 8in (20.5cm) diam.

£175–210 HAD

A Clarice Cliff Fantasque fruit bowl, decorated with Xavier pattern, printed mark, 1932–34, 7in (18cm) diam.

£370–440 N

A Clarice Cliff Bizarre bowl, decorated with Green Erin pattern, slight damage, 1933–34, 7¾in (19.5cm) diam.

£300–360 CHTR

Clarice Cliff (1899–1972)

Clarice Cliff started work in the Staffordshire potteries at the age of 13 and in 1916 was apprenticed to A. J. Wilkinson, later becoming art director at the Royal Staffordshire works and subsidiary Newport Pottery. At the latter she was given her own studio and in 1928/9 launched her famous Bizarre wares, distinguished by use of geometric blocks of bright colours. They were aimed at brightening the lives of 'the British housewives (who) deserved more colour in their lives'. She was a talented and innovative designer and pieces from the factories bore her facsimile signature until 1964. In 1940 she married her boss, Colley Shorter, and their business partnership was highly successful for both parties. Following his death in 1963 she sold the factory to Midwinter and retired in 1965.

A Clarice Cliff Bizarre table centrepiece, decorated with Rhodanthe pattern, slight damage, printed marks, 1934–41, 20in (51cm) wide.

£590–700 RTo

► A Clarice Cliff bowl, decorated with Cherry Blossom pattern, printed mark, 1935–36, 9½in (24cm) diam.

£340–400 BAM(M)

A Clarice Cliff charger, based on an Original Bizarre pattern, c1930, 9¾in (25cm) diam.

£210–250 BAM(M)

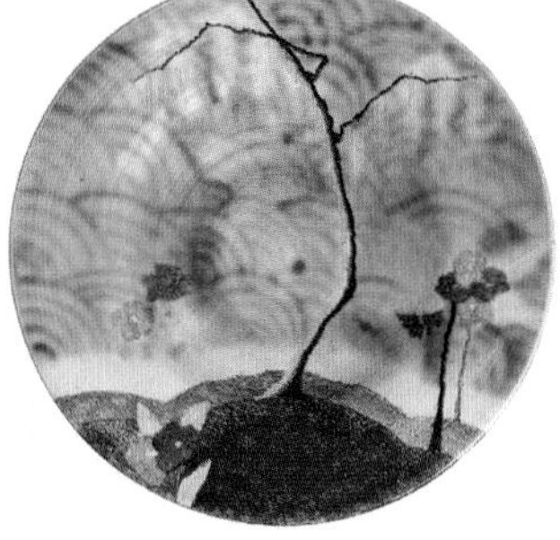

A Clarice Cliff charger, decorated with Inspiration Garden pattern, 1931, 13in (33cm) diam.

£900–1,000 TDG

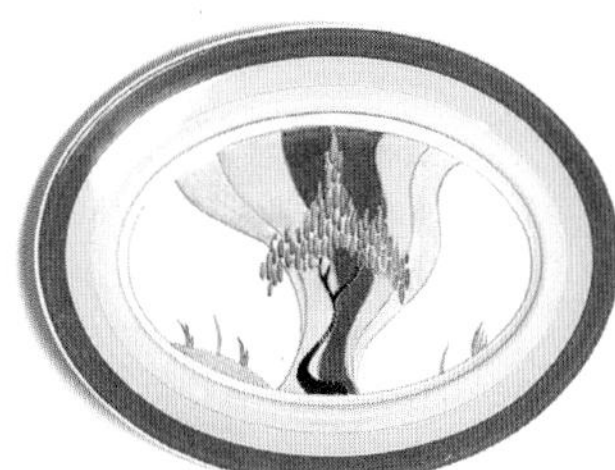

A Clarice Cliff charger, decorated with Windbells pattern, 1933–34, 12in (30.5cm) wide.

£450–500 BD

A Clarice Cliff Bizarre charger, decorated with Japan pattern, printed mark, 1933–44, 16½in (42cm) wide.

£750–900 AH

A Clarice Cliff Bizarre jardinière, decorated with Gay Day pattern, slight damage, 1930–34, 3½in (9cm) high.

£120–140 GTH

A Clarice Cliff jug and bowl set, decorated with Cherry pattern, gold mark, c1929, jug 10in (25.5cm) high.

£1,350–1,500 HEW

A Clarice Cliff Lotus jug, decorated with Secrets pattern, c1930, 12in (30.5cm) high.

£1,800–2,000 BD

A Clarice Cliff Bizarre Isis jug, decorated with Crest pattern, Newport mark, c1933, 9¾in (25cm) high.

£1,000–1,200 DN(HAM)

Only 12 pieces are known to have been produced in this experimental pattern.

A Clarice Cliff Bizarre honey pot, decorated with Nasturtium pattern, c1934, 4in (10cm) high.

£310–350 HUM

A Clarice Cliff Bizarre preserve pot, decorated with Autumn pattern, 1930–31, 3¾in (9.5cm) high.

£280–330 HAD

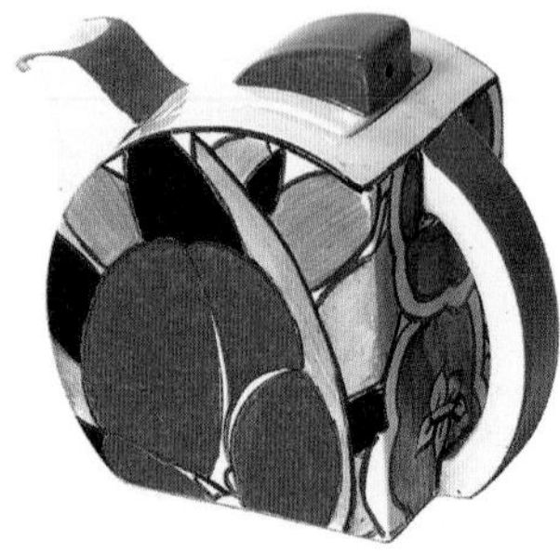

A Clarice Cliff Stamford tea pot, decorated with Gardenia pattern, 1932–33, 5in (12.5cm) high.

£2,050–2,300 HEW

LOCATE THE SOURCE

The source of each illustration in Miller's can be found by checking the code letters below each caption with the Key to Illustrations, pages 746–753.

A Clarice Cliff Bizarre coffee service, comprising 15 pieces, decorated with Sunshine pattern, c1930, coffee pot 7in (18cm) high.

£820–980 AH

A Clarice Cliff Original Bizarre coffee service, comprising 15 pieces, Newport mark, c1930.

£1,200–1,400 PFK

A Clarice Cliff Bizarre coffee service, decorated with House and Bridge pattern, comprising 13 pieces, 1931–33.

£1,750–2,100 E

A Clarice Cliff Bizarre tea-for-two, comprising eight pieces, decorated with Windbells pattern, early 1930s, teapot 4½in (11.5cm) high.

£3,400–3,800 GaL

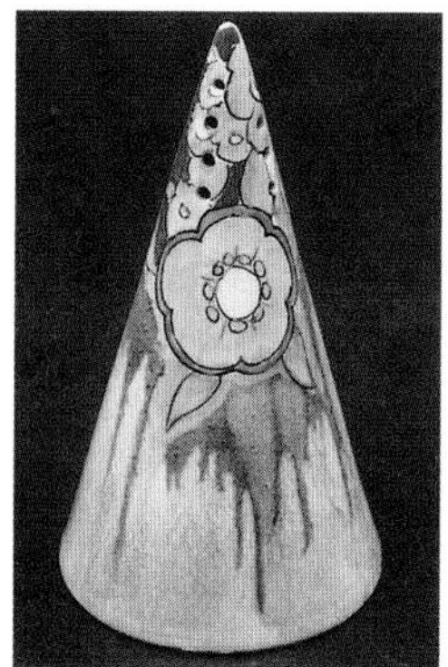

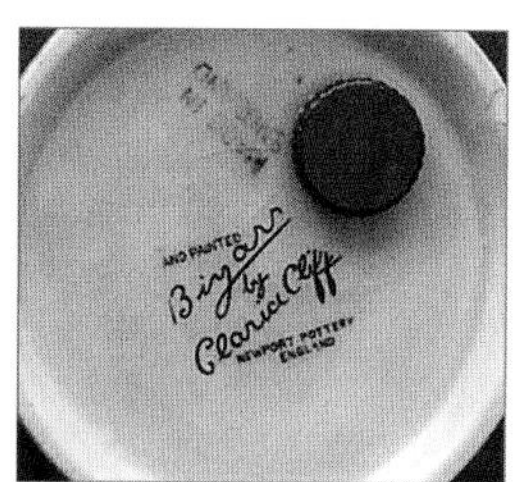

A Clarice Cliff Conical sugar sifter, decorated with Jonquil pattern, printed Newport Pottery mark, c1933, 5½in (14cm) high.

£370–440 DN(BR)

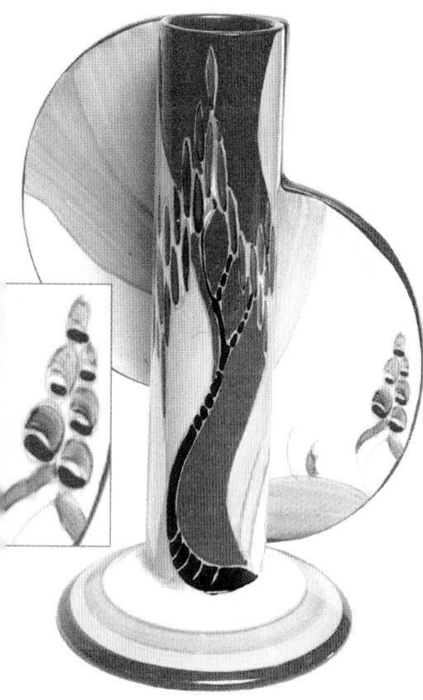

A Clarice Cliff vase, decorated with Windbells pattern, shape 465, c1930, 9½in (24cm) high.

£4,500–5,000 BD

The fact that this is a rare shape has significantly increased the value of this vase.

A Clarice Cliff Bizarre vase, shape 365, printed and impressed marks, c1930, 8¼in (21cm) high.

£260–310 Hal

A Clarice Cliff Isis vase, decorated with Melon pattern, 1930–31, 12in (30.5cm) high.

£2,700–3,000 HEW

The Melon pattern is also known as Picasso Fruit pattern.

Items in the Clarice Cliff section have been arranged in object order.

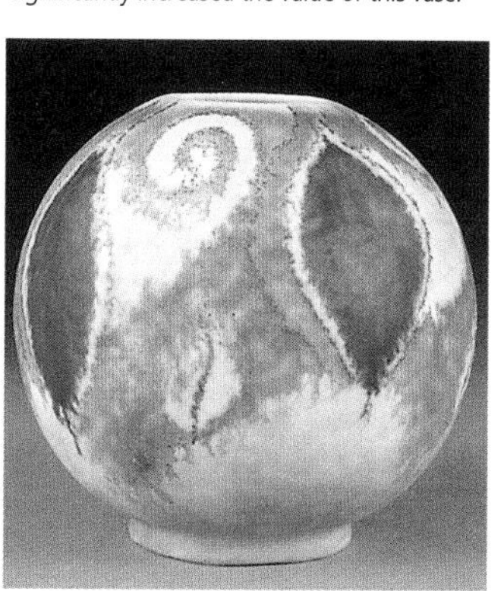

◀ **A Clarice Cliff Inspiration vase,** decorated with Persian pattern, shape 370, impressed mark, 1930–31, 6in (15cm) high.

£760–910 N

▶ **A Clarice Cliff vase,** Shape 635, decorated with Blue Firs pattern, 1933–37, 7in (18cm) high.

£800–960 LAY

ART DECO CLOCKS

An iron mantel timepiece, by Edgar Brandt, the case pierced with stylized flowers, leaves and scrolls, on a marble base with bronze feet, stamped mark, France, c1925, 11½in (29cm) high.

£12,000–14,400 S

► **A German School silver metal and enamel Poche Surprise timpiece,** stamped '0.935', '262914, 'Brevete' and maker's marks, c1930, 2in (5cm) long.

£2,000–2,400 S

A walnut mantel clock, the eight-day movement striking the hours and half-hours, the case inlaid with ebony and sycamore, Germany, c1930, 10in (25.5cm) wide.

£155–175 HEM

ART DECO FURNITURE

► **A birch and rosewood bookcase,** with three drawers, Sweden, 1930s, 47in (119.5cm) wide.

£720–800 PI

A Rowley Gallery lacquered cabinet, with combed decoration to the front and top, remains of label, c1935, 38¾in (98.5cm) wide.

£340–400 WW

◄ **A pair of karelian birch-veneered bedside cabinets,** each with a three-quarter gallery above two cupboard doors, c1940, 19in (48cm) wide.

£1,100–1,300 S

A pair of walnut-veneered bedside cabinets, 1930s, 26in (66cm) high.

£400–450 OCA

► **An Asprey mahogany cocktail cabinet,** c1925, 23in (58.5cm) high.

£950–1,100 TDG

A burr-walnut cocktail cabinet, with fluted front, on a plinth base, c1930, 64½in (164cm) high.

£4,500–5,000 TDG

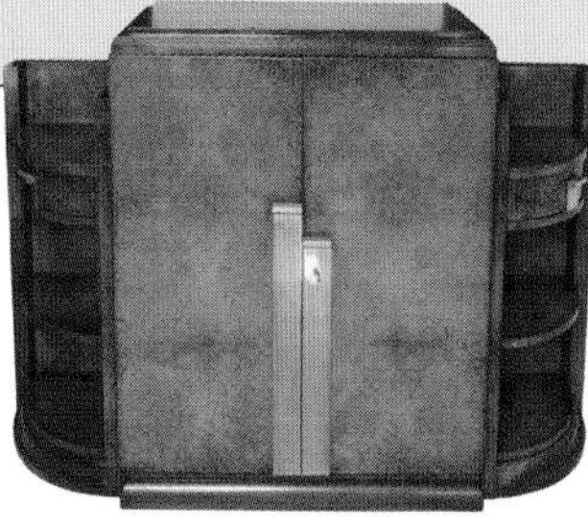

An amboyna side cabinet, with a marble top, France, c1930, 53¼in (135.5cm) wide.

£3,500–3,900 TDG

A teak, leather and brass easy chair, by Fritz Henningsen, Denmark, Copenhagen, 1930s.

£9,700–11,600 S(NY)

◀ **A pair of mahogany and gilt-bronze armchairs,** designed by Maurice Pré, manufactured by Neveu, Nelson and Bernaux, with original Jacquard tapestry by Cornille, France, c1934.

£15,600–18,700 S(NY)

These chairs were made for the first class dining room of SS Normandie.

A sycamore and leather club armchair, designed by Jean-Michel Frank, marked, manufactured by Chanaux & Co, 1930s.

£91,000–109,000 S(NY)

Jean-Michel Frank (1895–1941) was an interior decorator who also designed furniture. From 1927 he worked closely with fellow designer and craftsman, Adolphe Chanaux. Primarily concerned with form, his design and execution shows a strong respect for French traditionalism. Keen on earth tones, he worked mainly in sycamore and ebony and used ivory wherever possible. For decorative effect, exotic wood grains and sumptuous veneers such as sharkskin and vellum parchment were preferred to relief ornamentation. Over the past few years, pieces by Frank have been highly sought after by collectors and investors.

A rosewood, leather and metal swivel chair, by Jacques-Emile Ruhlmann, branded mark, France, c1925.

£24,400–29,200 S(NY)

◀ **A pair of painted and carved beech-wood and parcel-gilt bergères,** the carved stiles with gilt spiral detail, on toupie feet, upholstered in damask, France, 1925–1950.

£270–320 NOA

▶ **A pair of vinyl club armchairs,** France, 1930s.

£950–1,100 TREA

A walnut kneehole desk, by Heal & Son, the nine drawers with chrome-plated handles, ivorine label, c1930, 42½in (108cm) wide.

£500–600 DN

A bird's-eye maple pedestal desk, with three drawers and a cupboard door, c1930, 42in (106.5cm) wide.

£1,000–1,150 TDG

A bird's-eye maple dressing table, c1930, 48in (122cm) wide.

£450–500 BURA

A wrought-iron hall stand, the mirror plate surmounted by a basket of roses and flanked by pierced scrolls, France, c1930, 47¼in (120cm) wide.

£1,200–1,400 S

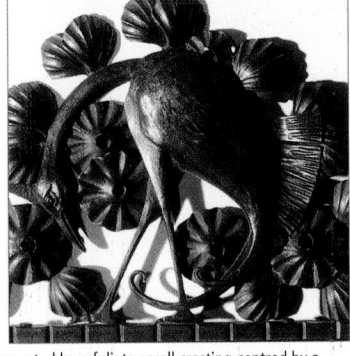

A wrought-iron mirror, by Raymond Subes, the plate surmounted by a foliate scroll cresting centred by a bird, France, c1925, 74½in (185cm) high.

£8,400–10,000 S

Raymond Subes (1893–1970) is one of the most renowned French metalworkers of the Art Deco period. In 1919 he became director of the metal workshop of Borderel et Robert, a major architectural construction company. Most of his work was on government commissions, notably a number of important ocean liners to which he contributed wall decorations and gilded metalwork. Despite their hand-finished look, his products were mainly mass-produced using industrial methods. This piece was manufactured by Borderel et Robert and was exhibited by Subes at the 1925 Paris Exposition Internationale des Arts Décoratifs et Industriels Modernes.

A pewter mirror, by Svenskt Tenn, surmounted by crossed laurel leaves, minor damage, stamped mark, Sweden, 1930, 24½ x 16¼in (62 x 41.5cm).

£1,550–1,850 BUK

A pair of chrome wall mirrors, the bevelled plates surrounded by four bands separated by balls, c1930, 26½in (67.5cm) diam.

£9,000–10,800 S

A lacquered wood and metal three-fold screen, by Jean Dunand, marked, France, c1923, 70½in (179cm) wide.

£21,100–25,300 S(NY)

Jean Dunand (1877–1942) was from Switzerland but lived in Paris from 1896. He was a prolific metalworker, lacquerist and furniture designer. He produced high-quality, hand-made pieces for the most exclusive end of the market, mainly to special commission. His early work featured naturalistic designs, but later his style became more geometric.

▶ **A wrought-iron fire screen,** by Edgar Brandt, stamped, France, 1929–32, 19¾in (50cm) wide.

£8,400–10,000 S(NY)

Edgar Brandt (1880–1960) was one of the leading metalworkers of the Art Deco period, both in Paris and New York, where he opened Ferrobrandt Inc, a company that executed commissions for several buildings and produced a range of metalwares. Brandt made great use of the decorative elements of wrought iron, and Art Deco-type scrolls are a common feature. His work was acclaimed in 1925 when he co-designed the Porte d'Honneur for the Paris Exhibition.

A burr-walnut cocktail sideboard, by H. & L. Epstein, with a fall-front compartment and fluted front, c1930, 42½in (108cm) high.

£2,950–3,300 TDG

◀ **A walnut and Macassar ebony sideboard,** c1930, 77in (195.5cm) wide.

£4,000–4,500 TDG

A burr-elm sideboard, with reeded ebonized columns, 1930s, 65in (165cm) wide.

£1,450–1,650 ⊞ OCA

A burr-walnut sofa, by Waring & Gillow, c1930, 97in (246.5cm) wide.

£3,150–3,500 ⊞ TDG

An amboyna and rosewood-veneered folio stand, the hinged side with gilt-metal supports, c1925, 18¼in (46.5cm) wide.

£5,000–6,000 S

◄ **A walnut and macassar ebony-inlaid dining suite,** c1930.

£5,300–5,900 ⊞ TDG

► **A Macassar ebony and ivory Colonette centre table,** by Jacques-Emile Ruhlmann, branded mark, France, c1923, 31¾in (80.5cm) diam.

£72,000–86,000 S(NY)

A model of this table was admired by millions of visitors at the Exposition Internationale des Arts Décoratifs *in Paris in 1925. It was situated in the salon of the famous Hotel du Collectionneur, Ruhlmann's own pavilion at the exhibition, with a bronze model of François Pompon's* Ours Blanc *placed on the top.*

Jacques-Emile Ruhlmann

Initially a painter, Jacques-Emile Ruhlmann (1879–1933) became the best known French cabinet-maker of his day. He designed for a rich and exclusive clientele, using exotic woods and other expensive materials. After WWI he took over his father's successful building firm, Ruhlmann et Laurent, and expanded it with workshops devoted to furniture and other aspects of interior design.

A satin-birch table, c1935, 23in (58.5cm) diam.

£470–530 ⊞ TDG

◄ **A Macassar ebony, nickel-plated-bronze, glass and leather swivel cocktail table,** by Paul Dupré-Lafon, France, c1935, 36½in (93cm) wide.

£26,000–31,000 S(NY)

A rosewood cocktail table, the top on four ebonized scroll supports, France, c1920, 27in (68.5cm) diam.

£950–1,100 NOA

► **A burr-maple console table,** with two short drawers, c1930, 46½in (118cm) wide.

£2,500–3,000 S

A mahogany, Macassar ebony and amboyna fold-over games table, with silvered-bronze mounts, the reverse fitted with a drawer and an extension leg, the baize top with a gilt-tooled leather edge, France, c1920, 31½in (80cm) wide.

£1,750–2,100 NOA

A walnut and satinwood games table, 1930s, 22in (56cm) diam.

£610–680 TDG

A burr-walnut nest of tables, the main table above four quarter-shaped tables, c1930, large table 22in (56cm) diam.

£210–240 HEM

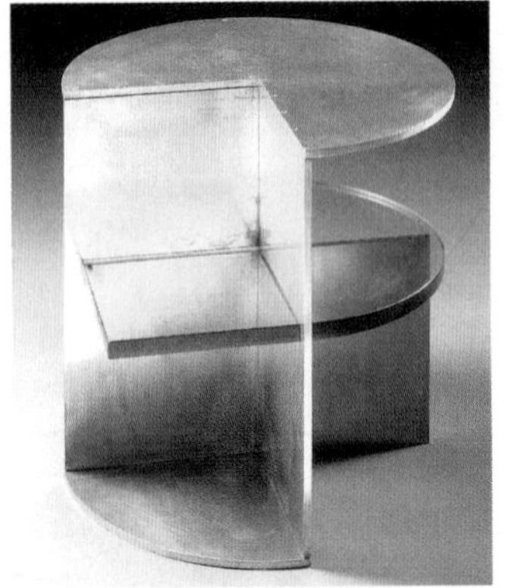

◄ **An aluminium and glass occasional table,** by Louis Sognot for Décoration Intérieure Moderne, the segmented top above a plate glass mid-tier, on an X-form support, France, c1928, 23¾in (60.5cm) diam.

£53,000–64,000 S

Décoration Intérieure Moderne (D.I.M.) was founded in 1919 by Philippe Joubert and René Petit. They started producing metal furniture in 1927 and by 1929 they exhibited at the 19th Salon des Artistes Décorateurs with a crystal glass dressing table of very avant-garde design to great acclaim. Their pieces were often made in small quantities of five or six items, but with reasonable prices that attracted a broad clientele. Louis Sognot was a highly accomplished designer and was innovative in his choice of materials and techniques of construction, maximizing the power of his designs. This piece comfortably straddles the Art Deco and Modernism periods with its right angles juxtaposed with the rounded edges creating an exciting visual impact. The lightness of the frame in aluminium balances beautifully with the transparency but sturdiness of the plate glass. Top-end French Art Deco pieces have a huge international following as well as naturally being keenly sought by the French themselves and it is this that enables them to command such high prices.

A wrought-iron and marble occasional table, on a foliate scroll pierced base, France, c1930, 19¼in (49cm) diam.

£3,100–3,700 S

A walnut side table, 1930s, 26in (66cm) wide.

£330–370 TDG

This table displays a playful use of geometric forms producing a quirky but practical piece of furniture.

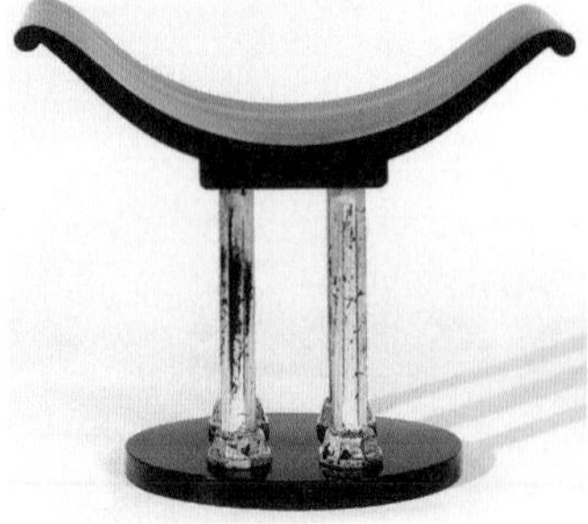

A lacquered and silvered wood tabouret, by Jules Leleu, France, 1930s, 21in (53.5cm) high.

£4,550–5,400 S(NY)

The design of this piece is based on native African examples, and has the appearance of an amalgam of Ashanti and Egyptian influences.

► **A walnut wardrobe,** with quarter-cut veneers, the three doors enclosing a fitted interior, 1930s, 56in (142cm) wide.

£690–770 OCA

◄ **A walnut wardrobe,** designed by Betty Joel, made by J. Penney, with an inlaid panel door, signed and dated 1928, 30½in (77.5cm) wide.

£350–420 MAL(O)

Betty Joel (1896–1984) established her furniture workshop in 1921 in Hayling Island, Hampshire. Joel's furniture is large in size, as it was intended for the spacious rooms of London mansion flats. It is usually highly practical and versatile, and mainly devoid of carved decoration and painted finishes. Some pieces are lacquered, but Joel had a strong preference for featuring the wood grain as the main, or sole, decorative element. All pieces are hand-finished and the quality of the craftsmanship is excellent.

ART DECO GLASS

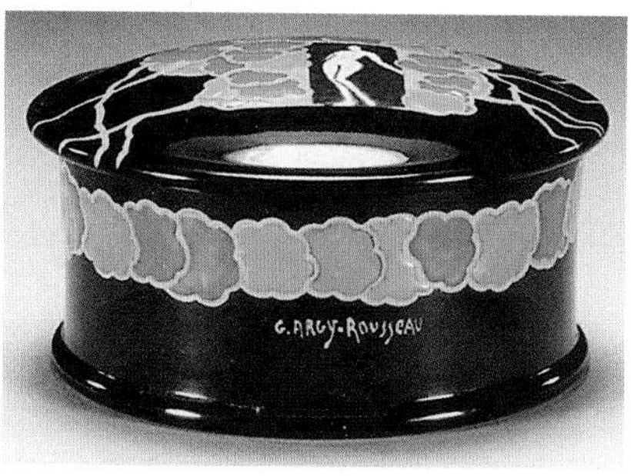

◀ **An Argy-Rousseau glass box and cover,** painted with a woman and stylized trees, painted mark, France, c1925, 6in (15cm) wide.
£1,050–1,250 S(O)

▶ **An Argy Rousseau *pâte-de-cristal* bud vase,** moulded with two eagles, signed, France, early 20thC, 5¼in (13.5cm) high.
£4,100–4,900 JDJ

Gabriel Argy-Rousseau

Gabriel Argy-Rousseau (1885–1953) first exhibited his *pâte-de-verre* designs in 1914, and his style evolved from Art Nouveau to Art Deco over the years. He produced vases decorated with stylized figures or geometric patterns in rich colours, as well as table lamps, plaques and some translucent *pâte-de-cristal* vessels. Popular vase designs were produced in large numbers, each one being hand-finished. Motifs included Egyptian and mythological subjects.

◀ **A Daum glass bowl,** with gold foil inclusions, on a wrought-iron stand by Louis Majorelle, France, Nancy, c1920, 5in (12.5cm) diam.
£630–700 CHAC

The glass in items such as this is blown into the wrought-iron armature, giving a swollen appearance.

A Daum glass bowl, with acid-etched decoration, France, Nancy, 1930s, 6in (15cm) high.
£490–550 MiW

A Daum glass comport, with gold foil inclusions, France, Nancy, 1920s, 10in (25.5cm) diam.
£720–800 MiW

A Daum glass vase, with two handles, France, Nancy, c1930, 10in (25.5cm) high.
£990–1,100 JSG

◀ **A Daum glass vase,** with acid-etched banding, France, Nancy, c1935, 9in (23cm) high.
£360–400 MiW

▶ **A Daum glass vase,** with acid-etched decoration, France, Nancy, 1930s, 13¼in (33.5cm) high.
£7,800–8,700 KK

A Daum glass vase, with acid-etched decoration, France, Nancy, 1930s, 6½in (16.5cm) high.
£6,800–7,600 KK

A Daum glass vase, with moulded decoration and applied motifs, France, Nancy, 1940s, 13½in (34.5cm) high.

£1,800–2,050 ⊞ KK

Two Degué glass vases, etched mark, France, c1930, 18¼in (46.5cm) high.

£1,800–2,150 ⚒ S

A Fanus glass vase, with cold-painted and enamel decoration, France, 1920–30, 10in (25.5cm) high.

£300–340 ⊞ CHAC

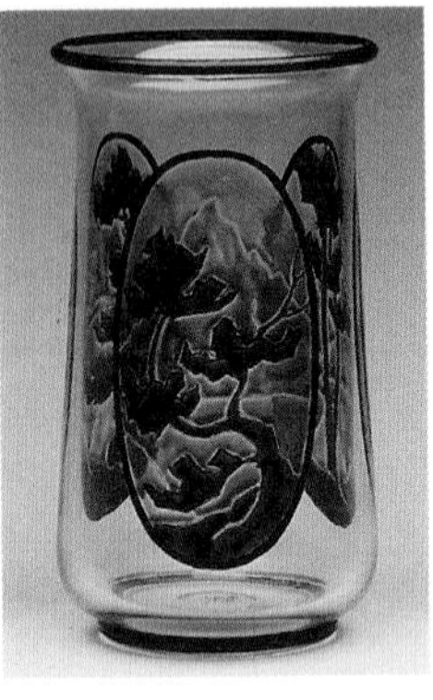

A Marcel Goupy glass vase, the three enamelled panels depicting stylized trees and mountains, signed, France, c1925, 9in (23cm) high.

£1,000–1,200 ⚒ JDJ

A Kosta glass vase, by Sven Erixson, slight damage, Sweden, 1930, 6in (15cm) high.

£1,700–2,000 ⚒ BUK

A Leerdam Serica glass vase, by A. D. Copier, Holland, c1930, 5½in (14cm) high.

£250–300 ⚒ AAT

The Serica range was small and items are therefore scarce.

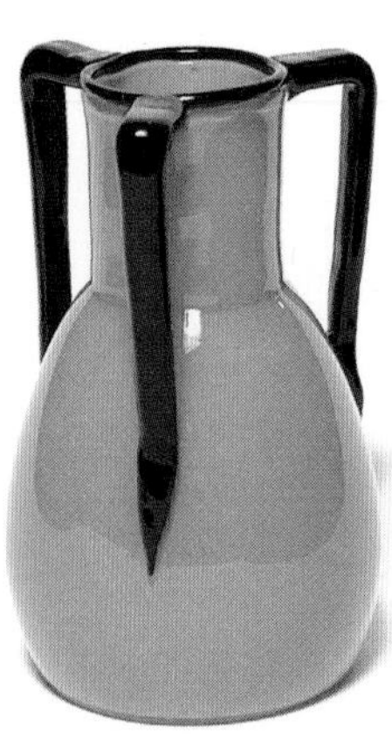

A Loetz glass vase, design attributed to Michael Powolny, Austria, c1920, 8in (20.5cm) high.

£310–350 ⊞ JSG

Items in the Decorative Arts section have been arranged alphabetically in factory order, with non-specific pieces appearing at the end of each sub-section.

A Loetz cameo glass vase, signed 'Richard', Austria, c1925, 9in (23cm) high.

£450–500 ⊞ MiW

Loetz signed some of their pieces 'Richard' in the 1920s, with the intention of making them seem French in origin.

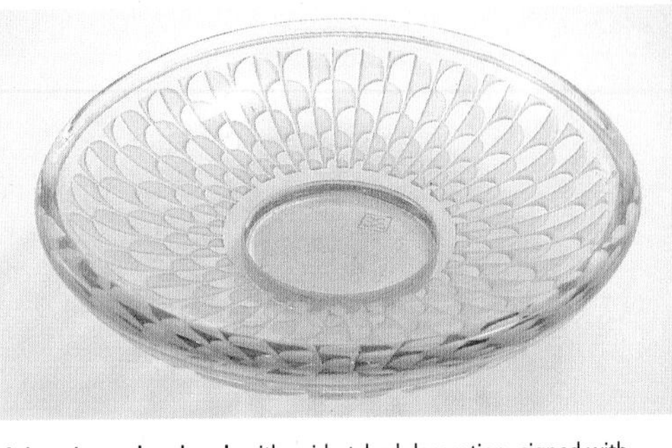

A Jean Luce glass bowl, with acid-etched decoration, signed with monogram, France, c1930, 9in (23cm) diam.

£250–300 ⚒ AAT

A Maurice Marinot glass bottle, internally decorated, etched signature, France, early 20thC, 8½in (21.5cm) high.

£3,900–4,650 ⚒ JDJ

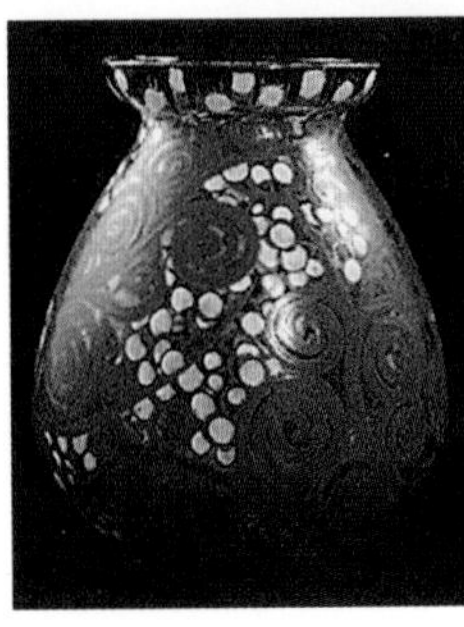

A Mazoyes glass vase, enamelled with flower sprays, signed, France, 8¼in (21cm) high.
£200–240 WW

A Myra-Kristall glass bowl, Germany, c1930, 14in (35.5cm) diam.
£170–190 CHAC

Myra-Kristall is iridescent glass produced by WMF. This bowl was made when Karl Wiedmann was manager of the WMF Glassworks. He recruited well-respected designers, architects and artists for technical research and artistic development purposes.

An Orrefors Graal glass vase, by Simon Gate, internally decorated with flowers, signed, Sweden, 1917, 8¼in (21cm) high.
£2,100–2,500 BUK

An Orrefors Graal glass vase, by Simon Gate, internally decorated, slight damage, signed, Sweden, 1927, 5¼in (13.5cm) high.
£1,650–1,950 BUK

◄ **An Orrefors glass vase,** by Vicke Lindstrand, engraved with a woman and a man holding a child, slight damage, signed, Sweden, 1937, 10½in (26.5cm) high.
£420–500 BUK

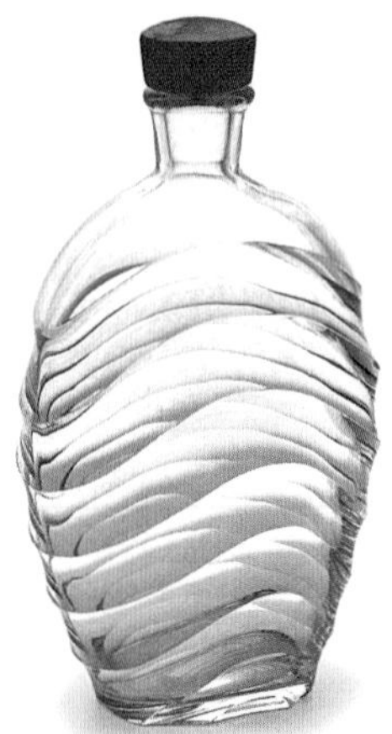

► **A Sabino glass vase,** press-moulded with a bee and honeycomb, signed, France, c1930, 7in (18cm) high.
£135–150 HEM

Marius-Ernest Sabino (1878–1961) was Italian by birth but established his glass company in Paris in 1919, where he produced metal-mounted lamps and architectural accessories. He adapted the techniques he used in the production of lamps and lighting devices to create decorative art glass of all kinds. His work was free-blown and moulded using primarily low-lead glass for its sculptural qualities. His unique opal-coloured glass became his signature, and was recognized worldwide.

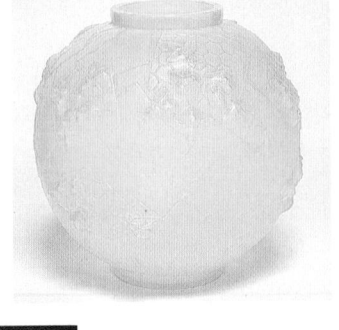

◄ **An Orrefors wheel-cut glass decanter,** by Simon Gate, marked, Sweden, c1934, 7¾in (19.5cm) high.
£90–100 Getc

◄ **A Sandvik Glassworks Astrid decanter,** by Simon Gate, Sweden, c1918, 15¼in (38.5cm) high.
£110–125 Getc

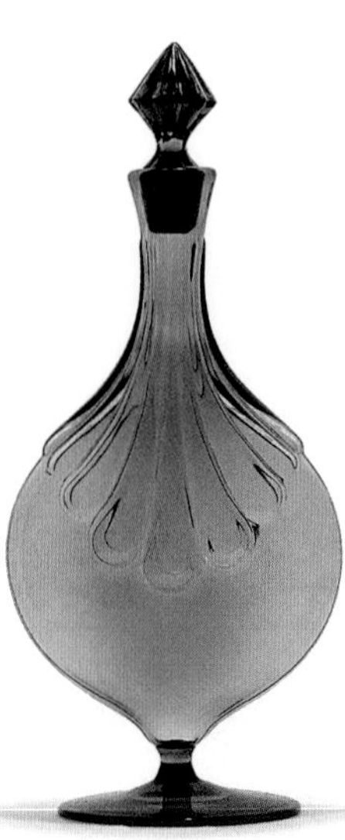

► **A Sandvik Glassworks decanter,** by Simon Gate, Sweden, c1923, 10¼in (26cm) high.
£400–450 Getc

A Schneider cameo glass vase, signed 'Charder', France, early 20thC, 19in (48.5cm) high.
£1,700–2,000 JDJ

A Schneider cameo glass vase, decorated with stylized palm trees, signed 'Charder', France, c1920, 10in (25.5cm) high.
£850–950 SAT

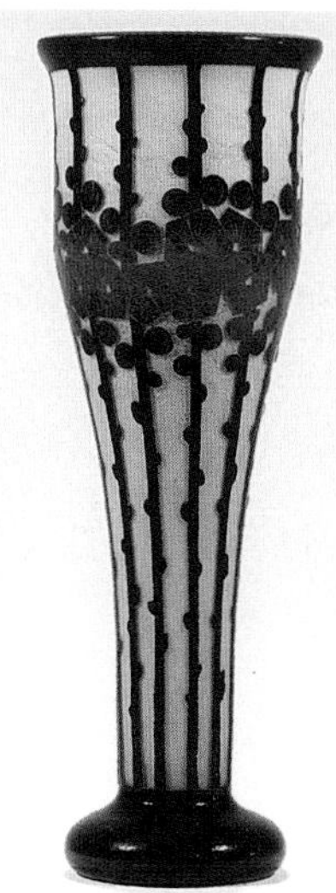

A Schneider Mirette cameo glass vase, signed 'Le Verre Français', France, 1925–26, 23¾in (60.5cm) high.

£7,800–9,300 S

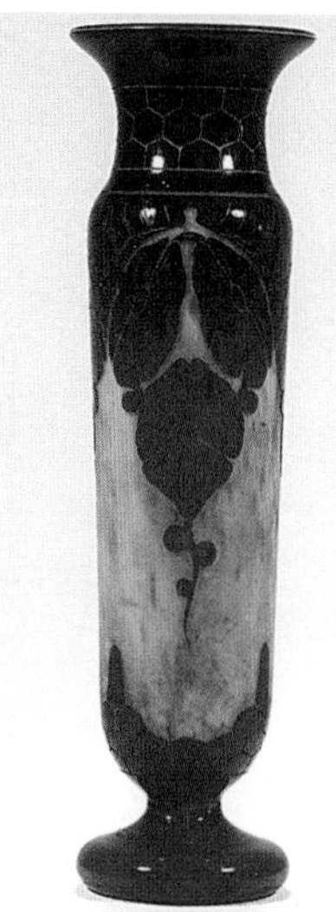

A Schneider cameo glass vase, overlaid and etched with flowers, marked 'Le Verre Français', France, 1925–30, 24¾in (63cm) high.

£4,800–5,700 S

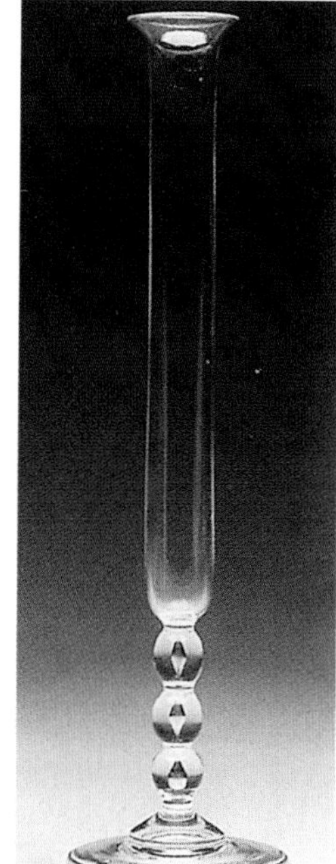

◄ **A pair of Steuben glass bud vases,** by Sidney Waugh and Frederick Carder, America, 1934, 11¾in (30cm) high.

£340–400 JDJ

Steuben was founded in 1903 in Corning, New York State, by members of the local glass-making Hawkes family and Frederick Carder, an Englishman who had previously established his reputation at Stevens & Williams. In the United States their work is regarded as the epitome of elegance in Art Deco glass. Before 1930 Carder designed many items himself, but from 1930 onwards the company employed a number of leading designers such as Sidney Waugh and Walter Dorwin Teague.

A Whitefriars Govette glass decanter, designed by Barnaby Powell, c1933, 15in (38cm) high.

£220–250 HUN

A Stuart glass vase, designed by Paul Nash for the 1934 Art in Industry Exhibition, engraved with geometric panels, marked, 1934, 8¼in (21cm) high.

£2,600–3,100 WW

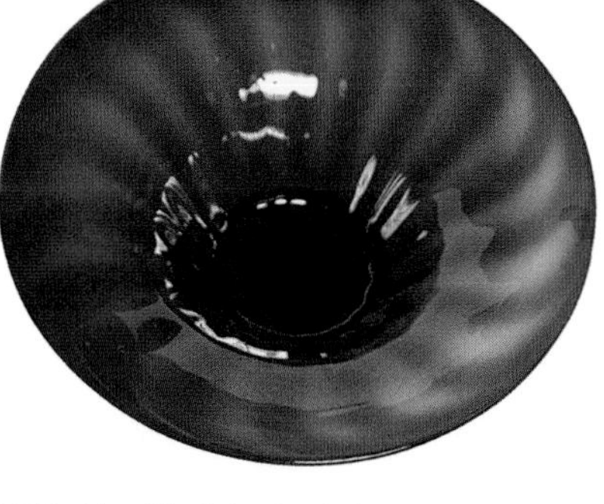

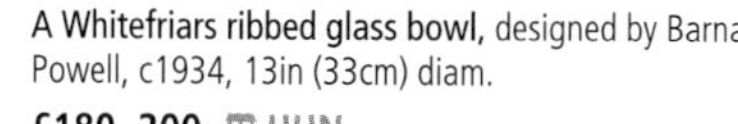

A Whitefriars ribbed glass bowl, designed by Barnaby Powell, c1934, 13in (33cm) diam.

£180–200 HUN

► **A Whitefriars Wave glass vase,** designed by William Butler, c1930, 5in (12.5cm) high.

£130–145 HUN

A frosted glass scent bottle, embossed with flowers, Czechoslovakia, c1920, 4in (10cm) high.

£105–120 BHA

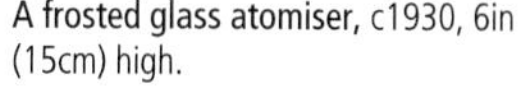

A frosted glass atomiser, c1930, 6in (15cm) high.

£120–135 BHA

◄ **A frosted glass wall panel,** Sweden, c1930, 38in (96.5cm) diam.

£720–800 PI

LALIQUE

A Lalique glass bowl, 'Gui', moulded with sprigs of mistletoe, France, 1920s, 8in (20.5cm) diam.

£630–700 MiW

◀ **A Lalique glass car mascot,** 'Moineau Coquet', France, 1930s, 9½in (24cm) high.

£350–390 VDA

▶ **A Lalique glass clock,** 'Deux Figurines', moulded with two figures, Marcilhac No. 726, engraved mark, France, after 1926, on an illuminated base, 14½in (37cm) high.

£9,600–11,500 S

A Lalique glass desk clock, 'Naiades', Marcilhac No. 764, France, c1924, 4½in (11.5cm) high.

£1,400–1,650 SK

Marcilhac Numbers

Marcilhac numbers were used to identify pieces referred to by Felix Marcilhac in his reference work *R. Lalique Catalogue Raisonne de l'Oeuvre de Verre*, published by Les Editions de l'Amateur, 1989.

◀ **A Lalique glass jardinière,** 'Acanthes', moulded with acanthus leaves, France, 1930s, 18in (45.5cm) wide.

£1,250–1,400 MiW

A pair of Lalique silvered-metal and glass lanterns, moulded with flowers, with later frosted glass panels, France, c1930, 54in (137cm) high.

£4,550–5,400 S

The panels on these lanterns, which do not appear separately in Marcilhac, are the same as those incorporated in the schemes for windows in a chapel in Douvres-la-Délivrande, Calvados, France, and the church of St Matthew, in Saint-Hélier, Jersey.

A Lalique glass scent bottle and stopper, 'Dahlia', with enamel and silver-stained decoration, marked, France, c1945, 5¼in (13.5cm) high.

£350–420 N

A Lalique glass vase, 'Grignon', France, c1930, 7in (18cm) high.

£270–320 AAT

◀ **A Lalique glass vase,** 'Feuilles', France, c1934, 8in (20.5cm) high.

£1,400–1,600 CHAC

▶ **A Lalique glass vase,** 'Medaillons', with six female portrait medallions, signed, France, late 1930s, 9in (23cm) high.

£3,200–3,800 E

A Lalique glass vase, 'Cerises', moulded with cherries, slight damage, signed, France, c1950, 8in (20.5cm) high.

£2,100–2,500 N

ART DECO JEWELLERY & WRISTWATCHES

An Egyptian revival silver-gilt expanding bracelet/armband, with enamelled decoration, signed 'Lotos', c1925.
£530–600 TDG

A diamond brooch, with central old-cut diamond, c1925.
£520–620 N

A diamond ribbon and bow brooch, c1930, 4in (10cm) wide.
£2,400–2,850 G(L)

A 18ct gold bow brooch, with diamond decoration, c1935, 3in (7.5cm) wide.
£1,650–1,850 WIM

A black opal and diamond pendant, c1930, 1¾in (4.5cm) high, in a fitted Wartski case.
£5,200–6,200 F&C

A silver and rock crystal pendant, by Wiwen Nilsson, Sweden, Lund, 1941, 1¾in (4.5cm) high.
£1,950–2,300 BUK

These pendants are seldom seen and when they appear on the market they usually fetch a high price.

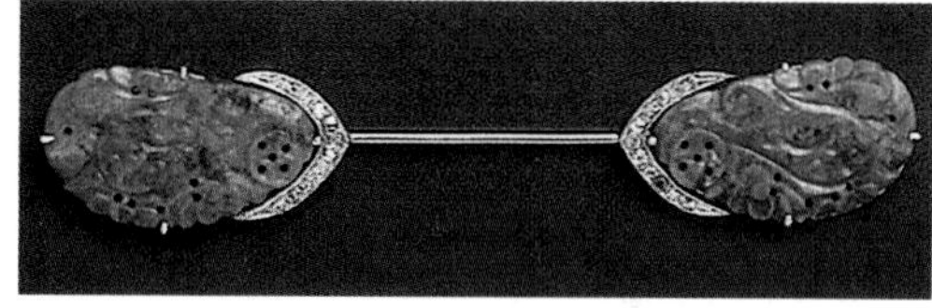

A platinum, jadeite and diamond jabot pin, c1930.
£510–610 SK

A platinum, diamond and sapphire ring, c1930.
£2,500–2,800 WIM

An 18ct gold wristwatch, with a silvered dial and 15-jewel lever movement, import marks for London 1928.
£230–270 DN(BR)

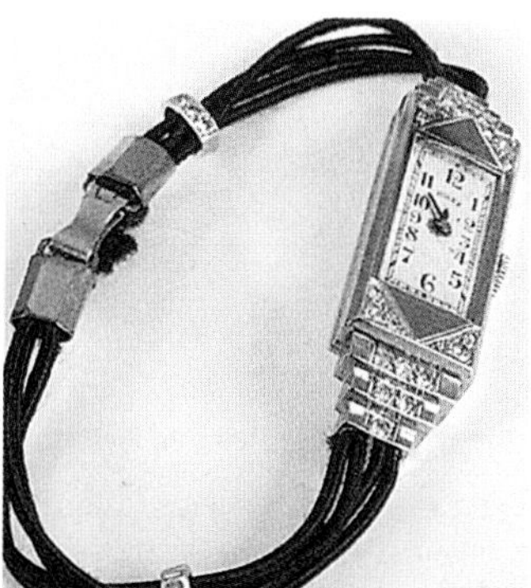

◀ **A Rolex 18ct gold cocktail watch,** with a 17-jewel movement, set with diamonds, marked, import marks for Glasgow 1930.
£1,000–1,200 FHF

The Rolex name attached to this watch makes all the difference to the price. Although some of the value is due to the quality of the movement, a similar piece by a lesser name might be a half or a third of the price.

◀ **A platinum and diamond bracelet watch,** with silvered dial and Swiss jewelled lever movement, c1935.
£820–980 DN

ART DECO LIGHTING

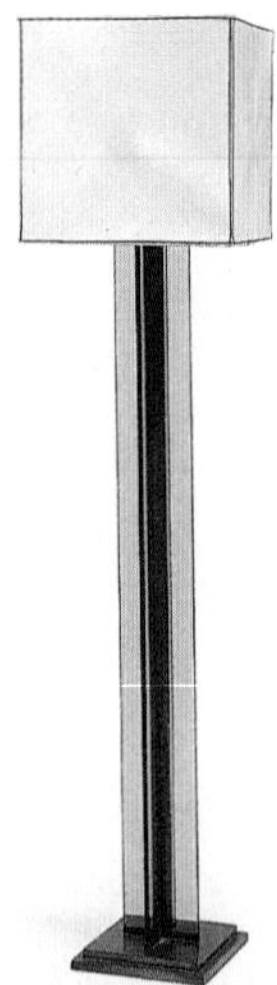

A pair of Baccarat glass and silvered-bronze table lamps, by Jacques Adnet, France, 1930s, 7½in (19cm) high.

£6,600–7,900 S

◀ **A Compagnie des Arts Français steel, copper and Lucite floor lamp,** by Jacques Adnet, France, 1930s, 68in (172.5cm) high.

£5,200–6,200 S(NY)

A wrought-iron and alabaster table lamp, by Edgar Brandt, stamped mark, France, c1929, 14¾in (37.5cm) wide.

£9,700–11,600 S(NY)

A C. G. Hallberg silvered-metal and glass ceiling light, by Elis Bergh, slight damage, Sweden, Stockholm, 1920s, 37½in (95.5cm) high.

£6,200–7,400 BUK

A silvered-bronze and alabaster chandelier, by Albert Cheuret, signed, France, c1925, 33¼in (84.5cm) wide.

£11,000–13,200 S(NY)

Cheuret's incredibly stylish and unusual design for this chandelier is what gives it its value.

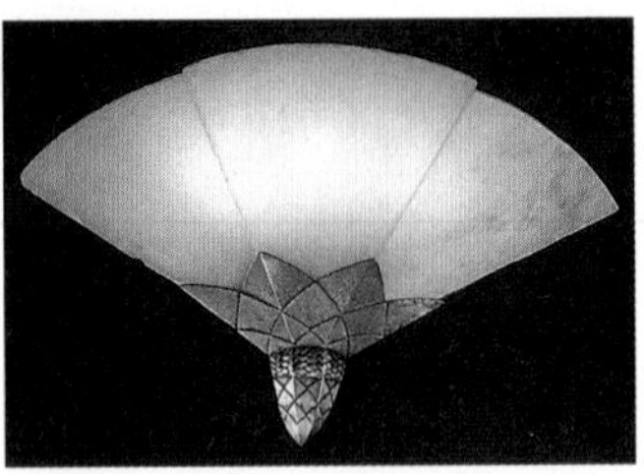

A pair of silvered-bronze and alabaster sconces, by Albert Cheuret, France, c1925, 18in (45.5cm) wide.

£14,600–17,500 S(NY)

A Daum glass ceiling light, signed, France, Nancy, c1920, 29½in (75cm) high.

£1,450–1,750 BUK

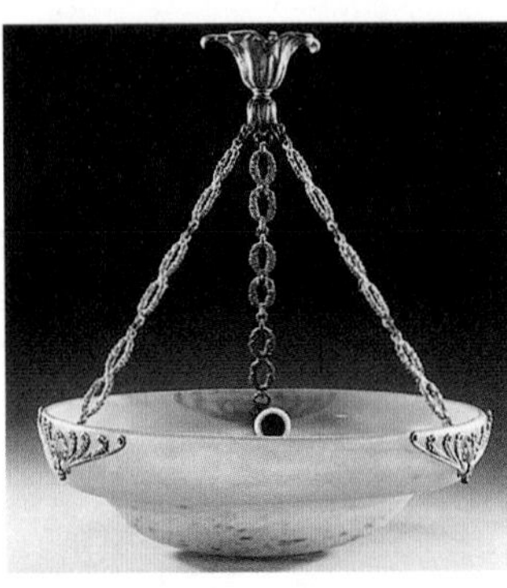

A Daum glass *plafonnier*, with gilt-metal mounts, engraved marks, France, Nancy, c1920, 19¼in (49cm) wide.

£1,050–1,250 S(O)

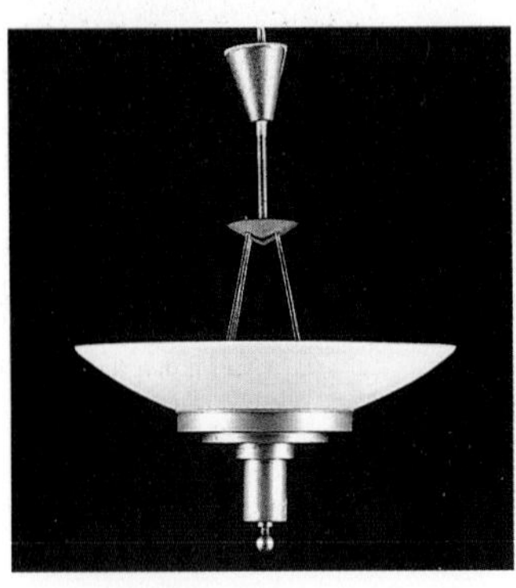

An Amsterdam School stained and leaded glass ceiling light, by De Honsel, decorated with Tuschinsky-style pattern, slight damage, Holland, 1921–23, 20in (51cm) diam.

£5,600–6,700 S(Am)

The Tuschinsky theatre in Amsterdam is famous for its exceptional interior decoration that includes beautiful murals, carpets, lamps and stained glass.

◀ **A Giso nickel-plated metal and milk glass Sonneveld ceiling light,** by W. H. Gispen, Holland, c1930, 22½in (57cm) high.

£2,400–2,850 S(Am)

▶ **A Glössner & Co brass and glass floor lamp,** designed by Kjell Löwenadler, the shade decorated with Neptune and a mermaid, signed, Sweden, Stockholm, 1940s, 66in (167.5cm) high.

£920–1,100 BUK

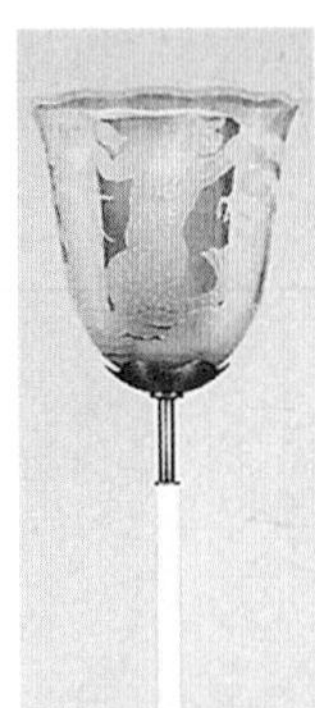

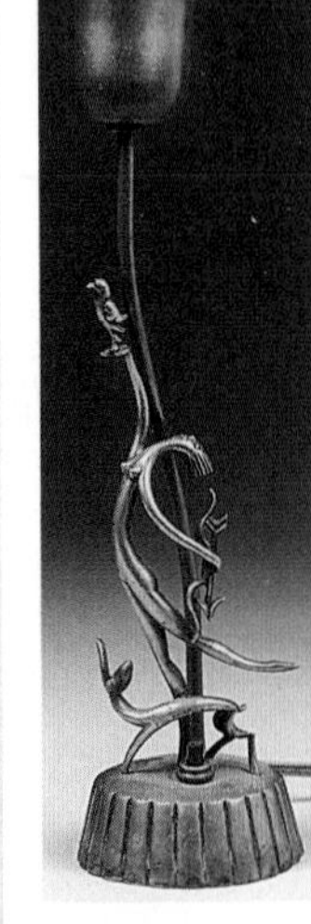

A Hagenauer brass table lamp, modelled with a stylized figure of Diana, a dog and a bird, slight damage, Austria, Vienna, prior to 1929, 12½in (32cm) high.

£2,700–3,200 DORO

A nickel-plated-bronze and frosted glass table lamp, by Boris Jean Lacroix, France, c1928, 11½in (29cm) high.

£4,550–5,400 S(NY)

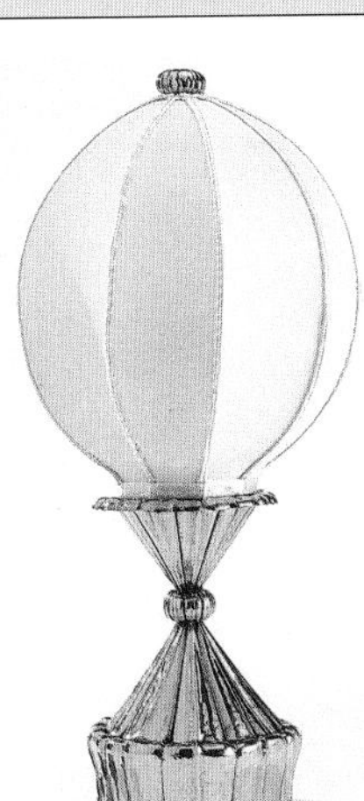

◄ **A Wiener Werkstätte wrought-brass Ballon table lamp,** by Dagobert Pêche, Austria, c1920, 17¾in (45cm) high.

£17,900–21,400 S(NY)

The amazing and somewhat frivolous nature of this design gives the piece great appeal. One could imagine it just floating off a piece of furniture.

A pair of Jacques Quinet-style frosted glass and bronze wall lights, France, 1925–50, 22in (56cm) high.

£2,400–2,850 S(O)

A silver lamp and clock, by Walker & Hall, Sheffield 1937, 5½in (14cm) wide.

£4,000–4,450 BEX

► **A figural table lamp,** in the form of Amelia Earhart on a map of North America, early 20thC, 18½in (47cm) high.

£230–270 JAA

The American aviator Amelia Earhart was the first woman to fly across the Atlantic in 1932. In an attempt to fly around the world in 1937 her plane was lost over the Pacific.

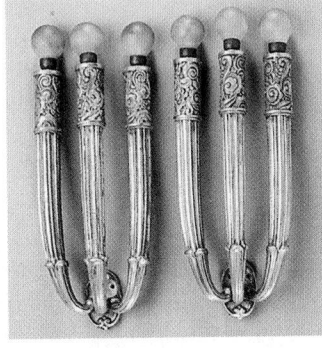

A pair of chrome and glass wall lights, c1930, 13¾in (35cm) high.

£340–380 TDG

A bronzed-spelter figural table lamp, in the form of a girl, with an alabaster shade, c1930, 23½in (59.5cm) high.

£500–600 G(L)

A wrought-iron and glass chandelier, moulded with grapes, c1930, 31½in (80cm) wide.

£1,800–2,150 S(O)

A pair of gilt-bronze wall lights, France, c1930, 13¼in (33.5cm) high.

£2,000–2,400 S(O)

A chrome chandelier, c1935, 38¼in (97cm) high.

£600–720 S

A pair of patinated-bronze and moulded glass ceiling lights, c1940, France, 11¾in (30cm) diam.

£7,800–9,300 S

A pair of chrome and frosted glass wall lights, decorated with star motifs, France, c1940, 26in (66cm) high.

£1,400–1,650 S(O)

ART DECO METALWARE

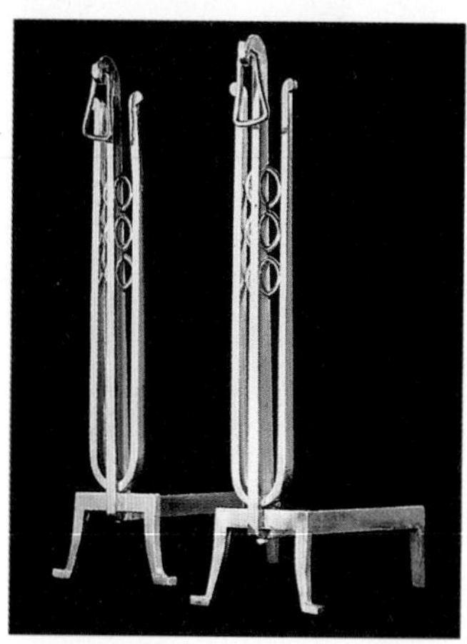

A pair of chrome metal andirons, c1935, 21in (53.5cm) high.

£780–930 S

A silver bowl, by Georg Jensen, Denmark, London import marks, 1933–34, 5in (12.5cm) diam.

£760–850 SHa

A hammered silver bowl, by A. E. Jones, with scrolled hardwood handles, Birmingham 1940, 6¾in (17cm) diam.

£840–1,000 S(O)

Georg Jensen

Georg Jensen (1866–1935) was born in Denmark. After working as a potter and sculptor he became a silversmith, winning first prize at the San Francisco World's Fair in 1915. As the popularity of his work increased he took on key designers such as Harald Nielsen, Henning Koppel and Johan Rohde to design for his retail outlets. His flatware designs are of particular interest to collectors, with an early design such as Magnolia Blossom selling at a premium price against more commonly seen designs such as the Acanthus or Acorn patterns. Collectors generally prefer his designs with pre-war import marks.

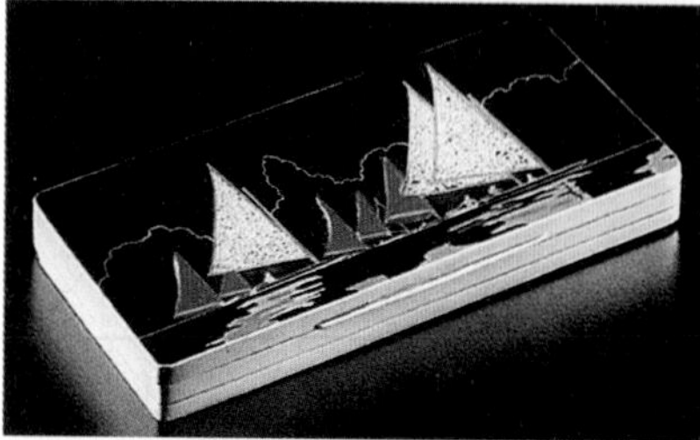

A silver and enamel box, by J. Trotain, the cover enamelled with a sailing scene, the background simulating tortoiseshell, France, Paris, c1930, 7¼in (18.5cm) wide.

£1,550–1,850 S(O)

This piece reflects the passion for sailing at this period and the triangular nature of the sails lend themselves perfectly to this striking geometric design.

A silver sugar caster, by Lee & Wigfull, the pierced cover with a finial, the body with stiff-leaf borders, Sheffield 1934, 7in (18cm) high.

£140–165 DN

◀ **A silver cutlery service,** by Georg Jensen, comprising 200 pieces, decorated with Lily of the Valley pattern, Denmark, Copenhagen, designed 1913, produced 1925–50, 226oz.

£7,100–8,500 S(NY)

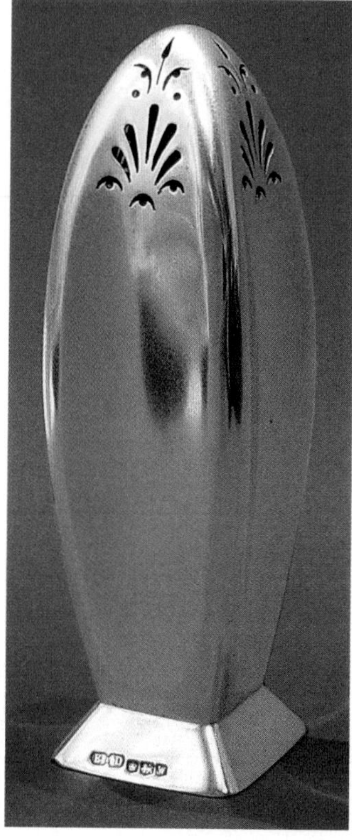

A silver sugar caster, maker's mark B&D, Sheffield 1939, 5½in (14cm) high, 5oz.

£1,100–1,250 BEX

A silver inkwell, by Walker & Hall, Sheffield 1931, 6in (15cm) wide.

£1,100–1,250 BEX

◀ **A silver photograph frame,** by Walker & Hall, Sheffield 1937, 8½in (21.5cm) high.

£400–450 BEX

A silver jug, by Johan Rohde for Georg Jensen, Swedish import marks, Denmark, Copenhagen, 1933–44, 9in (23cm) high, 20¼oz.

£2,300–2,750 BUK

Rohde designed this jug as early as 1920, but it was so advanced that it was not produced before 1925.

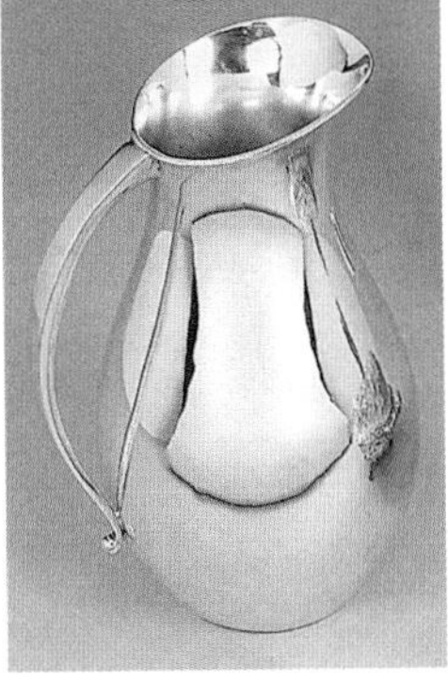

A silver wine jug, by K. Uyeba, marked, America, early 20thC, 10¾in (27.5cm) high.

£1,100–1,300 DORO

This design is very much influenced by Georg Jensen's design for Johan Rohde in 1920, shown on this page.

◀ **A silver and steel table lighter,** with engine-turned decoration, marks worn, Birmingham 1939, 4½in (11.5cm) high.

£290–330 BEX

A silver napkin ring, with engine-turned decoration, 1940, 2in (5cm) wide.

£115–130 ANC

A pair of pewter salt and pepper shakers, by Kem Weber for Porter Blanchard, stamped marks, America, Calabasas, 1930s, 3in (7.5cm) high.

£1,600–1,900 S(NY)

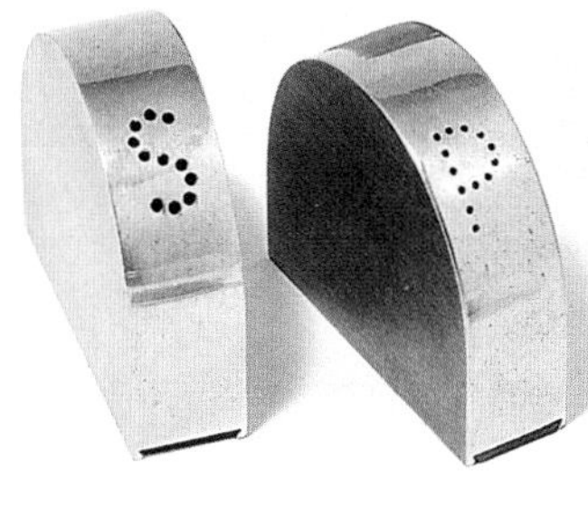

A pair of aluminium and plastic salt and pepper shakers, by William Lescaze for Revere Copper and Brass Co, stamped mark, America, New York State, Rome, c1935, 1¾in (4.5cm) high.

£390–460 S(NY)

A silver coffee service, comprising three pieces, each with a gilt interior, Sweden, Uppsala, 1927–28, coffee pot 8¼in (21cm) high, total weight 29¾oz.

£710–850 DORO

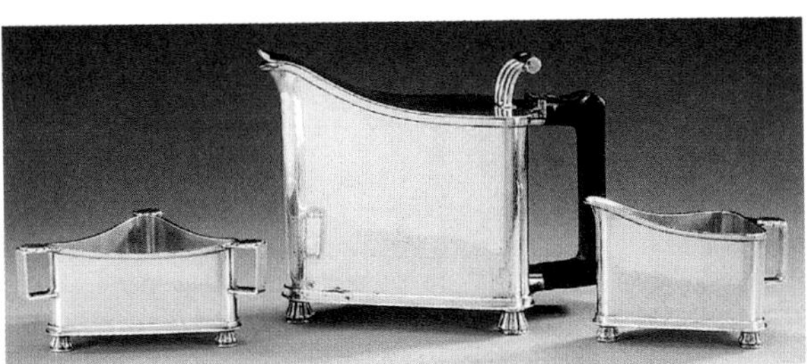

Further reading

Miller's Antiques Checklist: Art Deco, Miller's Publications, 2003

◀ **A silver coffee service,** by K. Andersson, comprising three pieces, the coffee pot with an ebonized handle, Sweden, Stockholm, 1930, coffee pot 6in (15cm) high.

£1,150–1,350 BUK

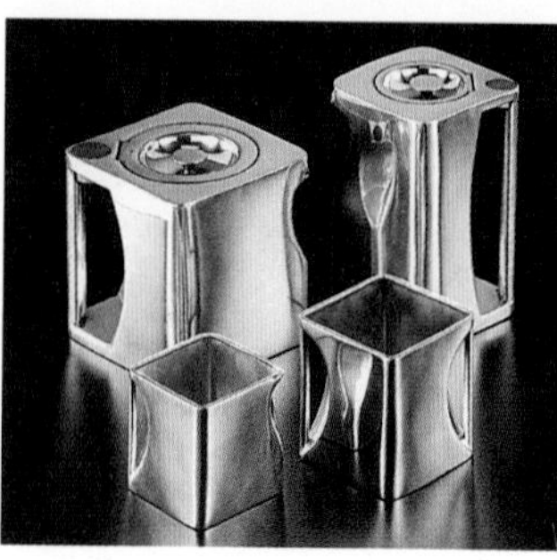

A silver-plated Cube tea and coffee service, by Elkington & Co, comprising four pieces, stamped marks, c1930, coffee pot 5¼in (13.5cm) high.

£1,550–1,850 S(O)

A silver tea service, comprising four pieces, the teapot and water jug with ivory handles and finials, each piece engraved with the initial 'D', 1933–34, teapot 9¾in wide.

£460–550 AH

A silver tea and coffee service, by Jean E. Puiforcat, comprising four pieces, with carved wooden handles, the wooden finials set with silver discs, France, Paris, c1935, coffee pot 7¼in (18.5cm) high, 73oz.

£3,250–3,900 S(NY)

A silver tea service, by Walker & Hall, comprising three pieces, the teapot with an ebonized finial and handle, Sheffield 1935–37, teapot 9½in (24cm) high.

£900–1,000 BEX

This service expresses the need to be modern and competitive with the stepped bases, handles and finial, but still without entirely letting go of the 'traditional' look.

A silver-mounted ivory tazza, by Elkington & Co, Birmingham 1936, 6in (15cm) diam.

£350–420 HYD

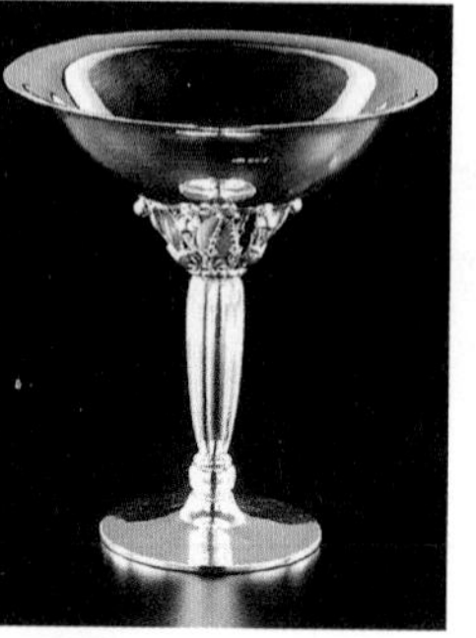

A silver tazza, by Georg Jensen, the lobed stem with stylized buds and leaves enclosing a bead, import mark for 1936, Denmark, Copenhagen, 7¾in (19.5cm) high.

£2,400–2,850 S(O)

A silver tray, with ivory handles, maker's mark 'FC', Sheffield 1934, 17¾in (45cm) wide, 36½oz.

£760–910 DN(HAM)

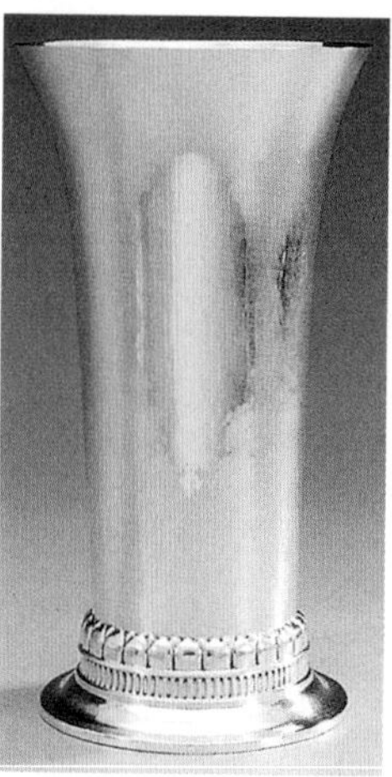

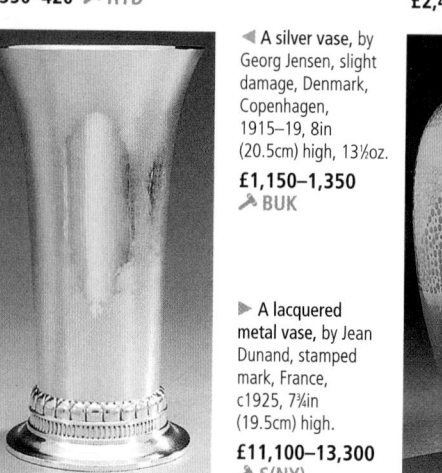

◄ **A silver vase,** by Georg Jensen, slight damage, Denmark, Copenhagen, 1915–19, 8in (20.5cm) high, 13½oz.

£1,150–1,350 BUK

► **A lacquered metal vase,** by Jean Dunand, stamped mark, France, c1925, 7¾in (19.5cm) high.

£11,100–13,300 S(NY)

A lacquered metal and eggshell vase, by Jean Dunand, signed, stamped marks, France, c1925, 5½in (14cm) high.

£16,300–19,600 S(NY)

ART DECO MODELS

A pair of ebonized models of stylized leaping antelopes, by S. Aguilar, signed, c1930, larger 27½in (70cm) high.

£1,550–1,850 S(O)

An Ashtead Pottery earthenware model of a seated woman, marked 'Allan G. Wyon 1927', 8in (20.5cm) high.

£540–640 AMB

A bronze model of a Russian dancer, by Marcel-André Bouraine, France, c1920, 8in (20.5cm) high.

£900–1,050 DuM

The influence in Europe of the Ballets Russes *may well have inspired the subject matter of this piece.*

A pair of bronze bookends modelled as gazelles, by Marcel-André Bouraine, each on a marble base, signed, France, c1930, 9in (23cm) high.

£1,800–2,150 S(O)

Marcel-André Bouraine

Marcel-André Bouraine exhibited at the *Salon des Artistes Français* in the early 1920s. His pieces were generally cast in bronze and often have enamelled or silvered surfaces. Female warriors, clowns, pierrots and harlequins were favourite subjects, often displaying a strong Cubist influence. Much of his work was produced by Etling in Paris.

► A painted bronze and ivory figure, by Demêtre Chiparus, entitled 'Actress', on an onyx base, signed, France, c1925, 17½in (44.5cm) high.

£11,500–13,800 S

Demêtre Chiparus was born in Romania. He lived in Paris and studied under A. Mercier and J. Boucher and exhibited at the Salon from 1914 to 1928.

A Royal Crown Derby figure of a woman with a dog, entitled 'Olga with Borzoi', printed mark, date code for 1932, 6¼in (16cm) high.

£280–330 BAM(M)

Pieces such as this are interesting in that they illustrate the fashion of the day rather than portraying a theatrical dancer in stage costume.

An earthenware figure of a nude woman, by Essevi, designed by Sandro Vachetti, Italy, Milan, 1930s, 16in (40.5cm) high.

£9,000–10,000 AnM

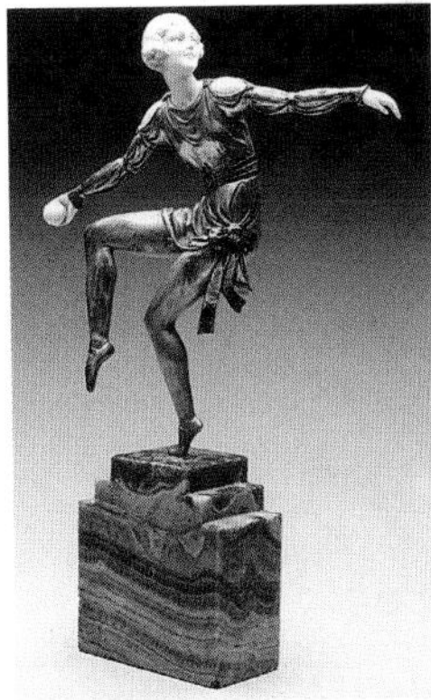

◄ A bronze and ivory figure of a dancer, by Joe Descomps, on an onyx base, etched signature, slight wear, France, 1930s, 17¾in (45cm) high.

£6,500–7,800 JDJ

A silvered bronze group of two running dogs, by Francisque, on a rosewood plinth, signed, seal mark, France, c1930, 33in (84cm) wide.

£1,900–2,250 S(O)

A terracotta study of the heads of a man and a horse, by Amadeo Gennarelli, signed, 1920s–30s, 31in (78.5cm) wide.

£880–980 ⊞ OCA

A Goldscheider ceramic figure of a dancer, by Josef Lorenzl, slight damage, Austria, Vienna, 1920s–30s, 18¼in (46.5cm) high.

£2,800–3,350 BUK

This figure by Lorenzl is also seen in bronze, *see page 440.*

Goldscheider

Founded in Vienna in 1885 by Friedrich Goldscheider, the company produced ceramic and stone reproductions of classical figures from local museums. By the 1920s, under the direction of Marcel and Walter Goldscheider, designs in bronze and ivory by sculptors Bruno Zach and Josef Lorenzl were produced in brightly-painted porcelain. African-inspired pottery wall masks were also produced to Lorenzl's designs.

A Goldscheider ceramic group, entitled 'The Dolly Sisters', Austria, Vienna, early 1930s, 16in (40.5cm) high.

£3,150–3,500 ⊞ GaL

A spelter figural group, by Gori, modelled as Diana and two hounds, on a marble base, signed, France, c1925, 31½in (80cm) wide.

£2,100–2,500 LJ

A chrome model of a giraffe, by Hagenauer, Austria, Vienna, c1925, 9in (23cm) high.

£530–590 ⊞ TDG

Hagenauer

The Hagenauer Werkstätte (workshops) were founded in Vienna in 1898 by Carl Hagenauer. Initially the firm specialized in practical and ornamental artefacts such as metal tablewares, lamps, mirrors and vases, but from 1910 to 1930 it became famous for the metal figures and groups that were exhibited throughout Europe. Carl Hagenauer's eldest son Karl joined the firm in 1919 and with his brother Franz, took over in 1928. In the 1930s their designs were at the forefront of the New Realism.

A silvered bronze figure, by Hagenauer, marked, Austria, Vienna, c1930, 4in (10cm) high.

£175–210 AAT

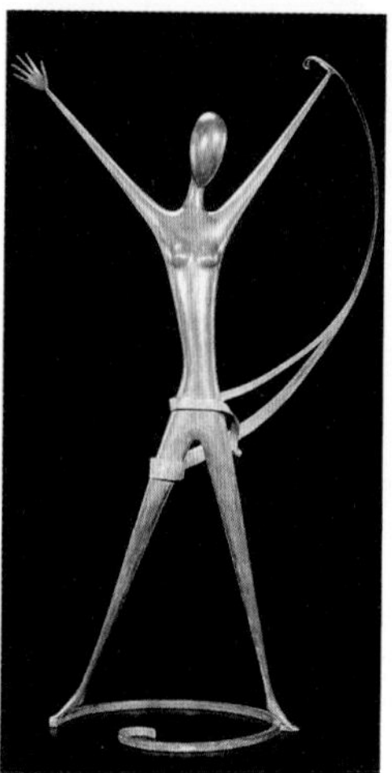

◀ **A brass figure of a female nude,** by Hagenauer, stamped, Austria, Vienna, c1930, 47in (119.5cm) high.

£12,000–14,400 S

▶ **A wood and bronze bust of a woman,** by Hagenauer, marked, Austria, Vienna, c1930, 14in (35.5cm) high.

£450–540 AAT

◄ **A Hutschenreuther porcelain figure of a woman,** by Karl Tutter, Germany, c1930, 11in (28cm) high.

£450–500 EAn

► **A Katzhütte ceramic figure of a woman and a deer,** Austria, c1934, 14in (35.5cm) wide.

£630–700 HEW

A bronze model of a golden pheasant, by Alex Kéléty, on an onyx base, signed, stamped, France, c1930, 23½in (59.5cm) wide.

£1,400–1,650 S

◄ **A silvered-bronze figure of a female archer,** by Georges Lavroff, signed, France, c1930, 15½in (39.5cm) wide.

£3,800–4,550 S(O)

A Keramos earthenware figure of a woman carrying a vase, Austria, c1930, 16in (440.5cm) high.

£1,050–1,200 AnM

A metal figure of a woman, by Max Le Verrier, on a marble base, France, Paris, 1920s, 7in (18cm) high.

£670–750 ANO

This piece was originally a car mascot.

A Lenci ceramic figure of Don Quixote on a horse, with a metal lance, Italy, Milan, c1937, 22in (56cm) high.

£5,800–6,500 AnM

Condition

The condition is absolutely vital when assessing the value of an antique. Damaged pieces on the whole appreciate much less than perfect examples. However, a rare desirable piece may command a high price even when damaged.

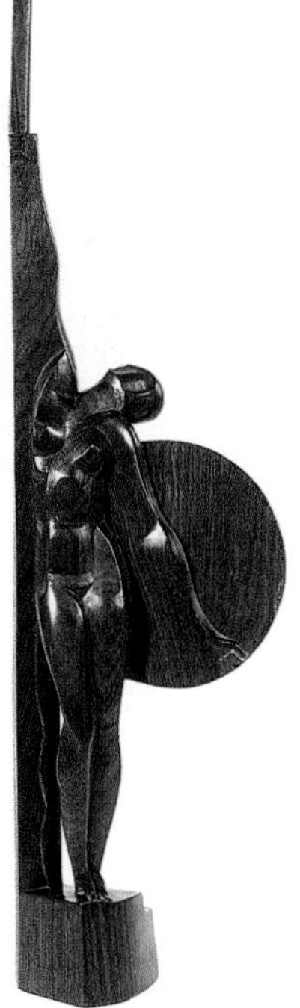

A carved rosewood figure of a female nude, by L. Leyritz, signed and marked, France, 1932, 33in (84cm) high.

£8,400–10,000 S

Josef Lorenzl

Josef Lorenzl was born and worked in Vienna and was one of the leading sculptors of the Art Deco period. He produced a range of figures in bronze, ivory and occasionally chryselephantine, the bases usually of onyx although black slate and marble were sometimes used. His female figures tend to be very slim and streamlined, with small breasts and realistic facial features with a serene, calm expression.

A bronze and ivory figure, by Josef Lorenzl, Austria, Vienna, 1920s, 9in (23cm) high.

£1,400–1,600 MiW

A bronze figure of a woman, by Josef Lorenzl, Austrian, 1929–30, 10in (25.5cm) high.
£1,500–1,700 ⊞ HEW

A bronze group of a mother and child, by A. Muller, signed and marked, France, Paris, c1930, 19in (48.5cm) high.
£2,400–2,850 S(O)

► **A bronze figure of a nude woman,** by F. Ouillon Carrère, entitled 'Sword Dancer', signed, France, dated 1919, 21¾in (55.5cm) high.
£2,900–3,450 DN

A bronze and ivory figure of Punchinello, by Roland Paris, on a marble base, signed, France, c1930, 13¾in (35cm) high.
£1,800–2,150 S(O)

A bronze and ivory figure of a woman, by Ferdinand Preiss, entitled 'Charleston Dancer', on a marble base, Germany, c1930, 15½in (39.5cm) high.
£9,600–11,500 S

Ferdinand Preiss formed the Preiss-Kassler Foundry in Berlin in 1906, designing most of the models himself, although by 1914 there were about six designers working for him including Dorothea Charol, Paul Philippe and Otto Poertzel.

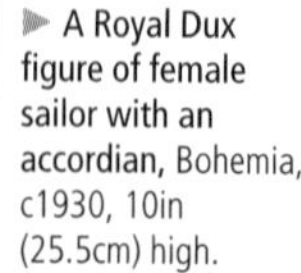

◄ **A Rosenthal figure of a dancing woman,** by Dorothea Charol, entitled 'Spring', Germany, c1930, 8in (20.5cm) high.
£360–400
⊞ CHO

► **A Royal Dux figure of female sailor with an accordian,** Bohemia, c1930, 10in (25.5cm) high.
£490–550
⊞ OAK

A Sabino glass panther group, engraved mark, France, Paris, c1925, 5¾in (14.5cm) high.
£420–500 G(L)

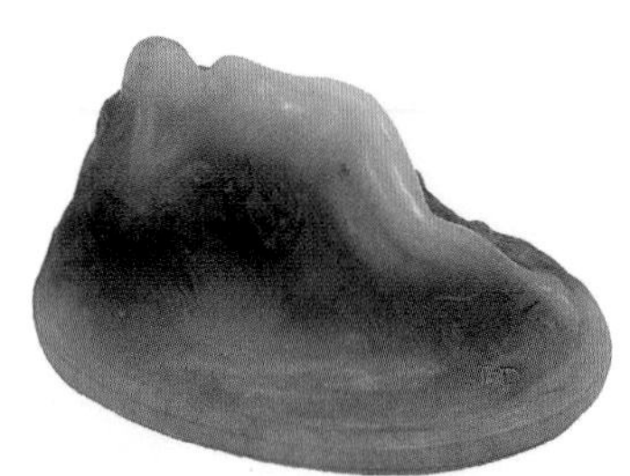

A ***pâte-de-verre*** **figural glass jewel tray,** by Joe Descomps, France, c1925, 6½in (16.5cm) wide.
£900–1,050 AAT

► **A patinated bronze figure of a seated woman,** by Bruno Zach, signed, Austria, c1930, 10¼in (26cm) high.
£2,600–3,100 S(O)

A spelter figure of a woman, entitled 'Girl with Doves', on a marble base, c1930, 14in (35.5cm) wide.
£360–400 ⊞ TDG

TWENTIETH-CENTURY DESIGN

DURING THE LAST DECADE, the rule when collecting 20th-century design was always to buy documented pieces by known designers. However, as this area of collecting has become more popular, there has been a noticeable move away from such thinking and demand for pieces by iconic core designers like Charles and Ray Eames, George Nelson and Edward Wormley has fallen, while items with character, but not necessarily pedigree, are becoming more popular with buyers.

In 2005 there was notable growth for the 1960s and 1970s segment of the market, which only partly accounts for the decline in popularity of the designers of the 1950s. Moulded plastics, stainless steel and foam-covered organic forms of the 1960s and 1970s by designers such as Verner Panton, Joe Colombo and Pierre Paulin have experienced a resurgence in popularity. Additionally, an entirely new collecting area has appeared; sales of branded luxury goods such as designer handbags and other accessories from this period have become very desirable. Other areas of strong growth include Scandinavian and Italian items by both known and unknown designers and include items such as flatware, rugs, jewellery and even kitchenware.

The online marketplace plays a key role in sales: eBay features prominently and most larger auction houses now offer online bidding. The anonymity of bidding online appeals to clients who prefer to reveal neither how much they spend nor that they need help in making selections.

Interior designers are also lending strong support to the market. At auction, dealers often stop bidding at a point well below that of a designer representing a well-heeled client. Interior designers also bring a new type of buyer to the marketplace: those who do not buy an item because it is a bargain, but because they love it. Must-have items are no longer solely defined by pedigree. Emotion and desire have come to play a larger role in buyers' choices.

Lisanne Dickson

Lisanne Dickson

Lisanne is head of 1950s Modern Design for Treadway/Toomey Auctions, a Chicago-based auction house established in 1987.

In seven years with the firm she has personally catalogued more than 6,000 examples of furniture, pottery, glass, sculpture, lighting, jewellery and textiles dating from 1930 to 1980.

CERAMICS

A Ruskin Pottery high-fired jardinière, impressed marks, dated 1925, 7½in (19cm) high.

£350–420 Hal

◄ A Ruskin Pottery high-fired vase, c1922, 6in (15cm) high.

£800–900 WAC

A Holyrood Pottery vase, by Henry Taylor Wyse, Scotland, 1920s, 9in (23cm) high.

£280–320 SDD

The Holyrood Pottery was set up by Henry Taylor Wyse, a former teacher, in Edinburgh 1918–27. Wyse is particularly known for the quality of his glazes.

A Ruskin Pottery pot, by William Howson Taylor, signed, 1931, 7in (18cm) high.

£350–400 WAC

Ruskin Pottery

Ruskin Pottery was founded in 1898 in West Smethwick, Birmingham, by William Howson Taylor and his father, Edward. Initially known as the Birmingham Tile & Pottery Works, it was renamed Ruskin Pottery some years later in honour of the artist John Ruskin. The range included high-fired stonewares, which are particularly sought after today, as well as lustre decorated or mottled monochrome 'soufflé' earthenwares, and crystalline glazed wares in eggshell-thin bone china.

A Paul Schreckengost earthenware teapot and cover, manufactured by Gem Clay Forming Co, impressed mark, America, Ohio, c1938, 7¼in (18.5cm) high.

£17,900–21,000 S(NY)

A Wedgwood model of a bull, by Arnold Machin, entitled 'Ferdinand', c1941, 12in (30.5cm) wide.

£450–500 RUSK

An Arne Bang Pottery jug, Denmark, 1940s, 5½in (14cm) high.

£115–130 RIWA

A Royal Copenhagen stoneware vase, by Gerd Bogelund, Denmark, 1940s–50s, 9in (23cm) high.

£270–300 RIWA

A Royal Copenhagen stoneware vase, by Axel Salto, decorated with stylized seed pods, painted and printed marks, Denmark, c1943, 7¼in (18.5cm) high.

£1,700–2,000 S(O)

A Gustavsberg Pottery faïence vase, by Stig Lindberg, slight damage, signed, Sweden, 1940s–50s, 15¾in (40cm) high.

£500–600 BUK

Stig Lindberg (1916–82) worked at Gustavsberg from 1937 and was made a director in 1978. For the last two years of his life he had his own studio in Italy.

A Gustavsberg Farsta ware jar and cover, by Wilhelm Kåge, signed, Sweden, 1951, 11½in (29cm) high.

£4,250–5,100 BUK

A ceramic vase, by Pablo Picasso, in the form of an owl, marked, France, 1951, 11¾in (30cm) high.

£4,800–5,700 S(O)

A painted terracotta plate, by Jean Cocteau, marked, signed and dated 1952, France, 12in (30.5cm) diam.

£1,300–1,550 S(O)

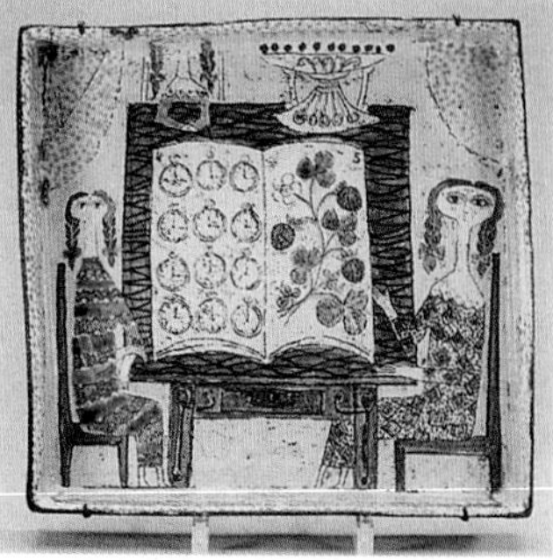

► **A Rörstrand stoneware dish,** by Birger Kaipiainen, painted with women seated at a table, signed, Sweden, 1954–58, 14½in (37cm) square.

£1,450–1,700 BUK

AUDREY STERNSHINE
AS Antique Galleries
26 Broad St
Pendleton, Salford
Manchester M6 5BY
Tel: 0161 737 5938
Fax: 0161 737 6626
Specialist in Art Nouveau & Art Deco.
www.artnouveau-artdeco.com
Email: as@artnouveau-artdeco.com

A Lucie Rie pottery footed bowl, c1955, 5in (12.5cm) diam.

£2,250–2,700 JNic

An earthenware bowl, by Herta Hillfon, decorated with representations of the sun, slight damage, Sweden, 1958, 20in (51cm) diam.

£350–420 BUK

A set of three Gustavsberg Pungo vases, by Stig Lindberg, Sweden, 1950s, largest 10in (25.5cm) high.

£720–800 PI

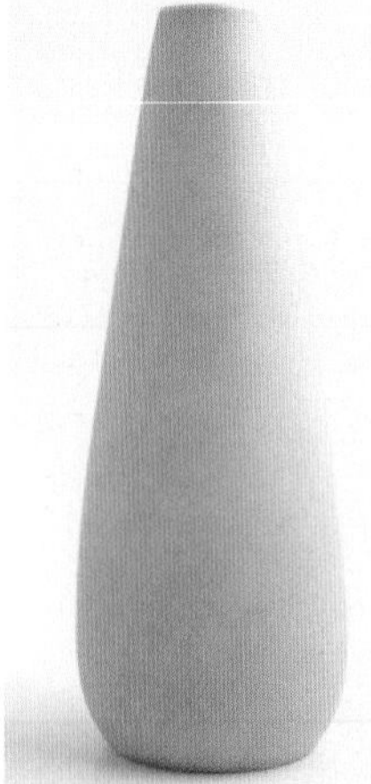

◄ **A Palshus tapered cylinder vase,** by Per Linneman-Schmidt, with hare's fur glaze, Denmark, 1950s, 9in (23cm) high.

£220–250 RIWA

Palshus was founded by Per and Annelise Linneman-Schmidt in 1948. Early pieces are simple in style with matt glazes. Later they experimented with rough glazes with incised decoration.

► **A Rörstrand pottery ewer,** by Gunnar Nylund, Sweden, 1950s, 9in (23cm) high.

£155–175 MARK

A porcelain charger, by Nino Strada, Italy, Milan, 1950s, 14in (35.5cm) diam.

£175–195 MARK

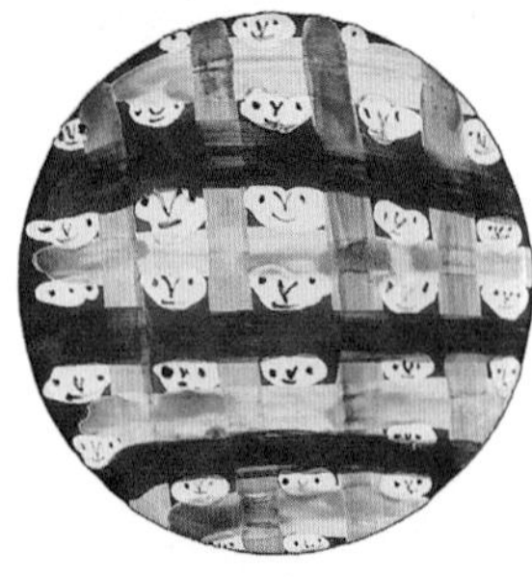

An earthenware plate, by Pablo Picasso, painted with faces, No. 57 of edition of 150, marked, France, 9¾in (25cm) diam.

£2,600–3,100 S(O)

A Portmeirion Jupiter coffee service, comprising 15 pieces, c1964, coffee pot 13in (33cm) high.

£340–380 CHI

A Troika wall plaque, painted marks, c1964, 10¾in (27.5cm) high.

£1,200–1,400 WW

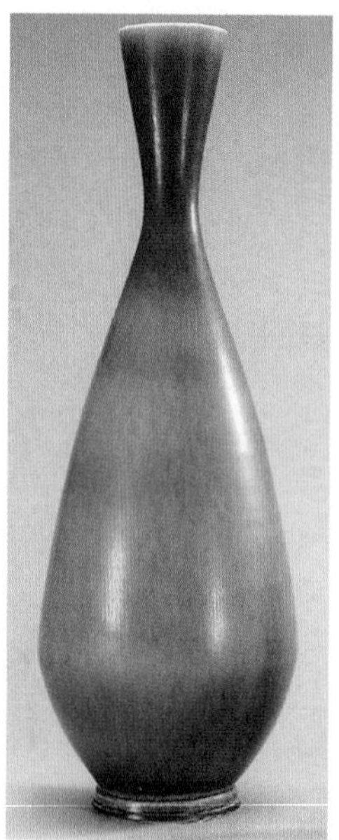

◄ **A Gustavsberg stoneware vase,** by Berndt Friberg, with hare's fur glaze, signed, Sweden, 1965, 21¾in (55.5cm) high.

£4,400–5,200 BUK

A descendant of many generations of potters, Berndt Friberg was born in Höganäs, Sweden, in 1899. He worked in the Höganäs pottery from the age of 13 until 18 and then for a number of Danish factories until 1934, when he found employment at Gustavsberg.

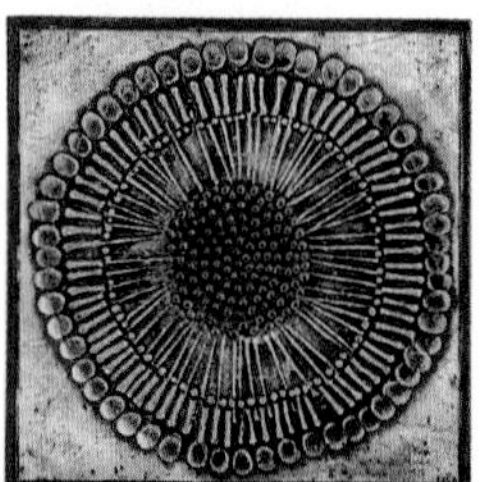

A Gustavsberg Unik Sunflower wall plaque, by Lisa Larson, 1967–86, 9in (23cm) square.

£80–90 RIWA

A painted terracotta tile, by Pablo Picasso, No. 5 of edition of 200, stamped and inscribed marks, France, 1968–69, 6¾in (17cm) square.

£1,050–1,250 S(O)

◄ **A Gustavsberg stoneware bowl,** by Berndt Friberg, signed, Sweden, 1969, 8¾in (22cm) diam.

£550–660 BUK

A Royal Copenhagen vase, by Berte Jessen, Denmark, 1969–74, 8in (20.5cm) high.

£95–110 RUSK

A stoneware bottle vase, by Finn Lyngaard, Denmark, 1960s, 15in (38cm) high.

£200–230 RIWA

An Aldermaston Pottery charger, by Alan Caiger-Smith, painted with a salamander, painted marks, 1960s, 10¾in (27.5cm) diam.

£120–140 DN

The Aldermaston Pottery was founded in 1955 by Alan Caiger-Smith. Drawing his influences from the pottery of the Middle East, the Hispano-Moresque period in Spain, the Italian Renaissance and 17th- and 18th-century European delftwares, Caiger-Smith developed a calligraphic style of painting that blended a modern approach with traditional handcraft techniques. Domestic wares were produced alongside one-off pieces, giving Aldermaston a stature beyond the conventional studio pottery. The pottery was closed in 1993 but was reopened some five years later by Caiger-Smith's son, Nick.

A Rörstrand stoneware dish, by Carl-Harry Stålhane, signed, Sweden, 1960s, 22½in (57cm) diam.

£1,450–1,700 BUK

Carl-Harry Stålhane was born in Mariestad, Sweden in 1920. He began work as an apprentice designer at Rörstrand in 1939 and stayed there until 1973, when he opened a studio with Kent Ericsson. They exported to the US, Japan and Germany among other countries.

A stoneware Ukul vessel, by Claude Conover, painted signature, America, Cleveland, 1960s, 21¾in (55.5cm) high.

£2,900–3,450 S(NY)

A Rörstrand plaque, by Sylvia Leuchovius, edition of 800, Sweden, 1960s, 17in (43cm) wide.

£105–120 PI

For more American wall clocks
see pages 349–353

An electric wall clock, mounted on a wood panel, with ceramic numerals and tiles by Harris Strong, manufacturer's label, America, 1960s, 42½in (108cm) wide.

£145–170 WW

A glazed earthenware plaque, by Robert Arneson, entitled 'Split Lick', signed, America, dated 1991, 14½in (37cm) high.

£17,900–21,400 S(NY)

Accused of racism by a colleague while working at the University of California, Robert Arneson created a series of works in the early 1990s that explored racial prejudices, specifically towards African Americans. The mask shown here not only conveys these ideas, but also marks the transition into his next body of work, an exhibition of self-portrait masks.

Arneson's work has always been controversial and his commission of a bust of Mayor George Moscone of San Francisco was rejected by the San Francisco Art Commission in 1881. He often used his own face as the subject of his art. His work, which has been widely exhibited, has sold for up to £38,000.

► **A stoneware and porcelain plate,** by Peter Voulkos, signed, America, 1973, 18½in (47cm) diam.

£7,800–9,300 S(NY)

A Lucie Rie stoneware bowl, impressed monogram, 1970s, 6in (15cm) diam.

£1,050–1,250 S(O)

► **A Bernard Rooke pottery vase,** 1970s, 14in (35.5cm) high.

£110–125 MARK

Bernard Rooke studied at Ipswich School of Art and opened a studio pottery in 1960 in south London. He relocated to Suffolk in 1967, where he opened a studio and workshop.

FURNITURE

A chrome and leather chaise longue, by Le Corbusier, model No. B306, France, 1928.

£1,500–1,800 LAY

Copyright

In the past, manufacturers had to pay a fee for the use of any furniture designs and the artist was paid a fee for each product that was produced. When a designer dies, the copyright protecting these designs belongs to his/her estate for 50 years, after which the designs belong to the public domain, and anyone can reproduce them without legal implications. However, buyers should be aware that some reproductions fall short of the works of the masters.

A leather and chrome Barcelona chair, by Ludwig Mies van der Rohe for Knoll, designed 1929, manufactured 1960s, America.

£1,600–1,800 MARK

The Barcelona chair was designed by the German architect and designer Ludwig Mies van der Rohe for the German pavilion at the 1929 Barcelona International Exhibition. Since this design is now in the public domain, inferior examples abound. The Knoll version features a one-piece steel frame, while lesser pieces have two-part frames that screw together at the top corners. The dimensions can also vary slightly.

A wrought-iron and painted metal table, by Warren McArthur, from the Arizona Biltmore Hotel, Phoenix, America, c1929, 27¾in (70.5cm) high.

£4,550–5,400 S(NY)

Having been apprenticed to Frank Lloyd Wright from 1907 to 1909, Albert McArthur opened an architectural firm in Chicago in 1912, and relocated his practice to Phoenix in 1925. While in Phoenix, McArthur was hired as the primary architect for the Arizona Biltmore Hotel commissioned in the late 1920s. McArthur collaborated with his former mentor, Frank Lloyd Wright, who served as a consultant on the project, and with his brother Warren, who designed all the interior furnishings, including tubular steel and wrought-iron furniture for the hotel's patios, terraces and bedrooms. The hotel opened its doors to the public in November 1929.

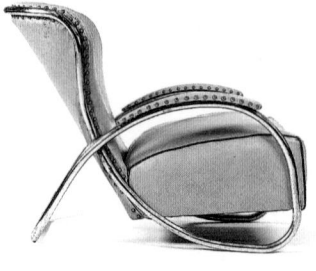

A pair of birch chairs, by Alvar Aalto for Finmar, Finland, c1932.

£1,600–1,800 EMH

Alvar Aalto

Alvar Aalto is one of the most significant figures in 20th-century design. Having trained as an architect in Finland, he received his first major architectural commission in the 1920s for a sanatorium in Paimio, Finland. He also designed the Finnish pavilions at the 1937 Paris Exhibition and the 1939 World's Fair in New York. In 1935 he established the Artek firm to manufacture and retail his furniture designs, as well as glassware and lighting. Aalto's designs were used widely in Finnish educational and healthcare establishments, the use of timber making for a more comfortable form of functionalist Modernism than that associated with metal or machine-age styling. These furniture designs could be economically manufactured and transported, and Artek exported to Britain through Finmar Ltd, and to America – Harvard University Library purchased Aalto tables for its reading rooms.

► **A chrome-plated steel and leatherette armchair,** by Kem Weber for Lloyd Manufacturing Co, America, Michigan.

£10,400–12,400 S(NY)

Karl Emanuel Martin, or Kem, Weber was born in Berlin in 1889, and trained as a cabinet-maker before travelling to San Francisco in 1914 where he was stranded due to the outbreak of WWI. Travelling to Europe in 1925, he was strongly influenced by the developments in French modern design and returned to California to put these ideas into effect.

◄ **A nest of three ebonized-wood and pewter tables,** by Nils Fougstedt for Svenskt Tenn, engraved with motifs depicting Noah's Ark, slight damage, stamped mark, Sweden, 1934, largest 26¼in (66.5cm) wide.

£17,000–20,400 BUK

A nest of two cast aluminium tables, by Frederick Kiesler for Alivar Museum, Italy, designed 1935, manufactured 1960s, larger 34in (86.5cm) wide.

£2,250–2,700 S(NY)

Lillian Kiesler licensed Alivar Museum to produce an edition of the biomorphic nesting table originally designed in 1935 by Frederick Kiesler for the New York apartment of the fabric designer Alma Mergentine.

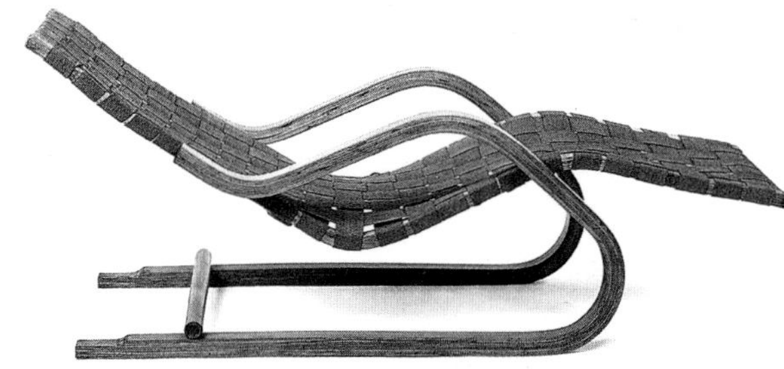

A laminated birch and canvas chaise longue, by Alvar Aalto for Artek, Finland, Helsinki, c1940.

£5,500–6,600 S(NY)

This chair model was first shown in the Finnish pavilion designed by Aalto for the Paris World's Fair in 1937.

A teak chair, designed by Finn Juhl for Niels Vodder, with retailer's label, Denmark, Copenhagen, 1945–46.

£9,100–10,900 S(NY)

Finn Juhl (1912–89) began his career in an architect's office and worked with the master cabinet-maker Niels Vodder on the construction of his furniture designs. By the late 1940s Juhl had opened his own design office and was also teaching at the Fredericksburg Technical School. International recognition came in the 1950s when he won five gold medals at the 1957 Milan Triennale. Juhl shared the love of organic, natural forms and materials of contemporaries such as Arne Jacobsen, but he relied more on traditional cabinet-making techniques to create his complicated designs.

A mahogany and leather elbow chair, by Gordon Russell, 1948.

£580–650 EMH

British furniture-maker and designer Gordon Russell (1892–1980) had no formal education in design, but he absorbed and treasured the ideas of the Arts & Crafts movement as a result of working in the Cotswolds where the architect and designers C. R. Ashbee and Ernest Gimson had established medieval-style guilds and rural communities to promote craftsmanship.

A fibreglass rocking chair, by Charles and Ray Eames, America, 1948.

£1,350–1,500 MARK

Charles and Ray Eames were the first designers to explore the use of the new materials developed in the mid-20th century and apply them to furniture design. Their designs moved away from the angular forms popular in the 1920s and 1930s to a more organic, sculptural appearance.

► **A plywood and cotton webbing chaise longue,** by Klaus Grabbe, America, New York, c1948.

£1,050–1,250 TREA

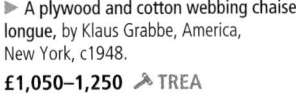

A bronze and travertine marble table, by Gio Ponti, Italy, c1948, 61in (155cm) diam.

£11,000–12,500 DeP

The architect and designer Gio Ponti embraced both tradition and modernity, working with both craft workshops and industrial manufacturers. He was involved in all areas of design, from town planning, buildings and interiors, to furniture, domestic machines and ornamental items.

◄ **A birch plywood day bed,** by Richard Stein for Knoll, reupholstered, America, c1948, 83in (211cm) wide.

£1,150–1,350 TREA

► **A set of four oak-veneered plywood Standard chairs,** by Jean Prouvé for Etablissements Vauconsant, France, 1940s.

£8,400–10,000 S(NY)

A pair of burr-maple chests of drawers, by Johan Tapp, marked, America, 1940s, 36in (91.5cm) wide.

£11,100–13,300 S(NY)

While much is known about the career of Johan Tapp (1888–1939), a Dutch-born designer and cabinet-maker whose Chicago-based firm produced expensive reproductions of Chippendale and Sheraton furniture, the enduring mystery is who in the firm designed the sensational 1940s pieces that rarely appear on the market. These tapering chests of drawers, the fronts carved with rustic oak leaves from which dangle bunches of acorn pulls, were apparently commissioned for the original owner's bedroom which was decorated by Alfred Messner.

A desk, designed for Gump's, with four drawers and a drop-leaf side, slight damage, signed, 1940s, 45in (114.5cm) extended.

£230–270 TREA

A pine console table, by Edward Wormley for Dunbar, carved with a shell, America, 1940s, 32in (81.5cm) wide.

£1,900–2,250 TREA

An ebonized-birch and steel Rudder stool, by Isamu Noguchi for Herman Miller, America, c1950, 16¾in (42.5cm) high.

£15,600–18,700 S(NY)

Isamu Noguchi (1904–88) was born in Los Angeles but his work is firmly rooted in the Japanese tradition, as he initially trained in cabinet-making c1917 in Japan. On returning to the US he trained in both medicine and sculpture, eventually giving up medicine altogether to concentrate on design. He won a Guggenheim fellowship in 1927 and worked in Paris for two years as assistant to the sculptor Constantin Brancusi. After travelling to Japan and Beijing in the early 1930s, he returned to New York where he practised as a sculptor. By the early 1940s he was working extensively in furniture, glassware and industrial product design. He became a consultant designer for Herman Miller after his work was brought to their attention by George Nelson.

An oak and painted chest of drawers, by G-Plan, with adjustable supports, c1950, 24in (61cm) wide.

£90–100 PI

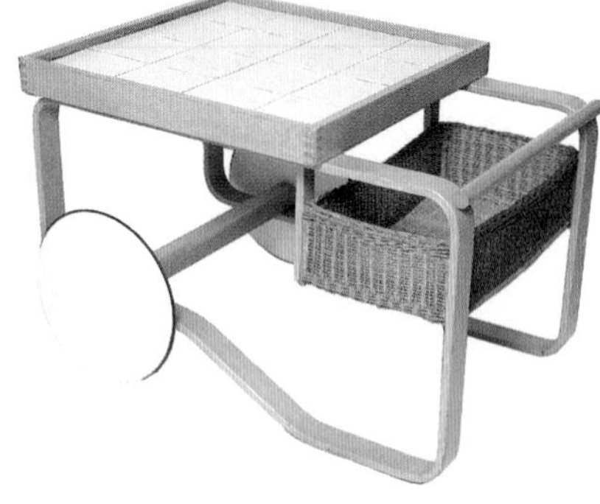

A birch tea trolley, by Alvar Aalto, No. 900, Finland,1950s, 36in (91.5cm) wide.

£1,300–1,450 DeP

▶ **A painted-iron and fabric Bowl chair,** by Lina Bo Bardi, Brazil, c1951, 29½in (75cm) high.

£24,500–29,400 S(NY)

Lina Bo Bardi ranks as one of the most prolific and successful female architects of her generation and her contributions are often compared to those of Charlotte Perriand, Lily Reich, Julia Morgan and Eileen Gray. Born and educated in Rome, she moved to Milan after her studies and worked on projects for the Gio Ponti office. Three years later, she and her husband Pietro Maria Bardi, a prominent art critic and gallery owner, moved to Brazil where the latter was invited to direct the Sao Paulo Museum of Art. Bo Bardi became a naturalized Brazilian citizen in 1951.

Throughout her career, Bo Bardi designed furnishings for numerous interiors, but perhaps her most famous chair, simply known as the Bowl chair, was designed for industrial production. Illustrated on the cover of the November 1953 issue of Interiors, *the chair was dubbed a 'free-tilting cuddle bowl'.*

Charlotte Perriand

Charlotte Perriand (1903–99) attended the *Ecole Centrale des Arts Décoratifs* in Paris in the early 1920s. In 1927, she began working with the architect Le Corbusier and together they designed modern furniture using tubular steel, sheet metal and aluminium. Perriand was inspired by the Machine Age and developed a great interest in creating furniture using industrial materials. She was well known for creating space-saving and storage furniture.

◀ **A tropical woods and aluminium cabinet,** by Charlotte Perriand in collaboration with Les Ateliers Jean Prouvé and André Chetaille, with 15 doors containing drawers and trays, France, 1952, 86½in (219.5cm) wide.

£11,700–14,000 S(NY)

This cabinet was designed to divide the kitchen and dining areas of the Air France apartments in Brazzaville.

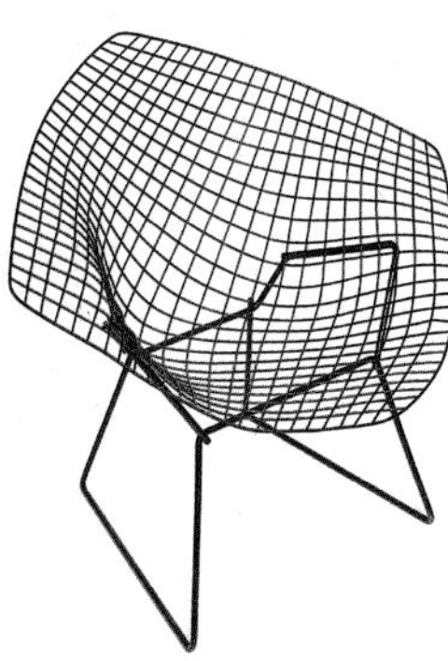

An enamelled metal Diamond chair, by Harry Bertoia for Knoll, America, 1952.
£180–200 FRD

A lacquered-steel and pine Mexique bookcase, by Charlotte Perriand and Jean Prouvé for Les Ateliers Jean Prouvé, France, c1953, 71¾in (182.5cm) wide.
£62,000–74,000 S(NY)

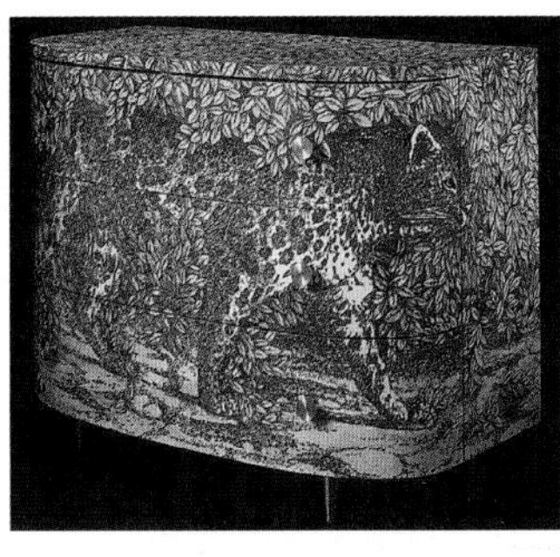

A wood and brass Leopard cabinet, by Piero Fornasetti, transfer-printed and painted with a leopard, No. 1 of edition of 8, Italy, designed 1953, manufactured 1992, 39¾in (101cm) wide.
£16,900–20,200 S(NY)

Piero Fornasetti worked from his house in Milan, where his son continues the studio today. His whimsical, dramatic decorations were based on the trompe l'oeil techniques of stage scene painters. They covered every surface of his furniture and featured on ceramics and a host of other household objects.

◀ A teak and oak Valet chair, by Hans Wegner for Johannes Hansen, the hinged seat revealing a compartment and forming a trouser stand, marked, Denmark, designed 1953, 37in (94cm) high.
£7,200–8,600 S

This chair was designed by Wegner for the 1953 Copenhagen Cabinet maker's Guild Exhibition. It was not intended for production but King Frederik IX saw the chair when he opened the exhibition and immediately ordered one. The chair proved popular and Hansen went on to produce further chairs but in limited numbers.

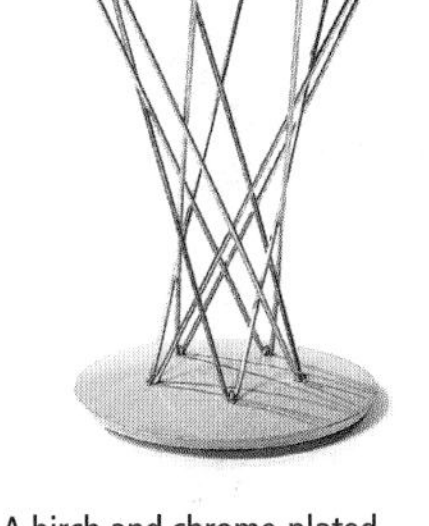

A birch and chrome-plated rocking stool, by Isamu Noguchi for Knoll, America, c1955, 16½in (42cm) high.
£13,000–15,600 S(NY)

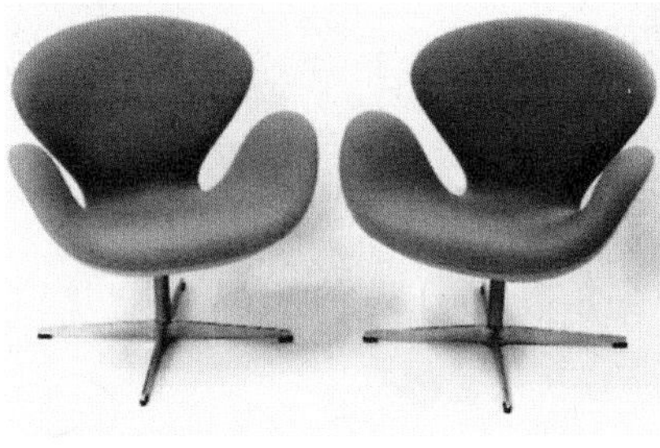

A pair of metal and upholstery Swan chairs, by Arne Jacobsen for Fritz Hansen, Denmark, designed 1956.
£1,500–1,800 JNic

The Swan, Ant and Egg chairs designed by Arne Jacobsen for the Danish furniture manufacturers Fritz Hansen helped define a characteristic Danish version of modern design and to continue a Scandinavian tradition of combining functionalism with softer, more organic shapes.

A metal and upholstery Lady chair, by Marco Zanuso, Italy, c1953.
£1,250–1,400 MARK

Zanuso was one of the first designers to experiment with materials such as foam rubber which had previously never been used in furniture manufacture. This material opened up a host of new design possibilities, since it could be shaped, moulded and upholstered to produce soft, curvaceous forms.

◀ A metal and upholstery Cone stool, by Verner Panton, Denmark, designed 1956, manufactured 1960s, 19in (48.5cm) diam.
£450–500 MARK

Verner Panton trained as an architect between 1950 and 1952, and after graduating from the Royal Academy of Fine Arts in Copenhagen, he spent some time working with Arne Jacobsen on designs including the Ant chair. He is arguably one of the most inventive and original designers of the Pop era, and is one of the most collected and admired modern designers today.

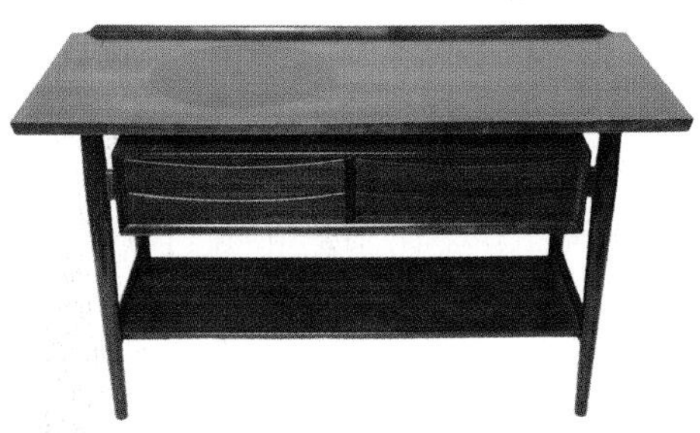

▶ A rosewood serving table, by Arne Vodder, Denmark, designed 1956, manufactured 1960s, 51in (129.5cm) wide.
£1,350–1,500 PI

An enamelled-steel and laminate telephone stand, by Eliot Noyes for IBM, America, c1957, 22½in (57cm) high.
£540–640 TREA

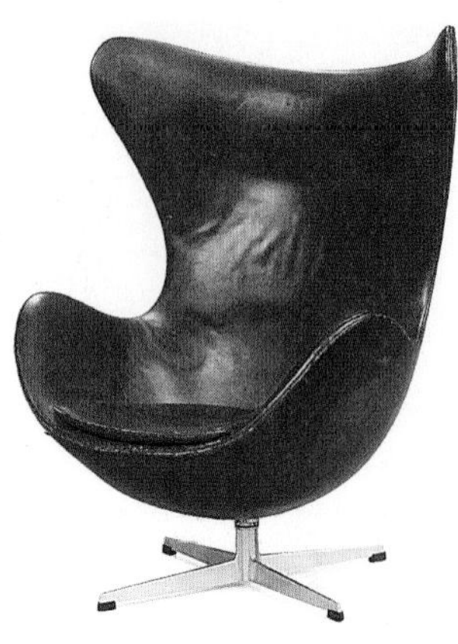

An aluminium and leather **Egg chair,** by Arne Jacobsen for Fritz Hansen, with label, Denmark, designed 1958, manufactured 1965.

£3,300–3,950 BUK

This chair was designed for the Royal Hotel, Copenhagen.

A copper-plated steel and leather Drop chair, by Arne Jacobsen for Fritz Hansen, Denmark.

£21,100–25,300 S(NY)

The Drop chair is a unique design only produced for the Royal Hotel, Copenhagen by Fritz Hansen. There were many versions of the Drop chair upholstered in fabric, which were used to decorate the rooms and approximately 50 chairs upholstered in leather for the snack bar. When the hotel was renovated, the leather Drop chairs were discarded. However, hotel employees salvaged some of the pieces, and today only approximately 30 examples of this iconic chair survive.

Arne Jacobsen

Arne Jacobsen (1902–71) originally trained as a mason but switched to architecture and by the early 1930s had founded his own design office specializing in architecture and interior design. He was committed to the Danish tradition of using natural materials but by the late 1950s he had embraced the new technology that enabled him to create the sculptural organic shapes that distinguish them from those of his contemporaries. He has become one of the most sought-after 20th century designers, thanks to his iconic designs such as the Egg, Ant and Swan chairs that epitomize Danish style in the mid-20th century.

An oak chest of drawers, by Stag, with four drawers, c1959, 30in (76cm) wide.

£670–750 BOOM

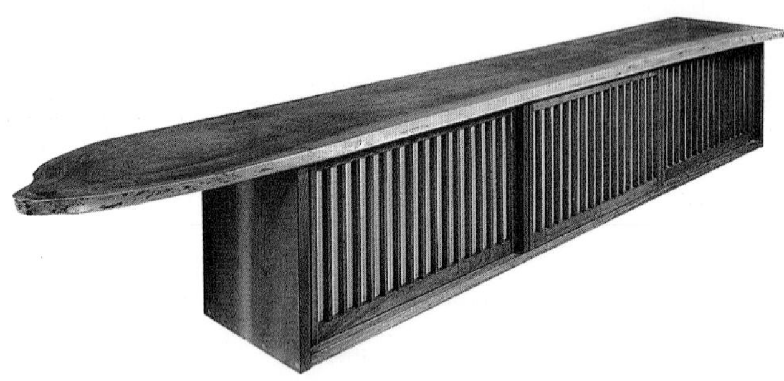

A walnut and pandanus cloth Hanging Wall Case, by George Nakashima, inscribed with client's name, America, 1959–60, 103½in (263cm) wide.

£52,000–62,000 S(NY)

The Hanging Wall Case shown here features a free-form slab top, which allows the natural personality of the wood to be expressed. The size, condition and Japanese-influenced sliding doors are major factors governing the price realized for this piece. The client's inclusion of the name is also important because it allows the piece to be dated and authenticated by Nakashima's studio.

A child's chrome and leatherette swivel armchair, in the style of Arne Jacobsen, c1950, 26in (66cm) high.

£120–140 Hal

A rosewood and leather chaise longue, by Joaquim Tenreiro, with a partial paper label, Brazil, c1950, 65in (165cm) long.

£21,100–25,300 S(NY)

The design for this chaise longue was inspired by the hammocks used in the northeast of Brazil.

A steel and rope Flag Halyard lounge chair, by Hans J. Wegner for Getama, with original cushion, Denmark, designed 1950, manufactured 1950s–60s.

£3,750–4,500 BUK

Hans Wegner

Hans Wegner (b1914) graduated in joinery from the Technological Institute in Copenhagen in 1938 at the age of 24. He made a name for himself in the 1950s when he won the prestigious Lunning prize and a gold medal at the 1951 Milan Triennale. One of his longest collaborations has been with the Copenhagen furniture manufacturer Johannes Hansen, with whom he first teamed up in 1940. Wegner was inspired by traditional furniture examples that he then updated with the use of newer materials such as teak and plywood. The Flag Halyard is one of Wegner's most futuristic designs, resembling a spacecraft, some ten years before the space age really began. The seat, sides and back are made from flag halyard and it came with a removable sheepskin cover and a pillow for a headrest. Wegner's chairs have sold throughout the world and were even used by the American President, John F. Kennedy, in a televised presidential debate.

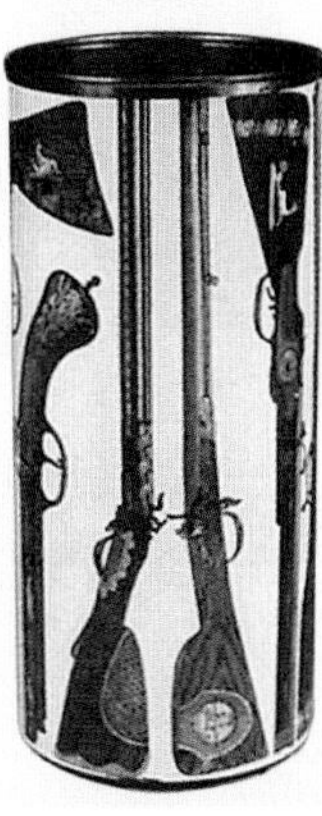

A metal umbrella stand, by Piero Fornasetti, decorated with lithograph images of rifles and pistols, printed marks, Italy, 1950s, 22½in (57cm) high.

£940–1,100 CGC

A teak daybed, by Hans Wegner for Getama, with wool upholstery, converts to a twin bed with a bedding storage area, signed, stamped mark, Denmark, 1950s, 77in (195.5cm) wide.

£900–1,050 TREA

A talosel and glass mirror, by Line Vautrin, signed and numbered, France, 1950s, 11¼in (28.5cm) diam.

£9,700–11,600 S(NY)

▶ **A walnut coffee table,** with metal label, by Trivia, NK-Design, Sweden, Nyköping, 1950s, 49¾in (126.5cm) wide.

£840–1,000 S(O)

A maplewood drop-leaf dining table and six chairs, by Heywood-Wakefield, America, c1950, table 40in (101.5cm) wide.

£750–900 JAA

◀ **A plywood, plastic laminate and painted steel ETR table,** by Charles and Ray Eames, for Herman Miller, America, 1950s, 89in (226cm) wide.

£2,250–2,700 S(NY)

This item is commonly referred to

A lacquered steel and reconstituted marble Granito table, by Jean Prouvé, France, 1950s, 81in (205.5cm) wide.

£18,200–21,800 S(NY)

Jean Prouvé

Jean Prouvé (1901–84) was a key designer working in the International Style in France, collaborating with other designers such as Le Corbusier and Charlotte Perriand. International Style pieces had sleek, clear lines with little or no decoration, and were generally not constructed of expensive materials. Prouvé trained in metalwork and opened his own workshop in Paris in 1923. In 1929 he founded with Le Corbusier the *Union des Artistes Modernes* and opened his own company, *Société des Ateliers Jean Prouvé*, in 1931. His designs were ideally suited for industial mass production and were used in schools and other public buildings throughout France.

A teak bureau, Sweden, c1960, 28in (71cm) wide.

£90–100 PI

◀ **A set of four teak and leather chairs,** by Ejvind Johansen, Denmark, c1960.

£1,050–1,200 MARK

▶ **A teak chest of drawers,** by Ib Kofod-Larsen for G-Plan, with six drawers, Denmark, c1960, 30in (76cm) wide.

£90–100 PI

A walnut and hickory Cross-Legged desk and New chair, by George Nakashima, both with the client's name on the underside, America, 1963, desk 47¼in (120cm) wide.

£14,300–17,100 S(NY)

▶ A leather and stainless steel Scimitar Lounge Chair, by Preben Fabricius and Jørgen Kastholm for Ivan Schlecter, branded mark, Denmark, designed 1963, 25½in (65cm) high.

£3,600–4,300 S

This chair was first presented at the Paris Furniture Fair of 1963 to international acclaim.

A rosewood table, by Silkborg, Denmark, c1963, 39½in (100.5cm) diam.

£720–800 BOOM

A tubular steel, urethane foam and nylon jersey Djinn sofa, by Olivier Mourgue for Airborne International, France, c1965, 47in (119.5cm) wide.

£1,350–1,500 MARK

A sofa of this design was used in 2001: A Space Odyssey. *The name 'Djinn' is derived from a spirit in Islamic mythology that can assume human or animal form and control men with supernatural powers.*

A set of four laminated walnut and vinyl side chairs, by Norman Cherner for Plycraft, America, labelled and dated 1964.

£1,450–1,700 TREA

A teak side cabinet, by Hans J. Wegner for Ry Möbler, slight damage, labelled, Denmark, 1965, 71in (180.5cm) wide.

£550–660 BUK

A foam ABCD chair and sofa, by Pierre Paulin, France, c1965, sofa 84in (213.5cm) wide.

£3,150–3,500 MARK

Pierre Paulin (b1927) studied sculpture in Paris and his classical training is reflected in the sculptural forms of his furniture from the 1960s. Having designed furniture for Thonet and Artifort in the 1950s, he opened his own industrial design office in Paris in 1965. By this time Paulin was breaking new ground with his inventive styling using foam, tubular steel, fibreglass and polyester.

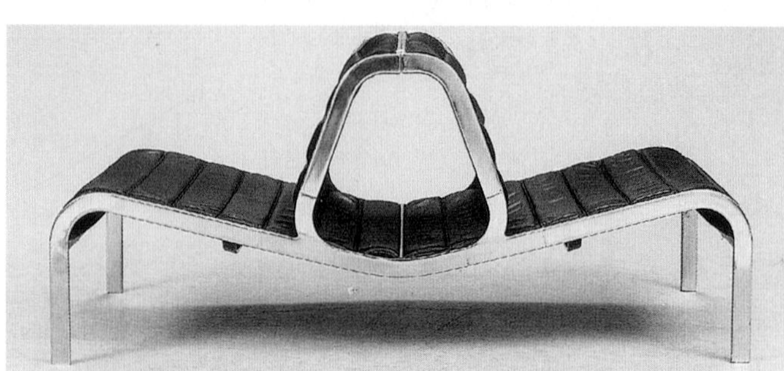

A leather and tubular steel Twinseat, by Olivier Mourgue for Airbourne International, France, 1960s, 57in (145cm) wide.

£1,200–1,400 BUK

Olivier Mourgue (b1939) is known for both his public and private commissions. He is most famous for his expressive, neo-organic furniture based on the shapes of the human body. Like Pierre Paulin he created fun, futuristic, comfortable and portable chairs out of tubular steel, foam and fabric.

◄ **A pair of rosewood-veneered side chairs,** designed by Dante La Torre for Pozzi e Verga, with ebonized legs, Italy, c1965.

£2,150–2,550 S(O)

A teak desk, by Hans Hansen, the kneehole flanked by eight drawers with open shelving to the reverse, Denmark, c1965, 60¼in (153cm) wide.

£1,450–1,650 BOOM

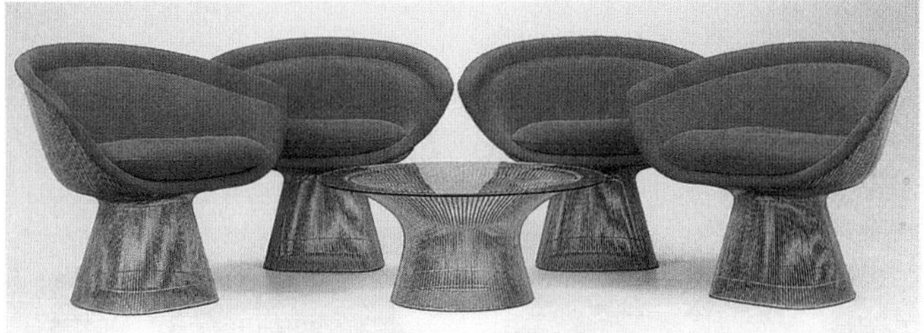

A nickel-plated tubular steel table and four armchairs, by Warren Platner for Knoll, the chairs with plush velvet upholstery, the table with a glass top, slight damage, America, 1960s–70s, table 35½in (90cm) diam.

£3,050–3,650 BUK

A walnut and hickory Harvest bench, by George Nakashima, signed, America, dated 1967, 59½in (151cm) wide.

£11,400–13,700 TREA

A wood and fabric Keyhole rocking chair, by Hans J. Wegner for Getama, Denmark, 1967.

£1,300–1,450 EMH

A rosewood, steel and chrome cabinet, by Merrow Associates, 1968, 36¼in (92cm) wide.

£1,300–1,450 BOOM

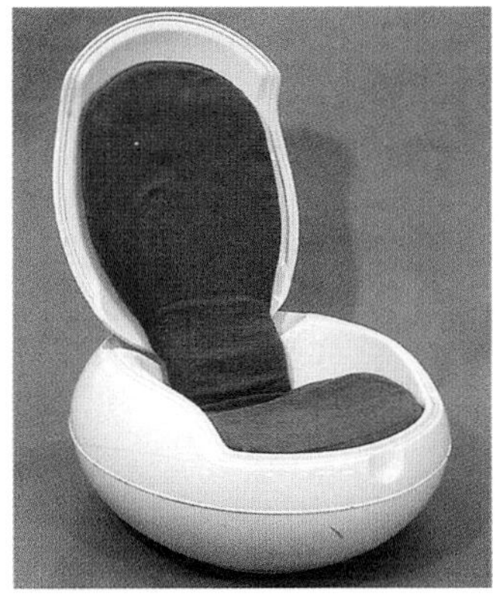

A moulded plastic Egg chair, by Peter Ghyzcy for Reuter Products, 1968.

£340–400 WilP

This organically-styled chair could be folded down into a plastic pod for protection against the elements when used outside, but it was equally popular inside the house. Examples were produced in a range of different coloured upholstery – bright Pop Art colours are the most desirable. Condition is also important – cracks, scratches or dents will affect the value.

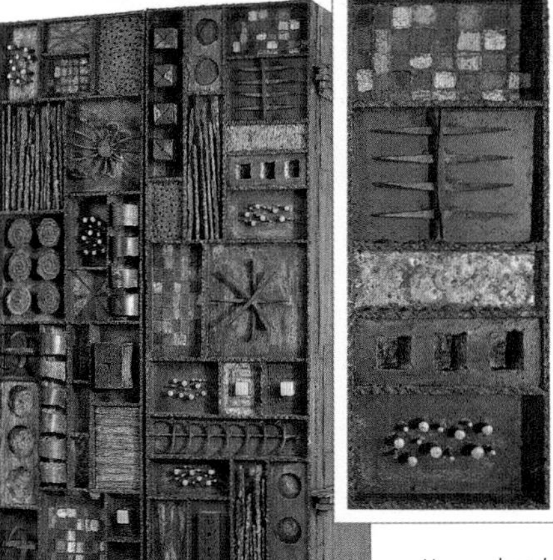

◄ **A patinated, painted and gilt-steel cabinet,** by Paul Evans, for Evans Studio, from the Sculpted Steel series, America, 1969, 42in (106.5cm) wide.

£45,000–54,000 S(NY)

Paul Evans (1931–87) was born in Pennsylvania and attended Cranbrook Academy of Art in Michigan on an art and design scholarship.

He returned to Pennsylvania and worked from a small studio in New Hope, where he produced his sculpted steel furniture with a staff of no more than eight or nine employees. This furniture was introduced in 1957 in New York, when he was only 26 years old, and met with great success.

In 1964, Evans teamed with Directional Furniture Co and his designs became much more widely available.

A pair of leather and steel Tulip chairs, by Jørgen Kastholm and Preben Fabricius for Alfred Kill, Germany, 1960s.

£1,100–1,300 JNic

A foam, vinyl, lacquered plastic, steel and rubber Tubo chair, by Joe Colombo, Italy, designed c1969, 24in (61cm) high.

£4,200–5,000 S(NY)

Joe Colombo

Joe Colombo (1930–71) was one of the most visionary designers of the 1960s. Born in Milan, he trained as a painter before progressing to architectural design, opening his own design office in Milan in 1962. In 1964 he received the IN-Arch prize for one of his hotel designs and in the same year produced his first chair design. He was hugely influential in advancing chair design, particularly the idea of multi-furniture, where a piece could work in a variety of different ways. The Tubo (tube) chair is a superb example of this, demonstrating Colombo's love of circular forms – a trend reflected across all strands of design in the 1960s, from architecture to textiles. The chair's ingenious design meant that each of the four interlocking plastic cylinders could be fitted together by steel and rubber joints to make curious configurations, whether as upright chairs, horizontal recliners or even just a single circular stool. It was also extremely comfortable, as the plastic shells were covered in polyurethane foam, and packaged in a drawstring bag so it could be stored away easily when not in use, the rings fitting inside one another.

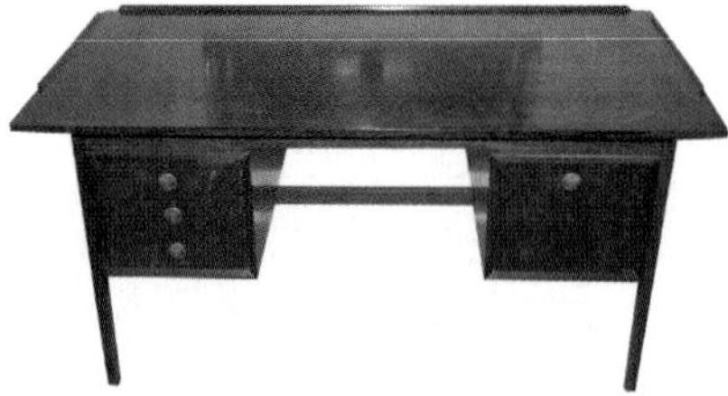

A rosewood desk, with three drawers and a cupboard flanking a kneehole, Denmark, 1960s.

£1,100–1,250 ALCH

◀ **A pair of chrome-plated chairs,** by Harry Bertoia, each with a leather cushion, America, 1960s.

£220–260 DN

Harry Bertoia (1915–78) was born in Italy and moved to the USA with his family in 1930. He studied at the Cranbrook Academy of Fine Arts in Michigan, where he met Charles and Ray Eames, and where he eventually became head of the metal-working department. Bertoia was primarily interested in sculpture and this is reflected in his futuristic wire mesh chairs from the early 1950s.

A chrome-plated steel and leather stool, by Poul Kjaerholm for E. Kold Christensen, model No. PK41, Denmark, 1960s, 14¾in (37.5cm) high.

£3,900–4,650 S(NY)

A leather sofa and two chairs, 1960s, sofa 54in (137cm) wide.

£900–1,000 OCA

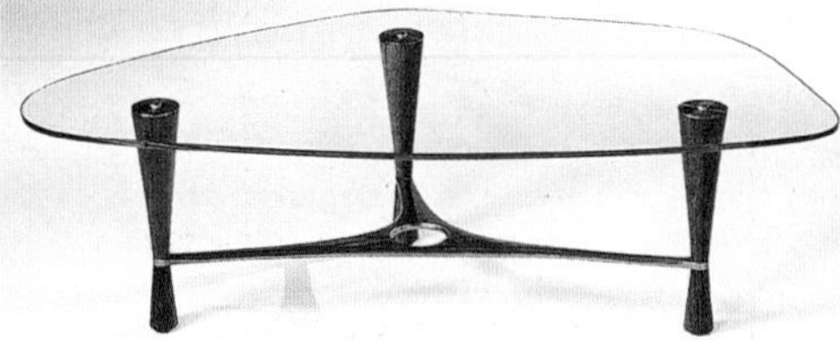

A rosewood, brass and glass coffee table, by Edward Wormley for Dunbar, model No. 5309A, America, 1960s, 57½in (146cm) wide.

£9,100–10,900 S(NY)

Edward Wormley was born in 1907 in a small farming community in Oswego, Illinois. He enrolled at the School of Art Institute in Chicago, but was forced to abandon his studies for financial reasons. His first job was in the interior design studio of the Marshall Field Department Store in Chicago. After a chance introduction to the head of Dunbar Furniture Co, Wormley began a forty-year collaboration with that firm, focusing on luxurious materials, historical allusion and superb construction. The 'Janus' Collection, introduced in 1957, that included 70 pieces and utilized tiles made by Tiffany & Co and Natzler, met with great success. He cited Greene & Greene and other designers and architects from the Arts & Crafts movement as sources of inspiration. He retired in 1967 and died in relative obscurity in 1995.

A nest of three teak occasional tables, by G-Plan, 1960s, largest 38in (96.5cm) wide.

£105–120 NWE

▶ **A palisander dining table and eight chairs,** by Grete Jalk for Poul Jeppesen, the chairs with leather seats, the table with two extra leaves, slight damage, marked, Denmark, 1960s, table 96½in (245cm) extended.

£1,450–1,700 BUK

A rosewood and chrome cocktail trolley, by Poul Norrekilt, Denmark, 1960s, 33in (84cm) wide.

£1,600–1,800 PI

A palisander and chrome writing table, by Bodil Kjaer for Hedensten Møbelfabrik/E. Pedersen, restored, slight damage, Denmark, 1960s, 84¾in (215.5cm) wide.

£3,400–4,050 BUK

In 1959, Kjaer was working for Polaroid in Boston, USA, for whom he designed a range of furniture. The furniture was produced in Denmark in 1961 and this writing table was particularly popular. It featured in the James Bond films From Russia with Love *and* You Only Live Twice, *and both Michael Caine and Prince Philip owned examples.*

A chrome and plastic dining table and six matching chairs, by Frank Wardle for Vono, 1970, table 57in (145cm) wide.

£450–500 FRD

A chair, by Charles and Ray Eames for Herman Miller, America, c1970.

£140–160 OCA

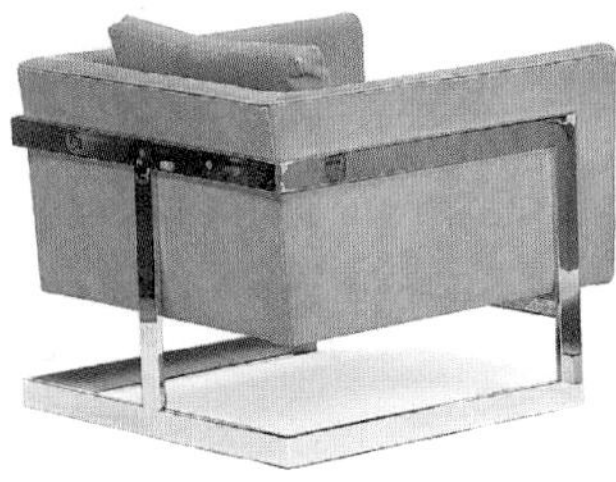

A pair of polished steel and vinyl lounge chairs, by Milo Baughman for Thayer Coggin, one with label, slight damage, America, c1970.

£1,600–1,900 TREA

A Lucite armchair, America, c1970.

£450–500 AGO

Lucite was created by DuPont in the 1930s and is also known as Plexiglas. It is a durable material and therefore resistant to damage and weathering and can be tinted to give it colour.

A pair of chrome-plated steel and leather chairs, by Poul Kjaerholm for E. Kold Christensen, model No. PK20, stamped mark, c1970, Denmark.

£4,200–5,000 S(NY)

Poul Kjaerholm (1929–80) studied at the School of Arts & Crafts in Copenhagen. He taught there from 1952 to 1956 and went on to become a lecturer and later professor in the furniture and interior design department at the Copenhagen Academy of Art. Much of his furniture used steel frames rather than traditional wood, but he did use natural materials such as canvas and leather for the seats of his chairs. A chrome, leather and steel chair that he designed won the Grand Prix at the Milan Trienniale in 1957. His designs were mainly manufactured by Fritz Hansen and, after 1955, E. Kold Christensen.

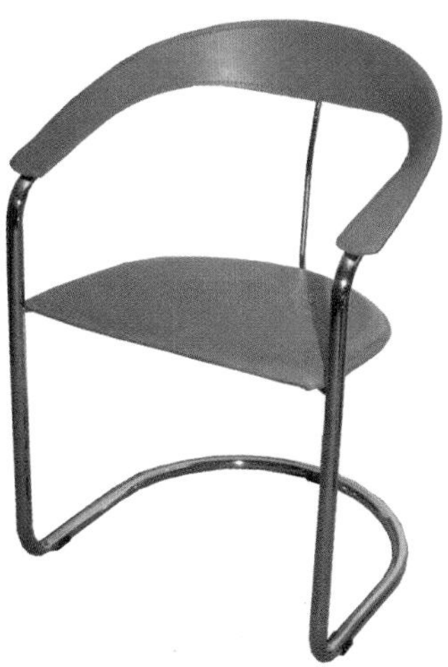

◀ **A set of six chrome and leather chairs,** c1970.

£450–500 OCA

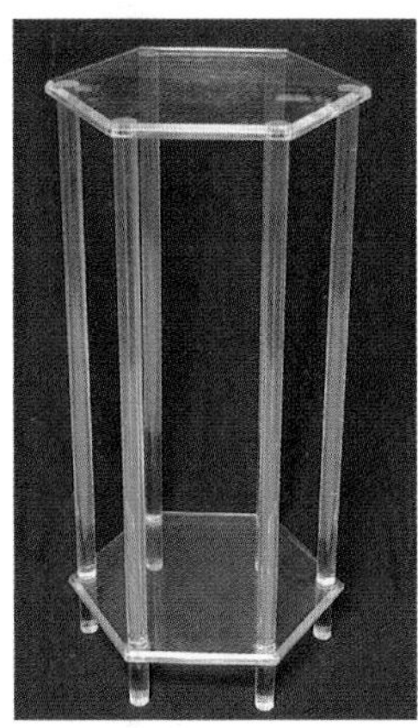

A Lucite stand, America, c1970, 30in (76cm) high.

£540–600 AGO

A set of six chrome-plated tubular steel chairs, by Charlotte Perriand, with leather sling seats, France, 1972.

£3,500–4,200 TREA

◄ **A leather, leatherette, brass, patinated metal and wood umbrella stand,** by Gucci, marked, c1972, 14¼in (36cm) high.

£3,550–4,250 S(NY)

This rare umbrella stand was exclusively designed for the Gucci store, New York, and was never produced for mass retail.

A black walnut, sapwood and rosewood Minguren II coffee table, by George Nakashima, marked with client's name, America, c1977, 76½in (194.5cm) wide.

£31,000–37,000 S(NY)

◄ **A steel, plastic and leather club chair and ottoman,** by Oscar Niemeyer with Anna Maria Niemeyer for Mobilier de France, France, 1970s, ottoman 30½in (77.5cm) wide.

£9,700–11,600 S(NY)

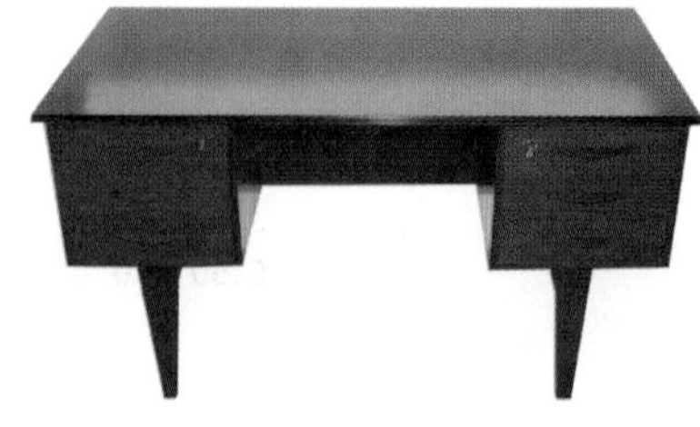

A rosewood double pedestal desk, with six short drawers and open shelving to the reverse, Denmark, 1970s, 52¾in (134cm) wide.

£1,100–1,250 BOOM

An aluminium and glass coffee table, possibly by Thayer Coggin, America, 1970s, 60½in (153.5cm) wide.

£280–330 TREA

A chrome and laminate writing table, by Preben Fabricius and Jørgen Kastholm for BO-EX, Denmark, 1970s, 70in (178cm) wide.

£3,400–4,050 BUK

Preben Fabricius (1931–84) was apprenticed as a cabinet-maker with Nils Vodder in 1952. Jørgen Kastholm (b1931) originally trained as a blacksmith and went on to become a professor of furniture design in Wuppertal, Germany in 1976. They worked together from 1962 to 1971.

A stainless-steel 'C' table, by Frank Gehry, America, 1980–81, 20in (51cm) wide.

£7,800–9,300 S(NY)

A metal Quinta chair, by Mario Botta for Alias, Italy, c1985.

£175–210 WilP

A plastic Jello table, by Marc Newson, Switzerland, 1980s, 23in (58.5cm) diam.

£720–800 MARK

◄ **A steel, teak and moose-leather Rex armchair,** by Mats Theselius for Källemo, No. 31 of edition of 200, with maker's and artist's labels, Sweden, 1990.

£3,900–4,650 S(NY)

► **A pair of tubular steel and leather Club armchairs,** by Peter Celsing for Galleri Stolen, marked, Sweden, 1996.

£16,400–19,600 BUK

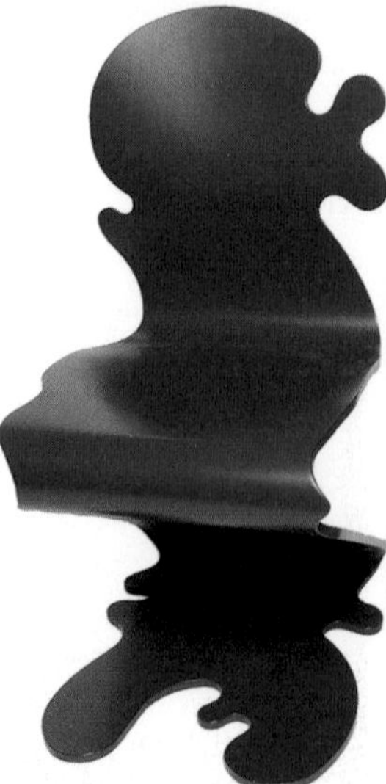

A painted wood Pantonic chair, by Verner Panton, Denmark, 1992.

£155–175 MARK

GLASS

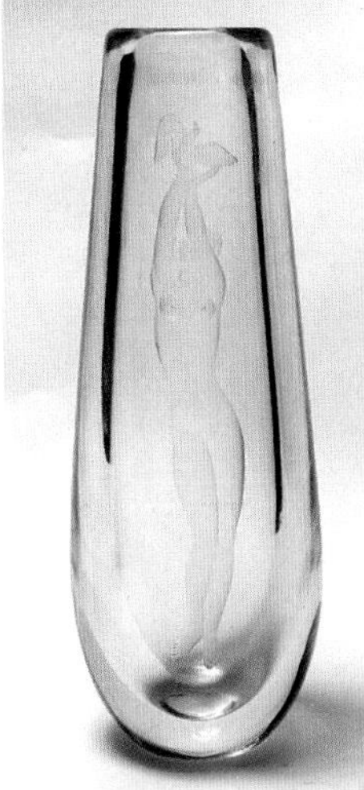

An Orrefors glass vase, by Vicke Lindstrand, Sweden, c1930, 11in (28cm) high.

£670–750 ⊞ JHa

Vicke Lindstrand (1904–83) worked for Orrefors until 1940, but his name has become synonymous with the firm of Kosta, which he joined in 1950.

A Whitefriars Wealdstone glass vase, with wave decoration, c1930, 8in (20.5cm) high.

£150–170 ⊞ RUSK

James Powell & Sons (1835–1980) was one of the foremost makers of studio glass in the Victorian period. James Powell bought the London company Whitefriars Glass Works in 1834 to produce Arts & Crafts-style goblets and wine glasses, carafes, decanters, table centrepieces, vases etc. This commitment to modern design continued throughout the lifetime of the factory.

An Orrefors glass bowl, Sweden, c1933, 9½in (24cm) diam.

£140–155 ⊞ MARK

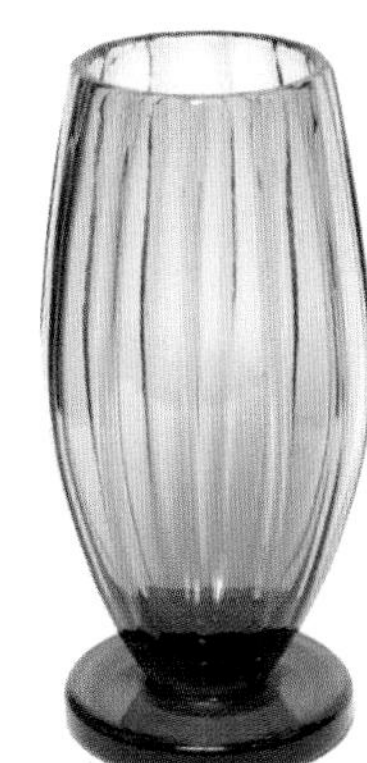

◄ **A Stevens & Williams Royal Brierley glass vase,** by Keith Murray, c1935, 10in (25.5cm) high.

£670–750 ⊞ JSG

Perhaps best known for the Modernist ceramic wares he made for Wedgwood, the New Zealander Keith Murray (1892–1981) was the only real exponent of Modernist glass in England. Influenced by the 1925 Paris Exhibition and the 1930 Swedish Exhibition, his work includes simple, minimalist, symmetrically-blown pieces and cut and engraved items, the best known of which is his Cactus series of vases.

An Orrefors Graal glass vase, by Edward Hald, decorated with fish, engraved mark, Sweden, 1930s, 4¾in (12cm) high.

£380–450 ⚒ CINN

◄ **A Whitefriars ribbed glass vase,** by Barnaby Powell, c1938, 6½in (16.5cm) high.

£85–95 ⊞ HUN

A pair of Webb Corbett glass vases, by Irene Stevens, c1946, 11in (28cm) high.

£1,350–1,500 ⊞ JSG

In 1897, Thomas and Herbert Webb and George Corbett acquired the White House Glassworks in Stourbridge and founded Thomas Webb & Corbett. The Webbs were sons of Thomas Wilkes Webb, the owner of Thomas Webb Glassworks. Webb Corbett was a progressive firm – actively seeking the leading designers of the period. By 1939 the company had grown, employing in excess of 500 staff. Irene Stevens (b1917) was appointed as chief designer in 1946 – she had trained at the Royal College of Art and was influenced by the simplicity and restraint of Georgian glass.

An Orrefors glass vase, by Vicke Lindstrand, Sweden, 1940s, 5¼in (13.5cm) high.

£90–100 ⊞ MARK

An Orrefors frosted glass decanter and three glasses, by Vicke Lindstrand, Sweden, 1940s, decanter 10in (25.5cm) high.

£105–120 ⊞ PI

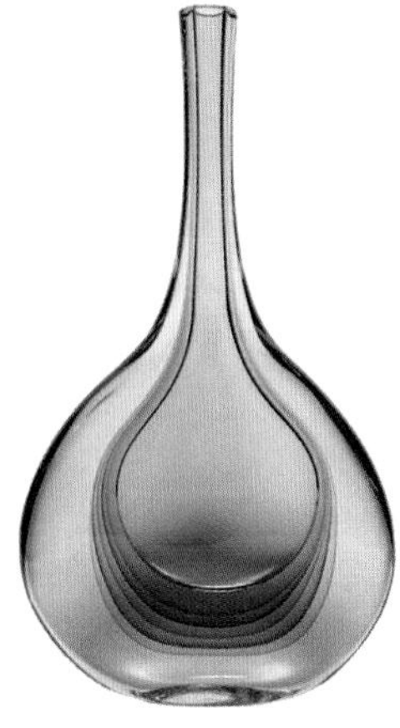

A Murano glass vase, attributed to Seguso, Italy, Venice, c1950, 19in (48.5cm) high.

£1,350–1,500 ⊞ JSG

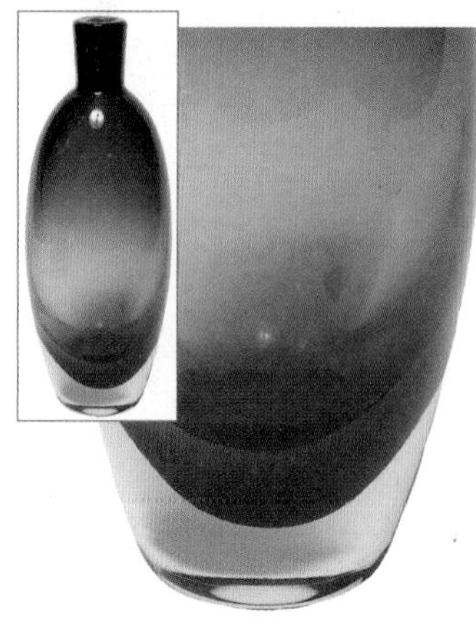

A Murano sommerso glass bottle, with a clear glass base, Italy, Venice, c1950, 10¼in (26cm) high.

£105–120 FD

Sommerso is a type of art glass characterized by a layer of coloured glass cased to the interior of a heavy, colourless or transparent vessel. It was made popular by Seguso Glassworks at Murano and by Scandinavian glass factories in the 1950s.

A Murano glass vase, decorated with dust inclusions, Italy, Venice, c1950, 13in (33cm) high.

£105–120 FD

A Gullaskruf glass bottle vase, by Arthur Percy, with original factory label, Sweden, 1954, 18¼in (46.5cm) high.

£90–100 Getc

► **An Orrefors Selina glass vase,** by Sven Palmqvist, signed, Sweden, 1954, 18¼in (46.5cm) high.

£155–175 Getc

A Whitefriars cut-glass vase, by Geoffrey Baxter, c1954, 9¾in (25cm) high.

£200–230 HUN

A Maastricht glass vase, by Max Verboeket, Holland, c1955, 8in (20.5cm) high.

£95–110 RUSK

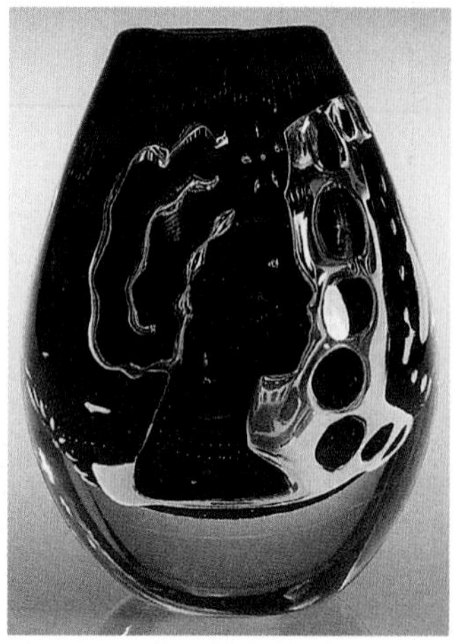

An Orrefors Ariel glass vase, by Edvin Ohrström, entitled 'The Girl and the Dove', signed, Sweden, 1956, 6¾in (17cm) high.

£1,700–2,000 BUK

A Whitefriars glass vase, by Geoffrey Baxter, 1957, 8in (20.5cm) high.

£850–950 COO

A Whitefriars cut-glass vase, by Geoffrey Baxter, c1958, 5½in (14cm) high.

£110–130 HUN

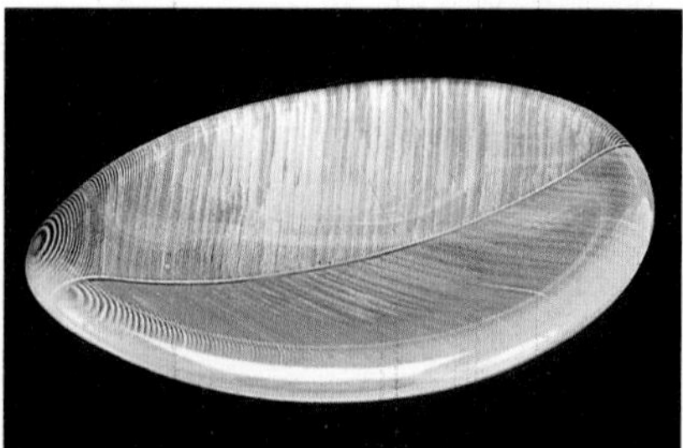

A comb-cut glass dish, by Tapio Wirkkala, signed, Finland, 1958, 10in (25.5cm) wide.

£470–560 BUK(F)

Tapio Wirkkala (1915–85) is perhaps best known for his work in glass, but he also created lighting, furniture and ceramics. His glass designs for Iittala, Venini and Rosenthal reflected his background as a sculptor. He was inspired by nature, leaves, seashells, ice formations and the natural movement of water and birds. His ice-like crystal forms and naturalistically- inspired shapes reflect the rugged Finnish landscape and make his work instantly recognizable.

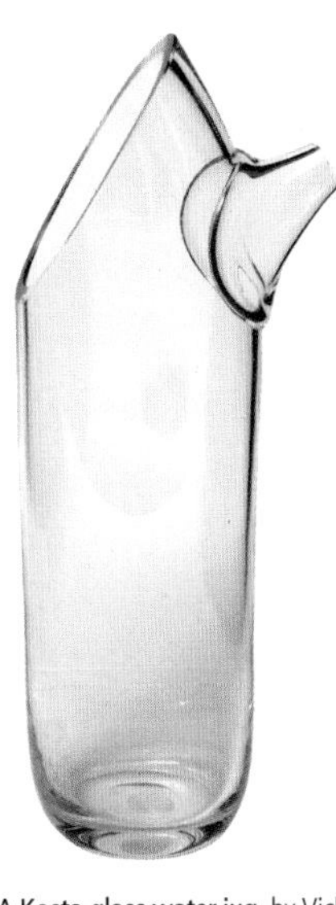
A Kosta glass water jug, by Vicke Lindstrand, No. 1523, Sweden, 1950s, 11¾in (30cm) high.
£135–150 MARK

A Venini Fascia Murrine glass vase, by Riccardo Licata, decorated with a central band of fused murrines, etched signature, Italy, 1950s, 7½in (19cm) high.
£1,950–2,300 BUK

► An Iitalia Kantarelli glass vase, by Tapio Wirkkala, signed, Finland, 1950s, 8¼in (21cm) high.
£720–860 BUK

A Murano sommerso glass vase, Italy, Venice, 1950s, 12in (30.5cm) high.
£105–120 FD

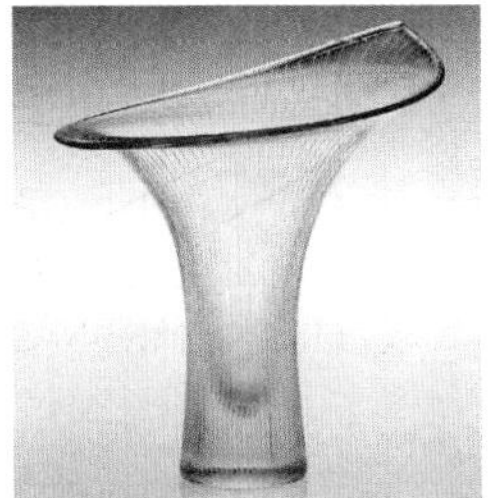

A Gullaskruf glass Martini carafe, by Kjell Blomberg, Sweden, 1959–60, 11in (28cm) high.
£110–125 Getc

A Holmegaard Greenland glass floor vase, by Per Lütken, engraved mark, Denmark, 1960, 7¾in (19.5cm) high.
£135–150 Getc

A Venini Occhi glass vase, by Tobia Scarpa, stamped mark, Italy, c1960, 12½in (32cm) high.
£1,250–1,500 TREA

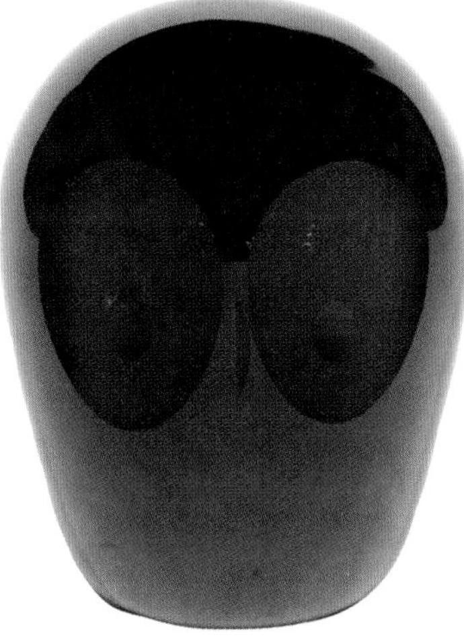
A Whitefriars Twilight Owl glass paperweight, by Harry Dyer, c1960, 4in (10cm) high.
£95–105 HUN

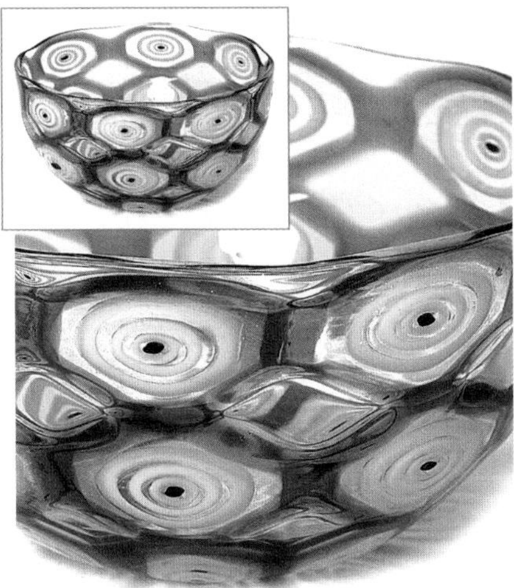
A Barovier & Toso Caccia glass bowl, by Ercole Barovier, decorated with applied bull's-eye murrines, Italy, c1960, 7in (18cm) diam.
£1,050–1,250 TREA

A Whitefriars Bark glass vase, by Geoffrey Baxter, No. 9674, 1967–69, 7in (18cm) high.
£155–175 MARK

The original designs for this series of vases were based on bark that Baxter collected and used to form a mould to make prototypes. Naturally this was too fragile to use for production, so three-part cast-iron moulds were made to produce the pieces.

A Whitefriars Banjo glass vase, by Geoffrey Baxter, No. 9861, 1967–73, 12½in (32cm) high.
£660–790 Hal

The Banjo vase, the largest and most imposing of the Textured series of vases, is generally regarded as the pinnacle of a Baxter collection.

A Whitefriars Banjo glass vase, by Geoffrey Baxter, c1969, 13in (33cm) high.

£2,850–3,200 HUN

Aubergine is one of the rarer colourways for the Banjo vase.

A Whitefriars Ears glass vase, by Geoffrey Baxter, No. 9416, c1969, 9in (23cm) high.

£165–185 HUN

A Whitefriars Pyramid vase, by Geoffrey Baxter, c1969, 7in (18cm) high.

£210–240 HUN

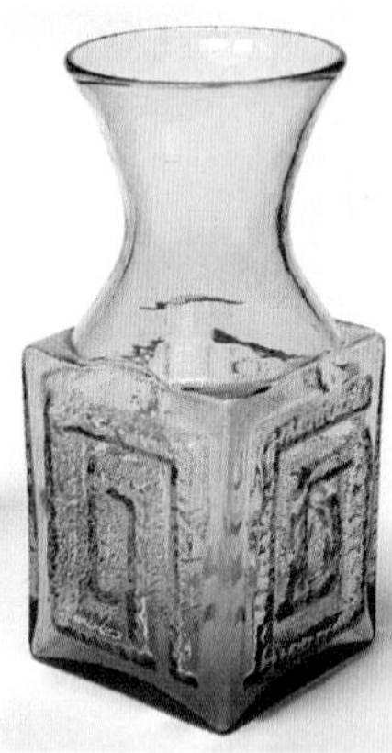

A Dartington glass vase, by Frank Thrower, 1969, 10in (25.5cm) high.

£90–100 COO

A Whitefriars Shoulder glass vase, by Geoffrey Baxter, c1969, 10in (25.5cm) high.

£310–350 HUN

A Whitefriars Cello glass vase, by Geoffrey Baxter, c1969, 7in (18cm) high.

£195–220 FRD

A Boda glass bottle, by Bertil Vallien, signed, Sweden, 1960s, 8½in (21.5cm) high.

£125–150 BUK

A Nuutajärvi Notsjö glass vase, by Kaj Franck, on a flint foot, marked, Finland, 1960s, 6in (15cm) high.

£175–195 RUSK

A set of three Arnolfo di Cambrio **glasses,** by Joe Colombo, Italy, 1960s, 5½in (14cm) high.

£195–220 MARK

A glass vase, by Sea Glasbruk, engraved signature, Sweden, 1960s–70s, 7in (18cm) high.

£55–65 RIWA

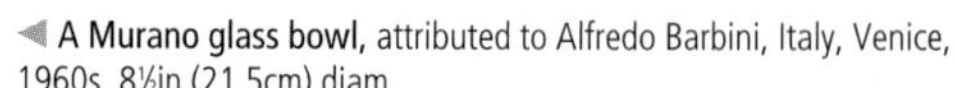

◄ **A Murano glass bowl,** attributed to Alfredo Barbini, Italy, Venice, 1960s, 8½in (21.5cm) diam.

£155–185 TREA

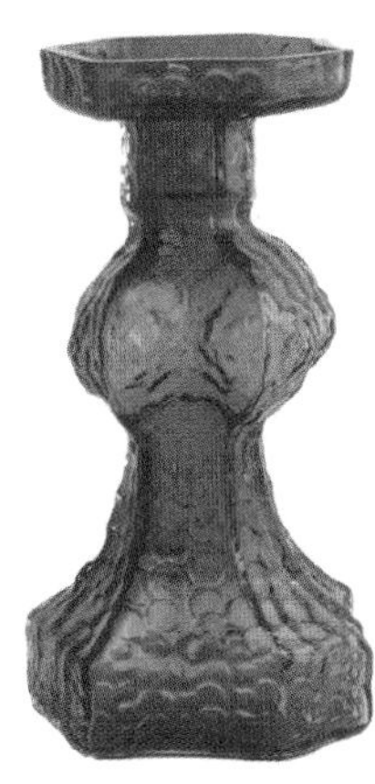

A Riihimaki Fenomena glass vase, by Nanni Still, Finland, 1968–72, 7½in (19cm) high.

£55–65 RIWA

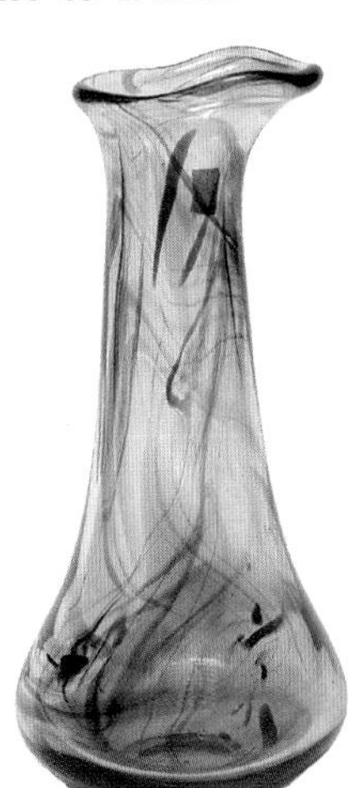

A Whitefriars Cirrus glass vase, by Geoffrey Baxter, 1974, 9in (23cm) high.

£135–150 COO

A glass Fairy Lantern vase, by Steven Lundberg, decorated with blossoms and foliage, signed, engraved marks, America, 1987, 5¼in (13.5cm) high.

£380–450 CINN

Steven Lundberg was born in Chicago in 1953, moving with his family to Santa Barbara, California in 1958. His career in glass began in 1972 when he was apprenticed to his older brother James, a pioneer in the studio glass movement. In August 1973, the brothers formed Lundberg Studios in Davenport, California.

A pair of Holmegaard Carnaby glass vases, by Per Lütken, Denmark, c1970, 6½in (16.5cm) high.

£135–150 PI

A Riihimaki Paukkiorauta glass bottle, by E. T. Siiroinen, Finland, 1970s–80s, 6¾in (17cm) high.

£75–85 RIWA

A Whitefriars Bubble vase, by Geoffrey Baxter, No. 9788, c1971, 7in (18cm) high.

£145–165 HUN

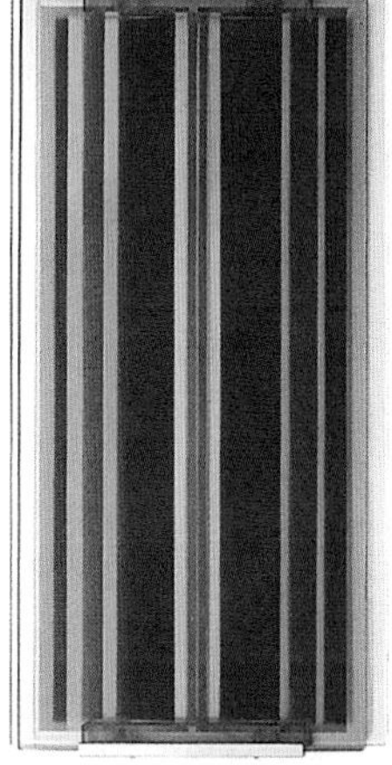

A glass plaque, by Eric H. Olson, entitled 'Optochromie', signed, Sweden, dated 1973, 15¾in (40cm) high.

£2,700–3,200 BUK

An Orrefors Ravenna glass bowl, by Sven Palmqvist, signed, Sweden, 1973, 8¼in (21cm) diam.

£970–1,150 BUK

The Ravenna technique was designed in 1948 after an inspirational visit to the Italian town of Ravenna, which is known for fine mosaics.

◄ **A Fenton glass rose bowl,** by Robert Barber, no. 245 of edition of 700, with original label, signed and dated 1975, America, 8in (20.5cm) high, with Fenton certificate.

£170–200 JDJ

A Holmegaard Carnaby glass vase, by Per Lütken, Denmark, 1970s, 13in (33cm) high.

£145–165 RIWA

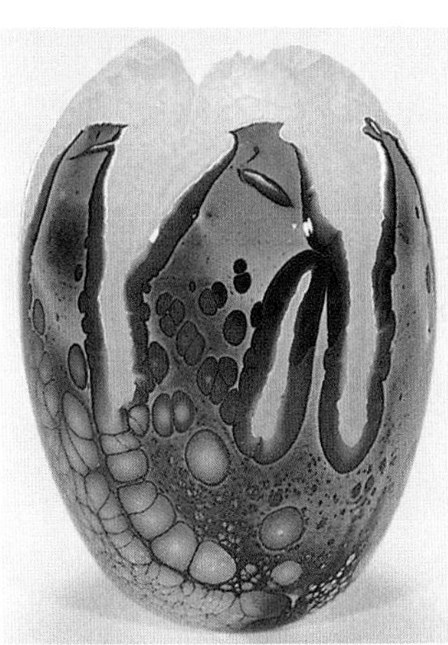

A Geode glass vase, by Noel Lane, signed, marked and dated 1991, 9¼in (23.5cm) high.

£1,100–1,300 CINN

A glass vase, by Charles Lotton, decorated with pods and stalks, signed and dated 1994, America, 7in (18cm) high.

£470–560 CINN

Charles Lotton's designs can be found in the Smithsonian Institution, Washington, the Corning Museum of Glass, New York, the High Museum of Art, Chicago and the Art Institute of Chicago.

JEWELLERY

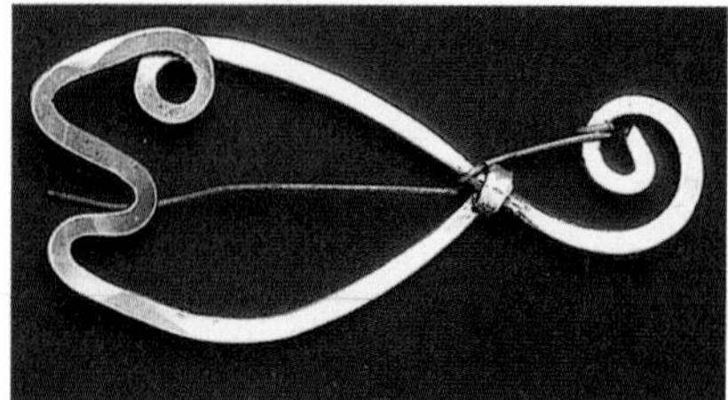

A silver fish brooch, by Alexander Calder, America, c1947, 4½in (11.5cm) wide.

£19,800–23,700 SK

While known primarily for his artwork and sculpture, Alexander Calder loved working with wire, and used brass, silver and gold. He only produced about 1,500 pieces of jewellery in his lifetime, and often gave examples to relatives and friends. He never intended them for mass production.

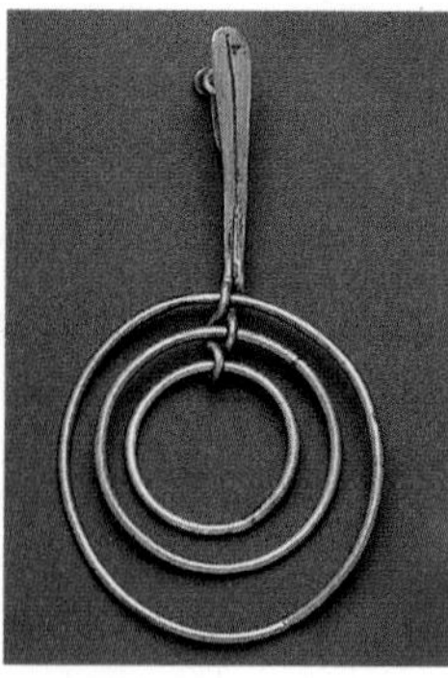

A pair of brass earrings, by Art Smith, signed, America, c1950, 3¼in (8.5cm) long.

£890–1,050 SK

A *pâte-de-verre* and paste necklace and earrings set, by Stanley Hagler, America, 1960s, necklace 18in (45.5cm) long.

£360–400 TDG

A silver and enamel necklace, bracelet, brooch and earrings set, by David Andersen, Norway, 1950s, with box.

£250–280 VDA

A pair of silver cufflinks, by Georg Jensen, Denmark, c1960, ½in (1cm) diam.

£140–160 SPE

A talosel resin and mirrored-glass necklace, by Line Vautrin, France, c1960, 11¾in (30cm) long.

£2,600–3,100 S(O)

A silver and parcel-gilt bangle, by Sigurd Persson and Peter Schmitt, Sweden, Stockholm 1963.

£400–480 BUK

A silver brooch, by Georg Jensen, decorated with butterflies and flowers, Denmark, import mark for London 1963, 2in (5cm) diam.

£390–440 BEX

A silver and amber bracelet, by N. E. From, Denmark, 1960s.

£135–150 VDA

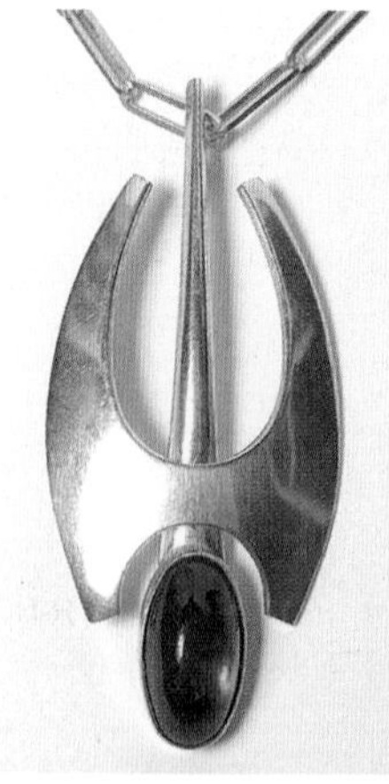

A silver and amber necklace, maker's mark N. E. From, Denmark, 1960s, pendant 2in (5cm) long.

£130–145 VDA

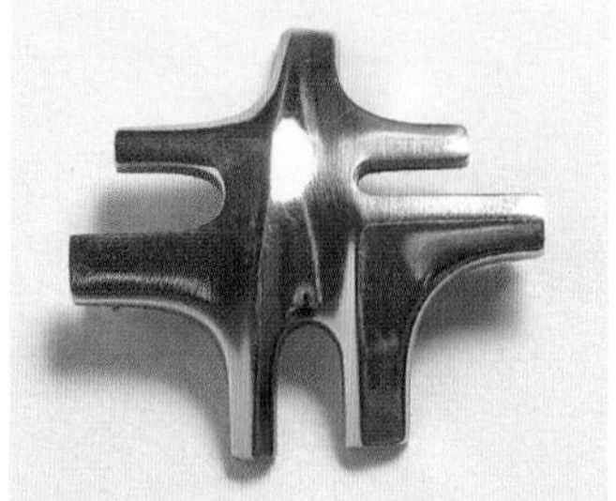

A silver brooch, by Georg Jensen, Denmark, c1969, 1½in (4cm) wide.

£135–150 SPE

A pair of silver cufflinks, by Georg Jensen, in the form of two cones, Denmark, 1960s, 1in (2.5cm) wide.

£135–150 SPE

► **A set of six 9ct gold and chrysoprase/ chalcedony rings,** by Wendy Ramshaw, London 1970.

£610–730 DN

A David Shackman & Sons silver and enamel watch, c1970.

£500–600 TEN

A Lapponia 14ct gold brooch, by Björn Weckström, Finland, c1972.

£360–430 BUK(F)

► **A Fireshine gold ring,** signed, 1970s.

£570–680 SK

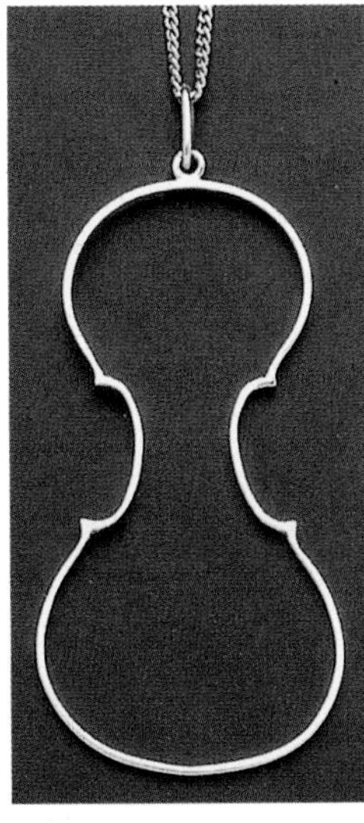

A pair of 18ct gold pendant necklaces, by Fernandez Arman, each forged in the outline of a violin body, stamped and hallmarked, France, c1973.

£1,050–1,250 SK

A 23ct gold pendant, designed by Max Ernst, decorated with an inscribed abstract design, No. 4 of edition of 6, signed, maker's mark for François Hugo, stamped, France, dated 1975, with original box.

£10,200–12,200 SK

Max Ernst (1891–1976) was a founding member of the Dada and Surrealist movements in Cologne and Paris. He worked in a wide range of styles and media. This work resembles his technique of 'grattage', which involved the scraping and trowelling of pigment from canvas.

A silver necklace, by Inga Lagervall, Sweden, Stockholm 1978, 20½in (52cm) long.

£380–450 BUK

Inga Lagervall pieces can be found in the collections of the National Museum in Stockholm and the Röhsska Museum, Gothenburg.

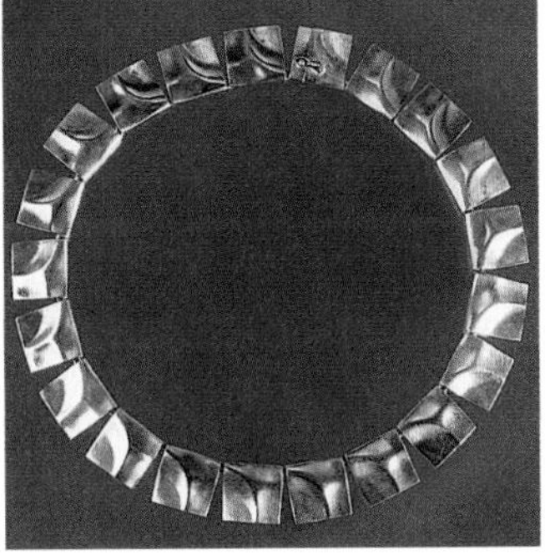

A Lapponia Galactic Peaks sterling silver necklace, by Björn Weckström, Finland, 1978, 15½in (39.5cm) long.

£470–560 BUK(F)

A silver ring, by Georg Jensen, No. 127, Denmark, import marks for London 1979.

£110–130 DN

A silver brooch, by Georg Jensen, Denmark, import marks for London 1979.

£240–280 DN

A silver and garnet brooch, by Georg Jensen, Denmark, c1980, 1½in (4cm) wide.

£160–180 SPE

A silver brooch, by Georg Jensen, Denmark, 1980s, 3in (7.5cm) high.

£270–300 SPE

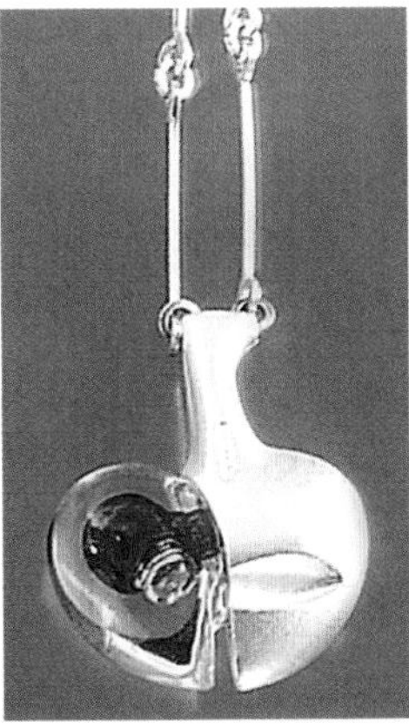

◄ **A Lapponia sterling silver and acrylic pendant,** by Björn Weckström, Finland, 1988.

£450–540 BUK(F)

◄ **An 18ct gold bangle,** c1990.

£290–330 SPE

LIGHTING

A steel table lamp, by Jean Perzel, in the form of a globe, globe later, signed, France, 1937, 24½in (62cm) high.

£11,000–13,200 S(NY)

In 1937, Henry Ford commissioned Jean Perzel to design lighting incorporating Ford auto parts to celebrate the manufacture of 25 million Ford cars at the River Rouge factory in Dearborn, Michigan. Created within 36 hours, the result was this lamp, incorporating a globe (once illuminated) and parts from the Ford V8 engine. Only a few examples were ever produced.

◀ **A crystal and Lucite seven-branch chandelier,** by J. & L. Lobmeyr, with silk shades, Austria, Vienna, c1940, 34in (86.5cm) wide.

£5,800–6,500 NART

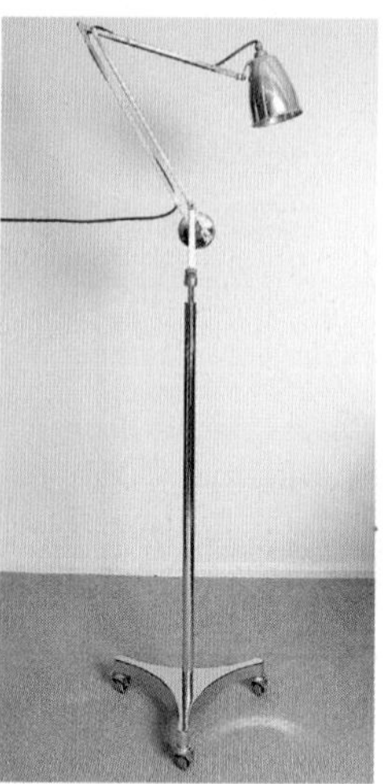

A chrome trolley lamp, by Hadrill & Horstmann, c1950, 85in (216cm) high.

£620–700 TDG

A near pair of Venini glass hanging lights, by Massimo Vignelli, Italy, c1956, 14¼in (36cm) high.

£2,600–3,100 S(O)

These lamps are part of a series which was originally designed to decorate the Oivetti shop in New York.

A pair of twelve-branch wall lights, attributed to Paavo Tynell, Finland, c1950, 95in (241.5cm) high.

£10,800–12,900 S

A pair of gilt-bronze and glass wall lights, by Max Ingrand for Fontana Arte, Italy, 1950s, 10¾in (27.5cm) diam.

£6,000–7,200 S

▶ **A pair of coated aluminium and chrome lights,** by Poul Henningsen for Louis Poulsen, Denmark, 1958, 23¾in (60.5cm) high.

£1,950–2,200 DeP

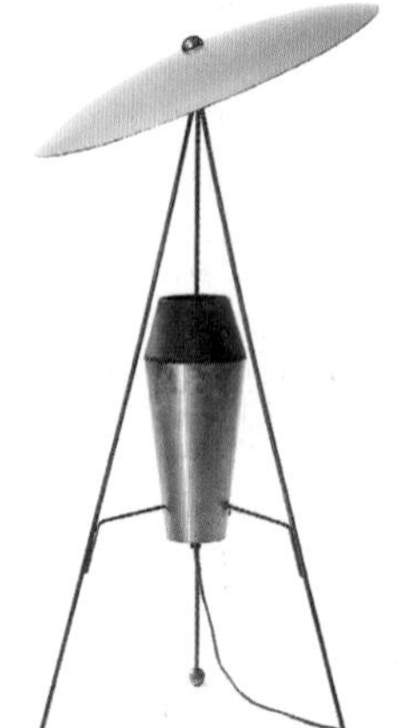

A brass, enamelled-metal and wood floor lamp, by A. W. & Marion Geller for Heifetz Co, America, 1950s, 36½in (92.5cm) high.

£5,200–6,200 S(NY)

This lamp model won an honourable mention in the 1951 lighting competition sponsored by the Museum of Modern Art, New York, and the Heifetz Company.

A brass and enamelled-metal three-branch table lamp, by Gino Sarfatti for Knoll, Italian, 1950s, 11in (28cm) high.

£920–1,100 TREA

A lacquered-metal and aluminium three-branch wall light, by Serge Mouille, France, 1950s, 136in (345.5cm) high.

£19,500–23,400 S(NY)

Serge Mouille (1922–88) studied as a silversmith and established his own studios in 1945. He designed his first prototype lamp in 1953 for the decorator and architect Jacques Adnet. In 1953 he participated in an exhibition at the Musée des Arts Décoratifs, Paris, before collaborating with Louis Sognot on lighting solutions and going on to be one of the avant-garde designers, including Jean Prouvé, whose modern designs were shown at the Steph Simon gallery, Paris, when it opened in 1956.

We invite you to visit our website to
order our new catalog, view our extensive
inventory, and become a member of our new
Designers Workshop.

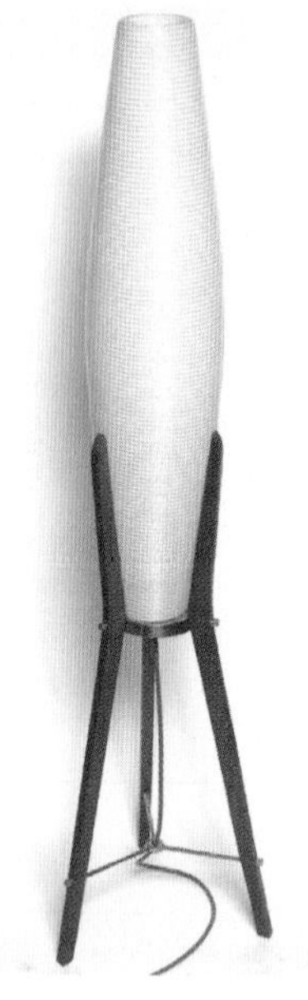

A plastic and teak Rocket lamp, 1950s, 48in (122cm) high.

£180–200 OCA

A chrome-plated steel, plastic and rubber Olook ceiling light, by Poltronova for Superstudio, Italy, c1968, 29in (73.5cm) high.

£1,600–1,900 S(NY)

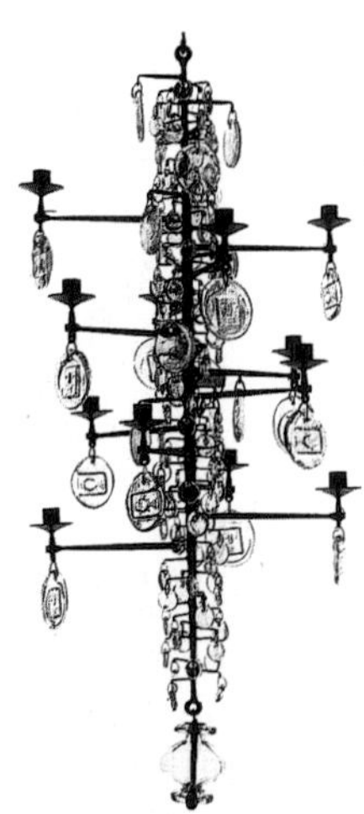

An iron and glass ceiling light, by Erik Höglund for Boda Glassworks, Sweden, 1960s, 41in (104cm) high.

£2,100–2,500 BUK

► **A pair of Venini glass table lamps,** with marble bases, silk shades later, Italy, 1960s, 33in (84cm) high.

£650–780 TREA

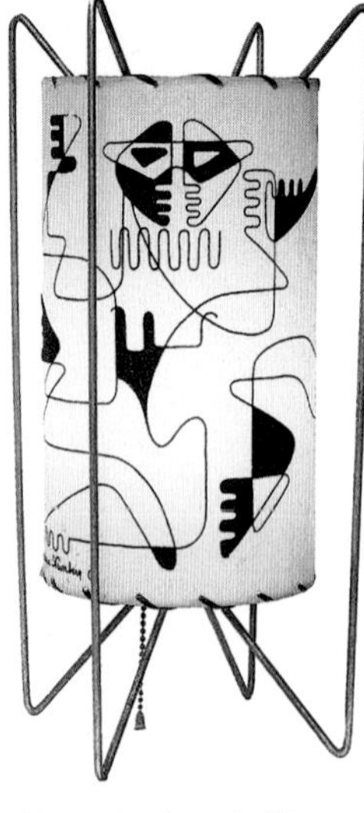

A brass-plated-metal table lamp, by Frederic Weinberg, the parchment shade with silkscreen decoration, signed, America, 1950s, 16in (40.5cm) high.

£510–610 TREA

A Murano glass and metal Giogali ceiling light, by Angelo Mangiarotti for Vistosi, Italy, 1960s, 17¾in (45cm) high.

£3,750–4,500 BUK

This is Mangiarotti's innovative take on the classical Venetian chandelier.

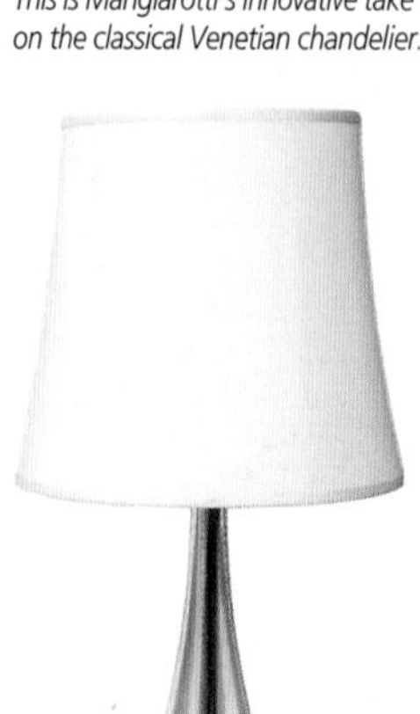

A Venini chrome and glass ceiling light, Italy, early 1960s, 30¾in (78cm) high.

£1,250–1,400 DeP

A marble table lamp, possibly by Knoll, with a silk shade, America, 1960s, 36½in (92cm) high.

£190–220 TREA

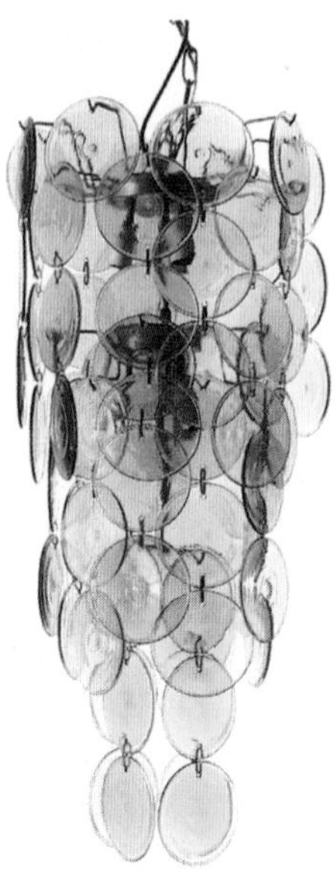

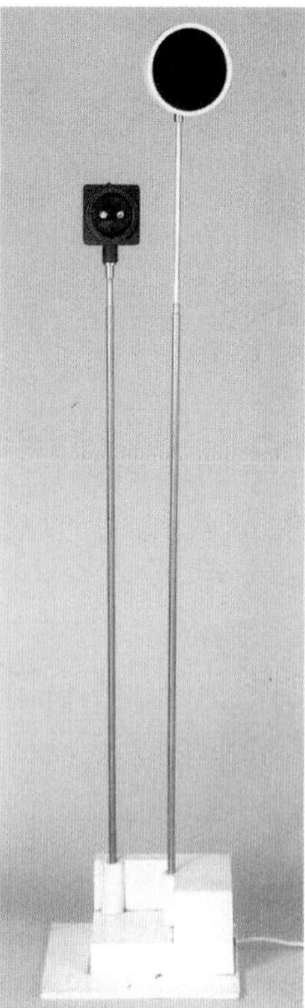

A painted metal Series 2 Signal lamp, by Vassilakis Takis for Unlimited, with label, 1967, 60in (152.5cm) high, extended.

£1,450–1,700 DN(HAM)

Vassilakis Takis was born in Athens in 1925, and moved to Paris in 1954. Since 1966 he has lived and worked in London. His kinetic experiments were started in 1954, and in that same year his first Signals were produced. This piece was given to the vendor by a former employee of Unlimited who was given them upon departure from the company. Unlimited was established c1966 by Jeremy Fry at Widcombe Manor, Bath, and ceased trading c1971.

A Murano glass ceiling light, by Barovier & Toso, Italy, Venice, 1960s–70s, 15½in (39.5cm) high.

£590–700 BUK

◄ **A Murano glass ceiling light,** by Mazzega marked, Italy, Venice, 1960s, 33½in (85cm) high.

£860–1,000 BUK

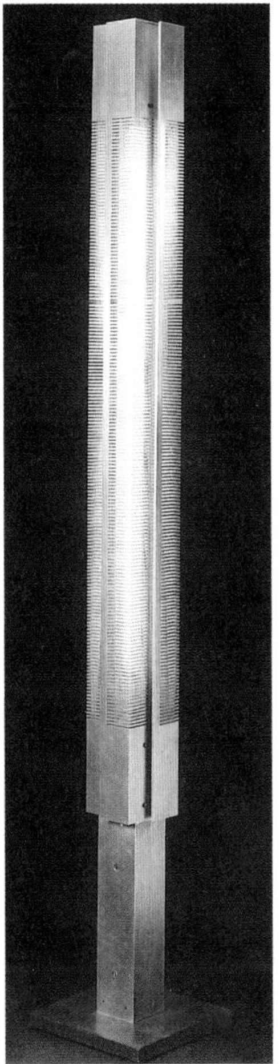

A steel Grand Signal floor lamp, by Serge Mouille, France, 1960s, 80in (203cm) high.
£42,000–50,000 S(NY)

Serge Moulle's lighting designs are very simple, yet entirely distinctive. They are highly prized both in Europe and the US, and often fetch more than £15,000 at auction. The 1990s reproduction of Grand Signal sells for about £4,500.

A Kosta glass lamp, by Warff, Sweden, c1970, 10in (25.5cm) high.
£155–175 MARK

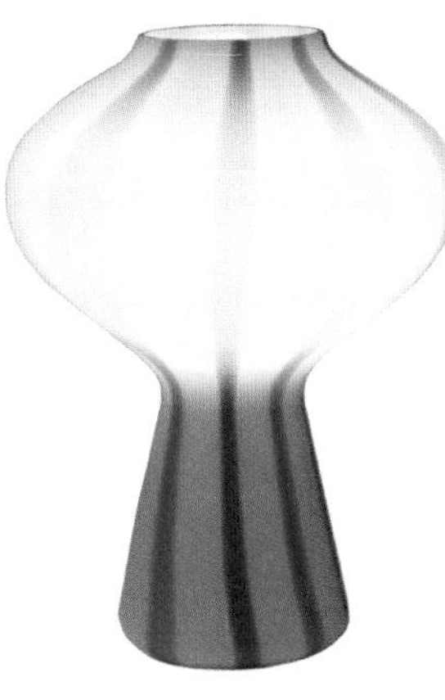

A Venini glass table lamp, Italy, 1960s, 14in (35.5cm) high.
£280–330 TREA

A metal ceiling light, 1960s, 23in (58.5cm) high.
£50–60 OCA

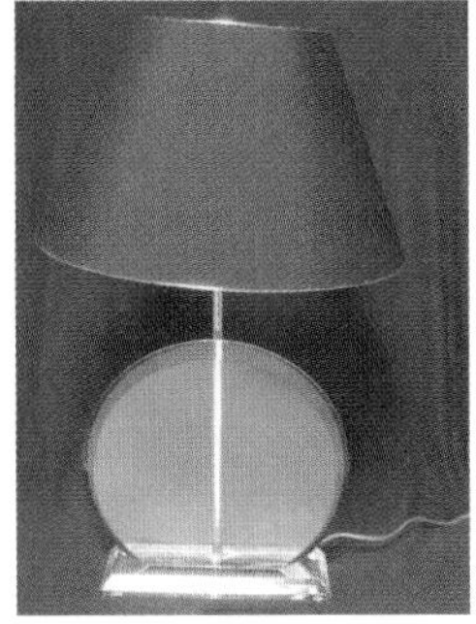

A pair of Lucite table lamps, America, 1970–75, 13½in (34.5cm) high.
£800–900 AGO

An adjustable chrome ceiling light, by Gino Sarfatti for Flos, Italy, designed 1958, manufactured 1960s, 29½in (75cm) high.
£760–850 DeP

A chrome floor lamp, 1960s, 61in (155cm) high.
£220–250 OCA

A copper ceiling light, by Raak, Holland, Amsterdam, 1960s, 29½in (75cm) diam.
£3,600–4,300 S

► **An Ateljé Lyktan chrome desk lamp,** Sweden, 1970s, 34in (86.5cm) long.
£270–300 PI

◄ **A plaster African table lamp,** by John Dickinson, model No. 101C, America, c1976, 29in (73.5cm) high.
£9,100–10,900 S(NY)

Many of Dickinson's designs were influenced by African vernacular furniture and he favoured unusual materials such as white plaster, faux bamboo and galvanized metal.

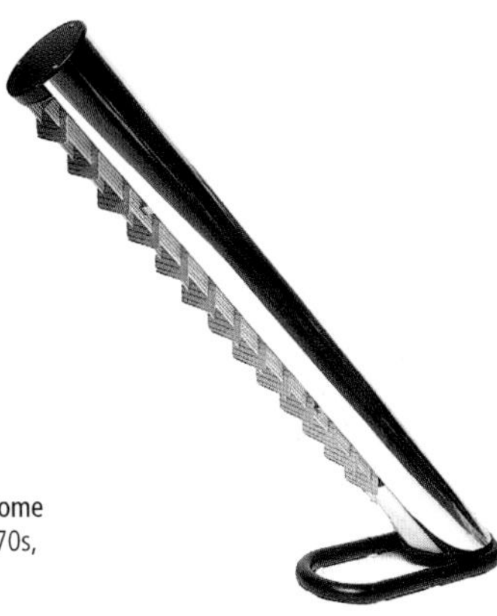

A metal and stained glass 12-branch chandelier, by Tom Dixon and André Dubreuil, 1984, 39½in (100.5cm) high.
£1,550–1,850 S(O)

METALWARE

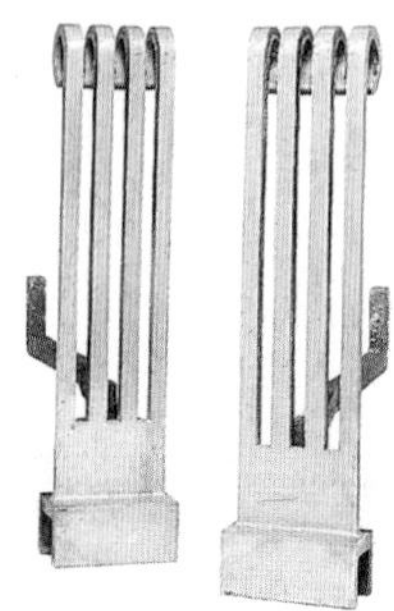

A pair of iron and aluminium andirons, by Donald Deskey for the Richard H. Mandel House, New York, stamped '1191', America, 1933–35, 17¾in (45cm) high.

£5,500–6,600 S(NY)

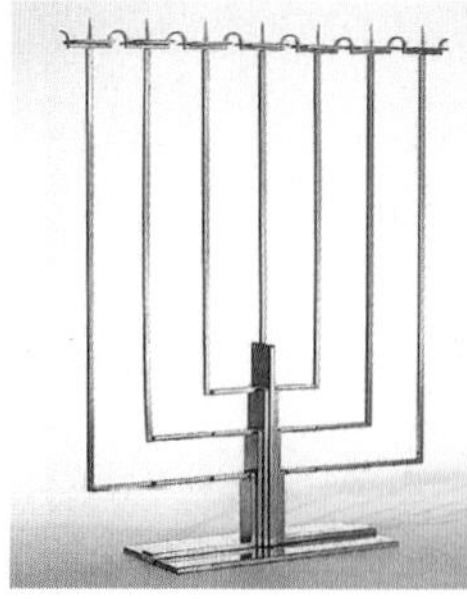

A chrome-plated brass candelabrum, by J. Robert F. Swanson for Saarinen-Swanson Group, America, designed 1935, manufactured by Cray, Boston, 1947, 21in (53.5cm) wide.

£1,950–2,350 S(NY)

A silver and Lucite cutlery service, by Porter Blanchard, comprising 108 pieces, signed and marked, America, c1950.

£10,400–12,400 S(NY)

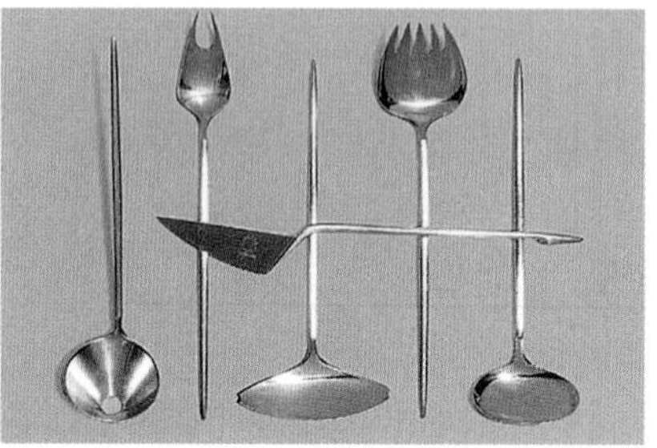

A sterling silver hors d'oeuvre set, by Vagn Åge Hemmingsen for Franz Hingelberg, comprising six pieces, Denmark, Århus, 1957–59.

£3,650–4,300 BUK

◀ **An enamelled-metal Saturnus cooking pot,** by Timo Sarpaneva, Finland, 1950s, 6in (15cm) diam.

£135–150 PI

Timo Sarpaneva studied at the Central School of Applied Arts in Helsinki. He is principally known for his glass designs.

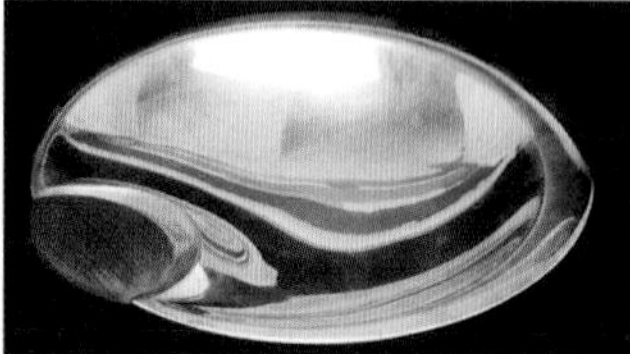

◀ **A silver and teak bread basket,** by Tapio Wirkkala for Kultakeskus, signed 'TW', Finland, 1961, 9¾in (25cm) diam.

£870–1,000 BUK(F)

A silver, walnut and plastic tea service, by Antonio Pineda, comprising four pieces, stamped, marked, Mexico, designed 1955, manufactured 1960s, teapot 7¼in (18.5cm) high.

£21,100–25,300 S(NY)

Legendary Mexican designer and former apprentice of William Spratling, Antonio Pineda opened his own silver workshop in 1941 in his home town of Taxco. His works have been exhibited internationally, beginning in 1944 when he participated in an exposition in San Francisco's Palace of the Legion of Honor. In 1953, he was awarded the Presidential Prize at the first National Silver Art Fair in Mexico. Designed c1955, this service shows the influence of the Italian Futurist movement.

▶ **A sterling silver Kungaskålen bowl,** by Wiwen Nilsson, Sweden, Lund, 1968, (23.5cm) wide.

£170–200 BUK

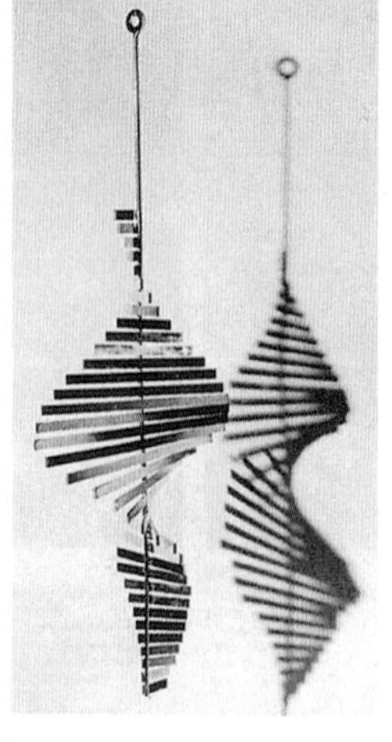

◀ **A chrome-plated steel Screw mobile,** by Kenneth Martin for Unlimited, c1970, 25¾in (65.5cm) high.

£1,950–2,300 DN(HAM)

Kenneth Martin was born in Sheffield in 1906, and studied at the Sheffield School of Art and the Royal College of Art, London. His first Screw mobiles were produced c1953.

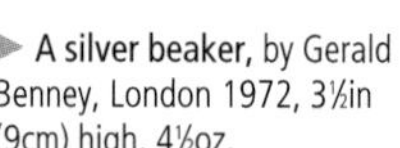

▶ **A silver beaker,** by Gerald Benney, London 1972, 3½in (9cm) high, 4½oz.

£400–480 DN(HAM)

A Perspex and chrome ashtray, by Pierre Cardin, France, 1970s, 7in (18cm) diam.

£180–200 MARK

SCULPTURE

◀ **A composition model of a reclining girl,** by Bror Hjorth, No. 3 of edition of 85, signed, Sweden, dated 1951, 10¼in (26cm) wide.
£1,100–1,300 BUK

A Murano glass sculpture, by Pablo Picasso for Francesco Martinuzzi, entitled 'Il Centauro', Italy, 1950s, 14in (35.5cm) high.
£5,400–6,000 KK

A gilt patinated bronze figure, by Eric Grate, entitled 'Esox Regina', No. 2 of edtion of 26, signed, marked, 1960s, 11in (28cm) high.
£940–1,100 BUK

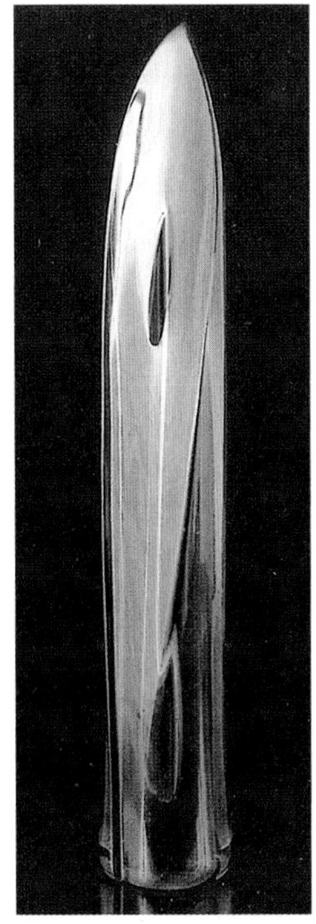

A glass sculpture, by Aimo Okkolin, entitled 'Iris', signed, Finland, 1957–62, 14½in (37cm) high.
£630–750 BUK(F)

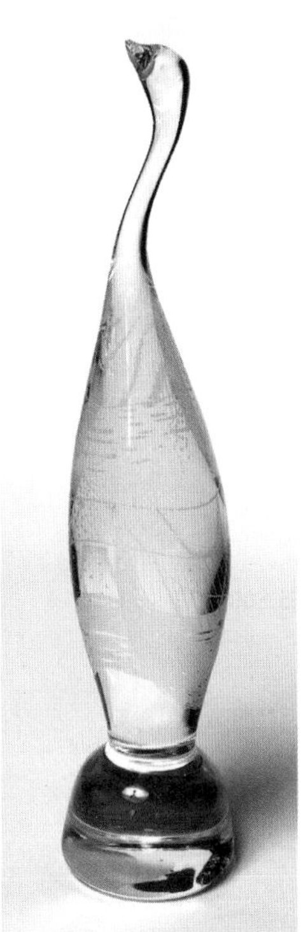

A glass model of a bird, by Vicke Lindstrand for Kosta, Sweden, 1950s, 9in (23cm) high.
£100–110 MARK

A glass sculpture, by Edvin Ohrström, on a wooden base, signed, Sweden, probably 1960s, 21¼in (54cm) high.
£1,400–1,650 BUK

A glass model of a bird, by Alessandro Pianon for Vistosi, entitled 'Pulcino', Italy, 1960s, 12½in (32cm) high.
£1,100–1,300 BUK

An aluminium sculpture, by Lygia Clark for Unlimited, entitled 'Animal LC1', c1969.
£1,050–1,250 DN(HAM)

▶ **A beryllium copper and brass Sound sculpture,** by Harry Bertoia, America, c1970, 30½in (77.5cm) high.
£16,300–19,500 S(NY)

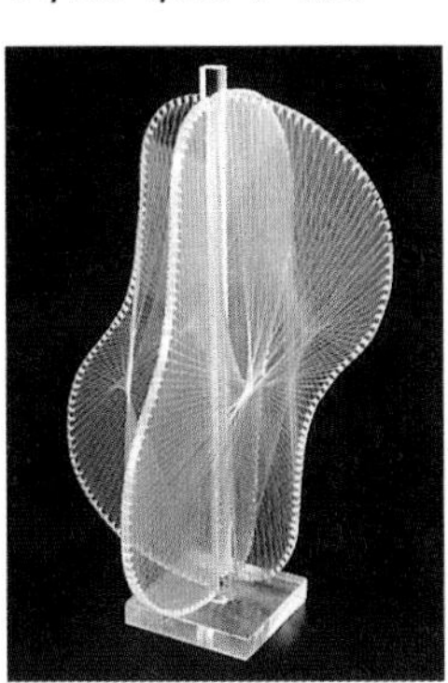

A Perspex and nylon thread sculpture, in the manner of Naum Gabo, probably retailed by Liberty, c1970, 11in (28cm) high.
£130–155 DN

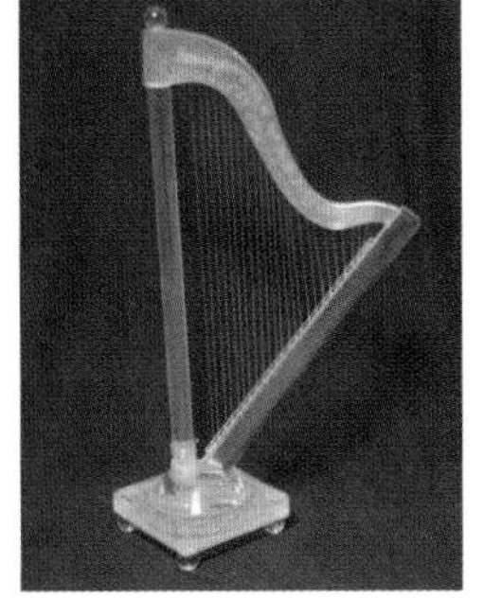

◀ **A Lucite harp sculpture,** America, early 1970s, 25in (63.5cm) high.
£580–650 AGO

A mixed media sculpture, by Ivor Abrahams, signed and dated 1975, 11½in (29cm) high.
£470–560 BUK

◀ **A stoneware Stack vessel,** by Peter Voulkos, signed and dated, America, 1977, 13¼in (33.5cm) diam.

£27,700–33,000 S(NY)

Peter Voulkos changed the face of ceramics in America, pushing the clay to the edge, testing it to see what it would do. He was the first of a new breed of artists who crossed and fused traditional lines between art and craft. The Stack form is a perfect example for Voulkos's unprecedented technical innovations. He was inspired by the stone-carved and bronze figurative sculptures of Austrian artist Fritz Wotruba. Wotruba's canted and finely-balanced volumetric sculptures deeply influenced Voulkos, suggesting to him a method of achieving mass and vertical thrust by anchoring an assemblage of piled elements to a central axis. Voulkos created this outstanding example of the Stack form in 1977 at a workshop in the Alice Martin Studio in Anchorage, Alaska.

A concrete and steel armchair, by Jonas Bohlin for Källemo AB, No. 69 of edition of 100, signed, Sweden, 1981.

£4,750–5,700 BUK

Jonas Bohlin created a stir with his concrete chair which he exhibited at the 1981 graduation show at Konstfack, the National College of Art & Design, in Stockholm. Intended as a piece of sculpture, rather than furniture, it epitomized the spirit of the 1980s, a freedom from the functionalism which characterized furniture design in the 1950s. This piece was issued in a limited edition and is now a collector's item.

A bronze sculpture, by Fernandez Arman, limited edition, signed and numbered, France, 1980s, 24in (61cm) high.

£3,600–4,000 MARK

TEXTILES

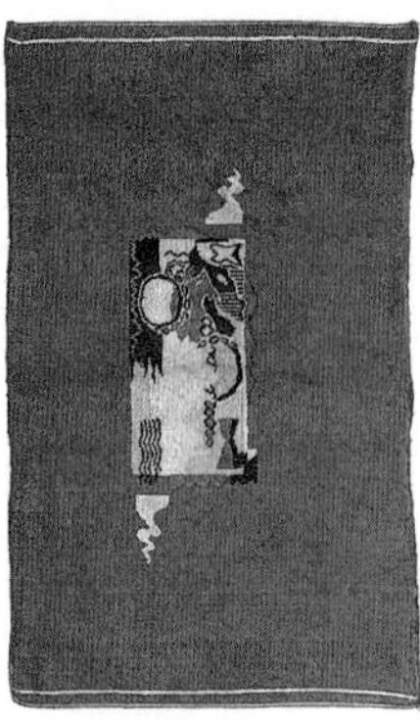

A woollen tapestry, by Jean Lurçat for Maison Myrbor's Workshop, Paris or Algiers, c1925, 106 x 66in (269 x 167.5cm).

£6,500–7,800 S(NY)

A hand-tufted rug, by Josef Frank for Kasthall Ateljé AB, entitled 'Rug No. 1', with label, Sweden, 1938, 135¾ x 102¾in (345 x 261cm).

£3,900–4,650 BUK

A tapestry, by René Perrot for Bordières Felletin, entitled 'La Corrida', signed, France, dated 1946, 76 x 111¾in (193 x 284cm).

£7,700–8,600 MI

◀ **A pair of screen-printed cotton satin curtains,** by John Piper for Sanderson Fabrics, entitled 'Stones of Bath', c1962, each 35¾ x 44in (91 x 112cm).

£175–210 CGC

A fabric panel, by Tibor Reich, entitled 'Age of Kings', c1964, in original wooden frame, 24 x 47in (61 x 119.5cm).

£270–300 FRD

▶ **A woollen rug,** by Verner Panton for Unika Vaev, entitled 'Geometri', slight damage, Denmark, 1960s, 89½ x 89¾in (227.5 x 228cm).

£1,400–1,650 BUK

A fabric panel, by Pierre Cardin for Dekko Plus, c1970, 236¼in (600cm) long.

£180–200 FRD

LAMPS & LIGHTING

CEILING & WALL LIGHTS

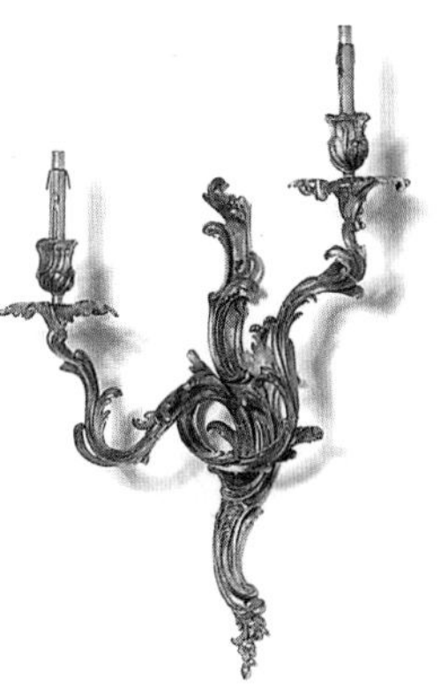

A pair of ormolu two-branch wall lights, fitted for electricity, France, c1750, 22in (56cm) high.

£5,200–6,200 S(NY)

A gilt and patinated bronze three-branch ceiling light, Sweden, 1800–50, 19¾in (50cm) high.

£1,050–1,250 BUK

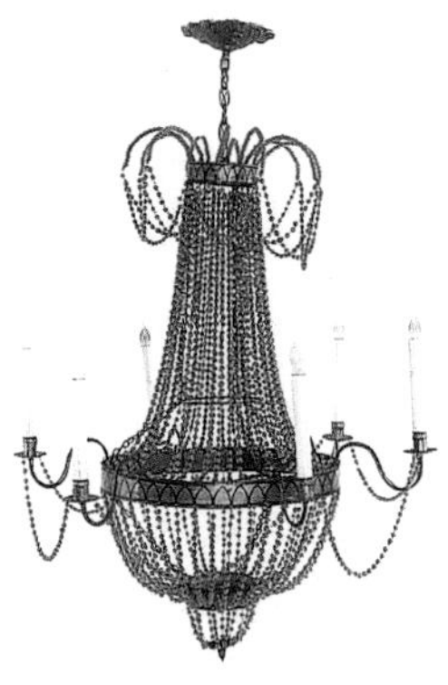

A *tôle peinte* and glass six-branch chandelier, fitted for electricity, France, 1800–50, 41½in (105.5cm) high.

£3,700–4,400 RIT

A patinated bronze eight-branch chandelier, cast with classical heads, one head missing, France, c1810, 33in (84cm) high.

£2,250–2,700 S(NY)

An alabaster and gilt-bronze ceiling light, with lion masks, 19thC, 15¾in (40cm) diam.

£5,600–6,700 S(P)

A bronze colza lamp-style chandelier, centred with a putto, Italy, 19thC, 17in (43cm) wide.

£640–760 DN

A gilt and patinated bronze 12-branch chandelier, decorated with leaves, Russia, c1840, 30¼in (77cm) high.

£750–900 BUK(F)

A brass and cut-glass lustre ceiling light, c1850, 13in (33cm) diam.

£230–260 EAL

◄ **A bronze carriage lantern,** with engraved bevelled glass, France, c1855, 30in (76cm) high.

£7,600–8,500 AUB

A Victorian Gothic-style brass ceiling light, pierced and cast with arches and leaves, with shaped chains, 15¾in (40cm) diam.

£680–810 DN

For more pieces in the Gothic revival style, please see our special feature on pages 102–104.

A Victorian brass and glass **ceiling lantern,** with coloured leaded panels, fitted for electricity, 38¼in (97cm) high.

£200–240 DD

A brass three-branch rise-and-fall ceiling **light,** with etched glass shades, pre-1883 registration mark, 27in (68.5cm) high.

£1,250–1,400 CHA

A brass and cut-glass six-branch chandelier, with etched-glass shades, fitted for electricity, America, 1875–1900, 31in (78.5cm) wide.

£3,050–3,650 NOA

Always check that electric lighting conforms to the current safety regulations before using.

A brass and cut-glass ceiling **light,** with original embossed brass ceiling canopy, fitted for electricity, America, 1875–1900, 14in (35.5cm) diam.

£1,250–1,500 NOA

A pair of ormolu and glass ceiling lights, the drops terminating in a foliate finial, late 19thC, 11in (28cm) diam.

£1,350–1,600 Bea

► **A wrought-iron and copper ceiling light,** with glass shade, c1890, 27in (68.5cm) high.

£250–280 EAL

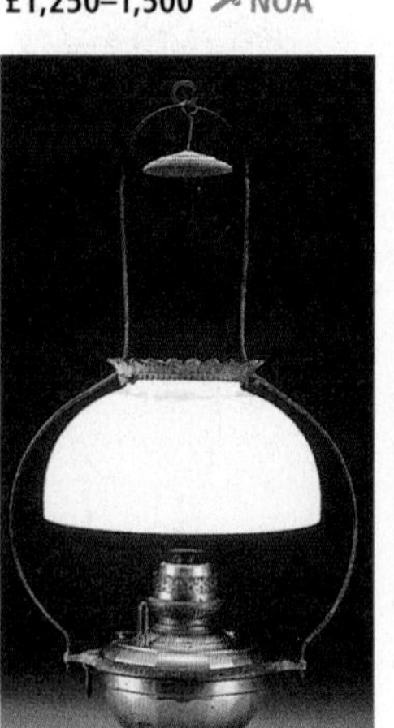

A brass and iron ceiling light, by Bradley & Hubbard, with glass shade, America, late 19thC, 33in (84cm) high.

£95–110 JAA

A gilt-bronze and glass chandelier, by E. F. Caldwell, America, New York, c1920, 30in (76cm) high.

£5,400–6,400 CHAM

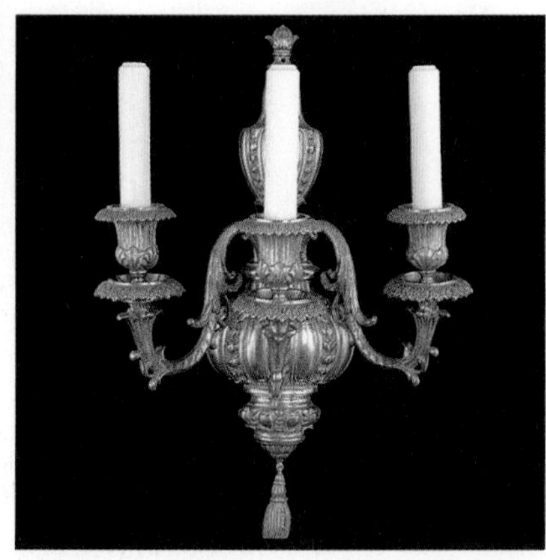

► **A pair of silvered-bronze wall lights,** by E. F. Caldwell, America, New York, c1900, 17in (43cm) high.

£6,800–7,600 CHAM

STANDARD & TABLE LAMPS

A pink quartz, giltwood and rock crystal lamp, the base with an Oriental figure beneath a tree, c1800, 18in (45.5cm) high.
£4,600–5,200 D&D

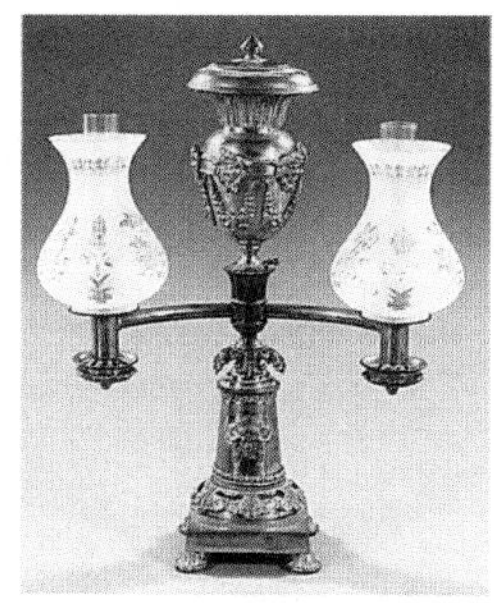

A gilt-bronze and brass two-branch lamp, decorated with masks and floral swags, with cut and etched glass shades, fitted for electricity, Anglo-American, 1825–50, 23in (58.5cm) high.
£1,100–1,300 NOA

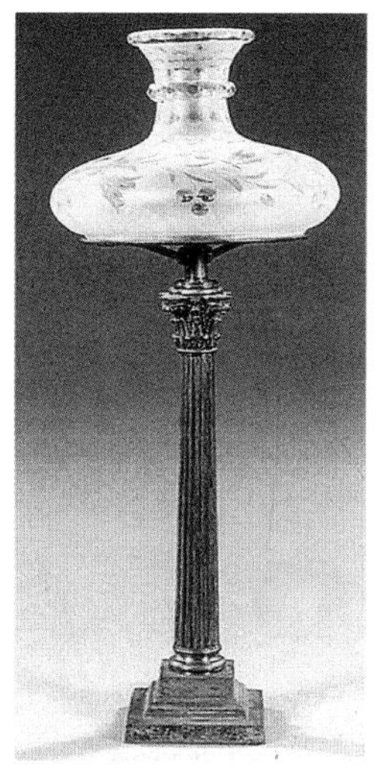

A pair of silvered-bronze and brass lamps, each with an etched and cut-glass shade on a Corinthian column, fitted for electricity, Anglo-American, 1825–50, 34½in (87.5cm) high.
£3,650–4,350 NOA

An ormolu-mounted cut-glass four-branch candelabrum, mounted as a lamp, with *tôle peinte* shade, Russia, c1850, 41in (104cm) high.
£5,800–6,900 S(NY)

A brass two-branch oil table lamp, the frosted glass shades with etched decoration, 19thC, 29in (73.5cm) high.
£165–195 GTH

◀ **A gilt-bronze table lamp,** with acanthus leaf decoration, 19thC, 26in (66cm) high.
£560–670 G(L)

A brass oil table lamp, with cranberry glass cabochons, reservoir and shade, the base with scroll and stylized floral decoration, 19thC, 31in (78.5cm) high.
£410–490 PF

A gilt-bronze and earthenware oil lamp, glass shade replaced, 19thC, 28in (71cm) high.
£560–670 S(P)

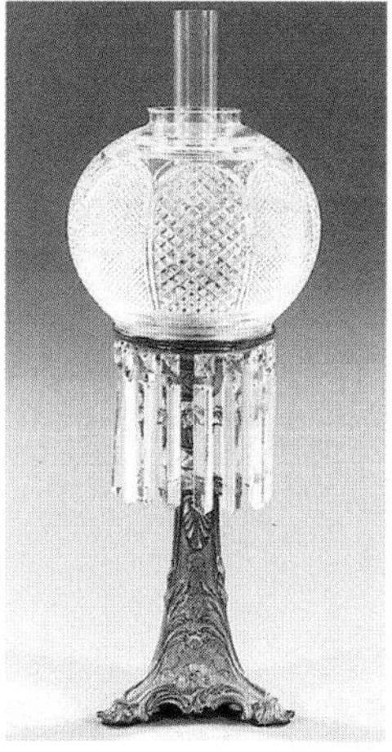

A pair of gilt and lacquered-bronze and glass table lamps, the base cast with foliate and shell decoration, fitted for electricity, labelled 'Cornelius & Co', America, Philadelphia, c1850, 27in (68.5cm) high.
£2,550–3,050 NOA

A tin and glass oil lamp, with label 'S. Sargents patent, September 17, 1861', America, 1860s, 14in (35.5cm) high.
£230–270 JDJ

▶ **An ormolu table lamp,** with frosted glass shade, fitted for electricity, c1860, 28in (71cm) high.
£400–450 EAL

A Victorian glass oil lamp, with brass fittings, fitted for electricity, 27in (68.5cm) high.

£890–1,050 WW

A Victorian ceramic oil lamp, the body painted with Grecian figures, with an etched glass shade, 15in (38cm) high.

£165–195 PF

A gilt-spelter figural lamp, the base with cherubs playing, the glass shade painted with flowers, the ring suspended with cut-glass drops, America, 1875–1900, 31in (78.5cm) high.

£270–320 NOA

A Gothic revival gilt-brass standard oil lamp, c1880, 59in (150cm) high.

£1,100–1,250 PVD

For more pieces in the Gothic revival style, please see our special feature on pages 102–104.

◄ An Edwardian silver table oil lamp, with a cut-glass reservoir and etched glass shade, on a Corinthium column, maker's mark 'B.B.', Birmingham 1906, 30½in (77.5cm) high.

£910–1,050 AG

A pair of giltwood figural candelabra, fitted for electricity, early 20thC, 82in (208.5cm) high.

£2,700–3,000 YOX

A cut-glass and metal table lamp, with floral-cut decoration, the ring suspended with drops, 1900–50, 18in (45.5cm) high.

£750–900 JDJ

A brass table lamp, the glass shade painted with roses, c1918, 16in (40.5cm) high.

£490–550 TOL

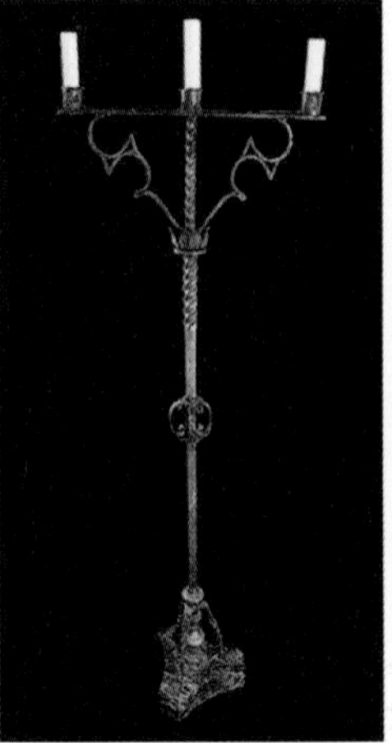

A wrought-iron and marble standard lamp, America, c1920, 62½in (159cm) high.

£2,950–3,300 CHAM

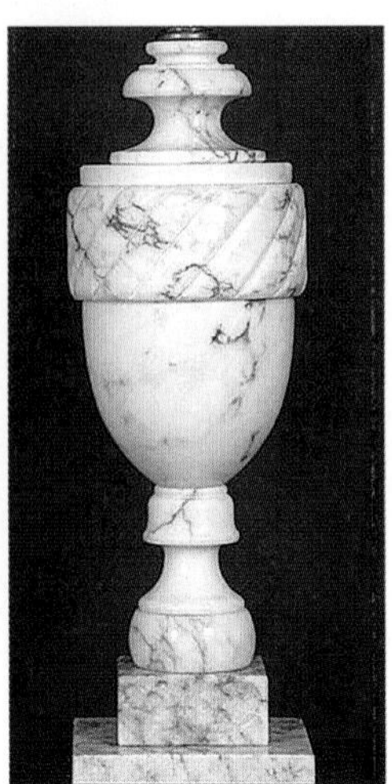

A pair of alabaster table lamps, c1920, 14½in (37cm) high.

£1,900–2,150 CHAM

A spelter and glass table lamp, with pull switch, 1920s, 22in (56cm) high.

£500–560 ALCH

RUGS & CARPETS

An Alcaraz carpet, Spain, 16thC, 129 x 67in (327.5 x 170cm).
£17,900–21,400 NAAW

◄ **A Savonnerie carpet,** Spain, early 20thC, 215 x 143in (546 x 363cm).
£2,750–3,300 FFAP

The rugs in this section have been arranged in geographical sequence from west to east, in the following order: Europe, Turkey, Anatolia, Caucasus, Persia, Turkestan, India and China.

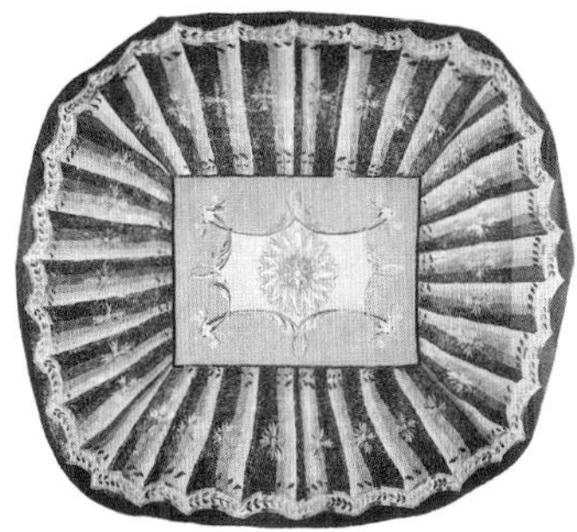

A fragment of an Aubusson carpet, rewoven and restored, France, c1790 and later, 137 x 155½in (348 x 393.5cm).
£4,800–5,700 S

A fragment of an Aubusson carpet, France, 1825–50, 113 x 74¾in (287 x 190cm).
£4,850–5,800 S(P)

An Aubusson rug, France, c1890, 63in (160cm) square.
£1,900–2,250 S(O)

A long-pile rug, Finland, dated 1826, 78¾ x 55¼in (200 x 140.5cm).
£1,050–1,250 BUK(F)

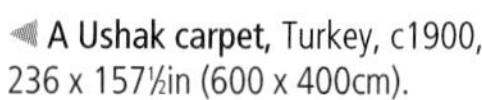

◄ **A Ushak carpet,** Turkey, c1900, 236 x 157½in (600 x 400cm).
£18,000–20,000 OR

This rug is of a very good size and has good colours – qualities that are attractive to interior designers.

A rug, Turkey, Yastik, c1900, 41 x 20½in (104 x 52cm).
£300–360 TREA

A silk prayer rug, Turkey, c1900, 64 x 49in (162.5 x 124.5cm).
£1,100–1,300 WAD

A prayer rug, repaired, Turkish, c1905, 62 x 43in (157.5 x 109cm).
£760–910 TREA

A Bezalel rug, Israel, Jerusalem, c1910, 35 x 52in (89 x 132cm).
£2,650–3,150 NSal

The Bezalel School of Arts & Crafts was founded in the early 20th century in Jerusalem by Boris Schaatz to forge a Jewish national style that would unify the Jews with their European counterparts and promote Zionist ideas.

An Akstafa prayer rug, southeast Caucasus, c1875, 61 x 38in (155 x 96.5cm).

£5,400–6,000 KNA

A Karabagh rug, south Caucasus, late 19thC, 124 x 61in (315 x 155cm).

£1,500–1,800 WW

A Karachov Kazak rug, southwest Caucasus, late 19thC, 72 x 48in (183 x 122cm).

£1,800–2,150 FFAP

These rugs are sometimes referred to as 'triple medallion' Karachov rugs.

A Kazak rug, southwest Caucasus, c1900, 104 x 62¼in (264 x 158cm).

£4,300–5,100 RIT

A Bordjalou Kazak rug, southwest Caucasus, c1910, 86 x 44in (218.5 x 112cm).

£3,550–4,250 WAD

A Kuba Chi-Chi rug, northeast Caucasus, late 19thC, 62 x 50in (157.5 x 127cm).

£570–680 NAAW

This is a very typical Chi-Chi design with its deep indigo field of stepped and hooked medallions within indigo slanted leaf and flowerhead borders.

A Moghan runner, south Caucasus, c1890, 97 x 43in (246.5 x 109cm).

£2,000–2,250 DNo

A Perepedil rug, slight losses, east Caucasus, c1910, 69 x 49in (175.5 x 124.5cm).

£470–560 TREA

A Seichur rug, with St Andrew's Cross motifs and running dog borders, slight damage, northeast Caucasus, c1875, 58 x 45in (147.5 x 114.5cm).

£5,300–6,300 SK

A Shirvan rug, with flowerheads and multiple guard borders, east Caucasus, c1900, 53 x 34in (134.5 x 86.5cm).

£530–630 WAD

For Decorative Arts and 20thC Design rugs see pages 390 and 470.

A *soumakh*, slight damage, Caucasus, c1900, 104½ x 64in (265.5 x 162.5cm).

£760–910 TREA

The technique of making a Soumakh involves wrapping wefts over four warps before drawing them back under the last two. The process is repeated from selvedge to selvedge. The weft strands on the underside may be left uncut and several inches long in order to provide extra warmth. Soumakhs tend to be finely woven and, although not as durable as piled carpets, they are stronger than kilims.

An Afshar rug, southwest Persia, c1875, 56 x 44in (142 x 112cm).

£2,700–3,000 KNA

The Afshar have been described as one of the great weaving tribes of Persia, weaving small Persian tribal rugs and also producing the finest grade of Bidjars.

An Afshar *soffreh*, southeast Persia, early 20thC, 46in (117cm) square.

£850–950 SAM

This is an unusual collector's piece with a design and colours that would appeal to many types of buyer. The price reflects its rarity. Soffreh were used as eating mats, where the food would be laid out and the diners would kneel to eat.

A Bidjar rug, slight damage, northwest Persia, c1910, 78 x 48in (198 x 122cm).

£1,600–1,900 TREA

This design is known as 'Mina Khani'.

A Dorush rug, east Persia, c1920, 70 x 47in (178 x 119.5cm).

£4,200–5,000 S(NY)

A Hamadan rug, northwest Persia, c1890, 83 x 52in (211 x 132cm).

£880–980 WADS

A Hamadan runner, northwest Persia, c1910, 172 x 40in (437 x 101.5cm).

£280–330 Hal

Hamadan rugs are coarsely woven but substantial rugs. They are notable for being single wefted, ie a single cotton weft, and made from good-quality wool.

A Karastan carpet, Persia, c1920, 77 x 41in (195.5 x 104cm).

£175–210 JAA

A Motasham Kashan rug, central Persia, late 19thC, 79 x 55in (200.5 x 139.5cm).

£2,400–2,850 WAD

Motasham is generally thought to refer to a master weaver who owned workshops in Kashan. They are among the most collectable of all Persian rugs.

A Motasham Kashan prayer rug, central Persia, late 19thC, 79 x 52in (200.5 x 132cm).

£2,900–3,450 FFAP

A Kashgai long rug, southwest Persia, c1880, 129 x 78in (327.5 x 198cm).

£2,250–2,500 WADS

► **A Kashgai long rug,** southwest Persia, 19thC, 112 x 46in (284.5 x 117cm).

£4,000–4,800 WAD

A Kashgai rug, southwest Persia, c1890, 73 x 47in (185.5 x 119.5cm).

£1,250–1,350 WADS

A Malayer *kelleh*, west Persia, 1900–20, 204 x 84in (518 x 213.5cm).

£1,200–1,400 NSal

Long, narrow rugs are more difficult to sell than pieces of more standard proportions.

► **A Tabriz silk rug,** some losses, fringes later, northwest Persia, c1880, 70 x 50in (178 x 127cm).

£1,750–2,100 S(NY)

A Senneh flatweave prayer rug, with applied fringe, slight damage, west Persia, late 19thC, 73 x 54in (185.5 x 137cm).

£4,750–5,700 TREA

► **A Senneh rug,** with Aubusson-style design, west Persia, early 20thC, 72 x 53in (183 x 134.5cm).

£1,700–2,000 WAD

A Khamseh rug, northwest Persia, slight damage and losses, c1900, 98 x 65in (249 x 165cm).

£760–910 TREA

A Sarouk carpet, inscribed, west Persia, c1920, 165 x 129in (419 x 327.5cm).

£3,850–4,600 FFAP

A Kirman rug, southeast Persia, c1920, 145 x 108in (368.5 x 274.5cm).

£950–1,100 TREA

A Senneh rug, west Persia, 1875–1900, 78 x 54in (198 x 137cm).

£4,950–5,500 KNA

A Tabriz silk carpet, northwest Persia, late 19thC, 151 x 103in (383.5 x 261.5cm).

£3,600–4,300 FFAP

This rug has excellent abrash from indigo to madder red.

A *soffreh* kilim, Persia, 1940s, 59 x 56¾in (150 x 144cm).

£580–650 SAMR

A Beshir runner, slight damage and restoration, Turkestan, 1850–1900, 419 x 78¾in (540 x 200cm).

£5,900–7,000 DORO

A Yomut Turkoman *ensi*, northwest Turkestan, late 19thC, 61 x 55in (155 x 155cm).

£1,200–1,400 FFAP

Not just for floors

Apart from their primary use as floor coverings, carpets were used as curtains, hangings, blankets, canopies and tomb covers. Small pieces of rug were woven for storage and saddle bags, as well as saddle cloths. In Europe they were used for wall hangings, table covers and celebratory balcony decorations.

► **A Tekke *chuval*,** west Turkestan, 19thC, 52 x 34in (132 x 86.5cm).

£540–640 WAD

A Saryk Turkoman *ensi*, south Turkestan, c1900, 55 x 47in (139.5 x 119.5cm).

£630–750 NSal

An Uzbek bag face, north Turkestan, late 19thC, 34 x 32in (86.5 x 81.5cm).

£290–330 KNA

► **A Yomut Turkoman *torba*,** northwest Turkestan, 1875–1900, 32 x 12in (81.5 x 30.5cm).

£900–1,000 KNA

A Timuri Balouch prayer rug, with soumakh panels, west Afghanistan, c1850, 54 x 31in (137 x 78.5cm).

£800–900 KNA

A Balouch rug, slight damage, Afghanistan, c1920, 72 x 41in (183 x 104cm).

£200–240 TREA

A Balouch rug, Afghanistan, c1920, 71¼ x 37in (181 x 94cm).

£760–850 SAMR

An Agra carpet, slight damage and repair, India, c1890, 202 x 148in (513 x 376cm).
£3,900–4,650 S(NY)

An Agra carpet, India, late 19thC, 142 x 106in (360.5 x 269cm).
£5,700–6,800 WAD

▶ **An Agra carpet,** India, c1890, 158 x 98in (401.5 x 249cm).
£13,200–15,800 S

An Amritsar carpet, c1900, 240 x 132in (609.5 x 335.5cm).
£5,800–6,900 FFAP

An Amritsar carpet, c1900, 127 x 114in (322.5 x 289.5cm).
£6,500–7,700 FFAP

▶ **A rug,** Tibet, c1920, 69 x 48in (175.5 x 122cm).
£350–420 TREA

A rug, decorated with peonies, Tibet, 64¼ x 36¼in (163 x 92cm).
£1,200–1,400 S

A silk velvet carpet, depicting two dragons chasing a flaming pearl, China, 18thC, 92¾ x 64¾in (235.5 x 164.5cm).
£5,200–6,200 S(NY)

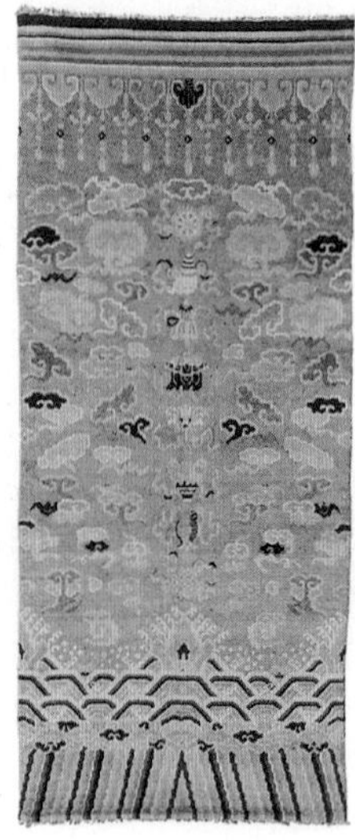

A Ninghsia pillar rug, depicting the Eight Buddhist Emblems above stylized waves and mountains, northwest China, c1875, 118 x 50in (299.5 x 127cm).
£3,900–4,650 S(NY)

Pillar rugs, as their name suggests, were made to decorate pillars in temples.

◀ **A rug,** China, c1930, 71 x 37½in (180.5 x 95.5cm).
£850–950 KW

TEXTILES

Patricia Herr

Patricia is a researcher, author, lecturer, and dealer in the field of American historic textiles.

She has written articles on textiles for Early American Life, The Quilt Digest, The Magazine Antiques *and other symposium and museum publications.*

AMERICAN QUILTS and other bed covers have been actively collected by a few individual connoisseurs and museums in the US since the late 19th century. By the early 20th century interest had increased and these textiles were being used for decorative purposes in the homes of well-to-do families. As the century progressed the hobby became more popular and organizations were founded to promote the study and collection of quilts and coverlets.

In the late 1960s a new breed of collector appeared with a fresh viewpoint: quilts became art. The 1971 exhibition 'Abstracts in American Design' at the Whitney Museum in New York City displayed quilts hung on the wall instead of on a period bedstead in the traditional manner. The quilts featured in this show were made in the early 20th century by Amish women living in Lancaster County, Pennsylvania. As a direct result values of Amish quilts rapidly increased and other examples identifiable with specific cultures and areas are now also widely collected and valued. Baltimore Album quilts made in the mid-19th century by groups of predominantly Methodist church women, increased significantly in value in the 1970s and '80s. Although these values have now levelled off, these types of quilt, and also bed rugs from New England, continue to sell for well over £5,000. Value is closely linked with condition, provenance and historic interest.

American collectors still appear to be the main consumers of American-made bedcovers. The traditional pieced and appliquéd varieties of quilts made throughout the US are the most popular pieces, but interest has increased in mid-19th century woven Jacquard-patterned coverlets, the earlier 18th-century whole-cloth quilted New England bedcovers and hand-worked bed rugs.

Textile collectors are able to find more information through the many museum exhibitions, lectures, and printed and online articles currently so popular throughout the country. Textile interest and collection is indeed alive and well as we move forward in the 21st century.

Patricia T. Herr

COVERS & QUILTS

A silk bedcover, embroidered in floss silks with a bird, slight restoration, lining later, Portugal, Castello Branco, 17thC, 92 x 66½in (234 x 169cm).

£12,100–13,500 MGa

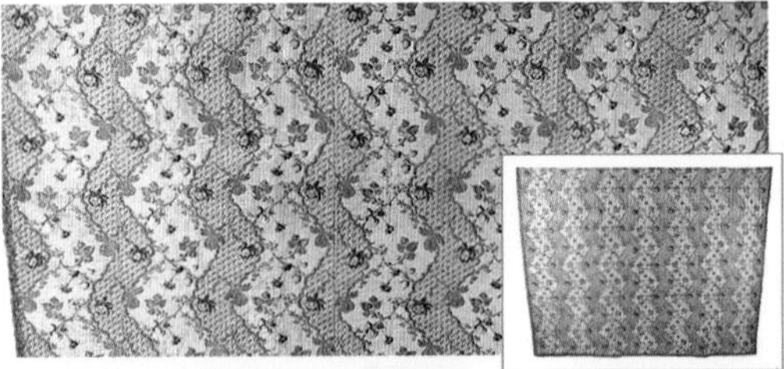

◄ **A silk coverlet,** brocaded with silk flowers, with metallic lace edging, cotton backing, slight damage, c1750, 69 x 81in (175.5 x 205.5cm).

£380–450 WHIT

► **A wool and hemp coverlet,** slight damage, America, Connecticut, c1830, 54 x 37in (137 x 94cm).

£125–150 WHIT

An appliqué cotton quilt, with double six-pointed star motif, with a cotton backing, slight damage, America, Baltimore, c1842, 134 x 125in (340.5 x 317.5cm).

£10,200–12,200 SK(B)

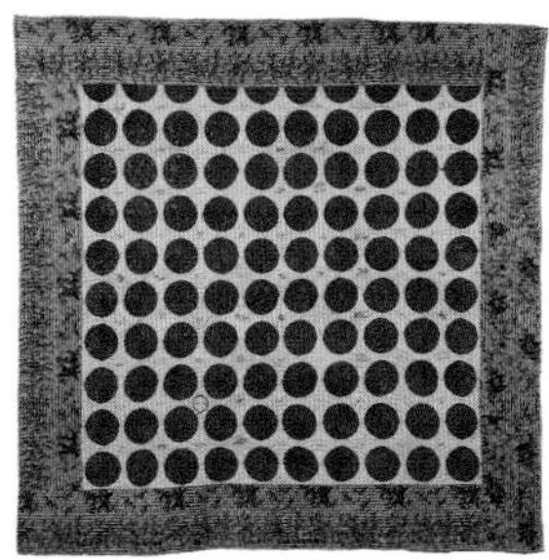

A pieced cotton and chintz Friendship quilt, comprising 81 cotton squares each centred with a pen and ink motif including clasped hands, sailing vessels and musical instruments, with a cotton backing, slight damage, America, Pennsylvania, many squares dated 1842, 96 x 92in (244 x 233.5cm).

£1,200–1,400 SK

An appliqué cotton Mariner's Compass quilt, slight damage, America, Pennsylvania or New Jersey, c1845, 107in (272cm) square.

£7,600–9,100 SK(B)

A Quaker Wistar Friendship quilt, comprising 100 blocks depicting a family tree, America, Philadelphia, individually dated, 1840s, 110in (279.5cm) square.

£17,100–19,000 TLD

Documentary pieces such as this are highly desirable.

A patchwork coverlet, slight damage, 19thC, 97in (246.5cm) square.

£220–260 PFK

A coverlet, by S. Hausman, losses, America, Pennsylvania, dated 1846, 99 x 77in (251.5 x 195.5cm).

£185–220 JAA

An appliqué cotton quilt, American, probably Pennsylvania, mid-19thC, 88in (223.5cm) square.

£5,400–6,000 HERR

An Eagle and Stars Album quilt, America, 1850–60, 100 x 96in (254 x 244cm).

£4,100–4,600 LFNY

Instead of a traditional arch of 13 stars to represent original colonies, a field of 30 five-point stars crown the spreadwing eagle central medallion. This may have been made to commemorate Wisconsin's admission into the Union in 1848. Appliqué quilt blocks in classic oak leaf and folded and cut-out designs surround the national symbol of America.

A wool coverlet, signed 'Jacob Sherman Attica Seneca Country Ohio 1853', America, 1853, 78 x 72in (198 x 183cm).

£120–140 WHIT

An appliqué pieced cotton quilt, with quilted monograms. America, dated 1854, 94 x 78in (239 x 198cm).

£890–1,050 WHIT

A patchwork quilt, America, Michigan, c1860, 72 x 57in (183 x 145cm).

£200–240 DuM

◀ **An appliqué pieced cotton American Flag quilt,** America, dated 1863, 54 x 78in (137 x 198cm).

£8,800–9,800 LFNY

Thirty-four stars arranged like a ship's anchor in the unusual canton, allude to the entry of Kansas into a Union that had broken. Made at the time of the Civil War, the quilt-maker expressed her anti-war sentiments in ink on white stars sewn on the blue backing: 'Never Falter While There is Still Treason Abroad', 'Union and Liberty Evermore', and 'One Flag, One Sword, One Heart, One Hand, One Nation Evermore'.

An appliqué pieced cotton Album quilt, the centre block depicts a spreadwing eagle over an anchor, an American shield flanked by flags, crossed cannon and cannonballs, bordered by various motifs signed in pen and ink by friends, family and makers of the blocks, America, New York, c1863, 82 x 66in (208.5 x 167.5).

£13,400–16,000 SK(B)

A woven table cover, with starburst medallion, 1869, 144 x 62in (366 x 157.5cm).

£410–490 WHIT

This table cover formed part of the dowry of the daughter of a Florentine marquis when she married a Genoan ship owner in 1869.

A quilt top, embroidered in wool with flowers, c1870, 84 x 78in (213.5 x 198cm).

£570–680 WHIT

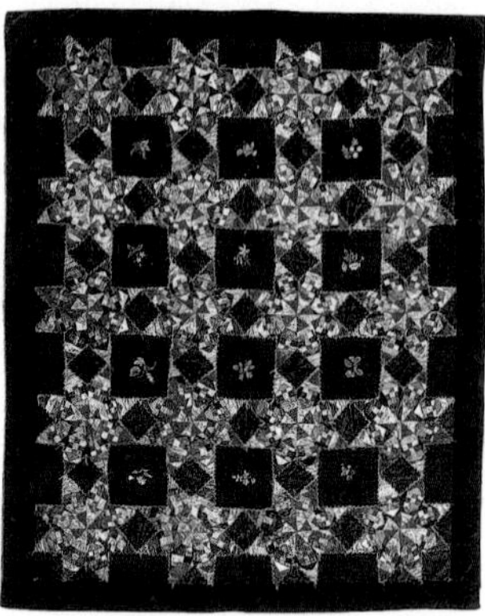

A pieced and embroidered silk and velvet Eight-Point Crazy Stars quilt, America, Ohio, 1880s, 64 x 54in (162 x 137cm).

£1,700–1,900 LFNY

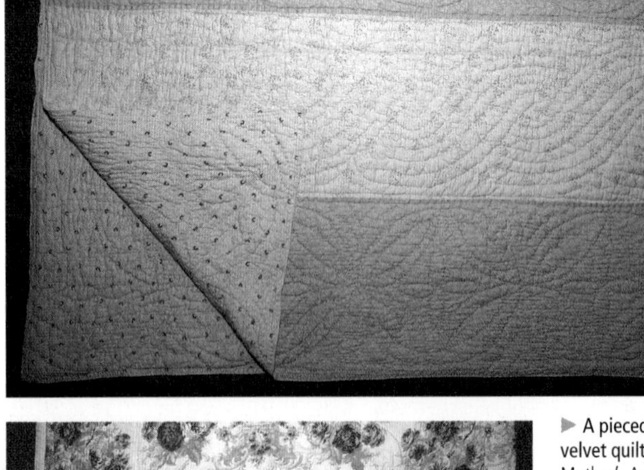

◀ **A cotton and satin Durham strip quilt,** c1880, 98 x 80in (249 x 203cm).

£410–460 JPr

A cotton and satin Durham quilt, c1890, 64in (162.5cm) square.

£260–290 JPr

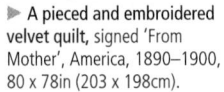

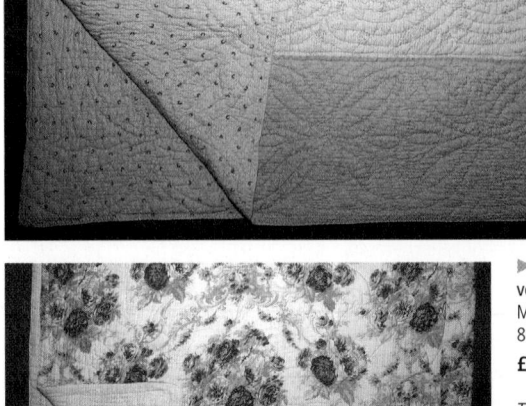

▶ **A pieced and embroidered velvet quilt,** signed 'From Mother', America, 1890–1900, 80 x 78in (203 x 198cm).

£880–980 LFNY

The randomly pieced blocks often referred to as 'crazy' were alternated with diamond-shaped blocks made of narrow strips. The contrast of linear diamonds with crazy blocks seems to reflect a turn-of-the-century aesthetic shift away from the elaborate towards the more streamlined effect.

A patchwork coverlet, slight damage, late 19thC, 102 x 88in (259 x 223.5cm).

£80–95 PFK

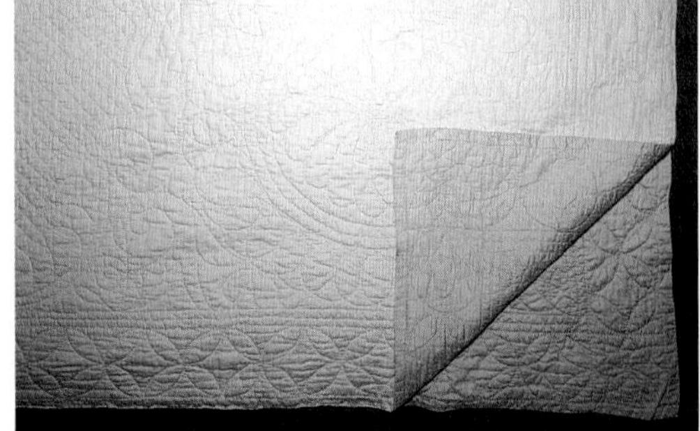

A cotton Durham quilt, 1890–1910, 84 x 80in (213.5 x 203cm).

£260–290 JPr

A Tashkent *susani*, Uzbekistan, late 19thC, 108¼ x 77¾in (275 x 197.5cm).

£900–1,050 S(O)

A blanket, hand-stitched in satin cotton, c1900, 84 x 64in (213.5 x 162.5cm).

£135–150 JPr

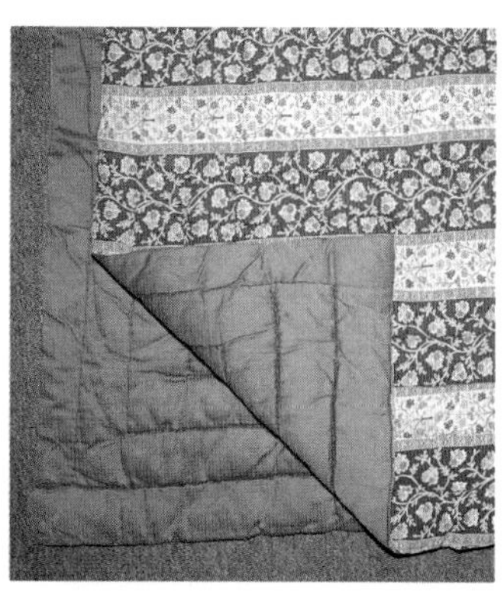

A quilt, France, c1900, 80 x 78in (203 x 198cm).

£170–190 JPr

An Amish cotton and wool Roman Stripe quilt, American, Ohio, 1910–20, 84x 64in (213.5 x 162.5cm).

£9,700–10,800 LFNY

A typical Amish pattern, this early example combines wool strips with the black cotton sateen characteristic of Holmes County settlement. The group, county, and state origin of an Amish quilt can often be discerned through the colours, materials and formats used. In Holmes County, this subdued earlier palette was superseded by saturated, jewel-like colours. The sawtooth border accentuates the design's three-dimensionality, as black triangles vie for visual dominance with the pieced segments.

A Crazy quilt, embroidered with flowers, slight damage, America, c1915, 83 x 70in (211 x 178cm).

£190–220 JDJ

This quilt won First Prize at the 9th Annual Vermont State Fair Exhibition in 1915.

A crewelwork appliqué coverlet, c1920, 74 x 60in (188 x 152.5cm).

£530–600 JPr

An Amish wool quilt, with cotton back, America, Pennsylvania, c1920, 91 x 84in (231 x 213cm).

£5,900–6,600 HERR

An appliqué cotton quilt, with embroidered decoration, America, 92 x 84in (233.5 x 213.5cm).

£19,600–21,800 LFNY

One of more than 33,000 entries in the Century of Progress quilt competition sponsored by Sears, Roebuck for the 1933–34 Chicago World's Fair, this imaginative work has 100 blocks depicting the quilt-maker's view of the significant technological, scientific, and social advances made during each year (1834–1933) of the preceding century. Each president and his party affiliation is noted along with such developments as the Emancipation 1863, Tubercle Bacillus (Koch) 1882, Movies 1894, First Transatlantic Flight (Alcock & Brown) 1919, Broadcasting 1920 and King Tutankhamen's Tomb 1922.

A pieced cotton quilt, with 24 American flags, America, 1939–45, 82 x 70in (208.5 x 178cm).

£1,850–2,100 LFNY

EMBROIDERY & NEEDLEWORK

A petit point runner, depicting butterflies, snakes, birds and foliage, Italy, 17thC, 101 x 72in (256.5 x 183cm).

£6,300–7,000 MGa

A needlework panel, depicting religious scenes, birds, animals and figures, backing later, slight damage, 17thC, 38 x 46in (96.5 x 117cm).

£1,250–1,500 CHTR

A ceremonial embroidered velvet and appliqué panel, worked in metal threads with flowers and a coat-of-arms, Italy, late 17thC, 87½ x 51¼in (222.5 x 130cm).

£3,350–4,000 S

An embroidered frieze, depicting obelisks, flowers and fruit, 18thC, 5¾ x 19¾in (14.5 x 50cm), in a Hogarth frame.

£560–670 SWO

An embroidered silk panel, depicting a spray of flowers, 18thC, in a giltwood frame, 15in (38cm) high.

£200–240 DN

Items in the Textiles section have been arranged in date order.

A needlework valance, worked in wool, France, 18thC, 79 x 22in (200.5 x 56cm).

£190–220 WHIT

A George III woolwork picture, worked in long and short stitch with a maiden playing a flute, with watercolour appliqués, 13in (33cm) high, in a gilt gesso frame.

£360–430 F&C

A woolwork picture, worked in tent stitch with a hunting scene, slight damage, America, Massachusetts, 1750–1800, 9 x 14in (23 x 35.5cm), in a giltwood frame.

£32,000–38,000 SK

Examples of American needlework such as this are very rare and therefore highly desirable.

An embroidered silk memorial picture, worked with threads and ink with a Gothic church and plinth, with inscription, America, New York, c1800.

£1,000–1,200 NAAW

An embroidered map of England and Wales, dated 1804, 23¼in (59cm) high.

£810–900 HIS

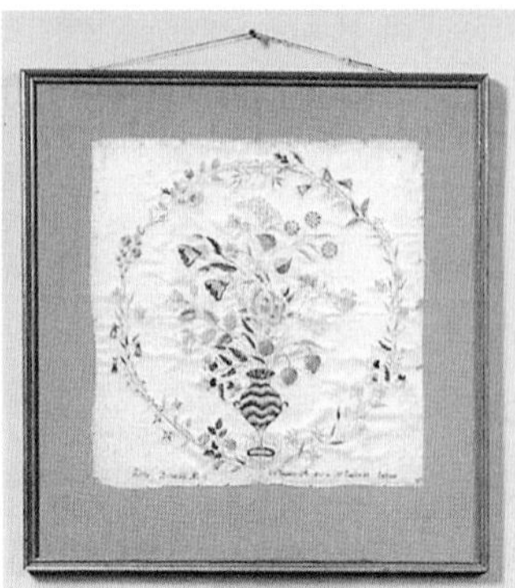

A silk needlework picture, worked in silk threads with an urn of flowers, slight damage, dated 1805, 14 x 14½in (35.5 x 37cm), in a giltwood frame.

£280–330 SK

An embroidered map of Europe, by Jenepher Fisher, Irish, dated 1809, 20¼in x 18in (52 x 45.5cm).

£780–930 WW

A needlework picture, c1830, 14 x 22in (35.5 x 56cm), framed.

£370–420 Fai

A beadwork and embroidered cushion, with wire trim, c1850, 15in (38cm) wide.

£240–270 DHA

A pair of embroidered satin curtains, with pelmet, c1880, 89 x 66in (226 x 167.5cm).

£440–490 JPr

A silk embroidered picture, early 19thC, 17 x 21in (43 x 53.5cm), framed.

£200–230 OD

A stumpwork picture, depicting Lancaster Castle Gate, 19thC, 13in (33in) square, in a rosewood frame.

£270–320 Mit

A Victorian needlework panel, worked in silks with various motifs, 9 x 6¾in (23 x 17cm), framed.

£320–380 Bea

A woolwork picture, c1880, 12 x 14in (30.5 x 35.5cm).

£140–160 NORTH

A needlework picture, worked in silk, chenille and metallic threads with Mount Vernon and the Potomac River, America, early 19thC, in a later moulded wood frame.

£1,650–1,950 SK

A needlework runner, composed of two joined panels, slight damage, losses, possibly shortened, France, c1850, 132 x 46in (335.5 x 117cm).

£4,200–5,000 S(NY)

An embroidered panel, c1890, 23in (59cm) square.

£130–145 HILL

LACE

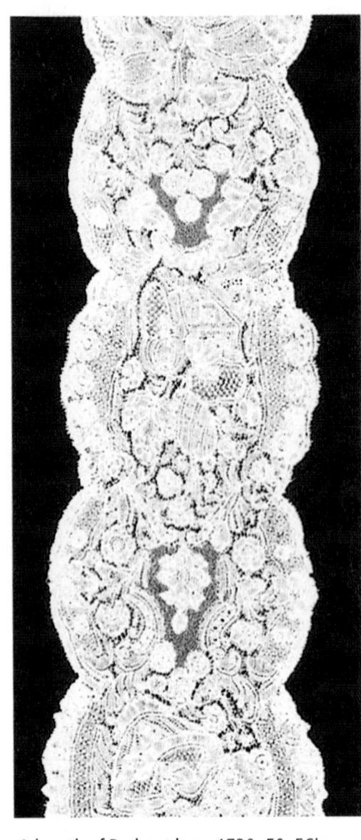

A length of Brabant lace, 1730–50, 56in (142cm) long.

£350–420 KTA

A flounce of Brussels bobbin lace, worked in *point-de-gaze* with floral bouquets, Belgium, 19thC, 16½ x 219in (42 x 556cm).

£410–490 WHIT

An ecru cotton lace tablecloth, early 20thC, 106 x 70in (269 x 178cm).

£250–300 WHIT

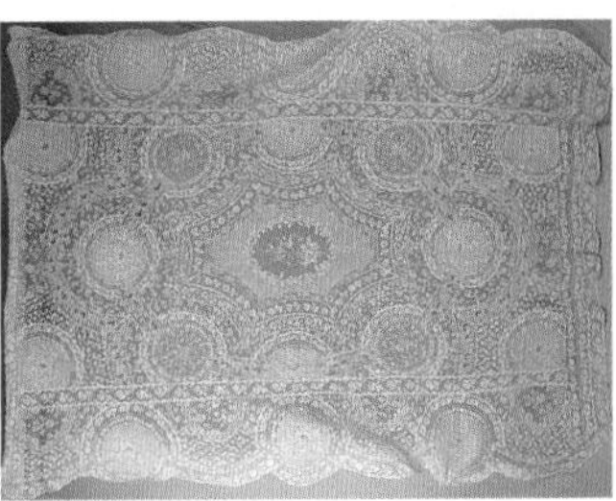

A Normandy lace bedspread, with embroidered medallions, France, 1910–20, 88 x 60in (223.5 x 152.5cm).

£470–560 WHIT

A Normandy lace bedspread, embroidered with floral medallions and an Oriental figure by the sea, France, 1910–20, 106 x 70in (269 x 178cm).

£440–520 WHIT

SAMPLERS

A sampler, worked with bands, alphabets and figures, framed, c1640, 21in (53.5cm) high.

£1,350–1,500 HIS

An alphabet sampler, worked with Adam and Eve, birds, animals and trees, 1781, 19 x 10in (48.5 x 25.5cm), in a painted wood frame.

£470–560 BAu

A sampler, by Lydia Gordon, worked in silk with alphabets, a verse, birds, flowers, fruit and animals, America, Massachusetts, 1797, 22¾ x 16¾in (58 x 42.5cm), framed.

£4,750–5,700 SK

▶ **A sampler,** by Hannah Lee, worked in silk with alphabets, a verse, trees and geometric borders, America, Massachusetts, 1793, 10¼ x 9½in (26 x 24cm), framed.

£830–990 SK(B)

A sampler, by Sarah Farmer, worked with a tree, birds, plants and a deer, with biblical verses, 1799, 12in (30.5cm) square.

£910–1,050 GIL

A sampler, by J. A. Coleman, entitled 'Wholesome Advice', c1800, 16¼ x 12¼in (41 x 31cm), in a wooden frame.

£440–520 MA&I

A Nine Partners Boarding School sampler, by Phebe Johnson, America, 1802, 7½in (19cm) high, in a wooden frame.

£1,050–1,200 HIS

◄ **A Quaker school sampler,** by Sarah Marchant, 1804, 12¼in (31cm) high.

£1,350–1,500 HIS

The script is very typical of Quaker Schools.

A sampler, by Nancy Lock, worked in silk threads with three alphabets, a verse and a vine of strawberries, America, 1806, 17in (43cm) square.

£4,150–4,950 SK(B)

◄ **A sampler,** by Susan Burson, worked in silk threads with an alphabet, a verse, flowers and sheep, America, 1812, 25 x 24½in (63.5 x 62cm), in a wooden frame.

£6,000–7,200 NAAW

► **A sampler,** by Martha Davis, worked in silk threads and metallic sequins with a verse, a view of Westtown School and flowers, America, New Jersey, 1813, 26 x 19in (66 x 48.5cm), in a mahogany-veneered frame.

£5,100–6,100 SK

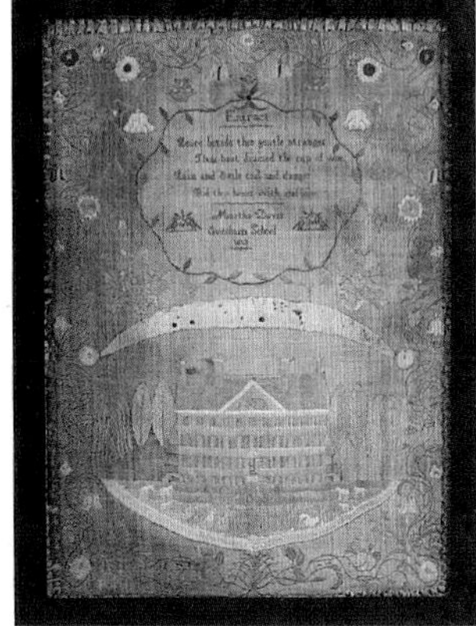

A miniature sampler, by Sally G. Lovejoy, America, New England, 1801, 6¼in (16cm) high, framed.

£630–700 HIS

An Ackworth School sampler, by L. Haworth, America, 1815, 15¾in (40cm) high.

£2,700–3,000 HIS

Quakers from Ackworth School in Yorkshire went on to set up, and teach at, Quaker schools in England and the US.

A Quaker sampler, by Lydia Smith, America, 1819, 13¾in (35cm) high.

£1,350–1,500 HIS

The half medallions embroidered on this example are typical of Quaker samplers.

A sampler, by Arianna H. Coles, worked in silk threads on a linen ground with verses, birds, trees and flowers, America, c1820, 18 x 13½in (45.5 x 34.5cm), in a mahogany-veneered frame.

£2,700–3,200 SK

A sampler, by Elizabeth Cobb, worked with three alphabets, America, New Jersey, dated 1824, framed, 17 x 12in (43 x 30.5cm).

£950–1,100 NAAW

A sampler, by Elizabeth Dibbs, worked with a religious verse and exotic animals and flowers, dated 1825, in a gesso moulded frame, 28 x 28½in (71 x 72.5cm).

£2,000–2,400 Hal

◄ **A sampler,** by Hannah Crary Brownell, worked in silk threads on a linen ground with alphabets and verses, bordered by trees and flowers, 1826, 13½ x 21½in (34.5 x 54.5cm), in a wooden frame.

£2,500–3,000 SK(B)

A sampler, by Jane Marsden, worked in silks with a verse, birds, flowers, figures, sheep and a church, 1826, 19½ x 18in (49.5 x 45.5cm), in a maple frame.

£540–640 AH

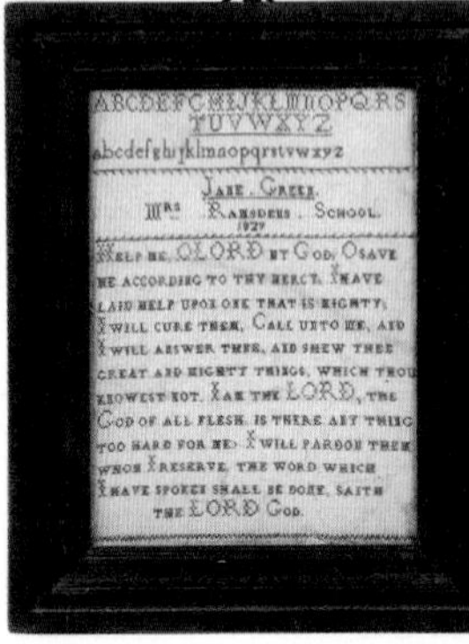

A sampler, by Jane Green, 1829, 7in (18cm) high, framed.

£270–300 HIS

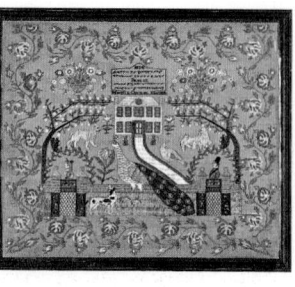

◄ **A sampler,** by Mary McVicker Hunter, worked in silks on a linen ground with an alphabet, initials, animals, birds, flowers, a figure and a house, Scotland, 1820s, 16¼ x 11in (41.5 x 28cm).

£350–420 F&C

Mary McVicker Hunter was the aunt of the Scottish painter James Paterson, (1854–1932).

A sampler, by Margaret Griffith, worked in silks on a gauze ground with a manor house, animals and figures and two verses in shorthand from the New Testament, probably Wales, dated 1834, 19¼ x 22¾in (49 x 58cm).

£14,000–16,800 KTA

This sampler is unusual for its size and has an extraordinarily ambitious and entertaining design. The brown wool gauze ground is also rare.

A sampler, by Kezia Howel, 1836, 36 x 29½in (91.5 x 75cm), in a rosewood frame.

£400–480 SWO

A memorial sampler, America, 1836, 17¼in (44cm) high, in a frame.

£720–800 HIS

A sampler, worked with an alphabet, a biblical verse, birds, animals, trees and houses, 1837, 19½ x 14¼in (49.5 x 36cm), in a gilt frame.

£1,000–1,200 BAu

A sampler, by Mary Headrick, worked with a verse, stag, trees, figures, a house and stylized flowerheads, 1837, 16½ x 11¾in (42 x 30cm), in a maple frame.

£270–320 BAM

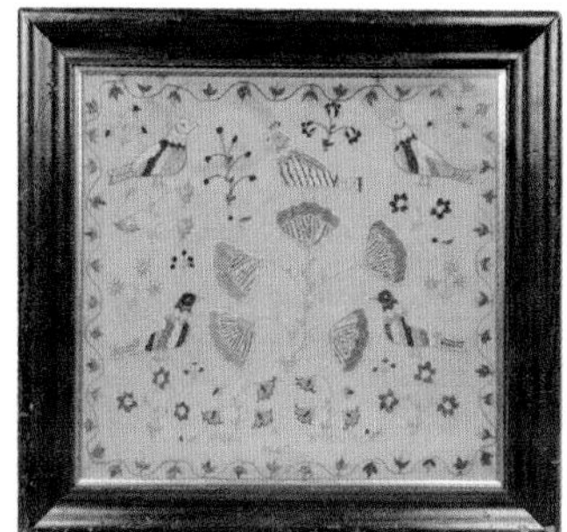

► **A sampler,** by Ellen Brotherton, America, Pennsylvania, 1840, 15½in (39.5cm) high, in a wooden frame.

£720–800 HIS

A sampler, by Mary Baildon, worked with angels, birds, figures, animals and a verse, 1845, 25 x 22in (63.5 x 56cm).

£670–800 DA

◄ **A sampler,** by Maria Taylor, worked in cotton and silk cross-stitch on linen with a house, a verse and a vine, America, Baltimore, 1841, in a wooden frame, 29¼ x 29¾in (74.5 x 75.5cm).

£1,150–1,350 SK(B)

A sampler, by Charlotte Bell, worked in silks with petit-point animals, birds, butterflies, flowers, a house and a verse, 1851, 16¼ x 11¾in (41.5 x 30cm).

£730–870 Bea

For more examples of American Folk Art, see pages 725–727.

A sampler, by Matilda Smith, worked with a house, trees, birds, dogs, butterflies, flowers and a house, 1852, 15¾ x 16¼in (40 x 41.5cm).

£200–240 WAD

A Bristol Orphanage sampler, by E. Moore, worked in silks with cross-stitch alphabets, numbers, biblical verses and motifs, 1881, 12¼ x 10¼in (31 x 26cm).

£3,400–4,000 DN

Samplers made by children in orphanages are particularly desirable.

TAPESTRIES

◄ **A tapestry fragment,** entitled 'Diana the Huntress', Continental, 17thC, 62 x 83in (157.5 x 211cm).

£2,400–2,850 FFAP

A tapestry, possibly Lambeth workshop, depicting Leander swimming across the Hellespont from Abydos to Sestos, from the mythological story of Hero and Leander, from a series of tapestries originally designed by Francis Cleyn, late 17thC, 81¾ x 132¼in (208 x 336cm).

£9,600–11,500 S

Francis Cleyn (1623–58) designed the Hero and Leander tapestry series of seven panels in 1620 for the Mortlake workshop, which was set up by James I.

A tapestry, after David Téniers, depicting a game of bowls, France, Beauvais, c1680, 98½ x 110¼in (250 x 280cm).

£9,600–11,500 S(NY)

The paintings of peasant scenes by David Téniers, popular in the Netherlands and used for cartoons for Flemish tapestries, were later copied by the weavers in Beauvais and Aubusson.

A Flanders tapestry, depicting trees and hills, 18thC, 112 x 105in (284.5 x 266.5cm).

£4,550–5,400 WAD

For more examples of 20thC textiles, see page 470.

A Flanders tapestry, after David Téniers, 18thC, 89½ x 100½in (227.5 x 255.5cm).

£8,900–10,600 S(P)

A Soho tapestry, worked with a chinoiserie scene, 19thC, 42½ x 78¾in (108 x 200cm).

£9,000–10,000 OR

A pair of Aubusson tapestry panels, depicting summer flowers and foliage, later selvedge, France, c1900, 39¼ x 120in (100 x 305cm).

£9,700–11,600 S(NY)

An Aubusson tapestry, depicting a game of Blind Man's Buff, 19thC, France, 100 x 111½in (254 x 283cm).

£1,900–2,250 S

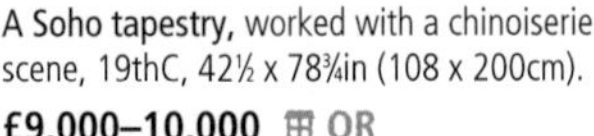

A tapestry, depicting a deer hunting scene and a castle, 19thC, 86¾ x 120in (220.5 x 305cm).

£3,000–3,600 BERN

COSTUME

A pair of silk damask wedding shoes, with linen lining and paper label to sole of one shoe 'Mrs Martin's Wedding Shoe, of West Moulton, Somerset Hall, 1736'.

£1,400–1,650 WHIT

A glazed cotton top hat, with John N. Genin label, with silk lining, America, New York, c1840, 8½in (21.5cm) high, with a wallpaper box.

£1,600–1,900 WHIT

◄ **A silk brocade robe,** the sleeves with ruched borders, later alterations, late 18thC.

£370–440 DN(HAM)

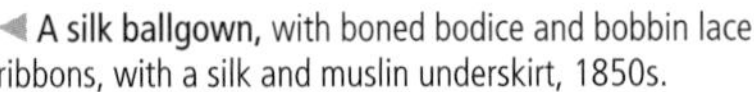

A Victorian paisley wool shawl, decorated with paisley pattern, 64 x 120in (162.5 x 305cm).

£490–550 Ech

◄ **A silk ballgown,** with boned bodice and bobbin lace ribbons, with a silk and muslin underskirt, 1850s.

£540–640 WHIT

A Victorian silk and lace parasol, with an ivory and coral-mounted handle, with a presentation box by W. & J. Sangster.

£840–1,000 AG

A silk mourning dress and bonnet, damaged, America, c1865.

£170–200 JDJ

A silk two-piece visiting dress, with parasol pocket, America, c1873.

£3,500–4,200 WHIT

A wool day suit, by Batz & Vogt, America, New York, 1880s.

£2,800–3,350 WHIT

A cotton sateen and lace corset, with embroidered decoration, 1880s.
£540–640 WHIT

► **A silk and velvet two-piece dress,** with beaded decoration, labelled 'Robes & Confections, G. Marchais, Nevers', France, 1892.
£510–610 WHIT

A lace and silk satin ribbon peignoir, slight damage, c1910.
£760–910 WHIT

A peignoir is a long nightgown for women, usually sheer and made of chiffon.

An embroidered coat, probably Tekke, west Turkmenistan, 19thC.
£9,100–10,900 BUK

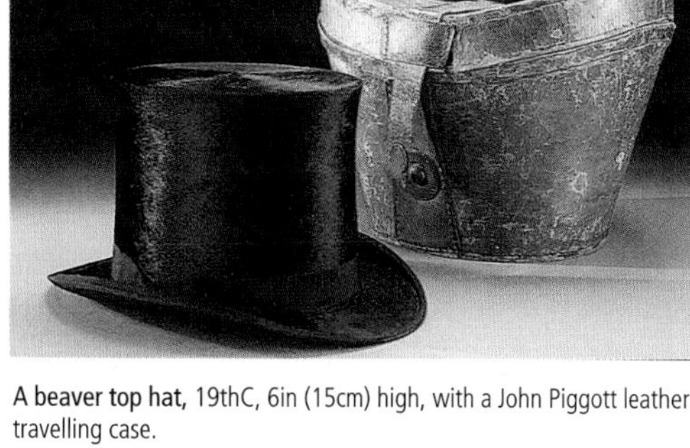

A beaver top hat, 19thC, 6in (15cm) high, with a John Piggott leather travelling case.
£90–105 JAA

◄ **A velvet piano dress,** by Lucile Ltd, with *crepe-de-Chine* borders and matching stole, France, c1919.
£1,200–1,400 KTA

Lucy Christiana, Lady Duff Gordon was a leading fashion designer in the early 20th century who opened branches of 'Lucile Ltd' in Paris, New York City and Chicago, dressing pillars of high society, the stage and early silent cinema. She is also famous for surviving the Titanic *disaster.*

► **An embroidered shawl,** late 19thC, 64in (162.5cm) square.
£180–200 JPr

An Edwardian child's lace dress.
£250–280 MARG

◄ **A silk taffeta two-piece tea gown,** by Nash, encrusted with sequins and beads simulating grapes and leaves, America, Philadelphia, c1900.
£510–610 WHIT

A lamé wrap, 1920s.
£140–165 Ech

FANS

A bone fan, the paper leaf painted in gouache with figures, damaged, France, c1800, 18½in (47cm) wide, with box.

£220–260 DORO

A bone fan, the lacquered card leaf painted to one side with 'Neopolitan girl with basket of flowers', slight damage, Italy, c1830, 12¼in (31cm) wide.

£175–210 DORO

An ivory fan, the leaf painted with a centaur and mythological figures, the sticks and guard pierced and carved with classical vignettes, France, 19thC, mounted in a gilt frame, 11¼ x 17¼in (28.5 x 44cm).

£250–300 WAD

An ivory fan, the leaf painted with figures in gardens, the sticks pierced with figures, China, Canton, mid-19thC, 11in (28cm) high, with a box.

£440–520 SWO

An ivory fan, the sticks and guards pierced and carved with figures and trees, China, Canton, mid-19thC, 10½in (26.5cm) high.

£260–310 SWO

An ivory fan, the paper leaf painted in watercolours with exotic birds and flowers, the ivory sticks decorated with flowers, birds and insects, with a lacquered ivory *ojime* and silk tassel, Japan, Meiji Period, 1868–1911, 12½in (32cm) high.

£1,500–1,800 G(B)

A lacquered ivory fan, decorated with Oriental figures, inscribed with a poem, with a lacquered ivory *ojime*, Japan, Meiji Period, 1868–1911, 23¾in (60.5cm) wide, with a fitted ivory box.

£7,400–8,800 S

A mother-of-pearl fan, the silk leaf painted with leaves, flowers and birds, repaired, c1890, 13½in (34.5cm) wide.

£155–185 WHIT

An advertising fan, the leaf depicting the route from Cherbourg to Florence by P. Clarey, the reverse title 'Western of France Railways', depicting French tourist scenes, the bone guards engraved with scrolling leaves and lozenge motif, France, dated 1893, 25½in (65cm) wide.

£120–140 Hal

► **A mother-of-pearl fan,** by Henri Dupras, the silk leaf painted with flowers and swallows, repaired, c1890, 11½in (29cm) high.

£155–185 WHIT

◄ **An ivory fan,** the leaf painted by Ding Yu with two herons, the reverse with an inscription, the sticks engraved in miniature, China, dated 1948, 12¼in (31cm) high.

£1,050–1,250 S

JEWELLERY

BANGLES & BRACELETS

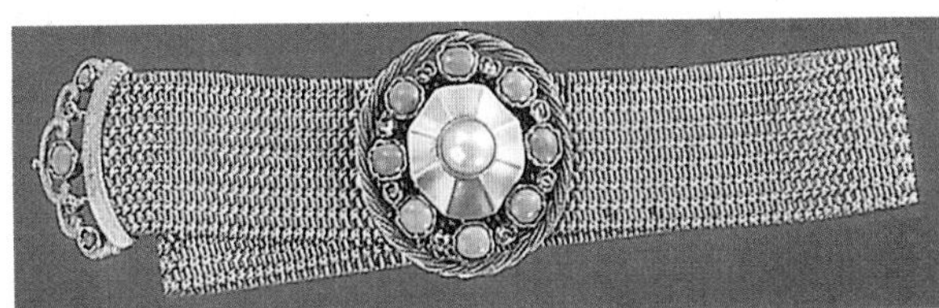

A gold bracelet, set with eight turquoises, diamonds and an Oriental pearl, maker's mark 'JB' probably for Jonas Bergström, slight damage, Russia, St Petersburg, 1764–1816.

£710–850 BUK(F)

◄ **A late George III gold and horsehair memorial bracelet,** with a gold locket inscribed 'W', enclosing a lock of hair thought to be from the first Duke of Wellington, the horse hair strap thought to be from the Duke's horse.

£300–360 DN

A Victorian 14ct gold bracelet, the bead-set clasp with diamonds and wirework, clasp later, 7in (18cm) long.

£250–300 SK

A Victorian gold bangle, set with pearls and diamonds.

£700–840 HYD

A Victorian Etruscan-style gold bracelet, chased with flowers and rocaille work, set with rubies and diamonds and a green glass panel.

£940–1,100 HYD

A seed pearl bracelet, with a gold and pearl clasp, c1800.

£490–550 SPE

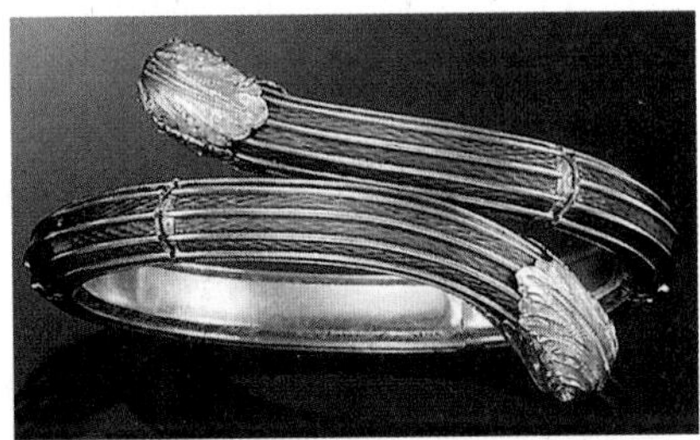

A gold bangle, decorated with guilloche enamel with acanthus-leaf terminals, 1840s, 2¼in (5.5cm) wide.

£2,500–3,000 S

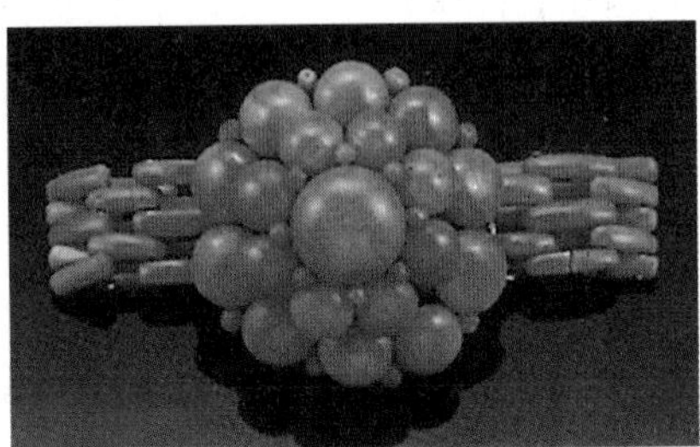

A 15ct gold bracelet, set with coral beads, c1860.

£300–360 LJ

◄ **A 15ct gold bracelet,** set with opals and diamonds, c1880.

£810–900 SPE

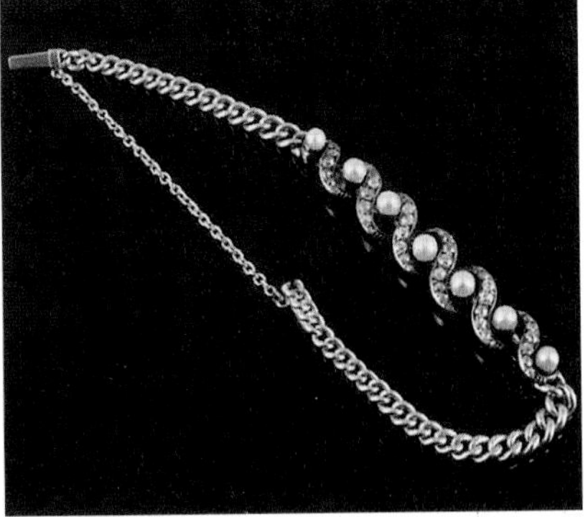

A gold and silver bracelet, set with pearls and diamonds, c1880.

£910–1,050 DN(HAM)

A 9ct gold curb bracelet, with three charms, c1880.
£190–220 SPE

A 15ct gold bangle, set with garnets and diamonds, c1890, with a Gunter's of Melbourne box.
£510–610 LJ

A 9ct gold gate bracelet, set with opals, c1890.
£310–350 SPE

A 15ct gold bangle, set with diamonds, hallmarked 'Denis', Australia, c1890.
£510–610 LJ

A 9ct gold bracelet, set with pearls and three amethysts, hallmarked, Birmingham 1907.
£165–195 GTH

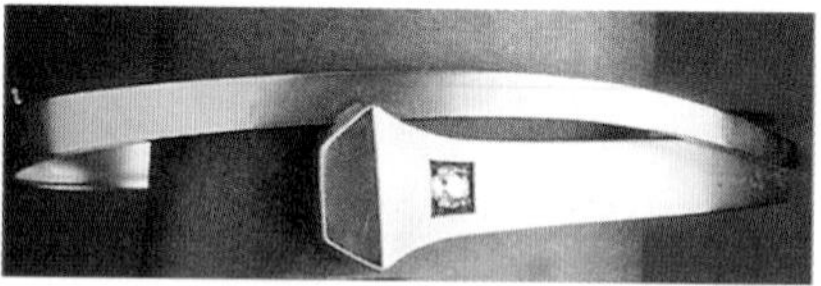

A 14ct gold bracelet, by L. Fritschze & Co, set with a diamond, America, c1908, 7in (18cm) long.
£950–1,100 SK

A 14ct gold bracelet, by L. Fritschze & Co, engraved with floral decoration, America, dated 1908, 7in (18cm) long.
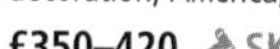
£350–420 SK

A 14ct gold bracelet, by Riker Bros, set with diamonds, America, early 20thC, 7¼in (18cm) long.
£1,000–1,200 SK

◀ **A 15ct gold and platinum curb bracelet,** c1910.
£630–700 SPE

▶ **An 18ct gold bracelet,** set with 14 pink spinels, maker's mark 'EB', France, c1910, 7in (18cm) long.

£540–640 SK

BROOCHES

A seed-pearl brooch, in the form of a butterfly, c1800, 1in (2.5cm) wide.
£320–370 ⊞ SPE

A gold and micro-mosaic brooch, depicting a view of Roman temple ruins, mid-19thC.
£660–790 JH

An amethyst and pearl brooch, slight damage, Continental, 19thC, 2¼in (5.5cm) high.
£350–420 G(L)

A silver Luckenbooth brooch, Scotland, c1840, 2½in (6.5cm) wide.
£190–220 ⊞ Aur

Luckenbooth brooches are in the form of a crowned heart or conjoined hearts. They were traditionally exchanged between sweethearts, but were also pinned to a child's clothing to ward off evil spirits. The name is said to derive from the 'locked booths' by St Giles Cathedral in Edinburgh from which they were first sold in the 17th century.

The language of jewellery

From the 18th to the early 20th century, jewellery was often used as a code from the giver to the receiver and it can be fun to unlock these secret messages. Hearts, cupids and lovebirds all represent love, of course, but clasped hands were another common device to symbolize everlasting love and friendship. A serpent – especially if it has its tail in its mouth – also represents eternal love; frogs and lizards denote wedded bliss and butterflies the soul. Certain flowers also conveyed a message, such as daisies for purity and innocence and pansies for 'thinking of you'. Even the combination of stones could be a code – a piece set with Rubies, Emeralds, Garnets, Amethysts, Rubies and Diamonds signified 'regard'.

A silver brooch, set with a Cairngorm stone and various agate stones, Scotland, c1860, 2in (5cm) diam.
£580–650 ⊞ Aur

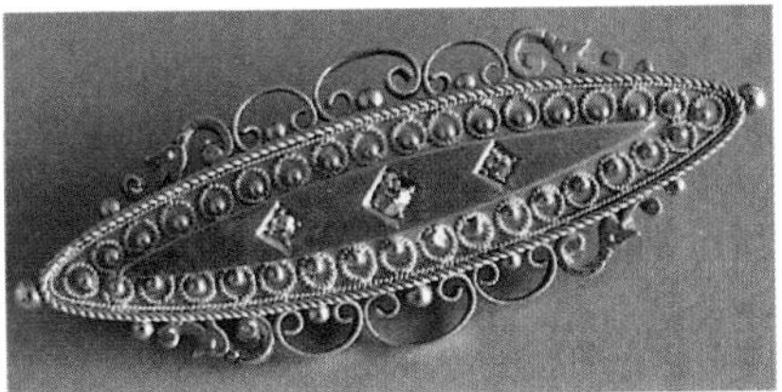

A Victorian gold brooch, set with diamonds, applied with beads and wirework, the back with a glazed locket compartment, with case.
£190–220 JBe

► A Victorian 18ct gold brooch, set with six diamonds and six emeralds, with a pendant set with diamonds and emeralds.
£450–540 WAD

A Victorian gold brooch, set with three diamonds, with a glazed locket back.
£440–520 DD

◄ A 15ct gold brooch, set with turquoises, c1860, 2in (5cm) high.
£620–690 ⊞ SGr

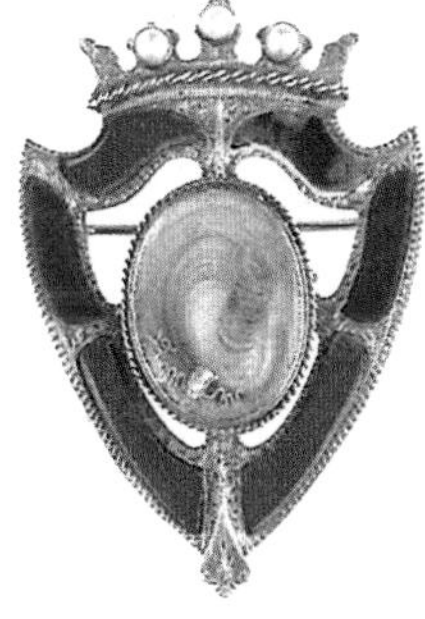

A 9ct gold brooch, in the form of a shield, set with carved hardstones and three pearls, centred with a glazed panel enclosing a lock of hair, Scotland, marks for1866.
£200–240 WAD

An 18ct brooch, set with rubies, c1870, 3in (7.5cm) wide.
£1,300–1,450 WIM

A gold brooch, set with quartz, a pearl and diamonds, Scotland, c1875, 2in (5cm) high.
£850–950 WIM

A Victorian 14ct gold brooch, set with 13 diamonds, with enamel highlights, 1¼in (3cm) wide.
£630–750 SK

▶ **A diamond brooch,** c1880, 2¼in (5.5cm) wide.
£6,200–6,900 SGr

An 18ct gold brooch, set with an enamel portrait and diamonds, c1880, 1¼in (3cm) diam.
£1,450–1,650 EXC

◀ **A silver brooch,** engraved with a basket of flowers, with gilt overlay, Birmingham 1883, 1½in (4cm) diam.
£145–165 Aur

A gold brooch, set with graduated opals and brilliant-cut diamonds, late 19thC.
£630–750 Bea

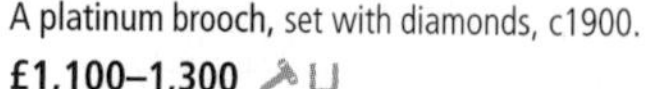

A platinum brooch, set with diamonds, c1900.
£1,100–1,300 LJ

◀ **An Edwardian 14ct gold brooch,** set with seed pearls and four diamonds, 1¼in (3cm) diam, in a J. E. Caldwell & Co box.
£350–420 SK

An Edwardian platinum and gold brooch, in the form of a winged insect, set with diamonds and an opal.
£1,700–2,000 DN

A Cartier diamond, turquoise and enamel brooch, in the form of a Native American wearing a headdress, France, 1920s.
£2,900–3,450 JH

A silver brooch, in the form of a butterfly, set with moonstones, c1920, 1¼in (3cm) wide.
£135–150 SGr

CAMEOS

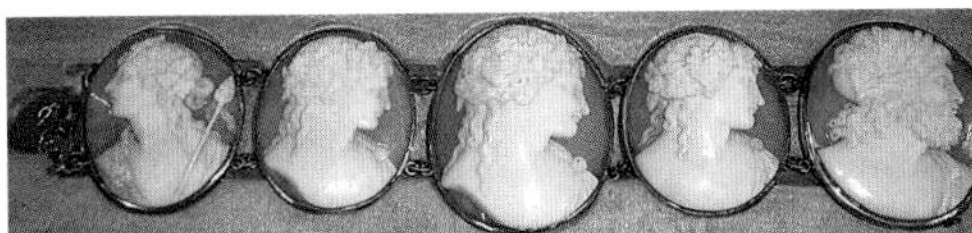

A gold cameo bracelet, with five plaques, each depicting classical figures, 19thC, 7in (18cm) long, with a fitted case.

£840–1,000 SWO

◄ **A gold cameo bracelet,** with seven plaques, c1875.

£1,550–1,750 WIM

A Victorian shell cameo brooch, carved with the bust of a female wearing a leopard skin, in a 15ct gold mount, the reverse with a hair/photograph compartment.

£440–520 LAY

A Victorian lava cameo brooch, carved in the form of Cupid with a bird of prey.

£240–280 JBe

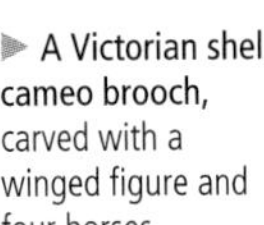

► **A Victorian shell cameo brooch,** carved with a winged figure and four horses.

£300–360 PF

An 18ct gold and carnelian agate pendant/locket, carved with a cherub with cymbals, the locket compartment enclosing a lock of hair worked as a sheaf of wheat, slight damage, with a 14ct gold chain.

£380–450 SK

A cameo brooch, carved with a portrait of Garibaldi, in a gold mount, c1880, 1in (2.5cm) high.

£175–195 AMC

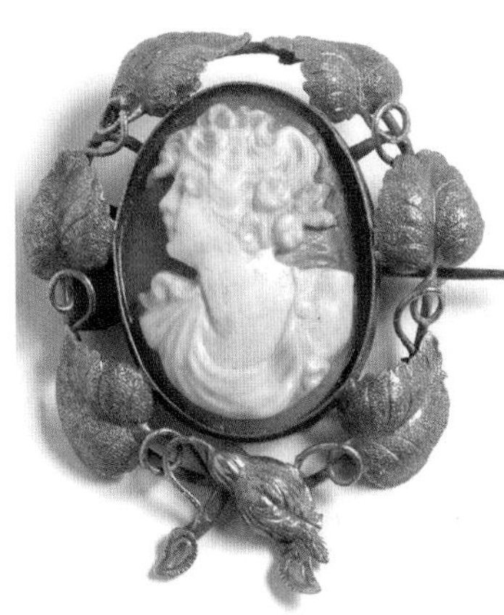

A shell cameo brooch, carved with a female portrait, in a 15ct gold mount and framed by ivy leaves, c1880, 2in (5cm) high.

£270–300 SPE

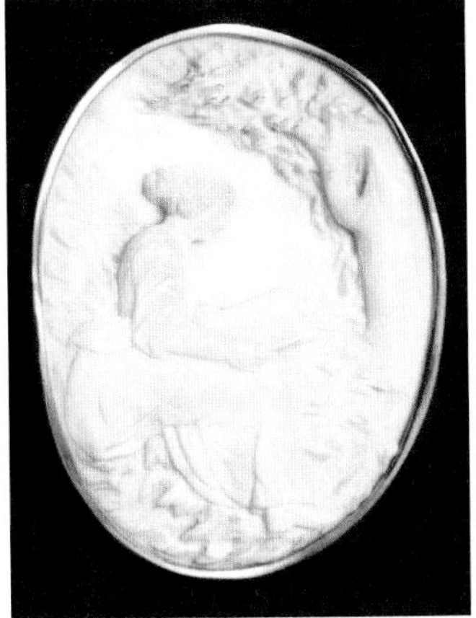

A cameo brooch, carved with the figure of a woman reading, c1890, 2¼in (5.5cm) high.

£340–380 AMC

A coral cameo brooch, carved with a classical maiden and framed by diamonds, in a platinum and 14ct gold mount, c1900, 1¾in (4.5cm) high.

£600–720 SK

A cameo brooch, carved with two thieves and two lovers, in a silver mount, c1920, 2¼in (5.5cm) high.

£220–250 AMC

CUFFLINKS

A pair of 18ct gold cufflinks, with engraved decoration, c1880.

£180–200 SPE

A pair of 18ct intaglio cufflinks, decorated with fox masks, c1890.

£2,450–2,750 WIM

A pair of Edwardian diamond cufflinks, set with diamonds, in 14ct gold and platinum mounts.

£200–240 SK

A pair of gold and enamel cufflinks, each set with a pearl, c1910.

£880–980 WIM

A pair of 18ct gold and mother-of-pearl cufflinks, each set with diamonds, early 20thC.

£260–310 GTH

A pair of silver cufflinks, enamelled with a crest, maker's mark 'TNS', 1930s.

£95–110 Aur

EARRINGS

A pair of silver and gold earrings, set with diamonds, c1840, 1in (2.5cm) long.

£2,450–2,750 WIM

A pair of tortoiseshell earrings, inlaid with silver and gold flowers and leaves, c1870.

£300–360 LJ

A pair of Victorian tortoiseshell earrings, decorated with scroll-engraved panels.

£350–420 DN

► **A pair of 18ct gold earrings,** set with blister pearls and diamonds, Continental hallmarks, early 20thC, 2¾in (7cm) high.

£2,700–3,200 SK

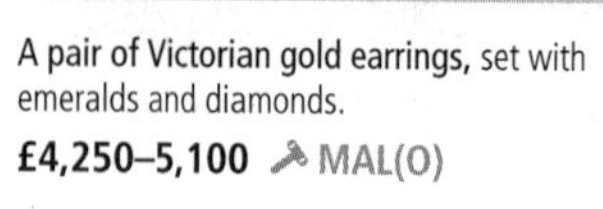

A pair of Victorian gold earrings, set with emeralds and diamonds.

£4,250–5,100 MAL(O)

► **A pair of gold, turquoise and pearl earrings,** c1880, 1in (2.5cm) high.

£135–150 SPE

◄ **A pair of 9ct gold earrings,** set with opals, early 20thC.

£120–140 GTH

NECKLACES

A Georgian seed pearl choker, the enamel clasp set with diamonds, 16in (40.5cm) long.

£1,300–1,450 SPE

A George III gold necklace, set with garnets, 16¼in (41.5cm) long, with a case.

£1,850–2,200 DN

A Whitby jet necklace, with carved beads, 1850–90, 26in (66cm) long.

£270–300 TDG

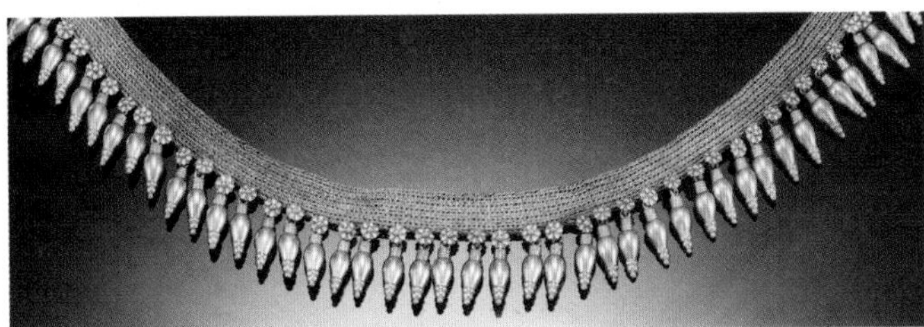

A Castellani Etruscan-style gold necklace, the woven band suspended with drops, each surmounted with an enamel flowerhead, maker's mark, Italy, 1860s, 15¾in (40cm) long.

£15,600–18,700 S

The Italian jewellery firm of Castellani was founded in Rome by Fortunato Pio Castellani. It is best known for developing a goldwork technique to mimic granulation found on Etruscan metalwork.

A silver choker, with engraved decoration, c1860, 16in (40.5cm) long.

£240–270 SPE

A jet necklace, 1860–70, 18in (45.5cm) long.

£340–380 Aur

A silver necklace, set with citrines, the drop engraved and pierced with thistle motifs, probably Scottish, c1880.

£420–500 JBe

◀ **A 22ct gold necklace,** chased and engraved with leaves and scrolls overlaid with blue enamel, hallmarked, Continental, c1880.

£270–320 LJ

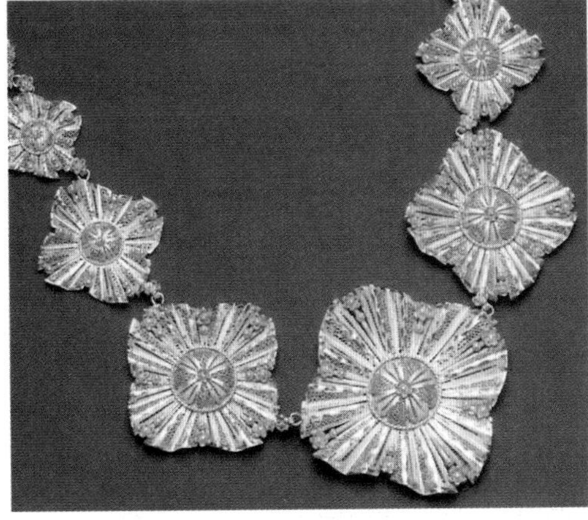

An 18ct gold filigree necklace, late 19thC, 16in (40.5cm) long.

£1,200–1,400 SK

◀ **An amethyst and seed pearl necklace,** 1890s, 16½in (42cm) long, with a fitted case.

£1,550–1,850 S

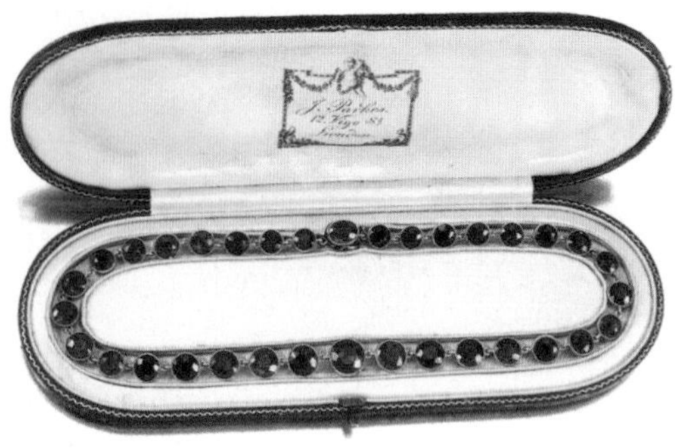

An amethyst *rivière*, early 20thC, 15¾in (40cm) long, with fitted case.
£3,350–4,000 S

An Edwardian platinum and gold necklace, set with aquamarines, seed pearls and diamonds, with a later 14ct white gold curb chain, 18½in (47cm) long.
£1,300–1,550 SK

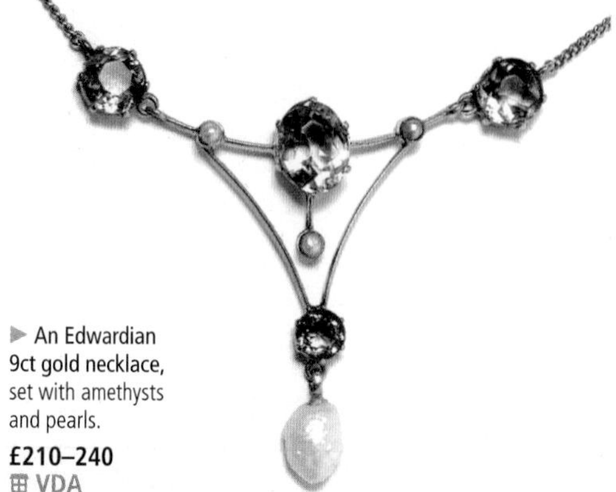

▶ **An Edwardian 9ct gold necklace,** set with amethysts and pearls.
£210–240 VDA

An Edwardian gold necklace, set with sapphires and pearls.
£1,200–1,400 MAL(O)

A 9ct gold necklace, set with tourmalines, with aquamarine and peridot drops, c1910, 15¾in (40cm) long.
£890–1,050 SK

A gold necklace, set with pearls and peridots, c1910.
£1,100–1,250 WIM

A diamond and seed pearl necklace, set with sapphires, early 20thC.
£5,000–6,000 Bea

◀ **A 14ct gold necklace,** set with citrines and seed pearls, maker's mark, America, c1915, 14¾in (37.5cm) long.
£2,350–2,800 SK

▶ **A platinum necklace,** set with diamonds and carved ruby beads, centred with a cameo of a woman, c1920, 15½in (39.5cm) long.
£12,100–14,500 SK

An 18ct gold necklace, set with aquamarines, France, 1940s, 16in (40.5cm) long.
£3,250–3,650 EXC

PARURES & SETS

◀ **A late Georgian 18ct gold and amethyst pendant necklace and earring set,** with detachable pendant/brooch, 13½in (34.5cm) long.
£2,200–2,600 SK

A Regency gold demi-parure, comprising a necklace, pendant/brooch and earrings, set with citrines, in a fitted case.
£3,750–4,500 HYD

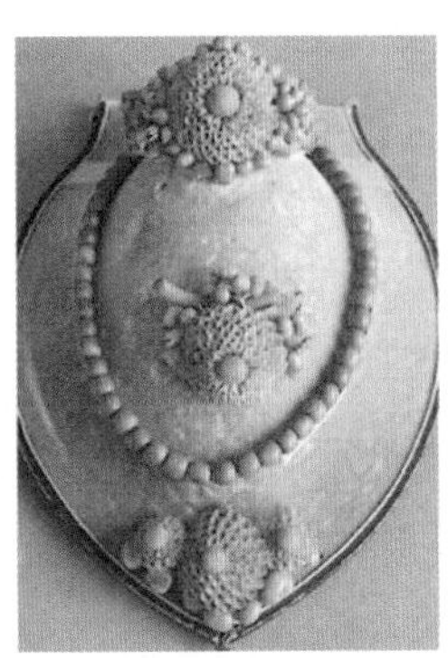

A coral demi-parure, comprising a necklace, brooch and the remains of a pair of earrings, damaged, probably Italy, 1825–50, with original case.
£840–1,000 JBe

An early Victorian gold brooch and earrings, set with opals and rubies, with original fitted velvet case inscribed 'Hunt & Roskell', brooch 2¼in (5.5cm) wide.
£3,500–4,200 F&C

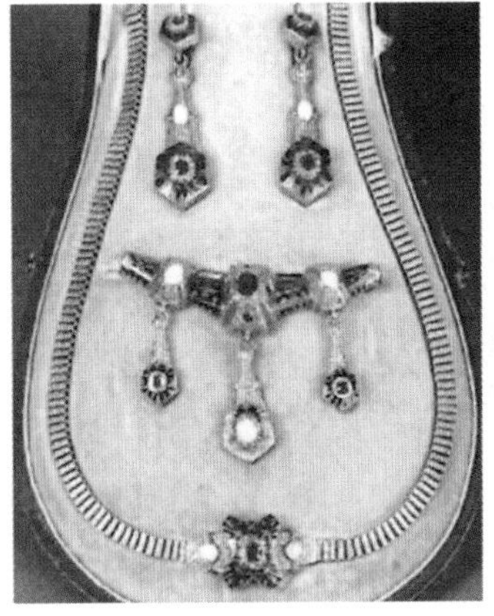

A Victorian 18ct gold parure, comprising a necklace, a brooch/pendant and earrings, set with rubies and decorated with enamel, in original fitted box.
£1,450–1,700 WAD

A 9ct gold brooch and earrings, set with amethysts, c1880, with a Tessiers Ltd leather box.
£850–1,000 LJ

For other Jewellery items
see pages 441–470

PENDANTS

A silver and gold pendant, set with diamonds, 18thC, with a fitted case.
£2,200–2,600 DN

A seed pearl star pendant, c1800, 1½in (4cm) diam.
£390–440 SPE

▶ **A late George III gold memorial pendant,** set with an amethyst within a border of fruiting vine, the reverse with a panel enclosing a lock of hair.
£370–440 DN

◀ **A gold cruciform pendant,** set with five garnets and turquoise, early 19thC.
£420–500 DN

A silver pendant/brooch, set with blue paste, with a pendant drop, losses, early 19thC, 4in (10cm) high, with a case.

£1,400–1,650 G(L)

A gold Maltese Cross pendant, set with an emerald with a surround of florets and chalcedony blades, the reverse with a glazed panel enclosing a lock of hair, with a curb chain, early 19thC.

£230–270 DN

A gold memorial pendant, with a mother-of-pearl and seed pearl classical monument in relief inscribed 'Sacred to the Memory of a Mother', with painted scenery, the glass cover painted with foliage, the reverse with an enamel cartouche with a seed pearl monogram within a hair border, damaged, 19thC, 1½in (4cm) diam, in a fitted case.

£500–600 SWO

A gold locket, the jade pendant surrounded by rubies and diamonds, the reverse with a glazed interior, indistinct marks, France, 19thC, 2½in (6.5cm) high.

£5,000–6,000 G(B)

A micro-mosaic pendant, depicting birds within a grapevine, converted from a brooch, Continental, 19thC.

£1,750–2,100 G(B)

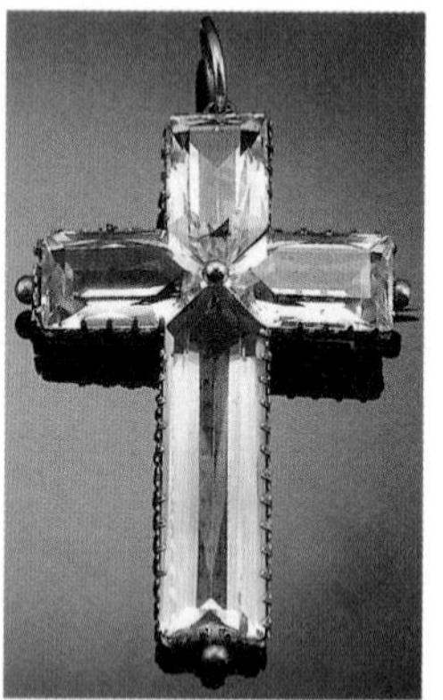

A rock crystal and 15ct gold cross pendant/brooch, c1870, in original fitted case.

£1,000–1,200 LJ

A silver locket, with engraved decoration, c1880, locket 2in (5cm) high.

£280–320 SPE

► **A 9ct gold locket,** set with a diamond, c1880, 1in (2.5cm) diam.

£90–100 SPE

A Victorian 14ct gold pendant/brooch, with foil-backed amethysts and chrysoberyls, the reverse with compartment enclosing a lock of hair and portrait of a boy, 2¾in (7cm) high.

£320–380 SK

A Victorian silver portrait pendant, hand-painted with a portrait of a gentleman, set with diamonds, gold backed.

£1,100–1,300 G(L)

◄ **A 9ct gold locket,** enclosing a photograph, set with turquoises and pearls, c1880, 1½in (4cm) diam.

£120–135 SPE

A Victorian 14ct gold locket, set with seed pearls, on a book chain with applied wirework, 18¼in (46.5cm) long.

£510–610 SK

A diamond, pearl and emerald pendant, with chain, damaged, c1890.

£730–870 N

Further reading

Miller's Costume Jewellery: How to Compare and Value, Miller's Publications, 2006

A 15ct gold pendant, set with turquoise and pearls, with chain, c1880, 1in (2.5cm) diam.

£230–260 SPE

A Victorian pendant, probably gold, set with garnets, 1in (2.5cm) diam.

£110–125 VDA

A 9ct gold locket, set with paste flowers, c1890, 1in (2.5cm) wide.

£90–110 SPE

A silver and gold pendant, set with emeralds and rose diamonds, centred with a baroque pearl drop and ribbon bow surmount, with a curb chain, France, late 19thC.

£470–560 DN

An Edwardian 15ct gold locket, set with a diamond, garnet and a synthetic sapphire, with a 9ct gold chain.

£470–560 BWL

A platinum and gold pendant, set with natural pearls and diamonds, c1910, 2½in (6.5cm) high.

£2,550–2,850 WIM

A platinum pendant, set with diamonds and pearls, with chain and brooch fitment, early 20thC, with original fitted case.

£1,950–2,300 Bea

A gold pendant, set with an opal, with chain, early 20thC, 1in (2.5cm) high.

£1,250–1,500 DN

A silver pendant/brooch, set with paste stones, 1920s–30s, 1½in (4cm) high.

£120–135 VDA

PINS

A gold stick pin, decorated with a salmon, early 19thC.
£360–430 Bea

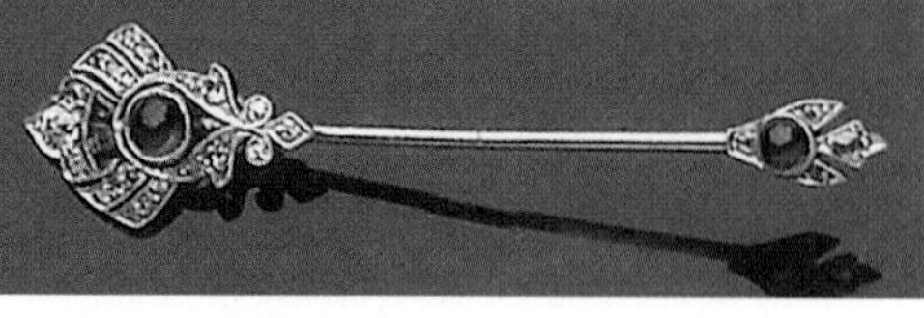

A pin, set with brilliant-cut diamonds and blue stones, c1910.
£560–670 TEN

A stick pin, painted with a horse's head, the reverse signed 'W. B. Ford, 1877', with case.
£220–260 GTH

A gold stick pin, the silver fox mask set with diamonds, with cabochon ruby eyes, late 19thC, with a fitted case.
£165–195 Bea

An Edwardian 14ct gold stick pin, with a carved moon-stone face, set with rose-cut diamonds and purple guilloche enamel collar and cap.
£1,550–1,850 SK

RINGS

A 22ct gold ring, inscribed 'I joy to find a constant mind', c1780.
£340–380 WELD

An 18ct gold mourning ring, inscribed 'Daniel Barnard 22/4/1780 aged 23', 1780.
£2,400–2,700 CVA

A Regency gold snuff ring, set with an emerald and diamonds, the mount pierced and chased with dolphins.
£940–1,100 ROS

An early Victorian gold dress ring, set with an emerald and diamonds.
£3,300–3,950 MAL(O)

An 18ct gold snake crossover ring, set with a ruby and diamond, late 19thC.
£280–330 Bea

An Edwardian platinum ring, set with three pearls and 33 diamonds.
£1,650–1,950 SK

◄ **A Victorian diamond and opal ring.**
£790–880 EXC

ENAMEL

◄ **An enamel box,** painted with figures, damaged, German, c1800, 3½in (9cm) wide.

£1,600–1,900 DN

An enamel and gilt-bronze box, the hinged cover and panelled sides decorated with roses enclosing a fitted interior, France, late 19thC, 10in (25.5cm) wide.

£770–920 FFAP

An Ovchinnikov silver-gilt and cloisonné enamel box, maker's and Imperial Warrant marks, Russia, Moscow, late 19thC, 7¾in (19.5cm) wide.

£8,400–10,000 S(O)

The Ovchinnikov firm was founded in 1853 by Pavel Akimovich Ovchinnikov, later run by his four sons, and remained in business until the Revolution. The operation was extensive, employing 300 workers by 1881 and establishing a school for craftsmen in Moscow with an enrolment of 130. The firm's enamel output was outstanding and won first prizes at every important Russian exhibition, including the All-Russian Exhibition of 1882 in Moscow. The company was granted the Imperial Warrant the following year.

An enamel box, by Ivan & Britzen, Russia, St Petersburg, 1908–17, 1in (2.5cm) diam.

£3,350–3,750 SHa

An enamel and bronze model of a carriage, Austria, Vienna, c1880, 12in (30.5cm) wide.

£4,900–5,500 ALEX

A silver and enamel cigarette case, decorated with scrolling foliage, Russia, c1900, 3¾ x 3in (9.5 x 7.5cm).

£590–700 JH

A silver-gilt and cloisonné enamel coffee pot, by Iwan Petrowitsch Chlebnikow, the spout in the form of a cockerel, Russia, late 19thC, 8¼in (21cm) high.

£4,250–5,100 DN

A silver-gilt and enamel scent bottle, late 19thC, 6in (15cm) high.

£470–560 BWL

A gilt-metal and enamel miniature tea caddy, painted with flowers and inscribed 'Green', 18thC, ¾in (2cm) high.

£330–390 G(L)

A Limoges 16thC-style enamel triptych, depicting a court scene, France, 19thC, centre panel 6¼ x 5¼in (16 x 13.5cm), with a velvet case.

£1,750–2,100 N

FABERGE

A Fabergé silver-mounted hardwood box, the cover and sides decorated with birds, stamped mark, Russia, Moscow, c1905, 3¼in (8.5cm) wide.

£6,600–7,900 S

A Fabergé silver-gilt and enamel belt buckle, by Henrik Wigström, marked, Russia, St Petersburg, 1908–17, 3in (7.5cm) wide, with original holly-wood box.

£10,200–12,200 S

A Fabergé silver-gilt and cloisonné enamel box, by Fedor Ruckert, the hinged cover decorated with 'A Knight at the Crossroads', after Viktor Vasnetsov, Fabergé and Imperial Warrant marks, London import marks, Russia, Moscow 1908–17,

£50,000–60,000 SWO

Viktor Mikhailovich Vasnetsov painted Russian Knight at the Crossroads *in 1882. It is now hanging in the State Russian museum in St Petersburg. The box was given to the vendor's husband by his grandfather, who lived in St Petersburg and had to leave after the Revolution in 1919.*

◄ **A Fabergé silver *charka*,** by Stephan Wäkeva, the exterior decorated with a band of palmettes, with a gilt interior, the handle inset with a coin depicting Catherine II, Russia, St Petersburg, 1896–1908, 3¼in (8.5cm) wide.

£4,750–5,700 BUK

A charka is a traditional Russian drinking vessel.

A Fabergé silver inkwell, by Stephan Wäkeva, set with medallions of Peter I, Anna, Elisabeth and Catherine II, with a glass liner, Russia, St Petersburg, 1896–1908, 6¼in (16cm) high.

£10,100–12,100 BUK

A Fabergé silver dressing mirror, surmounted with ribbon-tied swags enclosing a medallion, K Fabergé and Imperial Warrant marks, Russia, Moscow, 1896, 21½in (55cm) high.

£15,000–18,000 S

A Fabergé gold model of a mouse, by Henrik Wigström, with rose diamond eyes, Russia, early 20thC, ¾in (2cm) wide.

£12,400–14,800 F&C

A Fabergé silver teapot, decorated with cast and chased flowers, scrolls and bullrushes, the handle with two ivory bands, K Fabergé and Imperial Warrant marks, later control marks, Russia, Moscow, 1894, 6¼in (16cm) high.

£4,200–5,000 S(O)

A Fabergé silver tray, by Stephan Wäkeva, decorated with acanthus leaves, inset with a 1762 four-kopek coin, on ball feet, marked, Russia, St Petersburg, c1890, 4¾in (12cm) wide.

£4,200–5,000 S(NY)

◄ **A Fabergé silver-gilt and cloisonné enamel tea strainer,** with floral decoration, K Fabergé and Imperial Warrant marks, Russia, Moscow, c1900, 6¼in (16cm) high.

£2,400–2,800 S(O)

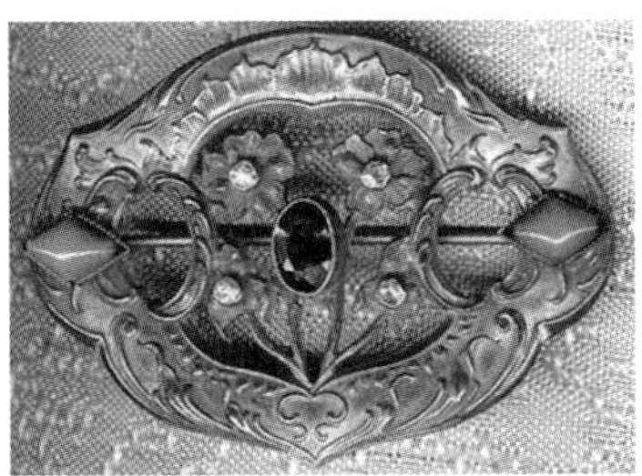

SHAPIRO & CO
Jewels • Silver • Objects d'Art

GRAYS
ANTIQUE MARKETS
Home to over two hundred of the country's leading antiques specialists, Grays is world renowned for the finest and most diverse selection of fine jewellery and antiques, ceramics, objects d'art, silver, paintings, and much more…
Open Mon-Fri 10am-6pm
020 7629 7034 www.graysantiques.com

SKINNER
Auctioneers and Appraisers of Antiques and Fine Art
ONE OF AMERICA'S LEADING AUCTION HOUSES
www.skinnerinc.com
63 Park Plaza Boston, MA 02116 Tel: 617-350-5400
357 Main Street Bolton, MA 01740 Tel: 978-779-6241

GOLD

A gold-mounted bloodstone egg bonbonnière, pierced and chased with birds and scrolls, the rim enamelled 'Dieu vous garde', early 20thC, 2¼in (6.5cm) high.

£1,550–1,850 S(O)

A gold *charka*, by T. Hesketh, with a talon handle, the base inset with a 1756 two-rouble coin, Russia, St Petersburg, c1880, 3½in (9cm) wide.

£9,000–10,800 S

A charka *is a traditional Russian drinking vessel.*

▶ **A 9ct gold cruet set,** Chester 1901, salt 2in (5cm) wide, in a fitted case.

£1,750–1,950 BHA

A gold cigarette case, applied with a diamond-set inscription in Cyrillic 'From Kadya', decorated with an enamel Russian Imperial ensign, an enamel badge and a jewelled horseshoe, with a cabochon sapphire thumbpiece, unidentified maker's mark, Russia, 1899–1908, 3½in (9cm) wide.

£5,800–6,900 S(NY)

◀ **An 18ct gold dish,** by George Howson, with a shell and gadrooned border and inscription, London 1899, 5in (12.5cm) diam.

£590–700 DN

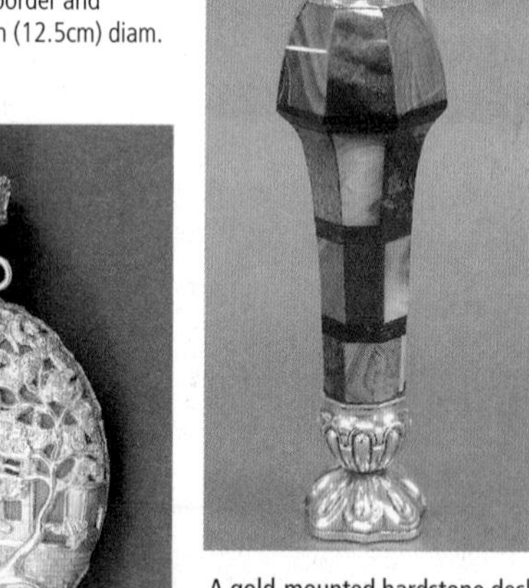

A gold-mounted hardstone desk seal, engraved with a crest and motto, Scotland, 19thC, 3¾in (9.5cm) high.

£2,450–2,900 HYD

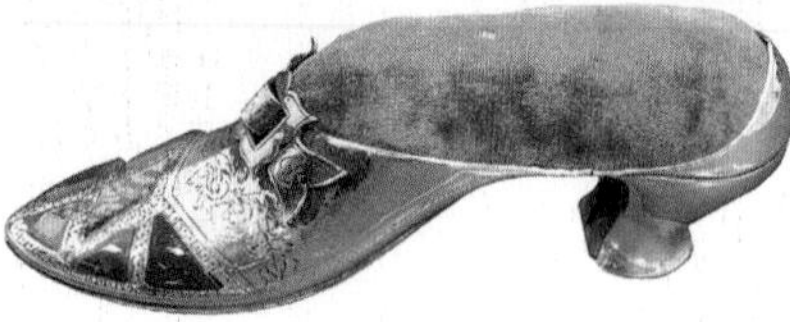

A 9ct gold pincushion, in the form of a lady's shoe, inset with stones, probably Birmingham 1897, 3¾in (9.5cm) wide.

£680–810 G(L)

A gold-mounted glass scent bottle, decorated with chinoiserie buildings, birds and blossoming trees, 18thC, 3in (7.5cm) high.

£2,900–3,450 G(L)

A late Victorian 9ct gold thimble, decorated with vine leaves.

£260–310 TEN

A Tiffany & Co 16ct gold dressing table set, comprising 17 pieces, America, New York, c1920, jewel box 6¼in (16cm) long, 28oz.

£7,100–8,500 S(NY)

A Regency gold-mounted agate vinaigrette, in the form of a barrel, with engraved decoration, the hinged cover enclosing a grille pierced with scrolls and thistles, 2¼in (5.5cm) high.

£4,000–4,800 HYD

ASIAN WORKS OF ART

CHINA'S BOOM ECONOMY has had a dramatic effect on the Asian works of art market. As with ceramics, rarity, condition and provenance all affect the prices attained and Imperial works continue to reach record prices.

The attractiveness of good-quality boulder jade ensures its continuing popularity. A Qianlong white jade brush washer carved as a peach sold at Christie's London in 2005 for £62,000 – double the price that it would have fetched 12 months earlier. The importance of provenance was illustrated with the sale of items from the Morrison collection, which had been purchased in 1861 directly from Lord Loch of Drylaw on his return from the sacking of the Summer Palace. Imperial enamels and cloisonné fetched record prices, including £300,000 for a pair of Qianlong cloisonné and enamel jardinières. This was an exceptional piece, but finely crafted cloisonné of the 18th and early 19th centuries continues to increase in value. Good-quality bronzes of all periods are still rising in value with record prices being paid for the very best pieces. A large lacquered gilt-bronze figure representing the Buddha Amitabha and dating to the 17th/18th century sold at Sotheby's London in 2005 for £170,000. Intricately carved lacquer work has also seen a strong market. An Imperial carved lacquer panel dated to 1788 was bid to £380,000 at Christie's, London. In New York a red lacquer Qianlong screen carved with an Imperial five-clawed dragon fetched £163,000. The market for Chinese furniture seems to have polarized with record prices paid for the best pieces. Provincial furniture is slowing down as it is no longer fashionable with interior decorators and poor-quality pieces are proving difficult to sell. In New York, a pair of Wanli period Imperial quality lacquer cabinets realized £545,000. New York is still the centre for first-rate *huanghuali* furniture, which shows a steady increase in value year-on-year. Good-quality Chinese silver and Indian jewellery are also finding a ready market in the West, with prices doubling in the last year.

Peter Wain

Peter is a leading specialist in Chinese and Japanese ceramics and works of art. He has also been the Chairman of the Oriental Vetting Committees for many of the top international antiques fairs.

He has written numerous books on this subject and given many lectures in the UK, USA and Australia.

The slight upturn in the Japanese economy has brought Japanese buyers back to the market, particularly for fine quality arms and armour. These have also attracted Russian enthusiasts, producing staggering results for well-provenanced pieces. The Museum of Japanese Sword Fittings sale was a sell-out with some pieces selling for triple their estimate. High quality Meiji metalwork and ivory *okimonos* have also been in great demand with the best pieces finding eager buyers at two or three times their estimate. After the stagnation of the past ten years, the market for Japanese antiques is looking healthier.

Peter Wain

CLOISONNE & ENAMEL

A cloisonné censer, each side decorated with a stylized *taotie* mask below two dragons, China, 18thC, 8¾in (22cm) wide.

£3,250–3,900 S(NY)

A cloisonné censer and cover, the cover pierced with cash and applied with leaves, with mask and ring handles, the body decorated with precious objects, China, 19thC, 4¾in (12cm) high.

£280–330 DN

A Canton enamel saucer dish, decorated with a dragon and clouds within a border of lotus and bats, the reverse with three dragons and clouds, phoenix medallion mark to the base, China, Qianlong period, 1736–95, 8½in (21.5cm) diam.

£3,600–4,300 S

A pair of cloisonné dishes, decorated with ducks, Japanese, c1900, 12in (30.5cm) diam.

£300–360 WW

A pair of cloisonné moon flasks, decorated with peony blooms, the base with Greek key pattern, with applied bronze dragon handles, probably Qing Dynasty, 18thC, 21in (53.5cm) high.

£13,200–15,800 GIL

Moon flasks are always popular and in demand. This fine pair of flasks date from the late 18th century and are of excellent quality.

◀ **A cloisonné garden seat,** decorated with lappets and bats' faces, China, early 20thC, 18½in (47cm) high.

£5,500–6,600 NAAW

◀ **A cloisonné jardinière,** decorated with lotus, peony, chrysanthemum and prunus, slight damage, China, 19thC, 13in (33cm) high.

£2,350–2,800 RTo

A set of four Canton *famille rose* enamel tea bowls, each painted with figures in a landscape, one damaged, China, Qianlong period, 1736–95, 2in (5cm) diam.

£560–670 DN(BR)

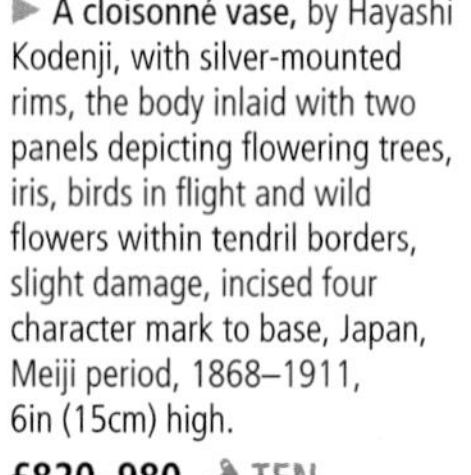

▶ **A cloisonné vase,** by Hayashi Kodenji, with silver-mounted rims, the body inlaid with two panels depicting flowering trees, iris, birds in flight and wild flowers within tendril borders, slight damage, incised four character mark to base, Japan, Meiji period, 1868–1911, 6in (15cm) high.

£820–980 TEN

Liberty imported a large quantity of pieces by Hayashi Kodenji into Britain in the late 19th and early 20th centuries.

Items in the Asian Works of Art section have been arranged in alphabetical order.

A Hayashi Kodenji-style cloisonné vase, decorated with chrysanthemum and cherry blossom and four birds in flight, with stiff-leaf borders, Japan, Meiji period, 1868–1911, 8½in (21.5cm) high.

£230–270 Hal

A cloisonné vase, decorated with flowers, Japan, late 19thC, 14½in (37cm) high.

£810–970 JDJ

A cloisonné vase, the mouth decorated with a flower and scroll collar, the body with a hawk on a rock amid rolling waves, with plated-copper mounts, Japan, c1915, 7in (18cm) high.

£350–420 WAD

A cloisonné bud vase, decorated with a kingfisher on irises, with bead and scroll mouth and base bands, with plated-brass mounts, Japan, c1915, 7½in (19cm) high.

£200–240 WAD

GLASS

▶ **A Peking glass bowl,** the exterior carved with a frieze of lotus, China, 18th/19thC, 6in (15cm) diam.

£960–1,150 WW

A glass bottle, the red overlay carved through to a pink ground with a meandering lotus scroll, China, 18thC, 10in (25.5cm) high.

£3,900–4,650 S(NY)

A Peking overlaid glass brush washer, carved with *shou* symbols, bats and endless knots, China, 19thC, 4in (10cm) wide.

£1,000–1,200 WW

A reverse painting on glass, after a print by Wheatley, China, late 18thC, 17 x 23in (43 x 58.5cm), framed.

£4,050–4,500 HUM

A pair of reverse paintings on glass, entitled 'October' and 'December', each depicting a bucolic scene and based on English prints, China, c1800, 26 x 20in (66 x 51cm), framed.

£11,100–13,300 NAAW

These pictures are very rare.

▶ **A pair of reverse paintings on glass,** depicting a dignitary and elegant figures on a terrace with a landscape beyond, China, in moulded hardwood frames, 13½ x 19¼thC, (34.5 x 49cm).

£940–1,100 HYD

A pair of paintings on glass, in the manner of George Morland, depicting European figures in country landscapes, China, 19thC, in cherrywood frames, one damaged, 16 x 21in (40.5 x 53.5cm).

£680–810 MAL(O)

A glass vase, carved with eight fluted facets, incised four character Qianlong mark within a square, 1736–95, 5½in (14cm) high.

£9,600–11,500 WW

JADE

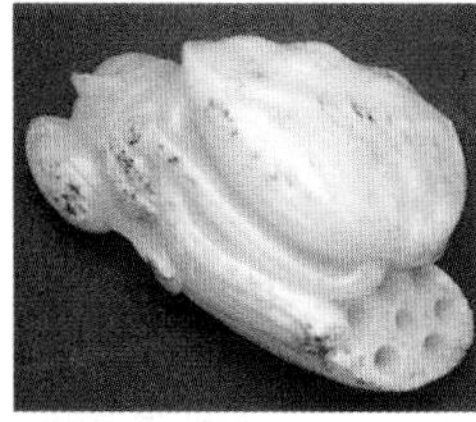

A russet and celadon jade boulder carving, in the form of a lily pad and flowers, Chinese, 19thC, 4¾in (12cm) wide.

£1,050–1,250 DN(BR)

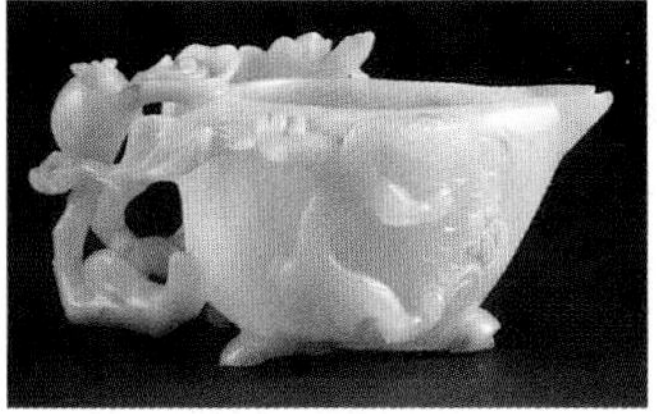

A carved white jade brush washer, in the form of a pomegranate, the handle carved as leafy branches, a fruit and a *chilong* to the side, China, probably 18thC, 4½in (11.5cm) wide.

£3,000–3,600 WW

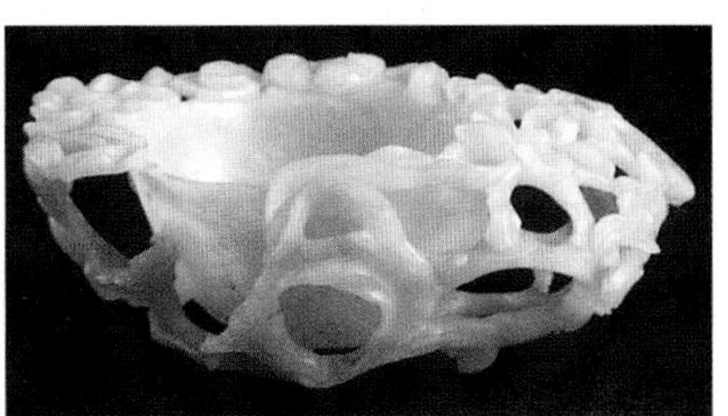

A jade cup, carved as a flowerhead surrounded by flowering openwork branches, the handle carved as a branch, 17th–18thC, 6¼in (16cm) wide.

£1,750–2,100 WW

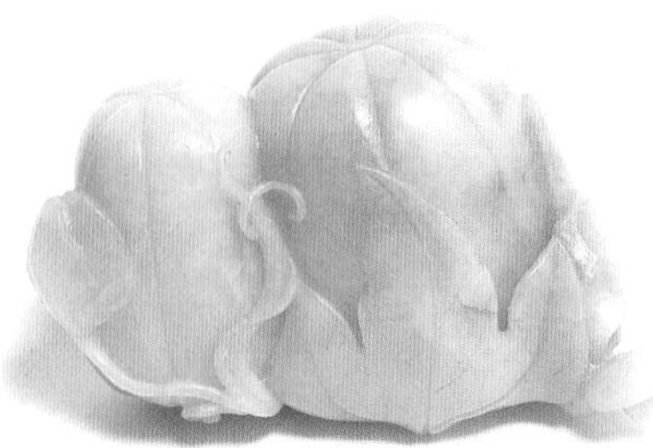

A jade carving, in the form of a fruit, 18thC, 3½in (9cm) wide.

£1,050–1,200 BOW

A pair of celadon jade perfumers, each perforated for incense, with black jade tops and bases, 18thC, 8in (20.5cm) high.

£9,000–10,000 BOW

A jade plaque, carved with *fu shou*, comprising four peaches, a blossom and a bat, China, 19thC, 5in (12.55cm) wide.

£400–480 WW

The fu shou (the bat and the peach) used together represent a wish for long life and happiness.

◄ **A celadon jade scent bottle,** carved in the form of two leaping carp, the celadon jade with caramel inclusions, China, Qing Dynasty, 19thC, 3in (7.5cm) wide.

£1,400–1,650 S

A jade vase, China, Ming Dynasty, 1368–1644, 6in (15cm) high.

£900–1,200 BOW

A celadon jade vase and cover, the body carved with a *taotie* band above a carved and pierced peony spray issuing from rockwork, the neck carved with a band of bosses, with bracket handles, the cover with a knop finial, China, Qianlong period, 1736–95, 7¼in (18.5cm) high, with a carved stand.

£6,600–7,900 S

A jade double vase, with brown inclusions, carved as citron on a branch, China, probably 18thC, 6¼in (16cm) wide.

£2,600–3,100 WW

► **A jadeite vase and cover,** of flattened vase form, with green inclusions, applied with blossoms and branches in high relief, China, c1800, 5in (12.5cm) high.

£630–750 WAD

LACQUER

A lacquer card case, decorated with a water pavilion amid mountains, the back and interior in *nashiji*, Japan, 19thC, 4in (10cm) high.

£570–680 WAD

A lacquer picnic set, containing a four-tiered *jubako*, the *nashiji* ground decorated with a lakeland landscape, the frame decorated with prunus blossoms in mother-of-pearl, Japan, 19thC, 12½in (32cm) wide.

£640–760 TEN

A lacquer tray, Burma, late 19thC, 18in (45.5cm) diam.

£130–145 SOO

► **A pair of lacquer vases,** carved with figures in rocky landscapes, slight damage, China, c1900, 12in (30.5cm) high.

£370–440 WW

METALWARE

A bronze altarpiece, dedicated to Svetambara, with inset silver eyes, inscribed to the reverse, India, Rajastan, 14thC, 18in (45.5cm) high.

£700–840 AG

A Chinese silver punchbowl, by Wang Hing, with a reeded border, embossed with chrysanthemums and peonies, stamped 'WH90', China, late 19thC, 8¼in (21cm) diam, on a hardwood stand.

£840–1,000 DN

A copper censer, by Hu-Wen-Ming, with relief decoration of mythical animals and stylized foliage on a wave and punch-decorated ground, the two bronze handles modelled as monsters' heads, incised vertical six character mark in a gilded rectangle to base, signed, China, Wanli period, c1600, 6¼in (16cm) diam.

£2,100–2,500 F&C

A silver censer, the cover in the form of a pagoda, the body with two flange handles, China, early 20thC, 12½in (32cm) high.

£270–320 WAD

A silver cigarette case, in the form of a book, engraved by Masahide with an Oriental lady against a mountainous landscape with temples, Japan, Kyoto, early 20thC, 5in (12.5cm) high, 6oz.

£110–130 WAD

A Japanese silver and copper cigarette case, engraved with an Oriental lady in a lakeside landscape, Japan, c1930, 4in (10cm) wide.

£360–400 BEX

A pair of silver sake decanters and covers, each decorated with a Shakudo *mon*, signed, Japan, Meiji period, 1868–1911, 8¼in (21cm) high, with original box.

£560–670 RTo

A *Shibayama* dish, the six lacquer panels set in a wire frame, with two character signature on a gold pad, slight damage, Japan, 19thC, 12¼in (31cm) diam.

£940–1,100 WW

A bronze koro and cover, relief-decorated with phoenix among stylized clouds, the cover pierced and moulded as a twining dragon, Japan, Meiji period, 1868–1911, 15½in (39.5cm) high.

£320–380 LJ

A set of four porcelain tea bowls and an ashtray with silver mounts, with silver saucers and spoons, silver Vietnam, porcelain China, c1890, cup 4in (10cm) diam.

£420–470 PCR

Chinese silver

Shanghai was the centre of fine silverwork during the 19th and early 20th centuries. Many of the makers became well known and were in great demand, their output including such objects as tea services, bowls, boxes and tankards.

A Chinese export silver four-piece tea and coffee service, with repoussé and engraved decoration and scroll handles, initialled, c1865, coffee pot 10in (25.5cm) high, 135oz.

£1,850–2,200 WAD

A Chinese silver three-piece tea service, decorated in low relief with prunus, the handles and finials formed as branches, China, early 20thC, teapot 4in (10cm) high.

£400–480 WAD

A Chinese silver three-piece tea service, embossed with figures and pavilions in a garden, bases marked '90KL' and a panel of Chinese script, China, early 20thC, teapot 4¾in (12cm) high.

£370–440 CAG

A pair of bronze vases, decorated with elephants on rocky outcrops, Japan, Meiji period, 1868–1911, 12in (30.5cm) high.

£280–330 MA&I

◄ **A bronze *usabata*,** the censer cover decorated with an eagle and serpent, loss to wing tip, Japan, Meiji period, 1868–1911, 23in (58.5cm) high.

£510–600 JAA

An usabata *is a large urn used for burning incense.*

A bottle vase, by Komai, decorated in gold *nunome* with two crows in the branches of a pine tree, the mouth decorated with cranes in flight, the base signed, Japan, late 19thC, 9½in (24cm) high.

£1,200–1,400 NSal

WOOD

A carved wood bowl, mounted with metal bands, the cover inlaid with hardstone carved with dragons and scrolls, damaged, Tibet, 17th–18thC, 8¼in (21cm) diam.

£630–750 WW

A bamboo needle case, China, Guanxu period, 1875–1908, 4½in (11.5cm) long.

£55–65 JCH

► **A bamboo brush pot,** carved with trees, huts and mountains below calligraphy, China, probably 18thC, 5¼in (13.5cm) high.

£300–360 WW

A carved wood panel, painted with flowers within an ivory border, India, Kashmir, 19thC, 20in (51cm) square.

£350–420 DN(HAM)

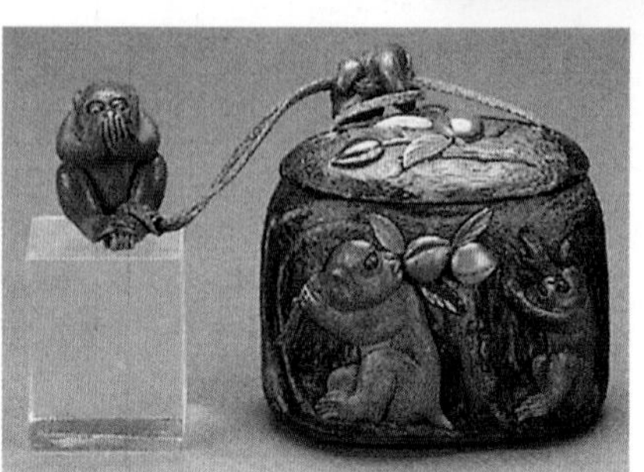

A carved paulownia tobacco pouch, decorated with three monkeys, the cover decorated with peaches, with *ojime* and *netsuke* in the form of monkeys, Japan, 19thC, 3¼in (8.5cm) high.

£260–310 WAD

A teak window frame, carved with flowers and stylized leaves, India, Rajasthan, c1700, 23½ x 16¾in (59.5 x 43cm).

£240–280 AG

ARMS & ARMOUR

A Samurai lacquered metal suit of armour, with engraved decoration and gilt highlights, Japan, Edo period, 1600–1868.
£5,600–6,700 E

A velvet and gilt-brass ceremonial suit of armour, embroidered and embossed with dragons, silver breast and back plate, velvet-covered bow case and pouch, slight damage, China, Qianlong period, 1736–95.
£12,500–15,000 WAL

This armour would have been worn by an officer of the Imperial Palace Guard.

An iron and fur helmet, with a cloth liner, Japan, c1830, 15in (38cm) high.
£1,850–2,100 MDL

◀ **An iron and lacquered plate *Tosei Gusoku* armour,** Japan, c1800.
£6,000–7,200 TDM

A *wakizashi*, with a silver-foiled blade collar and painted hilt, altered from a polearm, tang signed, Japan, 32¼in (82cm) long, with a burrwood scabbard.
£400–480 JDJ

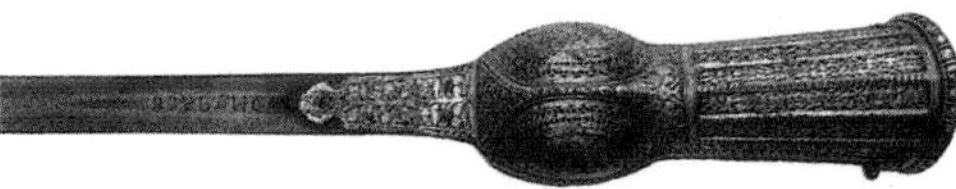

A *pata*, with a European blade, the pierced and chiselled hilt overlaid in silver and gold, India, c1700, 39¾in (101cm) long.
£2,050–2,450 F&C

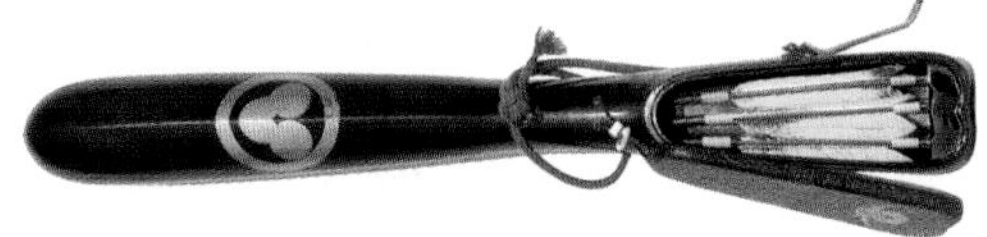

A lacquered quiver, decorated with a gilt *mon* of the Sanada family, the hide cover with ivory toggles, Japan, c1750, 38in (96.5cm) long, with three original arrows.
£1,300–1,450 FAC

◀ **A Samurai sword,** with a blade, signed, Japan, c1716, 38in (96.5cm) long, with a scabbard decorated with a pagoda.
£4,850–5,400 TLA

TSUBA

An iron *tsuba*, inlaid with geese and flowers, Japan, late Muromachi period, 1333–1568, 3¼in (8.5cm) diam.
£12,000–14,400 S

An Akasaka School iron *tsuba*, carved and pierced with insects and grasses, Japan, Edo period, 18thC, 3in (7.5cm) diam.
£6,000–7,200 S

This tsuba is almost certainly the work of the third generation of the Akasaka school.

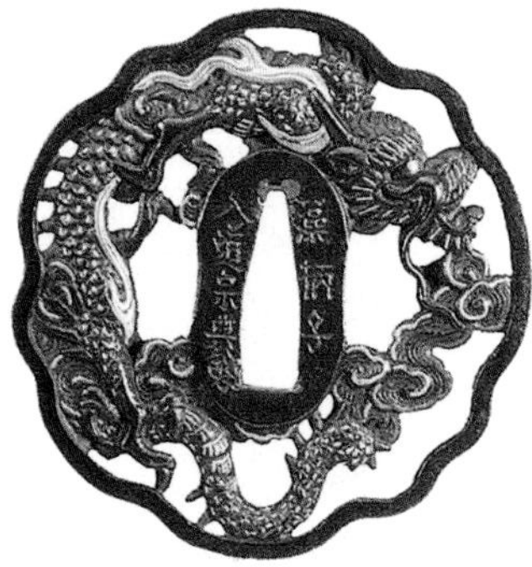

A Soten school iron *tsuba*, carved, pierced and inlaid in *hikone-bori* with a dragon and clouds, Japan, c1800, 3in (7.5cm), with a fitted wooden box.
£1,400–1,650 S

BOXES

A cinnabar lacquer box and cover, carved with two prunus branches on a brocade diaper ground, China, 18thC, 3in (7.5cm) diam.

£2,900–3,450 S(NY)

A rosewood table bureau, Anglo-Chinese, mid-18thC, 20in (51cm) wide.

£1,200–1,400 S(O)

MILLER'S COMPARES

I. **A cinnabar lacquer 'hundred boys' box and cover,** carved with boys at play, China, Qianlong period, 1736–95, 5in (12.5cm) diam.

£31,000–37,000 S

II. **A cinnabar lacquer box and cover,** carved with figures, fruit and foliage on a diaper ground, China, Qianlong period, 1736–95, 6¾in (17cm) diam.

£4,300–5,100 S

Item I is very deeply carved and relates to known Chinese Imperial examples. Although it is not marked, its quality and subject matter suggest it was manufactured in the Imperial workshops, thus making it highly desirable and therefore much more valuable than Item II which, although also of high quality, is not considered to be Imperial workmanship.

A rosewood knife case, inlaid with ivory stylized leaves and flowers, Anglo-Indian, Vizagapatam, 1760–70, 11½in (29cm) high.

£11,000–13,200 S(NY)

This is a rare item which accounts for the high price it achieved at auction.

A Chinese export lacquer needlework/ writing box, decorated in gilt and bronze with scenes of village and court life, the hinged cover enclosing a fitted interior with bone and ivory accessories, slight damage, early 19thC, 13½in (34.5cm) wide.

£210–250 N

An ivory work box, the hinged cover enclosing a satinwood and ivory fitted interior, with an ivory thimble and tape holder, India, Vizagapatam, early 19thC, 9¼in (23.5cm) wide.

£1,950–2,300 CAG

A Chinese export ivory box, carved with figures in a village, on ball feet, 19thC, 10½in (26.5cm) wide.

£1,950–2,300 S(NY)

◄ **A brass-mounted padouk dressing box,** the hinged cover enclosing a mirror, removable trays and secret drawers, Anglo-Indian, 19thC, 16in (40.5cm) wide.

£1,600–1,900 S(NY)

A mandarin's leather collar box, China, 19thC, 7½in (19cm) diam.

£60–70 MB

A coromandel work box, the hinged cover decorated with an ivory figure, enclosing a fitted interior with simulated tortoiseshell, ebony, ivory and coromandel with chevron borders, Anglo-Indian, 19thC, 17¾in (45cm) wide.

£700–840 CGC

A Japanese silver and enamel incense box, decorated with flowers and insects, with enamel highlights, two character mark, slight damage, Japan, 19thC, 3¼in (8.5cm) diam.

£1,850–2,200 WW

A Shibayama box and cover, in *togidashi* and *takamakie* and inlaid in *shibuichi*, *aogai* and horn, the interior of *nashiji* with a fitted tray, the rims mounted in silver, Japan, Meiji period, 1868–1911, 6in (15cm) wide.

£2,600–3,100 S

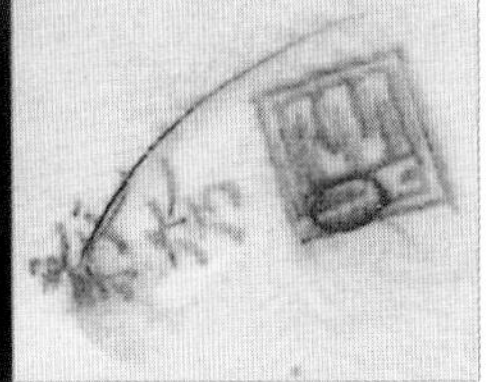

An ivory box and cover, carved in high relief with fish and an octopus, the cover signed with two character mark, the finial in the form of a cluster of shellfish, repaired, Japan, Meiji period, 1868–1911, 6¼in (16cm) high.

£610–730 DN(BR)

A lacquer box and cover, China, late 19thC, 20in (51cm) wide.

£195–220 SOO

An ivory and sandalwood work box, the fitted interior with compartments, a bottle and a watchstand, damaged, losses, India, late 19thC, 16¼in (41.5cm) wide.

£1,450–1,700 S(P)

A Japanese silver and *shibuichi* box and cover, decorated with a crane, marked, signed 'Rozan', Japan, c1900, 5in (12.5cm) high.

£300–360 SWO

A leather dome-topped document box, China, 1920s, 13in (33cm) wide.

£260–300 SOO

CLOCKS

A rosewood bracket clock, with a Canton enamel dial, ormolu mounts, English export fusee movement, China, 18thC, 15in (38cm) high.

£5,200–5,800 WALP

◀ **A rosewood stickclock,** with crown-verge escapement, key drawer missing, Japan, c1840, 17in (43cm) high.

£1,600–1,900 ROSc

▶ **A brass chamber clock,** the movement with twin-operating verges, crown wheels, foliate escapement and a bell, weights and hands missing, Japan, 19thC, 12in (30.5cm) high.

£2,250–2,700 G(L)

FIGURES & MODELS

A Khmer carved sandstone head, possibly Vishnu, slight damage, Cambodia, 7th/8thC, 6¼in (16cm) high.

£610–730 WW

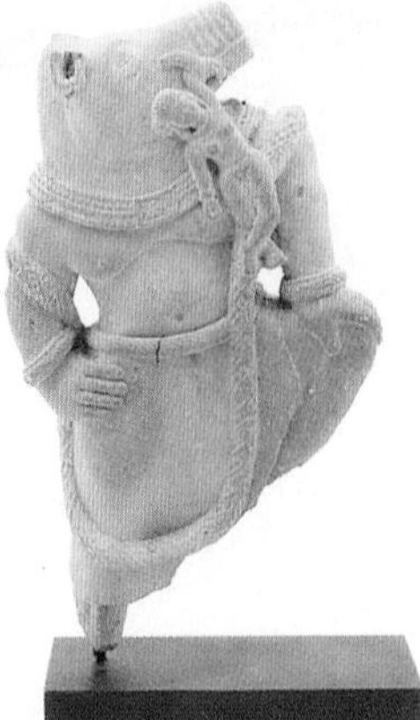

A sandstone figure of Varaha and Prithvi, damaged and repaired, India, possibly 10thC, 11½in (29cm) high.

£1,100–1,300 RIT

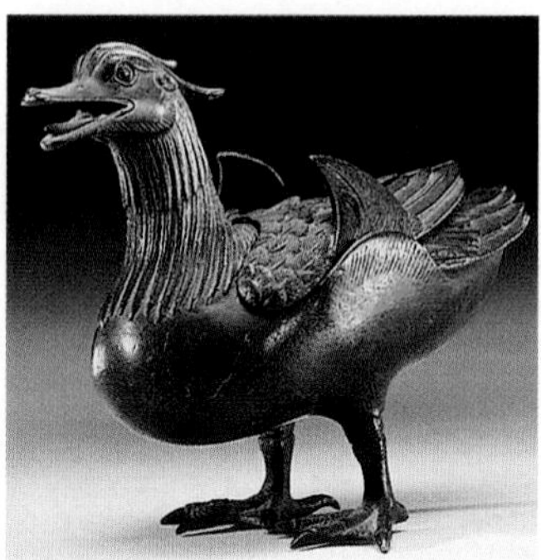

A jade model of two horses, China, Song Dynasty, 960–1279, 4in (15cm) wide.

£5,400–6,000 BOW

A bronze censer, with a removable cover, in the form of a duck, China, 17thC, 6in (15cm) wide.

£3,250–3,900 S(NY)

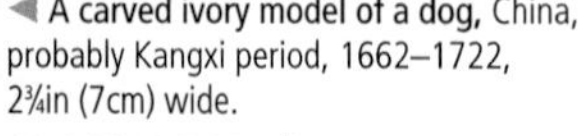

◄ **A carved ivory model of a dog,** China, probably Kangxi period, 1662–1722, 2¾in (7cm) wide.

£1,100–1,300 WW

A carved ivory figure of the Virgin Mary and child, the base carved with putti and a ribbon, India, Goa, 17thC, 8½in (21.5cm) high.

£3,600–4,300 S

A gilded teak figure of Buddha, Laos, 18thC, 37in (94cm) high.

£3,700–4,200 SOO

A jade model of a monkey, China, 18thC, 2½in (6.4cm) wide.

£1,400–1,600 BOW

► **A stone figure of Guanyin seated,** China, c1800, 37¾in (96cm) high.

£2,700–3,000 LOP

A pair of silvered-bronze models of dogs of *Fo*, the male with a brocade ball, the female with a cub, China, early 19thC, 10¾in (27.5cm) high.

£5,200–6,200 S(NY)

Dogs of *Fo*

Dogs of *Fo* are mythical lion-type animals resembling Pekinese dogs with large bushy tails, often playing with a brocaded ball to which ribbons are attached. In use from the 15th century, these dogs are normally placed each side of a statue of Buddha. In recent times it has become popular to place them each side of a main entrance to an establishment to ward off evil spirits.

A bronze model of a dog of *Fo*, with a brocade ball, China, early 19thC, 11in (28cm) high.

£150–180 NSal

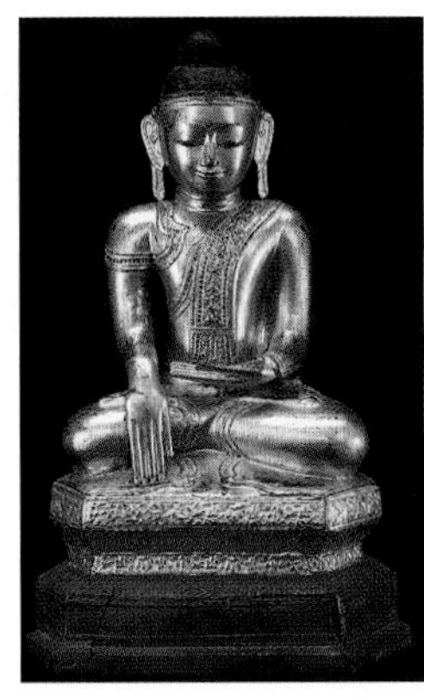

A gilt lacquer figure of Buddha, Burma, 19thC, 26¾in (68cm) high.

£2,650–2,950 LOP

A pair of Mandalay-style giltwood figures, the eyes inlaid with mother-of-pearl, the garment hems carved with a floral motif and mica inlay, Burma, 19thC, 26in (66cm) high.

£9,100–10,900 S(NY)

A coral carving of the Eight Immortals, on a wooden stand, China, 19thC, 9¾in (25cm) wide.

£2,000–2,400 WW

◄ **A gilded teak figure of Buddha,** Cambodia, 19thC, 52in (132cm) high.

£5,700–6,400 SOO

A jade model of a mythical beast, China, 19thC, 3¼in (8.5cm) wide.

£175–210 WW

The Eight Immortals

The Eight Immortals have been a common subject for Chinese artisans since the Song Dynasty. They are considered to be guardian figures representing virtue and the quest for eternity. Three of the Eight Immortals are historical figures and five are purely legendary.

- Zhongli Quan – carries a fan to revive the souls of the dead.
- He Xiangu – a graceful girl who carries a lotus blossom.
- Zhang Guolao – a bearded figure carrying a bamboo drum.
- Lu Dongbin – a dignified elderly figure with a sword.
- Han Xiangzi – the philosopher represented as a youthful figure carrying a flute.
- Cao Guojiu – the imperial brother-in-law, an elderly bearded figure carrying a pair of castanets.
- Li Tieguai – an emaciated deformed figure carrying a gourd that contains the elixir of immortality.
- Lan Caihe – a young girl or boy carrying a basket of flowers.

A silver-mounted jade box and cover, in the form of two ducks, China, 19thC, 7¾in (19.5cm) wide.

£2,150–2,550 S

◄ **A jadeite figure of a *meiren*,** China, 19thC, 7¾in (19.5cm) high.

£540–640 WAD

A meiren is a beautiful, elegant lady.

A bronze figure of Krishna, on a pedestal, southern India, 19thC, 9¾in (25cm) high.

£145–175 WAD

An ivory *okimono* of a monkey, with an *inro*, Japan, 19thC, 1½in (4cm) high.

£260–310 WAD

A pair of cloisonné enamel models of elephants, each with a howdah supporting a candle sconce, on wooden stands, China, 19thC, 12¼in (31cm) high.

£4,800–5,700 S

A carved bamboo model of a three-legged toad, China, 19thC, 4in (10cm) high.

£150–180 WW

A bronze *okimono* of a turtle with young, signed, Japan, 19thC, 5½in (14cm) wide.

£290–330 K&M

A carved ivory *okimono* of sumo wrestlers, inscribed, Japan, Meiji period, 1868–1911, 2¾in (7cm) high.

£700–840 HYD

A carved ivory figure of a lady, Japan, 19thC, 4in (10cm) high.

£990–1,100 BOW

A Tokyo School ivory figure of a boy catching a bird, 19thC, 5in (12.5cm) high.

£990–1,100 K&M

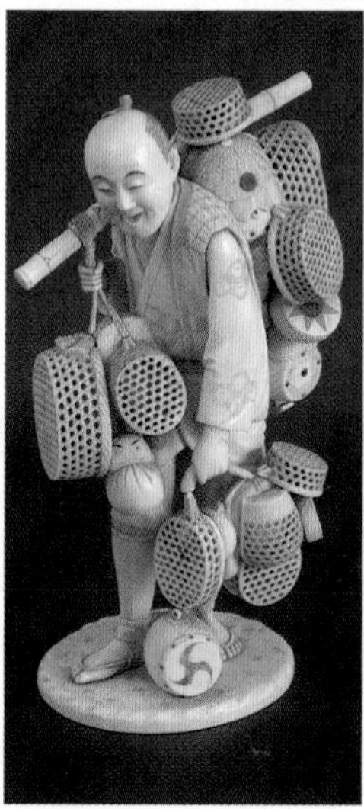

A carved ivory figure of a trader, signed, Japan, Meiji period, 1868–1911, 7in (18cm) high.

£1,700–2,000 BWL

A carved ivory group of a farmer and his son, Japan, Meiji period, 1868–1911, 9in (23cm) high.

£3,700–4,200 LBO

◀ **A carved ivory figure of a man with chickens,** Japan, 19thC, 5in (12.5cm) high.

£2,600–2,900 BOW

▶ **An ivory *okimono* of Daikoku,** Japan, 19thC, 2in (5cm) wide.

£580–650 K&M

Daikoku is one of the seven Gods of good fortune. His attributes are rice bags, rats and a magic mallet from which all sorts of riches shower. He is to be found in the household shrines of farmers and merchants.

A carved ivory figure of a man and a boy, by Toshimitsu, with engraved detail, signed, Japan, Meiji period, 1868–1911, 5¾in (14.5cm) high.

£440–520 G(L)

A carved ivory figure of a warrior god, Japan, Meiji period, 1868–1911, 5in (12.5cm) high.

£2,100–2,400 BOW

A bronze figure of a *Diamyo*, on a wooden stand, Japan, Meiji period, 1868–1911, 14½in (36cm) high.

£820–980 TEN

A Diamyo is a Samurai governor of a province.

A bronze group of a mother and child, marked, slight damage, Japan, Meiji period, 1868–1911, 15in (38cm) high.

£590–700 TEN

A bronze group of elephants, signed, Japan, Meiji period, 1868–1911, 21¾in (55.5cm) wide.

£1,250–1,500 HAD

A bronze model of a tiger, with *shakudo*-inlaid stripes and glass eyes, one eye missing, signed, Japan, Meiji period, 1868–1911, 17¾in (45cm) long, on a softwood stand.

£560–670 PFK

◀ **A bronze censer,** in the form of an elephant, with ivory tusks, the harness inlaid with glass beads, the lantern pierced with *aoi-mon*, signed 'Gyokko', Japan, Meiji period, 1868–1911, 17¾in (45cm) high.

£2,850–3,400 S

A carved ivory and *Shibayama okimono* of three monkeys, signed, Japan, Meiji period, 1868–1911, 17¾in (45cm) high.

£3,300–3,900 HYD

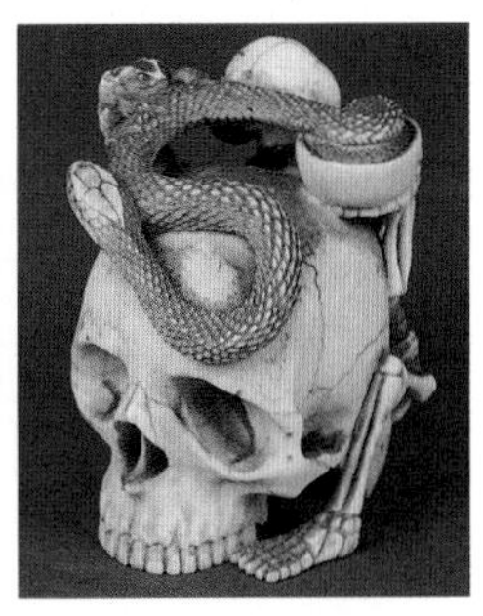

An ivory *okimono* of a skull, a toad, a skeleton and a snake, Japan, Meiji period, 1868–1911, 2½in (6.5cm) high.

£800–960 HYD

A pair of lacquered figures of Jo and Uba, on a wooden stand, slight damage, Japan, c1880, larger 15½in (39.5cm) high.

£1,200–1,400 SWO

Jo and Uba are Japanese figures of longevity and fidelity.

A bronze group of puppies, with *shakudo* eyes, signed, Japan, c1900, 12in (30.5cm) wide.

£2,300–2,600 LBO

A carved ivory group of a ploughman and a buffalo, on a carved wood stand, Japan, c1900, 14½in (37cm) wide.

£700–840 TEN

A carved ivory figure of a traveller, seated on a bench with his belongings, marked 'Mune', Japan, c1900, 8¼in (21cm) wide.

£2,200–2,600 WAD

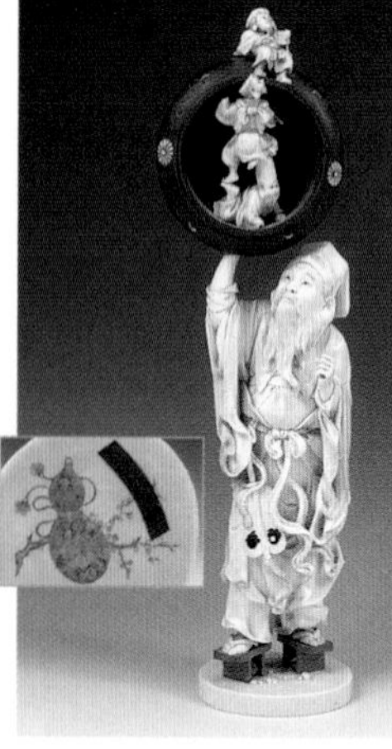

An ivory figure of Jurojin, supporting a wooden bowl with figures of Hotei, Diakoku and Fukurokuju, Japan, late 19thC, 12¼in (31cm) high.

£2,200–2,600 SWO

These characters are all Immortals.

A carved ivory figure of a woman, wearing gold lacquer and *aogai* robes, signed 'Chikusai', Japan, c1900, 17in (43cm) high.

£510–610 WAD

A carved ivory group of a *bijin* and two attendants, head repaired, signed 'Akikane', Japan, c1900, 8¼in (21cm) high.

£610–730 DN

A carved ivory *okimono* of a monkey trainer, two monkeys and a boy, Japan, c1900, 6½in (16.5cm) high.

£370–440 WAD

A carved bamboo figure of *Shoulao*, seated with a deer, China, c1900, 5½in (14cm) high.

£370–440 WW

Shoulao is the Star God of Longevity.

A carved ivory figure of a fisherman, Japan, early 20thC, 6¼in (16cm) high.

£150–180 WilP

◄ **A padouk model of a Madras elephant,** with ivory toenails, eyes and tusks, India, early 20thC, 18½in (47cm) high.

£1,700–2,000 DN(BR)

A bronze figure of a fisherman, by Seiya, probably Kyoto School, on a carved wood stand, signed, Japan, early 20thC, 52¼in (132.5cm) high.

£5,600–6,700 RTo

FURNITURE

A padouk three-tier buffet, Anglo-Indian, 1845–50, 38in (96.5cm) wide.
£2,600–2,900 YOX

A padouk bureau, with a fitted interior and paktong handles, Anglo-Chinese, 18thC, 38in (96.5cm) wide.
£3,300–3,950 WW

A hardwood bureau, with a fitted interior and three panelled drawers, India, Goa, 1725–50, 37in (94cm) wide.
£3,500–4,200 SK

A satinwood and ebony cabinet, the upper section with a pierced frieze above two panelled doors, the base with three frieze drawers and two doors, Anglo-Indian, 19thC, 82½in (209.5cm) high.
£1,200–1,400 DN

A hardwood cabinet, inlaid with ivory figures and flowers, Japan, late 19thC, 37in (94cm) wide.
£1,050–1,250 S(O)

A burr-elm cabinet, with three pairs of locking panelled doors, Korea, 19thC, 44in (112cm) wide.
£2,050–2,450 MAL(O)

A carved wood corner cabinet, the three cupboards with sliding doors, the lacquered panels inlaid with bone and ivory birds and flowers, Japan, 19thC, 65¾in (167cm) high.
£270–320 TRM(E)

► **A hardwood altar cabinet,** with three frieze drawers above two panelled doors, carved with dragons, China, late 19thC, 80¾in (205cm) wide.
£2,200–2,600 SWO

A padouk cocktail cabinet, the hinged top enclosing a fitted interior containing decanters, glasses, silver-plated cigarette boxes and ashtrays, with a glass undertier, Japan, early 20thC, 22in (56cm) wide.
£610–730 AH

This cabinet was made for export to the West.

A hardwood cabinet-on-chest, with two panelled doors enclosing shelves, above three long drawers, Anglo-Indian, 19thC, 53in (134.5cm) wide.
£3,500–4,200 NAAW

A lacquer cabinet-on-stand, China, c1800, 40¼in (102cm) wide.
£3,350–4,000 S

Anglo-Asian Furniture

Anglo-Indian and Anglo-Chinese furniture was made not for export but specifically for ex-patriot order and use.

Export furniture from Japan and China was limited to lacquered and inlaid pieces such as display cabinets, screens, work and games boxes. Jardinière stands became a popular import in the West during the late 19th century.

◄ **A coromandel cabinet-on-stand,** with inlaid decoration, Anglo-Indian, early 19thC, 23¾in (60.5cm) wide.
£1,800–2,150 S

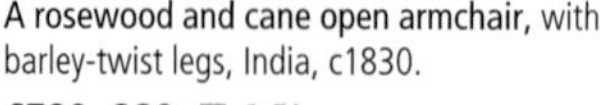

A rosewood and cane open armchair, with barley-twist legs, India, c1830.
£780–880 AGI

A pair of elm open armchairs, China, 19thC.
£850–950 AQ

A pair of bamboo open armchairs, each with a lacquer seat, China, mid-19thC.
£1,300–1,500 SOO

A hardwood open armchair, carved with entwined dragons, Japan, c1900.
£440–520 SWO

◄ **A pair of carved padouk hall chairs,** the backs with marble panels, China, c1900.
£850–950 PWA

This piece was made for the European market.

► **A rosewood nursery chair,** India, 19thC.
£350–420 HOLL

A pair of elm scholars' chairs, cane seats reworked, China, mid-19thC.
£1,350–1,500 SOO

A pair of coromandel side chairs, Anglo-Indian, early 19thC.
£1,250–1,500 WW

◄ **A teak side chair,** carved and pierced with leaves, Burma, late 19thC.
£350–420 DN

A padouk chest of drawers, Anglo-Chinese, late 18thC, 27½in (70cm) wide.

£3,800–4,500 S

A lacquer secretaire chest, with ten drawers, painted with vines and butterflies and inlaid with mother-of-pearl, Japan, c1600, 22½in (57cm) wide.

£1,600–1,900 WAD

A wooden coffer, painted in gold lacquer with mandarin orange trees, animals and a chariot, damaged, Japan, late 16thC, 38¼in (97cm) wide, on a later stand.

£12,800–15,300 BERN

A rosewood coffer, with brass mounts, Anglo-Indian, c1850, 55in (139.5cm) wide.

£850–950 PENH

A six-fold screen, painted with a landscape and Mount Fuji, Japan, 19thC, 151in (384cm) wide.

£560–670 WW

A coromandel 12-fold floor screen, in two sections, decorated in lacquer with a palace scene and animals, China, 1800–20, 42¼in (107.5cm) high.

£8,900–10,600 NOA

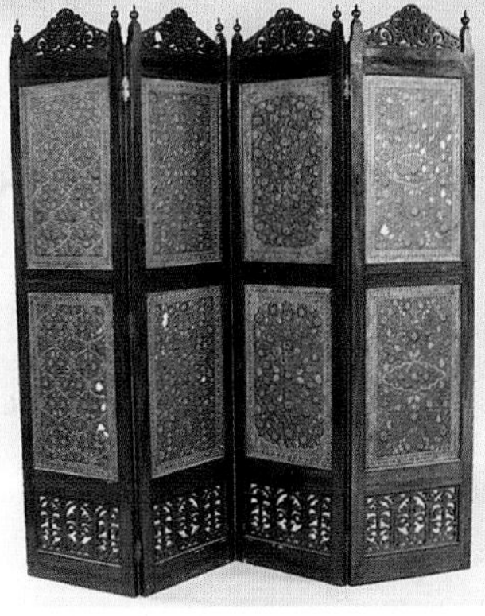

A carved rosewood four-fold screen, painted with flowers, Anglo-Indian, late 19thC, each panel 75½ x 18¾in (192 x 47.5cm).

£1,650–1,950 WW

A wooden screen, comprising four panels, carved with mythical animals and figures, with gilt highlights, China, late 19thC, 84½in (214.5cm) wide.

£1,200–1,500 NOA

A rosewood table screen, inlaid with an Immortal and plaques, China, 19thC, 14 x 20in (35.5 x 51cm).

£540–640 WAD

A wooden eight-fold table screen, inlaid with marble panels, painted with figures and calligraphy, China, 19thC, 22in (56cm) high.

£430–510 WAD

A pair of carved hardwood table screens, each inset with a jade panel carved with dragons, stands damaged, China, late 19thC, 71in (180.5cm) wide.

£2,900–3,450 SWO

A carved wood screen, the porcelain plaque decorated in the Qianjiang palette with figures and pine trees, China, early 20thC, 23 x 16in (58.5 x 40.5cm).

£370–440 RIT

A carved and ebonized shesham wood settle, carved with a Moghul Tree of Life pattern, with a Franco-Belgian tapestry cushion, Anglo-Indian, 1875–1900, 60in (152.5cm) wide.

£410–490 NOA

Shesham wood is native to northern India.

A pair of padouk urn stands, each with a marble top, China, c1900, 18in (45.5cm) high.

£400–480 HOLL

A carved *hongmu* wood barrel stool, inset with a marble top, China, c1800, 20¾in (52.5cm) high.

£2,900–3,450 S(NY)

A pair of barrel stools, probably rosewood, each inset with a marble top, inlaid with mother-of-pearl, with openwork sides, China, late 19thC, 21in (53.5cm) high.

£880–1,050 DN(HAM)

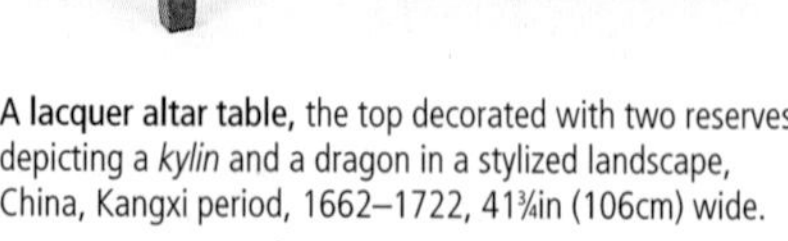

A lacquer altar table, the top decorated with two reserves depicting a *kylin* and a dragon in a stylized landscape, China, Kangxi period, 1662–1722, 41¾in (106cm) wide.

£3,700–4,400 S(P)

A Japanese export card table, the hinged top inlaid with mother-of-pearl flowers and birds and opening to reveal a landscape, Nagasaki, c1800, 36in (91.5cm) diam.

£2,550–3,050 NAAW

A Chinese export burr-walnut games table, inlaid with an amboyna and mother-of-pearl chessboard, opening to reveal a backgammon board and a well, the frieze with bone stringing, 19thC, 31½in (80cm) wide.

£8,900–10,600 NAAW

A Regency mahogany and satinwood drum library table, with seven ebony and ivory-strung frieze drawers, restored, leather top later, Anglo-Chinese, 48in (122cm) diam.

£5,400–6,400 S

A lacquer low table, inlaid with a tortoiseshell and mother-of-pearl dragon and stylized clouds, China, 19thC, 39in (99cm) wide.

£1,500–1,800 S(P)

A lacquer occasional table, decorated with birds and flowers, slight damage, China, late 18thC, 24¾in (63cm) diam.

£320–380 S(P)

A blackwood occasional table, in the form of a camel, India, c1880, 28½in (72.5cm) wide.

£3,800–4,250 ⊞ WALP

A hardwood occasional table, the top inlaid with ivory flowers, the borders with ebony stringing, on a folding stand with friezes and ivory inlay, India, late 19thC, 23in (59cm) diam.

£520–620 NSal

A Regency Chinese export hardwood pier table, the marble top above a mirror back, half-fluted columns and scrolls supports, with ebony inlay, 53in (134.5cm) wide.

£6,000–7,200 NAAW

A hardwood folding side table, the top and freeze carved with dragons above pierced folding supports, China, 19thC, 30in (76cm) wide.

£220–260 Mit

A hardwood and mother-of-pearl-inlaid side table, the inset marble top above a carved frieze, China, 19thC, 41¼in (105cm) wide.

£680–810 DN(HAM)

A lacquered elm table side table, China, 19thC, 15in (38cm) wide.

£260–290 ⊞ OE

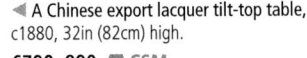

◄ **A Chinese export lacquer tilt-top table,** c1880, 32in (82cm) high.

£790–890 ⊞ CSM

An elm and ivory-inlaid two-tier table, c1860, 25in (63.5cm) wide.

£190–220 ⊞ NoC

A carved teak two-tier table, Anglo-Indian, c1880, 19in (48.5cm) diam.

£80–90 ⊞ ERA

◄ **A pair of Japanese export mahogany and lacquer work tables,** each with three sliding panels enclosing wells, on a tripod base with shoe-form feet, losses, 19thC, 20in (51cm) diam.

£5,200–6,200 S(NY)

► **A carved rosewood tray-on-stand,** Anglo-Indian, 1900–25, 32in (81.5cm) wide.

£410–490 NOA

INRO

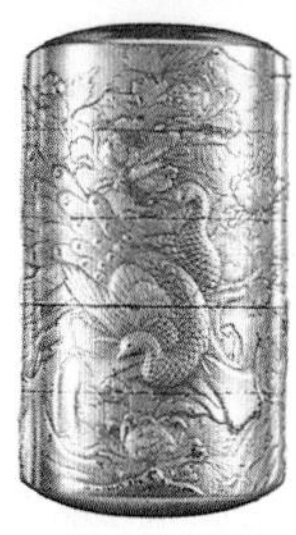

A lacquer four-case *inro*, by Masayasu, decorated with birds and peonies, signed, Japan, 19thC, 3½in (9cm) high, with an ivory *netsuke* of Hotei.

£1,200–1,400 S

◄ A lacquer five-case *inro*, decorated with Samurai warriors, Japan, Meiji period, 1868–1911, 3¼in (8.5cm) high, with an ivory *netsuke* carved in the form of a boat, with a hardwood toggle.

£1,400–1,650 HYD

► A lacquer five-case *inro*, decorated in *nashiji* and *hiramakie* with a landscape, slight damage, Japan, c1900, 4in (10cm) high.

£350–420 DN

A lacquer five-case *inro*, decorated with bamboo and rocks, Japan, Meiji period, 1868–1911, 3½in (9cm) high.

£470–560 TEN

A lacquer five-case *inro*, decorated with a cockerel, hen and chicks, Japan, Meiji period, 1868–1911, 4in (10cm) high, with a stained ivory *ojime* and an ivory and metal *netsuke*.

£590–700 TEN

JEWELLERY

A Victorian 15ct gold brooch, set with rubies, emeralds and seed pearls, Anglo-Indian, 1½in (4cm) wide.

£510–610 SK

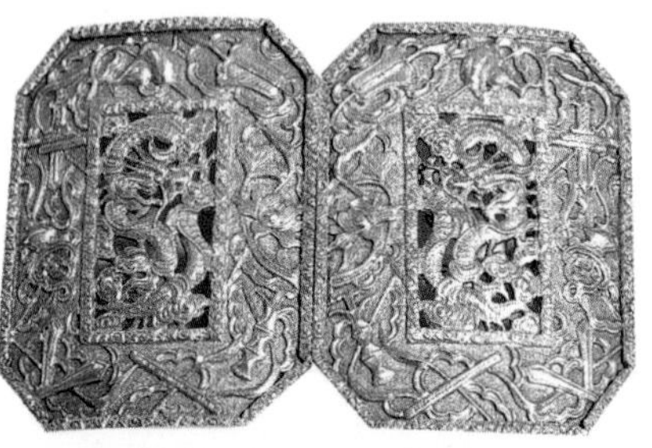

A Chinese silver buckle, China, c1925, 4in (10cm) wide.

£50–55 EXC

A gold filigree locket, India, Chittaurgarh, 19thC, 2in (5cm) high.

£135–150 VDA

A gold necklace, set with seven glass panels inlaid with gold hunting scenes, flowers and animals, India, Partabargh, 1860–70, 18in (45.5cm) long, in a Phillips Bros & Son fitted box.

£2,800–3,350 DN

◄ An 18ct gold necklace, set with sapphires, seed pearls, chrysoberyls, emeralds and yellow sapphires, six gilt beads replaced, India, c1900, 15½in (39.5cm) long.

£1,000–1,200 SK

► A gold parure, set with fruitwood panels carved with figures, maker's mark CW, China, late 19thC.

£280–330 BWL

A jadeite archer's ring, carved with a Buddhist lion, a bat and fungus, China, 19thC.

£330–390 WW

NETSUKE

◀ An ivory *netsuke* of a farmer and his family, signed, Japan, Edo period, 1600–1868, 2in (5cm) high.

£720–800 AMC

▶ An ivory *netsuke* of a fish, Japan, late 18thC, 2¼in (5.5cm) wide.

£1,900–2,250 S

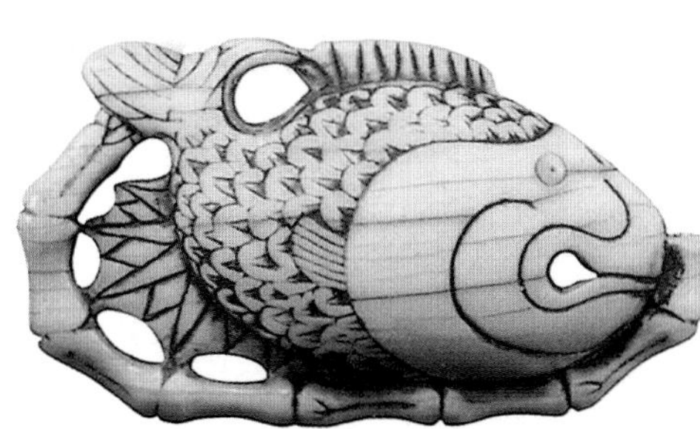

A wooden netsuke of Okame, by Ittan, signed, Japan, 1820–77, 2in (5cm) high.

£2,150–2,550 S

Okame, also known as Otafuku or Uzume, is the primitive Shinto goddess of mirth.

A wooden *netsuke* of a monkey, by Koichi, Japan, 19thC, 1½in (4cm) high.

£1,600–1,800 BOW

An ivory *okimono*-style *netsuke* of a warrior, horse and attendant, Japan, 19thC, 1¼in (3cm) high.

£670–750 K&M

An ivory *netsuke* of a monkey holding a glass, by Masatomo, Japan, 19thC, 1½in (4cm) high.

£2,150–2,400 BOW

A wooden *netsuke* of three turtles, by Tadakazu, Japan, 19thC, 2in (5cm) high.

£2,150–2,550 S

An ivory *netsuke* of two wrestling *oni*, Japan, 19thC, 2in (5cm) wide.

£1,100–1,250 K&M

Prices

The price ranges quoted in this book reflect the average price a purchaser might expect to pay for a similar item. The price will vary according to the condition, rarity, size, popularity, provenance, colour and restoration of the item, and this must be taken into account when assessing values. Don't forget that if you are selling it is quite likely that you will be offered less than the price range.

A boxwood *netsuke* of a man, by Kosai, Japan, 19thC, 1in (2.5cm) high.

£1,050–1,200 BOW

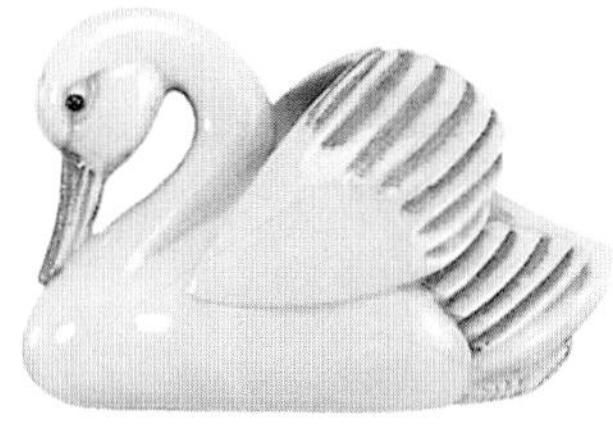

An ivory *netsuke* of a swan, by Seikichi, signed, Japan, 19thC, 2in (5cm) wide.

£2,400–2,850 S

An ivory *netsuke* of an actor wearing a mask to one side, Japan, Meiji period, 1868–1911, 2in (5cm) high.

£700–840 HYD

ROBES & COSTUME

◄ **A gypsy bridal dress,** southern India, c1915, together with a quantity of jewellery.
£280–330 Mit

► **A silk and brocade sash,** decorated with chrysanthemums and butterflies, slight damage, Japan, 19thC, 212in (538.5cm) long.
£230–270 WHIT

An embroidered robe, decorated with dragons, China, mid-19thC.
£360–430 KTA

An Ainu cotton and plant fibre robe, Japan, c1900.
£160–190 WAD

Ainu is an area in northern Japan, famed for its cotton.

An embroidered robe and skirt, decorated with cranes, flowers, butterflies, mountains and waves, slight damage, China, c1900.
£5,100–6,100 BUK

A silk robe, embroidered with five dragons, China, early 20thC.
£1,000–1,200 S

A pair of silk shoes, China, c1880, 4in (10cm) long.
£85–95 JPr

◄ **A Japanese export silk crepe kimono,** embroidered with chrysanthemums, with Takashimaya label, early 20thC.
£350–420 WHIT

A pair of silk shoes, China, c1880, 4in (10cm) long.
£85–95 JPr

SNUFF BOTTLES

◄ **A jade snuff bottle,** China, 18thC, 3½in (9cm) high.
£2,700–3,000 BOW

► **A jade snuff bottle,** China, 18thC, 3in (7.5cm) high.
£2,150–2,400 BOW

An amethyst glass snuff bottle, carved with squirrels and fruit vines, probably 18thC, China, 2in (5cm) high.
£980–1,150 WW

A smoked crystal snuff bottle, by Ye Zhongsan, China, 19thC, 2¼in (5.5cm) high.
£900–1,000 BOW

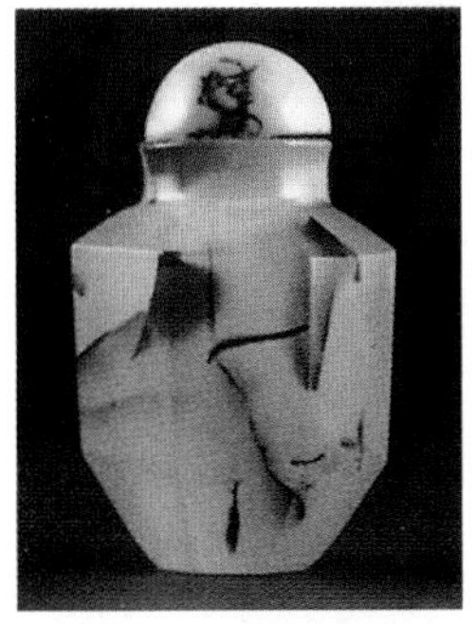

An agate snuff bottle, with a turquoise stopper, China, probably 19thC, 2½in (6.5cm) high.
£175–210 WW

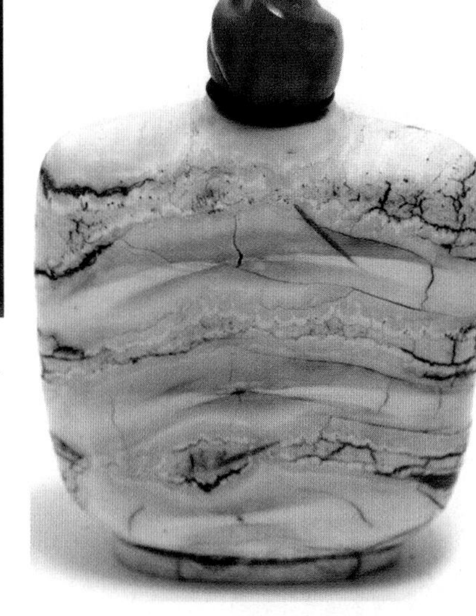

A mammoth tooth snuff bottle, China, c1850, 2½in (6.5cm) high.
£160–180 BOW

► **A cinnabar snuff bottle,** China, 19thC, 3in (7.5cm) high.
£540–600 BOW

LOCATE THE SOURCE

The source of each illustration in Miller's can be found by checking the code letters below each caption with the Key to Illustrations, pages 746–753.

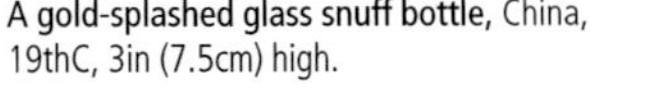

A gold-splashed glass snuff bottle, China, 19thC, 3in (7.5cm) high.
£2,150–2,400 BOW

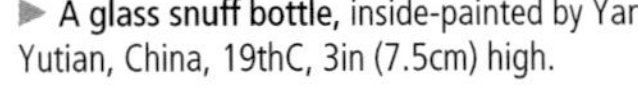

► **A glass snuff bottle,** inside-painted by Yan Yutian, China, 19thC, 3in (7.5cm) high.
£720–800 BOW

A coral glass snuff bottle, relief-decorated with pine trees, deer and a pavilion, stopper missing, China, 19thC, 2½in (6.5cm) high.
£200–240 WAD

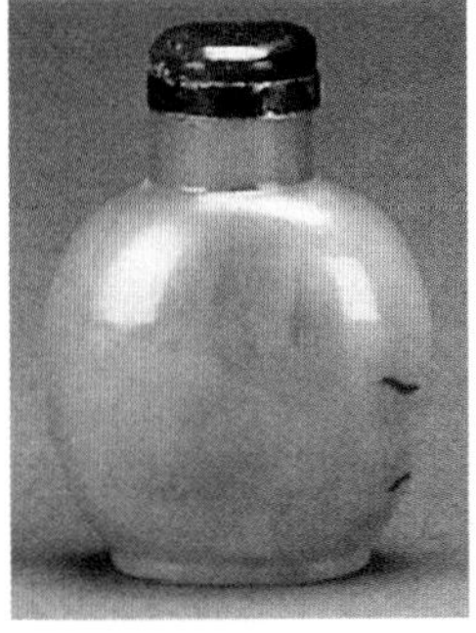

An agate snuff bottle, with an amethyst stopper, China, 19thC, 2¾in (7cm) high.
£75–90 WAD

A glass snuff bottle, overlaid with flowers and fruit above a bat, China, Beijing, 19thC, 3in (7.5cm) high.
£270–320 WAD

An ivory snuff bottle, decorated with dragons, China, early 20thC, 3in (7.5cm) high.
£160–190 WAD

TEXTILES

A Dai woven cotton baby carrier, China, early 20thC, 28in (71cm) wide.
£230–260 Wai

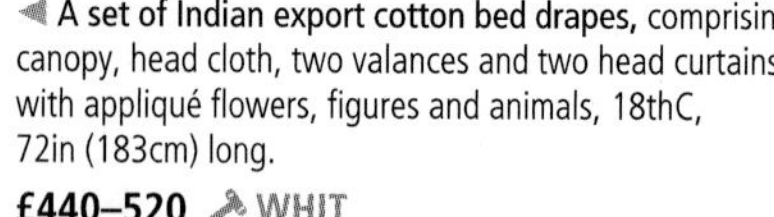

◄ **A set of Indian export cotton bed drapes,** comprising canopy, head cloth, two valances and two head curtains, with appliqué flowers, figures and animals, 18thC, 72in (183cm) long.
£440–520 WHIT

A silk satin coverlet, embroidered with birds and flowers, China, early 20thC, 108in (274.5cm) wide.
£950–1,100 WHIT

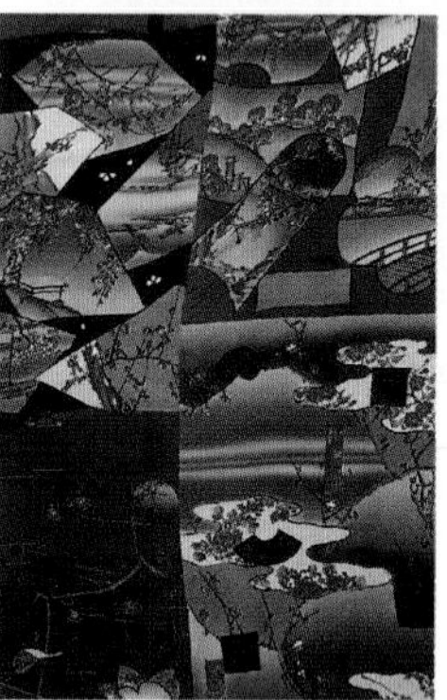

A silk crepe coverlet, made from kimono panels, Japan, 1920s, 51in (129.5cm) wide.
£105–120 JCH

A silk coverlet, embroidered with flowers and birds, China, c1930, 60in (152.5cm) wide.
£450–500 JPr

► **A tapestry throne cushion cover,** decorated with bats, precious emblems, flowers and fruit, China, early 19thC, 41 x 50½in (104 x 128.5cm).
£970–1,100 S(NY)

A silk tapestry panel, embroidered with a dragon, Japan, c1900, 75 x 52in (190.5 x 132cm).
£1,450–1,700 WHIT

◄ **A pair of silk rank badges,** worked in metal threads with a quail, within borders of bats and *shou* medallions, China, 19thC, 11½ x 12¼in (29 x 31cm).
£90–105 WAD

A gauze rank badge, worked in tent stitch, China, c1900, 11¼in (28.5cm) wide.
£530–600 JCH

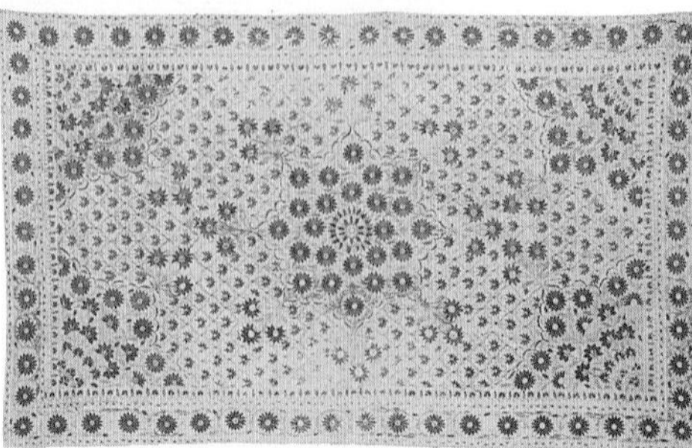

A silk panel, embroidered with a medallion within flowers, trellis and a scrolling vine, India, Punjab, c1820, 91¾ x 56in (233 x 142cm).
£6,600–7,900 S

This textile panel was formerly the property of the guardian of Maharajah Duleep Singh, King of the Sikh Empire, who was deposed in 1849 by the East India Company and sent to England, where he became a favourite of Queen Victoria.

A silk wall hanging, worked in silver and gold thread with a mythological dragon and a tiger, Japan, 19thC, 76 x 53in (193 x 134.5cm), in a bamboo frame.
£750–900 MAL(O)

A cotton seat cover, China, Beijing, c1880, 28in (71cm) square.
£880–980 WADS

ISLAMIC WORKS OF ART

ARMS & ARMOUR

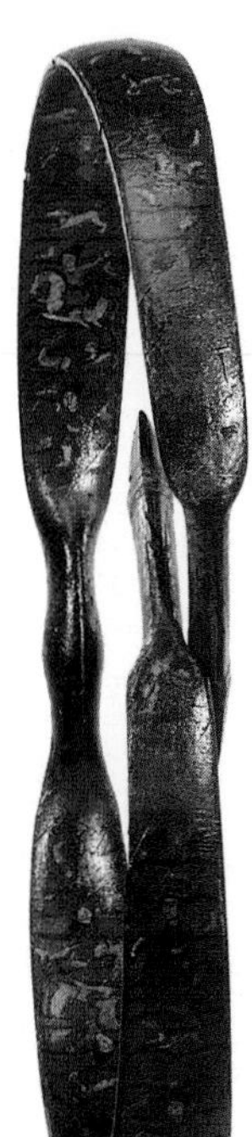

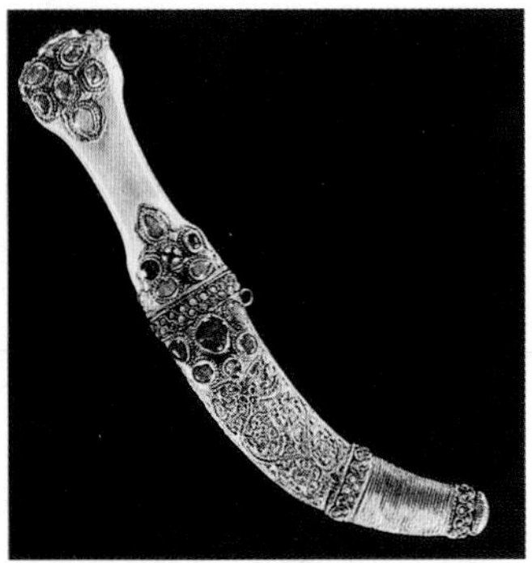

A child's steel dagger, the ivory hilt inlaid with semi-precious stones and gems, central Asia, Samarkand, 18thC, 9½in (24cm) long, with a gold scabbard.

£4,200–5,000 S

◄ **A bow,** painted with hunting scenes and scrolling foliage, slight damage, Persia, c1800, 19¾in (50cm) long.

£2,400–2,850 TDM

► **A steel *kard*,** the jade hilt set with a garnet, Turkey, 18thC, 13½in (34.5cm) long, with a gold-mounted wood scabbard.

£1,050–1,250 TDM

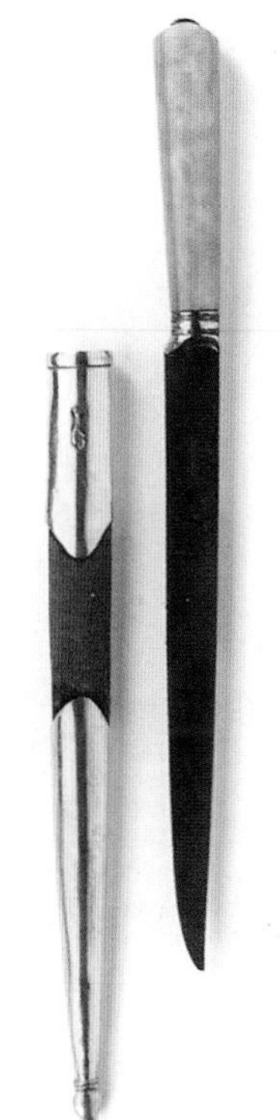

A *kindjal*, the horn grip with gold mounts, inscribed 'Allah's help and victory is very near', signed, 'Ali Hussain', Caucasus, 19thC, 15½in (39.5cm) long, with a leather scabbard.

£700–840 F&C

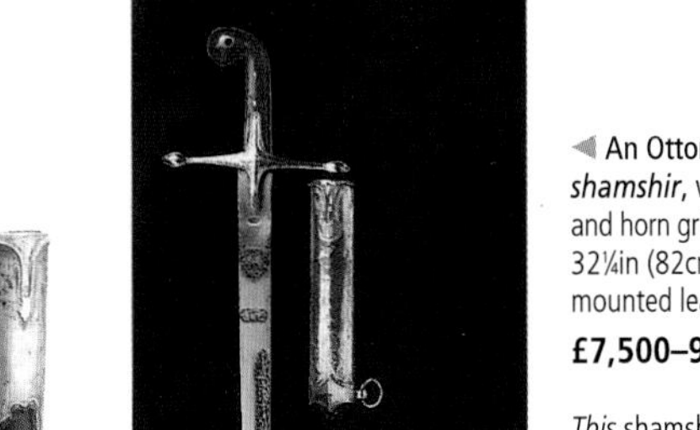

◄ **A silver-mounted toe-lock musket,** engraved with scrollwork, inset with chased silver panels, the engraved brass butt plate inlaid with coral, with wooden ramrod, Algeria, 1825–50, barrel 36¾in (92.5cm) long.

£3,200–3,800 TDM

► **A silver-mounted hardwood flintlock musket,** inlaid in silver wire with flowers and scrolls, with steel ramrod, dated 1844, 50in (127cm) long.

£4,000–4,800 F&C

A *khula khud*, etched with Islamic decoration, with a chainmail neck guard, Persia, c1850, 11in (28cm) high.

£700–790 MDL

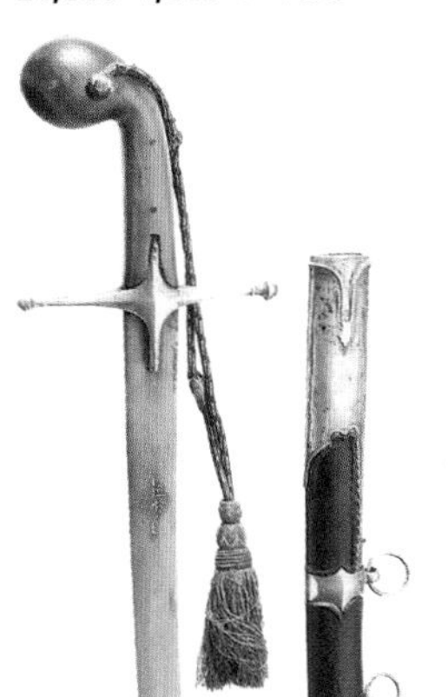

► **A silver-mounted *shamshir*,** Egypt, c1800, 37½in (95.5cm) long, with a silver-mounted leather-covered wooden scabbard.

£2,850–3,400 Herm

◄ **An Ottoman silver-mounted *shamshir*,** with Arabic inscription and horn grip, Turkey, c1807, blade 32¼in (82cm) long, with a silver-mounted leather-covered scabbard.

£7,500–9,000 TDM

This shamshir *was presented to Captain Colin Mackay by Mohammed Ali Pasha of Egypt in 1807, following his command of the Grenadier Company of the 2nd Battalion of the 78th Regiment of Foot at El Hamet in 1807.*

CERAMICS

A ceramic bowl, damaged and repaired, Persia, 12thC, 18½in (47cm) diam.

£310–350 G&G

A glazed and painted pottery bowl, decorated with a band of pseudo calligraphy, Spain, 12thC, 8¾in (22cm) diam.

£8,400–10,000 S

This bowl has the distinctive green and manganese palette associated with the Umayyad and post-Umayyad period in Muslim Spain. This particular example is probably from Valencia and uses the unusual combination of the cuerda seca *technique with light green enamel.*

A pottery vase, painted with stylized motifs, probably 15thC, Syria, 10½in (26.5cm) high.

£410–490 WW

A Safavid *kendi*, painted with birds, butterflies and flowers, with pseudo Chinese mark, Persia, probably Mashhad, 17thC, 7in (18cm) high.

£1,400–1,650 S(O)

For further information on Ceramics see pages 232–259

A hanging ornament, painted with strapwork, interlocking palmettes and coronet motifs, Turkey, Kütahya, 19thC, 7½in (19cm) high.

£6,000–7,200 S

These ornaments were often hung from the same chain as mosque lamps to deter rodents from climbing down the chains and drinking the oil from the lamps. The spherical form is reminiscent of the ostrich eggs brought back by pilgrims from Mecca.

A Qajar vase, Persia, 19thC, 9½in (24cm) high.

£120–140 ROS

JEWELLERY

A Qajar gold and enamel brooch, in the form of a bird, set with emeralds and rubies, with pendant pearls, Persia, 19thC, 2¾in (7cm) high.

£8,400–10,000 S

◄ **A pair of Qajar gold and enamel earrings,** set with emeralds and rubies within seed pearls, the reverse decorated with a bird and a rose, Persia, 19thC, 2½in (6.5cm) high.

£4,200–5,000 S

A gold nephrite seal, inscribed with extracts of Koranic verse, later mounted as a ring, 17thC, 1¼in (3cm) wide.

£540–640 F&C

Ayat ul kursi *is a verse used as a prayer to help one seek solace, patience and well being.*

◄ **A silver signet ring,** incised with Arabic script 'The slave (possession) of Ali Ahmad son of Al-íAndarus', India, dated 1872.

£310–350 MANO

METALWARE

A tinned copper bowl, decorated with floral and character panels, damaged, Persia, 19thC, 20in (51cm) diam.

£1,200–1,400 Hal

A cast-bronze mirror, cast with a horse and rider and other animals, within a border of Kufic inscriptions, Persia, Khorasan, 11th–13thC, 6½in (16.5cm) diam.

£720–860 S

An Ilkhanid parcel-gilt silver breastplate for a horse, engraved and chased with a lotus blossom in a ribbon cartouche and cats, enclosed by a repeating inscription 'Perpetual Glory, Prosperity and Wealth and Long-Life to its owner', Persia, 14thC, 5¼in (13.5cm) wide.

£4,800–5,700 S

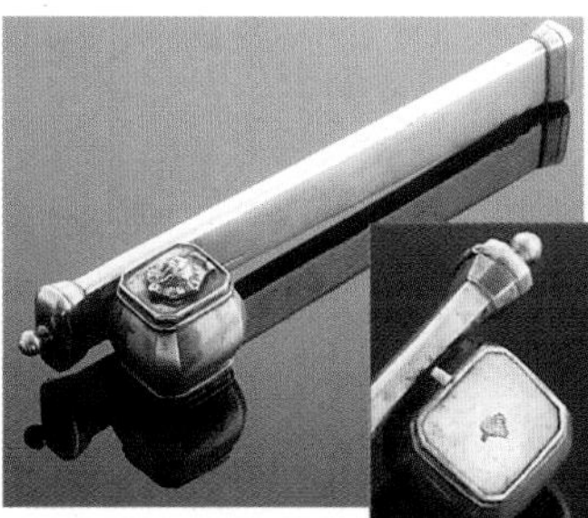

An Ottoman silver travelling pen case, with an inkwell, marked, Turkey, 19thC, 9¼in (23.5cm) long, 8½oz.

£940–1,100 SWO

A Seljuq bronze oil lamp, the hinged cover incised and inscribed with a band of animals, the handle with a bird finial, Anatolia, 12thC, 6in (15cm) high.

£450–540 WAD

A bronze plaque, in the form of a lion, Spain or Sicily, 10th–12thC, 20in (51cm) wide.

£6,600–7,900 S

This plaque may have been mounted on a throne or other grand piece of furniture. The lion is part of the iconography of royalty in many cultures, but has a notable ubiquity in Muslim culture in medieval Spain and southern Italy.

TEXTILES

An Ottoman linen coverlet, comprising three panels embroidered in silks with bands of stylized pomegranates and carnations, panels joined with lace ribbon, mounted on a stretcher, lined, Turkey, west Anatolia, late 17thC, framed, 65½in (166.5cm) wide.

£10,800–12,000 MANO

◄ **An Ottoman velvet coverlet,** worked in gold, Turkey, c1870, 46in (117cm) square.

£580–650 JPr

► **An Ottoman silk panel,** embroidered with a vase of flowers flanked by two candlesticks, Turkey, 18thC, 75½ x 54in (192 x 137cm).

£840–1,000 DN

An Ottoman silk tomb cover, worked with calligraphy within chevron bands, Turkey, 17th–18thC, 26in (66cm) square.

£2,400–2,850 S

ARCHITECTURAL ANTIQUES

BRONZE

A bronze call bell, clapper missing, c1900, 12½in (32cm) high.

£220–250 RML

A gilt-bronze jardinière, embossed with classical figures, France, early 19thC, 16in (40.5cm) wide.

£2,700–3,200 MAL(O)

A bronze vessel, c1900, 42in (106.5cm) diam.

£2,600–3,100 S(S)

For further metalware items
see pp 561–565

CERAMICS

A Victorian ceramic chimney pot, 37in (94cm) high.

£105–120 WRe

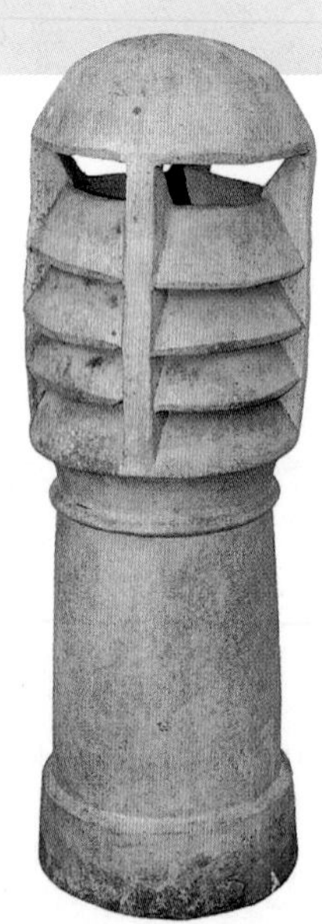

A Victorian ceramic louvred chimney pot, 39in (99cm) high.

£55–65 WRe

A pair of stoneware pedestals, c1860, 30in (76cm) high.

£4,200–5,000 S

A collection of 600 stoneware garden edging tiles, c1840, 9in (23cm) wide.

£4,300–5,000 S(S)

A pair of stoneware urns, c1870, 21in (53.5cm) high.

£2,150–2,550 S(S)

A tiled wall plaque, 1860–80, 36in (91.5cm) wide.

£300–340 CLAR

IRON

A wrought-iron garden bench, on paw feet, c1820, 42½in (108cm) wide.

£550–660 BAM

◄ A Mott Foundry cast-iron garden bench, cast with Laurel pattern, America, c1870, 43in (109cm) wide.

£3,600–4,300 S

J. L. Mott & Co was founded in the early 19th century as the Mott Iron Works stove business on Water Street, New York. The business was so successful that it was worth approximately £550,000 by 1870. From 1875 to 1878 the company had a showroom on Sixth Avenue, and by 1882 another had opened on Broadway.

A Coalbrookdale cast-iron garden bench, c1880, 38in (96.5cm) wide.

£490–550 AIN

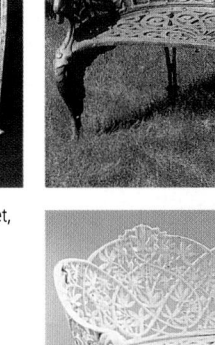

A cast-iron garden bench, cast with Passion Flower pattern, inscribed 'Hinderer's Iron Works New Orleans', America, c1900, 42in (106.5cm) wide.

£2,300–2,750 NOA

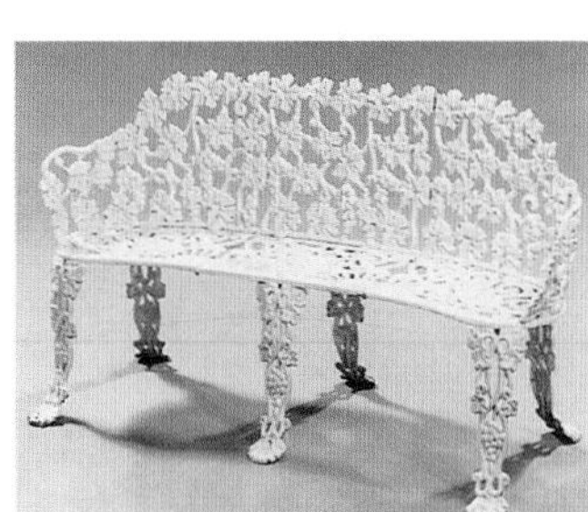

A cast-iron garden bench, cast with Vintage pattern, America, early 20thC, 56½in (143.5cm) wide.

£220–260 NOA

A cast-iron boot scraper, with griffin supports, early 19thC, 13in (33cm) wide.

£230–270 DN

A pair of William IV cast-iron boot scrapers, on paw feet, 18¼in (46.5cm) wide.

£2,600–3,100 S

► A pair of Regency iron chairs.

£250–280 AQ

A pair of cast-iron garden chairs, cast with Morning Glory pattern, Anglo-American, late 19thC.

£630–750 NOA

► A set of four cast-iron garden chairs, cast with Ram's Head pattern, c1900.

£720–800 HOP

A cast-iron Royal coat-of-arms, c1880, 59in (150cm) wide.
£5,700–6,800 S

A pair of wrought-iron gates, c1890, 164in (416.5cm) wide.
£7,600–8,500 WRe

A cast-iron gate, with scrollwork and a Tudor rose, late 19thC, 45in (114.5cm) wide.
£520–620 JBe

An Edwardian cast-iron radiator, with a detachable grille and feet, 26in (66cm) wide.
£200–240 SWO

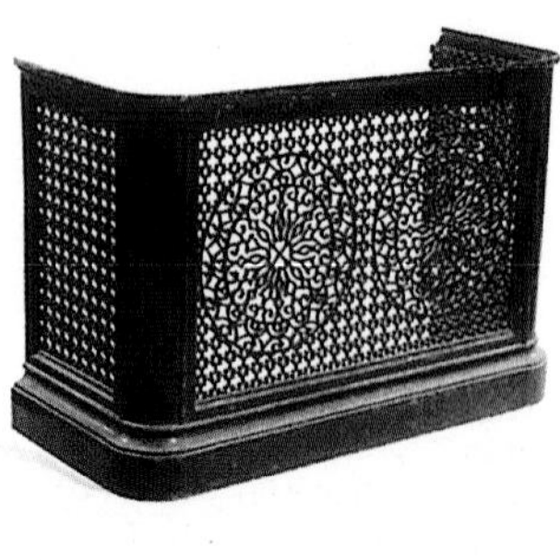

A Victorian cast-iron radiator cover, with a marble top, 51½in (131cm) wide.
£470–560 DN

A pair of wrought-iron room dividers, c1900, 58in (146cm) wide.
£5,400–6,400 S

A set of four cast-iron urns, each painted to resemble porphyry and with a flame finial, France, late 19thC, 45¼in (115cm) high.
£10,400–12,400 S(NY)

A pair of Victorian cast-iron garden urns, with floral swags, the handles with mask terminals, on pedestals, 18¼in (46.5cm) diam.
£1,250–1,500 N

A cast-iron garden urn, decorated with grapes and leaves, on a pedestal, America, late 19thC, 41in (104cm) wide.
£2,400–2,800 NOA

A near pair of painted cast-iron garden urns, each pedestal with three cranes, America, late 19thC, 22in (56cm) diam.
£1,400–1,650 NOA

A pair of cast-iron garden urns, early 20thC, 19in (48.5cm) diam.
£170–200 JAA

MARBLE

A marble font, on a later *faux* marble plinth, probably Italy, 18thC, 32½in (82.5cm) diam.

£7,100–8,500 S(NY)

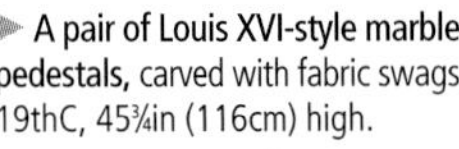

▶ **A pair of Louis XVI-style marble pedestals,** carved with fabric swags, 19thC, 45¾in (116cm) high.

£7,800–9,300 S(NY)

Two carved marble urns, reproductions of the Medici Urn and the Borghese Urn, with lead liners, Italy, 19thC, 42in (106.5cm) high.

£9,600–11,500 S(S)

The Medici Urn was first recorded in 1598 in the inventory of the Villa Medici, Rome, although there is evidence that it was there at least 30 years earlier. In 1780 it was removed to Florence and soon entered the Uffizi where it remains today. The vase was one of the most popularly reproduced antiquities and was commonly paired with the similarly shaped Borghese Urn. It is believed that the original was executed in the second half of the first century AD. The Borghese Urn was first recorded in 1594 and by 1645 had found its way into the Villa Borghese where it stayed until it was purchased by Napoleon in 1807. By 1811 it was on display in the Louvre, Paris, where it remains today. It is believed that the original was executed in the second half of the first century AD.

STONE

A stone birdbath, surmounted by a lead cherub, c1920, 30in (76cm) wide.

£760–850 WRe

A set of 12 composition stone columns, 1850–1900, 114in (289.5cm) high.

£9,600–11,500 S

These columns were made for Queen Victoria's visit to Weston-super-Mare, Somerset, and stood in the Winter Gardens.

A limestone gate finial, c1790, 24in (61cm) high.

£260–290 OLA

A pair of composition stone lions' heads, 1920s, 26in (66cm) square.

£3,150–3,500 OLA

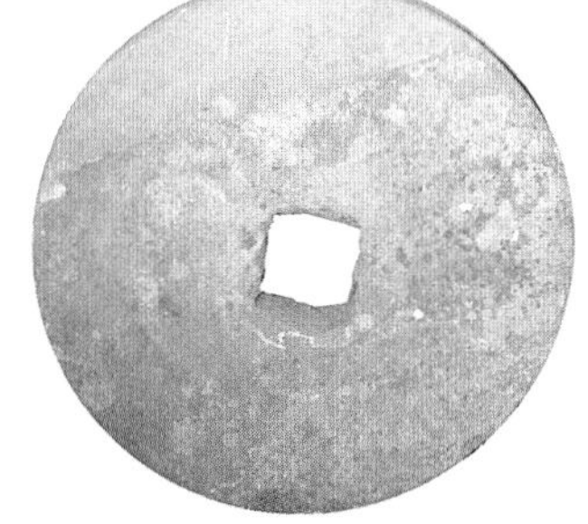

A sandstone millstone, 19thC, 25in (63.5cm) diam.

£165–185 HOP

A composition stone planter, in the form of a swan, 1920s, 32in (81.5cm) high.

£960–1,150 S

A carved stone trough, France, 19thC, 46½in (118cm) wide.

£1,050–1,250 S

◀ **A stone trough,** c1850, 28in (71cm) wide.

£310–350 WRe

Sets/pairs

Unless otherwise stated, any description which refers to 'a set' or 'a pair' includes a guide price for the entire set or the pair, even though the illustration may show only a single item.

A sandstone garden trough, with a central boss, 19thC, 26½in (67.5cm) diam.

£500–600 AH

A George III stone urn, on a plinth, 82¼in (209cm) high.

£8,800–10,500 DN

◀ **A pair of carved Cotswold stone urns,** 18th–19thC, 25in (63.5cm) diam.

£1,650–1,950 S

A set of three composition stone urn finials, c1920, 26in (66cm) high.

£1,050–1,200 OLA

TERRACOTTA

A terracotta roof finial, France, c1860, 24in (61cm) high.

£85–95 ALCH

A Gothic-style terracotta finial, c1880, 32in (81.5cm) high.

£105–120 RML

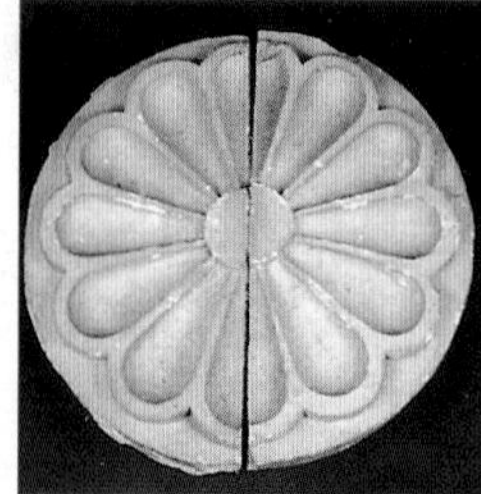

A terracotta roundel, cast with flutes, 19thC, 25¼in (64cm) diam.

£260–310 DN

◀ **A Victorian terracotta rhubarb forcing pot,** 27in (68.5cm) high.

£175–195 HOP

WOOD

A pair of carved oak brackets, c1720, 27in (68.5cm) wide.

£1,350–1,500 OLA

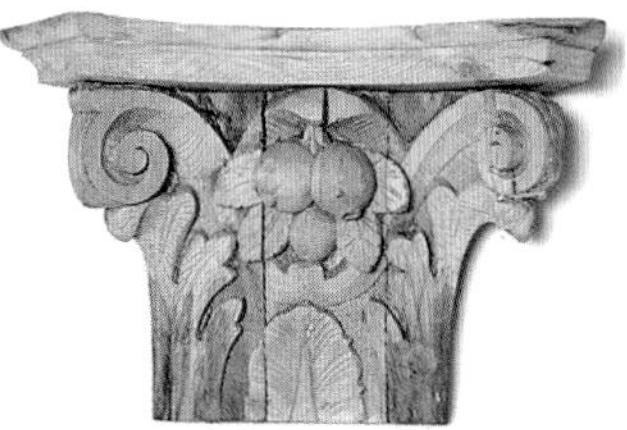

Ten carved pine capitals, c1880, 14in (35.5cm) high.

£1,800–2,000 RML

◄ **A pair of Louis XVI painted wood capitals,** France, late 18thC, 15in (38cm) wide.

£4,550–5,400 S(NY)

A pair of carved oak newel post finials, each in the form of a lion rampant, on marble bases, tails later, 17thC, 23in (58.5cm) high.

£1,700–2,000 AH

A carved eucalyptus panel, by John K. Blogg, carved with a Golden Wattle branch, signed, Australia, dated 1925, 20 x 11½in (51 x 30cm).

£6,000–7,200 LJ

A Victorian oak overmantel, carved with figures, incorporating 16th-century Franco-Flemish fragments, 63in (160cm) wide.

£1,300–1,550 S(O)

◄ **A set of four oak panels,** by Edward Pearce, carved with leaves and fruit, 1650–1700, largest 37½ x 10¼in (95.5 x 26cm).

£7,800–9,300 S

These panels are originally from the magnificent Charles II staircase at Wolseley Hall in Staffordshire. Edward Pearce (1635–95) worked with the leading architects of his day, including Christopher Wren with whom he worked on the chapel at Emmanuel College, Cambridge, supplying drawings for the ground plan, wainscot and seats. In London, Pearce was the master mason, or main building contractor, for four of Wren's churches and for parts of St Paul's Cathedral. He also worked at Chatsworth, Derbyshire, being named as a mason contractor in Wren's report of 1692 to the fifth earl of Devonshire on the costs of the south and east fronts, and at Hampton Court.

A carved and painted wood pediment, in the form of the Royal coat-of-arms, slight damage, early 19thC, 50½in (128.5cm) wide.

£940–1,100 DN(BR)

► **A carved and painted oak pew end,** the terminal in the form of a hare, inscribed 'Swallows' and 'Remember on Ye Mr Dales of Olde', early 16thC, 29¾in (75.5cm) high.

£2,850–3,400 S(O)

A set of pine niche shelves, c1775, 39in (99cm) wide.

£1,550–1,750 OLA

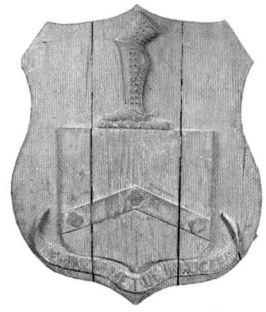

An oak armorial, carved with a coat-of-arms and the motto 'Neminem Metu E Innocens', 19thC, 51¼in (130cm) high.

£1,650–1,950 SWO

BATHROOM FITTINGS

A Victorian toleware bath, with a brass tap, on casters, 59in (150cm) wide.
£350–420 HOLL

► **A Shanks & Co ceramic canopy bath,** with chrome fittings, restored, c1900, 91in (231cm) high.
£8,100–9,000 DRU

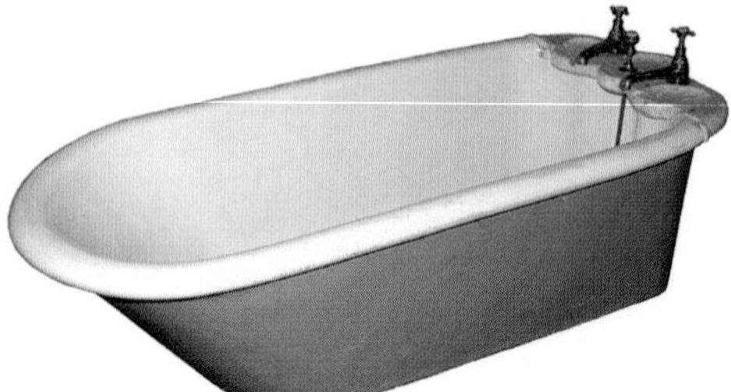

A Shanks & Co ceramic bath, with brass fittings and marble soap dish, c1900, 75in (190.5cm) wide.
£3,350–3,750 DRU

An iron bateau bath, on feet, c1900, 64in (162.5cm) wide.
£900–1,000 C&R

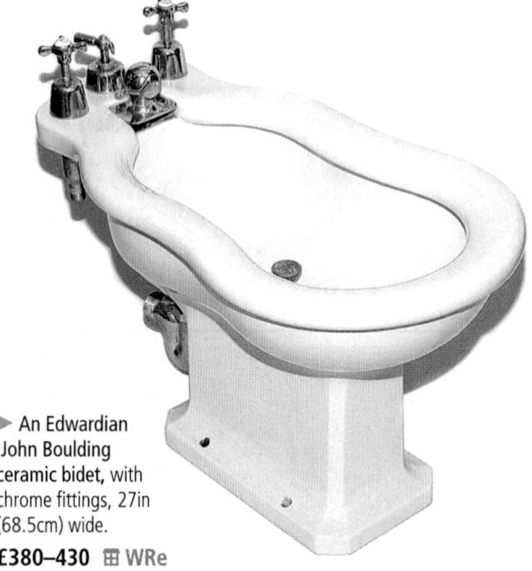

► **An Edwardian John Boulding ceramic bidet,** with chrome fittings, 27in (68.5cm) wide.
£380–430 WRe

A ceramic lavatory pan, commemorating Queen Victoria's Diamond Jubilee, with floral decoration, dated 1897, 17in (43cm) high.
£1,650–1,850 DRU

◄ **A Morrison Ingram & Co Triton Patent ceramic lavatory pan,** c1900, 17in (43cm) high.
£810–900 WRe

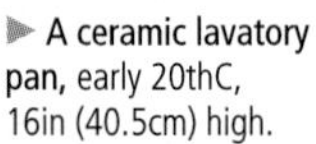

► **A ceramic lavatory pan,** early 20thC, 16in (40.5cm) high.
£760–850 OLA

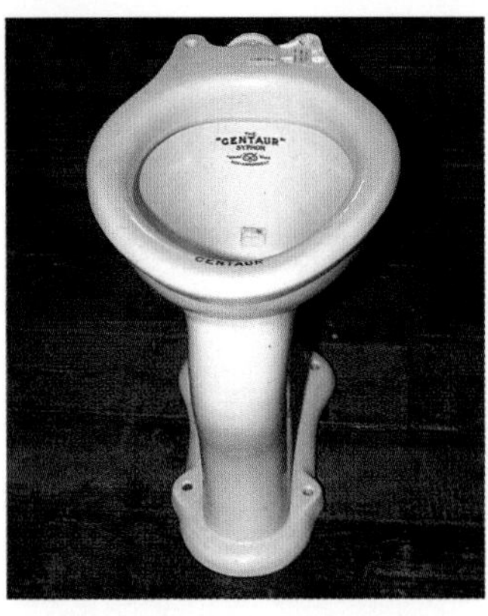

A Vitrina Ware ceramic Centaur Syphon lavatory pan, 1930s, 16in (40.5cm) high.

£790–880 ⊞ DRU

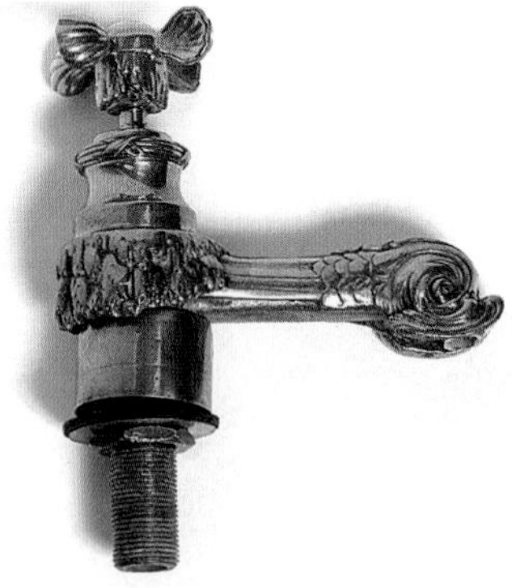

A pair of brass taps, with scallop shell handles and dolphin spouts, France, 19thC, 8in (20.5cm) high.

£1,600–1,800 ⊞ AUB

A pair of bronze taps, with swan neck handles, France, late 19thC, 10in (25.5cm) high.

£1,200–1,400 S

A pair of brass and copper bath taps, c1920, 8in (20.5cm) high.

£180–200 ⊞ WRe

A Victorian ceramic wash basin, with bracket, 30in (76cm) wide.

£1,250–1,400 ⊞ WRe

An Edwardian ceramic wash basin, decorated with flowers, with a cast-iron mirror frame, on a cast-iron stand, 75in (190.5cm) high.

£2,000–2,250 ⊞ DRU

► A ceramic wash basin, on a pedestal, with nickel taps and plunger waste, France, c1900, 33in (84cm) wide.

£1,750–1,950 ⊞ DRU

A marble wash basin, c1930, 27in (68.5cm) wide.

£580–650 ⊞ OLA

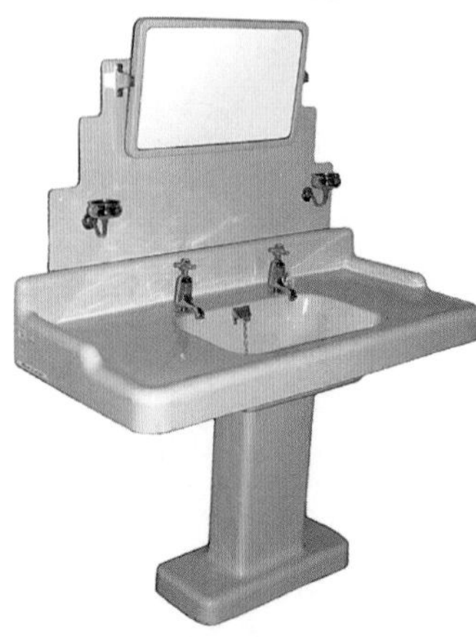

An Art Deco-style cast-iron and enamel wash basin, with a mirror, 1930s, 48in (122cm) wide.

£4,150–4,650 ⊞ DRU

For more Art Deco items, please see the Decorative Arts section on pages 367–440.

DOORS & DOOR FURNITURE

A pair of Louis XVI-style carved oak doors, with later stained wood architrave, 19thC, 45in (115cm) wide.

£2,400–2,850 S

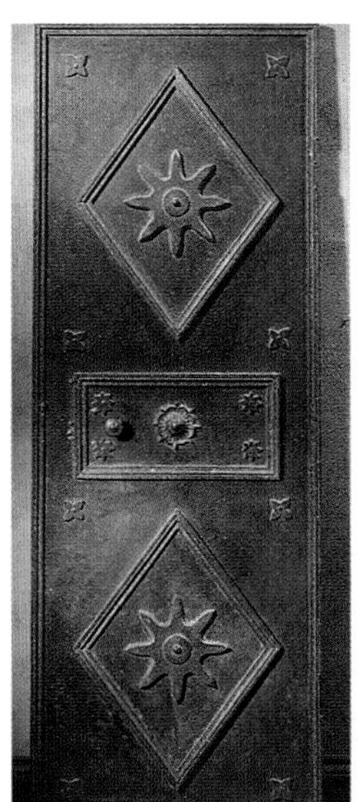

A cast-iron cellar door, France, early 19thC, 27in (68.5cm) wide.

£2,000–2,400 S

A painted pine door, c1840, 37in (94cm) wide.

£190–220 WRe

A pine entrance hall door and surround, with stained-glass windows depicting birds, c1890, 98½in (250cm) high.

£4,050–4,500 RML

A pair of pine doors, with stained-glass windows, c1890, 51in (129.5cm) wide.

£900–1,000 WRe

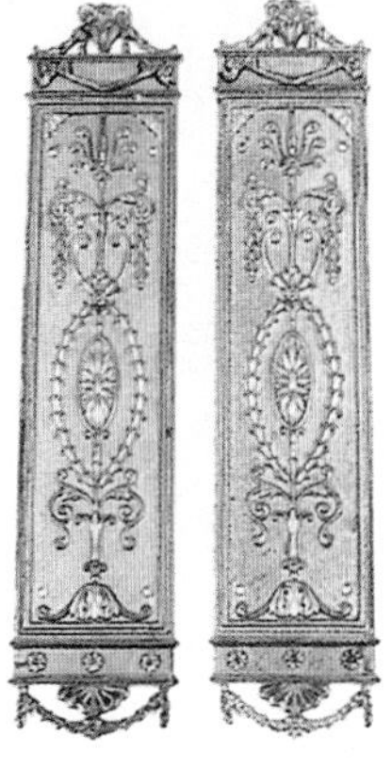

A pair of gilt-brass finger plates, by William Tonks, each cast with garrya, foliate scrolls and a ram's head, c1900, 13in (33cm) high.

£150–180 DN

A set of four Arts & Crafts copper hinges, c1900, largest 6in (15cm) wide.

£110–125 WAC

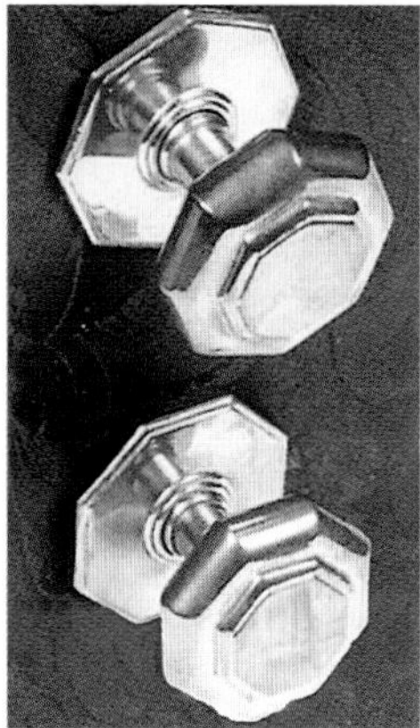

A pair of brass door handles, mid-19thC, 3¼in (8.5cm) high.

£210–250 DN

A steel door knocker, Italy, early 18thC, 11½in (29cm) high.

£2,900–3,450 S(NY)

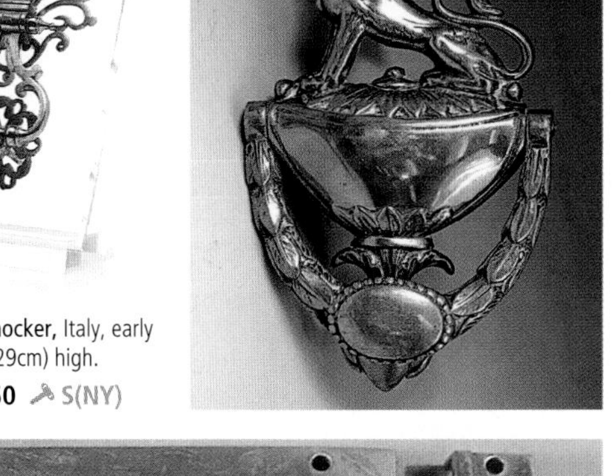

A George III brass door knocker, cast in the form of a sphinx on an urn, 8¾in (22cm) high.

£165–195 SWO

A Kendrick brass door knocker, after a design by Christopher Dresser, registration mark for 1877, 8in (20.5cm) high.

£210–250 DN

A brass door lock and keeper, engraved with scrolls, the keyhole with a swivel cover, 18thC, 7¾in (19.5cm) wide.

£320–380 PFK

FIREPLACES

A stone fire surround, France, Nancy, late 18thC, 56in (142cm) wide.
£9,100–10,900 S(P)

A George III marble fire surround, carved with classical maidens bathing a baby, with raised fruit pendants, 55in (139.5cm) wide.
£43,000–52,000 DMC

A Victorian mahogany fire surround, with a carved frieze above a mirror flanked by wrythen-turned columns, 70in (178cm) wide.
£640–760 AH

A stained oak fire surround, with a mirror above a serpentine shelf, c1900, 61in (155.5cm) wide.
£230–270 PFK

A Pugin-style iron fire grate, with brass finials, 19thC, 30in (76cm) wide.
£330–390 SWO

A Victorian brass and steel fire grate, by T. Elsley, decorated with a griffin, 23½in (59.5cm) wide.
£540–640 WW

A cast-iron fire grate, the ceramic tiles decorated with leaves, c1880, 38in (96.5cm) wide.
£470–530 WRe

► **A cast-iron and brass stove,** c1830, 32in (81.5cm) wide.
£3,150–3,500 OLA

◄ **A Fiala Stoveworks Radstädter Keramic oven,** the tiles decorated with stags, trees and the Virgin and Child, Austria, c1880, 39in (99cm) wide.
£17,500–21,000 DORO

FIREPLACE ACCESSORIES

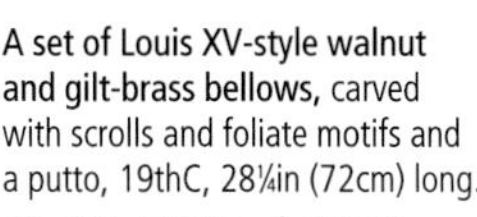

A set of Louis XV-style walnut and gilt-brass bellows, carved with scrolls and foliate motifs and a putto, 19thC, 28¼in (72cm) long.
£2,600–3,100 S(NY)

An oak and brass coal scuttle, c1900, 13in (33cm) wide.
£220–250 PWS

A cast-iron fireback, cast with a giraffe and its keeper, France, c1830, 29½in (75cm) wide.
£9,700–11,600 S(P)

The design on this fireback commemorates the gift to France in 1827 of a giraffe by Mehmet Ali, pasha of Egypt.

A cast-iron fireback, cast with the French Royal coat-of-arms and foliage, France, c1900, 32in (81.5cm) wide.
£3,250–3,900 S(NY)

◀ **A set of oak and brass Westmorland breezer bellows,** with a leather pulley, 19thC, 24in (61cm) long.
£260–310 Mit

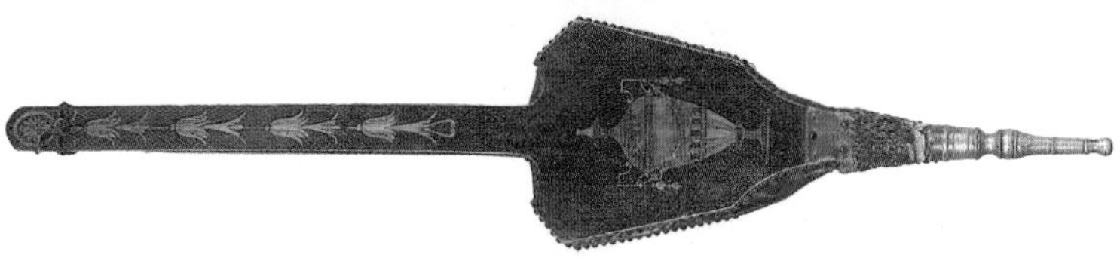

An Edwardian set of mahogany and brass bellows, inlaid with an urn and harebells, 45½in (115.5cm) long.
£120–140 DA

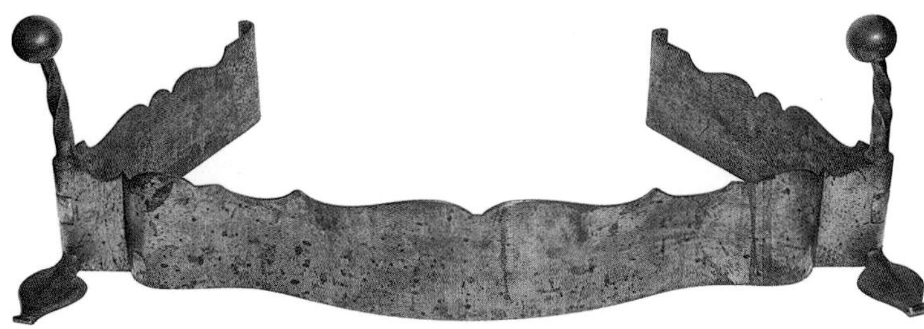

A Thomas Hadden & Sons wrought-iron fender, designed by Sir Robert Lorimer, c1906, 26in (66cm) wide.
£1,550–1,750 JSG

The firm of Thomas Hadden & Sons was founded in Scotland in 1901 and specialized in high quality wrought-iron work. Hadden's most significant professional relationship was with Sir Robert Lorimer, Scotland's premier architect and designer who worked in the Arts & Crafts style with particular reference to Scotland's vernacular traditions.

A pair of brass andirons, by R. Wittingham, stamped mark, America, New York, 18th–19thC, 23in (58.5cm) high.
£4,850–5,800 NAAW

Richard Wittingham worked in New York from 1785 to 1818.

A pair of brass andirons, c1900, 27in (68.5cm) high.
£1,600–1,800 RML

A set of steel fire irons, comprising a pair of tongs, shovel and poker, Russia, possibly Tula, c1800, 30in (76cm) high.
£8,400–10,000 S(NY)

▶ **An Adam revival brass hearth suite,** comprising a fender and a pair of andirons, cast with rams' masks, swags, pendants and rosettes, early 20thC, fender 52in (132cm) wide.
£220–260 N

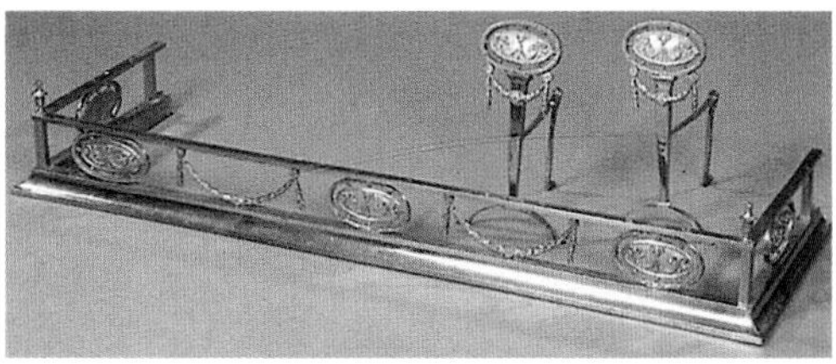

FOUNTAINS

A lead fountain head, in the form of a Bacchus mask, 19thC, 9in (23cm) wide.

£560–670 DN

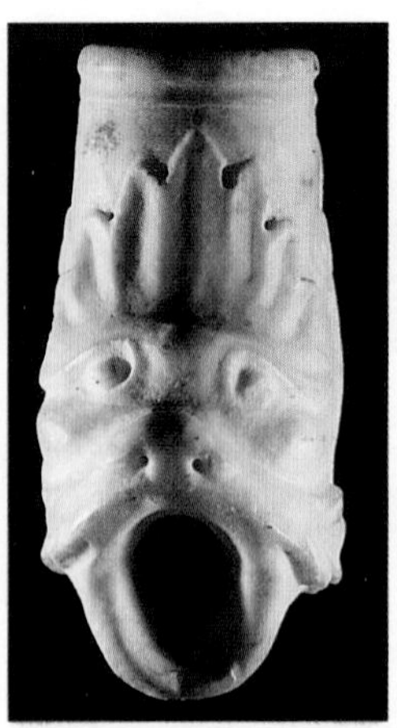

◄ **A marble fountain spout,** Italy, 19thC, 9in (23cm) high.

£900–1,050 S

► **A Coalbrookdale cast-iron fountain,** with a brass rose, stamped mark, c1870, 28in (71cm) high.

£2,250–2,700 S(S)

This rare fountain is illustrated in the 1875 Coalbrookdale catalogue.

A cast-iron fountain, decorated with a mask, France, c1870, 51in (129.5cm) high.

£5,000–6,000 S

A Blanchard stoneware fountain, carved in the form of Triton, shells and dolphins, c1870, 51in (129.5cm) high.

£17,400–20,800 S(S)

Mark Henry Blanchard served his apprenticeship with the Coade Company and established his own manufactory in London around 1839. By the middle of the 19th century he had emerged as the leading manufacturer of terracotta in Britain, and was awarded prizes for his exhibit at the Great Exhibition of 1851. It is believed that in 1883 he moved his workshops to Bishop's Waltham, Hampshire, to be nearer the source of clay that he used.

STATUARY

A carved sandstone bust of a gentleman, 19thC, 25in (63.5cm) high.

£680–810 BWL

A marble figure of Pulcinella, from the Commedia dell'Arte, with an associated stone plinth, probably Continental, 19thC, 48in (122cm) high.

£1,650–1,950 TEN

The Commedia dell'Arte was a form of comedy performed in Italy from the 16th to the 18th centuries.

◄ **A carved stone bust of a city father,** inscribed 'Pickering', 19thC, 23in (58.5cm) high.

£560–670 Hal

A marble bust, c1855, 45in (114.5cm) high.

£1,300–1,450 NORTH

A cast-iron figure of Venus bathing, after Falconet, France, c1870, 67in (170cm) high.

£5,700–6,800 S(S)

Etienne Maurice Falconet studied under Lemoyne and was elected as a member of the Paris Academy in 1754, becoming professor in 1761. He was the director of sculpture for the Sèvres porcelain factory between 1757 and 1766 and counted Madame Pompadour among his patrons.

Two cast-iron herons, probably by Fiske, America, 1875–1900, 22in (56cm) high.

£1,550–1,850 S

The Fiske Foundry was set up by Joseph Winn Fiske in New York in 1858. It was one of the first foundries to popularize the use of alloys and zinc for fountain figures since, unlike iron, they are not susceptible to rust. Not all wares are marked.

An Austin & Seeley composition stone Mansion House dwarf, c1900, 29in (73.5cm) high.

£7,200–8,600 S

Austin & Seeley, founded in 1828, were probably the earliest manufacturers of artificial stone, which they declared 'requires no painting or colouring, and will not sustain injury from the severest winter'.

A lead figure of Mercury, c1910, 55in (139.5cm) high.

£1,300–1,450 OLA

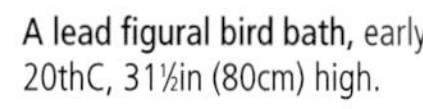

A lead figural bird bath, early 20thC, 31½in (80cm) high.

£300–360 SWO

WINDOWS

An oak mullioned window frame, with pegged joints, late 16thC, 16½ x 39¾in (42 x 101cm).

£700–840 PFK

A pair of stained glass window panels, possibly by Williams Gamon & Co, comprising three panes depicting bishops, soldiers, damsels and Middle Eastern merchants, 1900–10, framed 35 x 60in (89 x 152.5cm).

£2,350–2,800 Hal

A pair of Swaine Bourne stained glass and leaded windows, representing dusk and dawn, one decorated with an owl and bat, the other with a crane and dragonfly, c1900, each panel 19½in (49.5cm) square, in a wooden frame.

£2,800–3,350 PFK

◄ **A stained glass window panel,** in two parts, decorated with a pair of stylized fish and flowers, early 20thC, each panel 57 x12in (145 x 30.5cm).

£260–310 G(L)

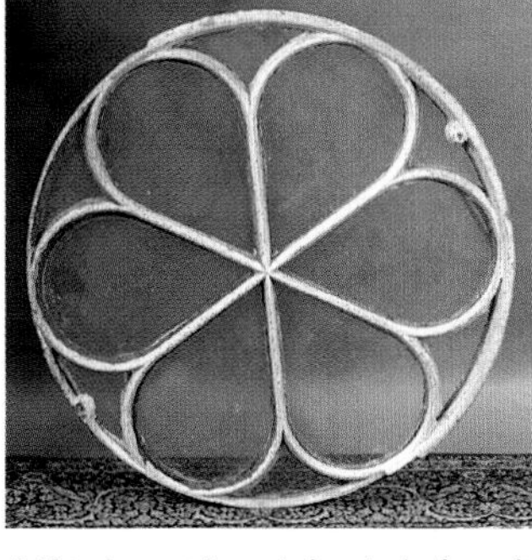

A Victorian cast-iron window, in the form of a flowerhead, 37½in (95.5cm) diam.

£730–870 SWO

A Gothic-style Bath stone window, late 19thC, 56½in (145.5cm) wide.

£1,400–1,650 S

► **A stained glass window,** by Henry Keck, entitled 'Holy Mary', c1920, 79 x 27½in (200.5 x 70cm).

£1,750–2,100 JAA

Born in Germany in 1873, Keck emigrated to America at an early age and was apprenticed at the stained glass workshop of Louis Comfort Tiffany for 15 years. Eventually, Keck opened his own stained glass studio in 1903 and by 1920 he had earned a reputation as one of the foremost designers of stained glass.

SCULPTURE

A carved and gilt figure of an **apostle,** with painted decoration, Belgium, Antwerp, early 16thC, 11½in (29cm) high.

£1,050–1,250 S(O)

A pair of alabaster figures of soldiers astride lions, with gilt and painted decoration, restored, Sicily, 17thC, 8½in (21.5cm) high.

£4,200–5,000 S(NY)

A bronze model of a toad carrying its young, restored, north Italy, 17thC, 3½in (8.5cm) high.

£2,150–2,550 S

◄ **A bronze group of Leda and the Swan,** after a model by Massimiliano Soldani-Benzi, repaired, Italy, Florence, early 18thC, 11½in (29cm) high.

£8,400–10,000 S(NY)

Soldani-Benzi studied in Rome where he executed portrait medals for several influential royal and papal patrons. After a ten-month sojourn with King Louis XIV in France, he returned to his native Florence, where his work included a commission for John Churchill, 1st Duke of Marlborough. His body of work, incorporating unusual compositions and delicate castings and chasing, made Soldani one of the most sought-after sculptors of the late 17th and early 18th centuries.

Market Information

Sculpture is a category of fine art and therefore often purchased by those who also collect paintings. Demand is steady and enthusiastic and, therefore, sculpture currently represents a prudent investment, as the field does not appear to have suffered the same misfortunes as other areas, such as brown furniture for instance.

A terracotta half-figure of the 'river god' Tiber, some losses, Italy or France, 18thC, 14in (35.5cm) high.

£5,200–6,200 S(NY)

This model, paired with a figure of the River Nile, became popular when the famous colossal antique Roman marbles were excavated in 1512 in Rome. Various reproductions are known, particularly bronzes made in France in the 17th and 18th centuries.

A stained wood group of St Rochus and a dog, Spain, c1800, 33in (84cm) high.

£2,000–2,400 BERN

A terracotta bust of Beaumarchais, France, c1800, 34¼in (87cm) high.

£5,200–6,200 S(NY)

Pierre Augustin Caron de Beaumarchais (1732–99) was the son of a watchmaker and learned the same trade, eventually producing watches for Mme de Pompadour and other members of the court. Passionate about music, Beaumarchais later rose up in society by writing some of the most famous comedies of the period, including Le Barbier de Seville *and* Le Marriage de Figaro.

◄ **A terracotta bust of the sculptor's daughter,** after Jean Antoine Houdon, entitled 'Sabine', c1860, 19in (48.5cm) high.

£1,950–2,200 CRU

◄ **A marble bust of Caesar Augustus,** socle repaired, early 19thC, 22in (56cm) high.

£2,350–2,650 LGr

A bronze figure of Cleopatra, reclining on a day bed, 19thC, 13in (33cm) wide.

£520–620 G(L)

A bronze and gilt figure of a putto, with gilt flowers, on a marble base, 19thC, 14in (35.5cm) wide.

£1,200–1,350 SPUR

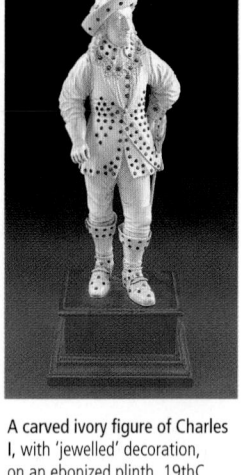

A carved ivory figure of Charles I, with 'jewelled' decoration, on an ebonized plinth, 19thC, 15in (38cm) high.

£3,750–4,500 G(L)

A carved ivory figure of Napoleon Bonaparte, France, 19thC, 4¾in (12cm) high.

£300–360 ROS

A cold-painted spelter figure of an Arab, by Louis Hottot, France, 19thC, 29¼in (74.5cm) high.

£1,650–1,950 S(O)

A carved marble figure of a young woman seated on a cushion, slight damage, signed, Italy, 19thC, 15½in (39.5cm) high.

£1,700–2,000 CAG

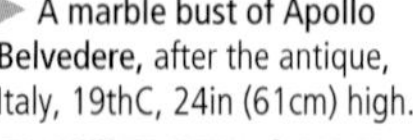

► **A marble bust of Apollo Belvedere,** after the antique, Italy, 19thC, 24in (61cm) high.

£3,300–3,950 WAD

◄ **A Russian School bronze group of a Cossack on horseback leading a packhorse,** on a marble plinth, signed in Cyrillic, Russia, 19thC, 18in (45.5cm) wide.

£2,300–2,750 CAG

A bronze figure of a boy, by Jose Cardona, entitled 'Newsboy', stamped and numbered, signed, Spain, 19thC, 13in (33cm) high.

£280–330 JAA

A plaster bust of the Reverend Thomas Chalmers, by Sir John Steel, signed, dated 1846, 20½in (52cm) high.

£340–400 WW

The Reverend Chalmers was a Scottish preacher and social reformer. There is a similar bust of Chalmers in the Scottish National Portrait Gallery.

A patinated bronze group, in the manner of J. J. Pradier, entitled 'Maternité', base signed 'Moreau', France, c1875, 10in (25.5cm) high.

£1,050–1,250 NOA

A patinated bronze figure of a female lute player, on a slate base, Germany, 1850–75, 6½in (16.5cm) high.

£600–720 NOA

◄ **A bronze model of a tiger slaying a young camel,** by Christophe Fratin, signed, France, 19thC, 15¾in (40cm) wide.

£1,400–1,650 JAA

A bronze classical figural group of a mother and child, France, c1870, 16in (40.5cm) high.

£1,900–2,250 TEN

A bronze bust of Napoleon, by Emile Placide Lambert, the base with an eagle, France, c1875, 4½in (11.5cm) high.

£1,050–1,200 HAZ

A plaster of Paris classical bust of a man, by Evelyn Pickering, slight damage, signed and dated 1873, 30½in (77.5cm) high.

£2,050–2,450 DN

Evelyn Pickering, perhaps better known as the wife of the eminent potter William de Morgan (1839–1917), was herself a very accomplished artist. Painting in the Pre-Raphaelite style, her work was full of allegory and symbolism. She studied at the Slade School where she was one of the first female students and her uncle, the artist Roddam Spencer Stanhope, a member of the Pre-Raphaelite Brotherhood, helped to shape her style. He lived in Florence and she made frequent visits to him to study the Renaissance masters. G. F. Watts said of her 'I look upon her as the first woman artist of the day – if not of all time'. The date of this piece would indicate its creation during her Slade years.

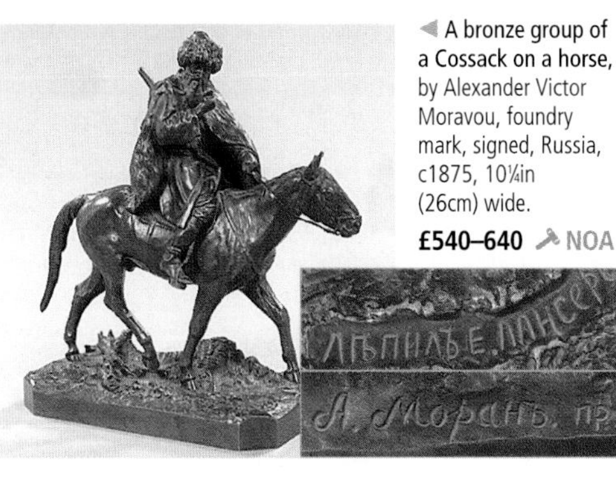

◀ **A bronze group of a Cossack on a horse,** by Alexander Victor Moravou, foundry mark, signed, Russia, c1875, 10¼in (26cm) wide.

£540–640 NOA

A gilt-bronze model of a fox and a rabbit, by Clovis Masson, on a marble base, France, c1890, 5in (12.5cm) wide.

£990–1,100 HAZ

◀ **A pair of gilt-bronze figures of a Samurai and *bijin*,** attributed to Emile-Coriolan Hippolyte Guillemin, France, c1875, 24¾in (63cm) high.

£10,600–12,700 TEN

Emile-Coriolan Hippolyte Guillemin was a leading Parisian sculptor who often collaborated with furniture-makers and designers. He exhibited at the Salon from 1870 onwards and won an honourable mention in 1897.

A bronze figural group, by Grachev (probably Vassili Yacovlevitch), entitled 'A Troika Driver and His Passenger', signed and marked, Russia, c1875, 10¾in (27.5cm) wide.

£3,300–3,950 JAA

An alabaster figure of a boy fishing, by Raffaello Romanelli, signed and dated 1876, Italy, 24½in (62cm) high.

£2,400–2,850 S(O)

A bronze figure of a woman carrying a basket of fruit, by Emile Pinedo, entitled 'L'Esclave', France, c1880, 30in (76cm) high.

£4,050–4,500 HAZ

A patinated bronze figure of a man, on a wood plinth, by Emma-Marie Cadwallader Guild, on a bronze base and wood plinth, signed and dated 1887, America, 17½in (44.5cm) high.

£1,750–2,100 S(P)

A terracotta bust of a Native American girl, by Henri-Louis Cordier, on a later granite base, signed, France, dated 1893, 14¼in (36cm) high.

£960–1,150 S

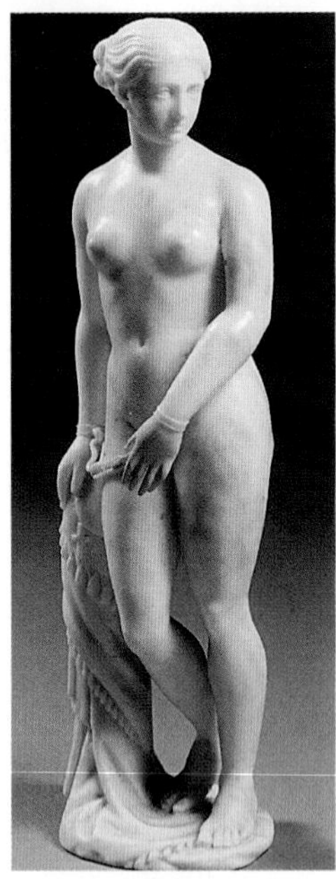

An alabaster figure of a woman, after Hiram Powers, entitled 'The Greek Slave', late 19thC, 28in (71cm) high.

£1,800–2,150 S(O)

The American sculptor Hiram Powers established himself in Florence in 1837 and made busts and statues of prominent personages including Longfellow and General Sheridan. The Greek Slave, which was exhibited at the Great Exhibition of 1851, received great acclaim and was one of the most talked about statues of the 19th century.

A gilt-bronze model of a lioness, by Clovis Masson, on a marble base, France, c1895, 5in (12.5cm) high.

£940–1,050 HAZ

A bronze model of a cat seated on a pile of books concealing a mouse, by Jean Carrit, cat's eyes light up, electrified, France, signed, late 19thC, 27½in (70cm) high.

£4,700–5,600 DN(HAM)

◄ **A bronze group of lovers in a carriage drawn by three horses,** by G. Guradze, on a marble base, signed, late 19thC, 18¼in (46.5cm) wide.

£870–1,000 BERN

A bronze figure of a young woman standing by an amphora, by Georges Charles Coudray, entitled 'Kidda', signed, France, c1895, 29½in (75cm) high.

£5,400–6,000 BeF

A bust of a boy, by Prince Paul Troubetzkoy, signed, Italy, Milan, dated 1897, 19¾in (50cm) high.

£11,500–12,800 BeF

A marble figure of a classical maiden sitting on a bench, late 19thC, 28in (71cm) high.

£1,750–2,100 BWL

A figure of St Ignatius, c1900, 43in (109cm) high.

£670–750 RML

► **A bronze figure of a woman with a butterfly,** by Professor V. H. Seifert, on a marble base, Austria, c1900, 18¾in (47.5cm) high.

£3,150–3,500 HAZ

A bronze figure of a woodland dryad playing a pipe, by E. Drouot, entitled 'Muse des Bois', signed, France, c1900, 27in (68.5cm) high.

£2,250–2,700 PFK

LOCATE THE SOURCE

The source of each illustration in Miller's can be found by checking the code letters below each caption with the Key to Illustrations, pages 746–753.

A gilt-bronze figure of a Cossack with a borzoi, on a malachite base, Russia, c1900, 3½in (9cm) high.

£260–310 FFAP

A figure of a boy mariner sitting on a capstan, by Antoine Bofill, Spain, c1900, 16½in (42cm) high.

£2,250–2,500 HAZ

A painted plaster figure of St Francis, c1900, 46in (117cm) high.

£670–750 RML

◄ **A carved wood model of a stag,** Switzerland, c1900, 14in (35.5cm) wide.

£400–450 WB

◄ **A bronze model of a seal,** by Frederick George Richard Roth, stamped and inscribed 'Roman Bronze Works N.Y. 1904', America, 6½in (16.5cm) wide.

£2,550–3,050 JAA

A carved alabaster model of a heron, France, early 20thC, 22½in (57cm) high.

£2,150–2,550 S

A bronze bust of a woman, by Alfred Drury, entitled 'Griselda', on a marble plinth, signed and dated 1901, 14½in (37cm) high.

£1,800–2,150 S

A bronze figure of a crouching man, by Paul Wayland Bartlett, signed, America, late 19thC, 8½in (21.5cm) high.

£1,900–2,250 S(P)

An identical statue, signed and dated '96' is in the Musée d'Orsay in Paris.

A pair of marble busts, one depicting Bacchus, the other a Roman noblewoman, Italy, early 20thC, 35½in (90cm) high.

£11,000–13,200 S(NY)

A cold-painted and gilt-bronze group of a Native American and a horse, by T. Curts, tomahawk head missing, Austria, early 20thC, 13in (33cm) high.

£4,000–4,800 RTo

An Italian School carved alabaster bust of a woman, entitled 'Beatrice', c1920, 8in (20.5cm) wide.

£160–190 JAA

A cold-painted bronze model of an Alsatian, Austria, Vienna, c1920, 5½in (14cm) high.

£360–400 RdeR

A cold-painted bronze model of a pheasant, Austria, Vienna, c1920, 8in (20.5cm) wide.

£270–300 RdeR

MARBLE & MINERALS

A pair of agate candlesticks, with silver metal mounts, damaged and repaired, late 17thC, 6¼in (16cm) high.
£2,600–3,100 S(O)

► **A pair of Ashford marble candlesticks,** inlaid with specimen marbles, c1870, 13in (33cm) high.
£500–600 BAM

◄ **A marble obelisk,** carved with hieroglyphics, engraved 'Obelisk called Cleopatra's Needle at Alexandria', 19thC, 10¾in (27.5cm) high.
£175–210 DN

A blue john column, with a brass capital, on a marble base, slight damage, 19thC, 6¼in (41.5cm) high.
£1,750–2,100 DN

A blue john goblet, 19thC, 4¾in (12cm) high.
£1,450–1,700 DN

A blue john tazza, repaired, 19thC, 9½in (24cm) wide.
£1,400–1,650 MAL(O)

◄ **A pair of marble tazze,** Continental, 19thC, 13in (33cm) diam.
£4,850–5,800 S(NY)

◄ **A blue john urn,** attributed to Richard Brown of Derby, on an Ashford marble base, c1790, 10¼in (26cm) high.
£3,000–3,600 BAM

From its distinct neo-classical shape, its obvious quality and the absence of ormolu, this piece can probably be attributed to Richard Brown of Derby, trading as Brown, Son & Maw, possibly from the period just prior to his move to purpose-built marble works in Kings Street in 1801–02.

► **A porphyry urn,** Sweden, 1800–50, 9¾in (25cm) high.
£1,750–2,100 BUK

A Cornish serpentine urn, early 20thC, 8¼in (21cm) diam.
£200–240 DN

METALWARE

BRASS

A brass tobacco box, with a lion-mask cover, c1810, 4in (10cm) high.

£145–165 PeN

A set of six Goldsmiths of Lyon gilt-brass candlesticks, by Pierre Ballay, stamped 'Ballay', France, c1740, 36¼in (92cm) high.

£7,200–8,600 S

A pair of brass candlesticks, c1880, 18in (45.5cm) high.

£180–200 WAC

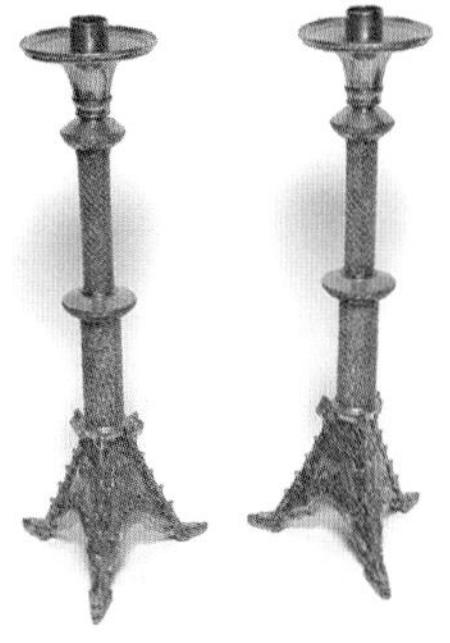

A pair of Gothic revival brass candlesticks, c1890, 22in (56cm) high.

£220–250 TOP

A pair of C. H. Grun brass candlesticks, Poland, Warsaw, early 20thC, 14½in (37cm) high.

£330–390 WAD

A gilt-brass and enamel dressing table set, comprising nine pieces, France, c1900.

£1,150–1,350 WAD

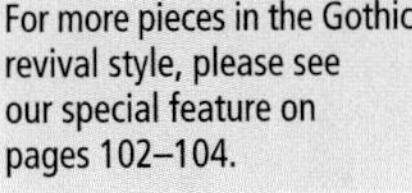

For more pieces in the Gothic revival style, please see our special feature on pages 102–104.

► A brass soap dish, the hinged cover with pierced decoration, mid-18thC, 3½in (9cm) wide.

£700–840 DN

A Victorian brass snuff box, in the form of a coffin, with iron mounts, 3½in (9cm) long.

£145–170 PFK

A brass stick stand, c1890, 32in (81.5cm) high.

£260–290 PICA

A brass teapot, with a ceramic finial, on leafy pad feet, 19thC, 8¼in (21cm) high.

£105–125 DN

◄ A pair of brass vases, c1900, 25in (63.5cm) high.

£760–850 RML

◄ A late George III brass wax jack, 5¼in (13.5cm) high.

£330–390 WW

BRONZE

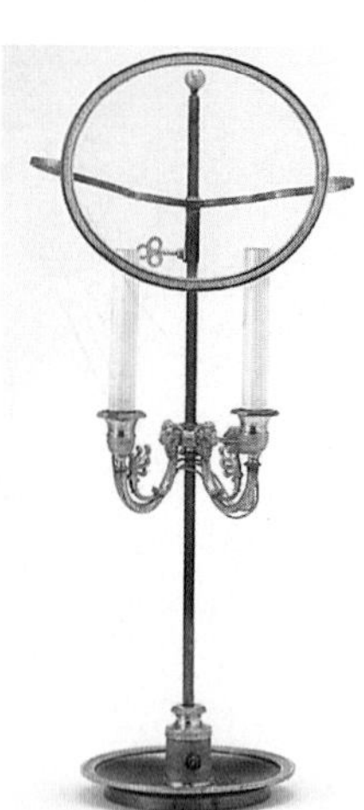

◄ **An ormolu and patinated bronze candelabrum,** fitted for electricity, Russia, late 18thC, 23in (58.5cm) high.
£4,550–5,400 S(NY)

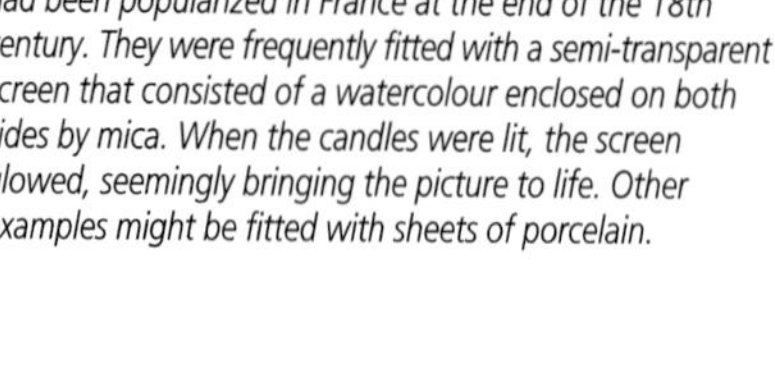

Lamps of this type were found in the drawing rooms of fashionable Russian society in the early 19th century and they seem to be a development of the bouillotte *lamp that had been popularized in France at the end of the 18th century. They were frequently fitted with a semi-transparent screen that consisted of a watercolour enclosed on both sides by mica. When the candles were lit, the screen glowed, seemingly bringing the picture to life. Other examples might be fitted with sheets of porcelain.*

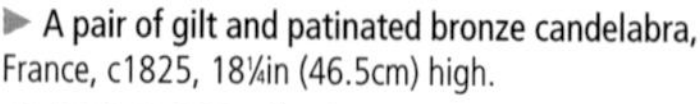

► **A pair of gilt and patinated bronze candelabra,** France, c1825, 18¼in (46.5cm) high.
£2,900–3,450 S(NY)

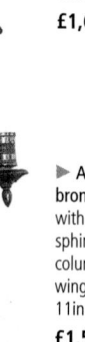

◄ **A pair of bronze sconces,** France, 1815–30, 8in (20.5cm) high.
£1,600–1,800 AUB

► **A pair of bronze and gilt-bronze incense burners,** each with a bowl supported on three sphinx-headed monopodia on columns shouldered with winged sceptres, France, 19thC, 11in (28cm) high.
£1,500–1,800 G(L)

A bronze and brass samovar, c1820, 17in (43cm) high.
£300–340 SPUR

COPPER

◄ **A copper coffee pot,** with a yew-wood handle, c1740, 10in (25.5cm) high.
£220–250 PeN

A copper and wrought-iron jardinière, c1910, 26in (66cm) high.
£230–270 PICA

A copper jug, with silver-plated mounts, the hinged cover applied with the head of a moose, America, c1900, 18in (45.5cm) high.
£880–1,050 AH

◄ **A copper samovar,** with a brass tap, early 19thC, 13½in (34.5cm) high.
£90–105 GTH

► **A Victorian copper hot water jug,** impressed mrks, 17¼in (44cm) high.
£120–140 PFK

IRON

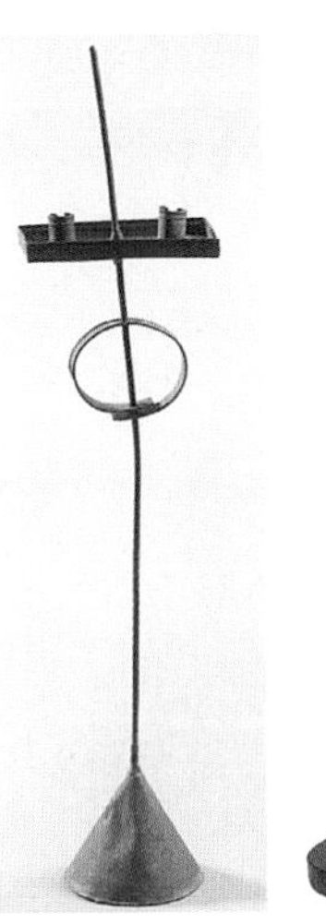

An iron and tin candlestick, America, New England, 18thC, 32½in (83cm) high.

£650–780 NAAW

A cast-iron pricket candlestick, c1880, 23in (58.5cm) high.

£310–350 PeN

A Tula steel chamberstick, engraved with foliage, the handle and nozzle with a beaded border, Russia, early 19thC, 8in (20.5cm) high.

£4,550–5,400 S(NY)

The Tula Arms Manufactory was established in 1712 and rapidly became the centre of the Russian arms industry. By the second quarter of the century the craftsmen of Tula began to create distinctive works of art for domestic use in polished and cut steel. Many such items, including steel furniture, were provided for the Imperial palaces, especially the palace of Pavlovsk. A large collection of works by the Tula masters can be found preserved in the collection of the State Hermitage Museum, St Petersburg. Tula pieces are highly sought after.

A Regency cast-iron casket, the hinged cover with foliate decoration, above a panel decorated with figures, with lion-mask handles, brass lock stamped 'T. Davis, London', 26½in (67.5cm) wide.

£1,400–1,650 DMC

◄ **A Victorian painted cast-iron doorstop,** decorated with scrolling leaves, 13¾in (35cm) high.

£220–260 WW

► **A cast-iron doorstop,** c1850, 15in (38cm) high.

£140–165 PeN

A cast-iron umbrella stand, France, c1890, 30in (76cm) high.

£1,300–1,450 WAA

ORMOLU

A pair of ormolu figural candelabra, France, c1820, 25¼in (64cm) high.

£5,200–6,200 S(NY)

A pair of Louis XV-style ormolu and porcelain urns, the Sèvres-style panels painted with figures, indistinctly stamped, c1870, 11in (28cm) high.

£175–210 Hal

An ormolu urn, decorated in relief with cherubs and fauns, on an openwork base, Continental, c1900, 20in (51cm) high.

£860–1,000 LCM

PEWTER

A set of four pewter footed **beakers,** Continental, dated 1841, 4in (10cm) high.

£175–195 PeN

A set of three pewter candelabra, c1880, 15in (38cm) high.

£940–1,050 PeN

A pewter chalice, inscribed 'This is the Communion Cup, Church of St James, Kinnieborough 1742', 8in (20.5cm) high.

£280–330 GIL

Condition

The condition is absolutely vital when assessing the value of an antique. Damaged pieces on the whole appreciate much less than perfect examples. However, a rare desirable piece may command a high price even when damaged.

A Charles II pewter charger, the rim engraved with wrigglework, oak leaves and acorns, the centre a coat-of-arms and initials, stamped marks, damaged, 20¼in (51.5cm) diam.

£13,800–16,500 WW

A pewter rose-water bowl, with a central boss, stamped 'I.C.', 1600–25, 17¼in (44cm) diam.

£3,600–4,300 S(O)

Rose-water bowls appear from the 16th century onwards. They were used as finger bowls to rinse the grease from diners' fingers while seated at the table. A fine example such as this would have belonged to a wealthy owner.

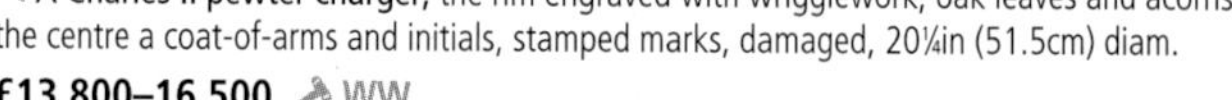

MILLER'S COMPARES

I. **A set of four pewter chargers,** by Adam Bankes, Chester, two damaged, marked, c1700, 18in (45.5cm) diam.

£940–1,100 Hal

II. **A set of four pewter chargers,** by Robert Baldwin, Wigan, one damaged, marked, c1700, 16¾in (42.5cm) diam.

£370–440 Hal

Pieces by Adam Bankes, the maker of the chargers shown in Item I, are much rarer than those by Robert Baldwin, the maker of the pieces shown in Item II. Also, the patina of Item I is a better colour and has built up over a very long time, whereas the chargers in item II are not of such a good colour. It is worth noting that if the patina has been removed it can reduce the value of a piece by as much as 90 per cent.

A set of four pewter plates, by J. Spackman, London, c1760, 10in (25.5cm) diam.

£850–950 PeN

A pewter ale jug, c1820, 6in (15cm) high.

£140–155 PeN

A Victorian pewter ale jug, 6½in (16.5cm) high.

£65–75 LGr

TOLEWARE

A toleware pierced cake basket, painted with flowers, early 19thC, 14½in (37cm) wide.

£2,350–2,800 DN

A George III toleware coffee pot, with vermicelli decoration, 10¾in (27.5cm) high.

£300–360 DN

A toleware snuff box, the hinged cover decorated with a harvest trophy, 19thC, 3¼in (8.5cm) wide.

£190–220 DN

A toleware snuff box, Wales, Pontypool, 1850, 3in (7.5cm) wide.

£135–150 HUM

► **A toleware tea canister and cover,** later painted with an Oriental man, converted for use as a table lamp, early 19thC, 17in (43cm) high.

£150–180 MAL(O)

A toleware tea canister and cover, decorated in gilt with Chinese characters, converted for use as a table lamp, early 19thC, 17¾in (45cm) high.

£290–340 LFA

A parcel-gilt toleware tray, painted with a pair of exotic birds and flowers, America, 1850–75, 21in (53.5cm) diam.

£95–110 NOA

► **A toleware tray,** decorated with flowers and Christ carrying the cross, 19thC, 28¼in (72cm) wide.

£130–155 WW

A lacquer and gilt toleware tray set, comprising five pieces, c1890, 26in (66cm) wide.

£660–740 PICA

A Regency toleware coffee urn and a pair of chestnut urns, coffee urn 14¼in (36cm) high.

£1,200–1,400 S(O)

A toleware watch holder, in the form of a Christopher Wren-style church, 19thC, 11¾in (30cm) wide.

£1,650–1,950 DN

PAPIER-MACHE

A Victorian papier-mâché book stand, decorated with flowers, 11in (28cm) wide.
£430–480 ⊞ DHA

A papier-mâché box, c1780, 3in (7.5cm) diam.
£220–250 ⊞ MB

A papier-mâché card case, by Spiers & Son, painted with a scene of Christchurch College, Oxford, c1860, 4in (10cm) high.
£1,350–1,550 ⊞ SiA

A papier-mâché and lacquer card case, one side painted with a boat, the other with a lakeside scene, 19thC, 3¼in (8.5cm) wide.
£440–520 ⚒ DN

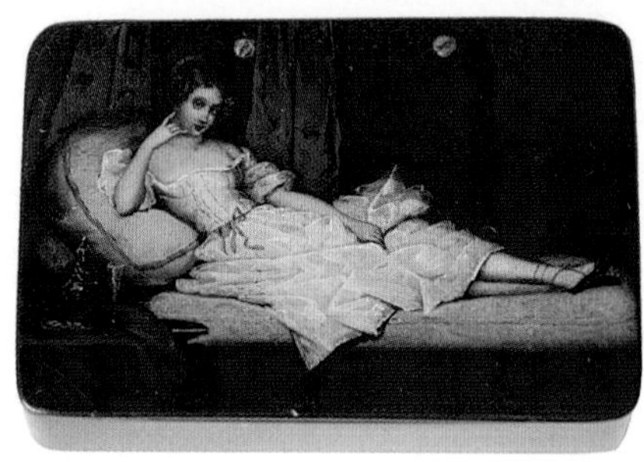

A papier-mâché snuff box, signed 'Stobwasser', German, c1830, 4in (10cm) wide.
£1,600–1,800 ⊞ RdeR

A papier-mâché and lacquer snuff box, hand-painted with a face, c1855, 3¼in (8.5cm) high.
£380–430 ⊞ EUA

◄ **A papier-mâché snuff box,** 19thC, 3in (7.5cm) wide.
£110–125 ⊞ WB

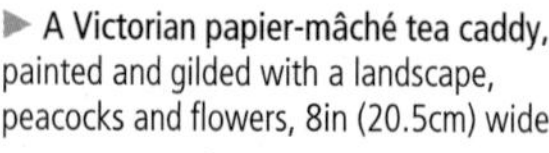

► **A Victorian papier-mâché tea caddy,** painted and gilded with a landscape, peacocks and flowers, 8in (20.5cm) wide.
£210–250 ⚒ BWL

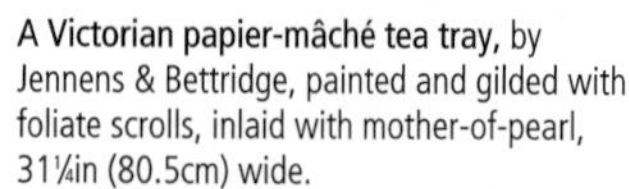

A Victorian papier-mâché tea tray, by Jennens & Bettridge, painted and gilded with foliate scrolls, inlaid with mother-of-pearl, 31¾in (80.5cm) wide.
£400–480 ⚒ AH

A Victorian papier-mâché tea tray, by Jennens & Bettridge, painted with a flower spray, inlaid with mother-of-pearl, stamped mark, possibly painted later, 31¼in (79.5cm) wide.
£210–250 ⚒ DN

A set of three papier-mâché vases, painted with flowers and birds, with lappet rims, early 19thC, largest 10¼in (26cm) high.
£560–670 ⚒ DN

A papier-mâché work box, by Jennens & Bettridge, c1850, 9½in (24cm) wide.
£960–1,150 ⚒ S(O)

TREEN

A lignum vitae box and cover, with a moulded base, 19thC, 8¼in (21cm) high.
£420–500 DN

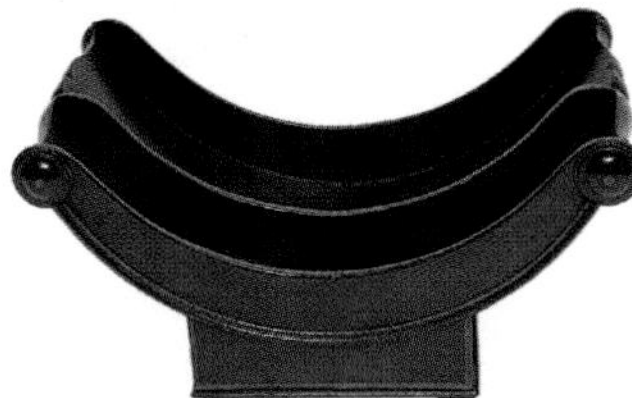

A mahogany and satinwood-inlaid cheese coaster, c1850, 16in (40.5cm) wide.
£710–790 PICA

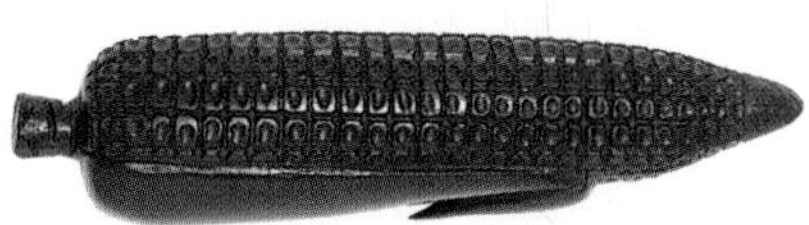

A carved mahogany corn cob, c1900, 7in (18cm) long.
£120–135 PeN

A lignum vitae cup, with engine-turned decoration, on a turned knopped stem and moulded foot, early 17thC, 5½in (14cm) high.
£4,100–4,900 WW

A pair of mahogany cutlery urns, each with a rise-and-fall cover above a fitted interior, the body with lion-head handles, on lion-paw feet, c1850, 23in (58.5cm) high.
£5,600–6,200 YOX

A pine distaff, with carved and painted decoration, Russia, 19thC, 41in (104cm) high.
£280–330 JAA

A set of six fruitwood egg cups, on a stand, c1880, 8in (20.5cm) high.
£105–120 GSA

A George IV rosewood inkstand, by G. C. Diller, the two hinged covers enclosing a pen rest and two cut-glass bottles with silver-plated covers, one end with a frieze drawer, with a paper trade label, 9in (23cm) wide.
£330–390 WW

George Christian Diller was at 5 Chandos Street, Covent Garden, London, as a portable writing and dressing case maker from 1819 to 1837, when the business was passed to D. and J. Diller.

A turned lignum vitae tobacco jar, c1860, 8in (20.5cm) high.
£170–190 SPUR

A coquilla nut inkwell, with carved decoration, on a brass base, France, 19thC, 5in (12.5cm) high.
£670–750 WB

A walnut double inkstand, with a pen rest and pen drawer, brass mounts and handle, c1890, 12in (30.5cm) wide.
£250–280 PEZ

A pair of turned wood ginger jars and covers, decorated with foliage and butterflies, signed, late 19thC, 6in (15cm) high.
£250–300 WW

◀ A wood *kasa*, in the form of a crested serpent, the exterior and interior painted with foliate scrolls, with inscription and dated 1858, Norway, 15½in (39.5cm) wide.

£9,600–11,500 DN

A kasa is a drinking vessel.

A carved wood *kasa*, in the form of a duck, with chip-carved decoration, Norway, 19thC, 8½in (21.5cm) wide.

£60–70 JAA

A Victorian mahogany lazy Susan, the moulded edge top with linked circles and carved with flowers, 23in (58.5cm) diam.

£410–490 AH

▶ **A mahogany *necessaire*,** in the form of a grand piano, fitted with a musical movement, the mirrored cover enclosing a fitted interior with accessories, 19thC, 12in (30.5cm) wide.

£700–840 BWL

A carved wood snuff box, in the form of a ship, with pen and ink decoration, c1810, 3½in (9cm) wide.

£500–560 GAU

A wooden box, in the form of a shoe, with brass inlay, the toe decorated with a floral motif, the arch inscribed 'Isaac Ward McEward 1878', 1875–1900, 4in (10cm) wide.

£145–170 WAD

A birch and pine ale tankard, with carved and painted decoration and initials 'K.T.S.', Norway, dated 1748, 9½in (24cm) high.

£3,400–3,800 RYA

An ebony teapot, 19thC, 5in (12.5cm) diam.

£360–400 WB

◀ **A cherrywood wall box,** the pierced shaped backboard and thumb-moulded front panel above a drawer with a brass pull, America, Connecticut or Rhode Island, c1800, 22in (56cm) high, together with five clay pipes.

£2,600–3,100 SK(B)

A carved wood wall plaque, depicting a hunter with a gun and an eagle, 19thC, 35¾in (91cm) high.

£1,500–1,800 MA&I

A lignum vitae double-ended whistle, 19thC, 5in (12.5cm) long.

£220–250 WB

▶ **A George III mahogany wig stand,** the reeded and leaf-carved turned column on a moulded base, 9in (23cm) high.

£1,250–1,500 DN

An oak writing cabinet, by Asprey, London, the bowfronted top with a collection plaque and delivery slot with a plaque inscribed 'Letters', the glass door with a crest, above a telegram slide, flanked by four open stationery compartments, with an inscription 'Lieut. Col. L. Gordon-Cumming, August 1912', 22¾in (58cm) wide.

£640–760 BAM

TUNBRIDGE WARE

A Tunbridge ware coromandel book stand, inlaid with a mosaic bird, slight damage and losses, c1840, 9½ x 12¼in (24 x 31cm).

£560–670 DN(BR)

A Tunbridge ware bough pot, in the manner of Wise, the top with three recesses, the sides with parquetry bands and stylized marbling, with ebony handles, possibly adapted from a tea caddy, early 19thC, 11in (28cm) wide.

£350–420 DN(BR)

A Tunbridge ware box, painted with a scene of Brighton Pavilion, c1820, 5in (12.5cm) wide.

£270–300 RdeR

A Tunbridge ware box, painted with a seashell and coral, c1820, 4in (10cm) square.

£220–250 RdeR

A Tunbridge ware box, inlaid with a mosaic of a seated child, the interior with a watch holder, c1860, 3¼in (8.5cm) square.

£380–430 AMH

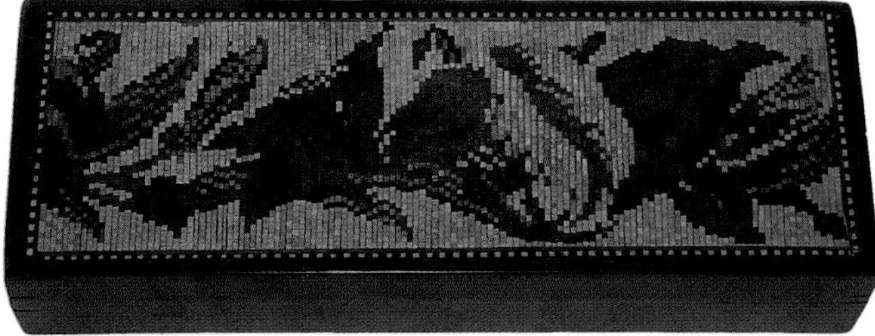

A Tunbridge ware box, inlaid with a floral mosaic, c1870, 6in (15cm) wide.

£220–250 AMH

A Tunbridge ware rosewood-veneered cribbage box, inlaid with a mosaic of roses and fuchsias, the frieze with a floral border, c1860, 10in (25.5cm) wide.

£400–450 AMH

A Tunbridge ware clamp, with a tape measure and pin cushion, c1820, 3½in (9cm) diam.

£180–200 RdeR

A Tunbridge ware glove box, by William Upton, inlaid with a cube mosaic, with original label, 1838–59, 9½in (24cm) wide.

£540–600 AMH

A Tunbridge ware rosewood jewellery box, inlaid with a mosaic view of Battle Abbey gatehouse, c1865, 9in (23cm) wide, with key.

£700–780 ⊞ PAST

A Tunbridge ware mahogany sewing/jewellery box, c1870, 12in (30.5cm) wide.

£670–750 ⊞ GSA

A Tunbridge ware coromandel jewellery box, by Thomas Barton, inlaid with a floral mosaic, the base with a printed label and inscription 'from Grandmama 15th September 1880', 8in (20.5cm) wide.

£290–340 ⚒ DN(BR)

A Tunbridge ware boxwood and burr-walnut mirror and cover, c1820, 5in (12.5cm) diam.

£270–300 ⊞ RdeR

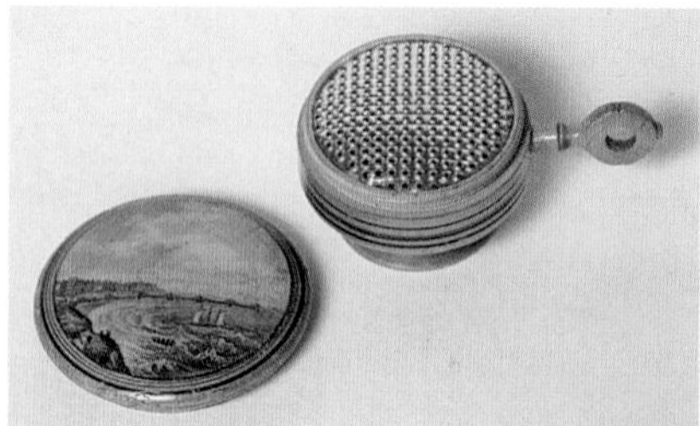

◄ **A Tunbridge ware nutmeg grater,** inlaid with a view of Chain Pier, Brighton, c1820, 3½in (9cm) diam.

£400–450 ⊞ RdeR

A Tunbridge ware obelisk thermometer stand, c1860, 8in (20.5cm) high.

£310–350 ⊞ EUA

A Tunbridge ware obelisk thermometer stand, by Hollamby, the needle inlaid with flower sprays, the ivory vernier scale engraved 'Hollamby Tunbridge Wells', the plinth inlaid with a dog and perspective cube panels, damaged, late 19thC, 7in (18cm) high.

£590–700 ⚒ DN(BR)

A Tunbridge ware paperweight, inlaid with a view of Buckhurst Park, East Sussex, c1850, 6in (15cm) wide.

£470–530 ⊞ AMH

► **A Tunbridge ware coromandel-veneered scent bottle box,** attributed to Thomas Barton, inlaid with floral mosaic, containing three cut-glass bottles, c1870, 8¼in (21cm) wide.

£810–900 ⊞ AMH

A Tunbridge ware rosewood stamp box, inlaid with a mosaic of a cat, 19thC, 2¼in (5.5cm) wide.

£110–130 ⚒ DN(BR)

A Tunbridge ware walnut stationery box, 19thC, 10in (25.5cm) wide.

£460–550 ⚒ PBA

A Victorian Tunbridge ware stationery box, inlaid with panels of flowers and foliage within geometric borders, the hinged cover enclosing a fitted interior, 8¼in (21cm) wide.

£560–670 ⚒ Bea

A Tunbridge ware rosewood wine table, probably by Wise, the top inlaid with a parquetry star within half-square and marquetry bandings and van dyke crossbanding, mid-19thC, 18in (45.5cm) square.

£1,950–2,300 DN(BR)

A Tunbridge ware tea caddy, inlaid with a stylized floral motif, c1870, 5in (12.5cm) wide.

£650–730 AMH

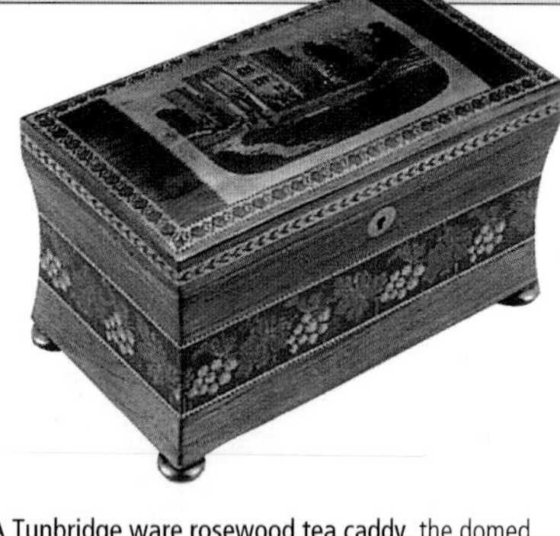

A Tunbridge ware rosewood tea caddy, the domed hinged cover inlaid with a panel of Battle Abbey gatehouse, East Sussex, within geometric borders, the box with a band of fruiting vine, 19thC, 9in (23cm) wide.

£390–460 N

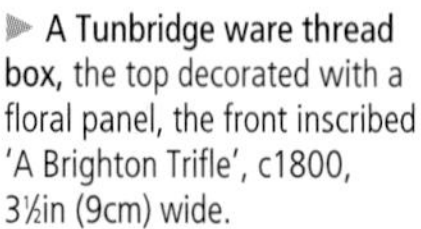

► **A Tunbridge ware thread box,** the top decorated with a floral panel, the front inscribed 'A Brighton Trifle', c1800, 3½in (9cm) wide.

£180–200 PAST

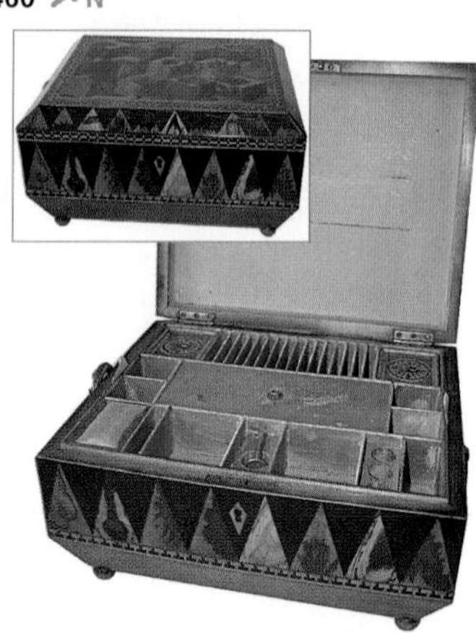

A Regency Tunbridge ware work box, inlaid with cube mosaic decoration and a van dyke border, the interior with a lift-out tray, c1820, 12in (30.5cm) wide.

£1,600–1,800 AMH

A Tunbridge ware work box, inlaid with half cube mosaic, with rosewood ring handles, c1845, 11½in (29cm) wide.

£1,350–1,500 AMH

◄ **A Tunbridge ware ebony work box,** inlaid with a panel of Bayham Abbey, East Sussex, c1860, 9½in (24cm) wide.

£630–700 AnB

► **A Tunbridge ware work box,** inlaid with a mosaic of two mice within a floral and geometric border, c1860, 12½in (32cm) wide.

£2,200–2,450 AMH

► **A Tunbridge ware work box,** inlaid with a view of Battle Abbey within floral scroll borders and sides, with label for T. Barton, late Nye, 19thC, 9½in (24cm) wide.

£1,850–2,200 SPF

A Tunbridge ware work box, inlaid with a cottage within zig-zag banding, the sides decorated with a band of foliage, with a fitted interior, 19thC, 8¼in (21cm) wide.

£330–390 AH

BOXES

A William and Mary ivory and *piqué* work box, with silver mounts, worked with flowers and rockwork, thumbpiece associated, 3½in (9cm) wide.

£300–360 HYD

An etched and pierced bone casket, incised with foliate motifs and pierced panels, Russia, Archangel, 18thC, 5in (12.5cm) high.

£1,500–1,700 RGa

A walnut lap desk, the burr-walnut panels inlaid with herringbone banding and crossbanding, the slope enclosing a fitted interior with pigeonholes and five drawers, above one long drawer, carrying handles later, 18thC, 14in (35.5cm) wide.

£980–1,150 CAG

A George III inlaid and crossbanded mahogany knife box, converted into a stationery box, 9in (23cm) high.

£230–270 WilP

A tortoiseshell snuff box, decorated with gold inlay, c1770, 3in (7.5cm) wide.

£200–230 MB

A satinwood-veneered tea caddy, with kingwood crossbanding and line and floral inlay decoration, c1780, 4½in (11.5cm) high.

£2,250–2,500 RGa

A mahogany box, decorated with shell inlay and boxwood stringing, c1780, 20in (51cm) wide.

£340–380 AGI

A harewood and marquetry tea caddy, by Gillows of Lancaster, the top inlaid with a floral panel, the front with convolvulus and an ivory escutcheon, stamped mark, c1790, 6in (15cm) high.

£1,750–2,100 G(L)

A curled paper tea caddy, with satinwood and ebony crossbanding and an ivory escutcheon, c1795, 7in (18cm) wide.

£1,400–1,600 AnB

A mahogany snuff box, the cover with a boxwood patera, late 18thC, 4in (10cm) wide.

£135–150 WB

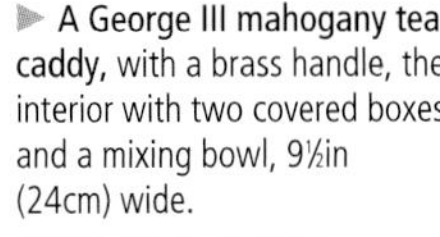

A George III mahogany tea caddy, with a brass handle, the interior with two covered boxes and a mixing bowl, 9½in (24cm) wide.

£220–260 BWL

A Spa ware work box, decorated with penwork drawings of views of the town of Spa, Belgium, c1800, 3½in (9cm) high.

£1,000–1,150 RGa

◀ **A copper-mounted brass document box,** the top and two sides each with a bail handle, with inscription, feet later, c1825, 19¼in (49cm) wide.

£600–720 NOA

A sycamore sewing box, with penwork decoration and gilt-brass fittings, c1815, 9in (23cm) wide.

£470–530 SAT

A rosewood tea caddy, with parquetry decoration and kingwood banding, the interior with two compartments, early 19thC, 8¼in (21cm) wide.

£560–670 CGC

An ebony tea caddy, with cut-steel mounts and handle, each facet set with a jasper ware medallion within cut-steel mounts, early 19thC, 4in (10cm) wide.

£6,000–7,200 S

Birmingham was the largest centre for fashioned steel and iron production in England during the late 18th and early 19th centuries and it is therefore highly probable that the mounts on this caddy were produced there. One of the most celebrated, and also the largest, manufacturers of decorative metalwares at that time were Matthew Boulton and John Fothergill whose factory was in Soho, Birmingham. Boulton and Fothergill are known to have purchased cameos from Wedgwood to mount in cut steel for jewellery from 1772. Another link between Boulton and Wedgwood was their membership of the Lunar Society whose aims included the application of scientific ideas to the processes of industry.

A tooled leather casket, the rising top opened by a secret button, the two doors enclosing a sewing drawer and a writing drawer, c1820, 9½in (24cm) high.

£1,750–1,950 RGa

A rosewood sewing box, with a drawer and turned handle, c1820, 10in (25.5cm) wide.

£270–300 SAT

A mahogany lap desk, inlaid with cut-brass and ebony foliate decoration, with two links, candle sconces, a reading bar and a riser, original skiver and keys, c1820, 20in (51cm) wide.

£2,150–2,400 AnB

◀ **A boulle casket,** inlaid with ormolu and mother-of-pearl, the four glass perfume bottles with cut panels, gilded decoration and ormolu tops, c1830, 5in (12.5cm) wide.

£2,200–2,450 BHA

A Gothic-style oak casket, carved with Gothic tracery, 19thC, 14½in (37cm) wide.

£2,000–2,400 S

For more pieces in the Gothic revival style, please see our special feature on pages 102–104.

A coromandel tea caddy, c1835, 10in (25.5cm) wide.

£380–430 GSA

A rosewood travelling case, the hinged cover with a mother-of-pearl plaque inscribed 'Annie' revealing a fitted interior with a mirror and accessories, with a drawer to the side and a jewellery drawer to the base, 19thC, 12in (30.5cm) wide.

£260–310 AH

A flame maple and ebony tea caddy, of temple form, with two removable hinged compartments, sugar bowl missing, slight damage, c1850, 14¼in (36cm) wide.

£2,150–2,550 RIT

A Victorian coromandel dressing box, by W. Leuchars, with brass handles and banding, the fitted interior with silver-mounted cut-glass containers, marked 'T.J.' and London 1873, 13½in (34.5cm) wide.

£2,300–2,600 AnB

A carved limewood jewel casket, the lid crested with a dove and chick, with a satin-lined interior, Germany, c1875, 7¾in (19.5cm) wide, with steel key.

£300–360 NOA

A gold-mounted tortoiseshell workbox, the fitted interior including scissors in a silver-plated scabbard, thimble, awl, larger awl and a mechanical pencil set with a bloodstone, France, c1875, 8in (20.5cm) wide.

£1,100–1,300 NOA

A gilt-brass-mounted and gilt-tooled leather jewel box, with moiré silk lined necklace and ring compartments, the fall-front revealing three drawers, France, c1875, 15in (38cm) wide.

£1,500–1,800 NOA

A burr-holly lap desk, the cover inlaid with specimen marbles, Austria, c1880, 13in (33cm) wide.

£310–350 MB

A gilt-brass-mounted oak casket, by Brook & Son, Scotland, Edinburgh, the cover decorated with a heraldic crest, c1880, 11in (28cm) wide.

£1,050–1,200 AnB

An inlaid bird's-eye maple lap desk, with mahogany moulding, the fitted interior with a mahogany inkstand, two glass reservoirs and a case containing a brass compass and sewing and writing implements, slight damage, America, late 19thC, 13¼in (33.5cm) wide.

£570–680 SK

A burr-walnut stationery/writing box, the two doors revealing tiered racks, with a secret drawer to the base, c1880, 14in (35.5cm) high.

£540–600 PSA

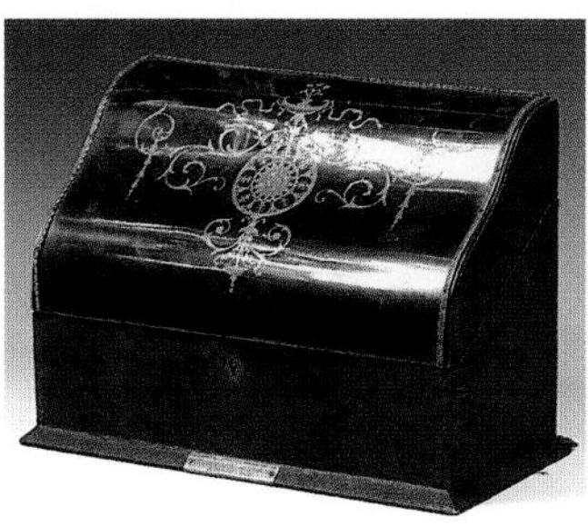

A tortoiseshell and silver-inlaid stationery box, late 19thC, 12¼in (31cm) wide.

£370–440 SWO

◄ **A burr-walnut box,** decorated with panels of mosaic, Italy, Sorrento, late 19thC, 6in (15cm) diam.

£380–430 WB

A brass-mounted oak stationery box, the fall-front enclosing an interior fitted with racks and a drawer above a writing surface, with cut-brass handles, c1900, 16in (40.5cm) wide, with steel key.

£350–420 NOA

MUSIC

CYLINDER MUSICAL BOXES

◄ **A cylinder musical box,** by LeCoultre & Falconnet, playing overtures by Bellini, Rossini, Auber and Herold, with a two-piece comb, the walnut-veneered case with a Hungarian ash panel, stamped mark, Switzerland, c1840, 23¼in (59cm) wide.

£15,600–18,700 S

► **A cylinder musical box,** by Nicole Frères, playing four airs of 'Musique de Genève', the mahogany case with inlaid stringing, Switzerland, Geneva, 1850–75, 14½in (37cm) wide.

£760–910 NOA

A cylinder musical box, by Nicole Frères, playing six airs, in a rosewood case, Switzerland, Geneva, c1870, 20in (51cm) wide.

£2,250–2,500 MB

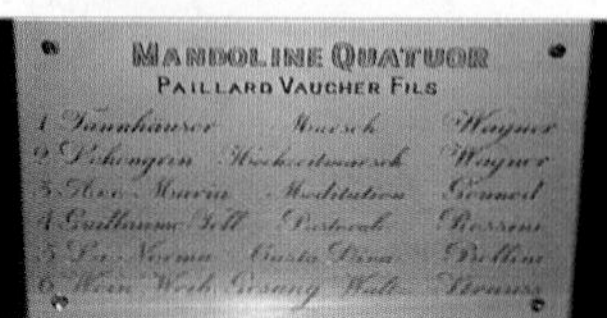

A cylinder musical box, by Paillard, playing six airs, in a rosewood-veneered, kingwood-crossbanded and marquetry-inlaid case with an ebonized interior and a silvered plaque, on a stand, Switzerland, c1884, 45in (114.5cm) wide.

£19,800–22,000 VHA

◄ **An Amobean cylinder musical box,** by Paillard, No. 700–711, in a rosewood case with stringing and a floral panel, Switzerland, 1880s, 38½in (98cm) wide, with two cylinders.

£470–560 TRM(D)

A cylinder musical box, playing 12 airs, with a drum and rack of six bells, the rosewood case with marquetry inlay, Switzerland, c1870, 28in (71cm) wide.

£1,900–2,250 WAD

A cylinder musical box, with a steel comb playing on a brass cylinder, the wooden case with inlaid decoration, Switzerland, c1880, 23in (58.5cm) wide.

£880–1,050 PF

◄ **A cylinder musical box,** playing eight airs on two combs, the lacquer case with chinoiserie decoration, Switzerland, c1880, 22in (56cm) wide.

£3,150–3,500 VHA

► **A cylinder musical box,** playing six airs, the rosewood case inlaid with a bird on a flowering branch, Switzerland, late 19thC, 17½in (44.5cm) wide.

£470–560 BWL

A cylinder musical box, playing eight airs, with six bells, the wooden case with marquetry-inlaid decoration, Switzerland, c1890, 19in (48.5cm) wide.

£1,600–1,800 K&D

DISC MUSICAL BOXES

An Ariosa Polyphon disc musical box, with 45 discs, in an ebonized wood case, with retailer's label, Germany, late 19thC.

£250–300 DORO

An Ariston 24 organette, with nine discs, in an ebonized case, Germany, c1890, 16in (40.5cm) wide.

£810–900 VHA

A Nichole Frères Regina disc musical box, with one disc, the parcel-gilt wood and composition case decorated with motifs and classical figures, with label, Switzerland, c1897, 21¼in (54cm) wide.

£1,400–1,650 TEN

A Polyphon disc musical box, by Nicole Frères, the coin-operated mechanism with 32 discs, with two steel combs, in a walnut case, Switzerland, 19thC, 27in (68.5cm) wide.

£4,100–4,900 CAG

◄ **A Polyphon disc musical box,** by Nicole Frères, the coin-operated mechanism with 60 19¾in (50cm) discs, in a walnut case, Switzerland, late 19thC, 50¾in (129cm) high.

£460–550 Bea

A Polyphon disc musical box, in a mahogany and walnut case, Germany, late 19thC, 50in (127cm) high.

£3,300–3,950 BWL

A Polyphon disc musical box and glockenspiel, with 18 22in (56cm) discs, in a beech and walnut cabinet, on a later disc bin, Germany, c1905, 85in (216cm) high.

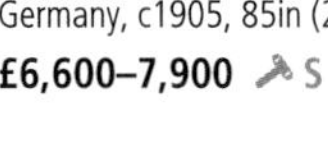

£6,600–7,900 S

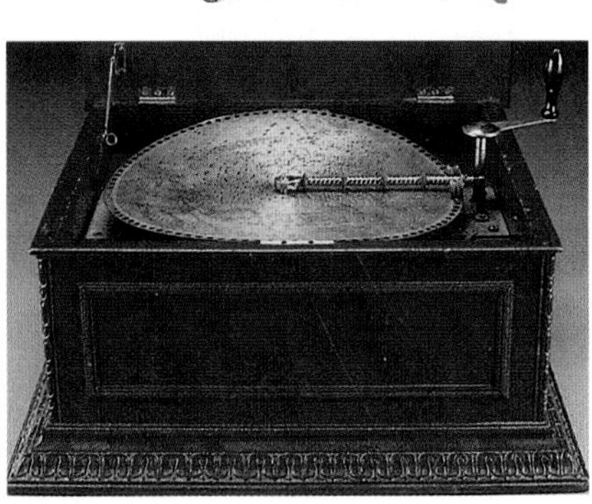

A Regina disc musical box, with 19 15½in (39.5cm) discs, in a mahogany case, America, late 19thC, 21in (53.5cm) wide.

£2,100–2,500 JAA

◄ **A Symphonion disc musical box,** with 10 12in (30.5cm) discs, the wooden case carved with cherubs playing musical instruments, Germany, c1890, 19in (48.5cm) wide.

£1,700–2,000 BWL

A Junghan's Symphonion disc musical mantel clock, with a twin-train balance wheel movement, in a beech case, Germany, late 19thC, 11in (28cm) high.

£470–560 DMC

GRAMOPHONES

◀ **An Edison Diamond gramophone,** model No. 250, the mahogany case with a drawer, early 20thC, 50in (127cm) high.

£185–220 JAA

▶ A Larg & Sons **gramophone,** on an oak base, dated 1911, 28in (71cm) wide.

£630–700 ET

An HMV gramophone, model No. 460, with a pleated diaphragm by Lumière, in an oak case, 1925, 17¼in (44cm) wide.

£2,400–2,850 KOLN

This model was produced for the English market only between 1924 and 1925 and is therefore very rare.

A G&T Monarch gramophone, with a brass horn, on an oak base, c1902, 10in (25.5cm) wide.

£1,350–1,500 ET

◀ An Edwardian Perophone **gramophone,** in a satinwood cabinet with a leaded glazed door above a record cupboard, 20in (51cm) wide.

£350–420 G(B)

MECHANICAL MUSIC

A key-wound musical box, in the form of an ebonized wood chalet, with 11in (28cm) cylinder playing eight airs, Switzerland, c1880, 27in (68.5cm) wide.

£3,600–4,000 VHA

◀ **A painted satinwood grand pianola,** by John Broadwood & Sons, with original paper rolls, c1920, 57¾in (146.5cm) wide.

£7,200–8,600 S(O)

The pianola, or self playing piano, was a popular form of home entertainment in the early 20th century until the advent of the wireless in the 1930s. The player mechanism is powered by suction created by the use of the two foot pedals. The music can be selected from a large choice of interchangeable paper rolls which have perforations to represent the notes.

An oak pianola, by Autopiano Co, America, New York, c1920, 64in (162.5cm) wide.

£570–680 JAA

A mahogany baby grand pianola, by A. B. Chase, restored, America, c1925, 60in (152.5cm) wide, and a collection of 65 QRS musical rolls.

£950–1,100 JAA

MUSICAL INSTRUMENTS

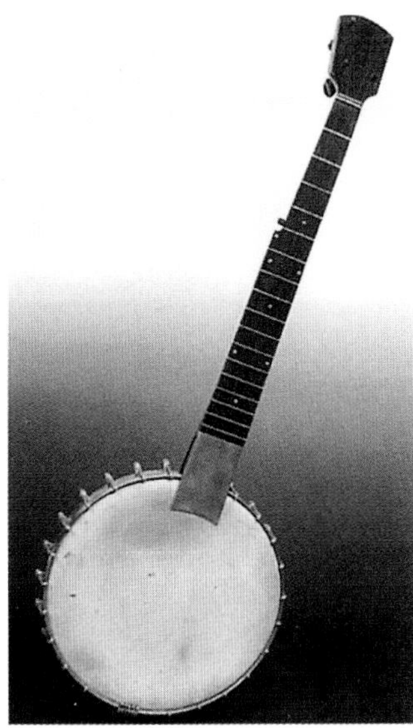

A fretless banjo, by H. C. Dobson, c1885.
£175–210 BAM

A silver bugle, engraved 'For Valour, First Eastern Siberian Sapper Battalion', applied with a badge of the Imperial Order of St George, maker's mark 'IB', Russia, St Petersburg, 1904–05, 16¼in (41.5cm) long.
£9,700–11,600 S(NY)

► **A cello,** with a two-piece back, stamped 'Alan Warrick', c1810, length of back 29in (73.5cm).
£3,750–4,500 E

A three-quarter cello, Continental, late 19thC, length of back 30in (76cm).
£640–760 MAL(O)

◄ **A brass contrabassoon,** by Giuseppe Pelitti, with nickel mounts stamped with honeysuckle motifs, Italy, Milan, c1840, 179½in (456cm) long.
£5,400–6,400 S

► **A cornet,** 19thC, with a wooden case, together with a manuscript music book.
£350–420 JDJ

A boxwood and ivory flageolet, by Hastrick, c1820, 19in (48.5cm) long.
£800–890 ANGE

◄ **A Martin rosewood and mahogany guitar,** the ebony fingerboard with diamond pearl inlay, America, 1933, length of back 19¼in (49cm), cased.
£10,200–12,200 SK

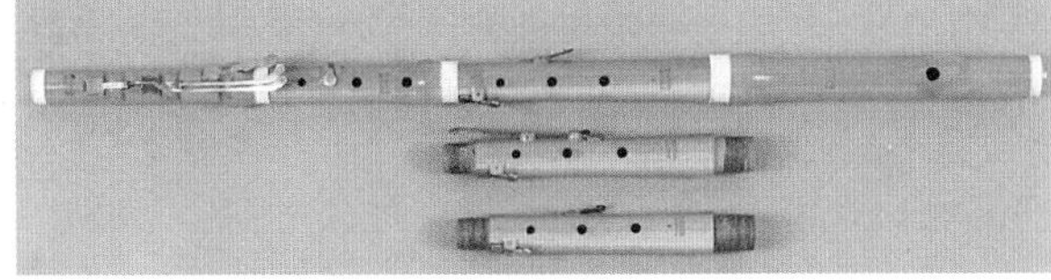

A boxwood and ivory flute, by William Henry & Richard Potter, with silver keys, stamped marks, early 19thC, 24in (61cm) long.
£3,600–4,300 S

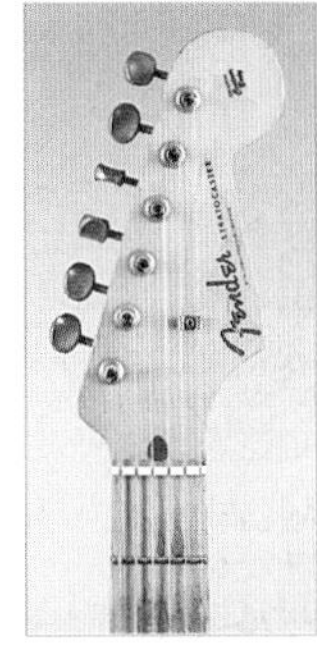

A maple and alder Fender Stratocaster electric guitar, with synchronized tremolo and Bakelite inlay, America, 1958, length of back 15¾in (40cm), cased.
£10,800–12,900 SK

◀ **A rosewood and mahogany classical guitar,** by Ignacio Fleta, with an ebony fingerboard, Spain, Barcelona, 1960, length of back 19½in (49.5cm), cased.

£11,500–13,800 SK

▶ **A fruitwood harmonium,** the ebony-strung hinged top with a burr-walnut panel, Continental, 19thC, 26½in (67.5cm) wide.

£410–490 DN

A giltwood and *vernis Martin* harp, decorated with chinoiserie scenes, slight damage, signed 'Cousineau, supplier of string instruments to the Queen', late 18thC, 62½in (159cm) high.

£12,900–15,400 S(P)

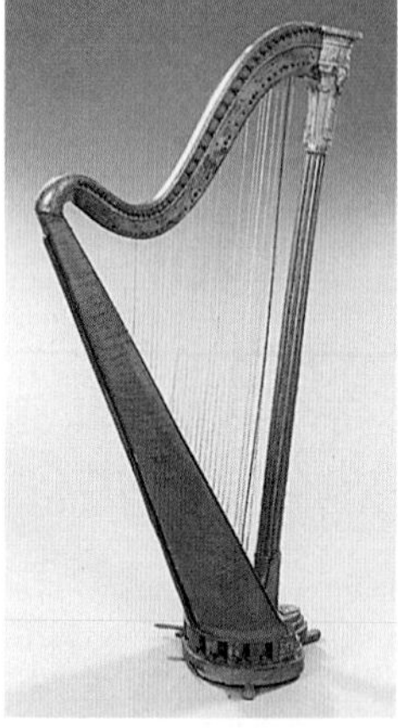

A carved giltwood harp, by Erard Frères, with gilt-brass mounts, signed, France, Paris, dated 1806, 62in (157.5cm) high.

£1,900–2,250 NOA

Erard Frères held an imperial warrant as instrument makers to the Empress Josephine.

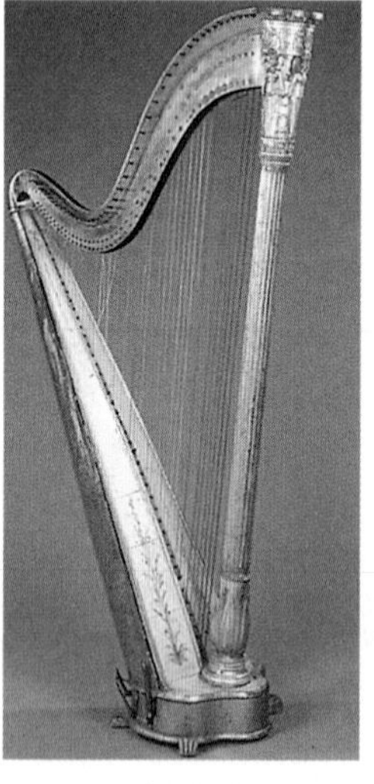

A Regency gilt salon harp, by T. Dodd & Sons, decorated with mermaids and mermen, painted with floral sprays, 66¼in (168.5cm) high.

£1,450–1,700 N

A painted wood harp, carved with the head of a Native American, America, c1890, 48¾in (124cm) high.

£9,000–10,000 GIAM

A lacquered wood harpsichord, the interior painted with a gentleman and animals, 1700–50 and later, 82in (208.5cm) wide.

£12,000–14,000 S

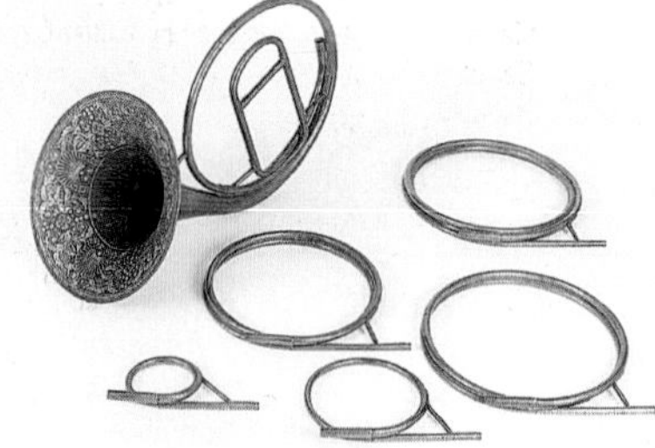

◀ **A brass horn,** by Courtoise Neveu Aîne, the bell interior lacquered and gilded with shells, oak leaves and floral motifs, stamped mark, France, Paris, c1825, bell 11½in (29cm) diam.

£3,000–3,600 S

▶ **An oak parlour organ,** by Beckwith Organ Co, with applied carvings and tiered shelves, America, c1900, 80in (203cm) high.

£120–140 JAA

▶ **A mandolino,** with an ebony fingerboard and pierced rose, late 18thC, 36in (91.5cm) high.

£960–1,150 S

A rosewood-banded mahogany piano, by Lord & Brothers, decorated with gilt stencilling, with ormolu mounts, America, Philadelphia, early 19thC, 70in (178cm) wide.

£1,000–1,200 NOA

A mahogany square piano, by John Broadwood & Sons, on turned legs, c1801, 60in (152.5cm) wide.

£4,650–5,200 WAA

A mahogany square piano, by Uzio Clementi & Co, with parquetry decoration, restored, marked, early 19thC, 66½in (169cm) wide.

£230–270 WW

A Regency mahogany and rosewood-crossbanded square piano, by Dettmer & Son, with brass stringing and gilt foliate decoration, on turned and fluted legs, 68in (172.5cm) wide.

£350–420 G(L)

A rosewood bichord cottage grand piano, by John Broadwood & Sons, c1856, 74in (188cm) wide.

£3,150–3,500 RBM

An Arts & Crafts-style mahogany grand piano, by Bechstein, designed by Walter Cave, Germany, Berlin, c1905, 61in (155cm) wide.

£2,100–2,500 M

A rosewood piano, by Bechstein, Germany, dated 1907, 57¾in (146.5cm) wide.

£500–600 MAL(O)

For more items in the Arts & Crafts style, please see the Decorative Arts section on pages 367–440.

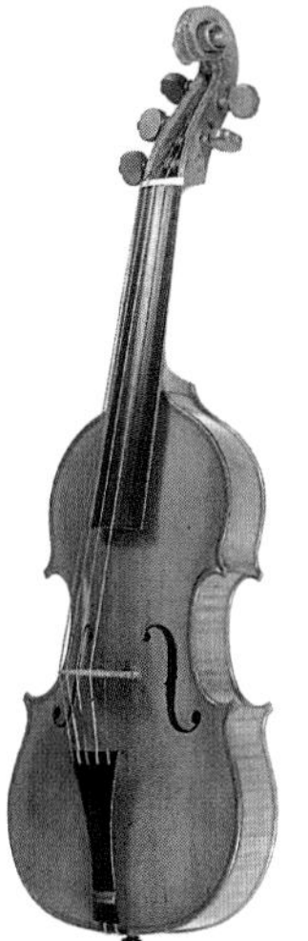

◄ **A quinton,** by Louis Guersan, France, Paris, 1752, length of back 13½in (34.5cm).

£3,600–4,300 S

► **A Martin koa and mahogany soprano ukulele,** model 5K, with ivory, abalone and mother-of-pearl decoration, stamped, America, c1928, length of back 9½in (24cm), with original case.

£5,400–6,400 SK

A viola, by Joseph Kloz, Germany, Mittenwald, c1800, length of back 15¼in (38.5cm), cased.

£4,450–5,300 SK

A viola, by Georges Chanot, France, Paris, dated 1850, length of back 15¼in (38.5cm), cased.

£10,200–12,200 SK

A violin, probably from the Testore School, Italy, 18thC, length of back 14in (35.5cm), with three nickel-mounted bows, cased.

£4,800–5,700 LAY

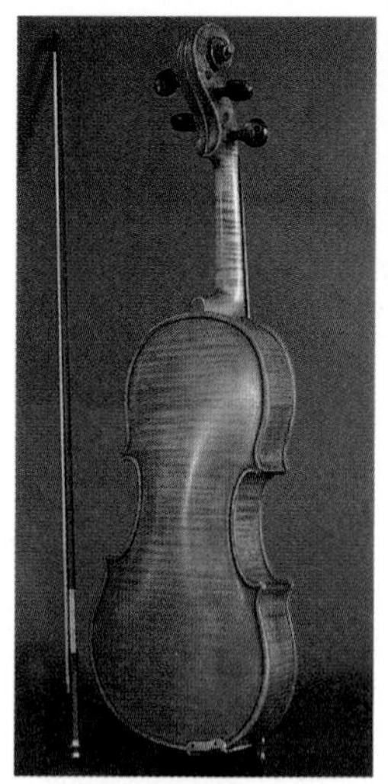

A violin, by P. James Stevens, 1919, length of back 13¾in (35cm).

£630–750 BWL

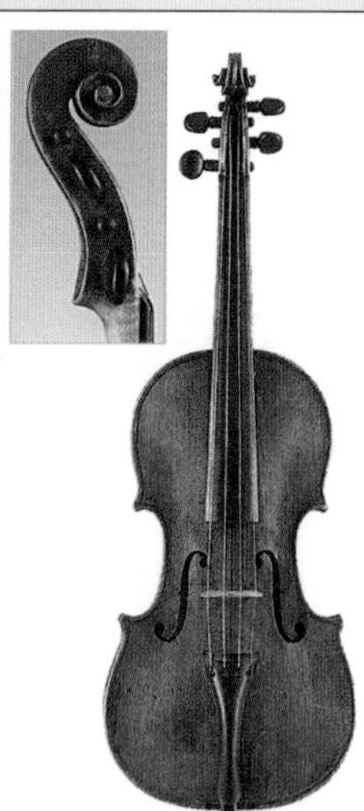

A violin, by Joseph & Antonio Gagliano, Italy, Naples, c1780, length of back 14in (35.5cm), cased.

£11,500–13,800 SK

A violin, by Gabriel Magniere, France, dated 1888, length of back 14½in (37cm), with two bows and a later case.

£590–700 PF

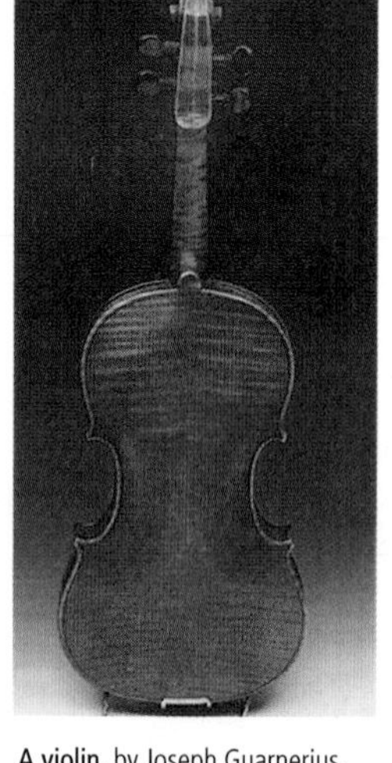

A violin, by Joseph Guarnerius, with mother-of-pearl inlay, Continental, 19thC, length of back 14¼in (36cm), and a bow, cased.

£350–420 MAL(O)

A maple violin, by Collin-Mezin, stamped, France, Paris, dated 1899, length of back 14in (35.5cm), and a bow.

£4,250–5,100 E

A violin, strings missing, early 20thC, length of back 14in (35.5cm), and a bow, cased.

£165–195 BWL

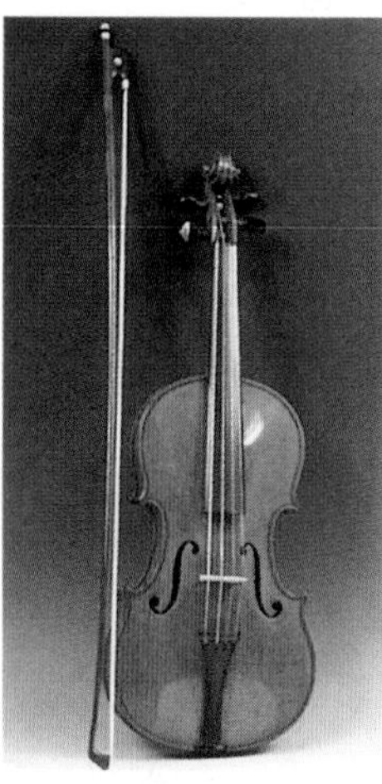

A sycamore violin, by Charles Brugère, France, Paris, c1920, length of back 23¼in (59cm), with a silver-mounted bow stamped 'Carrodus', cased.

£1,050–1,250 SWO

A violin, by Ernesto Pevere, Italy, Ferrara, dated 1928, length of back 14in (35.5cm), cased.

£10,200–12,200 SK

A violin, by Pallinotti Pietro, Italy, dated 1933, length of back 14in (35.5cm), cased.

£4,450–5,300 SK

A French School silver-mounted violin bow, the later ebony frog with a pearl eye, the later silver and ebony adjuster with a pearl eye, stamped 'Vuillaume', late 19thC, 59 grams.

£1,150–1,350 SK

ICONS

An icon of Saint Alexander Svirsky, Russia, c1625, 12½ x 9½in (32 x 24cm).
£1,900–2,250 JAA

An icon of Christ Pantocrator, Crete, 17thC, 17¾ x 12½in (45 x 32cm).
£7,200–8,600 S(O)

An icon of The Smolensk Mother of God, Russia, c1680, 12¼ x 10¾in (31 x 27.5cm).
£2,050–2,450 JAA

An icon of Saint Boniface, Russia, 17thC, 4¼ x 3in (11 x 7.5cm).
£670–750 TeG

An icon of Saint John the Forerunner, with scenes showing his beheading and the discovery of his head, Russia, c1700, 12½ x 10½in (32 x 26.5cm).
£890–1,050 JAA

A triptych icon of the Forty Martyrs of Sebaste, Greece, 18thC, 17¾ x 12¼in (45 x 31cm) open.
£2,250–2,700 S(O)

The Forty Martyrs of Sebaste were soldiers persecuted for their faith. Having openly confessed to being Christians the Prefect ordered them to stand naked in a freezing lake overnight. One of the soldiers defected and went to the warm pool provided for any who might prove inconstant. However, the guard keeping watch was so impressed by this act of faith that he threw off his garments and joined the martyrs keeping the number to 40.

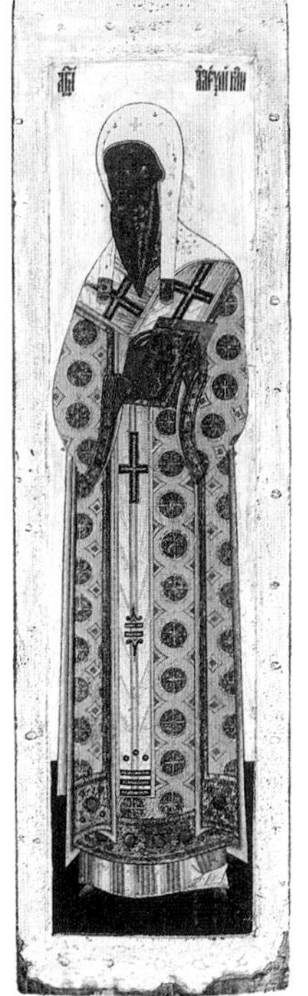

◀ **An icon of Metropolitan Alexei of Moscow,** Russia, c1750, 41¾ x 13½in (106 x 34.5cm).
£4,050–4,500 TeG

In medieval times, the highest religious office in Russia was that of Metropolitan of Moscow 'and all the Russias'. In 1589 this was changed to the Russian Patriarchate. Saint Alexei is one of four great 14th- and 15th-century metropolitans, the others being Saint Philippe, Saint Ioan and Saint Peter. Sometimes all four are shown together, at other times they are shown individually. Metropolitans are dressed like bishops in the Greek and Russian Orthodox tradition but instead of the bishop's crown, they wear the distinctive white cowl seen in this icon. Alexei was consecrated as Metropolitan of Moscow in 1354.

◀ **A triptych icon of the Theotokos, Saint George Slaying the Dragon and Saint Demetrius,** Greece, 18thC, 11½ x 15¾in (29 x 39.5cm).
£760–910 JAA

LOCATE THE SOURCE

The source of each illustration in Miller's can be found by checking the code letters below each caption with the Key to Illustrations, pages 746–753.

▶ **A carved and pierced icon of Saint Dionysus,** Greek, late 18thC, 20 x 10¼in (51 x 26cm).
£1,650–1,950 S(O)

An icon of Christ Pantocrator the Saviour, Russia, c1800, 17¾ x 14½in (45 x 37cm).

£520–580 TeG

These small half-length or shoulder-length images are for private prayer and would be used in a domestic setting. A traditional Russian Orthodox house would have a special shrine in the main room on which were placed the family icons: Christ, the Mother of God, Saint Nicholas, name saints of family members and other icons of special significance to that particular family. A person entering would bow towards icons and cross themselves before greeting the people in the room.

An icon of The Mother of God of the Sign, Russia, c1800, 8 x 6½in (20.5 x 16.5cm).

£670–750 TeG

The image of the Virgin with hands raised in prayer is one of the oldest in Christian art; examples are found dating from 3rd-century sarcophagi. Since the 14th century, Russian churches place the image at the centre of the upper row on the icon screen 'iconastasis' where the Virgin is flanked by Old Testament prophets. This refers to the prophecies, particularly that of Isaiah: 'Behold a Virgin shall conceive and bear a son, and this shall be a sign unto you'. Consequently the icon is known in Russia as 'of the Sign'.

An icon of the Virgin Mary and Child, Greece, 19thC, 12¼ x 10½in (31 x 26.5cm).

£230–270 MAL(O)

An icon of Seven Sleepers of Ephesus, Russia, 19thC, 12 x 10½in (30.5 x 26.5cm).

£760–850 TeG

Decius (AD 249–251) once came to Ephesus to enforce his laws against Christians. Here he found seven noble young men who were Christians. They were tried and given a short time for consideration. Refusing to give up their faith they gave their property to the poor, and went into a cave to pray and prepare for death. Decius returned and the imperial forces buried the men alive while they slept. Years passed, the empire became Christian, and the men awoke, thinking they had slept only one night, and sent one of their number to the city to buy food. He came into Ephesus and was amazed to see crosses over the churches. The bishop and the prefect went to the cave with him, where they found the six others and the saints told their story. Everyone rejoiced at this proof of the resurrection of the body.

A folding icon of the Deisis, Russia, 19thC, 2½ x 7in (6.5 x 18cm) open.

£1,150–1,350 JAA

An icon of Saint Marina, Russia, 19thC, 12¼ x 10¼in (31 x 26cm).

£670–750 TeG

Saint Marina was born into a high-ranking pagan family in the 3rd century. Converting to Christianity she refused, against the orders of her family and of the king, to marry. For this she was tortured, imprisoned and finally beheaded but she preached and prayed until the very last moment and many were converted.

An icon of The Baptism of Christ, with an engraved oklad, Russia, 19thC, 12 x 10½in (30.5 x 26.5cm).

£230–270 JAA

Icons were frequently clad in metal covers known as an oklad or more traditionally, riza, which means robe. They were often of gilt or silvered metal and could be set with artificial, semi-precious or precious stones and pearls.

▶ **An icon of Saint Michael of Tver,** Russia, 19thC, 10¾ x 9in (27.5 x 23cm).

£100–120 JAA

An icon of the Mother of God of Kazan, Russia, 19thC, 12¼ x 10¼in (31 x 26cm).

£450–500 TeG

According to church tradition, a vision of the Virgin in the form depicted here appeared to a young girl in the city of Kazan in 1579. From that time onwards Kazan became the most widely venerated image of the Mother of God in Russia. It became extremely popular in the 19th century and many hundreds of copies of the icon were made.

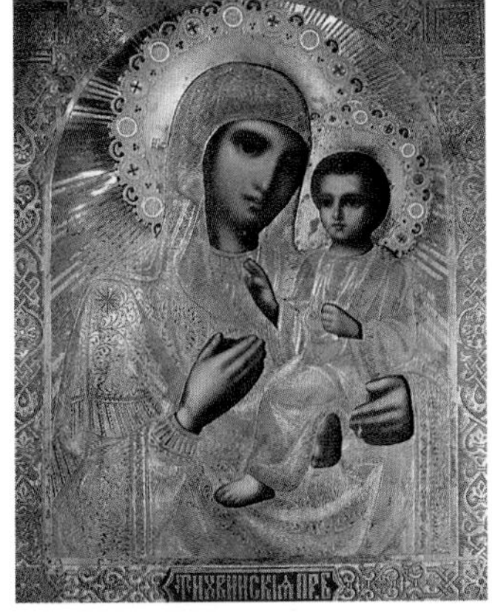

An icon of the Mother of God, with a silver-gilt engraved and enamelled oklad, Russia, 19thC, 10¾ x 9in (27.5 x 23cm).

£330–390 ROS

► **An icon of Saints Florus and Laurus,** overlaid with a beaded oklad, Russia, 19thC, 13 x 11in (33 x 28cm).

£1,650–1,950 JAA

An icon of the Madonna and Child, with an embossed and gilt-brass oklad, Russia, 19thC, 7 x 5½in (18 x 14cm).

£230–270 CAG

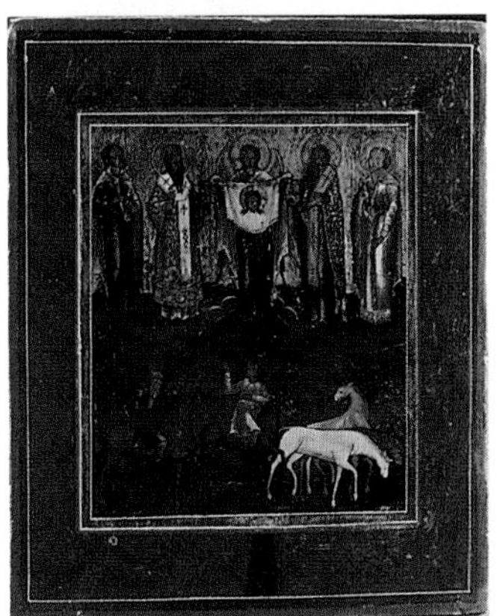

An icon of Saint Nil Stolbenski, Russia, 19thC, 12¼ x 10½in (31 x 26.5cm).

£1,100–1,250 TeG

Saint Nil Stolbenski is depicted on this icon in front of the monastery he founded on the island of Stolbny in the middle of Lake Seliger. As a young man, Nil spent ten years in the Krypetsk Monastery, later founding a hermitage on the bank of the Cheremkha river where for the next 12 years he devoted his life entirely to prayer. His reputation as a holy man attracted crowds of pilgrims and so to avoid unwanted attention he moved to Stolbny Island where he lived for the last 26 years of his life in total silence. He is reputed to have slept standing upright supported by crutches.

◄ **An icon of the Image of Christ,** with a silvered-metal oklad, Mexico, 19thC, 12½ x 10¾in (32 x 27.5cm).

£650–780 LCM

An icon of the Mother of God of Tikhvine, Russia, c1850, 9 x 7in (23 x 18cm).

£700–780 TeG

The Tikhvine Mother of God protected the city of Tikhvine.

An icon of The Pochaevskaya Mother of God, with a silver-gilt repoussé and chased oklad, Russia, St Petersburg, dated 1856, 10½ x 8¾in (26.5 x 22cm).

£900–1,050 JAA

An icon of The Virgin and Child, with a brass, enamel and parcel-gilt oklad, Russia, c1875, 12 x 10½in (30.5 x 26.5cm).

£220–260 NOA

An icon of The Lord Almighty, in a silver-gilt repoussé and chased oklad, Russia, Moscow 1888, 12½ x 10½in (32 x 26.5cm).

£1,250–1,500 JAA

◄ A 16thC-style icon of Saint Basil the Great, Russia, late 19thC, 28 x 9¾in (71 x 25cm).
£1,550–1,750 ⊞ TeG

Born in Caesarea in Cappadocia in AD 329, Saint Basil was educated in Athens and Constantinople and travelled in Egypt, the country widely regarded at that time as the source of all knowledge and wisdom. He was of great intellect and also had many influential connections, but he gave up what would have been a dazzling career in public life to become a monk. Rather than the solitary life he had seen in Egypt, he founded the communal brotherhoods in Cappadocia and gave rules for the life of communal work and prayer for both monks and nuns that profoundly influenced the subsequent development of Christian monasticism. He became bishop of Caesarea in AD 370 where he died in AD 379.

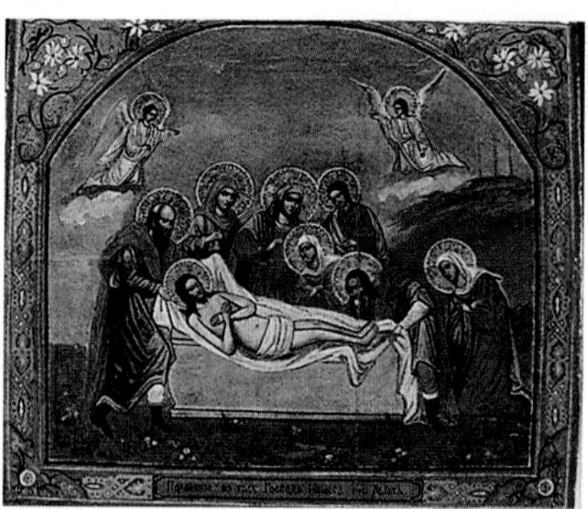

An icon of The Placing in the Tomb, Russia, c1890, 17½ x 21in (44.5 x 53.5cm).
£200–240 JAA

An icon of The Raising of the Cross, Russia, late 19thC, 12¼ x 10½in (31 x 26.5cm).
£850–950 ⊞ TeG

It was Constantine the Great's mother Helena who excavated the site of Golgotha and found three crosses, but the sign which had been placed on Christ's cross had fallen off, and it was impossible to decide which was His. Only after miracles occurred at one cross did it become known which was the true Cross. Then crowds of people flocked to the place and begged the Patriarch to raise it so that all could see. On the site where the cross was found, Saint Helen built the church of the Holy Sceptre and the cross was kept in it. The main part of the cross is now kept in the Greek church museum in Jerusalem and other parts of it were carried all over the Christian world.

An icon of the Kazan Mother of God, with a silver oklad, Russia, Moscow 1896–1905, 5½ x 4½in (14 x 11.5cm).
£310–370 WAD

An icon of the Kazan Mother of God, with a silver oklad, Russia, St Petersburg, late 19thC, 12½ x 10½in (32 x 26.5cm).
£600–720 WAD

An icon of 'Dostoino Est' Mother of God, Russia, c1890, 13½ x 12in (34.5 x 30.5cm).
£1,250–1,500 JAA

◄ An icon of the Venerable Martha, the Holy Martyr Ephraim Bishop and the Holy Martyr Anthysa, with *faux* enamel borders, Russia, c1890, 12¼ x 10½in (31 x 26.5cm).
£570–680 JAA

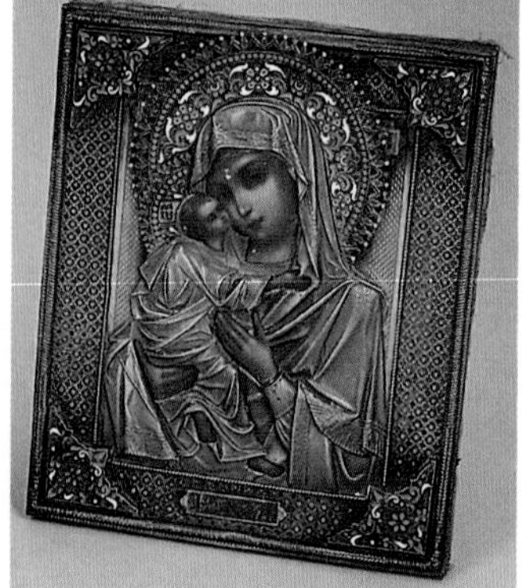

An icon of the Virgin and Child, with a silver and cloisonné enamel oklad, master's mark A. Tsch, Russia, Moscow 1893, 10¾ x 8¾in (27.5 x 22cm).
£3,150–3,750 DORO

◄ An icon of The Venerable Job, Abbot of Pochaev Monastery, Russia, c1910, 9 x 7in (23 x 18cm).
£340–400 JAA

ARTISTS' MATERIALS

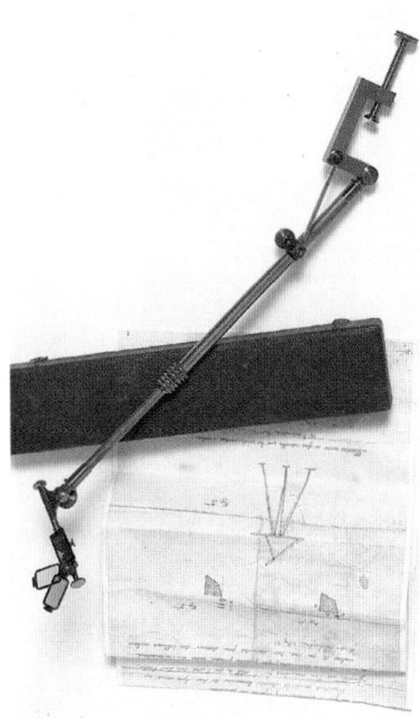

◀ **A brass camera lucida,** retailed by Maison Lerebours & Secretan, France, c1850, 10in (25.5cm) long.

£180–200 ET

A camera lucida is an artist's optical aid to drawing and painting.

▶ **A Victorian oak adjustable easel,** the painting support shelf with a turn crank, marked 'Weber', 70in (178cm) high.

£400–480 JDJ

A late Victorian ebonized easel, by Howard & Sons, the supports with rondel terminals, stamped, 44½in (113cm) high.

£140–165 WW

A carved wood artist's lay figure, c1820, 15½in (39.5cm) high.

£900–1,000 F&F

This would be used to study the effects of drapery when it was arranged on the model.

▶ **An artist's brass-bound mahogany paint box,** by Ackermann, c1880, 12½in (32cm) wide.

£1,050–1,200 AnB

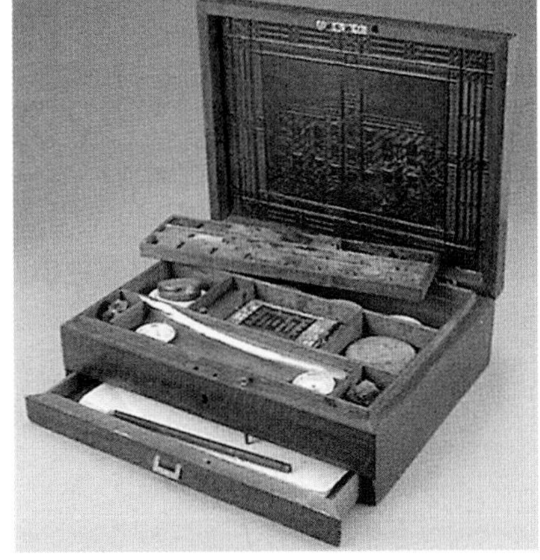

A Victorian watercolourist's mahogany paint box, the underside of the lid with an embossed morocco panel of a Gothic mansion, the fitted interior with some original paint tablets, the base with a drawer, stamped 'J. Newman's Manufactory', 12¼in (31cm) wide.

£165–195 N

An artist's mahogany and ebony-strung paint box, by G. Rowney & Co, the hinged top enclosing a lift-out paint tray and two palettes and recesses above a concealed drawer, with paper label, 19thC, 9¼in (23.5cm) wide.

£200–240 DN

An artist's painted and decorated pigment chest, with three rows of four short drawers over two drawers and a long drawer, America, 19thC, 22½in (57cm) wide.

£6,500–7,800 NAAW

An artist's folding yew-wood stool, with woven horsehair fabric, c1825, 22½in (57cm) high.

£660–740 F&F

SILHOUETTES

◄ **A pair of silhouettes,** Sweden, late 18thC, 5¾in (14.5cm) high.
£1,000–1,200 BUK(F)

► **A silhouette of a boy,** c1810, 2in (5cm) high.
£105–120 PSC

A pair of silhouettes of young ladies, by Mrs Watkins, c1820, 2¼in (5.5cm) high, in lacquered frames.
£350–420 TEN

An American School double silhouette portrait of a lady and gentleman, hollow-cut paper over fabric, flanking a figure of Cupid and hearts, America, 19thC, 7½in (19cm) wide, in original gilt stencilled frame.
£7,700–9,200 SK

An American School silhouette of a family group, hollow-cut paper over fabric, slight damage, America, 19thC, 8½in (21.5cm) wide, in a wooden frame.
£700–840 SK

A silhouette of a man with a hat, by Augustin Edouart, cut-out on paper, signed, dated 1827, 12¼in (31cm) high.
£780–930 NAAW

A silhouette profile portrait of a gentleman, by Henry Albert Frith, signed and dated 1852, Ireland, Limerick, 12in (30.5cm) high.
£380–450 MEA

A pair of full length silhouette portraits of a gentleman and his wife, by Hill's Gallery of Arts, c1830, 9in (23cm) high, in rosewood frames.
£520–620 CAG

An English School silhouette on glass of a stagecoach, 19thC, 15¾in (40cm) wide.
£440–520 DN

► **A Victorian full-length silhouette portrait of a gentleman,** indistinctly signed, 9¾in (25cm) high, framed.
£50–60 NSal

PORTRAIT MINIATURES

A portrait miniature of a young man, oil on copper, Holland, c1680, in a gilt-metal frame, 3½in (9cm) high.

£260–310 Hal

A portrait miniature of Cardinal Aloysius Estensis, oil on card on a panel, c1700, 5in (12.5cm) high.

£400–480 G(B)

A portrait miniature of Mrs Lee Ellis, oil on copper, c1720, in a gilt-metal frame, 3¾in (9.5cm) high.

£410–490 Hal

An enamel portrait miniature of a gentleman, mounted as a brooch, fastener damaged, c1720, in a gold frame, 1¾in (4.5cm) high.

£640–760 TEN

A pair of portrait miniatures of a military gentleman and a young woman, by Filippo Castelli, watercolour on ivory, one signed, Italy, 18thC, 2in (5cm) diam.

£750–900 JAd

▶ **A portrait miniature of a young man,** School of Devis, c1730, in a silvered frame, 2in (5cm) high.

£440–520 Hal

A pair of portrait miniatures of a gentleman and his wife, on metal panels, 18thC, in silvered-metal frames, 3¼in (8.5cm) diam.

£630–750 CAG

▶ **An In Memoriam portrait miniature for Fanny Spence,** depicted cuddling a lamb, the reverse with three angels crowning a vase altar inscribed 'To Y Memory of a Beloved Child Fanny Spence', c1785, in a gold frame, 1¼in (3cm) high.

£590–700 TEN

A pair of portrait miniatures of Captain John Page and his wife, attributed to Joseph Dunkerley, watercolour on ivory, one signed 'I.D.', America, Boston, 1784–88, in gilt-copper frames, 1¼in (3cm) high.

£5,400–6,400 SK(B)

Joseph Dunkerley was born in England and arrived in America with the British Army, but deserted soon after to serve as a lieutenant in a Massachusetts artillery regiment. Later he became a civilian and a resident of Boston, and rented a house from Paul Revere, who probably made many of his miniature cases. A portrait of Mrs Revere by Dunkerley is in the Museum of Fine Arts, Boston. In 1788, Dunkerley moved to Jamaica.

A portrait miniature of Mr Wigston, by George Engleheart, on ivory, the reverse with hair locket, c1786, in a gold frame, 2¾in (7cm) high.

£3,750–4,500 TEN

A Mr Wigston appears in the list of people who sat for George Engleheart from 1755–1813.

► **A portrait miniature of a lady,** attributed to George Engleheart, late 18thC, in a gilt-metal frame, 2½in (6.5cm) high, in a leather case.

£3,750–4,500 CGC

George Engleheart

George Engleheart (1752-1829) trained under George Barret and later Sir Joshua Reynolds, exhibiting at the Royal Academy in 1773. That same year he began his illustrious career as a painter of portrait miniatures and came to have a wide circle of prestigious clients including George III, whom he painted 25 times. He also made copies in miniature of many of Sir Joshua Reynold's portraits. His fee book, which lists his sitters and the prices charged, is still in existence.

A portrait miniature of a Sea Captain holding a telescope, watercolour, America, late 18thC, 4½in (11.5cm) high.

£12,700–15,200 NAAW

The sitter's hair and clothing and the presence of a Chippendale chair date this fine, early watercolour to the 1790s. Very few American portraits of sea captains exist before 1800 and this is one of the earliest known.

A pair of portrait miniatures *en grisaille*, by Jacob Spornberg of Bath, watercolour on ivory, c1790, 3in (7.5cm) high.

£1,050–1,200 PSC

A portrait miniature of a gentleman, by Frederick Buck, Ireland, Cork, c1795, framed, 4in (10cm) square.

£1,000–1,150 SIL

A portrait miniature of a gentleman, ivory on wood, possibly French, c1800, the frame with 18ct gold rim, 4¼in (11cm) square.

£670–750 SHa

◄ **An enamel portrait miniature of a young girl,** by Joseph Lee, early 19thC, 2in (5cm) high.

£3,550–3,950 BHa

A portrait miniature of a lady, by Daniel Saint, c1810, 3in (7.5cm) high.

£4,500–5,000 BHa

◄ **A portrait miniature of a lady,** by Hurter, Switzerland, c1798, in an 18ct gold frame, 2¾in (7cm) high.

£670–750 SHa

A portrait miniature of William Hull, possibly by Anson Dickinson, watercolour on ivory, the reverse with a lock of hair and sitter's name on a piece of paper, America, c1810, 2½in (6.5cm) high.

£3,800–4,550 SK(B)

A portrait miniature of a girl with a basket of flowers, watercolour on ivory, damaged, c1820, in a moulded wood frame, 3¼in (8.5cm) high.

£540–640 SK

A portrait miniature of a lady, on ivory, early 19thC, in a silver-gilt frame, 2¼in (5.5cm) high.

£195–220 HUM

A portrait miniature of a young girl, watercolour on paper, reverse inscribed in pencil 'Daughter of Minister Mallery New England 1827', slight damage, America, in a Victorian gilt gesso frame, 4in (10cm) high.

£2,550–3,050 SK

Condition

The condition is absolutely vital when assessing the value of an antique. Damaged pieces on the whole appreciate much less than perfect examples. However, a rare desirable piece may command a high price even when damaged.

A portrait miniature of a young gentleman, by Frederick Buck, watercolour on ivory, Ireland, c1820, 3in (7.5cm) high.

£360–410 PSC

A portrait miniature of a lady seated on a chair, English School, on ivory, early 19thC, in a papier-mâché frame, 3½in (9cm) high.

£240–280 AH

◀ **A primitive portrait miniature of a lady,** watercolour, early 19thC, 5in (12.5cm) high.

£135–150 HUM

◀ **A portrait miniature of Moses Waterhouse Esquire,** watercolour on paper, reverse with pencil inscription and date, damaged, America, dated 1839, 4½in (11.5cm) high.

£4,750–5,700 SK(B)

A portrait miniature of a lady, on ivory, the reverse with a plaited lock of hair, France, c1820, in a gold frame set with peridots and diamonds, ¾in (2cm) high.

£2,450–2,750 SHa

A portrait miniature of a gentleman, the reverse with his silhouette, c1825, 2½in (6.5cm) high.

£400–480 Mit

A portrait miniature of a young lady, on ivory, probably Germany, early 19thC, in an ebonized frame, 5in (12.5cm) high.

£175–210 PFK

A portrait miniature of a young lady, attributed to Alekseij Vasilijevich Tiranov, signed 'A.T.', Russia, 19thC, 3¼in (8.5cm) high.

£400–480 BUK(F)

A portrait miniature of a lady, on ivory, 19thC, in a chatelaine frame set with three diamonds, 2in (5cm) high.

£270–320 FFAP

A portrait miniature of a boy, English School, the reverse with a plaited lock of hair and monogram 'J.H.O.D.', 19thC, 2¾in (7cm) high.

£1,400–1,650 HYD

A portrait miniature of a gentleman, c1840, in original frame, 4in (10cm) high.

£185–220 JDJ

A portrait miniature of a gentleman, in a twisted-leaf frame with a suspension loop, late 19thC, 3¼in (8cm) high.

£150–180 FHF

A double portrait miniature of Lord Horatio Nelson and Lady Emma Hamilton, c1850, 2in (5cm) high.

£340–400 BAM

◀ **A portrait miniature of a young gentleman,** English School, in a pierced giltwood frame, c1850, 4½in (11.5cm) high.

£190–220 N

▶ **A portrait miniature of an early Victorian Naval Officer,** by A. Dixon, on board, reverse inscribed and dated 1851, 4in (10cm) high, with leather case.

£1,000–1,200 GIL

A portrait miniature of Mary Queen of Scots, watercolour on ivory, late 19thC, 3in (7.5cm) high.

£310–350 LGr

A portrait miniature of a young woman, the card backing inscribed 'Eadyth Violet Maclear Oakes-Jones', probably the sitter, late 19thC, 5¼in (13.5cm) high.

£350–420 PFK

A portrait miniature of a young girl, English School, watercolour on porcelain, early 20thC, 4¼in (11cm) high.

£200–240 DN

A portrait miniature of a lady, by A. Hole, watercolour on ivory, c1930, 3in (7.5cm) high.

£230–270 BAM

ANTIQUITIES

An alabaster ushabti, with inscriptions to the front, sides and back, Egypt, 19th Dynasty, 1292–1190 BC, 7in (18cm) high.
£4,850–5,800 S(NY)

A glazed composition ushabti, inscribed with bands of hieroglyphics, Egypt, 1000 BC, 7in (18cm) high.
£470–560 MA&I

Egyptian funerary practices

The artefacts found in Egyptian tombs tell us a great deal about their complex belief system. Canopic jars stored the organs and viscera essential for the dead person's existence in the afterlife. The jars took the form of the Four Sons of Horus: human-headed Imsety responsible for the liver; baboon-headed Hapy responsible for the lungs; jackal-headed Duamutef responsible for the stomach and falcon-headed Qebhesenuef responsible for the viscera of the lower body. The heart was considered to be 'ka', the soul of the body and was the only organ not removed. The canopic jars were preserved with the sarcophagus of the deceased in order to preserve the integrity of the body. Ushabti figures were buried with the deceased. They are generally depicted carrying implements such as the pick, the hoe and the flail, that would enable them to complete necessary tasks in the afterlife.

◄ **A limestone canopic jar,** the cover in the form of Qebhesenuef, one of the Four Sons of Horus, Egypt, 27th–30th Dynasty, 656–332 BC, 11½in (29cm) high.
£680–810 WAD

The items in this section have been arranged chronologically in sequence of civilizations, namely, Egyptian, Near Eastern, Greek, Roman, Byzantine, western Europe, British, Anglo-Saxon and Medieval.

A granite head of a man, Egypt, 7th–5thC BC, 7½in (19cm) high.
£3,600–4,300 S(Am)

◄ **A limestone head of a king,** Egypt, early Ptolemaic Period, 305–200 BC, 4¼in (11cm) high.
£3,050–3,650 S(NY)

◄ **A bronze figure of Harpocrates,** wearing the nemes headdress and the hem-hem crown, Late Period, c600 BC, 5½in (14cm) high.
£1,100–1,250 MIL

A stone fragment, depicting Isis and Harpocrates, Egypt, 350 BC, 5½in (14cm) high.
£1,150–1,350 BERN

LOCATE THE SOURCE

The source of each illustration in Miller's can be found by checking the code letters below each caption with the Key to Illustrations, pages 746–753.

A cartonnage mummy pectoral, with painted decoration, Egypt, Later Ptolemaic Period, 200–30 BC, 14in (35.5cm) wide.
£5,800–6,900 S(NY)

A faience figure of Harpocrates, Egypt, Roman Period, c1stC AD, 3in (7.5cm) wide.
£650–780 S(NY)

A Coptic textile panel, Egypt, 5th–6thC AD, 11¼ x 9¾in (28.5 x 25cm).
£2,400–2,850 S(NY)

A clay tablet, incised with cuneiform script, Sumer, c3000 BC, 7in (18cm) high.
£600–720 BERN

A pottery bust of a mother goddess, Syria, 2400–1850 BC, 10in (25.5cm) wide.
£470–560 BERN

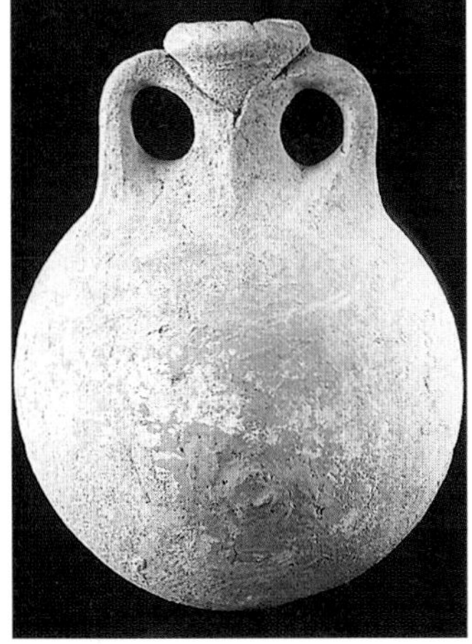
A pottery double-handled pilgrim jug, Phonecia, 11thC BC, 7in (18cm) high.
£470–560 BERN

A bronze spearhead, Persia, Luristan, c800 BC, 15in (38cm) wide.
£135–150 PASM

A Sasanian bronze bowl, 6–7thC AD, 14in (35.5cm) diam.
£470–560 BERN

A pottery Painted Ware cup, with painted decoration, Cyprus, 11th–8thC BC, 3¾in (9.5cm) diam.
£110–125 ANG

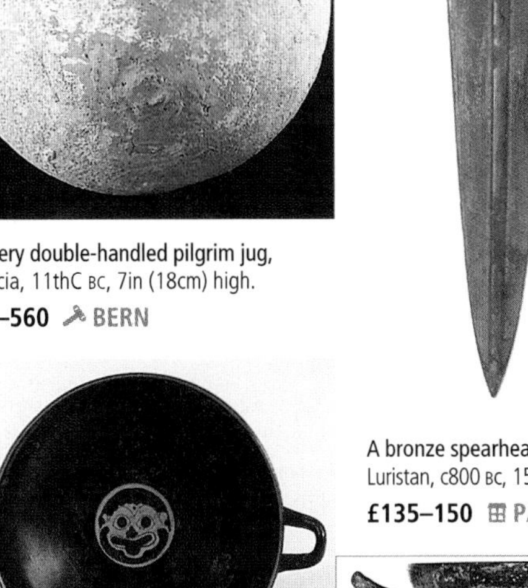

◄ **An Attic Black-Figure stemless cup,** with painted decoration, Greece, c510–490 BC, 6½in (16.5cm) diam.
£1,950–2,300 S(NY)

An Attic Red-Figure skyphos, with painted decoration, Greece, c460–450 BC, 7in (18cm) diam.

£1,950–2,300 S(NY)

Black- and Red-Figure decoration

On Greek Black-Figure vases, the decorative motifs were applied with a slip which turned black during firing, while the background was left the natural clay colour. Detail was then added to the motifs by incising the slip or by adding white and purple slip. In contrast, the decorative motifs of Red-Figure vases were the natural clay colour, while the background was filled with slip that turned black when fired. The detail was then added by using additional glaze applied using a brush. The Red-Figure technique was invented around 530 BC and gradually replaced the earlier Black-Figure technique. It is believed that it was felt that the use of a brush to delineate detail rather than incision could provide greater accuracy.

A pottery ewer, the body with combwork decoration beneath incised bands, with trefoil lip and strap handle, Cyprus, 5th–4thC BC, 9in (23cm) high.

£280–330 WAD

A silver *phiale mesomphalos*, with flaring rim, the relief-cast body with radiating petals, Greece, 5th–4thC BC, 7½in (19cm) diam.

£2,600–3,100 S(NY)

► **An Apulian Gnathian ware bell krater,** Greek South Italy, late 4thC BC, 12½in (32cm) high.

£2,250–2,700 S(NY)

A Hellenistic terracotta female figure, holding a fan, wearing a *polos* headdress and close-fitting *chiton*, 400–300 BC, 8¼in (21cm) high.

£810–970 BERN

◄ **A Gnathian ware *prochous*,** decorated with bands of applied design, small heads where the handle meets the body, handle repaired, Greek South Italy, 4thC BC, 7½in (19cm) high.

£380–430 MIL

A Red-Figure *pelike*, the body decorated with a lady seated on a pile of rocks, presenting a casket to a winged figure, objects in the field, a band of palmettes around the neck, Greek South Italy, 4thC BC, 12in (30.5cm) high.

£2,000–2,400 DN

A Roman marble herm head of a young maenad, wearing a wreath of vine leaves and a gold earring dating from 2nd–3rdC AD, 4¾in (12cm) high.

£6,600–7,900 S(P)

A Roman amber glass bottle, the translucent matrix decorated with festoons, c1stC AD, 7in (18cm) high.

£3,900–4,600 S(NY)

◄ **A Roman marble head of a woman,** probably from a herm, c1st–2ndC AD, 8½in (21.5cm) high.

£3,600–4,300 S(NY)

► **A bronze figure of Isis-Aphrodite,** her vulture headdress surmounted by a crown with sun-disk, horns and feathers, holding an apple in one hand and a wreath in the other, on a stepped dais, Roman, c2ndC AD, 8¼in (21cm) high.

£4,600–5,500 S(NY)

Prices

The price ranges quoted in this book reflect the average price a purchaser might expect to pay for a similar item. The price will vary according to the condition, rarity, size, popularity, provenance, colour and restoration of the item, and this must be taken into account when assessing values. Don't forget that if you are selling it is quite likely that you will be offered less than the price range.

A Roman fragment of a marble head of a youth, Antonine Period, mid-2ndC AD, 9½in (24cm) high.

£4,400–5,300 S(P)

A Roman glass cinerarium, with overhanging rim above a pyriform body, lead cover, late 1st–2ndC AD, 10in (25.5cm) high.

£2,300–2,700 S(NY)

A Rpman gold bracelet, the terminals drawn into cylindrical wires, each wound into a spiral around the opposite shoulder, Egypt, c2nd–3rdC AD, 2¾in (7cm) diam.

£9,100–10,900 S(NY)

◄ **A Roman mosaic,** depicting various species of fish and a lobster, set among stylized waves, Eastern Empire, 4thC AD, 42in (106.5cm) square.

£18,600–22,300 S

► **A Roman glass jar,** the rim and shoulder connected by four handles, with iridescence, c4thC AD, 8¾in (9.5cm) high.

£1,300–1,550 S(NY)

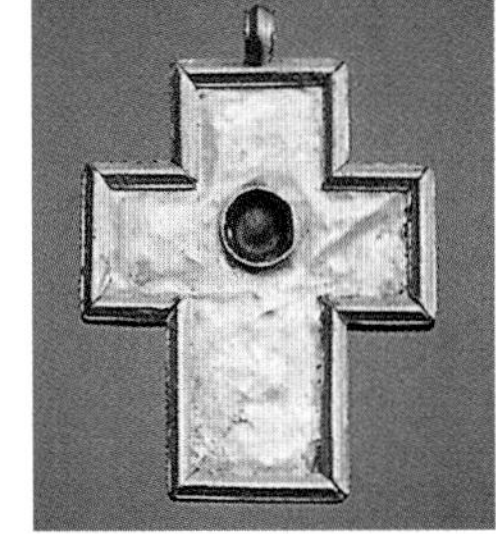

A Latin-style gold cross, with centrally-ribbed suspension loop, the arms with carinated edge to front, centred by a red disc in a gold perimeter, Byzantium, c6th–7thC AD, 1½in (4cm) high.

£3,100–3,700 S(NY)

A Neolithic polished jadeite axe head, Scotland, 3000–2000 BC, 5in (12.5cm) long.
£200–230 PASM

A stone axe head, with cylindrical shaft hole and narrow cutting edge, Denmark, c2000 BC, 4in (10cm) long.
£135–150 PASM

An Iron Age gold finger or toe ring, modelled from coiled twisted wire with pointed terminals, 2nd–1stC AD, 1in (2.5cm) diam.
£870–1,000 F&C

A bronze latch key, the openwork bow handle modelled with animals, East Anglia, 9th–11thC AD, 2¼in (5.5cm) long.
£65–75 ANG

A pilgrim's bronze badge, 'The Annunciation', depicting Mary and Gabriel, flanking a central lily, 14thC, 1in (2.5cm) high.
£95–110 MIL

◀ **A bronze heraldic horse pendant,** with enamelled owl design, 13thC, 1¾in (4.5cm) wide.
£170–190 MIL

A bronze mirror case, decorated on both sides with a cross, 14thC, 1½in (4cm) long.
£65–75 ANG

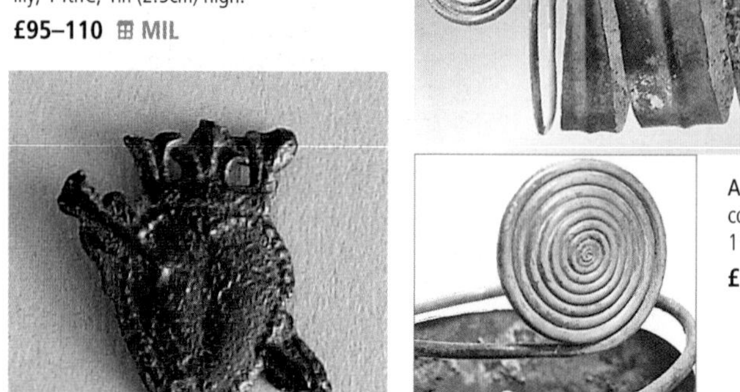

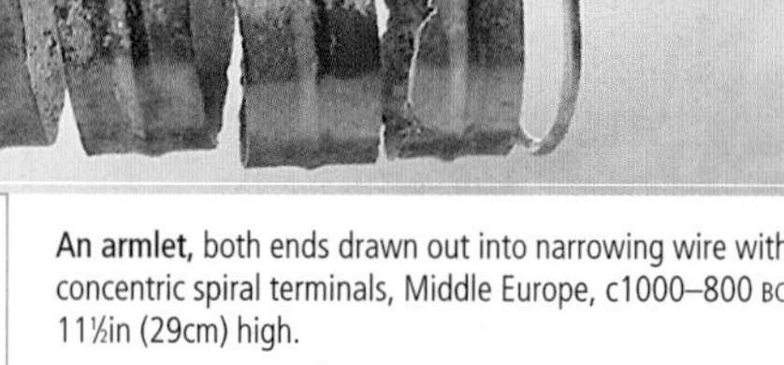

An armlet, both ends drawn out into narrowing wire with concentric spiral terminals, Middle Europe, c1000–800 BC, 11½in (29cm) high.
£1,000–1,200 Herm

A pilgrim's pewter sacred heart badge, c1350, 1in (2.5cm) high.
£85–95 MIL

For more examples of helmets
see Militaria page 706

▶ **An iron helmet,** with curved neck-guard and raised rib, the crown with reinforced finial, cheek guards missing, slight damage, probably Eastern Europe, 3rd–2ndC BC, 7½in (19cm) high.
£5,800–6,900 Herm

TRIBAL ART

◄ A Native American Acoma **pottery jar,** with painted decoration and a moulded base, New Mexico, c1930, 11in (28cm) high.

£1,050–1,250 JAA

► A Native American Algonquian carved **wood walking stick,** the finial in the form of the head of a deer with inlaid metal eyes, with a carved spiral-twist shaft, slight damage and losses, Eastern Woodlands, c1850, 36in (91.5cm) high.

£470–560 F&C

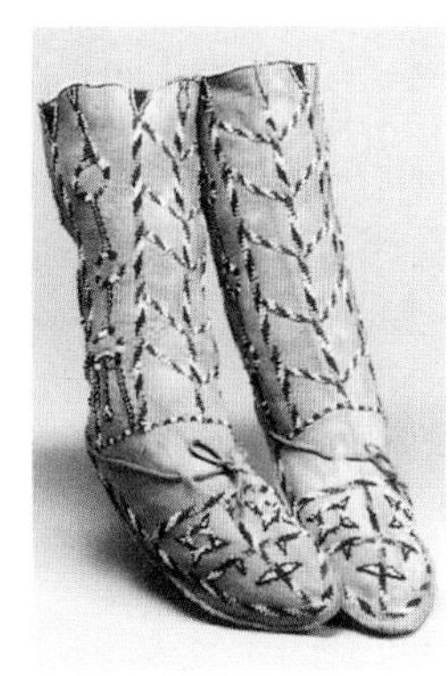

A pair of Native American **Apache hide moccasins,** the buckskin uppers beaded with symbolic and geometric devices, slight bead loss, c1900, 12in (30.5cm) high.

£1,050–1,250 SK

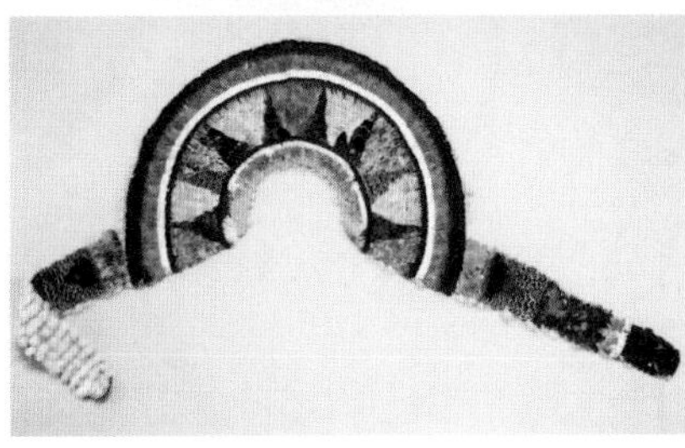

A Native American **feathered cape,** the feathers sewn on cloth in a geometric pattern, some losses, Great Lakes c1850, 26in (66cm) wide.

£1,100–1,300 SK

Simpler versions of this type of cape sell for around £300 at auction in Europe.

Items in the Tribal Art section have been arranged in geographical sequence from west to east starting with Native American artefacts.

► A Native American Ojibwa **beaded cloth outfit,** comprising bibbed shirt, half leggings and breech cloth, all decorated with glass and metallic beaded floral devices, slight bead loss, Great Lakes, c1900, shirt 33in (84cm) long.

£1,600–1,900 SK

A Native American **wood, lead and steel crooked knife,** carved with a bending figure, Great Lakes, c1865.

£13,500–16,200 GIAM

Hopi *kachina* dolls

Kachina dolls are made from cottonwood root and are the embodiments of spirits and act as intermediaries between the Hopi people and their gods who dwell in the San Francisco Peaks. The *kachina* spirits are also represented by dancers and the subjects they personify include animals, plants, mountains, storms and skies. During the *kachina* season that lasts for the six months of autumn and winter, ceremonial dances take place to promote the wellbeing, prosperity and fertility of the community. Dolls have an instructional purpose and were often given to young women to hang from the walls of the home. By the late 19th century, anthropologists and traders began to collect the great variety of dolls, which encouraged them to be made specifically for the trade as well as for sacred purposes. Most of the dolls seen on the market today date from after the 1930s and 1940s.

A Native American **Hopi cottonwood root Palhik Mana *kachina* doll,** with painted decoration, late 19thC, 11in (28cm) high.

£3,500–4,200 SK

Palhik Mana or the Butterfly Maiden is one of the most popular kachina *dolls.*

◄ A Native American **Hopidoll cottonwood root *kachina* doll,** possibly the Star Kachina, painted with cross motifs on the case mask, slight damage, early 20thC, 8½in (21.5cm) high.

£1,100–1,300 JDJ

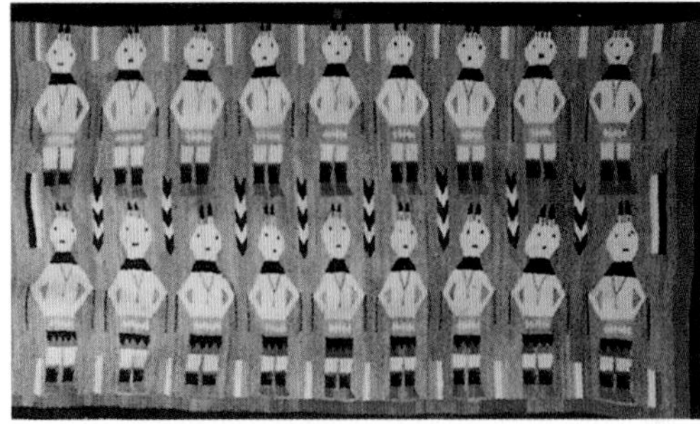

A Native American Navajo *yei* rug, hand-woven with a double row of figures, c1925, 40 x 69in (101.5 x 175.5cm).

£750–900 JAA

Yei refers to the dancers represented on such rugs. The dancers imitate the Navajo gods *(yeis).*

A Native American Navajo weaving, with an Eye-Dazzler pattern, fringe losses, Southwest Germantown, 1875–1900, 36 x 54in (91.5 x 137cm).

£2,350–2,800 SK

A Native American Navajo dyed wool pictorial weaving, c1930, 58½in (148.5cm) wide.

£6,800–8,100 GIAM

A Native American carved wood fish club, with a carved fish surmount, slight damage, Northwest Coast, c1900, 25½in (65cm) long.

£930–1,100 JDJ

► **A Native American carved and painted wood totem pole,** with a flat back, Northwest Coast, c1900, 59in (150cm) high.

£4,450–5,300 SK

This is a particularly large totem. Small models can fetch anything from £300 to £400, depending on age and quality.

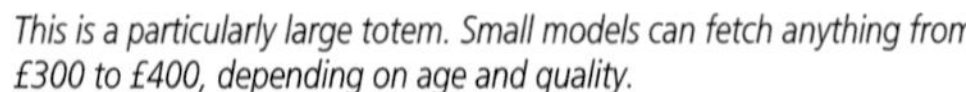

A Native American painted wood and hide drum, decorated with sunbursts, with beater, Plains, early 20thC, 18in (45.5cm) diam.

£300–360 SK

A Native American catlinite pipe, carved in the form of a man on a horse, Plains, c1880, 6½in (16.5cm) wide.

£6,800–8,100 GIAM

A Native American beaded handbag, the front decorated with a shield and flag motif, with a metal clasp, Plateau region, c1930, 9¾in (25cm) wide.

£210–250 JDJ

A Native American Pomo coiled basketwork bowl, the outside decorated with shells, abalone and glass beads, slight damage, California, 19thC, 10in (25.5cm) diam.

£3,500–4,200 SK

◀ A Native American Salish coiled basketwork cradle, with carved wood head bar and woven straps, slight damage and losses, Northwest region, late 19thC, 28in (71cm) wide.

£280–330 SK

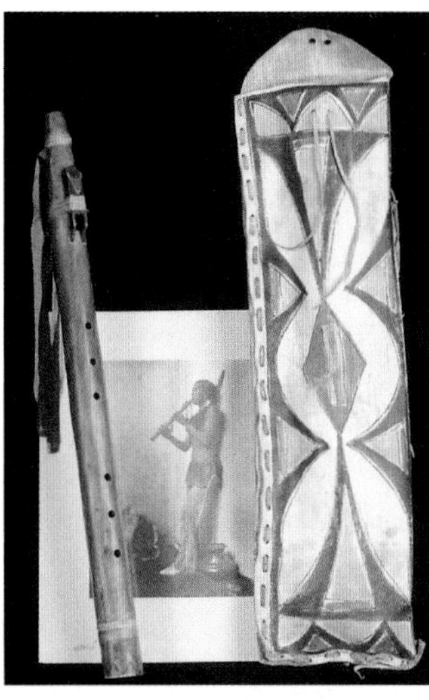

A Native American Sioux cedar and sinew flute, with ribbon streamers, the painted stop carved in low relief with a buffalo's head, with a rawhide case, late 19thC, case 23½in (59.5cm) long, with a black and white photograph of a Native American.

£5,700–6,800 JDJ

In the photograph this flute is being played by Geronimo Gomez, in Taos, New Mexico in 1914. The photograph is entitled Love Song.

Local interest

Most of the pictures of Native American artefacts shown here have been sourced in the United States where they naturally attract a considerable amount of interest. When similar pieces are sold in Europe the prices are often lower. For example, some of the Sioux moccasins shown here would sell for about half the price.

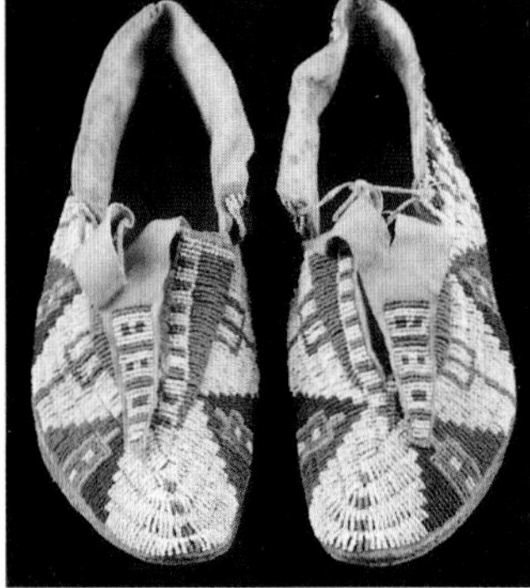

A pair of Native American Sioux cowhide and rawhide beaded moccasins, late 19thC, 10¼in (26cm) long.

£750–900 JDJ

◀ A Native American Ute beaded hide and wood model cradle, the cloth doll with a beaded necklace and cloth-wrapped hood, Central Plains, c1875, 21in (53.5cm) high.

£4,800–5,800 SK

A Native American Yokut woven storage basket, decorated with a diamond design, central California, c1920, 12in (30.5cm) diam.

£620–740 JAA

A Native American Zia pottery dough bowl, hand-painted with a leaf and berry design, New Mexico, 1900–50, 12in (30.5cm) diam.

£460–550 JAA

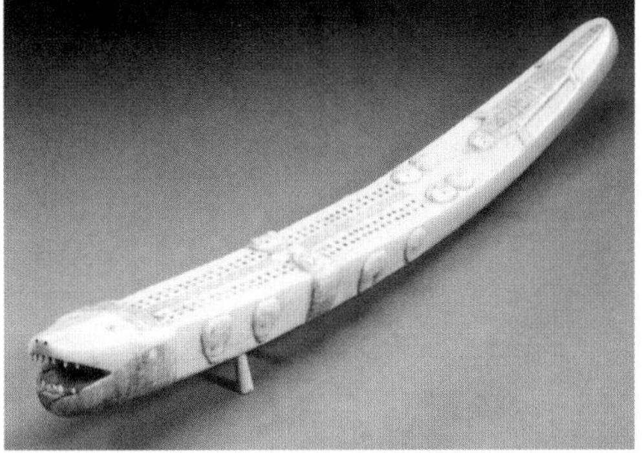

An Inuit scrimshaw walrus tusk cribbage board, in the form of a wolf, with applied teeth, carved and incised with beaver forms and stylized walrus masks, on three legs, c1900, 24in (61cm) long.

£2,000–2,400 S(O)

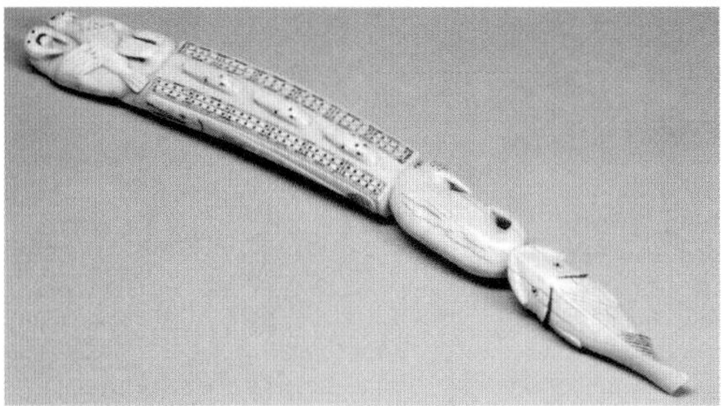

◀ An Inuit carved ivory cribbage board, in the form of a water monster attacking a family of walrus, carved fish to the sides, the reverse engraved with a kayak and seal on an ice floe, Nunivak Island, 1900–25, 25in (63.5cm) long.

£3,000–3,600 SK

◀ **An Inuit carved wood mask,** traces of red pigment at the mouth, label to reverse inscribed 'Eskimo, St Michaels, Kuskokwim Alaska', early 20thC, 8in (20.5cm) high.

£1,650–1,950 SK

▶ **An Inuit carved soapstone model of an Inuit mother and child,** by Osuitok Ipeelee, Cape Dorset, c1955, 4½in (11.5cm) high.

£1,550–1,850 WAD

Outside Canada and America, the vast majority of soapstone carvings have a value of less than £100 as decorative pieces. This carving sold particularly well as it is by a recognized artist.

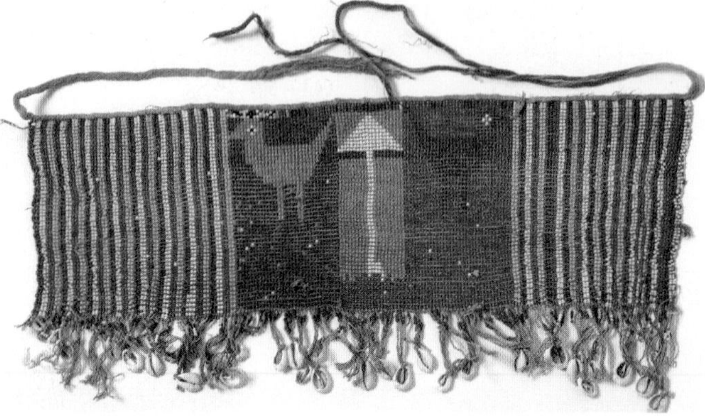

A beaded cache-sexe, decorated with a pattern of birds and a tree, Africa, Cameroon, c1950, 12in (30.5cm) wide.

£160–180 EG

A Kumu wood and fibre mask, Africa, Democratic Republic of Congo, early 20thC, 8in (20.5cm) high.

£580–650 Trib

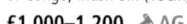

◀ **A Lega wooden *lukwakongo*,** with punched decoration, on a metal stand, Africa, Democratic Republic of Congo, mask 6in (15cm) high.

£1,000–1,200 AG

Lega masks are used in Bwami initiation rites and are divided into five types according to material, size and form, of which lukwakongo is one. They serve as an important mark of rank identifying the owners as members of specific Bwami levels. They can be assigned different uses and meanings depending on the context of the performance.
In Bwami ceremonies, masks are attached to different parts of the body, piled in stacks, hung on fences, displayed, dragged on the ground, and occasionally worn on the forehead.

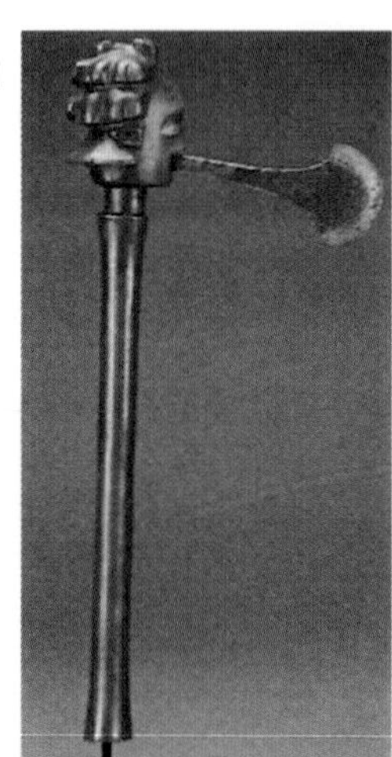

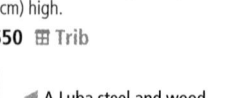

◀ **A Luba steel and wood ceremonial hatchet,** the blade emerging from the mouth of a carved head with layered hair, Africa, Democratic Republic of Congo, 19in (48.5cm) high.

£970–1,150 WAD

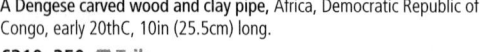

A Dengese carved wood and clay pipe, Africa, Democratic Republic of Congo, early 20thC, 10in (25.5cm) long.

£310–350 Trib

▶ **A Baule wooden heddle pulley,** the body, head and neck with decorative scarification, with roller, Africa, Ivory Coast, 7½in (19cm) high.

£250–300 WAD

A heddle pulley is a weaving implement.

A Baule wooden figure of a horse and rider, with some traces of colour, Africa, Ivory Coast, 24½in (62cm) high.

£910–1,050 WAD

A Makonde terracotta jar, Africa, Mozambique, early 20thC, 11in (28cm) high.

£410–460 Trib

A pair of Yoruba carved hardwood *ibeji* male figures, decorated with bead ringlets, Africa, Nigeria, 11½in (29cm) high.

£610–730 AG

A Yoruba carved wood mask, slight damage and repair, Africa, Nigeria, collected in the 1940s, 14in (35.5cm) high.

£440–520 SK

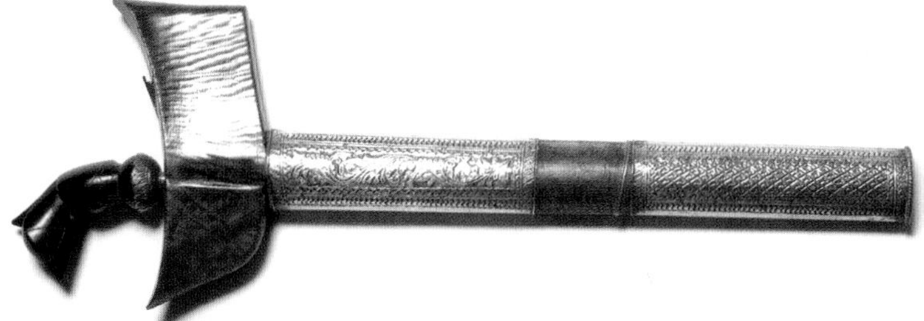

A meteorite iron *kris*, with decorated silver mounts, remounted, blade earlier, Indonesia, 19thC, 18½in (47cm) long.

£300–340 TLA

A carved and pierced lime spatula, New Guinea, Trobriand Island, 14½in (37cm) high.

£260–310 ROS

A Sepik wood figure of a woman, with a shell and fibre bracelet, New Guinea, Highlands, 7½in (19cm) high.

£630–750 WAD

A carved wood mask, with painted decoration, protruding tongue and one upturned ear, with plant fibre hair, some damage and losses, Papua New Guinea, New Ireland, late 19thC, 15½in (39.5cm) high.

£4,450–5,300 SK

► **A hardwood club,** with a greenstone mace head, Papua New Guinea, Gazelle Peninsula, 1800–50, 51in (129.5cm) long.

£370–440 F&C

► **A nokonoko wood *ula*,** with a chip-carved grip, Fiji Islands, 1800–50, 14in (35.5cm) long.

£820–980 F&C

Fiji throwing clubs, or ula, are relatively common and survive in large quantities. An average club will fetch between £100 and £300 at auction but this example is particularly finely carved – see the butt detail – and has an attractive glossy patina.

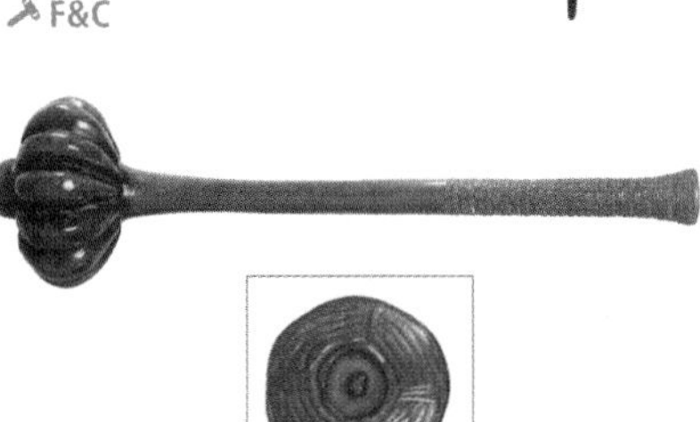

A wooden shark god, inset with mother-of-pearl, the humanoid body holding a second shark between its legs, standing on two small sharks, Solomon Islands, 19½in (49.5cm) high.

£400–480 WAD

BOOKS & BOOK ILLUSTRATIONS

Dr Philip W. Errington

Philip is Deputy Director of Printed Books and Manuscripts at Sotheby's, London and an Honorary Research Fellow of the Department of English Language and Literature, University College of London.

His specialist areas include Children's Books, Illustrated Books and Drawings and English Literature.

WITHIN THE ANTIQUES WORLD, the popularity of books and book illustrations continues to thrive. The following pages illustrate a number of collecting areas, including travel, natural history, private press, special bindings, illustrated books, children's books and modern first editions. The term 'first edition' generally means the first commercial appearance of the work published in its own right. Modern firsts focuses on books of the 20th and 21st centuries.

There are a number of important factors and trends to identify. Firstly make sure your terminology is sound: 'first edition' should not strictly be applied to an edition published in the United States that had been previously published in England, and vice-versa. It is also taken to be the first impression of the first edition.

In the book world age does not always equate to value and, in modern firsts, age is even less of a factor; all-important here is condition, and the presence of the dust jacket, now taken to be an integral part of the book. Huge prices are being paid for the protective cover that was commonly discarded only a few generations ago.

Classic authors such as Joyce, Hemingway and Woolf continue to sell well and speculative buying of works by new authors creates interesting trends – Tracy Chevalier and Kazuo Ishiguro feature in these pages this year. These last two highlight one collecting field currently in vogue: books turned into films, and a number of auction houses have held specifically themed sales in this area. John Masefield, the former Poet Laureate, expressed his exasperation with modern firsts back in 1928. In private correspondence he stated '... I do not understand the passion for first editions. I conclude that it is fostered by those who deal in the article.' Collecting modern first editions can allow the collector to choose a budget – they can be bought from second-hand and antiquarian bookshops, auction houses and, in the case of new books, from your local bookshop.

Dr Philip W. Errington

Hans Christian Andersen, *Fairy Tales*, illustrated by Kay Nielsen, published by Hodder & Stoughton, London, 1924, 12 x 9in (30.5 x 23cm).

£670–750 BAY

C. D. Arfwedson, *The United States and Canada*, first edition, 1834, 8°, 2 vols, calf with gilt spine.

£190–220 BBA

Items in the Books & Book Illustrations section have been arranged in alphabetical order.

◄ Martin Amis, *The Rachel Papers*, published by Jonathan Cape, first edition, slight damage, 1973, 8°, cloth, dust jacket.

£160–190 DW

This is the author's first novel. As with most modern first editions, value is largely dependent upon condition. The black and yellow dust jacket is notorious for fading on the spine.

Isaac Asimov, *I, Robot*, published by Gnome Press, New York, 1950, first edition, 8°, cloth, dust jacket.

£840–1,000 S

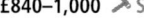

Jane Austen, *The Complete Novels*, London, 2°, 1813–18, 5 works in 16 vols, gilt morocco, bound by Riviere & Sons.

£23,000–27,600 N

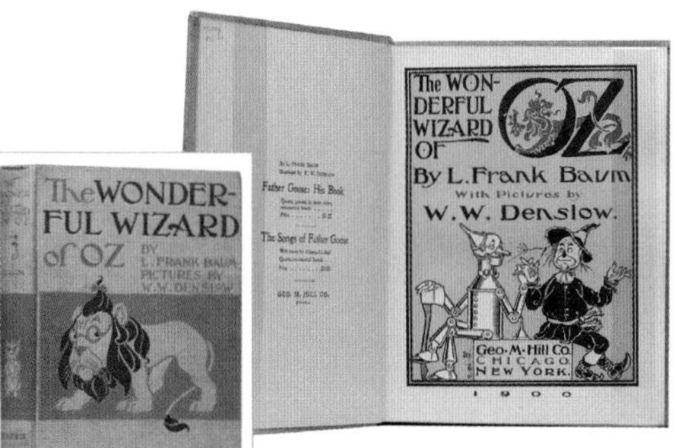

L. Frank Baum, *The Wonderful Wizard of Oz*, illustrated by W. W. Denslow, published by George M. Hill, Chicago and New York, first edition, 8°, 1900, cloth.

£10,800–12,000 BRB

Friedrich, Graf von Berchtold and Jan Swatopluk Presl, Prague, 1823–25, 4°, 2 vols, 160 lithographed botanical plates, gilt morocco.

£1,200–1,450 DW

This is a rare hand-coloured botany from 19th century-Prague. The first edition from 1820 did not include plates, but this second edition has 160 plates.

► **Samuel Beckett**, *Waiting for Godot*, published by Faber & Faber, first edition, 8°, 1956, cloth, dust jacket.

£390–460 DW

◄ **Robert Bloch**, *Psycho*, first edition, New York, 1959, 8°, cloth, dust jacket.

£1,050–1,250 BBA

This book was published one year before the classic Hitchcock thriller, starring Anthony Perkins and Janet Leigh, was released.

François Boucher, *Deuxième Livre de Figures, d'après les Porcelaines de la Manufacture Royal de France, Paris,* 1757, 2°, 12 plates engraved by Tardien, half morocco.

£1,900–2,250 LAY

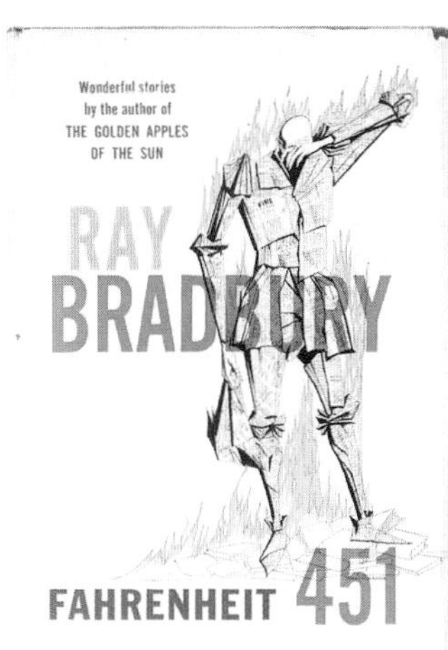

► **Ray Bradbury**, *Fahrenheit 451*, published by Ballantine Books, New York, first edition, inscribed by the author, 1988, cloth, dust jacket.

£2,150–2,550 S

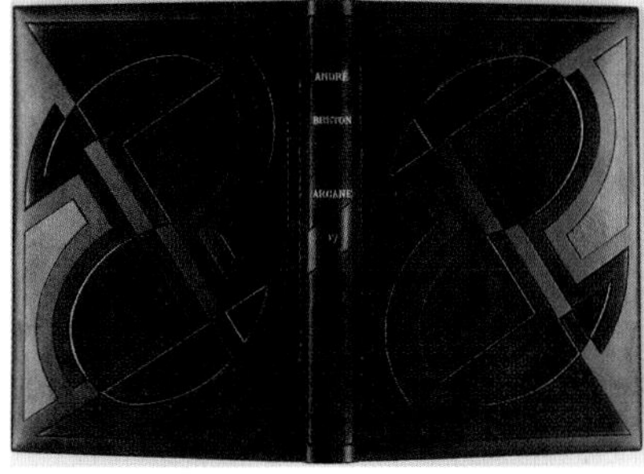

André Breton, *Arcane 17*, published by Brentano's, New York, first edition presentation copy, 1944, 8°, with a signed etched aquatint frontispiece by Matta, four plates designed after Matta, calf with strapwork, sunken sectors and gilt lettering and edges, chemise and slipcase.

£4,550–5,450 S(NY)

Arcane 17 *was Breton's only book written and published in America, and one of the earliest Surrealist collaborations with Matta. This copy is inscribed by Breton to Alexander Malitsky on the half-title, and on the justification by Robert Tenger, who directed the project through the press. The frontispiece, signed but not numbered by Matta, is additionally annotated in pencil, 'one of the first sample proof'; the half title is also signed by Matta.*

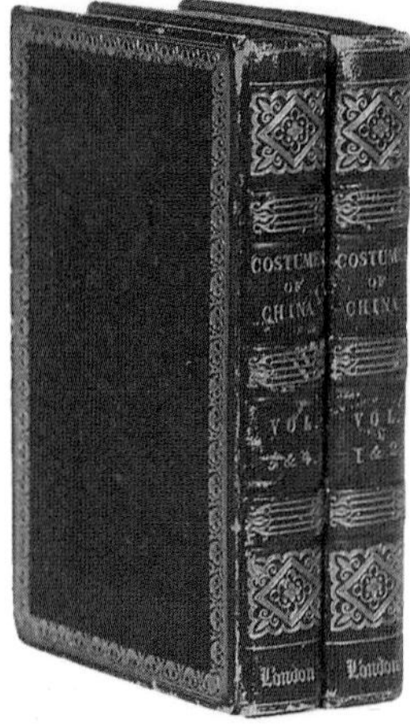

Jean Baptiste Joseph Breton de la Martiniere, *China: Its Costume, Arts, Manufactures Etc*, 1824, 12°, 4 vols in 2, 80 hand-coloured plates, gilt morocco.

£1,500–1,800 BBA

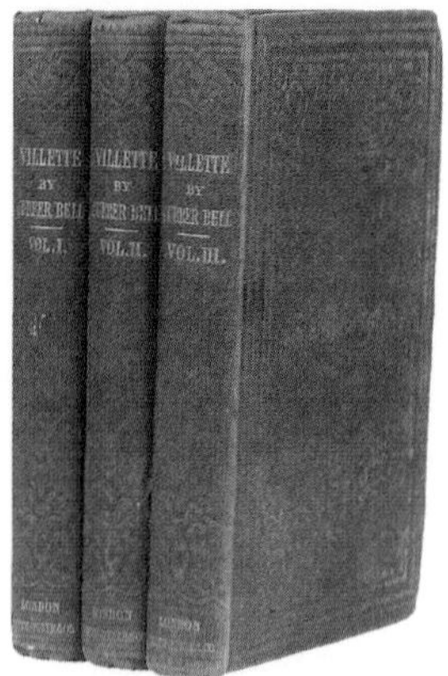

Charlotte Brontë, *Villette*, published by Smith, Elder & Co, first edition, 1853, 8°, cloth, with cloth folding box.

£6,600–7,900 S

Charlotte Brontë wrote her novels under the pseudonym of Currer Bell.

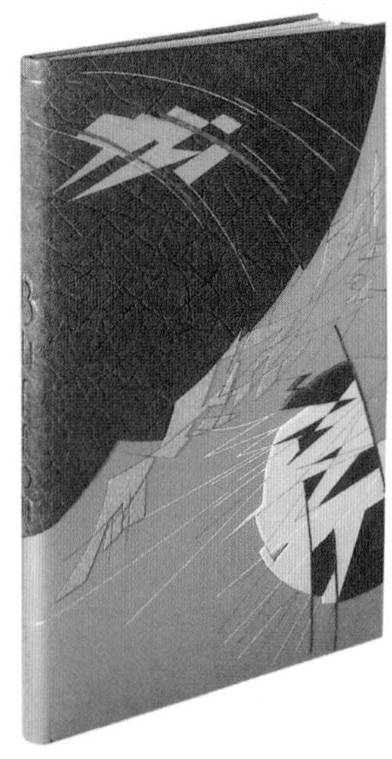

Georges-Louis Leclerc de Buffon, *Histoire Naturelle*, signed, Paris, 1951, 2°, No. 5 of 5 numbered copies of edition of 115, 30 hand-printed engravings in Chinese ink by Germaine de Coster, calf with inlaid elephant hide, with an extra suite of plates, a *suite de décomposition* and a signed Chinese ink drawing of a dove.

£4,550–5,450 S(NY)

Anthony Burgess, *A Clockwork Orange*, published by William Heinemann, first edition, 1962, 8°, cloth, dust jacket.

£910–1,050 DW

Paul Cain (Peter Ruric), *Fast One*, published by Doubleday, Doran & Co, New York, first edition, 1933, 8°, cloth, dust jacket.

£3,800–4,550 S

► Italo Calvino, *Adam, One Afternoon*, published by Collins, London, first edition, 1957, 8 x 5½in (20.5 x 14cm), dust jacket.

£280–320 BB

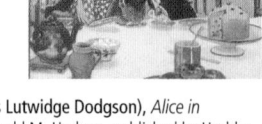

Lewis Carroll (Reverend Charles Lutwidge Dodgson), *Alice in Wonderland*, illustrated by Gwynedd M. Hudson, published by Hodder & Stoughton, London, 1932, 10in (25.5cm) high.

£120–135 VAN

Copyright for Alice in Wonderland *ran out in 1907 and a large number of publishers immediately brought out newly-illustrated editions with work by Arthur Rackham, Harry Rountree, Mabel Lucie Attwell etc. The edition illustrated by Gwynedd M. Hudson was first published in 1922. The 'Centenary Edition' stamp on the upper cover would imply a publication date for this edition of 1932.*

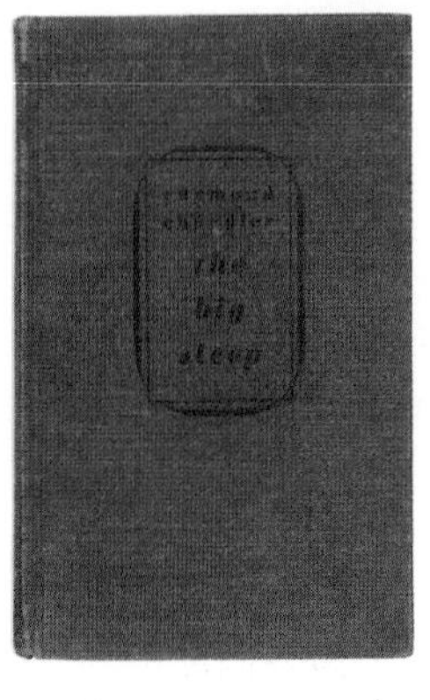

Raymond Chandler, *The Big Sleep*, first edition, 1939, 8°, America, New York, cloth, with library stickers.

£380–450 BBA

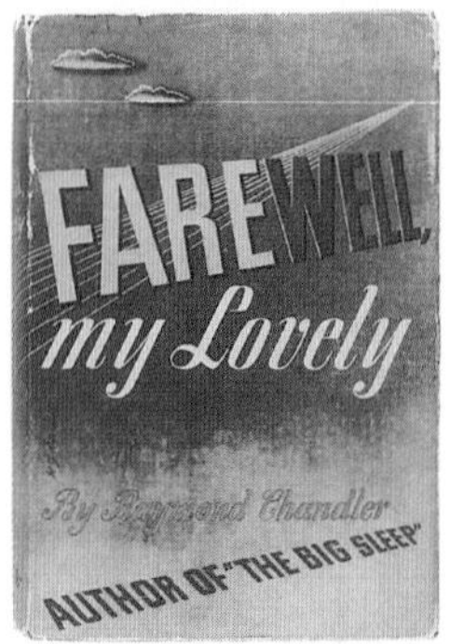

Raymond Chandler, *Farewell, My Lovely*, published by Alfred A. Knopf, New York, first edition, presentation copy, signed and inscribed by author, 1940, 8°, cloth, dust jacket.

£6,600–7,900 S

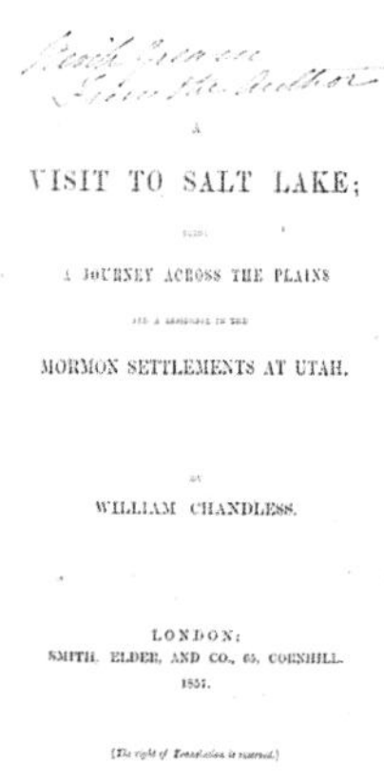
A
VISIT TO SALT LAKE;
A JOURNEY ACROSS THE PLAINS
MORMON SETTLEMENTS AT UTAH.
WILLIAM CHANDLESS.
LONDON:
SMITH, ELDER, AND CO., 65, CORNHILL.
1857.

William Chandless, *A Visit to Salt Lake; Being a Journey Across the Plains and a Residence in the Mormon Settlements at Utah*, published by Smith, Elder & Co, first edition, 1857, 8°, presentation inscription, lithographed frontispiece map, gilt spine, cloth.

£420–500 BBA

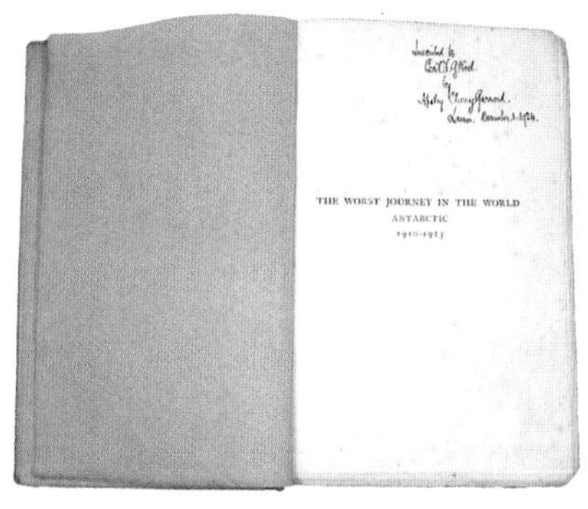
THE WORST JOURNEY IN THE WORLD
ANTARCTIC
1910–1913

Apsley Cherry-Garrard, *The Worst Journey in the World. Antarctic 1910–1913*, first edition, 1922, 8°, 2 vols, presentation inscription, plates, folding panoramas and maps, cloth, together with newspaper cuttings relating to the author, cloth-backed boards.

£2,250–2,700 F&C

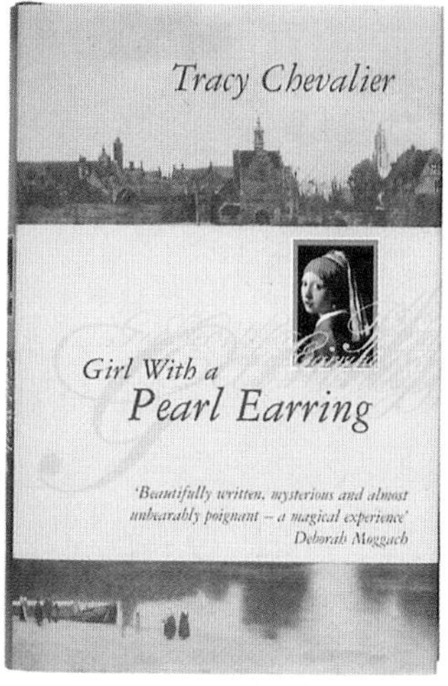

Tracy Chevalier, *Girl with a Pearl Earring*, published by Harper Collins, first edition, 1999, 8°, original boards, dust jacket.

£200–240 BBA

This book is from the first issue with the misspelling of 'Earing' on the lower panel.

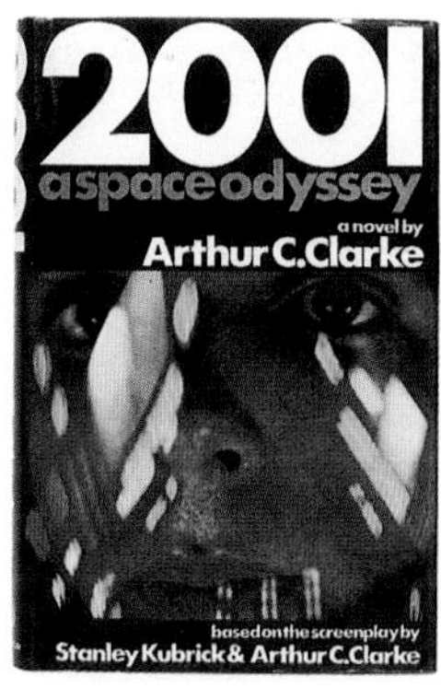

► **Arthur C. Clarke**, *2001: A Space Odyssey*, first English edition, 1968, 8°, original boards, dust jacket.

£130–155 BBA

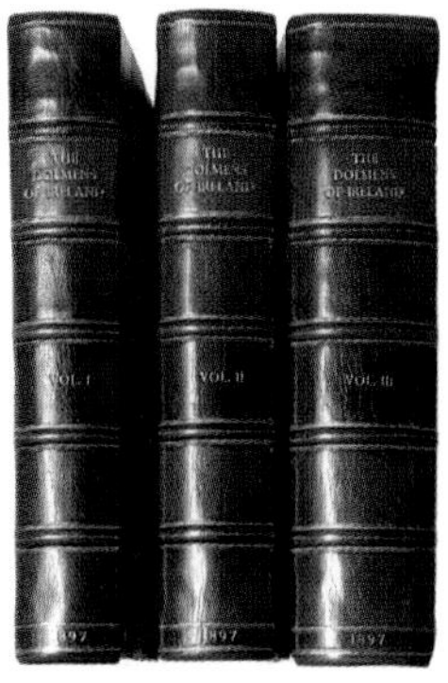

◄ **William Copeland**, *The Dolmens of Ireland*, published by Chapman & Hall, London, first edition, 1897, 9in (23cm) high, 3 vols.

£2,400–2,700 VAN

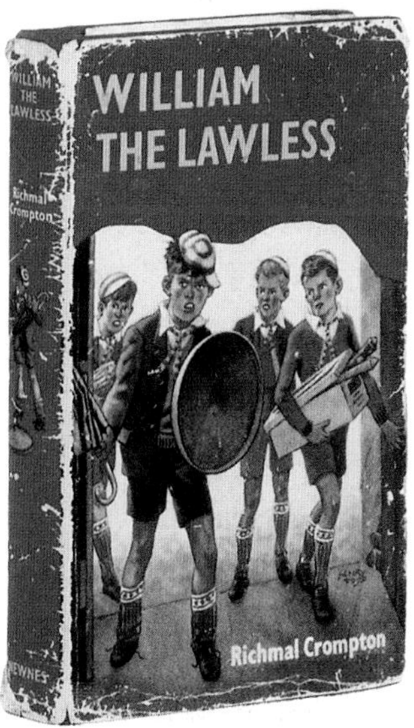

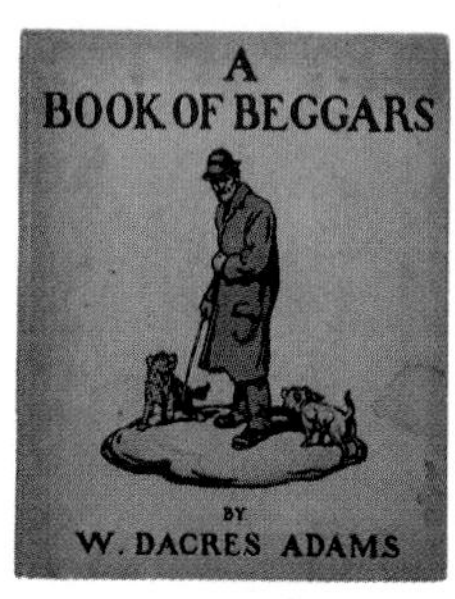

W. Dacres Adams, *A Book of Beggars*, published by J. B. Lippincott Co, Philadelphia, 1912, 12in (30.5cm) high.

£120–135 VAN

Richmal Crompton, *William the Lawless*, published by Newnes, first edition, 1970, 8°, illustrated, cloth, dust jacket.

£400–480 DW

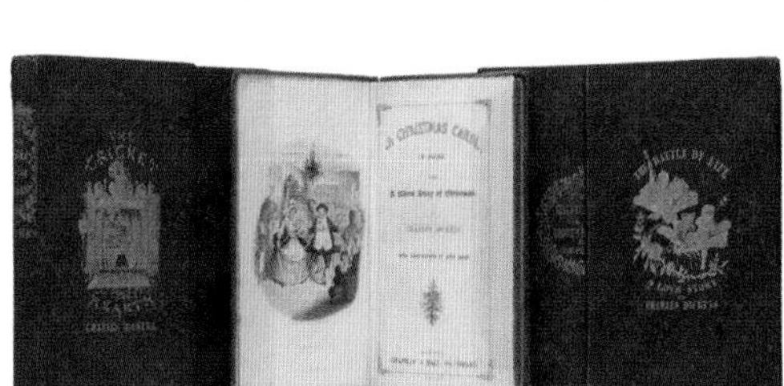

Charles Dickens, *The Christmas Books: A Christmas Carol*, published by Chapman & Hall, first edition, 1843; *The Chimes*, published by Chapman & Hall, first edition, 1845; *The Cricket on the Hearth*, published by Chapman & Hall, first edition, 1846; *The Battle of Life*, published by Bradbury & Evans, 1846, and *The Haunted Man and the Ghost's Bargain*, published by Bradbury & Evans, first edition, 1848, small 8°, 5 vols, original cloth, gilt-decorated covers and spine, gilt edges, in a cloth chemise and slip case.

£12,200–13,600 BRB

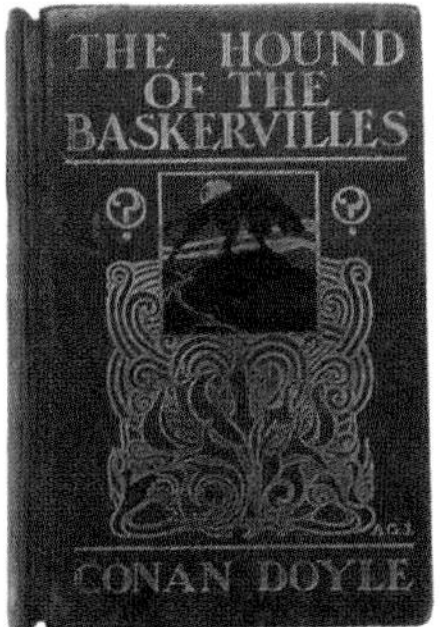

Sir Arthur Conan Doyle, *The Hound of the Baskervilles*, published by George Newnes, London, first edition, 1902, 6¾ x 5¾in (17 x 14.5cm).

£520–580 BB

Daniel Giraud Elliot, *The New and Heretofore Unfigured Species of the Birds of North America*, New York, first edition, 1869, 2°, 2 vols, 72 hand-coloured lithographed plates, 21 mounted wood-engraved illustrations, half-morocco.

£13,600–16,300 S(NY)

William Faulkner, *The Sound and the Fury*, published by Jonathan Cape and Harrison Smith, New York, first edition, 1929, 8°, cloth, dust jacket.

£4,800–5,700 S

Lt Col G. A. Fitzclarence, *Journal of a Route Across India, Through Egypt, to England,* first edition, 4°, 12 plates, 9 hand-coloured, 5 plans and 2 maps, most with tissue guards, cloth.

£2,000–2,400 BBA

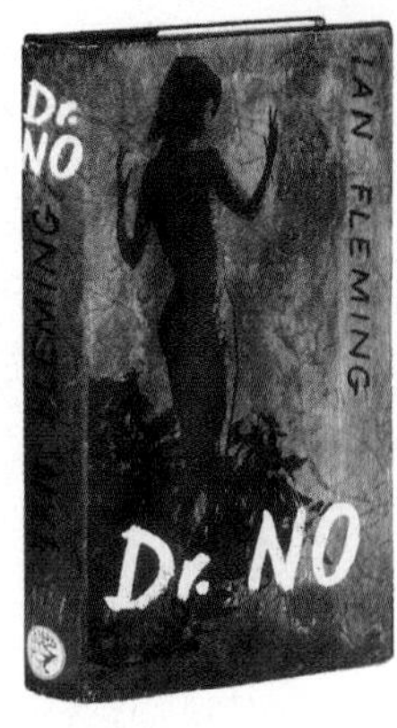

Ian Fleming, *Dr. No*, published by Jonathan Cape, first edition, 1958, 8°, cloth, dust jacket.

£150–180 DW

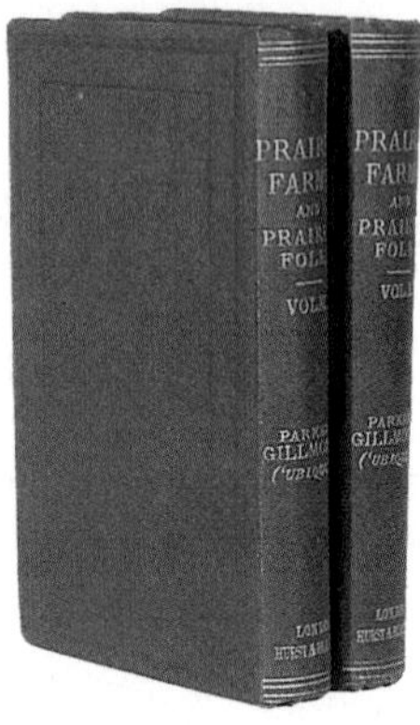

Parker Gillmore, *Prairie Farms and Prairie Folk*, published by Hurst & Blackett, London, 1872, 8°, 2 vols, wood-engraved frontispieces, cloth.

£165–195 BBA

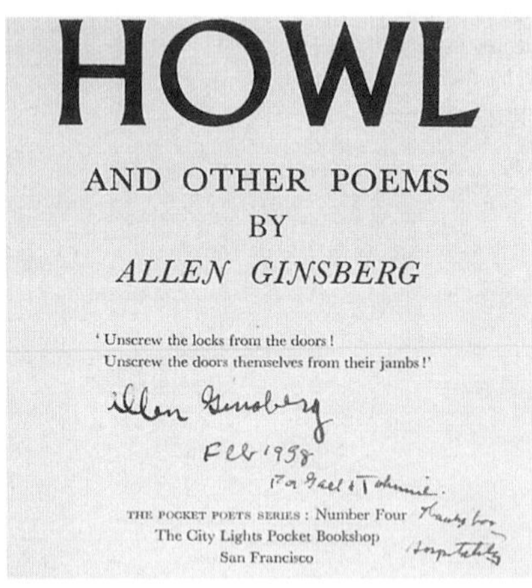

HOWL

AND OTHER POEMS

BY

ALLEN GINSBERG

'Unscrew the locks from the doors!
Unscrew the doors themselves from their jambs!'

THE POCKET POETS SERIES : Number Four
The City Lights Pocket Bookshop
San Francisco

Allen Ginsberg, *Howl and other poems*, published by City Lights Bookshop, San Francisco, first edition, inscribed by author to Gael Turnbull, 1956, 16°, dust jacket.

£2,150–2,550 S

Eliza Eve Gleadall, *The Beauties of Flora with Botanic and Poetic Illustrations: Being a Selection of Flowers drawn from Nature, Arranged Emblematically, with Directions for Colouring them*, published by Eliza Eve Gleadall at Heath Hall, 1834, 2°, Vol. 1 of 2, 20 hand-coloured plates, morocco.

£1,200–1,400 DW

Edward Gorey (illustrator), original pen and ink drawing for the dust jacket illustration for *Cobweb Castle*, by Jan Wahl, watercolour, c1968, 12 x 18in (30.5 x 45.5cm).

£1,950–2,300 S(NY)

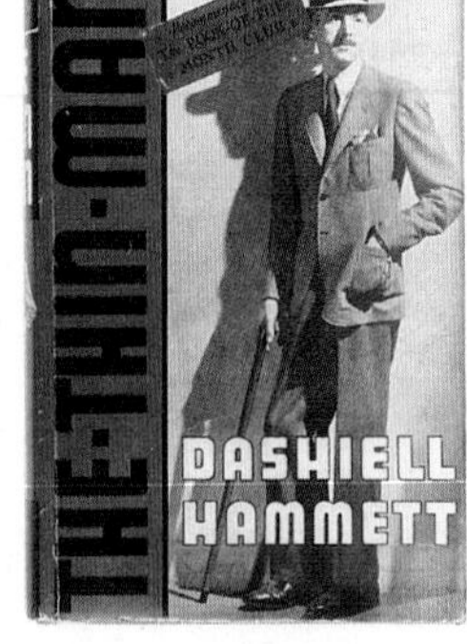

◀ **Dashiell Hammett,** *The Thin Man*, published by Alfred A. Knopf, New York, first edition, 1934, 8°, cloth, dust jacket, slight damage.

£2,850–3,400 S

▶ **Helene Hanff,** *84, Charing Cross Road*, published by Grossman, New York, first edition, 1970, 8¼ x 6in (21 x 15cm), cloth, dust jacket.

£145–165 ⊞ BB

First published in New York by Grossman in 1970, this is the true first edition. The 1971 Andre Deutsch publication in London is the first English edition. Collectors should always be familiar with 'first edition' terminology – if in doubt, do a little bibliographical research!

Thomas Hardy, *Under the Greenwood Tree – A Rural Painting of the Dutch School,* published by Tinsley Brothers, London, first edition, 1872, 8°, 2 vols, marbled boards, gilt spines and edges, cloth.

£1,900–2,250 S

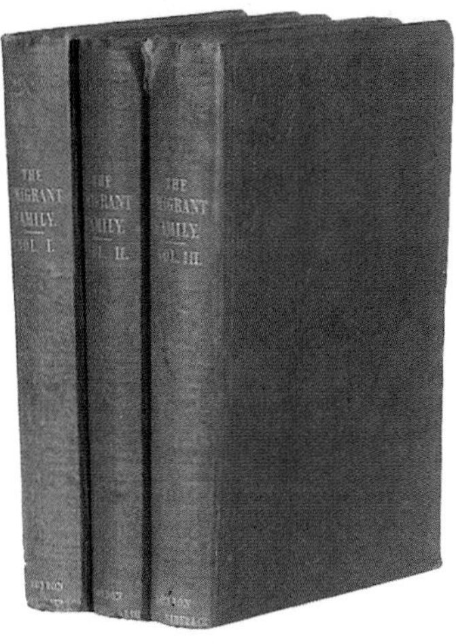

Alexander Harris, *The Emigrant Family; or, The Story of an Australian Settler,* first edition, 1849, 8°, 3 vols, gilt spines.
£1,900–2,250 BBA

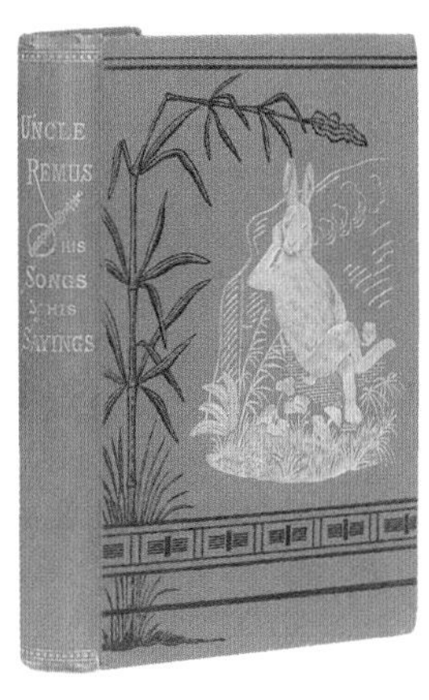

Joel Chandler Harris, *Uncle Remus. His Songs and His Sayings. The Folk-Lore of the Old Plantation,* published by D. Appleton & Co, New York, first edition, 1881, 8°, wood-engraved illustrations by Frederick S. Church and James H. Moser, gilt spine and gilt and black decoration, cloth.
£5,400–6,400 S

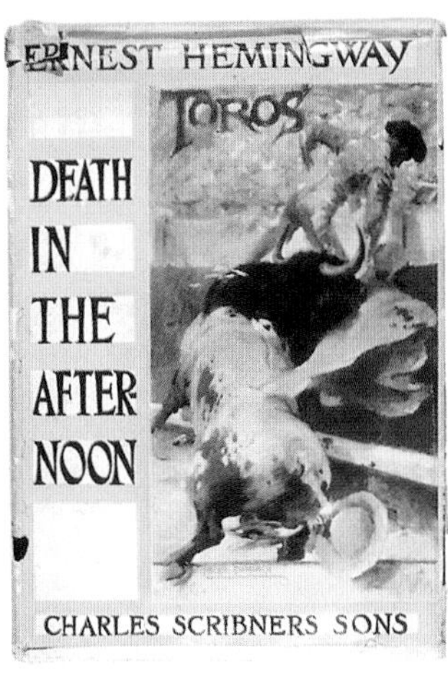

Ernest Hemingway, *Death in the Afternoon,* published by Charles Scribner's Sons, New York, first edition, 1932, large 8°, colour frontispiece, black and white photographic plates, cloth, dust jacket.
£830–990 BBA

Ernest Hemingway, *The Old Man and the Sea,* published by Charles Scribner's Sons, New York, presentation inscribed to the American Ambassador to Cuba, 1956, 8°, cloth, dust jacket.
£3,900–4,350 BRB

HUTCHINGS' CALIFORNIA MAGAZINE.

GRIZZLY BEAR.

THE GRIZZLY BEAR.

This animal has ever been represented by the trappers and mountaineers of the American continent, as the most formidable and ferocious of wild beasts. His home is among the solitary fastnesses of the mountain, and whenever the footsteps of the hunter has invaded it, it has been at the peril of his life. Who has not heard of the hairbreadth escapes, the severe wounds, and often fatal results of such rencounters in the Rocky Mountains? And often, in the early history of mountain adventure in California, after the discovery of gold, has the pioneer miner, with rifle and pickaxe, his blankets and pan, encountered this stern tenant of the forest, while in search of the precious metal.

We remember very well that during the winter of 1849 a colored man was passing through the underbrush, in the vicinity of Mud Springs, (now Eldorado,) then a very sparsely populated mining district, when he came suddenly upon a large grizzly bear, which immediately raised upon and struck him, tearing off his clothing and making a few gashes in his flesh with the blow. The man had presence of mind to draw his knife, and, fortunately, with one blow he stabbed his antagonist in the heart, when he immediately fell with a groan. The man concluded to run, and when he returned to the spot, with assistance, the bear was dead. It was eventually taken to camp, and sold at one dollar and a quarter per pound, and as it weighed, when dressed, some little over eleven hundred pounds, it netted him about thirteen hundred dollars. He has many times since confessed that "it was the best prospect that he ever got!"

If a grizzly bear is suddenly disturbed, he will immediately make an attack upon the cause, whether it be man or beast. An acquaintance of ours when descending a brushy hill near Bird's Valley, in the spring of 1850, unfortunately came suddenly upon one, when it attacked and tore him so fearfully that for several months his life was despaired of, and though living, he is very badly disfigured in person.

◀ **James Mason Hutchings,** *Hutchings' Illustrated California Magazine,* published by Hutchings & Rosenfield, San Francisco, 1857–61, 8°, 5 vols, steel-engraved illustrations, gilt spine, half-leather.
£970–1,150 S(NY)

Hutchings (1820–1902) organized and led the first tourist party to Yosemite Valley, bringing along the artist Thomas Ayres to record their finds in 1855. The following year he began to publish this illustrated magazine to record the natural wonders of California, its economic development, and to promote tourism and settlement. His Illustrated Magazine *records some of the earliest images of Yosemite Valley and other sites, as well as of native peoples. An image of the Grizzly Bear that appeared in the September 1856 issue by Charles Nahl became the model for the grizzly on California's state flag.*

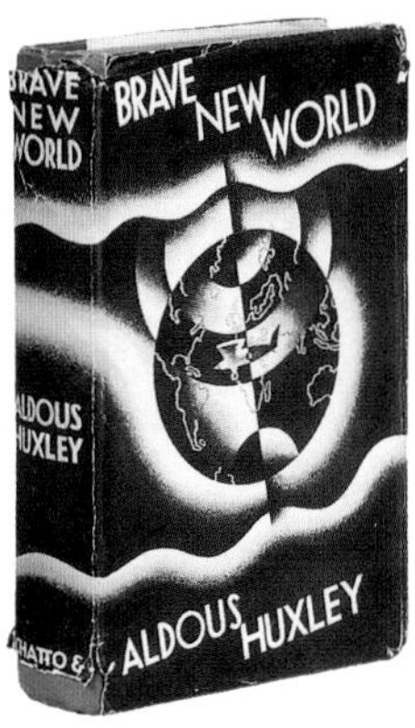

Aldous Huxley, *Brave New World,* published by Chatto & Windus, first edition, 1931, 8°, gilt, cloth, dust jacket.
£800–960 DW

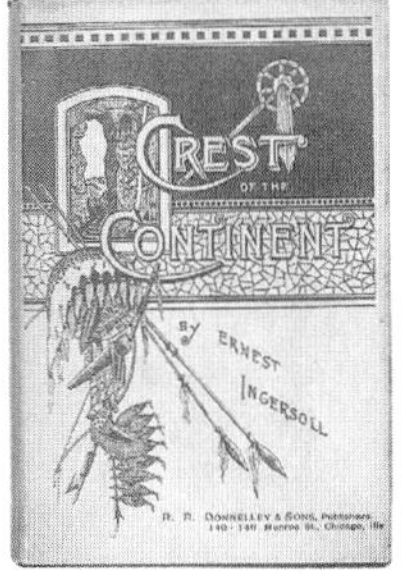

Ernest Ingersoll, *The Crest of the Continent: A Record of a Summer's Ramble in the Rocky Mountains and Beyond,* published by R. R. Donnelley & Sons, Chicago, first edition, pencil inscription, 1885, 8°, illustrations and folding map, gilt cloth, dust jacket.
£650–780 BBA

◀ **Kazuo Ishiguro,** *The Remains of the Day,* published by Faber & Faber, first edition, signed, 1989, 8°, original boards, dust jacket.
£280–330 BBA

▶ **T. Gwynn Jones,** *Detholiad o Ganiadau,* published by The Gregynog Press, Newtown, 1926, 8°, No. 7 of edition of 500, one of 30 copies specially bound, signed 'Gregynog Press Bindery', 9 wood-engraved head- and tail-pieces by R. A. Maynard, gilt spine and covers, morocco, original slipcase.
£1,550–1,850 S

In addition to the standard binding, a small number of Gregynog Press books were also available in a special binding. This copy was from a collection of the controller of the press, R. A. Maynard, who, it appears, always secured copy number 7.

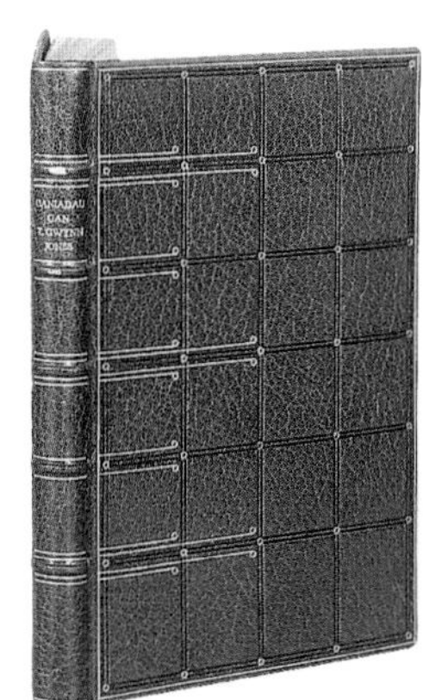

James Joyce, *Ulysses,* illustrated by Henri Matisse, published by The Limited Editions Club, New York, first illustrated edition, signed by Matisse, 1935, 4°, No. 732 of edition of 1,500.
£4,050–4,500 BRB

Although Joyce was to have signed the entire edition, he only signed 250 copies. Apparently, he felt incensed that Matisse had taken Homer's Odyssey *as inspiration for the illustrations.*

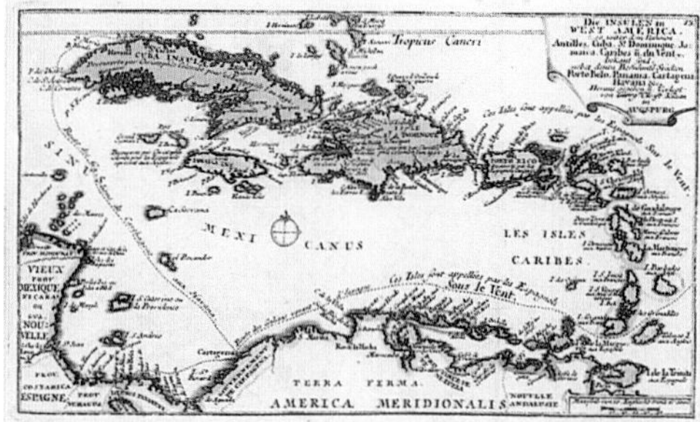

Georg Christoph Kilian, *Americanische Urquelle derer innerlichen Kriege des bedrängten Teutschlands...*, published by Georg Christoph Kilian, Augsburg, 1760, 4°, 60 maps, plans and plates on 59 leaves, mostly folding and hand-coloured, half-calf, some damage and losses.

£4,800–5,700 S

This is a rare work detailing events of the Seven Years' War outside Europe up to 1762, and hence charting the beginning of France's decline as a colonial power in North America and India, and prefiguring the rise of the United States. Eleven of the maps relate to America.

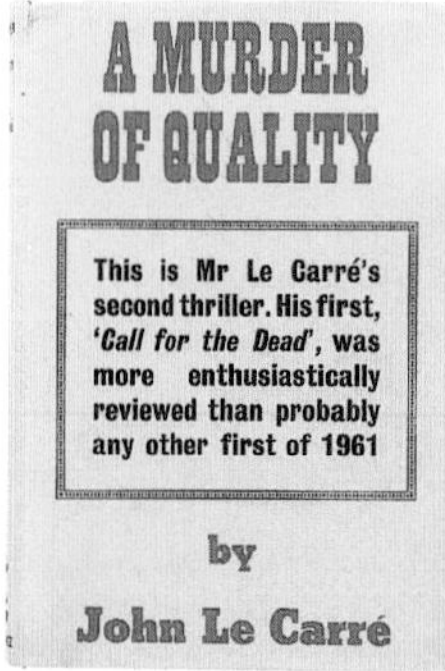

John Le Carré, *A Murder of Quality*, published by Victor Gollancz, first edition, signed, repaired, 1962, 8°, cloth, dust jacket.

£1,300–1,550 S

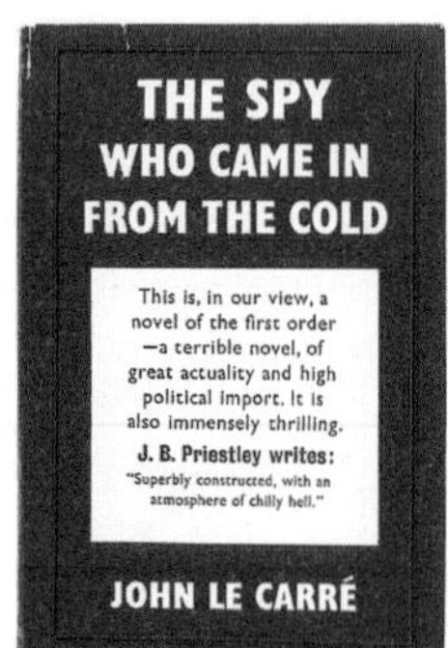

John Le Carré, *The Spy Who Came in from the Cold*, published by Victor Gollancz, first edition, 1963, 8°, original boards, dust jacket.

£770–920 BBA

► **Ted Lewis**, *Jack's Return Home*, published by Michael Joseph, London, first edition, 1970, 8°, dust jacket.

£770–860 BB

This is the novel that was made into the film Get Carter.

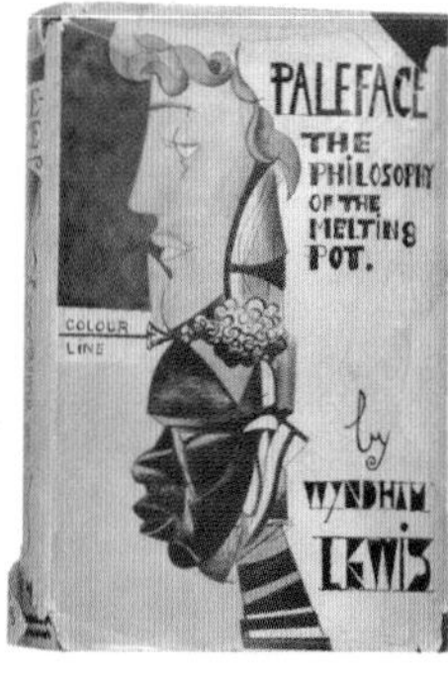

Wyndham Lewis, *Paleface – The Philosophy of the Melting Pot*, published by Chatto & Windus, London, first edition, 1929, 8°, dust jacket.

£110–125 BB

THE
True Method
OF
BREWING
STRONG ALE;
Such as
York, Nottingham, Lincoln, &c.
With a true way of Refining them.

LONDON,
Printed for *John Everingham*, at the *Star* in *Ludgate-street*, 1694.

◄ **James Lightbody**, *The Gauger and Measurer's Companion... to Which is Added...the True Method of Brewing Strong Ale*, published by John Everingham, London, 1694, 12°, three parts in one, contemporary sheep.

£1,300–1,550 BBA

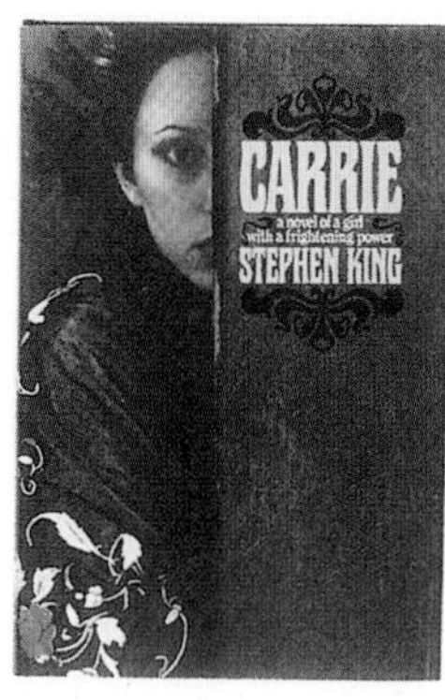

Stephen King, *Carrie*, published by Doubleday & Co, first edition, presentation inscription, 1974, 8°, cloth, dust jacket.

£1,550–1,850 S

Rudyard Kipling, *The Five Nations*, 1903, 8°, contemporary vellum by Chivers, decorated in inks and gilt with mother-of-pearl onlays.

£620–740 S

MILLER'S COMPARES

I. C.S. Lewis, *The Lion, the Witch and the Wardrobe*, illustrated by Pauline Baynes, published by Geoffrey Bles, first edition, 1950, 8°, cloth, dust jacket.

£5,900–7,000 DW

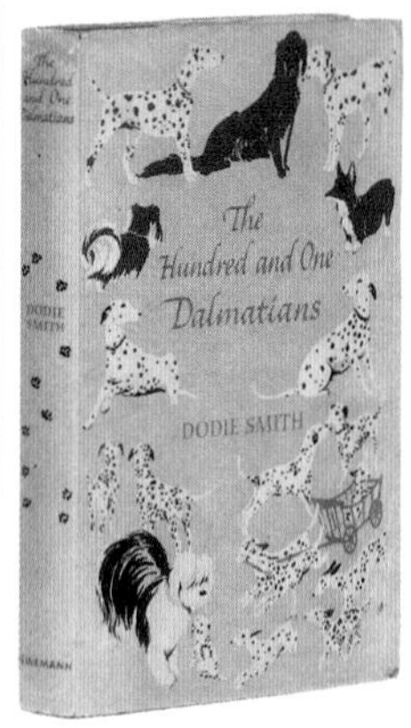

II. Dodie Smith, *The Hundred and One Dalmatians*, illustrated by Janet and Anne Grahame-Johnston, published by William Heinemann, first edition, 1956, 8°, cloth, dust jacket.

£240–280 DW

Although these two classic examples of children's literature were published within six years of each other, Item I realized over 24 times more at auction than Item II. Both were in original bindings and had their dust-jackets and both have been adapted into highly successful films. However, works by C. S. Lewis have always commanded higher prices than those by Dodie Smith. Lewis's *Chronicles of Narnia* have a cult following, and although there is a sequel to Smith's first novel it has never been highly regarded. Although Item I would always have realized more at auction than Item II, the recent film has added further to the value.

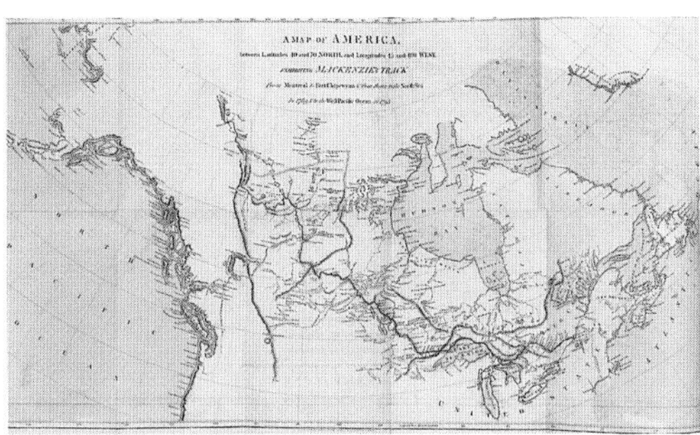

Alexander Mackenzie, *Voyages from Montreal, on the River St Laurence, through the Continent of North America, to the Frozen and Pacific Oceans; in the years 1789 and 1793. With a Preliminary Account of the Rise, Progress and Present State of the Fur Trade of that Country,* published by R. Noble, first edition, 1801, 4°, engraved frontispiece and three folded maps, contemporary calf, restored, with cloth folding case.

£2,250–2,700 S(NY)

This is a classic account of the first crossing of the continent north of Mexico by a European. Mackenzie's dual expeditions were intended to expand the field of trade for the North West Company, of which he was a member. His travel narrative is renowned for the accuracy of his investigation and observation. Brief vocabularies of the Cree, Algonquian, and Chipewyan tribes – all of whom Mackenzie traded with – are included.

Alistair MacLean, *H.M.S. Ulysses*, published by Collins, London, first edition, signed, 1955, 8°, gilt spine, cloth, dust jacket.

£160–180 BB

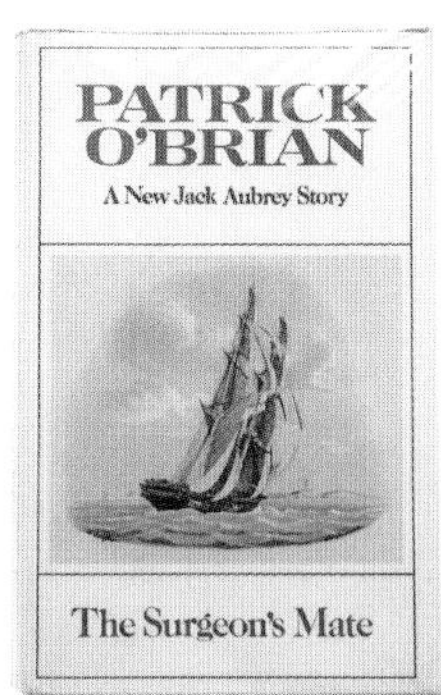

Patrick O'Brian, *The Surgeon's Mate*, published by Collins, London, first edition, 1980, 8°.

£560–630 BB

This is the seventh Jack Aubrey novel and it was printed in a comparatively small print run.

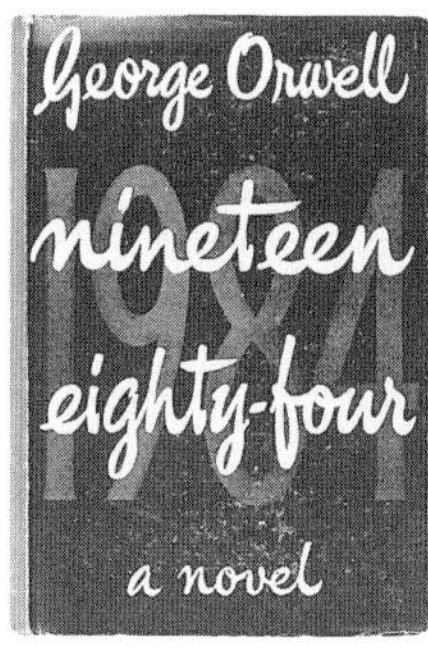

George Orwell, *Nineteen Eighty-Four*, published by Secker & Warburg, London, first edition, 1949, 8°, cloth, dust jacket.

£770–920 BBA

MILLER'S COMPARES

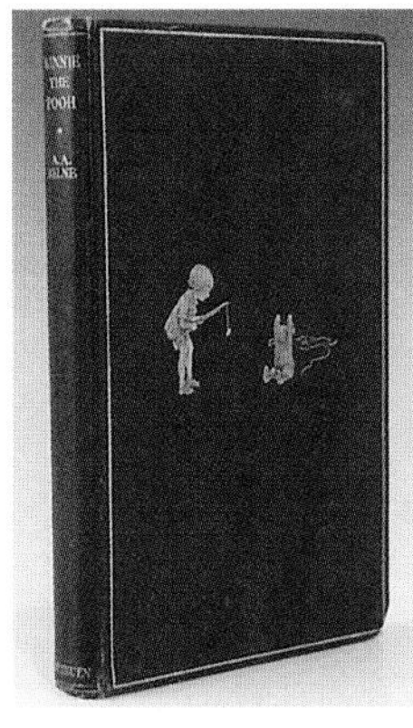

I. A. A. Milne, *Winnie-the-Pooh*, illustrated by E. H. Shepard, published by Methuen, first edition, 1926, 8°,original cloth.

£190–220 Rto

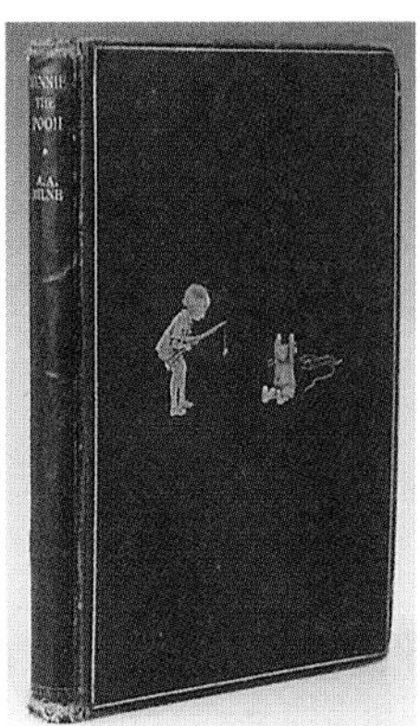

II. A. A. Milne, *Winnie-the-Pooh*, illustrated by E. H. Shepard, published by Methuen, first edition, 1926, 8°, original cloth.

£105–125 Rto

There are a great number of reasons why two apparently similar examples of the same edition may sell for different amounts in the same auction: provenance, competition and condition, for example. Condition appears to be the major factor here. Although Item I is damaged at the head and foot of the spine, Item II has a frayed spine. There may also have been internal factors – one may have had an ugly ownership signature or show browning and spotting.

The *Old Testament*, Low Countries, dated 29 July 1637, 8°, tooled leather.

£440–520 JAA

This book bears the bookplate of the artist Sir Lawrence Alma Tadema.

◀ **Boris Pasternak,** *Doctor Zhivago*, published by Feltrinelli, Milan, first authorized Russian language edition, 1957, 8°, dust jacket.

£300–360 BBA

Sir Arthur Quiller-Couch, *In Powder and Crinoline*, illustrated by Kay Nielsen, published by Hodder & Stoughton, 1913, 4°, No. 107 of edition of 500, 26 coloured plates, illustrated end papers, gilt-vellum, silk ties later.

£2,250–2,700 S

▶ **Ramon Reventos,** *Dos Contes, El centaure Picador, El capvespre d'un Faune,* illustrated by Pablo Picasso, published by Editions Albor Paris & Barcelona, 1947, 4°, loose leaves with 4 original engravings, limited Catalan edition of 250, ribbon fastening.

£3,600–4,300 S(P)

The Reventos brothers were among the friends of the young Picasso when he lived in Barcelona. Ramon, the writer, died prematurely in 1923. When Ferran Canyameres made known his intention to publish Catalan texts in France, Picasso thought of his old friend and suggested publishing Dos Contes, *for which he would provide the illustrations.*

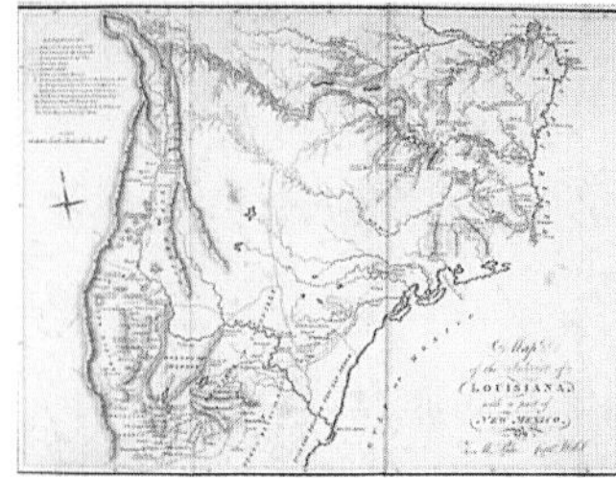

Zebulon Montgomery Pike, *Exploratory Travels through the Western Territories of North America,* first edition, 1811, 4°, parchment-backed marbled boards, slight damage.

£1,400–1,650 BBA

For further information on American Maps see pages 616–621

To Ivan Lebedeff —
Ayn Rand

Дорогой Старик,
От „маленькой девочки с испуганными глазами", на память о „гардеробе" и многом другом — мое первое оправдание Вашей доброты, помощи и веры в меня.
С глубокой благодарностью
Ваша
Старуха

3-19-1936

Ayn Rand, *We the Living,* published by Macmillan & Co, first edition, 1936, 8°, inscribed and signed in English and Russian, cloth, dust jacket, slight damage and repair.

£2,250–2,700 S(NY)

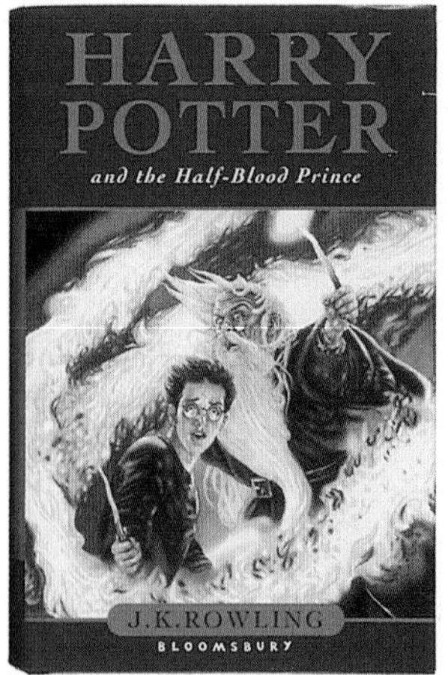

J. K. Rowling, *Harry Potter and the Half-Blood Prince,* published by Bloomsbury, first edition, signed, 2005, 8°, original picture boards, dust jacket.

£2,850–3,400 BBA

With the high financial value now attached to the author's signature, potential collectors should buy from recognized sources and enquire about provenance.

▶ **Alexander Pope Jr and Ernest Ingersoll,** *Upland Game Birds and Water Fowl of the United States,* published by Charles Scribner's Sons, New York, first edition, 1878, oblong 2°, in ten parts, loose as issued, 20 plates, some finished by hand, half morocco gilt portfolio/display easel, ribbon ties missing, some repair.

£4,850–5,800 S(NY)

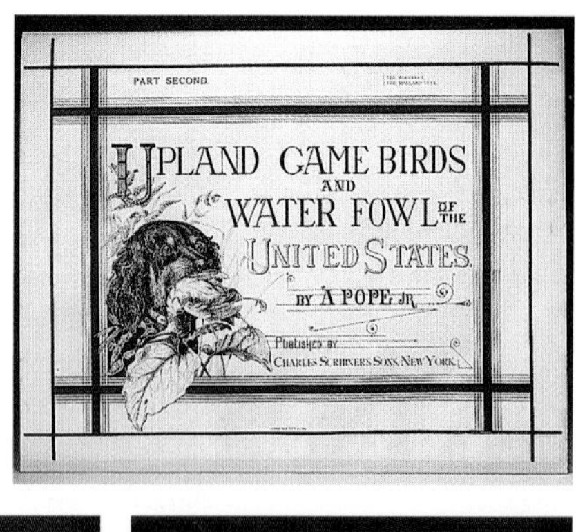

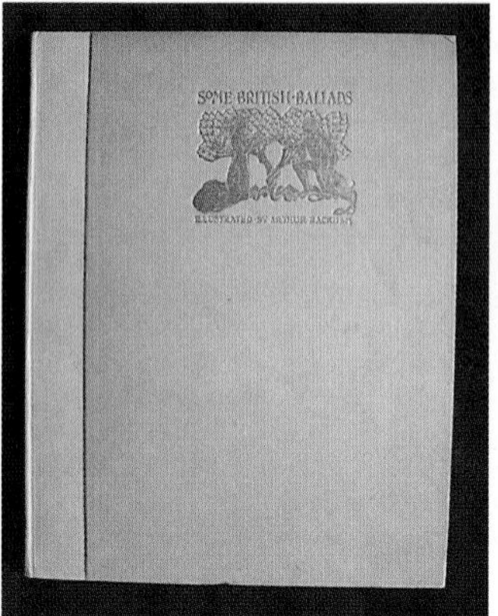

Arthur Rackham (illustrator), *Some British Ballads,* published by Constable, 1919, 4° edition of 575, signed by the illustrator.

£1,350–1,500 BI

THE FLOOD
Ian Rankin

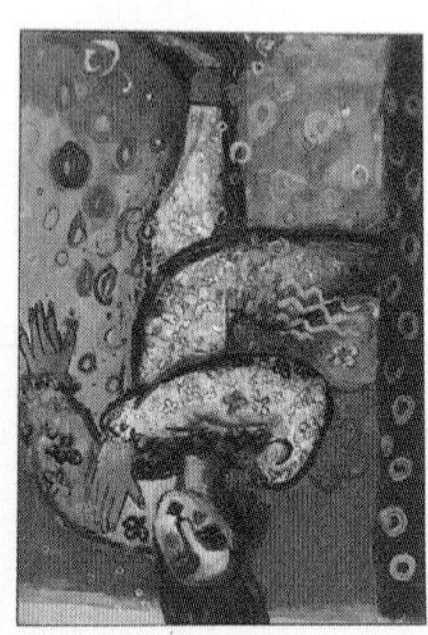

POLYGON
New Fiction

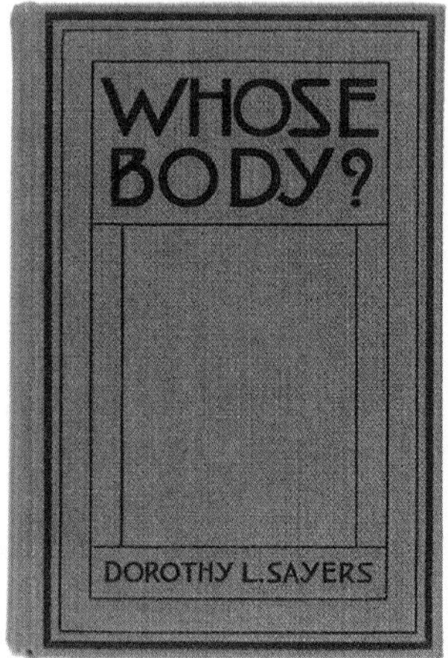

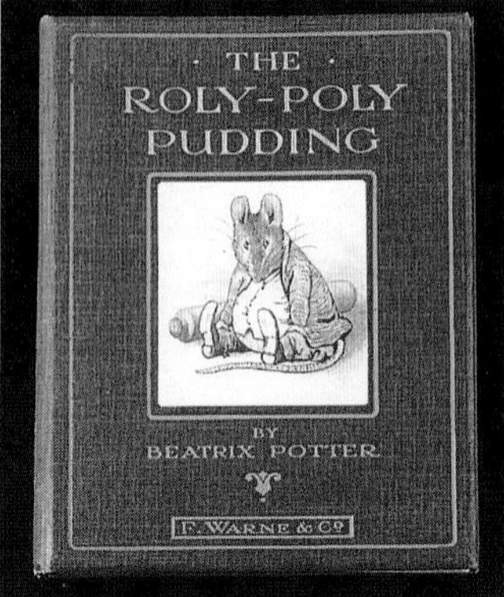

Beatrix Potter, *The Roly-Poly Pudding,* published by Frederick Warne & Co, London, first edition, 1908, 8°, 18 colour plates, pictorial endpapers, gilt letter and colour outlay of Samuel Whiskers on cloth upper cover.

£240–280 DN

◀ **Ian Rankin,** *The Flood,* published by Polygon, Edinburgh, first edition, signed, 1986, 8°.

£500–560 BB

This is the author's first book.

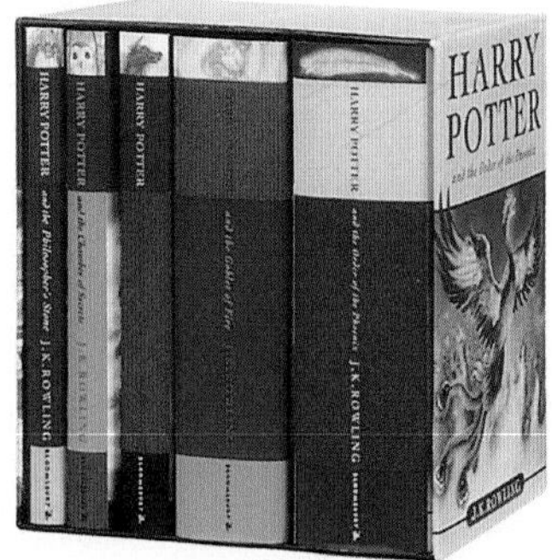

J. K. Rowling, *Harry Potter and the Philosopher's Stone, Harry Potter and the Chamber of Secrets, Harry Potter and the Prisoner of Azkaban, Harry Potter and the Goblet of Fire, Harry Potter and the Order of the Phoenix,* published by Bloomsbury, boxed set, all signed on the half-title, c2000, 8°, pictorial boards, dust jackets, slipcase.

£2,350–2,800 DW

◀ **Dorothy L. Sayers,** *Whose Body?,* published by Boni and Liveright, New York, first edition, 1923, 8°, cloth.

£1,900–2,250 S

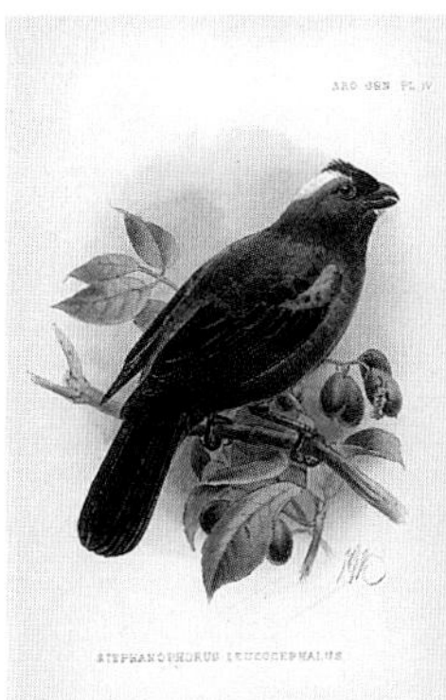

Philip Lutley Sclater and William Henry Hudson, *Argentine Ornithology. A Descriptive Catalogue of the Birds of the Argentine Republic,* published by R. H. Porter, London, first edition, 1888–89, 8°, 2 vols, 20 hand-coloured plates by Keulemans, printed boards.

£1,950–2,300 S(NY)

Alan Sillitoe, *Saturday Night and Sunday Morning,* published by W. H. Allen, first edition, 1958, 8°, cloth, dust jacket.

£190–220 BBA

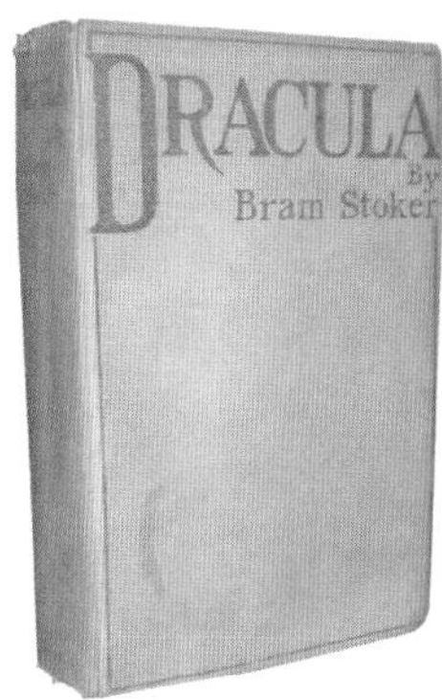

Bram Stoker, *Dracula,* published by Archibald Constable & Co, first American edition, 1897, 8°, cloth.

£1,650–1,950 G(L)

LOCATE THE SOURCE

The source of each illustration in Miller's can be found by checking the code letters below each caption with the Key to Illustrations, pages 746–753.

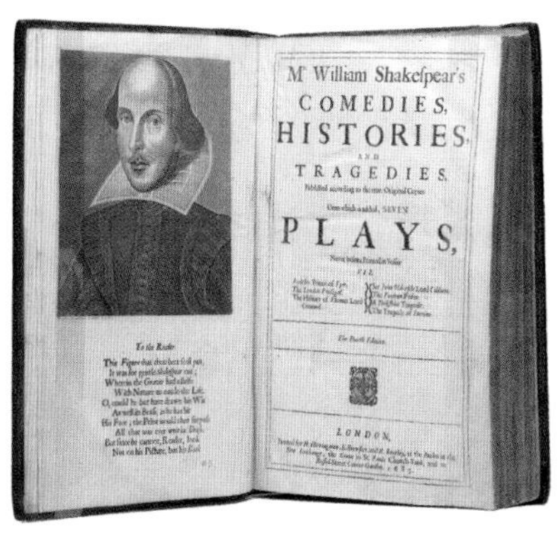

William Shakespeare, *Mr William Shakespeare's Comedies, Histories and Tragedies, published according to the true Original Copies. Unto which is added Seven Plays, Never Before Printed in Folio... The Fourth Edition,* 1685, 2°, morocco spine label, calf, in a morocco box.

£122,000–136,000 BRB

The four Folios of Shakespeare are the first four editions of Shakespeare's collected plays, which were the only collected editions printed in the 17th century. At that time, plays were not considered 'serious literature', they were to be performed and attended, not read, and thus they were not routinely printed.

This fourth folio 'contains the additional seven plays that first appeared in 1663 (third folio) edition (none of which, with the exception of Pericles, is now considered to be written by Shakespeare), as well as a good deal of correction and modernization of the text designed to make it easier to read and understand'. It was the last edition of Shakespeare's plays printed in the 17th century.

Sir George Thomas Staunton, *An Authentic Account of an Embassy from the King of Great Britain to the Emperor of China,* 1798, 4° and 2°, 3 vols, engraved portrait frontispieces and illustrations, atlas with 44 plates and maps, gilt spines, morocco.

£4,750–5,700 BBA

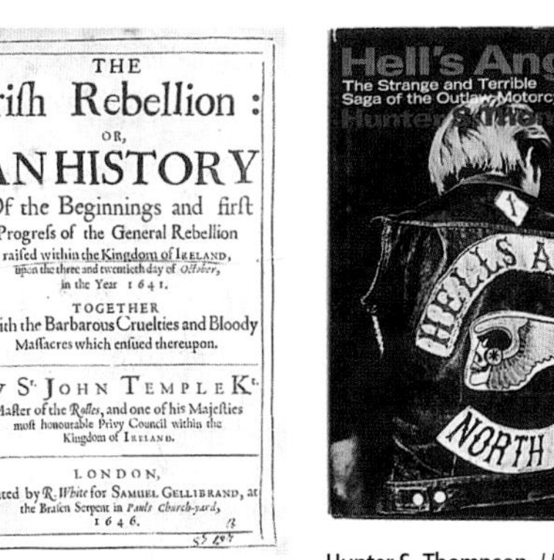

THE
Irish Rebellion:
OR,
AN HISTORY
Of the Beginnings and first
Progress of the General Rebellion
raised within the Kingdom of IRELAND,
upon the three and twentieth day of October,
in the Year 1641.
TOGETHER
With the Barbarous Cruelties and Bloody
Massacres which ensued thereupon.
By Sr JOHN TEMPLE Kt.
Master of the Rolles, and one of his Majesties
most honourable Privy Council within the
Kingdom of IRELAND.
LONDON,
Printed by R. White for SAMUEL GELLIBRAND, at
the Brasen Serpent in Pauls Church-yard,
1646.

Sir John Temple, *The Irish Rebellion: or, An History of the Beginnings and first Progress of the General Rebellion,* published by R. White for Samuel Gellibrand, first edition, 1646, small 4°, gilt calf.

£770–920 BBA

Hunter S. Thompson, *Hell's Angels,* published by Random House, first edition, New York, 1967, 8°, pictorial cloth, dust jacket.

£400–480 BBA

E. H. Shepard (illustrator), *Mole and Rat Sleepily Retiring to Bed with Candles,* ink drawing signed with initials, 1931, 4½ x 4¼in (11.5 x 11cm), framed and glazed.

£9,600–11,500 S

E. H. Shepard was a prolific artist and although most value has been realized by his Winnie-the-Pooh *illustrations, his other work is now beginning to be financially reassessed. This charming ink drawing was the tailpiece for the 1931 edition of Kenneth Grahame's* The Wind in the Willows *and exhibits all of Shepard's skill and charm.*

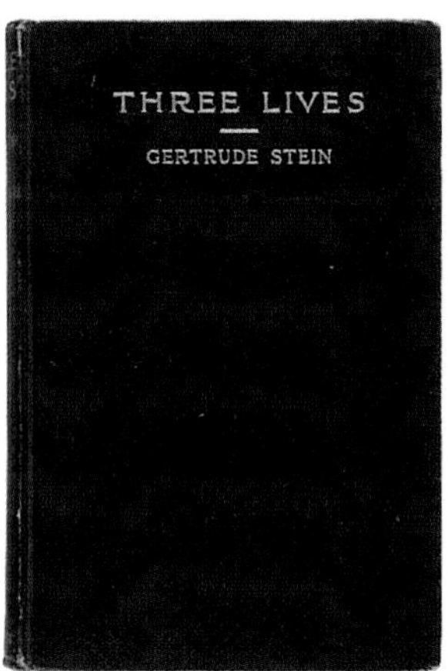

Gertrude Stein, *Three Lives: Stories of the Good Anna, Melanctha and the Gentle Lena,* published by Grafton Press, New York, first edition, 1909, 8°, cloth.

£380–450 BBA

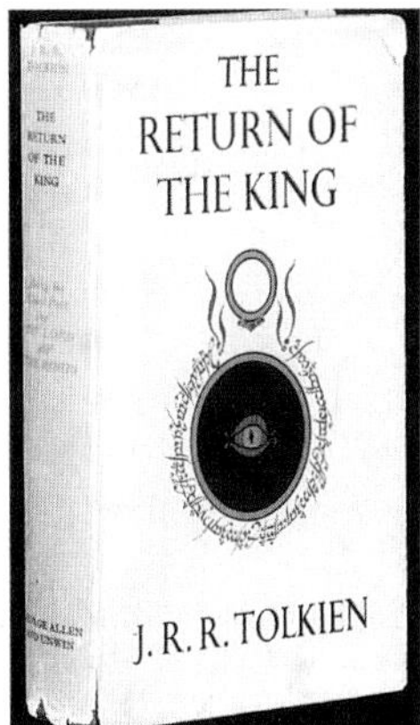

J. R. R. Tolkien, *The Return of the King,* published by Allen & Unwin, first edition, 1955, 8°, folding map, cloth, dust jacket.

£350–420 DW

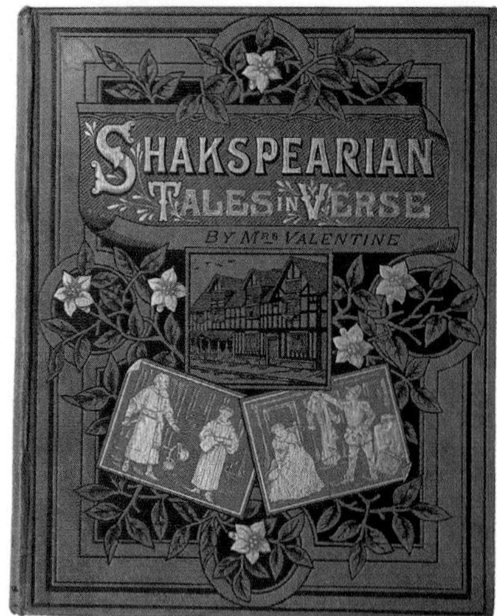

Mrs Valentine, *Shakespearian Tales in Verse*, illustrated by R. Andre, published by McLoughlin Bros, New York, 1880, 4°.

£140–160 ⊞ VAN

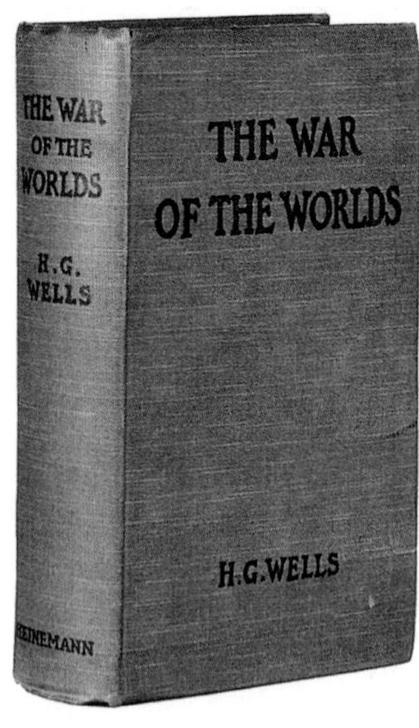

H. G. Wells, *The War of the Worlds*, published by William Heinemann, first edition, 1898, 8°, cloth, slight damage.

£750–900 DW

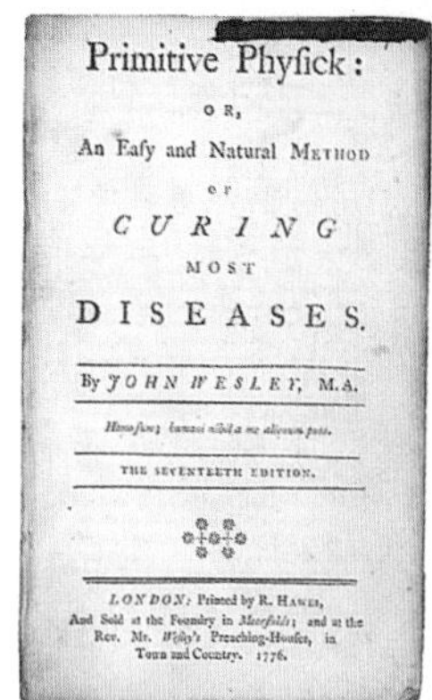

Primitive Phyfick:

OR,

An Eafy and Natural METHOD

OF

CURING

MOST

DISEASES.

By JOHN WESLEY, M.A.

THE SEVENTEENTH EDITION.

LONDON: Printed by R. HAWES,
And Sold at the Foundry in Moorfields; and at the Rev. Mr. Wesley's Preaching-Houses, in Town and Country. 1776.

John Wesley, *Primitive Physick: or, An Easy and Natural Method of Curing Most Diseases*, 1776, 12°, contemporary sheep, losses and damage.

£350–420 BBA

◄ **William Westall,** *Views of Australian Scenery*, 1814, oblong 2°, 9 engraved hand-coloured plates, gilt spine, slight damage and repair.

£1,400–1,650 BBA

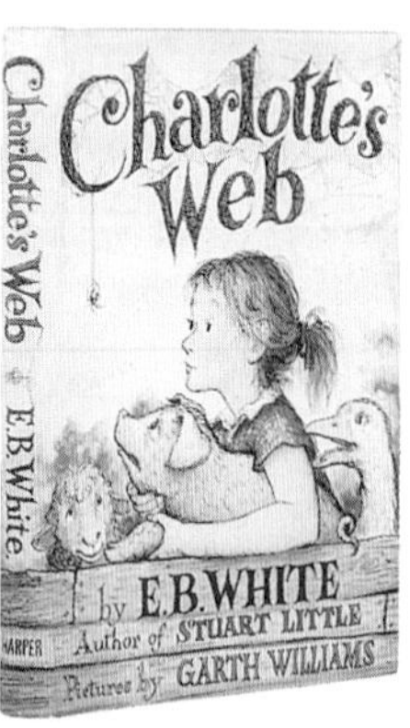

E. B. White, *Charlotte's Web*, illustrated by Garth Williams, published by Harper & Brothers, New York, first edition, 1952, 8°, illustrated endpapers, cloth, first issue dust jacket.

£780–930 S

◄ **William R. Wilde,** *Wilde's Loch Coirib*, 1936, 8°, dust jacket.

£95–105 ⊞ VAN

John White, *Journal of a Voyage to New South Wales*, first edition, 1790, 4°, engraved vignette title, 65 hand-coloured engraved plates, marbled boards, later half-diced russia.

£4,750–5,700 BBA

Alexander Wilson, *American Ornithology, or The Natural History of the Birds of the United States*, published by Robert Carr for Bradford and Inskeep, Philadelphia, first edition, 1808–14, 4°, 9 vols, 76 hand-coloured engraved plates, half calf.

£4,550–5,400 S(Am)

As a result of this comprehensive work depicting the majority of birds known in America at the time, Wilson became known as the father of American ornithology.

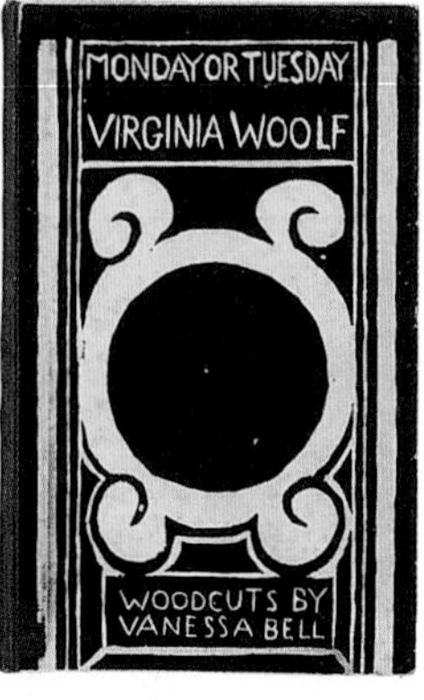

Virginia Woolf, *Monday or Tuesday*, 4 woodcuts by Vanessa Bell, published by Hogarth Press, first edition, 1921, 8°, cloth-backed boards.

£500–600 DW

W. B. Yeats, *The Secret Rose*, illustrated by J. B. Yeats, published by Lawrence & Bullen, first edition, 1897, 8°, black and white frontispiece and six plates, gilt cloth.

£800–960 DW

This copy is in superb condition and shows the sumptuous design by Althea Gyles in full glory.

MAPS & ATLASES

WORLD MAPS

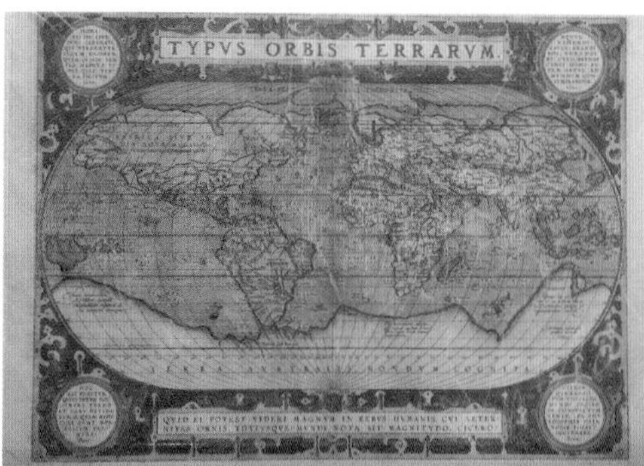

Abraham Ortelius, a hand-coloured map of the world, Belgium, Antwerp, 1588–1602, 20 x 22in (51 x 56cm).

£5,800–6,500 JT

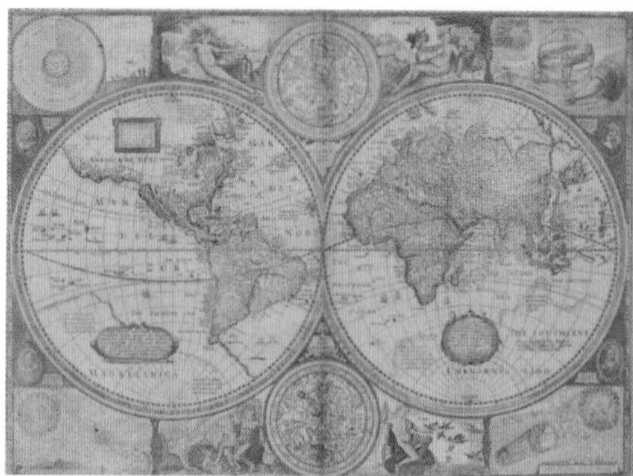

John Speed, a coloured map of the world, 1651, 16 x 21in (40.5 x 53.5cm).

£5,000–6,000 HYD

Justus Dankerts, an engraved and coloured map of the world, Holland, Amsterdam, 1685, 15 x 20in (38 x 51cm).

£4,900–5,500 JT

◀ **G. Bailleul,** a coloured copperplate map of the world, France, Paris, c1750, 20 x 24in (51 x 61cm).

£7,600–8,500 JOP

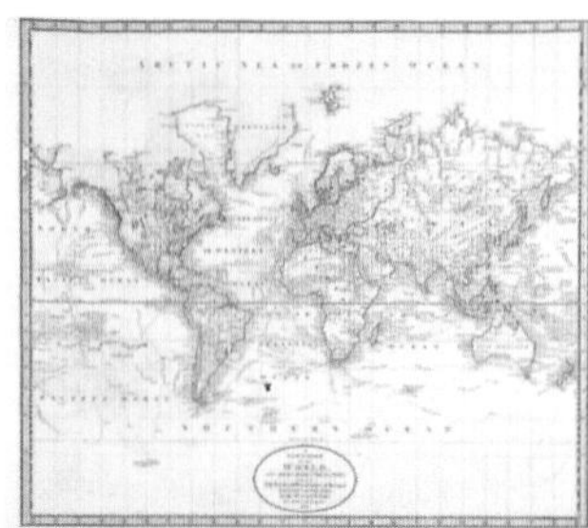

John Cary, *Cary's New Universal Atlas,* 60 coloured maps, 1799–1807, 21 x 23¾in (53.5 x 60.5cm).

£1,400–1,650 N

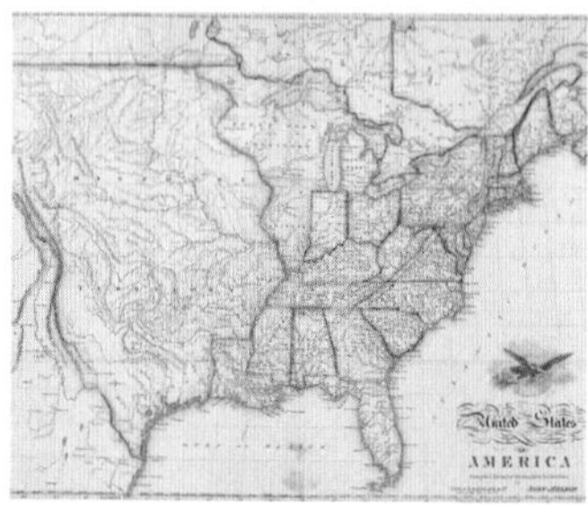

▶ **Abraham Rees,** *The Ancient and Modern Atlas, Containing Twenty Two Ancient and Forty Modern Maps,* published by Samuel F. Bradford and Murray, Fairman & Co, 1818, 2°, Philadelphia, 62 engraved hand-coloured maps, slight damage.

£900–1,050 FFAP

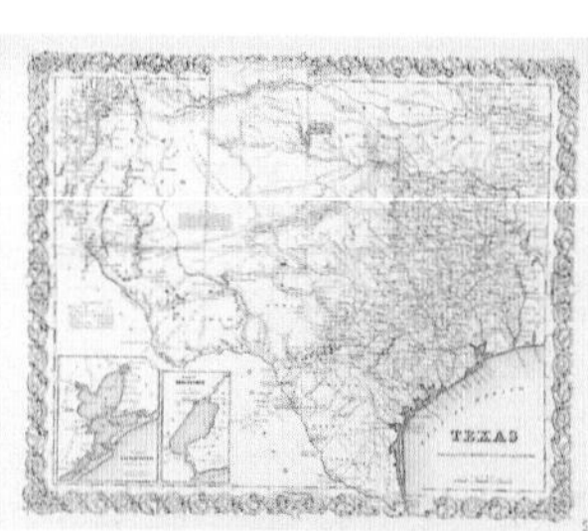

Richard Swainson Fischer, *Colton's Atlas of the World,* published by J. H. Colton & Co, New York and Trübner & Co, London, 1855, 2°, 2 vols, 103 engraved maps with original hand-coloured outlines, plans and plates, slight damage.

£2,600–3,100 S

The first edition of this important American atlas, Vol I is entirely devoted to the American continent and was sometimes issued separately. It includes 14 town plans and 32 state maps. Vol II covers the rest of the world.

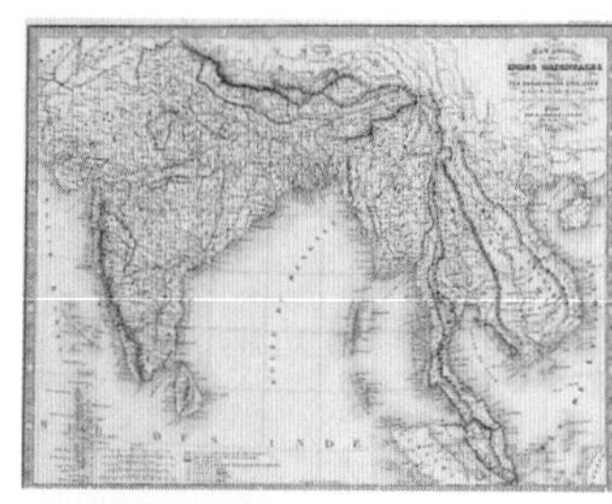

▶ **Eugene Andriveau-Goujon,** an atlas with 15 engraved maps with original hand-coloured outlines, damaged, France, c1850, large 2°.

£230–270 BBA

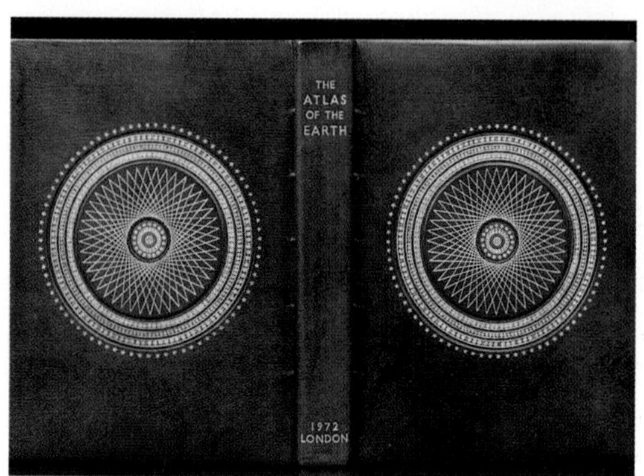

◀ ***The Atlas of the Earth,*** published by Mitchell Beazley with George Philip & Son, first edition, signed, 1972, 2°, gilt-tooled morocco by Bernard Middleton.

£4,800–5,700 S

AMERICAS

Abraham Ortelius, *Maris Pacifici*, a coloured copperplate map of the Pacific Ocean showing north and south America and New Guinea, Belgium, Antwerp, 1590–1606, 14 x 20in (35.5 x 51cm).

£7,200–8,000 JOP

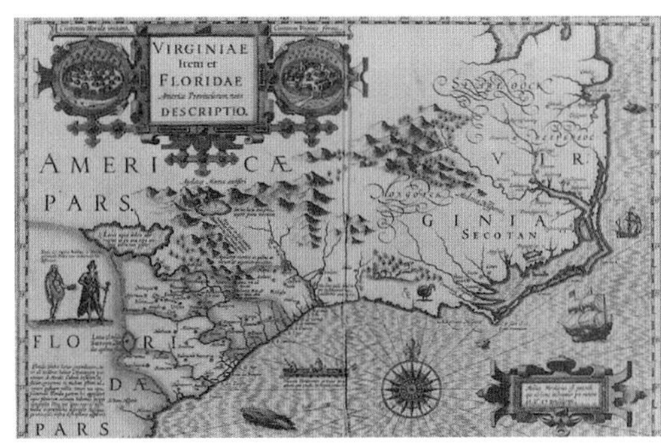

Gerard Mercator and Jocodus Hondius, *Virginiae item ed Floridae Americae provinciarum*, hand-coloured map incorporating vignettes of native villages typical of Florida and Virginia, Holland, Amsterdam, 1610 and later, framed 14 x 19¼in (35.5 x 49cm).

£1,750–2,100 S(NY)

◀ **Henricus Hondius,** *Nova Virginiae*, copperplate map with original outline colouring, Holland, Amsterdam, 1630–47, 15 x 20in (38 x 51cm).

£2,150–2,400 JOP

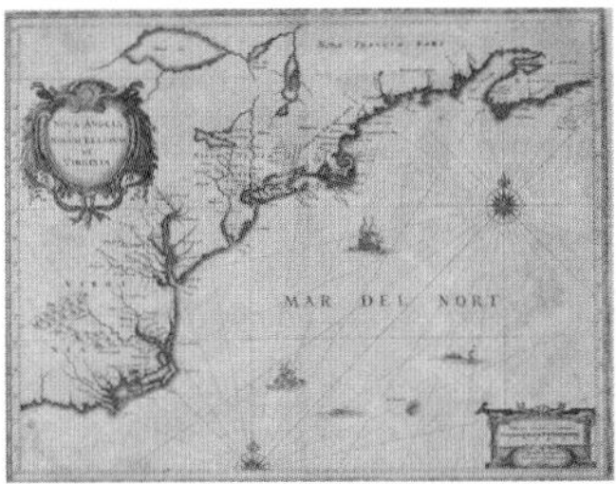

Jan Jansson, *Nova Anglia, Nova Belgium et Virginia*, copperplate map with original outline colouring, Holland, Amsterdam, 1636–47, 15 x 20in (38 x 51cm).

£2,150–2,400 JOP

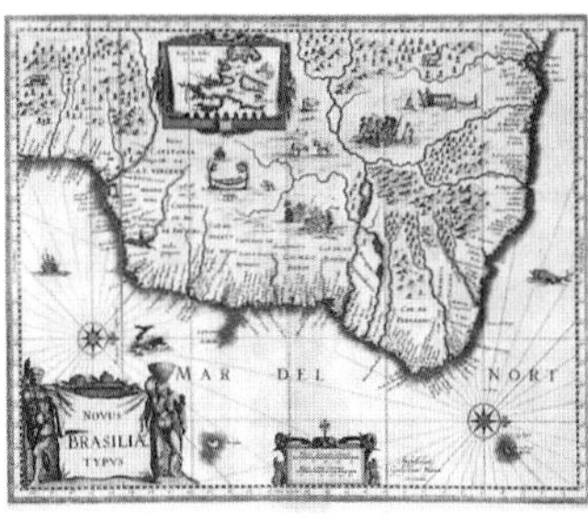

Henricus Hondius and Willem Blaeu, *Novus Brasiliae Typus*, hand-coloured with animals, birds and native scenes, Holland, Amsterdam, 1635, 15 x 19½in (38 x 49.5cm).

£350–420 BBA

This map was originally engraved by Hondius and acquired by Blaeu in 1629.

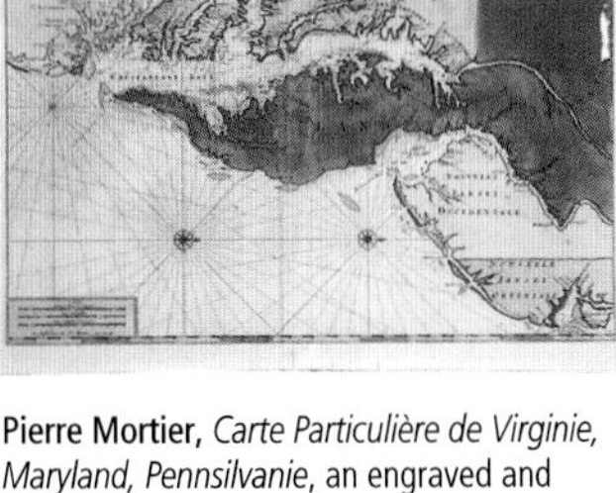

Pierre Mortier, *Carte Particulière de Virginie, Maryland, Pennsilvanie*, an engraved and hand-coloured chart, damaged, Holland, Amsterdam, 1693, 21¼ x 31½in (54 x 80cm).

£520–620 BBA

▶ **John Senex,** *America*, an engraved map, depicting California as an island, America, early 18thC, 8 x 10in (20.5 x 25.5cm).

£220–260 DW

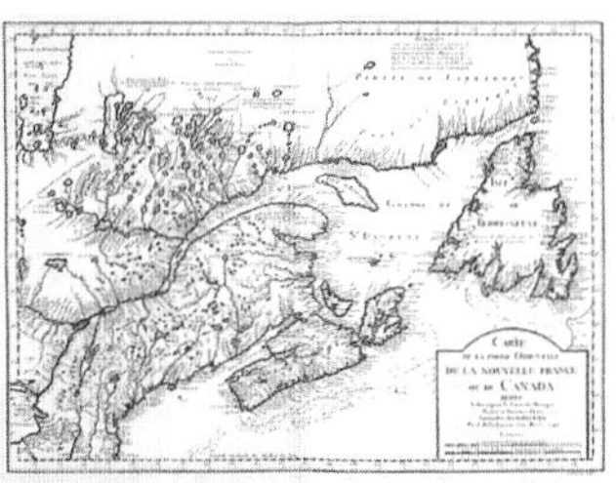

Guillaume de l'Isle, a coloured copperplate map of Louisiana and the course of the Mississippi, published by Covens & Mortimer, Holland, Amsterdam, 1718–30, 18 x 23in (45.5 x 58.5cm).

£2,150–2,400 JOP

Georg Matthäus Seutter, *United States – New England*, a hand-coloured engraved map inset with a view of New York, Germany, c1740, 19¾ x 22¾in (50 x 58cm).

£1,850–2,200 DW

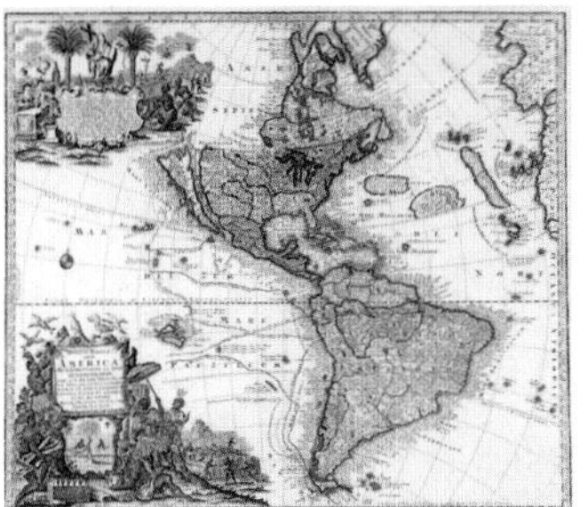

Georg Matthäus Seutter, *America*, a hand-coloured engraved map, depicting California as an island, slight damage, Germany, c1740, 19¾ x 22¾in (50 x 58cm).

£800–960 DW

J. N. Bellin, *Carte de la Partie Orientale de la Nouvelle France ou du Canada*, engraved map, slight damage, France, Paris, 1744, 15¾ x 22in (40 x 56cm).

£210–250 BBA

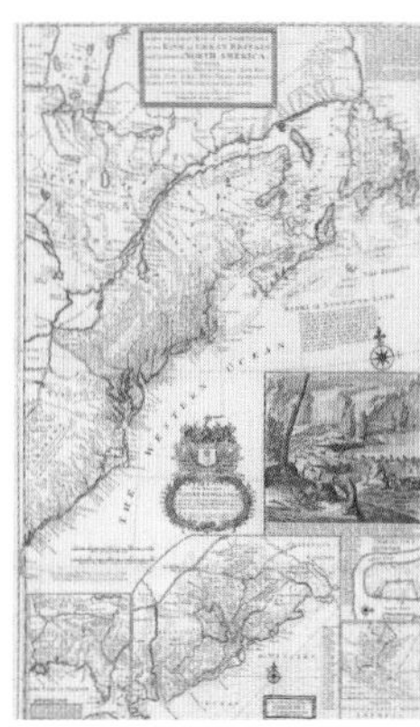

◀ **Herman Moll,** *A New and Exact Map of the Dominions of the King of Great Britain on Ye Continent of North America*, published by Thomas & John Bowles, London, 1755, 40 x 24in (101.5 x 61cm).

£7,800–9,300 FFAP

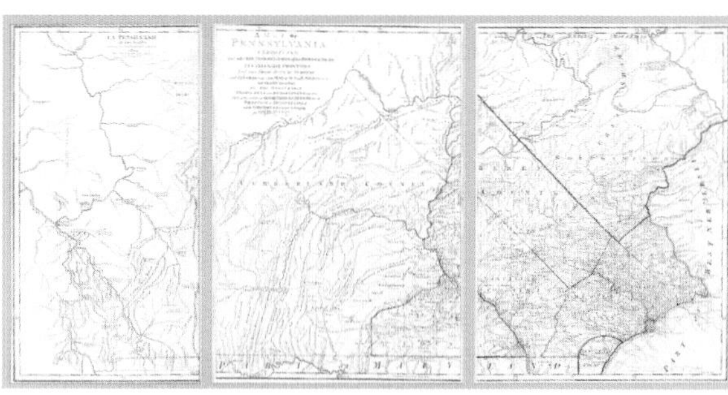

William Scull, *Pennsylvania*, a hand-coloured engraved map with original outline colouring, France, Paris, 1777, 53 x 27¼in (134.5 x 69cm), framed.

£2,250–2,700 FFAP

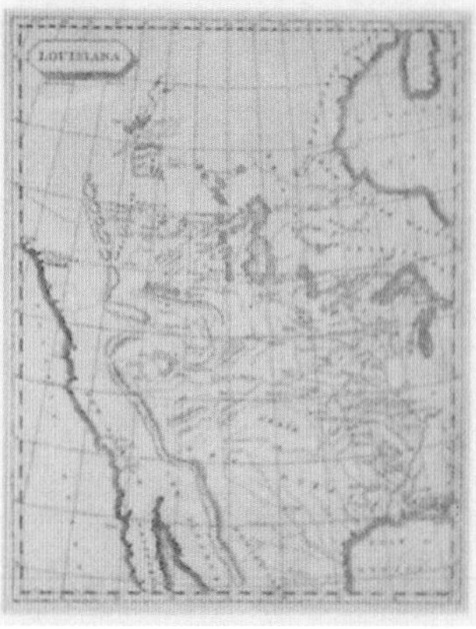

S. Lewis, *Louisiana*, engraved by Tanner, early 19thC, 10¼ x 8¼in (26 x 21cm), framed.

£250–300 NOA

Louis Delarochette, *Colombia Prima, or South America*, an engraved map with coloured outline on two sheets, joined, published by W. Faden, slight damage, 1811, 42¼ x 29¾in (107.5 x 75.5cm).

£130–155 BBA

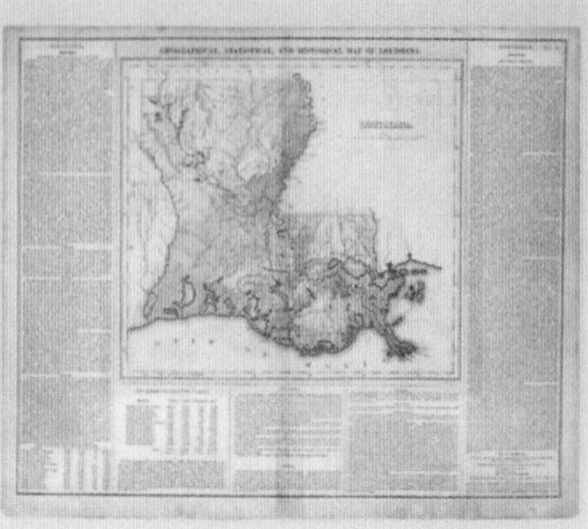

Geographical, Statistical and Historical Map of Louisiana, printed by Kneass, America, Philadelphia, 1825–50, 17½ x 21¾in (44.5 x 55.5cm), framed.

£350–420 NOA

ASIA & AUSTRALIA

Abraham Ortelius, *Indiae Orientalis*, engraved map of southeast Asia, hand-coloured, Belgium, Antwerp, 1570 or later, 13¾ x 19½in (35 x 49.5cm).

£2,100–2,500 BBA

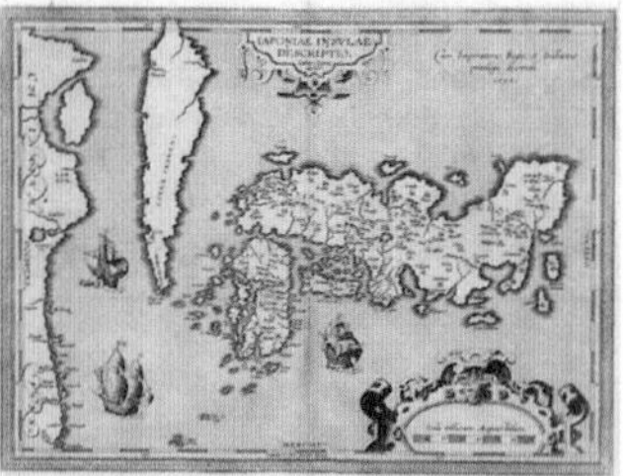

Abraham Ortelius, *Japoniae Insulae Descriptio*, after Ludoico Teisera, an engraved map showing the east coast of China and Korea, illustrated with galleons, some restoration, Belgium, Antwerp, 1595, 14 x 19in (35.5 x 48.5cm).

£1,150–1,350 BBA

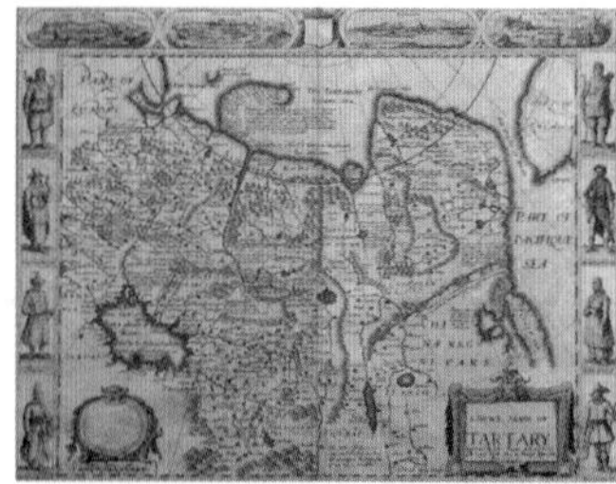

John Speed, *Map of Tartary*, engraved by D. Gryp, with later colouring, c1627, 16 x 20in (40.5 x 51cm).

£810–900 JT

Tobias Conrad Lotter, *Asia*, a hand-coloured engraved map, damaged and repaired, Germany, Augsburg, 1740 or later, 19 x 23in (48.5 x 58.5cm).

£160–190 BBA

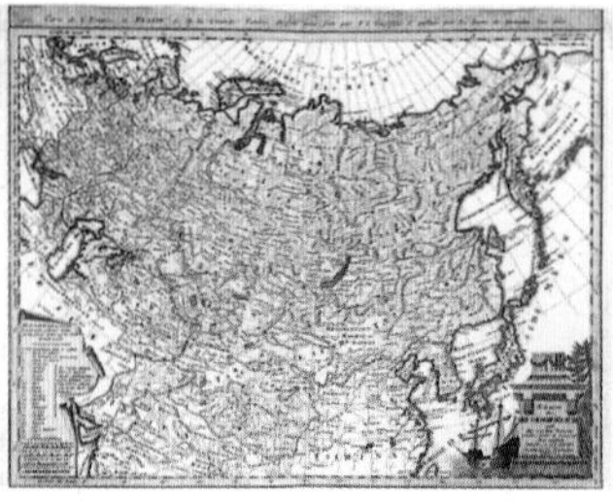

Franz Ludwig Gussefeld, an engraved and hand-coloured map of Russia, with northern China and Japan, slight damage and repair, Germany, Nuremberg, 1786, 18¼ x 24in (46.5 x 61cm).

£200–240 BBA

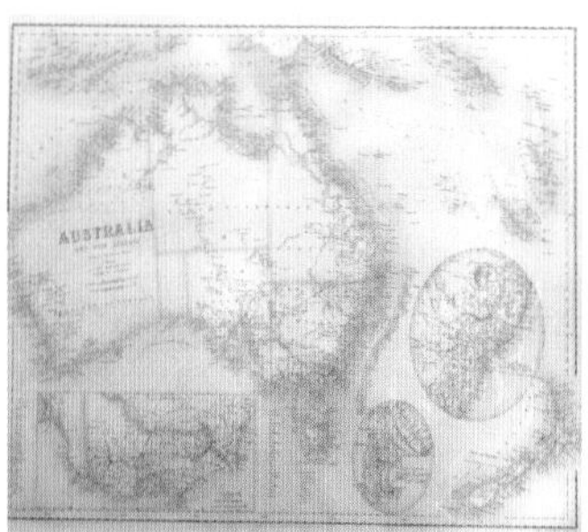

A. Fullerton, *Australia*, engraved by G. H. Swanston, with original hand colouring, c1850, 17 x 21in (43 x 53.5cm).

£140–155 JT

EUROPE & THE MIDDLE EAST

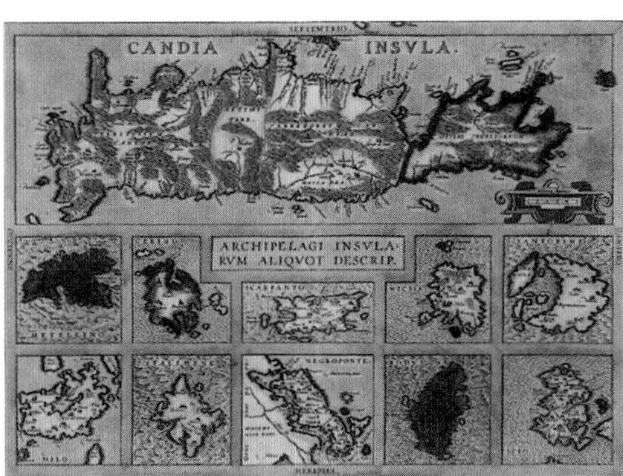

Abraham Ortelius, *Candia Insula,* an engraved map of Crete, with original hand colouring and ten inset maps of other islands, slight damage, Belgium, Antwerp, 1570 or later, 14¼ x 20in (36 x 51cm).

£300–360 BBA

Abraham Ortelius, *Terra Sancta*, an engraved and hand-coloured map of the Holy Land, slight damage and repair, Belgium, Antwerp, 1584 or later, 14½ x 20in (37 x 51cm).

£540–640 BBA

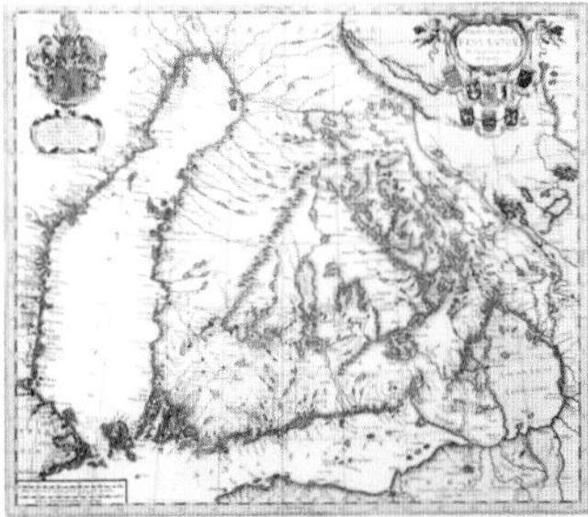

Jan Jansson, a map of Finland, Holland, Amsterdam, c1680, 17 x 20½in (43.5 x 52cm).

£1,400–1,650 BUK(F)

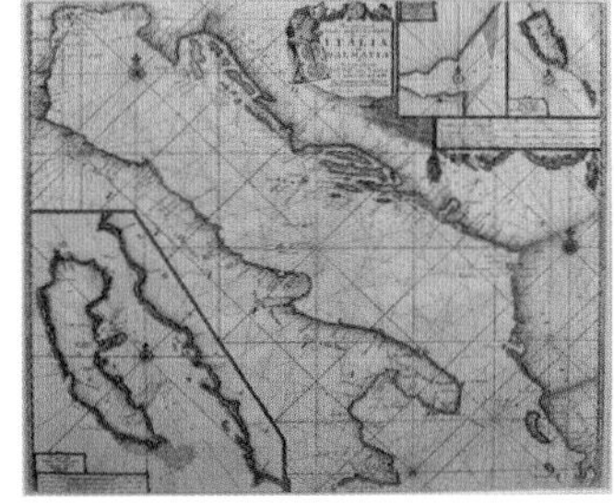

J. Van Keulen, a coloured copperplate chart of Italy and Dalmatia, Holland, Amsterdam, c1680, 21 x 24in (53.5 x 61cm).

£760–850 JOP

Philip Lea, an engraved map of Europe, with later hand colouring, c1690, 19 x 22in (48.5 x 56cm).

£760–850 JT

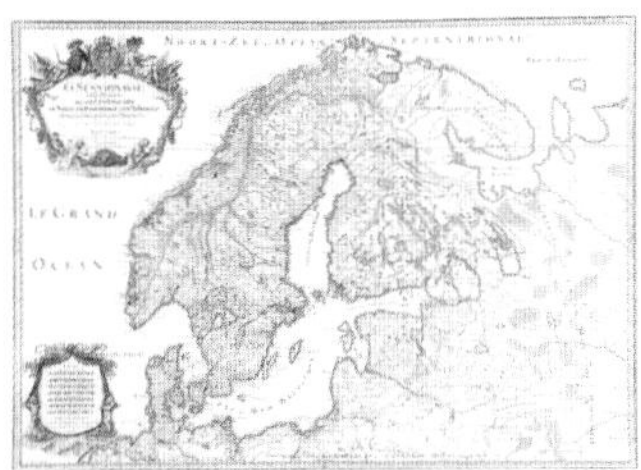

Nicolas Sanson, a map of Scandinavia, France, 1708, 18¾ x 25½in (47.5 x 65cm).

£750–900 BUK(F)

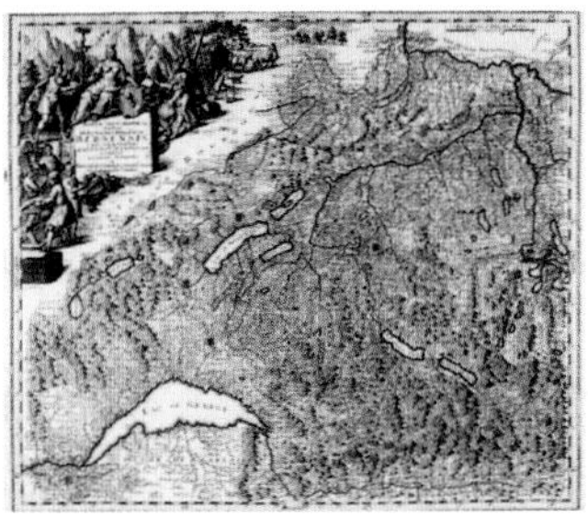

Georg Matthäus Seutter, an engraved and hand-coloured map of Switzerland, slight damage, Germany, 1730s, 19¾ x 22¾in (50 x 58cm).

£105–125 DW

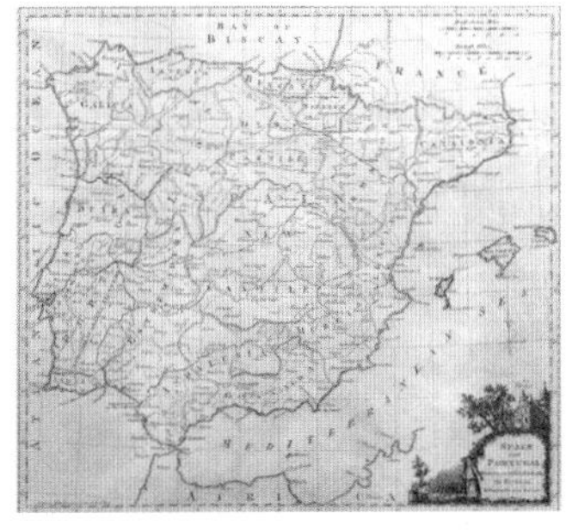

T. Kitchin, *Spain and Portugal*, a copperplate map with original hand colouring, c1780, 14 x 15in (35.5 x 38cm).

£70–80 JT

◀ **A road map of France for automobiles,** published by De Dion-Bouton, mounted on canvas, France, Paris, c1900, 61¾ x 50¾in (157 x 129cm).

£2,750–3,300 S(P)

De Dion-Bouton was one of the largest and most prestigious car manufacturers of the early 20th century. Count Albert de Dion contributed greatly to the development of the automobile, and in particular by founding the Automobile Club of France in 1895. It was around 1900 that De Dion-Bouton began using road maps as a promotion vehicle. The company took advantage of the festivities organized for the beginning of the new century by producing a one-page map of France commemorating De Dion-Bouton's history since its creation in 1882. The map shown here is surrounded by drawings of models produced prior to that date, accompanied by explanatory notes.

GREAT BRITAIN & IRELAND

◀ **Abraham Ortelius,** an engraved and hand-coloured map of England and Wales, based on earlier maps by Humphrey Lhuyd and Mercator, the title cartouche flanked by two figures, Belgium, Antwerp, 1573, 15¾ x 19¼in (40 x 49cm).

£260–310 DN

Christopher Saxton and William Kip, *Devoniae Comitatus*, an engraved and hand-coloured map, c1607, 11¾ x 13½in (30 x 34.5cm).

£130–155 BBA

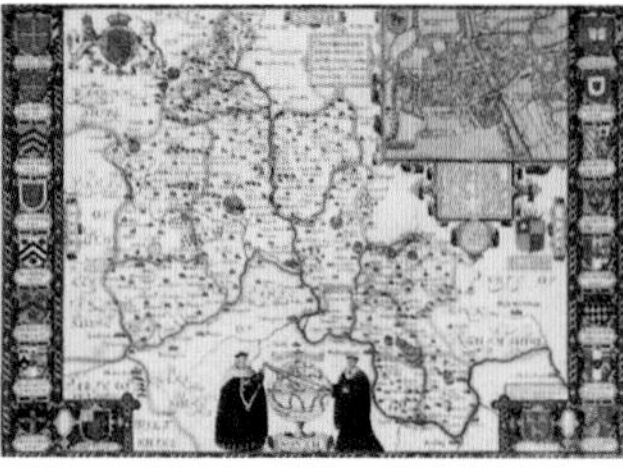

John Speed, *Oxfordshire Described*, engraved and hand-coloured map, with an inset street plan of Oxford, decorated with figures and armorials, repaired, 1611 or later, 15 x 20in (38 x 51cm).

£1,350–1,600 DW

Michael Drayton, a hand-coloured map of Kent, 1612–22, 11 x 13in (28 x 33cm).

£310–350 JT

William Camden *Britannia,* 46 engraved maps, 1617, bound with Thomas Smith, *De Rupublica et administratione Anglorum libri tres*, France, Strasbourg, 1625, 8°.

£1,650–1,950 S

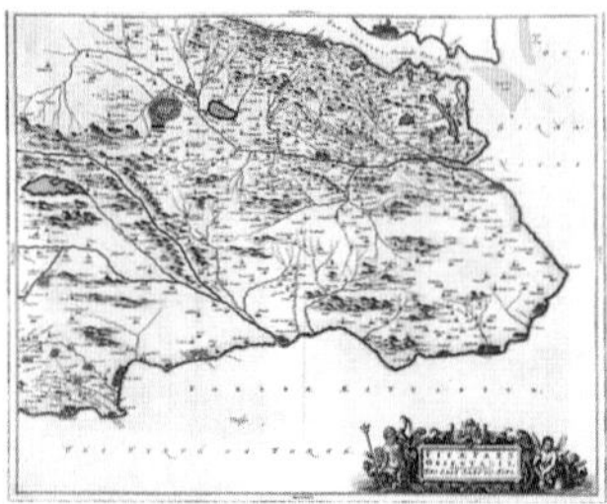

Joan and Willem Blaeu, *Fifae Pars Orientalis*, engraved and hand-coloured map of Fife and the Firth of Forth, Holland, Amsterdam, c1650, 16½ x 21in (42 x 53.5cm).

£390–460 BBA

◀ **Joan Blaeu,** *Wallia*, a map of Wales, Holland, 1662, 5 x 19½in (38 x 49.5cm), framed.

£640–760 PF

▶ **Nicolas Visscher,** a map of Great Britain, with original colouring, 1693, 21 x 24in (53.5 x 61cm).

£900–1,000 VHA

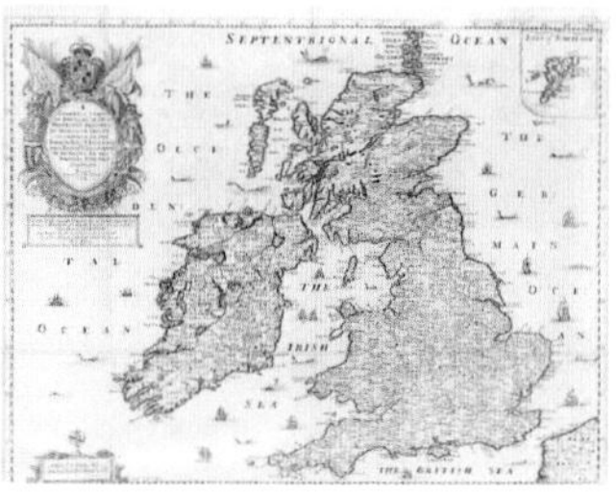

Richard Blome, *Britannia*, 1673, 2°, 24 engraved leaves, engraved map of British Isles, 49 double-page engraved county maps, single-page plan of London, repaired.

£8,400–10,000 S

Robert Morden, a map of Ireland, from *Camden's Britannia*, 1722, 14 x 16in (35.5 x 40.5cm).

£200–230 NEP

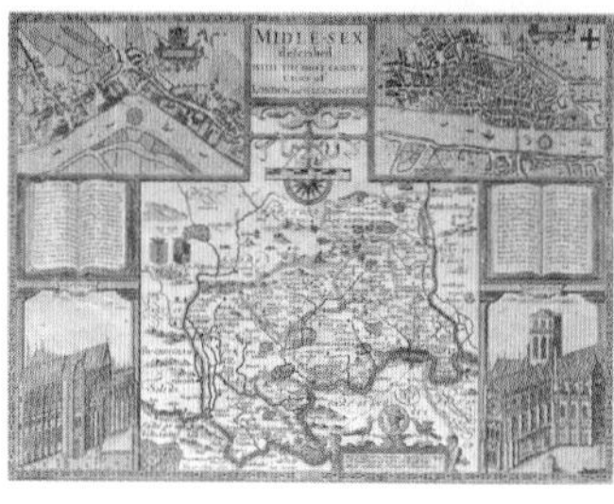

Jodocus Hondius, *Middlesex Described*, an engraved map after John Speed, with later hand colouring, 1743, 16 x 21in (40.5 x 53.5cm).

£1,100–1,250 JT

John Harrison, *A New Map of Ireland*, with later colouring, 1787, 16 x 14in (40.5 x 35.5cm).

£140–160 NEP

POLAR MAPS

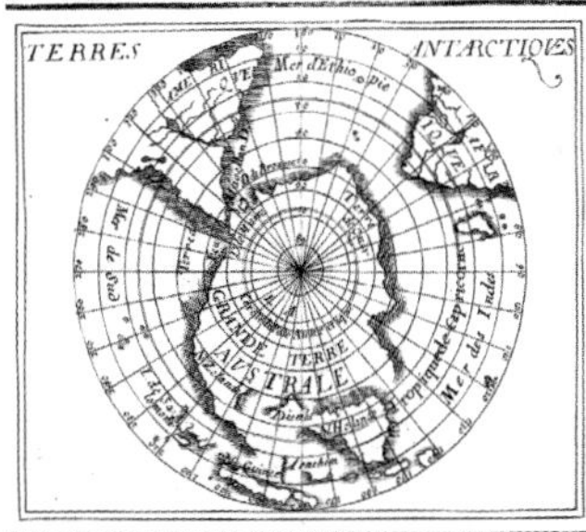

Pierre du Val, *Terres Antarctiques,* a copperplate map of the Antarctic, from the miniature volume *La Géographie Universelle,* France, 1661, 4 x 4½in (10 x 11.5cm).

£280–320 JOP

This map was first published in 1661 and then republished at a later date. There is no way of knowing whether this particular map is from the original date or later.

▶ **Lewis Hebert and John Pinkerton,** an engraved copperplate map of the southern hemisphere, engraved by Neele, from *Pinkerton's Modern Atlas,* published by Cadell & Davies, Longman, Hurst, Rees, Orme & Brown, 1812, 22 x 20in (56 x 51cm).

£300–340 JOP

Frederick de Wit, an engraved map of the North Pole with original colouring, with vignettes of whaling scenes, damaged, Holland, Amsterdam, c1680, 17¼ x 19½in (44 x 49.5cm).

£380–450 BBA

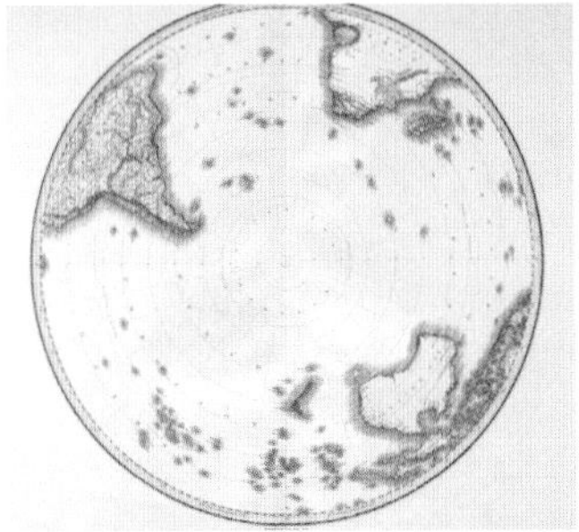

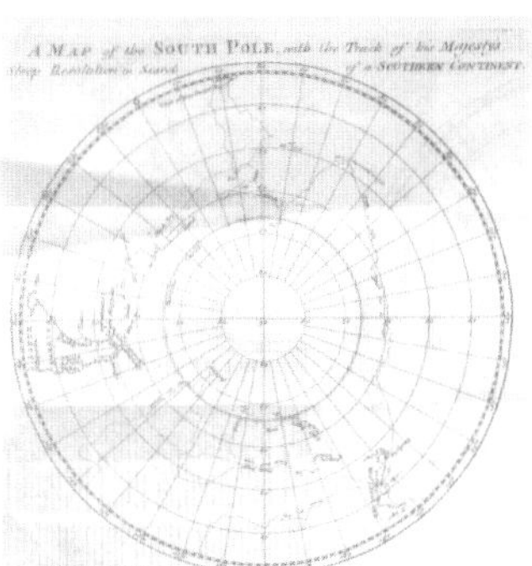

Thomas Bowen, *The South Pole, with Track of His Majesty's Sloop, Resolution,* a copperplate map, published by the *Gentleman's Magazine,* London, 1776, 9½in (24cm) square.

£270–300 JOP

The Resolution *was Captain James Cook's ship for his second major voyage to the Pacific and its tracks of 1772 to 1775 are marked on this map. Sandwich Land and the Isle of Georgia are named, and the Capes of Horn and Good Hope are depicted along with New Zealand, but there is no Antarctic landmass.*

TOWN & CITY PLANS

Georg Braun and Frans Hogenberg, an engraved plan of Algiers, with original hand colouring, damaged, Germany, Cologne, c1575, 13¾ x 19¾in (35 x 50cm).

£155–185 BBA

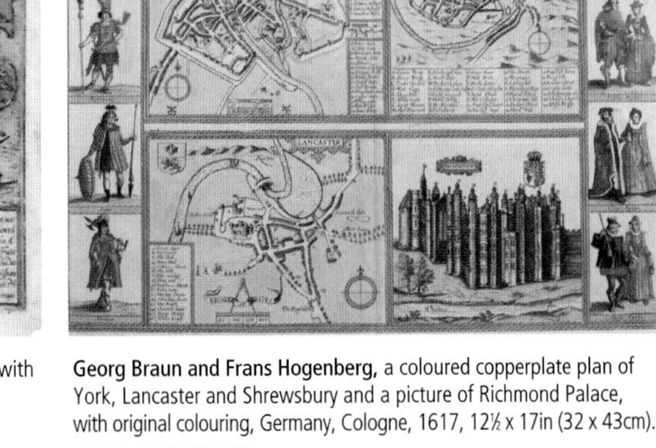

Georg Braun and Frans Hogenberg, a coloured copperplate plan of York, Lancaster and Shrewsbury and a picture of Richmond Palace, with original colouring, Germany, Cologne, 1617, 12½ x 17in (32 x 43cm).

£720–800 JOP

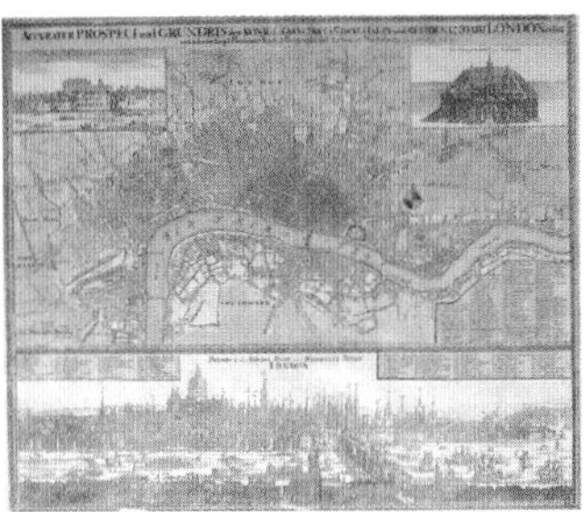

Johann Baptist Homann, an engraved plan of London, with original hand colouring, Germany, c1700, 20 x 23in (51x 58.5cm).

£1,350–1,500 JT

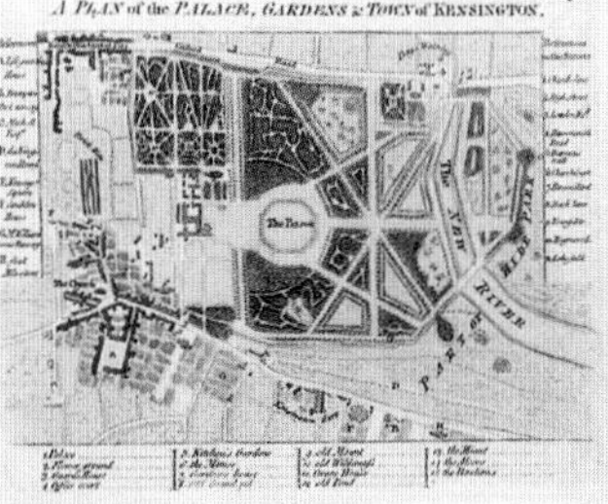

◀ **Andrew Dury,** *A Collection of Plans of the Principal Cities of Great Britain and Ireland,* 22 double-page engraved and hand-coloured maps by J. Ellis, 19 double-page engraved and hand-coloured city plans, first edition, 1764, 8°.

£1,900–2,250 S

▶ **A plan of St Petersburg,** 1844, 14¼ x 19in (36 x 48.5cm).

£710–850 BUK(F)

SOFT TOYS

A Chad Valley velveteen **Bonzo dog**, jointed, with button, c1930, 7in (18cm) high.
£780–870 ⊞ DOAN

A **Dean's Rag Book Co velveteen Pluto the Dog**, c1930, 9in (23cm) long.
£360–400 ⊞ DOAN

A Schuco plush hump-back cat, Germany, c1930, 6in (15cm) high.
£75–85 ⊞ DOAN

A Schuco Big Foot rabbit, Germany, c1950, 4in (10cm) high.
£145–165 ⊞ NAW

A Schuco mohair Yes/No monkey, with glass eyes, Germany, 1950s, 8½in (21.5cm) high.
£135–150 ⊞ BWH

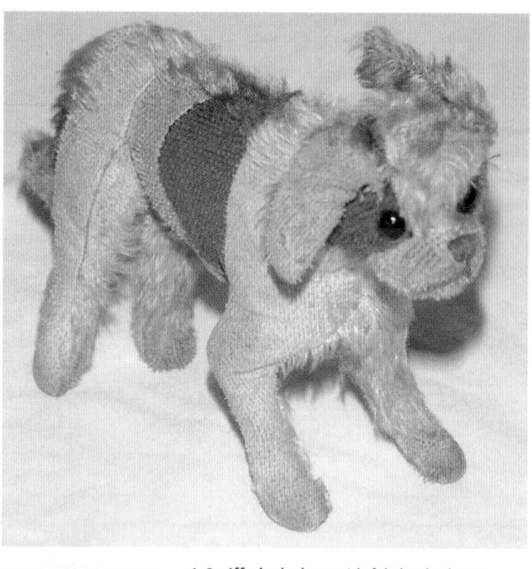

A Steiff plush dog, with felt-backed eyes, Germany, c1906, 10in (25.5cm) long.
£220–250 ⊞ BaN

This three-coloured example is rare.

A Steiff mohair Cocoli monkey, the felt face with painted features, jointed rubber body, wearing original costume, original button, tag and paper label, Germany, c1950, 4in (10cm) high.
£145–170 ⚒ THE

A straw-filled mohair Felix the Cat, with boot-button eyes, late 1920s, 10in (25.5cm) high.
£135–150 ⊞ BaN

A tabby cat, c1918, 10in (25.5cm) high.
£170–190 ⊞ NAW

TEDDY BEARS

A Bing tumbling teddy bear, not operative, Germany, c1910, 19in (48.5cm) high.

£1,100–1,250 ⊞ BBe

A mohair teddy bear, possibly Bing, with boot-button eyes, jointed limbs, pads replaced, Germany, c1915, 12½in (32cm) high.

£540–640 G(L)

A Chad Valley miniature teddy bear, with glass eyes, label on inner leg, c1930, 4in (10cm) high.

£110–125 ⊞ SAAC

A Chiltern Bellows musical teddy bear, with glass eyes, 1950s, 15in (38cm) high.

£260–300 ⊞ BWH

A Dean's Rag Book Co mouse-eared teddy bear, 1930s, 18in (45.5cm) high.

£450–500 ⊞ BBe

A Farnell mohair teddy bear, with original pads, c1920, 20in (51cm) high.

£1,600–1,800 ⊞ BBe

◄ **A Schuco Janus two-faced teddy bear,** with jointed limbs and rotating head, Germany, 1954, 3½in (9cm) high.

£230–270 MA&I

A Steiff teddy bear, with button in ear, Germany, c1900, 28in (71cm) high.

£4,900–5,500 ⊞ BBe

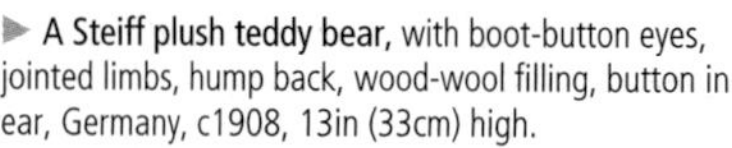

► **A Steiff plush teddy bear,** with boot-button eyes, jointed limbs, hump back, wood-wool filling, button in ear, Germany, c1908, 13in (33cm) high.

£1,500–1,800 G(L)

A Steiff mohair Smuggers teddy bear, with boot-button eyes, original ear tag, Germany, c1905, 11½in (29cm) high.

£2,900–3,450 CAG

A Steiff teddy bear, Germany, c1910, 11in (28cm) high.

£1,200–1,350 DOAN

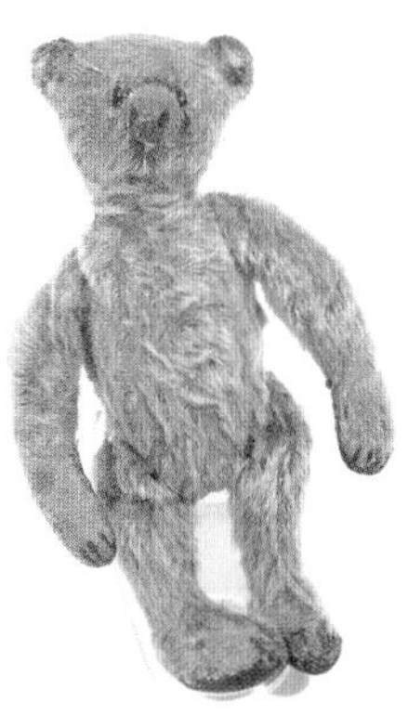

A Steiff plush teddy bear, with boot-button eyes, jointed limbs, hump back, button in ear, Germany, c1910, 10in (25.5cm) high.

£420–500 G(L)

A mohair teddy bear, probably Steiff, with boot-button eyes, worn, squeaker not operative, Germany, pre-1914, 14in (35.5cm) high.

£710–850 Bert

A mohair teddy bear, possibly Steiff, with boot-button eyes, original felt pads, minor wear, left ear torn, button missing, Germany, pre-1914, 16in (41cm) high.

£840–1,000 JDJ

A plush teddy bear, probably Steiff, with hump back, eyes replaced, Germany, early 20thC, 29½in (75cm) high.

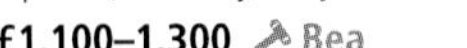

£1,100–1,300 Bea

A Steiff paper plush teddy bear, with glass eyes, button, worn, Germany, 1918–22, 11½in (29cm) high.

£650–780 Bert

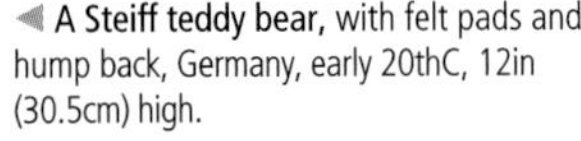

◄ **A Steiff teddy bear,** with felt pads and hump back, Germany, early 20thC, 12in (30.5cm) high.

£200–240 JAA

A mohair teddy bear, with boot-button eyes, original pads, slight wear, Germany, pre-1914, 13in (33cm) high.

£660–790 Bert

A mohair teddy bear, with glass eyes, jointed, straw stuffing, damage and repairs, early 20thC, 18in (45.5cm) high.

£65–75 WHIT

◄ **A plush teddy bear,** with felt pads, hump back, early 20thC, 15in (38cm) high.

£330–390 GTH

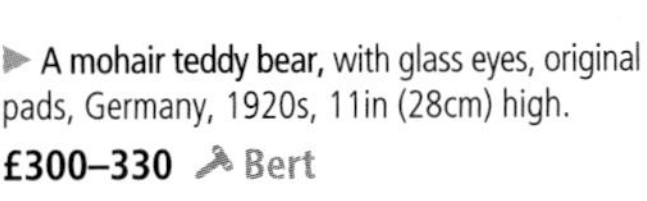

► **A mohair teddy bear,** with glass eyes, original pads, Germany, 1920s, 11in (28cm) high.

£300–330 Bert

DOLLS

Florence Theriault

Florence is a well-known lecturer and seminar leader in the study of dolls and is the author of a number of doll books.

She has been researching, cataloguing and appraising dolls for 30 years and, with her husband George, founded Theriault's the Dollmasters, an auction house specializing in antique dolls in the US.

DOLLS, THE SIGNAL ARTEFACTS of our childhood culture, have seen values continue to rise during the past two or three years, with record after record being achieved. In 2004 a French Albert Marque doll, c1915, brought a record £120,000, a far cry from the £19,000 it realized in 1982. The landmark auction of Lucy Morgan's antique doll collection in 2006 emphatically underscored the surging values that until now have seemed to many collectors to be simple aberrations.

This shift in collector attitude, a willingness to spend big figures on rare dolls, has had an ironic result. Suddenly antiques collectors are taking a new look at the subject and seem willing to add a doll treasure or two to their eclectic collections of rare paintings, furniture and decorative arts. Even toy and automaton collectors who previously thought of dolls as 'just girl things' are easing their hard-edged attitude and adding a doll or two to their childhood nostalgia collections; of course, they only want the best. All of this has a definite and defining impact on rising values for the very rarest dolls.

Another category of rapidly growing collector interest – and hence rising prices – can be labeled simply 'the unusual'. Contemporary artist dolls in materials ranging from cloth to porcelain, beguiling handmade dolls of native cultures, and folk art dolls ranging from simplistically carved wood or wishbone to corn husk figures with painted faces, are categories where interest, if not yet seismic, is certainly on the increase.

Conversely, the common doll, defined as a doll that is fairly easily found especially if in worn or damaged condition, is declining somewhat in value. As more collectors seek the very best in dolls, they are willing to leave common dolls in the dust no matter how low the price may be. Which, of course, makes this an excellent time for a savvy collector to buy in this category. What's common today can become rare tomorrow and prices can escalate.

Florence Theriault

◄ **An Alexander Doll Co set of Dionne quintuplets,** with socket heads, painted hair and eyes, on five-piece composition bodies, wearing original piqué costumes, one with minor damage, marked, America, c1935, 8in (20.5cm) high.

£810–970 THE

◄ **An Alexander Doll Co composition doll,** McGuffey Ana, with weighted eyes, wearing original costume, America, c1937, 12½in (32cm) high.

£135–150 BWH

An Alt, Beck & Gottschalck bisque-headed boy doll, Germany, c1920, 14in (35.5cm) high.

£310–350 PSA

◄ **A C. M. Bergmann composition doll,** with fixed eyes, Germany, Waltershausen early 20thC, 18in (45.5cm) high.

£150–180 JAA

A Carl Bergner bisque three-faced doll, with glass eyes, the head enclosed in a papier-mâché hood above a muslin body, costume probably original, marked 'C.B.', Germany, c1890, 11in (28cm) high.

£540–640 THE

A Leon Casimir Bru bisque-headed doll, with glass eyes, mohair wig, on a kid-edged bisque shoulder plate, wearing original costume, marked 'B', France, c1870, 12in (30.5cm) high.

£1,400–1,650 THE

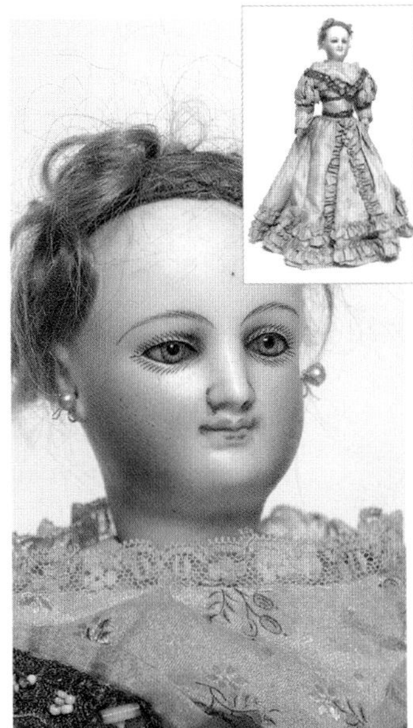

A Cameo Doll Co Kewpie composition doll, wearing a replica costume, America, c1925, 9in (23cm) high seated.

£135–150 BWH

◀ **A Bru bisque fashion doll,** with swivel neck and painted features, on a gusseted kid body, France, c1875, 16in (40.5cm) high.

£3,150–3,500 DOAN

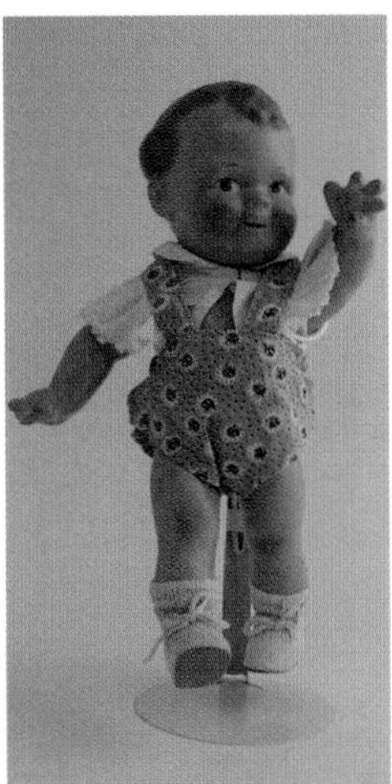

A Cameo Doll Co Skootles composition doll, wearing original costume, slight restoration, America, c1925, 11½in (29cm) high.

£150–170 BWH

A Chad Valley cotton and velveteen doll, with glass eyes, wearing original costume, label on foot, c1935, 10in (25.5cm) high.

£175–195 RRe

Items in the Dolls section have been arranged in maker order with unknown makers at the end.

A Martha Chase oil cloth doll, with painted features, stitch-jointed limbs, wearing antique costume, America, c1950, 14in (35.5cm) high.

£155–185 THE

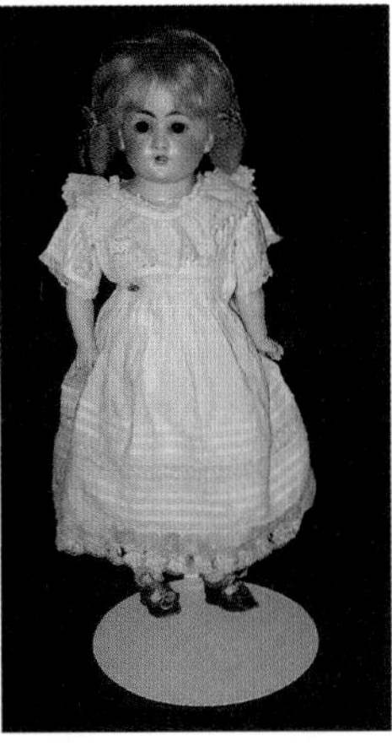

A Cuno & Otto Dressel bisque shoulder-headed doll, with weighted eyes, on a cloth body with composition lower limbs, wearing original costume, Germany, c1900, 17in (43cm) high.

£220–250 BaN

A François Gaultier bisque poupée doll, with a swivel head, glass eyes, human hair wig, on a kid gusset-jointed fashion body, the hands with stitched and separated fingers, marked 'F.G.' and 'O', France, c1880, 12in (30.5cm) high.

£760–910 THE

A François Gaultier composition *bébé* doll, with weighted eyes, replacement sheepskin wig, fully-jointed body, minor damage, France, 1890s, 16½in (42cm) high.

£1,750–2,100 JDJ

▶ **A François Gaultier bisque-headed doll,** with closed mouth, pierced ears and composition body, slight damage, France, early 20thC, 18in (45.5cm) high.

£870–1,000 JAA

A Hertel, Schwab & Co bisque-headed character doll, mould No. 152, with hair wig, jointed body, Germany, c1930, 20in (51cm) high.

£580–650 DOAN

A Gebrüder Heubach ceramic boy doll, Germany, c1910, 7in (18cm) high.

£270–300 PSA

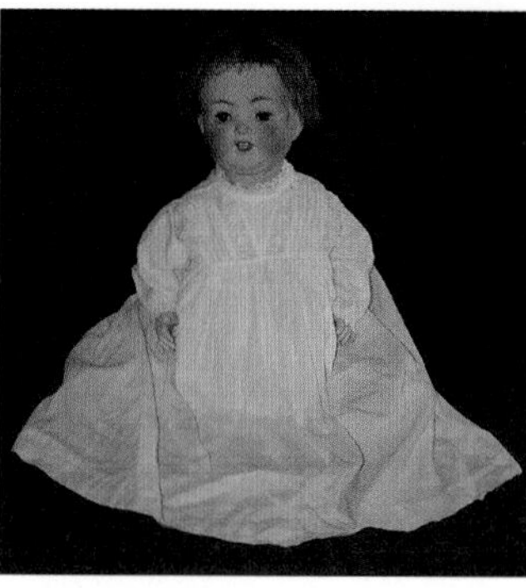

A Heubach Koppelsdorf bisque-headed character doll, mould No. 3427, with weighted eyes, on a bent limb baby body, Germany, c1915, 23in (58.5cm) high.

£250–280 BaN

A Heubach Koppelsdorf bisque-headed doll, mould No. 300, with weighted eyes, Germany, c1920, 15in (38cm) high, seated.

£290–330 PSA

► **An E. I. Horsman Rosebud composition doll,** with swivel head and shoulder plate, cloth body with articulated arms, possibly wearing original costume designed by Bernard Lippert, America, 1930s, 20in (51cm) high.

£115–130 BWH

An Ideal composition Shirley Temple doll, with mohair wig, minor damage, America, 1930s, 18in (45.5cm) high.

£125–150 JDJ

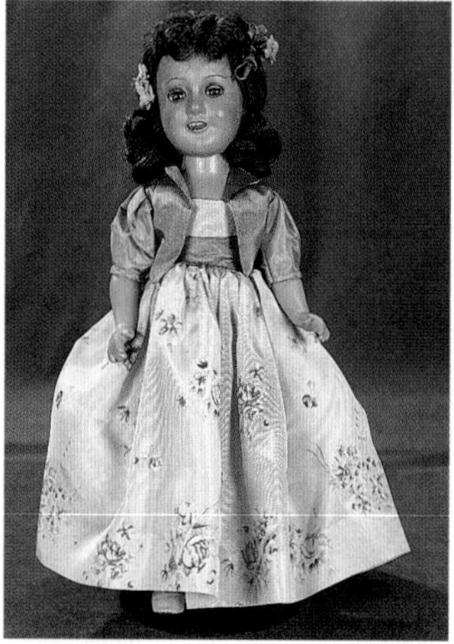

An Ideal Deanna Durbin composition doll, with socket head, weighted eyes, mohair lashes, human hair wig, five-piece body, wearing original costume, America, c1940, 14in (35.5cm) high.

£650–780 THE

Insurance values

Always insure your valuable antiques for the cost of replacing them with similar items, regardless of the original price paid. Both dealers and auctioneers can provide a valuation service for a fee.

A Jumeau bisque-headed *bébé* doll, with weighted eyes, lambswool wig, the wooden body with ball-jointed limbs, France, c1880, 18in (45.5cm) high.

£6,750–7,500 DOAN

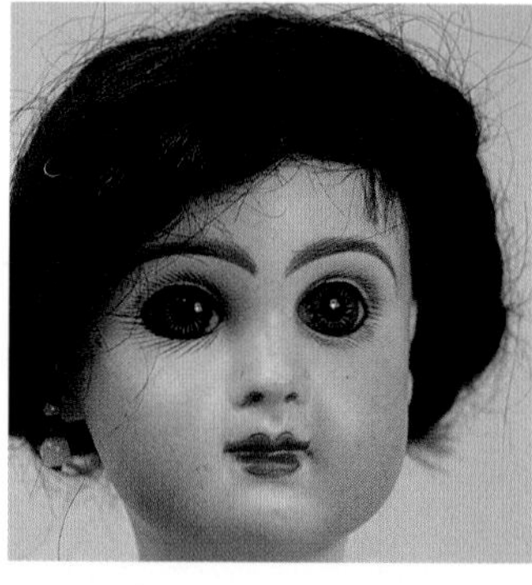

A Jumeau bisque-headed Mama Papa talking doll, with weighted glass eyes, human hair wig, jointed wood body, voice mechanism not operative, marked, France, c1884, 17in (43cm) high.

£2,150–2,550 WHIT

► **A Jumeau bisque *bébé* doll,** with weighted glass eyes, human hair wig, jointed wood body with working crier, France, marked, c1890, 26in (66cm) high.

£1,200–1,400 THE

A Jumeau bisque-headed doll, with fixed eyes, original wig, France, late 19thC, 20in (51cm) high.

£990–1,100 BaN

A Jumeau *bébé* doll, minor damage, France, early 20thC, 24in (61cm) high.

£750–900 JAA

◄ A Jumeau bisque-headed doll, with weighted eyes, pierced ears, France, c1890, 22in (56cm) high.

£1,350–1,500 GLEN

KÄMMER & REINHARDT / SIMON & HALBIG

As well as producing entire dolls, Simon & Halbig (c1869–c1930) was one of the most prolific manufacturers of bisque and china shoulder heads, which they supplied to other manufacturers such as Kämmer & Reinhardt, Schmidt & Dressel, Jumeau and Roullet & Descamps. These dolls will usually bear the marks of both companies and also a mould number, which can be important as it will identify rare or desirable series.

A Kämmer & Reinhardt doll, with a Simon & Halbig bisque head, with weighted glass eyes, mohair wig, Germany, c1910, 23in (58.5cm) high.

£630–700 DOAN

A Kämmer & Reinhardt bisque-headed soldier doll, with intaglio eyes, Germany, c1910, 11in (28cm) high.

£1,050–1,200 DOAN

A Kämmer & Reinhardt bisque-headed walking doll, with weighted eyes, mohair wig, composition body, with head turning/walking mechanism, Germany, early 20thC, 21in (53.5cm) high.

£520–580 BaN

A Kestner bisque child doll, with weighted glass eyes, possibly human hair wig, repaired, incised mark and stamp, Germany, c1914, 27in (69cm) high.

£280–330 Bert

A Kestner character baby doll, mould No. 150, with weighted eyes, minor wear, Germany, early 20thC, 17in (43cm) high.

£200–240 JAA

A Kley & Hahn Walküre bisque doll, with weighted eyes, Germany, early 20thC, 28in (71cm) high.

£220–260 JAA

► A Käthe Kruse doll, the sewn-on muslin head with painted hair and features, the cloth body with wide, disc-jointed hips, signed, Germany, 1910–29, 14in (35.5cm) high.

£1,650–1,950 G(L)

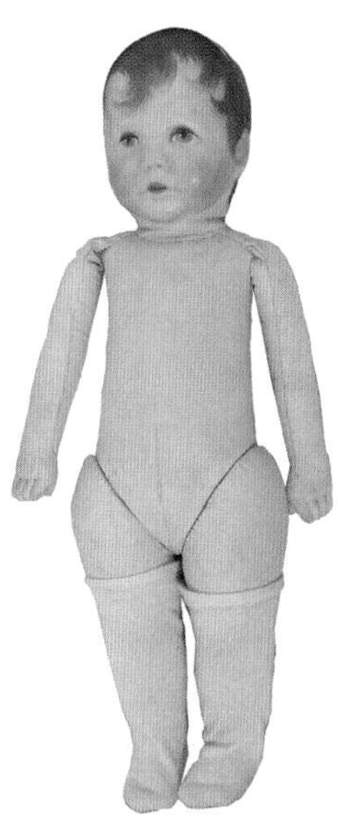

A Lenci felt peasant girl doll, Italy, c1930, 14in (35.5cm) high.

£340–380 DOAN

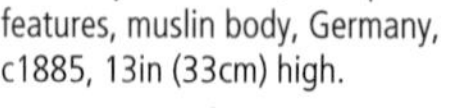

A Limbach bisque shoulder-headed portrait doll, with painted features, muslin body, Germany, c1885, 13in (33cm) high.

£290–340 THE

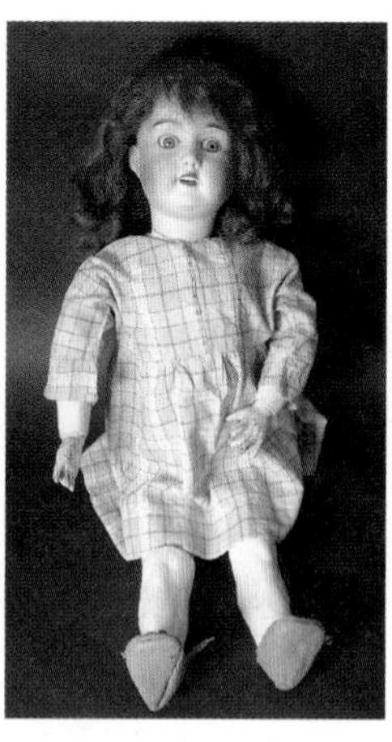

A Limoges bisque-headed composition Cherie II doll, with weighted eyes, France, c1915, 25½in (65cm) high.

£210–250 ROS

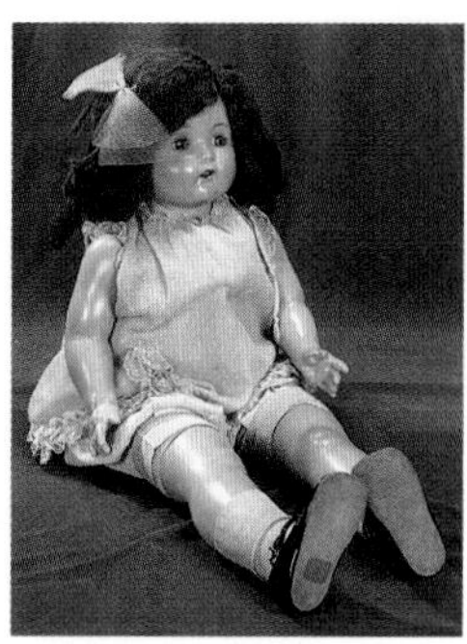

A Mae Starr composition phonograph doll, wearing original costume, marked, America, c1930, 29in (73.5cm) high.

£220–260 THE

An Armand Marseille bisque Flora Dora doll, with natural wig and eyebrows, Germany, c1920, 16in (40.5cm) high.

£155–175 RRe

An Armand Marseille bisque-headed Dream Baby doll, Germany, c1920, 17in (43cm) high.

£320–360 GLEN

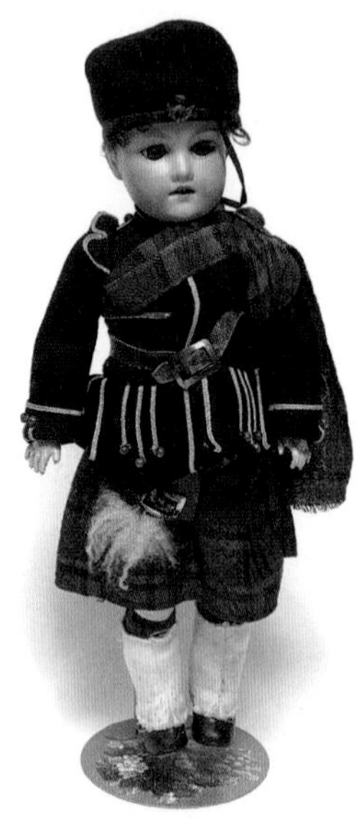

An Armand Marseille bisque-headed composition doll, dressed in Scottish costume, Germany, c1920, 16in (40.5cm) high.

£270–300 GLEN

◄ **An Armand Marseille-style Dream Baby doll,** mould No. 500, Japan, 1940s, 18in (45.5cm) high.

£200–220 UD

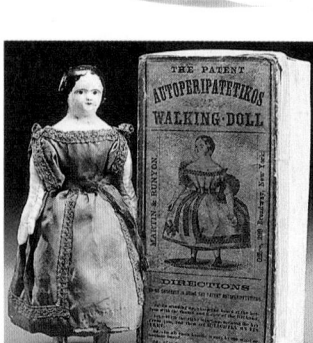

A Martin & Runyon Autoperipatetikos clockwork doll, America, c1862, 10in (25.5cm) high, with original box.

£1,500–1,800 JAA

► **A Mattel Barbie Fashion Queen doll,** wearing an American Airlines stewardess outfit, America, c1963, 11¾in (30cm) high.

£110–125 BWH

A Pedigree hard plastic bent knee walking doll, with original wig, 1950s, 22in (56cm) high.

£120–135 BWH

A Pintel & Godchaux bisque-headed doll, France, c1880, 20in (51cm) high.

£1,600–1,800 DOL

▶ **A Rabery & Delphieu bisque-headed composition *bébé* doll,** with weighted glass eyes, mohair wig, ball-jointed body, marked, France, c1885, 13in (33cm) high.

£3,050–3,650 THE

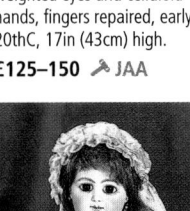

◀ **A Bye Lo Baby doll,** with weighted eyes and celluloid hands, fingers repaired, early 20thC, 17in (43cm) high.

£125–150 JAA

Bébés

Bébés are dolls that are an idealized version of a young girl, with chubby limbs and a rounded stomach. They are probably the most popular of all dolls – early examples, which usually had closed mouths and fixed wrists, can command extremely high prices if in exceptional condition. The French company Jumeau produced the first *bébé* in 1855 but the golden age of French production was from c1860 to the 1890s. After 1899 the quality declined due to the proliferance of less expensive examples from Germany, leading to the formation of the S. F. B. J. (Société Française de Bébés et Jouets).

◀ **A Schmitt *bébé* doll,** with weighted eyes, antique mohair wig, minor damage, incised and stamped marks, France, early 1880s, 15in (38cm) high.

£9,100–10,900 JDJ

A Schönau & Hoffmeister bisque-headed doll, mould No. 1909, with weighted eyes, mohair wig, jointed composition body, Germany, c1910, 23in (58.5cm) high.

£370–420 BaN

A Schoenhut wooden character doll, with later costume and wig, minor damage, America, early 20thC, 15in (38cm) high.

£140–160 JAA

◀ **An S. F. B. J. character doll,** No. 236, with weighted eyes, mohair wig, bent-limb papier-mâché body, France, early 20thC, 12½in (32cm) high.

£490–550 BaN

A Simon & Halbig bisque doll, mould No. 939, Germany, c1880, 14in (35.5cm) high.

£760–850 SAAC

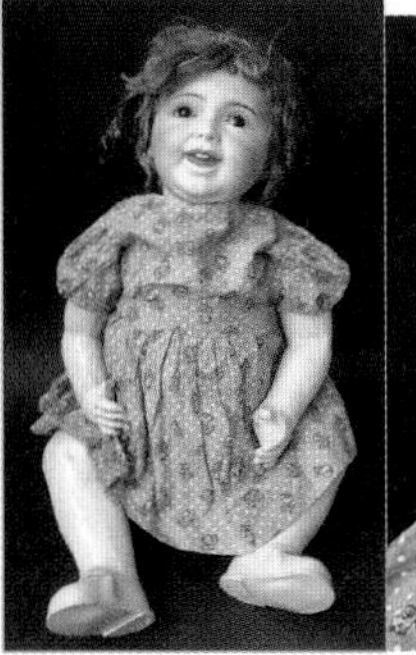

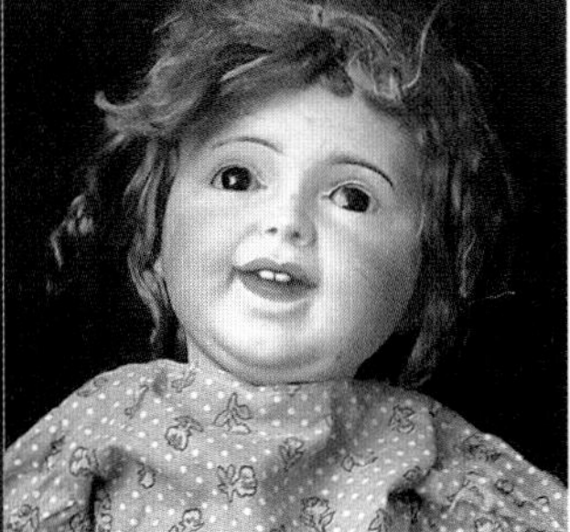

◀ **An S. F. B. J. bisque-headed composition doll,** No. 236, with weighted eyes, jointed composition body, wearing a later costume, impressed mark, France, c1930, 23¾in (60.5cm) high.

£165–195 ROS

A Simon & Halbig bisque-headed doll, mould No. 1009, with original dress Germany, c1900, 17in (43cm) high.

£610–680 PSA

A Simon & Halbig bisque doll, mould No. 1248, Germany, c1900, 15in (38cm) high.

£720–800 DOL

► **A Simon & Halbig bisque-headed swimming doll,** wearing original silk costume, Germany, c1910, 16in (40.5cm) long.

£1,200–1,350 BaN

A Simon & Halbig shoulder-headed doll, mould No. 1250, with leather body, Germany, early 20thC, 23in (58.5cm) high.

£260–310 JAA

A Sonneberg bisque doll, with glass eyes, human hair wig, five-piece papier-mâché body, marked '2', Germany, c1885, 10in (25.5cm) high.

£440–520 THE

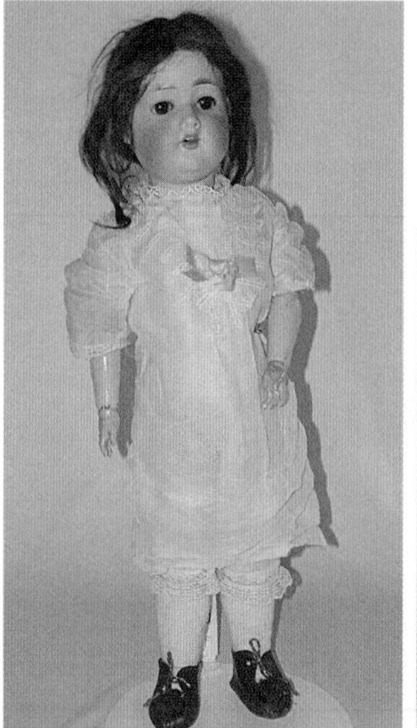

A Hermann Steiner bisque-headed doll, with weighted eyes, mohair wig, jointed body, Germany, c1920, 19in (48.5cm) high.

£290–330 BaN

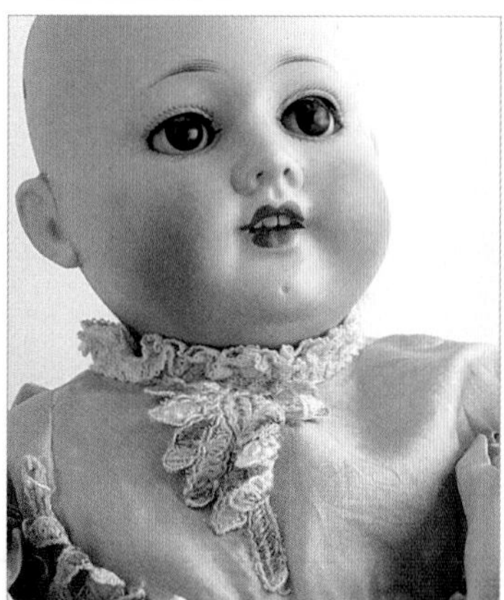

A Hermann Steiner bisque doll, with weighted glass eyes, natural eyelashes, firing fault, Germany, c1920, 22in (56cm) high.

£165–185 RRe

◄ **A Walther & John composition doll,** No. 120, with weighted glass eyes and fur eyelashes, slight wear, Germany, early 20thC, 23½in (59.5cm) high.

£280–330 JAA

A pair of Norah Wellings cloth character dolls, c1930, 8in (20.5cm) high.

£160–180 DOAN

UNKNOWN MAKERS

A papier-maché shoulder-headed doll, with leather body and wooden arms and legs, slight damage, 1830s, 12in (30.5cm) high.

£440–480 JDJ

A wax shoulder-headed doll, with fixed glass eyes, mohair wig, stuffed fabric body and wax-covered arms, hands and lower legs, wearing original silk-trimmed muslin dress, c1860, 30in (76cm) high.

£2,250–2,700 AH

A bisque-headed doll, the body with impressed mark 'DEP 1875', c1875, 15in (38cm) high.

£450–500 SAAC

A Parian shoulder-headed doll, with moulded and painted features, on a stuffed muslin body, leather forearms, leather boots sewn to legs, slight damage and losses, 1870s, 19½in (49.5cm) high.

£230–270 JDJ

A wax-headed doll, with a soft body, c1880, 23in (58.5cm) high.

£300–330 PSA

◄ **A wax shoulder-headed doll,** with a cloth body, wax lower limbs, c1880, 17in (43cm) high.

£540–600 DOAN

► **A bisque-headed doll,** with mohair wig, muslin body and bisque arms, wearing original costume, Germany, c1885, 15in (38cm) high.

£300–360 THE

A bisque doll, with glass eyes and original wig, on a kid and bisque body, with original muslin costume, one arm missing, France, c1885, 5in (12.5cm) high.

£680–800 THE

► **A papier-mâché shoulder-headed miniature doll,** with glass eyes, articulated mouth, papier mâché hollow body, composition arms and legs, wearing original costume, Germany, c1885, 9in (23cm) high.

£140–160 THE

A papier-mâché doll, with glass eyes and painted features, mohair wig, stitch-jointed muslin body, wearing original costume with undergarments, Germany, c1885, 16in (40.5cm) high.

£320–380 THE

A wax Little Red Riding Hood doll, c1890, 9in (23cm) high.

£905–100 PSA

► **A bisque-headed fashion doll,** with a leather body, possibly France, late 19thC, 11in (28cm) high.

£340–400 MAL

A bisque child doll, the weighted glass eyes with silk lashes, human hair wig, fully-articulated body, head incised 'DEP4', France, c1900, 12in (30.5cm) high.

£270–320 Bert

A carved wood doll, the skirt enclosing the frame, Germany, late 19thC, 16in (40.5cm) high.

£140–160 JAA

► **A bisque doll,** with fixed glass eyes, wearing original costume, marked, Germany, c1900, 8in (20.5cm) high.

£270–300 RRe

A wax-headed doll, on a kid leather body, Germany, c1900, 16in (40.5cm) high.

£310–350 DOAN

A wax doll, probably Germany, c1900, 32in (81.5cm) high.

£95–115 JAA

A squeaker doll, with fixed glass eyes, Germany, c1900, 11in (28cm) high.

£310–350 RRe

An Edwardian porcelain shoulder-headed doll, with porcelain arms and leather body, beneath a glass dome, 28in (71cm) high.

£230–270 PF

A bisque-headed doll, wearing Scottish costume, Germany, c1910, 19in (48.5cm) high.

£680–750 DOAN

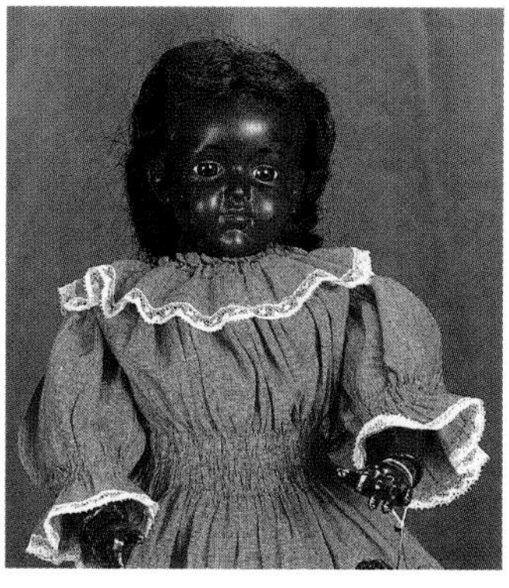

A bisque character doll with glass eyes, mohair wig, wooden fully-jointed body, marked 'F1', France or Germany, c1910, 19in (48.5cm) high.

£510–610 THE

◀ **A bisque shoulder-headed doll,** with fixed millefiori eyes, on a kid body with bisque arms, marked '3', c1910, 14½in (37cm) high.

£540–640 AH

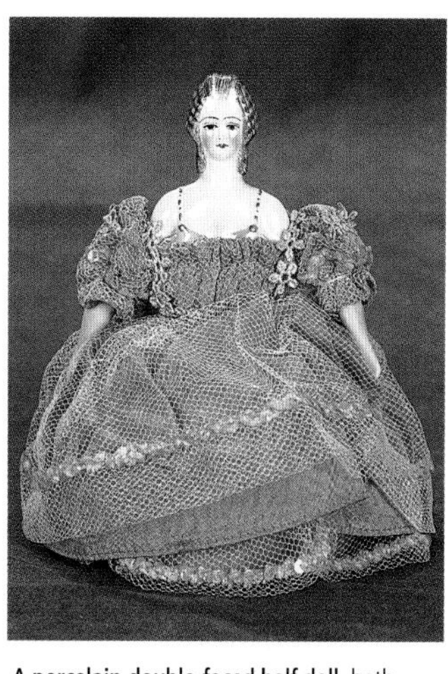

A porcelain double-faced half doll, both faces identical, painted shoulder straps and bodice, on a silk and tulle pin-cushion base, Germany, c1910, 6in (15cm) high.

£145–170 THE

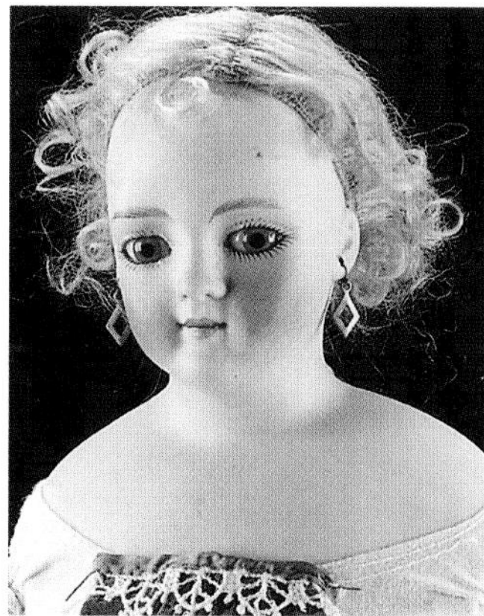

A shoulder-headed fashion doll, with glass eyes, solid dome head, replacement body, France, early 20thC.

£380–450 JAA

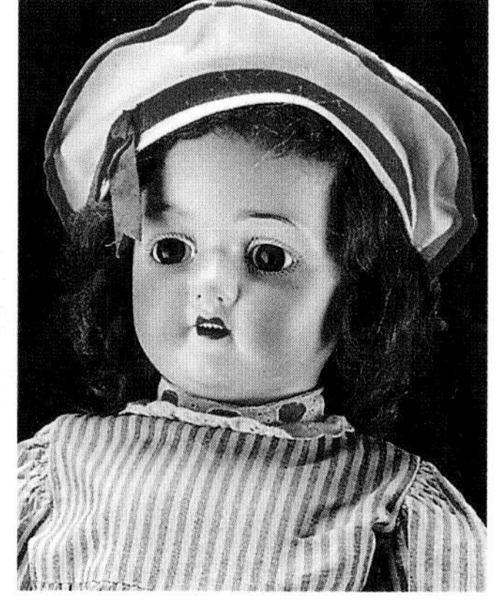

A mechanical talking doll, with fixed eyes, mohair wig, losses, marked 'LC', France, early 20thC, 24in (61cm) high.

£270–320 JAA

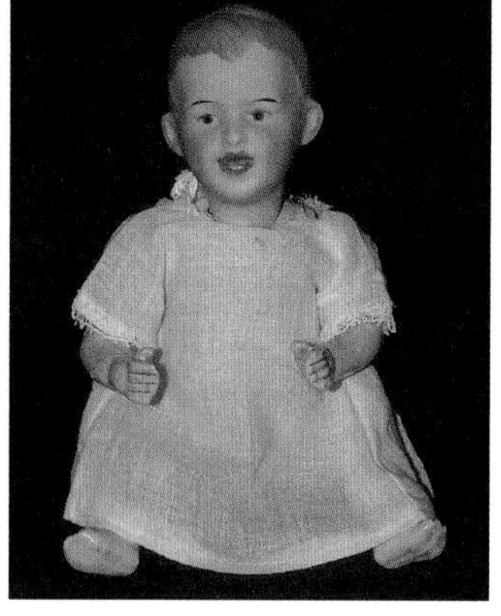

A baby doll, with intaglio eyes, open/closed mouth, painted hair, on a bent-limb body, Germany, early 20thC, 8in (20.5cm) high.

£200–220 BaN

A miniature bisque-headed doll, with fixed eyes, mohair wig, wearing Scottish costume, Germany, c1920, 5½in (14cm) high.

£130–150 BaN

▶ **A bisque-headed baby doll,** with weighted eyes, cloth body, with celluloid hands, Germany, c1920, 15in (38cm) high.

£220–250 BaN

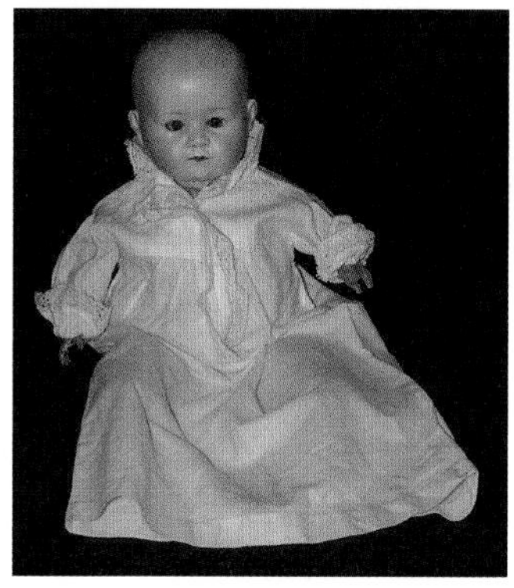

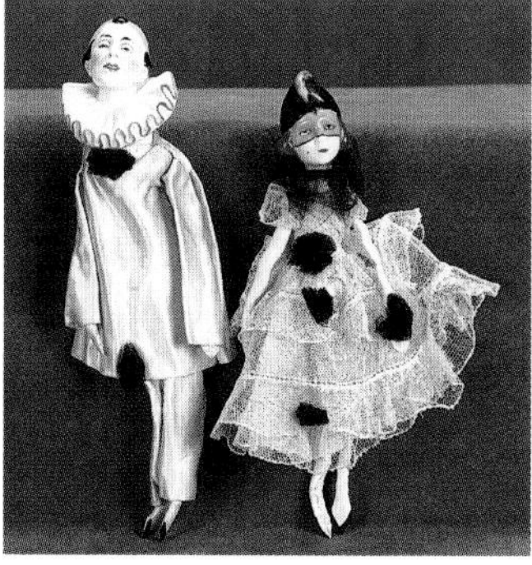

A pair of porcelain flapper dolls, Pierrot and Pierrette, with flanged-neck heads, on hand-made silk bodies, wearing original costumes, Germany, c1920, 7in (18cm) high.

£270–320 THE

▶ **A bisque-headed doll,** with weighted eyes, Germany, c1920, 10in (25.5cm) high.

£90–100 PSA

DOLLS' HOUSES & ACCESSORIES

A Victorian double-fronted dolls' house, with opening doors and gables, furnished, 34in (86.5cm) high.

£350–420 GTH

A painted pine dolls' house, c1880, 22in (56cm) high.

£670–750 SPUR

A G. J. Lines wooden dolls' house, with opening front, original fireplaces and wallpaper, c1900, 31in (78.5cm) high.

£720–800 HOB

A painted pine dolls' house, early 20thC, 28in (71cm) high.

£430–480 SPUR

A Georgian-style dolls' house, with dentil cornice and balconied windows, detachable front panel, c1920, 38½in (98cm) high.

£330–390 ROS

A Tri-Ang Princess Elizabeth dolls' house, 1930s, 23¾in (60.5cm) high.

£280–320 LIT

This is a copy of a Wendy house given by the people of Wales to the Queen as a young girl.

A bisque-headed dolls' house doll, with weighted eyes, mohair wig, wearing original silk costume, Germany, c1880, 5¼in (13.5cm) high.

£200–230 BaN

A bisque shoulder-headed dolls' house doll, with muslin body, bisque lower limbs, wearing original costume, Germany, c1885, 5in (12.5cm) high.

£145–170 THE

A bisque shoulder-headed dolls' house chauffeur, muslin body, bisque limbs, Germany, c1890, 5½in (14cm) high.

£210–250 THE

TOYS

AEROPLANES & AIRSHIPS

A Dinky Toys diecast Spitfire Mk II, c1969, 6in (15cm) long, with box.

£145–165 MILI

A Dinky Toys Thunderbirds set, comprising Thunderbirds 2 and 4, No. 101, c1973.

£290–340 E

A Märklin hand-painted tin clockwork Zeppelin, Germany, c1910, 12in (30.5cm) long.

£2,250–2,700 Bert

◄ **A Steelcraft pressed-steel Pursuit pedal aeroplane,** with later paint, c1946, 48in (122cm) long.

£140–160 JAA

A Tipp & Co tinplate clockwork bomber, tail fin later, slight damage, Germany, c1930, 14½in (37cm) long.

£830–990 Bert

BOATS

◄ **A Bing clockwork speed cruiser,** Germany, c1912, 18½in (47cm) long.

£1,350–1,600 JDJ

A Bowman painted wood and tinplate speedboat, with spirit-fired single screw steam engine, c1928, 23in (58.5cm) long.

£290–340 AH

A Bliss cardboard and paper Sachem schooner, America, 1880s, 42½in (108cm) long.

£1,600–1,900 Bert

► **A Reed wooden Pilgrim sidewheeler passenger boat,** with lithographed paper detail, stacks, flags and figures later, America, c1895, 28in (71cm) long.

£2,000–2,400 Bert

A Sutcliffe tinplate clockwork *Bluebird* motorboat, c1937, 11in (28cm) long.

£145–165 GEOH

This Sutcliffe tinplate toy is based on Sir Malcolm Campbell's Bluebird *K3 boat in which he first took the water speed record in 1937 at 126.32mph. He subsequently raised the record twice more in this boat in 1937 and 1938 before finally breaking the record in 1939 at 141.74 mph in* Bluebird *K4. All his cars and boats were called* Bluebird.

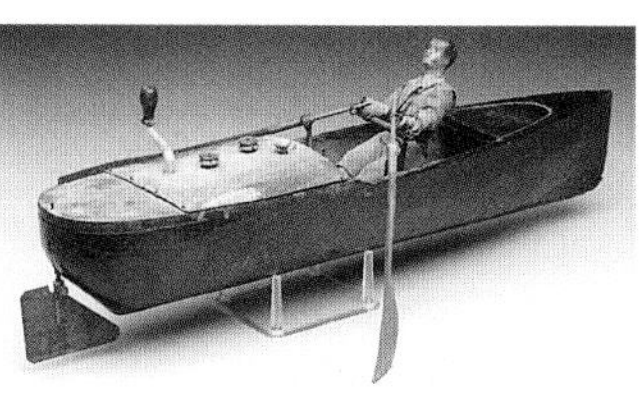

◄ **A wooden clockwork boat and oarsman,** France, c1900, 22in (56cm) long.

£1,400–1,650 JDJ

FIGURES & MODELS

A Cotswold Toys carved pine hunting set, comprising huntsman, hounds and foxes, one hound damaged, 1930s, huntsman 7in (18cm) high.

£330–380 KLH

A CBG Mignot lead figure of the Earl of Huntingdon, France, c1950, 3in (7.5cm) high.

£55–65 SAAC

A CBG Mignot lead figure of Cardinal Richelieu, France, c1950, 3in (7.5cm) high.

£60–70 SAAC

MECHANICAL TOYS

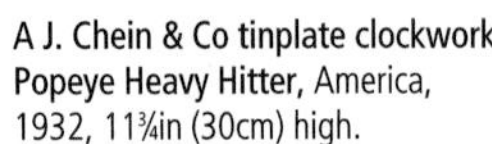

A J. Chein & Co tinplate clockwork Popeye Heavy Hitter, America, 1932, 11¾in (30cm) high.

£1,900–2,250 Bert

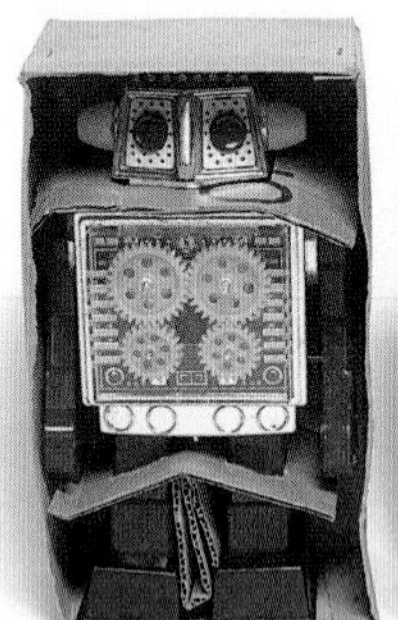

An Einco plastic clockwork Gear Robot, Japan, c1960, 8½in (21.5cm) high, with original box.

£65–75 SAAC

A tinplate clockwork Staggering Butler, possibly Günthermann, Germany, early 20thC, 7½in (19cm) high.

£540–640 Bea

A Horikawa battery-operated Roto-Robot, Japan, c1950, 8½in (21.5cm) high, with original box.

£90–105 JAA

A tinplate battery-operated Attacking Martian robot, possibly by Horikawa, chest opens to reveal flashing guns, impressed mark, Japan, 1960s, 11½in (29cm) high.

£90–105 JBe

A Leopold Lambert clockwork musical Oriental woman, with a bisque head and glass eyes, the music box with velvet cover and key, France, c1890, 14½in (37cm) high.

£3,900–4,650 JDJ

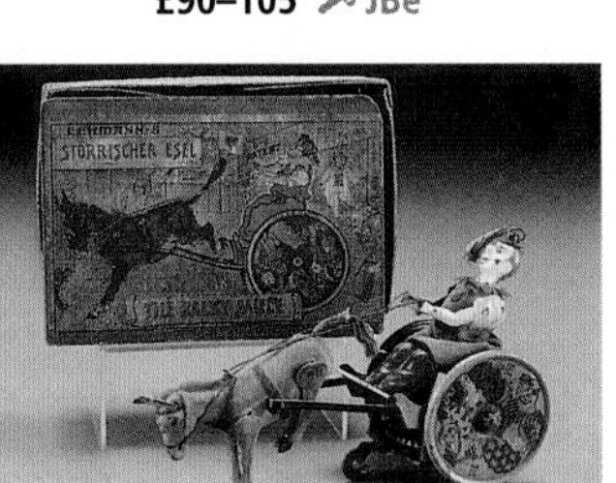

► A Lehmann tinplate clockwork Balky Mule, Germany, c1900, 7½in (19cm) wide, with original box.

£250–300 JAA

► A Lehmann tinplate clockwork Dancing Sailor, Germany, c1903, 7½in (19cm) high.

£830–990 JAA

A Roullet & Decamps clockwork drinking bear, France, Paris, c1930, 14in (35.5cm) high.

£1,650–1,850 AUTO

A Roullet & Decamps clockwork cat in a milk churn, France, Paris, c1945, 9in (23cm) high.

£1,450–1,600 AUTO

A Schuco clockwork drumming clown, Germany, c1930, 5in (12.5cm) high.

£105–120 SAAC

A Schuco clockwork drumming pig, Germany, 1930s, 5in (12.5cm) high.

£140–160 HAL

A set of Vichy wall-mounted clockwork musical ballroom dancers, France, Paris, c1870, 14in (35.5cm) wide.

£6,700–7,500 AUTO

A papier-mâché clockwork bulldog, with opening mouth and nodding head, the feet on wheels, France, late 19thC, 21¾in (55.5cm) long.

£560–670 RTo

MONEY BANKS

A Hubley Manufacturing Co mechanical money bank, with a clown and a dog, America, 1930s, 8in (20.5cm) wide.

£190–220 JDJ

A Kyser & Rex cast-iron money bank, in the form of an apple with leaves, America, c1882, 5¼in (13.5cm) wide.

£2,350–2,800 Bert

A Kyser & Rex metal mechanical money bank, with a boy stealing a watermelon, trap later, America, c1894.

£950–1,100 Bert

A J. & E. Stevens cast-iron mechanical Columbus money bank, c1893, America, 8¼in (21cm) wide.

£600–720 JAA

A J. & E. Stevens cast-iron mechanical Boy Scout Camp money bank, designed by Charles A. Bailey, America, c1915.

£2,400–2,850 Bert

A tinplate mechanical Automatic Coin Savings Bank, with window depicting fortune, c1890.

£1,500–1,800 Bert

NOAH'S ARKS

A Victorian painted wood Noah's Ark, with carved and painted wood animals and figures, 18in (45.5cm) wide.
£140–165 MAL(O)

A painted wood Noah's Ark, with celluloid and carved wood animals, late 19thC, 24in (61cm) wide.
£760–910 G(L)

A painted wood Noah's Ark, with 30 painted wood animals and a figure of Noah, slight damage, Germany, c1900, 19½in (49.5cm) wide.
£280–330 JDJ

ROCKING HORSES

An F. H. Ayres carved wood rocking horse, on a bow rocker, 19thC, 89in (226cm) long.
£5,800–6,500 SPUR

A painted wood rocking horse, with original horse hair mane and tail, on a pine trellis stand, 19thC, 64in (162.5cm) long.
£700–840 MEA

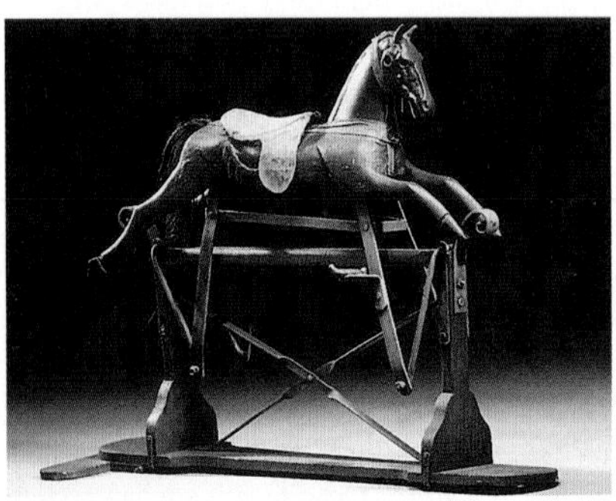

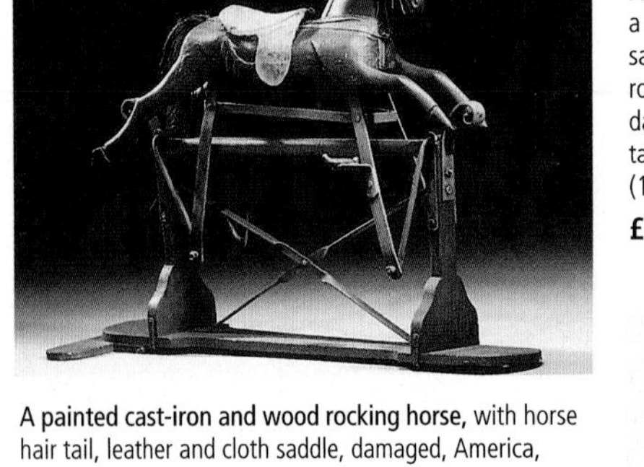

A painted cast-iron and wood rocking horse, with horse hair tail, leather and cloth saddle, damaged, America, 1850–1900, 39½in (100.5cm) long.
£970–1,150 S(Am)

► **A Victorian painted wood rocking horse,** with a leather and cloth saddle, on a bow rocker, slight damage, mane and tail missing, 61½in (156cm) long.
£530–630 JDJ

◄ **A carved wood and cast-iron rocking horse,** on a bow rocker, with wheel conversion, France, c1880, 38in (96.5cm) long.
£1,400–1,600 CRU

A carved wood rocking horse, on a bow rocker, c1880, 83in (211cm) long.
£2,050–2,300 SPUR

► **A carved and painted pine rocking horse,** Continental, late 19thC, 49in (124.5cm) long.
£175–210 NOA

A carved wood rocking horse, c1890, 67in (170cm) long.
£1,000–1,150 TRED

A carved wood rocking horse, c1900, 56in (142cm) long.
£2,250–2,500 NoC

A painted pine rocking horse, France, c1900, 26in (66cm) long.
£180–200 TOP

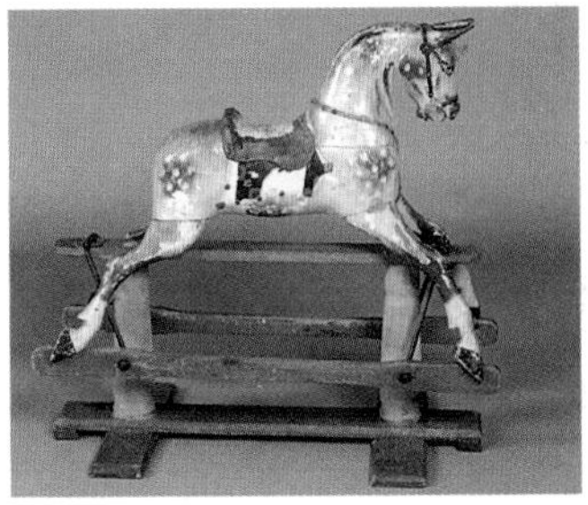

An Edwardian carved wood rocking horse, damaged, mane and tail missing, 59in (150cm) high.
£400–480 M

A carved wood rocking horse, c1910, 40in (101.5cm) long.
£400–450 ALCH

A G. & J. Lines carved wood rocking horse, c1910, 33in (84cm) long.
£790–880 SPUR

A carved wood carousel horse, with a horse hair tail, now on a bow rocker, inscribed 'Margaret', early 20thC, 40in (102cm) long.
£560–670 HOLL

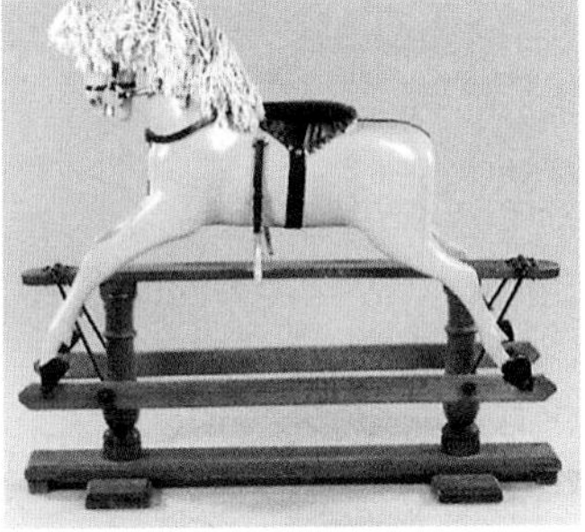

A carved wood rocking horse, on a pine safety rocker, restored, early 20thC, 56in (142cm) long.
£470–560 PFK

A painted gesso rocking horse, mane missing, 1920s, 36¾in (93.5cm) long.
£500–600 SWO

SOLDIERS

A Britains Mounted Life Guard Band set, No. 9406, comprising 12 musicians, c1950, in original fitted box, 12 x 15in (30.5 x 38cm).
£220–260 WAL

◄ A B. & T. mounted guardsmen set, c1949, 3in (7.5cm) high, with box.
£90–100 SAAC

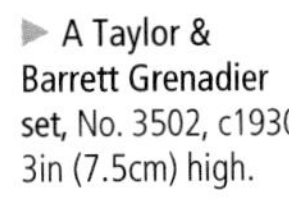

► A Taylor & Barrett Grenadier set, No. 3502, c1930, 3in (7.5cm) high.
£80–90 SAAC

TRAINS

An American Flyer gauge 0 Hiawatha train set, comprising locomotive, tender and three cars, America, c1936, with box.

£1,100–1,300 Bert

A Bassett-Lowke gauge 0 electric 0–6–0 Southern Railway tank locomotive, No. 5305/0 and No. 78, 1930s, with original box.

£500–600 CAG

A Bassett-Lowke gauge 0 clockwork Midland Compound 4–4–0 locomotive and tender, 1930s.

£820–980 WAL

A Bassett-Lowke gauge 0 electric three-rail Princess Coronation 4–6–2 locomotive and tender, No. RN6232, 'Duchess of Montrose', 1939–49.

£1,300–1,550 WAL

A Bassett-Lowke gauge 0 three-rail locomotive and tender, 'Deltic', 1959–63.

£5,000–5,800 AG

It is believed that fewer than 10 of these locomotives were manufactured.

MILLER'S COMPARES

I. A Bassett-Lowke gauge 0 three-rail locomotive and tender, 'Flying Scotsman', in blue livery, 1950–52, with original box.

£2,200–2,600 AG

II. A Bassett-Lowke gauge 0 three-rail electric locomotive and tender, 'Flying Scotsman', in green livery, 1953–58, with original box.

£1,700–2000 AG

Although these trains are similar in appearance and date, Item I was only produced for two years and is therefore much rarer than Item II, which was produced for five years.

A Bing for Bassett-Lowke gauge 0 clockwork 4–4–2 L&NWR locomotive, No. RN44, early 1900s.

£230–270 WAL

A Bing gauge 1 LNRW locomotive and tender, 'Jupiter', slight damage, some paint later, Germany, 1920–30, 15in (38cm) long.

£420–470 AH

◀ **A hand-painted brass scale model 4–4–0 locomotive,** 'The America', America, late 19thC.

£6,500–7,800 Bert

A Carette for Bassett-Lowke gauge 1 Anglo-American Oil Co tank wagon, c1910, with original box.

£730–870 VEC

An Exley gauge 0 LMS Royal Mail coach, c1957.
£370–440 AG

A Hornby gauge 0 clockwork 4–4–0 LMS No. 2 Special Tender locomotive and tender, No. 1185, late 1920s.
£230–270 WAL

◄ **A Hornby Series gauge 0 tinplate station platform,** 'Windsor', 1926–28, 17in (43cm) wide.
£290–330 VIN

► **A Hornby Series gauge 0 tinplate LNER No. 1 Special Tank locomotive,** c1932, 8in (20.5cm) long.
£360–400 VIN

A Hornby gauge 0 4–4–0 electric SR locomotive and tender, No. 4, 'Eton', two wheels damaged and pony track frame later, late 1930s.
£870–1,000 WAL

A Hornby gauge 0 tinplate No. 2 GWR corridor coach, 1937–38, 11½in (29cm) long.
£290–330 VIN

◄ **A Hornby Dublo three-rail locomotive and tender,** 'Duchess of Athol', 1940–50, with box.
£90–100 HAL

A Hornby gauge 0 electric 4–4–2 locomotive and tender, No. 850, 'Lord Nelson', with Pullman coach 'Loraine' and brake end coach 'Alberta', with 12 pieces of tinplate two-rail track, c1935, with original box.
£1,050–1,250 VEC

An Ives gauge 0 train set, comprising 0–4–0 locomotive, two parlour coaches and an observation coach, America, c1929, with boxes.
£870–1,050 Bert

An Ives gauge 0 electric train set, comprising 4–4–0 locomotive, coaches, pullman coach, baggage coach and observation coach, America, c1932, with box.
£5,000–6,000 Bert

A Lionel gauge 0 electric train set, comprising engine and two coaches, engine wheels replaced, America, 1920s, with original box.
£280–330 JDJ

◄ **A Märklin gauge 1 teak buffet coach,** 'Mitropa', the hinged roof enclosing a fitted interior, Germany, 1920–30, 12in (30.5cm) long.
£470–560 AH

VEHICLES

An Arcade cast-iron taxi cab, radiator missing, America, early 20thC, 9in (23cm) long.

£220–260 JAA

An Arcade cast-iron Mack Wrecker, with nickel spoke wheels, America, 1930s, 10½in (26.5cm) long.

£650–780 Bert

A Bing tinplate tourer, with rubber tyres, chauffeur later, Germany, early 20thC, 10in (25.5cm) long.

£1,700–2,000 JDJ

A Brimtoy tinplate clockwork painter's and decorator's van, with ladder, 1950s, 7in (18cm) long, with original box.

£85–95 SAAC

A Britains die-cast Napier *Bluebird* car, No. 1400, c1937, 6¼in (16cm) long, with original box.

£240–280 DW

► **A Budgie *Wagon Train* set,** comprising three wagons and horses and figures, cardboard packaging depicting Robert Horton as Flint McCullogh and Ward Bond as Major Seth Williams from the TV series, 1960s.

£190–220 WAL

◄ **A Chad Valley tinplate van,** 1930s, 10in (25.5cm) long.

£360–400 JUN

A Citroën clockwork B2 Torpedo tourer, with nickel-plated grille, France, 1920s, 14¼in (36cm) long.

£950–1,100 Bert

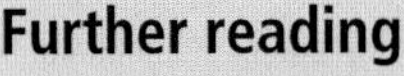

Further reading

Miller's Toys & Games Buyer's Guide, Miller's Publications, 2004

A Corgi Toys diecast Standard Vanguard III Saloon, No. 207, late 1950s, 4in (10cm) long, with box.

£95–110 PAST

A Corgi Toys diecast Euclid TC12 Tractor, 1960s, 7in (18cm) long, with box.

£70–80 HAL

◀ **A Dinky Toys diecast gift set,** No. 5, comprising tank, transport wagon, reconnaissance car, jeep and gun on trailer, 1949–50, with box, 9in (23cm) square.

£5,200–5,900 ⊞ MILI

This set was made for export to the US and did not appear in any catologue. It was sold mainly through mail order stores such as FOA Schwarz for one year only.

A Dinky Toys diecast Foden Flat Truck, No. D905, with chains, c1955, with box, 8in (20.5cm) long.

£95–110 ⊞ PAST

MILLER'S COMPARES

I. A Dinky Toys diecast Big Bedford Van, No. D923, advertising Heinz Tomato Ketchup, 1958–59, with original box, 6in (15cm) long.

£540–600 ⊞ PAST

II. A Dinky Toys diecast Big Bedford Van, No. D923, advertising Heinz Baked Beans, 1955–58, with original box, 6in (18cm) long.

£200–230 ⊞ PAST

These two Dinky lorries date from similar periods and are both in their original boxes, but Item I is worth more than Item II because it was only made for a very short time. Item II was produced over four years and is therefore more commonly seen. Another very important factor governing value is that Item I has its original box showing an image of the lorry decorated with the tomato ketchup bottle.

A Dinky Supertoys diecast Platform Servicing Vehicle, No. 977, 1960–64, with original box, 8½in (21.5cm) long.

£290–330 ⊞ MILI

A Dinky Supertoys diecast Berliet Transformer Carrier Alsthom, No. 898, France, c1961, with box, 11½in (29cm) long.

£530–600 ⊞ MILI

A Hubley Manufacturing Co taxi cab, with rubber tyres and wooden hubs, America, 1939, 7¾in (19.5cm) long.

£185–220 ⚒ JDJ

A JEP clockwork Hispano Suiza, with nickel headlights and grille, restored, France, 1930s, 18½in (47cm) long.

£2,800–3,350 ⚒ Bert

A Kenton cast-iron four-door limousine, America, 1960s, 12in (30.5cm) long.

£590–700 ⚒ Bert

This toy was made exclusively for Sears Department stores.

◀ **A Kilgore cast-iron truck,** with three interchangeable bodies: Arctic Ice Cream, livestock stake and dump bed, America, c1930, 6½in (16.5cm) long.

£260–310 ⚒ Bert

▶ **A Kingsbury tinplate *Bluebird* car,** America, c1931, 19in (48.5cm) long.

£540–600 ⊞ GEOH

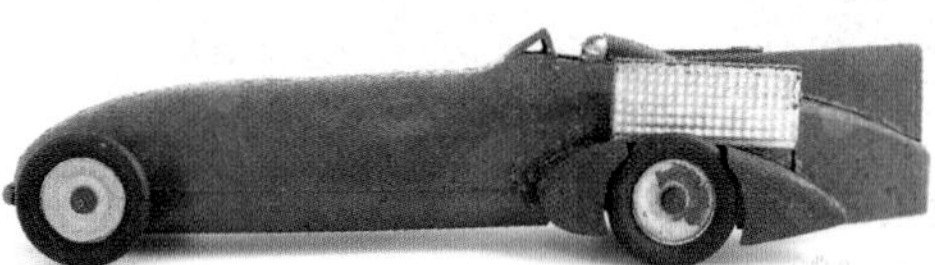

A Mar Toys tinplate clockwork tank, No. 3, America, c1940, 8in (20.5cm) long.

£90–100 JUN

A Western Models tinplate Sunbeam, 1927, 5½in (14cm) long.

£90–100 GEOH

This car was produced to celebrate Sir Henry Segrave's land speed record of 203.792 mph at Daytona Beach in Florida in 1927. It was issued with the children's comic The Modern Boy, No. 4.

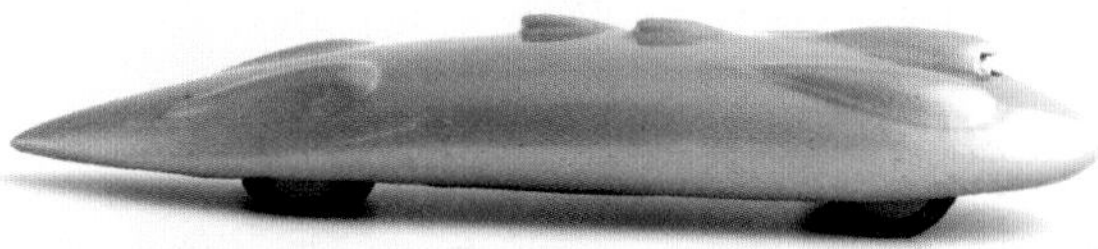

A Jo Hill Co lead *Golden Arrow*, c1929, 5¼in (13.5cm) long.

£135–150 GEOH

Sir Henry Segrave set a new landspeed record of 231.4mph in the Golden Arrow *at Daytona Beach in Florida in 1929.*

A Mettoy tinplate battery-powered searchlight lorry, slight damage, c1940, 14¼in (36cm) long.

£100–120 WAL

A Structo clockwork dump truck, slight damage, losses, America, early 20thC, 19in (48.5cm) long.

£200–240 JAA

Structo Manufacturing Company was founded by Louis Strohacker in Freeport, Illinois in 1908. In 1918 they began producing bolt-together model cars in kit form with clockwork motors that were wound up with a hand crank like the real cars of the time.

A lithographed tinplate horse-drawn US mail wagon, America, c1900, 14in (35.5cm) long.

£250–280 JDJ

◄ A lithographed tinplate horse-drawn Klondlike Ice wagon, America, c1900, 17in (43cm) long.

£250–280 JDJ

A painted pine toy truck, c1910, 26in (66cm) long.

£165–185 ALCH

A painted tin pedal Baby Dacota rocket, with rubber tyres, mid-20thC, 47¼in (120cm) long.

£150–180 MA&I

An Austin Junior Forty Roadster pedal car, 1960s, 39½in (100.5cm) long.

£530–630 GTH

MISCELLANEOUS

A Voyage of Discovery board game, published by William Spooner, hand-coloured lithograph on linen, 1836, 22½ x 18½in (57 x 47cm).

£550–660 DW

► **A Train for Boston board game,** published by Parker Bros, America, c1900, 16½ x 14¾in (42 x 37.5cm).

£460–550 JDJ

An American Boys board game, published by McLoughlin Bros, America, 1913, 10½ x 19½in (26.5 x 49.5cm).

£150–180 JDJ

A set of five wooden building blocks, each illustrated with children, numbers and letters, slight damage, c1880, largest 3½in (9cm) square.

£80–95 DW

An ebony and boxwood weighted Staunton chess set, by Jaques, London, c1890, king 4½in (11.5cm) high, in a mahogany case.

£1,250–1,400 TMi

A pack of domino playing cards, in a silver case, c1900, 3in (7.5cm) high.

£210–240 SKA

A roll-up wooden draughts board, by H. C. Small of East Lemington, Maine, with wooden draughts and box, slight damage, America, patented 1862.

£930–1,100 JDJ

A set of Les Anamorphoses optical game cards, comprising 11 hand-coloured lithographed cards, printed by Walter Frères, France, 1840s–50s, cards 8 x 6½in (20.5 x 16.5cm), in original case.

£230–270 LAY

◄ **A Victorian mahogany games compendium,** containing a cribbage board, dominoes, draughts, folding board and a later boxwood chess set, 12in (30.5cm) wide.

£410–490 MAL(O)

A Victorian carved and painted wood toy, in the form of a man and a serpent, fitted with a metal pipe to emit smoke from serpent, America, 15in (38cm) high.

£6,500–7,800 NAAW

A wooden Superior Dissected Maps jigsaw, published by Gall & Inglis, Edinburgh, one piece later, Scotland, c1870, with original box, 18½ x 15in (47 x 38cm).

£170–200 DW

A pull-along tinplate Dexter Horse platform toy, by George Brown, on cast-iron wheels, America, c1880, 12in (30.5cm) long.

£590–700 JDJ

A Victorian *faux* tortoiseshell Little Conjurer magician's set, with turned wood pieces, boxed, 17in (43cm) wide.

£220–260 ROS

A Steiff pull-along bear, with button eyes and stitched nose, button in ear, with iron wheels, Germany, c1910, 14¾in (37.5cm) long.

£370–440 DMC

A Steiff pull-along donkey, button missing, Germany, c1915, 14in (35.5cm) high.

£155–175 BaN

An Uncle Remus Shooting Gallery game, by B&B Novelties, America, c1920, boxed, 20¼ x 13½in (51.5 x 34.5cm).

£370–440 JDJ

A turned mahogany solitaire board, with 32 hand-made mica marbles, 19thC, 10in (25.5cm) diam.

£175–210 PFK

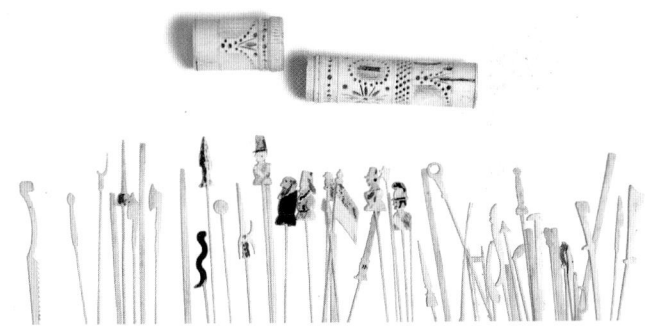

A Prisoner of War bone spillikins game, early 19thC, 4½in (11.5cm) long.

£310–350 ET

A Transformation game, containing 15 wooden pieces decorated with hand-painted figures, slight damage, c1850, each figure 7 x 4in (18 x 10cm).

£100–120 BBA

A wood and metal tricycle, in the form of a horse, France, c1900, 29in (73.5cm) long.

£1,150–1,300 PICA

▶ **A ventriloquist's carved and painted wood puppet,** with fabric and leather costume, America, c1900, 38½in (98cm) high.

£7,800–8,700 GIAM

EPHEMERA

ANNUALS, BOOKS & COMICS

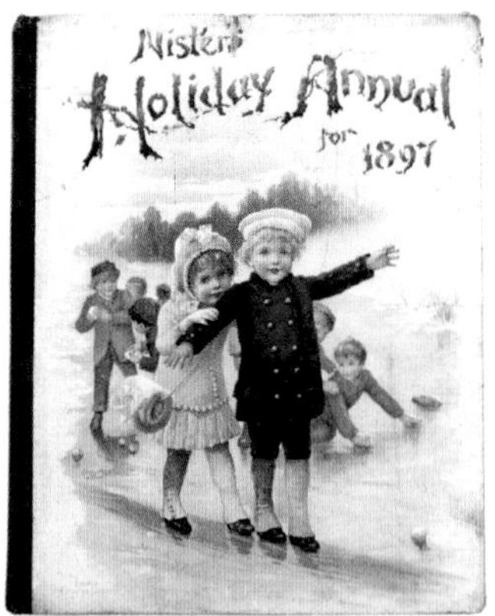

Nister's Holiday Annual, by Lewis Wayne Prints, 1897, 10in (25.5cm) high.

£75–90 NGL

Triumph comic, No. 772, 5 August, 1939.

£900–1,050 VAU

This edition features the first Superman story to appear in a British comic.

Batman comic book, No. 1, restored, spring 1940.

£3,500–4,200 JAA

Detective Comics comic book, No. 38, April 1940.

£1,250–1,500 JAA

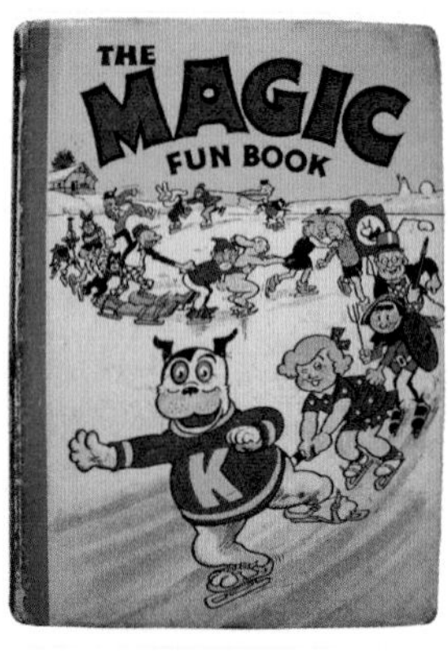

The Magic Fun Book, 1941, 11¼ x 8¼in (28.5 x 21cm).

£450–500 PSH

The Magic *comic began in 1939 and ran for only 80 issues, being a victim of wartime shortages. Two* Magic Fun Books *were produced before the title and characters were amalgamated with the* Beano. Magic *comics and books rarely come onto the market.*

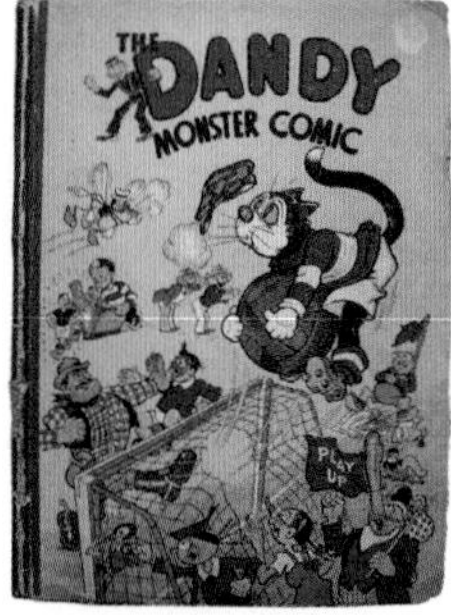

The Dandy Monster Comic annual, 1944, 11½ x 8½in (29 x 21.5cm).

£360–400 PSH

The first Dandy *annual, entitled* The Dandy Monster Comic, *was a large book and would have been the centrepiece of any child's Christmas stocking in 1939. The title continued until 1952 whereafter it was called* The Dandy Book. *War year annuals such as this 1944 book are rare and highly sought after by collectors.*

The Magic-Beano Book, 1948, 10¾ x 8in (27.5 x 20.5cm).

£220–250 PSH

The first Beano Book *of 1940 was a huge success. The title changed in 1943 to* The Magic-Beano Book *with the amalgamation of the* Magic *comic.*

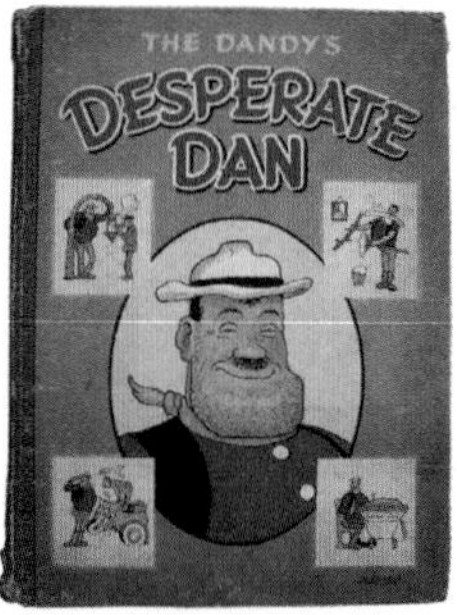

The Dandy's Desperate Dan book, 1954, 12 x 9in (30.5 x 23cm).

£90–100 PSH

Desperate Dan, drawn by Dudley Watkins, appeared in every issue from No. 1 in 1937 but, despite being a national hero, only ever had five of his own annuals – in 1954, 1979, 1991, 1992 and 1993. This first issue of 1954 comprised reprints of earlier strips. Due to its large format it was prone to wear.

Justice League of America comic book, No. 1, 1960.

£75–85 JAA

AUTOGRAPHS

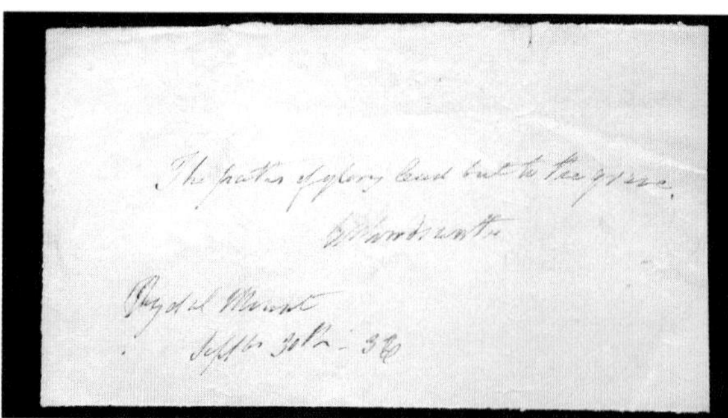

◀ **William Wordsworth,** an autograph and quotation from 'Elegy Written in a Country Churchyard', by Thomas Gray, signed and dated 30 September 1836, 8°.

£790–880 CFSD

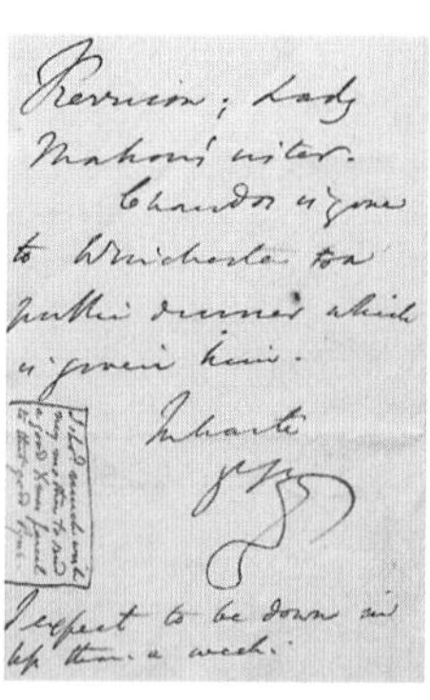

Benjamin Disraeli, a signed letter to his sister Sarah, informing her of the latest political news of Irish affairs, eight pages, 17 December 1836, 8°.

£840–1,000 S

This detailed letter to a close confidante, written in the early period of Disraeli's full involvement in politics and the year before he entered the Commons, gives a strong impression of political events in late 1836.

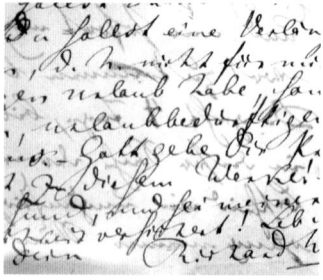

Theodor Uhlig, a letter from the German composer to Franz Schubert, with addendum written by Richard Wagner, two pages, dated 19 July 1851, 16¾ x 10½in (42.5 x 26.5cm).

£1,750–2,100 AH

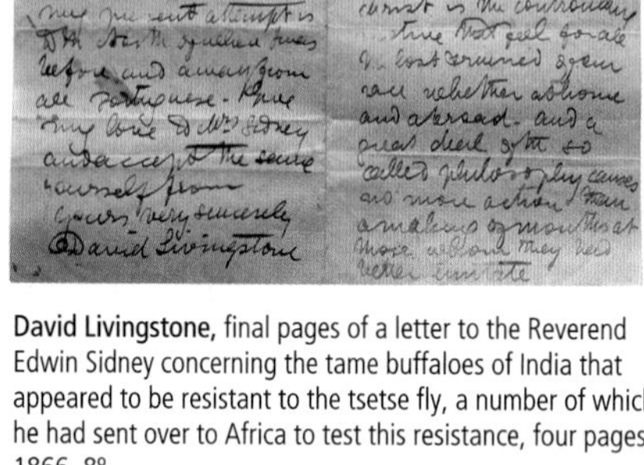

David Livingstone, final pages of a letter to the Reverend Edwin Sidney concerning the tame buffaloes of India that appeared to be resistant to the tsetse fly, a number of which he had sent over to Africa to test this resistance, four pages, 1866, 8°.

£2,450–2,750 CFSD

Robert E. Lee, signed *carte de visite*, America, photograph 2½in (6.5cm) high.

£3,900–4,600 JDJ

John Ruskin, two signed letters to Mr Schütz Wilson, each three pages, dated 12 March 1879 and 25 March 1879, 8°.

£760–910 RTo

Queen Victoria, a signed photograph on the occasion of her Diamond Jubilee, dated 1897, in a leather and brass frame, 8 x 6in (20.5 x 15cm).

£1,650–1,850 AEL

Grand Duke Vladimir Alexandrovich, a signed photograph, Russia, c1900, 20½ x 16¼in (52 x 41.5cm), in a wooden frame.

£1,200–1,400 S(O)

Grand Duke Vladimir Alexandrovich was the second surviving son of Tsar Alexander II.

John Philip Sousa, a signed photograph, 1905.

£220–260 VS

The American composer and band leader John Philip Sousa (1854–1932) was often known as The March King.

▶ **Nicholas II,** signed decree document, in Russian with translation, countersigned by Vladimir Sukhomlinov, 1914, 2°.

£1,120–1,250 CFSD

Nicholas succeeded his father in 1894. He was to be the last Emperor of Russia and his reign was marked by the alliance with France, entente with Britain, and the war with Japan (1904–05). He took command of the Russian armies against the Central Powers in 1915. At the Revolution he was forced to abdicate and the Red Guards shot him and his entire family at Yekaterinburg in July 1918.

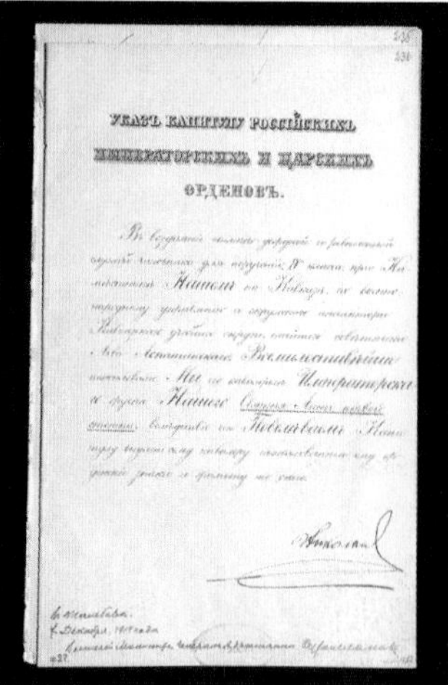

УКАЗЪ КАПИТУЛУ РОССІЙСКИХЪ ИМПЕРАТОРСКИХЪ И ЦАРСКИХЪ ОРДЕНОВЪ.

Edward, Prince of Wales, a signed photograph inscribed 'Cottesmore Hounds Jan 22nd 1921, Stapleford Park', 8 x 10in (20.5 x 25.5cm), in a leather frame.

£680–810 GTH

◀ **Buffalo Bill,** a signed letter to Dr Richard Tanner (Diamond Dick) describing a trip with Deadwood Dick in Wyoming, c1927.

£125–145 JAA

The letter is accompanied by news clippings regarding Deadwood Dick and Diamond Dick's visit to Norfolk, Nebraska. Diamond Dick was an author and performer for Buffalo Bill and other Wild West shows.

WITH BEST WISHES FOR CHRISTMAS AND THE NEW YEAR 1948

George R Elizabeth R

◀ **King George VI and Queen Elizabeth,** a signed Christmas card with a photograph of the couple with their daughters, Princess Elizabeth and Princess Margaret, 1948, 6 x 14in (15 x 35.5cm).

£450–500 AEL

Christ Church,
Oxford.
21st May 1932.

Dear Mr Jacob,

I thank you for your letter of the 20th. I am quite willing for your publishers to quote the remarks I made in my letter to you of the 16th.

Yours truly,

A. Einstein.

A.J.Jacob Esq.,
16 Brondesbury Park,
London, N.W.6.

Albert Einstein, a signed letter to A. J. Jacob, 21 May 1932.

£960–1,150 VS

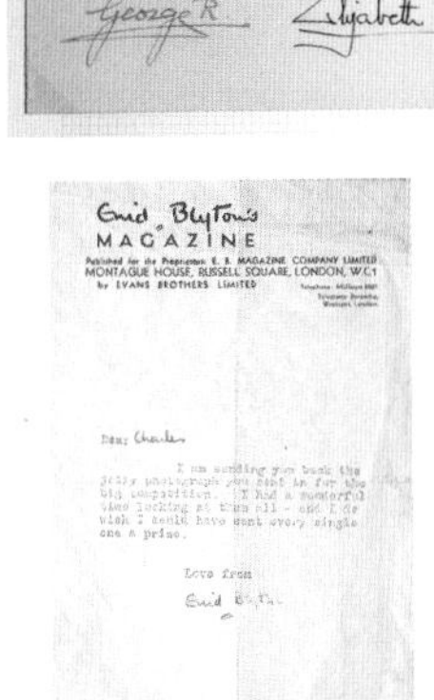

Enid Blyton's MAGAZINE
Published for the Proprietors E. B. MAGAZINE COMPANY LIMITED
MONTAGUE HOUSE, RUSSELL SQUARE, LONDON, W.C.1
by EVANS BROTHERS LIMITED

Dear Charles

I am sending you back the jolly photograph you sent in for the big competition. I had a wonderful time looking at them all - and I do wish I could have sent every single one a prize.

Love from

Enid Blyton

E. B. MAGAZINE COMPANY LIMITED

◀ **Enid Blyton,** a signed letter to 'Charles', returning a photograph sent by him for a competition, 8°.

£110–125 CFSD

▶ **Stan Laurel and Oliver Hardy,** a signed page from an autograph book, 1950s.

£280–330 AH

CIGARETTE CARDS

Carreras, Film Favourites, set of 50, 1939.

£80–90 SAT

John Player & Sons, Life on Board a Man of War 1805, set of 50, 1905.

£105–120 SAT

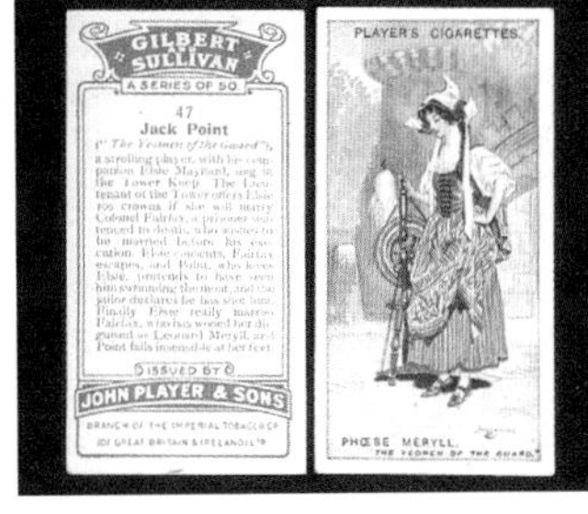

John Player & Sons, Gilbert and Sullivan, set of 50, 1929.

£45–50 MUR

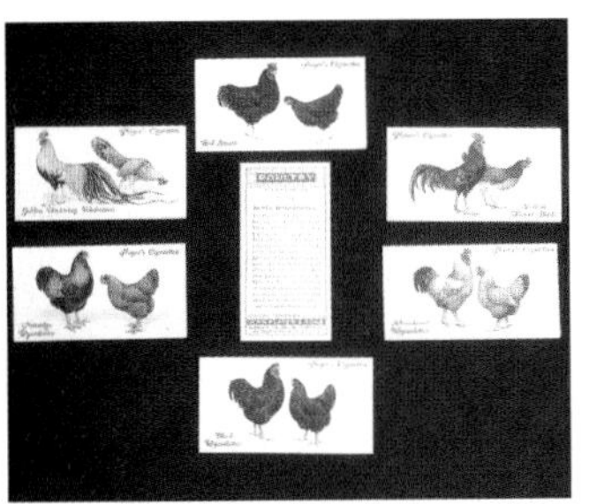

◀ **John Player & Sons,** Poultry, set of 50, 1931.

£70–80 MUR

▶ **W. D. & H. O. Wills,** Allied Army Badges, set of 50, 1917.

£70–80 SOR

POSTCARDS

A Waverley Cycles postcard, by Alphonse Mucha, France, c1898.

£6,800–8,100 JAA

Originally produced as a poster in 1897, the Waverley Cycles postcard is regarded as the most famous postcard in existence. It is widely believed that very few, perhaps less than six, are known to exist. Several of these known examples have considerable writing on the message portion as well as having been postally used.

A postcard, depicting the Socialist Drum Corps, Syracuse, New York, America, c1908.

£400–480 JAA

A postcard, depicting the Exhibition of Munich poster art, signed, Germany, 1914.

£140–165 JAA

An Art Nouveau postcard, depicting the painting La Liseron/La Capucine, by Jack Abeille, 1899.

£50–60 VS

An Algiers postcard, c1900.

£15–20 S&D

A postcard, depicting Warren Halt train station, Folkestone, 1910.

£20–25 M&C

A postcard, depicting a soldier with a machine gun, America, early 20thC.

£155–185 JAA

◄ **A postcard,** depicting a California corrugated car, America, April 1915.

£140–165 JAA

A postcard, depicting a Gloucester shop front, c1900.

£20–25 M&C

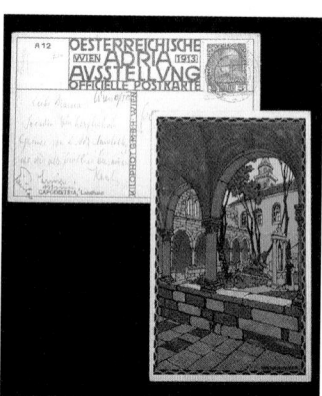

A postcard, depicting the first American car in Kearney, Nebraska, America, c1908.

£110–130 JAA

A postcard, by Hans Kalmsteiner, depicting a design for the Adria Exhibition in Vienna, Austria, 1913.

£25–30 S&D

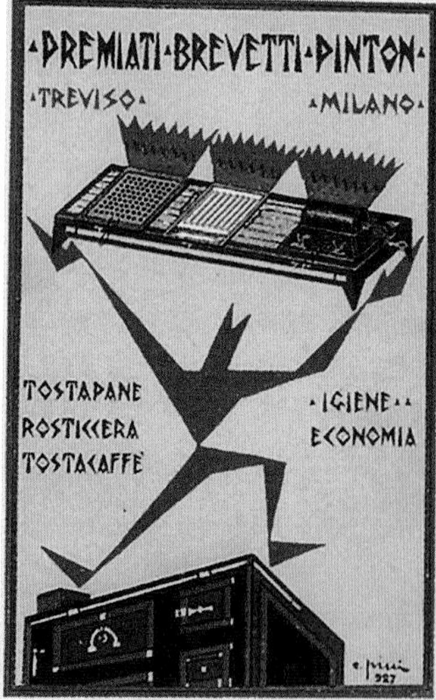

A postcard, advertising a stove company, signed 'Pissi', Italy, 1927.

£110–130 JAA

POSTERS

A Ménagerie du Cap poster, France, 1885, 33 x 24in (84 x 61cm).

£510–580 Do

A Vittel Vosges poster, by F. Hugo d'Alési, France, c1890, 42½ x 31in (107.5 x 78.5cm).

£300–360 VSP

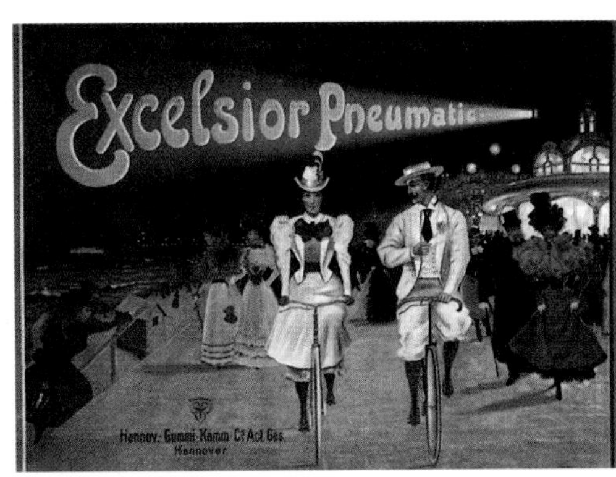

An Excelsior Pneumatic poster, Germany, c1890, 32 x 41½in (81.5 x 105cm).

£1,300–1,550 VSP

A Bruant au Mirliton poster, by Henri de Toulouse-Lautrec, France, 1893, 31½ x 23½in (80 x 59.5cm).

£5,500–6,600 S(NY)

A Cycles Decauville poster, by Alfred Choubras, on linen, France, c1895, 58½ x 42in (149 x 106.5cm).

£970–1,150 VSP

A May Milton poster, by Henri de Toulouse-Lautrec, on wove paper, France, 1895, 31¼ x 24¼in (79.5 x 61.5cm).

£4,500–5,400 S(NY)

A Salon des Cent poster, by Alphonse Mucha, on japan paper, France, 1896, 24¾ x 17in (63 x 43cm).

£7,000–8,400 VSP

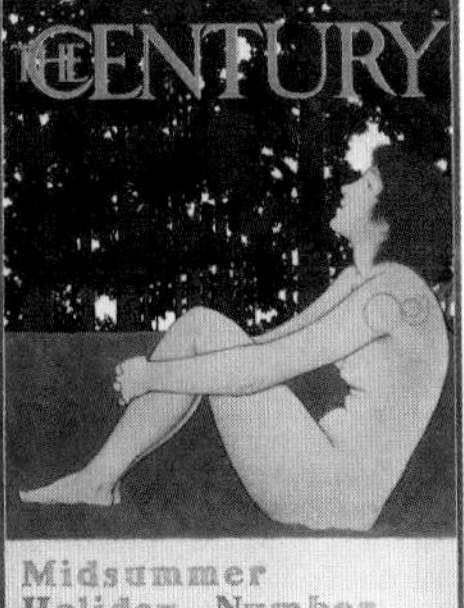

► **A promotional poster,** by Maxfield Parris, 'The Century Midsummer Holiday Number. August', America, 1897, 22¼ x 15¼in (56.5 x 38.5cm).

£1,350–1,600 FFAP

An Adlake Camera poster, by Maxfield Parrish, America, 1897, 11 x 17in (28 x 43cm).

£1,950–2,300 FFAP

◄ **A poster,** promoting Concarneau, on board, France, c1900, 62 x 46½in (157.5 x 118cm).

£270–320 NOA

► **A Levensverzekering Maatschappij Arnhem poster,** by Jan Th. Toorop, on linen, Holland, 1900, 39¾ x 28½in (101 x 72cm).

£2,350–2,800 VSP

The Bookman Christmas Number **poster,** by Louis Rhead, slight damage, America, c1900, 19 x 11½in (48.5 x 29cm).

£195–230 FFAP

A Kodak Christmas poster, by Edward Penfield, slight damage, America, c1905, 14¼ x 9in (36 x 23cm).

£1,500–1,800 FFAP

A promotional poster, 'Kellar – The Witch, The Sailor and The Enchanted Monkey, America, 1905, 28 x 38in (71 x 96.5cm), framed.

£1,150–1,350 NOA

Harry Kellar (1849–1922) was known as the Dean of the American Magicians and was a close friend and mentor to Harry Houdini.

LOCATE THE SOURCE

The source of each illustration in Miller's can be found by checking the code letters below each caption with the Key to Illustrations, pages 746–753.

A Col W. F. Cody ***Buffalo Bill*** **poster,** on linen, America, 1908, 81½ x 38½in (207 x 98cm).

£4,050–4,850 VSP

A Die Kornfranck-Tante poster, by Ludwig Hohlwein or Louis Oppenheim, on japan paper, Germany, c1913, 28¾ x 19in (73 x 48.5cm).

£970–1,150 VSP

A Hamburg-Amerika Linie poster, by Hans Bohrdt, 'Ostasien', Germany, c1915, 27½ x 20½in (70 x 52cm).

£480–570 VSP

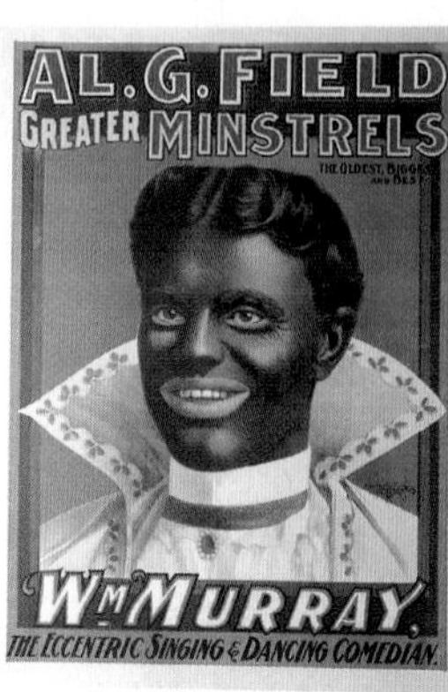

An Al. G. Field Greater Minstrels poster, on paper, 1920, 28 x 21in (71 x 53.5cm).

£450–500 Do

◄ **A promotional poster,** by John Hassel, *The Weekly Telegraph*, on paper, 1920, 35 x 20in (89 x 51cm).

£290–330 Do

An Aérobus de L'Eau des Récolletes poster, by Emilio Vilá, original gouache poster design, slight damage, signed, France, c1920, 65 x 47in (165 x 119.4cm).

£1,250–1,500 DW

Emilio Vilá was born in Barcelona but lived in France for many years.

An LNER poster, by Fred Tayler, 'Cambridge', on linen, c1925, 40¼ x 25in (102 x 63.5cm).

£280–330 VSP

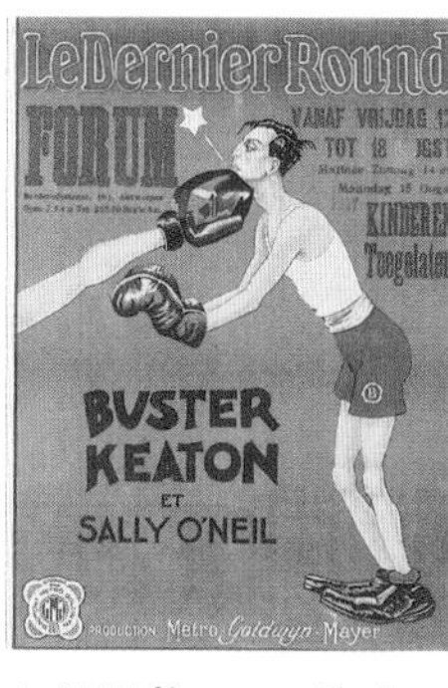

An MGM film poster, *The Last Round*, starring Buster Keaton and Sally O'Neil at the Forum, Belgium, Antwerp, dated 1927, 33 x 24in (84 x 61cm).

£360–430 BERN

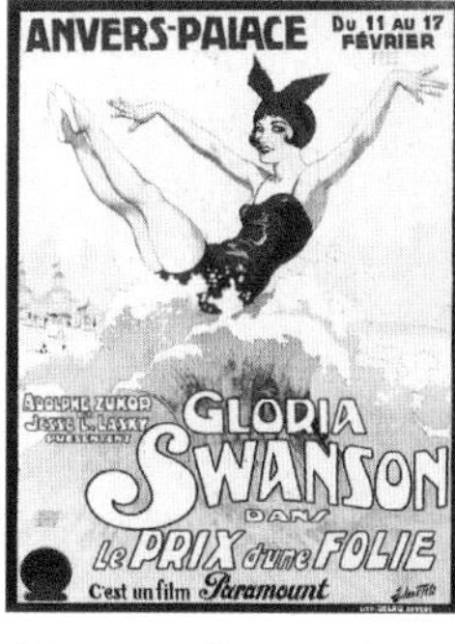

A Paramount film poster, by Julien 't Felt, starring Gloria Swanson in *The Price of a Folly*, signed, Belgium, 1927, 34¾ x 26¾in (88.5 x 68cm), framed.

£870–1,000 BERN

A Marco Polo Tee poster, by Ludwig Hohlwein, on cardboard, Germany, 1929, 11¾ x 7¾in (30 x 19.5cm).

£85–100 VSP

◄ **A BP advertising poster,** by Edward McKnight Kauffer, 'BP Plus – Plus a Little Something that Some Others Haven't Got' original gouache poster design, signed and dated 1932, 31 x 21in (78.5 x 53.5cm), framed.

£3,600–4,300 S

A film poster, *I Dream too Much*, starring Lily Pons and Henry Fonda, on japan paper, America, 1935, 41 x 27¼in (104 x 69cm).

£360–430 VSP

A Dodge Cars promotional poster, on japan paper, America, c1935, 50 x 38in (127 x 96.5cm).

£2,250–2,700 VSP

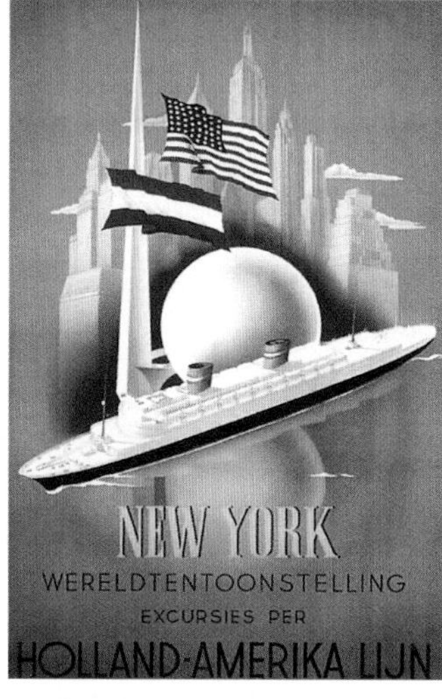

A Holland-Amerika Lijn poster, by Willem F. ten Broek, 'New York', Holland, 1938, 38 x 24½in (96.5 x 62cm).

£2,700–3,250 VSP

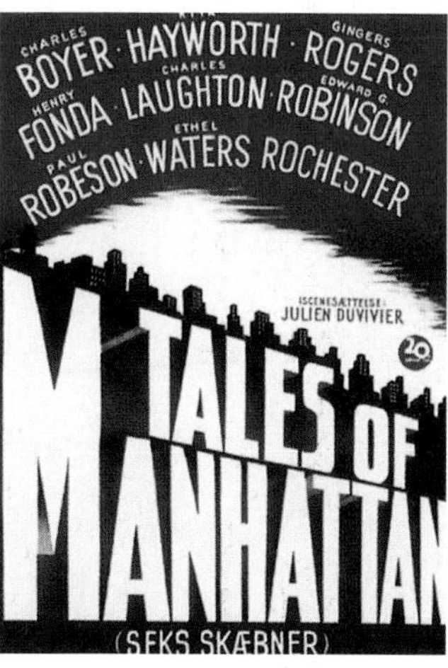

A 20th Century-Fox film poster, *Tales of Manhattan*, starring Ginger Rogers and Henry Fonda, Denmark, Copenhagen, 1942, 33¼ x 24¼in (84.5 x 61.5cm).

£240–280 VSP

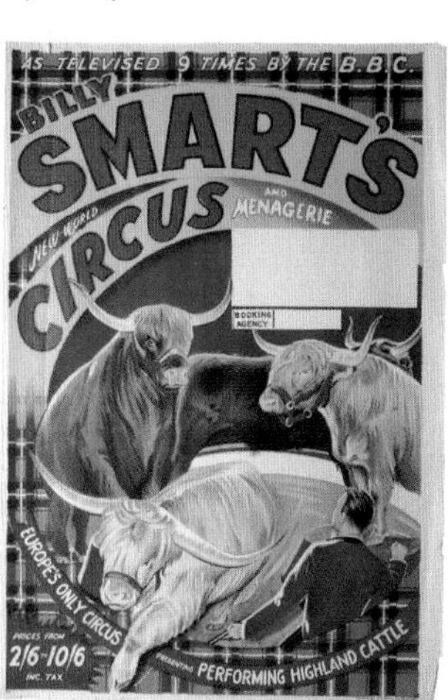

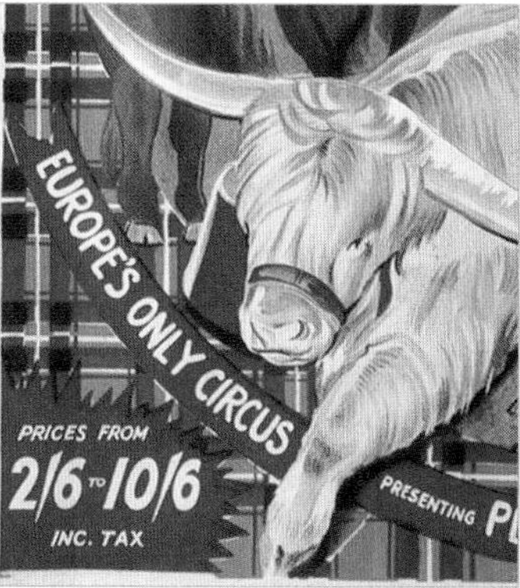

◄ **A Billy Smart's Circus poster,** on paper, 1950, 30 x 20in (76 x 51cm).

£135–150 Do

A Canadian Pacific poster, by H. Simpkins, 'Canada for Fishing', c1950, 36 x 24in (91.5 x 61cm).

£280–330 VSP

A Universal International Pictures film poster, *Lost in Alaska*, starring Bud Abbott and Lou Costello, linen-backed, America, 1950, 41 x 27in (104 x 68.5cm).

£430–480 Lim

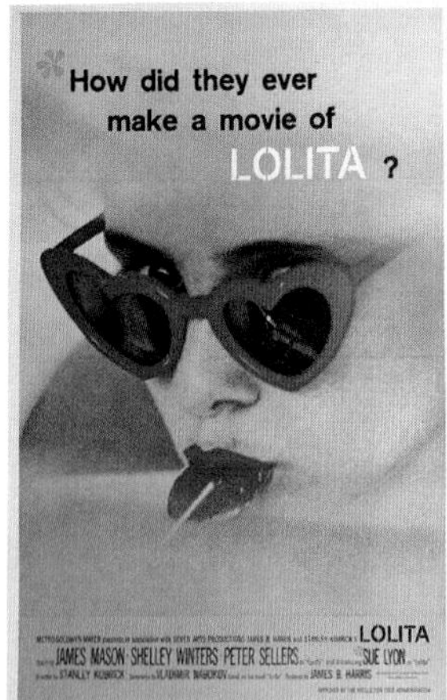

An A. A. Productions film poster, *Lolita*, starring James Mason, Shelley Winters and Peter Sellers, America, 1952, 40 x 26in (101.5 x 66cm).

£760–850 CINE

A *Ville de Honfleur Societé des Artistes* poster, 'Hommage à Raoul Dufy', France, 1954, 30¾ x 20¾in (78 x 52.5cm), framed.

£175–210 SK

A Paramount Pictures film poster, Alfred Hitchcock's *Rear Window*, starring James Stewart and Grace Kelly, America, 1954, 22 x 28in (56 x 71cm).

£3,150–3,500 CINE

◄ **A travel poster,** by Martin Peikert, promoting Rigi, Switzerland, 1954, 40¼ x 25¼in (102 x 64cm).

£300–360 VSP

► **A film poster,** *The Wages of Fear*, starring Yves Montand, 1955, 30 x 40in (76 x 101.5cm).

£760–850 CINE

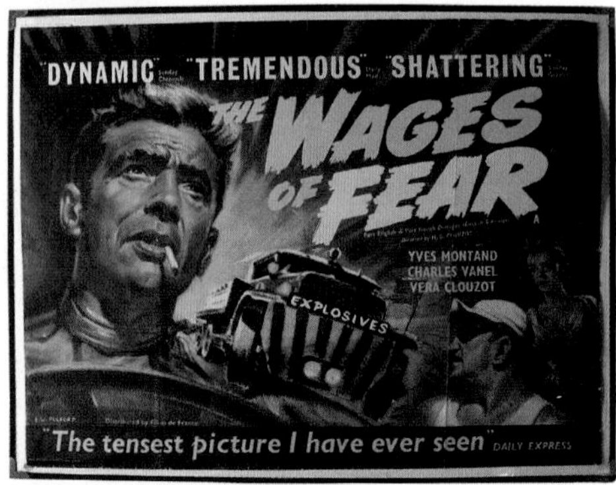

A Berggruen & Cie poster, 'Klee', France, Paris, 1955, 26½ x 20¼in (67.5 x 51.5cm), framed.

£220–260 SK

► **A Musée Galliéra poster,** *Les Peintres Témoins de Leur Temps*, France, Paris, 1957, 30½ x 21in (77.5 x 53.5cm), framed.

£220–260 SK

◄ **A Galerie Lorenceau poster,** 'Gerard Singer' France, 1957, 26½ x 18in (67.5 x 45.5cm).

£200–240 SK

A British Railways poster, by Frank Sherwin, promoting the Pass of Glencoe, Western Highlands, slight damage, Scotland, Glasgow, 1950s, 39½ x 45in (100.5 x 114.5cm).

£420–500 SWO

A MacBrayne's Services poster, by Norman Wilkinson, promoting the Western Highlands and Islands, Scotland, c1960, 48½ x 39½in (123 x 100.5cm).

£590–600 SWO

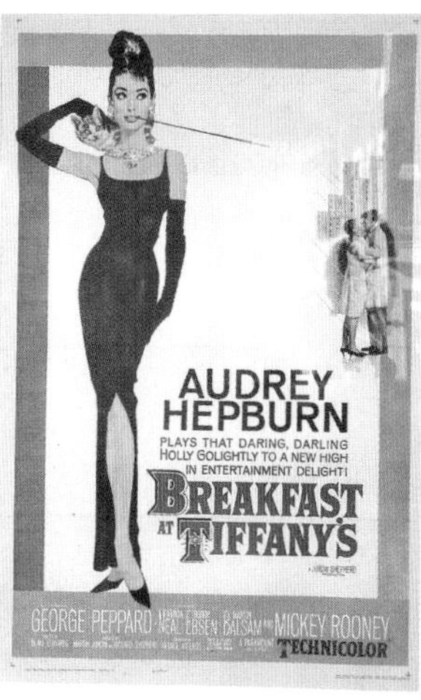

A Paramount film poster, *Breakfast at Tiffany's*, starring Audrey Hepburn, America, 1961, 41 x 27in (104 x 68.5cm).

£4,250–4,750 CINE

A United Artists film poster, *Dr No*, starring Sean Connery, 1962, 30 x 40in (76 x 101.5cm).

£4,050–4,500 CINE

▶ **A Colombia Pictures Corporation film poster,** by Saul Bass, *Advise & Consent*, starring Henry Fonda, America, 1962, 36 x 14in (91.5 x 35.5cm).

£360–400 Lim

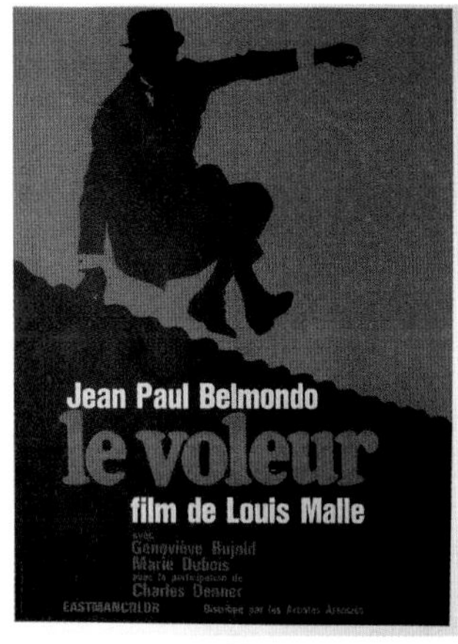

A film poster, *Le Voleur*, starring Jean Paul Belmondo, linen-backed, France, 1967, 30 x 23in (76 x 58.5cm).

£270–300 Lim

◀ **A Warner Brothers and Seven Arts film poster,** *Bullitt*, starring Steve McQueen, Italy, 1969, 78 x 55in (198 x 139.5cm).

£1,600–1,800 CINE

A Locandina film poster, *A Fistful of Dollars*, starring Clint Eastwood, Italy, 1968, 28 x 13in (71 x 33cm).

£990–1,100 Lim

▶ **A United Artists film poster,** *Thunderball*, starring Sean Connery, Italy, 1972, 78 x 55in (198 x 139.5cm).

£1,050–2,000 CINE

A film poster, *The Last Remake of Beau Geste*, starring Marty Feldman, Ann-Margret, Michael York, Peter Ustinov and James Earl Jones, linen-backed, America, 1977, 41 x 27in (104 x 68.5cm).

£115–130 Lim

ROCK & POP

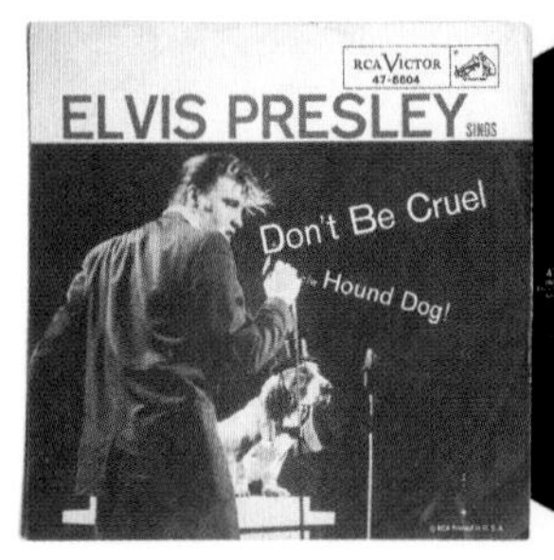

◄ Elvis Presley 'Don't Be Cruel' and 'Hound Dog', by RCA Victor, c1959, EP record, with sleeve.

£110–125 SDR

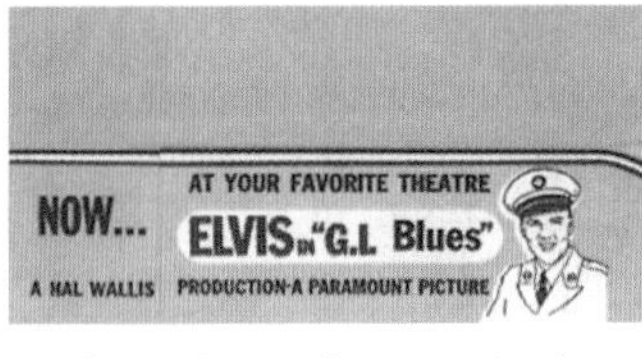

An Elvis Presley *G.I. Blues* promotional paper hat, 1960.

£175–210 CO

WHAT'S ON ON MERSEYSIDE

MERSEY BEAT

Guitar Contest at Crane Theatre

FRANK HESSY Ltd
62 STANLEY STREET
LIVERPOOL 1

BANDS IN THE PARKS

OPEN-AIR THEATRE

PHILHARMONIC CONCERT

Merseybeat, Vol. 1 No. 1, 1961.

£350–420 CO

THE FOLKLORE CENTER
Presents
BOB DYLAN
IN HIS FIRST NEW YORK CONCERT
SAT. NOV. 4, 1961 8:40pm
CARNEGIE CHAPTER HALL
154 WEST 57th STREET • NEW YORK CITY
All seats $2.00

A Bob Dylan concert programme, Carnegie Chapter Hall, New York, America, 1961.

£350–420 CO

The Beatles, four photographs by Hatami, entitled 'Fab Four (Beatles)', signed and numbered AP 0305, 1962, 39½ x 30in (100.5 x 76cm), framed.

£6,500–7,800 S(NY)

The Beatles 'Please Please Me', by Parlophone, LP record, 1963.

£90–100 SDR

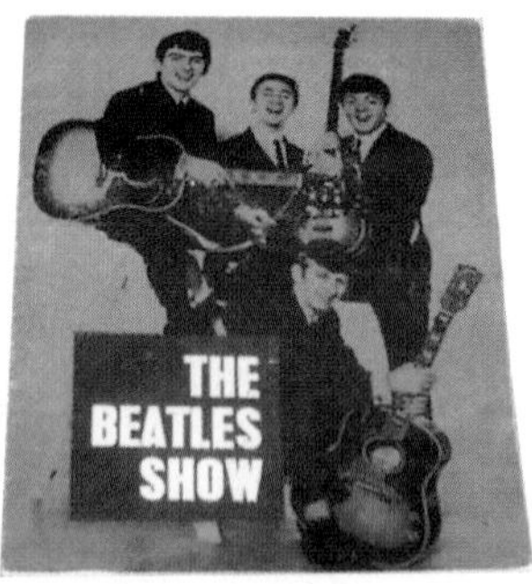

A Beatles show programme, for the Odeon, Llandudno, 1963.

£105–125 GTH

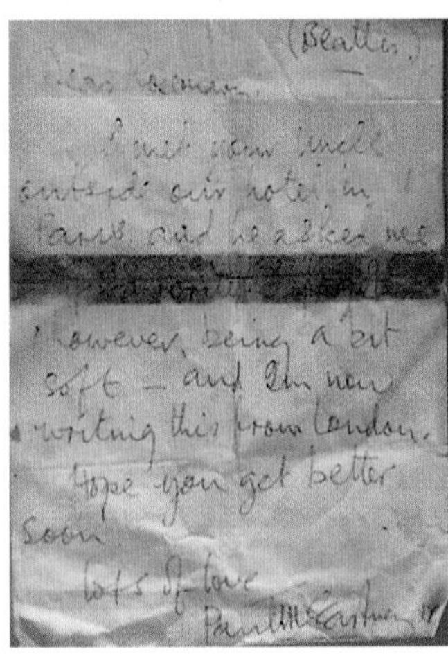

(Beatles)
Dear Rosemary,
I met your uncle outside our hotel in Paris and he asked me
...
however, being a bit soft — and I'm now writing this from London.
Hope you get better soon.
Lots of love
Paul McCartney

A handwritten letter by Paul McCartney, damaged and repaired, c1964, 17 x 4½in (43 x 11.5cm).

£820–980 Hal

When the recipient, Rosemary, took this letter to school her teacher tore it in half and threw it in the wastepaper bin, only for Rosemary to retrieve it and Sellotape it back together again.

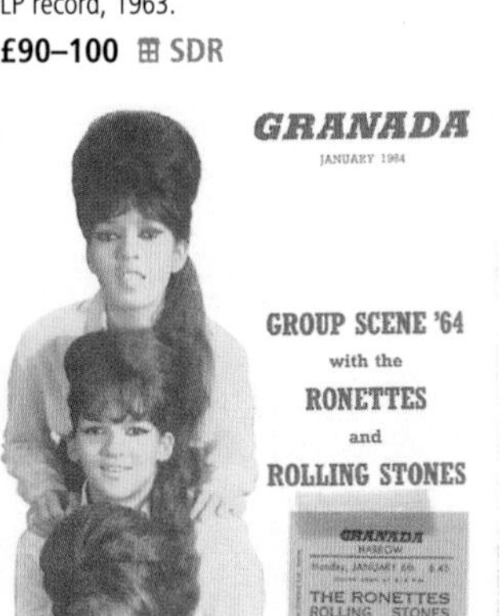

◄ A Rolling Stones Second UK Tour programme and ticket stub, 1964, programme 9¼ x 7in (23.5 x 18cm).

£165–195 CO

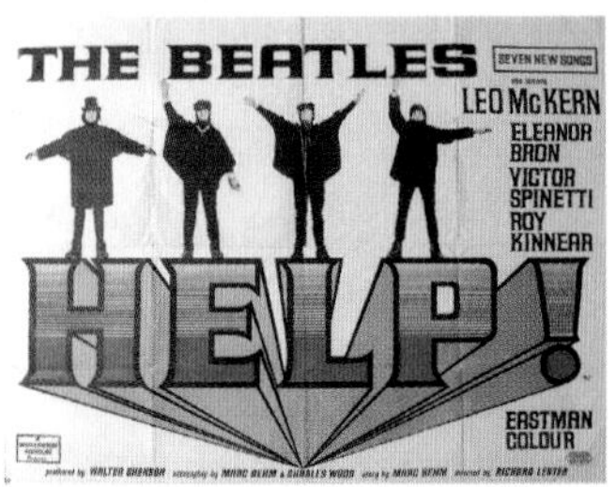

◄ A film poster, *Help!*, starring The Beatles, 1965, 30 x 40in (76 x 101.5cm).

£850–950 CINE

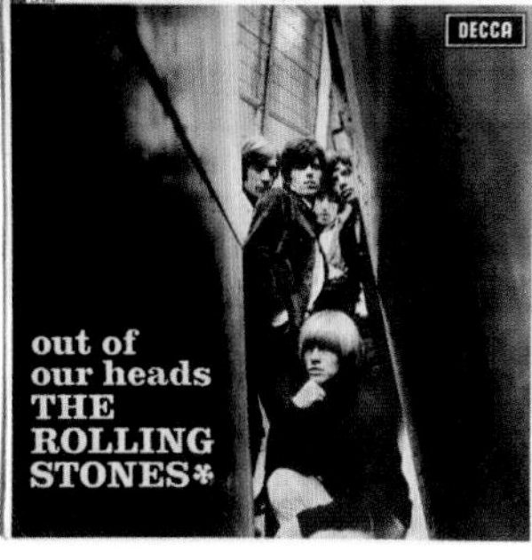

The Rolling Stones, 'Out of Our Heads', by Decca, LP record, 1965, boxed.

£70–80 SDR

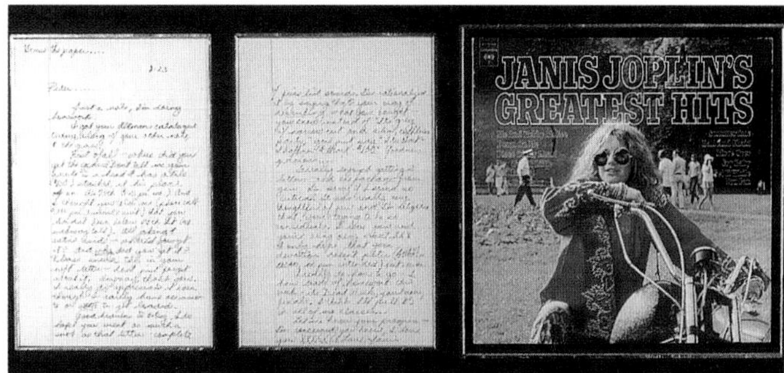

A handwritten letter by Janis Joplin, to her boyfriend Peter DuBlanc, together with a copy of the LP cover 'Janis Joplin's Greatest Hits', 1965, framed and glazed, overall 20 x 39in (51 x 99cm).

£940–1,100 CO

An Easy Beats LP record, 'Good Friday', by UK Artists, 1966.

£65–75 SDR

A poster, by Theo van de Boogaard, advertising The Mothers of Invention record 'Absolutely Free', 1967, 24½ x 18in (62 x 45.5cm).

£125–150 VSP

A United Artists poster, The Beatles in *Yellow Submarine*, America, 1968, 78¾ x 41in (200 x 104cm).

£360–430 VSP

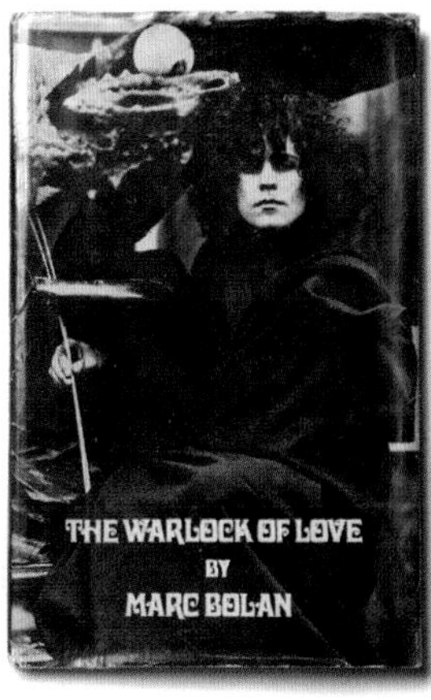

Marc Bolan, *The Warlock of Love*, published by Lupus Music, London, first edition, 1969, signed, 8¾ x 5½in (22 x 14cm).

£750–840 BB

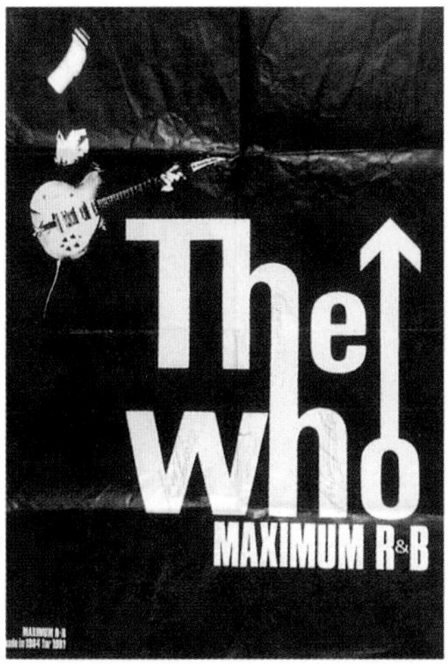

◄ **A poster,** advertising The Who 'Maximum R&B', signed by John Entwistle, Roger Daltrey, Pete Townshend and Kenny Jones, slight damage, c1981, 36 x 26½in (91.5 x 67.5cm).

£560–670 CO

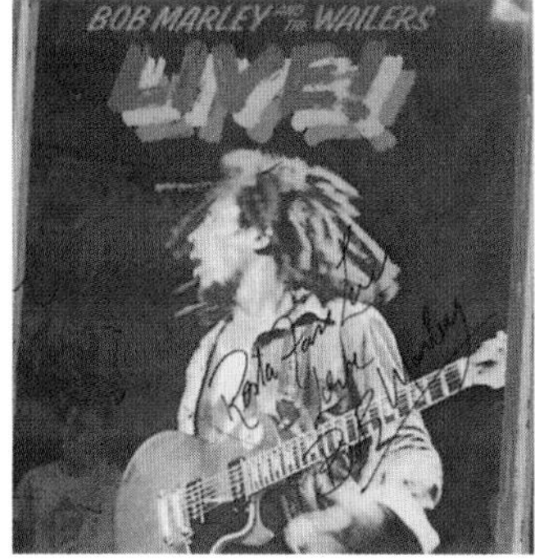

Bob Marley, 'Bob Marley and the Wailers Live!', LP record, signed, 1975.

£1,750–2,100 CO

A set of four Royal Doulton Beatles character jugs, by Stanley James Taylor, marked and numbered, 1984–91, 5½in (14cm) high.

£500–600 BAM

SCIENTIFIC INSTRUMENTS

CALCULATING INSTRUMENTS & MACHINES

◀ **A mahogany Thatcher's calculator and slide rule,** patented 1881, America, 1900–25, 24in (61cm) wide.

£400–480 NOA

Slide rules

John Napier (1550–1617) invented a system to simplify multiplication and division that he called logarithms. These were used by Edmund Gunter to develop what is known as Gunter's Rule, which was further extended by William Oughtred in 1621 to produce the first slide rule. Slide rules in their different formats were used until the early 1970s when the first hand-held electronic calculators were manufactured for general use. There is a growing and vibrant market for slide rules worldwide, with collectors keen to find examples that perform a vast variety of calculations.

A Farmar boxwood slide rule, early 19thC, 23in (58.5cm) long.

£190–220 ET

A boxwood Gunter's rule, by Edward Fage, with a brass folding hinge, marked with Lines, Solids, Tangents, Numbers, Sines, Metals, the Zodiac and Equatorial Bodies, together with Dry, Wine and Ale Measure, signed, dated 1669, 18in (45.5cm) long.

£4,700–5,600 F&C

Edward Fage, the maker of this piece, is recorded as a mathematical instrument maker working at the Sign of the Sugar Loaf in Hosier Lane, West Smithfield, who was admitted to the Clockmaker's Company in 1667. Although he made all manner of instruments he was particularly noted for his engraved scales. This extremely early, dated example of a Gunter's rule is, in addition to the usual scales, also marked for wine and ale measures, which may indicate that Thomas Hatton, for whom the scale had been made, was perhaps a wine merchant.

COMPASSES & DIALS

A painted tole hanging compass, in the form of a crown, inscribed 'Benjamin Scott, St Petersburg', Russia, 18thC, 8¾in (22cm) high.

£1,600–1,900 S(NY)

◀ **A late Victorian mahogany and brass dry card compass,** with a printed card and steel needle, 6¾in (17cm) diam.

£175–210 ROS

▶ **A silver folding pocket equinoctial dial,** the latch in the form of an exotic bird, the compass with engraved rose, engraved with 68 Spanish, European and South American places and their latitudes, signed 'Juan Matheo de Mendoza', Spain/South America, 18thC, 2½in (6.5cm) wide.

£4,800–5,700 S

A brass universal equinoctial dial, by Koni, with folding, spring-loaded gnomon, inscribed in Cyrillic with positions for St Petersburg, Tobol'sk, Irkutsk and Moscow, latitude arc, inset compass rose, on three levelling screws, Russia, 19thC, 4½in (11.5cm) diam.

£910–1,100 F&C

GLOBES & TELLURIONS

A pocket globe, the terrestrial globe labelled 'A Correct Globe with the New Discoveries', the shagreen case lined with a celestial map labelled 'A Correct Globe with New Constellations of Dr Halley etc', c1775, 7¾in (19.5cm) diam.

£3,400–4,000 CGC

A George III papier-mâché terrestrial pocket globe, by Halley & Co, entitled 'The Correct Globe with the New Discoveries', with a snakeskin-covered case lined with a hand-coloured a celestial map entitled 'A Correct Globe with Ye New Constellations', slight damage, c1800, 3in (7.5cm) diam.

£3,900–4,600 CAG

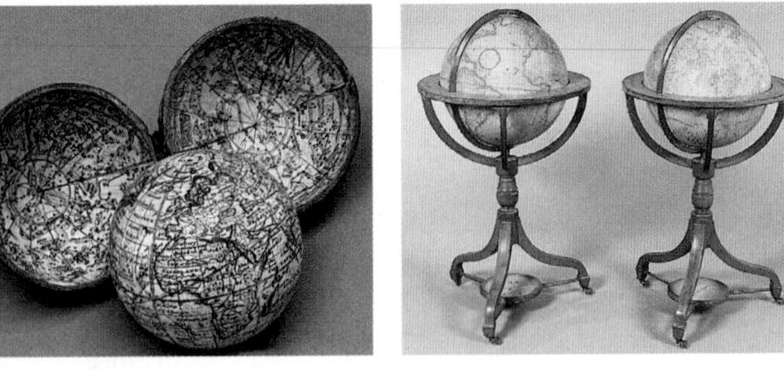

A pair of library globes, by John & William Cary, the terrestrial globe depicting the tracks and discoveries made by Captain Cook, the celestial globe with constellations depicted as mythical beasts and figures, each on a mahogany support with a glazed compass, London, 1816, 18in (45.5cm) diam.

£46,000–55,000 TEN

◄ **A pair of terrestrial and celestial globes,** by Josiah Loring, America, c1841, 12in (30.5cm) diam, each on a cast-iron stand.

£52,000–58,000 RGa

American collectors are very keen to regain their cultural heritage and will usually pay a premium for exceptional pieces such as these globes, which would have been just as prestigious at the time of manufacture. The wooden frames would have been made in a high quality cabinet-maker's workshop and finished to the same standard as a piece of finely crafted furniture. The cast-iron stands reflect the growing industrial industry in America, which sparked a fashion for ornate cast-iron wares for the home. As this medium is brittle by nature, it is unusual that these are in such good condition.

A terrestrial library globe, by Gilman Joslin, with a calibrated brass ring, America, Boston, 19thC, 15in (38cm) diam, on a mahogany stand.

£13,400–14,900 RGa

► **A cast-iron candlelit sun and moon tellurion,** by J. Felkl, Czech Republic, Prague, c1850, 31in (78.5cm) wide.

£2,250–2,500 ET

A tellurion shows how the movement of the earth on its axis and its revolution around the sun causes day and night and the seasons.

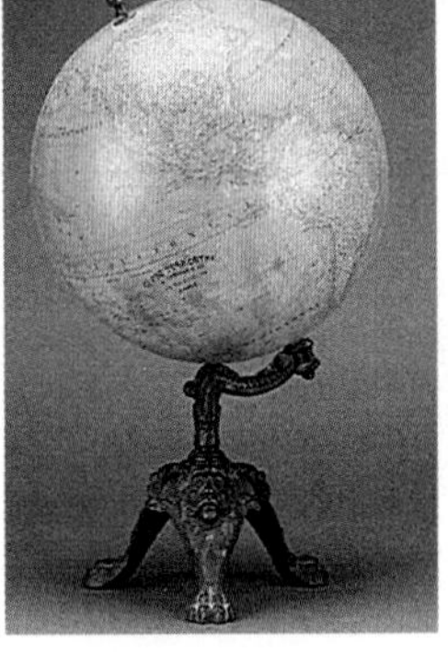

◄ **A terrestrial globe,** by J. Lebègue & Cie, on a cast-iron stand, France, late 19thC, 21½in (54.5cm) high.

£360–430 WAD

A terrestrial globe, by Malby, with gilt-metal meridian, on a mahogany stand inset with a compass, late 19thC, 34in (86.5cm) high.

£3,400–4,000 G(L)

A Parkes & Hadley's battery-powered Salter's Improved tellurion, c1900, 17in (43cm) wide.

£1,600–1,800 ET

◄ **A terrestrial globe,** by W. Violet, on a wooden base inset with a compass, Germany, Stuttgart, c1905, 12½in (32cm) diam.

£240–280 KOLN

MEDICAL & DENTAL

THERE ARE MANY AREAS of specialist interest for the collector within the field of scientific instruments, including medical and dental antiques. Dental history as we know it is still quite young; the first dental surgery is recorded as being undertaken in Egypt in the 3rd century bc, but for centuries dentistry was practised by just about anyone who had the skills to do so, such as blacksmiths, horse doctors and barbers. Early dental instruments were quite crude, their principal function being to remove teeth. Engineering and ingenuity combined over time to create more refined and ingenious devices such as tooth keys and pelicans, so-called because it resembles a pelican's beak.

The beginning of modern dentistry dates back to the 17th century. 'Operators for the teeth' extracted rotten molars, and fabricated dentures for those wealthy enough to pay for the treatment. In 1764, James Rae gave the first lectures on teeth at the Royal College of Surgeons in Edinburgh and in 1780 William Addis manufactured the first modern toothbrush.

Collectors today have an array of different styles and ages of implements to choose from. As time progressed, tools became more uniform and by 1900 were commonly made from sterile steels. The earlier pieces are generally far more interesting and hence valuable. As the majority of dental instruments were not as invasive as other medical implements they could be far more grandiose in design and form; tools can be found in solid silver and gold, mounted with ivory or tortoiseshell and in exquisite fitted cases. The better your reputation the higher your fee and the more elaborate your tools would be in order to impress your clients. Today a set of iron forceps would cost very little whereas solid gold bridges mounted with ivory, or a set of porcelain dentures, would fetch a four-figure sum.

Prices are still climbing steadily for the most interesting and complete items. The older and more gruesome the instrument, the higher its market appeal will be, although with the current trend for more flamboyant and showy items, values of early porcelain apothecary jars have risen sharply. Today's fashion-conscious may have gold teeth encrusted with diamonds but the Georgians were there before us!

Bill Higgins

Bill Higgins

Bill has been a specialist dealer in Antique Scientific and Medical instruments for many years and has supplied collectors, dealers and museums as well as individual buyers throughout the world.

His real interest lies in the ingenuity and engineering of old instruments and the skills of those who made them.

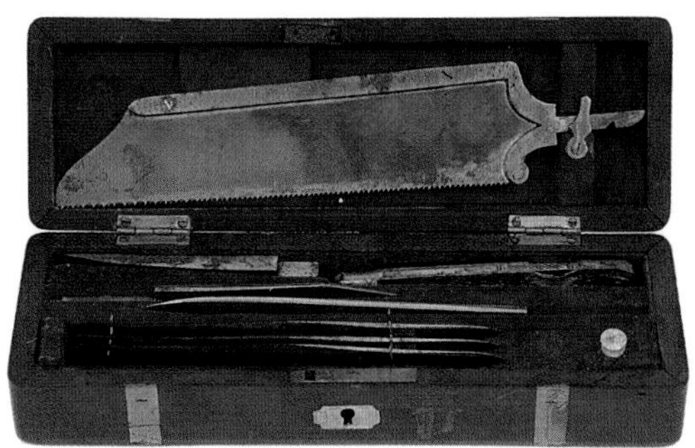

An amputation set, one implement stamped 'J. Dick, Glasgow', in a brass-bound mahogany case, 19thC, 9in (23cm) wide.

£240–280 CHTR

A mahogany apothecary box, hinged to reveal sliding compartments and two banks of short drawers, containing glass bottles, 1775–1800, 12in (30.5cm) wide.

£800–960 WAD

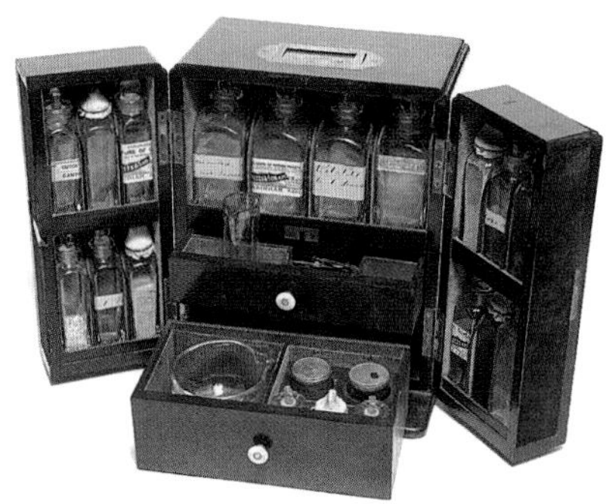

An apothecary box, attributed to N. B. Drewry, containing bottles, spring-loaded fleam, glass cupping device, pestle, ivory spoon, corkscrews, America, Georgia, c1863, 12in (30.5cm) wide.

£2,150–2,550 JDJ

The 30th Regiment of Georgia Volunteers lists N. B. Drewry as a regimental surgeon in 1863.

A mahogany apothecary box, by Thompson of London, containing glass bottles, pestle and mortar, scales and a secret poison compartment, c1840, 11in (28cm) high.

£2,450–2,750 AnB

Two banks of mahogany apothecary drawers, the 42 drawers with brass labels, possibly Continental, c1840, 41in (104cm) wide.

£6,200–6,900 WALP

A silver-plated auriscope, in a leather-covered pine box, c1890, 4in (10cm) wide.

£220–250 CuS

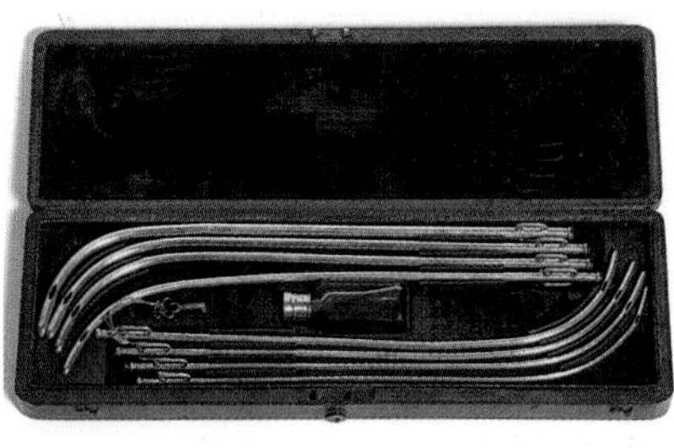

A set of silver catheters, with a glass bottle, 1870, boxed, 13in (33cm) wide.

£490–550 CuS

A three-piece chiropody set, by J. Richardson, Leicester, with ivory handles, c1820, boxed, 7½in (19cm) long.

£200–230 FOF

A nickel-plated-brass lithotrite, c1880, 16in (40.5cm) long.

£310–350 CuS

A lithotrite would have been used to crush bladder stones.

A wooden dentist's chair, by White Dental Manufacturing Co, with a caned seat and back, America, c1900, 51in (129.5cm) high.

£300–360 JAA

◄ **An oak dental dispensing set,** by Lynch for Hamilton Lony, Ireland, Dublin, 19thC, 10½in (26.5cm) high.

£1,100–1,250 PCR

Dental items from Ireland are rare.

◄ **A mahogany dentist's cabinet,** with a glazed top over an arrangement of drawers, late 19thC, 18in (45.5cm) wide.

£440–520 JBe

An electric copper belt, America, patented 1904, 20in (51cm) long.

£310–350 ET

These belts were used to cure rheumatism They were tailor-made to the individual's requirements and were worn next to the skin. Perspiration reacted with the copper to form a magnetic field.

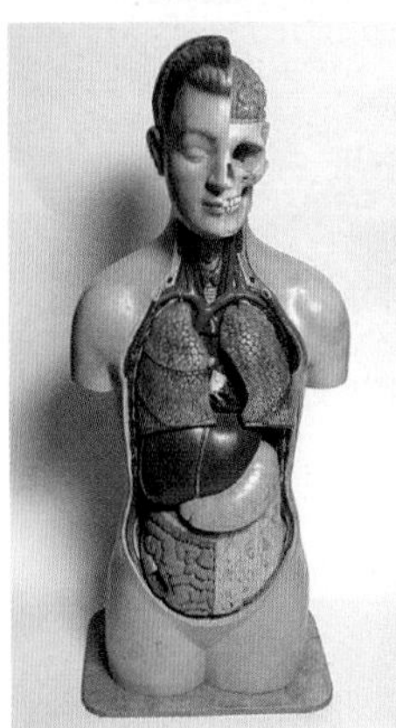

A plaster teaching dummy, c1920, 38in (96.5cm) high.

£580–650 CuS

◄ **An electro-therapeutic battery-powered apparatus,** in a mahogany box, 1873, 12in (30.5cm) wide.

£630–700 ET

This piece of apparatus was reputed to ease rheumatic pains and toothache. It would have been used by private practitioners on their patients, either in their surgeries or in the patient's own home.

An electro-medical machine, by Société Electrogénique, with scale and two electrodes, in a mahogany case, France, c1900.

£160–190 KOLN

This type of instrument was produced in fairly large numbers, principally for home use.

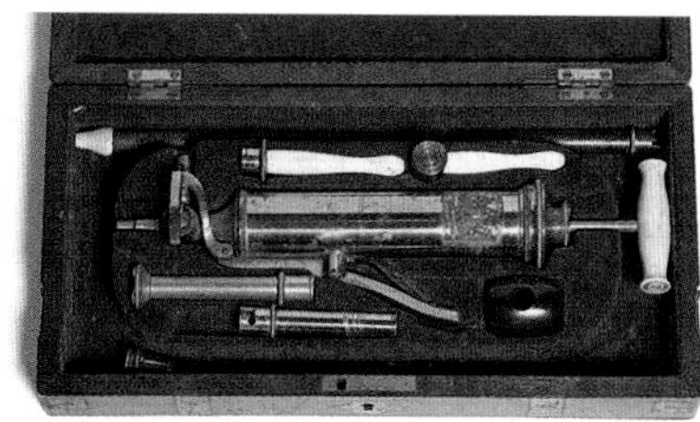

A brass and ivory stomach pump and enema set, in a mahogany box, c1880, 12in (30.5cm) wide.
£310–350 ⊞ CuS

A tortoiseshell and silver veterinary pocket fleam set, c1840, 3in (7.5cm) high.
£290–330 ⊞ EUA

► **A nickel surgical inhaler,** by Stratford-Cookson, America, 1905, 8in (20.5cm) long.
£220–250 ⊞ ET

A pair of apothecary glass display jars, each printed and decorated with a royal coat-of-arms, one inscribed 'Pure Drugs', the other 'Toilet Articles', late 19thC, 26in (66cm) high.
£1,500–1,800 CAG

A silver ophthalmic syringe, by Charrière Collin, in a fitted case, France, Paris, c1880, 4½in (11.5cm) wide.
£310–350 ⊞ CuS

A card and paper telescopic hearing aid, France, c1860, 22in (56cm) long.
£850–950 ⊞ CuS

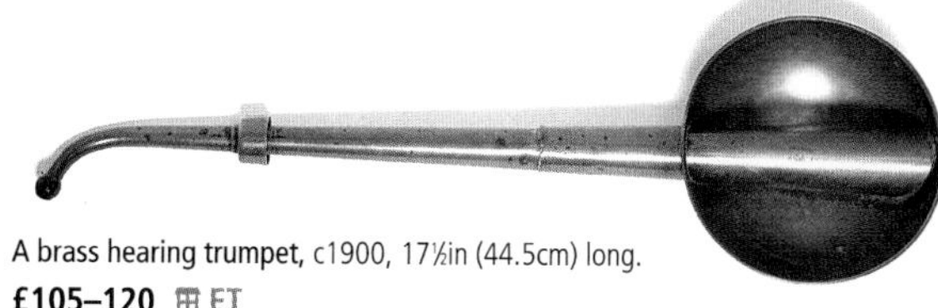

A brass hearing trumpet, c1900, 17½in (44.5cm) long.
£105–120 ⊞ ET

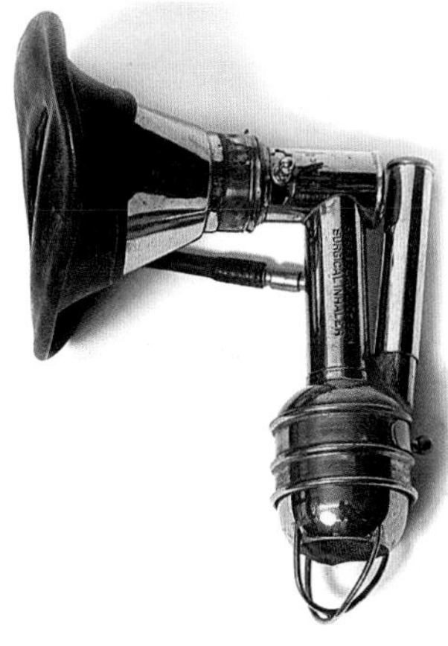

► **A cut-glass apothecary display jar,** 18thC, 31in (78.5cm) high.
£330–380 ⊞ GMI

A pharmacist's ceramic jar, inscribed 'Opium', France, c1900, 11in (28cm) high.
£135–150 ⊞ CuS

A leather medicine box, c1890, 10in (25.5cm) wide.
£580–650 ⊞ CuS

◄ **An optician's mahogany lens case,** with a roller shutter, c1910, 22in (56cm) wide.
£450–500 ⊞ ET

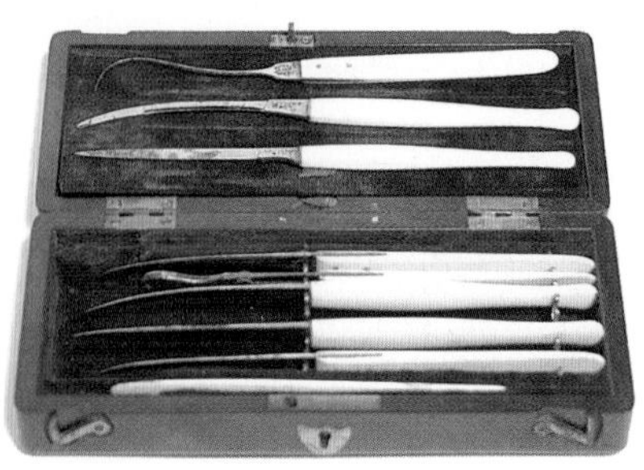

A scalpel set, with ivory handles, slight staining, c1830, in a mahogany case, 8½in (21.5cm) wide.

£360–400 ⊞ AnB

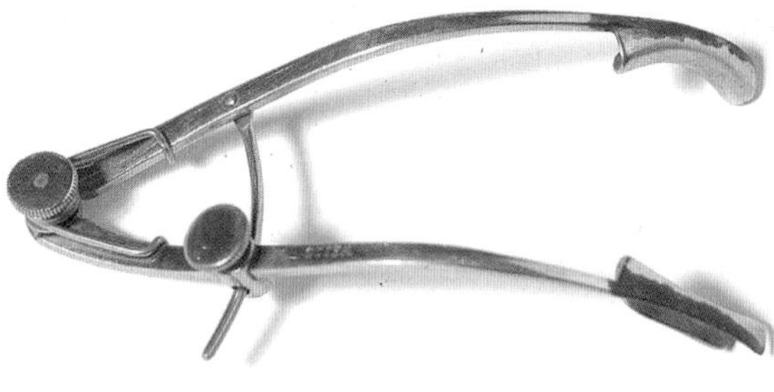

A brass optical speculum, c1890, 4in (10cm) long.

£85–95 ⊞ CuS

A speculum was used to hold open both the upper and lower eyelids enabling the eyeball to be examined.

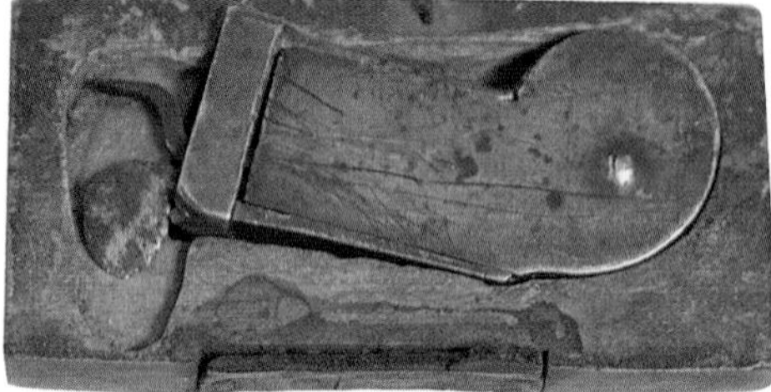

◀ **A brass spring-lancet,** with a steel blade, in a wooden case, 18thC, 2½in (6.5cm) wide.

£160–180 ⊞ ET

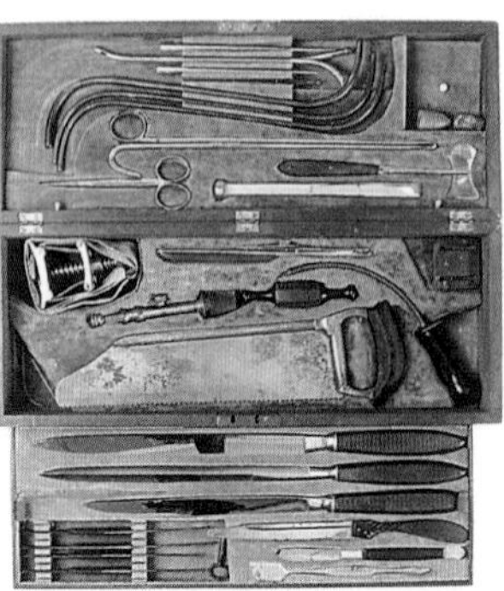

▶ **A surgeon's set,** with 17 implements, some later, America, c1863, in a fitted case.

£2,650–3,150 ⚒ JDJ

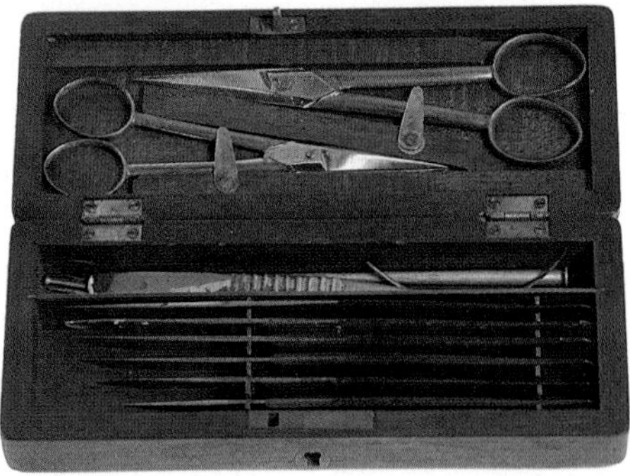

A surgeon's field set, instruments stamped 'Durroch, Bigg & Milkin and Arnold', 19thC, in a mahogany box, 7½in (19cm) wide.

£480–540 ⊞ PCR

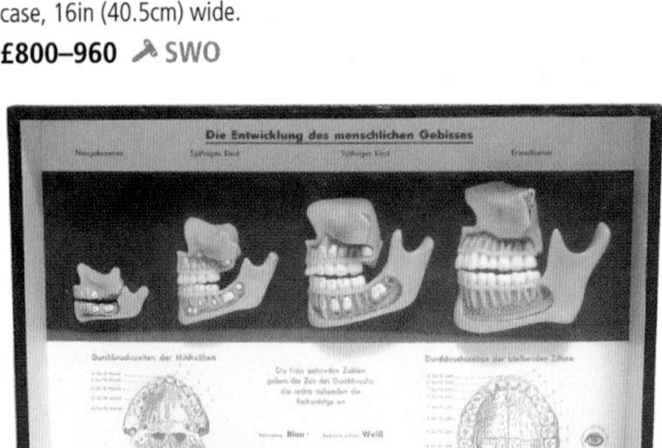

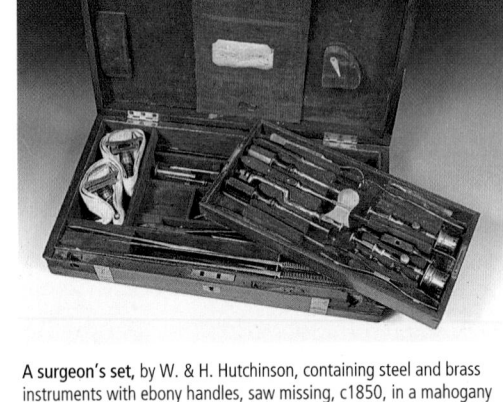

A surgeon's set, by W. & H. Hutchinson, containing steel and brass instruments with ebony handles, saw missing, c1850, in a mahogany case, 16in (40.5cm) wide.

£800–960 ⚒ SWO

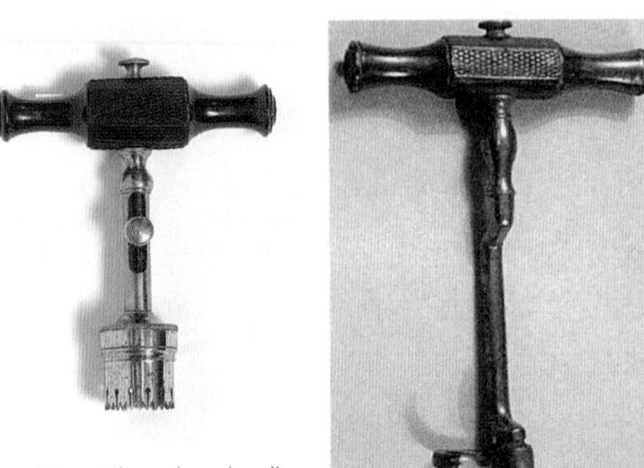

A trephine, with an ebony handle, c1850, 5in (12.5cm) long.

£110–125 ⊞ ET

A trephine would be used for boring holes into a skull.

A steel tooth key, with a carved ebony handle, 19thC, 6in (15cm) long.

£190–220 ⚒ PFK

A wax display of the development of human teeth, German, c1910, 17in (43cm) wide.

£760–850 ⊞ CuS

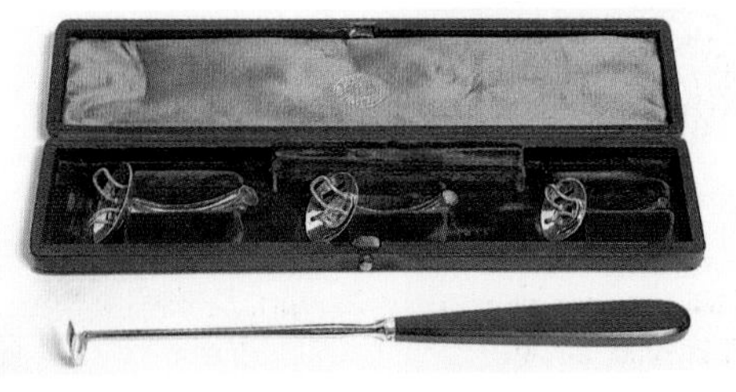

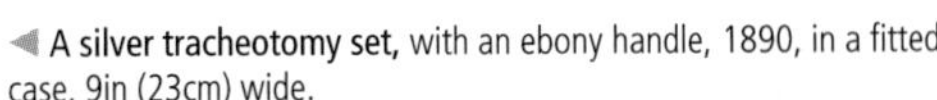

◀ **A silver tracheotomy set,** with an ebony handle, 1890, in a fitted case, 9in (23cm) wide.

£31 0–350 ⊞ CuS

METEOROLOGICAL INSTRUMENTS

A brass portable anemometer, Germany, c1890, 2½in (6.5cm) diam.

£580–650 ⊞ CuS

This is a desirable piece because of its robust housing and its main and subsidiary dials which make it easier to use than one with tenths and units on the same dial. Items like this are not often seen.

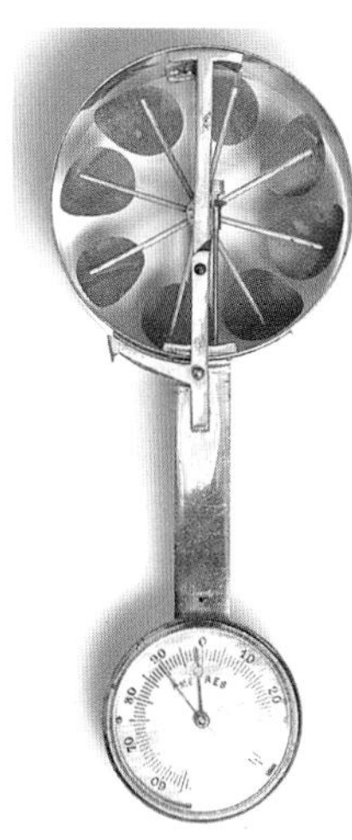

► **A thermometer,** by Robert Banks, with a silvered Fahrenheit scale, c1800, 16in (40.5cm) long.

£2,050–2,300 ⊞ AW

This thermometer is unusual as it records temperatures as high as 225°, although the wooden case would not stand up to being immersed in boiling water.

Anemometers

The use of anemometers in coal and tin mines was essential to monitor the freshness of air levels at great depths. They were also used to measure the efficiency of fan-assisted ventilation systems. They originally measured in feet per second in the UK, but litres per minute elsewhere in Europe.

◄ **A chrome anemometer,** by Richard, France, Paris, c1900, 9in (23cm) long.

£310–350 ⊞ ET

A copper electric rain gauge, by Negretti & Zambra, c1900, 28in (71cm) high.

£1,800–2,000 ⊞ RTW

Negretti & Zambra were one of the greatest manufacturers of weather recording and measuring devices in the UK, often commissioned by the government and state-run industries. The instruments they produced are therefore keenly sought after by collectors.

A glass, bronze and slate Campbell-Stokes sun recorder, c1900, 11in (28cm) wide.

£1,350–1,500 ⊞ ET

The Campbell-Stokes sunshine recorder was invented by John Francis Campbell in 1853 and later modified in 1879 by Sir George Gabriel Stokes. It consists of a spherical lens which burns an image of the sun onto a chemically-impregnated card. The resulting scorch mark is an indication of the sun's strength at certain points in the day. When not in use, the card should be kept out of natural light as it degrades over time.

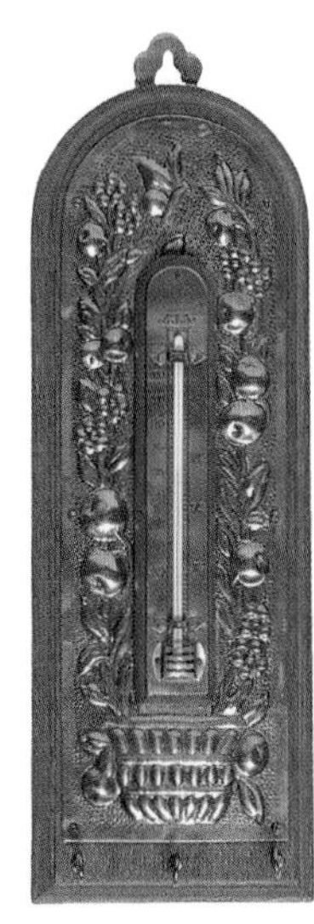

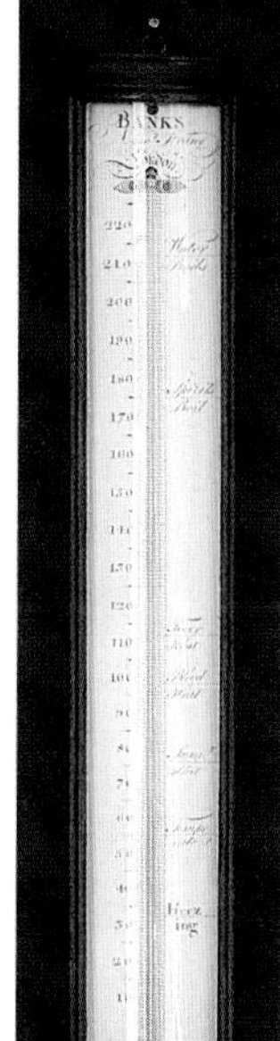

◄ **An oak and brass thermometer,** c1900, 14in (35.5cm) long.

£120–140 ⊞ TOP

A painted brass Weather Foreteller, by Negretti & Zambra, in an oak case, c1925, 10in (25.5cm) diam.

£360–400 ⊞ RTW

MICROSCOPES

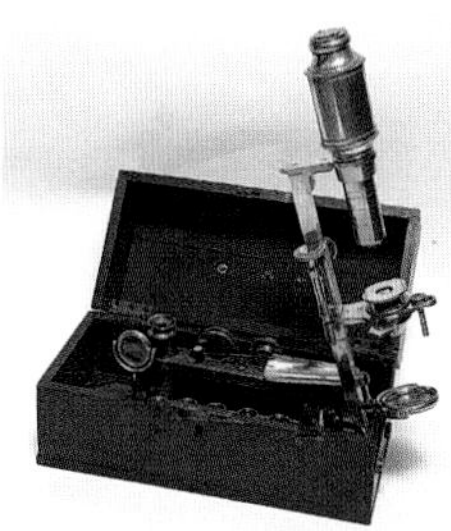

A chest microscope, by Nairne, c1750, 15in (38cm) high.

£2,700–3,000 ⊞ GMI

A brass microscope, by John Browning, early 19thC, 14in (35.5cm) high, with original mahogany case.

£580–650 ⊞ GMI

A brass miniature microscope, c1850, 5in (12.5cm) high, with a case.

£220–250 ⊞ GMI

◄ **A microscope,** by G. & S. Merz, with two eyepieces, signed, Germany, 1858, 10¾in (27.5cm) high.

£1,200–1,400 KOLN

Shedding light on the matter

The viewing of objects under early microscopes was dependent on the amount of reflected light available beneath the object. The invention of the bull's-eye lens in the 17th century helped to improve the intensity of the light from an oil lamp placed nearby, or a device known as a condensing lens was used to illuminate a transparent object from beyond it. In the 18th century Culpeper devised a microscope with a concave mirror below the viewing plate in order to reflect lamplight through it. Further developments utilized a subsidiary lens to help gather and condense received light from the mirror below, and in Victorian times a lens system, known as a condenser unit, was designed to fit below the specimen to provide illumination.

A brass binocular microscope, by W. C. Hughes, c1860, 14in (35.5cm) high, with original mahogany case.

£600–680 GMI

A brass compound microscope, by Smith, Beck & Beck, London, with a Wenham binocular body tube and rack-and-pinion focusing above a mechanical stage plate, c1860, with accessories and a fitted mahogany case.

£2,600–3,100 AG

A brass and anodized medical microscope, by J. Parkes & Sons, 19thC, 10in (25.5cm) high, with accessories and original fitted case.

£125–150 DMC

A spelter and brass microscope, the stand in the form of a monkey, arm repaired, c1880, 6¾in (17cm) high.

£500–550 ET

► **A lacquered-brass compound monocular Van Heurck microscope,** by William Watson & Sons, with rack-and-pinion focusing, the circuit stage with thumb wheel micrometer adjustment, signed and numbered, London, c1900, 13¼in (33.5cm) high, with two oculars, five objectives and a mahogany case.

£1,650–1,950 S

This microscope contains elements devised by Van Heurck, hence its name.

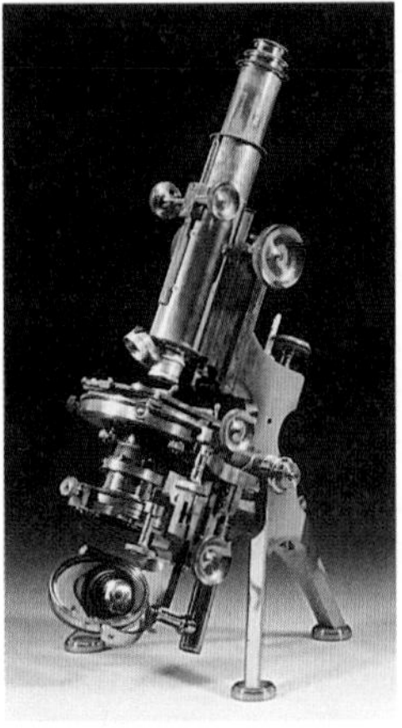

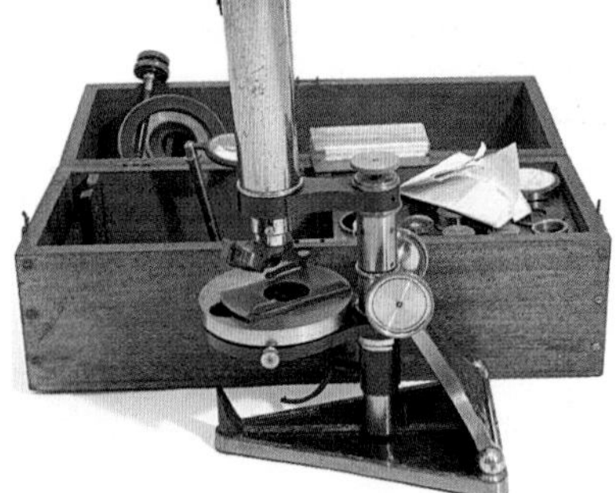

A compound binocular microscope, by R. & J. Beck, with rack-and-pinion focusing, late 19thC, 15in (38cm) high, with objectives, bull's-eye lens, eyepieces and a mahogany case.

£440–520 G(L)

A microscope, by Hunter Sands, London, c1900, 10in (25.5cm) high, with accessories and original mahogany box.

£330–380 GMI

◄ **A brass and enamelled monocular microscope,** by William Watson & Sons, with rack-and-pinion focusing, c1925, 11½in (29cm) high, with three oculars, four objectives, condenser light and a mahogany box.

£190–220 GTH

SURVEYING & DRAWING INSTRUMENTS

A gun metal and brass clinometer, c1910, 7in (15cm) high.

£310–350 CuS

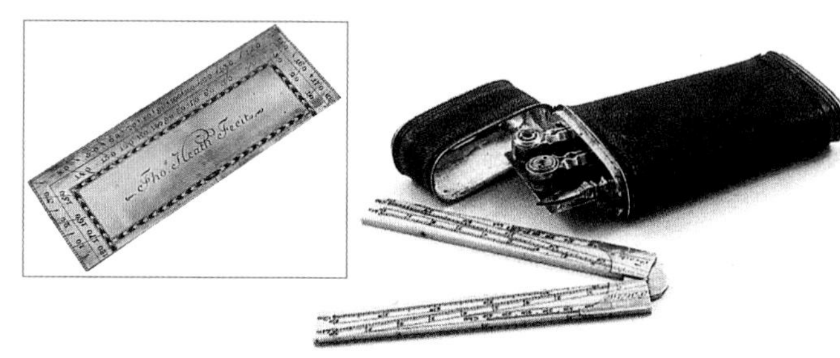

A set of draughtsman's instruments, by Thomas Heath, London, comprising two pairs of dividers, ink extension tool, ivory folding rule, scale rule and protractor, in a silver-mounted shagreen case, c1740, 4½in (11.5cm) high.

£1,000–1,200 WW

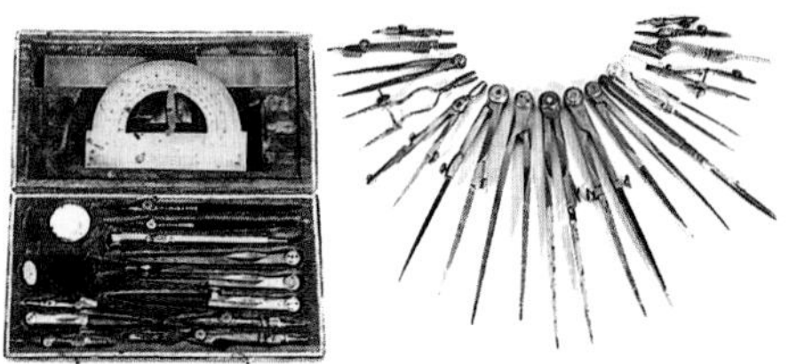

A set of drawing instruments, with a transversal scale and protractor, Germany, c1800, in a leather-covered case.

£180–210 KOLN

A late Victorian brass-mounted fruitwood surveyor's rule, by Negretti & Zambra, inset with a compass, spirit level and folding eyepiece, 6¾in (17cm) folded.

£150–180 ROS

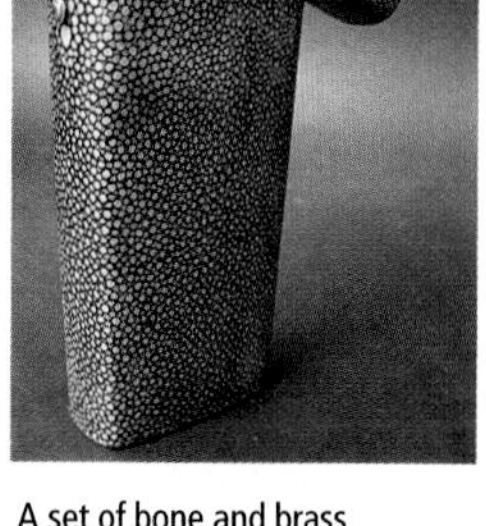

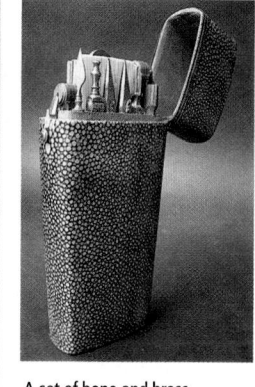

A set of bone and brass draughtsman's instruments, in a silver-mounted shagreen case, c1815, 6¾in (17cm) high.

£730–870 ROS

A set of silver draughtsman's instruments, by Dollond, London, in a silver-bound rosewood-veneered case, slight damage, losses, signed, early 19thC.

£6,000–7,200 S

A surveyor's brass level, with a double sight, with a walnut bracket and on a wooden base, Germany, c1780, 18½in (47cm) long.

£1,400–1,650 KOLN

This instrument comprises a telescope and a spirit level on a rotating axis that would have been used to view the distances of opposite points and calculate the relative heights of the land.

TELESCOPES

A brass-mounted mahogany single-draw telescope, c1770, 30in (76cm) long.

£310–350 GMI

An ivory and metal single-draw pocket telescope, early 19thC, 3¼in (8.5cm) long, with a fitted box.

£300–360 CAG

A miniature brass and shagreen telescope, by Newman, London, c1835, 13in (33cm) long.

£180–200 GMI

A mahogany and brass four-draw telescope, by Cary, London, engraved 'Lady Campbell', 19thC, 36in (91.5cm) extended.

£80–95 PFK

A 1¾in three-draw brass telescope, by G. & C. Dixey, London, signed, 19thC, 2in (5cm) unextended.

£560–670 S(Am)

▶ **A lacquered brass single-draw table telescope,** by F. Westley, London, 19thC, 20in (51cm) high.

£440–520 CAG

A gilt-brass six-draw pocket telescope, by W. & S. Jones, with engine-turned and acanthus-leaf decoration, signed, 19thC, 4in (10cm) extended.

£190–220 DN(HAM)

Seventeenth-century inventions

It is a little known fact that no less than six important scientific instruments that continue to play a major role in modern day life were invented in the space of 30 years in the 17th century. These were the telescope, microscope, pendulum clock, barometer, thermometer and air pump. All these instruments enabled the rapid execution of scientific experiments and measurements that were, until then, either impossible or extremely time-consuming, and the invention of the barometer and telescope directly challenged the doctrines of the time.

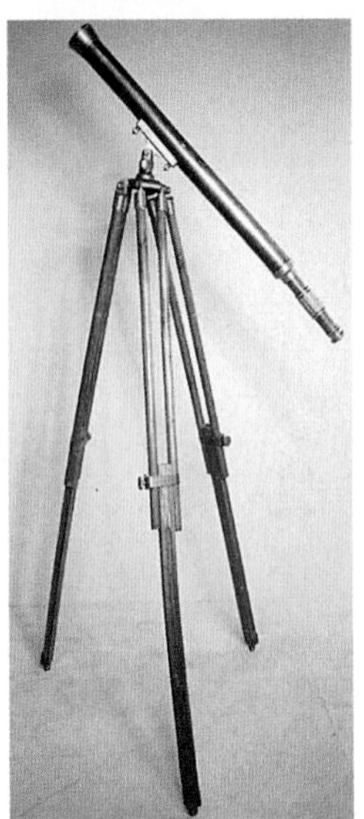

▶ **A brass refracting telescope,** by Stanley, London, 1902, 42in (106.5cm) long, on a wooden tripod with brass mounts.

£470–560 Hal

WEIGHTS & MEASURES

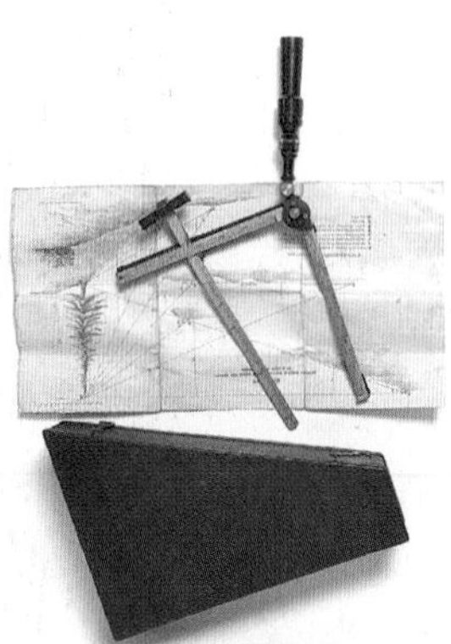

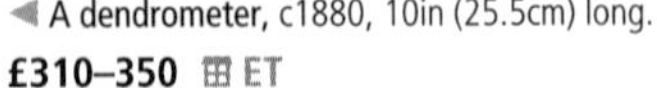

◀ **A dendrometer,** c1880, 10in (25.5cm) long.

£310–350 ET

The dendrometer played a very important part in the harvesting of trees for the timber industry. It was also used by foresters to gather data to evaluate tree growth which enabled them to produce national tables indicating where specific trees grew best.

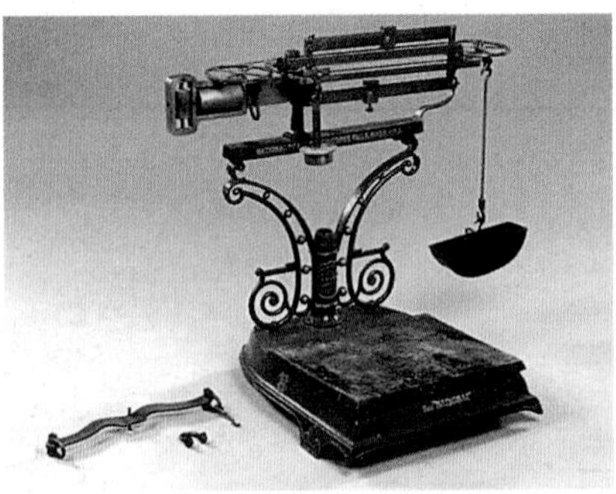

▶ **A set of cast-iron and brass sack scales,** by National Scale Co, stamped mark, America, Massachusetts, early 20thC, 30¾in (78cm) wide.

£140–165 PFK

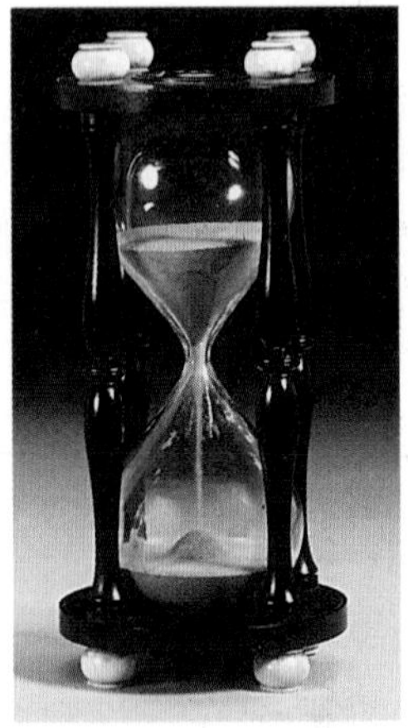

An ebony and ivory sand glass, late 18thC, 7½in (19cm) high.

£1,050–1,250 S

A set of Galileo scales, in a glazed oak case, Italy, Milan, c1920, 20in (51cm) high.

£90–100 ET

◀ **A Victorian mahogany Waywiser,** by G. & C. Dixey, London, with brass spanner, 54in (137cm) high.

£2,350–2,650 ALS

This instrument would have been used to measure distances between points on roads or racecourses in miles, furlongs, poles and yards.

A brass and steel well measure, c1940, 18in (45.5cm) long.

£50–60 ET

MARINE

BAROMETERS

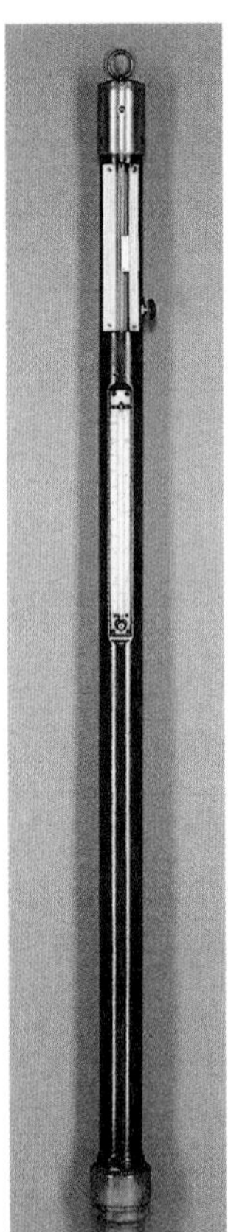

◄ **A mahogany marine barometer,** by Matthew Berge, with a brass top, mercury thermometer, ivory scale and a boxwood cistern cover, gimbal fitting missing, signed 'Berge, London, late Ramsden', c1805, 37½in (95.5cm) high.

£6,000–7,200 S

Matthew Berge was the workshop manager to Jesse Ramsden (1731–1800), a highly-respected English instrument maker. Berge took over the business on the death of Ramsden and continued it at 199 Piccadilly, London until his own death in 1819.

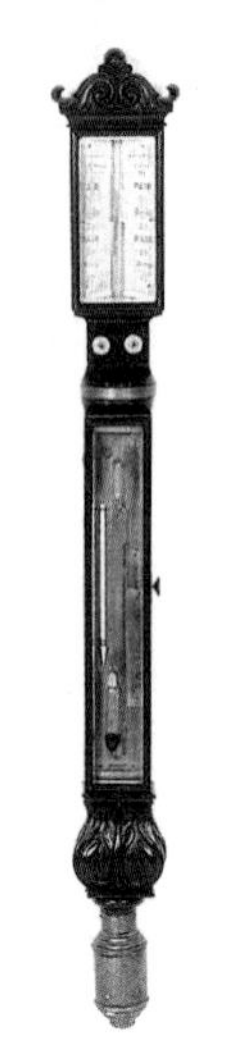

An early Victorian marine barometer, by Atkin of Newcastle, with an engraved ivory scale, the Improved Sympiesometer thermometer and dial graduated from 28–30, above leaf-carved decoration and brass-capped reservoir, 38½in (98cm) high.

£1,500–1,800 HYD

A mahogany marine barometer, with bone scales, signed 'Moralee', c1860, 34in (86.5cm) high.

£4,000–4,500 RAY

A rosewood marine barometer, with mother-of-pearl inlay, signed 'Smith & Hind, Hartlepool', c1860, 34in (86.5cm) high.

£4,500–5,000 RAY

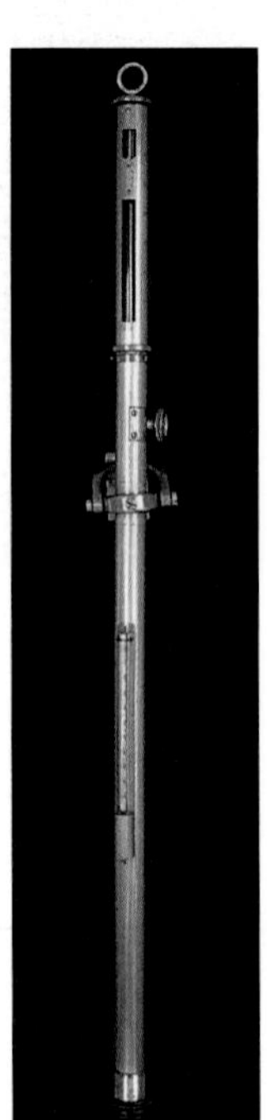

A brass Kew Pattern marine stick barometer, by Henry Hughes, London, c1880, 35in (89cm) long.

£1,350–1,500 AW

CHRONOMETERS

A brass-bound mahogany marine two-day chronometer, by Richard Hornby & Sons, Liverpool, the silvered dial with subsidiary seconds dial in a brass gimbal, 19thC, dial 4in (10cm) diam.

£1,750–2,100 E

Richard Hornby & Sons are recorded as working in Liverpool from 1837 until 1851.

► **A mahogany deck chronometer,** by J. Calame Robert, the silvered dial with subsidiary seconds dial in a brass gimbal bowl, the keywind gilt bar movement with going barrel, polished steel regulator, compensation balance with silver overcoil hairspring, Switzerland, c1860, dial 3½in (9cm) diam.

£1,100–1,250 PT

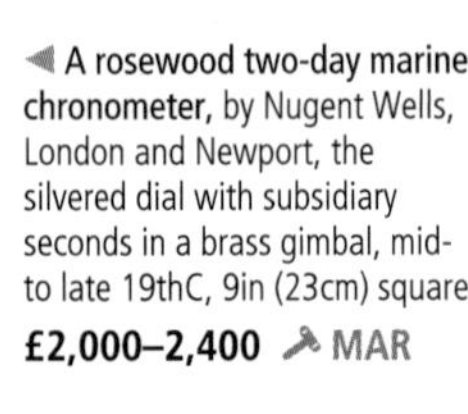

◄ **A rosewood two-day marine chronometer,** by Nugent Wells, London and Newport, the silvered dial with subsidiary seconds in a brass gimbal, mid- to late 19thC, 9in (23cm) square.

£2,000–2,400 MAR

Nugent Wells are recorded as working in Newport 1858–99.

An ebonized two-day marine chronometer, by Henry Daniels, Liverpool, the silvered dial with subsidiary seconds dial in a brass gimbal bowl, the fusee movement with Earnshaw's spring detent escapement, blued helical spring maintaining power, c1860, 7¼in (18.5cm) wide.

£2,750–3,300 S

MODEL SHIPS

A bone prisoner of war model of a ship, France, c1800, 10¼in (26cm) wide.
£3,500–4,200 BERN

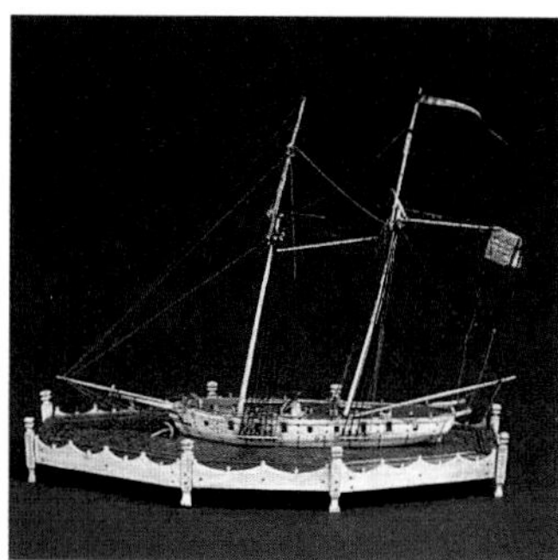

◄ **A bone prisoner of war model of a Baltimore clipper,** on a straw work platform with a bone gallery, in a glass case, America, c1812, 11¾in (30cm) wide.
£9,500–11,400 NAAW

The war of 1812 was fought between the United States and Great Britain as a result of simmering disputes, particularly the impressment of American sailors into the British Navy. The war was mainly fought along the Canadian borders. This ship was made by an American prisoner of war inmate of Dartmoor prison in Devon and is the only such piece known.

► **A prisoner of war bone model of a three-masted ship,** the masts with standing and running rigging, the deck with capstan, wheel and hatch covers, early 19thC, 36in (91.5cm) wide.
£16,300–19,500 NAAW

A model of a Revenue Cutter, with cloth sails and a fitted deck, on an associated plinth, c1850, 45¼in (115cm) wide.
£1,150–1,350 MA&I

A carved and painted wood shipping diorama, c1850, in a maplewood frame, 28 x 38in (71 x 96.5cm).
£2,500–2,800 WALP

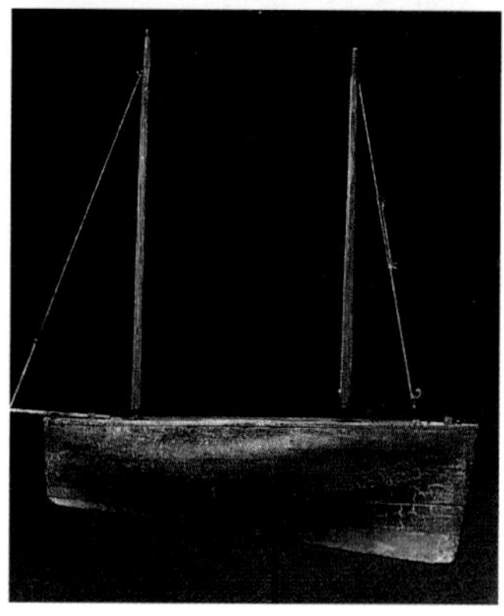

A painted pine twin-masted pond yacht, c1880, 19in (48.5cm) wide.
£850–950 RYA

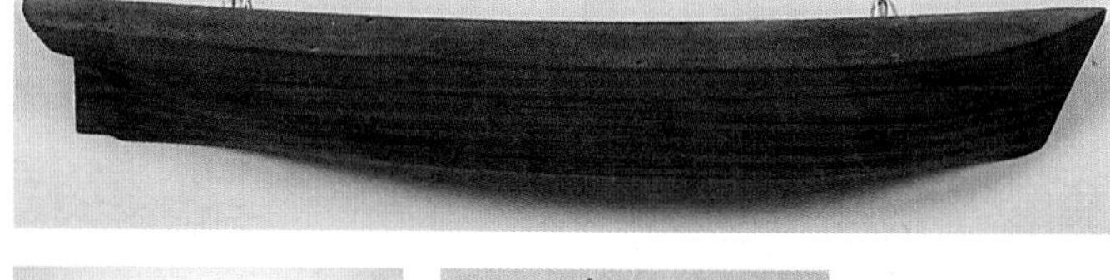

◄ **A laminated wood half-model of a ship's hull,** damaged, America, c1900, 47in (119.5cm) wide.
£1,450–1,700 SK(B)

An Edwardian pine pond yacht, with canvas sails, 61in (155cm) high.
£1,100–1,250 MINN

A wood and brass pond yacht, with linen sails, early 20thC, 25in (63.5cm) wide.
£175–210 HOLL

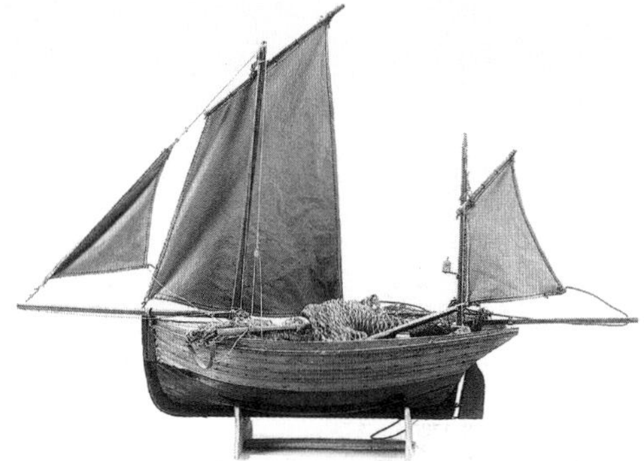

A wooden model of a fishing yacht, by W. R. Hilder, c1937, 21¾in (55.5cm) wide.
£310–350 BERN

NAUTICAL HANDCRAFTS

A painted and carved wood figure of a sailor, inscribed 'Dat Smaakt', Holland, 19thC, 23¾in (60.5cm) high.

£8,100–9,700 NAAW

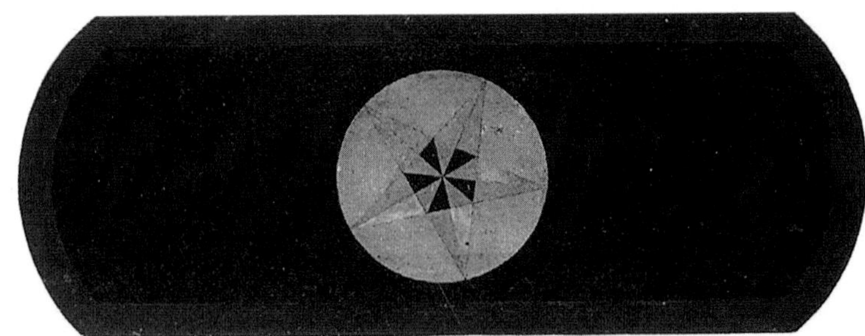

A printed canvas mat, decorated with a five-pointed star, 19thC, 18¼ x 48in (46.5 x 122cm).

£950–1,150 NAAW

◀ **A pair of painted glass silhouette pictures,** one entitled 'USS *Constitution* 1800' the other 'USS *Perseverance*, New York, 1799', with gilt highlights, America, 1850–75, 16¾ x 19½in (42.5 x 49.5cm), in bird's-eye maple frames.

£1,300–1,550 S(O)

The American market for nautical items is currently very strong and will probably remain so for some time to come as more people recognize the importance of the history of the shipping trade along America's vast coastline.

A pair of painted glass silhouette pictures, one entitled 'HMS *Hogue*' the other 'HMS *Euryalus*', each depicted at sea with another warship, early 19thC, 6¼ x 8in (16 x 20.5cm), in maple frames.

£940–1,100 HOLL

The frigate HMS Euryalus *served with Lord Nelson at the Battle of Trafalgar under the command of Captain Blackwood.*

A woolwork picture of HMS *Hero*, 19thC, framed, 9 x 11½in (23 x 29cm).

£440–520 CHTR

A woolwork picture, decorated with a Prince of Wales crest, Royal Marines, Gibraltar crest, flags and flowers, signed 'T. Moon', 1825–1850, 23 x 30in (58.5 x 76cm).

£1,100–1,300 RIT

A pair of ink and watercolour pictures, by George E. Dunham, one entitled 'Ship David Paddack', the other 'The Flurry', depicting whaling scenes, signed and dated 1858, America, Massachussetts, 11½ x 14½in (29 x 37cm).

£15,700–18,800 NAAW

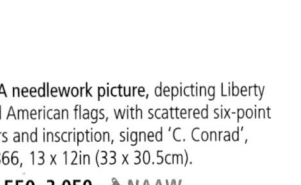

▶ **A needlework picture,** depicting Liberty and American flags, with scattered six-point stars and inscription, signed 'C. Conrad', c1866, 13 x 12in (33 x 30.5cm).

£2,550–3,050 NAAW

A woolwork picture, depicting an American ship and a lighthouse beneath an eagle and flags, 1840–50, 18½ x 20½in (47 x 52cm).

£39,000–47,000 NAAW

Sailors experienced at sailmaking and mending turned their skills with a needle to producing woolwork items for their wives and families in their spare time. The great majority of these depicted British vessels and were made by British seamen; it is rare to find an example of the craft with an American ship and motifs.

For further information on
Textiles see pages 482–495

A woolwork picture of a three-masted sailing ship, 19thC, 20 x 24in (51 x 61cm).

£350–420 JAA

◀ **A scrimshaw whale's tooth,** engraved with the Nantucket whaleship *Pacific*, signed 'Edward Burdett', early 19thC, 4¾in (12cm) long.

£108,000–130,000 NAAW

Edward Burdett was born in Nantucket in 1805, joined the island's legendary whale hunters and died at sea in 1833. He is the earliest known American scrimshander, his work dating from the mid-1820s to 1833. In 1991 there were only six whale's teeth known to have been signed by Burdett, four of which are in museum collections. This tooth, previously unknown, brings the total to seven. The Pacific *tooth, thought to have been a gift from the artist to his sister, is the only known example of Burdett's work to have remained in the artist's family.*

MILLER'S COMPARES

I. **A scrimshaw whale's tooth,** inscribed 'South Sea Fishery', with a whaling bark and three boats, the reverse with 'Port Owharre, Huahene' and a sperm whale, early to mid-19thC, 8¼in (21cm) long.

£38,000–45,000 SK

▶ II. **A scrimshaw whale's tooth,** depicting a ship in full sail, the reverse depicting a woman and an anchor, America, c1835, 5in (12.5cm) high.

£8,900–10,600 SK

Item I realized a much higher price than Item II because it has a unique design and historic connections with British Naval exploits. Huahene is probably best known as having Captain James Cook as its first European visitor in 1769 and being the last stop of HMS *Bounty* before its fateful mutiny in 1789. Item II displays the type of scrimshaw decoration executed by seamen universally.

A scrimshaw **whalebone busk,** engraved with motifs and geometric banding, 19thC, 13¾in (35cm) long.

£340–400 LJ

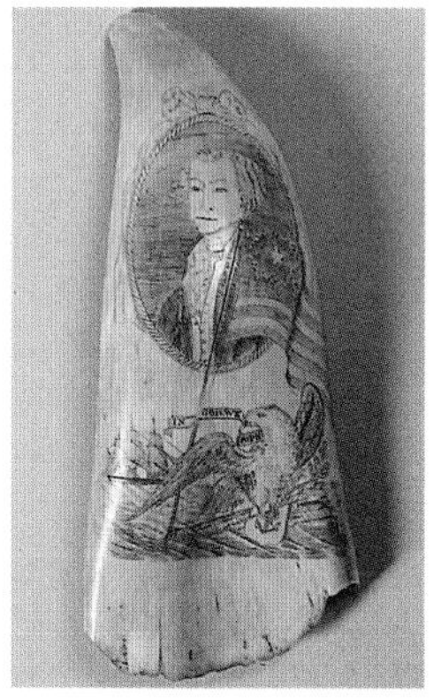

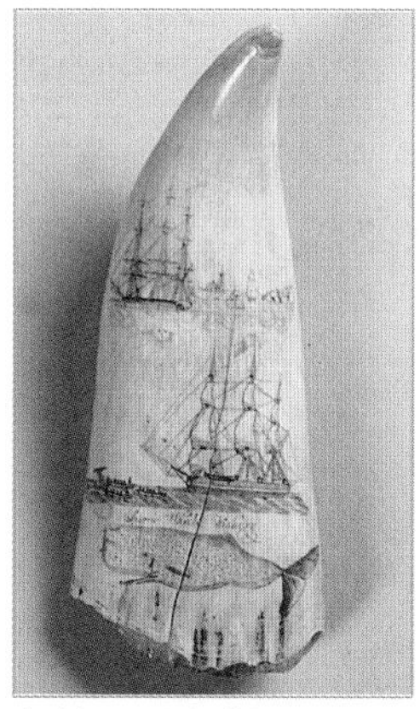

A scrimshaw whale's tooth, engraved with a portrait of George Washington, the American flag and an eagle, the reverse with ships and a whale, slight damage, America, 19thC, 7½in (19cm) high.

£14,600–17,500 SK(B)

A scrimshaw whalebone and whale ivory sewing basket, America, Massachusetts, c1860, 9½in (24cm) high.

£9,000–10,100 GIAM

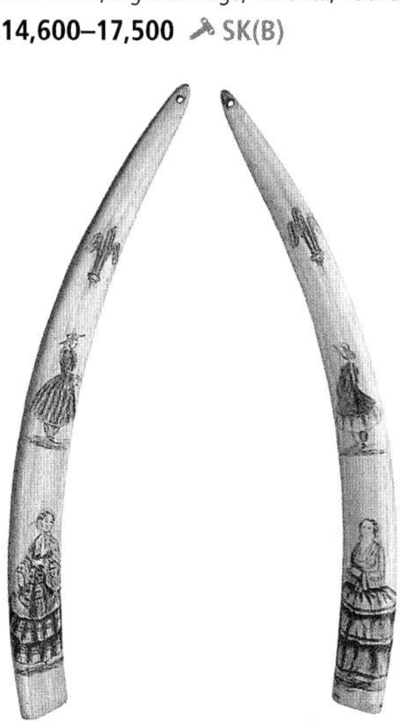

◀ **A pair of scrimshaw walrus tusks,** decorated with Prince of Wales feathers and female figures, c1860, 18½in (47cm) high.

£590–700 F&C

Walrus tusks were traded by Alaskan Inuits to the whale hunters, who created the scrimshaw decoration.

A wooden seaman's chest lid, painted with Masonic emblems and drapery, 19thC, 20¾ x 36in (52.5 x 91.5cm).

£3,450–4,100 NAAW

NAVIGATIONAL INSTRUMENTS

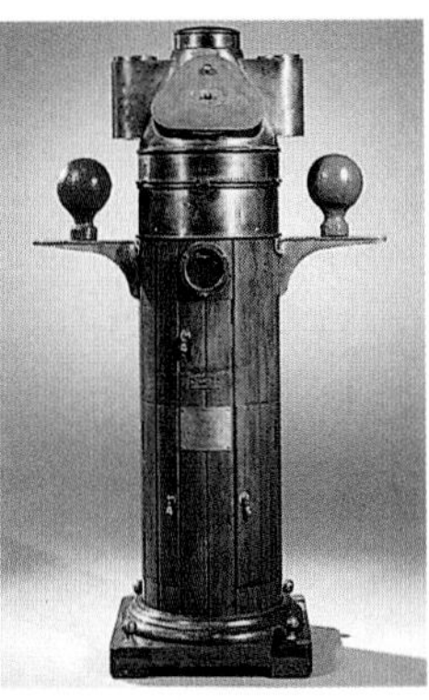

A brass and teak binnacle compass, by Kelvin Bottomley & Baird, with a brass cover and a floating compass card, Scotland, Glasgow, 1850–1900, 53½in (136cm) high.

£640–760 S(Am)

A brass and wood binnacle compass, 19thC, 61½in (156cm) high.

£610–730 JAd

A George III ebony and brass Hadley's Quadrant octant, by Gilbert Wright & Hooke, London, with an engraved ivory scale, 14½in (37cm) wide.

£480–570 F&C

John Hadley's quadrant, invented in 1731, measures solar altitude by reflection.

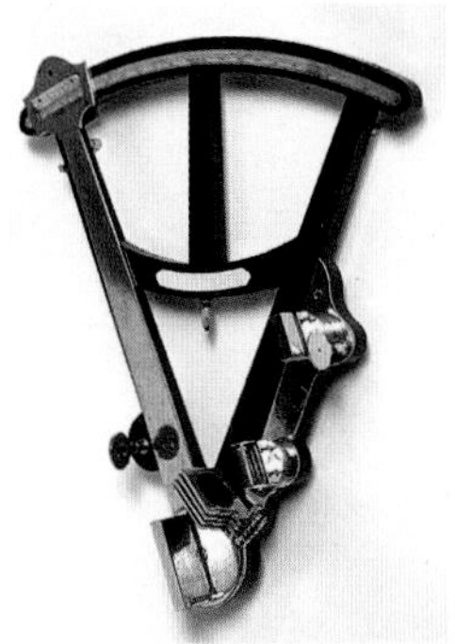

An octant, by Spencer Browning & Rust, 19thC, 13in (33cm) high.

£1,250–1,500 PCR

◄ **An ebony and brass sextant,** by William de Silva, Liverpool, with an ivory vernier scale, early 19thC, 9¾in (25cm) wide, with a teak case.

£430–510 CAG

► **A brass sextant,** by Imray Son & Co, London, with a telescopic eyepiece, 1846–51, 11in (28cm) high, with a mahogany case.

£380–430 GMI

SHIPS' FITTINGS

A carved pine ship's figurehead, possibly from the *Cynthia Watkins*, America, c1835, 23¼in (59cm) high.

£10,300–12,300 NAAW

A carved and painted pine ship's figurehead, America, 1840–60, 25in (63.5cm) high.

£11,400–13,600 NAAW

A carved and painted pine ship's figurehead, in the form of a woman, America, 1840–50, 25½in (65cm) high.

£10,300–12,300 NAAW

A carved wood ship's figurehead, in the form of Jenny Lind, America, c1850, 38in (96.5cm) high.

£1,150–1,300 CGA

Jenny Lind (1820–87) was a Swedish opera singer.

► **A copper ship's port oil light,** c1890, 14in (35.5cm) high.

£200–230 GMI

◄ **A ship's lifebelt,** from SS *Garryvale*, Glasgow', c1907, 31in (78.5cm) diam.

£150–170 CGA

MISCELLANEOUS

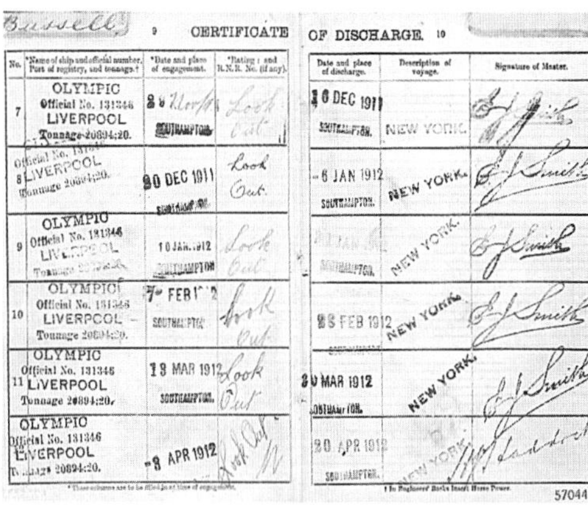

Bussell 9 CERTIFICATE OF DISCHARGE 10

No.	Name of ship and official number, Port of registry, and tonnage	Date and place of engagement	Rating; and R.N.R. No. (if any)	Date and place of discharge	Description of voyage	Signature of Master
7	OLYMPIC Official No. 131346 LIVERPOOL Tonnage 20894:20.	SOUTHAMPTON	Look Out	16 DEC 1911 SOUTHAMPTON	NEW YORK	
8	Official No. 131346 LIVERPOOL Tonnage 20894:20.	20 DEC 1911 SOUTHAMPTON	Look Out	6 JAN 1912 SOUTHAMPTON	NEW YORK	E J Smith
9	OLYMPIC Official No. 131346 LIVERPOOL	10 JAN 1912 SOUTHAMPTON	Look Out	SOUTHAMPTON	NEW YORK	E J Smith
10	OLYMPIC Official No. 131346 LIVERPOOL Tonnage 20894:20.	7 FEB 12 SOUTHAMPTON	Look Out	28 FEB 1912	NEW YORK	E J Smith
11	OLYMPIC Official No. 131346 LIVERPOOL Tonnage 20894:20.	13 MAR 1912 SOUTHAMPTON	Look Out	30 MAR 1912 SOUTHAMPTON	NEW YORK	E J Smith
	OLYMPIC Official No. 131346 LIVERPOOL Tonnage 20894:20.	8 APR 1912	Look Out	20 APR 1912 SOUTHAMPTON	NEW YORK	

570444

A certificate of discharge, for the seaman Samuel Bussell serving as 'Look Out', comprising 14 pages of a book issued by the Board of Trade, with stamped signature of Captain E. J. Smith, in a cloth wallet cover, slight damage, 1909–14, 8°.

£1,800–2,150 S

This evocative seaman's discharge certificate records a discharge by Captain Smith on his last command of SS Olympic *just before he assumed command of RMS* Titanic.

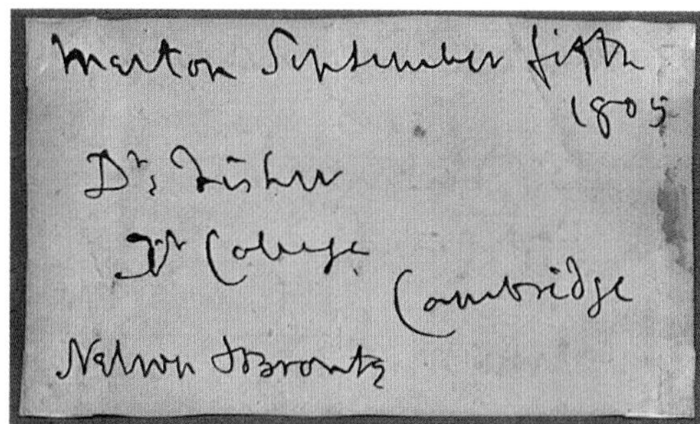

Merton September fifth 1805

Dr. Fisher

V. College

Cambridge

Nelson & Bronte

Admiral Lord Nelson, a handwritten envelope addressed to 'Dr Fisher, V. College, Cambridge' and 'Merton September Fifth 1805', signed 'Nelson & Bronte', slight damage, c1805, framed, 2½ x 4¼in (6.5 x 11cm).

£660–790 CAG

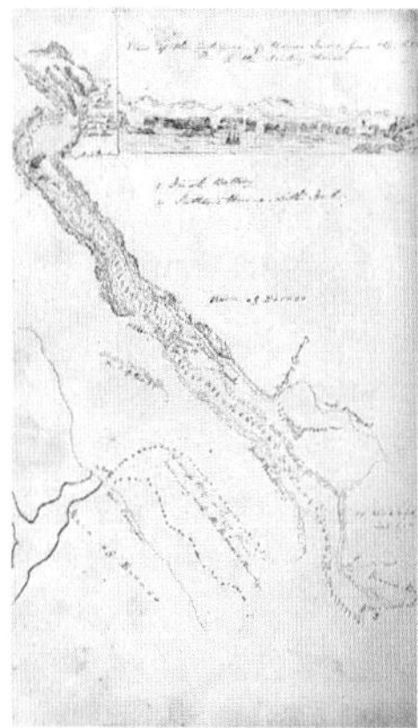

A British Navy log book, by Frederick Williams, with hand-drawn illustrations and charts, 1846–48.

£570–680 NAAW

This log book was kept aboard HMS Wolverine *and HMS* Daedalus *and includes entries from ports such as Penang, Singapore, Hong Kong and Amoy.*

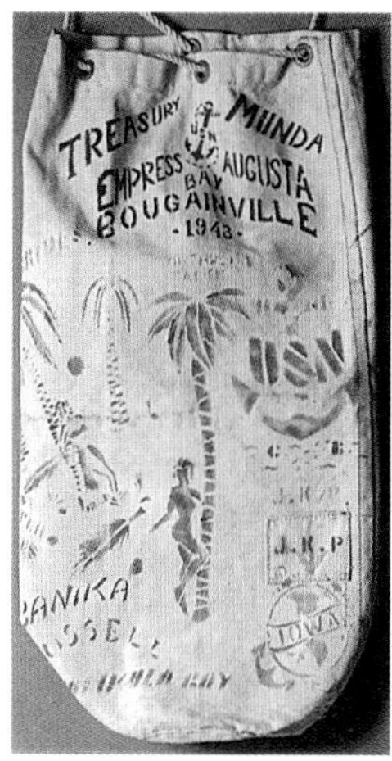

A Seabee canvas sea bag, stencilled with images, names, locations and dates, America, dated 1943, 32in (81.5cm) high.

£120–140 JAA

A Seabee was a member of one of the construction battalions in the US Navy.

A silver-plated coffee and tea service, engraved with Castle Packet Shipping Line company crest, 1876–81, coffee pot 9in (23cm) high.

£720–800 CGA

A Haviland porcelain ship's part dinner service, comprising 85 pieces, from the yacht *Iris*, each painted with the flag of the New York Yacht Club, America, c1910.

£650–780 NAAW

◀ **A fragment of Admiral Lord Nelson's funeral flag,** the battle ensign of HMS *Victory*, mounted on a signed declaration of authenticity, 1812, framed, 12½ x 8in (32 x 20.5cm), together with a portrait of Philip Holdsworth and a ceremonial sword.

£9,400–11,200 LAY

This fragment was obtained by Rowden Holdsworth, son of Philip Holdsworth, Marshall of the City of London, when he attended the funeral of Admiral Lord Nelson at St Paul's Cathedral.

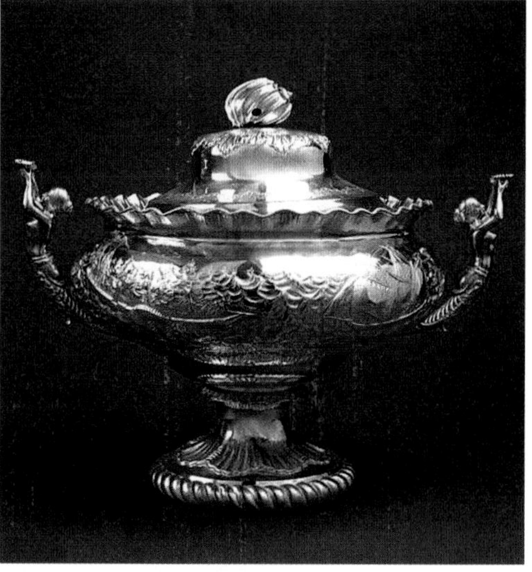

A silver trophy, by R. & W. Wilson, depicting the burning of the *San Francisco* and the rescue of the passengers, with two handles in the form of mermaids holding shells, the knop in the form of a shell, with inscription, America, c1853, 17½in (44.5cm) wide, 102oz.

£38,000–45,600 NAAW

CAMERAS

An Agfa Standard Luxury rollfilm camera, with CRF, Solinar f4.5/10.5 lens, Compur shutter, Germany, 1929.

£450–540 KOLN

An Ihagee VP Exakta camera, with Tessar f2.8/7.5cm lens, Germany, 1934.

£230–270 KOLN

◄ **A wooden camera,** with telescopic lens and linen bellows, on a wood and cast-iron stand, damaged, marked 'Gordens', America, 1860s.

£1,200–1,400 JDJ

A Kodak camera, with bellows and chrome-mounted mahogany slide, Goerz lens later, America, early 20thC.

£80–95 ROS

A Kodak Bantam Special camera, America, 1936.

£180–210 KOLN

A Lancaster Kapawl mahogany folding camera, with brass lens, c1885.

£1,650–1,950 KOLN

◄ **A Mackenstein walnut folding strut camera,** with Goerz lens and shutter, France, 1894.

£1,100–1,300 KOLN

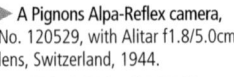

► **A Pignons Alpa-Reflex camera,** No. 120529, with Alitar f1.8/5.0cm lens, Switzerland, 1944.

£1,450–1,700 KOLN

A Voigtländer Bergheil Deluxe camera, with Helier f4.5/10.5cm lens, Compur shutter, Germany, 1933.

£370–440 KOLN

A Zeiss Ikon Contax I camera, No. AU 65.704, with Tessar f3.5/5cm lens, relacquered, Germany, 1932.

£560–670 KOLN

A Zeiss Ikon Super Ikonta 531/2 camera, with Tessar f3.5/10.5cm lens, Compur rapid shutter, Germany, 1950.

£165–195 KOLN

OPTICAL DEVICES & VIEWERS

A Brewster's Patent table **kaleidoscope,** by Robert Brettell Bate, London, No. 25, engraved with royal coat-of-arms, on a tripod stand, signed, c1817, 12¼in (31cm) high.

£24,000–28,800 S

Sir David Brewster (1781–1868), Fellow of the Royal Society, was one of the leading natural philosophers of 19th-century Britain. He is particularly noted for his work on optics and was awarded the Royal Society's Copley Medal in 1815. Brewster invented the kaleidoscope in 1816 and patented it in the following year. Robert Brettell Bate was a noted optician and instrument maker working in London between 1808 and 1847. The inscription 'Brewster's Patent' on this instrument shows that it was manufactured by Bate under license from Brewster during the period when his patent was still in force.

A Phantasmagorian Magic Lantern **dissolving projector,** probably by Liesegang, Düsseldorf, with both lenses and condensers, losses, Germany, c1870, 21in (53.5cm) wide.

£3,600–4,300 KOLN

A wooden **Perspective Peepshow box,** with six slots and 86 hand-coloured copperplate cards by Martin Engelbrecht, slight damage, Germany, c1750, 21¼in (54cm) high.

£7,600–9,100 KOLN

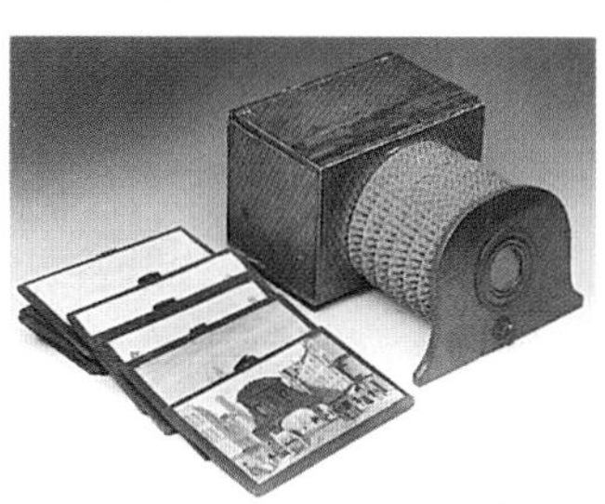

A mahogany **day/night viewer,** with paper bellows, France, 1880s, 6½in (16.5cm) wide, together with nine London scenes.

£370–440 MAL(O)

◄ A walnut and ebony **stereoscope,** with foliate ormolu handles, France, late 19thC, 46½in (118cm) high, with a number of stereoviews.

£2,600–3,100 S(NY)

A chestnut **Megalithoscope,** by Carlo Ponti, the hinged back containing printed English pictorial instructions, stamped mark, Italy, 1860s, 35in (89cm) wide, together with albumen print of St Peters and the Vatican.

£3,800–4,500 BBA

A walnut **stereo graphoscope,** by Watson & Sons, with hinged eyepieces, fold-over magnifying lens, glass and fretwork card stand, fretwork adjustable support, ivory plaque, 1860s–70s, 16in (40.5cm) wide.

£170–200 BBA

An Edwardian carved mahogany **Kinora picture viewer,** 13in (33cm) wide, damaged, with six picture reels.

£1,750–2,100 G(L)

Insurance values

Always insure your valuable antiques for the cost of replacing them with similar items, regardless of the original price paid. Both dealers and auctioneers can provide a valuation service for a fee.

PHOTOGRAPHS

Berenice Abbott, 'Nadeau's Store, Maine', America, 1960s, 19½ x15½in (49.5 x 39.5cm).
£400–480 JDJ

Berenice Abbott, 'Gunsmith Opposite Police Department, Centre Street, New York City', matted, mounted, signed in pencil, studio stamp, America, 1937, 7½ x19½in (19 x 49.5cm).
£5,200–6,200 S(NY)

Ansel Adams, 'Oak Tree, Snowstorm', mounted, signed and titled in ink, America, 1948, printed later 9½ x 7½in (24 x 19cm).
£2,900–3,400 S(NY)

Fratelli Alinari, dilute albumen print, Italy, Sienna, 1855, 12 x 10in (30.5 x 25.5cm).
£180–200 RMe

Diane Arbus, 'Teenage Couple on Hudson Street, NYC', matted, signed, titled, dated and numbered 13/75 in ink by photographer's daughter, America, 1963, printed later by Neil Selkirk, 14¾in (37.5cm) square, framed.
£15,600–18,700 S(NY)

Richard Avedon, 'Sunny Harnett, Evening Dress by Gres, Casino, Le Touquet', matted, signed and numbered 31/75 in pencil, America, 1954, printed 1978, 17¾ x 14¼in (44 x 36cm), framed.
£7,100–8,500 S(NY)

Felice Beato, 'Nautsh Dancers, India', albumen print, 1858, 8 x 6in (20.5 x 15cm).
£310–350 RMe

◀ **Bernard Bruce,** 'Francis Bacon in his studio', gelatin silver print, signed and dated, with inscription, 1984, 11¾ x 8in (30 x 20.5cm).
£450–540 BBA

▶ **Lev Borodulin,** 'Swallow', silver print, titled and dated in pencil to reverse, photographer's wetstamp, Russia, Moscow, 1960, printed later 11¾ x 8¼in (30 x 21cm).
£1,650–1,950 S

◀ **Margaret Bourke-White,** 'The Chrysler Building Announcement', matted, signed by photographer in pencil on the mount, America, 1930, 5¼ x 4in (13.5 x 10cm), framed.
£20,800–24,900 S(NY)

Bourke-White was commissioned by the Chrysler Corporation to photograph their new skyscraper in 1930, while it was still under construction. She was much taken with the building: with its status as the tallest building in the world and its gleaming stainless steel gargoyles, she decided it would be the perfect place for her studio. When the building's landlord expressed doubt about renting such prime real estate to a woman, Fortune *magazine intervened on her behalf.*

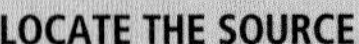

LOCATE THE SOURCE

The source of each illustration in Miller's can be found by checking the code letters below each caption with the Key to Illustrations, pages 746–753.

Margaret Bourke-White, 'In British Honduras', silver print, pencil annotations, wetstamp, America, c1954, 14 x 11in (35.5 x 28cm).
£480–570 S

Manuel Alvarez Bravo, 'El Ensueño', platinum print, matted, signed and annotated 'Mexico' by the photographer in pencil on reverse, Mexico, 1931, printed later, 9¾ x 7¾in (25 x 19.5cm), framed.
£2,750–3,300 S(NY)

► **Francis Bruguière,** 'Multiple Exposure', silver print, mounted on board, signed on reverse, America, c1925, 10½ x 13¼in (26.5 x 33.5cm), framed and glazed.
£720–860 S

Bruguière, best known for his light abstractions, also experimented in the 1920s with multiple exposures.

Bob Carlos Clarke, 'Charlotte', toned gelatin, silver print, mounted on board, signed and titled in ink, signed by photographer on reverse, 1986, 20 x 15¾in (51 x 40cm).
£690–820 BBA

Bourne & Shepherd, 'Shipping in the River Hooghly Calcutta', albumen print, c1875, 10 x 12 in (25.5 x 30.5cm).
£180–200 RMe

Brassaï, Gyula Halasz, 'Transmutation 8, Tentations de Saint-Antoine', ferrotyped, matted, hinged to a mount, titled by photographer in red ink, studio stamp, France, 1934–35, printed later, 6¾ x 9¼in (17 x 23.5cm).
£5,200–6,200 S(NY)

► **Henry Cartier-Bresson,** 'Ascot', silver print, signed in ink, photographer's blindstamp, France, 1955, printed later, 15¾ x 11¾in (40 x 30cm).
£2,250–2,700 S

Jean Claudet, 'Portrait of a young man', stereo daguerreotype with hand tinting and highlights, label to reverse, France, 1850s, 3¼ x 7in (8.5 x 18cm).
£280–330 BBA

► **Howard Coster,** 'T. E. Lawrence', silver print, signed in pencil on mount, photographer's label to reverse, 1931, 10¾ x 7¾in (27.5 x 19.5cm).
£1,300–1,550 S

Bill Brandt, 'Coalminer's Child', silver print, titled in pencil, wetstamp, probably 1937, 14¼ x 11¾in (36 x 30cm).
£8,400–10,000 S

The hanging loop on the reverse of this print and the unusually large format suggests that it was intended as an exhibition print. It may be that this is the same print that was shown in Brandt's first exhibition 'Modern Photography' held at Marx House, London, in 1940.

Julia Margaret Cameron, 'The Clogstoun Sisters', albumen print, 1864, 12 x 15in (30.5 x 38cm).
£1,000–1,200 RMe

◄ **William, Earl of Craven,** 'Trees under snow', salt print, mounted on card, 1856–57, 14½ x 11¾in (37 x 30cm).

3,800–4,550 S

Nearly all of the Earl of Craven's photographs were taken at Ashdown Park, Berkshire, the family seat, and so it is likely that this study is no exception. It is generally thought that the photographer was only active between 1854 and 1857. Despite such a brief period of activity the Earl of Craven's photographs, only recently rediscovered, have been acknowledged as some of the finest works of the important English amateur period.

Robert Doisneau, 'Le Petit Balcon', silver print, signed in ink, titled and dated to reverse, France, 1953, printed later, 11¾ x 16in (30 x 40.5cm).

£1,400–1,650 S

Terence Donovan, 'Ritz', gelatin silver print, signed to reverse, titled and numbered '1/10', c1985, 15 x 12¼in (38 x 31cm).

£300–360 BBA

Alfred Eisenstaedt, 'Headwaiter René Breguet serving drinks on Grand Hotel ice ring, St Moritz', matted, signed by photographer in ink, credit stamp to reverse, titled and dated in ink, Germany, 1932, printed later, 12½ x 9½in (32 x 24cm).

£4,200–5,000 S(NY)

William English, 'Portrait of Vivienne Westwood', colour print, signed by subject in gold ink, signed by photographer to reverse, 1975, printed later, 11½ x 7½in (29 x 19cm).

£200–240 BBA

Walker Evans, 'Landlord, Hale County, Alabama', numbered 111 and 244, matted, America, 1936, 9 x 7½in (23 x 19cm).

£9,100–10,900 S(NY)

Roger Fenton, 'Algerian Zouaves, Crimea', albumen print, 1855, 5½ x 8in (14 x 20.5cm).

£420–500 BBA

Roger Fenton, 'Officers of the 90th Regiment, Crimea', salt print, 1856, 5 x 7in (12.5 x 18cm).

£630–700 RMe

► **Thomas H. G. Fermor,** 'Lady Anna Maria Arabella Fermor tending flowers', salt print, mounted on card, later pencil inscription, 1850s, 10 x 6¾in (25.5 x 17cm).

£960–1,150 S

Frederick Fiebig, 'A Monument, Calcutta', salt print, India, c1850, 7¼ x 9¼in (18.5 x 23.5cm).

£2,300–2,750 BBA

◀ **Arnold Genthe,** 'Street of the Gamblers (Chinatown, San Francisco)', signed and annotated in ink, matted, framed, America, c1896, 22½ x 16¾in (57 x 42.5cm).

£13,000–15,600 S(NY)

Mario Giacomelli, 'Fiamme Sul Campo' silver print, ferrotyped, titled and numbered '1015' to reverse, photographer's wetstamp, Italy, c1954, 6½ x 9½in (16.5 x 24cm).

£600–720 S

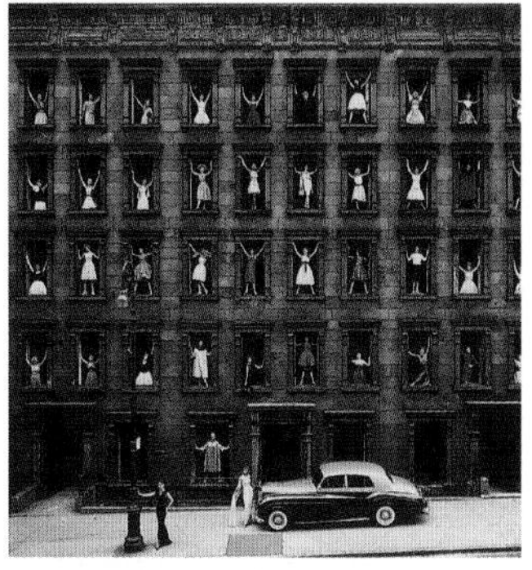

Ormond Gigli, 'New York City (Models in Windows)', chromogenic print, mounted, signed, titled, dated and numbered '11/12' by photographer in ink on mount and reverse, 1960, printed later, 46in (117cm) square.

£15,600–18,700 S(NY)

Laura Gilpin, 'Flower Detail', platinum print, signed by photographer on mount, printed studio label to reverse, matted, framed, c1930, America, 9½ x 7½in (24 x 19cm).

£11,000–13,200 S(NY)

A student of the Clarence White School of Photography, Laura Gilpin developed an affection for the expressive qualities of printing in platinum, and she continued to use this paper of choice long after other photographers switched to the more affordable silver gelatin.

Laura Gilpin, 'Sand Dunes', bromide print, signed and dated by photographer in pencil, 1931–33, America, 7½ x 9½in (19 x 24cm).

£9,700–11,600 S(NY)

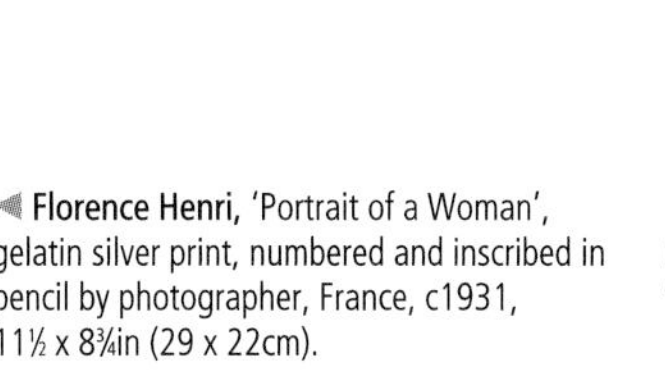

◀ **Florence Henri,** 'Portrait of a Woman', gelatin silver print, numbered and inscribed in pencil by photographer, France, c1931, 11½ x 8¾in (29 x 22cm).

£2,350–2,800 BBA

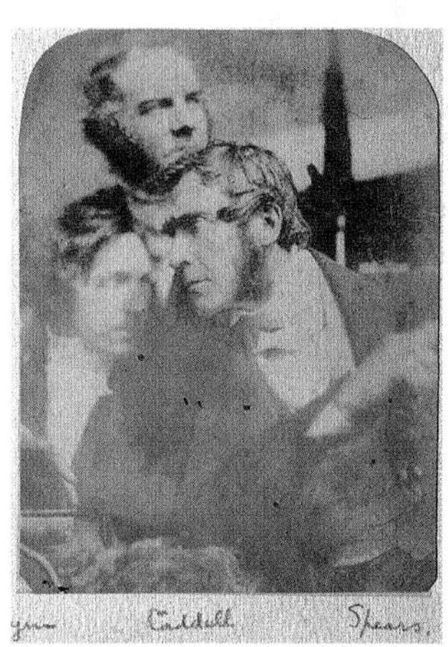

David Octavius Hill and Robert Adamson, 'Rev. Fyvie, Mr Cadell and Mr Spiers', salt print, 1840s, printed later, 5 x 4in (12.5 x 10cm).

£310–350 RMe

◀ **David Octavius Hill and Robert Adamson,** 'Portrait of Elizabeth Rigby, Lady Eastlake', carbon print from calotype negative, 1840s, pobably printed by Thomas Annan, c1880, 8 x 6¼in (20.5 x 16cm).

£190–220 BBA

Lady Eastlake was the first president of the Photographic Society of London.

▶ **Yousuf Karsh,** 'Georgia O'Keefe', mounted, signed by photographer in ink, matted, Canada, 1956, printed later, 23¾ x 19¼in (60.5 x 49cm), framed.

£4,550–5,400 BBA

André Kertész, 'Melancholic Tulip', signed and dated by photographer to reverse, matted, France, 1939, printed later, 13¾ x 9¾in (35 x 25cm), framed.
£5,500–6,600 S(NY)

◀ **Professor Rudolf Koppitz,** 'Mädchen', bromoil print, signed by photographer in pencil in the margin, dated and annotated by photographer in pencil, studio and reproduction stamps to reverse, matted, Austria, 1923, 13 x 7¾in (33 x 19.5cm), framed.
£8,400–10,000 S(NY)

In 1923 Koppitz undertook a series of movement and figure studies that would culminate in his famous 'Bewegungsstudie'. The image offered here is one of the first in which he explored the compositional possibilities of stylized models in a studio setting. As in 'Bewegungsstudie', the subjects are contingent upon each other for balance, while distanced from each other emotionally.

◀ **Heinrich Kühn,** 'The Photographer's Children, Hans and Lotte, in a meadow', platinum or bromoil transfer print on tissue, annotated in pencil, matted, Austria, c1910, 9¼ x 11½in (23.5 x 29cm).
£3,250–3,900 S(NY)

Heinrich Kühn, 'Still Life with Horse Statuette and Hydrangeas', brown-toned bromoil print on tissue, titled in German in an unidentified hand in pencil to the reverse, matted, framed, c1910, 11¾ x 14¼in (30 x 36cm).
£3,250–3,900 S(NY)

◀ **Lafayette Ltd,** 'Portrait of the Actress Emilie Charlotte (Lillie) Langtry', paper print, mounted on board, photographer's credit on mount, Ireland, Dublin, c1899, 8¾ x 11½in (22 x 29cm).
£540–640 S

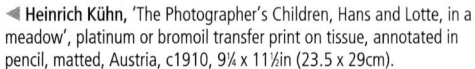

Annie Leibovitz, 'Self Portrait', gelatin silver print, signed in ink, America, 1990, 6 x 8¾in (15 x 22cm).
£710–850 BBA

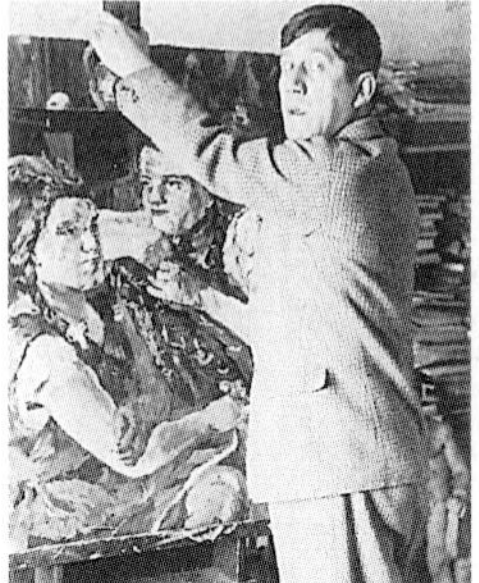

Felix H. Man, 'Oskar Kokoschka in Vienna' gelatin silver print, signed, titled and dated by photographer, inkstamp and monogram to reverse, Germany, 1930, 8¼ x 6¼in (21 x 16cm).
£190–220 DW

Baron Adolf de Meyer, 'Still Life with Lilies', platinum print, matted, c1910, 8½ x 6in (21.5 x 15in), framed.
£7,100–8,500 S(NY)

Léonard Misonne, 'Les Ornières', oil print, signed and dated by photographer in pencil, Belgium, 1932, 11½ x 15¼in (29 x 38.5cm).
£5,800–6,900 S(NY)

LOCATE THE SOURCE
The source of each illustration in Miller's can be found by checking the code letters below each caption with the Key to Illustrations, pages 746–753.

Albert Renger-Patzsch, 'Cactus Flower: *Cactaceae Astrophytum*', gelatin silver print, photographer's printed credit, Germany, 1920s, printed c1950, 9 x 6½in (23 x 16.5cm).
£420–500 BBA

► **Art Sinsabaugh,** 'Bal. La. 43', signed, titled and dated by photographer in pencil, matted, mounted on Strathmore illustration board, America, 1967, 10¼ x 19½in (26 x 49.5cm).
£3,900–4,650 S(NY)

Aaron Siskind, 'New York', mounted, signed, titled and dated by photographer in ink to reverse, matted, America, 1951, 16½ x 13¾in (42 x 35cm).
£5,200–6,200 S(NY)

Herbert G. Ponting, 'Mr Ponting Developing a Plate', magenta-toned silver print, photographer's blindstamp, Fine Art Society label to reverse, numbered 55, 1910–12, 17¾ x 13¼in (45 x 33.5cm), framed.
£2,400–2,850 S

F. A. Rinehart, 'Afraid of Eagle', silver gelatin sepiatone, mounted on card, America, 1898, 9¼ x 7¼in (23.5 x 18.5cm).
£160–190 JAA

O. G. Rejlandler, 'Two Figures Drawing Water from a Well', albumen salt print, 1825–50, 8 x 6½in (20.5 x 16.5cm).
£2,150–2,550 S

O. G. Rejlander, the 'father of art photography', is well known for including himself in his artistic figure studies taken from the mid-1850s through to the early 1980s.

William Saunders, 'Bride and Groom', albumen print, China, c1875, 10 x 8in (25.5 x 20.5cm).
£310–350 RMe

◄ **Ralph Steiner,** 'American Rural Baroque', mounted, signed and inscribed 'with overpowering affection' by photographer in pencil, matted, America, 1929, printed later, 7½ x 9½in (19 x 24cm).
£6,200–7,400 S(NY)

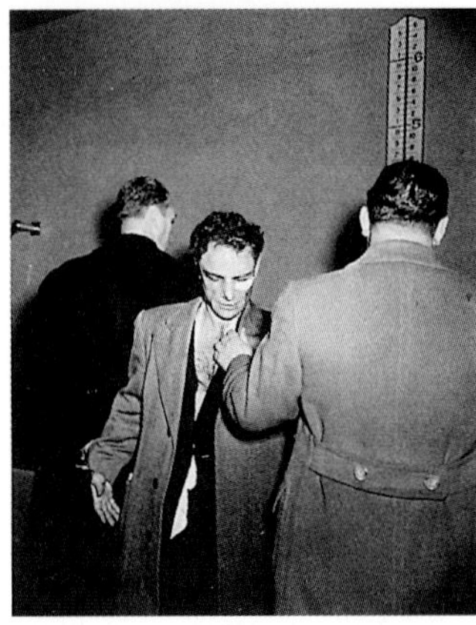

Weegee (Arthur Fellig), 'Cop Killer, Anthony Esposito in the Line-up Room', silver print, photographer's wetstamp to reverse, America, 1939, printed later 10 x 8in (25.5 x 20.5cm), framed.

£1,650–1,950 S

Brett Weston, 'Rock and Pebbles', mounted on board, signed and dated by photographer in pencil, matted, America, 1966, 7½ x 9½in (19 x 24cm).

£5,200–6,200 S(NY)

Minor White, 'Devil's Slide, San Mateo County, California', mounted, matted, America, c1958, 6½ x 8½in (16.5 x 21.5cm).

£3,550–4,250 S(NY)

Anon, a whole-plate daguerreotype of a gentleman wearing a top hat, in a gilt frame, America, c1850, 8½ x 6½in (21.5 x 16.5cm).

£760–910 SK

Anon, a sixth-plate daguerreotype of the 13th US president, Millard Fillmore, in a gilded-brass frame and a leather and pressed paper case, slight damage, America, c1850, 3½ x 3¼in (9 x 8.5cm).

£5,700–6,800 SK(B)

Anon, half-plate daguerreotype of two young men, France, c1850, 8 x 5½in (20.5 x 14cm).

£720–800 RMe

◀ **Anon,** a sixth-plate ambrotype portrait of three brothers in US Army uniform, with light hand-tinting and gilt highlights, in a gilt mount and leather case, 1860s, 2½ x 3½in (6.5 x 9cm)

£220–260 BBA

Anon, 'African Tribesman by a Kraal, with a Boer', ambrotype, with hand tinting, in a gilt mount, c1860, 4¼ x 5½in (11 x 14cm), in a leather case.

£4,280–5,100 BBA

Condition

The condition is absolutely vital when assessing the value of an photograph. Damaged pieces on the whole appreciate much less than perfect examples. However, a rare desirable piece may command a high price even when damaged.

◀ **Anon,** 'Building and Construction Work of a Canal Lock, possibly Leeds, Yorkshire', albumen print, in three sections, mounted, 1860s, 10¾ x 31½in (27.5 x 80cm).

£130–155 DW

Anon, an albumen print of a Siamese musician, 1874, 8 x 6in (20.5 x 15cm).

£360–400 RMe

ARMS & ARMOUR

ARMOUR

A half-suit of armour, Germany, c1600.

£6,600–7,900 Herm

A composite cuirassier's armour, comprising Flemish helmet, German collar, breastplate, backplate and pauldrons, northern Europe, 1620–30.

£9,000–10,800 Herm

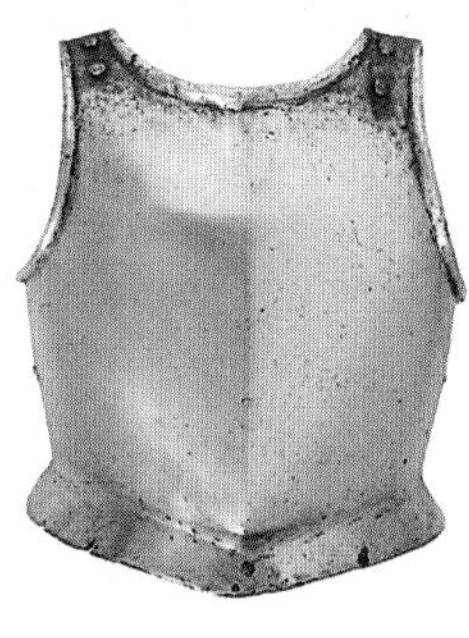

A siege weight breastplate, Europe, c1600.

£2,000–2,250 FAC

This breastplate, which was probably used during the Thirty Years War and English Civil War, weighs over 16lbs (7kg) and protected the wearer from anything short of cannon fire.

A Staff officer's iron cuirass breastplate, with brass rivets, gilt crowned monogram 'AR' of the Saxon Elector and Polish King Friedrich August I surrounded by trophies, traces of red paint, lined with chamois leather, Germany, c1720.

£6,300–7,500 Herm

A cuirassier's steel breastplate and backplate, with brass rivets, France, c1812.

£810–900 ARB

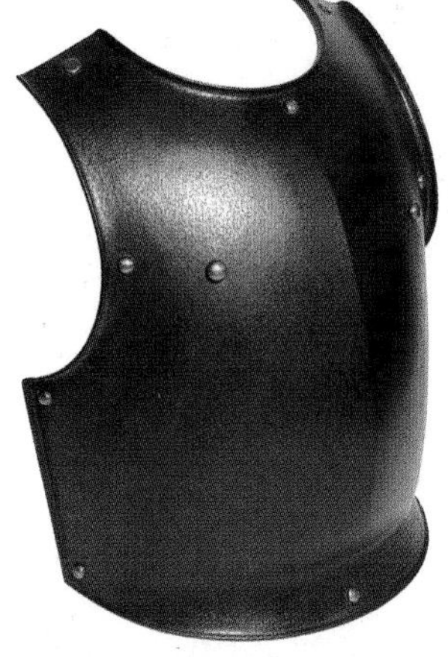

A cuirassier's steel breastplate, with brass rivets, France, c1845.

£310–350 ARB

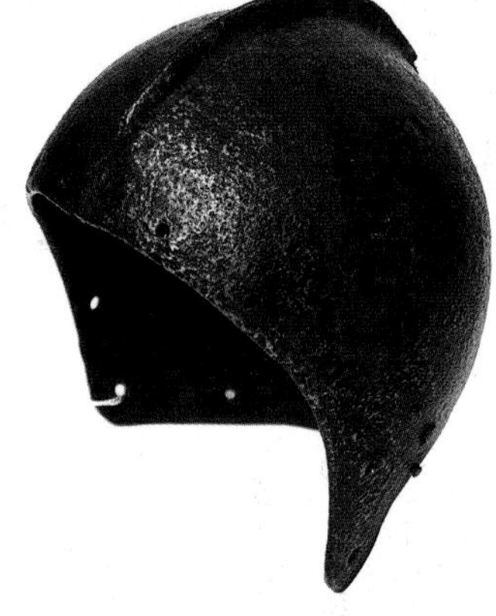

An iron burgonet, formed in two sections, Europe, c1450.

£1,750–1,950 MDL

This burgonet is a fine early example of heavy armour, designed for use by engineers and other besieging troops for advanced protection from enemy fire.

A burgonet, with articulated neck guard, two maker's marks, Germany, c1570.

£2,700–3,000 FAC

◄ **A lobster-tail helmet,** with articulated earflaps, regimental control marks, Europe, c1625.

£2,150–2,400 FAC

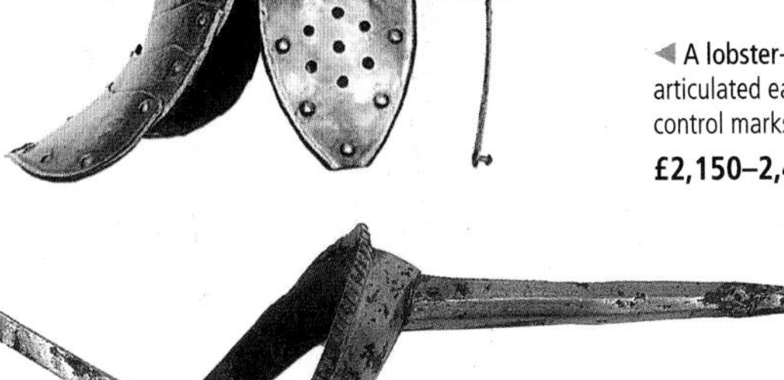

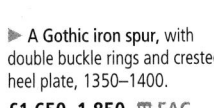

► **A Gothic iron spur,** with double buckle rings and crested heel plate, 1350–1400.

£1,650–1,850 FAC

AXES

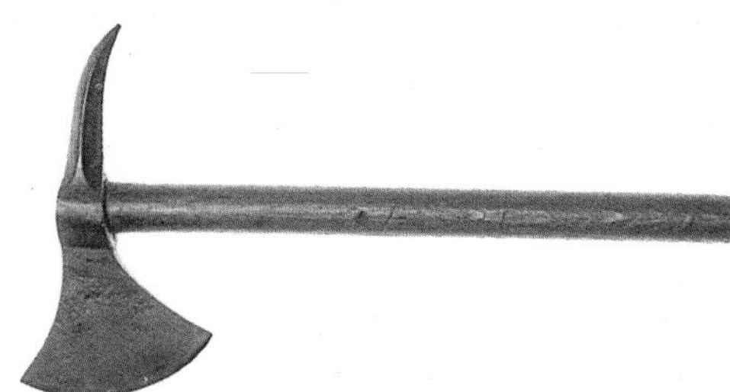

A naval boarding or fire axe, stamped 'M' surmounted by a stylized crown, with an oak haft, Europe, 1800–40, face 5½in (14cm) wide.

£560–670 JDJ

A naval boarding axe, c1810, 32in (81.5cm) long.

£310–350 GMI

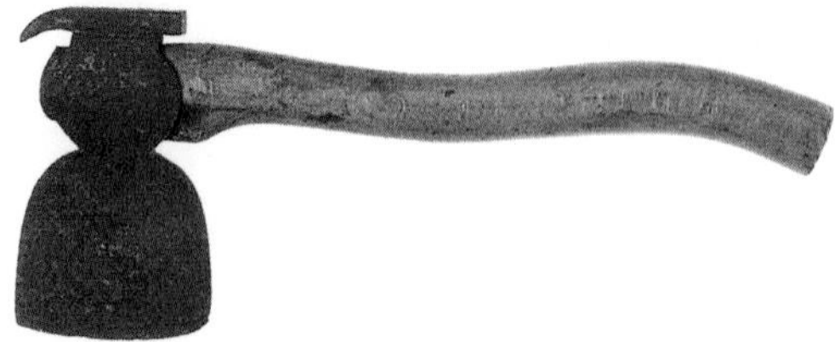

◄ **An axe,** the butt-end with a two-pronged claw, Spain, late 19thC, 15¾in (40cm) long.

£190–220 JDJ

This hatchet has a hand-written paper label with the inscription 'This hatchet was taken from the arsenal, at Cavetae, Manilla when Dewey took that place from the Spanish in May, 1898. Presented by the Gunner of the USS Raleigh *when she was dismantled at this navy yard after the war with Spain. Kittery Maine, Oct 11th 189-, Wm. M. C. Philabrick'.*

CANNONS

◄ **An iron breech-loaded cannon,** with a log cassion, enlarged breech, breech block missing, Germany, c1500, barrel 58¼in (148cm) long.

£4,000–4,800 Herm

A pair of bronze saluting cannons, each cast with a shield with three fleur-de-lys with a crown above, and stylized dolphin lifting handles, on oak carriages, France, 18thC, barrels 30in (76cm) wide.

£14,900–17,800 WW

► **A pair of iron cannons,** each stamped 2-2-20 by the touch hole, early 19thC, 49in (124.5cm) long.

£2,400–2,850 S

An iron cannon, with two six-spoked wheels, c1880, barrel 22½in (57cm) long.

£880–1,050 BAM

A pair of bronze signalling cannons, on bronze-mounted mahogany carriages, c1875, barrels 27½in (70cm) long.

£6,600–7,900 SWO

Garth Vincent
Antique Arms, Armour & Medals
LAPADA MEMBER
THE GUN TRADE ASSOCIATION
I have customers worldwide and I am interested in purchasing single items or complete collections, advice freely given
Dealer in antique and reproduction arms and armour for the collector, investor and interior decorator
Commission buying at auction
Access & Visa accepted
Brochure available
The Old Manor House
Allington, Nr Grantham
Lincolnshire NG32 2DH
Telephone: 01400 281358
Fax: 01400 282658
Mobile: 07785 352151
Email: garthvincent@aol.com
Website: http://www.guns.uk.com

EDGED WEAPONS

A naval cutlass, with walnut grip, the early French blade stamped with a fleur-de-lys surmounted by a three-leafed figure, America, 1740–80, blade 27in (68.5cm) long.

£2,500–3,000 JDJ

A naval dirk, with a silver-mounted ivory handle and gilt-mounted scabbard, c1810, 14in (35.5cm) long.

£760–850 GV

A dirk, with extra pieces *en suite,* the carved bogwood handles set with foil-backed gems, the leather scabbard with pressed-silver mounts, maker's mark 'DF', Scotland, Glasgow 1870, 19in (48.5cm) long.

£880–1,050 MAL(O)

A Cameron Highlanders dirk, the handle set with a Cairngorm, the scabbard decorated with a family crest and mounted with a Cairngorm, Scotland, c1880, 16in (40.5cm) long.

£1,250–1,400 GV

◄ **A hanger,** with a copper wire and band-wrapped grip and iron hilt, the pierced shell guard chiselled with relief portraits of King Charles I and Queen Henrietta Maria, the blade chiselled with a running wolf mark, c1635, blade 27¼in (69cm) long.

£3,350–3,750 FAC

Swords of this form are sometimes known as Hounslow Hangers as many were assembled in Hounslow, west of London. This example was probably made in London. It is dated to the early part of the period for its type, based on the rolled quillon and form of the knuckle bow.

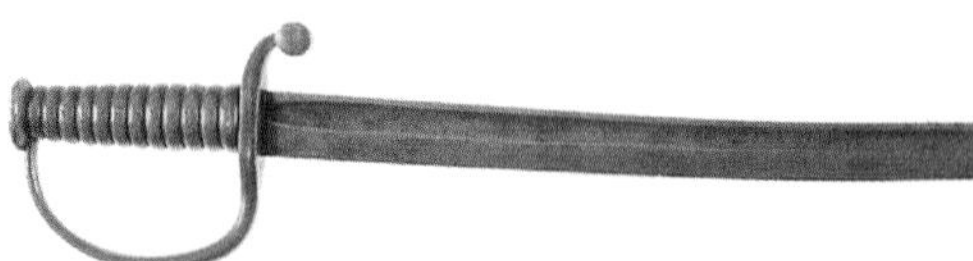

A hanger, with a brass hilt, America, blade 22in (56cm) long.

£560–670 JDJ

A Bowie knife, by Cerise Johnson & Co, Sheffield, with a stag-horn grip and brass crossguard, c1830, 14in (35.5cm) long.

£350–390 MDL

A folding knife, by Henry Hobson, with a stag-horn grip and nickel fittings, marked, America, 19thC, blade 4in (10cm) long.

£380–430 MDL

A Bowie knife, with a chequered ebony grip and brass ferrule and pommel, probably America, 19thC, 11¾in (30cm) long.

£1,300–1,550 JDJ

An attached tag written in ink says 'Taken from a prisoner of war Jan 6, 1865 at Colombia South Car by Henry Hescock and later sold to Second Lieutenant Joseph McClure of Co C 15th Kentucky.'

An officer's side knife, the grip with an engraved inscription 'A. H. Embler', the blade stamped 'G. Woodhead, 36 Howard Street, Sheffield', in a tooled leather scabbard decorated with gold embossed scrollwork, c1860, blade 5½in (14cm) long.

£5,000–6,000 JDJ

Captain Andrew H. Embler was awarded the Congressional Medal of Honour on October 19, 1893.

► **A rapier,** the iron hilt with a double ring guard incorporating a thumb ring, the pommel guard and pommel with chiselled foliate scrolls, the blade etched with scrolls, mottos and military motifs, Holland, 1610–20, blade 34in (86.5cm) long.

£2,900–3,250 FAC

A chiselled rapier, the iron hilt with flower quillon finials and a pineapple grip, the blade inlaid with a copper wolf, Italy, Brescia, c1650, 42¼in (107.5cm) long.

£3,150–3,750 Herm

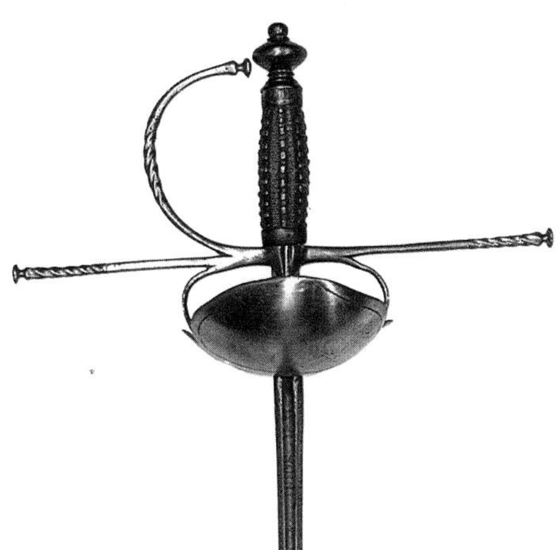

A cup-hilt rapier, with an iron hilt, the blade etched with scrolling foliage and inscribed with cutler's name and mark: Johannes Coll, Spain, c1650, blade 35in (89cm) long.

£2,450–2,750 FAC

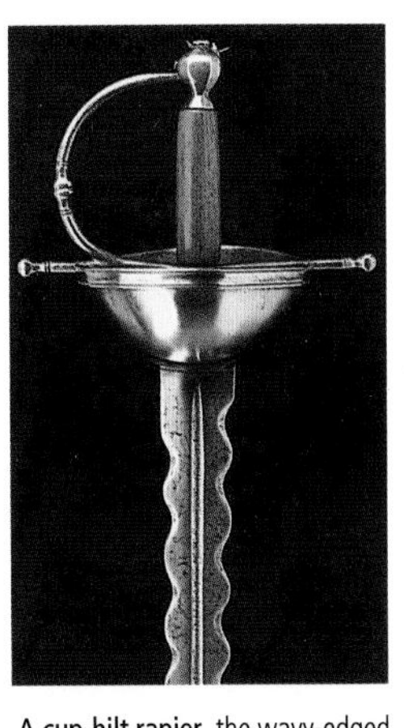

A cup-hilt rapier, the wavy-edged blade engraved with trophies and stamped 'Santisimo Chrusufisio', grip replaced, Spain, 18thC, blade 37¼in (94.5cm) long.

£800–960 TDM

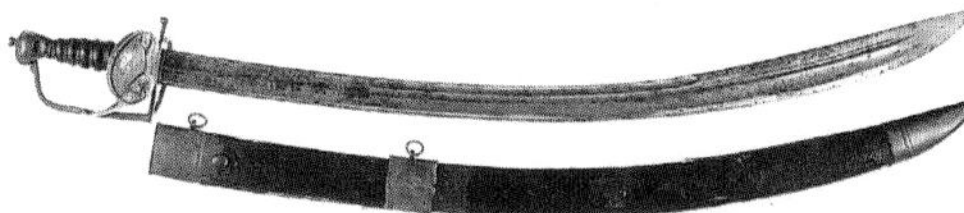

A horseman's sabre, with a spiral-turned wooden grip, the clamshell counter guard etched and embossed with a design of a Hanoverian running horse, the blade etched with a panel depicting a naval battle, with a wood and leather scabbard, damage to scabbard, America, c1780, blade 33in (84cm) long.

£2,300–2,750 JDJ

A sabre, the fire-gilt hilt with a lion's head pommel and fish skin grip, with a pierced and chased guard, the blade engraved with the royal arms and crowned 'GR' cypher within floral scrolls, inlaid with gold, the leather scabbard with gilt-metal mounts, c1820, 35in (89cm) long.

£2,650–2,950 MDL

A horseman's broadsword, the iron hilt decorated with chiselled stylized foliage and bands, carved wood grip, South German, c1650, blade 30¼in (77cm) long.

£1,750–1,950 FAC

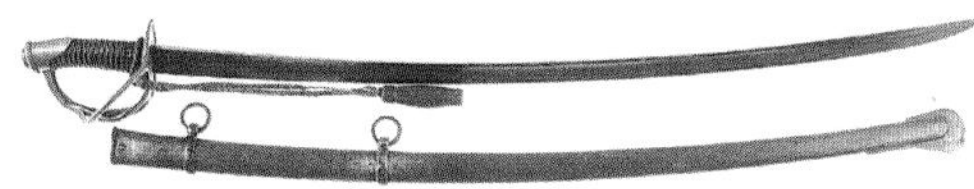

A cavalry sabre, with a three-branch hilt and iron scabbard, America, early 1860s, blade 36½in (92.5cm) long.

£310–370 JDJ

A silver smallsword, the hilt with a ball pommel and twisted silver wire grip, London 1721, the blade 30in (76cm) long.

£1,650–1,950 F&C

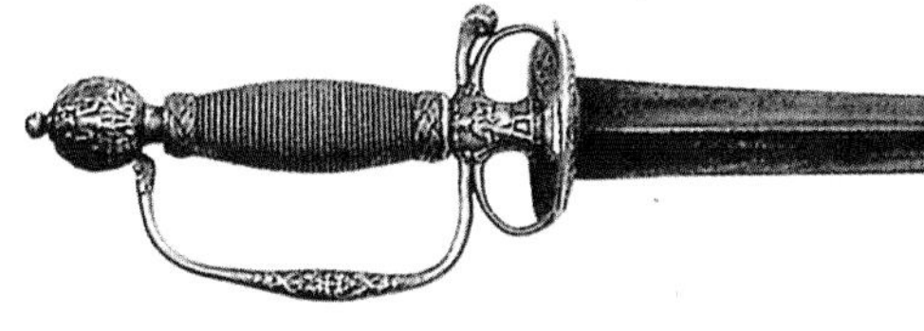

A silver-gilt smallsword, the hilt cast and chased with masks and military trophies on a punched ground, with a ball pommel and twisted silver wire grip, France, probably Paris, 1700–25, blade 22¾in (58cm) long.

£480–570 F&C

The size of this sword would suggest that it was made for a child.

A smallsword, with a hallmarked silver hilt, 18thC, 38in (96.5cm) long.

£1,700–1,900 ARB

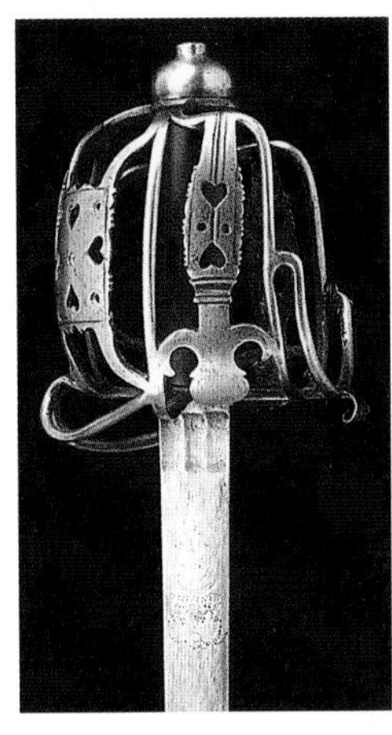

A basket-hilt backsword, the iron basket guard pierced with hearts and circles, the blade engraved with a crown and the royal cypher 'GR' on each side and the maker's name 'Harvey', grip later, 1775–80, 34½in (87.5cm) long.

£1,300–1,550 TDM

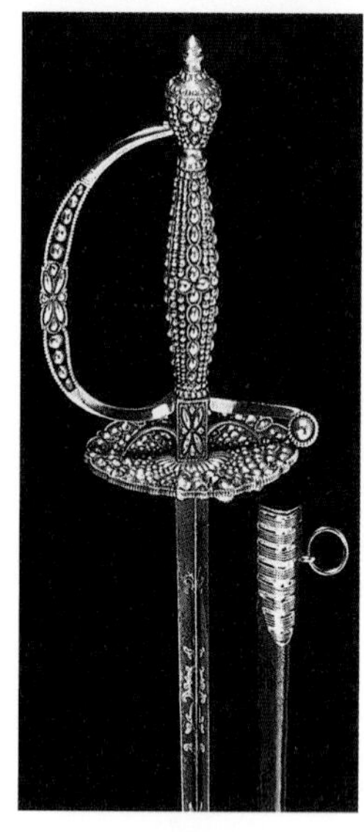

A light cavalry sword, blade marked 'Kanfield, Dublin', scabbard marked 'Oakfarn & Co', Ireland, 1788, 36in (91.5cm) long.

£1,100–1,250 MDL

◄ **A smallsword,** by William Gray, London, with a decorative cut-steel hilt, the blade etched and gilt with scrolls, with original leather-covered wood scabbard, 1780–90, blade 32½in (82.5cm) long.

£1,400–1,650 TDM

► **A smallsword,** the silver hilt with pierced and chased decoration, marked 'L.R., London', the blade with engraved scroll decoration, London 1791, 38in (96.5cm) long.

£1,100–1,250 MDL

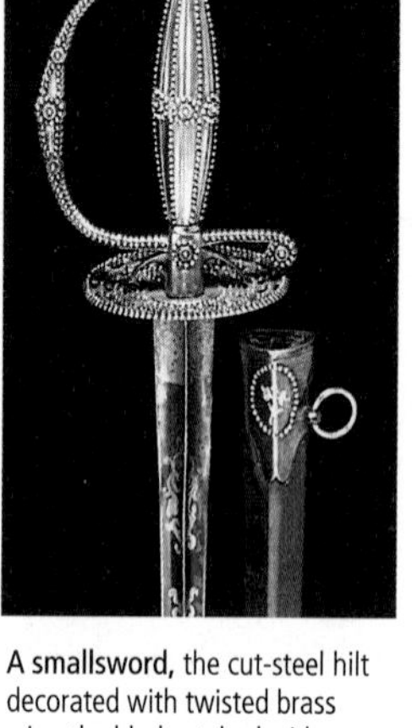

An officer's sword, by J. Lamprey, Dublin, the pommel formed as a lion's head with a chequered ivory grip, the blade etched and gilt with foliage and crowned royal cypher, the leather scabbard with a signed gilt-brass locket, chape missing, Ireland, c1800, blade 30½in (77.5cm) long.

£2,200–2,600 TDM

A cuirassier officer's sword, with a gold-plated hilt and knuckle guard with eagle, with an etched Montmorency blade, leather grip possibly restored, Germany, late 18thC, 42½in (108cm) long.

£5,000–6,000 Herm

A smallsword, the cut-steel hilt decorated with twisted brass wire, the blade etched with scrolls, trophies and an angelic figure, with a leather-covered wood scabbard, Russia, Tula, c1790, blade 29½in (75cm) long.

£2,800–3,350 TDM

A broadsword, the hilt chiselled with scrolling foliage, America, c1800, blade 33in (84cm) long.

£2,900–3,250 FAC

This is an exceptional example of a distinctively Mexican form of the broadsword, distinguished by its elegant crossguard. The construction and decorative theme of the hilt is related to other Mexican and southwestern metalwork, particularly spurs, and is therefore likely to be a product of the same industry.

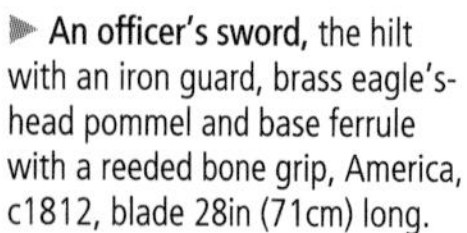

► **An officer's sword,** the hilt with an iron guard, brass eagle's-head pommel and base ferrule with a reeded bone grip, America, c1812, blade 28in (71cm) long.

£1,000–1,150 FAC

Mixed metal hilts are very rarely encountered but this example was clearly made under the pressure of war and combines the strength of an iron guard with the workability of a cast pommel.

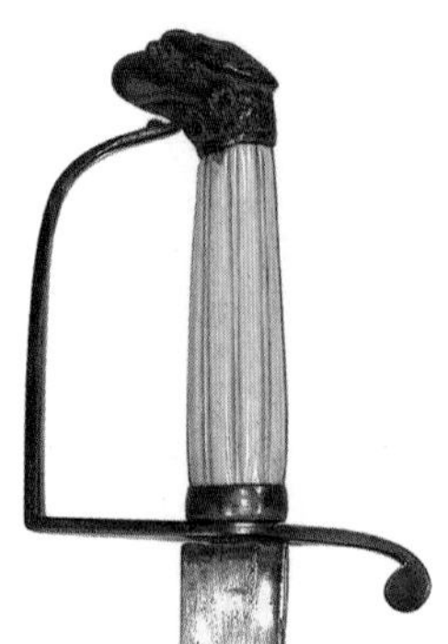

A cavalry officer's sword, with a gilt hilt and blade, c1800, 38in (96.5cm) long.

£530–590 ARB

A sword, the gilt basket hilt with leaf decoration and musketeer badge with fleur-de-lys, the blade engraved with maker's mark and date, with a steel scabbard, France, 1815, 45in (114.5cm) long.

£2,700–3,000 MDL

A cavalry sword, with a brass three-bar guard, the blade engraved 'Klingenthal' and dated, with a steel scabbard guard, grip releathered, France, 1831, 45in (114.5cm) long.

£850–950 MDL

◀ **A pair of French shortswords,** with brass hilts, the pommels cast with foliate decoration, stamped 'Agier-Fondu, Charrière à Paris', with leather scabbards, France, 19thC, 26½in (67.5cm) long.

£260–310 G(L)

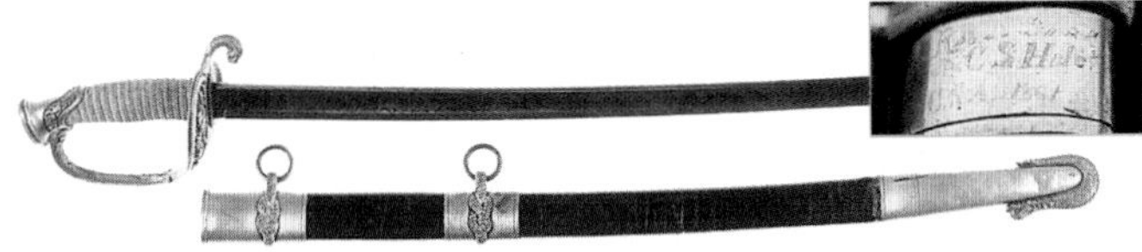

A naval officer's sword, the blade decorated with etched panels of patriotic naval motifs with remnants of green paint and inscribed 'Ames Mfg. Co. Chicopee, Mass 1852', scabbard mount inscribed 'Rebels.....C.S. Hale, CSA 1861', America, 1852, blade 26in (66cm) long.

£2,800–3,350 JDJ

A court sword, the hilt with diamond steel-cut decoration, c1850, blade 31in (78.5cm) long.

£270–300 Q&C

A staff and field officer's sword, the German silver scabbard with an inscription, the blade etched with military and patriotic motifs, America, 1861, blade 30¾in (78cm) long.

£3,750–4,500 JDJ

An infantry officer's sword, with a brass hilt and scabbard, c1855, 38in (96.5cm) long.

£450–500 ARB

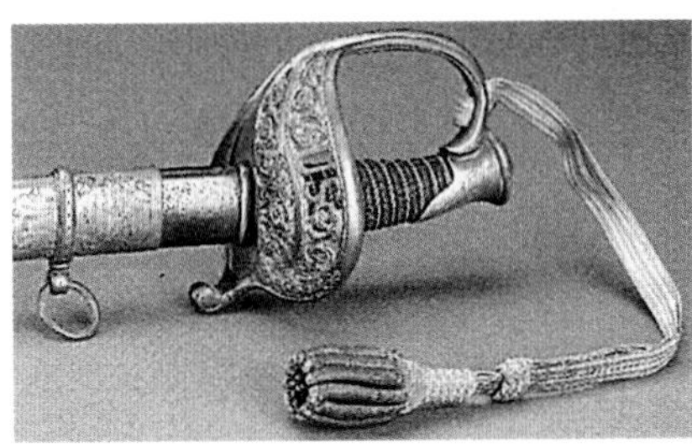

A staff and field officer's sword, the blade with a presentation inscription, with steel scabbard, America, early 1860s, blade 32in (81.5cm) long.

£1,100–1,300 WAD

An infantry officer's sword, the blade etched 'Savage & Lyman, Montreal', with a Victoria crown and cypher, the leather scabbard with an engraved dedication, Canada, 1866, blade 32in (81.5cm) long.

£1,000–1,200 WAD

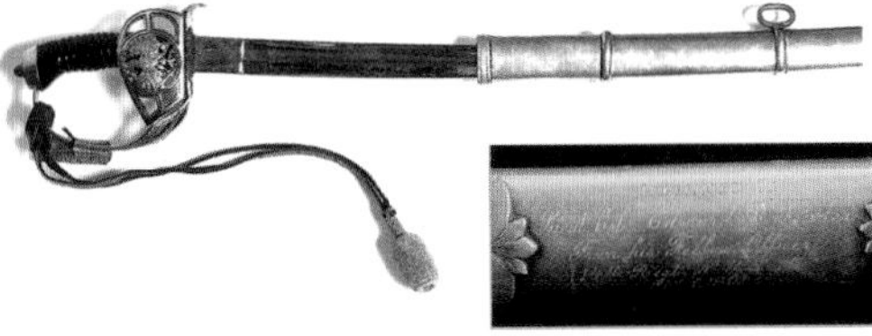

A Prussian Army senior NCO's sword, Germany, c1880, blade 28in (71cm) long.

£200–230 Q&C

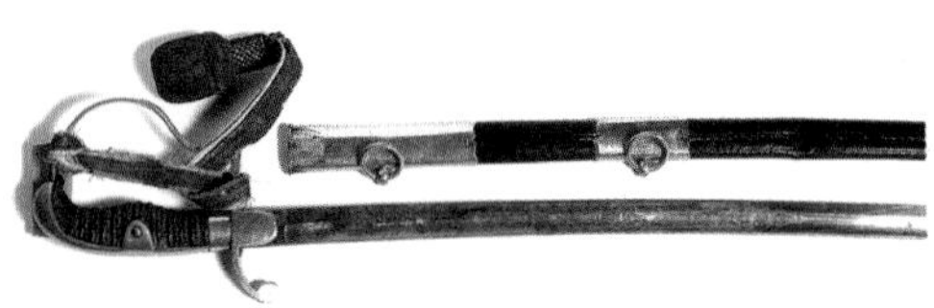

An officer's sword, Germany, c1890, blade 34in (86.5cm) long.

£130–145 Q&C

A cavalry officer's sword, by Wilkinson & Co, 1912 pattern, c1915, blade 34in (86.5cm) long.

£400–450 Q&C

▶ **An RAF officer's sword,** by Wilkinson & Co, the blade engraved with a George V cypher, No. 63321, with a leather-covered scabbard, scabbard worn, early 20thC, blade 32in (81.5cm) long.

£370–440 WAD

FIREARMS

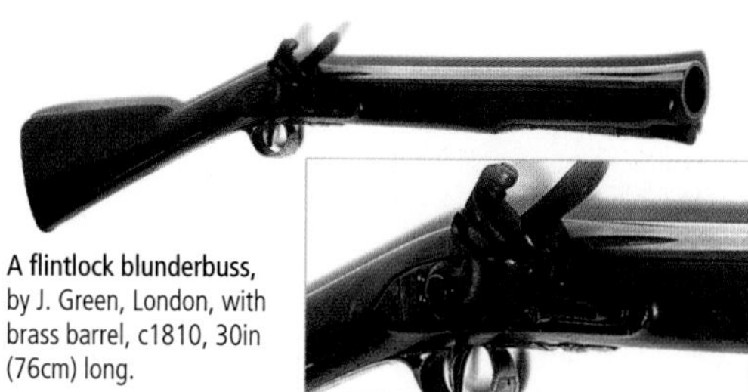

A flintlock blunderbuss, by J. Green, London, with brass barrel, c1810, 30in (76cm) long.
£2,000–2,250 GV

A flintlock blunderbuss, with brass barrel, spring bayonet and walnut full stock with chequered wrist, the plate inscribed 'Alley', ramrod missing, c1815, 29¾in (75.5cm) long.
£2,000–2,400 WAL

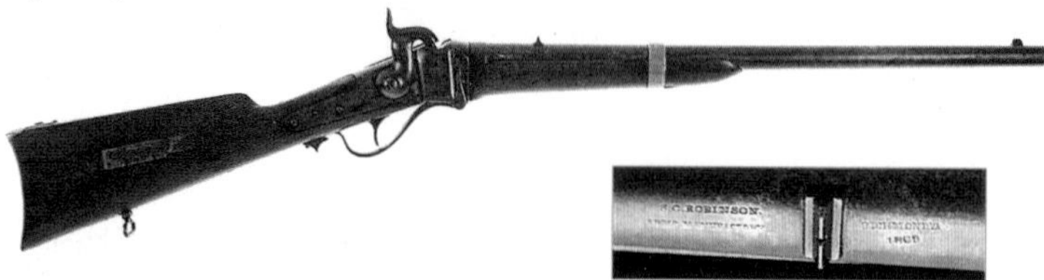

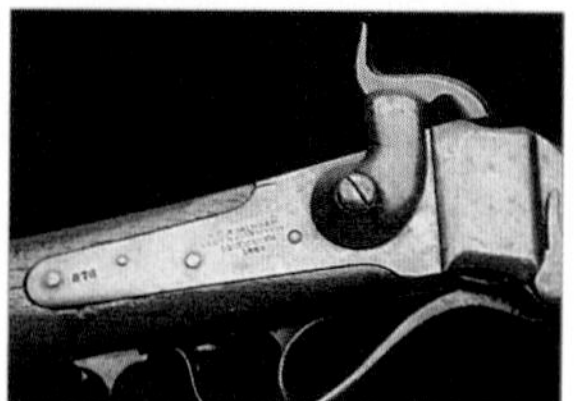

A .52 Sharps carbine, by S. C. Robinson, with a brass buttplate, marked, America, 1862, barrel 21in (53.5cm) long.
£7,500–9,000 JDJ

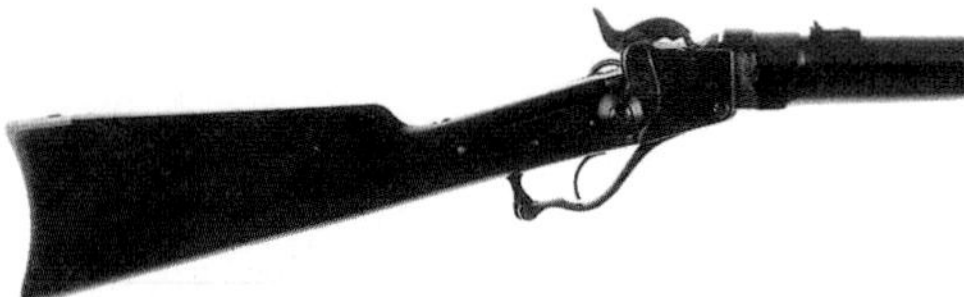

A .54 Starr carbine, with a brass buttplate, marked, America, 1860s, barrel 21in (53.5cm) long.
£1,000–1,200 JDJ

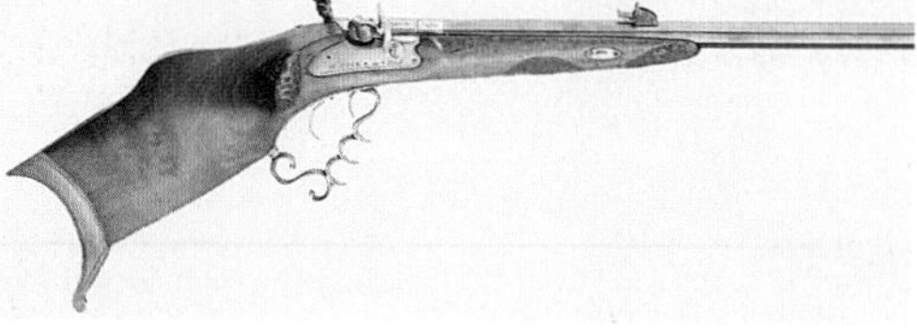

A carbine, by C. Mang, with carved walnut stock and iron plates, the floral-engraved lock with rebounding hammer, Austria, Graz, c1870, 47in (119.5cm) long.
£1,750–2,100 Herm

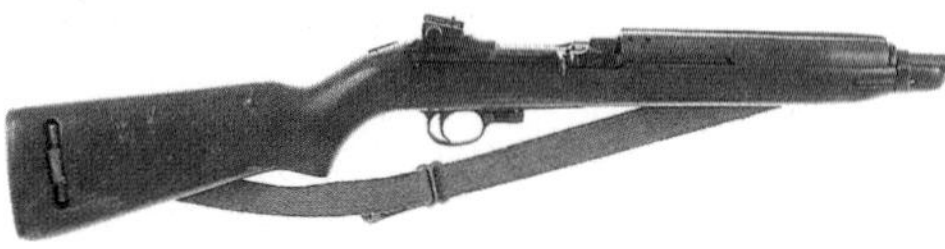

A .30 M1 carbine, by Standard Products, with walnut stock and ordnance wheel, with canvas sling and oiler, America, dated 1944.
£350–420 JDJ

A volunteer sergeant's .65 flintlock fusil, by Wilson, c1780, 43in (109cm) long.
£2,550–2,850 MDL

This is basically a scaled down Brown Bess with 28in barrel of carbine calibre made with a pistol-size lock. Its smaller size was intended to give a sergeant greater mobility while giving out orders.

A .75 Tower short Land Pattern Brown Bess flintlock musket, the walnut full stock with ordnance store keeper's mark on butt, regulation brass mounts, sling swivels, steel ramrod, slight damage, c1775, 58in (147.5cm) long.
£4,700–5,600 WAL

A naval musket, with brass barrel and walnut full stock, c1780, 40in (101.5cm) long.
£900–1,000 GMI

A Harper Ferry .69 model 1816 flintlock musket, inscribed 'AD', 'JPC', and 'AT', marked, America, dated 1819, barrel 41¾in (106cm) long.
£1,750–2,100 JDJ

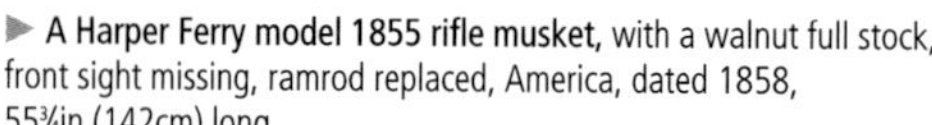

▶ **A Harper Ferry model 1855 rifle musket,** with a walnut full stock, front sight missing, ramrod replaced, America, dated 1858, 55¾in (142cm) long.
£950–1,100 NOA

A .58 Springfield model 1863 musket, the stock with cartouches inscribed 'HGH' and 'ESA', ramrod replaced, America, dated 1863, 40in (101.5cm) long, with associated bayonet and scabbard.

£1,550–1,850 JDJ

A .50 model 1863 rifle musket, by E. Robinson, America, New York, dated 1864, barrel 40in (101.5cm) long.

£500–600 JDJ

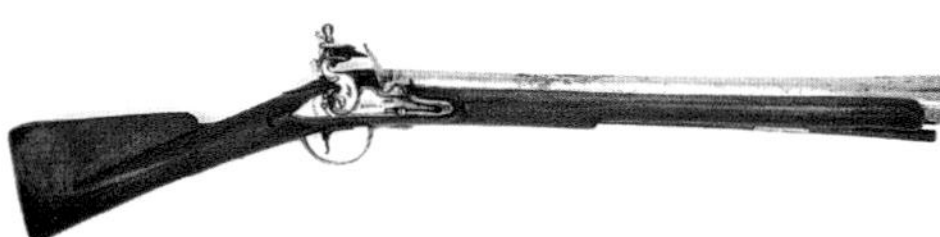

A flintlock sea service musketoon, by Brooks, the iron barrel with Ordnance view, with figured walnut full stock and brass mounts, brass and wood ramrod, stamped 'Tower', c1790, barrel 40½in (103cm) long.

£4,600–5,500 TDM

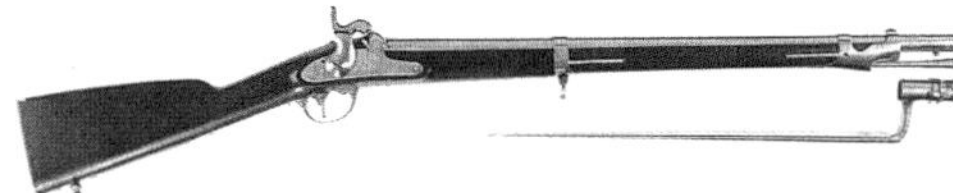

A .69 Springfield musketoon, with modified bayonet, America, dated 1853 and 1854, barrel 26in (66cm) long.

£2,000–2,400 JDJ

A ship-to-shore firing percussion gun, with walnut full stock, c1860, 23in (58.5cm) long.

£450–500 GMI

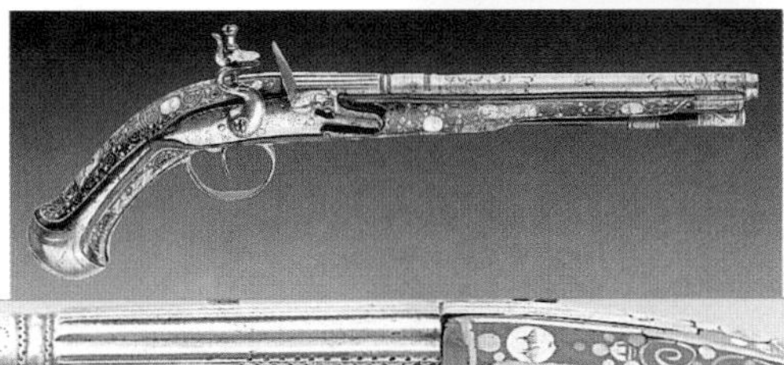

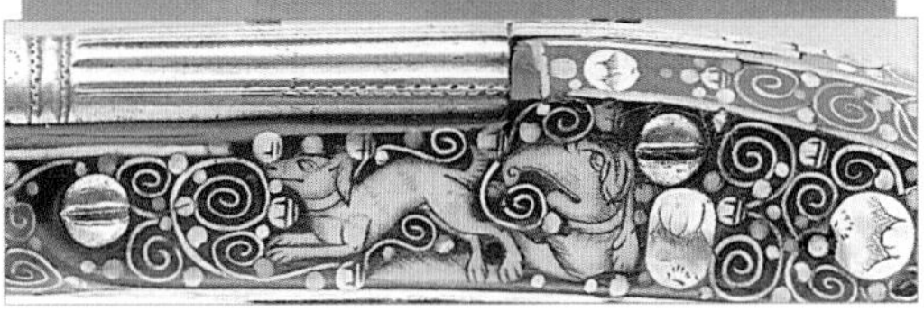

A pair of flintlock pistols, the walnut full stocks inlaid with mother-of-pearl dogs, mythical creatures and game, the wooden ramrods with bone tips, one stock damaged, Bohemia, 1670–80, 17¼in (44cm) long.

£9,800–11,700 Herm

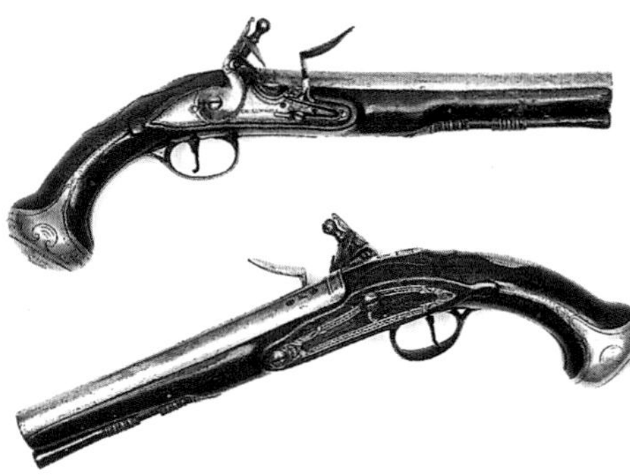

A pair of .20 flintlock holster pistols, by Collumbell, London, each with a walnut full stock and brass mounts, with baluster ramrod pipes and engraved escutcheons, c1740, 13½in (34cm) long.

£1,300–1,550 WAL

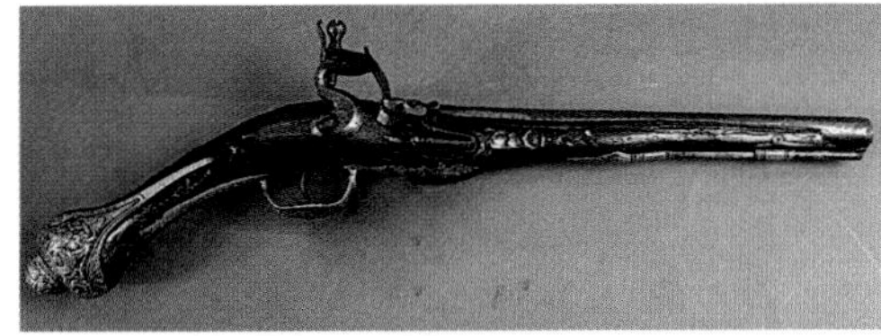

A flintlock pistol, with a steel barrel and carved walnut full stock, with a cast-brass pommel, damaged, losses, France, 18thC, 20½in (52cm) long.

£350–420 CAG

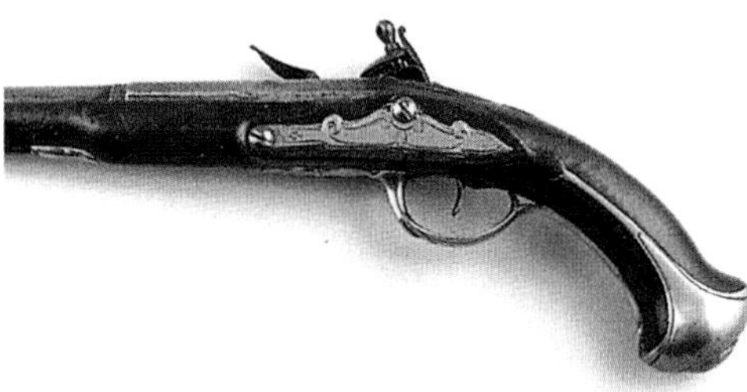

A flintlock pistol, with steel barrel and walnut full stock, with brass mounts, 18thC, 17in (43cm) long.

£640–760 WW

A cannon barrel flintlock pistol, by Henshaw, Cambridge, engraved with a garniture of arms, the slab-sided butt with silver wire inlay and grotesque mask butt cap, c1760, 13in (33cm) long.

£1,100–1,250 MDL

► **A pair of pistols,** by T. Hughes, Cork, with brass barrels and walnut full stocks, the silver-plated trigger guards with acorn finials and grotesque mask butt caps, marked, Ireland, 18thC, 14in (35.5cm) long.

£3,200–3,800 MEA

A Tower sea service pistol, with Board of Ordnance mark, shortened, 1760s, 16in (40.5cm) long.

£1,650–1,850 ⊞ TLA

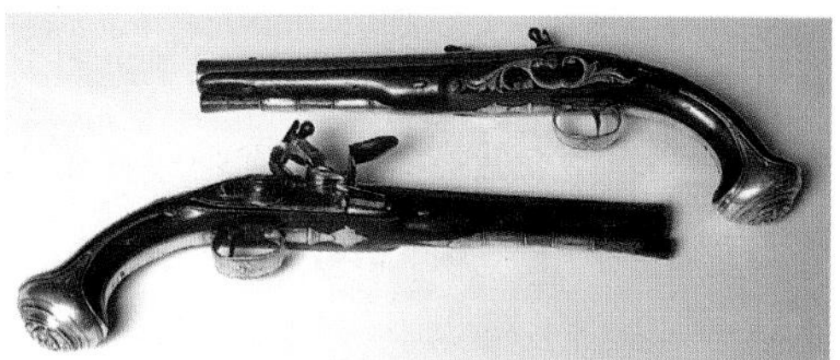

A pair of flintlock holster pistols, by John Twigg, with silver mounts by Jeremiah Ashley, London 1763, 14in (35.5cm) long.

£6,800–7,600 ⊞ WSA

A pair of flintlock pistols, with walnut full stocks and gold mounts depicting hunting scenes, Germany, c1770, 17¼in (44cm) long.

£3,100–3,450 ⊞ MDL

A .28 flintlock duelling pistol, by Wogdon, with walnut full stock and part-chequered butt, steel mounts and horn-tipped ramrod, c1775, 14in (35.5cm) long.

£1,900–2,250 WAL

A pair of flintlock pocket pistols, by Lamotte, with carved walnut full stocks and silver mounts, France, c1780, 7in (18cm) long.

£2,650–2,950 ⊞ ARB

A pair of percussion pistols, by H. W. Mortimer, with walnut full stocks and chequered butts, engraved steel mounts and trigger guards, one ramrod replaced, converted from flintlocks, c1790, in a later fitted oak case, 15in (38cm) wide.

£1,800–2,150 TDM

◀ **A pair of officer's flintlock pistols,** by J. Scudamore, with accessories, c1800, in a fitted case, 14in (35.5cm) wide.

£7,200–8,000 ⊞ Q&C

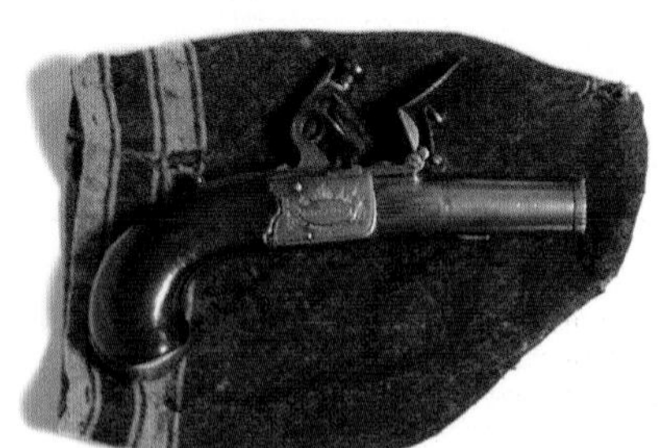

A box flintlock pistol, by Twigg, with silver butt plate, c1805, 6in (15cm) long, with original bag.

£720–800 ⊞ ARB

A cavalry pistol, France, year XIII (1809), 14in (35.5cm) long.

£940–1,050 ⊞ TLA

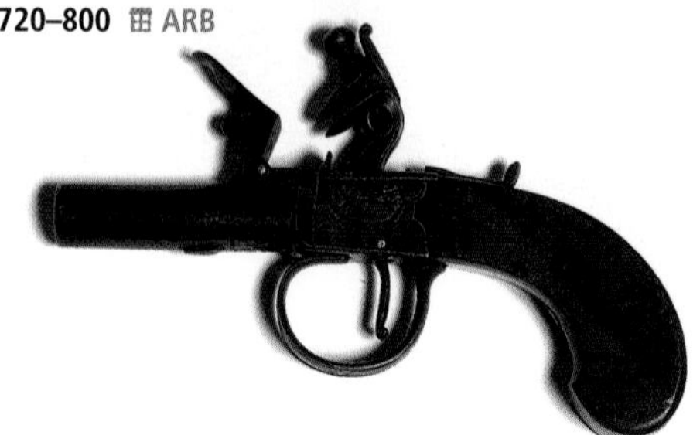

A flintlock muff pistol, by H. Nock, c1810, 5in (12.5cm) long.

£610–680 ⊞ GV

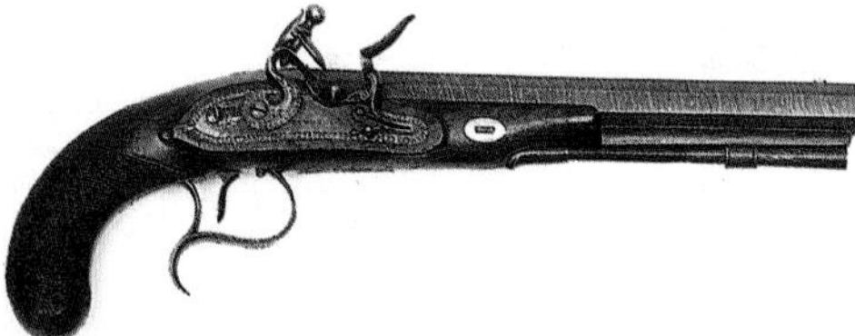

◀ **A pair of flintlock duelling pistols,** by Symonds, Blandford, with walnut half stocks, chequered butts and horn fore-end caps, steel spurred trigger guards and ramrods with screw-off powder measures, restored, c1810, 15in (38cm) long.

£3,900–4,650 WAL

A double-barrel flintlock pistol, by Hughes, c1815, 9in (23cm) long.

£1,350–1,500 GV

A pair of flintlock pocket pistols, by Wood, York, with walnut butts and silver escutcheons, c1815, 7in (18cm) long.

£1,650–1,850 ARB

◀ **A pair of flintlock overcoat pistols,** by Hutchinson, Dublin, with engraved silver butt caps, trigger guards and escutcheons, Ireland, c1820, 11in (28cm) long.

£3,100–3,450 MDL

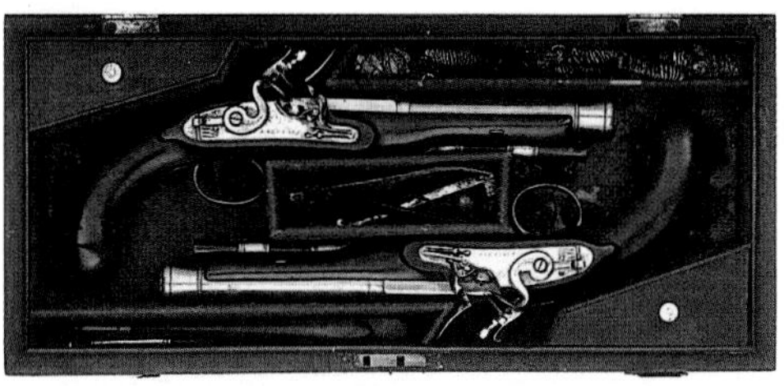

A pair of flintlock blunderbuss pistols, by Sargeant, Abergavenny, each with three-stage brass barrel belled at muzzle, walnut full stocks, engraved brass trigger guards and moulded ramrod pipes, with horn-tipped ramrod, Wales, c1820, in a fitted mahogany case with some accessories, 13½in (34.5cm) wide.

£6,000–7,200 TDM

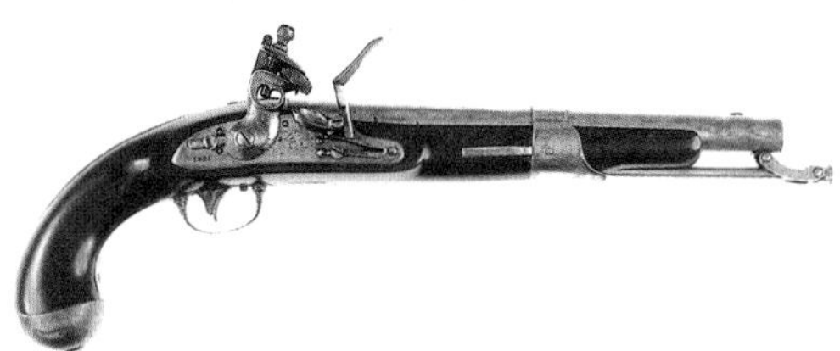

A North model 1819 martial pistol, with 'ET' cartouche, reconverted, slight damage, ramrod replaced, America, dated 1821, 10in (25.5cm) long.

£620–740 JDJ

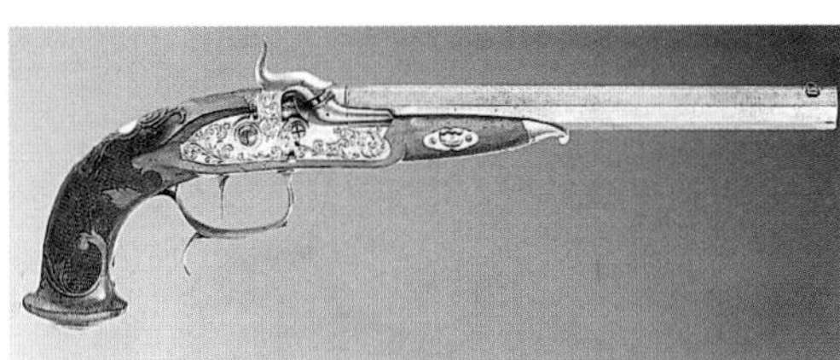

A pair of percussion pistols, by Bartolomaeus Joseph Kuchenreuter, with patent breechblocks, inset front sights, walnut half stocks, chequered butts, upper barrels signed in silver and numbered '1' and '2' respectively, Germany, c1830, 15¾in (40cm) long.

£3,200–3,800 Herm

A flintlock target pistol, by Jean Baptiste Missilieur, with saw-handle half stock, barrel engraved with maker's name and with silver inlet Vienne proof mark, France, c1830, 16¾in (42.5cm) long.

£1,550–1,750 MDL

A pair of flintlock travelling pistols, by Coland, Chelmsford, with silver masks, folding triggers and safety slides, c1830, 6in (15cm) long.

£1,900–2,150 ARB

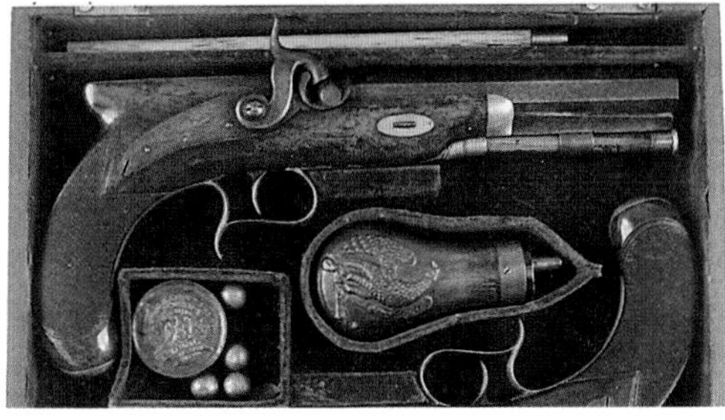

A pair of travelling pistols, by W. T. Howell & Co, Philadelphia, lockplates marked with maker's name, America, mid-19thC, barrels 6½in (15.5cm) long, in a velvet-lined fitted case.

£2,800–3,350 JDJ

▶ **A flintlock pistol,** by Drury & Wilde, with walnut full stock, ramrod and bayonet, 19thC, 14in (35.5cm) long.

£870–1,050 PBA

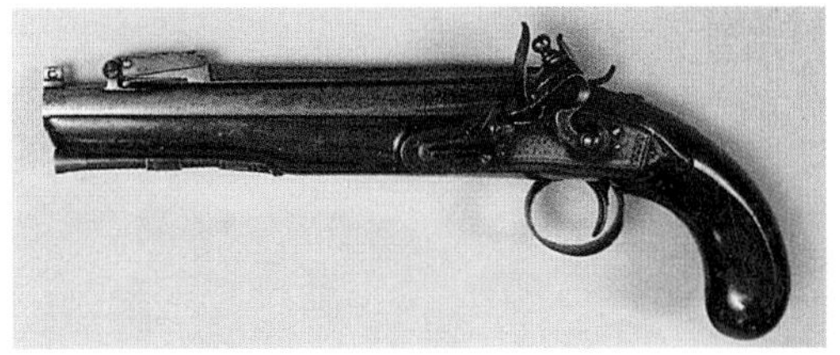

A Tower flintlock Customs and Excise pistol, c1840, 9in (23cm) long.

£450–500 ⊞ GMI

A pair of belt pistols, by Smith, London, restored, 1840–60, barrels 8in (20.5cm) long.

£900–1,000 ⊞ SPA

A Garrett confederate pistol, by A. H. Waters & Co, engraved with maker's name, America, dated 1852, barrels 8½in (21.5cm) long.

£2,950–3,500 JDJ

A Victorian percussion cap pistol, the brass fittings with lanyard ring and belt clip, Tower lock stamped with VR cypher and dated 1844, 11in (28cm) long.

£370–440 G(L)

◀ **A percussion punt gun,** smoothbore, muzzle loading, with walnut stock, Birmingham proof marks, late 19thC, barrel 84in (213.5cm) long.

£680–810 AG

A seven-barrelled flintlock pepperbox revolver, by J. H. Bolton, Birmingham, c1800, 9in (23cm) long.

£8,900–9,900 ⊞ WSA

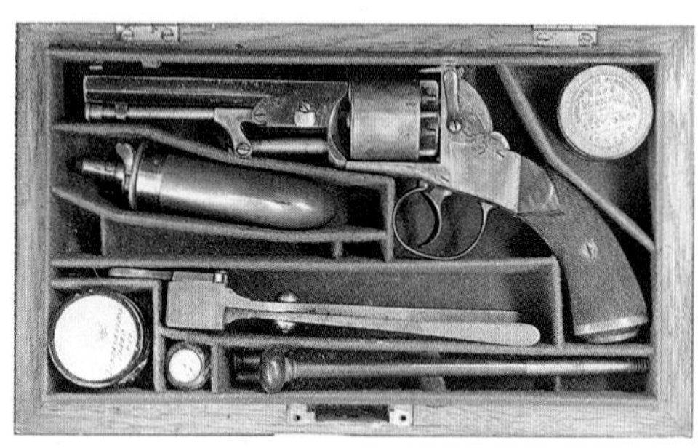

An 80-bore six-shot percussion revolver, by Moore & Harris, Birmingham, with self-cocking wedge frame, chequered walnut grip, c1845, barrel 4¾in (12cm) long, in a fitted oak case with accessories.

£2,350–2,800 Hal

◀ **A six-shot percussion pepperbox revolver,** by George and John Deane, London, with case-hardened self-cocking action, chequered walnut butt with scroll-engraved butt cap, 1846–51, 9in (23cm) long, in original brass-bound mahogany fitted case and accessories.

£2,800–3,350 TDM

George and John Deane were appointed gunsmiths to Prince Albert in 1848 and exhibited an electroplated silver revolving pistol at the Great Exhibition of 1851. They were succeeded at the same address by Deane, Adams & Deane.

▶ **A Colt model 1849 New York percussion pistol,** No. 97561, traces of original silver finish, America, 1854, 8¾in (22cm) long.

£380–450 TDM

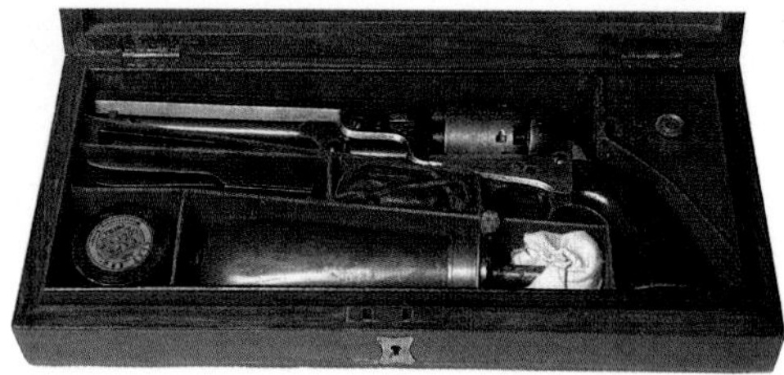

A Colt Hartford London Navy revolver, No. 37498, c1855, in a fitted case, 14in (35.5cm) long.

£5,800–6,500 WSA

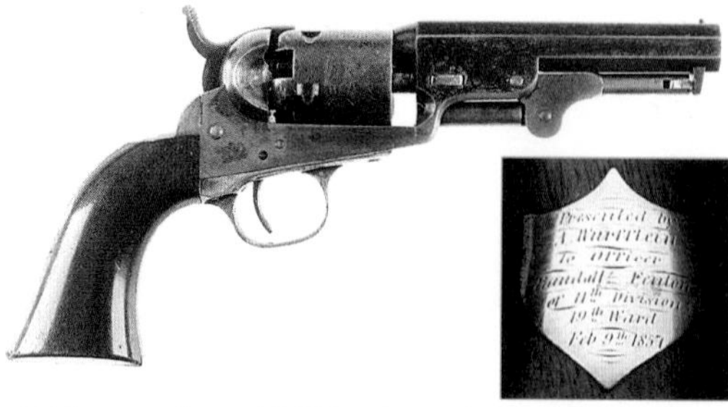

A Colt presentation model 1849 pocket revolver, No. 130360, with 4in octagonal barrel, brass pin-front sight, silver-plated grip and frame, walnut grip with presentation inscription 'A. Wurfflein, to officer Randall Fenton of 11th Division, 19th Ward, Feb 9th 1857', America, mid-19thC.

£3,900–4,650 JDJ

Andrew Wurfflein is listed as a maker of percussion derringers and double-barrelled shotguns in Philadelphia, Pa, between 1835 and 1860. He was the father of William, who was the proprietor of the famous W. Wurfflein Gun Company.

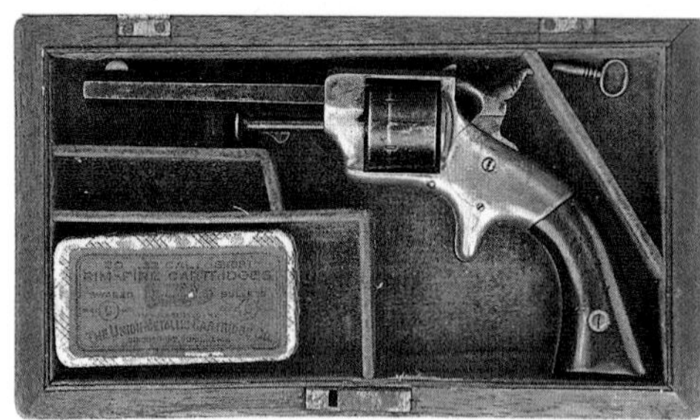

A Remington-Beals .36 six-shot percussion Navy revolver, with single-winged cylinder pin, two walnut grips with retaining screw, trigger guard inscribed 'G. W. Burke', America, 1860s, barrel 7½in (19cm) long.

£1,600–1,900 JDJ

A 54-bore five-shot percussion revolver, by Deane, Adams & Deane, No. 8608R, with self-cocking action, chequered butt with engraved trap, Adams patent rammer, barrel shortened, c1855, barrel 3¾in (9.5cm), in a fitted oak case with accessories.

£1,300–1,550 Hal

A Manhattan five-shot percussion Navy-type revolver, with chased cylinder and walnut grips, barrel signed 'Manhattan Fire Arms Co, Newark, NJ', America, mid-19thC, 10¼in (26cm) long, with a brass-mounted copper flask.

£700–840 N

The Manhattan Navy-type revolver was made between 1859 and 1868, and bore close resemblance to the Colt model 1851 Navy and the Colt 1849 pocket revolver. A number of these guns were privately purchased and carried by officers and men of both the army and navy during the American Civil War. The Manhattan Co was founded in 1856 and moved to Newark, New Jersey, in 1859. The company was in production for only 20 years and in total 150,000 guns of various calibre and function were produced.

◄ **A revolver,** by E. A. Prescott, with brass frame, America, c1860, barrel 4in (10cm) long, in a fitted wood case with cartridges.

£430–510 JDJ

A .34 six-shot needle-fire revolver, by F. Dreyse, Sömmerda, No. 593, frame with silver inlay, chequered grip, Germany, c1860, 11½in (29cm) long.

£4,450–5,300 Herm

This is a very early type with a low serial number. Only 13,000 revolvers of this type, including civil and military models, were made .

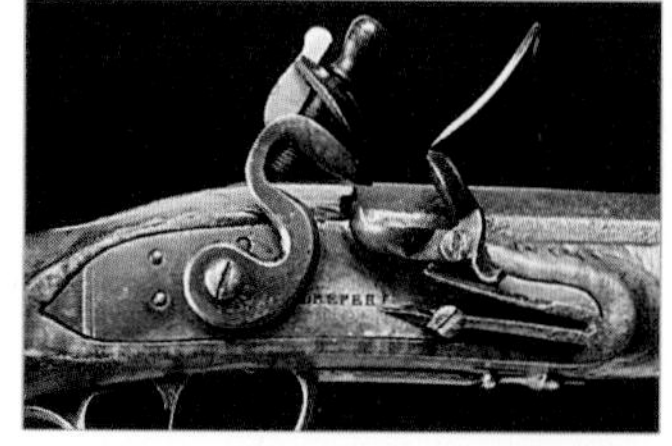

A Kentucky-style .54 flintlock smoothbore rifle, lock plate stamped 'Dreppert', barrel inscribed 'M. Fordney', America, mid-19thC, barrel 48in (122cm) long.

£3,900–4,650 JDJ

Fordney appears on the tax list of Lancaster City in 1805 and was a gunsmith until about 1846 when he was murdered by a neighbour.

A .73 rifle, by Samuel Shillito & Son, rear sight altered, America, mid-19thC, barrel 30in (76cm) long.

£1,200–1,400 JDJ

Samuel Shillito worked in South Central Pa from 1819 until his death in 1852; the firm only operated from 1850 to 1852.

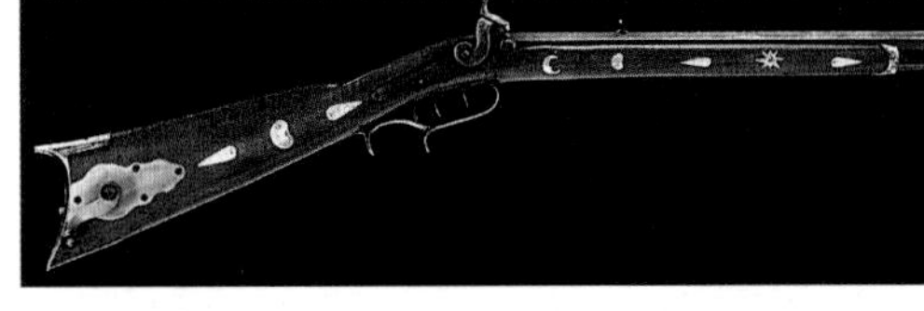

A percussion plains rifle, with silver foresight, double set trigger, figured hardwood half stock applied with engraved silver plaques, butt with 'coffee grinder' for black powder, later ramrod, America, c1840, barrel 37½in (95.5cm) long.

£1,200–1,400 TDM

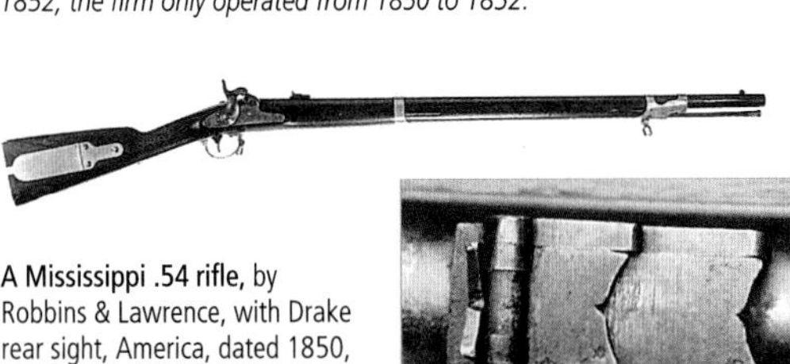

A Mississippi .54 rifle, by Robbins & Lawrence, with Drake rear sight, America, dated 1850, barrel 33in (84cm) long.

£5,300–6,300 JDJ

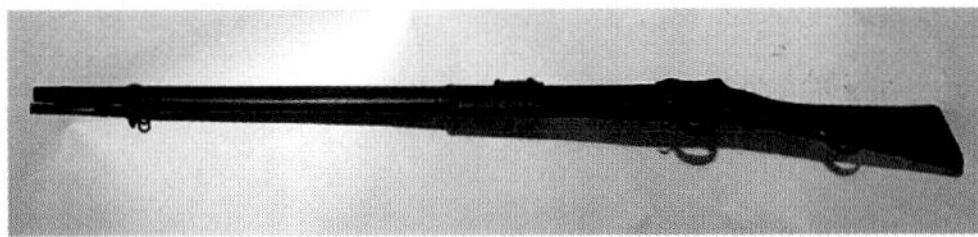

A Henry Mark IV Long Lever .577 military rifle, by Henry Martini, c1887, 50in (127cm) long.

£510–570 PASM

A Springfield model 1892 Krag rifle, stock with 1896 conversion with filled ramrod channel, America, dated 1894, barrel 30in (76cm) long.

£780–930 JDJ

◄ **A .23 flintlock smoothbore wall gun,** wooden half stock, Germany, c1700, 67¼in (171cm) long.

£2,350–2,800 Herm

POLEARMS

A halberd, on a wooden haft fitted with moulded iron shoe, Italy, probably Venice, c1600, head 43in (109cm) long.

£1,600–1,900 TDM

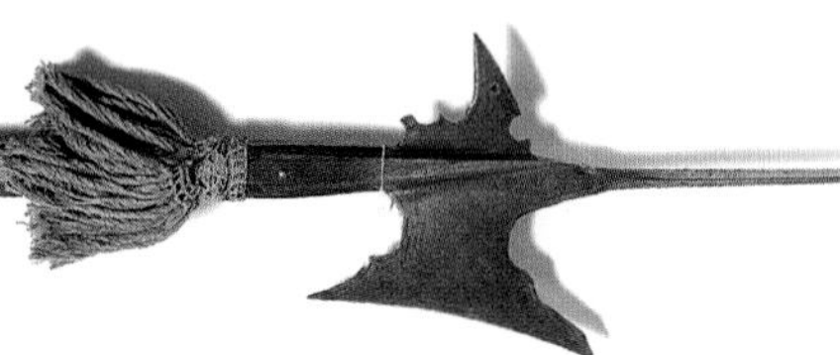

A forged steel halberd, made for the Graf von Stolberg, with engraved crest, Germany, early 17thC, 96in (244cm) long.

£3,400–3,800 ARB

There are three basic types of halberd: the standard halberd is a flat axe with a long spike at the front; the Austrian halberd has a finer, longer spike, the axe blade is in the shape of a crescent moon, the blade is the concave edge and is curved inwards; the German halberd has a knife-like spike and the axe is small, this halberd also has a conclave blade but the arc is a half circle. All three have a small hook at the rear end of the axe blade.

A forged steel halberd, made for the Guard of Queen Isabella II, Spain, dated 1845, 87in (221cm) long.

£2,250–2,500 ARB

A gilt-iron ceremonial mace, c1800, 32in (78.5cm) long.

£1,800–2,000 GV

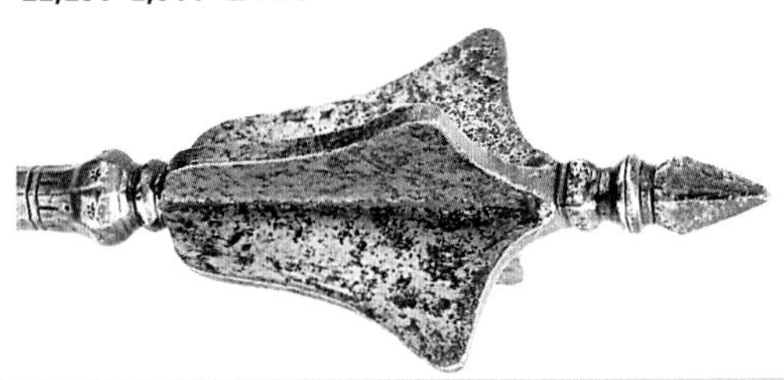

A Gothic iron mace, the head with four flanges, Germany, 1450–1500, 22in (56cm) long.

£2,700–3,200 Herm

A state partisan of the Yeoman of the Guard, the head with remains of engraved decoration of crowned Royal Arms and cypher GR, on a wooden haft, 1820–30, head 34½in (86.5cm) long.

£1,000–1,200 TDM

MILITARIA

BADGES & PLATES

A Semenovsky Regiment of the Imperial Guard silver and enamel badge, screw-backed, marked, Russia, St Petersburg, 1908–17, 2in (5cm) high.

£3,000–3,600 DNW

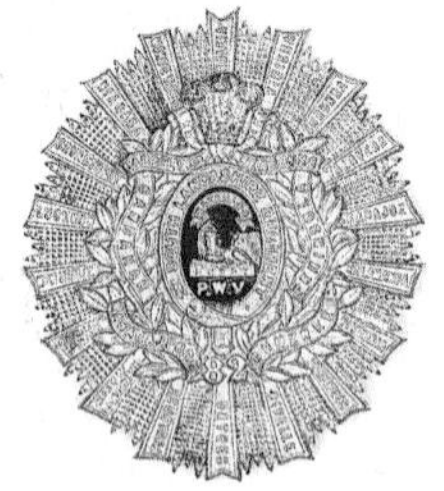

A 2nd Battalion The South Lancashire Regiment gilt and silver-plated colour belt badge, with Sphinx and Egypt within a scroll marked 'Waterloo' and 'PWV', rays bearing battle honours to South Africa, 1899–1902, 7½in (19cm) high.

£210–250 WAL

A 5th (Royal Irish) Lancers officer's gilt and silver-plated lance cap plate, with Royal Arms and supporters, four battle honours 'Blenheim' to 'Malplaquet', 19thC.

£710–850 WAL

A County Carlow Rifles officer's cross belt plate, Ireland, c1880, 4in (10cm) high.

£450–500 Q&C

A Waterford Artillery gilt-metal helmet badge, with Royal cipher and cannon, Ireland, 19thC, 4in (10cm) high.

£630–750 MEA

A Victorian Ordnance Stores Corps officer's gilt helmet plate, with silver-plated monogram, minor dents.

£420–500 WAL

A 10th County of London Battalion (Hackney) officer's full dress helmet plate, KC gilt star with silver title scroll, 1912–20.

£360–420 DNW

◄ **A Victorian 7th (the Princess Royal's) Dragoon Guards officer's gilt and silver-plated undress sabretache badge,** in the form of an 1869 pattern shako plate.

£550–660 WAL

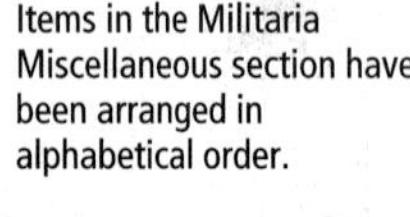

Items in the Militaria Miscellaneous section have been arranged in alphabetical order.

► **A Royal Marine Light Infantry officer's gilt shako plate,** with silver overlays, 1866–78.

£960–1,150 DNW

A brass regimental shoulder belt plate, 'Fingaul', engraved with crowned heart and inscription, Ireland, 18thC, 2½in (6.5cm) high.

£810–970 MEA

An Ouse & Derwent Volunteers (Yorkshire) officer's gilt shoulder belt plate, with silver mount, impressed maker's mark 'Linwood', 1803–08.

£650–770 DNW

COSTUME

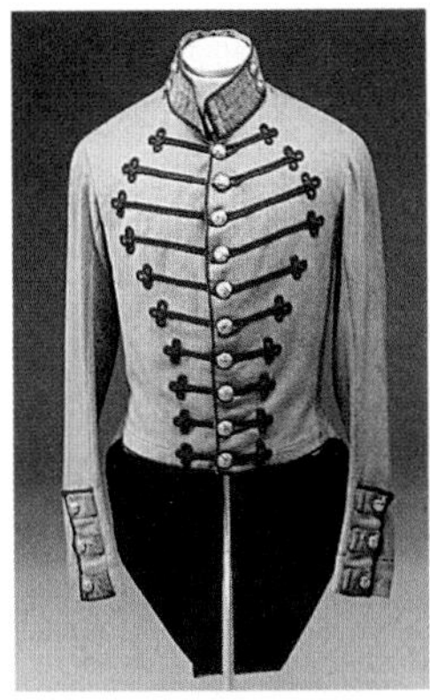

An American Militia Artillery Company officer's coatee, with US eagle 'A' cuff buttons, the collar with gold bullion facings, minor damage, America, c1845.

£1,450–1,700 JDJ

A regulation coatee and bicorn hat, owned by Lieutenant-General Alexander Graham Stirling, with post-1812 aiguillette, 1820–30.

£3,200–3,800 TDM

A Union Civil War artillery wool shell jacket, with plaid lining, America, early 1860s.

£1,700–2,000 JDJ

A gentleman's military wool jacket, with wool braid and brass buttons, homespun wool lining, name in right sleeve, some period repairs, America, 1860s.

£1,750–2,100 WHIT

A Finnish Sharpshooter Battalion Lieutenant-Colonel's pair of epaulettes, c1860.

£1,300–1,550 BUK(F)

◄ **A Confederate veteran's wool frock coat,** America, 1875–1925.

£980–1,150 JDJ

► **A mantle,** bearing the Order of St Patrick for King Ernst August of Hanover, early 19thC.

£3,900–4,650 S(Han)

Ex-Royal House of Hanover sale. For further information on this sale please see p205.

A Victorian Yorkshire Dragoons officer's full dress cloth pouch, with silver lace border and tin liner, minor wear.

£420–500 WAL

A Prince of Wales' Own Royal Wiltshire Yeomanry officer's sabretache, c1860, 13in (33cm) high.

£540–600 GMI

◄ **A Victorian Sherwood Rangers Yeomanry officer's leather full dress flap pouch,** with central St. Edward's crown, bottom stud, side mounts and rings missing, patent to reverse.

£210–250 DNW

A George III army officer's wool tunic, with brocade trim and brass buttons, epaulettes missing, minor wear.

£910–1,050 WAD

HELMETS & HEADDRESSES

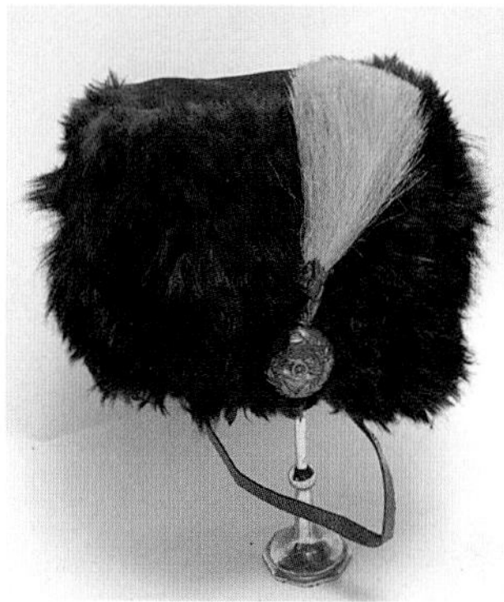

A Royal Horse Artillery **busby,** c1900.

£150–170 GMI

A Civil War enlisted **forage cap,** minor wear and section of headband missing, America, early 1860s.

£3,750–4,500 JDJ

A Cromwellian triple bar **lobster-tail helmet,** ear flaps missing, minor dents.

£1,650–1,950 WAL

A 1st West Yorkshire Yeomanry Cavalry **officer's silver-plated full dress helmet,** replacement plate, 1876–97.

£1,800–2,150 DNW

A Royal Berkshire Yeomanry **white metal and gilt helmet,** c1880.

£850–950 GMI

A **cavalry helmet,** with velvet-covered cork body, horse-hair plume, maker's logo to leather sweatband, America, c1880, 12in (30.5cm) high.

£420–470 MDL

◄ An **officer's wool kepi,** with gold bullion decoration and bullion cord chinstrap with Indian war period eagle buttons, marked quilted liner, minor damage, America, 1866–90.

£300–360 JDJ

A 17th Lancers **officer's foul weather lance cap,** by Sanderson & Sons, London, c1870, 8in (20.5cm) high.

£3,550–3,950 MDL

► An **officer's leather *Picklehaube*,** with brass spike and spread eagle mount, Germany, 1914–18, 11in (28cm) high.

£300–360 G(L)

◄ A Napoleonic 100th Foot Regiment **other ranks' shako,** with felt body and leather top, minor wear, France.

£2,250–2,700 WAL

ORDERS & MEDALS

A Military General Service medal, awarded to Tier Isioriwa, with one clasp, Chateauguay, 1793–1814.

£4,700–5,600 DNW

A Naval General Service medal, awarded to James MacDonald, with clasp 1st June 1794.

£3,600–4,000 Q&C

James McDonald served on HMS Royal Sovereign, *flagship of Admiral Lord Howe. Only four medals to officers and 22 other ranks were awarded.*

A Royal Order of Merit of St Michael, Bavaria, gold and silver breast star of the Grand Cross, with chiselled motto, Germany, 1837–1918, 3¼in (8.5cm) diam.

£1,550–1,850 Herm

◄ **A Crimea medal,** awarded to Private Henry Campbell, 2nd Dragoons, with one clasp, 1854–56.

£6,400–7,700 DNW

Private Henry Campbell was killed in action at Balaklava on 25 October 1854, one of only two fatalities suffered by the Scots Greys in this historic action. Indeed, the entire Heavy Brigade had only nine men killed in action at Balaklava. He is also entitled to the clasp for Sebastopol which would have been issued separately as a loose clasp.

A group of three, awarded to Lieutenant W. R. Boulton, Royal Navy: Baltic 1854–55, Crimea 1854–56, one clasp Sebastopol, Turkish Crimea 1855, British issue.

£590–700 DNW

These medals were presented personally to Lieutenant Boulton by Queen Victoria in St James's Park on 18 May 1855.

A second Anglo-China war medal, awarded to Lieutenant R. V. Dillon, The Royal Artillery, with one clasp Canton 1857.

£400–480 MAL(O)

A Canada General Service medal, awarded to Private W. J. Munshaw, 1st Battalion, with one clasp Fenian Raid 1866 bar.

£310–370 WAD

A South Africa medal, awarded to Sergeant W. Lyne, F. A. Military Police, with clasp 1877–8–9.

£320–380 JBe

An Order of St Andrew silver, silver-gilt and enamel breast star, by Keibel, St Petersburg, minor damage, Russian, marks for 1896–1908.

£5,900–7,000 DNW

◄ **A group of eleven,** awarded to William Brereton: Distinguished Conduct Medal; British Empire Medal civil division; 1914–15 Star; British War and Victory Medals; 1939–45 Star; Africa Star; Defence Medal; War Medal 1939–45; Police Long Service and Good Conduct Medal; Russian Cross of St George, 4th Class.

£4,700–5,600 Bea

A group of seven, awarded to Quarter-Master and Lieutenant J. Clay, Leicestershire Regiment, late Grenadier Guards: Military Cross, GVR; Queen's South Africa 1899–1902, three clasps, Cape Colony, Transvaal, Wittebergen; King's South Africa 1901–02, two clasps, South Africa 1901, South Africa 1902; 1914–15 Star; British War and Victory Medals; Russian Medal of St George for Bravery, 1st Class, gold.

£4,450–5,300 DNW

Lieutenant Clay was decorated for his bravery on the Somme as a Company Sergeant-Major.

A group of five, awarded to Captain F. W. Gransmore, Welch Regiment: George V Military Cross; 1914–15 Star; 1914–18 British War and Victory medals; India General Service medal with clasp Waziristan 1921–24; with miniatures, including MID spray.

£3,000–3,600 JBe

A group of seven, awarded to E. Cains: Distinguished Conduct medal; 1914–15 Star; 1914–18 British War and Victory medals; India General Service medal with bar Waziristan 1919–21; General Service medal; George V Long Service and Good Conduct medal.

£1,050–1,250 L

A group of five, awarded to Lieutenant-Colonel Stephen John Guest Gornall, Loyal Regiment (North Lancashire): General Service medal 1918–62, one clasp Palestine with MiD oak leaf; 1939–45 and Italy Stars; Defence and War medals, latter with MiD oak leaf, mounted for wearing.

£850–1,000 WW

A group of four, awarded to Dvr-A.Bmbr M. Casey, 77/Bde R.F.A., Military Medal, George V first type; 1914 Star; British War and Victory medals.

£410–490 WAL

A group of four, awarded to Sergeant J. T. Hollis, ASC: 1914–18 British War and Victory medals; Victory medal; 1914–15 Star; Queen's South Africa Medal with clasps, Modder River and Belmont.

£280–330 DMC

Further reading

Interested in campaign medals?
See our *Miller's Collectables Price Guides*

A group of three, awarded to Private H. Pike, 3rd Battalion Grenadier Guards: Military Medal, British War and Victory medals, 1914–15.

£630–700 Q&C

A group of four, awarded to Sergeant W. Brueton, 2nd Lancashire Fusiliers: Distinguished Conduct Medal; 1914 Star (with Mentioned in Dispatches dated 8 October 1914); War and Victory medals, with photographs, newspaper cutting and leather dispatch case.

£3,000–3,600 CAG

A George V Military medal with bar, awarded to Private C. E. Cornwell, 8th Suffolk Regiment.

£880–1,050 G(L)

A group of six, awarded to Lieutenant-Commander R. H. Bartlett, Royal Navy Volunteer Reserve: 1939–45 Star; Atlantic Star with clasp France and Germany; 1939–45 War medal with oak leaf clasp; Naval General Service medal with clasp for Minesweeping 1945–51; the Queen Elizabeth II Coronation medal; Royal Naval Volunteer Reserve Long Service and Good Conduct medal (George VI issue); with miniatures, a Royal Naval Reserve Decoration dated 1959, photographs and assorted memorabilia.

£590–700 MCA

POWDER FLASKS & HORNS

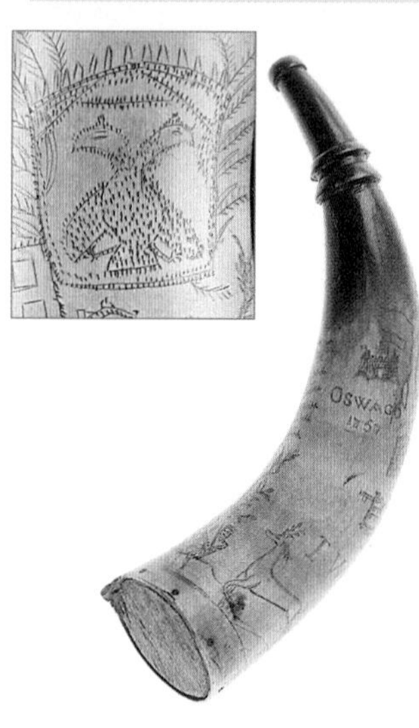

A Fort Oswago scrimshaw powder horn, with turned mouth and two neck rings, marked 'T. Wakefield/1760', America, 18thC, 12¾in (32.5cm) long.

£2,500–3,000 JDJ

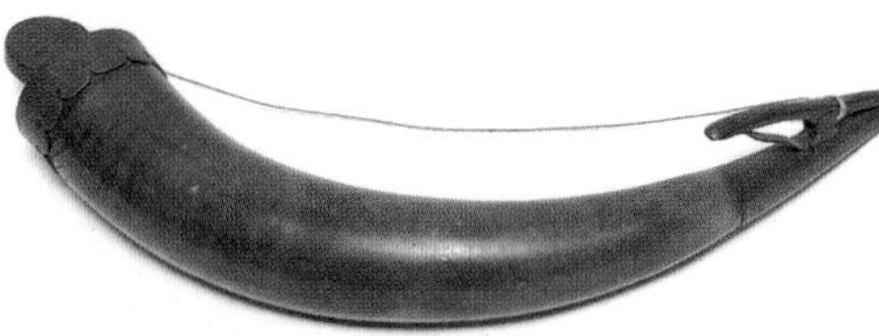

A powder horn, c1830, 16in (40.5cm) long.

£125–150 GMI

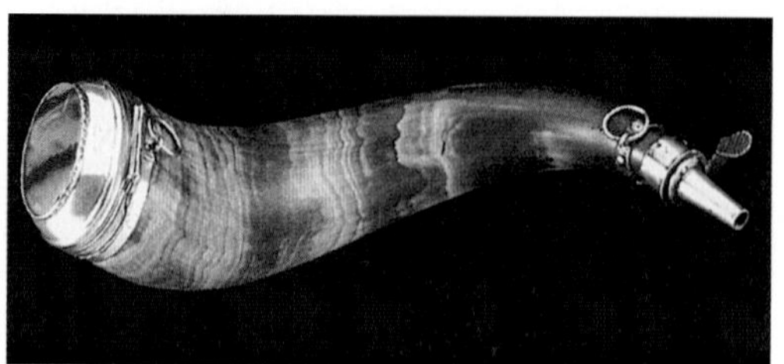

A cow horn powder flask, with silver mounts, quartz plaque, and suspension ring, cap missing, mounts rubbed, Scotland, 19thC, 11½in (29cm) long.

£1,600–1,900 TDM

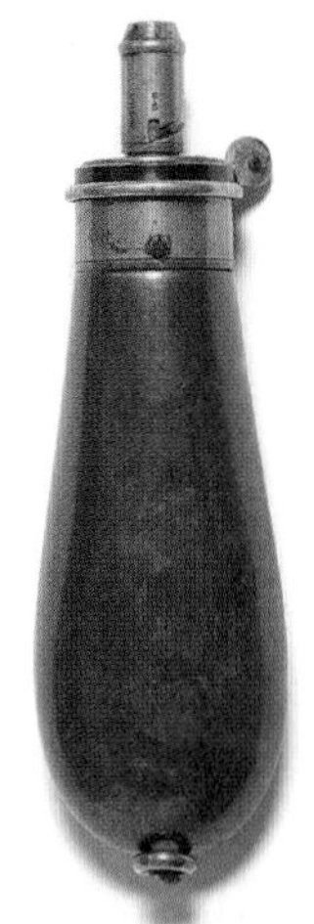

A brass and copper pistol powder flask, by J. Dixon & Son, c1860, 6in (15cm) long.

£360–400 ARB

MISCELLANEOUS

A Grand Army of the Republic drum, with the emblem of Massachusetts, America, 19thC, 17in (43cm) high.

£3,000–3,600 NAAW

LOCATE THE SOURCE

The source of each illustration in Miller's can be found by checking the code letters below each caption with the Key to Illustrations, pages 746–753.

A woolwork picture of The Soldier's Return, c1890, in original maple frame, 29 x 27in (73.5 x 68.5cm).

£2,950–3,250 WALP

A Bunting Company press-dyed US Navy boat flag, manufactured in accordance with the 1867 and 1870 patents, minor damage and repairs, 19thC, 74in (188cm) wide.

£1,850–2,200 JDJ

A wool patchwork quilt, 1880s, 95¾ x 98½in (243 x 250cm).

£5,700–6,400 AV

This quilt was made by Francis Brayley with the Devonshire Regiment in India, from materials used to make army uniforms. The Devonshire Regiment 2nd Battalion was stationed in Bengal throughout the 1880s, in the second Afghan War 1878–80 and Burma 1890–92.

A Civil War 1st Arkansas Regiment battle flag, minor wear, America, 33½ x 35in (85 x 89cm), with attached note.

£2,200–2,600 WAD

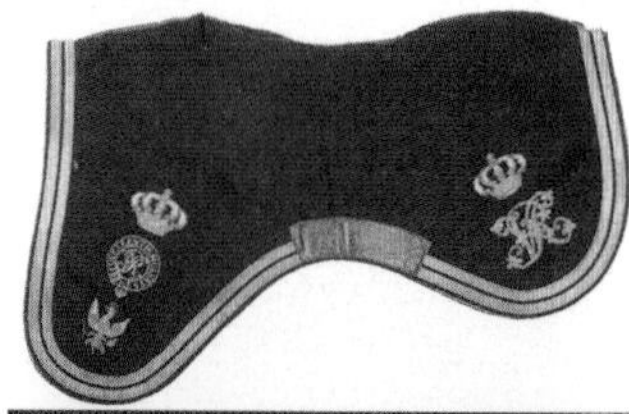

A Victorian 14th (King's) Hussars officer's cloth saddle blanket, with Guelphic crown and Prussian eagle, minor wear and faults.

£1,200–1,400 WAL

SPORT

BASEBALL

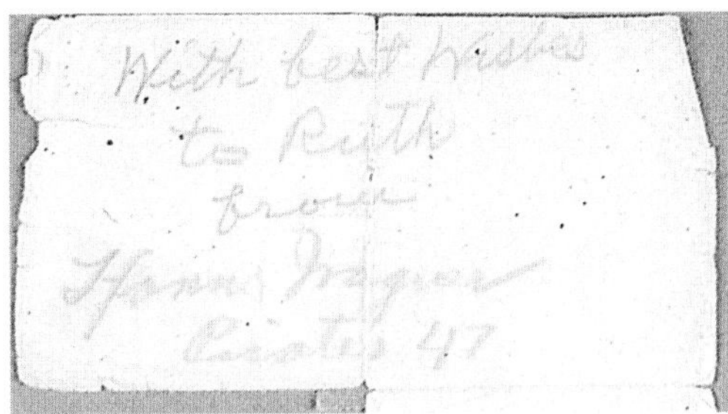

Honus Wagner, an autograph, on paper, incscribed 'to Ruth', c1947.
£300–360 JAA

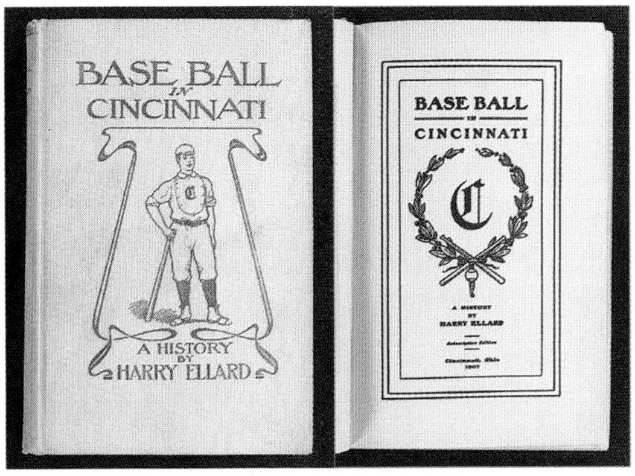

Harry Ellard, *Baseball in Cincinnati*, America, 1907, hardback.
£500–600 MN

A signed photograph of New York Giants National League Champions, 1937, 9¼ x 16½in (23.5 x 42cm).
£1,600–1,900 MN

A World Series Game 5 ticket, for Comiskey Park, Chicago, 1917.
£1,100–1,300 MN

BASKETBALL

◀ **A Spalding Detroit Pistons basketball,** signed, c1990.
£80–95 DuM

A metal and glass coin-operated basketball arcade game, restored, 1940s, 22in (56cm) high.
£420–500 MN

◀ **A Bob Houbregs cotton jersey,** worn at the Fort Wayne Zollner Pistons game, 1955–56.
£1,600–1,900 MN

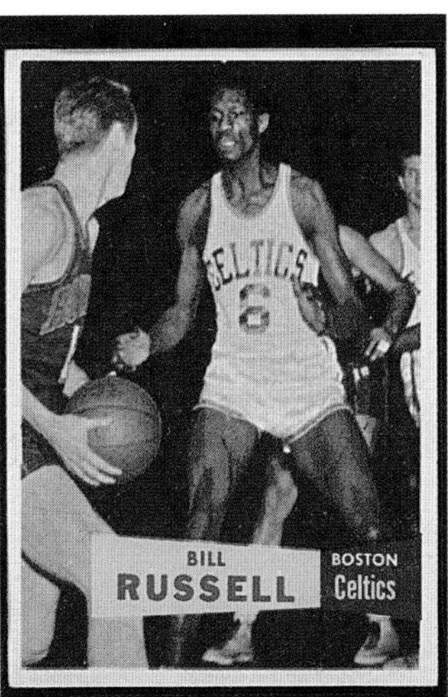

Topps bubble gum, a Bill Russell Rookie 1st trade card, No. 77, 1957–58.
£1,950–2,300 MN

This is one of the most important basketball cards ever made.

BILLIARDS

A Hobson & Sons military outfitters advertisement card, by Harry Payne, c1900, 5 x 4in (12.5 x 10cm).

£240–280 VS

A set of full-size billiard balls, with triangle, c1940s, in a mahogany case, 15in (38cm) wide.

£490–550 MSh

A mahogany billiards cabinet, with revolving carved fruitwood panel, the interior with a scoreboard, c1890, 77in (195.5cm) high.

£5,200–5,800 AGI

A mahogany billiard cue stand, with 18 cues and four bridges, 1850–75, 22in (56cm) diam.

£1,000–1,200 NOA

◄ **A mahogany billiard cue stand,** with cast-iron cue holder, c1890, 38in (96.5cm) high.

£850–950 GEO

► **Michael Phelan,** *The Game of Billiards*, fourth edition, America, New York, 1959, 8º.

£190–220 DW

An ivory and mahogany wall-mounted billiards scoreboard, maker's label 'Cox and Yeman, London', 1850–75, 39in (99cm) wide.

£760–910 NOA

A wall-mounted wooden billiards and snooker scoreboard, with a set of 15 composition snooker balls and extra brown ball, c1900, 40¼in (102cm) wide.

£4,500–5,400 S

A carved mahogany snooker table, with maker's plaque for Cox & Yeman, with later felt top, 1825–50, 140in (355.5cm) long.

£2,300–2,750 NOA

A walnut bar billiards table, with rosewood crossbanding, maker's stamp for Mechi, London, with bridge, cues and eight balls, 19thC, 95½in (242.5cm) open.

£440–520 DA

◄ **A mahogany snooker/dining table,** c1880, 92in (233.5cm) long.

£2,500–2,800 Fai

A mahogany quarter size billiards/dining table, with four leaves, inscribed 'Stevens & Son', early 20thC, 64½in (164cm) wide, with accessories.

£530–630 DN(BR)

BOXING

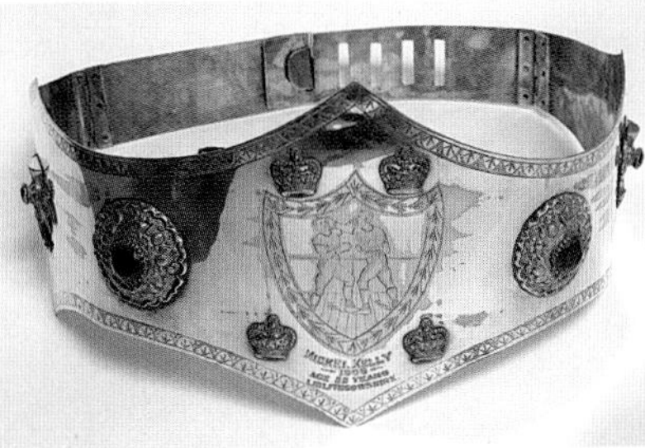

A silver-plated boxing belt, won by Mickel Kelly, set with cairngorms, with engraved inscription, 1905, 12in (30.5cm) diam.

£1,200–1,350 PCR

A 9ct gold and enamel Lonsdale Challenge belt, by Mappin & Webb, won by Tancy Lee in the featherweight division, with cloth backing and baize-lined leather carrying pouch, 1919, 33in (84cm) long.

£19,000–22,800 BUDD

► **Old Judge,** Boxers, set of 3 cigarette cards, 1886.

£4,200–5,000 MN

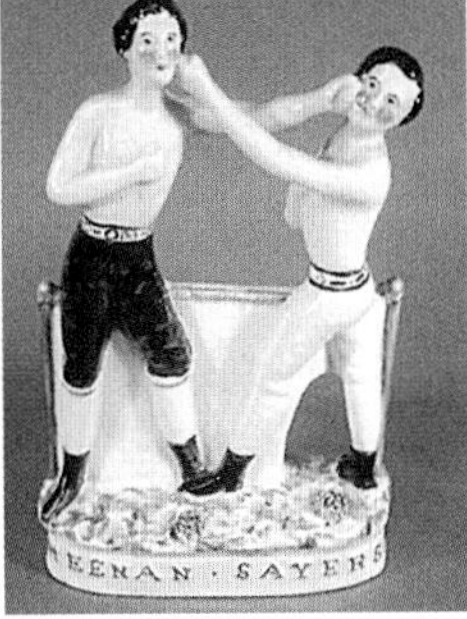

A Staffordshire pottery figural group of the bare-knuckle boxers Heenan and Sayers, 19thC, 8½in (21.5cm) high.

£175–210 PFK

The fight between John Carmel Heenan ('The Benicia Boy') of New York State and Tom Sayers of Pimlico, Champion of England, took place at Farnborough on 17 April 1860. Attended by 12,000 spectators, the fight lasted 37 rounds totalling two hours and six minutes. In the fourth round, Sayers dislocated his right arm and fought the remainder of the fight one-handed. The amazing fight ended in a draw, with each fighter awarded the champion's belt.

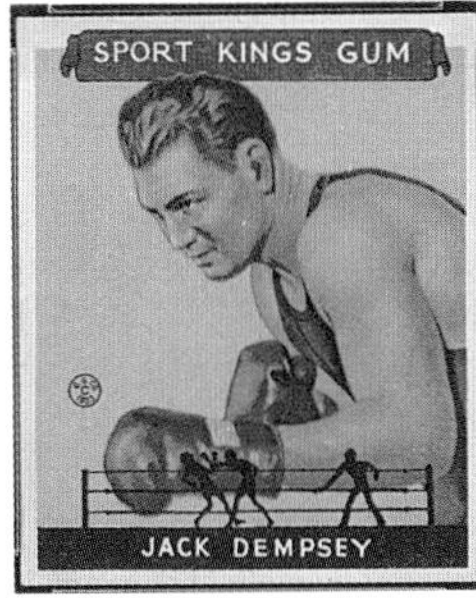

Goudey Gum, Sport Kings series, No. 17, Jack Dempsey card, 1933.

£980–1,150 MN

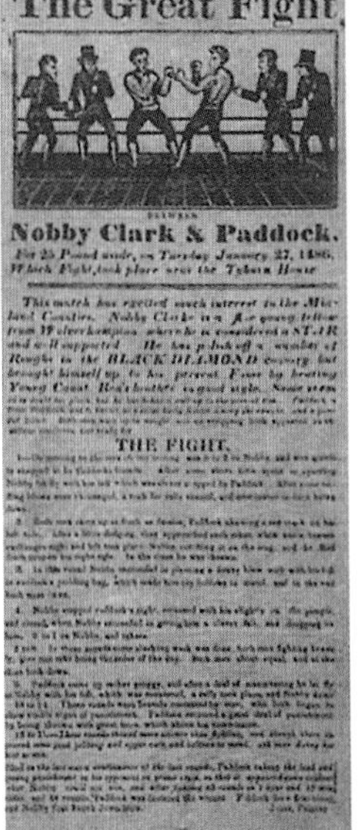

The Great Fight

Nobby Clark & Paddock.

THE FIGHT.

► **A printed handbill,** with an account of the Great Fight between Nobby Clark and Paddock at Tyburn House on 27 January 1846, 16½ x 8½in (42 x 21.5cm), framed.

£550–650 BUDD

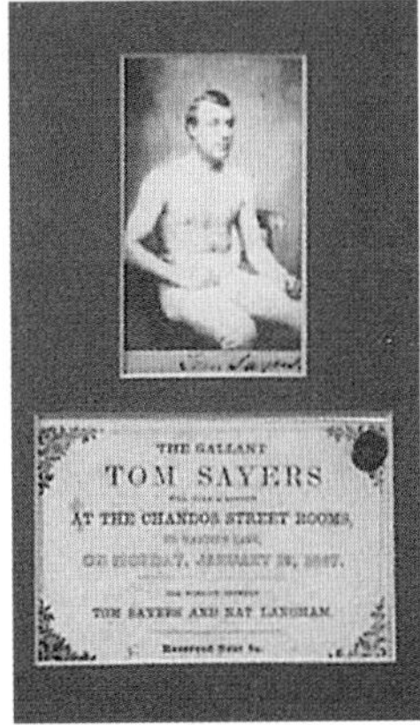

THE GALLANT

TOM SAYERS

AT THE CHANDOS STREET ROOMS,

ON MONDAY, JANUARY 19, 1857.

TOM SAYERS AND NAT LANGHAM.

Tom Sayers, a photograph mounted above a handbill advertising a Sayers v Langham benefit bout at the Chandos Street Rooms, London, 19 January 1857, 12½ x 9¼in (32 x 23.5cm), framed.

£420–500 BUDD

A cabinet card, with a photograph of John L. Sullivan, 1880s, 6½ x 4½in (16.5 x 11cm).

£750–900 MN

A cabinet card, with a photograph of a boxer, late 19thC, 6½ x 4½in (16.5 x 11.5cm).

£220–260 JAA

◄ **A World Heavyweight Championship souvenir programme and ticket stub,** for the first fight between Sonny Liston and Cassius Clay, with ticket stub, 25 February 1964, 9 x 12in (23 x 30.5cm).

£730–870 MN

EQUESTRIAN

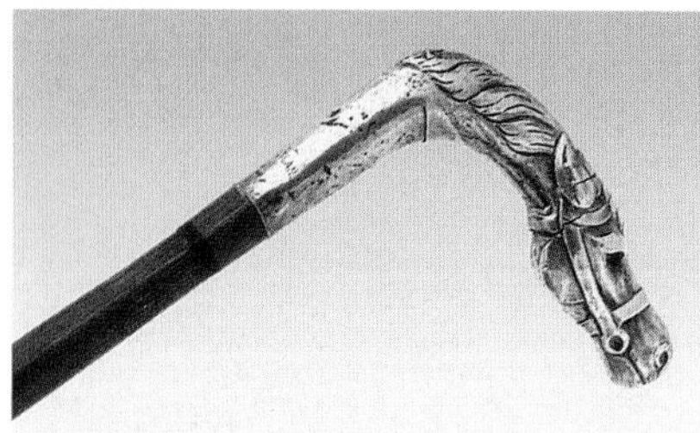

A silver-topped bamboo walking cane, the handle modelled as the head of a racehorse, with glass bead eyes, engraved 'W. Blair, Blisland', marks rubbed, c1900.

£300–360 Bea

A silver cigarette case, by The Goldsmiths & Silversmiths Co, the cover hand-painted with an enamel hunting scene, the interior engraved and dated 1928, case London 1927, 6in (15cm) wide.

£850–950 MSh

A pair of 15ct gold cufflinks, in the form of a hunting horn and riding crop, c1880, ½in (2cm) long.

£320–370 SPE

A pair of 14ct gold cufflinks, depicting a steeplechase scene, Continental, c1910.

£890–1,050 SK

◄ **A Victorian silver-plated novelty egg cruet,** each egg cup in the form of a riding boot, two spoons with whip handles resting on spurs, two spoons missing, 6¾in (17cm) high.

£370–430 SWO

A brass and copper hunting horn, by Köhler and Son, London, c1890, 10in (25.5cm) long.

£120–140 MSh

► **A ceramic and enamel portrait of Fred Archer,** by G. S. Furnivall, Stoke-on-Trent, with facsimile signature, c1887, in a velvet-lined frame, 16 x 12in (40.5 x 30.5cm).

£1,300–1,550 BUDD

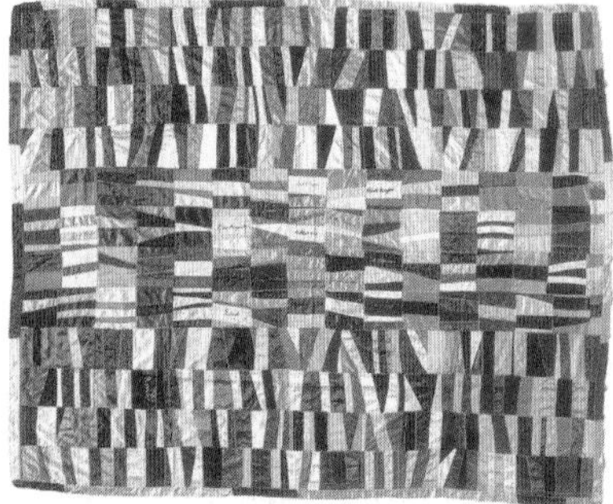

A quilt, made from jockeys' silks, with signatures and names of winners, 1950–60, 88 x 92in (223.5 x 233.5cm).

£2,200–2,450 LFNY

A Derby Day racecard, with Dorling's List of Epsom Races, 1851.

£250–300 BUDD

A silver stirrup cup, by John Samuel Hunt, in the form of a fox's head with plain collar, London 1864, 5¼in (13.5cm) high, c12oz.

£6,200–7,400 HYD

◄ **A silver-gilt and enamel scent flask,** by H. W. Dee, in the form of a horseshoe, with jockey's cap cover, London 1870, 3¼in (8.5cm) high.

£1,950–2,300 N

A late Victorian enamelled vesta case, decorated with horse racing scenes, 2in (5cm) wide.

£1,500–1,800 G(L)

FISHING

A wicker and oilcloth boat creel, the brass clasp with registration mark dated 1880, 24in (61cm) wide.

£210–250 GTH

A Native American hand-made creel and landing net, 19thC, net 26in (66cm) long.

£650–780 DuM

A pigskin fly wallet, by Hardy Brothers, 1930s, 5in (12.5cm) wide.

£145–165 MSh

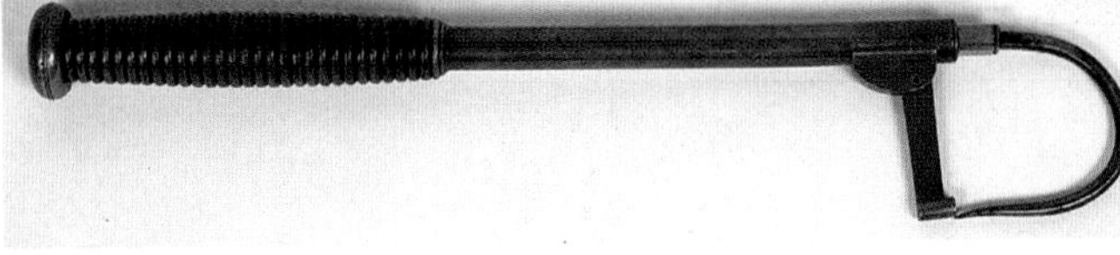

A wood and brass telescopic salmon gaff, c1900, 15in (38cm) long.

£145–165 MSh

► **A Wedgwood ceramic plate,** depicting a fishing scene, inscribed 'He Whipped Day In, He Whipped Day Out, But What He Caught Was Not A Trout', 1891–1910, 10in (25.5cm) diam.

£130–145 BtoB

An Eaton & Deller 5in salmon reel, with ebonite plate and leather thumb brake, c1880.

£270–300 OTB

Reels in this large size are rare.

A brass multiplier 2in trout reel, with ebonized handles, early 19thC.

£220–250 MSh

A Dreadnought Casting Reel Co Meteor alloy and brass 3½in reel, Newport, c1920.

£540–600 OTB

A walnut and brass 8¼in sea reel, with wooden handles, c1930.

£250–280 MSh

A Mullock alloy 5in sidecasting reel, Scotland, Perth, c1930.

£125–140 MSh

◄ **A Hardy Perfect alloy 3½in trout reel,** with agate line ring, perforated drum and chromium foot, original receipt and box, dated 1966.

£105–125 Hal

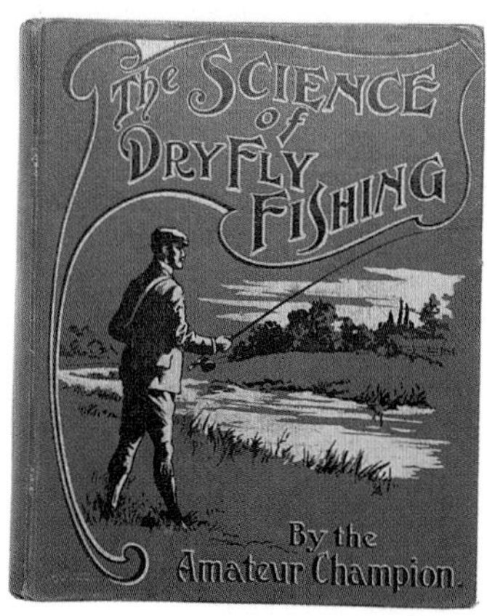

◄ Fred G. Shaw (The Amateur Champion), *The Science of Dry Fly Fishing*, published by Bradburn Agnew & Co, London, first edition, 1906, 9½in (24cm) high.

£210–240 VAN

A stuffed and mounted roach, in a bowfronted glazed case, caught by H. M. Saunders at Boxstead Mills, August 1904, restored, case 17¼in (44cm) wide.

£500–600 JBe

◄ **A stuffed and mounted barbel,** in a glazed case, caught by R. J. C. James in the River Severn, August 1948, case 30in (76cm) wide.

£165–190 PF

A carved wood trophy, by C. Farlow & Co, inscribed 'Rainbow Trout, caught by G. Fothergill on the Kennet, May 1922', stamped mark to reverse, 27¾in (70.5cm) wide.

£940–1,100 GTH

◄ **A stuffed and mounted tench,** in a bowfronted glazed case, caught by G. Krohn at Theale, July 1934, case 24½in (62cm) wide.

£700–840 Hal

FOOTBALL

◄ **A pair of leather football boots,** by CERT, c1930.

£130–145 MSh

A pair of leather football boots, worn by Sir Stanley Matthews, 1965.

£660–790 LT

When Sir Stanley Matthews played football for Stoke City the vendor's father worked at the North Stafford Hotel as a Hall Porter and looked after the needs of Sir Stan. In return, Sir Stan would always ensure that he had tickets for the best seats in the ground and gave him mementos. After his last match for Stoke City Sir Stan gave him the boots he had been wearing.

An FA Cup international trial cap, with monogram, inscribed '1901–2'.

£900–1,050 BUDD

◄ **A metal figural clock,** by Jennings Brothers Manufacturing Co, Connecticut, with a figure of an American football player, America, 1920s, 7¼in (18.5cm) high.

£360–430 MN

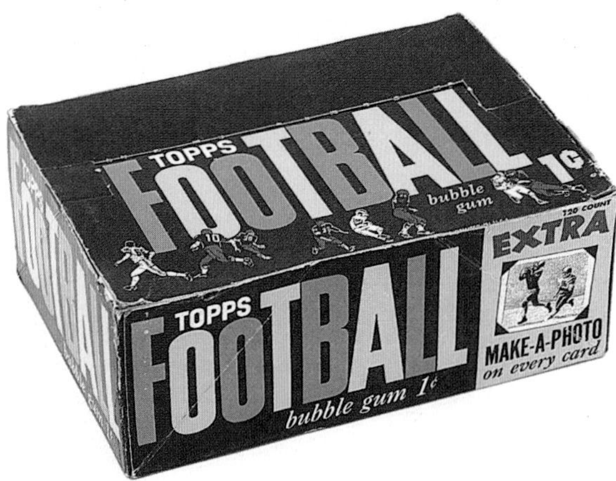

A Topps bubble gum display box, American Football, holds 120 wax packs, America, 1961, 7½in (19cm) wide.

£650–780 MN

A plaster figural group of four American football players, by John Rogers, America, c1891, 16in (40.5cm) high.

£2,350–2,800 MN

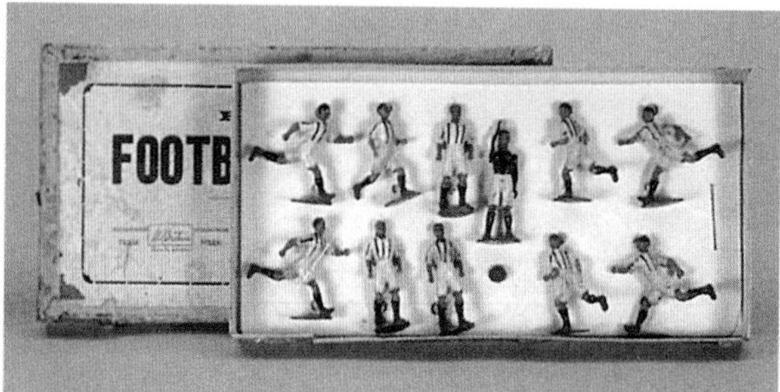

◄ **A set of Britains painted lead Huddersfield Town figures,** comprising 10 players and a goalkeeper, 1930s.

£400–480 BUDD

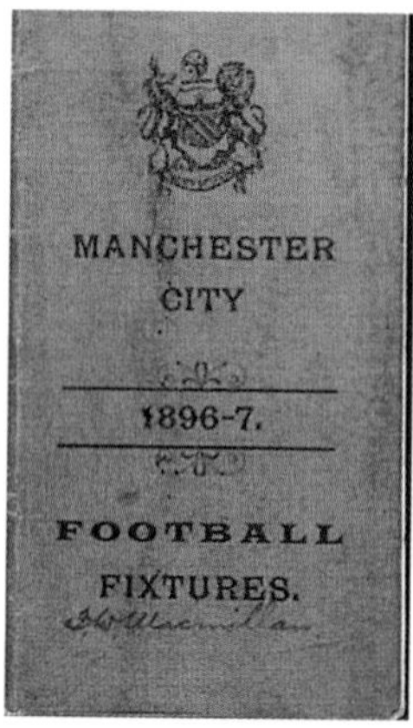

► **A Manchester City fixture list,** with cloth covers, the interior with printed first and second team fixtures in ink, 1896–97.

£340–400 BUDD

A World Cup first day cover cover, signed in biro by 11 England players, with four England Winners stamps, dated 1966.

£1,800–2,150 BUDD

A World Cup fixture card, published by Francisco Susena e Hijos, the interior with printed fixtures, 1930.

£300–360 BUDD

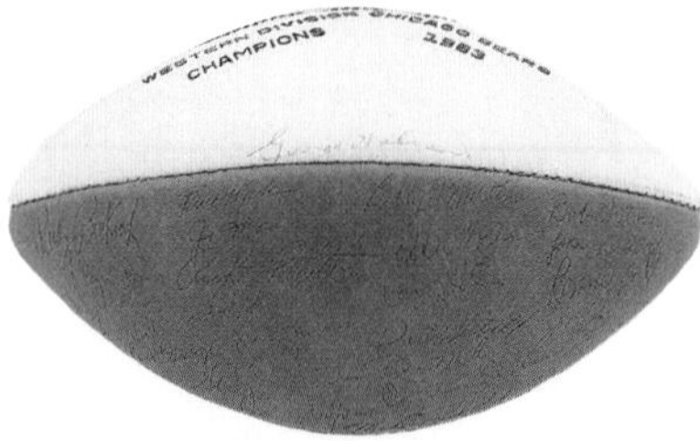

A Wilson American football, with 44 ink signatures of the Chicago Bears World Champions, America, 1963.

£1,050–1,250 MN

◄ **A leather football,** c1930.

£75–85 MSh

Prices

The price ranges quoted in this book reflect the average price a purchaser might expect to pay for a similar item. The price will vary according to the condition, rarity, size, popularity, provenance, colour and restoration of the item, and this must be taken into account when assessing values. Don't forget that if you are selling it is quite likely that you will be offered less than the price range.

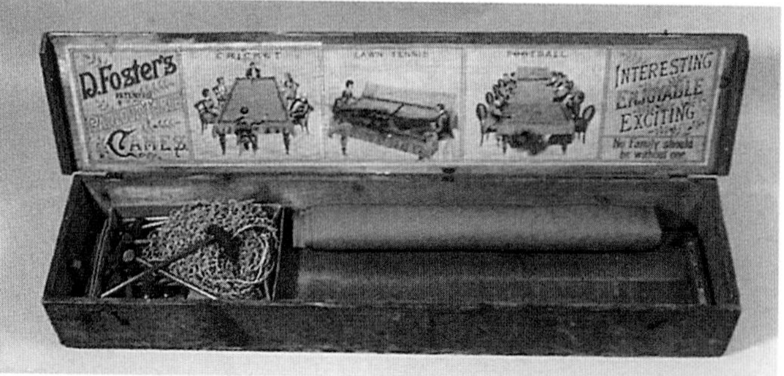

A D. Foster's Patented Parlour Table game, originally for football, cricket and lawn tennis, only football pieces remaining, in a pine box, later green baize, patented 1890, 45¾in (116cm) wide.

£1,200–1,400 BUDD

An American Football woollen jumper, by W. H. Brine, with leather elbow pads, damaged, America, early 20thC.

£560–670 MN

A Staffordshire pottery jug, commemorating Bristol City Football Club, with silver lustre rim, handle repaired, 1905, 12¼in (31cm) high.

£1,300–1,550 BUDD

A 9ct gold winner's medal, awarded to Malachi O'Brien, inaugural All-Ireland football final, 1887.

£18,000–21,600 BUDD

Malachi O'Brien was born in Ballinvrina, Emly, where he lived until he was 14 years old. After living in Dublin for a while he moved to America where he remained for 32 years, returning to his native Ballinvrina from 1929 until his death on 2 August 1953.

A Clyde Pottery mug, commemorating Dan Doyle and W. J. Bassett, inscribed the 'International Heroes', c1890, 4in (10cm).

£890–1,000 RdV

A ceramic plate, inscribed 'Les Grands Moments Du Sport Français', c1921, 7½in (19cm) diam.

£115–130 NLS

A colour photograph, signed by the England World Cup team members including Bobby Moore, 1966, 5¾ x 8¼in (14.5 x 21cm).

£1,100–1,300 BUDD

W. H. Smith & Son's
SOUVENIR CARD
OF THE
ENGLISH CUP FINAL
1909

W. Meredith

MANCHESTER UNITED v. BRISTOL CITY
PLAYED AT THE
CRYSTAL PALACE
Saturday, April 24th
PRICE: ONE PENNY

A W. H. Smith & Sons FA Cup Final souvenir programme, for Bristol City v Manchester United, played at Crystal Palace, 1909.

£4,400–5,200 BUDD

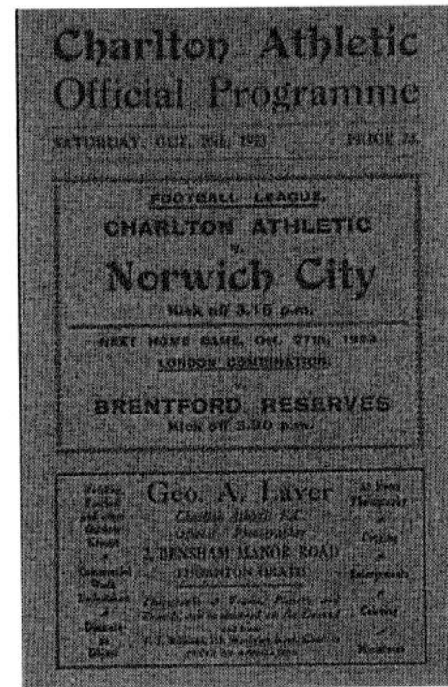

Charlton Athletic
Official Programme

FOOTBALL LEAGUE.
CHARLTON ATHLETIC
Norwich City

BRENTFORD RESERVES

Geo. A. Laver

A football programme, for Charlton Athletic v Norwich City, 20 October 1923.

£480–570 BUDD

► **An FA Cup Final programme,** for Bolton Wanderers v Portsmouth, held at Wembley, 27 April 1929.

£420–500 JBe

LOCATE THE SOURCE

The source of each illustration in Miller's can be found by checking the code letters below each caption with the Key to Illustrations, pages 746–753.

► **An FA Cup Final programme,** for Arsenal v Newcastle United, 23 April 1932.

£500–600 BUDD

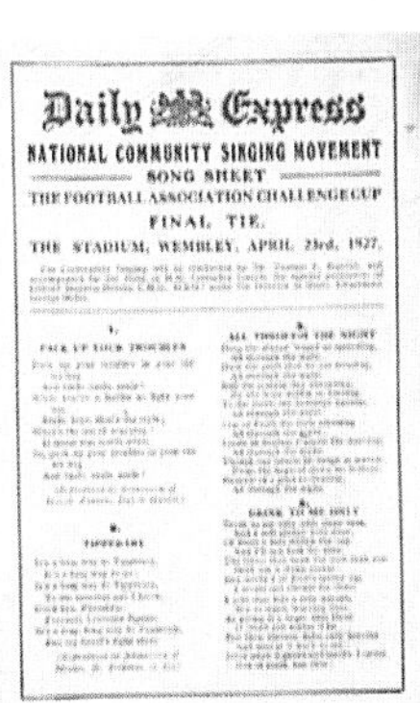

Daily Express
NATIONAL COMMUNITY SINGING MOVEMENT
SONG SHEET
THE FOOTBALL ASSOCIATION CHALLENGE CUP
FINAL TIE,
THE STADIUM, WEMBLEY, APRIL 23rd, 1927.

An FA Cup Final songsheet, for Arsenal v Cardiff City, Wembley, 23 April 1927.

£400–480 BUDD

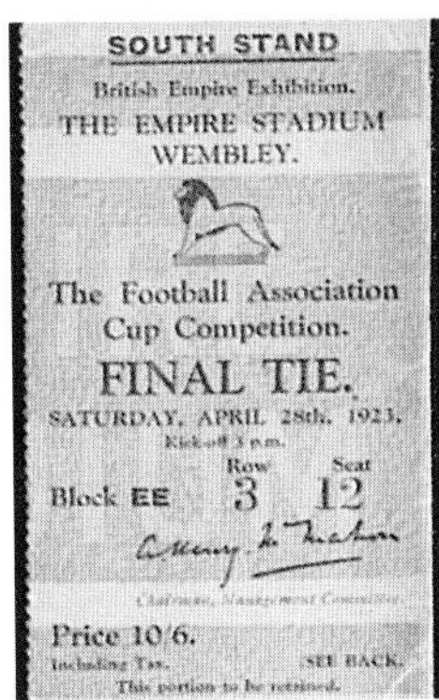

SOUTH STAND
British Empire Exhibition.
THE EMPIRE STADIUM
WEMBLEY.

The Football Association
Cup Competition.
FINAL TIE.
SATURDAY, APRIL 28th, 1923.
Kick-off 3 p.m.
Block EE Row 3 Seat 12

Price 10/6.
Including Tax. SEE BACK
This portion to be retained.

An FA Cup Final ticket stub, for Bolton Wanderers v West Ham United, 1923.

£1,600–1,900 BUDD

GOLF

A hand-hammered gutta-percha ball, c1855.
£250–300 BUDD

A box of Spalding Top-Flite rubber core golf balls, c1935, in original box.
£240–280 BUDD

A Morrison ware bowl, decorated with a golfer, 1890s, 8in (20.5cm) diam.
£1,300–1,450 MSh

Horace G. Hutchinson, *British Golf Links*, first edition, 1897, slight damage and repair, in a later morocco case, 4°.
£1,150–1,350 BBA

A pair of brass candlesticks, in the form of sword handles, inscribed 'Golf Handicap 1905 Officer's Second ERYRCA Vols, Winner Captain H. B. Allen', c1905, 12½in (32cm) high.
£140–165 DA

A left-handed long nose spoon golf club, with sheepskin grip, c1850, 45in (114.5cm) long.
£2,300–2,600 MSh

Sets/pairs

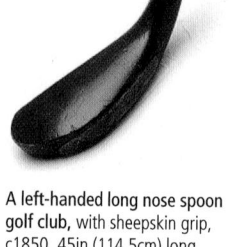

Unless otherwise stated, any description which refers to 'a set' or 'a pair' includes a guide price for the entire set or the pair, even though the illustration may show only a single item.

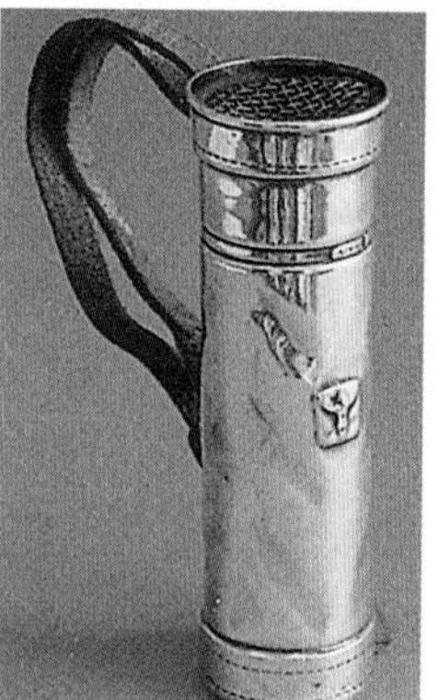

A novelty silver container, in the form of a golf club bag, Birmingham 1912, 3in (7.5cm) high.
£175–210 JBe

A silver-plated cruet set, comprising three pieces in the form of golf balls and clubs, 1930s, 3in (7.5cm) high.
£130–145 MSh

A Copeland Spode jug, decorated with a golfing scene, c1890, 5½in (14cm) high.
£480–540 MSh

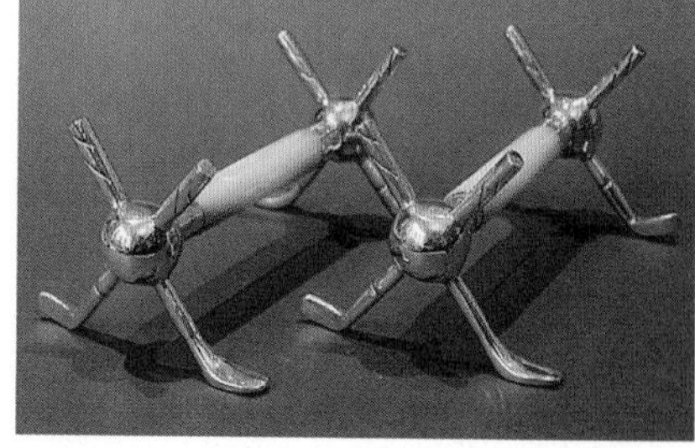

A pair of silver and mother-of-pearl golf club knife rests, by George Butler & Co, Sheffield 1907, 3½in (9cm) wide.
£600–680 BEX

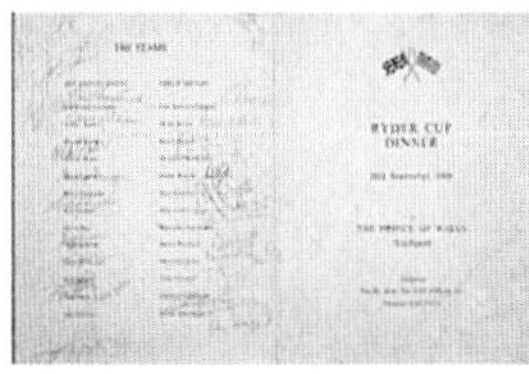

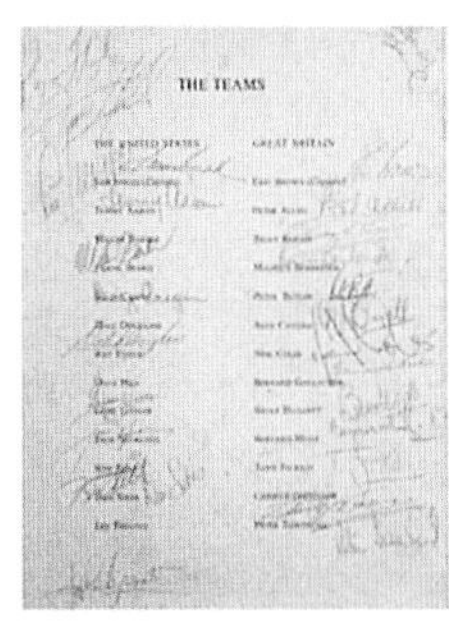

A spring-loaded Birdie Putt money box, with a golfer and a caddie, America, c1960, 8¼in (21cm) wide.

£250–300 BUDD

◀ **A Ryder Cup dinner menu,** signed in ink by 26 members of the US and Great Britain teams, 1969, 12½ x 18in (32 x 45.5cm) open, framed.

£1,100–1,300 BUDD

A pottery mug, decorated with a golfing cartoon, with Masonic crest for Tuscan Lodge, 1900–26, 7in (18cm) high.

£120–135 BtoB

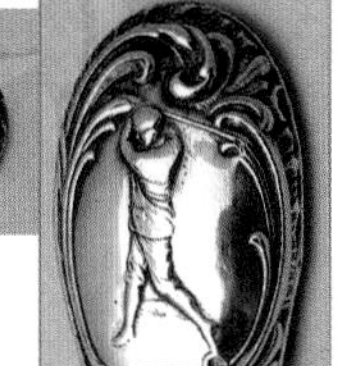

A silver and ivory paper knife, the handle embossed with a golfer, Birmingham 1902, 14in (35.5cm) long.

£850–950 MSh

▶ **A silver pen holder,** by Deakin & Francis, in the form of a golf bag, Birmingham 1907, 5½in (14cm) high, with a silver pen in the form of a golf club, by Sampson Mordan & Co, inscribed 'Stringer Trophy 1939', London 1933.

£640–760 HYD

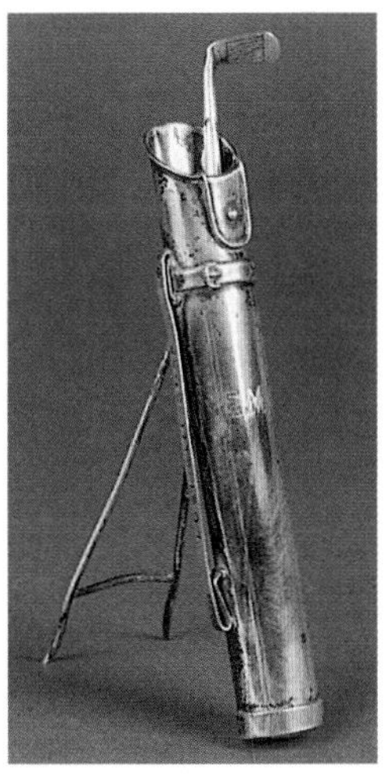

A Grimwades plate, entitled 'The Indispensable Caddie!', 1910–20, 10in (25.5cm) diam.

£220–250 BtoB

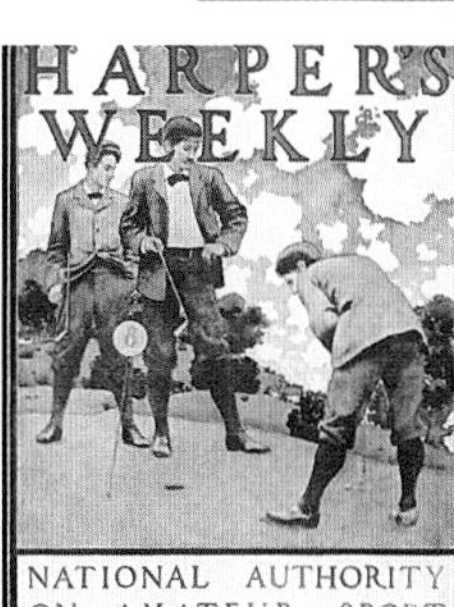

A Harper's Weekly lithograph and screen poster, *National Authority on Amateur Sport*, illustrated by Maxfield Parrish, slight damage, America, 1896, 18¼ x 14in (46.5 x 35.5cm).

£1,600–1,900 FFAP

A promotional poster, 'Come to Britain for Golf', illustrated by Rowland Hilder, printed by W. S. Cowell, London & Ipswich, c1935, 27½ x 20in (70 x 51cm).

£330–390 VSP

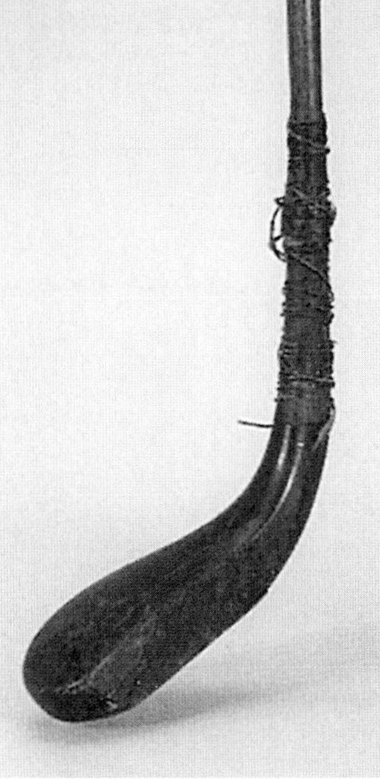

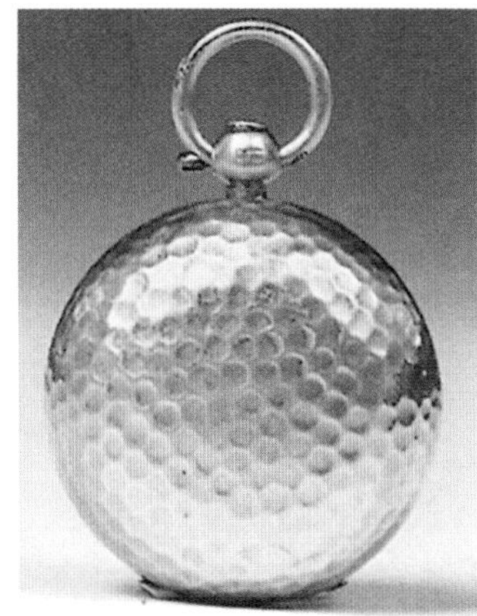

A Victorian 9ct gold sovereign case, in the form of a golf ball, ¼in (3cm) diam.

£530–630 TEN

◀ **A Hugh Philp long nosed putter,** with thorn head and hickory shaft, slight damage, St Andrews, Scotland, c1850, 37½in (95.5cm) long.

£2,800–3,350 BUDD

ROWING & SAILING

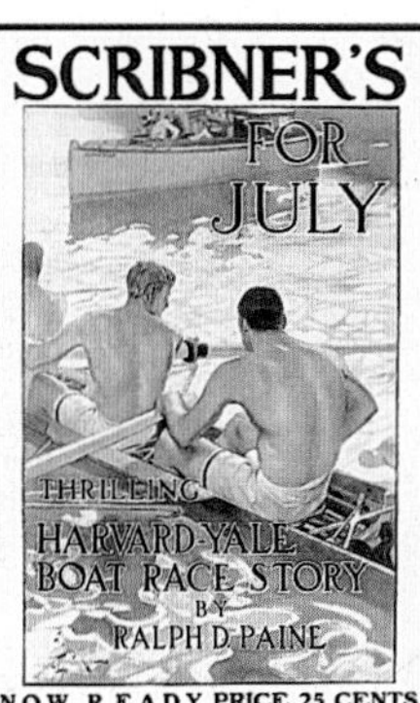

A promotional colour screen poster, 'Scribner's for July, Harvard-Yale Boat Race', illustrated by J. C. Leyendecker, slight damage, America, 1905, 22½ x 14¼in (57 x 36cm).

£900–1,050 FFAP

A silver-plated and gilded timepiece, in the form of a lifebelt and two oars, with French brass movement, c1890, 11in (28cm) high.

£880–980 WALP

A silver-plated and gilt timepiece, mounted with two rudders and two oars, French movement, on an oak base, c1890, 10¾in (27.5cm) wide.

£780–880 WALP

► **A silver-gilt trophy cup,** by Edward & John Barnard, chased and embossed with flowers, with presentation inscription 'Lough Corrib Regatta 1838', London 1837, 7¼in (18.5cm) high, 14oz.

£350–420 DN

RUGBY

A Staffordshire bisque figure of a rugby player, c1890, 9¾in (25cm) high.

£130–145 BtoB

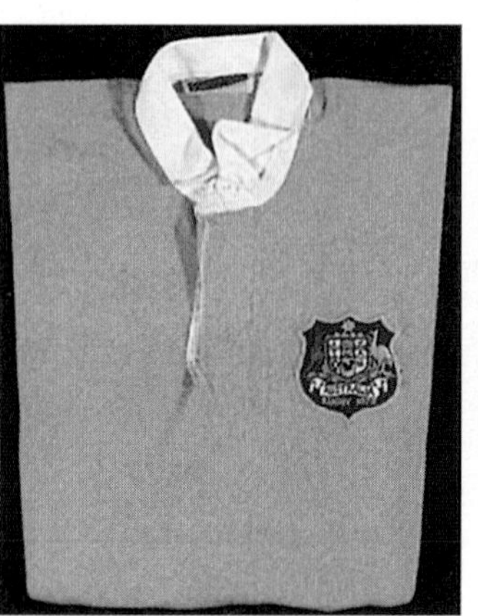

A long-sleeved Australia No. 10 International rugby shirt, as worn by G. C. Richardson, 1973.

£350–420 BUDD

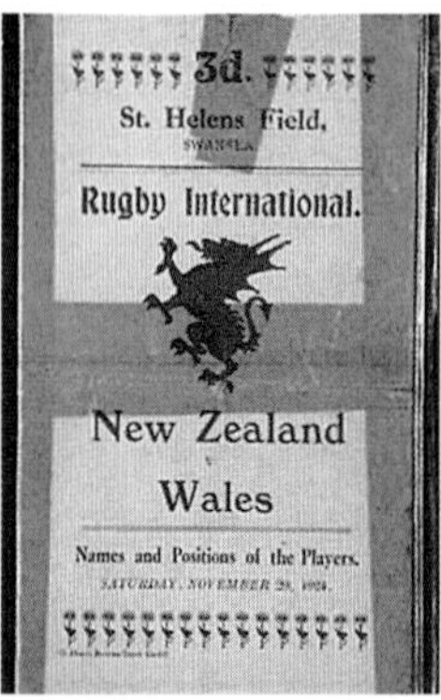

A Rugby International programme, for New Zealand v Wales, St Helens Field, Swansea, repaired, 1924.

£180–210 BUDD

SHOOTING

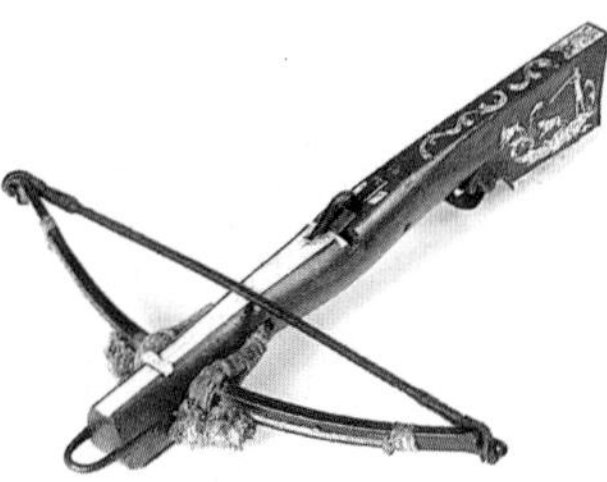

A steel crossbow, with figured walnut tiller, inlaid with a staghorn hunting scene, brass trigger guard, steel bolt clip, iron loop, twisted cord later, Germany, c1750, 27¾in (70.5cm) long.

£1,800–2,150 TDM

A .75 Hudson Valley-type flintlock fowling piece, repaired, 18thC, 56in (142cm) long.

£1,550–1,850 JDJ

A Paradox revolving sporting gun, with two shotgun barrels and a rifle barrel, the stock with a nickel patch box, America, c1850, 47in (119.5cm) long.

£880–990 MDL

A silver powder flask, decorated with a sporting scene, Continental, 19thC, 10in (25.5cm) high.

£1,400–1,600 ARB

A brass-mounted powder horn, decorated with a family crest, c1810, 12in (30.5cm) long.

£370–420 ARB

A powder horn, carved with hounds chasing deer, with ivory carrying eyelets, Germany, c1850, 10¾in (27.5cm) long.

£1,500–1,800 Herm

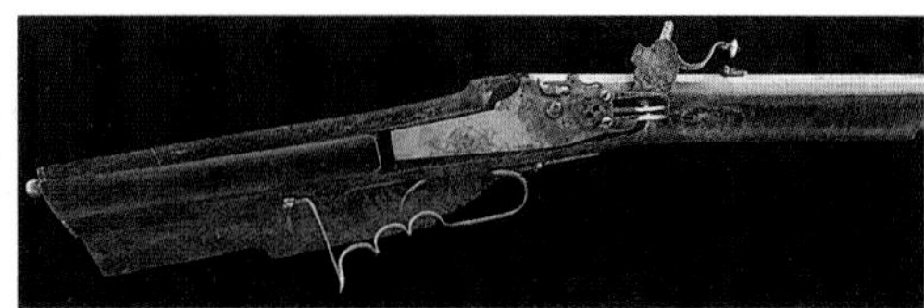

A wheel-lock sporting rifle, by Johannes Will, the barrel lock engraved with scrolling foliage and garlands of flowers, the burrwood butt inlaid with a bone panel and horn butt plate, ramrod missing, Germany, Hanau, c1680, barrel 23¾in (60.5cm) long.

£2,200–2,600 TDM

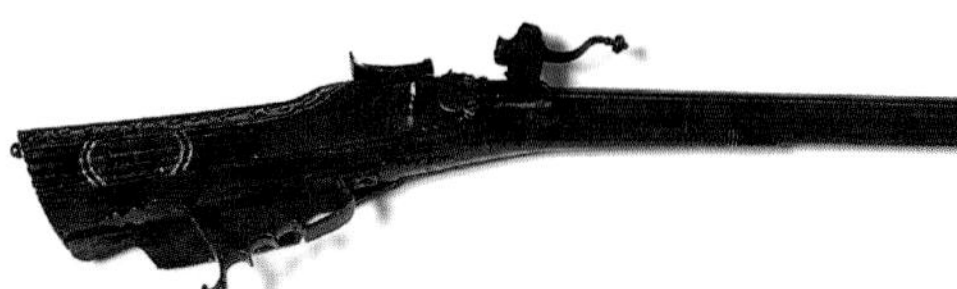

A wheel-lock sporting rifle, with walnut stock and patch box, Europe, c1700, 44in (112cm) long.

£3,800–4,250 MDL

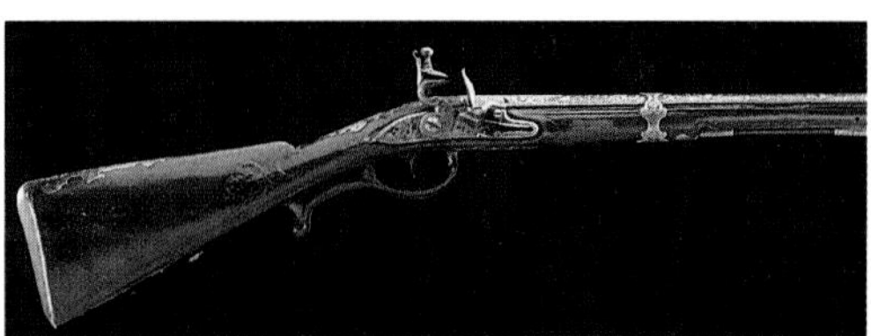

A flintlock sporting gun, by Joseph Stockl, the barrel with silver scrollwork and brass bands, the figured walnut half stock carved with scrollwork, with brass-tipped wooden ramrod, Austria, Neustadt, c1770, barrel 39½in (99.5cm) long.

£1,400–1,650 TDM

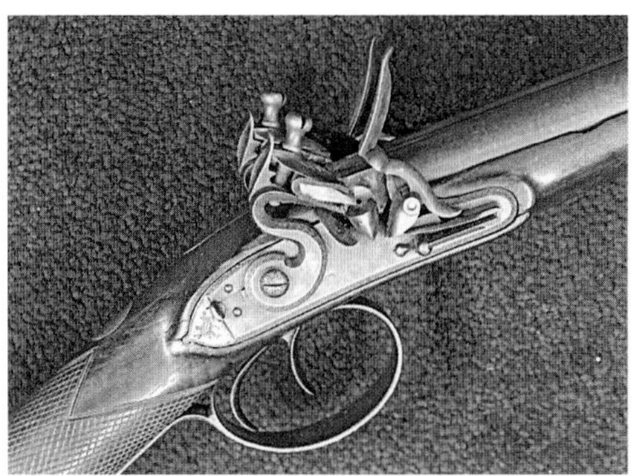

A flintlock sporting gun, by Joseph Manton, No. 1451, with Damascus barrels, chequered half stock and brass-tipped wooden ramrod, 1800, barrel 32in (81.5cm) long.

£3,000–3,600 Hal

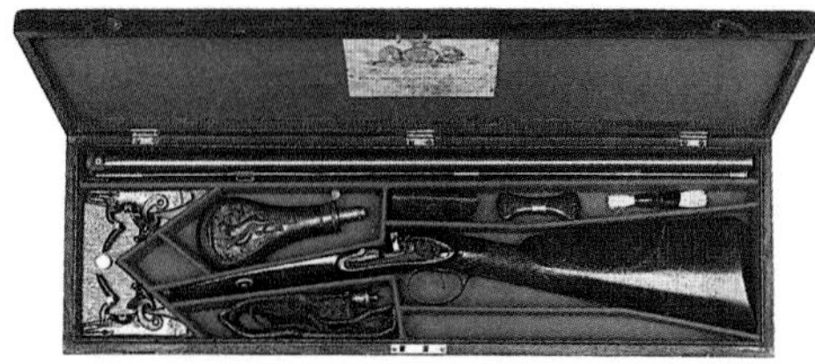

A flintlock sporting gun, by John Manton & Son, London, with walnut half stock, engraved steel mounts, 1817, 46in (117cm) long.

£3,300–3,950 WAL

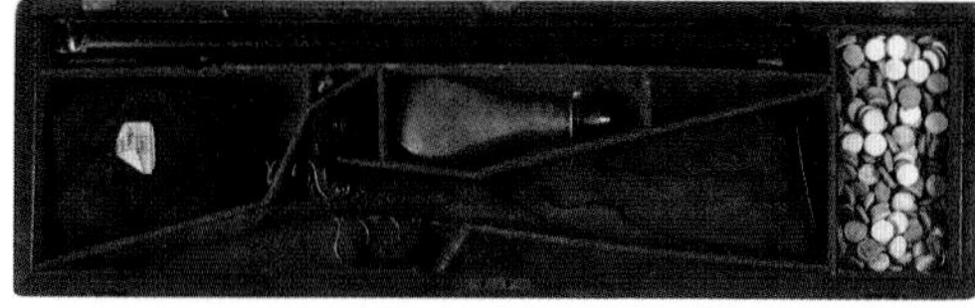

A percussion sporting gun, by Hollis, No. 3757, with walnut half stock and engraved steel mounts, c1850, in a brass-bound mahogany case with accessories, barrel 25in (63.5cm) long.

£1,300–1,550 TDM

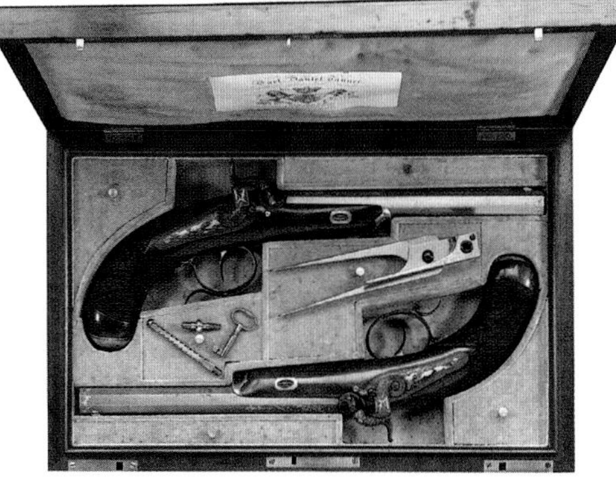

◄ **A pair of Hanoverian Royal percussion target pistols,** by C. D. Tanner, engraved with cypher of George IV, 1829–30, 15in (38cm) long.

£25,300–30,300 S(Han)

Ex-Royal House of Hanover sale.
For information about this sale please see p205.

TENNIS

An ivory and patinated bronze figure of a tennis player, by Ferdinand Preiss, on an onyx base, signed, Germany, c1930, 12in (30.5cm) wide.

£12,600–15,000 S

For more Arts & Crafts items, please see the Decorative Arts section on pages 367–440.

An Edwardian diamond and ruby pin, in the form of a tennis racket, with a seed pearl ball, on a platinum-topped 18ct gold mount, two rubies missing, 1½in (4cm) long.

£540–640 SK

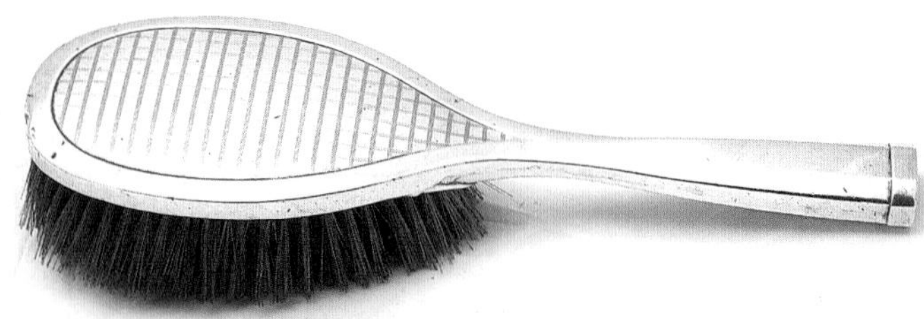

A silver hairbrush, in the shape of a tennis racket, Chester 1910, 11in (28cm) long.

£410–460 MSh

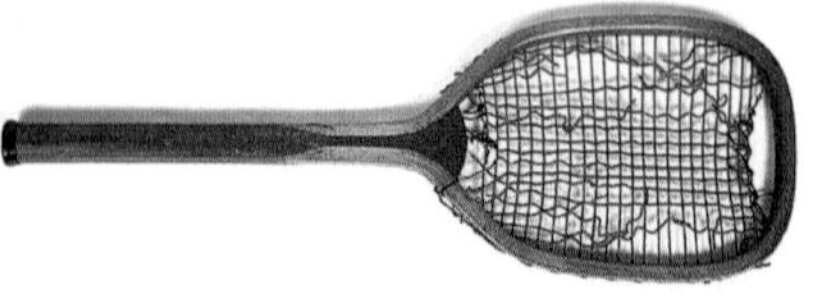

A Slazenger Renshaw wooden tennis racket, 1880s, 27in (68.5cm) long.

£640–800 MSh

► **An Arts & Crafts-style silver tennis trophy,** inscribed 'Spillmann & Sickert, Grand Hotel Du Lac, Lucerne, Tennis Tournament 1914', marked '800 A Burber', 7¼in (18.5cm) high, 4½oz.

£150–180 DN(HAM)

WINTER SPORTS

Hamilton bubble gum, Ice Hockey, set of 21, all except three cards feature either Toronto or the Canadians, Canada, 1933–34.

£1,450–1,700 MN

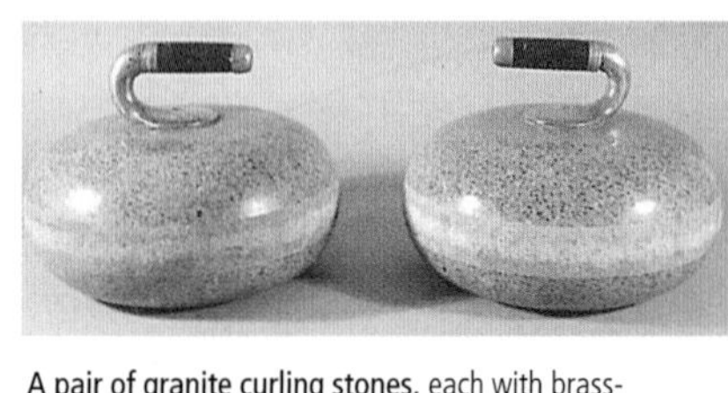

A pair of granite curling stones, each with brass-mounted ebony handles and initials 'A. F.', Scotland, early 20thC, 11in (28cm) diam.

£120–140 PFK

◄ **O-Pee-Chee bubble gum,** Ice Hockey, Eddie Shore, trade card, America, 1936–37.

£960–1,150 MN

An ivory and bronze figure of a girl skating, by Ferdinand Preiss, base signed, Germany, c1930, 13in (33cm) high.

£6,800–8,100 CAu

A wooden table-top ice hockey game, legs and backboard detached, America, 1930s, table 42½in (108cm) long.

£1,200–1,400 MN

A Royal Caledonian Curling Club silver medal, Scotland, 1838, 2in (5cm) diam.

£320–360 MSh

AMERICAN FOLK ART

◀ **A painted tin document box,** possibly by Oliver Filley Tin Decorating Shop, Bloomfield, Connecticut, the front decorated with a bird on a branch, the top and sides with pinwheels, the lid with a wire handle, slight paint loss, early 19thC, 9½in (24cm) wide.
£2,200–2,600 SK(B)

▶ **A carved wood bust of Abraham Lincoln,** varnished, 1900–50, 10in (25.5cm) high.
£95–110 JAA

Folk Art is a very broad term, encompassing many collecting areas. For other examples refer to the sections on Kitchenware, Marine, Metalware, Treen, Boxes, Textiles and Toys.

A carved and painted Cigar Store Indian, repainted, slight damage, minor repairs, 78in (198cm) high.
£8,700–10,400 JDJ

A painted and gilded wood Cigar Store Indian, Rhode Island, c1875, 76¼in (193.5cm) high .
£32,000–36,000 GIAM

A carved and painted decoy duck, by Ward Bros, Chrisfield, Maryland, maker's signature and later signature 'Lem', 1929, 16in (40.5cm) long.
£2,950–3,500 JDJ

A carved giltwood pilot house eagle, 19thC, 28½in (72.5cm) high.
£11,900–14,200 NAAW

A carved giltwood eagle, regilded, c1900, 27in (68.5cm) high.
£1,900–2,250 SK

▶ **A carved and painted wood figure of a soldier,** slight damage, probably 1900–50, 68½in (172.5cm) high.
£2,600–3,100 JDJ

A 38-star American flag, c1880, 71 x 94½in (180 x 240cm).
£330–390 SWO

The 38-star Stars and Stripes became the official United States flag on 4 July 1877, after a star was added for the admission of Colorado in 1876, and was to last for 13 years.

A painted metal Eureka floating bicycle, New York City, c1917, 51in (129.5cm) high.
£6,100–6,800 GIAM

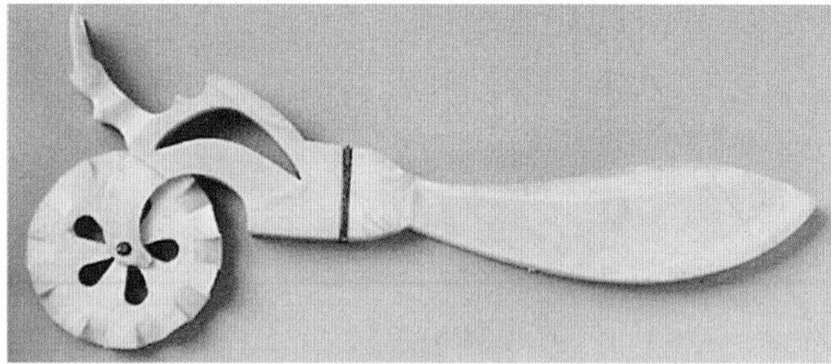

◀ **A carved ivory jagging wheel,** with a silver band, slight damage, 19thC, 7½in (19cm) long.

£700–840 SK

A jagging wheel is used for cutting pastry.

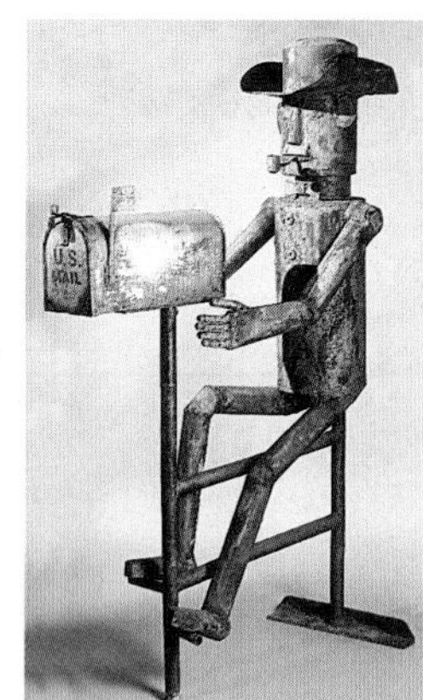

▶ **A painted tin and steel mail box figure,** Connecticut, c1935, 68in (172.5cm) high.

£7,800–8,100 GIAM

A pen and ink map of the United States, by Maria Philpot, 1819, 20 x 25in (51 x 63.5cm).

£5,700–6,800 NAAW

This map was executed under the direction of Miss Lucinda Gridley at Franklin Academy, Dover, New Hampshire. Franklin Academy was established in 1818 and continued until 1896.

A carved and painted wood American Eagle wall plaque, attributed to George Stapf, Harrisburg and Lancaster, Pennsylvania, slight damage, late 19thC, 22½in (57cm) high.

£12,100–14,500 JDJ

A carved and painted wooden eagle plaque, attributed to John Haley Bellamy, late 19thC, 24¼in (61.5cm) wide.

£17,900–21,400 S(NY)

Ex-Estate of Laurance S. Rockefeller.
For more information on this sale please see p20.
John Haley Bellamy (1836–1914), was a wood-carver from Kittery Point, Maine. For many years, following his apprenticeship to a Boston wood-carver, he carved figureheads and ornamental work for sterns, panels and various other forms of ship decoration. Bellamy eagles were enormously popular, with imitations made during his own lifetime.

A hooked rug, worked with flowerheads, monogrammed 'S.E.A.', dated 1866, 36 x 58in (91.5 x 147.5cm).

£950–1,100 NAAW

A painted and varnished wood sewing box and spool holder, in the form of a book with sliding drawer, decorated with hearts and carved birds, possibly New York State, 19thC, 12in (30.5cm) high.

£3,100–3,700 WAD

▶ **A child's painted bird's-eye maple and pine sled,** decoration attributed to Henry A. Gage, Manchester, New Hampshire, with an American Eagle and initials 'A.R.S.', one runner signed 'Gage Painter', base inscribed 'Simmons', dated 1858, 43¾in (111cm) long.

£440–520 SK

A painted and gilded wood tavern sign, with original iron brackets, Connecticut, 1805, 59½in (151cm) high.

£61,000–68,000 GIAM

A gilded trade sign, for E. G. Wood, inscribed 'Garfield & Co', late 19thC, 49½in (125.5cm) wide.
£640–760 SK

◄ **A painted cast-iron, zinc and tin Father Time trade sign,** c1875, 47½in (120.5cm) high.
£24,000–27,200 GIAM

A painted wood trade sign, for Central Sign Co, Point Murray, New Jersey, c1925, 47½in (120.5cm) wide.
£9,800–10,900 GIAM

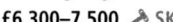

A carved and painted weather vane, in the form of a fish, 19thC, 12½in (32cm) wide.
£5,700–6,800 NAAW

A moulded copper and cast-zinc weather vane, attributed to A. L. Jewell & Co, Waltham, Massachusetts, in the form of a running horse, traces of gilding, 1852–67, 29in (73.5cm) wide.
£6,300–7,500 SK

A moulded copper and cast-lead weather vane, attributed to A. L. Jewell & Co, Waltham, Massachusetts, in the form of a centaur, traces of yellow sizing, gilt, verdigris and black paint, repaired, 1852–67, 39¼in (99.5cm) wide.
£28,100–33,000 SK(B)

A moulded copper weather vane, in the form of a rooster, decorated with gold leaf, c1880, 25¾in (65.5cm) wide.
£6,100–6,800 GIAM

A carved wood weather vane, in the form of a rooster, c1900, 26in (66cm) wide.
£5,900–6,600 GIAM

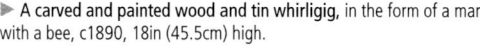

► **A carved and painted wood and tin whirligig,** in the form of a man with a bee, c1890, 18in (45.5cm) high.
£8,800–9,800 GIAM

A carved and painted wood, tin and leather whirligig, in the form of a flagman, c1910, 18½in (47cm) high.
£12,200–13,600 GIAM

GLOSSARY

abrash: Slight shift in colour tone in a rug or carpet, due to a new batch of yarn being used – each batch of a natural dye will differ slightly from the others.

agate ware: 18thC pottery, veined or marbled to resemble the mineral agate.

***albarello*:** Drug jar, usually of waisted cylindrical form, used in most major European countries from the 15thC.

album quilt: Quilt designed by those that have worked it, in the same way as an autograph album.

anchor escapement: Said to have been invented c1670 by Robert Hooke or William Clement. A type of escape mechanism shaped like an anchor, which engages at precise intervals with the toothed escape wheel. The anchor permits the use of a pendulum (either long or short), and gives greater accuracy than was possible with the verge escapement.

***anhua*:** Hidden decoration on Chinese porcelain.

***aogai*:** Japanese lacquer technique.

argyle: Silver gravy-warmer shaped like a coffee pot with a central well for the gravy and an outer casing for hot water, said to have been invented by one of the Dukes of Argyll.

associated: Term used in antiques, in which one part of an item is of the same design but not originally made for it. See *marriage* and *made up*.

automaton: Any moving toy or decorative object, usually powered by a clockwork mechanism.

aventurine: Brown or blue quartz with gold inclusions, hence anything that resembles the mineral, such as aventurine glass, that is flecked with gold-coloured mica or other metals, or lacquer work of gold strands on a red or black background.

barbotine: Painting on pottery using coloured kaolin pastes, invented in 1865 by Ernest Chaplet.

bezel: Ring, usually brass, surrounding the dial of a clock, and securing the glass dial cover.

***bianco-sopra-bianco*:** Literally white-on-white. Used in ceramics to describe an opaque white pattern painted on an off-white background.

Biedermeier: Style of furniture made principally in the 1820s and '30s in Austria, Germany and parts of Scandinavia and characterized by simple, heavy Classical forms. It is named after a fictional character who symbolized the German bourgeoisie of the early 19thC.

biggin: Form of coffee percolator invented c1799 by George Biggin.

***bijin*:** Japanese term for a beautiful woman.

bisque: French term for biscuit ware, or unglazed porcelain.

***blanc-de-Chine*:** Translucent white Chinese porcelain, unpainted and with a thick glaze, made in kilns in Dehua in the Fujian province from the Song Dynasty and copied in Europe.

***bleu de Nevers*:** A brilliant blue glaze first found on pottery from Nevers in France from the 17th or early 18th century.

Bodhisattva: Attendant of Buddha.

***bombé*:** Bulbous, curving form, a feature often seen on wares produced during the rococo period.

***bonbonnière*:** Sweet jar or box.

***bordalou*:** Lady's portable commode.

***boteh*:** Stylized design of a floral bush found on rugs, similar to a Paisley design.

Britannia standard: Higher standard of silver required between 1697 and 1720. Denoted by Britannia and a lion's head in profile on the hallmark.

***bureau de dame*:** Writing desk of delicate appearance and designed for use by ladies. Usually raised above slender cabriole legs and with one or two external drawers.

***bureau plat*:** French writing table with a flat top and drawers in the frieze.

cabaret set: Tea set on a tray for three or more people.

calamander: Hardwood, imported from Sri Lanka (of the same family as ebony), used in the Regency period for making small articles of furniture, as a veneer and for crossbanding.

cameo glass: Two or more layers of coloured glass in which the top layers are then cut or etched away to create a multi-coloured design in relief. An ancient technique popular with Art Nouveau glassmakers in the early 20thC.

cannetille: Extremely thin gold wirework decoration.

cartouche: Ornate tablet or shield surrounded by scrollwork and foliage, often bearing an inscription, monogram or coat-of-arms.

cash motif: Chinese ceramic pattern based on the design of Chinese coins with a square central hole.

catlinite: Red stone composed of compressed clay, often used by Native Americans to make pipes.

celadon: Chinese stoneware with an opaque grey-green glaze, first made in the Song Dynasty and still made today, principally in Korea.

cellaret: Lidded container on legs designed to hold wine. The interior is often divided into sections for individual bottles.

***champlevé*:** Enamelling on copper or bronze, similar to cloisonné, in which a glass paste is applied to the hollowed-out design, fired and ground smooth.

character doll: One with a naturalistic face, especially laughing, crying, pouting, etc.

***chilong*:** Small lizard, often portrayed on Chinese ceramics.

Chinese Imari: Chinese imitations of Japanese blue, red and gold painted Imari wares, made from the early 18thC.

chinoiserie: The fashion, prevailing in the late 18thC, for Chinese-style ornamentation on porcelain, wall-papers, fabrics, furniture and garden architecture.

chryselephantine: Combination of ivory and a metal, usually bronze; used for Art Deco figures.

chrysoprase: opaque green glass.

***chuval*:** Turkic word meaning bag.

cistern tube: Mercury tube fitted into stick barometers, the lower end of which is sealed into a boxwood cistern.

Cizhou: Chinese porcelain wares characterized by bold shapes and decoration on a slip-covered body. They were named after the most important centre of production, Cixian (Cizhou), but were also produced in many different places in northern China.

clock garniture: Matching group of clock and vases or candelabra made for the mantel shelf. Often highly ornate.

cloisonné: Enamelling on metal with divisions in the design separated by lines of fine metal wire. A speciality of the Limoges region of France in the Middle Ages, and of Chinese craftsmen to the present day.

close-concentric paperweight: One which consists of concentric circles of canes arranged tightly together so that the clear glass cannot be seen between the rings of canes.

close-pack paperweight: One which is characterized by canes closely packed together without a pattern.

***coffor bach*:** Small Welsh coffer.

***coiffeuse*:** French dressing table.

coin silver: Silver of the standard used for coinage, ie .925 or sterling.

colza lamp: Lamp that burned a thick heavy oil made from rapeseed that was stored to one side in a reservoir shaped like a classical urn.

coromandel: Imported wood from the Coromandel coast of India, of similar blackish appearance to calamander and used from c1780 for banding, and for small pieces of furniture.

countwheel: Wheel with segments cut out of the edge or with pins fitted to one face, which controls the striking of a clock. Also known as a locking plate.

***craquelé* glass:** Technique used to decorate some Venetian glass in the 17thC and revived in the 19thC, particularly in Britain and France. A fine network of cracks was created on the surface of a vessel during the process of blowing, by plunging it into cold water. The resulting finish resembled the cracks on the surface of ice and so it is also known as 'ice glass' in England.

***crespina*:** Shallow Italian dish with a fluted border.

***cuerda seca*:** Technique of tile-making, developed in Iran in the 15thC, whereby the colours of the design were separated by an oily substance which leaves a brownish outline.

***cwpwrdd deuddarn*:** Welsh variety of the press cupboard with two tiers.

***cwpwrdd tridarn*:** Welsh variety of the press cupboard with three tiers.

cyma: Double-carved moulding. Cyma recta is concave above and convex below; cyma reversa the other way round. Also known as ogee and reverse ogee moulding. Popular with 18thC cabinet makers.

Cymric: Trade-name used by Liberty & Co for a mass-produced range of silverware inspired by Celtic art, introduced in 1899 and often incorporating enamelled pictorial plaques.

deadbeat escapement: Type of anchor escapement, possibly invented by George Graham and used in precision pendulum clocks.

Dehua: Town in southern China where much *blanc-de-Chine* was produced.

Delft: Dutch tin-glazed earthenwares named after the town of Delft, the principal production centre, from the 16thC onwards. Similar pottery made in England from the late 16thC is also termed 'delft' or 'delftware'.

dentils: Small rectangular blocks applied at regular intervals as a decorative feature.

***deutsche Blumen*:** Naturalistically painted flowers, either single or tied into bunches, used as a popular decorative motif on 18thC pottery and porcelain.

***dhurrie*:** Cotton flatweave rug or carpet from India.

diaper: Surface decoration composed of repeated diamonds or squares, often carved in low relief.

dog of *Fo*: Buddhist guardian lion.

***doucai*:** Decoration on Chinese porcelain using five colours.

***duchesse brisée*:** Type of chaise longue of French origin, consisting of one or two tub-shaped chairs and a stool to extend the length. Popular in Britain during the late 18thC.

Durham quilt: A type of quilt with fancy stitching on a plain background, made in the northeast of England.

***encre-de-Chine*:** Indian ink.

***en grisaille*:** Painted decoration using a mainly black and grey palette and resembling a print.

***ensi*:** Rug used as a tent door by Turkoman tribes.

escapement: Means or device which regulates the release of the power of a timepiece to its pendulum or balance.

***façon de Venise*:** Literally 'in the Venetian style', used to describe high quality, Venetian-influenced glassware made in Europe during the 16th to 17thC.

***fahua*:** Type of sancai (Chinese three-coloured ware). Usually has a turquoise or purple-blue ground and dates from the late 15th/early 16th centuries.

faïence: Tin-glazed earthenware named after the town of Faenza in Italy, but actually used to describe products made anywhere but Italy, where they are called maiolica.

***famille jaune/noire/rose/verte*:** Chinese porcelain in which yellow, black, pink or green respectively are the predominant ground colours.

***fauteuil*:** French open-armed drawing room chair.

fielded panel: Panel with bevelled or chamfered edges.

Fitzhugh pattern: Design in Chinese ceramics characterized by a border of four split pomegranates and butterflies. Made for the American market and named after the person who first ordered it.

flambé: Glaze made from copper, usually deep crimson, flecked with blue or purple, and often faintly crackled.

flatware (1): Collective name for flat pottery and porcelain, such as plates, dishes and saucers.

flatware (2): Cutlery.

flatweave: Term sometimes used to describe kilims and *soumakhs.*

flow blue: Process used principally after 1840 in which powder is added to the dye used in blue and white transfer-printed ceramics so that the blue flows beyond the edges of the transfer, making the pattern less sharply defined. Items using this process were made primarily for the American market.

fluted: Border that resembles a scalloped edge, used as a decoration on furniture, glass, silver and porcelain items.

***fuku*:** Chinese term for happiness.

***fu shou*:** Chinese decorative motif meaning happiness and longevity.

fusee: 18thC clockwork invention; a cone-shaped drum, linked to the spring barrel by a length of gut or chain. The shape compensates for the declining strength of the mainspring thus ensuring constant timekeeping.

gadroon: Border or ornament comprising radiating lobes of either curbed or straight form. Used from the late Elizabethan period.

garrya: Catkin-bearing evergreen shrub used as carved or inlaid decoration, usually on furniture in the styles of Hepplewhite or Adam.

girandole: Carved and gilt candle sconce incorporating a mirror.

Gnathian ware: A unique style of ancient Greek pottery from the town of Gnathia, characterized by painted decoration on a black gloss body.

Guanyin: Buddhist Bodhisattva of Compassion.

***guéridon*:** Small circular table designed to carry some form of lighting.

guglet: Type of water bottle, often accompanied by a small basin and used for minor ablutions.

***guilloche*:** Decorative motif of interlacing circles forming a continuous figure-of-eight pattern.

***gul*:** From the Persian word for flower – usually used to describe a geometric flowerhead on a rug.

***guttus*:** Ancient Greek closed vessel with a spout and handle for pouring oil into lamps.

halberd: Spear fitted with a double axe.

hard paste: True porcelain made of china stone (petuntse) and kaolin; the formula was long known to, and kept secret by, Chinese potters but only discovered in the 1720s at Meissen, Germany, from where it spread to the rest of Europe and the Americas. Recognized by its hard, glossy feel.

***hatchli*:** Rug used as a door by Turkomans on their tents.

***hiramakie*:** Japanese term for sponged gold applied level with the surface.

***hongmu*:** Type of wood used in the manufacture of Chinese furniture.

***ho-o*:** Mythical Chinese bird, similar to a phoenix, symbolizing wisdom and energy.

Hotei: Japanese Shinto god of Luck, Happiness, Laugher and Wisdom of Contentment.

***hu*:** Bronze Chinese ritual vessel.

***huanghuali*:** Type of Oriental wood, much admired for its colour.

***ibeji*:** Nigerian cult whereby if a twin died a wooden figure of it would be commissioned and the mother would feed, clothe and care for it, look after it and prevent it from taking the surviving twin. If both twins died a pair would be carved.

Imari: Export Japanese porcelain of predominantly red, blue and gold decoration which, although made in Arita, is called Imari after the port from which it was shipped.

impasto: Technique of applying paint thickly to ceramics so that the brush or palette knife marks are visible.

***indianische Blumen*:** German for 'indian flowers'; painting on porcelain in the Oriental style, especially on mid-18thC Meissen.

***inro*:** Japanese multi-compartmental medicine or seal container, carried suspended from the sash of a kimono.

***intarsio*:** Dramatic form of underglaze decoration featured on wares designed and decorated by Frederick Rhead.

ironstone: Stoneware, patented 1813 by Charles James Mason, containing ground glassy slag, a by-product of iron smelting, for extra strength.

***jubako*:** Japanese term for food box.

***kachina*:** Native American supernatural ancestor figure.

Kakiemon: Family of 17thC Japanese porcelain decorators who produced wares decorated with flowers and figures on a white ground in distinctive colours: azure, yellow, turquoise and soft red. Widely imitated in Europe.

***kasa*:** Scandinavian drinking vessel.

***katana*:** Long Japanese sword.

***kelleh*:** Long narrow carpets which are wider than runners.

***kendi*:** Chinese or Japanese globular drinking vessel which is filled through the neck, the liquid being drunk through the spout.

***khula khud*:** Indo-Persian term for helmet.

kilim: Flat woven rug without a pile.

***klapmuts*:** Chinese dish with rounded wall and flattened rim, said to resemble a type of woollen hat of this name worn by the Dutch in the 16th and 17th centuries.

knop: Knob, protuberance or swelling in the stem of a wine glass, of various forms which can be used as an aid to dating and provenance.

***Komai*:** Style of Japanese lacquerwork made famous by the Komai family.

***koro*:** Japanese incense burner.

***kotile*:** Ancient Greek vessel in the form of a bowl.

***kovsh*:** Russian vessel used for measuring drink, often highly decorated for ornamental purposes.

***kozuka*:** Small Japanese utility knife.

kraak porselein: Dutch term for porcelain raided from Portuguese ships, used to describe the earliest Chinese export porcelain.

krater: Ancient Greek vessel for mixing water and wine in which the mouth is always the widest part.

***kris*:** Indonesian or Malaysian dagger with a scalloped edge.

***kylin*:** Chinese mythical beast.

***laque burgauté*:** Asian lacquer wares, inlaid with mother-of-pearl, gold or precious stones.

***latticinio*:** Fine threads of white or clear glass forming a filigree mesh effect enclosed in clear glass.

***lattimo*:** from the Italian *latte* meaning milk; an opaque white glass made by adding bone ash or tin oxide to the glass batch.

lekythos: Ancient Greek flask used for oil or perfume.

***lingzhi*:** Type of fungus or mushroom, used as a motif on Chinese works of art.

***lishui*:** Chinese term for vertical water. A traditional border design normally used on Imperial Chinese garments.

loaded: Term used for a silver candlestick with a hollow stem filled with pitch or sand for weight and stability.

Longquan: Chinese ceramics with a pale grey body covered by a thick, opaque, bluish-green, slightly bubbly glaze.

Lucite: Type of solid, transparent plastic, often used instead of glass.

made up: Piece of furniture that has been put together from parts of other pieces of furniture. See *associated* and *marriage*.

maiolica: Tin-glazed earthenware produced in Italy from the 15thC to the present day.

majolica: Heavily-potted, moulded ware covered in transparent glazes in distinctive, often sombre colours, developed by the Minton factory in the mid-19thC.

marriage: Joining together of two unrelated parts to form one piece of furniture. See *associated* and *made up*.

***martelé*:** Term for silverware with a fine, hammered surface, first produced in France and later revived by the American silversmiths Gorham Manufacturing Co during the Art Nouveau period.

matched pair: Two items that are very similar in appearance and give the appearance of being a pair.

***meiping*:** Chinese for cherry blossom, used to describe a tall vase with high shoulders, small neck and narrow mouth, used to display flowering branches.

***meiren*:** Chinese term for a beautiful, elegant lady.

merese: Flat disc of glass which links the bowl and stem, and sometimes the stem and foot, of a drinking glass.

***mihrab*:** Prayer niche with a pointed arch; the motif which distinguishes a prayer rug from other types.

milk glass: (*milchglass*) Term for glass made with tin oxide, which turns it an opaque white. Developed in Venice in the late 15thC.

millefiori: Italian term meaning 'thousand flowers'. A glassmaking technique whereby canes of coloured glass are arranged in bundles so that the cross-section creates a pattern. Commonly used in paperweights.

***minogame*:** Mythical Japanese character, half turtle, half beast.

***mon*:** Japanese crest or coat-of-arms.

monteith: Large bowl with detachable collar and scalloped rim from which wine glasses were suspended to cool over iced water.

***nashiji*:** Multitude of gold flakes in Japanese lacquer.

near pair: Two items that are very similar in appearance and give the appearance of being a pair. Also known as a matched pair.

***netsuke*:** Japanese carved toggles made to secure *sagemono* (hanging things) to the *obi* (waist belt) from a cord; usually of ivory, lacquer, silver or wood, from the 16thC.

***nonome*:** Japanese term for false damascening or inlay.

niello: Black metal alloy or enamel used for filling in engraved designs on silverware.

nulling (knulling): Decorative carving in the form of irregular fluting, usually found on early oak furniture.

ogee: Double curve of slender S shape.

oinochoe: Ancient Greek small jug with handles.

***ojime*:** Japanese word meaning bead.

***okimono*:** Small, finely carved Japanese ornament.

oklad: Silver or gold icon cover, applied as a tribute or in gratitude for a prayer answered. Also known as a riza or basma.

olla: Ancient earthenware pot for cooking or carrying water.

***oni*:** Chinese devil.

opaline: Semi-translucent glass.

ormolu: Strictly, gilded bronze but used loosely for any yellow metal. Originally used for furniture handles and mounts but, from the 18thC, for inkstands, candlesticks etc.

overlay: In cased glass, the top layer, usually engraved to reveal a different coloured layer beneath.

palmette: Stylized palm-leaf motif.

paper plush: Type of plush fabric used in the manufacture of soft toys, made from nettle plant derivatives due to a lack of mohair and other quality materials in the 1920s.

***pardah*:** A rug which is suspended in a tent doorway.

***pâte-de-cristal*:** Glass that is crushed into fine crystals and then bound together so that it can be moulded rather than having to be worked in its molten state.

***pâte-sur-pâte*:** 19thC Sèvres porcelain technique, much copied, of applying coloured clay decoration to the body before firing.

***pâte-de-verre* (glass paste) :** Transluscent glass created by melting and applying powdered glass in layers or by casting it in a mould.

***pavé*:** Setting that has been paved with snugly fitting gemstones, so that little or no metal shows through.

penwork: Type of decoration applied to japanned furniture, principally in England in the late 18th/early 19thC. Patterns in white japan were applied to a piece which had already been japanned black, and then the details and shading were added using black Indian ink with a fine quill pen.

***phiale mesomphalos*:** an ancient Greek metal vessel used for pouring libations and also for making offerings at religious sanctuaries. The mesomphalos is the raised central boss.

pier glass: Mirror designed to be fixed to the pier, or wall, between two tall window openings, often partnered by a matching pier table. Made from the mid-17thC.

***pietra dura*:** Italian term for hardstone, applied to a mosaic pattern of semi-precious stones and marble.

***piqué*:** Technique in which a material such as tortoiseshell is inlaid with metal decoration.

***plique-à-jour*:** Enamelling technique in which a structure of metal strips is laid on a metal background to form enclosed areas which are then filled with transparent enamels. When the backing is removed, a transparent 'stained glass' effect is achieved.

plumbago: Another word for graphite.

plum pudding: Type of figuring in some veneers, produced by dark oval spots in the wood. Found particularly in mahogany.

***point-de-gaze*:** Type of lace developed in Belgium in the latter half of the 19thC, so-called because of its light, gauzy appearance.

pole screen: Small adjustable screen mounted on a pole and designed to stand in front of an open fire to shield a lady's face from the heat.

powder flask: Device for measuring out a precise quantity of priming powder, suspended from a musketeer's belt or bandolier and often ornately decorated. Sporting flasks are often made of antler and carved with hunting scenes.

powder horn: Cow horn hollowed out, blocked at the wide end with a wooden plug and fitted with a measuring device at the narrow end, used by musketeers for dispensing a precise quantity of priming powder.

prie-dieu: Chair with a low seat and a tall back designed for prayer. Usually dating from the 19thC.

printie/printy: Circular or oval hollow cut into glass for decorative effect, sometimes called a lens.

***prochous*:** Ancient Greek pitcher.

protome: Ancient Greek head and shoulders bust, often with a flat back.

proto-porcelain: Early high-fired stoneware that preceded true porcelain, developed in China as kilns became more efficient and capable of reaching higher temperatures.

prunt: Blob of glass applied to the stem of a drinking vessel both as decoration and to stop the glass from slipping in the hand. Sometimes impressed with a decorative stamp to form a 'raspberry'.

***punchong*:** Style of 15th-century Korean ceramics.

***Qianjian* palette:** Range of light brown colours used in the decoration of Chinese ceramics.

***qilin*:** Chinese mythical beast. Also spelt *kilin*.

Qingbai: White ware produced by potters in the Jingdezhen area of China throughout the Song Dynasty.

quarter-veneered: Four consecutively cut, and therefore identical, pieces of veneer laid at opposite ends to each other to give a mirrored effect.

***religieuse*:** Early clocks of the Louis XIV period in France, influenced by the sober Protestantism of the Dutch taste.

repoussé: Relief decoration on metal made by hammering on the reverse so that the decoration projects.

register plate: Scale of a barometer against which the mercury level is read.

regulator: Clock of great accuracy, thus sometimes used for controlling or checking other timepieces.

rocaille: Shell and rock motifs found in rococo work.

rouleau vase: Type of Chinese vase of cylindrical shape with a rolled over rim.

rummer: 19thC English low drinking goblet.

***ruyi*:** Chinese presentation sceptre.

***ruyi* clouds:** Cloud-like decorative feature often used as a design in Chinese art.

***sancai*:** Three-colour decoration on Chinese porcelain.

S. F. B. J.: *Société de Fabrication de Bébés et Jouets*; association of doll makers founded 1899 by the merger of Jumeau, Bru and others.

***sang-de-bouef*:** Bright red glaze used extensively on Chinese ceramics during the Qing Dynasty.

***Sennin*:** Japanese immortal.

sgraffito: Form of ceramic decoration incised through a coloured slip, revealing the ground beneath.

***shamshir*:** Indian sword.

***shakudo*:** Japanese term for an alloy of copper and gold.

***Shibayama*:** Japanese term for lacquer applied with semi-precious stones and ivory.

***Shibuichi*:** Japanese term for an alloy of copper and silver.

***shishi*:** Japanese mythical beast, a lion-dog.

***shou* symbol:** Chinese decorative motif, symbolizing longevity.

shoulder-head: Term for a doll's head and shoulders below the neck.

shoulderplate: Area of a doll's shoulder-head below the neck.

silver resist: Decorative technique normally found on pearlware ceramics c1800–20, whereby a design is painted in wax onto an object and then silver lustre is applied to the surface. When the wax is burnt off in the kiln, the painted design appears on a silver lustre ground.

siphon tube: U-shaped tube fitted into wheel barometers where the level of mercury in the short arm is used to record air pressure.

soft paste: Artificial porcelain made with the addition of ground glass, bone-ash or soap-stone. Used by most European porcelain manufacturers during the 18thC. Recognized by its soft, soapy feel.

spadroon: Cut-and-thrust sword.

spandrel: Element of design, closing off a corner.

spelter: Zinc treated to look like bronze and much used as an inexpensive substitute in Art Nouveau appliqué ornament and Art Deco figures.

strapwork: Repeated carved decoration suggesting plaited straps.

strip quilt ('strippy'): Quilt composed of alternating strips of different fabrics, either solid colours or prints. Very often used as the back of a patchwork or floral quilt.

stuff-over: Descriptive of upholstered furniture where the covering extends over the frame of the seat.

stumpwork: Embroidery which incorporates distinctive areas of raised decoration, formed by padding certain areas of the design.

***sugán*:** Twisted lengths of straw: referring to a type of Irish country chair that has a seat of this type.

***susani*:** Central Asian hand-embroidered bridal bed-cover.

***table ambulante*:** French term for a small, portable occasional table.

***takamakie*:** Technique used in Japanese lacquerware in which the design is built up and modelled in a mixture of lacquer and charcoal or clay dust, and then often gilded.

***taotie*:** Chinese mythical animal that devours wrong-doers.

tazza: Wide but shallow bowl on a stem with a foot; ceramic and metal tazzas were made in antiquity and the form was revived by Venetian glassmakers in the 15thC. Also made in silver from the 16thC.

teapoy: Piece of furniture in the form of a tea caddy on legs, with a hinged lid opening to reveal caddies, mixing bowl and other tea drinking accessories.

tear: Tear-drop-shaped air bubble in the stem of an early 18thC wine glass, from which the air-twist evolved.

tête-à-tête: Tea set for two people.

thuyawood: Reddish-brown wood with distinctive small 'bird's-eye' markings, imported from Africa and used as a veneer.

***tiki*:** Symbol of the procreative power of the Maori god Tane.

timepiece: Clock that does not strike or chime.

tin glaze: Glassy opaque white glaze of tin oxide; re-introduced to Europe in the 14thC by Moorish potters; the characteristic glaze of delftware, faïence and maiolica.

***togidashi*:** Japanese lacquer technique in which further layers of lacquer are added to *hiramake* (qv) then polished flush with the original surface.

***tôle-peinte*:** Polychrome painted metal.

toleware: Items made from tinplated sheet iron which is varnished and then decorated with brightly coloured paints.

tombak: Alloy of copper and zinc.

***Tosei Gusoku*:** Japanese term meaning 'modern equipment', used to describe a new style of armour introduced in the late 16thC.

touch: Maker's mark stamped on much, but not all, early English pewter. Their use was strictly controlled by the Pewterer's Company of London: early examples consist of initials, later ones are more elaborate and pictorial, sometimes including the maker's address.

Trafalgar chair: Type of dining chair with sabre legs and a ropetwist bar, made during the Regency period to commemorate the Battle of Trafalgar

***trembleuse*:** French term for a cup and saucer with a raised rim that holds the cup steady to avoid spillages.

trumeau: Section of wall between two openings; a pier mirror.

***tsuba*:** Guard of a Japanese sword, usually consisting of an ornamented plate.

Tudric: Range of Celtic-inspired Art Nouveau pewter of high quality, designed for mass-production by Archibald Knox and others, and retailed through Liberty & Co.

tyg: Three-handled mug.

***ushabti*:** Literally 'answerer'. Ancient Egyptian ceramic figure placed in a tomb to work in the afterworld in the place of the dead person it represented.

vaseline glass: Type of opalescent glass developed in Britain in the late 1870s and designed to resemble 15th- and 16thC Venetian glass.

***vase parlant*:** Glass vase of Art Nouveau design engraved or decorated in cameo with verses from French poetry.

verge escapement: Oldest form of escapement, found on clocks as early as 1300 and still in use in 1900. Consisting of a bar (the verge) with two flag-shaped pallets that rock in and out of the teeth of the crown or escape wheel to regulate the movement.

vernier scale: Short scale added to the traditional 3in (7.5cm) scale on stick barometers to give more precise readings than had previously been possible.

***vernis Martin*:** Type of japanning or imitation lacquerwork invented by the Martin family in Paris in the 18th century.

***verre églomisé*:** Painting on glass. Often the reverse side of the glass is covered in gold or silver leaf through which a pattern is engraved and then painted black.

vesta case: Ornate flat case of silver or other metal for carrying vestas, an early form of match. Used from the mid-19thC.

vitrine: French display cabinet which is often of *bombé* or serpentine outline and ornately decorated with marquetry and ormolu.

***wakizashi*:** Short Japanese sword.

WMF: Short for Württembergische Metallwarenfabrik, a German foundry that was one of the principal producers of Art Nouveau metalware.

***wucai*:** Type of five-colour Chinese porcelain decoration, executed in vigorous style.

***wufu*:** Chinese term meaning 'the five happinesses' (long life, riches, tranquility, love of virtue and a good end to one's life).

***yaki*:** Japanese term for ware.

***yen yen*:** Chinese term for a long-necked vase with a trumpet mouth.

Yingqing: Type of porcelain from Jingdezhen in China, first produced during the Song dynasty. Also known as Qingbai.

DIRECTORY OF SPECIALISTS

If you wish to be included in next year's directory, or if you have a change of address or telephone number, please contact Miller's Advertising Department on +44 (0) 1580 766411 by March 2007. We advise readers to make contact by telephone before visiting a dealer, therefore avoiding a wasted journey.

UK & REPUBLIC OF IRELAND

20TH DESIGN

Berkshire
Special Auction Services, Kennetholme, Midgham, Reading, RG7 5UX
Tel: 0118 971 2949
www.specialauctionservices.com
Specialist auctions of 20th Century designer furniture

Essex
20th Century Marks, Whitegates, Rectory Road, Little Burstead, Near Billericay, Essex, CM12 9TR
Tel: 01268 411 000
info@20thcenturymarks.co.uk
www.20thcenturymarks.co.uk

ANTIQUITIES

Dorset
Ancient & Gothic, P.O. Box 5390, Bournemouth, BH7 6XR
Tel: 01202 431721
Antiquities from before 3,000 BC to about 1500 AD

Lancashire
Millennia Antiquities
Tel: 01204 690175 or 07930 273998
millenniaant@aol.com
www.AncientAntiquities.co.uk

ARCHITECTURAL ANTIQUES

Kent
Catchpole & Rye, Saracens Dairy, Jobbs Lane, Pluckley, Ashford, TN27 0SA
Tel: 01233 840840
info@crye.co.uk
www.crye.co.uk

Somerset
Robert Mills Ltd, Narroways Road, Eastville, Bristol, BS2 9XB
Tel: 0117 955 6542
info@rmills.co.uk
www.rmills.co.uk

Wales
Drew Pritchard Ltd, St Georges Church, Church Walks, Llandudno, LL30 2HL
Tel: 01492 874004
info@drewpritchard.co.uk
www.drewpritchard.co.uk

ARMS & MILITARIA

Cheshire
Armourer - The Militaria Magazine, Published by Beaumont Publishing Ltd, P.O. BOX 161, Congleton, CW12 3PP
Tel: 01260 278 044
editor@armourer.co.uk
www.armourer.co.uk
A bi-monthly magazine for military antique collectors and military history enthusiasts offering hundreds of contacts for buying and selling, articles on all aspects of militaria collecting plus the dates of UK militaria fairs and auctions. Available on subscription

Gloucestershire
Q & C Militaria, 22 Suffolk Road, Cheltenham, Gloucestershire, GL50 2AQ
Tel: 01242 519815
qcmilitaria@btconnect.com
www.qcmilitaria.com

Lincolnshire
Garth Vincent, The Old Manor House, Allington, Nr Grantham, NG32 2DH
Tel: 01400 281358 or 07785 352151
garthvincent@aol.com
www.guns.uk.com

Somerset
Grimes Militaria, 13 Lower Park Row, Bristol, Somerset, BS1 5BN
Tel: 0117 929 8205

Surrey
West Street Antiques, 63 West Street, Dorking, RH4 1BS Tel: 01306 883487
weststant@aol.com
www.antiquearmsandarmour.com

East Sussex
Wallis & Wallis, West Street Auction Galleries, Lewes, BN7 2NJ
Tel: 01273 480208
auctions@wallisandwallis.co.uk
www.wallisandwallis.co.uk
Auctioneers of militaria, arms and armour and medals

Yorkshire
Andrew Spencer Bottomley, The Coach House, Thongsbridge, Holmfirth, HD9 3JJ Tel: 01484 685234 or 07770 398270
andrewbottomley@compuserve.com

BAROGRAPHS

Somerset
Richard Twort
Tel: 01934 641900 or 07711 939789

BAROMETERS

Berkshire
Alan Walker, Halfway Manor, Halfway, Newbury, Berkshire, RG20 8NR
Tel: 01488 657670
enquiries@alanwalker-barometers.com
www.alanwalker-barometers.com

Cheshire
Derek & Tina Rayment Antiques, Orchard House, Barton Road, Barton, Nr Farndon, Cheshire, SY14 7HT
Tel: 01829 270429
raymentantiques@aol.com
www.antique-barometers.com

BOOKS

Gloucestershire
Dominic Winter Book Auctions, Mallard House, Broadway Lane, South Cerney, GL7 5UQ
Tel: 01285 860006
info@dominicwinter.co.uk
www.dominicwinter.co.uk
Specialist book auctions

Somerset
George Bayntun, Manvers Street, Bath, Somerset, BA1 1JW
Tel: 01225 466000
ebc@georgebayntun.com

Tyne & Wear
Barter Books, Alnwick Station, Alnwick, Northumberland, NE66 2NP
Tel: 01665 604888
www.barterbooks.co.uk

Surrey
David Aldous-Cook,
P.O. Box 413,
Sutton, SM3 8SZ
Tel: 020 8642 4842
office@davidaldous-cook.co.uk
www.davidaldous-cook.co.uk
Reference books on antiques and collectables

BOXES
Mostly Boxes,
93 High Street, Eton,
Windsor, Berkshire, SL4 6AF
Tel: 01753 858470

CIGARETTE CARDS
London
Murray Cards (International) Ltd, 51 Watford Way,
Hendon Central, London,
NW4 3JH Tel: 020 8202 5688
murraycards@ukbusiness.com
www.murraycard.com/

East Sussex
Soldiers of Rye,
Mint Arcade, 71 The Mint,
Rye, East Sussex, TN31 7EW
Tel: 01797 225952
rameses@supanet.com
chris@johnbartholomewcards.co.uk
www.rameses.supanet.com

CLOCKS
Cheshire
Coppelia Antiques,
Holford Lodge, Plumley
Moor Road, Nr Knutsford,
Plumley, WA16 9RS
Tel: 01565 722197
www.coppeliaantiques.co.uk

Gloucestershire
Jeffrey Formby,
The Gallery, Orchard
Cottage, East Street,
Moreton-in-Marsh,
Gloucestershire, GL56 0LQ
Tel: 01608 650558
www.formby-clocks.co.uk

The Grandfather Clock Shop,
Styles of Stow, The Little
House, Sheep Street,
Stow-on-the-Wold, GL54 1JS
Tel: 01451 830455
info@stylesofstow.co.uk
www.stylesofstow.co.uk

Jillings Antique Clocks,
Croft House,
17 Church Street, Newent,
Gloucestershire, GL18 1PU
Tel: 01531 822100
clocks@jillings.com
www.jillings.com

Woodward Antique Clocks,
21 Suffolk Parade,
Cheltenham, GL50 2AE
Tel: 01242 245667
woodwardclocks@onetel.com
www.woodwardclocks.com

Hampshire
The Clock-Work-Shop
(Winchester), 6A Parchment
Street, Winchester,
SO23 8AT
Tel: 01962 842331 or
07885 954302
www.clock-work-shop.co.uk

Kent
Gaby Gunst,
140 High Street, Tenterden,
TN30 6HT Tel: 01580 765818
gabysclocks@tenterden140.wanadoo.co.uk
www.gabysclocks.com.uk

The Old Clock Shop,
63 High Street, West
Malling, ME19 6NA
Tel: 01732 843246
theoldclockshop@tesco.net
www.theoldclockshop.co.uk

Derek Roberts Antiques,
25 Shipbourne Road,
Tonbridge, TN10 3DN
Tel: 01732 358986
drclocks@clara.net
www.qualityantiqueclocks.com

London
The Clock Clinic Ltd,
85 Lower Richmond Road,
Putney, SW15 1EU
Tel: 020 8788 1407
clockclinic@btconnect.com
www.clockclinic.co.uk

Roderick Antique Clocks,
23 Vicarage Gate, W8 4AA
Tel: 020 7937 8517
rick@roderickantiqueclocks.com
www.roderickantiqueclocks.com

Somerset
Kembery Antique Clocks Ltd,
George Street Antique
Centre, 8 Edgar Buildings,
George Street,
Bath, BA1 2EH
Tel: 0117 956 5281
kembery@kdclocks.co.uk
www.kdclocks.co.uk

Surrey
Antique Clocks by Patrick
Thomas, 62a West Street,
Dorking, Surrey, RH4 1BS
Tel: 01306 743661
patrickthomas@btconnect.com
www.antiqueclockshop.co.uk

The Clock House,
75 Pound Street, Carshalton,
SM5 3PG Tel: 020 8773 4844
or 07850 363 317
markcocklin@theclockhouse.co.uk
www.theclockhouse.co.uk

The Clock Shop,
64 Church Street,
Weybridge, KT13 8DL
Tel: 01932 840407/855503
www.theclockshopweybridge.co.uk

Wiltshire
P. A. Oxley Antique Clocks &
Barometers, The Old
Rectory, Cherhill, Calne,
Wiltshire, SN11 8UX
Tel: 01249 816227
info@paoxley.com
www.british-antiqueclocks.com

Allan Smith Clocks,
Amity Cottage, 162
Beechcroft Road, Upper
Stratton, Swindon, SN2 7QE
Tel: 01793 822977 or
07778 834342
allansmithclocks@lineone.net
www.allansmithantiqueclocks.co.uk

COMICS
London
Comic Book Postal Auctions
Ltd, 40-42 Osnaburgh
Street, NW1 3ND
Tel: 020 7424 0007
comicbook@compalcomics.com www.compalcomics.com

East Sussex
phil-comics auctions,
P.O. Box 3433, Brighton,
BN50 9JA Tel: 01273 673462
or 07739 844703
phil@phil-comics.com
www.phil-comics.com
A collector and trader/auctioneer with fifteen years experience specialising in Beano and Dandy children's annuals and comics. phil-comics auctions will sell your single items to entire collections through live online auctions. We seek all types of children's books, annuals and comics, including: Beano, Beezer, Black Bob, Broons, Dandy, Giles, Hotspur, Knockout, Lion, Marvelman, Mickey Mouse, Oor Wullie, Superman, Rupert Bear, Radio Fun, Rover, Topper, Victor, Wizard and many, many more! Please quote single items to entire collections from 1900 to 1980. Books, annuals, comics, summer specials, free gifts, flyers, original artwork, ephemera, etc. Please see www.phil-comics.com for full details and write, telephone or email with any queries. We look forward to hearing from you and will provide a fast courteous response.

DECORATIVE ARTS
Greater Manchester
A. S. Antique Galleries,
26 Broad Street,
Pendleton, Salford,
M6 5BY
Tel: 0161 737 5938 or
07836 368230
as@artnouveau-artdeco.com
www.artnouveau-artdeco.com

London
Crafts Nouveau,
112 Alexandra Park Road,
Muswell Hill, N10 2AE
Tel: 0208 444 3300 or
07958 448 380
www.craftsnouveau.co.uk

Sylvia Powell Decorative Arts, Suite 400, Ceramic House, 571 Finchley Road, London, NW3 7BN
Tel: 020 8458 4543
dpowell909@aol.com

Republic of Ireland
Mitofsky Antiques, 8 Rathfarnham Road, Terenure, Dublin 6
Tel: 1 492 0033
info@mitofskyantiques.com
www.mitofskyantiques.com

Worcestershire
Art Nouveau Originals, The Bindery Gallery, 69 High Street, Broadway, Worcestershire, WR12 7DP
Tel: 01386 854645
cathy@artnouveauoriginals.com
www.artnouveauoriginals.com

Yorkshire
Muir Hewitt, Art Deco Originals, Halifax Antiques Centre, Queens Road Mills, Queens Road/Gibbet Street, Halifax, Yorkshire, HX1 4LR
Tel: 01422 347377
muir.hewitt@virgin.net
muir.hewitt@btconnect.com
www.muirhewitt.com

DOLLS

Cheshire
Dollectable, 53 Lower Bridge Street, Chester, CH1 1RS
Tel: 01244 344888/679195

London
Glenda - Antique Dolls, A18-A19 Grays Antique Market, Davies Mews, London, W1Y 2LP
Tel: 020 8367 2441/020 7629 7034
glenda@glenda-antiquedolls.com
www.glenda-antiquedolls.com

EPHEMERA

Nottinghamshire
T. Vennett-Smith, 11 Nottingham Road, Gotham, NG11 0HE
Tel: 0115 983 0541
info@vennett-smith.com
www.vennett-smith.com
Ephemera auctions

EXHIBITION & FAIR ORGANISERS

London
The Decorative Antiques & Textiles Fair, Harvey (Management Services) Ltd, P.O. Box 149, W9 1QN
Tel: 020 7624 5173
fairs@decorativefair.com
www.decorativefair.com

Nottinghamshire
DMG Fairs, P.O. Box 100, Newark, NG24 1DJ
Tel: 01636 702326
www.dmgantiquefairs.com

West Midlands
Antiques for Everyone Fair, NEC House, National Exhibition Centre, Birmingham, B40 1NT
Tel: 0121 780 4141
antiques@necgroup.co.uk

EXPORTERS

East Sussex
International Furniture Exporters Ltd, Old Cement Works, South Heighton, Newhaven, BN9 0HS
Tel: 01273 611251
ife555@aol.com
www.int-furniture-exporters.co.uk

Wiltshire
North Wilts. Exporters, Farm Hill House, Farm Hill House, SN15 5AJ
Tel: 01666 510876 or 07836 260730
mike@northwilts.demon.co.uk
www.northwiltsantiqueexporters.com

FISHING

Kent
The Old Tackle Box, P.O. Box 55, High Street, Cranbrook, TN17 3ZU
Tel: 01580 713979 or 07729 278 293
tackle.box@virgin.net

FURNITURE

Devon
Pugh's Antiques, Pugh's Farm, Monkton, Nr Honiton, EX14 9QH
Tel: 01404 42860
sales@pughsantiques.com
www.pughsantiques.com
(Relocating to: Portley House, Old Ludlow Road, Leominster H36 0AA Tel: 01568 616546)

Essex
Victor Hall & Sons Antiques
Tel: 01268 711777
www.victorhallantiques.com

Northamptonshire
Lorraine Spooner Antiques, 211 Watling Street West, Towcester, NN12 6BX
Tel: 01327 358777
lorraine@lsantiques.com
www.lsantiques.com
Period furniture, clocks, silver, porcelain, glass, paintings & prints, linens, books

Nottinghamshire
Newark Antiques Warehouse Ltd, Old Kelham Road, Newark, NG24 1BX
Tel: 01636 674869/07974 429185
enquiries@newarkantiques.co.uk
www.newarkantiques.co.uk

Oxfordshire
The Chair Set, 18 Market Place, Woodstock, Oxfordshire, OX20 1TA
Tel: 01428 707301
allanjames@thechairset.com
www.thechairset.com

Scotland
Jeremy Gow Antique Restoration, Pitscandly Farm, Forfar, Angus, DD8 3NZ
Tel: 01307 465342
jeremy@knowyourantiques.com
www.knowyourantiques.com
Antique furniture and restoration

West Sussex
British Antique Replicas, 22 School Close, Queen Elizabeth Avenue, Burgess Hill, RH15 9RX
Tel: 01444 245577
www.1760.com
Antique replica furniture

Warwickshire
Apollo Antiques Ltd, The Saltisford, Birmingham Road, Warwick, CV34 4TD Tel: 01926 494746/494666
mynott@apolloantiques.com

Wiltshire
Cross Hayes Antiques, Units 6–8 Westbrook Farm, Draycot Cerne, Chippenham, SN15 5LH
Tel: 01249 720033
david@crosshayes.co.uk
www.crosshayes.co.uk
Shipping furniture

Worcestershire
S.W. Antiques, Newlands (road), Pershore, WR10 1BP
Tel: 01386 555580
sales@sw-antiques.co.uk
www.sw-antiques.co.uk

GLASS

Cumbria
Just Glass, Cross House, Market Place, Alston, Cumbria, CA9 3HS
Tel: 01434 381263

Essex
F.W. Aldridge Ltd, Unit 3 St Johns Industrial Estate, Dunmow Road, Takeley, CM22 6SP
Tel: 01279 874000
angela@fwaldridge.abel.co.uk
www.fwaldridgeglass.com

London
Jeanette Hayhurst Fine Glass, 32a Kensington Church Street, London, W8 4HA
Tel: 020 7938 1539
www.antiqueglass-london.com

Norfolk
Brian Watson Antique Glass, BY APPOINTMENT, Foxwarren Cottage, High Street, Marsham, Norwich, Norfolk, NR10 5QA
Tel: 01263 732519
brian.h.watson@talk21.com

East Sussex
Glass etc, 18–22 Rope Walk, Rye, East Sussex, TN31 7NA
decanterman@freezone.co.uk www.decanterman.com

Wales
Drew Pritchard Ltd, St Georges Church, Church Walks, Llandudno, LL30 2HL
Tel: 01492 874004
info@drewpritchard.co.uk
www.drewpritchard.co.uk
Stained glass

JEWELLERY

London
Shapiro & Co, Stand 380, Gray's Antique Market, 58 Davies Street, W1Y 5LP Tel: 020 7491 2710
Faberge

Aurum, 310/311 Grays Antique Market, 58 Davies Street, London, W1K 5LP
Tel: 020 7409 0215
aurum@tinyworld.co.uk
www.graysantiques.com

LIGHTING

Devon
The Exeter Antique Lighting Co., Cellar 15, The Quay, Exeter, Devon, EX2 4AP
Tel: 01392 490848
www.antiquelightingcompany.com

Somerset
Joanna Proops Antique Textiles & Lighting, 34 Belvedere, Lansdown Hill, Bath, Somerset, BA1 5HR
Tel: 01225 310795
antiquetextiles@aol.co.uk
www.antiquetextiles.co.uk

MAPS

London
Jonathan Potter Ltd Antique Maps, 125 New Bond Street, London, W1S 1DY
Tel: 020 7491 3520
jpmaps@attglobal.net
www.jpmaps.co.uk

MARKETS & CENTRES

Lincolnshire
Hemswell Antique Centres, Caenby Corner Estate, Hemswell Cliff, Gainsborough, DN21 5TJ
Tel: 01427 668389
info@hemswell-antiques.com
www.hemswell-antiques.com

London
Antiquarius Antiques Centre, 131/141 King's Road, Chelsea, SW3 5ST
Tel: 020 7351 5353
info@antiquarius.co.uk
www.antiquarius.co.uk

Grays Antique Markets, South Molton Lane, W1K 5AB
Tel: 020 7629 7034
www.graysantiques.com
Over 200 specialist antique dealers selling beautiful and unusual antiques & collectables

East Sussex
Church Hill Antiques Centre, 6 Station Street, Lewes, BN7 2DA
Tel: 01273 474 842
churchhilllewes@aol.com
www.church-hill-antiques.com

MUSIC

Kent
Stephen T.P. Kember, Pamela Goodwin, 11 The Pantiles, Royal Tunbridge Wells, TN2 5TD
Tel: 01959 574067 or 07850 358067
steve.kember@btinternet.com
www.antique-musicboxes.co.uk
Antique cylinder & disc musical boxes

London
Robert Morley & Co Ltd, Piano and Harpsicord Showroom & Workshop, 34 Engate Street, London, SE13 7HA
Tel: 020 8318 5838
jvm@morley-r.u-net.com
www.morleypianos.com

Nottinghamshire
Turner Violins, 1-5 Lily Grove, Beeston, NG9 1QL
Tel: 0115 943 0333
info@turnerviolins.co.uk
Violins, double basses, violas, cellos & their bows

OAK & COUNTRY

Surrey
The Refectory, 38 West Street, Dorking, RH4 1BU
Tel: 01306 742111
www.therefectory.co.uk
Oak & country - refectory table specialist

Northamptonshire
Paul Hopwell Antiques, 30 High Street, West Haddon, NN6 7AP
Tel: 01788 510636
paulhopwell@antiqueoak.co.uk
www.antiqueoak.co.uk

PACKERS & SHIPPERS

Gloucestershire
The Shipping Company, Bourton Industrial Park, Bourton on the Water, Cheltenham, GL54 2HQ
Tel: 01451 822451
enquiries@theshippingcompanyltd.com
www.theshippingcompanyltd.com

Middlesex
Adam Crease Shipping Ltd, Cumberland House, Drake Avenue, Staines, TW18 2AP
Tel: 01784 461 300
sales@adamcreaseshipping.com
www.adamcreaseshipping.com

PAPERWEIGHTS

Cheshire
Sweetbriar Gallery Paperweights Ltd., 29 Beechview Road, Kingsley, WA6 8DF
Tel: 01928 788225
sales@sweetbriar.co.uk
www.sweetbriar.co.uk

PINE

Buckinghamshire
For Pine, 340 Berkhampstead Road, Chesham, Buckinghamshire, HP5 3HF Tel: 01494 776119

Nottingham
Harlequin Antiques, 79–81 Mansfield Road, Daybrook, Nottingham, NG5 6BH
Tel: 0115 967 4590
sales@antiquepine.net
www.antiquepine.net

Republic of Ireland
Honan's Antiques, Crowe Street, Gort, County Galway, Republic of Ireland
Tel: 00 353 91 631407
www.honansantiques.com

Somerset
Gilbert & Dale Antiques, The Old Chapel, Church Street, Ilchester, Nr Yeovil, BA22 8ZA
Tel: 01935 840464
roy@roygilbert.com
Painted pine & country furniture

Ministry of Pine, Timsbury Village Workshop, Unit 2, Timsbury Industrial Estate, Hayeswood Road, Timsbury, Bath, Somerset, BA2 0HQ
Tel: 01761 472297
ministryofpine.uk@virgin.net
www.ministryofpine.com

Wiltshire
North Wilts. Exporters, Farm Hill House, Brinkworth, SN15 5AJ
Tel: 01666 510876 or 07836 260730
mike@northwilts.demon.co.uk
www.northwiltsantiqueexporters.com

Yorkshire
Havelocks Pine & Antiques,
13, 15, 17 Westmoreland Street, Harrogate,
Yorkshire, HG1 5AY
Tel: 01423 506721

PORCELAIN

London
Guest & Gray,
1–7 Davies Mews,
London, W1K 5AB
Tel: 020 7408 1252
info@chinese-porcelain-art.com
www.chinese-porcelain-art.com

Mario's Antiques,
75 Portobello Road,
London, W11 2QB
Tel: 020 8902 1600 or 07919 254000
marwan@barazi.screaming.net
www.marios_antiques.com

Tablewhere Ltd,
4 Queens Parade Close,
N11 3FY Tel: UK local rate 0845 130 6111/ 020 8361 6111
www.tablewhere.co.uk
Tableware matching specialists.

East Sussex
Tony Horsley,
P.O. Box 3127,
Brighton, BN1 5SS
Tel: 01273 550770
Candle extinguishers, Royal Worcester and other fine porcelain

Warwickshire
Chinasearch, Ltd,
4 Princes Drive, Kenilworth,
Warwickshire, CV8 2FD
Tel: 01926 512402
info@chinasearch.co.uk
www.chinasearch.co.uk

POTTERY

Berkshire
Special Auction Services,
Kennetholme, Midgham,
Reading, RG7 5UX
Tel: 0118 971 2949
www.specialauctionservices.com
Specialist auctions of commemoratives, pot lids & Prattware, Fairings, Goss & Crested, Baxter & Le Blond prints

Buckinghamshire
Gillian Neale Antiques,
P.O. Box 247,
Aylesbury, HP20 1JZ
Tel: 01296 423754/ 07860 638700
gillianneale@aol.com
www.gillianneale antiques.co.uk
Blue & white transfer printed pottery 1780–1860

Gloucestershire
Styles of Stow,
The Little House,
Sheep Street, Stow-on-the-Wold, GL54 1JS
Tel: 01451 830455
www.stylesofstow.co.uk
Staffordshire figures

London
Aurea Carter,
P.O. Box 44134,
London, SW6 3YX
Tel: 020 7731 3486
aureacarter@englishceramics.com
www.englishceramics.com

Oxfordshire
John Howard at Heritage,
6 Market Place,
Woodstock,
Oxfordshire, OX20 1TA
Tel: 0870 4440678
john@johnhoward.co.uk
www.antiquepottery.co.uk

Winson Antiques,
Unit 11, Langston Priory Workshops, Kingham,
OX7 6UR
Tel: 01608 658856 or 07764 476776
clive.payne@virgin.net
www.clivepayne.co.uk
Mason's Ironstone china and period furniture

Surrey
Judi Bland Antiques
Tel: 01536 724145 or 01276 857576
18th & 19th century English Toby jugs

Julian Eade
Tel: 01865 300349 or 07973 542971
Doulton Lambeth stoneware and Burslem wares. Royal Worcester, Minton and Derby

London
Rogers de Rin,
76 Royal Hospital Road,
SW3 4HN
Tel: 020 7352 9007
rogersderin@rogersderin.co.uk
www.rogersderin.co.uk
Wemyss

Wales
Islwyn Watkins,
Offa's Dyke Antique Centre,
4 High Street, Knighton,
Powys, LD7 1AT, Wales
Tel: 01547 520145

Warwickshire
Chinasearch Ltd,
4 Princes Drive,
Kenilworth,
Warwickshire, CV8 2FD
Tel: 01926 512402
info@chinasearch.co.uk
www.chinasearch.co.uk

PUBLICATIONS

London
Antiques Trade Gazette,
115 Shaftesbury Avenue,
WC2H 8AD
Tel: 0207 420 6646
www.antiquestradegazette.com

West Midlands
Antiques Magazine,
H.P. Publishing,
2 Hampton Court Road,
Harborne, Birmingham,
B17 9AE
Tel: 0121 681 8000
Subs 01562 701001
subscriptions@antiquesmagazine.com

ROCK & POP

Cheshire
Collector's Corner,
P.O. Box 8, Congleton,
CW12 4GD
Tel: 01260 270429
dave.popcorner@ukonline.co.uk

Lancashire
Tracks,
P.O. Box 117,
Chorley, PR6 0UU
Tel: 01257 269726
sales@tracks.co.uk
www.tracks.co.uk
Beatles and rare pop memorabilia

RUGS & CARPETS

KENT
Desmond & Amanda North,
The Orchard, 186 Hale Street, East Peckham,
Kent, TN12 5JB
Tel: 01622 871353

London
Orientalist Rugs,
152–154 Walton Street,
London, SW3 2JJ
Tel: 020 7581 2332
mike@orientalist.demon.co.uk
www.orientalistrugs.com

West Sussex
Wadsworth's,
Marehill, Pulborough,
RH20 2DY
Tel: 01798 873555
www.wadsworthsrugs.com

SCIENTIFIC INSTRUMENTS

Cambridge
Fossack & Furkle,
P.O. Box 733, Abington,
Cambridgeshire, CB1 6BF
Tel: 01223 894296
fossack@btopenworld.com
www.fossackandfurkle.freeservers.com

Cheshire
Charles Tomlinson,
Chester Tel: 01244 318395
charlestomlinson@tiscali.co.uk

London
Curious Science,
307 Lillie Road, Fulham,
London, SW6 7LL
Tel: 020 7610 1175
props@curiousscience.com
www.curiousscience.com

Scotland
Early Technology,
Monkton House,
Old Craighall, Musselburgh,

Midlothian, EH21 8SF
Tel: 0131 665 5753 or 07831 106768
michael.bennett-levy@virgin.net
www.earlytech.com
www.rare78s.com
www.tvhistory.tv

SCULPTURE
London
David Hickmet,
75 Portobello Road,
W11 2QB
Tel: 07050 123450 or 0797 1850405
david@hickmet.com
www.hickmet.com

Kent
Hazlehurst Sculpture & Antiques, P.O. Box 128,
Cranbrook, Kent,
TN17 4WY Tel: 01580 241993
dirkpam.com@btopenworld.com
www.hazlehurstantiques.com

East Sussex
Garret & Hurst Sculpture,
P.O. Box 138,
Hailsham, BN27 1WX
Tel: 01323 848824 or 07976 247942
garhurst@btinternet.com
www.garretandhurst.co.uk

SERVICES
London
Antiques Hunting,
34B Chiswick Lane,
Chiswick, W4 2JQ
Tel: 01723 350163
enquiries@antiqueshunting.com
www.antiqueshunting.com
Antiques online

SILVER
London
Daniel Bexfield Antiques,
26 Burlington Arcade,
W1J 0PU
Tel: 020 7491 1720
antiques@bexfield.co.uk
www.bexfield.co.uk
Specialising in fine quality silver, jewellery and objects of vertu dating from the 17th to the 20thc

Lyn Bloom & Jeffrey Neal,
Vault 27, The London Silver Vaults, Chancery Lane,
London, WC2A 1QS
Tel: 020 8421 8848
jeffrey@bloomvault.com
www.bloomvault.com

West Sussex
Nicholas Shaw Antiques,
Virginia Cottage,
Lombard Street, Petworth,
West Sussex, GU28 0AG
Tel: 01798 345146/ 01798 345147
silver@nicholas-shaw.com
www.nicholas-shaw.com

SPORTS & GAMES
Nottinghamshire
T. Vennett-Smith,
11 Nottingham Road,
Gotham, NG11 0HE
Tel: 0115 983 0541
info@vennett-smith.com
www.vennett-smith.com
Sporting auctions

TEDDY BEARS
Oxfordshire
Teddy Bears of Witney,
99 High Street,
Witney, OX28 6HY
Tel: 01993 706616
jan@witneybears.co.uk
www.teddybears.co.uk

West Yorkshire
Bears of Windy Hill,
P.O. Box 51, Shipleg,
West Yorkshire, BD18 2YH
Tel: 01274 599175
info@bearsofwindyhill.co.uk
www.bearsofwindyhill.co.uk

TEXTILES
London
Elizabeth Gibbons Antique Textiles, By appointment only Tel: 020 7352 1615 & 01989 750243
elizabeth@egantiquetextiles.co.uk

Erna Hiscock & John Shepherd, Chelsea Galleries,
69 Portobello Road, W11
Tel: 01233 661407
erna@ernahiscockantiques.com
www.ernahiscockantiques.com
Antique samplers

Somerset
Joanna Proops Antique Textiles & Lighting,
34 Belvedere,
Lansdown Hill, Bath,
Somerset, BA1 5HR
Tel: 01225 310795
antiquetextiles@aol.co.uk
www.antiquetextiles.co.uk

Suffolk
Marilyn Garrow,
By appointment only
Tel: 01728 648671 or 07774 842074
marogarrow@aol.com
www.antiquesweb.co.uk/marilyngarrow

TOYS
Berkshire
Special Auction Services,
Kennetholme, Midgham,
Reading, RG7 5UX
Tel: 0118 971 2949
www.specialauctionservices.com
Specialist auctions of toys for the collector including Dinky, Corgi, Matchbox, lead soldiers and figures, tinplate and model railways.

East Sussex
Wallis & Wallis,
West Street Auction Galleries, Lewes, BN7 2NJ
Tel: 01273 480208
grb@wallisandwallis.co.uk
www.wallisandwallis.co.uk
Auctioneers of diecast toys, model railways, tin plate toys and models

Yorkshire
John & Simon Haley,
89 Northgate, Halifax,
Yorkshire, HX1 1XF
Tel: 01422 822148/ 360434
toysandbanks@aol.com
Toys and money boxes

WATCHES
London
Pieces of Time,
1–7 Davies Mews,
W1K 5AB
Tel: 020 7629 2422
info@antique-watch.com
www.antique-watch.com
www.cufflinksworld.com

WINE ANTIQUES
Buckinghamshire
Christopher Sykes,
The Old Parsonage,
Woburn, Milton Keynes,
Buckinghamshire,
MK17 9QM
Tel: 01525 290259
www.sykes-corkscrews.co.uk
Corkscrews

U.S.A.
AMERICANA
American West Indies Trading Co. Antiques & Art
Tel: 305 872 3948
awindies@att.net
www.goantiques.com/members/awindiestrading
Ethnographic, Folk, Tribal, Spanish Colonial, Santos & Retablos, American Indian, Indonesian Keris, southeast Asian antiquities, orientalia, Art Deco, Floridiana

Allan Katz Americana,
25 Old Still Road,
Woodbridge,
Connecticut 06525
Tel: 203 393 9356
Folk Art, trade signs and weather vanes

ANTIQUITIES
Hurst Gallery,
53 Mt. Auburn Street,
Cambridge,
MA 02138
Tel: 617 491 6888
manager@hurstgallery.com
www.hurstgallery.com
Art of the Pacific, Africa, Asia, The Americas and the ancient world

ARMS & MILITARIA
Faganarms,
Box 425,
Fraser, MI48026
Tel: 586 465 4637
info@faganarms.com
www.faganarms.com

BAROMETERS
Barometer Fair,
P.O. Box 25502,
Sarasota, Florida 34277
Tel: 941 923 6136
john@barometerfair.com
Buys, sells and restores antique barometers

BOOKS
Bauman Rare Books,
1608 Walnut Street,
19th Floor, Philadelphia,
PA 19104 Tel: 215 546 6466
brb@baumanrarebooks.com
www.baumanrarebooks.com

CLOCKS
R. O. Schmitt Fine Art,
Box 1941, Salem,
New Hampshire 03079
Tel: 603 432 2237
roschmittclocks@yahoo.com
www.antiqueclockauction.com
Specialist antique clock auctions

DOLLS
Sara Bernstein Antique Dolls
& Bears, Englishtown,
New Jersey 07726
Tel: 732 536 4101
santiqbebe@aol.com
www.sarabernsteindolls.com
Dolls and Teddy bears

Theriault's, P.O. Box 151,
Annapolis, MD 21404
Tel: 410 224 3655
info@theriaults.com
www.theriaults.com
Doll auctions

FURNITURE
American Art Display,
514 14th West Palm Beach,
Florida 33401
Tel: 561 379 9367
americanartdisplay@msn.com
Display stands

Antique Associates at West
Townsend, P.O. Box 129W,
473 Main Street,
West Townsend, MA 01474
Tel: 978 597 8084
drh@aaawt.com

Antiquebug,
Frank & Cathy Sykes,
85 Center Street, Wolfeboro,
New Hampshire 03894
Tel: 603 569 0000
dragonfly@antiquebug.com
www.antiquebug.com
Also Folk Art, mahogany speed boat models, maps and antiquarian books

Axe Antiques,
275 Alt. A1A (SR811)
Jupiter, Florida 33477,
Palm Beach County
Tel: 561 743 7888/
877 689 1730
www.axeantiques.com
Also stocks fine art, vintage pillows, seals, militaria and architectural elements

Douglas Hamel Antiques,
56 Staniels Road,
Chichester,
New Hampshire 03234
Tel: 603 798 5912
doughamel@shaker
antiques.com
www.shakerantiques.com
We buy, sell and locate Shaker antiques

LIGHTING
Chameleon Fine Lighting,
223 East 59th Street,
New York, NY 10022
Tel: 212 355 6300
mail@chameleon59.com
www.chameleon59.com

MARKETS & CENTRES
Chesapeake Antique Center,
Inc., Route 301,
P.O. Box 280, Queenstown,
MD 21658 Tel: 410 827 6640
admin@chesapeake
antiques.com
www.chesapeakantiques.com

Santa Monica Antique
Market, 1607 Lincoln
Boulevard, Santa Monica,
California 90404
Tel: 310 673 7048

ORIENTAL
Mimi's Antiques
Tel: 443 250 0930
mimisantiques@comcast.net
www.mimisantiques.com
www.trocadero.com/
mimisantiques
18th and 19th century Chinese export porcelain, American and English furniture, continental porcelain, paintings, Sterling, oriental rugs

PAPERWEIGHTS
The Dunlop Collection,
P.O. Box 6269,
Statesville, NC 28687
Tel: 704 871 2626 or
Toll Free Telephone
(800) 227 1996

PUBLICATIONS
Antique Collectors Club Ltd,
Market Street Industrial
Park, Wappinger Falls,
New York 12590
Tel: 1 914 297 0003

SERVICES
Go Antiques,
94 North Street, Suite 300,
Dublin, Ohio 43017
Tel: 614 923 4250
www.goantiques.com
Antiques online

SILVER
Alter Silver Gallery Corp.,
Gallery 49A & 50,
1050 Second Avenue,
New York, NY10022
Tel: 212 750 1928/
917 848 1713
altersilvergallery@mac.com

Antique Elegance
Tel: 617 484 7556
gloriab415@aol.com
Also jewelry, pottery, porcelain, orientalia, cut glass, paintings, rugs and furniture

Argentum,
The Leopard's Head,
472 Jackson Street,
San Francisco, CA 94111
Tel: 415 296 7757
info@argentum-the
leopard.com
www.argentum-the
leopard.com

Imperial Half Bushel,
831 North Howard Street,
Baltimore, Maryland 21201
Tel: 410 462 1192
patrick.duggan@world
net.att.net
www.imperialhalfbushel.com

SPORTS & GAMES
Hunt Auctions,
75 E. Uwchlan Avenue,
Suite 130, Exton,
Pennsylvania 19341
Tel: 610 524 0822
info@huntauctions.com
www.huntauctions.com

TEXTILES
Antique European Linens
& Decadence Down,
P.O. Box 789, Gulf Breeze,
Florida 32562-0789
Tel: 850 432 4777
sales@antiqueeuropean
linens.com
www.antiqueeuropean
linens.com
Hungarian goose down pillows & european duvets.

Laura Fisher at Fisher
Heritage, 305 East 61st
Street, 5th Floor,
New York, NY 10021,
U.S.A.
Tel: 212 838 2596
laurafisherquilts@yahoo.com
www.laurafisherquilts.com

TRIBAL ART
Hurst Gallery,
53 Mt. Auburn Street,
Cambridge,
MA 02138
Tel: 617 491 6888
manager@hurstgallery.com
www.hurstgallery.com
Art of the Pacific, Africa, Asia, The Americas and the ancient world

CANADA
FISHING
Juniper Fishing Camps Ltd,
The Old River Lodge,
40 Green Bye Road,
Blissfield, Nr Doaktown,
New Brunswick, E9C 1L4
Tel: 506 455 2005 or
506 365 7277
Jon@theoldriverlodge.net
www.theoldriverlodge.net

JEWELLERY
Fiona Kenny Antiques
Tel: 905 682 0090
merday@cogeco.ca
www.tocadero.com/merday.
fionakennyantiques.com
18th–20thC jewellery and antiques, sterling and silver plate, china and pottery, 20thC modern, collectibles and advertising.

LIGHTING
Andrew W. Zegers Antiques,
25 Rodman Street,
St Catherines,
Ontario, L2R 5C9
Tel: 905 685 4643
Also art and accessories, antique formal upholstered

DIRECTORY OF AUCTIONEERS

Auctioneers who hold frequent sales should contact the advertising department on +44 (0) 1580 766411 by March 2007 for inclusion in the next edition.

UK & REPUBLIC OF IRELAND

Bedfordshire

Sheffield Railwayana Auctions, 4 The Glebe, Clapham, Bedford, MK41 6GA Tel: 01234 325341 www.sheffieldrailwayana.co.uk

W&H Peacock, 26 Newnham Street, Bedford, MK40 3JR Tel: 01234 266366

Berkshire

Cameo Auctions, Kennet Holme Farm, Bath Road, Midgham, Reading, RG7 5UX Tel: 01189 713772 www.cameo-auctioneers.co.uk

Dreweatt Neate, Donnington Priory, Donnington, Newbury, RG14 2JE Tel: 01635 553553 www.dnfa.com/donnington

Law Fine Art Tel: 01635 860033 www.lawfineart.co.uk

Padworth Auctions, 30 The Broadway, Thatcham, RG19 3HX Tel: 01734 713772

Shiplake Fine Art, 31 Great Knollys Street, Reading, RG1 7HU Tel: 01734 594748

Special Auction Services, Kennetholme, Midgham, Reading, RG7 5UX Tel: 0118 971 2949 www.specialauctionservices.com

Buckinghamshire

Amersham Auction Rooms, Station Road, Amersham, HP7 0AH Tel: 01494 729292 info@amershamauctionrooms.co.uk

Bourne End Auction Rooms, Station Approach, Bourne End, SL8 5QH Tel: 01628 531500

Dickins Auctioneers Ltd, The Claydon Saleroom, Calvert Road, Middle Claydon, MK18 2EZ Tel: 01296 714434 www.dickinsauctioneers.com

Cambridgeshire

Cheffins, Clifton House, 1 & 2 Clifton Road, Cambridge, CB1 7EA Tel: 01223 271966 www.cheffins.co.uk

Rowley Fine Art, The Old Bishop's Palace, Little Downham, Ely, CB6 2TD Tel: 01353 699177 www.rowleyfineart.com

Willingham Auctions, 25 High Street, Willingham, CB4 5ES Tel: 01954 261252 www.willinghamauctions.com

Cheshire

Halls Fine Art Auctions, Booth Mansion, 30 Watergate Street, Chester, CH1 2LA Tel: 01244 312300/312112

Frank R. Marshall & Co, Marshall House, Church Hill, Knutsford, WA16 6DH Tel: 01565 653284

Maxwells of Wilmslow inc Dockree's, 133A Woodford Road, Woodford, SK7 1QD Tel: 0161 439 5182 www.maxwells-auctioneers.co.uk

Wright Manley, Beeston Castle Salerooms, Tarporley, CW6 9NZ Tel: 01829 262150 www.wrightmanley.co.uk

Cleveland

Vectis Auctions Ltd, Fleck Way, Thornaby, Stockton-on-Tees, TS17 9JZ Tel: 01642 750616 www.vectis.co.uk

Co. Durham

Addisons Auctions, The Auction Rooms, Staindrop Road, Barnard Castle, DL12 8TD Tel: 01833 690545 www.addisons-auctioneers.co.uk

Cornwall

Lambrays, Polmorla Walk Galleries, The Platt, Wadebridge, PL27 7AE Tel: 01208 813593

W.H. Lane & Son, Jubilee House, Queen Street, Penzance, TR18 2DF Tel: 01736 361447 graham.bazlet@excite.com

David Lay, ASVA, Auction House, Alverton, Penzance, TR18 4RE Tel: 01736 361414

Martyn Rowe, The Truro Auction Centre, Triplets Business Park, Poldice Valley, Nr Chacewater, Truro, TR16 5PZ Tel: 01209 822266 www.invaluable.com/martynrowe

Cumbria

Kendal Auction Rooms, Sandylands Road, Kendal, LA9 6EU Tel: 01539 720603 www.kendalauction.co.uk/furniture

The Mitchells Auction Company, Furniture Hall, 47 Station Road, Cockermouth, CA13 9PZ Tel: 01900 827800 info@mitchellsfineart.com

Penrith Farmers' & Kidd's plc, Skirsgill Salerooms, Penrith, CA11 0DN Tel: 01768 890781 info@pfkauctions.co.uk www.pfkauctions.co.uk

Thomson, Roddick & Medcalf Ltd, Coleridge House, Shaddongate, Carlisle, CA2 5TU Tel: 01228 528939 www.thomsonroddick.com

Derbyshire

Bamfords Ltd, The Matlock Auction Gallery, The Old Picture Palace, 133 Dale Road, Matlock, DE4 3LU Tel: 01629 57460 www.bamfords-auctions.co.uk

Bamfords Ltd, The Derby Auction House, Chequers Road, off Pentagon Island, Derby, DE21 6EN Tel: 01332 210000 www.bamfords-auctions.co.uk

Devon

Bearnes, St Edmund's Court, Okehampton Street, Exeter, EX4 1DU Tel: 01392 207000 www.bearnes.co.uk

Michael J. Bowman, 6 Haccombe House, Nr Netherton, Newton Abbott, TQ12 4SJ Tel: 01626 872890

Dreweatt Neate, 205 High Street, Honiton, EX14 1LQ Tel: 01404 42404 www.dnfa.com/honiton

Eldreds Auctioneers & Valuers, 13–15 Ridge Park Road, Plympton, Plymouth, PL7 2BS Tel: 01752 340066

S.J. Hales, 87 Fore Street, Bovey Tracey, TQ13 9AB Tel: 01626 836684

The Plymouth Auction Rooms, Edwin House, St John's Road, Cattedown, Plymouth, PL4 0NZ Tel: 01752 254740

Rendells, Stonepark, Ashburton, TQ13 7RH Tel: 01364 653017 www.rendells.co.uk

G.S. Shobrook & Co, 20 Western Approach, Plymouth, PL1 1TG Tel: 01752 663341

John Smale & Co, 11 High Street, Barnstaple, EX31 1BG Tel: 01271 42000/42916

Martin Spencer-Thomas, Bicton Street, Exmouth, EX8 2SN Tel: 01395 267403

Dorset

Chapman, Moore & Mugford, 9 High Street, Shaftesbury, SP7 8JB Tel: 01747 822244

Charterhouse, The Long Street Salerooms, Sherborne, DT9 3BS Tel: 01935 812277 www.charterhouse-auctions.co.uk

Cottees of Wareham, The Market, East Street, Wareham, BH20 4NR Tel: 01929 552826 www.auctionsatcottees.co.uk

Hy Duke & Son, The Dorchester Fine Art Salerooms, Weymouth Avenue, Dorchester, DT1 1QS Tel: 01305 265080 www.dukes-auctions.com

Onslow's Auctions Ltd, The Coach House, Manor Road, Stourpaine, DT8 8TQ Tel: 01258 488838

Riddetts of Bournemouth, 1 Wellington Road, Bournemouth, BH8 8JQ Tel: 01202 555686 www.riddetts.co.uk

Semley Auctioneers, Station Road, Semley, Shaftesbury, SP7 9AN Tel: 01747 855122/855222

Essex

Ambrose, Ambrose House, Old Station Road, Loughton, IG10 4PE Tel: 020 8502 3951

Cooper Hirst Auctions, The Granary Saleroom, Victoria Road, Chelmsford, CM2 6LH Tel: 01245 260535

Leigh Auction Rooms, John Stacey & Sons, 88–90 Pall Mall, Leigh-on-Sea, SS9 1RG Tel: 01702 477051

Saffron Walden Auctions, 1 Market Street, Saffron Walden, CB10 1JB Tel: 01799 513281 www.saffronwaldenauctions.com

Sworders, 14 Cambridge Road, Stansted Mountfitchet, CM24 8BZ Tel: 01279 817778 www.sworder.co.uk

Flintshire

Dodds Property World, Victoria Auction Galleries, 9 Chester Street, Mold, CH7 1EB Tel: 01352 752552

Gloucestershire

Bruton, Knowles & Co, 111 Eastgate Street, Gloucester, GL1 1PZ Tel: 01452 880000

Clevedon Salerooms, The Auction Centre, Kenn Road, Kenn, Clevedon, Bristol, BS21 6TT Tel: 01934 830111 www.clevedon-salerooms.com

The Cotswold Auction Company Ltd, incorporating Short Graham & Co and Hobbs and Chambers Fine Arts, The Coach House, Swan Yard, 9–13 West Market Place, Cirencester, GL7 2NH Tel: 01285 642420 www.cotswoldauction.co.uk

The Cotswold Auction Company Ltd, incorporating Short Graham & Co and Hobbs and Chambers Fine Arts, Chapel Walk Saleroom, Cheltenham, GL50 3DS Tel: 01242 256363 www.cotswoldauction.co.uk

The Cotswold Auction Company Ltd, incorporating Short Graham & Co and Hobbs and Chambers Fine Arts, 4–6 Clarence Street, Gloucester, GL1 1DX 01452 521177 www.cotswoldauction.co.uk

Dreweatt Neate, St John's Place, Apsley Road, Clifton, Bristol, BS8 2ST Tel: 0117 973 7201 www.dnfa.com/bristol

Mallams, 26 Grosvenor Street, Cheltenham, GL52 2SG Tel: 01242 235712

Moore, Allen & Innocent, The Salerooms, Norcote, Cirencester, GL7 5RH Tel: 01285 646050 www.mooreallen.co.uk

Specialised Postcard Auctions, 25 Gloucester Street, Cirencester, GL7 2DJ Tel: 01285 659057

Tayler & Fletcher, London House, High Street, Bourton-on-the-Water, Cheltenham, GL54 2AP Tel: 01451 821666 www.taylerfletcher.com

Dominic Winter Book Auctions, Mallard House, Broadway Lane, South Cerney, GL7 5UQ Tel: 01285 860006 info@dominicwinter.co.uk www.dominicwinter.co.uk

Wotton Auction Rooms, Tabernacle Road, Wotton-under-Edge, GL12 7EB Tel: 01453 844733 www.wottonauctionrooms.co.uk

Greater Manchester

Capes Dunn & Co, The Auction Galleries, 38 Charles Street, Off Princess Street, M1 7DB Tel: 0161 273 6060/1911 capesdunn@yahoo.co.uk

Hampshire

Evans & Partridge, Agriculture House, High Street, Stockbridge, SO20 6HF Tel: 01264 810702

Jacobs & Hunt, 26 Lavant Street, Petersfield, GU32 3EF Tel: 01730 233933 www.jacobsandhunt.co.uk

George Kidner Auctioneers and Valuers, The Lymington Saleroom, Emsworth Road, Lymington, SO41 9BL Tel: 01590 670070 info@georgekidner.co.uk www.georgekidner.co.uk *Free auction estimates, specialist and general sales, probate and insurance valuations*

May & Son Auctioneers & Valuers, Delta Works, Salisbury Road, Shipton Bellinger, SP9 7UN Tel: 01980 846000 www.mayandson.com

D.M. Nesbit & Co, Fine Art and Auction Department, Southsea Salerooms, 7 Clarendon Road, Southsea, PO5 2ED Tel: 023 9286 4321 www.nesbits.co.uk

Odiham Auction Sales, Unit 4, Priors Farm, West Green Road, Mattingley, RG27 8JU Tel: 01189 326824 auction@dircon.co.uk

Herefordshire

Brightwells Fine Art, The Fine Art Saleroom, Easters Court, Leominster, HR6 0DE Tel: 01568 611122 www.brightwells.com

Morris Bricknell, Stroud House, 30 Gloucester Road, Ross-on-Wye, HR9 5LE Tel: 01989 768320 www.morrisbricknell.com

Williams & Watkins, Ross Auction Rooms, Ross-on-Wye, HR9 7QF Tel: 01989 762225

Nigel Ward & Co, The Border Property Centre, Pontrilas, HR2 0EH Tel: 01981 240140 www.nigel-ward.co.uk

Hertfordshire

Sworders, The Hertford Saleroom, 42 St Andrew Street, Hertford, SG14 1JA Tel: 01992 583508 www.sworder.co.uk

Tring Market Auctions, The Market Premises, Brook Street, Tring, HP23 5EF Tel: 01442 826446 www.tringmarketauctions.co.uk

Kent

Bentley's Fine Art Auctioneers, The Old Granary, Waterloo Road, Cranbrook, TN17 3JQ Tel: 01580 715857 www.bentleysfineartauctioneers.co.uk

The Canterbury Auction Galleries, 40 Station Road West, Canterbury, CT2 8AN Tel: 01227 763337 www.thecanterburyauctiongalleries.com

Mervyn Carey, Twysden Cottage, Scullsgate, Benenden, Cranbrook, TN17 4LD Tel: 01580 240283

Dreweatt Neate, The Auction Hall, The Pantiles, Tunbridge Wells, TN2 5QL Tel: 01892 544500 www.dnfa.com/tunbridgewells

Gorringes, 15 The Pantiles, Tunbridge Wells, TN2 5TD Tel: 01892 619670 www.gorringes.co.uk

Ibbett Mosely, 125 High Street, Sevenoaks, TN13 1UT Tel: 01732 456731 www.ibbettmosely.co.uk

Lambert & Foster, 102 High Street, Tenterden, TN30 6HT
Tel: 01580 762083
saleroom@lambertandfoster.co.uk
www.lambertandfoster.co.uk

Lambert & Foster, 77 Commercial Road, Paddock Wood, TN12 6DR Tel: 01892 832325

B.J. Norris, The Quest, West Street, Harrietsham, Maidstone, ME17 1JD Tel: 01622 859515

Wealden Auction Galleries, Desmond Judd, 23 Hendly Drive, Cranbrook, TN17 3DY Tel: 01580 714522

Lancashire

Smythes Fine Art, Chattel & Property Auctioneers & Valuers, 174 Victoria Road West, Cleveleys, FY5 3NE Tel: 01253 852184

Tony & Sons, 4–8 Lynwood Road, Blackburn, BB2 6HP Tel: 01254 691748

Leicestershire

Gilding's Auctioneers and Valuers, 64 Roman Way, Market Harborough, LE16 7PQ Tel: 01858 410414 www.gildings.co.uk

Lincolnshire

Batemans Auctioneers, The Exchange Hall, Broad Street, Stamford, PE9 1PX Tel: 01780 766466 www.batemans-auctions.co.uk

DDM Auction Rooms, Old Courts Road, Brigg, DN20 8JD Tel: 01652 650172 www.ddmauctionrooms.co.uk

Thomas Mawer & Son, Dunston House, Portland Street, Lincoln, LN5 7NN Tel: 01522 524984 mawer.thos@lineone.net

Marilyn Swain Auction, The Old Barracks, Sandon Road, Grantham, NG31 9AS Tel: 01476 568861 www.marilynswainauctions.co.uk

Walter's, No 1 Mint Lane, Lincoln, LN1 1UD Tel: 01522 525454

London

Angling Auctions, P. O. Box 2095, W12 8RU Tel: 020 8749 4175 neil@anglingauctions.demon.co.uk

Auction Atrium, 56 Commercial St, Spitalfields, E1 6LT Tel: 07966188819 sales@fcrgallery.com

Bloomsbury, Bloomsbury House, 24 Maddox Street, W1S 1PP Tel: 020 7495 9494 www.bloomsburyauctions.com

Graham Budd Auctions Ltd, Auctioneers & Valuers gb@grahambuddauctions.co.uk

Comic Book Postal Auctions Ltd, 40–42 Osnaburgh Street, NW1 3ND Tel: 020 7424 0007 comicbook@compalcomics.com www.compalcomics.com

Criterion Salerooms, 53 Essex Road, Islington, N1 2BN Tel: 020 7359 5707

Dix-Noonan-Webb, 16 Bolton Street, W1J 8BQ Tel: 020 7016 1700 www.dnw.co.uk

Harmers of London, 111 Power Road, Chiswick, W4 5PY Tel: 020 8747 6100 www.harmers.com

Lloyds International Auction Galleries, Lloyds House, 9 Lydden Road, SW18 4LT Tel: 020 8788 7777 www.lloyds-auction.co.uk

Lots Road Auctions, 71–73 Lots Road, Chelsea, SW10 0RN Tel: 020 7351 7771 www.lotsroad.com

Morton & Eden Ltd in association with Sotheby's, 45 Maddox Street, W1S 2PE Tel: 020 7493 5344 info@mortonandeden.com

Piano Auctions Ltd, Sale room: Conway Hall, 25 Red Lion Square, Holborn, WC1R 4RL Tel: 01234 831742 www.pianoauctions.co.uk

Proud Oriental Auctions, Proud Galleries, 5 Buckingham St, WC2N 6BP Tel: 020 7839 4942

Rosebery's Fine Art Ltd, 74/76 Knights Hill, SE27 0JD Tel: 020 8761 2522 auctions@roseberys.co.uk

Sotheby's, 34–35 New Bond Street, W1A 2AA Tel: 020 7293 5000 www.sothebys.com

Sotheby's Hanover Sale, c/o 34–35 New Bond Street, W1A 2AA Tel: 020 7293 5000

Sotheby's Olympia, Hammersmith Road, W14 8UX Tel: 020 7293 5555

Spink & Son Ltd, 69 Southampton Road, Bloomsbury, WC1B 4ET Tel: 020 7563 4000 www.spink.com

Kerry Taylor Auctions in Association with Sotheby's, St George Street Gallery, Sotheby's New Bond Street, W1A 2AA Tel: 07785 734337 fashion.textiles@sothebys.com

Thomas Del Mar Ltd, c/o Sotheby's Olympia, Hammersmith Road, W14 8UX Tel: 020 7602 4805 www.thomasdelmar.com www.antiquestradegazette.com/thomasdelmar

Vault Auctions Ltd, P.O. Box 257, South Norwood, SE25 6JN Tel: 01342 300 900 www.vaultauctions.com

Merseyside

Cato Crane & Company, Antiques & Fine Art Auctioneers, 6 Stanhope Street, Liverpool, L8 5RF Tel: 0151 709 5559 www.cato-crane.co.uk

Outhwaite & Litherland, Kingsway Galleries, Fontenoy Street, Liverpool, L3 2BE Tel: 0151 236 6561

Middlesex

West Middlesex Auction Rooms, 113–114 High Street, Brentford, TW8 8AT Tel: 020 8568 9080

Norfolk

Garry M. Emms & Co. Ltd., Auctioneers, Valuers & Agents, Great Yarmouth Salerooms, Beevor Road (off South Beach Parade), Great Yarmouth, NR30 3PS Tel: 01493 332668 www.greatyarmouthauctions.com

Thomas Wm Gaze & Son, Diss Auction Rooms, Roydon Road, Diss, IP22 4LN Tel: 01379 650306 www.twgaze.com

Horners Professional Valuers & Auctioneers, incorporating Howlett & Edrich and Jonathan Howlett, North Walsham Salerooms, Midland Road, North Walsham, NR28 9JR Tel: 01692 500603

Keys Aylsham Salerooms
Antiques, Pictures, Books, Collectables and General Auctioneers
Palmers Lane, Aylsham, Norfolk
NR11 6JA Tel: 01263 733195
Fax 01263 732140
www.aylshamsalerooms.co.uk

Northamptonshire

Denise E. Cowling, FGA Tel: 01604 686219 northants@peacockauction.co.uk

J.P. Humbert Auctioneers Ltd, The Salerooms, Unit 2A Burcote Road Estate, Towcester, NN12 6TF Tel: 01327 359595 www.invaluable.com/jphumbert www.jphumbertauctioneers.co.uk

Northern Ireland

Anderson's Auction Rooms Ltd, Unit 7, Prince Regent Business Park, Prince Regent Road, Castereagh, Belfast, BT5 6QR Tel: 028 9040 1888

Northumberland
Jim Railton, Nursery House, Chatton, Alnwick, NE66 5PY Tel: 01668 215323 www.jimrailton.com

Nottinghamshire
Arthur Johnson & Sons Ltd, The Nottingham Auction Centre, Meadow Lane, Nottingham, NG2 3GY Tel: 0115 986 9128 antiques@arthurjohnson.co.uk

Mellors & Kirk, The Auction House, Gregory Street, Lenton Lane, Nottingham, NG7 2NL Tel: 0115 979 0000

Neales, Nottingham Salerooms, 192 Mansfield Road, Nottingham, NG1 3HU Tel: 0115 962 4141 www.dnfa.com/nottingham

Scotarms Ltd, formerly Weller & Dufty Ltd, The White House, Primrose Hill, Besthorpe, Newark, NG23 7HR Tel: 01636 893 946/947

C.B. Sheppard & Son, The Auction Galleries, Chatsworth Street, Sutton-in-Ashfield, NG17 4GG Tel: 01623 556310

T. Vennett-Smith, 11 Nottingham Road, Gotham, NG11 0HE Tel: 0115 983 0541 info@vennett-smith.com www.vennett-smith.com

Oxfordshire
Holloway's, 49 Parsons Street, Banbury, OX16 5NB Tel: 01295 817777 www.hollowaysauctioneers.co.uk

Jones & Jacob, The Barn Ingham Lane, Watlington, OX49 5EJ Tel: 01491 612810 www.jonesandjacob.com

Mallams, Bocardo House, 24 St Michael's Street, Oxford, OX1 2EB Tel: 01865 241358 oxford@mallams.co.uk

Soames County Auctioneers, Pinnocks Farm Estates, Northmoor, OX8 1AY Tel: 01865 300626

Republic of Ireland
James Adam & Sons, 26 St Stephen's Green, Dublin 2 Tel: 1 676 0261 www.jamesadam.ie/

Hamilton Osborne King, 4 Main Street, Blackrock, Co. Dublin Tel: 1 288 5011 www.hok.ie

Mealy's, Chatsworth Street, Castle Comer, Co Kilkenny Tel: 564 441 229 www.mealys.com

Whyte's Auctioneers, 38 Molesworth Street, Dublin 2 Tel: 1 676 2888 www.whytes.ie

Scotland
William Hardie Ltd, 15a Blythswood Square, Glasgow, G2 4EW Tel: 0141 221 6780

Loves Auction Rooms, 52 Canal Street, Perth, PH2 8LF Tel: 01738 633337

Lyon & Turnbull, 33 Broughton Place, Edinburgh, EH1 3RR Tel: 0131 557 8844 info@lyonandturnbull.com

Macgregor Auctions, 56 Largo Road, St Andrews, Fife, KY16 8RP Tel: 01334 472431

Shapes Fine Art Auctioneers & Valuers, Bankhead Avenue, Sighthill, Edinburgh, EH11 4BY Tel: 0131 453 3222 www.shapesauctioneers.co.uk

L.S. Smellie & Sons Ltd, Within the Furniture Market, Lower Auchingramont Road, Hamilton, ML10 6BE Tel: 01698 282007 or 01357 520211

Sotheby's, 112 George Street, Edinburgh, EH2 4LH Tel: 0131 226 7201 www.sothebys.com

Thomson, Roddick & Medcalf Ltd, 60 Whitesands, Dumfries, DG1 2RS Tel: 01387 279879 www.thomsonroddick.com

Thomson, Roddick & Medcalf Ltd, 43/44 Hardengreen Business Park, Eskbank, Edinburgh, EH22 3NX Tel: 0131 454 9090

Shropshire
Halls Fine Art Auctions, Welsh Bridge, Shrewsbury, SY3 8LA Tel: 01743 231212

McCartneys, Ox Pasture, Overture Road, Ludlow, SY8 4AA Tel: 01584 872251

Mullock & Madeley, The Old Shippon, Wall-under-Heywood, Nr Church Stretton, SY6 7DS Tel: 01694 771771 www.mullockmadeley.co.uk

Nock Deighton, Livestock & Auction Centre, Tasley, Bridgnorth, WV16 4QR Tel: 01746 762666

Walker, Barnett & Hill, Cosford Auction Rooms, Long Lane, Cosford, TF11 8PJ Tel: 01902 375555 www.walker-barnett-hill.co.uk

Welsh Bridge Salerooms, Welsh Bridge, Shrewsbury, SY3 8LH Tel: 01743 231212

Somerset
Aldridges, Newark House, 26–45 Cheltenham Street, Bath, BA2 3EX TeL: 01225 462830

Greenslade Taylor Hunt Fine Art, Magdelene House, Church Square, Taunton, TA1 1SB Tel: 01823 332525

Lawrence Fine Art Auctioneers, South Street, Crewkerne, TA18 8AB Tel: 01460 73041 www.lawrences.co.uk

Tamlyn & Son, 56 High Street, Bridgwater, TA6 3BN Tel: 01278 458241

Gardiner Houlgate, The Bath Auction Rooms, 9 Leafield Way, Corsham, Nr Bath, SN13 9SW Tel: 01225 812912 www.invaluable.com/gardiner-houlgate

Staffordshire

Louis Taylor Auctioneers & Valuers, Britannia House, 10 Town Road, Hanley, Stoke on Trent, ST1 2QG Tel: 01782 214111 louis.taylor@ukonline.co.uk www.louistaylorfineart.co.uk

Potteries Specialist Auctions, 271 Waterloo Road, Cobridge, Stoke on Trent, ST6 3HR Tel: 01782 286622 www.potteriesauctions.com

Wintertons Ltd, Lichfield Auction Centre, Fradley Park, Lichfield, WS13 8NF Tel: 01543 263256 www.wintertons.co.uk

Suffolk
Abbotts Auction Rooms, Campsea Ashe, Woodbridge, IP13 0PS Tel: 01728 746323

Boardman Fine Art Auctioneers, P.O. Box 99, Haverhill, CB9 7YF Tel: 01440 730414

Diamond Mills & Co, 117 Hamilton Road, Felixstowe, IP11 7BL Tel: 01394 282281

Durrants, The Old School House, Peddars Lane, Beccles, NR34 9UE Tel: 01502 713490 www.durrantsauctionrooms.com

Dyson & Son, The Auction Room, Church Street, Clare, CO10 8PD Tel: 01787 277993 www.dyson-auctioneers.co.uk

Lacy Scott and Knight, Fine Art Department, The Auction Centre, 10 Risbygate Street, Bury St Edmunds, IP33 3AA Tel: 01284 763531

Neal Sons & Fletcher, 26 Church Street, Woodbridge, IP12 1DP Tel: 01394 382263

Olivers, Olivers Rooms, Burkitts Lane, Sudbury, CO10 1HB Tel: 01787 880305 oliversauctions@btconnect.com

Vost's, Newmarket, CB8 9AU Tel: 01638 561313

Surrey
Clarke Gammon Wellers, The Sussex Barn, Loseley Park, Guildford, GU3 1HS Tel: 01483 880915

Cooper Owen, 74 Station Road, Egham, TW20 9LF Tel: 01784 434 900 www.cooperowen.com

Dreweatt Neate, Baverstock House, 93 High Street, Godalming, GU7 1AL Tel: 01483 423567 www.dnfa.com/godalming

Ewbank Auctioneers, Burnt Common Auction Rooms, London Road, Send, Woking, GU23 7LN Tel: 01483 223101 www.ewbankauctions.co.uk

Lawrences Auctioneers Limited, Norfolk House, 80 High Street, Bletchingley, RH1 4PA Tel: 01883 743323 www.lawrencesbletchingley.co.uk

John Nicholson, The Auction Rooms, Longfield, Midhurst Road, Fernhurst, GU27 3HA Tel: 01428 653727 sales@johnnicholsons.com

P.F. Windibank, The Dorking Halls, Reigate Road, Dorking, RH4 1SG Tel: 01306 884556/876280 www.windibank.co.uk

Richmond & Surrey Auctions Ltd, Richmond Station, Kew Road, Old Railway Parcels Depot, Richmond, TW9 2NA Tel: 020 8948 6677 rsatrading.richmond@virgin.net

East Sussex

Burstow & Hewett, Abbey Auction Galleries, Lower Lake, Battle, TN33 0AT Tel: 01424 772374 www.burstowandhewett.co.uk

Dreweatt Neate, 46–50 South Street, Eastbourne, BN21 4XB Tel: 01323 410419 www.dnfa.com/eastbourne

Gorringes Auction Galleries, Terminus Road, Bexhill-on-Sea, TN39 3LR Tel: 01424 212994 www.gorringes.co.uk

Gorringes inc Julian Dawson, 15 North Street, Lewes, BN7 2PD Tel: 01273 478221 www.gorringes.co.uk

Raymond P. Inman, 98a Coleridge Street, Hove, BN3 5AA Tel: 01273 774777 www.invaluable.com/raymondinman

phil-comics auctions, P.O. Box 3433, Brighton, BN50 9JA Tel: 01273 673462 or 07739 844703 phil@phil-comics.com www.phil-comics.com

Rye Auction Galleries, Rock Channel, Rye, TN31 7HL Tel: 01797 222124 sales@ryeauction.fsnet.co.uk

Wallis & Wallis, West Street Auction Galleries, Lewes, BN7 2NJ Tel: 01273 480208 auctions@wallisandwallis.co.uk grb@wallisandwallis.co.uk www.wallisandwallis.co.uk

West Sussex

Henry Adams Auctioneers, Baffins Hall, Baffins Lane, Chichester, PO19 1UA Tel: 01243 532223 enquiries@henryadamsfineart.co.uk

Bellmans Auctioneers & Valuers, New Pound, Wisborough Green, Billingshurst, RH14 0AZ Tel: 01403 700858 www.bellmans.co.uk

Peter Cheney, Western Road Auction Rooms, Western Road, Littlehampton, BN17 5NP Tel: 01903 722264 & 713418

Denham's, The Auction Galleries, Warnham, Nr Horsham, RH12 3RZ Tel: 01403 255699 or 253837 www.denhams.com

R.H. Ellis & Sons, 44–46 High Street, Worthing, BN11 1LL Tel: 01903 238999

Scarborough Fine Arts, Unit 2, Grange Industrial Estate, Albion Street, Southwick, BN42 4EN Tel: 01273 870371 www.scarboroughfinearts.co.uk

Sotheby's Sussex, Summers Place, Billingshurst, RH14 9AD Tel: 01403 833500 www.sothebys.com

Stride & Son, Southdown House, St John's Street, Chichester, PO19 1XQ Tel: 01243 780207

Toovey's Antique & Fine Art Auctioneers & Valuers, Spring Gardens, Washington, RH20 3BS Tel: 01903 891955 auctions@tooveys.com www.tooveys.com
Monthly three day specialist sales of Antiques, Fine Art and Collectors' Items. Regular specialist sales of Books and Ephemera, Toys & Dolls and Automobilia & Aeronautica

Worthing Auction Galleries Ltd, Fleet House, Teville Gate, Worthing, BN11 1UA Tel: 01903 205565 www.worthing-auctions.co.uk

Tyne & Wear

Anderson & Garland (Auctioneers), Marlborough House, Marlborough Crescent, Newcastle-upon-Tyne, NE1 4EE Tel: 0191 430 3000

Boldon Auction Galleries, 24a Front Street, East Boldon, NE36 0SJ Tel: 0191 537 2630

Sneddons, Sunderland Auction Rooms, 30 Villiers Street, Sunderland, SR1 1EJ Tel: 0191 514 5931

Wales

Anthemion Auctions, 2 Llandough Trading Park, Penarth Road, Cardiff, CF11 8RR Tel: 029 2071 2608

Peter Francis, Curiosity Sale Room, 19 King Street, Carmarthen, SA31 1BH Tel: 01267 233456 www.peterfrancis.co.uk

Morgan Evans & Co Ltd, 30 Church Street, Llangefni, Anglesey, LL77 7DU Tel: 01248 723303/ 421582 www.morganevans.com

Rogers Jones & Co, The Saleroom, 33 Abergele Road, Colwyn Bay, LL29 7RU Tel: 01492 532176 www.rogersjones.co.uk

J. Straker Chadwick & Sons, Market Street Chambers, Abergavenny, Monmouthshire, NP7 5SD Tel: 01873 852624

Wingetts Auction Gallery, 29 Holt Street, Wrexham, Clwyd, LL13 8DH Tel: 01978 353553 www.wingetts.co.uk

Warwickshire

Bigwood Auctioneers Ltd, The Old School, Tiddington, Stratford-upon-Avon, CV37 7AW Tel: 01789 269415

Locke & England, 18 Guy Street, Leamington Spa, CV32 4RT Tel: 01926 889100 www.auctions-online.com/locke

West Midlands

Biddle and Webb Ltd, Ladywood, Middleway, Birmingham, B16 0PP Tel: 0121 455 8042 www.biddleandwebb.co.uk

Fellows & Sons, Augusta House, 19 Augusta Street, Hockley, Birmingham, B18 6JA Tel: 0121 212 2131 www.fellows.co.uk

Fieldings Auctioneers Ltd, Mill Race Lane, Stourbridge, DY8 1JN Tel: 01384 444140 www.fieldingsauctioneers.co.uk

Wiltshire

Henry Aldridge & Son Auctions, Unit 1, Bath Road Business Centre, Devizes, SN10 1XA Tel: 01380 729199 www.henry-aldridge.co.uk

Dreweatt Neate, Hilliers Yard, High Street, Marlborough, SN8 1AA Tel: 01672 515161 www.dnfa.com/marlborough

Finan & Co, The Square, Mere, BA12 6DJ Tel: 01747 861411 www.finanandco.co.uk

Kidson Trigg, Estate Office, Friars Farm, Sevenhampton, Highworth, Swindon, SN6 7PZ Tel: 01793 861000

Netherhampton Salerooms, Salisbury Auction Centre, Netherhampton, Salisbury, SP2 8RH Tel: 01722 340 041

Woolley & Wallis, Salisbury Salerooms, 51–61 Castle Street, Salisbury, SP1 3SU Tel: 01722 424500/411854 www.woolleyandwallis.co.uk

Worcestershire

Andrew Grant, St Mark's House, St Mark's Close, Cherry Orchard, Worcester, WR5 3DL Tel: 01905 357547 www.andrew-grant.co.uk

Philip Laney, The Malvern Auction Centre, Portland Road, off Victoria Road, Malvern, WR14 2TA Tel: 01684 893933 philiplaney@aol.com

Yorkshire

BBR, Elsecar Heritage Centre, Elsecar, Nr Barnsley, S74 8HJ Tel: 01226 745156 sales@onlinebbr.com www.onlinebbr.com

Boulton & Cooper, St Michael's House, Market Place, Malton, YO17 7LR Tel: 01653 696151 www.boultoncooper.co.uk

H.C. Chapman & Son, The Auction Mart, North Street, Scarborough, YO11 1DL Tel: 01723 372424

Cundalls, 15 Market Place, Malton, YO17 7LP Tel: 01653 697820 jackie.barker@cundalls.co.uk

Dee, Atkinson & Harrison, The Exchange Saleroom, Driffield, YO25 6LD Tel: 01377 253151 info@dahauctions.com

David Duggleby, The Vine St Salerooms, Scarborough, YO11 1XN Tel: 01723 507111 www.davidduggleby.com

ELR Auctions Ltd, The Nichols Building, Shalesmoor, Sheffield, S3 8UJ Tel: 0114 281 6161

Andrew Hartley, Victoria Hall Salerooms, Little Lane, Ilkley, LS29 8EA Tel: 01943 816363 www.andrewhartleyfinearts.co.uk

Lithgow Sons & Partners, The Auction Houses, Station Road, Stokesley, Middlesbrough, TS9 7AB Tel: 01642 710158 www.lithgowsauctions.com

Malcolm's No. 1 Auctioneers & Valuers Tel: 01977 684971 info@malcolmsno1auctions.co.uk www.malcolmsno1auctions.co.uk

Christopher Matthews, 23 Mount Street, Harrogate, HG2 8DQ Tel: 01423 871756

Morphets of Harrogate, 6 Albert Street, Harrogate, HG1 1JL Tel: 01423 530030

Paul Beighton, Woodhouse Green, Thurcroft, Rotherham, S66 9AQ Tel: 01709 700005 www.paulbeightonauctioneers.co.uk

Tennants, The Auction Centre, Harmby Road, Leyburn, DL8 5SG Tel: 01969 623780 www.tennants.co.uk

Tennants, 34 Montpellier Parade, Harrogate, HG1 2TG Tel: 01423 531661 www.tennants.co.uk

Wilkinson & Beighton Auctioneers, Woodhouse Green, Thurcroft, Rotherham, SY3 8LA Tel: 01709 700005

Wilkinson's Auctioneers Ltd, The Old Salerooms, 28 Netherhall Road, Doncaster, DN1 2PW Tel: 01302 814884 www.wilkinsons-auctioneers.co.uk

Wombell's Antiques & General Auction, The Auction Gallery, Northminster Business Park, Northfield Lane, Upper Poppleton, York, YO26 6QU Tel: 01904 790777 www.invaluable.com/wombell

AUSTRALIA

Leonard Joel Auctioneers, 333 Malvern Road, South Yarra, Victoria 3141 Tel: 03 9826 4333 www.ljoel.com.au

Shapiro Auctioneers, 162 Queen Street, Woollahra, Sydney, NSW 2025 Tel: 612 9326 1588

AUSTRIA

Dorotheum, Palais Dorotheum, A-1010 Wien, Dorotheergasse 17, 1010 Vienna Tel: 515 60 229 client.services@dorotheum.at

BELGIUM

Bernaerts, Verlatstraat 18–22, 2000 Antwerpen/Anvers Tel: +32 (0)3 248 19 21 www.auction-bernaerts.com

CANADA

Bailey's Auctioneers & Appraisers Tel: 519 823 1107 www.BaileyAuctions.com

Robert Deveau Galleries Fine Art Auctioneers, 297–299 Queen Street, Toronto, Ontario, M5A 1S7 Tel: 416 364 6271

Ritchies Inc., Auctioneers & Appraisers of Antiques & Fine Art, 288 King Street East, Toronto, Ontario, M5A 1K4 Tel: (416) 364 1864 www.ritchies.com

Sotheby's, 9 Hazelton Avenue, Toronto, Ontario, M5R 2El Tel: (416) 926 1774 www.sothebys.com

A Touch of Class Auction & Appraisal Service Tel: 705 726 2120 www.atouchofclassauctions.com

Waddington's Auctions, 111 Bathurst Street, Toronto, M5V 2R1 Tel: 416 504 9100 info@waddingtons.ca www.waddingtons.ca

When the Hammer Goes Down, 440 Douglas Avenue, Toronto, Ontario, M5M 1H4 Tel: 416 787 1700 TOLL FREE 1 (866) BIDCALR (243 2257) www.bidcalr.com

CHINA

Sotheby's, Suites 3101–3106, One Pacific Place, 88 Queensway, Hong Kong Tel: (852) 2524 8121 www.sothebys.com

DENMARK

Bruun Rasmussen-Havnen, Pakhusvej 12, DK-2100, Copenhagen Tel: +45 70 27 60 80 www.bruun-rasmussen.dk

FINLAND

Bukowskis, Horhammer, Iso Roobertink, 12 Stora Robertsg, 00120 Helsinki Helsingfors Tel: 00 358 9 668 9110 www.bukowskis.fi

Hagelstam, Bulevardi 9 A, II kerros, 00120 Helsinki Tel: 358 (0)9 680 2300 www.hagelstam.fi

FRANCE

A La Façon de Venise, 65, rue Saint Andre d'Arts, 75006 Paris sylvie.lhermite.expert@wanadoo.fr

Chochon-Barré Allardi, 15 rue de la Grange-Bateliere, 75009 Paris Tel: 01 47 70 72 51 www.allardi.com

Gros & Delettrez, 22 rue Drout, 75009 Paris Tel: 01 47 70 83 04 www.gros-delettrez.com

Sotheby's France SA, 76 rue du Faubourg, Saint Honore, Paris 75008 Tel: 33 1 53 05 53 05 www.sothebys.com

Tajan, 37 rue des Mathurins, 75008 Paris Tel: 01 53 30 30 30 www.tajan.com

GERMANY

Auction Team Koln, Postfach 50 11 19, 50971 Koln Tel: 00 49 0221 38 70 49 auction@breker.com

Hermann Historica OHG, Postfach 201009, 80010 Munchen Tel: 00 49 89 5237296

Sotheby's Berlin, Palais anmFestungsgraben, Unter den Linden, Neue Wache D-10117 Tel: 49 (30) 201 0521 www.sothebys.com

Sotheby's Munich, Odeonsplatz 16, D-80539 Munchen Tel: 49 (89) 291 31 51

ISRAEL

Sotheby's Israel, 46 Rothschild Boulevard, Tel Aviv 66883 Tel: 972 3 560 1666 www.sothebys.com

ITALY

Sotheby's, Palazzo Broggi, Via Broggi, 19, Milan 20129 Tel: 39 02 295 001 www.sothebys.com

Sotheby's Rome, Piazza d'Espana 90, Rome 00186 Tel: 39(6) 69941791/ 6781798

MEXICO

Galeria Louis C. Morton, GLC A7073L IYS, Monte Athos 179, Col. Lomas de Chapultepec CP11000 Tel: 52 5520 5005 www.lmorton.com

MONACO

Sotheby's Monaco, B.P. 45 Le Sporting d'Hiver, Place du Casino, Monte Carlo, Cedex, MC 98001 Tel: 377 93 30 88 80 www.sothebys.com

NETHERLANDS

Sotheby's Amsterdam, De Boelelaan 30, Amsterdam 1083 HJ Tel: 31 20 550 2200 www.sothebys.com

Van Sabben Poster Auctions,
Appelsteeg 1-B, NL-1621 BD, Hoorn
Tel: 31 (0)229 268203
www.vansabbenauctions.nl

NEW ZEALAND

Webb's, 18 Manukau Rd, Newmarket,
P.O. Box 99251, Auckland
Tel: 09 524 6804 www.webbs.co.nz

SINGAPORE

Sotheby's (Singapore) Pte Ltd,
1 Cuscaden Road, 01-01 The Regent,
249715 Tel: 65 6732 8239
www.sothebys.com

SOUTH AFRICA

Rudd's Auctioneers, 87 Bree Street, Cape
Town, 8001 Tel: (021) 426 0384/6/7
info@rudds.co.za

SWEDEN

Bukowskis, Arsenalsgatan 4,
Stockholm Tel: +46 (8) 614 08 00
www.bukowskis.se

SWITZERLAND

Sotheby's, 13 Quai du Mont Blanc,
Geneva CH-1201 Tel: 41 22 908 4800
www.sothebys.com

Sotheby's Zurich, Gessneralee 1,
CH-8021 Zurich

Taiwan R.O.C.
Sotheby's Taipei, 1st Floor, No 79 Secl,
An Ho Road, Taipei Tel: 886 2 755 2906

U.S.A.

Bertoia Auctions, 2141 DeMarco Drive,
Vineland, New Jersey 08360 Tel: 856
692 1881 www.bertoiaauctions.com

Bloomington Auction Gallery,
300 East Grove St, Bloomington,
Illinois 61701 Tel: 309 828 5533
joyluke@verizon.net www.joyluke.com

Frank H. Boos Gallery, 420 Enterprise
Court, Bloomfield Hills, Michigan 48302
Tel: 248 332 1500
www.boosgallery.com

Braswell Galleries, 125 West Ave,
Norwalk, CT06854 Tel: 203 899 7420

Cincinnati Art Galleries, LLC, 225 East
6th Street, Cincinnati, Ohio 45202
Tel: 513 381 2128
www.cincinnatiartgalleries.com

Cobbs Auctioneers LLC, Noone Falls
Mill, 50 Jaffrey Rd, Peterborough,
NH 03458 Tel: 603 924 6361
www.thecobbs.com

Copake Auction, Inc., 266 RT. 7A,
Copake, NY 12516 Tel: 518 329 1142
www.copakeauction.com

Doyle New York, 175 East 87th Street,
New York, NY 10128 Tel: 212 427 2730
www.doylenewyork.com

Du Mouchelles, 409 East Jefferson,
Detroit, Michigan 48226
Tel: 313 963 6255
info@dumouchelles.com

Eldred's, Robert C. Eldred Co Inc.,
1475 Route 6A, East Dennis,
Massachusetts 0796
Tel: 508 385 3116
www.eldreds.com

Freeman's Fine Art Of Philadelphia Inc.,
Samuel T. Freeman & Co., 1808
Chestnut Street, Philadelphia, PA 19103
Tel: 215 563 9275
www.freemansauctions.com
Photographer Elizabeth Field

The Great Atlantic Auction Company,
2 Harris & Main Street, Putnam,
CT 06260 Tel: 860 963 2234
www.thegreatatlanticauction.com

Green Valley Auctions, Inc.,
2259 Green Valley Lane, Mt. Crawford,
VA 22841 Tel: 540 434 4260
www.greenvalleyauctions.com

Gene Harris Antique Auction Center,
203 S. 18th Avenue, P.O. Box 476,
Marshalltown, Iowa 50158
Tel: 641 752 0600
geneharrisauctions.com

Leslie Hindman, Inc., 122 North
Aberdeen Street, Chicago, Illinois 60607
Tel: 312 280 1212
www.lesliehindman.com

Hunt Auctions, 75 E. Uwchlan Avenue,
Suite 130, Exton, Pennsylvania 19341
Tel: 610 524 0822
www.huntauctions.com

Randy Inman Auctions Inc., P.O. Box 726,
Waterville, Maine 04903-0726
Tel: 207 872 6900
www.inmanauctions.com

Jackson's International Auctioneers &
Appraisers of Fine Art & Antiques,
2229 Lincoln Street, Cedar Falls,
IA 50613 Tel: 319 277 2256
www.jacksonsauction.com

James D. Julia, Inc., P.O. Box 830,
Rte.201 Skowhegan Road, Fairfield,
ME 04937 Tel: 207 453 7125
jjulia@juiaauctions.com
www.juliaauctions.com

Mastro Auctions, 7900 South Madison
Street, Burr Ridge, Illinois 60527
Tel: 630 472 1200
www.mastroauctions.com

Paul McInnis Inc Auction Gallery,
21, Rockrimmon Road, Northampton,
New Hampshire
Tel: +1 603 964 1301

New Orleans Auction Galleries, Inc.,
801 Magazine Street, AT 510 Julia,
New Orleans, Louisiana 70130
Tel: 504 566 1849
info@neworleansauction.com

Northeast Auctions, 93 Pleasant St,
Portsmouth, NH 03801-4504
Tel: 603 433 8400
www.northeastauctions.com

R.O. Schmitt Fine Art, Box 1941,
Salem, New Hampshire 03079
Tel: 1 603 432 2237
www.antiqueclockauction.com

Skinner Inc., 357 Main Street, Bolton,
MA 01740 Tel: 978 779 6241
www.skinnerinc.com

Skinner Inc., The Heritage On The
Garden, 63 Park Plaza, Boston,
MA 02116 Tel: 617 350 5400

Sloan's & Kenyon, 4605 Bradley
Boulevard, Bethesda, Maryland 20815
Tel: +1 301 634 2330
www.sloansandkenyon.com

Sotheby's, 1334 York Avenue at 72nd
St, New York, NY 10021
Tel: +1 212 606 7000
www.sothebys.com

Sotheby's, 9665 Wilshire Boulevard,
Beverly Hills, California 90212
Tel: 310 274 0340

Sotheby's, 215 West Ohio Street,
Chicago, Illinois 60610
Tel: 312 670 0010

Sprague Auctions, Inc., Route 5,
Dummerston, VT 05301
Tel: 802 254 8969
bob@spragueauctions.com
www.spragueauctions.com

Stair Galleries, P.O. Box 418, 33 Maple
Avenue, Claverack, NY 12513
Tel: 212 860 5446/518 851 2544
www.stairgalleries.com

Strawser Auctions, Michael G. Strawser,
200 North Main Street, Wolcottville,
Indiana 46795 Tel: 260 854 2859
www.strawserauctions.com
www.majolicaauctions.com

Swann, 104 East 25th Street, New York
10010 Tel: 212 254 4710
swann@swanngalleries.com

Theriault's, P.O. Box 151, Annapolis,
MD 21404 Tel: 410 224 3655
www.theriaults.com

Treadway Gallery, Inc., 2029 Madison
Road, Cincinnati, Ohio 45208
Tel: 513 321 6742
www.treadwaygallery.com

TreasureQuest Auction Galleries, Inc.,
2690 S.E. Willoughby Blvd, Stuart,
Florida 34994 Tel: 772 781 8600
www.TQAG.com

Weschler's Auctioneers & Appraisers,
909 E Street, NW, Washington DC2004
Tel: 202 628 1281/800 331 1430
www.weschlers.com

Charles A. Whitaker Auction Company,
1002 West Cliveden St, Philadelphia,
PA 19119 Tel: 215 817 4600
caw@whitakerauction.com
www.whitakerauction.com

Wolfs Gallery, 1239 W 6th Street,
Cleveland, OH 44113 Tel: 216 575 9653

KEY TO ILLUSTRATIONS

Each illustration and descriptive caption is accompanied by a letter code. By referring to the following list of auctioneers (denoted by ⚒) and dealers (⊞) the source of any item may be immediately determined. Inclusion in this edition in no way constitutes or implies a contract or binding offer on the part of any of our contributors to supply or sell the goods illustrated, or similar articles, at the prices stated. Advertisers in this year's directory are denoted by †.

If you require a valuation for an item, it is advisable to check whether the dealer or specialist will carry out this service and if there is a charge. Please mention Miller's when making an enquiry. Having found a specialist who will carry out your valuation it is best to send a photograph and description of the item to the specialist together with a stamped addressed envelope for the reply. A valuation by telephone is not possible.

Most dealers are only too happy to help you with your enquiry; however, they are very busy people and consideration of the above points would be welcomed.

A&C ⊞ Ancient & Classic Inc., 54 Franklin St., New York, NY 10013, U.S.A. Tel: 212 393 9696/646 812 3693 info@ancientclassic.com www.ancientclassic.com

AAT ⚒ Auction Atrium, 56 Commercial St, Spitalfields, London, E1 6LT Tel: 07966188819 sales@fcrgallery.com

ACAC ⊞ Afonwen Craft & Antique Centre, Afonwen, Nr Caerwys, Nr Mold, Flintshire, CH7 5UB, Wales Tel: 01352 720965 www.afonwen.co.uk

AEL ⊞ Argyll Etkin Ltd, 1-9 Hills Place, Oxford Circus, London, W1F 7SA Tel: 020 7437 7800 philatelists@argyll-etkin.com www.argyll-etkin.com

AG ⚒ Anderson & Garland (Auctioneers), Marlborough House, Marlborough Crescent, Newcastle-upon-Tyne, Tyne & Wear, NE1 4EE Tel: 0191 430 3000

AGI ⊞ Andy Gibbs, 29 Brookend Street, Ross-on-Wye, Herefordshire, HR9 7EE Tel: 01989 566833 andy.gibbs@clara.co.uk www.andygibbs-antiques.co.uk

AGO ⊞ Ashton Gower Antiques, 9 Talbot Court, Market Square, Stow-on-the-Wold, Gloucestershire, GL54 1BQ Tel: 01451 870699 ashtongower@aol.com

AH ⚒ Andrew Hartley, Victoria Hall Salerooms, Little Lane, Ilkley, Yorkshire, LS29 8EA Tel: 01943 816363 info@andrewhartleyfinearts.co.uk www.andrewhartleyfinearts.co.uk

AIN ⊞ Antiques Within Ltd, incorporating A.W.L. Packing & Shipping, Ground Floor, Compton Mill, Leek, Staffordshire, ST13 5NJ Tel: 01538 387848 antiques.within@virgin.net www.antiques-within.com

ALCH ⊞ Alchemy Antiques, The Old Chapel, Long Street, Tetbury, Gloucestershire, GL8 8AA Tel: 01666 505281

ALEX ⊞ Alexander's Antiques Inc., 1050 Second Avenue, Galleries 43 & 85, New York, NY 10022, U.S.A. Tel: 212 935 9386 alex@alexantiques.com

ALS ⊞† Allan Smith Clocks, Amity Cottage, 162 Beechcroft Road, Upper Stratton, Swindon, Wiltshire, SN2 7QE Tel: 01793 822977 allansmithclocks@lineone.net www.allansmithantiqueclocks.co.uk

ALT ⊞ Alter Silver Gallery Corp., Gallery 49A & 50, 1050 Second Avenue, New York, NY 10022, U.S.A. Tel: 212 750 1928/917 848 1713 altersilvergallery@mac.com

AMB ⚒ Ambrose, Ambrose House, Old Station Road, Loughton, Essex, IG10 4PE Tel: 020 8502 3951

AMC ⊞ Amelie Caswell Tel: 0117 9077960

AMG ⊞ Amphora Galleries, 16–20 Buchanan Street, Balfron, Glasgow, G63 0TT, Scotland Tel: 01360 440329

AMH ⊞ Amherst Antiques, Monomark House, 27 Old Gloucester Street, London, WC1N 3XX Tel: 01892 725552 info@amherstantiques.co.uk www.amherstantiques.co.uk

AnB ⊞ Antique Boxes Tel: 01694 722735 bevstella@whistons.freeserve.co.uk

ANC ⊞ Andrew Campbell, 83 Fern Avenue, Jesmond, Newcastle-upon-Tyne, Tyne & Wear, NE2 2RA Tel: 0191 281 5065 andrewcampbell@acsilver.biz www.acsilver.biz

ANG ⊞† Ancient & Gothic, P.O. Box 5390, Bournemouth, Dorset, BH7 6XR Tel: 01202 431721

ANGE ⊞ Angelo Tel: 01753 864657

AnM ⊞ Andrew Muir Tel: 07976 956208 andrewmuir@blueyonder.co.uk www.andrew-muir.com

ANO ⊞ Art Nouveau Originals, The Bindery Gallery, 69 High Street, Broadway, Worcestershire, WR12 7DP Tel: 01386 854645 cathy@artnouveauoriginals.com www.artnouveauoriginals.com

APO ⊞ Apollo Antiques Ltd, The Saltisford, Birmingham Road, Warwick, CV34 4TD Tel: 01926 494746/494666 mynott@apolloantiques.com

AQ ⊞ Antiquated, 10 New Street, Petworth, West Sussex, GU28 0AS Tel: 01798 344011

ARB ⊞ Arbour Antiques, Poet's Arbour, Sheep Street, Stratford-on-Avon, Warwickshire, CV37 6EF Tel: 01789 293453

ARCA ⊞ Arcadia Antiques, 30 Long Street, Tetbury, Gloucestershire, GL8 8AQ Tel: 01666 500236 jackharness1@aol.com www.arcadiaantiques.co.uk

ARG ⊞ Argentum, The Leopard's Head, 472 Jackson Street, San Francisco, CA 94111, U.S.A. Tel: 415 296 7757 info@argentum-theleopard.com www.argentum-theleopard.com

AUB ⊞ Brandt Antiques, Augustus, Media House, Pound Street, Petworth, West Sussex, GU28 0DX Tel: 01798 344722 brandt@easynet.co.uk www.augustus-brandt-antiques.co.uk

AUC ⊞ Aurea Carter, P.O. Box 44134, London, SW6 3YX Tel: 020 7731 3486 aureacarter@englishceramics.com www.englishceramics.com

Aur ⊞ Aurum, 310/311 Grays Antique Market, 58 Davies Street, London, W1K 5LP Tel: 020 7409 0215 aurum@tinyworld.co.uk www.graysantiques.com

AUTO ⊞ AutomatomaniA, Logie Steading, Forres, Morayshire, IV36 2QN Scotland Tel: 01309 694828 magic@automatomania.com www.automatomania.com

AV ⊞ Avon Antiques, 25-26-27 Market Street, Bradford on Avon, Wiltshire, BA15 1LL Tel: 01225 862052 avonantiques@aol.com www.avon-antiques.co.uk

AW ⊞ Alan Walker, Halfway Manor, Halfway, Newbury, Berkshire, RG20 8NR Tel: 01488 657670 enquiries@alanwalker-barometers.com www.alanwalker-barometers.com

B2W ⊞ Back 2 Wood, The Old Goods Shed, Station Road, Appledore, Ashford, Kent, TN26 2DF Tel: 01233 758109 pine@back2wood.com www.back2wood.com

BAC ⊞ The Brackley Antique Cellar, Drayman's Walk, Brackley, Northamptonshire, NN13 6BE Tel: 01280 841841 antiquecellar@tesco.net

BAM ⚒ Bamfords Ltd, The Derby Auction House, Chequers Road, off Pentagon Island, Derby, DE21 6EN Tel: 01332 210000 bamfords-auctions@tiscali.co.uk www.bamfords-auctions.co.uk

BAM(M) ⚒ Bamfords Ltd, The Matlock Auction Gallery, The Old Picture Palace, 133 Dale Road, Matlock, Derbyshire, DE4 3LU Tel: 01629 57460 bamfords-matlock@tiscali.co.uk www.bamfords-auctions.co.uk

BaN ⊞ Barbara Ann Newman Tel: 07850 016729

BAY ⊞ George Bayntun, Manvers Street, Bath, Somerset, BA1 1JW Tel: 01225 466000 ebc@georgebayntun.com

BB ⊞ Barter Books, Alnwick Station, Alnwick, Northumberland, NE66 2NP Tel: 01665 604888 www.barterbooks.co.uk

BBA ⚒ Bloomsbury, Bloomsbury House, 24 Maddox Street, London, W1S 1PP Tel: 020 7495 9494 info@bloomsburyauctions.com www.bloomsburyauctions.com

BBe ⊞ Bourton Bears Tel: 01993 824756 help@bourtonbears.co.uk www.bourtonbears.com

BBR ⚒ BBR, Elsecar Heritage Centre, Elsecar, Nr Barnsley, South Yorkshire, S74 8HJ Tel: 01226 745156 sales@onlinebbr.com www.onlinebbr.com

BD ⊞ Banana Dance Ltd, 155A Northcote Road, Battersea, London, SW11 6QT Tel: 01634 364539 jonathan@bananadance.com www.bananadance.com

Bea ⚒ Bearnes, St Edmund's Court, Okehampton Street, Exeter, Devon, EX4 1DU Tel: 01392 207000 enquiries@bearnes.co.uk www.bearnes.co.uk

BeF ⊞ Bevan Fine Art, P.O. Box 60, Uckfield, East Sussex, TN22 1ZD Tel: 01825 766649 bevanfineart@quista.net

BeFA ⚒ Bentley's Fine Art Auctioneers, The Old Granary, Waterloo Road, Cranbrook, Kent, TN17 3JQ Tel: 01580 715857 BentleysKent@aol.com www.bentleysfineartauctioneers.co.uk

BELL ⊞ Bellhouse Antiques Tel: 01268 710415 Bellhouse.Antiques@virgin.net

BERN ⚒ Bernaerts, Verlatstraat 18-22, 2000 Antwerpen/Anvers, Belgium Tel: +32 (0)3 248 19 21 info@bernaerts.be www.auction-bernaerts.com

Bert ⚒† Bertoia Auctions, 2141 DeMarco Drive, Vineland, New Jersey 08360, U.S.A. Tel: 856 692 1881 toys@bertoiaauctions.com www.bertoiaauctions.com

BEV ⊞ Beverley, 30 Church Street, Marylebone, London, NW8 8EP Tel: 020 7262 1576

BEX ⊞† Daniel Bexfield Antiques, 26 Burlington Arcade, London, W1J 0PU Tel: 020 7491 1720 antiques@bexfield.co.uk www.bexfield.co.uk

BGe ⊞ Bradley Gent Tel: 07711 158005 www.antiques-shop.co.uk

BHa ⊞ Judy & Brian Harden, P.O. Box 14, Bourton on the Water, Cheltenham, Gloucestershire, GL54 2YR Tel: 01451 810684 harden@portraitminiatures.co.uk www.portraitminiatures.co.uk

BHA ⊞ Bourbon-Hanby Antiques Centre, 151 Sydney Street, Chelsea, London, SW3 6NT Tel: 020 7352 2106

BI ⊞ Books Illustrated Tel: 0777 1635 777 booksillustrated@aol.com www.booksillustrated.com

BKJL ⊞ Brenda Kimber & John Lewis, The Victoria Centre, 3-4 Victoria Road, Saltaire, Shipley, West Yorkshire Tel: 01274 611478 or 01482 442265

BLm ⊞ Lyn Bloom & Jeffrey Neal, Vault 27, The London Silver Vaults, Chancery Lane, London, WC2A 1QS Tel: 020 8421 8848 jeffrey@bloomvault.com www.bloomvault.com

BOOM ⊞ Boom Interiors, 115-117 Regents Park Road, Primrose Hill, London, NW1 8UR Tel: 020 7722 6622 info@boominteriors.com www.boominteriors.com

BOW ⊞ David Bowden, 304/306 Grays Antique Market, 58 Davies Street, London, W1K 5LP Tel: 020 7495 1773

BRB ⊞ Bauman Rare Books, 1608 Walnut Street, 19th Floor, Philadelphia, PA 19104, U.S.A. Tel: 215 546 6466 brb@baumanrarebooks.com www.baumanrarebooks.com

BRT ⊞ Britannia, Grays Antique Market, Stand 101, 58 Davies Street, London, W1Y 1AR Tel: 020 7629 6772 britannia@grays.clara.net

BrW ⊞ Brian Watson Antique Glass, BY APPOINTMENT, Foxwarren Cottage, High Street, Marsham, Norwich, Norfolk, NR10 5QA Tel: 01263 732519 brian.h.watson@talk21.com

BtoB ⊞ Bac to Basic Antiques Tel: 07787 105609 bcarruthers@waitrose.com

BUDD ⚒ Graham Budd Auctions Ltd, Auctioneers & Valuers gb@grahambuddauctions.co.uk

BUK ⚒ Bukowskis, Arsenalsgatan 4, Stockholm, Sweden Tel: +46 (8) 614 08 00 info@bukowskis.se www.bukowskis.se

BUK(F) ⚒ Bukowskis, Horhammer, Iso Roobertink, 12 Stora Robertsg, 00120 Helsinki Helsingfors, Finland Tel: 00 358 9 668 9110 www.bukowskis.fi

BURA ⊞ Burford Antiques Centre, at the Roundabout, Cheltenham Road, Burford, Oxfordshire, OX8 4JA Tel: 01993 823227

BWDA ⊞ Brightwells Decorative Arts Tel: 01744 24899 stanmoore@brightwells.demon.co.uk

BWH ⊞ Bears of Windy Hill, P.O. Box 51, Shipleg, West Yorkshire, BD18 2YH Tel: 01274 599175 info@bearsofwindyhill.co.uk www.bearsofwindyhill.co.uk

BWL ⚒ Brightwells Fine Art, The Fine Art Saleroom, Easters Court, Leominster, Herefordshire, HR6 0DE Tel: 01568 611122 fineart@brightwells.com www.brightwells.com

CaF ⊞ Caren Fine, 11603 Gowrie Court, Potomac, Maryland 20854, U.S.A. Tel: 301 854 6262 caren4antiques@yahoo.com

CAG ⚒ The Canterbury Auction Galleries, 40 Station Road West, Canterbury, Kent, CT2 8AN Tel: 01227 763337 auctions@thecanterburyauctiongalleries.com www.thecanterburyauctiongalleries.com

CAu ⚒ The Cotswold Auction Company Ltd, incorporating Short Graham & Co and Hobbs and Chambers Fine Arts, The Coach House, Swan Yard, 9-13 West Market Place, Cirencester, Gloucestershire, GL7 2NH Tel: 01285 642420 info@cotswoldauction.co.uk www.cotswoldauction.co.uk

CDC ⚒ Capes Dunn & Co, The Auction Galleries, 38 Charles Street, Off Princess Street, Greater Manchester, M1 7DB Tel: 0161 273 6060/1911 capesdunn@yahoo.co.uk

CFSD ⊞ Clive Farahar & Sophie Dupre, Horsebrook House, XV The Green, Calne, Wiltshire, SN11 8DQ Tel: 01249 821121 post@farahardupre.co.uk www.farahardupre.co.uk

CGA ⊞ Castlegate Antiques Centre, 55 Castlegate, Newark, Nottinghamshire, NG24 1BE Tel: 01636 700076

CGC ⚒ Cheffins, Clifton House, 1 & 2 Clifton Road, Cambridge, CB1 7EA Tel: 01223 271966 www.cheffins.co.uk

CHA ⊞ Chislehurst Antiques, 7 Royal Parade, Chislehurst, Kent, BR7 6NR Tel: 020 8467 1530

CHAC ⊞† Church Hill Antiques Centre, 6 Station Street, Lewes, East Sussex, BN7 2DA Tel: 01273 474 842 churchhilllewes@aol.com www.church-hill-antiques.com

CHAM ⊞† Chameleon Fine Lighting, 223 East 59th Street, New York, NY 10022, U.S.A. Tel: 212 355 6300 www.chameleon59.com

CHar ⊞ C. Hart Tel: 01922 457985

CHI ⊞ Chinasearch, Ltd, 4 Princes Drive, Kenilworth, Warwickshire, CV8 2FD Tel: 01926 512402 info@chinasearch.co.uk www.chinasearch.co.uk

CHO ⊞ Candice Horley Antiques Tel: 01883 716056 cjhorleyantiques@aol.com

ChS ⊞ The Chair Set, 18 Market Place, Woodstock, Oxfordshire, OX20 1TA Tel: 01428 707301 allanjames@thechairset.com www.thechairset.com

CHTR ⚒ Charterhouse, The Long Street Salerooms, Sherborne, Dorset, DT9 3BS Tel: 01935 812277 enquiry@charterhouse-auctions.co.uk www.charterhouse-auctions.co.uk

CINE ⊞ Cine Art Gallery, 759 Fulham Road, London, SW6 5UU Tel: 020 7384 0728 info@cineartgallery.com www.cineartgallery.com

CINN ⚒ Cincinnati Art Galleries, LLC, 225 East 6th Street, Cincinnati, Ohio 45202, U.S.A. Tel: 513 381 2128 info@cincinnatiartgalleries.com www.cincinnatiartgalleries.com

CLAR ⊞ Clarenbridge Antiques, Limerick Road, Clarenbridge, Co Galway, Republic of Ireland Tel: 091 796522 clarenbridgeantiques@tinet.ie

CO ⚒ Cooper Owen, 74 Station Road, Egham, Surrey, TW20 9LF Tel: 01784 434 900 customerservice@cooperowen.com www.cooperowen.com

CoHA ⊞ Corner House Antiques and Ffoxe Antiques, Gardners Cottage, Broughton Poggs, Filkins, Lechlade-on-Thames, Gloucestershire, GL7 3JH Tel: 01367 252007 www.corner-house-antiques.co.uk

COO ⊞ Graham Cooley Tel: 07968 722269

CPC ⊞ Carnegie Paintings & Clocks, 15 Fore Street, Yealmpton, Plymouth, Devon, PL8 2JN Tel: 01752 881170 info@paintingsandclocks.com www.paintingsandclocks.com

CRU ⊞ Mary Cruz Antiques, 5 Broad Street, Bath, Somerset, BA1 5LJ Tel: 01225 334174

CS ⊞ Christopher Sykes, The Old Parsonage, Woburn, Milton Keynes, Buckinghamshire, MK17 9QM Tel: 01525 290259 www.sykes-corkscrews.co.uk

CSM ⊞ C. S. Moreton Antiques, Inchmartine House, Inchture, Perth, PH14 9QQ, Scotland Tel: 01828 686412 moreton@inchmartine.freeserve.co.uk

CuS ⊞ Curious Science, 307 Lillie Road, Fulham, London, SW6 7LL Tel: 020 7610 1175 props@curiousscience.com www.curiousscience.com

CVA Courtville Antiques, Powerscourt Townhouse Centre, South William Street, Dublin 2, Republic of Ireland Tel: 01 679 4042 courtville@eircom.net

D&D D & D Antiques Gallery, Fine Antiques & Objects d'Art, 226 East 59th St, New York, NY 10022, U.S.A. Tel: 212 319 9323

DA Dee, Atkinson & Harrison, The Exchange Saleroom, Driffield, East Yorkshire, YO25 6LD Tel: 01377 253151 info@dahauctions.com www.dahauctions.com

DAD decorative arts @ doune, Scottish Antique & Arts Centre, By Doune, Stirling, Scotland, FK16 6HD Tel: 01786 834401 decorativearts.doune@btinternet.com www.decorativearts-doune.com

DAP David Phillips Antiques, Westbank, Pontypridd, Mid Glamorgan, CF37 2HS, Wales Tel: 01443 404646

DAV Hugh Davies, The Packing Shop, 6-12 Ponton Road, London, SW8 5BA Tel: 020 7498 3255

DD David Duggleby, The Vine St Salerooms, Scarborough, Yorkshire, YO11 1XN Tel: 01723 507111 auctions@davidduggleby.com www.davidduggleby.com

DeA Delphi Antiques, Powerscourt Townhouse Centre, South William Street, Dublin 2, Republic of Ireland Tel: 00 353 1 679 0331

DEB Debden Antiques, Elder Street, Debden, Saffron Walden, Essex, CB11 3JY Tel: 01799 543007 info@debden-antiques.co.uk www.debden-antiques.co.uk

DeP De Parma, Core One, The Gasworks, 2 Michael Road, London, SW6 2AN Tel: 0207 736 3384 info@deparma.com www.deparma.com

DHA Durham House Antiques, Sheep Street, Stow-on-the-Wold, Gloucestershire, GL54 1AA Tel: 01451 870404 DurhamHouseGB@aol.com www.DurhamHouseGB.com

DLP † The Dunlop Collection, P.O. Box 6269, Statesville, NC 28687, U.S.A. Tel: 00 1 704 871 2626 or Toll Free Telephone (800) 227 1996

DMa David March, Abbots Leigh, Bristol, Gloucestershire, BS8 Tel: 0117 937 2422

DMC Diamond Mills & Co, 117 Hamilton Road, Felixstowe, Suffolk, IP11 7BL Tel: 01394 282281

DN Dreweatt Neate, Donnington Priory, Donnington, Newbury, Berkshire, RG14 2JE Tel: 01635 553553 donnington@dnfa.com www.dnfa.com/donnington

DN(BR) Dreweatt Neate, The Auction Hall, The Pantiles, Tunbridge Wells, Kent, TN2 5QL Tel: 01892 544500 tunbridgewells@dnfa.com www.dnfa.com/tunbridgewells

DN(HAM) Dreweatt Neate, Baverstock House, 93 High Street, Godalming, Surrey, GU7 1AL Tel: 01483 423567 godalming@dnfa.com www.dnfa.com/godalming

DNo Desmond & Amanda North, The Orchard, 186 Hale Street, East Peckham, Kent, TN12 5JB Tel: 01622 871353

DNW Dix-Noonan-Webb, 16 Bolton Street, London, W1J 8BQ Tel: 020 7016 1700 coins@dnw.co.uk medals@dnw.co.uk www.dnw.co.uk

Do Liz Farrow T/As Dodo, Stand F071/73, Alfie's Antique Market, 13-25 Church Street, London, NW8 8DT Tel: 020 7706 1545

DOA Dorchester Antiques, 3 High Street, Dorchester-on-Thames, Oxfordshire, OX10 7HH Tel: 01865 341 373

DOAN Doll Antiques Tel: 0121 449 0637

DOL Dollectable, 53 Lower Bridge Street, Chester, CH1 1RS Tel: 01244 344888/679195

DORO Dorotheum, Palais Dorotheum, A-1010 Wien, Dorotheergasse 17, 1010 Vienna, Austria Tel: 515 60 229 client.services@dorotheum.at

DRA † Derek Roberts Antiques, 25 Shipbourne Road, Tonbridge, Kent, TN10 3DN Tel: 01732 358986 drclocks@clara.net www.qualityantiqueclocks.com

DRO(C) Craftsman Auctions, Rago Arts & Auction Center, 333 North Main Street, Lambertville, New Jersey 08530, U.S.A. Tel: 609 397 9374 info@ragoarts.com www.ragoarts.com

DuM Du Mouchelles, 409 East Jefferson, Detroit, Michigan 48226, U.S.A. Tel: 313 963 6255 info@dumouchelles.com

DW † Dominic Winter Book Auctions, Mallard House, Broadway Lane, South Cerney, Gloucestershire, GL7 5UQ Tel: 01285 860006 info@dominicwinter.co.uk www.dominicwinter.co.uk

E Ewbank Auctioneers, Burnt Common Auction Rooms, London Road, Send, Woking, Surrey, GU23 7LN Tel: 01483 223101 antiques@ewbankauctions.co.uk www.ewbankauctions.co.uk

EAL The Exeter Antique Lighting Co., Cellar 15, The Quay, Exeter, Devon, EX2 4AP Tel: 01392 490848 www.antiquelightingcompany.com

EAn Era Antiques ikar66@aol.com

EG Elizabeth Gibbons Antique Textiles, By appointment only Tel: 020 7352 1615 & 01989 750243 elizabeth@egantiquetextiles.co.uk

EMH Eat My Handbag Bitch, 37 Drury Lane, London, WC2B 5RR Tel: 020 7836 0830 gallery@eatmyhandbagbitch.co.uk www.eatmyhandbagbitch.co.uk

ERA English Rose Antiques, 7 Church Street, Coggeshall, Essex, CO6 1TU Tel: 01376 562683 or 07770 880790 & 0049 (0)1719 949541 englishroseantiques@hotmail.com www.englishroseantiques.co.uk www.Delta-Line-Trading.com

ET † Early Technology, Monkton House, Old Craighall, Musselburgh, Midlothian, Scotland, EH21 8SF Tel: 0131 665 5753 michael@rare78s.com www.earlytech.com www.rare78s.com www.tvhistory.tv

EUA Eureka Antiques, Saturdays: 105 Portobello Road, London, W11 2QB Tel: 020 7229 5577

EXC Excalibur Antiques, Taunton Antique Centre, 27-29 Silver Street, Taunton, Somerset, TA13DH Tel: 01823 289327/07774 627409 pwright777@btopenworld.com www.excaliburantiques.com

F&C Finan & Co, The Square, Mere, Wiltshire, BA12 6DJ Tel: 01747 861411 post@finanandco.co.uk www.finanandco.co.uk

F&F Fenwick & Fenwick, 88-90 High Street, Broadway, Worcestershire, WR12 7AJ Tel: 01386 853227/841724

FAC Faganarms, Box 425, Fraser MI48026, U.S.A. Tel: 586 465 4637 info@faganarms.com www.faganarms.com

Fai Fair Finds Antiques, Rait Village Antiques Centre, Rait, Perthshire, PH2 7RT, Scotland Tel: 01821 670379

FD Frank Dux Antiques, 33 Belvedere, Bath, Somerset, BA1 5HR Tel: 01225 312367

FFAP Freeman's Fine Art Of Philadelphia, Inc., Samuel T. Freeman & Co., 1808 Chestnut Street, Philadelphia, PA 19103, U.S.A. Tel: 215 563 9275 www.freemansauctions.com *Photographer Elizabeth Field*

FHF Fellows & Sons, Augusta House, 19 Augusta Street, Hockley, Birmingham, West Midlands, B18 6JA Tel: 0121 212 2131 info@fellows.co.uk www.fellows.co.uk

FLDA Fieldings Auctioneers Ltd, Mill Race Lane, Stourbridge, West Midlands, DY8 1JN Tel: 01384 444140 info@fieldingsauctioneers.co.uk www.fieldingsauctioneers.co.uk

FOF Fossack & Furkle, P.O. Box 733, Abington, Cambridgeshire, CB1 6BF Tel: 01223 894296 fossack@btopenworld.com www.fossackandfurkle.freeservers.com

FP For Pine, 340 Berkhampstead Road, Chesham, Buckinghamshire, HP5 3HF Tel: 01494 776119

FRD Fragile Design, 8 The Custard Factory, Digbeth, Birmingham, West Midlands, B9 4AA Tel: 0121 693 1001 info@fragiledesign.com www.fragiledesign.com

G(B) Gorringes Auction Galleries, Terminus Road, Bexhill-on-Sea, East Sussex, TN39 3LR Tel: 01424 212994 bexhill@gorringes.co.uk www.gorringes.co.uk

G(L) Gorringes inc Julian Dawson, 15 North Street, Lewes, East Sussex, BN7 2PD Tel: 01273 478221 clientservices@gorringes.co.uk www.gorringes.co.uk

G&G Guest & Gray, 1-7 Davies Mews, London, W1K 5AB Tel: 020 7408 1252 info@chinese-porcelain-art.com www.chinese-porcelain-art.com

GaL Gazelles Ltd, Stratton Audley, Ringwood Road, Stoney Cross, Lyndhurst, Hampshire, SO43 7GN Tel: 023 8081 1610 allan@gazelles.co.uk www.gazelles.co.uk

GAN Greene's Antiques Galleries, Seagrave House, Dunany, Co. Louth, Republic of Ireland Tel: 041 68 52440 hugo@greenesantiques.com www.greenesantiques.com

GD † Gilbert & Dale Antiques, The Old Chapel, Church Street, Ilchester, Nr Yeovil, Somerset, BA22 8ZA Tel: 01935 840464 roy@roygilbert.com

gdblay@gdblayantiques.com www.gdblayantiques.com

GEO ⊞ Georgian Antiques, 10 Pattinson Street, Leith Links, Edinburgh, EH6 7HF, Scotland Tel: 0131 553 7286 info@georgianantiques.net www.georgianantiques.net

GEOH ⊞ Geoff Holden Tel: 020 8891 6525 Geoff.Holden@ukonline.co.uk

Getc ⊞ Glass etc, 18–22 Rope Walk, Rye, East Sussex, TN31 7NA decanterman@freezone.co.uk www.decanterman.com

GGD ⊞ Great Grooms Antiques Centre, 51/52 West Street, Dorking, Surrey, RH4 1BU Tel: 01306 887076 dorking@greatgrooms.co.uk www.greatgrooms.co.uk

GH Gardiner Houlgate, The Bath Auction Rooms, 9 Leafield Way, Corsham, Nr Bath, Somerset, SN13 9SW Tel: 01225 812912 www.invaluable.com/gardiner-houlgate

GIAM ⊞ Giampietro, 1531/2 Bradley Street, Newhaven, CT 06511, U.S.A. Tel: (203) 787 3851 fredgiampietro@earthlink.net www.fredgiampietro.com

GIL Gilding's Auctioneers and Valuers, 64 Roman Way, Market Harborough, Leicestershire, LE16 7PQ Tel: 01858 410414 sales@gildings.co.uk www.gildings.co.uk

GLD ⊞ Glade Antiques, P.O. Box 873, High Wycombe, Buckinghamshire, HP14 3ZQ Tel: 01494 882818 sonia@gladeantiques.com www.gladeantiques.com

GLEN ⊞ Glenda - Antique Dolls, A18-A19 Grays Antique Market, Davies Mews, London, W1Y 2LP Tel: 020 8367 2441/020 7629 7034 glenda@glenda-antiquedolls.com www.glenda-antiquedolls.com

GMI ⊞ Grimes Militaria, 13 Lower Park Row, Bristol, Somerset, BS1 5BN Tel: 0117 929 8205

GN ⊞† Gillian Neale Antiques, P.O. Box 247, Aylesbury, Buckinghamshire, HP20 1JZ Tel: 01296 423754/07860 638700 gillianneale@aol.com www.gilliannealeantiques.co.uk

GOv ⊞ Glazed Over Tel: 0773 2789114

GRe ⊞ Greystoke Antiques, 4 Swan Yard, (off Cheap Street), Sherborne, Dorset, DT9 3AX Tel: 01935 812833

GSA ⊞ Graham Smith Antiques, 83 Fern Avenue, Jesmond, Newcastle upon Tyne, Tyne & Wear, NE2 2RA Tel: 0191 281 5065 gsmithantiques@aol.com

GTH Greenslade Taylor Hunt Fine Art, Magdelene House, Church Square, Taunton, Somerset, TA1 1SB Tel: 01823 332525

GV ⊞† Garth Vincent, The Old Manor House, Allington, Nr Grantham, Lincolnshire, NG32 2DH Tel: 01400 281358 garthvincent@aol.com www.guns.uk.com

HA ⊞ Hallidays, The Old College, Dorchester-on-Thames, Oxfordshire, OX10 7HL Tel: 01865 340028/68 antiques@hallidays.com www.hallidays.com

HAD Henry Adams Auctioneers, Baffins Hall, Baffins Lane, Chichester, West Sussex, PO19 1UA Tel: 01243 532223 enquiries@henryadamsfineart.co.uk

HAL ⊞ John & Simon Haley, 89 Northgate, Halifax, Yorkshire, HX1 1XF Tel: 01422 822148/360434 toysandbanks@aol.com

Hal Halls Fine Art Auctions, Welsh Bridge, Shrewsbury, Shropshire, SY3 8LA Tel: 01743 231212

HAV ⊞ Havelocks Pine & Antiques, 13, 15, 17 Westmoreland Street, Harrogate, Yorkshire, HG1 5AY Tel: 01423 506721

HAZ ⊞ Hazlehurst Sculpture & Antiques, P.O. Box 128, Cranbrook, Kent, TN17 4WY Tel: 01580 241993 dirkpam.com@btopenworld.com www.hazlehurstantiques.com

HEM ⊞† Hemswell Antique Centres, Caenby Corner Estate, Hemswell Cliff, Gainsborough, Lincolnshire, DN21 5TJ Tel: 01427 668389 info@hemswell-antiques.com www.hemswell-antiques.com

HeR ⊞ Heritage Restorations, Maes Y Glydfa, Llanfair Caereinion, Welshpool, Powys, SY21 0HD, Wales Tel: 01938 810384 www.heritagerestorations.co.uk

Herm Hermann Historica OHG, Postfach 201009, 80010 Munchen, Germany Tel: 00 49 89 5237296

HERR ⊞ The Herrs Antiques, 2363 Henbird Lane, Lancaster, PA 17601, U.S.A. Tel: 717 569 2268 trishherr@aol.com donmherr@aol.com

HEW ⊞ Muir Hewitt, Art Deco Originals, Halifax Antiques Centre, Queens Road Mills, Queens Road/Gibbet Street, Halifax, Yorkshire, HX1 4LR Tel: 01422 347377 muir.hewitt@virgin.net muir.hewitt@btconnect.com www.muirhewitt.com

HiA ⊞ Rupert Hitchcox Antiques, Warpsgrove, Nr Chalgrove, Oxford, OX44 7RW Tel: 01865 890241 www.ruperthitchcoxantiques.co.uk

HILL ⊞ Hillhaven Antique Linen & Lace Tel: 0121 358 4320

HIS ⊞† Erna Hiscock & John Shepherd, Chelsea Galleries, 69 Portobello Road, London, W11 Tel: 01233 661407 erna@ernahiscockantiques.com www.ernahiscockantiques.com

HKW ⊞ Hawkswood Antiques, P.O. Box 156, Goole, DN14 7FW Tel: 01757 638630 jenny@hawkswood.fsbusiness.co.uk

HOK Hamilton Osborne King, 4 Main Street, Blackrock, Co. Dublin, Republic of Ireland Tel: 353 1 288 5011 blackrock@hok.ie www.hok.ie

HOLL Holloway's, 49 Parsons Street, Banbury, Oxfordshire, OX16 5NB Tel: 01295 817777 enquiries@hollowaysauctioneers.co.uk www.hollowaysauctioneers.co.uk

HON ⊞ Honan's Antiques, Crowe Street, Gort, County Galway, Republic of Ireland Tel: 00 353 91 631407 www.honansantiques.com

HOW ⊞ John Howard at Heritage, 6 Market Place, Woodstock, Oxfordshire, OX20 1TA Tel: 0870 4440678 john@johnhoward.co.uk www.antiquepottery.co.uk

HRQ ⊞ Harlequin Antiques, 79-81 Mansfield Road, Daybrook, Nottingham, NG5 6BH Tel: 0115 967 4590 sales@antiquepine.net www.antiquepine.net

HTE ⊞ Heritage, 6 Market Place, Woodstock, Oxfordshire, OX20 1TA Tel: 01993 811332/0870 4440678 dealers@atheritage.co.uk www.atheritage.co.uk

HUM ⊞ Humbleyard Fine Art, Unit 32 Admiral Vernon Arcade, Portobello Road, London, W11 2DY Tel: 01362 637793

HUN ⊞ The Country Seat, Huntercombe Manor Barn, Henley-on-Thames, Oxfordshire, RG9 5RY Tel: 01491 641349 ferry&clegg@thecountryseat.com www.thecountryseat.com

HYD Hy Duke & Son, The Dorchester Fine Art Salerooms, Weymouth Avenue, Dorchester, Dorset, DT1 1QS Tel: 01305 265080 www.dukes-auctions.com

IW ⊞ Islwyn Watkins, Offa's Dyke Antique Centre, 4 High Street, Knighton, Powys, LD7 1AT, Wales Tel: 01547 520145

JAA † Jackson's International Auctioneers & Appraisers of Fine Art & Antiques, 2229 Lincoln Street, Cedar Falls, IA 50613, U.S.A. Tel: 319 277 2256/800 665 6743 sandim@jacksonsauctions.com www.jacksonsauction.com

JAd James Adam & Sons, 26 St Stephen's Green, Dublin 2, Republic of Ireland Tel: 00 3531 676 0261 www.jamesadam.ie/

JAK ⊞ Clive & Lynne Jackson Tel: 01242 254375

JAS ⊞ Jasmin Cameron, Antiquarius, 131-141 King's Road, London, SW3 4PW Tel: 020 7351 4154 or 077 74 871257 jasmin.cameron@mail.com

JBe Bellmans Auctioneers & Valuers, New Pound, Wisborough Green, Billingshurst, West Sussex, RH14 0AZ Tel: 01403 700858 enquiries@bellmans.co.uk www.bellmans.co.uk

JBL ⊞† Judi Bland Antiques Tel: 01536 724145 or 01276 857576

JBT ⊞ Joan Bogart Antiques, P.O. Box 21, Rockville Centre, NY 11571, U.S.A. Tel: 516 764 5712 www.joanbogart.com

JC ⊞ J. Collins & Son, P.O. Box No 119, Bideford, Devon, EX39 1WX Tel: 01237 473103 biggs@collinsantiques.co.uk www.collinsantiques.co.uk

JCH ⊞ Jocelyn Chatterton Tel: 07798 804 853 jocelyn@cixi.demon.co.uk www.cixi.demon.co.uk

JDJ † James D. Julia, Inc., P.O. Box 830, Rte.201 Skowhegan Road, Fairfield, ME 04937, U.S.A. Tel: 207 453 7125 www.juliaauctions.com

JeF ⊞ Jeffrey Formby, The Gallery, Orchard Cottage, East Street, Moreton-in-Marsh, Gloucestershire, GL56 0LQ Tel: 01608 650558 www.formby-clocks.co.uk

JG ⊞ Just Glass, Cross House, Market Place, Alston, Cumbria, CA9 3HS Tel: 01434 381263

JH Jacobs & Hunt, 26 Lavant Street, Petersfield, Hampshire, GU32 3EF Tel: 01730 233933 www.jacobsandhunt.co.uk

JHa ⊞ Jeanette Hayhurst Fine Glass, 32a Kensington Church Street, London, W8 4HA Tel: 020 7938 1539 www.antiqueglass-london.com

JIL ⊞ Jillings Antique Clocks, Croft House, 17 Church Street, Newent, Gloucestershire, GL18 1PU Tel: 01531 822100 clocks@jillings.com www.jillings.com

JNic John Nicholson, The Auction Rooms, Longfield, Midhurst Road, Fernhurst, Surrey, GU27 3HA Tel: 01428 653727 sales@johnnicholsons.com

Street, London, W1S 1DY Tel: 020 7491 3520 jpmaps@attglobal.net www.jpmaps.co.uk

JOR ⊞ John Rogers Tel: 01643 863170 or 07710 266136 johnrogers024@btinternet.com

JPr ⊞ Joanna Proops Antique Textiles & Lighting, 34 Belvedere, Lansdown Hill, Bath, Somerset, BA1 5HR Tel: 01225 310795 antiquetextiles@aol.co.uk www.antiquetextiles.co.uk

JSG ⊞ James Strang Tel: 01334 472 566 or 07950 490088 james@mod-i.com www.mod-i.com

JuA ⊞ Julian's Antiques, By appointment only Tel: 01904 796248 or 07798 840994

JUN ⊞ Junktion, The Old Railway Station, New Bolingbroke, Boston, Lincolnshire, PE22 7LB Tel: 01205 480068/480087 junktionantiques@hotmail.com

JUP ⊞ Jupiter Antiques, P.O. Box 609, Rottingdean, East Sussex, BN2 7FW Tel: 01273 302865

K&D ⊞† Kembery Antique Clocks Ltd, George Street Antique Centre, 8 Edgar Buildings, George Street, Bath, Somerset, BA1 2EH Tel: 0117 956 5281 kembery@kdclocks.co.uk www.kdclocks.co.uk

K&M ⊞ K & M Antiques, 369-370 Grays Antique Market, 58 Davies Street, London, W1K 5LP Tel: 020 7491 4310 Kandmantiques@aol.com

KEY ⊞ Key Antiques of Chipping Norton, 11 Horsefair, Chipping Norton, Oxfordshire, OX7 5AL Tel: 01608 644992/643777 info@keyantiques.com www.keyantiques.com

KK ⊞ Karl Kemp & Assoc., Ltd. Antiques, 36 East 10th Street, New York, NY 10003, U.S.A. Tel: 212 254 1877 info@karlkemp.com www.karlkemp.com

KLH ⊞ KLH Collects Tel: 01502 582572

KNA ⊞ Knights Antiques, 5 Friday Street, Henley-on-Thames, Oxfordshire, RG9 1AN Tel: 01491 414124 simon@knightsantiques.co.uk www.knightsantiques.co.uk

KOLN ⚒ Auction Team Koln, Postfach 50 11 19, 50971 Koln, Germany Tel: (49) 0221 38 70 49 auction@breker.com

KTA ⚒ Kerry Taylor Auctions in Association with Sotheby's, St George Street Gallery, Sotheby's New Bond Street, London, W1A 2AA Tel: 07785 734337 fashion.textiles@sothebys.com

KUR ⊞ William R. & Teresa F. Kurau, P.O. Box 457, Lampeter, PA 17537, U.S.A. Tel: 717 464 0731 lampeter@epix.net www.historicalchina.com

KW ⊞ Karel Weijand, Lion & Lamb Courtyard, Farnham, Surrey, GU9 7LL Tel: 01252 726215 carpets@karelweijand.com

L ⚒ Lawrence Fine Art Auctioneers, South Street, Crewkerne, Somerset, TA18 8AB Tel: 01460 73041 www.lawrences.co.uk

L&E ⚒ Locke & England, 18 Guy Street, Leamington Spa, Warwickshire, CV32 4RT Tel: 01926 889100 info@leauction.co.uk www.auctions-online.com/locke

LAY ⚒ David Lay ASVA, Auction House, Alverton, Penzance, Cornwall, TR18 4RE Tel: 01736 361414

LBO ⊞ Laura Bordignon Antiques, P.O. Box 6247, Finchingfield, Essex, CM7 4ER Tel: 01371 811 791 laurabordignon@hotmail.com

LCM ⚒ Galeria Louis C. Morton, GLC A7073L IYS, Monte Athos 179, Col. Lomas de Chapultepec CP11000, Mexico Tel: 52 5520 5005 glmorton@prodigy.net.mx www.lmorton.com

LFA ⚒ Law Fine Art Tel: 01635 860033 info@lawfineart.co.uk www.lawfineart.co.uk

LFNY ⊞ Laura Fisher at Fisher Heritage, 305 East 61st Street, 5th Floor, New York, NY 10021, U.S.A. Tel: 212 838 2596 laurafisherquilts@yahoo.com www.laurafisherquilts.com

Lfo ⊞ Lorfords, 57 Long Street, Tetbury, Gloucestershire, GL8 8AA Tel: 01666 505111 toby@lorfordsantiques.co.uk www.lorfordsantiques.co.uk

LGr ⊞ Langton Green Antiques, Langton Road, Langton Green, Tunbridge Wells, Kent, TN3 0HP Tel: 01892 862004 antiques@langtongreen.fsbusiness.co.uk www.langtongreenantiques.co.uk

Lim ⊞ Limelight Movie Art, N13-16 Antiquarius Antiques Centre, 131-141 King's Road, Chelsea, London, SW3 4PJ Tel: 01273 206919 info@limelightmovieart.com www.limelightmovieart.com

LJ ⚒ Leonard Joel Auctioneers, 333 Malvern Road, South Yarra, Victoria 3141, Australia Tel: 03 9826 4333 decarts@ljoel.com.au or jewellery@ljoel.com.au www.ljoel.com.au

LOP ⊞ Lopburi Art & Antiques, 5/8 Saville Row, Bath, Somerset, BA1 2QP Tel: 01225 322947 mail@lopburi.co.uk www.lopburi.co.uk

LT ⚒ Louis Taylor Auctioneers & Valuers, Britannia House, 10 Town Road, Hanley, Stoke on Trent, Staffordshire, ST1 2QG Tel: 01782 214111 clivehillier@ukonline.co.uk

LUH ⊞ Lucy Harris Antiques, By appointment Tel: 0207 405 0505 or 07957 144492 lucy@vault39.com

M ⚒ Morphets of Harrogate, 6 Albert Street, Harrogate, Yorkshire, HG1 1JL Tel: 01423 530030

MA&I ⚒ Moore, Allen & Innocent, The Salerooms, Norcote, Cirencester, Gloucestershire, GL7 5RH Tel: 01285 646050 fineart@mooreallen.co.uk www.mooreallen.co.uk

MAA ⊞ Mario's Antiques, 75 Portobello Road, London, W11 2QB Tel: 020 8902 1600 or 07919 254000 marwan@barazi.screaming.net www.marios_antiques.com

MAL(O) ⚒ Mallams, Bocardo House, 24 St Michael's Street, Oxford, OX1 2EB Tel: 01865 241358 oxford@mallams.co.uk

MALT ⊞ The Old Malthouse, 15 Bridge Street, Hungerford, Berkshire, RG17 0EG Tel: 01488 682209 hunwick@oldmalthouse30.freeserve.co.uk

MANO ⊞ Millner Manolatos, 2 Campden Street, Off Kensington Church Street, London, W8 7EP Tel: 020 7229 3268 info@millnermanolatos.com www.millnermanolatos.com

MAR ⚒ Frank R. Marshall & Co, Marshall House, Church Hill, Knutsford, Cheshire, WA16 6DH Tel: 01565 653284

MARK ⊞ 20th Century Marks, Whitegates, Rectory Road, Little Burstead, Near Billericay, Essex, CM12 9TR Tel: 01268 411 000 info@20thcenturymarks.co.uk www.20thcenturymarks.co.uk

MB ⊞ Mostly Boxes, 93 High Street, Eton, Windsor, Berkshire, SL4 6AF Tel: 01753 858470

MCA ⚒ Mervyn Carey, Twysden Cottage, Scullsgate, Benenden, Cranbrook, Kent, TN17 4LD Tel: 01580 240283

MCB ⊞ McBains of Exeter, Exeter Airport, Clyst, Honiton, Exeter, Devon, EX5 2BA Tel: 01392 366261 mcbains@netcom.co.uk

MDL ⊞ Michael D. Long Ltd, 96-98 Derby Road, Nottingham, NG1 5FB Tel: 0115 941 3307 sales@michaeldlong.com www.michaeldlong.com

MEA ⚒ Mealy's, Chatsworth Street, Castle Comer, Co Kilkenny, Republic of Ireland Tel: 00 353 564 441 229 info@mealys.com www.mealys.com

MGa ⊞ Marilyn Garrow, By appointment only Tel: 01728 648671 or 07774 842074 marogarrow@aol.com www.antiquesweb.co.uk/marilyngarrow

MI ⊞† Mitofsky Antiques, 8 Rathfarnham Road, Terenure, Dublin 6, Republic of Ireland Tel: 00 3531 492 0033 info@mitofskyantiques.com www.mitofskyantiques.com

MIL ⊞ Millennia Antiquities Tel: 01204 690175 or 07930 273998 millenniaant@aol.com www.AncientAntiquities.co.uk

MILI ⊞ Militaryman Tel: 01473 274367 militaryman@peace41.fsnet.co.uk www.dinkycollector.com

MIN ⊞ Ministry of Pine, Timsbury Village Workshop, Unit 2, Timsbury Industrial Estate, Hayeswood Road, Timsbury, Bath, Somerset, BA2 0HQ Tel: 01761 472297 ministryofpine.uk@virgin.net www.ministryofpine.com

MINN ⊞ Geoffrey T. Minnis, Hastings Antique Centre, 59–61 Norman Road, St Leonards-on-Sea, East Sussex, TN38 0EG Tel: 01424 428561

Mit ⚒ Mitchells Auction Company, The Furniture Hall, 47 Station Road, Cockermouth, Cumbria, CA13 9PZ Tel: 01900 827800 info@mitchellsfineart.com

MiW ⊞ Mike Weedon, 7 Camden Passage, Islington, London, N1 8EA Tel: 020 7226 5319 or 020 7609 6826 info@mikeweedonantiques.com www.mikeweedonantiques.com

MLL ⊞ Millers Antiques Ltd, Netherbrook House, 86 Christchurch Road, Ringwood, Hampshire, BH24 1DR Tel: 01425 472062 mail@millers-antiques.co.uk www.millers-antiques.co.uk

MMc ⊞ Marsh-McNamara Tel: 07790 759162

MN ⚒ Mastro Auctions, 7900 South Madison Street, Burr Ridge, Illinois 60527, U.S.A. Tel: 630 472 1200 jmarren@mastroauctions.com

MRA ⊞ Millroyale Antiques Tel: 01902 375006 www.whiteladiesantiques.com

MSh ⊞ Manfred Schotten, 109 High Street, Burford, Oxfordshire, OX18 4RG Tel: 01993 822302 sport@schotten.com www.schotten.com

MTay ⊞ Martin Taylor Antiques, 323 Tettenhall Road, Wolverhampton, West Midlands, WV6 0JZ Tel: 01902 751166 enquiries@mtaylor-antiques.co.uk www.mtaylor-antiques.co.uk

MUR ⊞ Murray Cards (International) Ltd, 51 Watford Way, Hendon Central, London, NW4 3JH Tel: 020 8202 5688 murraycards@ukbusiness.com www.murraycard.com/

N Neales, Nottingham Salerooms, 192 Mansfield Road, Nottingham, NG1 3HU Tel: 0115 962 4141 fineart@neales-auctions.com www.dnfa.com/nottingham

NAAW † Northeast Auctions, 93 Pleasant St, Portsmouth, NH 03801-4504, U.S.A. Tel: 603 433 8400 rbourgeault@northeastauctions.com www.northeastauctions.com

NART ⊞ Newel Art Galleries, Inc., 425 East 53rd Street, New York 10022, U.S.A. Tel: 212 758 1970 info@newel.com www.Newel.com

NAW ⊞† Newark Antiques Warehouse Ltd, Old Kelham Road, Newark, Nottinghamshire, NG24 1BX Tel: 01636 674869 enquiries@newarkantiques.co.uk www.newarkantiques.co.uk

NEP ⊞ Neptune Gallery Tel: 086 8064542 or 01 2353920 www.Neptuneonline.ie

NEW ⊞ Newsum Antiques, 2 High Street, Winchcombe, Gloucestershire, GL54 5HT Tel: 01242 603446 mark@newsumantiques.co.uk www.newsumantiques.co.uk

NGL ⊞ Noble Gold Ltd Tel: 01275 464152 james.cole1@btinternet.com

NLS ⊞ Lenson-Smith, 153 Portobello Road, London, W11 2DY Tel: 020 8340 8767

NOA † New Orleans Auction Galleries, Inc., 801 Magazine Street, New Orleans, Louisiana 70130, U.S.A. Tel: 504 566 1849 www.neworleansauction.com

NoC ⊞ No.1 Castlegate Antiques, 1-3 Castlegate, Newark, Nottinghamshire, NG24 1AZ Tel: 01636 701877

NORTH ⊞ Northiam Antiques & Interiors, Station Road, Northiam, East Sussex, TN31 6QT Tel: 01797 252523 robert.bingham2@btconnect.com

NS ⊞ Nicholas Shaw Antiques, Virginia Cottage, Lombard Street, Petworth, West Sussex, GU28 0AG Tel: 01798 345146/01798 345147 silver@nicholas-shaw.com www.nicholas-shaw.com

NSal Netherhampton Salerooms, Salisbury Auction Centre, Netherhampton, Salisbury, Wiltshire, SP2 8RH Tel: 01722 340 041

NSF Neal Sons & Fletcher, 26 Church Street, Woodbridge, Suffolk, IP12 1DP Tel: 01394 382263

NWE ⊞† North Wilts. Exporters, Farm Hill House, Brinkworth, Wiltshire, SN15 5AJ Tel: 01666 510876 mike@northwilts.demon.co.uk www.northwiltsantiqueexporters.com

OAK ⊞ Oakwood Antiques Tel: 01204 304309 or 07813 386415

OCA ⊞ The Old Cinema, 160 Chiswick High Road, London, W4 1PR Tel: 020 8995 4166 theoldcinema@antiques-uk.co.uk www.antiques-uk.co.uk/theoldcinema

OCH ⊞ Gillian Shepherd, Old Corner House Antiques, 6 Poplar Road, Wittersham, Kent, TN30 7PG Tel: 01797 270236

OD ⊞ Offa's Dyke Antique Centre, 4 High Street, Knighton, Powys, Wales, LD7 1AT Tel: 01547 528635/520145

OE ⊞ Orient Expressions, Landsdown Place East, Bath, Somerset, BA1 5ET Tel: 01225 425446 www.orientexpressions.com

Oli Olivers, Olivers Rooms, Burkitts Lane, Sudbury, Suffolk, CO10 1HB Tel: 01787 880305 oliversauctions@btconnect.com

OR ⊞ Orientalist Rugs, 152–154 Walton Street, London, SW3 2JJ Tel: 020 7581 2332 mike@orientalist.demon.co.uk www.orientalistrugs.com

OTB ⊞† The Old Tackle Box, P.O. Box 55, High Street, Cranbrook, Kent, TN17 3ZU Tel: 01580 713979 tackle.box@virgin.net

PAO ⊞ P. A. Oxley Antique Clocks & Barometers, The Old Rectory, Cherhill, Calne, Wiltshire, SN11 8UX Tel: 01249 816227 info@paoxley.com www.british-antiqueclocks.com

PASM ⊞ Pastimes (OMRS), 22 Lower Park Row, Bristol, Gloucestershire, BS1 5BN Tel: 0117 929 9330

PAST ⊞ Past Caring Tel: 01924 848119 chrisbates@lineone.net

PBA Paul Beighton, Woodhouse Green, Thurcroft, Rotherham, Yorkshire, S66 9AQ Tel: 01709 700005 www.paulbeightonauctioneers.co.uk

PCR ⊞ Paul Cranny Antiques, Bank Square Gallery, 63 Maghera Street, Kilrea, Co. Derry, BT51 5QL, Northern Ireland Tel: 028 2954 0279 paulcrannyantiques@yahoo.co.uk

PEC ⊞ Peter Campbell Antiques, 59 Bath Road, Atworth, Nr. Melksham, Wiltshire, SN12 8JY Tel: 01225 709742

PeN ⊞ Peter Norden Antiques, 61 Long Street, Tetbury, Gloucestershire, GL8 8AA Tel: 01666 503 854 peternorden_antiques@lineone.net www.peter-norden-antiques.co.uk

PENH ⊞ Pennard House Antiques, Pennard House, East Pennard, Shepton Mallet, Somerset, BA4 6TP Tel: 01749 860731 www.pennardantiques.com

PEZ ⊞ Alan Pezaro, 62a West Street, Dorking, Surrey, RH4 1BS Tel: 01306 743661

PF Peter Francis, Curiosity Sale Room,19 King Street, Carmarthen, SA31 1BH, Wales Tel: 01267 233456 nigel@peterfrancis.co.uk www.peterfrancis.co.uk

PFK Penrith Farmers' & Kidd's plc, Skirsgill Salerooms, Penrith, Cumbria, CA11 0DN Tel: 01768 890781 info@pfkauctions.co.uk www.pfkauctions.co.uk

PFS ⊞ Period Furniture Showrooms, 49 London End, Beaconsfield, Buckinghamshire, HP9 2HW Tel: 01494 674112 sales@periodfurniture.net www.periodfurniture.net www.englishoak.com

PI ⊞ Pure Imagination, P.O. Box 140, South Shields, Tyne & Wear, NE33 3WU Tel: 0191 4169090 or 0771 5054919 www.pureimaginations.co.uk

PICA ⊞ Piccadilly Antiques, 280 High Street, Batheaston, Bath, Somerset, BA1 7RA Tel: 01225 851494 piccadillyantiques@ukonline.co.uk

POW ⊞ Sylvia Powell Decorative Arts, Suite 400, Ceramic House, 571 Finchley Road, London, NW3 7BN Tel: 020 8458 4543 dpowell909@aol.com

PSA ⊞ Pantiles Spa Antiques, 4, 5, 6 Union House, The Pantiles, Tunbridge Wells, Kent, TN4 8HE Tel: 01892 541377 psa.wells@btinternet.com www.antiques-tun-wells-kent.co.uk

PSC ⊞ Peter & Sonia Cashman, Bath, Somerset Tel: 01225 469497 or 0780 8609860 pete@doubleflint.freeserve.co.uk soniacashman@hotmail.com www.cashman-antiques.co.uk

PSH ⊞ phil-comics auctions, P.O. Box 3433, Brighton, East Sussex, BN50 9JA Tel: 01273 673462 or 07739 844703 phil@phil-comics.com www.phil-comics.com

PT ⊞† Pieces of Time, 1-7 Davies Mews, London, W1K 5AB Tel: 020 7629 2422 info@antique-watch.com www.antique-watch.com www.cufflinksworld.com

PTh ⊞ Antique Clocks by Patrick Thomas, 62a West Street, Dorking, Surrey, RH4 1BS Tel: 01306 743661 patrickthomas@btconnect.com www.antiqueclockshop.co.uk

PVD ⊞ Puritan Values at the Dome, St Edmunds Business Park, St Edmunds Road, Southwold, Suffolk, IP18 6BZ Tel: 01502 722211 sales@puritanvalues.com www.puritanvalues.com

PWA ⊞ Paul Weatherell Antiques, 30–31 Montpellier Parade, Harrogate, Yorkshire, HG1 2TG Tel: 01423 507810 paul@weatherells.com www.weatherells.com

PWS ⊞ Pine Workshop, 28 Priestpopple, Hexham, Northumberland, NE46 1PQ Tel: 01434 601121

Q&C ⊞ Q & C Militaria, 22 Suffolk Road, Cheltenham, Gloucestershire, GL50 2AQ Tel: 01242 519815 qcmilitaria@btconnect.com www.qcmilitaria.com

QA ⊞ Quayside Antiques, 9 Frankwell, Shrewsbury, Shropshire, SY3 8JY Tel: 01743 360490 www.quaysideantiques.co.uk www.quaysideantiquesshrewsbury.co.uk

RAY ⊞ Derek & Tina Rayment Antiques, Orchard House, Barton Road, Barton, Nr Farndon, Cheshire, SY14 7HT Tel: 01829 270429 raymentantiques@aol.com www.antique-barometers.com

RBA ⊞ Roger Bradbury Antiques, Church Street, Coltishall, Norfolk, NR12 7DJ Tel: 01603 737444

RBM ⊞ Robert Morley & Co Ltd, Piano and Harpsicord Showroom & Workshop, 34 Engate Street, London, SE13 7HA Tel: 020 8318 5838 jvm@morley-r.u-net.com www.morleypianos.com

RCA ⊞ Raccoon Creek Antiques Tel: 856 224 1282 raccooncreek@msn.com raccooncreekantiques.com

RdeR ⊞† Rogers de Rin, 76 Royal Hospital Road, London, SW3 4HN Tel: 020 7352 9007

RdV ⊞ Roger de Ville Antiques, Bakewell Antiques Centre, King Street, Bakewell, Derbyshire, DE45 1DZ Tel: 01629 812496 or 07798 793857 contact@rogerdeville.co.uk www.rogerdeville.co.uk

RED ⊞ Red Lion Antiques, New Street, Petworth, West Sussex, GU28 0AS Tel: 01798 344485 www.redlion-antiques.com

REF ⊞† The Refectory, 38 West Street, Dorking, Surrey, RH4 1BU Tel: 01306 742111 www.therefectory.co.uk

ReN ⊞ Rene Nicholls, 56 High Street, Malmesbury, Wiltshire, SN16 9AT Tel: 01666 823089

RGa ⊞ Richard Gardner Antiques, Swanhouse, Market Square, Petworth, West Sussex, GU28 0AN Tel: 01798 343411 www.richardgardnerantiques.co.uk

RICC ⊞ Riccardo Sansoni

RIT ⚒ Ritchies Inc., Auctioneers & Appraisers of Antiques & Fine Art, 288 King Street East, Toronto, Ontario M5A 1K4, Canada Tel: (416) 364 1864 auction@ritchies.com www.ritchies.com

RIWA ⊞ Richard Wallis Antiks Tel: 020 8529 1749 www.richardwallisantiks.com

RMe ⊞ Jubilee Photographica, 10 Pierrepoint Row, Camden Passage, London, N1 8EE Tel: 07860 793707 meara@btconnect.com

RML ⊞† Robert Mills Ltd, Narroways Road, Eastville, Bristol, BS2 9XB Tel: 0117 955 6542 info@rmills.co.uk www.rmills.co.uk

ROH ⊞ Roy C. Harris Tel: 01283 520355 or 0771 8500961 rchclocks@aol.com www.rch-antique-clocks.com

ROS ⚒ Rosebery's Fine Art Ltd, 74/76 Knights Hill, London, SE27 0JD Tel: 020 8761 2522 auctions@roseberys.co.uk

ROSc ⚒ R. O. Schmitt Fine Art, Box 1941, Salem, New Hampshire 03079, U.S.A. Tel: 603 432 2237 roschmittclocks@yahoo.com www.antiqueclockauction.com

RRe ⊞ Rita Reeves Tel: 01978 810140 tintoy.net@boltblue.com

RTo ⚒ Toovey's, Spring Gardens, Washington, West Sussex, RH20 3BS Tel: 01903 891955 auctions@tooveys.com www.tooveys.com

RTW ⊞ Richard Twort Tel: 01934 641900 or 07711 939789

RUSK ⊞ Ruskin Decorative Arts, 5 Talbot Court, Stow-on-the-Wold, Cheltenham, Gloucestershire, GL54 1DP Tel: 01451 832254 william.anne@ruskindecarts.co.uk

RYA ⊞ Robert Young Antiques, 68 Battersea Bridge Road, London, SW11 3AG Tel: 020 7228 7847 office@robertyoungantiques.com www.robertyoungantiques.com

S ⚒ Sotheby's, 34-35 New Bond Street, London, W1A 2AA Tel: 020 7293 5000 www.sothebys.com

S(Am) ⚒ Sotheby's Amsterdam, De Boelelaan 30, Amsterdam 1083 HJ, Netherlands Tel: 31 20 550 2200 www.sothebys.com

S(Han) ⚒ Sotheby's Hanover Sale, c/o 34-35 New Bond Street, London, W1A 2AA Tel: 020 7293 5000 www.sothebys.com

S(NY) ⚒ Sotheby's, 1334 York Avenue at 72nd St, New York, NY 10021, U.S.A. Tel: 212 606 7000 www.sothebys.com

S(O) ⚒ Sotheby's Olympia, Hammersmith Road, London, W14 8UX Tel: 020 7293 5555 www.sothebys.com

S(P) ⚒ Sotheby's France SA, 76 rue du Faubourg, Saint Honore, Paris 75008, France Tel: 33 1 53 05 53 05 www.sothebys.com

SAAC ⊞ Scottish Antique Centre, Abernyte, Perthshire, PH14 9SJ, Scotland Tel: 01828 686401 sales@scottish-antiques.com www.scottish-antiques.com

SAM ⊞ Samarkand Galleries, 16 Howe Street, Edinburgh, EH3 6TD, Scotland Tel: 0131 225 2010 howe@samarkand.co.uk www.samarkand.co.uk

SAMR ⊞ Samarkand Rugs, 7 & 8 Brewery Yard, Sheep Street, Stow-on-the-Wold, Gloucestershire, GL54 1AA Tel: 01451 832322 samarkandrugs@tiscali.co.uk

SAS ⚒† Special Auction Services, Kennetholme, Midgham, Reading, Berkshire, RG7 5UX Tel: 0118 971 2949 www.specialauctionservices.com

SAT ⊞ The Swan at Tetsworth, High Street, Tetsworth, Nr Thame, Oxfordshire, OX9 7AB Tel: 01844 281777 antiques@theswan.co.uk www.theswan.co.uk

SCH ⊞ Scherazade Tel: 01708 641117 or 07855 383996 scherz1@yahoo.com

SCO ⊞ Peter Scott Tel: 0117 986 8468 or 07850 639770

Scot ⊞ Scottow Antiques, Green Street Green, Orpington, Kent Tel: 07860 795909

SDD ⊞ Sandra D. Deas Tel: 01333 360 214 or 07713 897 482

SDR ⊞ Spinna Disc Records, 2B Union Street, Aldershot, Hampshire, GU11 1EG Tel: 01252 327261 sales@spinnadiscrecords.com www.spinnadiscrecords.com

SEA ⊞ Mark Seabrook Antiques, P.O. Box 396, Huntingdon, Cambridgeshire, PE28 0ZA Tel: 01480 861935 enquiries@markseabrook.com www.markseabrook.com

SER ⊞ Serendipity, 125 High Street, Deal, Kent, CT14 6BB Tel: 01304 369165/01304 366536 dipityantiques@aol.com

SGr ⊞ Sarah Groombridge, Saturdays only: Silver Fox Gallery, 121 Portobello Road, London, W11 2DY By appt Tel: 07770 920277 sarah.groombridge@totalise.co.uk

SHa ⊞† Shapiro & Co, Stand 380, Gray's Antique Market, 58 Davies Street, London, W1Y 5LP Tel: 020 7491 2710

SiA ⊞ Simply Antiques, Windsor House, High Street, Moreton-in-Marsh, Gloucestershire, GL56 0AD Tel: 07710 470877 info@callingcardcases.com www.callingcardcases.com

SIL ⊞ The Silver Shop, Powerscourt Townhouse Centre, St Williams Street, Dublin 2, Republic of Ireland Tel: 01 679 4147 ianhaslam@eircom.net

SK ⚒† Skinner Inc., The Heritage On The Garden, 63 Park Plaza, Boston, MA 02116, U.S.A. Tel: 617 350 5400 www.skinnerinc.com

SK(B) ⚒† Skinner Inc., 357 Main Street, Bolton, MA 01740, U.S.A. Tel: 978 779 6241 www.skinnerinc.com

SKA ⊞ Sue Killinger Antiques Tel: 01494 862975 or 07836684815

SMI ⊞ Skip & Janie Smithson Antiques Tel: 01754 810265 or 07831 399180 smithsonantiques@hotmail.com

SOO ⊞ Soo San, 598a Kings Road, London, SW6 2DX Tel: 020 7731 2063 enquiries@soosan.co.uk www.soosan.co.uk

SOR ⊞ Soldiers of Rye, Mint Arcade, 71 The Mint, Rye, East Sussex, TN31 7EW Tel: 01797 225952 rameses@supanet.com chris@johnbartholomewcards.co.uk www.rameses.supanet.com

SOS ⊞† The Grandfather Clock Shop, Styles of Stow, The Little House, Sheep Street, Stow-on-the-Wold, Gloucestershire, GL54 1JS Tel: 01451 830455 info@stylesofstow.co.uk www.stylesofstow.co.uk

SPA ⊞ Sporting Antiques, 10 Union Square, The Pantiles, Tunbridge Wells, Kent, TN4 8HE Tel: 01892 522661

SPE ⊞ Sylvie Spectrum, Stand 372, Grays Market, 58 Davies Street, London, W1K 5LB Tel: 020 7629 3501

SPF ⚒ Scarborough Fine Arts, Unit 2 Grange Industrial Estate, Albion Street, Southwick, West Sussex, BN42 4EN Tel: 01273 870371 info@scarboroughfinearts.co.uk www.scarboroughfinearts.co.uk

SPUR ⊞ Spurrier-Smith Antiques, 39 Church Street, Ashbourne, Derbyshire, DE6 1AJ Tel: 01335 342198/343669 ivan@spurrier-smith.fsnet.co.uk

StB ⊞ Steven Bishop Antiques & Decorative Arts Tel: 07761563095 meridian34all@btinternet.com www.meridiangallery.co.uk

STRA ⊞ Strachan Antiques, 40 Darnley Street, Pollokshields, Glasgow, G41 2SE, Scotland Tel: 0141 429 4411 alex.strachan@btconnect.com www.strachanantiques.co.uk

SWA ⊞† S.W. Antiques, Newlands (road), Pershore, Worcestershire, WR10 1BP Tel: 01386 555580 catchall@sw-antiques.co.uk www.sw-antiques.co.uk

SWB ⊞† Sweetbriar Gallery Paperweights Ltd., 29 Beechview Road, Kingsley, Cheshire, WA6 8DF Tel: 01928 788225 sales@sweetbriar.co.uk www.sweetbriar.co.uk

SWO ⚒ Sworders, 14 Cambridge Road, Stansted Mountfitchet, Essex, CM24 8BZ Tel: 01279 817778 auctions@sworder.co.uk www.sworder.co.uk

TA2 ⊞ Time Antiques, The Antique Centre, 2nd floor, 142 Northumberland Street, Newcastle-upon-Tyne, Tyne & Wear, NE1 7DQ Tel: 0191 232 9832 timeantiques@talktalk.net

TDG ⊞ The Design Gallery 1850–1950, 5 The Green, Westerham, Kent, TN16 1AS Tel: 01959 561234 sales@thedesigngalleryuk.com www.thedesigngalleryuk.com

TDM ⚒ Thomas Del Mar Ltd, c/o Sotheby's Olympia, Hammersmith Road, London, W14 8UX Tel: 020 7602 4805 enquiries@thomasdelmar.com www.thomasdelmar.com www.antiquestradegazette.com/thomasdelmar

info@templegallery.com www.templegallery.com

TEM Tempus Tel: 01344 874007 www.tempus-watches.co.uk

TEN Tennants, The Auction Centre, Harmby Road, Leyburn, Yorkshire, DL8 5SG Tel: 01969 623780 enquiry@tennants-ltd.co.uk www.tennants.co.uk

TEN Tennants, 34 Montpellier Parade, Harrogate, Yorkshire, HG1 2TG Tel: 01423 531661 enquiry@tennants-ltd.co.uk www.tennants.co.uk

THE Theriault's, P.O. Box 151, Annapolis, MD 21404, U.S.A. Tel: 410 224 3655 info@theriaults.com www.theriaults.com

TIM S & S Timms, 2-4 High Street, Shefford, Bedfordshire, SG17 5DG Tel: 01462 851051 info@timmsantiques.com www.timmsantiques.com

TLA The Lanes Armoury, 26 Meeting House Lane, The Lanes, Brighton, East Sussex, BN1 1HB Tel: 01273 321357 enquiries@thelanesarmoury.co.uk www.thelanesarmoury.co.uk

TLD T. L. Dwyer Antiques, 121 Old Company Road, Barto, PA 19504, U.S.A. Tel: 215 679 5036 tleed@enter.net

TMA Tring Market Auctions, The Market Premises, Brook Street, Tring, Hertfordshire, HP23 5EF Tel: 01442 826446 sales@tringmarketauctions.co.uk www.tringmarketauctions.co.uk

TMi T. J. Millard Antiques, 59 Lower Queen Street, Penzance, Cornwall, TR18 4DF Tel: 01736 333454 or 07773 776086 chessmove@btinternet.com

TOL Turn On Lighting, Antique Lighting Specialists, 116/118 Islington High St, Camden Passage, Islington, London, N1 8EG Tel: 020 7359 7616

TOP The Top Banana Antiques Mall, 1 New Church Street, Tetbury, Gloucestershire, GL8 8DS Tel: 0871 288 1102 info@topbananaantiques.com www.topbananaantiques.com

TPAS Times Past Antiques, Broadfold Farm, Auchterarder, Perthshire, PH3 1DR, Scotland Tel: 01764 663166

TPC Pine Cellars, 39 Jewry Street, Winchester, Hampshire, SO23 8RY Tel: 01962 867014 or 01962 777546

TREA † Treadway Gallery, Inc., 2029 Madison Road, Cincinnati, Ohio 45208, U.S.A. Tel: 513 321 6742 www.treadwaygallery.com

TRED Tredantiques, The Antiques Complex, Exeter Airport Industrial Complex, Exeter, Devon, EX5 2BA Tel: 01392 447082 j.tredant@btinternet.com www.tredantiques.com

TRI Trident Antiques, 2 Foundry House, Hall Street, Long Melford, Suffolk, CO10 9JR Tel: 01787 883388 tridentoak@aol.com

Trib Tribal Gathering, No 1 Westbourne Grove Mews, Notting Hill, London, W11 2RU Tel: 020 7221 6650 bryan@tribalgathering.com www.tribalgatheringlondon.com

TRM(C) Thomson, Roddick & Medcalf Ltd, Coleridge House, Shaddongate, Carlisle, Cumbria, CA2 5TU Tel: 01228 528939 www.thomsonroddick.com

TRM(D) Thomson, Roddick & Medcalf Ltd, 60 Whitesands, Dumfries, DG1 2RS, Scotland Tel: 01387 279879 trmdumfries@btconnect.com www.thomsonroddick.com

TRM(E) Thomson, Roddick & Medcalf Ltd, 43/44 Hardengreen Business Park, Eskbank, Edinburgh, EH22 3NX, Scotland Tel: 0131 454 9090 www.thomsonroddick.com

TUR W. F. Turk, 355 Kingston Road, Wimbledon Chase, London, SW20 8JX Tel: 020 8543 3231 sales@wfturk.com www.wfturk.com

TYE Typically English Antiques Tel: 01249 721721 or 07818 000704 typicallyeng@ukonline.co.uk

UD Upstairs Downstairs, 40 Market Place, Devizes, Wiltshire, SN10 1JG Tel: 01380 730266 or 07974 074220 devizesantiques@btconnect.com

VAN Vanessa Parker Rare Books, The Old Rectory, Polranny, Achill Sound, Co Mayo, Republic of Ireland Tel: (098) 20984 or (087) 2339221

VAU Vault Auctions Ltd, P.O. Box 257, South Norwood, London, SE25 6JN Tel: 01342 300 900 contact@vaultauctions.com www.vaultauctions.com

VDA Vetta Decorative Arts, P.O. Box 247, Oxford, OX1 5XH Tel: 0780 905 4969 vettaatam@aol.com

VEC Vectis Auctions Ltd, Fleck Way, Thornaby, Stockton-on-Tees, Cleveland, TS17 9JZ Tel: 01642 750616 admin@vectis.co.uk www.vectis.co.uk

VHA Vanbrugh House Antiques, Park Street, Stow-on-the-Wold, Gloucestershire, GL54 1AQ Tel: 01451 830797 johnsands@vanbrughhouse.co.uk www.vanbrughhouse.co.uk

VIN Vintage Toys Tel: 01993 840064

VS † T. Vennett-Smith, 11 Nottingham Road, Gotham, Nottinghamshire, NG11 0HE Tel: 0115 983 0541 info@vennett-smith.com www.vennett-smith.com

VSP Van Sabben Poster Auctions, Appelsteeg 1-B, NL-1621 BD, Hoorn, Netherlands Tel: 31 (0)229 268203 uboersma@vansabbenauctions.nl www.vansabbenauctions.nl

WAA Woburn Abbey Antiques Centre, Woburn, Bedfordshire, MK17 9WA Tel: 01525 290666 antiques@woburnabbey.co.uk www.discoverwoburn.co.uk

WAC Worcester Antiques Centre, Reindeer Court, Mealcheapen Street, Worcester, WR1 4DF Tel: 01905 610680 ZACATWORCS@aol.com

WAD † Waddington's Auctions, 111 Bathurst Street, Toronto, M5V 2R1, Canada Tel: 416 504 9100 info@waddingtons.ca www.waddingtons.ca

WADS † Wadsworth's, Marehill, Pulborough, West Sussex, RH20 2DY Tel: 01798 873555 info@wadsworthsrugs.com www.wadsworthsrugs.com

Wai Peter Wain, Mor Awel, Marine Terrace, Camaes Bay, Anglesey, LL67 0ND Tel: 01407 710077 peterwain@supanet.com

WAL † Wallis & Wallis, West Street Auction Galleries, Lewes, East Sussex, BN7 2NJ Tel: 01273 480208 auctions@wallisandwallis.co.uk grb@wallisandwallis.co.uk www.wallisandwallis.co.uk

WALP Walpoles, 18 Nelson Road, Greenwich, London, SE10 9JB Tel: 07831 561042 info@walpoleantiques.com www.walpoleantiques.com

WAn † Winson Antiques, Unit 11, Langston Priory Workshops, Kingham, Oxfordshire, OX7 6UR Tel: 01608 658856 clive.payne@virgin.net www.clivepayne.co.uk

WB Wooden Bygones Tel: 01442 842992

WELD J. W. Weldon, 55 Clarendon Street, Dublin 2, Republic of Ireland Tel: 00 353 1 677 1638

WHIT † Courtesy of Whitakerauction.com, Charles A. Whitaker Auction Company, 1002 West Cliveden St, Philadelphia, PA 19119, U.S.A. Tel: 215 817 4600 www.whitakerauction.com

WiB Wish Barn Antiques, Wish Street, Rye, East Sussex, TN31 7DA Tel: 01797 226797

WilP W&H Peacock, 26 Newnham Street, Bedford, MK40 3JR Tel: 01234 266366

WIM Wimpole Antiques, Stand 349, Grays Antique Market, 58 Davies Street, London, W1K 5LP Tel: 020 7499 2889 WimpoleAntiques@compuserve.com lynn@wimpoleantiques.plus.com

WSA West Street Antiques, 63 West Street, Dorking, Surrey, RH4 1BS Tel: 01306 883487 weststant@aol.com www.antiquearmsandarmour.com

WV Westville House Antiques, Westville House, Littleton, Nr Somerton, Somerset, TA11 6NP Tel: 01458 273376 info@westville.co.uk www.westville.co.uk

WW Woolley & Wallis, Salisbury Salerooms, 51-61 Castle Street, Salisbury, Wiltshire, SP1 3SU Tel: 01722 424500/411854 enquiries@woolleyandwallis.co.uk www.woolleyandwallis.co.uk

WWH Westwood House Antiques, 29 Long Street, Tetbury, Gloucestershire, GL8 8AA Tel: 01666 502328 www.westwoodhouseantiques.com

YA Yvonne Adams, The Coffee House, 3-4 Church Street, Stow-on-the-Wold, Gloucestershire, GL54 1BB Tel: 01451 832015 antiques@adames.demon.co.uk www.antiquemeissen.com

YOX Yoxall Antiques, 68 Yoxall Road, Solihull, West Midlands, B90 3RP Tel: 0121 744 1744 sales@yoxallantiques.co.uk www.yoxall-antiques.co.uk

INDEX TO ADVERTISERS

INDEX

Bold page numbers refer to information and pointer boxes

J

K

L

Q

R

S

T